THE PENGUIN COMP
# GEORGE C

PENGUIN BOOKS

PENGUIN BOOKS

Published by the Penguin Group
27 Wrights Lane, London W8 5TZ, England
Viking Penguin Inc., 40 West 23rd Street, New York, New York 10010, USA
Penguin Books Australia Ltd, Ringwood, Victoria, Australia
Penguin Books Canada Ltd, 2801 John Street, Markham, Ontario, Canada L3R 1B4
Penguin Books (NZ) Ltd, 182–190 Wairau Road, Auckland 10, New Zealand

Penguin Books Ltd, Registered Offices: Harmondsworth, Middlesex, England

*Animal Farm* first published in Great Britain by Martin Secker & Warburg Ltd 1945
Published in Penguin Books 1951
Copyright 1945 by Eric Blair

*Burmese Days* first published in Great Britain by Victor Gollancz 1935
Published in Penguin Books 1944
This edition published by Martin Secker & Warburg Ltd 1949
Published in Penguin Books 1967
Copyright 1934 by Eric Blair

*A Clergyman's Daughter* first published in Great Britain by Victor Gollancz 1935
Published by Martin Secker & Warburg Ltd 1960
Published in Penguin Books 1964
Copyright 1935 by Eric Blair

*Coming up for Air* first published in Great Britain by Victor Gollancz 1939
Published by Martin Secker & Warburg Ltd 1954
Published in Penguin Books 1962
Copyright 1939 by Eric Blair

*Keep the Aspidistra Flying* first published in Great Britain by Victor Gollancz 1936
Published by Martin Secker & Warburg Ltd 1954
Published in Penguin Books 1962
Copyright 1936 by Eric Blair

*Nineteen Eighty-Four* first published in Great Britain by Martin Secker & Warburg Ltd 1949
Published in Penguin Books 1954
Copyright 1949 by Eric Blair

This edition first published by Martin Secker & Warburg Ltd in association
with Octopus Books Ltd 1976
Published in Penguin Books 1983
3 5 7 9 10 8 6 4

Copyright © the Estate of Eric Blair, 1976, 1983
All rights reserved

Made and printed in Great Britain by
BPCC Hazell Books Ltd
Member of BPCC Ltd
Aylesbury, Bucks, England

# CONTENTS

# INTRODUCTION

The novels of George Orwell, like his great essays, reflect, as in a mirror, constantly crystal-clear and frequently sharp with menace, the extensive changes of outlook and the shifts of values in British and indeed much of human society in the first half of the twentieth century.

Orwell was born Eric Blair in 1903 in an India that still seemed firmly fixed in an immutable Empire on which the sun never set. He attended Eton, his first publication was a patriotic poem printed by a provincial newspaper during the 1914–18 war, and in 1922 he joined the Indian Imperial Police and served in Burma for the next five years. On leave to England in 1927 he decided not to return to the Far East and resigned. From that time his life, until then seemingly cast in an upper middle-class mould and pointing towards a conventional career in Imperial service, took an entirely fresh course. Determined to become a writer, he lived in a succession of mean rooms on next to nothing in London and Paris, and it was in the latter city that his first article as a professional writer was published. He worked there as a kitchen porter in a luxury hotel and tramped and picked hops in Kent, later both conjured up so vividly in *Down and Out in Paris and London*. During this time, 1930–33, Orwell picked up a meagre living as well as he could, whether by reviewing or teaching, and he continued to write *Burmese Days*, completing it before going down with a bout of recurrent pneumonia. When the book came out in the U.S.A. (as no English publisher had bought it) Orwell had taken a job as a part-time assistant in a London bookshop. *Burmese Days* eventually appeared in England, a few months after *A Clergyman's Daughter* came out in 1935. Early in the following year Orwell was reviewing fiction for the *New English Weekly* and was also gathering material for a book on the depressed areas of the industrial North of England, *The Road to Wigan Pier*.

When the Spanish Civil War began in 1936, Orwell foresaw the importance of its outcome to the future of Europe and before the year ended he had enlisted in Barcelona. While in the front line as a Republican militiaman with the P.O.U.M., the anarchists and the Trotskyites, he was shot in the throat by a sniper. He survived and returned to England to write one of the most forthright and fearless books on the Spanish struggle, *Homage to Catalonia*, which came out in April 1938, one of the first books to denounce the Communists for exploiting the struggle for their own ends. He was repeatedly rejected on medical grounds when he tried to enlist in the British Army in 1939 on the outbreak of war. He subsequently served in the Home Guard, worked in the B.B.C. and became Literary Editor of *Tribune*. *Coming up for Air* was written immediately before the war, prophesying the war, and *Inside the Whale* and *The Lion and the Unicorn* followed in wartime. Just after the war ended and as Orwell rounded off a stint as *Observer* war correspondent in Europe, *Animal Farm*, that outstanding political satire against tyranny in general and the Stalinist betrayal of the Revolution in particular, was published and he began work on *Nineteen Eighty-Four*. Thanks to the money earned by the book in America Orwell found himself, for the first time in his life, free from money worries, able to live on the island of Jura off the West of Scotland and to drop much of his journalistic work to concentrate on his book and a few last essays. But his health deteriorated progressively and seven months after the publication of *Nineteen Eighty-Four* he died in 1950 at the age of 46.

George Orwell holds a unique place in contemporary English literature. He used facts and his own observation and when there was no actual reporting to be done, invention took over, as in *Animal Farm* and *Nineteen Eighty-Four*, and his clear vision, realistic deduction and profound understanding of human behaviour enabled him to reach the inner recesses of the reader's mind and startle him to reflection and self-examination. He said that one of his motives for writing was a 'desire to see things as they are, to find out true facts and store them up for the use of posterity . . . In a peaceful age I might have written ornate or merely descriptive books . . . When I sit down to write a book, I do not say to myself "I am going to produce a work of art." I write it because there is some lie I want to expose, some fact to which I want to draw attention, and my initial concern is to get a hearing.'

George Orwell certainly got his hearing and a constantly-increasing worldwide audience. Honesty, vigour and relevance to today are present in all these novels. Read any newspaper and *Animal Farm* is never far away and *Nineteen Eighty-Four* remains as true a description of the abuse of power as when he wrote it.

# ANIMAL FARM

A FAIRY STORY

# I

Mr Jones, of the Manor Farm, had locked the hen-houses for the night, but was too drunk to remember to shut the pop-holes. With the ring of light from his lantern dancing from side to side, he lurched across the yard, kicking off his boots at the back door, drew himself a last glass of beer from the barrel in the scullery, and made his way up to bed, where Mrs Jones was already snoring.

As soon as the light in the bedroom went out there was a stirring and a fluttering all through the farm buildings. Word had gone round during the day that old Major, the prize Middle White boar, had had a strange dream on the previous night and wished to communicate it to the other animals. It had been agreed that they should all meet in the big barn as soon as Mr Jones was safely out of the way. Old Major (so he was always called, though the name under which he had been exhibited was Willingdon Beauty) was so highly regarded on the farm that everyone was quite ready to lose an hour's sleep in order to hear what he had to say.

At one end of the big barn, on a sort of raised platform, Major was already ensconced on his bed of straw, under a lantern which hung from a beam. He was twelve years old and had lately grown rather stout, but he was still a majestic-looking pig, with a wise and benevolent appearance in spite of the fact that his tushes had never been cut. Before long the other animals began to arrive and make themselves comfortable after their different fashions. First came the three dogs, Bluebell, Jessie, and Pincher, and then the pigs who settled down in the straw immediately in front of the platform. The hens perched themselves on the window-sills, the pigeons fluttered up to the rafters, the sheep and cows lay down behind the pigs and began to chew the cud. The two cart-horses, Boxer and Clover, came in together, walking very slowly and setting down their vast hairy hoofs with great care lest there should be some small animal concealed in the straw. Clover was a stout motherly mare approaching middle life, who had never quite got her figure back after her fourth foal. Boxer was an enormous beast, nearly eighteen hands high, and as strong as any two ordinary horses put together. A white stripe down his nose gave him a somewhat stupid appearance, and in fact he was not of first-rate intelligence, but he was universally respected for his steadiness of character and tremendous powers of work. After the horses came Muriel, the white goat, and Benjamin, the donkey. Benjamin was the oldest animal on the farm, and the worst tempered. He seldom talked, and when he did it was usually to make some cynical remark—for instance, he would say that God had given him a tail to keep the flies off, but that he would sooner have had no tail and no flies. Alone among the animals on the farm he never laughed. If asked why, he would say that he saw nothing to laugh at. Nevertheless, without openly admitting it, he was devoted to Boxer; the two of them usually spent their Sundays together in the small paddock beyond the orchard, grazing side by side and never speaking.

The two horses had just lain down when a brood of ducklings, which had lost their mother, filed into the barn, cheeping feebly and wandering from side to side to find some place where they would not be trodden on. Clover made a sort of wall round them with her great foreleg, and the ducklings nestled down inside it, and promptly fell asleep. At the last moment Mollie, the foolish, pretty white mare who drew Mr Jones's trap, came mincing daintily in, chewing at a lump of sugar. She took a place near the front and began flirting her white mane, hoping to draw attention to the red ribbons it was plaited with. Last of all came the cat, who looked round, as usual, for the warmest place, and finally squeezed herself in between Boxer and Clover; there she purred contentedly throughout Major's speech without listening to a word of what he was saying.

All the animals were now present except Moses, the tame raven, who slept on a perch behind the back door. When Major saw that they had all made themselves comfortable and were waiting attentively, he cleared his throat and began:

'Comrades, you have heard already about the strange dream that I had last night. But I will come to the dream later. I have something else to say first. I do not think, comrades, that I shall be with you for many months longer, and before I die, I feel it my duty to pass on to you such wisdom as I have acquired. I have had a long life, I have had much time for thought as I lay alone in my stall, and I think I may say that I understand the nature of life on this earth as well as any animal now living. It is about this that I wish to speak to you.

'Now, comrades, what is the nature of this life of ours? Let us face it: our lives are miserable, laborious, and short. We are born, we are given just so much food as will keep the breath in our bodies, and those of us who are capable of it are forced to work to the last atom of our strength; and the very instant that our usefulness has come to an end we are slaughtered with hideous cruelty. No animal in England knows the meaning of happiness or leisure after he is a year old. No animal in England is free. The life of an animal is misery and slavery: that is the plain truth.

'But is this simply part of the order of nature? Is it because this land of ours is so poor that it cannot afford a decent life to those who dwell upon it? No, comrades, a thousand times no! The soil of England is fertile, its climate is good, it is capable of affording food in abundance to an enormously greater number of animals than now inhabit it. This single farm of ours would support a dozen horses, twenty cows, hundreds of sheep—and all of them living in a comfort and a dignity that are now almost beyond our imagining. Why then do we continue in this miserable condition? Because nearly the whole of the produce of our labour is stolen from us by human beings. There, comrades, is the answer to all our problems. It is summed up in a single word—Man. Man is the only real enemy we have. Remove Man from the scene, and the root cause of hunger and overwork is abolished for ever.

'Man is the only creature that consumes without producing. He does not give milk, he does not lay eggs, he is too weak to pull the plough, he cannot run fast enough to catch rabbits. Yet he is lord of all the animals. He sets them to work, he gives back to them the bare minimum that will prevent them from starving, and the rest he keeps for himself. Our labour tills the soil, our dung fertilizes it, and yet there is not one of us that owns more than his bare skin. You cows that I see before me, how many thousands of gallons of milk have you given during this last year? And what has happened to that milk which should have been breeding up sturdy calves? Every drop of it has gone down the throats of our enemies. And you hens, how many eggs have you laid this year, and how many of those eggs ever hatched into chickens? The rest have all gone to market to bring in money for Jones and his men. And you, Clover, where are those four foals you bore, who should have been the support and pleasure of your old age? Each was sold at a year old—you will never see one of them again. In return for your four confinements and all your labour in the field, what have you ever had except your bare rations and a stall?

'And even the miserable lives we lead are not allowed to reach their natural span. For myself I do not grumble, for I am one of the lucky ones. I am twelve years old and have had over four hundred children. Such is the natural life of a pig. But no animal escapes the cruel knife in the end. You young porkers who are sitting in front of me, every one of you will scream your lives out at the block within a year. To that horror we all must come—cows, pigs, hens, sheep, everyone. Even the horses and the dogs have no better fate. You, Boxer, the very day that those great muscles of yours lose their power, Jones will sell you to the knacker, who will cut your throat and boil you down for the fox-hounds. As for the dogs, when they grow old and toothless, Jones ties a brick round their necks and drowns them in the nearest pond.

'Is it not crystal clear, then, comrades, that all the evils of this life of ours spring from the tyranny of human beings? Only get rid of Man, and the produce of our labour would be our own. Almost overnight we could become rich and free. What then must we do? Why, work night and day, body and soul, for the overthrow of the human race! That is my message to you, comrades: Rebellion! I do not know when that Rebellion will come, it might be in a week or in a hundred years, but I know, as surely as I see this straw beneath my feet, that sooner or later justice will be done. Fix your eyes on that, comrades, throughout the short remainder of your lives! And above all, pass on this message of mine to those who come after you, so that future generations shall carry on the struggle until it is victorious.

'And remember, comrades, your resolution must never falter. No argument must lead you astray. Never listen when they tell you that Man and the animals have a common interest, that the prosperity of the one is the prosperity of the others. It is all lies. Man serves the interests of no creature except himself. And among us animals let there be perfect unity, perfect comradeship in the struggle. All men are enemies. All animals are comrades.'

At this moment there was a tremendous uproar. While Major was speaking four large rats had crept out of their holes and were sitting on their hind-quarters listening to him. The dogs had suddenly caught sight of them, and it was only by a swift dash for their holes that the rats saved their lives. Major raised his trotter for silence.

'Comrades,' he said, 'here is a point that must be settled. The wild creatures, such as rats and rabbits—are they our friends or our enemies? Let us put it to the vote. I propose this question to the meeting: Are rats comrades?'

The vote was taken at once, and it was agreed by an overwhelming majority that rats were comrades. There were only four dissentients, the three dogs and the cat, who was afterwards discovered to have voted on both sides. Major continued:

'I have little more to say. I merely repeat, remember always your duty of enmity towards Man and all his ways. Whatever goes upon two legs, is an enemy. Whatever goes upon four legs, or has wings, is a friend. And remember also that in fighting against Man, we must not come to resemble him. Even when you have conquered him, do not adopt his vices. No animal must ever live in a house, or sleep in a bed, or wear clothes, or drink alcohol, or smoke tobacco, or touch money, or engage in trade. All the habits of Man are evil. And, above all, no animal must ever tyrannize over his own kind. Weak or strong, clever or simple, we are all brothers. No animal must ever kill any other animal. All animals are equal.

'And now, comrades, I will tell you about my dream of last night. I cannot describe that dream to you. It was a dream of the earth as it will be when Man has vanished. But it reminded me of something that I had long forgotten. Many years ago, when I was a little pig, my mother and the other sows used to sing an old song of which they knew only the tune and the three first words. I had known that tune in my infancy, but it had long since passed out of my mind. Last night, however, it came back to me in my dream. And what is more, the words of the song also came back—words, I am certain, which were sung by the animals of long ago and have been lost to memory for generations. I will sing you that song now, comrades. I am old and my voice is hoarse, but when I have taught you the tune, you can sing it better for yourselves. It is called "Beasts of England".'

Old Major cleared his throat and began to sing. As he had said, his voice was hoarse, but he sang well enough, and it was a stirring tune, something between 'Clementine' and 'La Cucuracha'. The words ran:

> Beasts of England, beasts of Ireland,
> Beasts of every land and clime,
> Hearken to my joyful tidings
> Of the golden future time.
>
> Soon or late the day is coming,
> Tyrant Man shall be o'erthrown,
> And the fruitful fields of England
> Shall be trod by beasts alone.

Rings shall vanish from our noses,
And the harness from our back,
Bit and spur shall rust forever,
Cruel whips no more shall crack.

Riches more than mind can picture,
Wheat and barley, oats and hay,
Clover, beans, and mangel-wurzels
Shall be ours upon that day.

Bright will shine the fields of England,
Purer shall its water be,
Sweeter yet shall blow its breezes
On the day that sets us free.

For that day we all must labour,
Though we die before it break;
Cows and horses, geese and turkeys,
All must toil for freedom's sake.

Beasts of England, beasts of Ireland,
Beasts of every land and clime,
Hearken well and spread my tidings
Of the golden future time.

The singing of this song threw the animals into the wildest excitement. Almost before Major had reached the end, they had begun singing it for themselves. Even the stupidest of them had already picked up the tune and a few of the words, and as for the clever ones, such as the pigs and dogs, they had the entire song by heart within a few minutes. And then, after a few preliminary tries, the whole farm burst out into 'Beasts of England' in tremendous unison. The cows lowed it, the dogs whined it, the sheep bleated it, the horses whinnied it, the ducks quacked it. They were so delighted with the song that they sang it right through five times in succession, and might have continued singing it all night if they had not been interrupted.

Unfortunately, the uproar awoke Mr Jones, who sprang out of bed, feeling sure that there was a fox in the yard. He seized the gun which always stood in a corner of his bedroom, and let fly a charge of number 6 shot into the darkness. The pellets buried themselves in the wall of the barn and the meeting broke up hurriedly. Everyone fled to his own sleeping place. The birds jumped on to their perches, the animals settled down in the straw, and the whole farm was asleep in a moment.

## 2

Three nights later old Major died peacefully in his sleep. His body was buried at the foot of the orchard.

This was early in March. During the next three months there was much secret activity. Major's speech had given to the more intelligent animals on the farm a completely new outlook on life. They did not know when the Rebellion predicted by Major would take place, they had no reason for thinking that it would be within their own lifetime, but they saw clearly that it was their duty to prepare for it. The work of teaching and organizing the others fell naturally upon the pigs, who were generally recognized as being the cleverest of the animals. Pre-eminent among the pigs were two young boars named Snowball and Napoleon, whom Mr Jones was breeding up for sale. Napoleon was a large, rather fierce-looking Berkshire boar, the only Berkshire on the farm, not much of a talker, but with a reputation for getting his own way. Snowball was a more vivacious pig than Napoleon, quicker in speech and more inventive, but was not considered to have the same depth of character. All the other male pigs on the farm were porkers. The best known among them was a small fat pig named Squealer, with very round cheeks, twinkling eyes, nimble movements, and a shrill voice. He was a brilliant talker, and when he was arguing some difficult point he had a way of skipping from side to side and whisking his tail which was somehow very persuasive. The others said of Squealer that he could turn black into white.

These three had elaborated old Major's teachings into a complete system of thought, to which they gave the name of Animalism. Several nights a week, after Mr Jones was asleep, they held secret meetings in the barn and expounded the principles of Animalism to the others. At the beginning they met with such stupidity and apathy. Some of the animals talked of the duty of loyalty to Mr Jones, whom they referred to as 'Master', or made elementary remarks such as 'Mr Jones feeds us. If he were gone, we should starve to death.' Others asked such questions as 'Why should we care what happens after we are dead?' or 'If this rebellion is to happen anyway, what difference does it make whether we work for it or not?', and the pigs had great difficulty in making them see that this was contrary to the spirit of Animalism. The stupidest questions of all were asked by Mollie, the white mare. The very first question she asked Snowball was: 'Will there still be sugar after the Rebellion?'

'No,' said Snowball firmly. 'We have no means of making sugar on this farm. Besides, you do not need sugar. You will have all the oats and hay you want.'

'And shall I still be allowed to wear ribbons in my mane?' asked Mollie.

'Comrade,' said Snowball, 'those ribbons that you are so devoted to are the badge of slavery. Can you not understand that liberty is worth more than ribbons?'

Mollie agreed, but she did not sound very convinced.

The pigs had an even harder struggle to counteract the lies put about by Moses, the tame raven. Moses, who was Mr Jones's especial pet, was a spy and a tale-bearer, but he was also a clever talker. He claimed to know of the existence of a mysterious country called Sugarcandy Mountain, to which all animals went when they died. It was situated somewhere up in the sky, a little distance beyond the clouds, Moses said. In Sugarcandy Mountain it was Sunday seven days a week, clover was in season all the year round, and lump sugar and linseed cake grew on the hedges. The animals hated Moses because he told tales and did not work, but some of them believed in Sugarcandy Mountain, and the pigs had to argue very hard to persuade them that there was no such place.

Their most faithful disciples were the two carthouses, Boxer and Clover. These two had great difficulty in thinking anything out for themselves, but having once accepted the pigs as their teachers, they absorbed everything that they were told, and passed it on to the other animals by simple arguments. They were unfailing in their attendance at the secret meetings in the barn, and led the singing of 'Beasts of England', with which the meetings always ended.

Now, as it turned out, the Rebellion was achieved much earlier and more easily than anyone had expected. In the past years Mr Jones, although a hard master, had been a capable farmer, but of late he had fallen on evil days. He had become much disheartened after losing money in a lawsuit, and had taken to drinking more than was good for him. For whole days at a time he would lounge in his Windsor chair in the kitchen, reading the newspapers, drinking, and occasionally feeding Moses on crusts of bread soaked in beer. His men were idle and dishonest, the fields were full of weeds, the buildings wanted roofing, the hedges were neglected, and the animals were underfed.

June came and the hay was almost ready for cutting. On Midsummer's Eve, which was a Saturday, Mr Jones went into Willingdon and got so drunk at the Red Lion that he did not come back till midday on Sunday. The men had milked the cows in the early morning and then had gone out rabbiting, without bothering to feed the animals. When Mr Jones got back he immediately went to sleep on the drawing-room sofa with the *News of the World* over his face, so that when evening came, the animals were still unfed. At last they could stand it no longer. One of the cows broke in the door of the store-shed with her horns and all the animals began to help themselves from the bins. It was just then that Mr Jones woke up. The next moment he and his four men were in the store-shed with whips in their hands, lashing out in all directions. This was more than the hungry animals could bear. With one accord, though nothing of the kind had been planned beforehand, they flung themselves upon their tormentors. Jones and his men suddenly found themselves being butted and kicked from all sides. The situation was quite out of their control. They had never seen animals behave like this before, and this sudden uprising of creatures whom they were used to thrashing and maltreating just as they chose, frightened them almost out of their wits. After only a moment or two they gave up trying to defend themselves and took to their heels. A minute later all five of them were in full flight down the cart-track that led to the main road, with the animals pursuing them in triumph.

Mrs Jones looked out of the bedroom window, saw what was happening, hurriedly flung a few possessions into a carpet bag, and slipped out of the farm by another way. Moses sprang off his perch and flapped after her, croaking loudly. Meanwhile the animals had chased Jones and his men out on to the road and slammed the five-barred gate behind them. And so, almost before they knew what was happening, the Rebellion had been successfully carried through: Jones was expelled, and the Manor Farm was theirs.

For the first few minutes the animals could hardly believe in their good fortune. Their first act was to gallop in a body right round the boundaries of the farm, as though to make quite sure that no human being was hiding anywhere upon it; then they raced back to the farm buildings to wipe out the last traces of Jones's hated reign. The harness-room at the end of the stables was broken open; the bits, the nose-rings, the dog-chains, the cruel knives with which Mr Jones had been used to castrate the pigs and lambs, were all flung down the well. The reins, the halters, the blinkers, the degrading nosebags, were thrown on to the rubbish fire which was burning in the yard. So were the whips. All the animals capered with joy when they saw the whips going up in flames. Snowball also threw on to the fire the ribbons with which the horses' manes and tails had usually been decorated on market days.

'Ribbons,' he said, 'should be considered as clothes, which are the mark of a human being. All animals should go naked.'

When Boxer heard this he fetched the small straw hat which he wore in summer to keep the flies out of his ears, and flung it on to the fire with the rest.

In a very little while the animals had destroyed everything that reminded them of Mr Jones. Napoleon then led them back to the store-shed and served out a double ration of corn to everybody, with two biscuits for each dog. Then they sang 'Beasts of England' from end to end seven times running, and after that they settled down for the night and slept as they had never slept before.

But they woke at dawn as usual, and suddenly remembering the glorious thing that had happened, they all raced out into the pasture together. A little way down the pasture there was a knoll that commanded a view of most of the farm. The animals rushed to the top of it and gazed round them in the clear morning light. Yes, it was theirs—everything that they could see was theirs! In the ecstasy of that thought they gambolled round and round, they hurled themselves into the air in great leaps of excitement. They rolled in the dew, they cropped mouthfuls of the sweet summer grass, they kicked up clods of the black earth and snuffed its rich scent. Then they made a tour of inspection of the whole farm and surveyed with speechless admiration the ploughland, the hayfield, the orchard, the pool, the spinney. It was as though they had never seen these things before, and even now they could hardly believe that it was all their own.

Then they filed back to the farm buildings and halted in silence outside the door of the farmhouse. That was theirs too, but they were frightened to go inside. After a moment, however, Snowball and Napoleon butted the door open with their shoulders and the animals entered in single file, walking with the utmost care for fear of disturbing anything. They tiptoed from room to room, afraid to speak above a whisper and gazing with a kind of awe at the unbelievable luxury, at the beds with their feather mattresses, the looking-glasses, the horsehair sofa, the Brussels carpet, the lithograph of Queen Victoria over the drawing-room mantelpiece. They were just coming down the stairs when Mollie was discovered to be missing. Going back, the others found that she had remained behind in the best bedroom. She had taken a piece of blue ribbon from Mrs Jones's dressing-table, and was holding it against her shoulder and admiring herself in the glass in a very foolish manner. The others reproached her sharply, and they went outside. Some hams hanging in the kitchen were taken out for burial, and the barrel of beer in the scullery was stove in with a kick from Boxer's hoof, otherwise nothing in the house was touched. A unanimous resolution was passed on the spot that the farmhouse should be preserved as a museum. All were agreed that no animal must ever live there.

The animals had their breakfast, and then Snowball and Napoleon called them together again.

'Comrades,' said Snowball, 'it is half past six and we have a long day before us. Today we begin the hay harvest. But there is another matter that must be attended to first.'

The pigs now revealed that during the past three months they had taught themselves to read and write from an old spelling book which had belonged to Mr Jones's children and which had been thrown on the rubbish heap. Napoleon sent for pots of black and white paint and led the way down to the five-barred gate that gave on to the main road. Then Snowball (for it was Snowball who was best at writing) took a brush between the two knuckles of his trotter, painted out MANOR FARM from the top bar of the gate and in its place painted ANIMAL FARM. This was to be the name of the farm from now onwards. After this they went back to the farm buildings, where Snowball and Napoleon sent for a ladder which they caused to be set against the end wall of the big barn. They explained that by their studies of the past three months the pigs had succeeded in reducing the principles of Animalism to Seven Commandments. These Seven Commandments would now be inscribed on the wall; they would form an unalterable law by which all the animals on Animal Farm must live for ever after. With some difficulty (for it is not easy for a pig to balance himself on a ladder) Snowball climbed up and set to work, with Squealer a few rungs below him holding the paint-pot. The Commandments were written on the tarred wall·in great white letters that could be read thirty yards away. They ran thus:

THE SEVEN COMMANDMENTS
1. Whatever goes upon two legs is an enemy.
2. Whatever goes upon four legs, or has wings, is a friend.
3. No animal shall wear clothes.
4. No animal shall sleep in a bed.
5. No animal shall drink alcohol.
6. No animal shall kill any other animal.
7. All animals are equal.

It was very neatly written, and except that 'friend' was written 'freind' and one of the 'S's' was the wrong way round, the spelling was correct all the way through. Snowball read it aloud for the benefit of the others. All the animals nodded in complete agreement, and the cleverer ones at once began to learn the Commandments by heart.

'Now, comrades,' said Snowball, throwing down the paint-brush, 'to the hayfield! Let us make it a point of honour to get in the harvest more quickly than Jones and his men could do.'

But at this moment the three cows, who had seemed uneasy for some time past, set up a loud lowing. They had not been milked for twenty-four hours, and their udders were almost bursting. After a little thought, the pigs sent for buckets and milked the cows fairly successfully, their trotters being well adapted to this task. Soon there were five buckets of frothing creamy milk at which many of the animals looked with considerable interest.

'What is going to happen to all that milk?' said someone.

'Jones used sometimes to mix some of it in our mash,' said one of the hens.

'Never mind the milk, comrades!' cried Napoleon, placing himself in front of the buckets. 'That will be attended to. The harvest is more important. Comrade Snowball will lead the way. I shall follow in a few minutes. Forward, comrades! The hay is waiting.'

So the animals trooped down to the hayfield to begin the harvest, and when they came back in the evening it was noticed that the milk had disappeared.

# 3

How they toiled and sweated to get the hay in! But their efforts were rewarded, for the harvest was an even bigger success than they had hoped.

Sometimes the work was hard; the implements had been designed for human beings and not for animals, and it was a great drawback that no animal was able to use any tool that involved standing on his hind legs. But the pigs were so clever that they could think of a way round every difficulty. As for the horses, they knew every inch of the field, and in fact understood the business of mowing and raking far better than Jones and his men had ever done. The pigs did not actually work, but directed and supervised the others. With their superior knowledge it was natural that they should assume the leadership. Boxer and Clover would harness themselves to the cutter or the horse-rake (no bits or reins were needed in these days, of course) and tramp steadily round and round the field with a pig walking behind and calling out 'Gee up, comrade!' or 'Whoa back, comrade!' as the case might be. And every animal down to the humblest worked at turning the hay and gathering it. Even the ducks and hens toiled to and fro all day in the sun, carrying tiny wisps of hay in their beaks. In the end they finished the harvest in two days' less time than it had usually taken Jones and his men. Moreover, it was the biggest harvest that the farm had ever seen. There was no wastage whatever; the hens and ducks with their sharp eyes had gathered up the very last stalk. And not an animal on the farm had stolen so much as a mouthful.

All through that summer the work of the farm went like clockwork. The animals were happy as they had never conceived it possible to be. Every mouthful of food was an acute positive pleasure, now that it was truly their own food, produced by themselves and for themselves, not doled out to them by a grudging master. With the worthless parasitical human beings gone, there was more for everyone to eat. There was more leisure too, inexperienced though the animals were. They met with many difficulties—for instance, later in the year, when they harvested the corn, they had to tread it out in the ancient style and blow away the chaff with their breath, since the farm possessed no threshing machine—but the pigs with their cleverness and Boxer with his tremendous muscles always pulled them through. Boxer was the admiration of everybody. He had been a hard worker even in Jones's time, but now he seemed more like three horses than one; there were days when the entire work of the farm seemed to rest upon his mighty shoulders. From morning to night he was pushing and pulling, always at the spot where the work was hardest. He had made an arrangement with one of the cockerels to call him in the mornings half an hour earlier than anyone else, and would put in some volunteer labour at whatever seemed to be most needed, before the regular day's work began. His answer to every problem, every setback, was 'I will work harder!'—which he had adopted as his personal motto.

But everyone worked according to his capacity. The hens and ducks, for instance, saved five bushels of corn at the harvest by gathering up the stray grains. Nobody stole, nobody grumbled over his rations, the quarrelling and biting and jealousy which had been normal features of life in the old days had almost disappeared. Nobody shirked—or almost nobody. Mollie, it was true, was not good at getting up in the morning, and had a way of leaving work early on the ground that there was a stone in her hoof. And the behaviour of the cat was somewhat peculiar. It was soon noticed that when there was work to be done the cat could never be found. She would vanish for hours on end, and then reappear at meal-times, or in the evening after work was over, as though nothing had happened. But she always made such excellent excuses, and purred so affectionately, that it was impossible not to believe in her good intentions. Old Benjamin, the donkey, seemed quite unchanged since the Rebellion. He did his work in the same slow obstinate way as he had done it in Jones's time, never shirking, and never volunteering for extra work either. About the Rebellion and its results he would express no opinion. When asked whether he was not happier now that Jones was gone, he would say only 'Donkeys live a long time. None of you has ever seen a dead donkey,' and the others had to be content with this cryptic answer.

On Sundays there was no work. Breakfast was an hour later than usual, and after breakfast there was a ceremony which was observed every week without fail. First came the hoisting of the flag. Snowball had found in the harness-room an old green tablecloth of Mrs Jones's and had painted on it a hoof and a horn in white. This was run up the flagstaff in the farmhouse garden every Sunday morning. The flag was green, Snowball explained, to represent the green fields of England, while the hoof and horn signified the future Republic of the Animals which would arise when the human race had been finally overthrown. After the hoisting of the flag all the animals trooped into the big barn for a general assembly which was known as the Meeting. Here the work of the coming week was planned out and resolutions were put forward and debated. It was always the pigs who put forward the resolutions. The other animals understood how to vote, but could never think of any resolutions of their own. Snowball and Napoleon were by far the most active in the debates. But it was noticed that these two were never in agreement: whatever suggestion either of them made, the other could be counted on to oppose it. Even when it was resolved—a thing no one could object to in itself—to set aside a small paddock behind the orchard as a home of rest for animals who were past work, there was a stormy debate over the correct retiring age for each class of animal. The meeting always ended with the singing of 'Beasts of England', and the afternoon was given up to recreation.

The pigs had set aside the harness-room as a headquarters for themselves. Here, in the evening, they studied blacksmithing, carpentering, and other necessary arts from books which they had brought out of the farmhouse. Snowball also busied himself with organizing the other animals into what he called Animal Committees. He was indefatigable at this. He formed the Egg Production Committee for the hens, the Clean Tails League for the cows, the Wild Comrades' Re-education Committee (the object of this was to tame the rats and rabbits), the Whiter Wool Movement for the sheep, and various others, besides instituting classes in reading and writing. On the whole, these projects were a failure. The attempt to tame the wild creatures, for instance, broke down almost immediately. They continued to behave very much as before, and when treated with generosity, simply took advantage of it. The cat joined the Re-education Committee and was very active in it for some days. She was seen one day sitting on a roof and talking to some sparrows who were just out of her reach. She was telling them that all animals were now comrades and that any sparrow who chose could come and perch on her paw; but the sparrows kept their distance.

The reading and writing classes, however, were a great success. By the autumn almost every animal on the farm was literate in some degree.

As for the pigs, they could already read and write perfectly. The dogs learned to read fairly well, but were not interested in reading anything except the Seven Commandments. Muriel, the goat, could read somewhat better than the dogs, and sometimes used to read to the others in the evenings from scraps of newspaper which she found on the rubbish heap. Benjamin could read as well as any pig, but never exercised his faculty. So far as he knew, he said, there was nothing worth reading. Clover learnt the whole alphabet, but could not put words together. Boxer could not get beyond the letter D. He would trace out A, B, C, D, in the dust with his great hoof, and then would stand staring at the letters with his ears back, sometimes shaking his forelock, trying with all his might to remember what came next and never succeeding. On several occasions, indeed, he did learn E, F, G, H, and by the time he knew them, it was always discovered that he had forgotten A, B, C, and D. Finally he decided to be content with the first four letters, and used to write them out once or twice every day to refresh his memory. Mollie refused to learn any but the six letters which spelt her own name. She would form these very neatly out of pieces of twig, and would then decorate them with a flower or two and walk round them admiring them.

None of the other animals on the farm could get further than the letter A. It was also found that the stupider animals, such as the sheep, hens, and ducks, were unable to learn the Seven Commandments by heart. After much thought Snowball declared that the Seven Commandments could in effect be reduced to a single maxim, namely: 'Four legs good, two legs bad.' This, he said, contained the essential principle of Animalism. Whoever had thoroughly grasped it would be safe from human influences. The birds at first objected, since it seemed to them that they also had two legs, but Snowball proved to them that this was not so.

'A bird's wing, comrades,' he said, 'is an organ of propulsion and not of manipulation. It should therefore be regarded as a leg. The distinguishing mark of Man is the *hand*, the instrument with which he does all his mischief.'

The birds did not understand Snowball's long words, but they accepted his explanation, and all the humbler animals set to work to learn the new maxim by heart. FOUR LEGS GOOD, TWO LEGS BAD, was inscribed on the end wall of the barn, above the Seven Commandments and in bigger letters. When they had once got it by heart, the sheep developed a great liking for this maxim, and often as they lay in the field they would all start bleating 'Four legs good, two legs bad! Four legs good, two legs bad!' and keep it up for hours on end, never growing tired of it.

Napoleon took no interest in Snowball's committees. He said that the education of the young was more important than anything that could be done for those who were already grown up. It happened that Jessie and Bluebell had both whelped soon after the hay harvest, giving birth between them to nine sturdy puppies. As soon as they were weaned, Napoleon took them away from their mothers, saying that he would make himself responsible for their education. He took them up into a loft which could only be reached by a ladder from the harness-room, and there kept them in such seclusion that the rest of the farm soon forgot their existence.

The mystery of where the milk went to was soon cleared up. It was mixed every day into the pigs' mash. The early apples were now ripening, and the grass of the orchard was littered with windfalls. The animals had assumed as a matter of course that these would be shared out equally; one day, however, the order went forth that all the windfalls were to be collected and brought to the harness-room for the use of the pigs. At this some of the other animals murmured, but it was no use. All the pigs were in full agreement on this point, even Snowball and Napoleon. Squealer was sent to make the necessary explanation to the others.

'Comrades!' he cried. 'You do not imagine, I hope, that we pigs are doing this in a spirit of selfishness and privilege? Many of us actually dislike milk and apples. I dislike them myself. Our sole object in taking these things is to preserve our health. Milk and apples (this has been proved by Science, comrades) contain substances absolutely necessary to the well-being of a pig. We pigs are brain-workers. The whole management and organization of this farm depend on us. Day and night we are watching over your welfare. It is for your sake that we drink that milk and eat those apples. Do you know what would happen if we pigs failed in our duty? Jones would come back! Yes, Jones would come back! Surely, comrades,' cried Squealer almost pleadingly, skipping from side to side and whisking his tail, 'surely there is no one among you who wants to see Jones come back?'

Now if there was one thing that the animals were completely certain of, it was that they did not want Jones back. When it was put to them in this light, they had no more to say. The importance of keeping the pigs in good health was all too obvious. So it was agreed without further argument that the milk and the windfall apples (and also the main crop of apples when they ripened) should be reserved for the pigs alone.

# 4

By the late summer the news of what had happened on Animal Farm had spread across half the country. Every day Snowball and Napoleon sent out flights of pigeons whose instructions were to mingle with the animals on neighbouring farms, tell them the story of the Rebellion, and teach them the tune of 'Beasts of England'.

Most of this time Mr Jones had spent sitting in the taproom of the Red Lion at Willingdon, complaining to anyone who would listen of the monstrous injustice he had suffered in being turned out of his property by a pack of good-for-nothing animals. The other farmers sympathized in principle, but they did not at first give him much help. At heart, each of them was secretly wondering whether he could not somehow turn Jones's misfortune to his own advantage. It was lucky that the owners of the two farms which adjoined Animal Farm were on permanently bad terms. One of them, which was named Foxwood, was a large, neglected, old-fashioned farm, much overgrown by woodland, with all its pastures worn out and its hedges in a disgraceful condition. Its owner, Mr Pilkington, was an easy-going gentleman farmer who spent most of his time in fishing or hunting according to the season. The other farm, which was called Pinchfield, was smaller and better kept. Its owner was a Mr Frederick, a tough, shrewd man, perpetually involved in lawsuits and with a name for driving hard bargains. These two disliked each other so much that it was difficult for them to come to any agreement, even in defence of their own interests.

Nevertheless they were both thoroughly frightened by the rebellion on

Animal Farm, and very anxious to prevent their own animals from learning too much about it. At first they pretended to laugh to scorn the idea of animals managing a farm for themselves. The whole thing would be over in a fortnight, they said. They put it about that the animals on the Manor Farm (they insisted on calling it the Manor Farm; they would not tolerate the name 'Animal Farm') were perpetually fighting among themselves and were also rapidly starving to death. When time passed and the animals had evidently not starved to death, Frederick and Pilkington changed their tune and began to talk of the terrible wickedness that now flourished on Animal Farm. It was given out that the animals there practised cannibalism, tortured one another with red-hot horseshoes, and had their females in common. This was what came of rebelling against the laws of Nature, Frederick and Pilkington said.

However, these stories were never fully believed. Rumours of a wonderful farm, where the human beings had been turned out and the animals managed their own affairs, continued to circulate in vague and distorted forms, and throughout that year a wave of rebelliousness ran through the countryside. Bulls which had always been tractable suddenly turned savage, sheep broke down hedges and devoured the clover, cows kicked the pail over, hunters refused their fences and shot their riders on to the other side. Above all, the tune and even the words of 'Beasts of England' were known everywhere. It had spread with astonishing speed. The human beings could not contain their rage when they heard this song, though they pretended to think it merely ridiculous. They could not understand, they said, how even animals could bring themselves to sing such contemptible rubbish. Any animal caught singing it was given a flogging on the spot. And yet the song was irrepressible. The blackbirds whistled it in the hedges, the pigeons cooed it in the elms, it got into the din of the smithies and the tune of the church bells. And when the human beings listened to it, they secretly trembled, hearing in it a prophecy of their future doom.

Early in October, when the corn was cut and stacked and some of it was already threshed, a flight of pigeons came whirling through the air and alighted in the yard of Animal Farm in the wildest excitement. Jones and all his men, with half a dozen others from Foxwood and Pinchfield, had entered the five-barred gate and were coming up the cart-track that led to the farm. They were all carrying sticks, except Jones, who was marching ahead with a gun in his hands. Obviously they were going to attempt the recapture of the farm.

This had long been expected, and all preparations had been made. Snowball, who had studied an old book of Julius Caesar's campaigns which he had found in the farmhouse, was in charge of the defensive operations. He gave his orders quickly, and in a couple of minutes every animal was at his post.

As the human beings approached the farm buildings, Snowball launched his first attack. All the pigeons, to the number of thirty-five, flew to and fro over the men's heads and muted upon them from mid-air; and while the men were dealing with this, the geese, who had been hiding behind the hedge, rushed out and pecked viciously at the calves of their legs. However, this was only a light skirmishing manœuvre, intended to create a little disorder, and the men easily drove the geese off with their sticks. Snowball now launched his second line of attack. Muriel, Benjamin, and all the sheep, with Snowball at the head of them, rushed forward and prodded and butted the men from every side, while Benjamin turned round and lashed at them with his small hoofs. But once again the men, with their sticks and their hobnailed boots, were too strong for them; and suddenly, at a squeal from Snowball, which was the signal for retreat, all the animals turned and fled through the gateway into the yard.

The men gave a shout of triumph. They saw, as they imagined, their enemies in flight, and they rushed after them in disorder. This was just what Snowball had intended. As soon as they were well inside the yard, the three horses, the three cows, and the rest of the pigs, who had been lying in ambush in the cowshed, suddenly emerged in their rear, cutting them off. Snowball now gave the signal for the charge. He himself dashed straight for Jones. Jones saw him coming, raised his gun, and fired. The pellets scored bloody streaks along Snowball's back, and a sheep dropped dead. Without halting for an instant Snowball flung his fifteen stone against Jones's legs. Jones was hurled into a pile of dung and his gun flew out of his hands. But the most terrifying spectacle of all was Boxer, rearing up on his hind legs and striking out with his great iron-shod hoofs like a stallion. His very first blow took a stable-lad from Foxwood on the skull and stretched him lifeless in the mud. At the sight, several men dropped their sticks and tried to run. Panic overtook them and the next moment all the animals together were chasing them round and round the yard. They were gored, kicked, bitten, trampled on. There was not an animal on the farm that did not take vengeance on them after his own fashion. Even the cat suddenly leapt off a roof on to a cowman's shoulders and sank her claws in his neck, at which he yelled horribly. At a moment when the opening was clear, the men were glad enough to rush out of the yard and make a bolt for the main road. And so within five minutes of their invasion they were in ignominious retreat by the same way as they had come, with a flock of geese hissing after them and pecking at their calves all the way.

All the men were gone except one. Back in the yard Boxer was pawing with his hoof at the stable-lad who lay face down in the mud, trying to turn him over. The boy did not stir.

'He is dead,' said Boxer sorrowfully. 'I had no intention of doing that. I forgot that I was wearing iron shoes. Who will believe that I did not do this on purpose?'

'No sentimentality, comrade!' cried Snowball, from whose wounds the blood was still dripping. 'War is war. The only good human being is a dead one.'

'I have no wish to take life, not even human life,' repeated Boxer, and his eyes were full of tears.

'Where is Mollie?' exclaimed somebody.

Mollie was in fact missing. For a moment there was great alarm; it was feared that the men might have harmed her in some way, or even carried her off with them. In the end, however, she was found hiding in her stall with her head buried among the hay in the manger. She had taken to flight as soon as the gun went off. And when the others came back from looking for her, it was to find that the stable-lad, who in fact was only stunned, had already recovered and made off.

The animals had now reassembled in the wildest excitement, each recounting his own exploits in the battle at the top of his voice. An impromptu celebration of the victory was held immediately. The flag was run up and 'Beasts of England' was sung a number of times, then the sheep who had been killed was given a solemn funeral, a hawthorn bush being planted on her grave. At the graveside Snowball made a little speech, emphasizing the need for all animals to be ready to die for Animal Farm if need be.

The animals decided unanimously to create a military decoration, 'Animal Hero, First Class', which was conferred there and then on Snowball and Boxer. It consisted of a brass medal (they were really some old horse-brasses which had been found in the harness-room), to be worn on Sundays and holidays. There was also 'Animal Hero, Second Class', which was conferred posthumously on the dead sheep.

There was much discussion as to what the battle should be called. In the end, it was named the Battle of the Cowshed, since that was where the ambush had been sprung. Mr Jones's gun had been found lying in the mud, and it was known that there was a supply of cartridges in the farmhouse. It was decided to set the gun up at the foot of the flagstaff, like a piece of artillery, and to fire it twice a year—once on October the twelfth, the anniversary of the Battle of the Cowshed, and once on Midsummer Day, the anniversary of the Rebellion.

# 5

As winter drew on, Mollie became more and more troublesome. She was late for work every morning and excused herself by saying that she had overslept, and she complained of mysterious pains, although her appetite was excellent. On every kind of pretext she would run away from work and go to the drinking pool, where she would stand foolishly gazing at her own reflection in the water. But there were also rumours of something more serious. One day as Mollie strolled blithely into the yard, flirting her long tail and chewing at a stalk of hay, Clover took her aside.

'Mollie,' she said, 'I have something very serious to say to you. This morning I saw you looking over the hedge that divides Animal Farm from Foxwood. One of Mr Pilkington's men was standing on the other side of the hedge. And—I was a long way away, but I am almost certain I saw this—he was talking to you and you were allowing him to stroke your nose. What does that mean, Mollie?'

'He didn't! I wasn't! It isn't true!' cried Mollie, beginning to prance about and paw the ground.

'Mollie! Look me in the face. Do you give me your word of honour that the man was not stroking your nose?'

'It isn't true!' repeated Mollie, but she could not look Clover in the face, and the next moment she took to her heels and galloped away into the field.

A thought struck Clover. Without saying anything to the others, she went to Mollie's stall and turned over the straw with her hoof. Hidden under the straw was a little pile of lump sugar and several bunches of ribbon of different colours.

Three days later Mollie disappeared. For some weeks nothing was known of her whereabouts, then the pigeons reported that they had seen her on the other side of Willingdon. She was between the shafts of a smart dogcart painted red and black, which was standing outside a public-house. A fat red-faced man in check breeches and gaiters, who looked like a publican, was stroking her nose and feeding her with sugar. Her coat was newly clipped and she wore a scarlet ribbon round her forelock. She appeared to be enjoying herself, so the pigeons said. None of the animals ever mentioned Mollie again.

In January there came bitterly hard weather. The earth was like iron, and nothing could be done in the fields. Many meetings were held in the big barn, and the pigs occupied themselves with planning out the work of the coming season. It had come to be accepted that the pigs, who were manifestly cleverer than the other animals, should decide all questions of farm policy, though their decisions had to be ratified by a majority vote. This arrangement would have worked well enough if it had not been for the disputes between Snowball and Napoleon. These two disagreed at every point where disagreement was possible. If one of them suggested sowing a bigger acreage with barley, the other was certain to demand a bigger acreage of oats, and if one of them said that such and such a field was just right for cabbages, the other would declare that it was useless for anything except roots. Each had his own following, and there were some violent debates. At the meetings Snowball often won over the majority by his brilliant speeches, but Napoleon was better at canvassing support for himself in between times. He was especially successful with the sheep. Of late the sheep had taken to bleating 'Four legs good, two legs bad' both in and out of season, and they often interrupted the Meeting with this. It was noticed that they were especially liable to break into 'Four legs good, two legs bad' at the crucial moments in Snowball's speeches. Snowball had made a close study of some back numbers of the *Farmer and Stockbreeder* which he had found in the farmhouse, and was full of plans for innovations and improvements. He talked learnedly about field-drains, silage, and basic slag, and had worked out a complicated scheme for all the animals to drop their dung directly in the fields, at a different spot every day, to save the labour of cartage. Napoleon produced no schemes of his own, but said quietly that Snowball's would come to nothing, and seemed to be biding his time. But of all their controversies, none was so bitter as the one that took place over the windmill.

In the long pasture, not far from the farm buildings , there was a small knoll which was the highest point on the farm. After surveying the ground, Snowball declared that this was just the place for a windmill, which could be made to operate a dynamo and supply the farm with electrical power. This would light the stalls and warm them in winter, and would also run a circular saw, a chaff-cutter, a mangel-slicer, and an electric milking machine. The animals had never heard of anything of this kind before (for the farm was an old-fashioned one and had only the most primitive machinery), and they listened in astonishment while Snowball conjured up pictures of fantastic machines which would do their work for them while they grazed at their ease in the fields or improved their minds with reading and conversation.

Within a few weeks Snowball's plans for the windmill were fully worked out. The mechanical details came mostly from three books which had belonged to Mr Jones—*One Thousand Useful Things to Do About the House, Every Man His Own Bricklayer*, and *Electricity for Beginners*. Snowball used as his study a shed which had once been used for incubators and had a smooth wooden floor suitable for drawing on. He was closeted there for hours at a time. With his books held open by a stone, and with a piece of chalk gripped between the knuckles of his trotter, he would move rapidly to and fro, drawing in line after line and uttering little whimpers of excitement. Gradually the plans grew into a complicated mass of cranks and cog-wheels, covering more than half the floor, which the other animals found completely unintelligible but very impressive. All of them came to look at Snowball's drawings at least once a day. Even the hens and ducks came, and were at pains not to tread on the chalk marks. Only Napoleon held aloof. He had declared himself against the windmill from the start. One day, however, he arrived unexpectedly to examine the plans. He walked heavily round the shed, looked closely at every detail of the plans and snuffed at them once or twice, then stood for a little while contemplating them out of the corner of his eye; then suddenly he lifted his leg, urinated over the plans, and walked out without uttering a word.

The whole farm was deeply divided on the subject of the windmill. Snowball did not deny that to build it would be a difficult business. Stone would have to be quarried and built up into walls, then the sails would have to be made and after that there would be need for dynamos and cables. (How these were to be procured, Snowball did not say.) But he maintained that it could all be done in a year. And thereafter, he declared, so much labour would be saved that the animals would only need to work three days a week. Napoleon, on the other hand, argued that the great need of the moment was to increase food production, and that if they wasted time on the windmill they would all starve to death. The animals formed themselves into two factions under the slogans, 'Vote for Snowball and the three-day week' and 'Vote for Napoleon and the full manger'. Benjamin was the only animal who did not side with either faction. He refused to believe either that food would become more plentiful or that the windmill would save work. Windmill or no windmill, he said, life would go on as it had always gone on—that is, badly.

Apart from the disputes over the windmill, there was the question of the defence of the farm. It was fully realized that though the human beings had been defeated in the Battle of the Cowshed they might make another and more determined attempt to recapture the farm and reinstate Mr Jones. They had all the more reason for doing so because the news of their defeat had spread across the countryside and made the animals on the neighbouring farms more restive than ever. As usual, Snowball and Napoleon were in disagreement. According to Napoleon, what the animals must do was to procure fire-arms and train themselves in the use of them. According to Snowball, they must send out more and more pigeons and stir up rebellion among the animals on the other farms. The one argued that if they could not defend themselves they were bound to be conquered, the other argued that if rebellions happened everywhere they would have no need to defend themselves. The animals listened first to Napoleon, then to Snowball, and could not make up their minds which was right; indeed, they always found themselves in agreement with the one who was speaking at the moment.

At last the day came when Snowball's plans were completed. At the Meeting on the following Sunday the question of whether or not to begin work on the windmill was to be put to the vote. When the animals had assembled in the big barn, Snowball stood up and, though occasionally interrupted by bleating from the sheep, set forth his reasons for advocating the building of the windmill. Then Napoleon stood up to reply. He said very quietly that the windmill was nonsense and that he advised nobody to vote for it, promptly sat down again; he had spoken for barely thirty seconds, and seemed almost indifferent as to the effect he produced. At this Snowball sprang to his feet, and shouting down the sheep, who had began bleating again, broke into a passionate appeal in favour of the windmill. Until now the animals had been about equally divided in their sympathies, but in a moment Snowball's eloquence had carried them away. In glowing sentences he painted a picture of Animal Farm as it might be when sordid labour was lifted from the animals' backs. His imagination had now run far beyond chaff-cutters and turnip-slicers. Electricity, he said, could operate threshing machines, ploughs, harrows, rollers, and reapers and binders, besides supplying every stall with its own electric light, hot and cold water, and an electric heater. By the time he had finished speaking, there was no doubt as to which way the vote would go. But just at this moment Napoleon stood up and, casting a peculiar sidelong look at Snowball, uttered a high-pitched whimper of a kind no one had ever heard him utter before.

At this there was a terrible baying sound outside, and nine enormous dogs wearing brass-studded collars came bounding into the barn. They dashed straight for Snowball, who only sprang from his place just in time to escape their snapping jaws. In a moment he was out of the door and they were after him. Too amazed and frightened to speak, all the animals crowded through the door to watch the chase. Snowball was racing across the long pasture that led to the road. He was running as only a pig can run, but the dogs were close on his heels. Suddenly he slipped and it seemed certain that they had him. Then he was up again, running faster than ever, then the dogs were gaining on him again. One of them all but closed his jaws on Snowball's tail, but Snowball whisked it free just in time. Then he put on an extra spurt and, with a few inches to spare, slipped through a hole in the hedge and was seen no more.

Silent and terrified, the animals crept back into the barn. In a moment the dogs came bounding back. At first no one had been able to imagine where these creatures came from, but the problem was soon solved: they were the puppies whom Napoleon had taken away from their mothers and reared privately. Though not yet full-grown, they were huge dogs, and as fierce-looking as wolves. They kept close to Napoleon. It was noticed that they wagged their tails to him in the same way as the other dogs had been used to do to Mr Jones.

Napoleon, with the dogs following him, now mounted on to the raised portion of the floor where Major had previously stood to deliver his speech. He announced that from now on the Sunday morning Meetings would come to an end. They were unnecessary, he said, and wasted time. In future all questions relating to the working of the farm would be settled by a special committee of pigs, presided over by himself. These would meet in private and afterwards communicate their decisions to the others. The animals would still assemble on Sunday mornings to salute the flag, sing 'Beasts of England', and receive their orders for the week; but there would be no more debates.

In spite of the shock that Snowball's expulsion had given them, the animals were dismayed by this announcement. Several of them would have protested if they could have found the right arguments. Even Boxer was vaguely troubled. He set his ears back, shook his forelock several times, and tried hard to marshal his thoughts; but in the end he could not think of anything to say. Some of the pigs themselves, however, were more articulate. Four young porkers in the front row uttered shrill squeals of disapproval, and all four of them sprang to their feet and began speaking at once. But suddenly the dogs sitting round Napoleon let out deep, menacing growls, and the pigs fell silent and sat down again. Then the sheep broke out into a tremendous bleating of 'Four legs good, two legs bad!' which went on for nearly a quarter of an hour and put an end to any chance of discussion.

Afterwards Squealer was sent round the farm to explain the new arrangements to the others.

'Comrades,' he said, 'I trust that every animal here appreciates the sacrifice that Comrade Napoleon has made in taking this extra labour upon himself. Do not imagine, comrade, that leadership is a pleasure! On the contrary, it is a deep and heavy responsibility. No one believes more firmly than Comrade Napoleon that all animals are equal. He would be only too happy to let you make your decisions for yourselves. But sometimes you might make the wrong decisions, comrades, and then where should we be? Suppose you had decided to follow Snowball, with his moonshine of windmills–Snowball, who, as we now know, was no better than a criminal?'

'He fought bravely at the Battle of the Cowshed,' said somebody.

'Bravery is not enough,' said Squealer. 'Loyalty and obedience are more important. And as to the Battle of the Cowshed, I believe the time will come when we shall find that Snowball's part in it was much exaggerated. Discipline, comrades, iron discipline! That is the watchword for today. One false step, and our enemies would be upon us. Surely, comrades, you do not want Jones back?'

Once again this argument was unanswerable. Certainly the animals did not want Jones back; if the holding of debates on Sunday mornings was liable to bring him back, then the debates must stop. Boxer, who had now had time to think things over, voiced the general feeling by saying: 'if Comrade Napoleon says it, it must be right'. And from then on he adopted the maxim, 'Napoleon is always right,' in addition to his private motto of 'I will work harder.'

By this time the weather had broken and the spring ploughing had begun. The shed where Snowball had drawn his plans of the windmill had been shut up and it was assumed that the plans had been rubbed off the floor. Every Sunday morning at ten o'clock the animals assembled in the big barn to receive their orders for the week. The skull of old Major, now clean of flesh, had been disinterred from the orchard and set up on a stump at the foot of the flagstaff, beside the gun. After the hoisting of the flag, the animals were required to file past the skull in a reverent manner before entering the barn. Nowadays they did not sit all together as they had done in the past. Napoleon, with Squealer and another pig named Minimus, who had a remarkable gift for composing songs and poems, sat on the front of the raised platform, with the nine young dogs forming a semicircle round them, and the other pigs sitting behind. The rest of the animals sat facing them in the main body of the barn. Napoleon read out the orders for the week in a gruff soldierly style, and after a single singing of 'Beasts of England', all the animals dispersed.

On the third Sunday after Snowball's expulsion, the animals were somewhat surprised to hear Napoleon announce that the windmill was to be built after all. He did not give any reasons for having changed his mind, but merely warned the animals that this extra task would mean very hard work; it might even be necessary to reduce their rations. The plans, however, had all been prepared, down to the last detail. A special committee of pigs had been at work upon them for the past three weeks. The building of the windmill, with various other improvements, was expected to take two years.

That evening Squealer explained privately to the other animals that Napoleon had never in reality been opposed to the windmill. On the contrary, it was he who had advocated it in the beginning, and the plan which Snowball had drawn on the floor of the incubator shed had actually been stolen from among Napoleon's papers. The windmill was, in fact, Napoleon's own creation. Why, then, asked somebody, had he spoken so strongly against it? Here Squealer looked very sly. That, he said, was Comrade Napoleon's cunning. He had *seemed* to oppose the windmill, simply as a manœuvre to get rid of Snowball, who was a dangerous character and a bad influence. Now that Snowball was out of the way, the plan could go forward without his interference. This, said Squealer, was something called tactics. He repeated a number of times, 'Tactics, comrades, tactics!' skipping round and whisking his tail with a merry laugh. The animals were not certain what the word meant, but Squealer spoke so persuasively, and the three dogs who happened to be with him growled so threateningly, that they accepted his explanation without further questions.

# 6

All that year the animals worked like slaves. But they were happy in their work; they grudged no effort or sacrifice, well aware that everything that they did was for the benefit of themselves and those of their kind who would come after them, and not for a pack of idle, thieving human beings.

Throughout the spring and summer they worked a sixty-hour week, and in August Napoleon announced that there would be work on Sunday afternoons as well. This work was strictly voluntary, but any animal who absented himself from it would have his rations reduced by half. Even so, it was found necessary to leave certain tasks undone. The harvest was a little less successful than in the previous year, and two fields which should have been sown with roots in the early summer were not sown because the ploughing had not been completed early enough. It was possible to foresee that the coming winter would be a hard one.

The windmill presented unexpected difficulties. There was a good quarry of limestone on the farm, and plenty of sand and cement had been found in one of the outhouses, so that all the materials for building were at hand. But the problem the animals could not at first solve was how to break up the stones into pieces of suitable size. There seemed no way of doing this except with picks and crowbars, which no animal could use, because no animal could stand on his hind legs. Only after weeks of vain effort did the right idea occur to somebody—namely, to utilize the force of gravity. Huge boulders, far too big to be used as they were, were lying all over the bed of the quarry. The animals lashed ropes round these, and then all together, cows, horses, sheep, any animal that could lay hold of the rope—even the pigs sometimes joined in at critical moments—they dragged them with desperate slowness up the slope to the top of the quarry, where they were toppled over the edge, to shatter to pieces below. Transporting the stone when it was once broken was comparatively simple. The horses carried it off in cartloads, the sheep dragged single blocks, even Muriel and Benjamin yoked themselves into an old governess-cart and did their share. By late summer a sufficient store of stone had accumulated, and then the building began, under the superintendence of the pigs.

But it was a slow, laborious process. Frequently it took a whole day of exhausting effort to drag a single boulder to the top of the quarry, and sometimes when it was pushed over the edge it failed to break. Nothing could have been achieved without Boxer, whose strength seemed equal to that of all the rest of the animals put together. When the boulder began to slip and the animals cried out in despair at finding themselves dragged down the hill, it was always Boxer who strained himself against the rope and brought the boulder to a stop. To see him toiling up the slope inch by inch, his breath coming fast, the tips of his hoofs clawing at the ground, and his great sides matted with sweat, filled everyone with admiration. Clover warned him sometimes to be careful not to overstrain himself, but Boxer would never listen to her. His two slogans, 'I will work harder' and 'Napoleon is always right', seemed to him a sufficient answer to all problems. He had made arrangements with the cockerel to call him three-quarters of an hour earlier in the morning instead of half an hour. And in his spare moments, of which there were not many nowadays, he would go alone to the quarry, collect a load of broken stone, and drag it down to the site of the windmill unassisted.

The animals were not badly off throughout that summer, in spite of the hardness of their work. If they had no more food than they had in Jones's day, at least they did not have less. The advantage of only having to feed themselves, and not having to support five extravagant human beings as well, was so great that it would have taken a lot of failures to outweigh it. And in many ways the animal method of doing things was more efficient and saved labour. Such jobs as weeding, for instance, could be done with a thoroughness impossible to human beings. And again, since no animal now stole, it was unnecessary to fence off pasture from arable land, which saved a lot of labour on the upkeep of hedges and gates. Nevertheless, as the summer wore on, various unforeseen shortages began to make themselves felt. There was need of paraffin oil, nails, string, dog biscuits, and iron for the horses' shoes, none of which could be produced on the farm. Later there would also be need for seeds and artificial manure, besides various tools and, finally, the machinery for the windmill. How these were to be procured, no one was able to imagine.

One Sunday morning, when the animals assembled to receive their orders, Napoleon announced that he had decided upon a new policy. From now onwards Animal Farm would engage in trade with the neighbouring farms: not, of course, for any commercial purpose, but simply in order to obtain certain materials which were urgently necessary. The needs of the windmill must override everything else, he said. He was therefore making arrangements to sell a stack of hay and part of the current year's wheat crop, and later on, if more money were needed, it would have to be made up by the sale of eggs, for which there was always a market in Willingdon. The hens, said Napoleon, should welcome this sacrifice as their own special contribution towards the building of the windmill.

Once again the animals were conscious of a vague uneasiness. Never to have any dealings with human beings, never to engage in trade, never to make use of money—had not these been among the earliest resolutions passed at that first triumphant Meeting after Jones was expelled? All the animals remembered passing such resolutions: or at least they thought that they remembered it. The four young pigs who had protested when Napoleon abolished the Meetings raised their voices timidly, but they were promptly silenced by a tremendous growling from the dogs. Then, as usual, the sheep broke into 'Four legs good, two legs bad!' and the momentary awkwardness was smoothed over. Finally Napoleon raised his trotter for silence and announced that he had already made all the arrangements. There would be no need for any of the animals to come in contact with human beings, which would clearly be most undesirable. He intended to take the whole burden upon his own shoulders. A Mr Whymper, a solicitor living in Willingdon, had agreed to act as intermediary between Animal Farm and the outside world, and would visit the farm every Monday morning to receive his instructions. Napoleon ended his speech with his usual cry of 'Long live Animal Farm!', and after the singing of 'Beasts of England' the animals were dismissed.

Afterwards Squealer made a round of the farm and set the animals' minds at rest. He assured them that the resolution against engaging in trade and using money had never been passed, or even suggested. It was pure imagination, probably traceable in the beginning to lies circulated by Snowball. A few animals still felt faintly doubtful, but Squealer asked them shrewdly, 'Are you certain that this is not something that you have dreamed, comrades? Have you any record of such a resolution? Is it written down anywhere?' And since it was certainly true that nothing of the kind existed in writing, the animals were satisfied that they had been mistaken.

Every Monday Mr Whymper visited the farm as had been arranged. He was a sly-looking little man with side whiskers, a solicitor in a very small way of business, but sharp enough to have realized earlier than anyone else that Animal Farm would need a broker and that the commissions would be worth having. The animals watched his coming and going with a kind of dread, and avoided him as much as possible. Nevertheless, the sight of Napoleon, on all fours, delivering orders to Whymper, who stood on two legs, roused their pride and partly reconciled them to the new arrangement. Their relations with the human race were now not quite the same as they had been before. The human beings did not hate Animal Farm any less now that it was prospering; indeed, they hated it more than ever. Every human being held it as an article of faith that the farm would go bankrupt sooner or later, and, above all, that the windmill would be a failure. They would meet in the public-houses and prove to one another by means of diagrams that the windmill was bound to fall down, or that if it did stand up, then that it would never work. And yet, against their will, they had developed a certain respect for the efficiency with which the animals were managing their own affairs. One symptom of this was that they had begun to call Animal Farm by its proper name and ceased to pretend that it was called the Manor Farm. They had also dropped their championship of Jones, who had given up hope of getting his farm back and gone to live in another part of the country. Except through Whymper, there was as yet no contact between Animal Farm and the outside world, but there were constant rumours that Napoleon was about to enter into a definite business agreement either with Mr Pilkington of Foxwood or with Mr Frederick of Pinchfield—but never, it was noticed, with both simultaneously.

It was about this time that the pigs suddenly moved into the farmhouse and took up their residence there. Again the animals seemed to remember that a resolution against this had been passed in the early days, and again Squealer was able to convince them that this was not the case. It was absolutely necessary, he said, that the pigs, who were the brains of the farm, should have a quiet place to work in. It was also more suited to the dignity of the Leader (for of late he had taken to speaking of Napoleon under the title of 'Leader') to live in a house than in a mere sty. Nevertheless, some of the animals were disturbed when they heard that the pigs not only took their meals in the kitchen and used the drawing-room as a recreation room but also slept in the beds. Boxer passed it off as usual with 'Napoleon is always right!', but Clover, who thought she remembered a definite ruling against beds, went to the end of the barn and tried to puzzle out the Seven Commandments which were inscribed there. Finding herself unable to read more than individual letters, she fetched Muriel.

'Muriel,' she said, 'read me the Fourth Commandment. Does it not say something about never sleeping in a bed?'

With some difficulty Muriel spelt it out.

'It says, "No animal shall sleep in a bed *with sheets*",' she announced finally.

Curiously enough, Clover had not remembered that the Fourth Commandment mentioned sheets; but as it was there on the wall, it must have done so. And Squealer, who happened to be passing at this moment, attended by two or three dogs, was able to put the whole matter in its proper perspective.

'You have heard then, comrades,' he said, 'that we pigs now sleep in the beds of the farmhouse? And why not? You did not suppose, surely, that there was ever a ruling against *beds*? A bed merely means a place to sleep in. A pile of straw in a stall is a bed, properly regarded. The rule was against *sheets,* which are a human invention. We have removed the sheets from the farmhouse beds, and sleep between blankets. And very comfortable beds they are too! But not more comfortable than we need, I can tell you, comrades, with all the brainwork we have to do nowadays. You would not rob us of our repose, would you, comrades? You would not have us too tired to carry out our duties? Surely none of you wishes to see Jones back?'

The animals reassured him on this point immediately, and no more was said about the pigs sleeping in the farmhouse beds. And when, some days afterwards, it was announced that from now on the pigs would get up an hour later in the mornings than the other animals, no complaint was made about that either.

By the autumn the animals were tired but happy. They had had a hard year, and after the sale of part of the hay and corn, the stores of food for the winter were none too plentiful, but the windmill compensated for everything. It was almost half built now. After the harvest there was a stretch of clear dry weather, and the animals toiled harder than ever, thinking it well worth while to plod to and fro all day with blocks of stone if by doing so they could raise the walls another foot. Boxer would even come out at nights and work for an hour or two on his own by the light of the harvest moon. In their spare moments the animals would walk round and round the half-finished mill, admiring the strength and perpendicularity of its walls and marvelling that they should ever have been able to build anything so imposing. Only old Benjamin refused to grow enthusiastic about the windmill, though, as usual, he would utter nothing beyond the cryptic remark that donkeys live a long time.

November came, with raging south-west winds. Building had to stop because it was now too wet to mix the cement. Finally there came a night when the gale was so violent that the farm buildings rocked on their foundations and several tiles were blown off the roof of the barn. The hens woke up squawking with terror because they had all dreamed simultaneously of hearing a gun go off in the distance. In the morning the animals came out of their stalls to find that the flagstaff had blown down and an elm tree at the foot of the orchard had been plucked up like a radish. They had just noticed this when a cry of despair broke from every animal's throat. A terrible sight had met their eyes. The windmill was in ruins.

With one accord they dashed down to the spot. Napoleon, who seldom moved out of a walk, raced ahead of them all. Yes, there it lay, the fruit of all their struggles, levelled to its foundations, the stones they had broken and carried so laboriously scattered all around. Unable at first to speak, they stood gazing mournfully at the litter of fallen stone. Napoleon paced to and fro in silence, occasionally snuffing at the ground. His tail had grown rigid and twitched sharply from side to side, a sign in him of intense mental activity. Suddenly he halted as though his mind were made up.

'Comrades,' he said quietly, 'do you know who is responsible for this? Do you know the enemy who has come in the night and overthrown our windmill? SNOWBALL!' he suddenly roared in a voice of thunder. 'Snowball has done this thing! In sheer malignity, thinking to set back our plans and avenge himself for his ignominious expulsion, this traitor has crept here under cover of night and destroyed our work of nearly a year. Comrades, here and now I pronounce the death sentence upon Snowball. "Animal Hero, Second Class", and half a bushel of apples to any animal who brings him to justice. A full bushel to anyone who captures him alive!'

The animals were shocked beyond measure to learn that even Snowball could be guilty of such an action. There was a cry of indignation and everyone began thinking out ways of catching Snowball if he should ever come back. Almost immediately the footprints of a pig were discovered in the grass at a little distance from the knoll. They could only be traced for a few yards, but appeared to lead to a hole in the hedge. Napoleon snuffed deeply at them and pronounced them to be Snowball's. He gave it as his opinion that Snowball had probably come from the direction of Foxwood Farm.

'No more delays, comrades!' said Napoleon when the footprints had been examined. 'There is work to be done. This very morning we begin rebuilding the windmill, and we will build all through the winter, rain or shine. We will teach this miserable traitor that he cannot undo our work so easily. Remember, comrades, there must be no alteration in our plans: they shall be carried out to the day. Forward, comrades! Long live the windmill! Long live Animal Farm!'

# 7

It was a bitter winter. The stormy weather was followed by sleet and snow, and then by a hard frost which did not break till well into February. The animals carried on as best as they could with the rebuilding of the windmill, well knowing that the outside world was watching them and that the envious human beings would rejoice and triumph if the mill were not finished on time.

Out of spite, the human beings pretended not to believe that it was Snowball who had destroyed the windmill: they said that it had fallen down because the walls were too thin. The animals knew that this was not the case. Still, it had been decided to build the walls three feet thick this time instead of eighteen inches as before, which meant collecting much larger quantities of stone. For a long time the quarry was full of snowdrifts and nothing could be done. Some progress was made in the dry frosty weather that followed, but it was cruel work, and the animals could not feel so hopeful about it as they had felt before. They were always cold, and usually hungry as well. Only Boxer and Clover never lost heart. Squealer made excellent speeches on the joy of service and the dignity of labour, but the other animals found more inspiration in Boxer's strength and his never-failing cry of 'I will work harder!'

In January food fell short. The corn ration was drastically reduced, and it was announced that an extra potato ration would be issued to make up for it. Then it was discovered that the greater part of the potato crop had been frosted in the clamps, which had not been covered thickly enough. The potatoes had become soft and discoloured, and only a few were edible. For days at a time the animals had nothing to eat but chaff and mangels. Starvation seemed to stare them in the face.

It was vitally necessary to conceal this fact from the outside world. Emboldened by the collapse of the windmill, the human beings were inventing fresh lies about Animal Farm. Once again it was being put about that all the animals were dying of famine and disease, and that they were continually fighting among themselves and had resorted to cannibalism and infanticide. Napoleon was well aware of the bad results that might follow if the real facts of the food situation were known, and he decided to make use of Mr Whymper to spread a contrary impression. Hitherto the animals had had little or no contact with Whymper on his weekly visits: now, however, a few selected animals, mostly sheep, were instructed to remark casually in his hearing that rations had been increased. In addition, Napoleon ordered the almost empty bins in the store-shed to be filled nearly to the brim with sand, which was then covered up with what remained of the grain and meal. On some suitable pretext Whymper was led through the store-shed and allowed to catch a glimpse of the bins. He was deceived and continued to report to the outside world that there was no food shortage on Animal Farm.

Nevertheless, towards the end of January it became obvious that it would be necessary to procure some more grain from somewhere. In these days Napoleon rarely appeared in public, but spent all his time in the farmhouse, which was guarded at each door by fierce-looking dogs. When he did emerge, it was in a ceremonial manner, with an escort of six dogs who closely surrounded him and growled if anyone came too near. Frequently he did not even appear on Sunday mornings, but issued his orders through one of the other pigs, usually Squealer.

One Sunday morning Squealer announced that the hens, who had just come in to lay again, must surrender their eggs. Napoleon had accepted, through Whymper, a contract for four hundred eggs a week. The price of these would pay for enough grain and meal to keep the farm going till summer came on and conditions were easier.

When the hens heard this, they raised a terrible outcry. They had been warned earlier that this sacrifice might be necessary, but had not believed that it would really happen. They were just getting their clutches ready for the spring sitting, and they protested that to take the eggs away now was murder. For the first time since the expulsion of Jones there was something resembling a rebellion. Led by three young Black Minorca pullets, the hens made a determined effort to thwart Napoleon's wishes. Their method was to fly up to the rafters and there lay their eggs, which smashed to pieces on the floor. Napoleon acted swiftly and ruthlessly. He ordered the hen's rations to be stopped, and decreed that any animal giving so much as a grain of corn to a hen should be punished by death. The dogs saw to it that these orders were carried out. For five days the hens held out, then they capitulated and went back to their nesting boxes. Nine hens had died in the meantime. Their bodies were buried in the orchard, and it was given out they had died of coccidiosis. Whymper heard nothing of this affair, and the eggs were duly delivered, a grocer's van driving up to the farm once a week to take them away.

All this while no more had been seen of Snowball. He was rumoured to be hiding on one of the neighbouring farms, either Foxwood or Pinchfield. Napoleon was by this time on slightly better terms with the other farmers than before. It happened that there was in the yard a pile of timber which had been stacked there ten years earlier when a beech spinney was cleared. It was well seasoned, and Whymper had advised Napoleon to sell it; both Mr Pilkington and Mr Frederick were anxious to buy it. Napoleon was hesitating between the two, unable to make up his mind. It was noticed that whenever he seemed on the point of coming to an agreement with Frederick, Snowball was declared to be in hiding at Foxwood, while, when he inclined towards Pilkington, Snowball was said to be at Pinchfield.

Suddenly, early in the spring, an alarming thing was discovered. Snowball was secretly frequenting the farm by night! The animals were so disturbed that they could hardly sleep in their stalls. Every night, it was said, he came creeping in under cover of darkness and performed all kinds of mischief. He stole the corn, he upset the milk-pails, he broke the eggs, he trampled the seed-beds, he gnawed the bark off the fruit trees. Whenever anything went wrong it became usual to attribute it to Snowball. If a window was broken or a drain blocked up, someone was certain to say that Snowball had come in the night and done it, and when the key of the store-shed was lost, the whole farm was convinced that Snowball had thrown it down the well. Curiously enough, they went on believing this even after the mislaid key was found under a sack of meal. The cows declared unanimously that Snowball crept into their stalls and milked them in their sleep. The rats, which had been troublesome that winter, were also said to be in league with Snowball.

Napoleon decreed that there should be a full investigation into Snowball's activities. With his dogs in attendance he set out and made a careful tour of inspection of the farm buildings, the other animals following at a respectful distance. At every few steps Napoleon stopped and snuffed the ground for traces of Snowball's footsteps, which, he said, he could detect by the smell. He snuffed in every corner, in the barn, in the cowshed, in the hen-houses, in the vegetable garden, and found traces of Snowball almost everywhere. He would put his snout to the ground, give several deep sniffs, and exclaim in a terrible voice, 'Snowball! He has been here! I can smell him distinctly!' and at the word 'Snowball' all the dogs let out blood-curdling growls and showed their side teeth.

The animals were thoroughly frightened. It seemed to them as though Snowball were some kind of invisible influence, pervading the air about them and menacing them with all kinds of dangers. In the evening Squealer called them together, and with an alarmed expression on his face told them that he had some serious news to report.

'Comrades!' cried Squealer, making little nervous skips, 'a most terrible thing has been discovered. Snowball has sold himself to Frederick of Pinchfield Farm, who is even now plotting to attack us and take our farm away from us! Snowball is to act as his guide when the attack begins. But there is worse than that. We had thought that Snowball's rebellion was caused by his vanity and ambition. But we were wrong, comrades. Do you know what the real reason was? Snowball was in league with Jones from the very start! He was Jones's secret agent all the time. It has all been proved by documents which he left behind him and which we have only just discovered. To my mind this explains a great deal, comrades. Did we not see for ourselves how he attempted—fortunately without success—to get us defeated and destroyed at the Battle of the Cowshed?'

The animals were stupefied. This was a wickedness far outdoing Snowball's destruction of the windmill. But it was some minutes before they could fully take it in. They all remembered, or thought they remembered, how they had seen Snowball charging ahead of them in the Battle of the Cowshed, how he had rallied and encouraged them at every turn, and how he had not paused for an instant even when the pellets from Jones's gun had wounded his back. At first it was a little difficult to see how this fitted in with his being on Jones's side. Even Boxer, who seldom asked questions, was puzzled. He lay down, tucked his forehoofs beneath him, shut his eyes, and with a hard effort managed to formulate his thoughts.

'I do not believe that,' he said. 'Snowball fought bravely at the Battle of the Cowshed. I saw him myself. Did we not give him "Animal Hero, First Class", immediately afterwards?'

'That was our mistake, comrade. For we know now—it is all written down in the secret documents that we have found—that in reality he was trying to lure us to our doom.'

'But he was wounded,' said Boxer. 'We all saw him running with blood.'

'That was part of the arrangement!' cried Squealer. 'Jones's shot only grazed him. I could show you this in his own writing, if you were able to read it. The plot was for Snowball, at the critical moment, to give the signal for flight and leave the field to the enemy. And he very nearly succeeded—I will even say, comrades, he *would* have succeeded if it had not been for our heroic Leader, Comrade Napoleon. Do you not remember how, just at the moment when Jones and his men had got inside the yard, Snowball suddenly turned and fled, and many animals followed him? And do you not remember, too, that it was just at that moment, when panic was spreading and all seemed lost, that Comrade Napoleon sprang foward with a cry of "Death to Humanity!" and sank his teeth in Jones's leg? Surely you remember *that,* comrades?' exclaimed Squealer, frisking from side to side.

Now when Squealer described the scene so graphically, it seemed to the animals that they did remember it. At any rate, they remembered that at the critical moment of the battle Snowball had turned to flee. But Boxer was still a little uneasy.

'I do not believe that Snowball was a traitor at the beginning,' he said finally. 'What he has done since is different. But I believe that at the Battle of the Cowshed he was a good comrade.'

'Our Leader, Comrade Napoleon,' announced Squealer, speaking very slowly and firmly, 'has stated categorically—categorically, comrade—that Snowball was Jones's agent from the very beginning—yes, and from long before the Rebellion was ever thought of.'

'Ah, that is different!' said Boxer. 'If Comrade Napoleon says it, it must be right.'

'That is the true spirit, comrade!' cried Squealer, but it was noticed he cast a very ugly look at Boxer with his little twinkling eyes. He turned to go, then paused and added impressively: 'I warn every animal on this farm to keep his eyes very wide open. For we have reason to think that some of Snowball's secret agents are lurking among us at this moment!'

Four days later, in the late afternoon, Napoleon ordered all the animals to assemble in the yard. When they were all gathered together, Napoleon emerged from the farmhouse, wearing both his medals (for he had recently awarded himself 'Animal Hero, First Class', and 'Animal Hero, Second Class'), with his nine huge dogs frisking round him and uttering growls that sent shivers down all the animals' spines. They all cowered silently in their places, seeming to know in advance that some terrible thing was about to happen.

Napoleon stood sternly surveying his audience; then he uttered a high-pitched whimper. Immediately the dogs bounded forward, seized four of the pigs by the ear and dragged them, squealing with pain and terror, to Napoleon's feet. The pigs' ears were bleeding, the dogs had tasted blood, and for a few moments they appeared to go quite mad. To the amazement of everybody, three of them flung themselves upon Boxer. Boxer saw them coming and put out his great hoof, caught a dog in mid-air, and pinned him to the ground. The dog shrieked for mercy and the other two fled with their tails between their legs. Boxer looked at Napoleon to know whether he should crush the dog to death or let it go. Napoleon appeared to change countenance, and sharply ordered Boxer to let the dog go, whereat Boxer lifted his hoof, and the dog slunk away, bruised and howling.

Presently the tumult died down. The four pigs waited, trembling, with guilt written on every line of their countenances. Napoleon now called upon them to confess their crimes. They were the same four pigs as had protested when Napoleon abolished the Sunday Meetings. Without any further prompting they confessed that they had been secretly in touch with Snowball ever since his expulsion, that they had collaborated with him in destroying the windmill, and that they had entered into an agreement with him to hand over Animal Farm to Mr Frederick. They added that Snowball had privately admitted to them that he had been Jones's secret agent for years past. When they had finished their confession, the dogs promptly tore their throats out, and in a terrible vóice Napoleon demanded whether any other animal had anything to confess.

The three hens who had been the ringleaders in the attempted rebellion over the eggs now came forward and stated that Snowball had appeared to them in a dream and incited them to disobey Napoleon's orders. They, too, were slaughtered. Then a goose came forward and confessed to having secreted six ears of corn during the last year's harvest and eaten them in the night. Then a sheep confessed to having urinated in the drinking pool—urged to do this, so she said, by Snowball—and two other sheep confessed to having murdered an old ram, an especially devoted follower of Napoleon, by chasing him round the bonfire when he was suffering from a cough. They were all slain on the spot. And so the tale of confessions and executions went on, until there was a pile of corpses lying before Napoleon's feet and the air was heavy with the smell of blood, which had been unknown there since the expulsion of Jones.

When it was all over, the remaining animals, except for the pigs and dogs, crept away in a body. They were shaken and miserable. They did not know which was more shocking—the treachery of the animals who had leagued themselves with Snowball, or the cruel retribution they had just witnessed. In the old days there had often been scenes of bloodshed equally terrible, but it seemed to all of them that it was far worse now that it was happening among themselves. Since Jones had left the farm, until today, no animal had killed another animal. Not even a rat had been killed. They had made their way on to the little knoll where the half-finished windmill stood, and with one accord they all lay down as though huddling together for warmth—Clover, Muriel, Benjamin, the cows, the sheep, and a whole flock of geese and hens—everyone, indeed, except the cat, who had suddenly disappeared just before Napoleon ordered the animals to assemble. For some time nobody spoke. Only Boxer remained on his feet. He fidgeted to and fro, swishing his long black tail against his sides, and occasionally uttering a little whinny of surprise. Finally he said:

'I do not understand it. I would not have believed that such things could happen on our farm. It must be due to some fault in ourselves. The solution, as I see it, is to work harder. From now onwards I shall get up a full hour earlier in the mornings.'

And he moved off at his lumbering trot and made for the quarry. Having got there, he collected two successive loads of stone and dragged them down to the windmill before retiring for the night.

The animals huddled about Clover, not speaking. The knoll where they were lying gave them a wide prospect across the countryside. Most of Animal Farm was within their view—the long pasture stretching down to the main road, the hayfield, the spinney, the drinking pool, the ploughed fields where the young wheat was thick and green, and the red roofs of the farm buildings with the smoke curling from the chimneys. It was a clear spring evening. The grass and the bursting hedges were gilded by the level rays of the sun. Never had the farm—and with a kind of surprise they remembered that it was their own farm, every inch of it their own property—appeared to the animals so desirable a place. As Clover looked down the hillside her eyes filled with tears. If she could have spoken her thoughts, it would have been to say that this was not what they had aimed at when they had set themselves years ago to work for the overthrow of the human race. These scenes of terror and slaughter were not what they had looked forward to on that night when old Major first stirred them to rebellion. If she herself had had any picture of the future, it had been of a society of animals set free from hunger and the whip, all equal, each working according to his capacity, the strong protecting the weak, as she had protected the last brood of ducklings with her foreleg on the night of Major's speech. Instead—she did not know why—they had come to a time when no one dared speak his mind, when fierce, growling dogs roamed everywhere, and when you had to watch your comrades torn to pieces after confessing to shocking crimes. There was no thought of rebellion or disobedience in her mind. She knew that, even as things were, they were far better off than they had been in the days of Jones, and that before all else it was needful to prevent the return of the human beings. Whatever happened she would remain faithful, work hard, carry out the orders that were given to her, and accept the leadership of Napoleon. But still, it was not for this that she and all the other animals had hoped and toiled. It was not for this that they had built the windmill and faced the bullets of Jones's guns. Such were her thoughts, though she lacked the words to express them.

At last, feeling this to be in some way a substitute for the words she was unable to find, she began to sing 'Beasts of England'. The other animals sitting round her took it up, and they sang it three times over–very tunefully, but slowly and mournfully, in a way they had never sung it before.

They had just finished singing it for the third time when Squealer, attended by two dogs, approached them with the air of having something important to say. He announced that, by a special decree of Comrade Napoleon, 'Beasts of England' had been abolished. From now onwards it was forbidden to sing it.

The animals were taken aback.

'Why?' cried Muriel.

'It is no longer needed, comrade,' said Squealer stiffly. '"Beasts of England" was the song of the Rebellion. But the Rebellion is now completed. The execution of the traitors this afternoon was the final act. The enemy both external and internal has been defeated. In "Beasts of England" we expressed our longing for a better society in days to come. But that society has now been established. Clearly this song has no longer any purpose.'

Frightened though they were, some of the animals might possibly have protested, but at this moment the sheep set up their usual bleating of 'Four legs good, two legs bad', which went on for several minutes and put an end to the discussion.

So 'Beasts of England' was heard no more. In its place Minimus, the poet, had composed another song which began:

> Animal Farm, Animal Farm,
> Never through me shalt thou come to harm!

and this was sung every Sunday morning after the hoisting of the flag. But somehow neither the words nor the tune ever seemed to the animals to come up to 'Beasts of England'.

# 8

A few days later, when the terror caused by the executions had died down, some of the animals remembered–or thought they remembered–that the Sixth Commandment decreed: 'No animal shall kill any other animal.' And though no one cared to mention it in the hearing of the pigs or the dogs, it was felt that the killings which had taken place did not square with this. Clover asked Benjamin to read her the Sixth Commandment, and when Benjamin, as usual, said that he refused to meddle in such matters, she fetched Muriel. Muriel read the Commandment for her. It ran: 'No animal shall kill any other animal *without cause.*' Somehow or other, the last two words had slipped out of the animals' memory. But they saw now that the commandment had not been violated; for clearly there was good reason for killing the traitors who had leagued themselves with Snowball.

Throughout that year the animals worked even harder than they had worked in the previous year. To rebuild the windmill, with walls twice as thick as before, and to finish it by the appointed date, together with the regular work of the farm, was a tremendous labour. There were times when it seemed to the animals that they worked longer hours and fed no better than they had done in Jones's day. On Sunday mornings Squealer, holding down a long strip of paper with his trotter, would read out to them lists of figures proving that the production of every class of foodstuff had increased by 200 per cent, 300 per cent, or 500 per cent, as the case might be. The animals saw no reason to disbelieve him, especially as they could no longer remember very clearly what conditions had been like before the Rebellion. All the same, there were days when they felt that they would sooner have had less figures and more food.

All orders were now issued through Squealer or one of the other pigs. Napoleon himself was not seen in public as often as once a fortnight. When he did appear, he was attended not only by his retinue of dogs but by a black cockerel who marched in front of him and acted as a kind of trumpeter, letting out a loud 'cock-a-doodle-doo' before Napoleon spoke. Even in the farmhouse, it was said, Napoleon inhabited separate apartments from the others. He took his meals alone, with two dogs to wait upon him, and always ate from the Crown Derby dinner service which had been in the glass cupboard in the drawing-room. It was also announced that the gun would be fired every year on Napoleon's birthday, as well as on the other two anniversaries.

Napoleon was now never spoken of simply as 'Napoleon'. He was always referred to in formal style as 'our Leader, Comrade Napoleon', and the pigs liked to invent for him such titles as Father of All Animals, Terror of Mankind, Protector of the Sheep-fold, Ducklings' Friend, and the like. In his speeches, Squealer would talk with the tears rolling down his cheeks of Napoleon's wisdom, the goodness of his heart, and the deep love he bore to all animals everywhere, even and especially the unhappy animals who still lived in ignorance and slavery on other farms. It had become usual to give Napoleon the credit for every successful achievement and every stroke of good fortune. You would often hear one hen remark to another, 'Under the guidance of our Leader, Comrade Napoleon, I have laid five eggs in six days'; or two cows, enjoying a drink at the pool, would exclaim, 'Thanks to the leadership of Comrade Napoleon, how excellent this water tastes!' The general feeling on the farm was well expressed in a poem entitled 'Comrade Napoleon', which was composed by Minimus and which ran as follows:

> Friend of the fatherless!
> Fountain of happiness!
> Lord of the swill-bucket! Oh, how my soul is on
> Fire when I gaze at thy
> Calm and commanding eye,
> Like the sun in the sky,
> Comrade Napoleon!

Thou art the giver of
All that thy creatures love,
Full belly twice a day, clean straw to roll upon;
Every beast great or small
Sleeps at peace in his stall,
Thou watchest over all,
Comrade Napoleon!

Had I a sucking-pig,
Ere he had grown as big
Even as a pint bottle or a rolling-pin,
He should have learned to be
Faithful and true to thee,
Yes, his first squeak should be
'Comrade Napoleon!'

Napoleon approved of this poem and caused it to be inscribed on the wall of the big barn, at the opposite end from the Seven Commandments. It was surmounted by a portrait of Napoleon, in profile, executed by Squealer in white paint.

Meanwhile, through the agency of Whymper, Napoleon was engaged in complicated negotiations with Frederick and Pilkington. The pile of timber was still unsold. Of the two, Frederick was the more anxious to get hold of it, but he would not offer a reasonable price. At the same time there were renewed rumours that Frederick and his men were plotting to attack Animal Farm and to destroy the windmill, the building of which had aroused furious jealousy in him. Snowball was known to be still skulking on Pinchfield Farm. In the middle of the summer the animals were alarmed to hear that three hens had come forward and confessed that, inspired by Snowball, they had entered into a plot to murder Napoleon. They were executed immediately, and fresh precautions for Napoleon's safety were taken. Four dogs guarded his bed at night, one at each corner, and a young pig named Pinkeye was given the task of tasting all his food before he ate it, lest it should be poisoned.

At about the same time it was given out that Napoleon had arranged to sell the pile of timber to Mr Pilkington; he was also going to enter into a regular agreement for the exchange of certain products between Animal Farm and Foxwood. The relations between Napoleon and Pilkington, though they were only conducted through Whymper, were now almost friendly. The animals distrusted Pilkington, as a human being, but greatly preferred him to Frederick, whom they both feared and hated. As the summer wore on, and the windmill neared completion, the rumours of an impending treacherous attack grew stronger and stronger. Frederick, it was said, intended to bring against them twenty men all armed with guns, and he had already bribed the magistrates and police, so that if he could once get hold of the title-deeds of Animal Farm they would ask no questions. Moreover, terrible stories were leaking out from Pinchfield about the cruelties that Frederick practised upon his animals. He had flogged an old horse to death, he starved his cows, he had killed a dog by throwing it into a furnace, he amused himself in the evenings by making cocks fight with splinters of razor-blade tied to their spurs. The animals' blood boiled with rage when they heard of these things being done to their comrades, and sometimes they clamoured to be allowed to go out in a body and attack Pinchfield Farm, drive out the humans, and set the animals free. But Squealer counselled them to avoid rash actions and trust in Comrade Napoleon's strategy.

Nevertheless, feeling against Frederick continued to run high. One Sunday morning Napoleon appeared in the barn and explained that he had never at any time contemplated selling the pile of timber to Frederick; he considered it beneath his dignity, he said, to have dealings with scoundrels of that description. The pigeons who were still sent out to spread tidings of the Rebellion were forbidden to set foot anywhere on Foxwood, and were also ordered to drop their former slogan of 'Death to Humanity' in favour of 'Death to Frederick'. In the late summer yet another of Snowball's machinations was laid bare. The wheat crop was full of weeds, and it was discovered that on one of his nocturnal visits Snowball had mixed weed seeds with the seed corn. A gander who had been privy to the plot had confessed his guilt to Squealer and immediately committed suicide by swallowing deadly nightshade berries. The animals now also learned that Snowball had never—as many of them had believed hitherto—received the order of 'Animal Hero, First Class'. This was merely a legend which had been spread some time after the Battle of the Cowshed by Snowball himself. So far from being decorated, he had been censured for showing cowardice in the battle. Once again some of the animals heard this with a certain bewilderment, but Squealer was soon able to convince them that their memories had been at fault.

In the autumn, by a tremendous, exhausting effort—for the harvest had to be gathered at almost the same time—the windmill was finished. The machinery had still to be installed, and Whymper was negotiating the purchase of it, but the structure was completed. In the teeth of every difficulty, in spite of inexperience, of primitive implements, of bad luck, and of Snowball's treachery, the work had been finished punctually to the very day! Tired out but proud, the animals walked round and round their masterpiece, which appeared even more beautiful in their eyes than when it had been built the first time. Moreover, the walls were twice as thick as before. Nothing short of explosives would lay them low this time! And when they thought of how they had laboured, what discouragements they had overcome, and the enormous difference that would be made in their lives when the sails were turning and the dynamos running—when they thought of all this, their tiredness forsook them and they gambolled round and round the windmill, uttering cries of triumph. Napoleon himself, attended by his dogs and his cockerel, came down to inspect the completed work; he personally congratulated the animals on their achievement, and announced that the mill would be named Napoleon Mill.

Two days later the animals were called together for a special meeting in the barn. They were struck dumb with surprise when Napoleon announced that he had sold the pile of timber to Frederick. Tomorrow Frederick's wagons would arrive and begin carting it away. Throughout the whole period of his seeming friendship with Pilkington, Napoleon had really been in secret agreement with Frederick.

All relations with Foxwood had been broken off; insulting messages had been sent to Pilkington. The pigeons had been told to avoid Pinchfield Farm and to alter their slogan from 'Death to Frederick' to 'Death to Pilkington'. At the same time Napoleon assured the animals that the stories of an impending attack on Animal Farm were completely untrue, and that the tales about Frederick's cruelty to his animals had been greatly exaggerated. All these rumours had probably originated with Snowball and his agents. It now appeared that Snowball was not, after all, hiding on Pinchfield Farm, and in fact had never been there in his life: he was living—in considerable luxury, so it was said—at Foxwood, and had in reality been a pensioner of Pilkington for years past.

The pigs were in ecstasies over Napoleon's cunning. By seeming to be friendly with Pilkington he had forced Frederick to raise his price by twelve pounds. But the superior quality of Napoleon's mind, said Squealer, was shown in the fact that he trusted nobody, not even Frederick. Frederick had wanted to pay for the timber with something called a cheque, which, it seemed, was a piece of paper with a promise to pay written upon it. But Napoleon was too clever for him. He had demanded payment in real five-pound notes, which were to be handed over before the timber was removed. Already Frederick had paid up; and the sum he had paid was just enough to buy the machinery for the windmill.

Meanwhile the timber was being carted away at high speed. When it was all gone, another special meeting was held in the barn for the animals to inspect Frederick's bank-notes. Smiling beatifically, and wearing both his decorations, Napoleon reposed on a bed of straw on the platform, with the money at his side neatly piled on a china dish from the farmhouse kitchen. The animals filed slowly past, and each gazed his fill. And Boxer put out his nose to sniff at the bank-notes, and the flimsy white things stirred and rustled in his breath.

Three days later there was a terrible hullabaloo. Whymper, his face deadly pale, came racing up the path on his bicycle, flung it down in the yard, and rushed straight into the farmhouse. The next moment a choking roar of rage sounded from Napoleon's apartments. The news of what had happened sped round the farm like wildfire. The bank-notes were forgeries! Frederick had got the timber for nothing!

Napoleon called the animals together immediately and in a terrible voice pronounced the death sentence upon Frederick. When captured, he said, Frederick should be boiled alive. At the same time he warned them that after this treacherous deed the worst was to be expected. Frederick and his men might make their long-expected attack at any moment. Sentinels were placed at all the approaches to the farm. In addition, four pigeons were sent to Foxwood with a conciliatory message, which it was hoped might re-establish good relations with Pilkington.

The very next morning the attack came. The animals were at breakfast when the look-outs came racing in with the news that Frederick and his followers had already come through the five-barred gate. Boldly enough the animals sallied forth to meet them, but this time they did not have the easy victory that they had had in the Battle of the Cowshed. There were fifteen men, with half a dozen guns between them, and they opened fire as soon as they got within fifty yards. The animals could not face the terrible explosions and the stinging pellets, and in spite of the efforts of Napoleon and Boxer to rally them, they were soon driven back. A number of them were already wounded. They took refuge in the farm buildings and peeped cautiously out from chinks and knot-holes. The whole of the big pasture, including the windmill, was in the hands of the enemy. For the moment even Napoleon seemed at a loss. He paced up and down without a word, his tail rigid and twitching. Wistful glances were sent in the direction of Foxwood. If Pilkington and his men would help them, the day might yet be won. But at this moment the four pigeons, who had been sent out on the day before, returned, one of them bearing a scrap of paper from Pilkington. On it was pencilled the words: 'Serves you right'.

Meanwhile Frederick and his men had halted about the windmill. The animals watched them, and a murmur of dismay went round. Two of the men had produced a crowbar and a sledge-hammer. They were going to knock the windmill down.

'Impossible!' cried Napoleon. 'We have built the walls far too thick for that. They could not knock it down in a week. Courage, comrades!'

But Benjamin was watching the movements of the men intently. The two with the hammer and the crowbar were drilling a hole near the base of the windmill. Slowly, and with an air almost of amusement, Benjamin nodded his long muzzle.

'I thought so,' he said. 'Do you not see what they are doing? In another moment they are going to pack blasting powder into that hole.'

Terrified, the animals waited. It was impossible now to venture out of the shelter of the buildings. After a few minutes the men were seen to be running in all directions. Then there was a deafening roar. The pigeons swirled into the air, and all the animals, except Napoleon, flung themselves flat on their bellies and hid their faces. When they got up again, a huge cloud of black smoke was hanging where the windmill had been. Slowly the breeze drifted it away. The windmill had ceased to exist!

At this sight the animals' courage returned to them. The fear and despair they had felt a moment earlier were drowned in their rage against this vile, contemptible act. A mighty cry for vengeance went up, and without waiting for further orders they charged forth in a body and made straight for the enemy. This time they did not heed the cruel pellets that swept over them like hail. It was a savage, bitter battle. The men fired again and again, and when the animals got to close quarters, lashed out with their sticks and their heavy boots. A cow, three sheep, and two geese were killed, and nearly everyone was wounded. Even Napoleon, who was directing operations from the rear, had the tip of his tail chipped by a pellet. But the men did not go unscathed either. Three of them had their heads broken by blows from Boxer's hoofs; another was gored in the belly by a cow's horn; another had his trousers nearly torn off by Jessie and Bluebell. And when the nine dogs of Napoleon's own bodyguard, whom he had instructed to make a detour under cover of the hedge, suddenly appeared on the men's flank, baying ferociously, panic overtook them. They saw that they were in danger of being surrounded. Frederick shouted to his men to get out while the going was good, and the next moment the cowardly enemy was running for dear life. The animals chased them right down to the bottom of the field, and got in some last kicks at them as they forced their way through the thorn hedge.

They had won, but they were weary and bleeding. Slowly they began to limp back towards the farm. The sight of their dead comrades stretched upon the grass moved some of them to tears. And for a little while they halted in sorrowful silence at the place where the windmill had once stood. Yes, it was gone; almost the last trace of their labour was gone! Even the foundations were partially destroyed. And in rebuilding it they could not this time, as before, make use of the fallen stones. This time the stones had vanished too. The force of the explosion had flung them to distances of hundreds of yards. It was as though the windmill had never been.

As they approached the farm Squealer, who had unaccountably been absent during the fighting, came skipping towards them, whisking his tail and beaming with satisfaction. And the animals heard, from the direction of the farm buildings, the solemn booming of a gun.

'What is that gun firing for?' said Boxer.

'To celebrate our victory!' cried Squealer.

'What victory?' said Boxer. His knees were bleeding, he had lost a shoe and split his hoof, and a dozen pellets had lodged themselves in his hindleg.

'What victory, comrade? Have we not driven the enemy off our soil—the sacred soil of Animal Farm?'

'But they have destroyed the windmill. And we had worked on it for two years!'

'What matter? We will build another windmill. We will build six windmills if we feel like it. You do not appreciate, comrade, the mighty thing that we have done. The enemy was in occupation of this very ground that we stand upon. And now—thanks to the leadership of Comrade Napoleon—we have won every inch of it back again!'

'Then we have won back what we had before,' said Boxer.

'That is our victory,' said Squealer.

They limped into the yard. The pellets under the skin of Boxer's leg smarted painfully. He saw ahead of him the heavy labour of rebuilding the windmill from the foundations, and already in imagination he braced himself for the task. But for the first time it occurred to him that he was eleven years old and that perhaps his great muscles were not quite what they had once been.

But when the animals saw the green flag flying, and heard the gun firing again—seven times it was fired in all—and heard the speech that Napoleon made, congratulating them on their conduct, it did seem to them after all that they had won a great victory. The animals slain in the battle were given a solemn funeral. Boxer and Clover pulled the wagon which served as a hearse, and Napoleon himself walked at the head of the procession. Two whole days were given over to celebrations. There were songs, speeches, and more firing of the gun, and a special gift of an apple was bestowed on every animal, with two ounces of corn for each bird and three biscuits for each dog. It was announced that the battle would be called the Battle of the Windmill, and that Napoleon had created a new decoration, the Order of the Green Banner, which he had conferred upon himself. In the general rejoicings the unfortunate affair of the bank-notes was forgotten.

It was a few days later than this that the pigs came upon a case of whisky in the cellars of the farmhouse. It had been overlooked at the time when the house was first occupied. That night there came from the farmhouse the sound of loud singing, in which, to everyone's surprise, the strains of 'Beasts of England' were mixed up. At about half past nine Napoleon, wearing an old bowler hat of Mr Jones's, was distinctly seen to emerge from the back door, gallop rapidly round the yard, and disappear indoors again. But in the morning a deep silence hung over the farmhouse. Not a pig appeared to be stirring. It was nearly nine o'clock when Squealer made his appearance, walking slowly and dejectedly, his eyes dull, his tail hanging limply behind him, and with every appearance of being seriously ill. He called the animals together and told them that he had a terrible piece of news to impart. Comrade Napoleon was dying!

A cry of lamentation went up. Straw was laid down outside the doors of the farmhouse, and the animals walked on tiptoe. With tears in their eyes they asked one another what they should do if their Leader was taken away from them. A rumour went round that Snowball had after all contrived to introduce poison into Napoleon's food. At eleven o'clock Squealer came out to make another announcement. As his last act upon earth, Comrade Napoleon had pronounced a solemn decree: the drinking of alcohol was to be punished by death.

By the evening, however, Napoleon appeared to be somewhat better, and the following morning Squealer was able to tell them that he was well on the way to recovery. By the evening of that day Napoleon was back at work, and on the next day it was learned that he had instructed Whymper to purchase in Willingdon some booklets on brewing and distilling. A week later Napoleon gave orders that the small paddock beyond the orchard, which it had previously been intended to set aside as a grazing-ground for animals who were past work, was to be ploughed up. It was given out that the pasture was exhausted and needed re-seeding; but it soon became known that Napoleon intended to sow it with barley.

About this time there occurred a strange incident which hardly anyone was able to understand. One night at about twelve o'clock there was a loud crash in the yard, and the animals rushed out of their stalls. It was a moonlight night. At the foot of the end wall of the big barn, where the Seven Commandments were written, there lay a ladder broken in two pieces. Squealer, temporarily stunned, was sprawling beside it, and near at hand there lay a lantern, a paint-brush, and an overturned pot of white paint. The dogs immediately made a ring round Squealer, and escorted him back to the farmhouse as soon as he was able to walk. None of the animals could form any idea as to what this meant, except old Benjamin, who nodded his muzzle with a knowing air, and seemed to understand, but would say nothing.

But a few days later Muriel, reading over the Seven Commandments to herself, noticed that there was yet another of them which the animals had remembered wrong. They had thought that the Fifth Commandment was 'No animals shall drink alcohol', but there were two words that they had forgotten. Actually the Commandment read: 'No animal shall drink alcohol *to excess.*'

# 9

Boxer's split hoof was a long time in healing. They had started the rebuilding of the windmill the day after the victory celebrations were ended. Boxer refused to take even a day off work, and made it a point of honour not to let it be seen that he was in pain. In the evening he would admit privately to Clover that the hoof troubled him a great deal. Clover treated the hoof with poultices of herbs which she prepared by chewing them, and both she and Benjamin urged Boxer to work less hard. 'A horse's lungs do not last for ever,' she said to him. But Boxer would not listen. He had, he said, only one real ambition left—to see the windmill well under way before he reached the age for retirement.

At the beginning, when the laws of Animal Farm were first formulated, the retiring age had been fixed for horses and pigs at twelve, for cows at fourteen, for dogs at nine, for sheep at seven, and for hens and geese at five. Liberal old age pensions had been agreed upon. As yet no animal had actually retired on pension, but of late the subject had been discussed more and more. Now that the small field beyond the orchard had been set aside for barley, it was rumoured that a corner of the large pasture was to be fenced off and turned into a grazing-ground for superannuated animals. For a horse, it was said, the pension would be five pounds of corn a day and, in winter, fifteen pounds of hay, with a carrot or possibly an apple on public holidays. Boxer's twelfth birthday was due in the late summer of the following year.

Meanwhile life was hard. The winter was as cold as the last one had been, and food was even shorter. Once again all rations were reduced, except those of the pigs and dogs. A too rigid equality in rations, Squealer explained, would have been contrary to the principles of Animalism. In any case he had no difficulty in proving to the other animals that they were *not* in reality short of food, whatever the appearances might be. For the time being, certainly, it had been found necessary to make a readjustment of rations (Squealer always spoke of it as a 'readjustment', never as a 'reduction'), but in comparison with the days of Jones, the improvement was enormous. Reading out the figures in a shrill, rapid voice, he proved to them in detail that they had more oats, more hay, more turnips than they had had in Jones's day, that they worked shorter hours, that their drinking water was of better quality, that they lived longer, that a larger proportion of their young ones survived infancy, and that they had more straw in their stalls and suffered less from fleas. The animals believed every word of it. Truth to tell, Jones and all he stood for had almost faded out of their memories. They knew that life nowadays was harsh and bare, that they were often hungry and often cold, and that they were usually working when they were not asleep. But doubtless it had been worse in the old days. They were glad to believe so. Besides, in those days they had been slaves and now they were free, and that made all the difference, as Squealer did not fail to point out.

There were many more mouths to feed now. In the autumn the four sows had all littered about simultaneously, producing thirty-one young pigs between them. The young pigs were piebald, and as Napoleon was the only boar on the farm, it was possible to guess at their parentage. It was announced that later, when bricks and timber had been purchased, a schoolroom would be built in the farmhouse garden. For the time being, the young pigs were given their instruction by Napoleon himself in the farmhouse kitchen. They took their exercise in the garden, and were discouraged from playing with the other young animals. About this time, too, it was laid down as a rule that when a pig and any other animal met on the path, the other animal must stand aside: and also that all pigs, of whatever degree, were to have the privilege of wearing green ribbons on their tails on Sundays.

The farm had had a fairly successful year, but was still short of money. There were the bricks, sand, and lime for the schoolroom to be purchased, and it would also be necessary to begin saving up again for the machinery for the windmill. Then there were lamp oil and candles for the house, sugar for Napoleon's own table (he forbade this to the other pigs, on the ground that it made them fat), and all the usual replacements such as tools, nails, string, coal, wire, scrap-iron, and dog biscuits. A stump of hay and part of the potato crop were sold off, and the contract for eggs was increased to six hundred a week, so that that year the hens barely hatched enough chicks to keep their numbers at the same level. Rations, reduced in December, were reduced again in February, and lanterns in the stalls were forbidden, to save oil. But the pigs seemed comfortable enough, and in fact were putting on weight if anything. One afternoon in late February, a warm, rich, appetizing scent, such as the animals had never smelt before, wafted itself across the yard from the little brewhouse, which had been disused in Jones's time, and which stood beyond the kitchen. Someone said it was the smell of cooking barley. The animals sniffed the air hungrily and wondered whether a warm mash was being prepared for their supper. But no warm mash appeared, and on the following Sunday it was announced that from now onwards all barley would be reserved for the pigs. The field beyond the orchard had already been sown with barley. And the news soon leaked out that every pig was now receiving a ration of a pint of beer daily, with half a gallon for Napoleon himself, which was always served to him in the Crown Derby soup tureen.

But if there were hardships to be borne, they were partly offset by the fact that life nowadays had a greater dignity than it had had before. There were more songs, more speeches, more processions. Napoleon had commanded that once a week there should be held something called a Spontaneous Demonstration, the object of which was to celebrate the struggles and triumphs of Animal Farm. At the appointed time the animals would leave their work and march round the precincts of the farm in military formation, with the pigs leading, then the horses, then the cows, then the sheep, and then the poultry. The dogs flanked the procession and at the head of all marched Napoleon's black cockerel. Boxer and Clover always carried between them a green banner marked with the hoof and the horn and the caption, 'Long Live Comrade Napoleon!' Afterwards there were recitations of poems composed in Napoleon's honour, and a speech by Squealer giving particulars of the latest increases in the production of foodstuffs, and on occasion a shot was fired from the gun. The sheep were the greatest devotees of the Spontaneous Demonstration, and if anyone complained (as a few animals sometimes did, when no pigs or dogs were near) that they wasted time and meant a lot of standing about in the cold, the sheep were sure to silence him with a tremendous bleating of 'Four legs good, two legs bad!' But by and large the animals enjoyed these celebrations. They found it comforting to be reminded that, after all, they were truly their own masters and that the work they did was for their own benefit. So that, what with the songs, the processions, Squealer's lists of figures, the thunder of the gun, the crowing of the cockerel, and the fluttering of the flag, they were able to forget that their bellies were empty, at least part of the time.

In April, Animal Farm was proclaimed a Republic, and it became necessary to elect a President. There was only one candidate, Napoleon, who was elected unanimously. On the same day it was given out that fresh documents had been discovered which revealed further details about Snowball's complicity with Jones. It now appeared that Snowball had not, as the animals had previously imagined, merely attempted to lose the Battle of the Cowshed by means of a stratagem, but had been openly fighting on Jones's side. In fact, it was he who had actually been the leader of the human forces, and had charged into battle with the words 'Long live Humanity!' on his lips. The wounds on Snowball's back, which a few of the animals still remembered to have seen, had been inflicted by Napoleon's teeth.

In the middle of the summer Moses the raven suddenly reappeared on the farm, after an absence of several years. He was quite unchanged, still did no work, and talked in the same strain as ever about Sugarcandy Mountain. He would perch on a stump, flap his black wings, and talk by the hour to anyone who would listen. 'Up there, comrades,' he would say solemnly, pointing to the sky with his large beak–'up there, just on the other side of that dark cloud that you can see–there lies Sugarcandy Mountain, that happy country where we poor animals shall rest for ever from our labours!' He even claimed to have been there on one of his higher flights, and to have seen the everlasting fields of clover and the linseed cake and lump sugar growing on the hedges. Many of the animals believed him. Their lives now, they reasoned, were hungry and laborious; was it not right and just that a better world should exist somewhere else? A thing that was difficult to determine was the attitude of the pigs towards Moses. They all declared contemptuously that his stories about Sugarcandy Mountain were lies, and yet they allowed him to remain on the farm, not working, with an allowance of a gill of beer a day.

After his hoof had healed up, Boxer worked harder than ever. Indeed, all the animals worked like slaves that year. Apart from the regular work of the farm, and the rebuilding of the windmill, there was the schoolhouse for the young pigs, which was started in March. Sometimes the long hours on insufficient food were hard to bear, but Boxer never faltered. In nothing that he said or did was there any sign that his strength was not what it had been. It was only his appearance that was a little altered; his hide was less shiny than it had used to be, and his great haunches seemed to have shrunken. The others said, 'Boxer will pick up when the spring grass comes on'; but the spring came and Boxer grew no fatter. Sometimes on the slope leading to the top of the quarry, when he braced his muscles against the weight of some vast boulder, it seemed that nothing kept him on his feet except the will to continue. At such times his lips were seen to form the words, 'I will work harder'; he had no voice left. Once again Clover and Benjamin warned him to take care of his health, but Boxer paid no attention. His twelfth birthday was approaching. He did not care what happened so long as a good store of stone was accumulated before he went on pension.

Late one evening in the summer, a sudden rumour ran round the farm that something had happened to Boxer. He had gone out alone to drag a load of stone down to the windmill. And sure enough, the rumour was true. A few minutes later two pigeons came racing in with the news: 'Boxer has fallen! He is lying on his side and can't get up!'

About half the animals on the farm rushed out to the knoll where the windmill stood. There lay Boxer, between the shafts of the cart, his neck stretched out, unable even to raise his head. His eyes were glazed, his sides matted with sweat. A thin stream of blood had trickled out of his mouth. Clover dropped to her knees at his side.

'Boxer!' she cried 'how are you?'

'It is my lung,' said Boxer in a weak voice. 'It does not matter. I think you will be able to finish the windmill without me. There is a pretty good store of stone accumulated. I had only another month to go in any case. To tell you the truth, I had been looking forward to my retirement. And perhaps, as Benjamin is growing old too, they will let him retire at the same time and be a companion to me.'

'We must get help at once,' said Clover. 'Run, somebody, and tell Squealer what has happened.'

All the other animals immediately raced back to the farmhouse to give Squealer the news. Only Clover remained, and Benjamin, who lay down at Boxer's side, and, without speaking, kept the flies off him with his long tail. After about a quarter of an hour Squealer appeared, full of sympathy and concern. He said that Comrade Napoleon had learned with the very deepest distress of this misfortune to one of the most loyal workers on the farm, and was already making arrangements to send Boxer to be treated in the hospital at Willingdon. The animals felt a little uneasy at this. Except for Mollie and Snowball, no other animals had ever left the farm, and they did not like to think of their sick comrade in the hands of human beings. However, Squealer easily convinced them that the veterinary surgeon in Willingdon could treat Boxer's case more satisfactorily than could be done on the farm. And about half an hour later, when Boxer had somewhat recovered, he was with difficulty got on to his feet, and managed to limp back to his stall, where Clover and Benjamin had prepared a good bed of straw for him.

For the next two days Boxer remained in his stall. The pigs had sent out a large bottle of pink medicine which they had found in the medicine chest in the bathroom, and Clover administered it to Boxer twice a day after meals. In the evenings she lay in his stall and talked to him, while Benjamin kept the flies off him. Boxer professed not to be sorry for what had happened. If he made a good recovery, he might expect to live another three years, and he looked forward to the peaceful days that he would spend in the corner of the big pasture. It would be the first time that he had had leisure to study and improve his mind. He intended, he said, to devote the rest of his life to learning the remaining twenty-two letters of the alphabet.

However, Benjamin and Clover could only be with Boxer after working hours, and it was in the middle of the day when the van came to take him away. The animals were all at work weeding turnips under the supervision of a pig, when they were astonished to see Benjamin come galloping from the direction of the farm buildings, braying at the top of his voice. It was the first time that they had ever seen Benjamin excited—indeed, it was the first time that anyone had ever seen him gallop. 'Quick, quick!' he shouted. 'Come at once! They're taking Boxer away!' Without waiting for orders from the pig, the animals broke off work and raced back to the farm buildings. Sure enough, there in the yard was a large closed van, drawn by two horses, with lettering on its side and a sly-looking man in a low-crowned bowler hat sitting on the driver's seat. And Boxer's stall was empty.

The animals crowded round the van. 'Good-bye, Boxer!' they chorused, 'good-bye!'

'Fools! Fools!' shouted Benjamin, prancing round them and stamping the earth with his small hoofs. 'Fools! Do you not see what is written on the side of that van?'

That gave the animals pause, and there was a hush. Muriel began to spell out the words. But Benjamin pushed her aside and in the midst of a deadly silence he read:

'"Alfred Simmonds, Horse Slaughterer and Glue Boiler, Willingdon. Dealer in Hides and Bone-Meal. Kennels Supplied." Do you not understand what that means? They are taking Boxer to the knacker's!'

A cry of horror burst from all the animals. At this moment the man on the box whipped up his horses and the van moved out of the yard at a smart trot.

All the animals followed, crying out at the tops of their voices. Clover forced her way to the front. The van began to gather speed. Clover tried to stir her stout limbs to a gallop, and achieved a canter. 'Boxer!' she cried. 'Boxer! Boxer! Boxer!' And just at this moment, as though he had heard the uproar outside, Boxer's face, with the white stripe down his nose, appeared at the small window at the back of the van.

'Boxer!' cried Clover in a terrible voice. 'Boxer! Get out! Get out quickly! They are taking you to your death!'

All the animals took up the cry of 'Get out, Boxer, get out!' But the van was already gathering speed and drawing away from them. It was uncertain whether Boxer had understood what Clover had said. But a moment later his face disappeared from the window and there was the sound of a tremendous drumming of hoofs inside the van. He was trying to kick his way out. The time had been when a few kicks from Boxer's hoofs would have smashed the van to matchwood. But alas! his strength had left him; and in a few moments the sound of drumming hoofs grew fainter and died away. In desperation the animals began appealing to the two horses which drew the van to stop. 'Comrades, comrades!' they shouted. 'Don't take your own brother to this death!' But the stupid brutes, too ignorant to realize what was happening, merely set back their ears and quickened their pace. Boxer's face did not reappear at the window. Too late, someone thought of racing ahead and shutting the five-barred gate; but in another moment the van was through it and rapidly disappearing down the road. Boxer was never seen again.

Three days later it was announced that he had died in the hospital at Willingdon, in spite of receiving every attention a horse could have. Squealer came to announce the news to the others. He had, he said, been present during Boxer's last hours.

'It was the most affecting sight I have ever seen!' said Squealer, lifting his trotter and wiping away a tear. 'I was at his bedside at the very last. And at the end, almost too weak to speak, he whispered in my ear that his sole sorrow was to have passed on before the windmill was finished. "Forward, comrades!" he whispered. "Forward in the name of the Rebellion. Long Live Animal Farm! Long live Comrade Napoleon! Napoleon is always right." Those were his very last words, comrades.'

Here Squealer's demeanour suddenly changed. He fell silent for a moment, and his little eyes darted suspicious glances from side to side before he proceeded.

It had come to his knowledge, he said, that a foolish and wicked rumour had been circulated at the time of Boxer's removal. Some of the animals had noticed that the van which took Boxer away was marked 'Horse Slaughterer', and had actually jumped to the conclusion that Boxer was being sent to the knacker's. It was almost unbelievable, said Squealer, that any animal could be so stupid. Surely, he cried indignantly, whisking his tail and skipping from side to side, surely they knew their beloved Leader, Comrade Napoleon, better than that? But the explanation was really very simple. The van had previously been the property of the knacker, and had been bought by the veterinary surgeon, who had not yet painted the old name out. That was how the mistake had arisen.

The animals were enormously relieved to hear this. And when Squealer went on to give further graphic details of Boxer's death bed, the admirable care he had received, and the expensive medicines for which Napoleon had paid without a thought as to the cost, their last doubts disappeared and the sorrow that they felt for their comrade's death was tempered by the thought that at least he had died happy.

Napoleon himself appeared at the meeting on the following Sunday morning and pronounced a short oration in Boxer's honour. It had not been possible, he said, to bring back their lamented comrade's remains for interment on the farm, but he had ordered a large wreath to be made from the laurels in the farmhouse garden and sent down to be placed on Boxer's grave. And in a few days' time the pigs intended to hold a memorial banquet in Boxer's honour. Napoleon ended his speech with a reminder of Boxer's two favourite maxims, 'I will work harder' and 'Comrade Napoleon is always right'—maxims, he said, which every animal would do well to adopt as his own.

On the day appointed for the banquet, a grocer's van drove up from Willingdon and delivered a large wooden crate at the farmhouse. That night there was the sound of uproarious singing, which was followed by what sounded like a violent quarrel and ended at about eleven o'clock with a tremendous crash of glass. No one stirred in the farmhouse before noon on the following day, and the word went round that from somewhere or other the pigs had acquired the money to buy themselves another case of whisky.

# 10

Years passed. The seasons came and went, the short animal lives fled by. A time came when there was no one who remembered the old days before the Rebellion, except Clover, Benjamin, Moses the raven, and a number of the pigs.

Muriel was dead; Bluebell, Jessie, and Pincher were dead. Jones too was dead—he had died in an inebriates' home in another part of the country. Snowball was forgotten. Boxer was forgotten, except by the few who had known him. Clover was an old stout mare now, stiff in the joints, and with a tendency to rheumy eyes. She was two years past the retiring age, but in fact no animal had ever actually retired. The talk of setting aside a corner of the pasture for superannuated animals had long since been dropped. Napoleon was now a mature boar of twenty-four stone. Squealer was so fat that he could with difficulty see out of his eyes. Only old Benjamin was much the same as ever, except for being a little greyer about the muzzle, and, since Boxer' death, more morose and taciturn than ever.

There were many more creatures on the farm now, though the increase was not so great as had been expected in earlier years. Many animals had been born to whom the Rebellion was only a dim tradition, passed on by word of mouth, and others had been bought who had never heard mention of such a thing before their arrival. The farm possessed three horses now besides Clover. They were fine upstanding beasts, willing workers and good comrades, but very stupid. None of them proved able to learn the alphabet beyond the letter B. They accepted everything that they were told about the Rebellion and the principles of Animalism, especially from Clover, for whom they had an almost filial respect; but it was doubtful whether they understood very much of it.

The farm was more prosperous now, and better organized: it had even been enlarged by two fields which had been bought from Mr Pilkington. The windmill had been successfully completed at last, and the farm possessed a threshing machine and a hay elevator of its own, and various new buildings had been added to it. Whymper had bought himself a dogcart. The windmill, however, had not after all been used for generating electrical power. It was used for milling corn, and brought in a handsome money profit. The animals were hard at work building yet another windmill; when that one was finished, so it was said, the dynamos would be installed. But the luxuries of which Snowball had once taught the animals to dream, the stalls with electric light and hot and cold water, and the three-day week, were no longer talked about. Napoleon had denounced such ideas as contrary to the spirit of Animalism. The truest happiness, he said, lay in working hard and living frugally.

Somehow it seemed as though the farm had grown richer without making the animals themselves any richer—except, of course, for the pigs and the dogs. Perhaps this was partly because there were so many pigs and so many dogs. It was not that these creatures did not work, after their fashion. There was, as Squealer was never tired of explaining, endless work in the supervision and organization of the farm. Much of this work was of a kind that the other animals were too ignorant to understand. For example, Squealer told them that the pigs had to expend enormous labours every day upon mysterious things called 'files', 'reports', 'minutes', and 'memoranda'. These were large sheets of paper which had to be closely covered with writing, and as soon as they were so covered, they were burnt in the furnace. This was of the highest importance for the welfare of the farm, Squealer said. But still, neither pigs nor dogs produced any food by their own labour; and there were very many of them, and their appetites were always good.

As for the others, their life, so far as they knew, was as it had always been. They were generally hungry, they slept on straw, they drank from the pool, they laboured in the fields; in winter they were troubled by the cold, and in the summer by the flies. Sometimes the older ones among them racked their dim memories and tried to determine whether in the early days of the Rebellion, when Jones's expulsion was still recent, things had been better or worse than now. They could not remember. There was nothing with which they could compare their present lives: they had nothing to go upon except Squealer's lists of figures, which invariably demonstrated that everything was getting better and better. The animals found the problem insoluble; in any case, they had little time for speculating on such things now. Only old Benjamin professed to remember every detail of his long life and to know that things never had been, nor ever could be much better or much worse–hunger, hardship, and disappointment being, so he said, the unalterable law of life.

And yet the animals never gave up hope. More, they never lost, even for an instant, their sense of honour and privilege in being members of Animal Farm. They were still the only farm in the whole county–in all England!–owned and operated by animals. Not one of them, not even the youngest, not even the newcomers who had been brought from farms ten or twenty miles away, ever ceased to marvel at that. And when they heard the gun booming and saw the green flag fluttering at the masthead, their hearts swelled with imperishable pride, and the talk always turned towards the old heroic days, the expulsion of Jones, the writing of the Seven Commandments, the great battles in which the human invaders had been defeated. None of the old dreams had been abandoned. The Republic of the Animals which Major had foretold, when the green fields of England should be untrodden by human feet, was still believed in. Some day it was coming: it might not be soon, it might not be within the lifetime of any animal now living, but still it was coming. Even the tune of 'Beasts of England' was perhaps hummed secretly here and there: at any rate, it was a fact that every animal on the farm knew it, though no one would have dared to sing it aloud. It might be that their lives were hard and that not all of their hopes had been fulfilled; but they were conscious that they were not as other animals. If they went hungry, it was not from feeding tyrannical human beings; if they worked hard, at least they worked for themselves. No creature among them went upon two legs. No creature called any other creature 'Master'. All animals were equal.

One day in early summer Squealer ordered the sheep to follow him, and led them out to a piece of waste ground at the other end of the farm, which had become overgrown with birch saplings. The sheep spent the whole day there browsing at the leaves under Squealer's supervision. In the evening he returned to the farmhouse himself, but, as it was warm weather, told the sheep to stay where they were. It ended by their remaining there for a whole week, during which time the other animals saw nothing of them. Squealer was with them for the greater part of every day. He was, he said, teaching them to sing a new song, for which privacy was needed.

It was just after the sheep had returned, on a pleasant evening when the animals had finished work and were making their way back to the farm buildings, that the terrified neighing of a horse sounded from the yard. Startled, the animals stopped in the tracks. It was Clover's voice. She neighed again, and all the animals broke into a gallop and rushed into the yard. Then they saw what Clover had seen.

It was a pig walking on his hind legs.

Yes, it was Squealer. A little awkwardly, as though not quite used to supporting his considerable bulk in that position, but with perfect balance, he was strolling across the yard. And a moment later, out from the door of the farmhouse came a long file of pigs, all walking on their hind legs. Some did it better than others, one or two were even a trifle unsteady and looked as though they would have liked the support of a stick, but every one of them made his way right round the yard successfully. And finally there was a tremendous baying of dogs and a shrill crowing from the black cockerel, and out came Napoleon himself, majestically upright, casting haughty glances from side to side, and with his dogs gambolling round him.

He carried a whip in his trotter.

There was a deadly silence. Amazed, terrified, huddling together, the animals watched the long line of pigs march slowly round the yard. It was as though the world had turned upside-down. Then there came a moment when the first shock had worn off and when, in spite of everything—in spite of their terror of the dogs, and of the habit, developed through long years, of never complaining, never criticizing, no matter what happened—they might have uttered some word of protest. But just at that moment, as though at a signal, all the sheep burst out into a tremendous bleating of—

'Four legs good, two legs *better*! Four legs good, two legs *better*! Four legs good, two legs *better*!'

It went on for five minutes without stopping. And by the time the sheep had quieted down, the chance to utter any protest had passed, for the pigs had marched back into the farmhouse.

Benjamin felt a nose nuzzling at his shoulder. He looked round. It was Clover. Her old eyes looked dimmer than ever. Without saying anything, she tugged gently at his mane and led him round to the end of the big barn, where the Seven Commandments were written. For a minute or two they stood gazing at the tarred wall with its white lettering.

'My sight is failing,' she said finally. 'Even when I was young I could not have read what was written there. But it appears to me that that wall looks different. Are the Seven Commandments the same as they used to be, Benjamin?'

For once Benjamin consented to break his rule, and he read out to her what was written on the wall. There was nothing there now except a single Commandment. It ran:

ALL ANIMALS ARE EQUAL

BUT SOME ANIMALS ARE MORE

EQUAL THAN OTHERS

After that it did not seem strange when next day the pigs who were supervising the work of the farm all carried whips in their trotters. It did not seem strange to learn that the pigs had bought themselves a wireless set, were arranging to install a telephone, and had taken out subscriptions to *John Bull*, *Tit-Bits*, and the *Daily Mirror*. It did not seem strange when Napoleon was seen strolling in the farmhouse garden with a pipe in his mouth—no, not even when the pigs took Mr Jones's clothes out of the wardrobes and put them on. Napoleon himself appearing in a black coat, ratcatcher breeches, and leather leggings, while his favourite sow appeared in the watered silk dress which Mrs Jones had been used to wear on Sundays.

A week later, in the afternoon, a number of dogcarts drove up to the farm. A deputation of neighbouring farmers had been invited to make a tour of inspection. They were shown all over the farm, and expressed great admiration for everything they saw, especially the windmill. The animals were weeding the turnip field. They worked diligently, hardly raising their faces from the ground, and not knowing whether to be more frightened of the pigs or of the human visitiors.

That evening loud laughter and bursts of singing came from the farmhouse. And suddenly, at the sound of the mingled voices, the animals were stricken with curiosity. What could be happening in there, now that for the first time animals and human beings were meeting on terms of equality? With one accord they began to creep as quietly as possible into the farmhouse garden.

At the gate they paused, half frightened to go on, but Clover led the way in. They tiptoed up to the house, and such animals as were tall enough peered in at the dining-room window. There, round the long table, sat half a dozen farmers and half a dozen of the more eminent pigs, Napoleon himself occupying the seat of honour at the head of the table. The pigs appeared completely at ease in their chairs. The company had been enjoying a game of cards, but had broken off for a moment, evidently in order to drink a toast. A large jug was circulating, and the mugs were being refilled with beer. No one noticed the wondering faces of the animals that gazed in at the window.

Mr Pilkington of Foxwood, had stood up, his mug in his hand. In a moment, he said, he would ask the present company to drink a toast. But before doing so, there were a few words that he felt it incumbent upon him to say.

It was a source of great satisfaction to him, he said—and, he was sure, to all others present—to feel that a long period of mistrust and misunderstanding had now come to an end. There had been a time—not that he, or any of the present company, had shared such sentiments—but there had been a time when the respected proprietors of Animal Farm had been regarded, he would not say with hostility, but perhaps with a certain measure of misgiving, by their human neighbours. Unfortunate incidents had occurred, mistaken ideas had been current. It had been felt that the existence of a farm owned and operated by pigs was somehow abnormal and was liable to have an unsettling effect in the neighbourhood. Too many farmers had assumed without due inquiry, that on such a farm a spirit of licence and indiscipline would prevail. They had been nervous about the effects upon their own animals, or even upon their human employees. But all such doubts were now dispelled. Today he and his friends had visited Animal Farm and inspected every inch of it with their own eyes, and what did they find? Not only the most up-to-date methods, but a discipline and an orderliness which should be an example to all farmers everywhere. He believed that he was right in saying that the lower animals on Animal Farm did more work and received less food than any animals in the county. Indeed, he and his fellow visitors today had observed many features which they intended to introduce on their own farms immediately.

He would end his remarks, he said, by emphasizing once again the friendly feelings that subsisted, and ought to subsist, between Animal Farm and its neighbours. Between pigs and human beings there was not, and there need not be, any clash of interests whatever. Their struggles and their difficulties were one. Was not the labour problem the same everywhere? Here it became apparent that Mr Pilkington was about to spring some carefully prepared witticism on the company, but for a moment he was too overcome by amusement to be able to utter it. After much choking, during which his various chins turned purple, he managed to get it out: 'If you have your lower animals to contend with,' he said, 'we have our lower classes!' This *bon mot* set the table in a roar; and Mr Pilkington once again congratulated the pigs on the low rations, the long working hours, and the general absence of pampering which he had observed on Animal Farm.

And now, he said finally, he would ask the company to rise on their feet and make certain that their glasses were full. 'Gentlemen,' concluded Mr Pilkington, 'gentlemen, I give you a toast: to the prosperity of Animal Farm!'

There was enthusiastic cheering and stamping of feet. Napoleon was so gratified that he left his place and came round the table to clink his mug against Mr Pilkington's before emptying it. When the cheering had died down, Napoleon, who had remained on his feet, intimated that he too had a few words to say.

Like all of Napoleon's speeches, it was short and to the point. He too, he said, was happy that the period of misunderstanding was at an end. For a long time there had been rumours—circulated, he had reason to think, by some malignant enemy—that there was something subversive and even re-volutionary in the outlook of himself and his colleagues. They had been credited with attempting to stir up rebellion among the animals on neighbouring farms. Nothing could be further from the truth! Their sole wish, now and in the past, was to live at peace and in normal business relations with their neighbours. This farm which he had the honour to control, he added, was a co-operative enterprise. The title-deeds, which were in his own possession, were owned by the pigs jointly.

He did not believe, he said, that any of the old suspicions still lingered, but certain changes had been made recently in the routine of the farm which should have the effect of promoting confidence still further. Hitherto the animals on the farm had had a rather foolish custom of addressing one another as 'Comrade'. This was to be suppressed. There had also been a very strange custom, whose origin was unknown, of marching every Sunday morning past a boar's skull which was nailed to a post in the garden. This, too, would be suppressed, and the skull had already been buried. His visitors might have observed, too, the green flag which flew from the masthead. If so, they would perhaps have noted that the white hoof and horn with which it had previously been marked had now been removed. It would be a plain green flag from now onwards.

He had only one criticism, he said, to make of Mr Pilkington's excellent and neighbourly speech. Mr Pilkington had referred throughout to 'Animal Farm'. He could not of course know—for he, Napoleon, was only now for the first time announcing it—that the name, 'Animal Farm' had been abolished. Henceforward the farm was to be known as the 'Manor Farm'—which, he believed, was its correct and original name.

'Gentlemen,' concluded Napoleon, 'I will give you the same toast as before, but in a different form. Fill your glasses to the brim. Gentlemen, here is my toast: To the prosperity of the Manor Farm!'

There was the same hearty cheering as before, and the mugs were emptied to the dregs. But as the animals outside gazed at the scene, it seemed to them that some strange thing was happening. What was it that had altered in the faces of the pigs? Clover's old dim eyes flitted from one face to another. Some of them had five chins, some had four, some had three. But what was it that seemed to be melting and changing. Then, the applause having come to an end, the company took up their cards and continued the game that had been interrupted, and the animals crept silently away.

But they had not gone twenty yards when they stopped short. An uproar of voices was coming from the farmhouse. They rushed back and looked through the window again. Yes, a violent quarrel was in progress. There were shoutings, bangings on the table, sharp suspicious glances, furious denials. The source of the trouble appeared to be that Napoleon and Mr Pilkington had each played an ace of spades simultaneously.

Twelve voices were shouting in anger, and they were all alike. No question, now, what had happened to the faces of the pigs. The creatures outside looked from pig to man, and from man to pig, and from pig to man again; but already it was impossible to say which was which.

November 1943–February 1944

# BURMESE DAYS

# BURMESE DAYS

'This desert inaccessible
Under the shade of melancholy boughs'

*As you like it.*

# I

U Po Kyin, Sub-divisional Magistrate of Kyauktada, in Upper Burma, was sitting in his veranda. It was only half past eight, but the month was April, and there was a closeness in the air, a threat of the long, stifling midday hours. Occasional faint breaths of wind, seeming cool by contrast, stirred the newly drenched orchids that hung from the eaves. Beyond the orchids one could see the dusty, curved trunk of a palm tree, and then the blazing ultramarine sky. Up in the zenith, so high that it dazzled one to look at them, a few vultures circled without the quiver of a wing.

Unblinking, rather like a great porcelain idol, U Po Kyin gazed out into the fierce sunlight. He was a man of fifty, so fat that for years he had not risen from his chair without help, and yet shapely and even beautiful in his grossness; for the Burmese do not sag and bulge like white men, but grow fat symmetrically, like fruits swelling. His face was vast, yellow and quite unwrinkled, and his eyes were tawny. His feet—squat, high-arched feet with the toes all the same length—were bare, and so was his cropped head, and he wore one of those vivid Arakanese *longyis* with green and magenta checks which the Burmese wear on informal occasions. He was chewing betel from a lacquered box on the table, and thinking about his past life.

It had been a brilliantly successful life. U Po Kyin's earliest memory, back in the eighties, was of standing, a naked pot-bellied child, watching the British troops march victorious into Mandalay. He remembered the terror he had felt of those columns of great beef-fed men, red-faced and red-coated; and the long rifles over their shoulders, and the heavy, rhythmic tramp of their boots. He had taken to his heels after watching them for a few minutes. In his childish way he had grasped that his own people were no match for this race of giants. To fight on the side of the British, to become a parasite upon them, had been his ruling ambition, even as a child.

At seventeen he had tried for a Government appointment, but he had failed to get it, being poor and friendless, and for three years he had worked in the stinking labyrinth of the Mandalay bazaars, clerking for the rice merchants and sometimes stealing. Then when he was twenty a lucky stroke of blackmail put him in possession of four hundred rupees, and he went at once to Rangoon and bought his way into a Government clerkship. The job was a lucrative one though the salary was small. At that time a ring of clerks were making a steady income by misappropriating Government stores, and Po Kyin (he was plain Po Kyin then: the honorific U came years later) took naturally to this kind of thing. However, he had too much talent to spend his life in a clerkship, stealing miserably in annas and pice. One day he discovered that the Government, being short of minor officials, were going to make some appointments from among the clerks. The news would have become public in another week, but it was one of Po Kyin's qualities that his information was always a week ahead of everyone else's. He saw his chance and denounced all his confederates before they could take alarm. Most of them were sent to prison, and Po Kyin was made an Assistant Township Officer as the reward of his honesty. Since then he had risen steadily. Now, at fifty-six, he was a Sub-divisional Magistrate, and he would probably be promoted still further and made an acting Deputy Commissioner, with Englishmen as his equals and even his subordinates.

As a magistrate his methods were simple. Even for the vastest bribe he would never sell the decision of a case, because he knew that a magistrate who gives wrong judgments is caught sooner or later. His practice, a much safer one, was to take bribes from both sides and then decide the case on strictly legal grounds. This won him a useful reputation for impartiality. Besides his revenue from litigants, U Po Kyin levied a ceaseless toll, a sort of private taxation scheme, from all the villages under his jurisdiction. If any village failed in its tribute U Po Kyin took punitive measures—gangs of dacoits attacked the village, leading villagers were arrested on false charges, and so forth—and it was never long before the amount was paid up. He also shared the proceeds of all the larger-sized robberies that took place in the district. Most of this, of course, was known to everyone except U Po Kyin's official superiors (no British officer will ever believe anything against his own men) but the attempts to expose him invariably failed; his supporters, kept loyal by their share of the loot, were too numerous. When any accusation was brought against him, U Po Kyin simply discredited it with strings of suborned witnesses, following this up by counter-accusations which left him in a stronger position than ever. He was practically invulnerable, because he was too fine a judge of men ever to choose a wrong instrument, and also because he was too absorbed in intrigue ever to fail through carelessness or ignorance. One could say with practical certainty that he would never be found out, that he would go from success to success, and would finally die full of honour, worth several lakhs of rupees.

And even beyond the grave his success would continue. According to Buddhist belief, those who have done evil in their lives will spend the next incarnation in the shape of a rat, a frog or some other low animal. U Po Kyin was a good Buddhist and intended to provide against this danger. He would devote his closing years to good works, which would pile up enough merit to outweigh the rest of his life. Probably his good works would take the form of building pagodas. Four pagodas, five, six, seven—the priests would tell him how many—with carved stonework, gilt umbrellas and little bells that tinkled in the wind, every tinkle a prayer. And he would return to the earth in male human shape—for a woman ranks at about the same level as a rat or a frog—or at best as some dignified beast such as an elephant.

All these thoughts flowed through U Po Kyin's mind swiftly and for the most part in pictures. His brain, though cunning, was quite barbaric, and it never worked except for some definite end; mere meditation was beyond him. He had now reached the point to which his thoughts had been tending. Putting his smallish, triangular hands on the arms of his chair, he turned himself a little way round and called, rather wheezily:

'Ba Taik! Hey, Ba Taik!'

Ba Taik, U Po Kyin's servant, appeared through the beaded curtain of the veranda. He was an under-sized, pock-marked man with a timid and rather hungry expression. U Po Kyin paid him no wages, for he was a convicted thief whom a word would send to prison. As Ba Taik advanced he shikoed, so low as to give the impression that he was stepping backwards.

'Most holy god?' he said.

'Is anyone waiting to see me, Ba Taik?'

Ba Taik enumerated the visitors upon his fingers: 'There is the headman of Thitpingyi village, your honour, who has brought presents, and two villagers who have an assault case that is to be tried by your honour, and they too have brought presents. Ko Ba Sein, the head clerk of the Deputy Commissioner's office, wishes to see you, and there is Ali Shah, the police constable, and a dacoit whose name I do not know. I think they have quarrelled about some gold bangles they have stolen. And there is also a young village girl with a baby.'

'What does she want?' said U Po Kyin.

'She says that the baby is yours, most holy one.'

'Ah. And how much has the headman brought?'

Ba Taik thought it was only ten rupees and a basket of mangoes.

'Tell the headman,' said U Po Kyin, 'that it should be twenty rupees, and there will be trouble for him and his village if the money is not here tomorrow. I will see the others presently. Ask Ko Ba Sein to come to me here.'

Ba Sein appeared in a moment. He was an erect, narrow-shouldered man, very tall for a Burman, with a curiously smooth face that recalled a coffee blancmange. U Po Kyin found him a useful tool. Unimaginative and hard-working, he was an excellent clerk, and Mr Macgregor, the Deputy Commissioner, trusted him with most of his official secrets. U Po Kyin, put in a good temper by his thoughts, greeted Ba Sein with a laugh and waved to the betel box.

'Well, Ko Ba Sein, how does our affair progress? I hope that, as dear Mr Macgregor would say'—U Po Kyin broke into English—'"eet ees making perceptible progress"?'

Ba Sein did not smile at the small joke. Sitting down stiff and long-backed in the vacant chair, he answered:

'Excellently, sir. Our copy of the paper arrived this morning. Kindly observe.'

He produced a copy of a bilingual paper called the *Burmese Patriot*. It was a miserable eight-page rag, villainously printed on paper as bad as blotting paper, and composed partly of news stolen from the *Rangoon Gazette,* partly of weak Nationalist heroics. On the last page the type had slipped and left the entire sheet jet black, as though in mourning for the smallness of the paper's circulation. The article to which U Po Kyin turned was of a rather different stamp from the rest. It ran:

In these happy times, when we poor blacks are being uplifted by the mighty western civilization, with its manifold blessings such as the cinematograph, machine-guns, syphilis, etc., what subject could be more inspiring than the private lives of our European benefactors? We think therefore that it may interest our readers to hear something of events in the up-country district of Kyauktada. And especially of Mr Macgregor, honoured Deputy Commissioner of said district.

Mr Macgregor is of the type of the Fine Old English Gentleman, such as, in these happy days, we have so many examples before our eyes. He is 'a family man' as our dear English cousins say. Very much a family man is Mr Macgregor. So much so that he has already three children in the district of Kyauktada, where he has been a year, and in his last district of Shwemyo he left six young progenies behind him. Perhaps it is an oversight on Mr Macgregor's part that he has left these young infants quite unprovided for, and that some of their mothers are in danger of starvation, etc., etc., etc.

There was a column of similar stuff, and wretched as it was, it was well above the level of the rest of the paper. U Po Kyin read the article carefully through, holding it at arm's length—he was long-sighted—and drawing his lips meditatively back, exposing great numbers of small, perfect teeth, blood-red from betel juice.

'The editor will get six months' imprisonment for this,' he said finally.

'He does not mind. He says that the only time when his creditors leave him alone is when he is in prison.'

'And you say that your little apprentice clerk Hla Pe wrote this article all by himself? That is a very clever boy—a most promising boy! Never tell me again that these Government High Schools are a waste of time. Hla Pe shall certainly have his clerkship.'

'You think then, sir, that this article will be enough?'

U Po Kyin did not answer immediately. A puffing, labouring noise began to proceed from him; he was trying to rise from his chair. Ba Taik was familiar with this sound. He appeared from behind the beaded curtain, and he and Ba Sein put a hand under each of U Po Kyin's armpits and hoisted him to his feet. U Po Kyin stood for a moment balancing the weight of his belly upon his legs, with the movement of a fish porter adjusting his load. Then he waved Ba Taik away.

'Not enough,' he said, answering Ba Sein's question, 'not enough by any means. There is a lot to be done yet. But this is the right beginning. Listen.'

He went to the rail to spit out a scarlet mouthful of betel, and then began to quarter the veranda with short steps, his hands behind his back. The friction of his vast thighs made him waddle slightly. As he walked he talked, in the base jargon of the Government offices—a patchwork of Burmese verbs and English abstract phrases:

'Now, let us go into this affair from the beginning. We are going to make a concerted attack on Dr Veraswami, who is the Civil Surgeon and Superintendent of the jail. We are going to slander him, destroy his reputation and finally ruin him for ever. It will be rather a delicate operation.'

'Yes, sir.'

'There will be no risk, but we have got to go slowly. We are not proceeding against a miserable clerk or police constable. We are proceeding against a high official, and with a high official, even when he is an Indian, it is not the same as with a clerk. How does one ruin a clerk? Easy; an accusation, two dozen witnesses, dismissal and imprisonment. But that will not do here. Softly, softly, softly is my way. No scandal, and above all no official inquiry. There must be no accusations that can be answered, and yet within three months I must fix it in the head of every European in Kyauktada that the doctor is a villain. What shall I accuse him of? Bribes will not do, a doctor does not get bribes to any extent. What then?'

'We could perhaps arrange a mutiny in the jail,' said Ba Sein. 'As superintendent, the doctor would be blamed.'

'No, it is too dangerous. I do not want the jail warders firing their rifles in all directions. Besides, it would be expensive. Clearly, then, it must be disloyalty—Nationalism, seditious propaganda. We must persuade the Europeans that the doctor holds disloyal, anti-British opinions. That is far worse than bribery; they expect a native official to take bribes. But let them suspect his loyalty even for a moment, and he is ruined.'

'It would be a hard thing to prove,' objected Ba Sein. 'The doctor is very loyal to the Europeans. He grows angry when anything is said against them. They will know that, do you not think?'

'Nonsense, nonsense,' said U Po Kyin comfortably. 'No European cares anything about proofs. When a man has a black face, suspicion *is* proof. A few anonymous letters will work wonders. It is only a question of persisting; accuse, accuse, go on accusing—that is the way with Europeans. One anonymous letter after another, to every European in turn. And then, when their suspicions are thoroughly aroused—' U Po Kyin brought one short arm from behind his back and clicked his thumb and finger. He added: 'We begin with this article in the *Burmese Patriot*. The Europeans will shout with rage when they see it. Well, the next move is to persuade them that it was the doctor who wrote it.'

'It will be difficult while he has friends among the Europeans. All of them go to him when they are ill. He cured Mr Macgregor of his flatulence this cold weather. They consider him a very clever doctor, I believe.'

'How little you understand the European mind, Ko Ba Sein! If the Europeans go to Veraswami it is only because there is no other doctor in Kyauktada. No European has any faith in a man with a black face. No, with anonymous letters it is only a question of sending enough. I shall soon see to it that he has no friends left.'

'There is Mr Flory, the timber merchant,' said Ba Sein. (He pronounced it 'Mr Porley'.) 'He is a close friend of the doctor. I see him go to his house every morning when he is in Kyauktada. Twice he has even invited the doctor to dinner.'

'Ah, now there you are right. If Flory were a friend of the doctor it could do us harm. You cannot hurt an Indian when he has a European friend. It gives him—what is that word they are so fond of?—prestige. But Flory will desert his friend quickly enough when the trouble begins. These people have no feeling of loyalty towards a native. Besides, I happen to know that Flory is a coward. I can deal with him. Your part, Ko Ba Sein, is to watch Mr Macgregor's movements. Has he written to the Commissioner lately—written confidentially, I mean?'

'He wrote two days ago, but when we steamed the letter open we found it was nothing of importance.'

'Ah well, we will give him something to write about. And as soon as he suspects the doctor, then is the time for that other affair I spoke to you of. Thus we shall—what does Mr Macgregor say? Ah yes, "kill two birds with one stone". A whole flock of birds—ha, ha!'

U Po Kyin's laugh was a disgusting bubbling sound deep down in his belly, like the preparation for a cough; yet it was merry, even childlike. He did not say any more about the 'other affair', which was too private to be discussed even upon the veranda. Ba Sein, seeing the interview at an end, stood up and bowed, angular as a jointed ruler.

'Is there anything else your honour wishes done?' he said.

'Make sure that Mr Macgregor has his copy of the *Burmese Patriot*. You had better tell Hla Pe to have an attack of dysentery and stay away from the office. I shall want him for the writing of the anonymous letters. That is all for the present.'

'Then I may go, sir?'

'God go with you,' said U Po Kyin rather abstractedly, and at once shouted again for Ba Taik. He never wasted a moment of his day. It did not take him long to deal with the other visitors and to send the village girl away unrewarded, having examined her face and said that he did not recognize her. It was now his breakfast time. Violent pangs of hunger, which attacked him punctually at this hour every morning, began to torment his belly. He shouted urgently:

'Ba Taik! Hey, Ba Taik! Kin Kin! My breakfast! Be quick, I am starving.'

In the living-room behind the curtain a table was already set out with a huge bowl of rice and a dozen plates containing curries, dried prawns and sliced green mangoes. U Po Kyin waddled to the table, sat down with a grunt and at once threw himself on the food. Ma Kin, his wife, stood behind him and served him. She was a thin woman of five and forty, with a kindly, pale brown, simian face. U Po Kyin took no notice of her while he was eating. With the bowl close to his nose he stuffed the food into himself with swift, greasy fingers, breathing fast. All his meals were swift, passionate and enormous; they were not meals so much as orgies, debauches of curry and rice. When he had finished he sat back, belched several times and told Ma Kin to fetch him a green Burmese cigar. He never smoked English tobacco, which he declared had no taste in it.

Presently, with Ba Taik's help, U Po Kyin dressed in his office clothes, and stood for a while admiring himself in the long mirror in the living-room. It was a wooden-walled room with two pillars, still recognizable as teak-trunks, supporting the roof-tree, and it was dark and sluttish as all Burmese rooms are, though U Po Kyin had furnished it 'Ingaleik fashion' with a veneered sideboard and chairs, some lithographs of the Royal Family and a fire-extinguisher. The floor was covered with bamboo mats, much splashed by lime and betel juice.

Ma Kin was sitting on a mat in the corner, stitching an *ingyi*. U Po Kyin turned slowly before the mirror, trying to get a glimpse of his back view. He was dressed in a *gaungbaung* of pale pink silk, an *ingyi* of starched muslin, and a *paso* of Mandalay silk, a gorgeous salmon-pink brocaded with yellow. With an effort he turned his head round and looked, pleased, at the *paso* tight and shining on his enormous buttocks. He was proud of his fatness, because he saw the accumulated flesh as the symbol of his greatness. He who had once been obscure and hungry was now fat, rich and feared. He was swollen with the bodies of his enemies; a thought from which he extracted something very near poetry.

'My new *paso* was cheap at twenty-two rupees, hey, Kin Kin?' he said.

Ma Kin bent her head over her sewing. She was a simple, old-fashioned woman, who had learned even less of European habits than U Po Kyin. She could not sit on a chair without discomfort. Every morning she went to the bazaar with a basket on her head, like a village woman, and in the evenings she could be seen kneeling in the garden, praying to the white spire of the pagoda that crowned the town. She had been the confidante of U Po Kyin's intrigues for twenty years and more.

'Ko Po Kyin,' she said, 'you have done very much evil in your life.'

U Po Kyin waved his hand. 'What does it matter? My pagodas will atone for everything. There is plenty of time.'

Ma Kin bent her head over her sewing again, in an obstinate way she had when she disapproved of something that U Po Kyin was doing.

'But, Ko Po Kyin, where is the need for all this scheming and intriguing? I heard you talking with Ko Ba Sein on the veranda. You are planning some evil against Dr Veraswami. Why do you wish to harm that Indian doctor? He is a good man.'

'What do you know of these official matters, woman? The doctor stands in my way. In the first place he refuses to take bribes, which makes it difficult for the rest of us. And besides—well, there is something else which you would never have the brains to understand.'

'Ko Po Kyin, you have grown rich and powerful, and what good has it ever done you? We were happier when we were poor. Ah, I remember so well when you were only a Township Officer, the first time we had a house of our own. How proud we were of our new wicker furniture, and your fountain-pen with the gold clip! And when the young English police-officer came to our house and sat in the best chair and drank a bottle of beer, how honoured we thought ourselves! Happiness is not in money. What can you want with more money now?'

'Nonsense, woman, nonsense! Attend to your cooking and sewing and leave official matters to those who understand them.'

'Well, I do not know. I am your wife and have always obeyed you. But at least it is never too soon to acquire merit. Strive to acquire more merit, Ko Po

Kyin! Will you not, for instance, buy some live fish and set them free in the
river? One can acquire much merit in that way. Also, this morning when
the priests came for their rice they told me that there are two new priests at the
monastery, and they are hungry. Will you not give them something, Ko Po
Kyin? I did not give them anything myself, so that you might acquire the merit
of doing it.'

U Po Kyin turned away from the mirror. The appeal touched him a little.
He never, when it could be done without inconvenience, missed a chance of
acquiring merit. In his eyes his pile of merit was a kind of bank deposit,
everlastingly growing. Every fish set free in the river, every gift to a priest, was
a step nearer Nirvana. It was a reassuring thought. He directed that the basket
of mangoes brought by the village headman should be sent down to the
monastery.

Presently he left the house and started down the road, with Ba Taik behind
him carrying a file of papers. He walked slowly, very upright to balance his vast
belly, and holding a yellow silk umbrella over his head. His pink *paso* glittered
in the sun like a satin praline. He was going to the court, to try his day's cases.

## 2

At about the time when U Po Kyin began his morning's business, 'Mr Porley'
the timber merchant and friend of Dr Veraswami, was leaving his house for the
Club.

Flory was a man of about thirty-five, of middle height, not ill made. He had
very black, stiff hair growing low on his head, and a cropped black moustache,
and his skin, naturally sallow, was discoloured by the sun. Not having grown
fat or bald he did not look older than his age, but his face was very haggard in
spite of the sunburn, with lank cheeks and a sunken, withered look round the
eyes. He had obviously not shaved this morning. He was dressed in the usual
white shirt, khaki drill shorts and stockings, but instead of a topi he wore a
battered Terai hat, cocked over one eye. He carried a bamboo stick with a
wrist-thong, and a black cocker spaniel named Flo was ambling after him.

All these were secondary expressions, however. The first thing that one
noticed in Flory was a hideous birthmark stretching in a ragged crescent down
his left cheek, from the eye to the corner of the mouth. Seen from the left side
his face had a battered, woebegone look, as though the birthmark had been a
bruise—for it was a dark blue in colour. He was quite aware of its hideousness.
And at all times, when he was not alone, there was a sidelongness about his
movements, as he manœuvred constantly to keep the birthmark out of sight.

Flory's house was at the top of the maidan, close to the edge of the jungle.
From the gate the maidan sloped sharply down, scorched and khaki-coloured,

with half a dozen dazzling white bungalows scattered round it. All quaked, shivered in the hot air. There was an English cemetery within a white wall half-way down the hill, and near by a tiny tin-roofed church. Beyond that was the European Club, and when one looked at the Club—a dumpy one-storey wooden building—one looked at the real centre of the town. In any town in India the European Club is the spiritual citadel, the real seat of the British power, the Nirvana for which native officials and millionaires pine in vain. It was doubly so in this case, for it was the proud boast of Kyauktada Club that, almost alone of Clubs in Burma, it had never admitted an Oriental to membership. Beyond the Club, the Irrawaddy flowed huge and ochreous glittering like diamonds in the patches that caught the sun; and beyond the river stretched great wastes of paddy fields, ending at the horizon in a range of blackish hills.

The native town, and the courts and the jail, were over to the right, mostly hidden in green groves of peepul trees. The spire of the pagoda rose from the trees like a slender spear tipped with gold. Kyauktada was a fairly typical Upper Burma town, that had not changed greatly between the days of Marco Polo and 1910, and might have slept in the Middle Ages for a century more if it had not proved a convenient spot for a railway terminus. In 1910 the Government made it the headquarters of a district and a seat of Progress—interpretable as a block of law courts, with their army of fat but ravenous pleaders, a hospital, a school and one of those huge, durable jails which the English have built everywhere between Gibraltar and Hong Kong. The population was about four thousand, including a couple of hundred Indians, a few score Chinese and seven Europeans. There were also two Eurasians named Mr Francis and Mr Samuel, the sons of an American Baptist missionary and a Roman Catholic missionary respectively. The town contained no curiosities of any kind, except an Indian fakir who had lived for twenty years in a tree near the bazaar, drawing his food up in a basket every morning.

Flory yawned as he came out of the gate. He had been half drunk the night before, and the glare made him feel liverish. 'Bloody, bloody hole!' he thought, looking down the hill. And, no one except the dog being near, he began to sing aloud, 'Bloody, bloody, bloody, oh, how thou art bloody' to the tune of 'Holy, holy, holy, oh how Thou art holy ' as he walked down the hot red road, swishing at the dried-up grasses with his stick. It was nearly nine o'clock and the sun was fiercer every minute. The heat throbbed down on one's head with a steady, rhythmic thumping, like blows from an enormous bolster. Flory stopped at the Club gate, wondering whether to go in or to go farther down the road and see Dr Veraswami. Then he remembered that it was 'English mail day' and the newspapers would have arrived. He went in, past the big tennis screen, which was overgrown by a creeper with starlike mauve flowers.

In the borders beside the path swaths of English flowers—phlox and larkspur, hollyhock and petunia—not yet slain by the sun, rioted in vast size and richness. The petunias were huge, like trees almost. There was no lawn, but instead a shrubbery of native trees and bushes—gold mohur trees like vast umbrellas of blood-red bloom, frangipanis with creamy, stalkless flowers, purple bougainvillea, scarlet hibiscus and the pink Chinese rose, bilious-green crotons, feathery fronds of tamarind. The clash of colours hurt one's eyes in the glare. A nearly naked *mali,* watering-can in hand, was moving in the jungle of flowers like some large nectar-sucking bird.

On the Club steps a sandy-haired Englishman, with a prickly moustache, pale grey eyes too far apart, and abnormally thin calves to his legs, was standing with his hands in the pockets of his shorts. This was Mr Westfield, the District Superintendent of Police. With a very bored air he was rocking himself backwards and forwards on his heels and pouting his upper lip so that his moustache tickled his nose. He greeted Flory with a slight sideways movement of his head. His way of speaking was clipped and soldierly, missing out every word that well could be missed out. Nearly everything he said was intended for a joke, but the tone of his voice was hollow and melancholy.

'Hullo, Flory me lad. Bloody awful morning, what?'

'We must expect it at this time of year, I suppose,' Flory said. He had turned himself a little sideways, so that his birthmarked cheek was away from Westfield.

'Yes, dammit. Couple of months of this coming. Last year we didn't have a spot of rain till June. Look at that bloody sky, not a cloud in it. Like one of those damned great blue enamel saucepans. God! What'd you give to be in Piccadilly now, eh?'

'Have the English papers come?'

'Yes. Dear old *Punch, Pink'un* and *Vie Parisienne.* Makes you homesick to read 'em, what? Let's come in and have a drink before the ice all goes. Old Lackersteen's been fairly bathing in it. Half pickled already.'

They went in, Westfield remarking in his gloomy voice, 'Lead on, Macduff.' Inside, the Club was a teak-walled place smelling of earth-oil, and consisting of only four rooms, one of which contained a forlorn 'library' of five hundred mildewed novels, and another an old and mangy billiard-table—this, however, seldom used, for during most of the year hordes of flying beetles came buzzing round the lamps and littered themselves over the cloth. There were also a card-room and a 'lounge' which looked towards the river, over a wide veranda; but at this time of day all the verandas were curtained with green bamboo chicks. The lounge was an unhomelike room, with coco-nut matting on the floor, and wicker chairs and tables which were littered with shiny illustrated papers. For ornament there were a number of 'Bonzo' pictures, and the dusty skulls of sambhur. A punkah, lazily flapping, shook dust into the tepid air.

There were three men in the room. Under the punkah a florid, fine-looking, slightly bloated man of forty was sprawling across the table with his head in his hands, groaning in pain. This was Mr Lackersteen, the local manager of a timber firm. He had been badly drunk the night before, and he was suffering for it. Ellis, local manager of yet another company, was standing before the notice-board studying some notice with a look of bitter concentration. He was a tiny wiry-haired fellow with a pale, sharp-featured face and restless movements. Maxwell, the acting Divisional Forest Officer, was lying in one of the long chairs reading the *Field*, and invisible except for two large-boned legs and thick downy forearms.

'Look at this naughty old man,' said Westfield, taking Mr Lackersteen half affectionately by the shoulders and shaking him. 'Example to the young, what? There but for the grace of God and all that. Gives you an idea what you'll be like at forty.'

Mr Lackersteen gave a groan which sounded like 'brandy'.

'Poor old chap,' said Westfield, 'regular martyr to booze, eh? Look at it oozing out of his pores. Reminds me of the old colonel who used to sleep without a mosquito net. They asked his servant why and the servant said: "At night, master too drunk to notice mosquitoes; in the morning, mosquitoes too drunk to notice master." Look at him—boozed last night and then asking for more. Got a little niece coming to stay with him, too. Due tonight, isn't she, Lackersteen?'

'Oh, leave that drunken sot alone,' said Ellis without turning round. He had a spiteful Cockney voice. Mr Lackersteen groaned again, '— the niece! Get me some brandy, for Christ's sake.'

'Good education for the niece, eh? Seeing uncle under the table seven times a week. Hey, butler! Bringing brandy for Lackersteen master!'

The butler, a dark, stout Dravidian with liquid, yellow-irised eyes like those of a dog, brought the brandy on a brass tray. Flory and Westfield ordered gin. Mr Lackersteen swallowed a few spoonfuls of brandy and sat back in his chair, groaning in a more resigned way. He had a beefy, ingenuous face, with a toothbrush moustache. He was really a very simple-minded man, with no ambitions beyond having what he called 'a good time'. His wife governed him by the only possible method, namely, by never letting him out of her sight for more than an hour or two. Only once, a year after they were married, she had left him for a fortnight, and had returned unexpectedly a day before her time, to find Mr Lackersteen, drunk, supported on either side by a naked Burmese girl, while a third up-ended a whisky bottle into his mouth. Since then she had watched him, as he used to complain, 'like a cat over a bloody mousehole'. However, he managed to enjoy quite a number of 'good times', though they were usually rather hurried ones.

'My Christ, what a head I've got on me this morning,' he said. 'Call that butler again, Westfield. I've got to have another brandy before my missus gets here. She says she's going to cut my booze down to four pegs a day when our niece gets here. God rot them both!' he added gloomily.

'Stop playing the fool, all of you, and listen to this,' said Ellis sourly. He had a queer wounding way of speaking, hardly ever opening his mouth without insulting somebody. He deliberately exaggerated his Cockney accent, because of the sardonic tone it gave to his words. 'Have you seen this notice of old Macgregor's? A little nosegay for everyone. Maxwell, wake up and listen!'

Maxwell lowered the *Field*. He was a fresh-coloured blond youth of not more than twenty-five or six—very young for the post he held. With his heavy limbs and thick white eyelashes he reminded one of a cart-horse colt. Ellis nipped the notice from the board with a neat, spiteful little movement and began reading it aloud. It had been posted by Mr Macgregor, who, besides being Deputy Commissioner, was secretary of the Club.

'Just listen to this. "It has been suggested that as there are as yet no Oriental members of this club, and as it is now usual to admit officials of gazetted rank, whether native or European, to membership of most European Clubs, we should consider the question of following this practice in Kyauktada. The matter will be open for discussion at the next general meeting. On the one hand it may be pointed out"—oh, well, no need to wade through the rest of it. He can't even write a notice without an attack of literary diarrhoea. Anyway, the point's this. He's asking us to break all our rules and take a dear little nigger-boy into this Club. *Dear* Dr Veraswami, for instance. Dr Very-slimy, I call him. That *would* be a treat, wouldn't it? Little pot-bellied niggers breathing garlic in your face over the bridge-table. Christ, to think of it! We've got to hang together and put our foot down on this at once. What do you say, Westfield? Flory?'

Westfield shrugged his thin shoulders philosophically. He had sat down at the table and lighted a black, stinking Burma cheroot.

'Got to put up with it, I suppose,' he said. 'B—s of natives are getting into all the Clubs nowadays. Even the Pegu Club, I'm told. Way this country's going, you know. We're about the last Club in Burma to hold out against 'em.'

'We are; and what's more, we're damn well going to go on holding out. I'll die in the ditch before I'll see a nigger in here.' Ellis had produced a stump of pencil. With the curious air of spite that some men can put into their tiniest action, he re-pinned the notice on the board and pencilled a tiny, neat 'B.F.' against Mr Macgregor's signature—'There, that's what I think of his idea. I'll tell him so when he comes down. What do *you* say, Flory?'

Flory had not spoken all this time. Though by nature anything but a silent man, he seldom found much to say in Club conversations. He had sat down at the table and was reading G. K. Chesterton's article in the *London News,* at the same time caressing Flo's head with his left hand. Ellis, however, was one of those people who constantly nag others to echo their own opinions. He repeated his question, and Flory looked up, and their eyes met. The skin round Ellis's nose suddenly turned so pale that it was almost grey. In him it was a sign of anger. Without any prelude he burst into a stream of abuse that would have been startling, if the others had not been used to hearing something like it every morning.

'My God, I should have thought in a case like this, when it's a question of keeping those black, stinking swine out of the only place where we can enjoy ourselves, you'd have the decency to back me up. Even if that pot-bellied greasy little sod of a nigger doctor *is* your best pal. *I* don't care if you choose to pal up with the scum of the bazaar. If it pleases you to go to Veraswami's house and drink whisky with all his nigger pals, that's your look-out. Do what you like outside the Club. But, by God, it's a different matter when you talk of bringing niggers in here. I suppose you'd like little Veraswami for a Club member, eh? Chipping into our conversation and pawing everyone with his sweaty hands and breathing his filthy garlic breath in our faces. By god, he'd go out with my boot behind him if ever I saw his black snout inside that door. Greasy, pot-bellied little–!' etc.

This went on for several minutes. It was curiously impressive, because it was so completely sincere. Ellis really did hate Orientals–hated them with a bitter, restless loathing as of something evil or unclean. Living and working, as the assistant of a timber firm must, in perpetual contact with the Burmese, he had never grown used to the sight of a black face. Any hint of friendly feeling towards an Oriental seemed to him a horrible perversity. He was an intelligent man and an able servant of his firm, but he was one of those Englishmen–common, unfortunately–who should never be allowed to set foot in the East.

Flory sat nursing Flo's head in his lap, unable to meet Ellis's eyes. At the best of times his birthmark made it difficult for him to look people straight in the face. And when he made ready to speak, he could feel his voice trembling–for it had a way of trembling when it should have been firm; his features, too, sometimes twitched uncontrollably.

'Steady on,' he said at last, sullenly and rather feebly. 'Steady on. There's no need to get so excited. *I* never suggested having any native members in here.'

'Oh, didn't you? We all know bloody well you'd like to, though. Why else do you go to that oily little babu's house every morning, then? Sitting down at table with him as though he was a white man, and drinking out of glasses his filthy black lips have slobbered over–it makes me spew to think of it.'

'Sit down, old chap, sit down,' Westfield said. 'Forget it. Have a drink on it. Not worth while quarrelling. Too hot.'

'My God,' said Ellis a little more calmly, taking a pace or two up and down, 'my God, I don't understand you chaps. I simply don't. Here's that old fool Macgregor wanting to bring a nigger into this Club for no reason whatever, and you all sit down under it without a word. Good God, what are we supposed to be doing in this country? If we aren't going to rule, why the devil don't we clear out? Here we are, supposed to be governing a set of damn black swine who've been slaves since the beginning of history, and instead of ruling them in the only way they understand, we go and treat them as equals. And you silly b—s take it for granted. There's Flory, makes his best pal a black babu who calls himself a doctor because he's done two years at an Indian so-called university. And you, Westfield, proud as Punch of your knock-kneed, bribe-taking cowards of policemen. And there's Maxwell, spends his time running after Eurasian tarts. Yes, you do, Maxwell; I heard about your goings-on in Mandalay with some smelly little bitch called Molly Pereira. I suppose you'd have gone and married her if they hadn't transferred you up here? You all seem to *like* the dirty black brutes. Christ, I don't know what's come over us all. I really don't.'

'Come on, have another drink,' said Westfield. 'Hey, butler! Spot of beer before the ice goes, eh? Beer, butler!'

The butler brought some bottles of Munich beer. Ellis presently sat down at the table with the others, and he nursed one of the cool bottles between his small hands. His forehead was sweating. He was sulky, but not in a rage any longer. At all times he was spiteful and perverse, but his violent fits of rage were soon over, and were never apologized for. Quarrels were a regular part of the routine of Club life. Mr Lackersteen was feeling better and was studying the illustrations in *La Vie Parisienne*. It was after nine now, and the room, scented with the acrid smoke of Westfield's cheroot, was stifling hot. Everyone's shirt stuck to his back with the first sweat of the day. The invisible *chokra* who pulled the punkah rope outside was falling asleep in the glare.

'Butler!' yelled Ellis, and as the butler appeared, 'go and wake that bloody *chokra* up!'

'Yes, master.'

'And butler!'

'Yes, master?'

'How much ice have we got left?'

''Bout twenty pounds, master. Will only last today, I think. I find it very difficult to keep ice cool now.'

'Don't talk like that, damn you—"I find it very difficult!" Have you swallowed a dictionary? "Please, master, can't keeping ice cool"—that's how you ought to talk. We shall have to sack this fellow if he gets to talk English too well. I can't stick servants who talk English. D'you hear, butler?'

'Yes, master,' said the butler, and retired.

'God! No ice till Monday,' Westfield said. 'You going back to the jungle, Flory?'

'Yes. I ought to be there now. I only came in because of the English mail.'

'Go on tour myself, I think. Knock up a spot of Travelling Allowance. I can't stick my bloody office at this time of year. Sitting there under the damned punkah, signing one chit after another. Paper-chewing. God, how I wish the war was on again!'

'I'm going out the day after tomorrow,' Ellis said. 'Isn't that damned padre coming to hold his service this Sunday? I'll take care not to be in for that, anyway. Bloody knee-drill.'

'Next Sunday,' said Westfield. 'Promised to be in for it myself. So's Macgregor. Bit hard on the poor devil of a padre, I must say. Only gets here once in six weeks. Might as well get up a congregation when he does come.'

'Oh, hell! I'd snivel psalms to oblige the padre, but I can't stick the way these damned native Christians come shoving into our church. A pack of Madrassi servants and Karen school-teachers. And then those two yellow-bellies, Francis and Samuel—they call themselves Christians too. Last time the padre was here they had the nerve to come up and sit on the front pews with the white men. Someone ought to speak to the padre about that. What bloody fools we were ever to let those missionaries loose in this country! Teaching bazaar sweepers they're as good as we are. "Please, sir, me Christian same like master." Damned cheek.'

'How about that for a pair of legs?' said Mr Lackersteen, passing *La Vie Parisienne* across. 'You know French, Flory; what's that mean underneath? Christ, it reminds me of when I was in Paris, my first leave, before I married.

Christ, I wish I was there again!'

'Did you hear that one about "There was a young lady of Woking"?' Maxwell said. He was rather a silent youth, but, like other youths, he had an affection for a good smutty rhyme. He completed the biography of the young lady of Woking, and there was a laugh. Westfield replied with the young lady of Ealing who had a peculiar feeling, and Flory came in with the young curate of Horsham who always took every precaution. There was more laughter. Even Ellis thawed and produced several rhymes; Ellis's jokes were always genuinely witty, and yet filthy beyond measure. Everyone cheered up and felt more friendly in spite of the heat. They had finished the beer and were just going to call for another drink, when shoes creaked on the steps outside. A booming voice, which made the floorboards tingle, was saying jocosely:

'Yes, most distinctly humorous. I incorporated it in one of those little articles of mine in *Blackwood's,* you know. I remember, too, when I was stationed at Prome, another quite—ah—diverting incident which—'

Evidently Mr Macgregor had arrived at the Club. Mr Lackersteen exclaimed, 'Hell! My wife's there,' and pushed his empty glass as far away from him as it would go. Mr Macgregor and Mrs Lackersteen entered the lounge together.

Mr Macgregor was a large, heavy man, rather past forty, with a kindly, puggy face, wearing gold-rimmed spectacles. His bulky shoulders, and a trick he had of thrusting his head forward, reminded one curiously of a turtle—the Burmans, in fact, nicknamed him 'the tortoise'. He was dressed in a clean silk suit, which already showed patches of sweat beneath the armpits. He greeted the others with a humorous mock-salute, and then planted himself before the notice-board, beaming, in the attitude of a schoolmaster twiddling a cane behind his back. The good nature in his face was quite genuine, and yet there was such a wilful geniality about him, such a strenuous air of being off duty and forgetting his official rank, that no one was ever quite at ease in his presence. His conversation was evidently modelled on that of some facetious schoolmaster or clergyman whom he had known in early life. Any long word, any quotation, any proverbial expression figured in his mind as a joke, and was introduced with a bumbling noise like 'er' or 'ah', to make it clear that there was a joke coming. Mrs Lackersteen was a woman of about thirty-five, handsome in a contourless, elongated way, like a fashion plate. She had a sighing, discontented voice. The others had all stood up when she entered, and Mrs Lackersteen sank exhaustedly into the best chair under the punkah, fanning herself with a slender hand like that of a newt.

'Oh dear, this heat, this heat! Mr Macgregor came and fetched me in his car. *So* kind of him. Tom, that wretch of a rickshaw-man is pretending to be ill again. Really, I think you ought to give him a good thrashing and bring him to his senses. It's too terrible to have to walk about in this sun every day.'

Mrs Lackersteen, unequal to the quarter-mile walk between her house and the Club, had imported a rickshaw from Rangoon. Except for bullock-carts and Mr Macgregor's car it was the only wheeled vehicle in Kyauktada, for the whole district did not possess ten miles of road. In the jungle, rather than leave her husband alone, Mrs Lackersteen endured all the horrors of dripping tents, mosquitoes and tinned food; but she made up for it by complaining over trifles while in headquarters.

'Really I think the laziness of these servants is getting too shocking,' she sighed. 'Don't you agree, Mr Macgregor? We seem to have no *authority* over the natives nowadays, with all these dreadful Reforms, and the insolence they learn from the newspapers. In some ways they are getting almost as bad as the lower classes at home.'

'Oh, hardly as bad as that, I trust. Still, I am afraid there is no doubt that the democratic spirit is creeping in, even here.'

'And such a short time ago, even just before the war, they were so *nice* and respectful! The way they salaamed when you passed them on the road—it was really quite charming. I remember when we paid our butler only twelve rupees a month, and really that man loved us like a dog. And now they are demanding forty and fifty rupees, and I find that the only way I can even *keep* a servant is to pay their wages several months in arrears.'

'The old type of servant is disappearing,' agreed Mr Macgregor. 'In my young days, when one's butler was disrespectful, one sent him along to the jail with a chit saying "Please give the bearer fifteen lashes". Ah well, *eheu fugaces*! Those days are gone for ever, I am afraid.'

'Ah, you're about right there,' said Westfield in his gloomy way. 'This country'll never be fit to live in again. British Raj is finished if you ask me. Lost Dominion and all that. Time we cleared out of it.'

Whereat there was a murmur of agreement from everyone in the room, even from Flory, notoriously a Bolshie in his opinions, even from young Maxwell, who had been barely three years in the country. No Anglo-Indian will ever deny that India is going to the dogs, or ever has denied it—for India, like *Punch*, never was what it was.

Ellis had meanwhile unpinned the offending notice from behind Mr Macgregor's back, and he now held it out to him, saying in his sour way:

'Here, Macgregor, we've read this notice, and we all think this idea of electing a native to the Club is absolute—' Ellis was going to have said 'absolute balls', but he remembered Mrs Lackersteen's presence and checked himself—'is absolutely uncalled for. After all, this Club is a place where we come to enjoy ourselves, and we don't want natives poking about in here. We like to think there's still one place where we're free of them. The others all agree with me absolutely.'

He looked round at the others. 'Hear, hear!' said Mr Lackersteen gruffly. He knew that his wife would guess that he had been drinking, and he felt that a display of sound sentiment would excuse him.

Mr Macgregor took the notice with a smile. He saw the 'B. F.' pencilled against his name, and privately he thought Ellis's manner very disrespectful, but he turned the matter off with a joke. He took as great pains to be a good fellow at the Club as he did to keep up his dignity during office hours. 'I gather,' he said, 'that our friend Ellis does not welcome the society of—ah—his Aryan brother?'

'No, I do not,' said Ellis tartly. 'Nor my Mongolian brother. I don't like niggers, to put it in one word.'

Mr Macgregor stiffened at the word 'nigger', which is discountenanced in India. He had no prejudice against Orientals; indeed, he was deeply fond of them. Provided they were given no freedom he thought them the most charming people alive. It always pained him to see them wantonly insulted.

'Is it quite playing the game,' he said stiffly, 'to call these people niggers—a term they very naturally resent—when they are obviously nothing of the kind? The Burmese are Mongolians, the Indians are Aryans or Dravidians, and all of them are quite distinct—'

'Oh, rot that!' said Ellis, who was not at all awed by Mr Macgregor's official status. 'Call them niggers or Aryans or what you like. What I'm saying is that we don't want to see any black hides in this Club. If you put it to the vote you'll find we're against it to a man—unless Flory wants his *dear* pal Veraswami,' he added.

'Hear, hear!' repeated Mr Lackersteen. 'Count on me to blackball the lot of 'em.'

Mr Macgregor pursed his lips whimsically. He was in an awkward position, for the idea of electing a native member was not his own, but had been passed on to him by the Commissioner. However, he disliked making excuses, so he said in a more conciliatory tone:

'Shall we postpone discussing it till the next general meeting? In the meantime we can give it our mature consideration. And now,' he added, moving towards the table, 'who will join me in a little—ah—liquid refreshment?'

The butler was called and the 'liquid refreshment' ordered. It was hotter than ever now, and everyone was thirsty. Mr Lackersteen was on the point of ordering a drink when he caught his wife's eye, shrank up and said sulkily 'No.' He sat with his hands on his knees, with a rather pathetic expression, watching Mrs Lackersteen swallow a glass of lemonade with gin in it. Mr Macgregor, though he signed the chit for drinks, drank plain lemonade. Alone of the Europeans in Kyauktada, he kept the rule of not drinking before sunset.

'It's all very well,' grumbled Ellis, with his forearms on the table, fidgeting with his glass. The dispute with Mr Macgregor had made him restless again. 'It's all very well, but I stick to what I said. No natives in this Club! It's by constantly giving way over small things like that that we've ruined the Empire. The country's only rotten with sedition because we've been too soft with them. The only possible policy is to treat 'em like the dirt they are. This is a critical moment, and we want every bit of prestige we can get. We've got to hang together and say, "*We are the masters,* and you beggars—" ' Ellis pressed his small thumb down as though flattening a grub—' "you beggars keep your place!" '

'Hopeless, old chap,' said Westfield. 'Quite hopeless. What can you do with all this red tape tying your hands? Beggars of natives know the law better than we do. Insult you to your face and then run you in the moment you hit 'em. Can't do anything unless you put your foot down firmly. And how can you, if they haven't the guts to show fight?'

'Our burra sahib at Mandalay always said,' put in Mrs Lackersteen, 'that in the end we shall simply *leave* India. Young men will not come out here any longer to work all their lives for insults and ingratitude. We shall just *go*. When the natives come to us begging us to stay, we shall say, "No, you have had your chance, you wouldn't take it. Very well, we shall leave you to govern yourselves." And then, what a lesson that will teach them!'

'It's all this law and order that's done for us,' said Westfield gloomily. The ruin of the Indian Empire through too much legality was a recurrent theme with Westfield. According to him, nothing save a full-sized rebellion, and the consequent reign of martial law, could save the Empire from decay. 'All this paper-chewing and chit-passing. Office babus are the real rulers of this country now. Our number's up. Best thing we can do is to shut up shop and let 'em stew in their own juice.'

'I don't agree, I simply don't agree,' Ellis said. 'We could put things right in a month if we chose. It only needs a pennyworth of pluck. Look at Amritsar. Look how they caved in after that. Dyer knew the stuff to give them. Poor old Dyer! That was a dirty job. Those cowards in England have got something to answer for.'

There was a kind of sigh from the others, the same sigh that a gathering of Roman Catholics will give at the mention of Bloody Mary. Even Mr Macgregor, who detested bloodshed and martial law, shook his head at the name of Dyer.

'Ah, poor man! Sacrificed to the Paget M.P.s. Well, perhaps they will discover their mistake when it is too late.'

'My old governor used to tell a story about that,' said Westfield. 'There was an old havildar in a native regiment—someone asked him what'd happen if the British left India. The old chap said—'

Flory pushed back his chair and stood up. It must not, it could not—no, it simply should not go on any longer! He must get out of this room quickly, before something happened inside his head and he began to smash the furniture and throw bottles at the pictures. Dull boozing witless porkers! Was it possible that they could go on week after week, year after year, repeating word for word the same evil-minded drivel, like a parody of a fifth-rate story in *Blackwood's*? Would none of them *ever* think of anything new to say? Oh, what a place, what people! What a civilization is this of ours—this godless civilization founded on whisky, *Blackwood's* and the 'Bonzo' pictures! God have mercy on us, for all of us are part of it.

Flory did not say any of this, and he was at some pains not to show it in his face. He was standing by his chair, a little sidelong to the others, with the half-smile of a man who is never sure of his popularity.

'I'm afraid I shall have to be off,' he said. 'I've got some things to see to before breakfast, unfortunately.'

'Stay and have another spot, old man,' said Westfield. 'Morning's young. Have a gin. Give you an appetite.'

'No, thanks, I must be going. Come on, Flo. Good-bye, Mrs Lackersteen.

Good-bye, everybody.'

'Exit Booker Washington, the niggers' pal,' said Ellis as Flory disappeared. Ellis could always be counted on to say something disagreeable about anyone who had just left the room. 'Gone to see Very-slimy, I suppose. Or else sloped off to avoid paying a round of drinks.'

'Oh, he's not a bad chap,' Westfield said. 'Says some Bolshie things sometimes. Don't suppose he means half of them.'

'Oh, a very good fellow, of course,' said Mr Macgregor. Every European in India is ex-officio, or rather ex-colore, a good fellow, until he has done something quite outrageous. It is an honorary rank.

'He's a bit *too* Bolshie for my taste. I can't bear a fellow who pals up with the natives. I shouldn't wonder if he's got a lick of the tar-brush himself. It might explain that black mark on his face. Piebald. And he looks like a yellow-belly, with that black hair, and skin the colour of a lemon.'

There was some desultory scandal about Flory, but not much, because Mr Macgregor did not like scandal. The Europeans stayed in the Club long enough for one more round of drinks. Mr Macgregor told his anecdote about Prome, which could be produced in almost any context. And then the conversation veered back to the old, never-palling subject—the insolence of the natives, the supineness of the Government, the dear dead days when the British Raj *was* the British Raj and please give the bearer fifteen lashes. This topic was never let alone for long, partly because of Ellis's obsession. Besides, you could forgive the Europeans a great deal of their bitterness. Living and working among Orientals would try the temper of a saint. And all of them, the officials particularly, knew what it was to be baited and insulted. Almost every day, when Westfield or Mr Macgregor or even Maxwell went down the street, the High School boys, with their young, yellow faces—faces smooth as gold coins, full of that maddening contempt that sits so naturally on the Mongolian face—sneered at them as they went past, sometimes hooted after them with hyena-like laughter. The life of the Anglo-Indian officials is not all jam. In comfortless camps, in sweltering offices, in gloomy dakbungalows smelling of dust and earth-oil, they earn, perhaps, the right to be a little disagreeable.

It was getting on for ten now, and hot beyond bearing. Flat, clear drops of sweat gathered on everyone's face, and on the men's bare forearms. A damp patch was growing larger and larger in the back of Mr Macgregor's silk coat. The glare outside seemed to soak somehow through the green-chicked windows, making one's eyes ache and filling one's head with stuffiness. Everyone thought with malaise of his stodgy breakfast, and of the long, deadly hours that were coming. Mr Macgregor stood up with a sigh and adjusted his spectacles, which had slipped down his sweating nose.

'Alas that such a festive gathering should end,' he said. 'I must get home to breakfast. The cares of Empire. Is anybody coming my way? My man is waiting with the car.'

'Oh, thank you,' said Mrs Lackersteen; 'if you'd take Tom and me. What a relief not to have to walk in this heat!'

The others stood up. Westfield stretched his arms and yawned through his nose. 'Better get a move on, I suppose. Go to sleep if I sit here any longer. Think of stewing in that office all day! Baskets of papers. Oh Lord!'

'Don't forget tennis this evening, everyone,' said Ellis. 'Maxwell, you lazy devil, don't you skulk out of it again. Down here with your racquet at four-thirty sharp.'

'*Après vous,* madame,' said Mr Macgregor gallantly, at the door.

'Lead on, Macduff,' said Westfield.

They went out into the glaring white sunlight. The heat rolled from the earth like the breath of an oven. The flowers, oppressive to the eyes, blazed with not a petal stirring, in a debauch of sun. The glare sent a weariness through one's bones. There was something horrible in it—horrible to think of that blue, blinding sky, stretching on and on over Burma and India, over Siam, Cambodia, China, cloudless and interminable. The plates of Mr Macgregor's waiting car were too hot to touch. The evil time of day was beginning, the time, as the Burmese say, 'when feet are silent'. Hardly a living creature stirred, except men, and the black columns of ants, stimulated by the heat, which marched ribbon-like across the path, and the tail-less vultures which soared on the currents of the air.

# 3

Flory turned to the left outside the Club gate and started down the bazaar road, under the shade of the peepul trees. A hundred yards away there was a swirl of music, where a squad of Military Policemen, lank Indians in greenish khaki, were marching back to their lines with a Gurkha boy playing the bagpipes ahead of them. Flory was going to see Dr Veraswami. The doctor's house was a long bungalow of earth-oiled wood, standing on piles, with a large unkempt garden which adjoined that of the Club. The back of the house was towards the road, for it faced the hospital, which lay between it and the river.

As Flory entered the compound there was a frightened squawk of women and a scurrying within the house. Evidently he had narrowly missed seeing the doctor's wife. He went round to the front of the house and called up to the veranda:

'Doctor! Are you busy? May I come up?'

The doctor, a little black and white figure, popped from within the house like a jack-in-the-box. He hurried to the veranda rail, exclaimed effusively:

'If you may come up! Of course, of course, come up this instant! Ah, Mr Flory, how very delightful to see you! Come up, come up. What drink will you have? I have whisky, beer, vermouth and other European liquors. Ah, my dear friend, how I have been pining for some cultured conversation!'

The doctor was a small, black, plump man with fuzzy hair and round, credulous eyes. He wore steel-rimmed spectacles, and he was dressed in a badly fitting white drill suit, with trousers bagging concertina-like over clumsy black boots. His voice was eager and bubbling, with a hissing of the s's. As Flory came up the steps the doctor popped back to the end of the veranda and rummaged in a big tin ice-chest, rapidly pulling out bottles of all descriptions. The veranda was wide and dark, with low eaves from which baskets of fern hung, making it seem like a cave behind a waterfall of sunlight. It was furnished with long, cane-bottomed chairs made in the jail, and at one end there was a book-case containing a rather unappetizing little library, mainly books of essays, of the Emerson-Carlyle-Stevenson type. The doctor, a great reader, liked his books to have what he called a 'moral meaning'.

'Well, doctor,' said Flory—the doctor had meanwhile thrust him into a long chair, pulled out the leg-rests so that he could lie down, and put cigarettes and beer within reach. 'Well, doctor, and how are things? How's the British Empire? Sick of the palsy as usual?'

'Aha, Mr Flory, she iss very low, very low! Grave complications setting in. Septicaemia, peritonitis and paralysis of the ganglia. We shall have to call in the specialists, I fear. Aha!'

It was a joke between the two men to pretend that the British Empire was an aged female patient of the doctor's. The doctor had enjoyed this joke for two years without growing tired of it.

'Ah, doctor,' said Flory, supine in the long chair, 'what a joy to be here after that bloody Club. When I come to your house I feel like a Nonconformist minister dodging up to town and going home with a tart. Such a glorious holiday from *them*'—he motioned with one heel in the direction of the Club—'from my beloved fellow Empire-builders. British prestige, the white man's burden, the pukka sahib *sans peur et sans reproche*—you know. Such a relief to be out of the stink of it for a little while.'

'My friend, my friend, now come, come, please! That iss outrageous. You must not say such things of honourable English gentlemen!'

'You don't have to listen to the honourable gentlemen talking, doctor. I stood it as long as I could this morning. Ellis with his "dirty nigger", Westfield with his jokes, Macgregor with his Latin tags and please give the bearer fifteen lashes. But when they got on to that story about the old havildar—you know, the dear old havildar who said that if the British left India there wouldn't be a rupee or a virgin between—you know; well, I couldn't stand it any longer. It's time that old havildar was put on the retired list. He's been saying the same thing ever since the Jubilee in 'eighty-seven.'

The doctor grew agitated, as he always did when Flory criticized the Club members. He was standing with his plump white-clad behind balanced against the veranda rail, and sometimes gesticulating. When searching for a word he would nip his black thumb and forefinger together, as though to capture an idea floating in the air.

'But truly, truly, Mr Flory, you must not speak so! Why iss it that always you are abusing the pukka sahibs, ass you call them? They are the salt of the earth. Consider the great things they have done—consider the great administrators who have made British India what it iss. Consider Clive,

Warren Hastings, Dalhousie, Curzon. They were such men—I quote your immortal Shakespeare—ass, take them for all in all, we shall not look upon their like again!'

'Well, do you want to look upon their like again? I don't.'

'And consider how noble a type iss the English gentleman! Their glorious loyalty to one another! The public school spirit! Even those of them whose manner iss unfortunate—some Englishmen are arrogant, I concede—have the great, sterling qualities that we Orientals lack. Beneath their rough exterior, their hearts are of gold.'

'Of gilt, shall we say? There's a kind of spurious good-fellowship between the English and this country. It's a tradition to booze together and swap meals and pretend to be friends, though we all hate each other like poison. Hanging together, we call it. It's a political necessity. Of course drink is what keeps the machine going. We should all go mad and kill one another in a week if it weren't for that. There's a subject for one of your uplift essayists, doctor. Booze as the cement of empire.'

The doctor shook his head. 'Really, Mr Flory, I know not what it iss that hass made you so cynical. It iss so most unsuitable! You—an English gentleman of high gifts and character—to be uttering seditious opinions that are worthy of the *Burmese Patriot*!'

'Seditious?' Flory said. '*I'm* not seditious. I don't want the Burmans to drive us out of this country. God forbid! I'm here to make money, like everyone else. All I object to is the slimy white man's burden humbug. The pukka sahib pose. It's so boring. Even those bloody fools at the Club might be better company if we weren't all of us living a lie the whole time.'

'But, my dear friend, what lie are you living?'

'Why, of course, the lie that we're here to uplift our poor black brothers instead of to rob them. I suppose it's a natural enough lie. But it corrupts us, it corrupts us in ways you can't imagine. There's an everlasting sense of being a sneak and a liar that torments us and drives us to justify ourselves night and day. It's at the bottom of half our beastliness to the natives. We Anglo-Indians could be almost bearable if we'd only admit that we're thieves and go on thieving without any humbug.'

The doctor, very pleased, nipped his thumb and forefinger together. 'The weakness of your argument, my dear friend,' he said, beaming at his own irony, 'the weakness appears to be, that you are *not* thieves.'

'Now, my dear doctor—'

Flory sat up in the long chair, partly because his prickly heat had just stabbed him in the back like a thousand needles, partly because his favourite argument with the doctor was about to begin. This argument, vaguely political in nature, took place as often as the two men met. It was a topsy-turvy affair, for the Englishman was bitterly anti-English and the Indian fanatically loyal. Dr Veraswami had a passionate admiration for the English, which a thousand snubs from Englishmen had not shaken. He would maintain with positive eagerness that he, as an Indian, belonged to an inferior and degenerate race. His faith in British justice was so great that even when, at the jail, he had to superintend a flogging or a hanging, and would come home with his black face faded grey and dose himself with whisky, his zeal did not falter. Flory's seditious opinions shocked him, but they also gave him a certain shuddering pleasure, such as a pious believer will take in hearing the Lord's Prayer repeated backwards.

'My dear doctor,' said Flory, 'how can you make out that we are in this country for any purpose except to steal? It's so simple. The official holds the Burman down while the businessman goes through his pockets. Do you suppose my firm, for instance, could get its timber contracts if the country weren't in the hands of the British? Or the other timber firms, or the oil companies, or the miners and planters and traders? How could the Rice Ring go on skinning the unfortunate peasant if it hadn't the Government behind it? The British Empire is simply a device for giving trade monopolies to the English—or rather to gangs of Jews and Scotchmen.'

'My friend, it iss pathetic to me to hear you talk so. It iss truly pathetic. You say you are here to trade? Of course you are. Could the Burmese trade for themselves? Can they make machinery, ships, railways, roads? They are helpless without you. What would happen to the Burmese forests if the English were not here? They would be sold immediately to the Japanese, who would gut them and ruin them. Instead of which, in your hands, actually they are improved. And while your businessmen develop the resources of our country, your officials are civilizing us, elevating us to their level, from pure public spirit. It is a magnificent record of self-sacrifice.'

'Bosh, my dear doctor. We teach the young men to drink whisky and play football, I admit, but precious little else. Look at our schools—factories for cheap clerks. We've never taught a single useful manual trade to the Indians. We daren't; frightened of the competition in industry. We've even crushed various industries. Where are the Indian muslins now? Back in the forties or thereabouts they were building sea-going ships in India, and manning them as well. Now you couldn't build a seaworthy fishing boat there. In the eighteenth century the Indians cast guns that were at any rate up to the European standard. Now, after we've been in India a hundred and fifty years, you can't make so much as a brass cartridge-case in the whole continent. The only Eastern races that have developed at all quickly are the independent ones. I won't instance Japan, but take the case of Siam—'

The doctor waved his hand excitedly. He always interrupted the argument at this point (for as a rule it followed the same course, almost word for word), finding that the case of Siam hampered him.

'My friend, my friend, you are forgetting the Oriental character. How iss it possible to have developed us, with our apathy and superstition? At least you have brought to us law and order. The unswerving British Justice and the Pax Britannica.'

'Pox Britannica, doctor, Pox Britannica is its proper name. And in any case, whom is it pax for? The money-lender and the lawyer. Of course we keep the peace in India, in our own interest, but what does all this law and order business boil down to? More banks and more prisons—that's all it means.'

'What monstrous misrepresentations!' cried the doctor. 'Are not prissons necessary? And have you brought us nothing but prissons? Consider Burma in the days of Thibaw, with dirt and torture and ignorance, and then look around you. Look merely out of this veranda—look at that hospital, and over to the right at that school and that police station. Look at the whole uprush of modern progress!'

'Of course I don't deny,' Flory said, 'that we modernize this country in certain ways. We can't help doing so. In fact, before we've finished we'll have wrecked the whole Burmese national culture. But we're not civilizing them, we're only rubbing our dirt on to them. Where's it going to lead, this uprush of modern progress, as you call it? Just to our own dear old swinery of gramophones and billycock hats. Sometimes I think that in two hundred years all this—' he waved a foot towards the horizon—'all this will be gone—forests, villages, monasteries, pagodas all vanished. And instead, pink villas fifty yards apart; all over those hills, as far as you can see, villa after villa, with all the gramophones playing the same tune. And all the forests shaved flat—chewed into wood-pulp for the *News of the World*, or sawn up into gramophone cases. But the trees avenge themselves, as the old chap says in *The Wild Duck*. You've read Ibsen, of course?'

'Ah, no, Mr Flory, alas! That mighty master-mind, your inspired Bernard Shaw hass called him. It iss a pleasure to come. But, my friend, what you do not see iss that your civilization at its very worst iss for us an advance. Gramophones, billycock hats, the *News of the World*—all iss better than the horrible sloth of the Oriental. I see the British, even the least inspired of them, ass—ass—' the doctor searched for a phrase, and found one that probably came from Stevenson—'ass torchbearers upon the path of progress.'

'I don't. I see them as a kind of up-to-date, hygienic, self-satisfied louse. Creeping round the world building prisons. They build a prison and call it progress,' he added rather regretfully—for the doctor would not recognize the allusion.

'My friend, positively you are harping upon the subject of prissons! Consider that there are also other achievements of your countrymen. They construct roads, they irrigate deserts, they conquer famines, they build schools, they set up hospitals, they combat plague, cholera, leprosy, smallpox, venereal disease—'

'Having brought it themselves,' put in Flory.

'No, sir!' returned the doctor, eager to claim this distinction for his own countrymen. 'No, sir, it wass the Indians who introduced venereal disease into this country. The Indians introduce diseases, and the English cure them. *There* iss the answer to all your pessimism and seditiousness.'

'Well, doctor, we shall never agree. The fact is that you like all this modern progress business, whereas I'd rather see things a little bit septic. Burma in the days of Thibaw would have suited me better, I think. And as I said before, if we are a civilizing influence, it's only to grab on a larger scale. We should chuck it quickly enough if it didn't pay.'

'My friend, you do not think that. If truly you disapprove of the British

Empire, you would not be talking of it privately here. You would be proclaiming from the house-tops. I know your character, Mr Flory, better than you know it yourself.'

'Sorry, doctor; I don't go in for proclaiming from the housetops. I haven't the guts. I "counsel ignoble ease", like old Belial in *Paradise Lost*. It's safer. You've got to be a pukka sahib or die, in this country. In fifteen years I've never talked honestly to anyone except you. My talks here are a safety-valve; a little Black Mass on the sly, if you understand me.'

At this moment there was a desolate wailing noise outside. Old Mattu, the Hindu *durwan* who looked after the European church, was standing in the sunlight below the veranda. He was an old fever-stricken creature, more like a grasshopper than a human being, and dressed in a few square inches of dingy rag. He lived near the church in a hut made of flattened kerosene tins, from which he would sometimes hurry forth at the appearance of a European, to salaam deeply and wail something about his 'talab', which was eighteen rupees a month. Looking piteously up at the veranda, he massaged the earth-coloured skin of his belly with one hand, and with the other made the motion of putting food into his mouth. The doctor felt in his pocket and dropped a four-anna piece over the veranda rail. He was notorious for his soft-heartedness, and all the beggars in Kyauktada made him their target.

'Behold there the degeneracy of the East,' said the doctor, pointing to Mattu, who was doubling himself up like a caterpillar and uttering grateful whines. 'Look at the wretchedness of hiss limbs. The calves of hiss legs are not so thick ass an Englishman's wrists. Look at hiss abjectness and servility. Look at hiss ignorance—such ignorance ass iss not known in Europe outside a home for mental defectives. Once I asked Mattu to tell me hiss age. "Sahib," he said, "I believe that I am ten years old." How can you pretend, Mr Flory, that you are not the natural superior of such creatures?'

'Poor old Mattu, the uprush of modern progress seems to have missed him somehow,' Flory said, throwing another four-anna piece over the rail. 'Go on, Mattu, spend that on booze. Be as degenerate as you can. It all postpones Utopia.'

'Aha, Mr Flory, sometimes I think that all you say iss but to—what iss the expression?—pull my leg. The English sense of humour. We Orientals have no humour, ass iss well known.'

'Lucky devils. It's been the ruin of us, our bloody sense of humour.' He yawned with his hands behind his head. Mattu had shambled away after further grateful noises. 'I suppose I ought to be going before this cursed sun gets too high. The heat's going to be devilish this year, I feel it in my bones. Well, doctor, we've been arguing so much that I haven't asked for your news. I only got in from the jungle yesterday. I ought to go back the day after tomorrow—don't know whether I shall. Has anything been happening in Kyauktada? Any scandals?'

The doctor looked suddenly serious. He had taken off his spectacles, and his face, with dark liquid eyes, recalled that of a black retriever dog. He looked away, and spoke in a slightly more hesitant tone than before.

'That fact iss, my friend, there iss a most unpleasant business afoot. You will perhaps laugh—it sounds nothing—but I am in serious trouble. Or rather, I am in danger of trouble. It iss an underground business. You Europeans will never hear of it directly. In this place'—he waved a hand towards the bazaar—'there iss perpetual conspiracies and plottings of which you do not hear. But to us they mean much.'

'What's been happening, then?'

'It iss this. An intrigue iss brewing against me. A most serious intrigue which iss intended to blacken my character and ruin my official career. Ass an Englishman you will not understand these things. I have incurred the enmity of a man you probably do not know, U Po Kyin, the Sub-divisional Magistrate. He iss a most dangerous man. The damage that he can do to me iss incalculable.'

'U Po Kyin? Which one is that?'

'The great fat man with many teeth. Hiss house iss down the road there, a hundred yards away.'

'Oh, that fat scoundrel? I know him well.'

'No, no, my friend, no, no!' exclaimed the doctor quite eagerly; 'it cannot be that you know him. Only an Oriental could know him. You, an English gentleman, cannot sink your mind to the depth of such ass U Po Kyin. He iss more than a scoundrel, he iss—what shall I say? Words fail me. He recalls to me a crocodile in human shape. He hass the cunning of the crocodile, its cruelty, its bestiality. If you knew the record of that man! The outrages he hass committed! The extortions, the briberies! The girls he hass ruined, raping them before the very eyes of their mothers! Ah, an English gentleman cannot imagine such a character. And thiss iss the man who hass taken hiss oath to ruin me.'

'I've heard a good deal about U Po Kyin from various sources,' Flory said. 'He seems a fair sample of a Burmese magistrate. A Burman told me that during the war U Po Kyin was at work recruiting, and he raised a battalion from his own illegitimate sons. Is that true?'

'It could hardly be so,' said the doctor, 'for they would not have been old enough. But of hiss villainy there iss no doubt. And now he iss determined upon ruining me. In the first place he hates me because I know too much about him; and besides, he iss the enemy of any reasonably honest man. He will proceed—such iss the practice of such men—by calumny. He will spread reports about me—reports of the most appalling and untrue descriptions. Already he iss beginning them.'

'But would anyone believe a fellow like that against you? He's only a low-down magistrate. You're a high official.'

'Ah, Mr Flory, you do not understand Oriental cunning. U Po Kyin hass ruined higher officials than I. He will know ways to make himself believed. And therefore—ah, it iss a difficult business!'

The doctor took a step or two up and down the veranda, polishing his glasses with his handkerchief. It was clear that there was something more which delicacy prevented him from saying. For a moment his manner was so troubled that Flory would have liked to ask whether he could not help in some way, but he did not, for he knew the uselessness of interfering in Oriental quarrels. No European ever gets to the bottom of these quarrels; there is always something impervious to the European mind, a conspiracy behind the conspiracy, a plot within the plot. Besides, to keep out of 'native' quarrels is one of the Ten Precepts of the pukka sahib. He said doubtfully:

'What is a difficult business?'

'It iss, if only–ah, my friend, you will laugh at me, I fear. But it iss this: if only I were a member of your European Club! If only! How different would my position be!'

'The Club? Why? How would that help you?'

'My friend, in these matters prestige iss everything. It iss not that U Po Kyin will attack me openly; he would never dare; it iss that he will libel me and backbite me. And whether he iss believed or not depends entirely upon my standing with the Europeans. It iss so that things happen in India. If our prestige iss good, we rise; if bad, we fall. A nod and a wink will accomplish more than a thousand official reports. And you do not know what prestige it gives to an Indian to be a member of the European Club. In the Club, practically he *iss* a European. No calumny can touch him. A Club member iss sacrosanct.'

Flory looked away over the veranda rail. He had got up as though to go. It always made him ashamed and uncomfortable when it had to be admitted between them that the doctor, because of his black skin, could not be received in the Club. It is a disagreeable thing when one's close friend is not one's social equal; but it is a thing native to the very air of India.

'They might elect you at the next general meeting,' he said. 'I don't say they will, but it's not impossible.'

'I trust, Mr Flory, that you do not think I am asking you to propose me for the Club? Heaven forbid! I know that that iss impossible for you. Simply I wass remarking that if I were a member of the Club, I should be forthwith invulnerable–'

Flory cocked his Terai hat loosely on his head and stirred Flo up with his stick. She was asleep under the chair. Flory felt very uncomfortable. He knew that in all probability, if he had the courage to face a few rows with Ellis, he could secure Dr Veraswami's election to the Club. And the doctor, after all, was his friend, indeed, almost the sole friend he had in Burma. They had talked and argued together a hundred times, the doctor had dined at his house, he had even proposed to introduce Flory to his wife–but she, a pious Hindu, had refused with horror. They had made shooting trips together–the doctor, equipped with bandoliers and hunting knives, panting up hillsides slippery with bamboo leaves and blazing his gun at nothing. In common decency it was his duty to support the doctor. But he knew also that the doctor would never ask for any support, and that there would be an ugly row before an Oriental was got into the Club. No, he could not face that row! It was not worth it. He said:

'To tell you the truth, there's been talk about this already. They were discussing it this morning, and that little beast Ellis was preaching his usual "dirty nigger" sermon. Macgregor has suggested electing one native member. He's had orders to do so, I imagine.'

'Yes, I heard that. We hear all these things. It wass that that put the idea into my head.'

'It's to come up at the general meeting in June. I don't know what'll happen—it depends on Macgregor, I think. I'll give you my vote, but I can't do more than that. I'm sorry, but I simply can't. You don't know the row there'll be. Very likely they will elect you, but they'll do it as an unpleasant duty, under protest. They've made a perfect fetish of keeping this Club all-white, as they call it.'

'Of course, of course, my friend! I understand perfectly. Heaven forbid that you should get into trouble with your European friends on my behalf. Please, please, never to embroil yourself! The mere fact that you are known to be my friend benefits me more than you can imagine. Prestige, Mr Flory, iss like a barometer. Every time you are seen to enter my house the mercury rises half a degree.'

'Well, we must try and keep it at "Set Fair". That's about all I can do for you, I'm afraid.'

'Even that iss much, my friend. And for that, there iss another thing of which I would warn you, though you will laugh, I fear. It iss that you yourself should beware of U Po Kyin. Beware of the crocodile! For sure he will strike at you when he knows that you are befriending me.'

'All right, doctor, I'll beware of the crocodile. I don't fancy he can do me much harm, though.'

'At least he will try. I know him. It will be hiss policy to detach my friends from me. Possibly he would even dare to spread hiss libels about you also.'

'About me? Good gracious, no one would believe anything against *me*. *Civis Romanus sum*. I'm an Englishman—quite above suspicion.'

'Nevertheless, beware of hiss calumnies, my friend. Do not underrate him. He will know how to strike at you. He iss a crocodile. And like the crocodile'—the doctor nipped his thumb and finger impressively; his images became mixed sometimes—'like the crocodile, he strikes always at the weakest spot!'

'Do crocodiles always strike at the weakest spot, doctor?'

Both men laughed. They were intimate enough to laugh over the doctor's queer English occasionally. Perhaps, at the bottom of his heart, the doctor was a little disappointed that Flory had not promised to propose him for the Club, but he would have perished rather than say so. And Flory was glad to drop the subject, an uncomfortable one which he wished had never been raised.

'Well, I really must be going, doctor. Good-bye in case I don't see you again. I hope it'll be all right at the general meeting. Macgregor's not a bad old stick. I dare say he'll insist on their electing you.'

'Let us hope so, my friend. With that I can defy a hundred U Po Kyins. A thousand! Good-bye, my friend, good-bye.'

Then Flory settled his Terai hat on his head and went home across the glaring maidan, to his breakfast, for which the long morning of drinking, smoking and talking had left him no appetite.

# 4

Flory lay asleep, naked except for black Shan trousers, upon his sweat-damp bed. He had been idling all day. He spent approximately three weeks of every month in camp, coming into Kyauktada for a few days at a time, chiefly in order to idle, for he had very little clerical work to do.

The bedroom was a large square room with white plaster walls, open doorways and no ceiling, but only rafters in which sparrows nested. There was no furniture except the big four-poster bed, with its furled mosquito net like a canopy, and a wicker table and chair and a small mirror; also some rough book-shelves, containing several hundred books, all mildewed by many rainy seasons and riddled by silver fish. A *tuktoo* clung to the wall, flat and motionless like a heraldic dragon. Beyond the veranda eaves the light rained down like glistening white oil. Some doves in a bamboo thicket kept up a dull droning noise, curiously appropriate to the heat—a sleepy sound, but with the sleepiness of chloroform rather than a lullaby.

Down at Mr Macgregor's bungalow, two hundred yards away, a *durwan*, like a living clock, hammered four strokes on a section of iron rail. Ko S'la, Flory's servant, awakened by the sound, went into the cookhouse, blew up the embers of the woodfire and boiled the kettle for tea. Then he put on his pink *gaungbaung* and muslin *ingyi* and brought the tea-tray to his master's bedside.

Ko S'la (his real name was Maung San Hla; Ko S'la was an abbreviation) was a short, square-shouldered, rustic-looking Burman with a very dark skin and a harassed expression. He wore a black moustache which curved downwards round his mouth, but like most Burmans he was quite beardless. He had been Flory's servant since his first day in Burma. The two men were within a month of one another's age. They had been boys together, had tramped side by side after snipe and duck, sat together in *machans* waiting for tigers that never came, shared the discomforts of a thousand camps and marches; and Ko S'la had pimped for Flory and borrowed money for him from the Chinese money-lenders, carried him to bed when he was drunk, tended him through bouts of fever. In Ko S'la's eyes Flory, because a bachelor, was a boy still; whereas Ko S'la had married, begotten five children, married again and become one of the obscure martyrs of bigamy. Like all bachelors' servants, Ko S'la was lazy and dirty, and yet he was devoted to Flory. He would never let anyone else serve Flory at table, or carry his gun or hold his pony's head while he mounted. On the march, if they came to a stream, he would carry Flory across on his back. He was inclined to pity Flory, partly because he thought

him childish and easily deceived, and partly because of the birthmark, which
he considered a dreadful thing.

Ko S'la put the tea-tray down on the table very quietly, and then went round
to the end of the bed and tickled Flory's toes. He knew by experience that this
was the only way of waking Flory without putting him in a bad temper. Flory
rolled over, swore, and pressed his forehead into the pillow.

'Four o'clock has struck, most holy god,' Ko S'la said. 'I have brought two
teacups, because *the woman* said that she was coming.'

*The woman* was Ma Hla May, Flory's mistress. Ko S'la always called her *the
woman*, to show his disapproval—not that he disapproved of Flory for keeping a
mistress, but he was jealous of Ma Hla May's influence in the house.

'Will the holy one play *tinnis* this evening?' Ko S'la asked.

'No, it's too hot,' said Flory in English. 'I don't want anything to eat. Take
this muck away and bring some whisky.'

Ko S'la understood English very well, though he could not speak it. He
brought a bottle of whisky, and also Flory's tennis racquet, which he laid in a
meaning manner against the wall opposite the bed. Tennis, according to his
notions, was a mysterious ritual incumbent on all Englishmen, and he did not
like to see his master idling in the evenings.

Flory pushed away in disgust the toast and butter that Ko S'la had brought,
but he mixed some whisky in a cup of tea and felt better after drinking it. He
had slept since noon, and his head and all his bones ached, and there was a taste
like burnt paper in his mouth. It was years since he had enjoyed a meal. All
European food in Burma is more or less disgusting—the bread is spongy stuff
leavened with palm-toddy and tasting like a penny bun gone wrong, the butter
comes out of a tin, and so does the milk, unless it is the grey watery catlap of the
dudh-wallah. As Ko S'la left the room there was a scraping of sandals outside,
and a Burmese girl's high-pitched voice said, 'Is my master awake?'

'Come in,' said Flory rather bad temperedly.

Ma Hla May came in, kicking off red-lacquered sandals in the doorway. She
was allowed to come to tea, as a special privilege, but not to other meals, nor to
wear her sandals in her master's presence.

Ma Hla May was a woman of twenty-two or -three, and perhaps five feet tall.
She was dressed in a *longyi* of pale blue embroidered Chinese satin, and a
starched white muslin *ingyi* on which several gold lockets hung. Her hair was
coiled in a tight black cylinder like ebony, and decorated with jasmine flowers.
Her tiny, straight, slender body was a contourless as a bas-relief carved upon a
tree. She was like a doll, with her oval, still face the colour of new copper, and
her narrow eyes; an outlandish doll and yet a grotesquely beautiful one. A
scent of sandalwood and coco-nut oil came into the room with her.

Ma Hla May came across to the bed, sat down on the edge and put her arms
rather abruptly round Flory. She smelled at his cheek with her flat nose, in the
Burmese fashion.

'Why did my master not send for me this afternoon?' she said.

'I was sleeping. It is too hot for that kind of thing.'

'So you would rather sleep alone than with Ma Hla May? How ugly you must think me, then! Am I ugly, master?'

'Go away,' he said, pushing her back. 'I don't want you at this time of day.'

'At least touch me with your lips, then. (There is no Burmese word for to kiss.) All white men do that to their women.'

'There you are, then. Now leave me alone. Fetch some cigarettes and give me one.'

'Why is it that nowadays you never want to make love to me? Ah, two years ago it was so different! You loved me in those days. You gave me presents of gold bangles and silk *longyis* from Mandalay. And now look'—Ma Hla May held out one tiny muslin-clad arm—'not a single bangle. Last month I had thirty, and now all of them are pawned. How can I go to the bazaar without my bangles, and wearing the same *longyi* over and over again? I am ashamed before the other women.'

'Is it my fault if you pawn your bangles?'

'Two years ago you would have redeemed them for me. Ah, you do not love Ma Hla May any longer!'

She put her arms round him again and kissed him, a European habit which he had taught her. A mingled scent of sandalwood, garlic, coco-nut oil and the jasmine in her hair floated from her. It was a scent that always made his teeth tingle. Rather abstractedly he pressed her head back upon the pillow and looked down at her queer, youthful face, with its high cheekbones, stretched eyelids and short, shapely lips. She had rather nice teeth, like the teeth of a kitten. He had bought her from her parents two years ago, for three hundred rupees. He began to stroke her brown throat, rising like a smooth, slender stalk from the collarless *ingyi*.

'You only like me because I am a white man and have money,' he said.

'Master, I love you, I love you more than anything in the world. Why do you say that? Have I not always been faithful to you?'

'You have a Burmese lover.'

'Ugh!' Ma Hla May affected to shudder at the thought. 'To think of their horrible brown hands, touching me! I should die if a Burman touched me!'

'Liar.'

He put his hand on her breast. Privately, Ma Hla May did not like this, for it reminded her that her breasts existed—the ideal of a Burmese woman being to have no breasts. She lay and let him do as he wished with her, quite passive yet pleased and faintly smiling, like a cat which allows one to stroke it. Flory's embraces meant nothing to her (Ba Pe, Ko S'la's younger brother, was secretly her lover), yet she was bitterly hurt when he neglected them. Sometimes she had even put love-philtres in his food. It was the idle concubine's life that she loved, and the visits to her village dressed in all her finery, when she could boast of her position as a 'bo-kadaw'—a white man's wife; for she had persuaded everyone, herself included, that she was Flory's legal wife.

When Flory had done with her he turned away, jaded and ashamed, and lay silent with his left hand covering his birthmark. He always remembered the birthmark when he had done something to be ashamed of. He buried his face disgustedly in the pillow, which was damp and smelt of coco-nut oil. It was horribly hot, and the doves outside were still droning. Ma Hla May, naked, reclined beside Flory, fanning him gently with a wicker fan she had taken from the table.

Presently she got up and dressed herself, and lighted a cigarette. Then, coming back to the bed, she sat down and began stroking Flory's bare shoulder. The whiteness of his skin had a fascination for her, because of its strangeness and the sense of power it gave her. But Flory twitched his shoulder to shake her hand away. At these times she was nauseating and dreadful to him. His sole wish was to get her out of his sight.

'Get out,' he said.

Ma Hla May took her cigarette from her mouth and tried to offer it to Flory. 'Why is master always so angry with me when he has made love to me?' she said.

'Get out,' he repeated.

Ma Hla May continued to stroke Flory's shoulder. She had never learned the wisdom of leaving him alone at these times. She believed that lechery was a form of witchcraft, giving a woman magical powers over a man, until in the end she could weaken him to a half-idiotic slave. Each successive embrace sapped Flory's will and made the spell stronger—this was her belief. She began tormenting him to begin over again. She laid down her cigarette and put her arms round him, trying to turn him towards her and kiss his averted face, reproaching him for his coldness.

'Go away, go away!' he said angrily. 'Look in the pocket of my shorts. There is money there. Take five rupees and go.'

Ma Hla May found the five-rupee note and stuffed it into the bosom of her *ingyi*, but she still would not go. She hovered about the bed, worrying Flory until at last he grew angry and jumped up.

'Get out of this room! I told you to go. I don't want you in here after I've done with you.'

'That is a nice way to speak to me! You treat me as though I were a prostitute.'

'So you are. Out you go,' he said, pushing her out of the room by her shoulders. He kicked her sandals after her. Their encounters often ended in this way.

Flory stood in the middle of the room, yawning. Should he go down to the Club for tennis after all? No, it meant shaving, and he could not face the effort of shaving until he had a few drinks inside him. He felt his scrubby chin and lounged across to the mirror to examine it, but then turned away. He did not want to see the yellow, sunken face that would look back at him. For several minutes he stood slack-limbed, watching the *tuktoo* stalk a moth above the bookshelves. The cigarette that Ma Hla May had dropped burned down with an acrid smell, browning the paper. Flory took a book from the shelves, opened it and then threw it away in distaste. He had not even the energy to read. Oh God, God, what to do with the rest of this bloody evening?

Flo waddled into the room, wagging her tail and asking to be taken for a walk. Flory went sulkily into the little stone-floored bathroom that gave on to the bedroom, splashed himself with lukewarm water and put on his shirt and shorts. He must take some kind of exercise before the sun went down. In India it is in some way evil to spend a day without being once in a muck-sweat. It gives one a deeper sense of sin than a thousand lecheries. In the dark evening, after a quite idle day, one's ennui reaches a pitch that is frantic, suicidal. Work, prayer, books, drinking, talking—they are all powerless against it; it can only be sweated out through the pores of the skin.

Flory went out and followed the road uphill into the jungle. It was scrub jungle at first, with dense stunted bushes, and the only trees were half-wild mangoes, bearing little turpentiny fruits the size of plums. Then the road struck among taller trees. The jungle was dried-up and lifeless at this time of year. The trees lined the road in close, dusty ranks, with leaves a dull olive-green. No birds were visible except some ragged brown creatures like disreputable thrushes, which hopped clumsily under the bushes; in the distance some other bird uttered a cry of '*Ah* ha ha! *Ah* ha ha!'—a lonely, hollow sound like the echo of a laugh. There was a poisonous, ivy-like smell of crushed leaves. It was still hot, though the sun was losing its glare and the slanting light was yellow.

After two miles the road ended at the ford of a shallow stream. The jungle grew greener here, because of the water, and the trees were taller. At the edge of the stream there was a huge dead pyinkado tree festooned with spidery orchids, and there were some wild lime bushes with white waxen flowers. They had a sharp scent like bergamot. Flory had walked fast and the sweat had drenched his shirt and dribbled, stinging, into his eyes. He had sweated himself into a better mood. Also, the sight of this stream always heartened him; its water was quite clear, rarest of sights in a miry country. He crossed the stream by the stepping stones, Flo splashing after him, and turned into a narrow track he knew, which led through the bushes. It was a track that cattle had made, coming to the stream to drink, and few human beings ever followed it. It led to a pool fifty yards upstream. Here a peepul tree grew, a great buttressed thing six feet thick, woven of innumerable strands of wood, like a wooden cable twisted by a giant. The roots of the tree made a natural cavern, under which the clear greenish water bubbled. Above and all around dense foliage shut out the light, turning the place into a green grotto walled with leaves.

Flory threw off his clothes and stepped into the water. It was a shade cooler than the air, and it came up to his neck when he sat down. Shoals of silvery *mahseer,* no bigger than sardines, came nosing and nibbling at his body. Flo had also flopped into the water, and she swam round silently, otter-like, with her webbed feet. She knew the pool well, for they often came here when Flory was at Kyauktada.

There was a stirring high up in the peepul tree, and a bubbling noise like pots boiling. A flock of green pigeons were up there, eating the berries. Flory gazed up into the great green dome of the tree, trying to distinguish the birds; they were invisible, they matched the leaves so perfectly, and yet the whole tree was alive with them, shimmering, as though the ghosts of birds were shaking it. Flo rested herself against the roots and growled up at the invisible creatures. Then a single green pigeon fluttered down and perched on a lower branch. It did not know that it was being watched. It was a tender thing, smaller than a tame dove, with jade-green back as smooth as velvet, and neck and breast of iridescent colours. Its legs were like the pink wax that dentists use.

The pigeon rocked itself backwards and forwards on the bough, swelling out its breast feathers and laying its coralline beak upon them. A pang went through Flory. Alone, alone, the bitterness of being alone! So often like this, in lonely places in the forest, he would come upon something—bird, flower, tree—beautiful beyond all words, if there had been a soul with whom to share it. Beauty is meaningless until it is shared. If he had one person, just one, to halve his loneliness! Suddenly the pigeon saw the man and dog below, sprang into the air and dashed away swift as a bullet, with a rattle of wings. One does not often see green pigeons so closely when they are alive. They are high-flying birds, living in the treetops, and they do not come to the ground, or only to drink. When one shoots them, if they are not killed outright, they cling to the branch until they die, and drop long after one has given up waiting and gone away.

Flory got out of the water, put on his clothes and recrossed the stream. He did not go home by the road, but followed a foot-track southward into the jungle, intending to make a detour and pass through a village that lay in the fringe of the jungle not far from his house. Flo frisked in and out of the undergrowth, yelping sometimes when her long ears caught in the thorns. She had once turned up a hare near here. Flory walked slowly. The smoke of his pipe floated straight upwards in still plumes. He was happy and at peace after the walk and the clear water. It was cooler now, except for patches of heat lingering under the thicker trees, and the light was gentle. Bullock-cart wheels were screaming peacefully in the distance.

Soon they had lost their way in the jungle, and were wandering in a maze of dead trees and tangled bushes. They came to an impasse where the path was blocked by large ugly plants like magnified aspidistras, whose leaves terminated in long lashes armed with thorns. A firefly glowed greenish at the bottom of a bush; it was getting twilight in the thicker places. Presently the bullock-cart wheels screamed nearer, taking a parallel course.

'Hey, *saya gyi, saya gyi!*' Flory shouted, taking Flo by the collar to prevent her running away.

'*Ba le-de?*' the Burman shouted back. There was the sound of plunging hooves and of yells to the bullocks.

'Come here, if you please, O venerable and learned sir! We have lost our way. Stop a moment, O great builder of pagodas!'

The Burman left his cart and pushed through the jungle, slicing the creepers with his *dah*. He was a squat middle-aged man with one eye. He led the way back to the track, and Flory climbed on to the flat, uncomfortable bullock cart. The Burman took up the string reins, yelled to the bullocks, prodded the roots of their tails with his short stick, and the cart jolted on with a shriek of wheels.

The Burmese bullock-cart drivers seldom grease their axles, probably because they believe that the screaming keeps away evil spirits, though when questioned they will say that it is because they are too poor to buy grease.

They passed a whitewashed wooden pagoda, no taller than a man and half hidden by the tendrils of creeping plants. Then the track wound into the village, which consisted of twenty ruinous wooden huts roofed with thatch, and a well beneath some barren date-palms. The egrets that roosted in the palms were streaming homewards over the treetops like white flights of arrows. A fat yellow woman with her *longyi* hitched under her armpits was chasing a dog round a hut, smacking at it with a bamboo and laughing, and the dog was also laughing in its fashion. The village was called Nyaunglebin—'the four peepul trees'; there were no peepul trees there now, probably they had been cut down and forgotten a century ago. The villagers cultivated a narrow strip of fields that lay between the town and the jungle, and they also made bullock carts which they sold in Kyauktada. Bullock-cart wheels were littered everywhere under the houses; massive things five feet across, with spokes roughly but strongly carved.

Flory got off the cart and gave the driver a present of four annas. Some brindled curs hurried from beneath the houses to sniff at Flo, and a flock of pot-bellied, naked children, with their hair tied in top-knots, also appeared, curious about the white man but keeping their distance. The village headman, a wizened, leaf-brown old man, came out of his house, and there were shikoings. Flory sat down on the steps of the headman's house and relighted his pipe. He was thirsty.

'Is the water in your well good to drink, *thugyi-min?*'

The headman reflected, scratching the calf of his left leg with his right big toenail. 'Those who drink it, drink it, *thakin*. And those who do not drink it, do not drink it.'

'Ah. That is wisdom.'

The fat woman who had chased the pariah brought a blackened earthenware teapot and a handleless bowl, and gave Flory some pale green tea, tasting of wood-smoke.

'I must be going, *thugyi-min*. Thank you for the tea.'

'God go with you, *thakin*.'

Flory went home by a path that led out on to the maidan. It was dark now. Ko S'la had put on a clean *ingyi* and was waiting in the bedroom. He had heated two kerosene tins of bath-water, lighted the petrol lamps and laid out a clean suit and shirt for Flory. The clean clothes were intended as a hint that Flory should shave, dress himself and go down to the Club after dinner. Occasionally he spent the evening in Shan trousers, loafing in a chair with a book, and Ko S'la disapproved of this habit. He hated to see his master behaving differently from other white men. The fact that Flory often came back from the Club drunk, whereas he remained sober when he stayed at home, did not alter Ko S'la's opinion, because getting drunk was normal and pardonable in a white man.

'The woman has gone down to the bazaar,' he announced, pleased, as he always was when Ma Hla May left the house. 'Ba Pe has gone with a lantern, to look after her when she comes back.'

'Good,' Flory said.

She had gone to spend her five rupees—gambling, no doubt.

'The holy one's bath-water is ready.'

'Wait, we must attend to the dog first. Bring the comb,' Flory said.

The two men squatted on the floor together and combed Flo's silky coat and felt between her toes, picking out the ticks. It had to be done every evening. She picked up vast numbers of ticks during the day, horrible grey things that were the size of pin-heads when they got on to her, and gorged themselves till they were as large as peas. As each tick was detached Ko S'la put it on the floor and carefully crushed it with his big toe.

Then Flory shaved, bathed, dressed, and sat down to dinner. Ko S'la stood behind his chair, handing him the dishes and fanning him with the wicker fan. He had arranged a bowl of scarlet hibiscus flowers in the middle of the little table. The meal was pretentious and filthy. The clever 'Mug' cooks, descendants of servants trained by Frenchmen in India centuries ago, can do anything with food except make it eatable. After dinner Flory walked down to the Club, to play bridge and get three parts drunk, as he did most evenings when he was in Kyauktada.

# 5

In spite of the whisky he had drunk at the Club, Flory had little sleep that night. The pariah curs were baying the moon—it was only a quarter full and nearly down by midnight, but the dogs slept all day in the heat, and they had begun their moon-choruses already. One dog had taken a dislike to Flory's house, and had settled down to bay at it systematically. Sitting on its bottom fifty yards from the gate, it let out sharp, angry yelps, one to half a minute, as regularly as a clock. It would keep this up for two or three hours, until the cocks began crowing.

Flory lay turning from side to side, his head aching. Some fool has said that one cannot hate an animal; he should try a few nights in India, when the dogs are baying the moon. In the end Flory could stand it no longer. He got up, rummaged in the tin uniform case under his bed for a rifle and a couple of cartridges, and went out on to the veranda.

It was fairly light in the quarter moon. He could see the dog, and he could see his foresight. He rested himself against the wooden pillar of the veranda and took aim carefully; then, as he felt the hard vulcanite butt against his bare shoulder, he flinched. The rifle had a heavy kick, and it left a bruise when one fired it. The soft flesh of his shoulder quailed. He lowered the rifle. He had not the nerve to fire it in cold blood.

It was no use trying to sleep. Flory got his jacket and some cigarettes, and began to stroll up and down the garden path, between the ghostly flowers. It was hot, and the mosquitoes found him out and came droning after him. Phantoms of dogs were chasing one another on the maidan. Over to the left the gravestones of the English cemetery glittered whitish, rather sinister, and one could see the mounds near by, that were the remains of old Chinese tombs. The hillside was said to be haunted, and the Club *chokras* cried when they were sent up the road at night.

'Cur, spineless cur,' Flory was thinking to himself; without heat, however, for he was too accustomed to the thought. 'Sneaking, idling, boozing, fornicating, soul-examining, self-pitying cur. All those fools at the Club, those dull louts to whom you are so pleased to think yourself superior—they are all better than you, every man of them. At least they are men in their oafish way. Not cowards, not liars. Not half-dead and rotting. But you—'

He had reason to call himself names. There had been a nasty, dirty affair at the Club that evening. Something quite ordinary, quite according to precedent; but still dingy, cowardly, dishonouring.

When Flory had arrived at the Club only Ellis and Maxwell were there. The Lackersteens had gone to the station with the loan of Mr Macgregor's car, to meet their niece, who was to arrive by the night train. The three men were playing three-handed bridge fairly amicably when Westfield came in, his sandy face quite pink with rage, bringing a copy of a Burmese paper called the *Burmese Patriot*. There was a libellous article in it, attacking Mr Macgregor. The rage of Ellis and Westfield was devilish. They were so angry that Flory had the greatest difficulty in pretending to be angry enough to satisfy them. Ellis spent five minutes in cursing and then, by some extraordinary process, made up his mind that Dr Veraswami was responsible for the article. And he had thought of a counterstroke already. They would put a notice on the board—a notice answering and contradicting the one Mr Macgregor had posted the day before. Ellis wrote it out immediately, in his tiny, clear handwriting:

'In view of the cowardly insult recently offered to our Deputy Commissioner, we the undersigned wish to give it as our opinion that this is the worst possible moment to consider the election of niggers to this Club,' etc., etc.

Westfield demurred to 'niggers'. It was crossed out by a single thin line and 'natives' substituted. The notice was signed 'R. Westfield, P. W. Ellis, C. W. Maxwell, J. Flory.'

Ellis was so pleased with his idea that quite half of his anger evaporated. The notice would accomplish nothing in itself, but the news of it would travel swiftly round the town, and would reach Dr Veraswami tomorrow. In effect, the doctor would have been publicly called a nigger by the European community. This delighted Ellis. For the rest of the evening he could hardly keep his eyes from the notice-board, and every few minutes he exclaimed in glee, 'That'll give little fat-belly something to think about, eh? Teach the little sod what we think of him. That's the way to put 'em in their place, eh?' etc.

Meanwhile, Flory had signed a public insult to his friend. He had done it for the same reason as he had done a thousand such things in his life; because he lacked the small spark of courage that was needed to refuse. For, of course, he could have refused if he had chosen; and, equally of course, refusal would have meant a row with Ellis and Westfield. And oh, how he loathed a row! The nagging, the jeers! At the very thought of it he flinched; he could feel his birthmark palpable on his cheek, and something happening in his throat that made his voice go flat and guilty. Not that! It was easier to insult his friend, knowing that his friend must hear of it.

Flory had been fifteen years in Burma, and in Burma one learns not to set oneself up against public opinion. But his trouble was older than that. It had begun in his mother's womb, when chance put the blue birthmark on his cheek. He thought of some of the early effects of his birthmark. His first arrival at school, aged nine; the stares and, after a few days, shouts of the other boys; the nickname Blueface, which lasted until the school poet (now, Flory remembered, a critic who wrote rather good articles in the *Nation*) came out with the couplet:

> New-tick Flory does look rum,
> Got a face like a monkey's bum,

whereupon the nickname was changed to Monkey-bum. And the subsequent years. On Saturday nights the older boys used to have what they called a Spanish Inquisition. The favourite torture was for someone to hold you in a very painful grip known only to a few illuminati and called Special Togo, while someone else beat you with a conker on a piece of string. But Flory had lived down 'Monkey-bum' in time. He was a liar, and a good footballer, the two things absolutely necessary for success at school. In his last term he and another boy held the school poet in Special Togo while the captain of the eleven gave him six with a spiked running shoe for being caught writing a sonnet. It was a formative period.

From that school he went to a cheap, third-rate public school. It was a poor, spurious place. It aped the great public schools with their traditions of High Anglicanism, cricket and Latin verses, and it had a school song called 'The Scrum of Life' in which God figured as the Great Referee. But it lacked the chief virtue of the great public schools, their atmosphere of literary scholarship. The boys learned as nearly as possible nothing. There was not enough caning to make them swallow the dreary rubbish of the curriculum, and the wretched, underpaid masters were not the kind from whom one absorbs wisdom unawares. Flory left school a barbarous young lout. And yet even then there were, and he knew it, certain possibilities in him; possibilities that would lead to trouble as likely as not. But, of course, he had suppressed them. A boy does not start his career nicknamed Monkey-bum without learning his lesson.

He was not quite twenty when he came to Burma. His parents, good people and devoted to him, had found him a place in a timber firm. They had had great difficulty in getting him the job, had paid a premium they could not afford; later, he had rewarded them by answering their letters with careless scrawls at intervals of months. His first six months in Burma he had spent in Rangoon, where he was supposed to be learning the office side of his business. He had lived in a 'chummery' with four other youths who devoted their entire energies to debauchery. And what debauchery! They swilled whisky which they privately hated, they stood round the piano bawling songs of insane filthiness and silliness, they squandered rupees by the hundred on aged Jewish whores with the faces of crocodiles. That too had been a formative period.

From Rangoon he had gone to a camp in the jungle, north of Mandalay, extracting teak. The jungle life was not a bad one, in spite of the discomfort, the loneliness, and what is almost the worst thing in Burma, the filthy, monotonous food. He was very young then, young enough for hero-worship, and he had friends among the men in his firm. There were also shooting, fishing, and perhaps once in a year a hurried trip to Rangoon—pretext, a visit to the dentist. Oh, the joy of those Rangoon trips! The rush to Smart and Mookerdum's bookshop for the new novels out from England, the dinner at Anderson's with beefsteaks and butter that had travelled eight thousand miles on ice, the glorious drinking-bout! He was too young to realize what this life was preparing for him. He did not see the years stretching out ahead, lonely, eventless, corrupting.

He acclimatized himself to Burma. His body grew attuned to the strange rhythms of the tropical seasons. Every year from February to May the sun glared in the sky like an angry god, then suddenly the monsoon blew westward, first in sharp squalls, then in a heavy ceaseless downpour that drenched everything until neither one's clothes, one's bed nor even one's food ever seemed to be dry. It was still hot, with a stuffy, vaporous heat. The lower jungle paths turned into morasses, and the paddy-fields were wastes of stagnant water with a stale, mousy smell. Books and boots were mildewed. Naked Burmans in yard-wide hats of palm-leaf ploughed the paddy-fields, driving their buffaloes through knee-deep water. Later, the women and children planted the green seedlings of paddy, dabbing each plant into the mud with little three-pronged forks. Through July and August there was hardly a pause in the rain. Then one night, high overhead, one heard a squawking of invisible birds. The snipe were flying southward from Central Asia. The rains tailed off, ending in October. The fields dried up, the paddy ripened, the Burmese children played hop-scotch with gonyin seeds and flew kites in the cool winds. It was the beginning of the short winter, when Upper Burma seemed haunted by the ghost of England. Wild flowers sprang into bloom everywhere, not quite the same as the English ones, but very like them—honeysuckle in thick bushes, field roses smelling of pear-drops, even violets in dark places of the forest. The sun circled low in the sky, and the nights and early mornings were bitterly cold, with white mists that poured through the valleys like the steam of enormous kettles. One went shooting after duck and snipe. There were snipe in countless myriads, and wild geese in flocks that rose from the jeel with a roar like a goods train crossing an iron bridge. The ripening paddy, breast-high and yellow, looked like wheat. The Burmans went to their work with muffled heads and their arms clasped across their breasts, their faces yellow and pinched with the cold. In the morning one marched through misty, incongruous wilderness, clearings of drenched, almost English grass and naked trees where monkeys squatted in the upper branches, waiting for the sun. At night, coming back to camp through the cold lanes, one met herds of buffaloes which the boys were driving home, with their huge horns looming through the mist like crescents. One had three blankets on one's bed, and game pies instead of the eternal chicken. After dinner one sat on a log by the vast camp-fire, drinking beer and talking about shooting. The flames danced like red holly, casting a circle of light at the edge of which servants and coolies squatted, too shy to intrude on the white men and yet edging up to the fire like dogs. As one lay in bed one could hear the dew dripping from the trees like large but gentle rain. It was a good life while one was young and need not think about the future or the past.

Flory was twenty-four, and due for home leave, when the War broke out. He had dodged military service, which was easy to do and seemed natural at the time. The civilians in Burma had a comforting theory that 'sticking by one's job' (wonderful language, English! 'Sticking *by*'—how different from 'sticking *to*') was the truest patriotism; there was even a covert hostility towards the men who threw up their jobs in order to join the Army. In reality, Flory had dodged the War because the East already corrupted him, and he did not want to exchange his whisky, his servants and his Burmese girls for the boredom of the parade ground and the strain of cruel marches. The War rolled on, like a storm beyond the horizon. The hot, blowsy country, remote from danger, had a lonely, forgotten feeling. Flory took to reading voraciously, and learned to live in books when life was tiresome. He was growing adult, tiring of boyish pleasures, learning to think for himself, almost willy-nilly.

He celebrated his twenty-seventh birthday in hospital, covered from head to foot with hideous sores which were called mud-sores, but were probably caused by whisky and bad food. They left little pits in his skin which did not disappear for two years. Quite suddenly he had begun to look and feel very much older. His youth was finished. Eight years of Eastern life, fever, loneliness and intermittent drinking, had set their mark on him.

Since then, each year had been lonelier and more bitter than the last. What was at the centre of all his thoughts now, and what poisoned everything, was the ever bitterer hatred of the atmosphere of imperialism in which he lived. For as his brain developed—you cannot stop your brain developing, and it is one of the tragedies of the half-educated that they develop late, when they are already committed to some wrong way of life—he had grasped the truth about the English and their Empire. The Indian Empire is a despotism—benevolent, no doubt, but still a despotism with theft as its final object. And as to the English of the East, the *sahiblog*, Flory had come so to hate them from living in their society, that he was quite incapable of being fair to them. For after all, the poor devils are no worse than anybody else. They lead unenviable lives; it is a poor bargain to spend thirty years, ill-paid, in an alien country, and then come home with a wrecked liver and a pine-apple backside from sitting in cane chairs, to settle down as the bore of some second-rate Club. On the other hand, the *sahiblog* are not to be idealized. There is a prevalent idea that the men at the 'outposts of Empire' are at least able and hardworking. It is a delusion. Outside the scientific services—the Forest Department, the Public Works Department and the like—there is no particular need for a British official in India to do his job competently. Few of them work as hard or as intelligently as the post-master of a provincial town in England. The real work of administration is done mainly by native subordinates; and the real backbone of the despotism is not the officials but the Army. Given the Army, the officials and the businessmen can rub along safely enough even if they are fools. And most of them *are* fools. A dull, decent people, cherishing and fortifying their dullness behind a quarter of a million bayonets.

It is a stifling, stultifying world in which to live. It is a world in which every word and every thought is censored. In England it is hard even to imagine such an atmosphere. Everyone is free in England; we sell our souls in public and buy them back in private, among our friends. But even friendship can hardly exist when every white man is a cog in the wheels of despotism. Free speech is unthinkable. All other kinds of freedom are permitted. You are free to be a drunkard, an idler, a coward, a backbiter, a fornicator; but you are not free to think for yourself. Your opinion on every subject of any conceivable importance is dictated for you by the pukka sahibs' code.

In the end the secrecy of your revolt poisons you like a secret disease. Your whole life is a life of lies. Year after year you sit in Kipling-haunted little Clubs, whisky to right of you, *Pink'un* to left of you, listening and eagerly agreeing while Colonel Bodger develops his theory that these bloody Nationalists should be boiled in oil. You hear your Oriental friends called 'greasy little babus', and you admit, dutifully, that they *are* greasy little babus. You see louts fresh from school kicking grey-haired servants. The time comes when you burn with hatred of your own countrymen, when you long for a native rising to drown their Empire in blood. And in this there is nothing honourable, hardly even any sincerity. For, *au fond*, what do you care if the Indian Empire is a despotism, if Indians are bullied and exploited? You only care because the right of free speech is denied you. You are a creature of the despotism, a pukka sahib, tied tighter than a monk or a savage by an unbreakable system of tabus.

Time passed and each year Flory found himself less at home in the world of the sahibs, more liable to get into trouble when he talked seriously on any subject whatever. So he had learned to live inwardly, secretly, in books and secret thoughts that could not be uttered. Even his talks with the doctor were a kind of talking to himself; for the doctor, good man, understood little of what was said to him. But it is a corrupting thing to live one's real life in secret. One should live with the stream of life, not against it. It would be better to be the thickest-skulled pukka sahib who ever hiccuped over 'Forty years on', than to live silent, alone, consoling oneself in secret, sterile worlds.

Flory had never been home to England. Why, he could not have explained, though he knew well enough. In the beginning accidents had prevented him. First there was the War, and after the War his firm were so short of trained assistants that they would not let him go for two years more. Then at last he had set out. He was pining for England, though he dreaded facing it, as one dreads facing a pretty girl when one is collarless and unshaven. When he left home he had been a boy, a promising boy and handsome in spite of his birthmark; now, only ten years later, he was yellow, thin, drunken, almost middle-aged in habits and appearance. Still, he was pining for England. The ship rolled westward over wastes of sea like rough-beaten silver, with the winter trade wind behind her. Flory's thin blood quickenened with the good food and the smell of the sea. And it occurred to him—a thing he had actually forgotten in the stagnant air of Burma—that he was still young enough to begin over again. He would live a year in a civilized society, he would find some girl who did not mind his birthmark—a civilized girl, not a pukka memsahib—and he would marry her and endure ten, fifteen more years of Burma. Then they would retire—he would be worth twelve or fifteen thousand pounds on retirement, perhaps. They would buy a cottage in the country, surround themselves with friends, books, their children, animals. They would be free for ever of the smell of pukka sahibdom. He would forget Burma, the horrible country that had come near ruining him.

When he reached Colombo he found a cable waiting for him. Three men in his firm had died suddenly of black-water fever. The firm were sorry, but would he please return to Rangoon at once? He should have his leave at the earliest possible opportunity.

Flory boarded the next boat for Rangoon, cursing his luck, and took the train back to his headquarters. He was not at Kyauktada then, but at another Upper Burma town. All the servants were waiting for him on the platform. He had handed them over *en bloc* to his successor, who had died. It was so queer to see their familiar faces again! Only ten days ago he had been speeding for England, almost thinking himself in England already; and now back in the old stale scene, with the naked black coolies squabbling over the luggage and a Burman shouting at his bullocks down the road.

The servants came crowding round him, a ring of kindly brown faces, offering presents. Ko S'la had brought a sambhur skin, the Indians some sweetmeats and a garland of marigolds, Ba Pe, a young boy then, a squirrel in a wicker cage. There were bullock carts waiting for the luggage. Flory walked up to the house, looking ridiculous with the big garland dangling from his neck. The light of the cold-weather evening was yellow and kind. At the gate an old Indian, the colour of earth, was cropping grass with a tiny sickle. The wives of the cook and the *mali* were kneeling in front of the servants' quarters, grinding curry paste on the stone slab.

Something turned over in Flory's heart. It was one of those moments when one becomes conscious of a vast change and deterioration in one's life. For he had realized, suddenly, that in his heart he was glad to be coming back. This country which he hated was now his native country, his home. He had lived here ten years, and every particle of his body was compounded of Burmese soil. Scenes like these—the sallow evening light, the old Indian cropping grass, the creak of the cartwheels, the streaming egrets—were more native to him than

England. He had sent deep roots, perhaps his deepest, into a foreign country.

Since then he had not even applied for home leave. His father had died, then his mother, and his sisters, disagreeable horse-faced women whom he had never liked, had married and he had almost lost touch with them. He had no tie with Europe now, except the tie of books. For he had realized that merely to go back to England was no remedy for loneliness; he had grasped the special nature of the hell that is reserved for Anglo-Indians. Ah, those poor prosing old wrecks in Bath and Cheltenham! Those tomb-like boarding-houses with Anglo-Indians littered about in all stages of decomposition, all talking and talking about what happened in Boggleywalah in '88! Poor devils, they know what it means to have left one's heart in an alien and hated country. There was, he saw clearly, only one way out. To find someone who would share his life in Burma—but really share it, share his inner, secret life, carry away from Burma the same memories as he carried. Someone who would love Burma as he loved it and hate it as he hated it. Who would help him to live with nothing hidden, nothing unexpressed. Someone who understood him: a friend, that was what it came down to.

A friend. Or a wife? That quite impossible she. Someone like Mrs Lackersteen, for instance? Some damned memsahib, yellow and thin, scandalmongering over cocktails, making kit-kit with the servants, living twenty years in the country without learning a word of the language. Not one of those, please God.

Flory leaned over the gate. The moon was vanishing behind the dark wall of the jungle, but the dogs were still howling. Some lines from Gilbert came into his mind, a vulgar silly jingle but appropriate—something about 'discoursing on your complicated state of mind'. Gilbert was a gifted little skunk. Did all his trouble, then, simply boil down to that? Just complicated, unmanly whinings; poor-little-rich-girl stuff? Was he no more than a loafer using his idleness to invent imaginary woes? A spiritual Mrs Wititterly? A Hamlet without poetry? Perhaps. And if so, did that make it any more bearable? It is not the less bitter because it is perhaps one's own fault, to see oneself drifting, rotting, in dishonour and horrible futility, and all the while knowing that somewhere within one there is the possibility of a decent human being.

Oh well, God save us from self-pity! Flory went back to the veranda, took up the rifle, and wincing slightly, let drive at the pariah dog. There was an echoing roar, and the bullet buried itself in the maidan, wide of the mark. A mulberry-coloured bruise sprang out on Flory's shoulder. The dog gave a yell of fright, took to its heels, and then, sitting down fifty yards farther away, once more began rhythmically baying.

# 6

The morning sunlight slanted up the maidan and struck, yellow as goldleaf, against the white face of the bungalow. Four black-purple crows swooped down and perched on the veranda rail, waiting their chance to dart in and steal the bread and butter that Ko S'la had set down beside Flory's bed. Flory crawled through the mosquito net, shouted to Ko S'la to bring him some gin, and then went into the bathroom and sat for a while in a zinc tub of water that was supposed to be cold. Feeling better after the gin, he shaved himself. As a rule he put off shaving until the evening, for his beard was black and grew quickly.

While Flory was sitting morosely in his bath, Mr Macgregor, in shorts and singlet on the bamboo mat laid for the purpose in his bedroom, was struggling with Numbers 5, 6, 7, 8 and 9 of Nordenflycht's 'Physical Jerks for the Sedentary'. Mr Macgregor never, or hardly ever, missed his morning exercises. Number 8 (flat on the back, raise legs to the perpendicular without bending knees) was downright painful for a man of forty-three; Number 9 (flat on the back, rise to a sitting posture and touch toes with tips of fingers) was even worse. No matter, one must keep fit! As Mr Macgregor lunged painfully in the direction of his toes, a brick-red shade flowed upwards from his neck and congested his face with a threat of apoplexy. The sweat gleamed on his large, tallowy breasts. Stick it out, stick it out! At all costs one must keep fit. Mohammed Ali, the bearer, with Mr Macgregor's clean clothes across his arm, watched through the half-open door. His narrow, yellow, Arabian face expressed neither comprehension nor curiosity. He had watched these contortions—a sacrifice, he dimly imagined, to some mysterious and exacting god—every morning for five years.

At the same time, too, Westfield, who had gone out early, was leaning against the notched and ink-stained table of the police station, while the fat Sub-inspector interrogated a suspect whom two constables were guarding. The suspect was a man of forty, with a grey, timorous face, dressed only in a ragged *longyi* kilted to the knee, beneath which his lank, curved shins were speckled with tick-bites.

'Who is this fellow?' said Westfield.

'Thief, sir. We catch him in possession of this ring with two emeralds very-dear. No explanation. How could he—poor coolie—own a emerald ring? He have stole it.'

He turned ferociously upon the suspect, advanced his face tomcat-fashion till it was almost touching the other's, and roared in an enormous voice:

'You stole the ring!'

'No.'

'You are an old offender!'

'No.'

'You have been in prison!'

'No.'

'Turn round!' bellowed the Sub-inspector on an inspiration. 'Bend over!'

The suspect turned his grey face in agony towards Westfield, who looked away. The two constables seized him, twisted him round and bent him over; the Sub-inspector tore off his *longyi*, exposing his buttocks.

'Look at this, sir!' He pointed to some scars. 'He have been flogged with bamboos. He is an old offender. *Therefore* he stole the ring!'

'All right, put him in the clink,' said Westfield moodily, as he lounged away from the table with his hands in his pockets. At the bottom of his heart he loathed running in these poor devils of common thieves. Dacoits, rebels—yes; but not these poor cringing rats! 'How many have you got in the clink now, Maung Ba?' he said.

'Three, sir.'

The lock-up was upstairs, a cage surrounded by six-inch wooden bars, guarded by a constable armed with a carbine. It was very dark, stifling hot, and quite unfurnished, except for an earth latrine that stank to heaven. Two prisoners were squatting at the bars, keeping their distance from a third, an Indian coolie, who was covered from head to foot with ringworm like a coat of mail. A stout Burmese woman, wife of a constable, was kneeling outside the cage ladling rice and watery *dahl* into tin pannikins.

'Is the food good?' said Westfield.

'It is good, most holy one,' chorused the prisoners.

The Government provided for the prisoners' food at the rate of two annas and a half per meal per man, out of which the constable's wife looked to make a profit of one anna.

Flory went outside and loitered down the compound, poking weeds into the ground with his stick. At that hour there were beautiful faint colours in everything—tender green of leaves, pinkish brown of earth and tree-trunks—like aquarelle washes that would vanish in the later glare. Down on the maidan flights of small, low-flying brown doves chased one another to and fro, and bee-eaters, emerald-green, curvetted like slow swallows. A file of sweepers, each with his load half hidden beneath his garment, were marching to some dreadful dumping-hole that existed on the edge of the jungle. Starveling wretches, with stick-like limbs and knees too feeble to be straightened, draped in earth-coloured rags, they were like a procession of shrouded skeletons walking.

The *mali* was breaking ground for a new flower-bed, down by the pigeon-cote that stood near the gate. He was a lymphatic, half-witted Hindu youth, who lived his life in almost complete silence, because he spoke some Manipur dialect which nobody else understood, not even his Zerbadi wife. His tongue was also a size too large for his mouth. He salaamed low to Flory, covering his face with his hand, then swung his *mamootie* aloft again and hacked at the dry ground with heavy, clumsy strokes, his tender back-muscles quivering.

A sharp grating scream that sounded like 'Kwaaa!' came from the servants' quarters. Ko S'la's wives had begun their morning quarrel. The tame fighting cock, called Nero, strutted zigzag down the path, nervous of Flo, and Ba Pe came out with a bowl of paddy and they fed Nero and the pigeons. There were more yells from the servants' quarters, and the gruffer voices of men trying to stop the quarrel. Ko S'la suffered a great deal from his wives. Ma Pu, the first wife, was a gaunt hard-faced woman, stringy from much child-bearing, and Ma Yi, the 'little wife', was a fat, lazy cat some years younger. The two women fought incessantly when Flory was in headquarters and they were together. Once when Ma Pu was chasing Ko S'la with a bamboo, he had dodged behind Flory for protection, and Flory had received a nasty blow on the leg.

Mr Macgregor was coming up the road, striding briskly and swinging a thick walking-stick. He was dressed in khaki pagri-cloth shirt, drill shorts and a pigsticker topi. Besides his exercises, he took a brisk two-mile walk every morning when he could spare the time.

'Top o' the mornin' to ye!' he called to Flory in a hearty matutinal voice, putting on an Irish accent. He cultivated a brisk, invigorating, cold-bath demeanour at this hour of the morning. Moreover, the libellous article in the *Burmese Patriot,* which he had read overnight, had hurt him, and he was affecting a special cheeriness to conceal this.

'Morning!' Flory called back as heartily as he could manage.

Nasty old bladder of lard! he thought, watching Mr Macgregor up the road. How his bottom did stick out in those tight khaki shorts. Like one of those beastly middle-aged scoutmasters, homosexuals almost to a man, that you see photographs of in the illustrated papers. Dressing himself up in those ridiculous clothes and exposing his pudgy, dimpled knees, because it is the pukka sahib thing to take exercise before breakfast–disgusting!

A Burman came up the hill, a splash of white and magenta. It was Flory's clerk, coming from the tiny office, which was not far from the church. Reaching the gate, he shikoed and presented a grimy envelope, stamped Burmese-fashion on the point of the flap.

'Good morning, sir.'

'Good morning. What's this thing?'

'Local letter, your honour. Come this morning's post. Anonymous letter, I think, sir.'

'Oh bother. All right, I'll be down to the office about eleven.'

Flory opened the letter. It was written on a sheet of foolscap, and it ran:

Mr John Flory,

Sir,–I the undersigned beg to suggest and warn to your honour certain useful pieces of information whereby your honour will be much profited, sir.

Sir, it has been remarked in Kyauktada your honour's great friendship and intimacy with Dr Veraswami, the Civil Surgeon, frequenting with him, inviting him to your house, etc. Sir, we beg to inform you that the said Dr Veraswami is not a good man and in no ways a worthy friend of European gentlemen. The doctor is eminently dishonest, disloyal and corrupt public servant.

Coloured water is he providing to patients at the hospital and selling drugs for own profit, besides many bribes, extortions, etc. Two prisoners has he flogged with bamboos, afterwards rubbing chilis into the place if relatives do not send money. Besides this he is implicated with the Nationalist Party and lately provided material for a very evil article which appeared in the *Burmese Patriot* attacking Mr Macgregor, the honoured Deputy Commissioner.

He is also sleeping by force with female patients at the hospital.

Wherefore we are much hoping that your honour will ESCHEW same Dr Veraswami and not consort with persons who can bring nothing but evil upon your honour.

And shall ever pray for your honour's long health and prosperity.

(Signed)    A FRIEND.

The letter was written in the shaky round hand of the bazaar letter-writer, which resembled a copybook exercise written by a drunkard. The letter-writer, however, would never have risen to such a word as 'eschew'. The letter must have been dictated by a clerk, and no doubt it came ultimately from U Po Kyin. From 'the crocodile', Flory reflected.

He did not like the tone of the letter. Under its appearance of servility it was obviously a covert threat. 'Drop the doctor or we will make it hot for you', was what it said in effect. Not that that mattered greatly; no Englishman ever feels himself in real danger from an Oriental.

Flory hesitated with the letter in his hands. There are two things one can do with an anonymous letter. One can say nothing about it, or one can show it to the person whom it concerns. The obvious, the decent course was to give the letter to Dr Veraswami and let him take what action he chose.

And yet—it was safer to keep out of this business altogether. It is so important (perhaps the most important of all the Ten Precepts of the pukka sahib) not to entangle oneself in 'native' quarrels. With Indians there must be no loyalty, no real friendship. Affection, even love—yes. Englishmen do often love Indians—native officers, forest rangers, hunters, clerks, servants. Sepoys will weep like children when their colonel retires. Even intimacy is allowable, at the right moments. But alliance, partisanship, never! Even to know the rights and wrongs of a 'native' quarrel is a loss of prestige.

If he published the letter there would be a row and an official inquiry, and, in effect, he would have thrown in his lot with the doctor against U Po Kyin. U Po Kyin did not matter, but there were the Europeans; if he, Flory, were too conspicuously the doctor's partisan, there might be hell to pay. Much better to pretend that the letter had never reached him. The doctor was a good fellow, but as to championing him against the full fury of pukká sahibdom—ah, no, no! What shall it profit a man if he save his own soul and lose the whole world? Flory began to tear the letter across. The danger of making it public was very slight, very nebulous. But one must beware of the nebulous dangers in India. Prestige, the breath of life, is itself nebulous. He carefully tore the letter into small pieces and threw them over the gate.

At this moment there was a terrified scream, quite different from the voices of Ko S'la's wives. The *mali* lowered his *mamootie* and gaped in the direction of the sound, and Ko S'la, who had also heard it, came running bareheaded from the servants' quarters, while Flo sprang to her feet and yapped sharply. The scream was repeated. It came from the jungle behind the house, and it was an

English voice, a woman's, crying out in terror.

There was no way out of the compound by the back. Flory scrambled over the gate and came down with his knee bleeding from a splinter. He ran round the compound fence and into the jungle, Flo following. Just behind the house, beyond the first fringe of bushes, there was a small hollow, which, as there was a pool of stagnant water in it, was frequented by buffaloes from Nyaunglebin. Flory pushed his way through the bushes. In the hollow an English girl, chalk-faced, was cowering against a bush, while a huge buffalo menaced her with its crescent-shaped horns. A hairy calf, no doubt the cause of the trouble, stood behind. Another buffalo, neck-deep in the slime of the pool, looked on with mild prehistoric face, wondering what was the matter.

The girl turned an agonized face to Flory as he appeared. 'Oh, do be quick!' she cried, in the angry, urgent tone of people who are frightened. 'Please! Help me! Help me!'

Flory was too astonished to ask any questions. He hastened towards her, and, in default of a stick, smacked the buffalo sharply on the nose. With a timid, loutish movement the great beast turned aside, then lumbered off followed by the calf. The other buffalo also extricated itself from the slime and lolloped away. The girl threw herself against Flory, almost into his arms, quite overcome by her fright.

'Oh, thank you, thank you! Oh, those dreadful things! What *are* they? I thought they were going to kill me. What horrible creatures! What *are* they?'

'They're only water-buffaloes. They come from the village up there.'

'Buffaloes?'

'Not wild buffaloes—bison, we call those. They're just a kind of cattle the Burmans keep. I say, they've given you a nasty shock. I'm sorry.'

She was still clinging closely to his arm, and he could feel her shaking. He looked down, but he could not see her face, only the top of her head, hatless, with yellow hair as short as a boy's. And he could see one of the hands on his arm. It was long, slender, youthful, with the mottled wrist of a schoolgirl. It was several years since he had seen such a hand. He became conscious of the soft, youthful body pressed against his own, and the warmth breathing out of it; whereat something seemed to thaw and grow warm within him.

'It's all right, they're gone,' he said. 'There's nothing to be frightened of.'

The girl was recovering from her fright, and she stood a little away from him, with one hand still on his arm. 'I'm all right,' she said 'It's nothing. I'm not hurt. They didn't touch me. It was only their looking so awful.'

'They're quite harmless really. Their horns are set so far back that they can't gore you. They're very stupid brutes. They only pretend to show fight when they've got calves.'

They had stood apart now, and a slight embarrassment came over them both immediately. Flory had already turned himself sidelong to keep his birthmarked cheek away from her. He said:

'I say, this is a queer sort of introduction! I haven't asked yet how you got here. Wherever did you come from—if it's not rude to ask?'

'I just came out of my uncle's garden. It seemed such a nice morning, I thought I'd go for a walk. And then those dreadful things came after me. I'm quite new to this country, you see.'

'Your uncle? Oh, of course! You're Mr Lackersteen's niece. We heard you were coming. I say, shall we get out on to the maidan? There'll be a path somewhere. What a start for your first morning in Kyauktada! This'll give you rather a bad impression of Burma, I'm afraid.'

'Oh no; only it's all rather strange. How thick these bushes grow! All kind of twisted together and foreign-looking. You could get lost here in a moment. Is that what they call jungle?'

'Scrub jungle. Burma's mostly jungle—a green, unpleasant land, I call it. I wouldn't walk through that grass if I were you. The seeds get into your stockings and work their way into your skin.'

He let the girl walk ahead of him, feeling easier when she could not see his face. She was tallish for a girl, slender, and wearing a lilac-coloured cotton frock. From the way she moved her limbs he did not think she could be much past twenty. He had not noticed her face yet, except to see that she wore round tortoise-shell spectacles, and that her hair was as short as his own. He had never seen a woman with cropped hair before, except in the illustrated papers.

As they emerged on to the maidan he stepped level with her, and she turned to face him. Her face was oval, with delicate, regular features; not beautiful, perhaps, but it seemed so there, in Burma, where all Englishwomen are yellow and thin. He turned his head sharply aside, though the birthmark was away from her. He could not bear her to see his worn face too closely. He seemed to feel the withered skin round his eyes as though it had been a wound. But he remembered that he had shaved that morning, and it gave him courage. He said:

'I say, you must be a bit shaken up after this business. Would you like to come into my place and rest a few minutes before you go home? It's rather late to be out of doors without a hat, too.'

'Oh, thank you, I would,' the girl said. She could not, he thought, know anything about Indian notions of propriety. 'Is this your house here?'

'Yes. We must go round the front way. I'll have the servants get a sunshade for you. This sun's dangerous for you, with your short hair.'

They walked up the garden path. Flo was frisking round them and trying to draw attention to herself. She always barked at strange Orientals, but she liked the smell of a European. The sun was growing stronger. A wave of blackcurrant scent flowed from the petunias beside the path, and one of the pigeons fluttered to the earth, to spring immediately into the air again as Flo made a grab at it. Flory and the girl stopped with one consent, to look at the flowers. A pang of unreasonable happiness had gone through them both.

'You really mustn't go out in this sun without a hat on,' he repeated, and somehow there was an intimacy in saying it. He could not help referring to her short hair somehow, it seemed to him so beautiful. To speak of it was like touching it with his hand.

'Look, your knee's bleeding,' the girl said. 'Did you do that when you were coming to help me?'

There was a slight trickle of blood, which was drying, purple, on his khaki stocking. 'It's nothing,' he said, but neither of them felt at that moment that it was nothing. They began chattering with extraordinary eagerness about the flowers. The girl 'adored' flowers, she said. And Flory led her up the path, talking garrulously about one plant and another.

'Look how these phloxes grow. They go on blooming for six months in this country. They can't get too much sun. I think those yellow ones must be almost the colour of primroses. I haven't seen a primrose for fifteen years, nor a wallflower, either. Those zinnias are fine, aren't they?—like painted flowers, with those wonderful dead colours. These are African marigolds. They're coarse things, weeds almost, but you can't help liking them, they're so vivid and strong. Indians have an extraordinary affection for them; wherever Indians have been you find marigolds growing, even years afterwards when the jungle has buried every other trace of them. But I wish you'd come into the veranda and see the orchids. I've some I must show that are just like bells of gold—but literally like gold. And they smell of honey, almost overpoweringly. That's about the only merit of this beastly country, it's good for flowers. I hope you're fond of gardening? It's our greatest consolation, in this country.'

'Oh, I simply adore gardening,' the girl said.

They went into the veranda. Ko S'la had hurriedly put on his *ingyi* and his best pink silk *gaungbaung,* and he appeared from within the house with a tray on which were a decanter of gin, glasses and a box of cigarettes. He laid them on the table, and, eyeing the girl half apprehensively, put his hands flat together and shikoed.

'I expect it's no use offering you a drink at this hour of the morning?' Flory said. 'I can never get it into my servant's head that *some* people can exist without gin before breakfast.'

He added himself to the number by waving away the drink Ko S'la offered him. The girl had sat down in the wicker chair that Ko S'la had set out for her at the end of the veranda. The dark-leaved orchids hung behind her head, with gold trusses of blossom, breathing out warm honey-scent. Flory was standing against the veranda rail, half facing the girl, but keeping his birthmarked cheek hidden.

'What a perfectly divine view you have from here,' she said as she looked down the hillside.

'Yes, isn't it? Splendid, in this yellow light, before the sun gets going. I love that sombre yellow colour the maidan has, and those gold mohur trees, like blobs of crimson. And those hills at the horizon, almost black. My camp is on the other side of those hills,' he added.

The girl, who was long-sighted, took off her spectacles to look into the distance. He noticed that her eyes were very clear pale blue, paler than a harebell. And he noticed the smoothness of the skin round her eyes, like a petal, almost. It reminded him of his age and his haggard face again, so that he turned a little more away from her. But he said on impulse:

'I say, what a bit of luck you coming to Kyauktada! You can't imagine the difference it makes to us to see a new face in these places. After months of our own miserable society, and an occasional official on his rounds and American globe-trotters skipping up the Irrawaddy with cameras. I suppose you've come straight from England?'

'Well, not England exactly. I was living in Paris before I came out here. My mother was an artist, you see.'

'Paris! Have you really lived in Paris? By Jove, just fancy coming from Paris to Kyauktada! Do you know, it's positively difficult, in a hole like this, to believe that there *are* such places as Paris.'

'Do you like Paris?' she said.

'I've never even seen it. But, good Lord, how I've imagined it! Paris—it's all a kind of jumble of pictures in my mind; cafés and boulevards and artists' studios and Villon and Baudelaire and Maupassant all mixed up together. You don't know how the names of those European towns sound to us, out here. And did you really live in Paris? Sitting in cafés with foreign art students, drinking white wine and talking about Marcel Proust?'

'Oh, that kind of thing, I suppose,' said the girl, laughing.

'What differences you'll find here! It's not white wine and Marcel Proust here. Whisky and Edgar Wallace more likely. But if you ever want books, you might find something you liked among mine. There's nothing but tripe in the Club library. But of course I'm hopelessly behind the times with my books. I expect you'll have read everything under the sun.'

'Oh no. But of course I simply adore reading,' the girl said.

'What it means to meet somebody who cares for books! I mean books worth reading, not that garbage in the Club libraries. I do hope you'll forgive me if I overwhelm you with talk. When I meet somebody who's heard that books exist, I'm afraid I go off like a bottle of warm beer. It's a fault you have to pardon in these countries.'

'Oh, but I love talking about books. I think reading is so wonderful. I mean, what would life be without it? It's such a—such a—'

'Such a private Alsatia. Yes—'

They plunged into an enormous and eager conversation, first about books, then about shooting, in which the girl seemed to have an interest and about which she persuaded Flory to talk. She was quite thrilled when he described the murder of an elephant which he had perpetrated some years earlier. Flory scarcely noticed, and perhaps the girl did not either, that it was he who did all the talking. He could not stop himself, the joy of chattering was so great. And the girl was in a mood to listen. After all, he had saved her from the buffalo, and she did not yet believe that those monstrous brutes could be harmless; for the moment he was almost a hero in her eyes. When one does get any credit in this life, it is usually for something that one has not done. It was one of those times when the conversation flows so easily, so naturally, that one could go on talking forever. But suddenly, their pleasure evaporated, they started and fell silent. They had noticed that they were no longer alone.

At the other end of the veranda, between the rails, a coal-black moustachioed face was peeping with enormous curiosity. It belonged to old Sammy, the 'Mug' cook. Behind him stood Ma Pu, Ma Yi, Ko S'la's four eldest children, an unclaimed naked child, and two old women who had come down from the village upon the news that an 'Ingaleikma' was on view. Like carved teak statues with footlong cigars stuck in their wooden faces, the two old creatures gazed at the 'Ingaleikma' as English yokels might gaze at a Zulu warrior in full regalia.

'Those people . . .' the girl said uncomfortably, looking towards them.

Sammy, seeing himself detected, looked very guilty and pretended to be rearranging his *pagri*. The rest of the audience were a little abashed, except for the two wooden-faced old women.

'Dash their cheek!' Flory said. A cold pang of disappointment went through him. After all, it would not do for the girl to stay on his veranda any longer. Simultaneously both he and she had remembered that they were total strangers. Her face had turned a little pink. She began putting on her spectacles.

'I'm afraid an English girl is rather a novelty to these people,' he said. 'They don't mean any harm. Go away!' he added angrily, waving his hand at the audience, whereupon they vanished.

'Do you know, if you don't mind, I think I ought to be going,' the girl said. She had stood up. 'I've been out quite a long time. They may be wondering where I've got to.'

'Must you really? It's quite early. I'll see that you don't have to go home bareheaded in the sun.'

'I ought really—' she began again.

She stopped, looking at the doorway. Ma Hla May was emerging on to the veranda.

Ma Hla May came forward with her hand on her hip. She had come from within the house, with a calm air that asserted her right to be there. The two girls stood face to face, less than six feet apart.

No contrast could have been stranger; the one faintly coloured as an apple-blossom, the other dark and garish, with a gleam almost metallic on her cylinder of ebony hair and the salmon-pink silk of her *longyi*. Flory thought he had never noticed before how dark Ma Hla May's face was, and how outlandish her tiny, stiff body, straight as a soldier's, with not a curve in it except the vase-like curve of her hips. He stood against the veranda rail and watched the two girls, quite disregarded. For the best part of a minute neither of them could take her eyes from the other; but which found the spectacle more grotesque, more incredible, there is no saying.

Ma Hla May turned her face round to Flory, with her black brows, thin as pencil lines, drawn together. 'Who is this woman?' she demanded sullenly.

He answered casually, as though giving an order to a servant:

'Go away this instant. If you make any trouble I will afterwards take a bamboo and beat you till not one of your ribs is whole.'

Ma Hla May hesitated, shrugged her small shoulders and disappeared. And the other, gazing after her, said curiously:

'Was that a man or a woman?'

'A woman,' he said. 'One of the servants' wives, I believe. She came to ask about the laundry, that was all.'

'Oh, is *that* what Burmese women are like? They *are* queer little creatures! I saw a lot of them on my way up here in the train, but do you know, I thought they were all boys. They're just like a kind of Dutch doll, aren't they?'

She had begun to move towards the veranda steps, having lost interest in Ma Hla May now that she had disappeared. He did not stop her, for he thought Ma Hla May quite capable of coming back and making a scene. Not that it mattered much, for neither girl knew a word of the other's language. He called to Ko S'la, and Ko S'la came running with a big oiled-silk umbrella with bamboo ribs. He opened it respectfully at the foot of the steps and held it over the girl's head as she came down. Flory went with them as far as the gate. They stopped to shake hands, he turning a little sideways in the strong sunlight, hiding his birthmark.

'My fellow here will see you home. It was ever so kind of you to come in. I can't tell you how glad I am to have met you. You'll make such a difference to us here in Kyauktada.'

'Good-bye, Mr—oh, how funny! I don't even know your name.'

'Flory, John Flory. And yours—Miss Lackersteen, is it?'

'Yes. Elizabeth. Good-bye, Mr Flory. And thank you *ever* so much. That awful buffalo. You quite saved my life.'

'It was nothing. I hope I shall see you at the Club this evening? I expect your uncle and aunt will be coming down. Good-bye for the time being, then.'

He stood at the gate, watching them as they went. Elizabeth—lovely name, too rare nowadays. He hoped she spelt it with a Z. Ko S'la trotted after her at a queer uncomfortable gait, reaching the umbrella over her head and keeping his body as far away from her as possible. A cool breath of wind blew up the hill. It was one of those momentary winds that blow sometimes in the cold weather in Burma, coming from nowhere, filling one with thirst and with nostalgia for cold sea-pools, embraces of mermaids, waterfalls, caves of ice. It rustled through the wide domes of the gold mohur trees, and fluttered the fragments of the anonymous letter that Flory had thrown over the gate half an hour earlier.

# 7

Elizabeth lay on the sofa in the Lackersteen's drawing-room, with her feet up and a cushion behind her head, reading Michael Arlen's *These Charming People*. In a general way Michael Arlen was her favourite author, but she was inclined to prefer William J. Locke when she wanted something serious.

The drawing-room was a cool, light-coloured room with lime-washed walls a yard thick; it was large, but seemed smaller than it was, because of a litter of occasional tables and Benares brassware ornaments. It smelt of chintz and dying flowers. Mrs Lackersteen was upstairs, sleeping. Outside, the servants lay silent in their quarters, their heads tethered to their wooden pillows by the death-like sleep of midday. Mr Lackersteen, in his small wooden office down the road, was probably sleeping too. No one stirred except Elizabeth, and the *chokra* who pulled the punkah outside Mrs Lackersteen's bedroom, lying on his back with one heel in the loop of the rope.

Elizabeth was just turned twenty-two, and was an orphan. Her father had been less of a drunkard than his brother Tom, but he was a man of similar stamp. He was a tea-broker, and his fortunes fluctuated greatly, but he was by nature too optimistic to put money aside in prosperous phases. Elizabeth's mother had been an incapable, half-baked, vapouring, self-pitying woman who shirked all the normal duties of life on the strength of sensibilities which she did not possess. After messing about for years with such things as Women's Suffrage and Higher Thought, and making many abortive attempts at literature, she had finally taken up with painting. Painting is the only art that can be practised without either talent or hard work. Mrs Lackersteen's pose was that of an artist exiled among 'the Philistines'—these, needless to say, included her husband—and it was a pose that gave her almost unlimited scope for making a nuisance of herself.

In the last year of the War Mr Lackersteen, who had managed to avoid service, made a great deal of money, and just after the Armistice they moved into a huge, new, rather bleak house in Highgate, with quantities of greenhouses, shrubberies, stables and tennis courts. Mr Lackersteen had engaged a horde of servants, even, so great was his optimism, a butler. Elizabeth was sent for two terms to a very expensive boarding-school. Oh, the joy, the joy, the unforgettable joy of those two terms! Four of the girls at the school were 'the Honourable'; nearly all of them had ponies of their own, on which they were allowed to go riding on Saturday afternoons. There is a short period in everyone's life when his character is fixed forever; with Elizabeth, it was those two terms during which she rubbed shoulders with the rich. Thereafter her whole code of living was summed up in one belief, and that a simple one. It was that the Good ('lovely' was her name for it) is synonymous with the expensive, the elegant, the aristocratic; and the Bad ('beastly') is the cheap, the low, the shabby, the laborious. Perhaps it is in order to teach this creed that expensive girls' schools exist. The feeling subtilized itself as Elizabeth grew older, diffused itself through all her thoughts. Everything from a pair of stockings to a human soul was classifiable as 'lovely' or 'beastly'. And unfortunately—for Mr Lackersteen's prosperity did not last—it was the 'beastly' that had predominated in her life.

The inevitable crash came late in 1919. Elizabeth was taken away from school, to continue her education at a succession of cheap, beastly schools, with gaps of a term or two when her father could not pay the fees. He died when she was twenty, of influenza. Mrs Lackersteen was left with an income of £150 a year, which was to die with her. The two women could not, under Mrs Lackersteen's management, live on three pounds a week in England. They moved to Paris, where life was cheaper and where Mrs Lackersteen intended to dedicate herself wholly to Art.

Paris! Living in Paris! Flory had been a little wide of the mark when he pictured those interminable conversations with bearded artists under the green plane trees. Elizabeth's life in Paris had not been quite like that.

Her mother had taken a studio in the Montparnasse quarter, and relapsed at once into a state of squalid, muddling idleness. She was so foolish with money that her income would not come near covering expenses, and for several months Elizabeth did not even have enough to eat. Then she found a job as visiting teacher of English to the family of a French bank manager. They called her *'notre mees Anglaise'*. The banker lived in the twelfth arrondissement, a long way from Montparnasse, and Elizabeth had taken a room in a pension near by. It was a narrow, yellow-faced house in a side street, looking out on to a poulterer's shop, generally decorated with reeking carcasses of wild boars, which old gentlemen like decrepit satyrs would visit every morning and sniff long and lovingly. Next door to the poulterer's was a fly-blown café with the sign 'Café de l'Amitié. Bock Formidable'. How Elizabeth had loathed that pension! The patroness was an old black-clad sneak who spent her life in tiptoeing up and down stairs in hopes of catching the boarders washing stockings in their hand-basins. The boarders, sharp-tongued bilious widows, pursued the only man in the establishment, a mild, bald creature who worked in La Samaritaine, like sparrows worrying a bread-crust. At meals all of them watched each others' plates to see who was given the biggest helping. The bathroom was a dark den with leprous walls and a rickety verdigrised geyser which would spit two inches of tepid water into the bath and then mulishly stop working. The bank manager whose children Elizabeth taught was a man of fifty, with a fat, worn face and a bald, dark yellow crown resembling an ostrich's egg. The second day after her arrival he came into the room where the children were at their lessons, sat down beside Elizabeth and immediately pinched her elbow. The third day he pinched her on the calf, the fourth day behind the knee, the fifth day above the knee. Thereafter, every evening, it was a silent battle between the two of them, her hand under the table, struggling and struggling to keep that ferret-like hand away from her.

It was a mean, beastly existence. In fact, it reached levels of 'beastliness' which Elizabeth had not previously known to exist. But the thing that most depressed her, most filled her with the sense of sinking into some horrible lower world, was her mother's studio. Mrs Lackersteen was one of those people who go utterly to pieces when they are deprived of servants. She lived in a restless nightmare between painting and housekeeping, and never worked at either. At irregular intervals she went to a 'school' where she produced greyish still-lifes under the guidance of a master whose technique was founded on dirty brushes; for the rest, she messed about miserably at home with teapots and frying-pans. The state of her studio was more than depressing to Elizabeth; it was evil, Satanic. It was a cold, dusty pigsty, with piles of books and papers littered all over the floor, generations of saucepans slumbering in their grease on the rusty gas-stove, the bed never made till afternoon, and everywhere—in every possible place where they could be stepped on or knocked over—tins of paint-fouled turpentine and pots half full of cold black tea. You would lift a cushion from a chair and find a plate holding the remains of a poached egg underneath it. As soon as Elizabeth entered the door she would burst out:

'Oh, Mother, Mother dearest, how *can* you? Look at the state of this room! It is so terrible to live like this!'

'The room, dearest? What's the matter? Is it untidy?'

'Untidy! Mother, *need* you leave that plate of porridge in the middle of your bed? And those saucepans! It does look so dreadful. Suppose anyone came in!'

The rapt, other-wordly look which Mrs Lackersteen assumed when anything like work presented itself, would come into her eyes.

'None of *my* friends would mind, dear. We are such Bohemians, we artists. You don't understand how utterly wrapped up we all are in our painting. You haven't the artistic temperament, you see, dear.'

'I must try and clean some of those saucepans. I just can't bear to think of you living like this. What have you done with the scrubbing-brush?'

'The scrubbing-brush? Now, let me think, I know I saw it somewhere. Ah yes! I used it yesterday to clean my palette. But it'll be all right if you give it a good wash in turpentine.'

Mrs Lackersteen would sit down and continue smudging a sheet of sketching paper with a Conté crayon while Elizabeth worked.

'How wonderful you are, dear. So practical! I can't think whom you inherit it from. Now with me, Art is simply *everything*. I seem to feel it like a great sea surging up inside me. It swamps everything mean and petty out of existence. Yesterday I ate my lunch off *Nash's Magazine* to save wasting time washing plates. Such a good idea! When you want a clean plate you just tear off a sheet,' etc., etc., etc.

Elizabeth had no friends in Paris. Her mother's friends were women of the same stamp as herself, or elderly ineffectual bachelors living on small incomes and practising contemptible half-arts such as wood-engraving or painting on porcelain. For the rest, Elizabeth saw only foreigners, and she disliked all foreigners *en bloc*; or at least all foreign men, with their cheap-looking clothes and their revolting table manners. She had one great solace at this time. It was to go to the American library in the rue de l'Elysée and look at the illustrated papers. Sometimes on a Sunday or her free afternoon she would sit there for hours at the big shiny table, dreaming, over the *Sketch*, the *Tatler*, the *Graphic*, the *Sporting and Dramatic*.

Ah, what joys were pictured there! 'Hounds meeting on the lawn of Charlton Hall, the lovely Warwickshire seat of Lord Burrowdean.' 'The Hon. Mrs Tyke-Bowlby in the Park with her splendid Alsatian, Kublai Khan, which took second prize at Cruft's this summer.' 'Sunbathing at Cannes. Left to right: Miss Barbara Pilbrick, Sir Edward Tuke, Lady Pamela Westrope, Captain "Tuppy" Benacre.'

Lovely, lovely, golden world! On two occasions the face of an old schoolfellow looked at Elizabeth from the page. It hurt her in her breast to see it. There they all were, her old schoolfellows, with their horses and their cars and their husbands in the cavalry; and here she, tied to that dreadful job, that dreadful pension, her dreadful mother! Was it possible that there was no escape? Could she be doomed forever to this sordid meanness, with no hope of ever getting back to the decent world again?

It was not unnatural, with the example of her mother before her eyes, that Elizabeth should have a healthy loathing of Art. In fact, any excess of intellect–'braininess' was her word for it–tended to belong, in her eyes, to the 'beastly'. Real people, she felt, decent people–people who shot grouse, went to Ascot, yachted at Cowes–were not brainy. They didn't go in for this nonsense of writing books and fooling with paintbrushes; and all these Highbrow ideas–Socialism and all that. 'Highbrow' was a bitter word in her vocabulary. And when it happened, as it did once or twice, that she met a veritable artist who was willing to work penniless all his life, rather than sell himself to a bank or an insurance company, she despised him far more than she despised the dabblers of her mother's circle. That a man should turn deliberately away from all that was good and decent, sacrifice himself for a futility that led nowhere, was shameful, degrading, evil. She dreaded spinsterhood, but she would have endured it a thousand lifetimes through rather than marry such a man.

When Elizabeth had been nearly two years in Paris her mother died abruptly of ptomaine poisoning. The wonder was that she had not died of it sooner. Elizabeth was left with rather less than a hundred pounds in the world. Her uncle and aunt cabled at once from Burma, asking her to come out and stay with them, and saying that a letter would follow.

Mrs Lackersteen had reflected for some time over the letter, her pen between her lips, looking down at the page with her delicate triangular face like a meditative snake.

'I suppose we must have her out here, at any rate for a year. *What* a bore! However, they generally marry within a year if they've any looks at all. What am I to say to the girl, Tom?'

'Say? Oh, just say she'll pick up a husband out here a damn sight easier than at home. Something of that sort, y'know.'

'My *dear* Tom! What impossible things you say!'

Mrs Lackersteen wrote:

Of course, this is a very small station and we are in the jungle a great deal of the time. I'm afraid you will find it dreadfully dull after the *delights* of Paris. But really in some ways these small stations have their advantages for a young girl. She finds herself quite a *queen* in the local society. The unmarried men are so lonely that they appreciate a girl's society in a quite wonderful way, etc., etc.

Elizabeth spent thirty pounds on summer frocks and set sail immediately. The ship, heralded by rolling porpoises, ploughed across the Mediterranean and down the Canal into a sea of staring, enamel-like blue, then out into the green wastes of the Indian Ocean, where flocks of flying fish skimmed in terror from the approaching hull. At night the waters were phosphorescent, and the wash of the bow was like a moving arrowhead of green fire. Elizabeth 'loved' the life on board ship. She loved the dancing on deck at nights, the cocktails which every man on board seemed anxious to buy for her, the deck games, of which, however, she grew tired at about the same time as the other members of the younger set. It was nothing to her that her mother's death was only two months past. She had never cared greatly for her mother, and besides, the people here knew nothing of her affairs. It was so lovely after those two graceless years to breathe the air of wealth again. Not that most of the people here were rich; but on board ship everyone behaves as though he were rich. She was going to love India, she knew. She had formed quite a picture of India, from the other passengers' conversation; she had even learned some of the more necessary Hindustani phrases, such as '*idher ao*', '*jaldi*', '*sahiblog*', etc. In anticipation she tasted the agreeable atmosphere of Clubs, with punkahs flapping and barefooted white-turbaned boys reverently salaaming; and maidans where bronzed Englishmen with little clipped moustaches galloped to and fro, whacking polo balls. It was almost as nice as being really rich, the way people lived in India.

They sailed into Colombo through green glassy waters, where turtles and black snakes floated basking. A fleet of sampans came racing out to meet the ship, propelled by coal-black men with lips stained redder than blood by betel juice. They yelled and struggled round the gangway while the passengers descended. As Elizabeth and her friends came down, two sampan-wallahs, their prows nosing against the gangway, besought them with yells.

'Don't you go with him, missie! Not with him! Bad wicked man he, not fit taking missie!'

'Don't you listen him lies, missie! Nasty low fellow! Nasty low tricks him playing. Nasty *native* tricks!'

'Ha, ha! He is not native himself! Oh no! Him European man, white skin all same, missie! Ha ha!'

'Stop your *bat,* you two, or I'll fetch one of you a kick,' said the husband of Elizabeth's friend—he was a planter. They stepped into one of the sampans and were rowed towards the sun-bright quays. And the successful sampan-wallah turned and discharged at his rival a mouthful of spittle which he must have been saving up for a very long time.

This was the Orient. Scents of coco-nut oil and sandalwood, cinnamon and turmeric, floated across the water on the hot, swimming air. Elizabeth's friends drove her out to Mount Lavinia, where they bathed in a lukewarm sea that foamed like Coca-Cola. She came back to the ship in the evening, and they reached Rangoon a week later.

North of Mandalay the train, fuelled with wood, crawled at twelve miles an hour across a vast, parched plain, bounded at its remote edges by blue rings of hills. White egrets stood poised, motionless, like herons, and piles of drying chilis gleamed crimson in the sun. Sometimes a white pagoda rose from the plain like the breast of a supine giantess. The early tropic night settled down, and the train jolted on, slowly, stopping at little stations where barbaric yells sounded from the darkness. Half-naked men with their long hair knotted behind their heads moved to and fro in torchlight, hideous as demons in Elizabeth's eyes. The train plunged into forest, and unseen branches brushed against the windows. It was about nine o'clock when they reached Kyauktada, where Elizabeth's uncle and aunt were waiting with Mr Macgregor's car, and with some servants carrying torches. Her aunt came forward and took Elizabeth's shoulders in her delicate, saurian hands.

'I suppose you are our niece Elizabeth? We are *so* pleased to see you,' she said, and kissed her.

Mr Lackersteen peered over his wife's shoulder in the torchlight. He gave a half-whistle, exclaimed, 'Well, I'll be damned!' and then seized Elizabeth and kissed her, more warmly than he need have done, she thought. She had never seen either of them before.

After dinner, under the punkah in the drawing-room, Elizabeth and her aunt had a talk together. Mr Lackersteen was strolling in the garden, ostensibly to smell the frangipani, actually to have a surreptitious drink that one of the servants smuggled to him from the back of the house.

'My dear, how really lovely you are! Let me look at you again.' She took her by the shoulders. 'I *do* think that Eton crop suits you. Did you have it done in Paris?'

'Yes. Everyone was getting Eton-cropped. It suits you if you've got a fairly small head.'

'Lovely! And those tortoise-shell spectacles—such a becoming fashion! I'm told that all the—er—demi-mondaines in South America have taken to wearing them. I'd no idea I had such a *ravishing* beauty for a niece. How old did you say you were, dear?'

'Twenty-two.'

'Twenty-two! How delighted all the men will be when we take you to the Club tomorrow! They get so lonely, poor things, never seeing a new face. And you were two whole years in Paris? I can't think what the men there can have been about to let you leave unmarried.'

'I'm afraid I didn't meet many men, Aunt. Only foreigners. We had to live so quietly. And I was working,' she added, thinking this rather a disgraceful admission.

'Of course, of course,' sighed Mrs Lackersteen. 'One hears the same thing on every side. Lovely girls having to work for their living. It is such a shame! I think it's so terribly selfish, don't you, the way these men remain unmarried while there are so *many* poor girls looking for husbands?' Elizabeth not answering this, Mrs Lackersteen added with another sigh, 'I'm sure if I were a young girl I'd marry anybody, literally *anybody!*'

The two women's eyes met. There was a great deal that Mrs Lackersteen wanted to say, but she had no intention of doing more than hint at it obliquely. A great deal of her conversation was carried on by hints; she generally contrived, however, to make her meaning reasonably clear. She said in a tenderly impersonal tone, as though discussing a subject of general interest:

'Of course, I must say this. There *are* cases when, if girls fail to get married it's *their own fault*. It happens even out here sometimes. Only a short time ago I remember a case—a girl came out and stayed a whole year with her brother, and she had offers from all kinds of men—policemen, forest officers, men in timber firms with *quite* good prospects. And she refused them all; she wanted to marry into the I.C.S., I heard. Well, what do you expect? Of course her brother couldn't go on keeping her forever. And now I hear she's at home, poor thing, working as a kind of lady help, practically a *servant*. And getting only fifteen shillings a week! Isn't it dreadful to think of such things?'

'Dreadful!' Elizabeth echoed.

No more was said on this subject. In the morning, after she came back from Flory's house, Elizabeth was describing her adventure to her aunt and uncle. They were at breakfast, at the flower-laden table, with the punkah flapping overhead and the tall stork-like Mohammedan butler in his white suit and *pagri* standing behind Mrs Lackersteen's chair, tray in hand.

'And oh, Aunt, such an interesting thing! A Burmese girl came on to the veranda. I'd never seen one before, at least, not knowing they were girls. Such a queer little thing—she was almost like a doll with her round yellow face and her black hair screwed up on top. She only looked about seventeen. Mr Flory said she was his laundress.'

The Indian butler's long body stiffened. He squinted down at the girl with his white eyeballs large in his black face. He spoke English well. Mr Lackersteen paused with a forkful of fish half-way from his plate and his crass mouth open.

'Laundress?' he said. 'Laundress! I say, dammit, some mistake there! No such thing as a laundress in this country, y'know. Laundering work's all done by men. If you ask me—'

And then he stopped very suddenly, almost as though someone had trodden on his toe under the table.

# 8

That evening Flory told Ko S'la to send for the barber—he was the only barber in the town, an Indian, and he made a living by shaving the Indian coolies at the rate of eight annas a month for a dry shave every other day. The Europeans patronized him for lack of any other. The barber was waiting on the veranda when Flory came back from tennis, and Flory sterilized the scissors with boiling water and Condy's fluid and had his hair cut.

'Lay out my best Palm Beach suit,' he told Ko S'la, 'and a silk shirt and my sambhur-skin shoes. Also that new tie that came from Rangoon last week.'

'I have done so, *thakin*,' said Ko S'la, meaning that he would do so. When Flory came into the bedroom he found Ko S'la waiting beside the clothes he had laid out, with a faintly sulky air. It was immediately apparent that Ko S'la knew why Flory was dressing himself up (that is, in hopes of meeting Elizabeth) and that he disapproved of it.

'What are you waiting for?' Flory said.

'To help you dress, *thakin.*'

'I shall dress myself this evening. You can go.'

He was going to shave–the second time that day–and he did not want Ko S'la to see him take shaving things into the bathroom. It was several years since he had shaved twice in one day. What providential luck that he had sent for that new tie only last week, he thought. He dressed himself very carefully, and spent nearly a quarter of an hour in brushing his hair, which was stiff and would never lie down after it had been cut.

Almost the next moment, as it seemed, he was walking with Elizabeth down the bazaar road. He had found her alone in the Club 'library', and with a sudden burst of courage asked her to come out with him; and she had come with a readiness that surprised him; not even stopping to say anything to her uncle and aunt. He had lived so long in Burma, he had forgotten English ways. It was very dark under the peepul trees of the bazaar road, the foliage hiding the quarter moon, but the stars here and there in a gap blazed white and low, like lamps hanging on invisible threads. Successive waves of scent came rolling, first the cloying sweetness of frangipani, then a cold putrid stench of dung or decay from the huts opposite Dr Veraswami's bungalow. Drums were throbbing a little distance away.

As he heard the drums Flory remembered that a *pwe* was being acted a little farther down the road, opposie U Po Kyin's house; in fact, it was U Po Kyin who had made arrangements for the *pwe,* though someone else had paid for it. A daring thought occurred to Flory. He would take Elizabeth to the *pwe!* She would love it–she must; no one with eyes in his head could resist a *pwe*-dance. Probably there would be a scandal when they came back to the Club together after a long absence; but damn it! what did it matter? She was different from that herd of fools at the Club. And it would be such fun to go to the *pwe* together! At this moment the music burst out with a fearful pandemonium–a strident squeal of pipes, a rattle like castanets and the hoarse thump of drums, above which a man's voice was brassily squalling.

'Whatever is that noise?' said Elizabeth, stopping. 'It sounds just like a jazz band!'

'Native music. They're having a *pwe*–that's a kind of Burmese play; a cross between a historical drama and a revue, if you can imagine that. It'll interest you, I think. Just round the bend of the road here.'

'Oh,' she said rather doubtfully.

They came round the bend into a glare of light. The whole road for thirty yards was blocked by the audience watching the *pwe*. At the back there was a raised stage, under humming petrol lamps, with the orchestra squalling and banging in front of it; on the stage two men dressed in clothes that reminded Elizabeth of Chinese pagodas were posturing with curved swords in their hands. All down the roadway it was a sea of white muslin backs of women, pink scarves flung round their shoulders and black hair-cylinders. A few sprawled on their mats, fast asleep. An old Chinese with a tray of peanuts was threading his way through the crowd, intoning mournfully, *'Myaype! Myaype!'*

'We'll stop and watch a few minutes if you like,' Flory said.

The blaze of lights and the appalling din of the orchestra had almost dazed Elizabeth, but what startled her most of all was the sight of this crowd of people sitting in the road as though it had been the pit of a theatre.

'Do they always have their plays in the middle of the road?' she said.

'As a rule. They put up a rough stage and take it down in the morning. The show lasts all night.'

'But are they *allowed* to—blocking up the whole roadway?'

'Oh yes. There are no traffic regulations here. No traffic to regulate, you see.'

It struck her as very queer. By this time almost the entire audience had turned round on their mats to stare at the 'Ingaleikma'. There were half a dozen chairs in the middle of the crowd, where some clerks and officials were sitting. U Po Kyin was among them, and he was making efforts to twist his elephantine body round and greet the Europeans. As the music stopped the pock-marked Ba Taik came hastening through the crowd and shikoed low to Flory, with his timorous air.

'Most holy one, my master U Po Kyin asks whether you and the young white lady will not come and watch our *pwe* for a few minutes. He has chairs ready for you.'

'They're asking us to come and sit down,' Flory said to Elizabeth. 'Would you like to? It's rather fun. Those two fellows will clear off in a moment and there'll be some dancing. If it wouldn't bore you for a few minutes?'

Elizabeth felt very doubtful. Somehow it did not seem right or even safe to go in among that smelly native crowd. However, she trusted Flory, who presumably knew what was proper, and allowed him to lead her to the chairs. The Burmans made way on their mats, gazing after her and chattering; her shins brushed against warm, muslin-clad bodies, there was a feral reek of sweat. U Po Kyin leaned over towards her, bowing as well as he could and saying nasally:

'Kindly to sit down, madam! I am most honoured to make your acquaintance. Good evening. Good morning, Mr Flory, sir! A most unexpected pleasure. Had we known that you were to honour us with your company, we would have provided whiskies and other European refreshments. Ha ha!'

He laughed, and his betel-reddened teeth gleamed in the lamplight like red tinfoil. He was so vast and so hideous that Elizabeth could not help shrinking from him. A slender youth in a purple *longyi* was bowing to her and holding out a tray with two glasses of yellow sherbet, iced. U Po Kyin clapped his hands sharply, '*Hey haung galay!*' he called to a boy beside him. He gave some instructions in Burmese, and the boy pushed his way to the edge of the stage.

'He's telling them to bring on their best dancer in our honour,' Flory said. 'Look, here she comes.'

A girl who had been squatting at the back of the stage, smoking, stepped forward into the lamplight. She was very young, slim-shouldered, breastless, dressed in a pale blue satin *longyi* that hid her feet. The skirts of her *ingyi* curved outwards above her hips in little panniers, according to the ancient

Burmese fashion. They were like the petals of a downward-pointing flower. She threw her cigar languidly to one of the men in the orchestra, and then, holding out one slender arm, writhed it as though to shake the muscles loose.

The orchestra burst into a sudden loud squalling. There were pipes like bagpipes, a strange instrument consisting of plaques of bamboo which a man struck with a little hammer, and in the middle there was a man surrounded by twelve tall drums of different sizes. He reached rapidly from one to another, thumping them with the heel of his hand. In a moment the girl began to dance. But at first it was not a dance, it was a rhythmic nodding, posturing and twisting of the elbows, like the movements of one of those jointed wooden figures on an old-fashioned roundabout. The way her neck and elbows rotated was precisely like a jointed doll, and yet incredibly sinuous. Her hands. twisting like snakeheads with the fingers close together, could lie back until they were almost along her forearms. By degrees her movements quickened. She began to leap from side to side, flinging herself down in a kind of curtsy and springing up again with extraordinary agility, in spite of the long *longyi* that imprisoned her feet. Then she danced in a grotesque posture as though sitting down, knees bent, body leaned forward, with her arms extended and writhing, her head also moving to the beat of the drums. The music quickened to a climax. The girl rose upright and whirled round as swiftly as a top, the pannier of her *ingyi* flying out about her like the petals of a snowdrop. Then the music stopped as abruptly as it had begun, and the girl sank again into a curtsy, amid raucous shouting from the audience.

Elizabeth watched the dance with a mixture of amazement, boredom and something approaching horror. She had sipped her drink and found that it tasted like hair oil. On a mat by her feet three Burmese girls lay fast asleep with their heads on the same pillow, their small oval faces side by side like the faces of kittens. Under cover of the music Flory was speaking in a low voice into Elizabeth's ear commenting on the dance.

'I knew this would interest you; that's why I brought you here. You've read books and been in civilized places, you're not like the rest of us miserable savages here. Don't you think this is worth watching, in its queer way? Just look at that girl's movements—look at that strange, bent-forward pose like a marionette, and the way her arms twist from the elbow like a cobra rising to strike. It's grotesque, it's even ugly, with a sort of wilful ugliness. And there's something sinister in it too. There's a touch of the diabolical in all Mongols. And yet when you look closely, what art, what centuries of culture you can see behind it! Every movement that girl makes has been studied and handed down through innumerable generations. Whenever you look closely at the art of these Eastern peoples you can see that—a civilization stretching back and back, practically the same, into times when we were dressed in woad. In some way that I can't define to you, the whole life and spirit of Burma is summed up in the way that girl twists her arms. When you see her you can see the rice fields, the villages under the teak trees, the pagodas, the priests in their yellow robes, the buffaloes swimming the rivers in the early morning, Thibaw's palace–'

His voice stopped abruptly as the music stopped. There were certain things, and a *pwe*-dance was one of them, that pricked him to talk discursively and incautiously; but now he realized that he had only been talking like a character in a novel, and not a very good novel. He looked away. Elizabeth had listened to him with a chill of discomfort. What *was* the man talking about? was her first thought. Moreover, she had caught the hated word Art more than once. For the first time she remembered that Flory was a total stranger and that it had been unwise to come out with him alone. She looked round her, at the sea of dark faces and the lurid glare of the lamps; the strangeness of the scene almost frightened her. What was she doing in this place? Surely it was not right to be sitting among the black people like this, almost touching them, in the scent of their garlic and their sweat? Why was she not back at the Club with the other white people? Why had he brought her here, among this horde of natives, to watch this hideous and savage spectacle?

The music struck up, and the *pwe* girl began dancing again. Her face was powdered so thickly that it gleamed in the lamplight like a chalk mask with live eyes behind it. With that dead-white oval face and those wooden gestures she was monstrous, like a demon. The music changed its tempo, and the girl began to sing in a brassy voice. It was a song with a swift trochaic rhythm, gay yet fierce. The crowd took it up, a hundred voices chanting the harsh syllables in unison. Still in that strange bent posture the girl turned round and danced with her buttocks protruded towards the audience. Her silk *longyi* gleamed like metal. With hands and elbows still rotating she wagged her posterior from side to side. Then—astonishing feat, quite visible through the *longyi*—she began to wriggle her two buttocks independently in time with the music.

There was a shout of applause from the audience. The three girls asleep on the mat woke up at the same moment and began clapping their hands wildly. A clerk shouted nasally 'Bravo! Bravo!' in English for the Europeans' benefit. But U Po Kyin frowned and waved his hand. He knew all about European women. Elizabeth, however, had already stood up.

'I'm going. It's time we were back,' she said abruptly. She was looking away, but Flory could see that her face was pink.

He stood up beside her, dismayed. 'But, I say! Couldn't you stay a few minutes longer? I know it's late, but—they brought this girl on two hours before she was due, in our honour. Just a few minutes?'

'I can't help it, I ought to have been back ages ago. I don't know *what* my uncle and aunt will be thinking.'

She began at once to pick her way through the crowd, and he followed her, with not even time to thank the *pwe* people for their trouble. The Burmans made way with a sulky air. How like these English people, to upset everything by sending for the best dancer and then go away almost before she had started! There was a fearful row as soon as Flory and Elizabeth had gone, the *pwe* girl refusing to go on with her dance and the audience demanding that she should continue. However, peace was restored when two clowns hurried on to the stage and began letting off crackers and making obscene jokes.

Flory followed the girl abjectly up the road. She was walking quickly, her head turned away, and for some moments she would not speak. What a thing to happen, when they had been getting on so well together! He kept trying to apologize.

'I'm so sorry! I'd no idea you'd mind–'

'It's nothing. What is there to be sorry about? I only said it was time to go back, that's all.'

'I ought to have thought. One gets not to notice that kind of thing in this country. These people's sense of decency isn't the same as ours–it's stricter in some ways–but–'

'It's not that! It's not that!' she exclaimed quite angrily.

He saw that he was only making it worse. They walked on in silence, he behind. He was miserable. What a bloody fool he had been! And yet all the while he had no inkling of the real reason why she was angry with him. It was not the *pwe* girl's behaviour, in itself, that had offended her; it had only brought things to a head. But the whole expedition–the very notion of *wanting* to rub shoulders with all those smelly natives–had impressed her badly. She was perfectly certain that that was not how white men ought to behave. And that extraordinary rambling speech that he had begun, with all those long words–almost, she thought bitterly, as though he were quoting poetry! It was how those beastly artists that you met sometimes in Paris used to talk. She had thought him a manly man till this evening. Then her mind went back to the morning's adventure, and how he had faced the buffalo barehanded, and some of her anger evaporated. By the time they reached the Club gate she felt inclined to forgive him. Flory had by now plucked up courage to speak again. He stopped, and she stopped too, in a patch where the boughs let through some starlight and he could see her face dimly.

'I say. I say, I do hope you're not really angry about this?'

'No, of course I'm not. I told you I wasn't.'

'I oughtn't to have taken you there. Please forgive me. Do you know, I don't think I'd tell the others where you've been. Perhaps it would be better to say you've just been out for a stroll, out in the garden–something like that. They might think it queer, a white girl going to a *pwe*. I don't think I'd tell them.'

'Oh, of course I won't!' she agreed with a warmness that surprised him. After that he knew that he was forgiven. But what it was that he was forgiven, he had not yet grasped.

They went into the Club separately, by tacit consent. The expedition had been a failure, decidedly. There was a gala air about the Club lounge tonight. The entire European community were waiting to greet Elizabeth, and the butler and the six *chokras*, in their best starched white suits, were drawn up on either side of the door, smiling and salaaming. When the Europeans had finished their greetings the butler came forward with a vast garland of flowers that the servants had prepared for the 'missiesahib'. Mr Macgregor made a very humorous speech of welcome, introducing everybody. He introduced Maxwell as 'our local arboreal specialist', Westfield as 'the guardian of law and order and–ah–terror of the local banditti', and so on and so forth. There was much laughter. The sight of a pretty girl's face had put everyone in such a good humour that they could even enjoy Mr Macgregor's speech–which, to tell the truth, he had spent most of the evening in preparing.

At the first possible moment Ellis, with a sly air, took Flory and Westfield by the arm and drew them away into the card-room. He was in a much better mood than usual. He pinched Flory's arm with his small, hard fingers, painfully but quite amiably.

'Well, my lad, everyone's been looking for you. Where have you been all this time?'

'Oh, only for a stroll.'

'For a stroll! And who with?'

'With Miss Lackersteen.'

'I knew it! So *you're* the bloody fool who's fallen into the trap, are you? *You* swallowed the bait before anyone else had time to look at it. I thought you were too old a bird for that, by God I did!'

'What do you mean?'

'Mean! Look at him pretending he doesn't know what I mean! Why, I mean that Ma Lackersteen's marked you down for her beloved nephew-in-law, of course. That is, if you aren't bloody careful. Eh, Westfield?'

'Quite right, ol' boy. Eligible young bachelor. Marriage halter and all that. They've got their eye on him.'

'I don't know where you're getting this idea from. The girl's hardly been here twenty-four hours.'

'Long enough for you to take her up the garden path, anyway. You watch your step. Tom Lackersteen may be a drunken sot, but he's not such a bloody fool that he wants a niece hanging round his neck for the rest of his life. And of course *she* knows which side her bread's buttered. So you take care and don't go putting your head into the noose.'

'Damn it, you've no right to talk about people like that. After all, the girl's only a kid–'

'My dear old ass'–Ellis, almost affectionate now that he had a new subject for scandal, took Flory by the coat lapel–'my dear, dear old ass, don't you go filling yourself up with moonshine. You think that girl's easy fruit: she's not. These girls out from home are all the same. "Anything in trousers but nothing this side the altar"–that's their motto, every one of them. Why do you think the girl's come out here?'

'Why? I don't know. Because she wanted to, I suppose.'

'My good fool! She come out to lay her claws into a husband, of course. As if it wasn't well known! When a girl's failed everywhere else she tries India, where every man's pining for the sight of a white woman. The Indian marriage-market, they call it. Meat market it ought to be. Shiploads of 'em coming out every year like carcasses of frozen mutton, to be pawed over by nasty old bachelors like you. Cold storage. Juicy joints straight from the ice.'

'You do say some repulsive things.'

'Best pasture-fed English meat,' said Ellis with a pleased air. 'Fresh consignments. Warranted prime condition.'

He went through a pantomime of examining a joint of meat, with goatish sniffs. This joke was likely to last Ellis a long time; his jokes usually did; and there was nothing that gave him quite so keen a pleasure as dragging a woman's name through mud.

Flory did not see much more of Elizabeth that evening. Everyone was in the lounge together, and there was the silly clattering chatter about nothing that there is on these occasions. Flory could never keep up that kind of conversation for long. But as for Elizabeth, the civilized atmosphere of the Club, with the white faces all round her and the friendly look of the illustrated papers and the 'Bonzo' pictures, reassured her after that doubtful interlude at the *pwe*.

When the Lackersteens left the Club at nine, it was not Flory but Mr Macgregor who walked home with them, ambling beside Elizabeth like some friendly saurian monster, among the faint crooked shadows of the gold mohur stems. The Prome anecdote, and many another, found a new home. Any newcomer to Kyauktada was apt to come in for rather a large share of Mr Macgregor's conversation, for the others looked on him as an unparalleled bore, and it was a tradition at the Club to interrupt his stories. But Elizabeth was by nature a good listener. Mr Macgregor thought he had seldom met so intelligent a girl.

Flory stayed a little longer at the Club, drinking with the others. There was much smutty talk about Elizabeth. The quarrel about Dr Veraswami's election had been shelved for the time being. Also, the notice that Ellis had put up on the previous evening had been taken down. Mr Macgregor had seen it during his morning visit to the Club, and in his fair-minded way he had at once insisted on its removal. So the notice had been suppressed; not, however, before it had achieved its object.

# 9

During the next fortnight a great deal happened.

The feud between U Po Kyin and Dr Veraswami was now in full swing. The whole town was divided into two factions, with every native soul from the magistrates down to the bazaar sweepers enrolled on one side or the other, and all ready for perjury when the time came. But of the two parties, the doctor's was much the smaller and less efficiently libellous. The editor of the *Burmese Patriot* had been put on trial for sedition and libel, bail being refused. His arrest had provoked a small riot in Rangoon, which was suppressed by the police with the death of only two rioters. In prison the editor went on hunger strike, but broke down after six hours.

In Kyauktada, too, things had been happening. A dacoit named Nga Shwe O had escaped from the jail in mysterious circumstances. And there had been a whole crop of rumours about a projected native rising in the district. The rumours—they were very vague ones as yet—centred round a village named

Thongwa, not far from the camp where Maxwell was girdling teak. A *weiksa*, or magician, was said to have appeared from nowhere and to be prophesying the doom of the English power and distributing magic bullet-proof jackets. Mr Macgregor did not take the rumours very seriously, but he had asked for an extra force of Military Police. It was said that a company of Indian infantry with a British officer in command would be sent to Kyauktada shortly. Westfield, of course, had hurried to Thongwa at the first threat, or rather hope, of trouble.

'God, if they'd only break out and rebel properly for once!' he said to Ellis before starting. 'But it'll be a bloody washout as usual. Always the same story with these rebellions—peter out almost before they've begun. Would you believe it, I've never fired my gun at a fellow yet, not even a dacoit. Eleven years of it, not counting the War, and never killed a man. Depressing.'

'Oh, well,' said Ellis, 'if they won't come up to the scratch you can always get hold of the ringleaders and give them a good bambooing on the Q.T. That's better than coddling them up in our damned nursing homes of prisons.'

'H'm, probably. Can't do it though, nowadays. All these kid-glove laws—got to keep them, I suppose, if we're fools enough to make 'em.'

'Oh, rot the laws. Bambooing's the only thing that makes any impression on the Burman. Have you seen them after they've been flogged? I have. Brought out of the jail on bullock carts, yelling, with the women plastering mashed bananas on their backsides. That's something they do understand. If I had my way I'd give it 'em on the soles of the feet the same as the Turks do.'

'Ah well. Let's hope they'll have the guts to show a bit of fight for once. Then we'll call out the Military Police, rifles and all. Plug a few dozen of 'em—that'll clear the air.'

However, the hoped-for opportunity did not come. Westfield and the dozen constables he had taken with him to Thongwa—jolly round-faced Gurkha boys, pining to use their kukris on somebody—found the district depressingly peaceful. There seemed not the ghost of a rebellion anywhere; only the annual attempt, as regular as the monsoon, of the villagers to avoid paying the capitation tax.

The weather was growing hotter and hotter. Elizabeth had had her first attack of prickly heat. Tennis at the Club had practically ceased; people would play one languid set and then fall into chairs and swallow pints of tepid lime-juice—tepid, because the ice came only twice weekly from Mandalay and melted within twenty-four hours of arriving. The Flame of the Forest was in full bloom. The Burmese women, to protect their children from the sun, streaked their faces with yellow cosmetic until they looked like little African witch-doctors. Flocks of green pigeons, and imperial pigeons as large as ducks, came to eat the berries of the big peepul trees along the bazaar road.

Meanwhile, Flory had turned Ma Hla May out of his house.

A nasty, dirty job! There was a sufficient pretext—she had stolen his gold cigarette-case and pawned it at the house of Li Yeik, the Chinese grocer and illicit pawnbroker in the bazaar—but still, it was only a pretext. Flory knew perfectly well, and Ma Hla May knew, and all the servants knew, that he was getting rid of her because of Elizabeth. Because of 'the Ingaleikma with dyed hair', as Ma Hla May called her.

Ma Hla May made no violent scene at first. She stood sullenly listening while he wrote her a cheque for a hundred rupees—Li Yeik or the Indian *chetty* in the bazaar would cash cheques—and told her that she was dismissed. He was more ashamed than she; he could not look her in the face, and his voice went flat and guilty. When the bullock cart came for her belongings, he shut himself in the bedroom skulking till the scene should be over.

Cartwheels grated on the drive, there was the sound of men shouting; then suddenly there was a fearful uproar of screams. Flory went outside. They were all struggling round the gate in the sunlight. Ma Hla May was clinging to the gatepost and Ko S'la was trying to bundle her out. She turned a face full of fury and despair towards Flory, screaming over and over, '*Thakin! Thakin! Thakin! Thakin! Thakin!*' It hurt him to the heart that she should still call him *thakin* after he had dismissed her.

'What is it?' he said.

It appeared that there was a switch of false hair that Ma Hla May and Ma Yi both claimed. Flory gave the switch to Ma Yi and gave Ma Hla May two rupees to compensate her. Then the cart jolted away, with Ma Hla May sitting beside her two wicker baskets, straight-backed and sullen, and nursing a kitten on her knees. It was only two months since he had given her the kitten as a present.

Ko S'la, who had long wished for Ma Hla May's removal, was not altogether pleased now that it had happened. He was even less pleased when he saw his master going to church—or as he called it, to the 'English pagoda'—for Flory was still in Kyauktada on the Sunday of the padre's arrival, and he went to church with the others. There was a congregation of twelve, including Mr Francis, Mr Samuel and six native Christians, with Mrs Lackersteen playing 'Abide with Me' on the tiny harmonium with one game pedal. It was the first time in ten years that Flory had been to church, except to funerals. Ko S'la's notions of what went on in the 'English pagoda' were vague in the extreme; but he did know that church-going signified respectability—a quality which, like all bachelors' servants, he hated in his bones.

'There is trouble coming,' he said despondently to the other servants. 'I have been watching him (he meant Flory) these ten days past. He has cut down his cigarettes to fifteen a day, he has stopped drinking gin before breakfast, he shaves himself every evening—though he thinks I do not know it, the fool. And he has ordered half a dozen new silk shirts! I had to stand over the *dirzi* calling him *bahinchut* to get them finished in time. Evil omens! I give him three months longer, and then good-bye to the peace in this house!'

'What, is he going to get married?' said Ba Pe.

'I am certain of it. When a white man begins going to the English pagoda, it is, as you might say, the beginning of the end.'

'I have had many masters in my life,' old Sammy said. 'The worst was Colonel Wimpole sahib, who used to make his orderly hold me down over the table while he came running from behind and kicked me with very thick boots for serving banana fritters too frequently. At other times, when he was drunk, he would fire his revolver through the roof of the servants' quarters, just above our heads. But I would sooner serve ten years under Colonal Wimpole sahib than a week under a memsahib with her kit-kit. If our master marries I shall leave the same day.'

'I shall not leave, for I have been his servant fifteen years. But I know what is in store for us when that woman comes. She will shout at us because of spots of dust on the furniture, and wake us up to bring cups of tea in the afternoon when we are asleep, and come poking into the cookhouse at all hours and complain over dirty saucepans and cockroaches in the flour bin. It is my belief that these women lie awake at nights thinking of new ways to torment their servants.'

'They keep a little red book,' said Sammy, 'in which they enter the bazaar-money, two annas for this, four annas for that, so that a man cannot earn a pice. They make more kit-kit over the price of an onion than a sahib over five rupees.'

'Ah, do I not know it! She will be worse than Ma Hla May. Women!' he added comprehensively, with a kind of sigh.

The sigh was echoed by the others, even by Ma Pu and Ma Yi. Neither took Ko S'la's remarks as a stricture upon her own sex, Englishwomen being considered a race apart, possibly not even human, and so dreadful that an Englishman's marriage is usually the signal for the flight of every servant in his house, even those who have been with him for years.

# 10

But as a matter of fact, Ko S'la's alarm was premature. After knowing Elizabeth for ten days, Flory was scarcely more intimate with her than on the day when he had first met her.

As it happened, he had her almost to himself during these ten days, most of the Europeans being in the jungle. Flory himself had no right to be loitering in headquarters, for at this time of year the work of timber-extraction was in full swing, and in his absence everything went to pieces under the incompetent Eurasian overseer. But he had stayed—pretext, a touch of fever—while despairing letters came almost every day from the overseer, telling of disasters. One of the elephants was ill, the engine of the light railway that was used for carrying teak logs to the river had broken down, fifteen of the coolies had deserted. But Flory still lingered, unable to tear himself away from Kyauktada while Elizabeth was there, and continually seeking—never, as yet, to much purpose—to recapture that easy and delightful friendship of their first meeting.

They met every day, morning and evening, it was true. Each evening they played a single of tennis at the Club—Mrs Lackersteen was too limp and Mr Lackersteen too liverish for tennis at this time of year—and afterwards they would sit in the lounge, all four together, playing bridge and talking. But though Flory spent hours in Elizabeth's company, and often they were alone together, he was never for an instant at his ease with her. They talked—so long as they talked of trivialities—with the utmost freedom, yet they were distant, like strangers. He felt stiff in her presence, he could not forget his birthmark; his twice-scraped chin smarted, his body tortured him for whisky and tobacco—for he tried to cut down his drinking and smoking when he was with her. After ten days they seemed no nearer the relationship he wanted.

For somehow, he had never been able to talk to her as he longed to talk. To talk, simply to talk! It sounds so little, and how much it is! When you have existed to the brink of middle age in bitter loneliness, among people to whom your true opinion on every subject on earth is blasphemy, the need to talk is the greatest of all needs. Yet with Elizabeth serious talk seemed impossible. It was as though there had been a spell upon them that made all their conversation lapse into banality; gramophone records, dogs, tennis racquets—all that desolating Club-chatter. She seemed not to *want* to talk of anything but that. He had only to touch upon a subject of any conceivable interest to hear the evasion, the 'I shan't play', coming into her voice. Her taste in books appalled him when he discovered it. Yet she was young, he reminded himself, and had she not drunk white wine and talked of Marcel Proust under the Paris plane trees? Later, no doubt, she would understand him and give him the companionship he needed. Perhaps it was only that he had not won her confidence yet.

He was anything but tactful with her. Like all men who have lived much alone, he adjusted himself better to ideas than to people. And so, though all their talk was superficial, he began to irritate her sometimes; not by what he said but by what he implied. There was an uneasiness between them, ill-defined and yet often verging upon quarrels. When two people, one of whom has lived long in the country while the other is a newcomer, are thrown together, it is inevitable that the first should act as cicerone to the second. Elizabeth, during these days, was making her first acquaintance with Burma; it was Flory, naturally, who acted as her interpreter, explaining this, commenting upon that. And the things he said, or the way he said them, provoked in her a vague yet deep disagreement. For she perceived that Flory, when he spoke of the 'natives', spoke nearly always *in favour* of them. He was forever praising Burmese customs and the Burmese character; he even went so far as to contrast them favourably with the English. It disquieted her. After all, natives were natives—interesting, no doubt, but finally only a 'subject' people, an inferior people with black faces. His attitude was a little *too* tolerant. Nor had he grasped, yet, in what way he was antagonizing her. He so wanted her to love Burma as he loved it, not to look at it with the dull, incurious eyes of a memsahib! He had forgotten that most people can be at ease in a foreign country only when they are disparaging the inhabitants.

He was too eager in his attempts to interest her in things Oriental. He tried to induce her, for instance, to learn Burmese, but it came to nothing. (Her aunt had explained to her that only missionary-women spoke Burmese; nice women found kitchen Urdu quite as much as they needed.) There were countless small disagreements like that. She was grasping, dimly, that his views were not the views an Englishman should hold. Much more clearly she grasped that he was asking her to be fond of the Burmese, even to admire them; to admire people with black faces, almost savages, whose appearance still made her shudder!

The subject cropped up in a hundred ways. A knot of Burmans would pass them on the road. She, with her still fresh eyes, would gaze after them, half curious and half repelled; and she would say to Flory, as she would have said to anybody:

'How *revoltingly* ugly these people are, aren't they?'

'*Are* they? I always think they're rather charming-looking, the Burmese. They have such splendid bodies! Look at that fellow's shoulders—like a bronze statue. Just think what sights you'd see in England if people went about half naked as they do here!'

'But they have such hideous-shaped heads! Their skulls kind of slope up behind like a tom-cat's. And then the way their foreheads slant back—it makes them look so *wicked*. I remember reading something in a magazine about the shape of people's heads; it said that a person with a sloping forehead is a *criminal type*.'

'Oh, come, that's a bit sweeping! Round about half the people in the world have that kind of forehead.'

'Oh, well, if you count *coloured* people, of course—!'

Or perhaps a string of women would pass, going to the well: heavy-set peasant-girls, copper-brown, erect under their water-pots with strong marelike buttocks protruded. The Burmese women repelled Elizabeth more than the men; she felt her kinship with them, and the hatefulness of being kin to creatures with black faces.

'Aren't they too simply dreadful? So *coarse*-looking; like some kind of animal. Do you think *anyone* could think those women attractive?'

'Their own men do, I believe.'

'I suppose they would. But that black skin—I don't know how anyone could bear it!'

'But, you know, one gets used to the brown skin in time. In fact they say—I believe it's true—that after a few years in these countries a brown skin seems more natural than a white one. And after all, it *is* more natural. Take the world as a whole, it's an eccentricity to be white.'

'You *do* have some funny ideas!'

And so on and so on. She felt all the while an unsatisfactoriness, an unsoundness in the things he said. It was particularly so on the evening when Flory allowed Mr Francis and Mr Samuel, the two derelict Eurasians, to entrap him in conversation at the Club gate.

Elizabeth, as it happened, had reached the Club a few minutes before Flory, and when she heard his voice at the gate she came round the tennis-screen to meet him. The two Eurasians had sidled up to Flory and cornered him like a pair of dogs asking for a game. Francis was doing most of the talking. He was a meagre, excitable man, and as brown as a cigar-leaf, being the son of a South Indian woman; Samuel, whose mother had been a Karen, was pale yellow with dull red hair. Both were dressed in shabby drill suits, with vast *topis* beneath which their slender bodies looked like the stalks of toadstools.

Elizabeth came down the path in time to hear fragments of an enormous and complicated autobiography. Talking to white men—talking, for choice, about himself—was the great joy of Francis's life. When, at intervals of months, he found a European to listen to him, his life-history would pour out of him in unquenchable torrents. He was talking in a nasal, sing-song voice of incredible rapidity:

'Of my father, sir, I remember little, but he was very choleric man and many whackings with big bamboo stick all knobs on both for self, little half-brother and two mothers. Also how on occasion of bishop's visit little half-brother and I dress in *longyis* and sent among the Burmese children to preserve incognito. My father never rose to be bishop, sir. Four converts only in twenty-eight years, and also too great fondness for Chinese rice-spirit very fiery noised abroad and spoil sales of my father's booklet entitled *The Scourge of Alcohol*, published with the Rangoon Baptist Press, one rupee eight annas. My little half-brother die one hot weather, always coughing, coughing,' etc., etc.

The two Eurasians perceived the presence of Elizabeth. Both doffed their *topis* with bows and brilliant displays of teeth. It was probably several years since either of them had had a chance of talking to an Englishwoman. Francis burst out more effusively than ever. He was chattering in evident dread that he would be interrupted and the conversation cut short.

'Good evening to you, madam, good evening, good evening! Most honoured to make your acquaintance, madam! Very sweltering is the weather these days, is not? But seasonable for April. Not too much you are suffering from prickly heat, I trust? Pounded tamarind applied to the afflicted spot is infallible. Myself I suffer torments each night. Very prevalent disease among we Europeans.'

He pronounced it Europian, like Mr Chollop in *Martin Chuzzlewit*. Elizabeth did not answer. She was looking at the Eurasians somewhat coldly. She had only a dim idea as to who or what they were, and it struck her as impertinent that they should speak to her.

'Thanks, I'll remember about the tamarind,' Flory said.

'Specific of renowned Chinese doctor, sir. Also, sir-madam, may I advise to you, wearing only Terai hat is not judicious in April, sir. For the natives all well, their skulls are adamant. But for us sunstroke ever menaces. Very deadly is the sun upon European skull. But is it that I detain you, madam?'

This was said in a disappointed tone. Elizabeth had, in fact, decided to snub the Eurasians. She did not know why Flory was allowing them to hold him in conversation. As she turned away to stroll back to the tennis court, she made a practice stroke in the air with her racquet, to remind Flory that the game was overdue. He saw it and followed her, rather reluctantly, for he did not like snubbing the wretched Francis, bore though he was.

'I must be off,' he said. 'Good evening, Francis. Good evening, Samuel.'

'Good evening, sir! Good evening, madam! Good evening, good evening!' They receded with more hat flourishes.

'Who *are* those two?' said Elizabeth as Flory came up with her. 'Such extraordinary creatures! They were in church on Sunday. One of them looks almost white. Surely he isn't an Englishman?'

'No, they're Eurasians—sons of white fathers and native mothers. Yellow-bellies is our friendly nickname for them.'

'But what are they doing here? Where do they live? Do they do any work?'

'They exist somehow or other in the bazaar. I believe Francis acts as clerk to an Indian money-lender, and Samuel to some of the pleaders. But they'd probably starve now and then if it weren't for the charity of the natives.'

'The natives! Do you mean to say—sort of *cadge* from the natives?'

'I fancy so. It would be a very easy thing to do, if one cared to. The Burmese won't let anyone starve.'

Elizabeth had never heard of anything of this kind before. The notion of men who were at least partly white living in poverty among 'natives' so shocked her that she stopped short on the path, and the game of tennis was postponed for a few minutes.

'But how awful! I mean, it's such a bad example! It's almost as bad as if one of *us* was like that. Couldn't something be done for those two? Get up a subscription and send them away from here, or something?'

'I'm afraid it wouldn't help much. Wherever they went they'd be in the same position.'

'But couldn't they get some proper work to do?'

'I doubt it. You see, Eurasians of that type—men who've been brought up in the bazaar and had no education—are done for from the start. The Europeans won't touch them with a stick, and they're cut off from entering the lower-grade Government services. There's nothing they can do except cadge, unless they chuck all pretension to being Europeans. And really you can't expect the poor devils to do that. Their drop of white blood is the sole asset they've got. Poor Francis, I never meet him but he begins telling me about his prickly heat. Natives, you see, are supposed not to suffer from prickly heat—bosh, of course, but people believe it. It's the same with sunstroke. They wear those huge topis to remind you that they've got European skulls. A kind of coat of arms. The bend sinister, you might say.'

This did not satisfy Elizabeth. She perceived that Flory, as usual, had a sneaking sympathy with the Eurasians. And the appearance of the two men had excited a pecular dislike in her. She had placed their type now. They looked like dagoes. Like those Mexicans and Italians and other dago people who play the *mauvais rôle* in so many a film.

'They looked awfully degenerate types, didn't they? So thin and weedy and cringing; and they haven't got at all *honest* faces. I suppose these Eurasians *are* very degenerate? I've heard that half-castes always inherit what's worst in both races. Is that true?'

'I don't know that it's true. Most Eurasians aren't very good specimens, and it's hard to see how they could be, with their upbringing. But our attitude towards them is rather beastly. We always talk of them as though they'd sprung up from the ground like mushrooms, with all their faults ready-made. But when all's said and done, we're responsible for their existence.'

'Responsible for their existence?'

'Well, they've all got fathers, you see.'

'Oh . . . Of course there's that. . . . But after all, *you* aren't responsible. I mean, only a very low kind of man would–er–have anything to do with native women, wouldn't he?'

'Oh, quite. But the fathers of both those two were clergymen in holy orders, I believe.'

He thought of Rosa McFee, the Eurasian girl he had seduced in Mandalay in 1913. The way he used to sneak down to the house in a *gharry* with the shutters down; Rosa's corkscrew curls; her withered old Burmese mother, giving him tea in the dark living-room with the fern pots and the wicker divan. And afterwards, when he had chucked Rosa, those dreadful, imploring letters on scented note-paper, which, in the end, he had ceased opening.

Elizabeth reverted to the subject of Francis and Samuel after tennis.

'Those two Eurasians–does anyone here have anything to do with them? Invite them to their houses or anything?'

'Good gracious, no. They're complete outcasts. It's not considered quite the thing to talk to them, in fact. Most of us say good morning to them–Ellis won't even do that.'

'But *you* talked to them.'

'Oh well, I break the rules occasionally. I meant that a pukka sahib probably wouldn't be seen talking to them. But you see, I try–just sometimes, when I have the pluck–*not* to be a pukka sahib.'

It was an unwise remark. She knew very well by this time the meaning of the phrase 'pukka sahib' and all it stood for. His remark had made the difference in their viewpoint a little clearer. The glance she gave him was almost hostile, and curiously hard; for her face could look hard sometimes, in spite of its youth and its flower-like skin. Those modish tortoise-shell spectacles gave her a very self-possessed look. Spectacles are queerly expressive things–almost more expressive, indeed, than eyes.

As yet he had neither understood her nor quite won her trust. Yet on the surface, at least, things had not gone ill between them. He had fretted her sometimes, but the good impression that he had made that first morning was not yet effaced. It was a curious fact that she scarcely noticed his birthmark at this time. And there were some subjects on which she was glad to hear him talk. Shooting, for example–she seemed to have an enthusiasm for shooting that was remarkable in a girl. Horses, also; but he was less knowledgeable about horses. He had arranged to take her out for a day's shooting, later, when he could make preparations. Both of them were looking forward to the expedition with some eagerness, though not entirely for the same reason.

# II

Flory and Elizabeth walked down the bazaar road. It was morning, but the air was so hot that to walk in it was like wading through a torrid sea. Strings of Burmans passed, coming from the bazaar, on scraping sandals, and knots of girls who hurried by four and five abreast, with short quick steps, chattering, their burnished hair gleaming. By the roadside, just before you got to the jail, the fragments of a stone pagoda were littered, cracked and overthrown by the strong roots of a peepul tree. The angry carved faces of demons looked up from the grass where they had fallen. Near by another peepul tree had twined itself round a palm, uprooting it and bending it backwards in a wrestle that had lasted a decade.

They walked on and came to the jail, a vast square block, two hundred yards each way, with shiny concrete walls twenty feet high. A peacock, pet of the jail, was mincing pigeon-toed along the parapet. Six convicts came by, head down, dragging two heavy handcarts piled with earth, under the guard of Indian warders. They were long-sentence men, with heavy limbs, dressed in uniforms of coarse white cloth with small dunces' caps perched on their shaven crowns. Their faces were greyish, cowed and curiously flattened. Their leg-irons jingled with a clear ring. A woman came past carrying a basket of fish on her head. Two crows were circling round it and making darts at it, and the woman was flapping one hand negligently to keep them away.

There was a din of voices a little distance away. 'The bazaar's just round the corner,' Flory said. 'I think this is a market morning. It's rather fun to watch.'

He had asked her to come down to the bazaar with him, telling her it would amuse her to see it. They rounded the bend. The bazaar was an enclosure like a very large cattle pen, with low stalls, mostly palm-thatched, round its edge. In the enclosure, a mob of people seethed, shouting and jostling; the confusion of their multi-coloured clothes was like a cascade of hundreds-and-thousands poured out of a jar. Beyond the bazaar one could see the huge, miry river. Tree branches and long streaks of scum raced down it at seven miles an hour. By the bank a fleet of sampans, with sharp beak-like bows on which eyes were painted, rocked at their mooring-poles.

Flory and Elizabeth stood watching for a moment. Files of women passed balancing vegetable baskets on their heads, and pop-eyed children who stared at the Europeans. An old Chinese in dungarees faded to sky-blue hurried by, nursing some unrecognizable, bloody fragment of a pig's intestines.

'Let's go and poke around the stalls a bit, shall we?' Flory said.

'Is it all right going in among the crowd? Everything's so horribly dirty.'

'Oh, it's all right, they'll make way for us. It'll interest you.'

Elizabeth followed him doubtfully and even unwillingly. Why was it that he always brought her to these places? Why was he forever dragging her in among the 'natives', trying to get her to take an interest in them and watch their filthy, disgusting habits? It was all wrong, somehow. However, she followed, not feeling able to explain her reluctance. A wave of stifling air met them; there was a reek of garlic, dried fish, sweat, dust, anise, cloves and turmeric. The crowd surged round them, swarms of stocky peasants with cigar-brown faces, withered elders with their grey hair tied in a bun behind, young mothers carrying naked babies astride the hip. Flo was trodden on and yelped. Low, strong shoulders bumped against Elizabeth, as the peasants, too busy bargaining even to stare at a white woman, struggled round the stalls.

'Look!' Flory was pointing with his stick to a stall, and saying something, but it was drowned by the yells of two women who were shaking their fists at each other over a basket of pineapples. Elizabeth had recoiled from the stench and din, but he did not notice it, and led her deeper into the crowd, pointing to this stall and that. The merchandise was foreign-looking, queer and poor. There were vast pomelos hanging on strings like green moons, red bananas, baskets of heliotrope-coloured prawns the size of lobsters, brittle dried fish tied in bundles, crimson chilis, ducks split open and cured like hams, green coco-nuts, the larvae of the rhinoceros beetle, sections of sugar-cane, *dahs,* lacquered sandals, check silk *longyis,* aphrodisiacs in the form of large, soap-like pills, glazed earthenware jars four feet high, Chinese sweetmeats made of garlic and sugar, green and white cigars, purple prinjals, persimmon-seed necklaces, chickens cheeping in wicker cages, brass Buddhas, heart-shaped betel leaves, bottles of Kruschen salts, switches of false hair, red clay cooking-pots, steel shoes for bullocks, papiermâché marionettes, strips of alligator hide with magical properties. Elizabeth's head was beginning to swim. At the other end of the bazaar the sun gleamed through a priest's umbrella, blood-red, as though through the ear of a giant. In front of a stall four Dravidian women were pounding turmeric with heavy stakes in a large wooden mortar. The hot-scented yellow powder flew up and tickled Elizabeth's nostrils, making her sneeze. She felt that she could not endure this place a moment longer. She touched Flory's arm.

'This crowd—the heat is so dreadful. Do you think we could get into the shade?'

He turned round. To tell the truth, he had been too busy talking—mostly inaudibly, because of the din—to notice how the heat and stench were affecting her.

'Oh, I say, I am sorry. Let's get out of it at once. I tell you what, we'll go along to old Li Yeik's shop—he's the Chinese grocer—and he'll get us a drink of something. It is rather stifling here.'

'All these spices—they kind of take your breath away. And what *is* that dreadful smell like fish?'

'Oh, only a kind of sauce they make out of prawns. They bury them and then dig them up several weeks afterwards.'

'How absolutely horrible!'

'Quite wholesome, I believe. Come away from that!' he added to Flo, who was nosing at a basket of small gudgeon-like fish with spines on their gills.

Li Yeik's shop faced the farther end of the bazaar. What Elizabeth had really wanted was to go straight back to the Club, but the European look of Li Yeik's shop-front—it was piled with Lancashire-made cotton shirts and almost incredibly cheap German clocks—comforted her somewhat after the barbarity of the bazaar. They were about to climb the steps when a slim youth of twenty, damnably dressed in a *longyi*, blue cricker blazer and bright yellow shoes, with his hair parted and greased 'Ingaleik fashion', detached himself from the crowd and came after them. He greeted Flory with a small awkward movement as though restraining himself from shikoing.

'What is it?' Flory said.

'Letter, sir.' He produced a grubby envelope.

'Would you excuse me?' Flory said to Elizabeth, opening the letter. It was from Ma Hla May—or rather, it had been written for her and she had signed it with a cross—and it demanded fifty rupees, in a vaguely menacing manner.

Flory pulled the youth aside. 'You speak English? Tell Ma Hla May I'll see about this later. And tell her that if she tries blackmailing me she won't get another pice. Do you understand?'

'Yes, sir.'

'And now go away. Don't follow me about, or there'll be trouble.'

'Yes, sir.'

'A clerk wanting a job,' Flory explained to Elizabeth as they went up the steps. 'They come bothering one at all hours.' And he reflected that the tone of the letter was curious, for he had not expected Ma Hla May to begin blackmailing him so soon; however, he had not time at the moment to wonder what it might mean.

They went into the shop, which seemed dark after the outer air. Li Yeik, who was sitting smoking among his baskets of merchandise—there was no counter—hobbled eagerly forward when he saw who had come in. Flory was a friend of his. He was an old bent-kneed man dressed in blue, wearing a pigtail, with a chinless yellow face, all cheekbones, like a benevolent skull. He greeted Flory with nasal honking noises which he intended for Burmese, and at once hobbled to the back of the shop to call for refreshments. There was a cool sweetish smell of opium. Long strips of red paper with black lettering were pasted on the walls, and at one side there was a little altar with a portrait of two large, serene-looking people in embroidered robes, and two sticks of incense smouldering in front of it. Two Chinese women, one old, and a girl were sitting on a mat rolling cigarettes with maize straw and tobacco like chopped horsehair. They wore black silk trousers, and their feet, with bulging, swollen insteps, were crammed into red-heeled wooden slippers no bigger than a doll's. A naked child was crawling slowly about the floor like a large yellow frog.

'Do look at those women's feet!' Elizabeth whispered as soon as Li Yeik's back was turned. 'Isn't it simply dreadful! How do they get them like that? Surely it isn't natural?'

'No, they deform them artificially. It's going out in China, I believe, but the people here are behind the times. Old Li Yeik's pigtail is another anachronism. Those small feet are beautiful according to Chinese ideas.'

'Beautiful! They're so horrible I can hardly look at them. These people must be absolute savages!'

'Oh no! They're highly civilized; more civilized than we are, in my opinion. Beauty's all a matter of taste. There are a people in this country called the Palaungs who admire long necks in women. The girls wear broad brass rings to stretch their necks, and they put on more and more of them until in the end they have necks like giraffes. It's no queerer than bustles or crinolines.'

At this moment Li Yeik came back with two fat, round-faced Burmese girls, evidently sisters, giggling and carrying between them two chairs and a blue Chinese teapot holding half a gallon. The two girls were or had been Li Yeik's concubines. The old man had produced a tin of chocolates and was prising off the lid and smiling in a fatherly way, exposing three long, tobacco-blackened teeth. Elizabeth sat down in a very uncomfortable frame of mind. She was perfectly certain that it could not be right to accept these people's hospitality. One of the Burmese girls had at once gone behind the chairs and begun fanning Flory and Elizabeth, while the other knelt at their feet and poured out cups of tea. Elizabeth felt very foolish with the girl fanning the back of her neck and the Chinaman grinning in front of her. Flory always seemed to get her into these uncomfortable situations. She took a chocolate from the tin Li Yeik offered her, but she could not bring herself to say 'thank you'.

'Is this *all right*?' she whispered to Flory.

'All right?'

'I mean, ought we to be sitting down in these people's house? Isn't it sort of—sort of *infra dig*?'

'It's all right with a Chinaman. They're a favoured race in this country. And they're very democratic in their ideas. It's best to treat them more or less as equals.'

'This tea looks absolutely beastly. It's quite green. You'd think they'd have the sense to put milk in it, wouldn't you?'

'It's not bad. It's a special kind of tea old Li Yeik gets from China. It has orange blossoms in it, I believe.'

'Ugh! It tastes exactly like earth,' she said, having tasted it.

Li Yeik stood holding his pipe, which was two feet long with a metal bowl the size of an acorn, and watching the Europeans to see whether they enjoyed his tea. The girl behind the chair said something in Burmese, at which both of them burst out giggling again. The one kneeling on the floor looked up and gazed in a naïve admiring way at Elizabeth. Then she turned to Flory and asked him whether the English lady wore stays. She pronounced it *s'tays*.

'Ch!' said Li Yeik in a scandalized manner, stirring the girl with his toe to silence her.

'I should hardly care to ask her,' Flory said.

'Oh, *thakin,* please do ask her! We are so anxious to know!'

There was an argument, and the girl behind the chair forgot fanning and joined in. Both of them, it appeared, had been pining all their lives to see a veritable pair of *s'tays*. They had heard so many tales about them; they were made of steel on the principle of a strait waistcoat, and they compressed a woman so tightly that she had no breasts, absolutely no breasts at all! The girls pressed their hands against their fat ribs in illustration. Would not Flory be so kind as to ask the English lady? There was a room behind the shop where she could come with them and undress. They had been so hoping to see a pair of *s'tays*.

Then the conversation lapsed suddenly. Elizabeth was sitting stiffly, holding her tiny cup of tea, which she could not bring herself to taste again, and wearing a rather hard smile. A chill fell upon the Orientals; they realized that the English girl, who could not join in their conversation, was not at her ease. Her elegance and her foreign beauty, which had charmed them a moment earlier, began to awe them a little. Even Flory was conscious of the same feeling. There came one of those dreadful moments that one has with Orientals, when everyone avoids everyone else's eyes, trying vainly to think of something to say. Then the naked child, which had been exploring some baskets at the back of the shop, crawled across to where the European sat. It examined their shoes and stockings with great curiosity, and then, looking up, saw their white faces and was seized with terror. It let out a desolate wail, and began making water on the floor.

The old Chinese woman looked up, clicked her tongue and went on rolling cigarettes. No one else took the smallest notice. A pool began to form on the floor. Elizabeth was so horrified that she set her cup down hastily, and spilled the tea. She plucked at Flory's arm.

'That child! Do look what it's doing! Really, can't someone—it's too awful!'

For a moment everyone gazed in astonishment, and then they all grasped what was the matter. There was a flurry and a general clicking of tongues. No one had paid any attention to the child—the incident was too normal to be noticed—and now they all felt horribly ashamed. Everyone began putting the blame on the child. There were exclamations of 'What a disgraceful child! What a disgusting child!' The old Chinese woman carried the child, still howling, to the door, and held it out over the step as though wringing out a bath sponge. And in the same moment, as it seemed, Flory and Elizabeth were outside the shop, and he was following her back to the road with Li Yeik and the others looking after them in dismay.

'If *that's* what you call civilized people—!' she was exclaiming.

'I'm sorry,' he said feebly. 'I never expected—'

'What absolutely *disgusting* people!'

She was bitterly angry. Her face had flushed a wonderful delicate pink, like a poppy bud opened a day too soon. It was the deepest colour of which it was capable. He followed her past the bazaar and back to the main road, and they had gone fifty yards before he ventured to speak again.

'I'm so sorry that this should have happened! Li Yeik is such a decent old chap. He'd hate to think that he'd offended you. Really it would have been better to stay a few minutes. Just to thank him for the tea.'

'Thank him! After *that!*'

'But honestly, you oughtn't to mind that sort of thing. Not in this country. These people's whole outlook is so different from ours. One has to adjust oneself. Suppose, for instance, you were back in the Middle Ages—'

'I think I'd rather not discuss it any longer.'

It was the first time they had definitely quarrelled. He was too miserable even to ask himself how it was that he offended her. He did not realize that this constant striving to interest her in Oriental things struck her only as perverse, ungentlemanly, a deliberate seeking after the squalid and the 'beastly'. He had not grasped even now with what eyes she saw the 'natives'. He only knew that at each attempt to make her share his life, his thoughts, his sense of beauty, she shied away from him like a frightened horse.

They walked up the road, he to the left of her and a little behind. He watched her averted cheek and the tiny gold hairs on her nape beneath the brim of her Terai hat. How he loved her, how he loved her! It was as though he had never truly loved her till this moment, when he walked behind her in disgrace, not even daring to show his disfigured face. He made to speak several times, and stopped himself. His voice was not quite ready, and he did not know what he could say that did not risk offending her somehow. At last he said, flatly, with a feeble pretence that nothing was the matter:

'It's getting beastly hot, isn't it?'

With the temperature at 90 degrees in the shade it was not a brilliant remark. To his surprise she seized on it with a kind of eagerness. She turned to face him, and she was smiling again.

'Isn't it simply *baking!*'

With that they were at peace. The silly, banal remark, bringing with it the reassuring atmosphere of Club-chatter, had soothed her like a charm. Flo, who had lagged behind, came puffing up to them dribbling saliva; in an instant they were talking, quite as usual, about dogs. They talked about dogs for the rest of the way home, almost without a pause. Dogs are an inexhaustible subject. Dogs, dogs! thought Flory as they climbed the hot hillside, with the mounting sun scorching their shoulders through their thin clothes, like the breath of fire—were they never to talk of anything except dogs? Or failing dogs, gramophone records and tennis racquets? And yet, when they kept to trash like this, how easily, how amicably they could talk!

They passed the glittering white wall of the cemetery and came to the Lackersteens' gate. Old mohur trees grew round it, and a clump of hollyhocks eight feet high, with round red flowers like blowsy girls' faces. Flory took off his hat in the shade and fanned his face.

'Well, we're back before the worst of the heat comes. I'm afraid our trip to the bazaar wasn't altogether a success.'

'Oh, not at all! I enjoyed it, really I did.'

'No—I don't know, something unfortunate always seems to happen.—Oh, by the way! You haven't forgotten that we're going out shooting the day after tomorrow? I hope that day will be all right for you?'

'Yes, and my uncle's going to lend me his gun. Such awful fun! You'll have to teach me all about shooting. I *am* so looking forward to it.'

'So am I. It's a rotten time of year for shooting, but we'll do our best. Good-bye for the present, then.'

'Good-bye, Mr Flory.'

She still called him Mr Flory though he called her Elizabeth. They parted and went their ways, each thinking of the shooting trip, which, both of them felt, would in some way put things right between them.

## 12

In the sticky, sleepy heat of the living-room, almost dark because of the beaded curtain, U Po Kyin was marching slowly up and down, boasting. From time to time he would put a hand under his singlet and scratch his sweating breasts, huge as a woman's with fat. Ma Kin was sitting on her mat, smoking slender white cigars. Through the open door of the bedroom one could see the corner of U Po Kyin's huge square bed, with carved teak posts, like a catafalque, on which he had committed many and many a rape.

Ma Kin was now hearing for the first time of the 'other affair' which underlay U Po Kyin's attack on Dr Veraswami. Much as he despised her intelligence, U Po Kyin usually let Ma Kin into his secrets sooner or later. She was the only person in his immediate circle who was not afraid of him, and there was therefore a pleasure in impressing her.

'Well, Kin Kin,' he said, 'you see how it has all gone according to plan! Eighteen anonymous letters already, and every one of them a masterpiece. I would repeat some of them to you if I thought you were capable of appreciating them.'

'But supposing the Europeans take no notice of your anonymous letters? What then?'

'Take no notice? Aha, no fear of that! I think I know something about the European mentality. Let me tell you, Kin Kin, that if there is one thing I *can* do, it is to write an anonymous letter.'

This was true. U Po Kyin's letters had already taken effect, and especially on their chief target, Mr Macgregor.

Only two days earlier than this, Mr Macgregor had spent a very troubled evening in trying to make up his mind whether Dr Veraswami was or was not guilty of disloyalty to the Government. Of course, it was not a question of any overt act of disloyalty—that was quite irrelevant. The point was, was the doctor the *kind* of man who would hold seditious opinions? In India you are not judged for what you do, but for what you *are*. The merest breath of suspicion against his loyalty can ruin an Oriental official. Mr Macgregor had too just a nature to condemn even an Oriental out of hand. He had puzzled as late as midnight over a whole pile of confidential papers, including the five anonymous letters he had received, besides two others that had been forwarded to him by Westfield, pinned together with a cactus thorn.

It was not only the letters. Rumours about the doctor had been pouring in from every side. U Po Kyin fully grasped that to call the doctor a traitor was not enough in itself; it was necessary to attack his reputation from every possible angle. The doctor was charged not only with sedition, but also with extortion, rape, torture, performing illegal operations, performing operations while blind drunk, murder by poison, murder by sympathetic magic, eating beef, selling death certificates to murderers, wearing his shoes in the precincts of the pagoda and making homosexual attempts on the Military Police drummer boy. To hear what was said of him, anyone would have imagined the doctor a compound of Machiavelli, Sweeny Todd and the Marquis de Sade. Mr Macgregor had not paid much attention at first. He was too accustomed to this kind of thing. But with the last of the anonymous letters U Po Kyin had brought off a stroke that was brilliant even for him.

It concerned the escape of Nga Shwe O, the dacoit, from Kyauktada jail. Nga Shwe O, who was in the middle of a well-earned seven years, had been preparing his escape for several months past, and as a start his friends outside had bribed one of the Indian warders. The warder received his hundred rupees in advance, applied for leave to visit the death-bed of a relative and spent several busy days in the Mandalay brothels. Time passed, and the day of the escape was postponed several times—the warder, meanwhile, growing more and more homesick for the brothels. Finally he decided to earn a further reward by betraying the plot to U Po Kyin. But U Po Kyin, as usual, saw his chance. He told the warder on dire penalties to hold his tongue, and then, on the very night of the escape, when it was too late to do anything, sent another anonymous letter to Mr Macgregor, warning him that an escape was being attempted. The letter added, needless to say, that Dr Veraswami, the superintendent of the jail, had been bribed for his connivance.

In the morning there was a hullabaloo and a rushing to and fro of warders and policemen at the jail, for Nga Shwe O had escaped. (He was a long way down the river, in a *sampan* provided by U Po Kyin.) This time Mr Macgregor was taken aback. Whoever had written the letter must have been privy to the plot, and was probably telling the truth about the doctor's connivance. It was a very serious matter. A jail superintendent who will take bribes to let a prisoner escape is capable of anything. And therefore—perhaps the logical sequence was not quite clear, but it was clear enough to Mr Macgregor—therefore the charge of sedition, which was the main charge against the doctor, became much more credible.

U Po Kyin had attacked the other Europeans at the same time. Flory, who was the doctor's friend and his chief source of prestige, had been scared easily enough into deserting him. With Westfield it was a little harder. Westfield, as a policeman, knew a great deal about U Po Kyin and might conceivably upset his plans. Policemen and magistrates are natural enemies. But U Po Kyin had known how to turn even this fact to advantage. He had accused the doctor, anonymously of course, of being in league with the notorious scoundrel and bribe-taker U Po Kyin. That settled Westfield. As for Ellis, no anonymous letters were needed in his case; nothing could possibly make him think worse of the doctor than he did already.

U Po Kyin had even sent one of his anonymous letters to Mrs Lackersteen, for he knew the power of European women. Dr Veraswami, the letter said, was inciting the natives to abduct and rape the European women—no details were given, nor were they needed. U Po Kyin had touched Mrs Lackersteen's weak spot. To her mind the words 'sedition', 'Nationalism,', 'rebellion', 'Home Rule', conveyed one thing and one only, and that was a picture of herself being raped by a procession of jet-black coolies with rolling white eyeballs. It was a thought that kept her awake at night sometimes. Whatever good regard the Europeans might once have had for the doctor was crumbling rapidly.

'So you see,' said U Po Kyin with a pleased air, 'you see how I have undermined him. He is like a tree sawn through at the base. One tap and down he comes. In three weeks or less I shall deliver that tap.'

'How?'

'I am just coming to that. I think it is time for you to hear about it. You have no sense in these matters, but you know how to hold your tongue. You have heard talk of this rebellion that is brewing near Thongwa village?'

'Yes. They are very foolish, those villagers. What can they do with their *dahs* and spears against the Indian soldiers? They will be shot down like wild animals.'

'Of course. If there is any fighting it will be a massacre. But they are only a pack of superstitious peasants. They have put their faith in these absurd bullet-proof jackets that are being distributed to them. I despise such ignorance.'

'Poor men! Why do you not stop them, Ko Po Kyin? There is no need to arrest anybody. You have only to go to the village and tell them that you know their plans, and they will never dare to go on.'

'Ah well, I could stop them if I chose, of course. But then I do not choose. I have my reasons. You see, Kin Kin—you will please keep silent about this—this is, so to speak, my own rebellion. I arranged it myself.'

'What!'

Ma Kin dropped her cigar. Her eyes had opened so wide that the pale blue white showed all round the pupil. She was horrified. She burst out:

'Ko Po Kyin, what are you saying? You do not mean it! You, raising a rebellion—it cannot be true!'

'Certainly it is true. And a very good job we are making of it. That magician whom I brought from Rangoon is a clever fellow. He has toured all over India as a circus conjurer. The bullet-proof jackets were bought at Whiteaway & Laidlaw's stores, one rupee eight annas each. They are costing me a pretty penny, I can tell you.'

'But, Ko Po Kyin! A rebellion! The terrible fighting and shooting, and all the poor men who will be killed! Surely you have not gone mad? Are you not afraid of being shot yourself?'

U Po Kyin halted in his stride. He was astonished. 'Good gracious, woman, what idea have you got hold of now? You do not suppose that *I* am rebelling against the Government? I–a Government servant of thirty years' standing! Good heavens, no! I said that I had *started* the rebellion, not that I was taking part in it. It is these fools of villagers who are going to risk their skins, not I. No one dreams that I have anything to do with it, or ever will, except Ba Sein and one or two others.'

'But you said it was you who were persuading them to rebel?'

'Of course. I have accused Veraswami of raising a rebellion against the Government. Well, I must have a rebellion to show, must I not?'

'Ah, I see. And when the rebellion breaks out, you are going to say that Dr Veraswami is to blame for it. Is that it?'

'How slow you are! I should have thought even a fool would have seen that I am raising the rebellion merely in order to crush it. I am–what is that expression Mr Macgregor uses? *Agent provocateur*–Latin, you would not understand. I am *agent provocateur*. First I persuade these fools at Thongwa to rebel, and then I arrest them as rebels. At the very moment when it is due to start, I shall pounce on the ringleaders and clap every one of them in jail. After that, I dare say there may possibly be some fighting. A few men may be killed and a few more sent to the Andamans. But, meanwhile, I shall be first in the field. U Po Kyin, the man who quelled a most dangerous rising in the nick of time! I shall be the hero of the district.'

U Po Kyin, justly proud of his plan, began to pace up and down the room again with his hands behind his back, smiling. Ma Kin considered the plan in silence for some time. Finally she said:

'I still do not see why you are doing this, Ko Po Kyin. Where is it all leading? And what has it got to do with Dr Veraswami?'

'I shall never teach you wisdom, Kin Kin! Did I not tell you at the beginning that Veraswami stands in my way? This rebellion is the very thing to get rid of him. Of course we shall never prove that he is responsible for it; but what does that matter? All the Europeans will take it for granted that he is mixed up in it somehow. That is how their minds work. He will be ruined for life. And his fall is my rise. The blacker I can paint him, the more glorious my own conduct will appear. Now do you understand?'

'Yes, I do understand. And I think it is a base, evil plan. I wonder you are not ashamed to tell it me.'

'Now, Kin Kin! Surely you are not going to start that nonsense over again?'

'Ko Po Kyin, why is it that you are only happy when you are being wicked? Why is it that everything you do must bring evil to others? Think of that poor doctor who will be dismissed from his post, and those villagers who will be shot or flogged with bamboos or imprisoned for life. Is it necessary to do such things? What can you want with more money when you are rich already?'

'Money! Who is talking about money? Some day, woman, you will realize that there are other things in the world besides money. Fame, for example.

Greatness. Do you realize that the Governor of Burma will very probably pin an Order on my breast for my loyal action in this affair? Would not even you be proud of such an honour as that?'

Ma Kin shook her head, unimpressed. 'When will you remember, Ko Po Kyin, that you are not going to live a thousand years? Consider what happens to those who have lived wickedly. There is such a thing, for instance, as being turned into a rat or a frog. There is even hell. I remember what a priest said to me once about hell, something that he had translated from the Pali scriptures, and it was very terrible. He said, "Once in a thousand centuries two red-hot spears will meet in your heart, and you will say to yourself, 'Another thousand centuries of my torment are ended, and there is as much to come as there has been before.'" Is it not very dreadful to think of such things, Ko Po Kyin?'

U Po Kyin laughed and gave a careless wave of his hand that meant 'pagodas'.

'Well, I hope you may still laugh when it comes to the end. But for myself, I should not care to look back upon such a life.'

She relighted her cigar with her thin shoulder turned disapprovingly on U Po Kyin while he took several more turns up and down the room. When he spoke, it was more seriously than before, and even with a touch of diffidence.

'You know, Kin Kin, there is another matter behind all this. Something that I have not told to you or to anyone else. Even Ba Sein does not know. But I believe I will tell it you now.'

'I do not want to hear it, if it is more wickedness.'

'No, no. You were asking just now what is my real object in this affair. You think, I suppose, that I am ruining Veraswami merely because I dislike him and his ideas about bribes as a nuisance. It is not only that. There is something else that is far more important, and it concerns you as well as me.'

'What is it?'

'Have you never felt in you, Kin Kin, a desire for higher things? Has it never struck you that after all our successes—all my successes, I should say—we are almost in the same position as when we started? I am worth, I dare say, two lakhs of rupees, and yet look at the style in which we live! Look at this room! Positively it is no better than that of a peasant. I am tired of eating with my fingers and associating only with Burmans—poor, inferior people—and living, as you might say, like a miserable Township Officer. Money is not enough; I should like to feel that I have risen in the world as well. Do you not wish sometimes for a way of life that is a little more—how shall I say—elevated?'

'I do not know how we could want more than what we have already. When I was a girl in my village I never thought that I should live in such a house as this. Look at those English chairs—I have never sat in one of them in my life. But I am very proud to look at them and think that I own them.'

'Ch! Why did you ever leave that village of yours, Kin Kin? You are only fit to stand gossiping by the well with a stone water-pot on your head. But I am more ambitious, God be praised. And now I will tell you the real reason why I am intriguing against Veraswami. It is in my mind to do something that is really magnificent. Something noble, glorious! Something that is the very highest honour an Oriental can attain to. You know what I mean, of course?'

'No. What do you mean?'

'Come, now! The greatest achievement of my life! Surely you can guess?'

'Ah, I know! You are going to buy a motor-car. But oh, Ko Po Kyin, please do not expect me to ride in it!'

U Po Kyin threw up his hands in disgust. 'A motor-car! You have the mind of a bazaar peanut-seller! I could buy twenty motor-cars if I wanted them. And what use would a motor-car be in this place? No, it is something far grander than that.'

'What, then?'

'It is this. I happen to know that in a month's time the Europeans are going to elect one native member to their Club. They do not want to do it, but they will have orders from the Commissioner, and they will obey. Naturally, they would elect Veraswami, who is the highest native official in the district. But I have disgraced Veraswami. And so—'

'What?'

U Po Kyin did not answer for a moment. He looked at Ma Kin, and his vast yellow face, with its broad jaw and numberless teeth, was so softened that it was almost child-like. There might even have been tears in his tawny eyes. He said in a small, almost awed voice, as though the greatness of what he was saying overcame him:

'Do you not see, woman? Do you not see that if Veraswami is disgraced I shall be elected to the Club myself?'

The effect of it was crushing. There was not another word of argument on Ma Kin's part. The magnificence of U Po Kyin's project had struck her dumb.

And not withour reason, for all the achievements of U Po Kyin's life were as nothing beside this. It is a real triumph—it would be doubly so in Kyauktada—for an official of the lower ranks to worm his way into the European Club. The European Club, that remote, mysterious temple, that holy of holies far harder of entry than Nirvana! Po Kyin, the naked gutter-boy of Mandalay, the thieving clerk and obscure official, would enter that sacred place, call Europeans 'old chap', drink whisky and soda and knock white balls to and fro on the green table! Ma Kin, the village woman, who had first seen the light through the chinks of a bamboo hut thatched with palm-leaves, would sit on a high chair with her feet imprisoned in silk stockings and high-heeled shoes (yes, she would actually wear shoes in that place!) talking to English ladies in Hindustani about baby-linen! It was a prospect that would have dazzled anybody.

For a long time Ma Kin remained silent, her lips parted, thinking of the European Club and the splendours that it might contain. For the first time in her life she surveyed U Po Kyin's intrigues without disapproval. Perhaps it was a feat greater even than the storming of the Club to have planted a grain of ambition in Ma Kin's gentle heart.

# 13

As Flory came through the gate of the hospital compound four ragged sweepers passed him, carrying some dead coolie, wrapped in sackcloth, to a foot-deep grave in the jungle. Flory crossed the brick-like earth of the yard between the hospital sheds. All down the wide verandas, on sheetless charpoys, rows of grey-faced men lay silent and moveless. Some filthy-looking curs, which were said to devour amputated limbs, dozed or snapped at their fleas among the piles of the buildings. The whole place wore a sluttish and decaying air. Dr Veraswami struggled hard to keep it clean, but there was no coping with the dust and the bad water-supply, and the inertia of sweepers and half-trained Assistant Surgeons.

Flory was told that the doctor was in the out-patients' department. It was a plaster-walled room furnished only with a table and two chairs, and a dusty portrait of Queen Victoria, much awry. A procession of Burmans, peasants with gnarled muscles beneath their faded rags, were filing into the room and queueing up at the table. The doctor was in shirt-sleeves and sweating profusely. He sprang to his feet with an exclamation of pleasure, and in his usual fussy haste thrust Flory into the vacant chair and produced a tin of cigarettes from the drawer of the table.

'What a delightful visit, Mr Flory! Please to make yourself comfortable – that iss, if one can possibly be comfortable in such a place ass this, ha, ha! Afterwards, at my house, we will talk with beer and amenities. Kindly excuse me while I attend to the populace.'

Flory sat down, and the hot sweat immediately burst out and drenched his shirt. The heat of the room was stifling. The peasants steamed garlic from all their pores. As each man came to the table the doctor would bounce from his chair, prod the patient in the back, lay a black ear to his chest, fire off several questions in villainous Burmese, then bounce back to the table and scribble a prescription. The patients took the prescriptions across the yard to the Compounder, who gave them bottles filled with water and various vegetable dyes. The Compounder supported himself largely by the sale of drugs, for the Government paid him only twenty-five rupees a month. However, the doctor knew nothing of this.

On most mornings the doctor had not time to attend to the out-patients himself, and left them to one of the Assistant Surgeons. The Assistant Surgeon's methods of diagnosis were brief. He would simply ask each patient, 'Where is your pain? Head, back or belly?' and at the reply hand out a prescription from one of three piles that he had prepared beforehand. The patients much preferred this method to the doctor's. The doctor had a way of asking them whether they had suffered from venereal diseases—an ungentlemanly, pointless question—and sometimes he horrified them still more by suggesting operations. 'Belly-cutting' was their phrase for it. The majority of them would have died a dozen times over rather than submit to 'belly-cutting'.

As the last patient disappeared the doctor sank into his chair, fanning his face with the prescription-pad.

'Ach, this heat! Some mornings I think that never will I get the smell of garlic out of my nose! It iss amazing to me how their very blood becomes impregnated with it. Are you not suffocated, Mr Flory? You English have the sense of smell almost too highly developed. What torments you must all suffer in our filthy East!'

'Abandon your noses, all ye who enter here, what? They might write that up over the Suez Canal. You seem busy this morning?'

'Ass ever. Ah but, my friend, how discouraging iss the work of a doctor in this country! These villagers—dirty, ignorant savages! Even to get them to come to hospital iss all we can do, and they will die of gangrene or carry a tumour ass large ass a melon for ten years rather than face the knife. And such medicines ass their own so-called doctors give to them! Herbs gathered under the new moon, tigers' whiskers, rhinoceros horn, urine, menstrual blood! How men can drink such compounds iss disgusting.'

'Rather picturesque, all the same. You ought to compile a Burmese pharmacopoeia, doctor. It would be almost as good as Culpeper.'

'Barbarous cattle, barbarous cattle,' said the doctor, beginning to struggle into his white coat. 'Shall we go back to my house? There iss beer and I trust a few fragments of ice left. I have an operation at ten, strangulated hernia, very urgent. Till then I am free.'

'Yes. As a matter of fact there's something I rather wanted to talk to you about.'

They recrossed the yard and climbed the steps of the doctor's veranda. The doctor, having felt in the ice-chest and found that the ice was all melted to tepid water, opened a bottle of beer and called fussily to the servants to set some more bottles swinging in a cradle of wet straw. Flory was standing looking over the veranda rail, with his hat still on. The fact was that he had come here to utter an apology. He had been avoiding the doctor for nearly a fortnight—since the day, in fact, when he had set his name to the insulting notice at the Club. But the apology had got to be uttered. U Po Kyin was a very good judge of men, but he had erred in supposing that two anonymous letters were enough to scare Flory permanently away from his friend.

'Look here, doctor, you know what I wanted to say?'

'I? No.'

'Yes, you do. It's about that beastly trick I played on you the other week. When Ellis put that notice on the Club board and I signed my name to it. You must have heard about it. I want to try and explain—'

'No, no, my friend, no, no!' The doctor was so distressed that he sprang across the veranda and seized Flory by the arm. 'You shall *not* explain! Please never mention it! I understand perfectly–but most perfectly.'

'No, you don't understand. You couldn't. You don't realize just what *kind* of pressure is put on one to make one do things like that. There was nothing to make me sign the notice. Nothing could have happened if I'd refused. There's no law telling us to be beastly to Orientals–quite the contrary. But–it's just that one daren't be loyal to an Oriental when it means going against the others. It doesn't *do*. If I'd stuck out against signing the notice I'd have been in disgrace at the Club for a week or two. So I funked it, as usual.'

'Please, Mr Flory, please! Possitively you will make me uncomfortable if you continue. Ass though I could not make all allowances for your position!'

'Our motto, you know is, "In India, do as the English do".'

'Of course, of course. And a most noble motto. "Hanging together", ass you call it. It iss the secret of your superiority to we Orientals.'

'Well, it's never much use saying one's sorry. But what I did come here to say was that it shan't happen again. In fact–'

'Now, now, Mr Flory, you will oblige me by saying no more upon this subject. It iss all over and forgotten. Please to drink up your beer before it becomes ass hot ass tea. Also, I have a thing to tell you. You have not asked for my news yet.'

'Ah, your news. What is your news, by the way? How's everything been going all this time? How's Ma Britannia? Still moribund?'

'Aha, very low, very low! But not so low ass I. I am in deep waters, my friend.'

'What? U Po Kyin again? Is he still libelling you?'

'If he iss libelling me! This time it iss–well, it iss something diabolical. My friend, you have heard of this rebellion that is supposed to be on the point of breaking out in the district?'

'I've heard a lot of talk. Westfield's been out bent on slaughter, but I hear he can't find any rebels. Only the usual village Hampdens who won't pay their taxes.'

'Ah yes. Wretched fools! Do you know how much iss the tax that most of them have refused to pay? Five rupees! They will get tired of it and pay up presently. We have this trouble every year. But ass for the rebellion–the *so-called* rebellion, Mr Flory–I wish you to know that there iss more in it than meets the eye.'

'Oh? What?'

To Flory's surprise the doctor made such a violent gesture of anger that he spilled most of his beer. He put his glass down on the veranda rail and burst out:

'It iss U Po Kyin again! That unutterable scoundrel! That crocodile deprived of natural feeling! That–that–'

'Go on. "That obscene trunk of humors, that swol'n parcel of dropsies, that bolting-hutch of beastliness"–go on. What's he been up to now?'

'A villainy unparalleled'–and here the doctor outlined the plot for a sham rebellion, very much as U Po Kyin had explained it to Ma Kin. The only detail not known to him was U Po Kyin's intention of getting himself elected to the European Club. The doctor's face could not accurately be said to flush, but it grew several shades blacker in his anger. Flory was so astonished that he remained standing up.

'The cunning old devil! Who'd have thought he had it in him? But how did you manage to find all this out?'

'Ah, I have a few friends left. But now do you see, my friend, what ruin he iss preparing for me? Already he hass calumniated me right and left. When this absurd rebellion breaks out, he will do everything in his power to connect my name with it. And I tell you that the slightest suspicion of my loyalty could be ruin for me, ruin! If it were ever breathed that I were even a sympathizer with this rebellion, there iss an end of me.'

'But, damn it, this is ridiculous! Surely you can defend yourself somehow?'

'How can I defend myself when I can prove nothing? I know that all this iss true, but what use iss that? If I demand a public inquiry, for every witness I produce U Po Kyin would produce fifty. You do not realize the influence of that man in the district. No one dare speak against him.'

'But why need you prove anything? Why not go to old Macgregor and tell him about it? He's a very fair-minded old chap in his way. He'd hear you out.'

'Useless, useless. You have not the mind of an intriguer, Mr Flory. *Qui s'excuse, s'accuse*, iss it not? It does not pay to cry that there iss a conspiracy against one.'

'Well, what are you going to do, then?'

'There iss nothing I can do. Simply I must wait and hope that my prestige will carry me through. In affairs like this, where a native official's reputation iss at stake, there iss no question of proof, of evidence. All depends upon one's standing with the Europeans. If my standing iss good, they will not believe it of me; if bad, they will believe it. Prestige iss all.'

They were silent for a moment. Flory understood well enough that 'prestige iss all'. He was used to these nebulous conflicts, in which suspicion counts for more than proof, and reputation for more than a thousand witnesses. A thought came into his head, an uncomfortable, chilling thought which would never have occurred to him three weeks earlier. It was one of those moments when one sees quite clearly what is one's duty, and, with all the will in the world to shirk it, feels certain that one must carry it out. He said:

'Suppose, for instance, you were elected to the Club? Would that do your prestige any good?'

'If I were elected to the Club! Ah, indeed, yes! The Club! It iss a fortress impregnable. Once there, and no one would listen to these tales about me any more than if it were about you, or Mr Macgregor, or any other European gentleman. But what hope have I that they will elect me after their minds have been poisoned against me?'

'Well now, look here, doctor, I tell you what. I'll propose your name at the next general meeting. I know the question's got to come up then, and if someone comes forward with the name of a candidate, I dare say no one except Ellis will blackball him. And in the meantime–'

'Ah, my friend, my dear friend!' The doctor's emotion caused him almost to choke. He seized Flory by the hand. 'Ah, my friend, that iss noble! Truly it iss noble! But it iss too much. I fear that you will be in trouble with your European friends again. Mr Ellis, for example–would he tolerate it that you propose my name?'

'Oh, bother Ellis. But you must understand that I can't promise to get you elected. It depends on what Macgregor says and what mood the others are in. It may all come to nothing.'

The doctor was still holding Flory's hand between his own, which were plump and damp. The tears had actually started into his eyes, and these, magnified by his spectacles, beamed upon Flory like the liquid eyes of a dog.

'Ah, my friend! If I should but be elected! What an end to all my troubles! But, my friend, ass I said before, do not be too rash in this matter. Beware of U Po Kyin! By now he will have numbered you among hiss enemies. And even for you hiss enmity can be a danger.'

'Oh, good Lord, he can't touch me. He's done nothing so far–only a few silly anonymous letters.'

'I would not be too sure. He hass subtle ways to strike. And for sure he will raise heaven and earth to keep me from being elected to the Club. If you have a weak spot, guard it, my friend. He will find it out. He strikes always at the weakest spot.'

'Like the crocodile,' Flory suggested.

'Like the crocodile,' agreed the doctor gravely. 'Ah but, my friend, how gratifying to me if I should become a member of your European Club! What an honour, to be the associate of European gentlemen! But there iss one other matter, Mr Flory, that I did not care to mention before. It iss–I hope this iss clearly understood–that I have no intention of *using* the Club in any way. Membership is all I desire. Even if I were elected, I should not, of course, ever presume to *come* to the Club.'

'Not come to the Club?'

'No, no! Heaven forbid that I should force my society upon the European gentlemen! Simply I should pay my subscriptions. That, for me, iss a privilege high enough. You understand that, I trust?'

'Perfectly, doctor, perfectly.'

Flory could not help laughing as he walked up the hill. He was definitely committed now to proposing the doctor's election. And there would be such a row when the others heard of it–oh, such a devil of a row! But the astonishing thing was that it only made him laugh. The prospect that would have appalled him a month back now almost exhilarated him.

Why? And why had he given his promise at all? It was a small thing, a small risk to take–nothing heroic about it–and yet it was unlike him. Why, after all these years–the circumspect, pukka sahib-like years–break all the rules so suddenly?

He knew why. It was because Elizabeth, by coming into his life, had so changed it and renewed it that all the dirty, miserable years might never have passed. Her presence had changed the whole orbit of his mind. She had brought back to him the air of England—dear England, where thought is free and one is not condemned forever to dance the *danse du pukka sahib* for the edification of the lower races. Where is the life that late I led? he thought. Just by existing she had made it possible for him, she had even made it natural to him, to act decently.

Where is the life that late I led? he thought again as he came through the garden gate. He was happy, happy. For he had perceived that the pious ones are right when they say that there is salvation and life can begin anew. Hé came up the path, and it seemed to him that his house, his flowers, his servants, all the life that so short a time ago had been drenched in ennui and homesickness, were somehow made new, significant, beautiful inexhaustibly. What fun it could all be, if only you had someone to share it with you! How you could love this country, if only you were not alone! Nero was out on the path, braving the sun for some grains of paddy that the *mali* had dropped, taking food to his goats. Flo made a dash at him, panting, and Nero sprang into the air with a flurry and lighted on Flory's shoulder. Flory walked into the house with the little red cock in his arms, stroking his silky ruff and the smooth, diamond-shaped feathers of his back.

He had not set foot on the veranda before he knew that Ma Hla May was in the house. It did not need Ko S'la to come hurrying from within with a face of evil tidings. Flory had smelled her scent of sandalwood, garlic, coco-nut oil and the jasmine in her hair. He dropped Nero over the veranda rail.

'*The woman* has come back,' said Ko S'la.

Flory had turned very pale. When he turned pale the birthmark made him hideously ugly. A pang like a blade of ice had gone through his entrails. Ma Hla May had appeared in the doorway of the bedroom. She stood with her face downcast, looking at him from beneath lowered brows.

'*Thakin,*' she said in a low voice, half sullen, half urgent.

'Go away!' said Flory angrily to Ko S'la, venting his fear and anger upon him.

'*Thakin,*' she said, 'come into the bedroom here. I have a thing to say to you.'

He followed her into the bedroom. In a week—it was only a week—her appearance had degenerated extraordinarily. Her hair looked greasy. All her lockets were gone, and she was wearing a Manchester *longyi* of flowered cotton, costing two rupees eight annas. She had coated her face so thick with powder that it was like a clown's mask, and at the roots of her hair, where the powder ended, there was a ribbon of natural-coloured brown skin. She looked a drab. Flory would not face her, but stood looking sullenly through the open doorway to the veranda.

'What do you mean by coming back like this? Why did you not go home to your village?'

'I am staying in Kyauktada, at my cousin's house. How can I go back to my village after what has happened?'

'And what do you mean by sending men to demand money from me? How

can you want more money already, when I gave you a hundred rupees only a
week ago?'

'How can I go back?' she repeated, ignoring what he had said. Her voice rose
so sharply that he turned round. She was standing very upright, sullen, with
her black brows drawn together and her lips pouted.

'Why cannot you go back?'

'After that! After what you have done to me!'

Suddenly she burst into a furious tirade. Her voice had risen to the
hysterical graceless scream of the bazaar women when they quarrel.

'How can I go back, to be jeered at and pointed at by those low, stupid
peasants whom I despise? I who have been a *bo-kadaw,* a white man's wife, to
go home to my father's house, and shake the paddy basket with old hags and
women who are too ugly to find husbands! Ah, what shame, what shame! Two
years I was your wife, you loved me and cared for me, and then without
warning, without reason, you drove me from your door like a dog. And I must
go back to my village, with no money, with all my jewels and silk *longyis* gone,
and the people will point and say, "There is Ma Hla May who thought herself
cleverer than the rest of us. And behold! her white man has treated her as they
always do." I am ruined, ruined! What man will marry me after I have lived
two years in your house? You have taken my youth from me. Ah, what shame,
what shame!'

He could not look at her; he stood helpless, pale, hang-dog. Every word she
said was justified, and how tell her that he could do no other than he had done?
How tell her that it would have been an outrage, a sin, to continue as her lover?
He almost cringed from her, and the birthmark stood on his yellow face like a
splash of ink. He said flatly, turning instinctively to money—for money had
never failed with Ma Hla May:

'I will give you money. You shall have the fifty rupees you asked me
for—more later. I have no more till next month.'

This was true. The hundred rupees he had given her, and what he had spent
on clothes, had taken most of his ready money. To his dismay she burst into a
loud wail. Her white mask puckered up and the tears sprang quickly out and
coursed down her cheeks. Before he could stop her she had fallen on her knees
in front of him, and she was bowing, touching the floor with her forehead in the
'full' shiko of utter abasement.

'Get up, get up!' he exclaimed. The shameful, abject shiko, neck bent, body
doubled up as though inviting a blow, always horrified him. 'I can't bear that.
Get up this instant.'

She wailed again, and made an attempt to clasp his ankles. He stepped
backwards hurriedly.

'Get up, now, and stop that dreadful noise. I don't know what you are crying
about.'

She did not get up, but only rose to her knees and wailed at him anew. 'Why
do you offer me money? Do you think it is only for money that I have come
back? Do you think that when you have driven me from your door like a dog it
is only because of money that I care?'

'Get up,' he repeated. He had moved several paces away, lest she should seize him. 'What do you want if it is not money?'

'Why do you hate me?' she wailed. 'What harm have I done you? I stole your cigarette-case, but you were not angry at that. You are going to marry this white woman, I know it, everyone knows it. But what does it matter, why must you turn me away? Why do you hate me?'

'I don't hate you. I can't explain. Get up, please get up.'

She was weeping quite shamelessly now. After all, she was hardly more than a child. She looked at him through her tears, anxiously, studying him for a sign of mercy. Then, a dreadful thing, she stretched herself at full length, flat on her face.

'Get up, get up!' he cried out in English. 'I can't bear that—it's too abominable!'

She did not get up, but crept, wormlike, right across the floor to his feet. Her body made a broad ribbon on the dusty floor. She lay prostrate in front of him, face hidden, arms extended, as though before a god's altar.

'Master, master,' she whimpered, 'will you not forgive me? This once, only this once! Take Ma Hla May back. I will be your slave, lower than your slave. Anything sooner than turn me away.'

She had wound her arms round his ankles, actually was kissing his toes. He stood looking down at her with his hands in his pockets, helpless. Flo came ambling into the room, walked to where Ma Hla May lay and sniffed at her *longyi*. She wagged her tail vaguely, recognizing the smell. Flory could not endure it. He bent down and took Ma Hla May by the shoulders, lifting her to her knees.

'Stand up, now,' he said. 'It hurts me to see you like this. I will do what I can for you. What is the use of crying?'

Instantly she cried out in renewed hope: 'Then you will take me back? Oh, master, take Ma Hla May back! No one need ever know. I will stay here when that white woman comes, she will think I am one of the servants' wives. Will you not take me back?'

'I cannot. It's impossible,' he said, turning away again.

She heard finality in his tone, and uttered a harsh, ugly cry. She bent forward again in a shiko, beating her forehead against the floor. It was dreadful. And what was more dreadful than all, what hurt in his breast, was the utter gracelessness, the lowness of the emotion beneath those entreaties. For in all this there was not a spark of love for him. If she wept and grovelled it was only for the position she had once had as his mistress, the idle life, the rich clothes and dominion over servants. There was something pitiful beyond words in that. Had she loved him he could have driven her from his door with far less compunction. No sorrows are so bitter as those that are without a trace of nobility. He bent down and picked her up in his arms.

'Listen, Ma Hla May,' he said; 'I do not hate you, you have done me no evil. It is I who have wronged you. But there is no help for it now. You must go home, and later I will send you money. If you like you shall start a shop in the bazaar. You are young. This will not matter to you when you have money and can find yourself a husband.'

'I am ruined!' she wailed again. 'I shall kill myself. I shall jump off the jetty into the river. How can I live after this disgrace?'

He was holding her in his arms, almost caressing her. She was clinging close to him, her face hidden against his shirt, her body shaking with sobs. The scent of sandalwood floated into his nostrils. Perhaps even now she thought that with her arms around him and her body against his she could renew her power over him. He disentangled himself gently, and then, seeing that she did not fall on her knees again, stood apart from her.

'That is enough. You must go now. And look, I will give you the fifty rupees I promised you.'

He dragged his tin uniform case from under the bed and took out five ten-rupee notes. She stowed them silently in the bosom of her *ingyi*. Her tears had ceased flowing quite suddenly. Without speaking she went into the bathroom for a moment, and came out with her face washed to its natural brown, and her hair and dress rearranged. She looked sullen, but not hysterical any longer.

'For the last time, *thakin*: you will not take me back? That is your last word?'

'Yes. I cannot help it.'

'Then I am going, *thakin*.'

'Very well. God go with you.'

Leaning against the wooden pillar of the veranda, he watched her walk down the path in the strong sunlight. She walked very upright, with bitter offence in the carriage of her back and head. It was true what she had said, he had robbed her of her youth. His knees were trembling uncontrollably. Ko S'la came behind him, silent-footed. He gave a little deprecating cough to attract Flory's attention.

'What's the matter now?'

'The holy one's breakfast is getting cold.'

'I don't want any breakfast. Get me something to drink—gin.'

Where is the life that late I led?

# 14

Like long curved needles threading through embroidery, the two canoes that carried Flory and Elizabeth threaded their way up the creek that led inland from the eastern bank of the Irrawaddy. It was the day of the shooting trip—a short afternoon trip, for they could not stay a night in the jungle together. They were to shoot for a couple of hours in the comparative cool of the evening, and be back at Kyauktada in time for dinner.

The canoes, each hollowed out of a single tree-trunk, glided swiftly, hardly rippling the dark brown water. Water hyacinth with profuse spongy foliage and blue flowers had choked the stream so that the channel was only a winding ribbon four feet wide. The light filtered, greenish, through interlacing boughs. Sometimes one could hear parrots scream overhead, but no wild creatures showed themselves, except once a snake that swam hurriedly away and disappeared among the water hyacinth.

'How long before we get to the village?' Elizabeth called back to Flory. He was in a larger canoe behind, together with Flo and Ko S'la, paddled by a wrinkly old woman dressed in rags.

'How far, grandmama?' Flory asked the canoe-woman.

The old woman took her cigar out of her mouth and rested her paddle on her knees to think. 'The distance a man can shout,' she said after reflection.

'About half a mile,' Flory translated.

They had come two miles. Elizabeth's back was aching. The canoes were liable to upset at a careless moment, and you had to sit bolt upright on the narrow backless seat, keeping your feet as well as possible out of the bilge, with dead prawns in it, that sagged to and fro at the bottom. The Burman who paddled Elizabeth was sixty years old, half naked, leaf-brown, with a body as perfect as that of a young man. His face was battered, gentle and humorous. His black cloud of hair, finer than that of most Burmans, was knotted loosely over one ear, with a wisp or two tumbling across his cheek. Elizabeth was nursing her uncle's gun across her knees. Flory had offered to take it, but she had refused; in reality, the feel of it delighted her so much that she could not bring herself to give it up. She had never had a gun in her hand until today. She was wearing a rough skirt with brogue shoes and a silk shirt like a man's, and she knew that with her Terai hat they looked well on her. She was very happy, in spite of her aching back and the hot sweat that tickled her face, and the large, speckled mosquitoes that hummed round her ankles.

The stream narrowed and the beds of water hyacinth gave place to steep banks of glistening mud, like chocolate. Rickety thatched huts leaned far out over the stream, their piles driven into its bed. A naked boy was standing between two of the huts, flying a green beetle on a piece of thread like a kite. He yelled at the sight of the Europeans, whereat more children appeared from nowhere. The old Burman guided the canoe to a jetty made of a single palm-trunk laid in the mud—it was covered with barnacles and so gave foothold—and sprang out and helped Elizabeth ashore. The others followed with the bags and cartridges, and Flo, as she always did on these occasions, fell into the mud and sank as deep as the shoulder. A skinny old gentleman wearing a magenta *paso*, with a mole on his cheek from which four yard-long grey hairs sprouted, came forward shikoing and cuffing the heads of the children who had gathered round the jetty.

'The village headman,' Flory said.

The old man led the way to his house, walking ahead with an extraordinary crouching gait, like a letter L upside down—the result of rheumatism combined with the constant shikoing needed in a minor Government official. A mob of children marched rapidly after the Europeans, and more and more dogs, all yapping and causing Flo to shrink against Flory's heels. In the

doorway of every hut clusters of moonlike, rustic faces gaped at the
'Ingaleikma'. The village was darkish under the shade of broad leaves. In the
rains the creek would flood, turning the lower parts of the village into a squalid
wooden Venice where the villagers stepped from their front doors into their
canoes.

The headman's house was a little bigger than the others, and it had a
corrugated iron roof, which, in spite of the intolerable din it made during the
rains, was the pride of the headman's life. He had foregone the building of a
pagoda, and appreciably lessened his chances of Nirvana, to pay for it. He
hastened up the steps and gently kicked in the ribs a youth who was lying
asleep on the veranda. Then he turned and shikoed again to the Europeans,
asking them to come inside.

'Shall we go in?' Flory said. 'I expect we shall have to wait half an hour.'

'Couldn't you tell him to bring some chairs out on the veranda?' Elizabeth
said. After her experience in Li Yeik's house she had privately decided that she
would never go inside a native house again, if she could help it.

There was a fuss inside the house, and the headman, the youth and some
women dragged forth two chairs decorated in an extraordinary manner with
red hibiscus flowers, and also some begonias growing in kerosene tins. It was
evident that a sort of double throne had been prepared within for the
Europeans. When Elizabeth had sat down the headman reappeared with a
teapot, a bunch of very long, bright green bananas, and six coal-black cheroots.
But when he had poured her out a cup of tea Elizabeth shook her head, for the
tea looked, if possible, worse even than Li Yeik's.

The headman looked abashed and rubbed his nose. He turned to Flory and
asked him whether the young *thakin-ma* would like some milk in her tea. He
had heard that Europeans drank milk in their tea. The villages should, if it
were desired, catch a cow and milk it. However, Elizabeth still refused the tea;
but she was thirsty, and she asked Flory to send for one of the bottles of soda-
water that Ko S'la had brought in his bag. Seeing this, the headman retired,
feeling guiltily that his preparations had been insufficient, and left the veranda
to the Europeans.

Elizabeth was still nursing her gun on her knees, while Flory leaned against
the veranda rail pretending to smoke one of the headman's cheroots. Elizabeth
was pining for the shooting to begin. She plied Flory with innumerable
questions.

'How soon can we start out? Do you think we've got enough cartridges?
How many beaters shall we take? Oh, I do so hope we have some luck! You do
think we'll get something, don't you?'

'Nothing wonderful, probably. We're bound to get a few pigeons, and
perhaps jungle fowl. They're out of season, but it doesn't matter shooting the
cocks. They say there's a leopard round here, that killed a bullock almost in the
village last week.'

'Oh, a leopard! How lovely if we could shoot it!'

'It's very unlikely, I'm afraid. The only rule with this shooting in Burma is
to hope for nothing. It's invariably disappointing. The jungles teem with

game, but as often as not you don't even get a chance to fire your gun.'

'Why is that?'

'The jungle is so thick. An animal may be five yards away and quite invisible, and half the time they manage to dodge back past the beaters. Even when you see them it's only for a flash of a second. And again, there's water everywhere, so that no animal is tied down to one particular spot. A tiger, for instance, will roam hundreds of miles if it suits him. And with all the game there is, they need never come back to a kill if there's anything suspicious about it. Night after night, when I was a boy, I've sat up over horrible stinking dead cows, waiting for tigers that never came.'

Elizabeth wriggled her shoulder-blades against the chair. It was a movement that she made sometimes when she was deeply pleased. She loved Flory, really loved him, when he talked like this. The most trivial scrap of information about shooting thrilled her. If only he would always talk about shooting, instead of about books and Art and that mucky poetry! In a sudden burst of admiration she decided that Flory was really quite a handsome man, in his way. He looked so splendidly manly, with his *pagri*-cloth shirt open at the throat, and his shorts and puttees and shooting boots! And his face, lined, sunburned, like a soldier's face. He was standing with his birthmarked cheek away from her. She pressed him to go on talking.

'*Do* tell me some more about tiger-shooting. It's so awfully interesting!'

He described the shooting, years ago, of a mangy old man-eater who had killed one of his coolies. The wait in the mosquito-ridden *machan*; the tiger's eyes approaching through the dark jungle, like great green lanterns; the panting, slobbering noise as he devoured the coolie's body, tied to a stake below. Flory told it all perfunctorily enough—did not the proverbial Anglo-Indian bore always talk about tiger-shooting?—but Elizabeth wriggled her shoulders delightedly once more. He did not realize how such talk as this reassured her and made up for all the times when he had bored her and disquieted her. Six shock-headed youths came down the path, carrying *dahs* over their shoulders, and headed by a stringy but active old man with grey hair. They halted in front of the headman's house, and one of them uttered a hoarse whoop, whereat the headman appeared and explained that these were the beaters. They were ready to start now, if the young *thakin-ma* did not find it too hot.

They set out. The side of the village away from the creek was protected by a hedge of cactus six feet high and twelve thick. One went up a narrow lane of cactus, then along a rutted, dusty bullock-cart track, with bamboos as tall as flagstaffs growing densely on either side. The beaters marched rapidly ahead in single file, each with his broad *dah* laid along his forearm. The old hunter was marching just in front of Elizabeth. His *longyi* was hitched up like a loin-cloth, and his meagre thighs were tattooed with dark blue patterns, so intricate that he might have been wearing drawers of blue lace. A bamboo the thickness of a man's wrist had fallen and hung across the path. The leading beater severed it with an upward flick of his *dah*; the prisoned water gushed out of it with a diamond-flash. After half a mile they reached the open fields, and everyone was sweating, for they had walked fast and the sun was savage.

'That's where we're going to shoot, over there,' Flory said.

He pointed across the stubble, a wide dust-coloured plain, cut up into patches of an acre or two by mud boundaries. It was horribly flat, and lifeless save for the snowy egrets. At the far edge a jungle of great trees rose abruptly, like a dark green cliff. The beaters had gone across to a small tree like a hawthorn twenty yards away. One of them was on his knees, shikoing to the tree and gabbling, while the old hunter poured a bottle of some cloudy liquid on to the ground. The others stood looking on with serious, bored faces, like men in church.

'What *are* those men doing?' Elizabeth said.

'Only sacrificing to the local gods. Nats, they call them—a kind of dryad. They're praying to him to bring us good luck.'

The hunter came back and in a cracked voice explained that they were to beat a small patch of scrub over to the right before proceeding to the main jungle. Apparently the Nat had counselled this. The hunter directed Flory and Elizabeth where to stand, pointing with his *dah*. The six beaters plunged into the scrub; they would make a detour and beat back towards the paddy-fields. There were some bushes of the wild rose thirty yards from the jungle's edge, and Flory and Elizabeth took cover behind one of these, while Ko S'la squatted down behind another bush a little distance away, holding Flo's collar and stroking her to keep her quiet. Flory always sent Ko S'la to a distance when he was shooting, for he had an irritating trick of clicking his tongue if a shot was missed. Presently there was a far-off echoing sound—a sound of tapping and strange hollow cries; the beat had started. Elizabeth at once began trembling so uncontrollably that she could not keep her gun-barrel still. A wonderful bird, a little bigger than a thrush, with grey wings and body of blazing scarlet, broke from the trees and came towards them with a dipping flight. The tapping and the cries came nearer. One of the bushes at the jungle's edge waved violently—some large animal was emerging. Elizabeth raised her gun and tried to steady it. But it was only a naked yellow beater, *dah* in hand. He saw that he had emerged and shouted to the others to join him.

Elizabeth lowered her gun. 'What's happened?'

'Nothing. The beat's over.'

'So there was nothing there!' she cried in bitter disappointment.

'Never mind, one never gets anything the first beat. We'll have better luck next time.'

They crossed the lumpy stubble, climbing over the mud boundaries that divided the fields, and took up their position opposite the high green wall of the jungle. Elizabeth had already learned how to load her gun. This time the beat had hardly started when Ko S'la whistled sharply.

'Look out!' Flory cried. 'Quick, here they come!'

A flight of green pigeons were dashing towards them at incredible speed, forty yards up. They were like a handful of catapulted stones whirling through the sky. Elizabeth was helpless with excitement. For a moment she could not move, then she flung her barrel into the air, somewhere in the direction of the birds, and tugged violently at the trigger. Nothing happened—she was pulling at the trigger-guard. Just as the birds passed overhead she found the triggers and pulled both of them simultaneously. There was a deafening roar and she was thrown backwards a pace with her collar-bone almost broken. She had fired thirty yards behind the birds. At the same moment she saw Flory turn and level his gun. Two of the pigeons, suddenly checked in their flight, swirled over and dropped to the ground like arrows. Ko S'la yelled, and he and Flo raced after them.

'Look out!' said Flory, 'here's an imperial pigeon. Let's have him!'

A large heavy bird, with flight much slower than the others, was flapping overhead. Elizabeth did not care to fire after her previous failure. She watched Flory thrust a cartridge into the breech and raise his gun, and the white plume of smoke leapt up from the muzzle. The bird planed heavily down, his wing broken. Flo and Ko S'la came running excitedly up, Flo with the big imperial pigeon in her mouth, and Ko S'la grinning and producing two green pigeons from his Kachin bag.

Flory took one of the little green corpses to show to Elizabeth. 'Look at it. Aren't they lovely things? The most beautiful bird in Asia.'

Elizabeth touched its smooth feathers with her finger-tip. It filled her with bitter envy, because she had not shot it. And yet it was curious, but she felt almost an adoration for Flory now that she had seen how he could shoot.

'Just look at its breast-feathers; like a jewel. It's murder to shoot them. The Burmese say that when you kill one of these birds they vomit, meaning to say, "Look, here is all I possess, and I've taken nothing of yours. Why do you kill me?" I've never seen one do it, I must admit.'

'Are they good to eat?'

'Very. Even so, I always feel it's a shame to kill them.'

'I wish I could do it like you do!' she said enviously.

'It's only a knack, you'll soon pick it up. You know how to hold your gun, and that's more than most people do when they start.'

However, at the next two beats, Elizabeth could hit nothing. She had learned not to fire both barrels at once, but she was too paralysed with excitement ever to take aim. Flory shot several more pigeons, and a small bronze-wing dove with back as green as verdigris. The jungle fowl were too cunning to show themselves, though one could hear them cluck-clucking all round, and once or twice the sharp trumpet-call of a cock. They were getting deeper into the jungle now. The light was greyish, with dazzling patches of sunlight. Whichever way one looked one's view was shut in by the multitudinous ranks of trees, and the tangled bushes and creepers that struggled round their bases like the sea round the piles of a pier. It was so dense, like a bramble bush extending mile after mile, that one's eyes were oppressed by it. Some of the creepers were huge, like serpents. Flory and Elizabeth struggled along narrow game-tracks, up slippery banks, thorns tearing at their clothes. Both their shirts were drenched with sweat. It was stifling hot, with a scent of crushed leaves. Sometimes for minutes together invisible cicadas would keep up a shrill, metallic pinging like the twanging of a steel guitar, and then, by stopping, make a silence that startled one.

As they were walking to the fifth beat they came to a great peepul tree in which, high up, one could hear imperial pigeons cooing. It was a sound like the far-off lowing of cows. One bird fluttered out and perched alone on the topmost bough, a small greyish shape.

'Try a sitting shot,' Flory said to Elizabeth. 'Get your sight on him and pull off without waiting. Don't shut your left eye.'

Elizabeth raised her gun, which had begun trembling as usual. The beaters halted in a group to watch, and some of them could not refrain from clicking their tongues; they thought it queer and rather shocking to see a woman handle a gun. With a violent effort of will Elizabeth kept her gun still for a second, and pulled the trigger. She did not hear the shot; one never does when it has gone home. The bird seemed to jump upwards from the bough, then down it came, tumbling over and over, and stuck in a fork ten yards up. One of the beaters laid down his *dah* and glanced appraisingly at the tree; then he walked to a great creeper, thick as a man's thigh and twisted like a stick of barley sugar, that hung far out from a bough. He ran up the creeper as easily as though it had been a ladder, walked upright along the broad bough, and brought the pigeon to the ground. He put it limp and warm into Elizabeth's hand.

She could hardly give it up, the feel of it so ravished her. She could have kissed it, hugged it to her breast. All the men, Flory and Ko S'la and the beaters, smiled at one another to see her fondling the dead bird. Reluctantly, she gave it to Ko S'la to put in the bag. She was conscious of an extraordinary desire to fling her arms round Flory's neck and kiss him; and in some way it was the killing of the pigeon that made her feel this.

After the fifth beat the hunter explained to Flory that they must cross a clearing that was used for growing pineapples, and would beat another patch of jungle beyond. They came out into sunlight, dazzling after the jungle gloom. The clearing was an oblong of an acre or two hacked out of the jungle like a patch mown in long grass, with the pineapples, prickly cactus-like plants, growing in rows, almost smothered by weeds. A low hedge of thorns divided the field in the middle. They had nearly crossed the field when there was a sharp cock-a-doodle-doo from beyond the hedge.

'Oh, listen!' said Elizabeth, stopping. 'Was that a jungle cock?'

'Yes. They come out to feed about this time.'

'Couldn't we go and shoot him?'

'We'll have a try if you like. They're cunning beggars. Look, we'll stalk up the hedge until we get opposite where he is. We'll have to go without making a sound.'

He sent Ko S'la and the beaters on, and the two of them skirted the field and crept along the hedge. They had to bend double to keep themselves out of sight. Elizabeth was in front. The hot sweat trickled down her face, tickling her upper lip, and her heart was knocking violently. She felt Flory touch her heel from behind. Both of them stood upright and looked over the hedge together.

Ten yards away a little cock the size of a bantam, was pecking vigorously at the ground. He was beautiful, with his long silky neck-feathers, bunched comb and arching, laurel-green tail. There were six hens with him, smaller brown birds, with diamond-shaped feathers like snake-scales on their backs. All this Elizabeth and Flory saw in the space of a second, then with a squawk and a whirr the birds were up and flying like bullets for the jungle. Instantly, automatically as it seemed, Elizabeth raised her gun and fired. It was one of those shots where there is no aiming, no consciousness of the gun in one's hand, when one's mind seems to fly behind the charge and drive it to the mark. She knew the bird was doomed even before she pulled the trigger. He tumbled, showered feathers thirty yards away. 'Good shot, good shot!' cried Flory. In their excitement both of them dropped their guns, broke through the thorn hedge and raced side by side to where the bird lay.

'Good shot!' Flory repeated, as excited as she. 'By Jove, I've never seen anyone kill a flying bird their first day, never! You got your gun off like lightning. It's marvellous!'

They were kneeling face to face with the dead bird between them. With a shock they discovered that their hands, his right and her left, were clasped tightly together. They had run to the place hand-in-hand without noticing it.

A sudden stillness came on them both, a sense of something momentous that must happen. Flory reached across and took her other hand. It came yieldingly, willingly. For a moment they knelt with their hands clasped together. The sun blazed upon them and the warmth breathed out of their bodies; they seemed to be floating upon clouds of heat and joy. He took her by the upper arms to draw her towards him.

Then suddenly he turned his head away and stood up, pulling Elizabeth to her feet. He let go of her arms. He had remembered his birthmark. He dared not do it. Not here, not in daylight! The snub it invited was too terrible. To cover the awkwardness of the moment he bent down and picked up the jungle cock.

'It was splendid,' he said. 'You don't need any teaching. You can shoot already. We'd better get on to the next beat.'

They had just crossed the hedge and picked up their guns when there was a series of shouts from the edge of the jungle. Two of the beaters were running towards them with enormous leaps, waving their arms wildly in the air.

'What is it?' Elizabeth said.

'I don't know. They've seen some animal or other. Something good, by the look of them.'

'Oh, hurrah! Come on!'

They broke into a run and hurried across the field, breaking through the pineapples and the stiff prickly weeds. Ko S'la and five of the beaters were standing in a knot all talking at once, and the other two were beckoning excitedly to Flory and Elizabeth. As they came up they saw in the middle of the group an old woman who was holding up her ragged *longyi* with one hand and gesticulating with a big cigar in the other. Elizabeth could hear some word that sounded like 'Char' repeated over and over again.

'What is it they're saying?' she said.

The beaters came crowding round Flory, all talking eagerly and pointing into the jungle. After a few questions he waved his hand to silence them and turned to Elizabeth:

'I say, here's a bit of luck! This old girl was coming through the jungle, and she says that at the sound of the shot you fired just now, she saw a leopard run across the path. These fellows know where he's likely to hide. If we're quick they may be able to surround him before he sneaks away, and drive him out. Shall we try it?'

'Oh, do let's! Oh, what awful fun! How lovely, how lovely if we could get that leopard!'

'You understand it's dangerous? We'll keep close together and it'll probably be all right, but it's never absolutely safe on foot. Are you ready for that?'

'Oh, of course, of course! I'm not frightened. Oh, do let's be quick and start!'

'One of you come with us, and show us the way,' he said to the beaters. 'Ko S'la, put Flo on the leash and go with the others. She'll never keep quiet with us. We'll have to hurry,' he added to Elizabeth.

Ko S'la and the beaters hurried off along the edge of the jungle. They would strike in and begin beating farther up. The other beater, the same youth who had climbed the tree after the pigeon, dived into the jungle, Flory and Elizabeth following. With short rapid steps, almost running, he led them through a labyrinth of game-tracks. The bushes trailed so low that sometimes one had almost to crawl, and creepers hung across the path like trip-wires. The ground was dusty and silent underfoot. At some landmark in the jungle the beater halted, pointed to the ground as a sign that this spot would do, and put his finger on his lips to enjoin silence. Flory took four SG cartridges from his pockets and took Elizabeth's gun to load it silently.

There was a faint rustling behind them, and they all started. A nearly naked youth with a pellet-bow, come goodness knows whence, had parted the bushes. He looked at the beater, shook his head and pointed up the path. There was a dialogue of signs between the two youths, then the beater seemed to agree. Without speaking all four stole forty yards along the path, round a bend, and halted again. At the same moment a frightful pandemonium of yells, punctuated by barks from Flo, broke out a few hundred yards away.

Elizabeth felt the beater's hand on her shoulder, pushing her downwards. They all four squatted down under cover of a prickly bush, the Europeans in front, the Burmans behind. In the distance there was such a tumult of yells and the rattle of *dahs* against tree-trunks that one could hardly believe six men could make so much noise. The beaters were taking good care that the leopard should not turn back upon them. Elizabeth watched some large, pale yellow ants marching like soldiers over the thorns of the bush. One fell on to her hand and crawled up her forearm. She dared not move to brush it away. She was praying silently, 'Please God, let the leopard come! Oh please, God, let the leopard come!'

There was a sudden loud pattering on the leaves. Elizabeth raised her gun, but Flory shook his head sharply and pushed the barrel down again. A jungle fowl scuttled across the path with long noisy strides.

The yells of the beaters seemed hardly to come any closer, and this end of the jungle the silence was like a pall. The ant on Elizabeth's arm bit her painfully and dropped to the ground. A dreadful despair had begun to form in her heart; the leopard was not coming, he had slipped away somewhere, they had lost him. She almost wished they had never heard of the leopard, the disappointment was so agonizing. Then she felt the beater pinch her elbow. He was craning his face forward, his smooth, dull yellow cheek only a few inches from her own; she could smell the coco-nut oil in his hair. His coarse lips were puckered as in a whistle; he had heard something. Then Flory and Elizabeth heard it too, the faintest whisper, as though some creature of air were gliding through the jungle, just brushing the ground with its foot. At the same moment the leopard's head and shoulders emerged from the undergrowth, fifteen yards down the path.

He stopped with his forepaws on the path. They could see his low, flat-eared head, his bare eye-tooth and his thick, terrible forearm. In the shadow he did not look yellow but grey. He was listening intently. Elizabeth saw Flory spring to his feet, raise his gun and pull the trigger instantly. The shot roared, and almost simultaneously there was a heavy crash as the brute dropped flat in the weeds. 'Look out!' Flory cried, 'he's not done for!' He fired again, and there was a fresh thump as the shot went home. The leopard gasped. Flory threw open his gun and felt in his pocket for a cartridge, then flung all his cartridges on to the path and fell on his knees, searching rapidly among them.

'Damn and blast it!' he cried. 'There isn't a single SG among them. Where in hell did I put them?'

The leopard had disappeared as he fell. He was thrashing about in the undergrowth like a great, wounded snake, and crying out with a snarling, sobbing noise, savage and pitiful. The noise seemed to be coming nearer. Every cartridge Flory turned up had 6 or 8 marked on the end. The rest of the large-shot cartridges had, in fact, been left with Ko S'la. The crashing and snarling were now hardly five yards away, but they could see nothing, the jungle was so thick.

The two Burmans were crying out 'Shoot! Shoot! Shoot!' The sound of 'Shoot! Shoot!' got farther away—they were skipping for the nearest climbable trees. There was a crash in the undergrowth so close that it shook the bush by which Elizabeth was standing.

'By God, he's almost on us!' Flory said. 'We must turn him somehow. Let fly at the sound.'

Elizabeth raised her gun. Her knees were knocking like castanets, but her hand was as steady as stone. She fired rapidly, once, twice. The crashing noise receded. The leopard was crawling away, crippled but swift, and still invisible.

'Well done! You've scared him,' Flory said.

'But he's getting away! He's getting away!' Elizabeth cried, dancing about in agitation. She made to follow him. Flory jumped to his feet and pulled her back.

'No fear! You stay here. Wait!'

He slipped two of the small-shot cartridges into his gun and ran after the sound of the leopard. For a moment Elizabeth could not see either beast or man, then they reappeared in a bare patch thirty yards away. The leopard was writhing along on his belly, sobbing as he went. Flory levelled his gun and fired at four yards' distance. The leopard jumped like a cushion when one hits it, then rolled over, curled up and lay still. Flory poked the body with his gun-barrel. It did not stir.

'It's all right, he's done for,' he called. 'Come and have a look at him.'

The two Burmans jumped down from their tree, and they and Elizabeth went across to where Flory was standing. The leopard—it was a male—was lying curled up with his head between his forepaws. He looked much smaller than he had looked alive; he looked rather pathetic, like a dead kitten. Elizabeth's knees were still quivering. She and Flory stood looking down at the leopard, close together, but not clasping hands this time.

It was only a moment before Ko S'la and the others came up, shouting with glee. Flo gave one sniff at the dead leopard, then down went her tail and she bolted fifty yards, whimpering. She could not be induced to come near him again. Everyone squatted down round the leopard and gazed at him. They stroked his beautiful white belly, soft as a hare's, and squeezed his broad pugs to bring out the claws, and pulled back his black lips to examine the fangs. Presently two of the beaters cut down a tall bamboo and slung the leopard upon it by his paws, with his long tail trailing down, and then they marched back to the village in triumph. There was no talk of further shooting, though the light still held. They were all, including the Europeans, too anxious to get home and boast of what they had done.

Flory and Elizabeth walked side by side across the stubble field. The others were thirty yards ahead with the guns and the leopard, and Flo was slinking after them a long way in the rear. The sun was going down beyond the Irrawaddy. The light shone level across the field, gilding the stubble stalks, and striking into their faces with a yellow, gentle beam. Elizabeth's shoulder was almost touching Flory's as they walked. The sweat that had drenched their shirts had dried again. They did not talk much. They were happy with that inordinate happiness that comes of exhaustion and achievement, and with which nothing else in life—no joy of either the body or the mind—is even able to be compared.

'The leopard skin is yours,' Flory said as they approached the village.

'Oh, but you shot him!'

'Never mind, you stick to the skin. By Jove, I wonder how many of the women in this country would have kept their heads like you did! I can just see them screaming and fainting. I'll get the skin cured for you in Kyauktada jail. There's a convict there who can cure skins as soft as velvet. He's doing a seven-year sentence, so he's had time to learn the job.'

'Oh well, thanks awfully.'

No more was said for the present. Later, when they had washed off the sweat and dirt, and were fed and rested, they would meet again at the Club. They made no rendezvous, but it was understood between them that they would meet. Also, it was understood that Flory would ask Elizabeth to marry him, though nothing was said about this either.

At the village Flory paid the beaters eight annas each, superintended the skinning of the leopard, and gave the headman a bottle of beer and two of the imperial pigeons. The skin and skull were packed into one of the canoes. All the whiskers had been stolen, in spite of Ko S'la's efforts to guard them. Some young men of the village carried off the carcass in order to eat the heart and various other organs, the eating of which they believed would make them strong and swift like the leopard.

# 15

When Flory arrived at the Club he found the Lackersteens in an unusually morose mood. Mrs Lackersteen was sitting, as usual, in the best place under the punkah, and was reading the Civil List, the Debrett of Burma. She was in a bad temper with her husband, who had defied her by ordering a 'large peg' as soon as he reached the Club, and was further defying her by reading the *Pink'un*. Elizabeth was alone in the stuffy little library, turning over the pages of an old copy of *Blackwood's*.

Since parting with Flory, Elizabeth had had a very disagreeable adventure. She had come out of her bath and was half-way through dressing for dinner when her uncle had suddenly appeared in her room—pretext, to hear some more about the day's shooting—and begun pinching her leg in a way that simply could not be misunderstood. Elizabeth was horrified. This was her first introduction to the fact that some men are capable of making love to their nieces. We live and learn. Mr Lackersteen had tried to carry the thing off as a joke, but he was too clumsy and too nearly drunk to succeed. It was fortunate that his wife was out of hearing, or there might have been a first-rate scandal.

After this, dinner was an uncomfortable meal. Mr Lackersteen was sulking. What rot it was, the way these women put on airs and prevented you from having a good time! The girl was pretty enough to remind him of the illustrations in *La Vie Parisienne*, and damn it! wasn't he paying for her keep? It was a shame. But for Elizabeth the position was very serious. She was penniless and had no home except her uncle's house. She had come eight thousand miles to stay here. It would be terrible if after only a fortnight her uncle's house were to be made uninhabitable for her.

Consequently, one thing was much surer in her mind than it had been: that if Flory asked her to marry him (and he would, there was little doubt of it), she would say yes. At another time it just possible that she would have decided differently. This afternoon, under the spell of that glorious, exciting, altogether 'lovely' adventure, she had come near to loving Flory; as near as, in his particular case, she was able to come. Yet even after that, perhaps, her doubts would have returned. For there had always been something dubious about Flory; his age, his birthmark, his queer, perverse way of talking—that 'highbrow' talk that was at once unintelligible and disquieting. There had been days when she had even disliked him. But now her uncle's behaviour had turned the scale. Whatever happened she had got to escape from her uncle's house, and that soon. Yes, undoubtedly she would marry Flory when he asked her!

He could see her answer in her face as he came into the library. Her air was gentler, more yielding than he had known it. She was wearing the same lilac-coloured frock that she had worn that first morning when he met her, and the sight of the familiar frock gave him courage. It seemed to bring her nearer to him, taking away the strangeness and the elegance that had sometimes unnerved him.

He picked up the magazine she had been reading and made some remark; for a moment they chattered in the banal way they so seldom managed to avoid. It is strange how the drivelling habits of conversation will persist into almost all moments. Yet even as they chattered they found themselves drifting to the door and then outside, and presently to the big frangipani tree by the tennis court. It was the night of the full moon. Flaring like a white-hot coin, so brilliant that it hurt one's eyes, the moon swam rapidly upwards in a sky of smoky blue, across which drifted a few wisps of yellowish cloud. The stars were all invisible. The croton bushes, by day hideous things like jaundiced laurels, were changed by the moon into jagged black and white designs like fantastic wood-cuts. By the compound fence two Dravidian coolies were walking down the road, transfigured, their white rags gleaming. Through the tepid air the scent streamed from the frangipani trees like some intolerable compound out of a penny-in-the-slot machine.

'Look at the moon, just look at it!' Flory said. 'It's like a white sun. It's brighter than an English winter day.'

Elizabeth looked up into the branches of the frangipani tree, which the moon seemed to have changed into rods of silver. The light lay thick, as though palpable, on everything, crusting the earth and the rough bark of trees like some dazzling salt, and every leaf seemed to bear a freight of solid light, like snow. Even Elizabeth, indifferent to such things, was astonished.

'It's wonderful! You never see moonlight like that at Home. It's so–so–' No adjective except 'bright' presenting itself, she was silent. She had a habit of leaving her sentences unfinished, like Rosa Dartle, though for a different reason.

'Yes, the old moon does her best in this country. How that tree does stink, doesn't it? Beastly, tropical thing! I hate a tree that blooms all the year round, don't you?'

He was talking half abstractedly, to cover the time till the coolies should be out of sight. As they disappeared he put his arm round Elizabeth's shoulder, and then, when she did not start or speak, turned her round and drew her against him. Her head came against his breast, and her short hair grazed his lips. He put his hand under her chin and lifted her face up to meet his. She was not wearing her spectacles.

'You don't mind?'

'No.'

'I mean, you don't mind my—this thing of mine?' he shook his head slightly to indicate the birthmark. He could not kiss her without first asking this question.

'No, no. Of course not.'

A moment after their mouths met he felt her bare arms settle lightly round his neck. They stood pressed together, against the smooth trunk of the frangipani tree, body to body, mouth to mouth, for a minute or more. The sickly scent of the tree came mingling with the scent of Elizabeth's hair. And the scent gave him a feeling of stultification, of remoteness from Elizabeth, even though she was in his arms. All that that alien tree symbolized for him, his exile, the secret, wasted years—it was like an unbridgeable gulf between them. How should he ever make her understand what it was that he wanted of her? He disengaged himself and pressed her shoulders gently against the tree, looking down at her face, which he could see very clearly though the moon was behind her.

'It's useless trying to tell you what you mean to me,' he said. '"What you mean to me!" These blunted phrases! You don't know, you can't know, how much I love you. But I've got to try and tell you. There's so much I must tell you. Had we better go back to the Club? They may come looking for us. We can talk on the veranda.'

'Is my hair very untidy?' she said.

'It's beautiful.'

'But has it got untidy? Smooth it for me, would you, please?'

She bent her head towards him, and he smoothed the short, cool locks with his hand. The way she bent her head to him gave him a curious feeling of intimacy, far more intimate than the kiss, as though he had already been her husband. Ah, he must have her, that was certain! Only by marrying her could his life be salvaged. In a moment he would ask her. They walked slowly through the cotton bushes and back to the Club, his arm still round her shoulder.

'We can talk on the veranda,' he repeated. 'Somehow, we've never really talked, you and I. My God, how I've longed all these years for somebody to talk to! How I could talk to you, interminably, interminably! That sounds boring. I'm afraid it will be boring. I must ask you to put up with it for a little while.'

She made a sound of remonstrance at the word 'boring'.

'No, it is boring, I know that. We Anglo-Indians are always looked on as bores. And we *are* bores. But we can't help it. You see, there's—how shall I say?—a demon inside us driving us to talk. We walk about under a load of memories which we long to share and somehow never can. It's the price we pay for coming to this country.'

They were fairly safe from interruption on the side veranda, for there was no door opening directly upon it. Elizabeth had sat down with her arms on the little wicker table, but Flory remained strolling back and forth, with his hands in his coatpockets, stepping into the moonlight that streamed beneath the eastern eaves of the veranda, and back into the shadows.

'I said just now that I loved you. Love! The word's been used till it's meaningless. But let me try to explain. This afternoon when you were there shooting with me, I thought, my God! here at last is somebody who can share my life with me, but really share it, really *live* it with me—do you see—'

He was going to ask her to marry him—indeed, he had intended to ask her without more delay. But the words were not spoken yet; instead, he found himself talking egoistically on and on. He could not help it. It was so important that she should understand something of what his life in this country had been; that she should grasp the nature of the loneliness that he wanted her to nullify. And it was so devilishly difficult to explain. It is devilish to suffer from a pain that is all but nameless. Blessed are they who are stricken only with classifiable diseases! Blessed are the poor, the sick, the crossed in love, for at least other people know what is the matter with them and will listen to their belly-achings with sympathy. But who that has not suffered it understands the pain of exile? Elizabeth watched him as he moved to and fro, in and out of the pool of moonlight that turned his silk coat to silver. Her heart was still knocking from the kiss, and yet her thoughts wandered as he talked. Was he going to ask her to marry him? He was being so slow about it! She was dimly aware that he was saying something about loneliness. Ah, of course! He was telling her about the loneliness she would have to put up with in the jungle, when they were married. He needn't have troubled. Perhaps you did get rather lonely in the jungle sometimes? Miles from anywhere, no cinemas, no dances, no one but each other to talk to, nothing to do in the evenings except read—rather a bore, that. Still, you could have a gramophone. What a difference it would make when those new portable radio sets got out to Burma! She was about to say this when he added:

'Have I made myself at all clear to you? Have you got some picture of the life we live here? The foreignness, the solitude, the melancholy! Foreign trees, foreign flowers, foreign landscapes, foreign faces. It's all as alien as a different planet. But do you see—and it's this that I so want you to understand—do you see, it mightn't be so bad living on a different planet, it might even be the most interesting thing imaginable, if you had even one person to share it with. One person who could see it with eyes something like your own. This country's been a kind of solitary hell to me—it's so to most of us—and yet I tell you it could be a paradise if one weren't alone. Does all this seem quite meaningless?'

He had stopped beside the table, and he picked up her hand. In the half-darkness he could see her face only as a pale oval, like a flower, but by the feeling of her hand he knew instantly that she had not understood a word of what he was saying. How should she, indeed? It was so futile, this meandering talk! He would say to her at once, Will you marry me? Was there not a lifetime to talk in? He took her other hand and drew her gently to her feet.

'Forgive me all this rot I've been talking.'

'It's all right,' she murmured indistinctly, expecting that he was about to kiss her.

'No, it's rot talking like that. Some things will go into words, some won't.

Besides, it was an impertinence to go belly-aching on and on about myself. But I was trying to lead up to something. Look, this is what I wanted to say. Will–'

'*Eliz*-a-beth!'

It was Mrs Lackersteen's high-pitched, plaintive voice, calling from within the Club.

'Elizabeth? Where are you, Elizabeth?'

Evidently she was near the front door–would be on the veranda in a moment. Flory pulled Elizabeth against him. They kissed hurriedly. He released her, only holding her hands.

'Quickly, there's just time. Answer me this. Will you–'

But that sentence never got any further. At the same moment something extraordinary happened under his feet–the floor was surging and rolling like a sea–he was staggering, then dizzily falling, hitting his upper arm a thump as the floor rushed towards him. As he lay there he found himself jerked violently backwards and forwards as though some enormous beast below were rocking the whole building on its back.

The drunken floor righted itself very suddenly, and Flory sat up, dazed but not much hurt. He dimly noticed Elizabeth sprawling beside him, and screams coming from within the Club. Beyond the gate two Burmans were racing through the moonlight with their long hair streaming behind them. They were yelling at the top of their voices:

'Nga Yin is shaking himself! Nga Yin is shaking himself!'

Flory watched them unintelligently. Who was Nga Yin? Nga is the prefix given to criminals. Nga Yin must be a dacoit. Why was he shaking himself? Then he remembered. Nga Yin was a giant supposed by the Burmese to be buried, like Typhaeus, beneath the crust of the earth. Of course! It was an earthquake.

'An earthquake!' he exclaimed, and he remembered Elizabeth and moved to pick her up. But she was already sitting up, unhurt, and rubbing the back of her head.

'Was that an earthquake?' she said in a rather awed voice.

Mrs Lackersteen's tall form came creeping round the corner of the veranda, clinging to the wall like some elongated lizard. She was exclaiming hysterically:

'Oh dear, an earthquake! Oh, what a dreadful shock! I can't bear it–my heart won't stand it! Oh dear, oh dear! An earthquake!'

Mr Lackersteen tottered after her, with a strange ataxic step caused partly by earth-tremors and partly by gin.

'An earthquake, dammit!' he said.

Flory and Elizabeth slowly picked themselves up. They all went inside, with that queer feeling in the soles of the feet that one has when one steps from a rocking boat on to the shore. The old butler was hurrying from the servants' quarters, thrusting his *pagri* on his head as he came, and a troop of twittering *chokras* after him.

'Earthquake, sir, earthquake!' he bubbled eagerly.

'I should damn well think it was an earthquake,' said Mr Lackersteen as he lowered himself cautiously into a chair. 'Here, get some drinks, butler. By God, I could do with a nip of something after that.'

They all had a nip of something. The butler, shy yet beaming, stood on one leg beside the table, with the tray in his hand. 'Earthquake, sir, *big* earthquake!' he repeated enthusiastically. He was bursting with eagerness to talk; so, for that matter, was everyone else. An extraordinary *joie de vivre* had come over them all as soon as the shaky feeling departed from their legs. An earthquake is such fun when it is over. It is so exhilarating to reflect that you are not, as you well might be, lying dead under a heap of ruins. With one accord they all burst out talking: 'My dear, I've never *had* such a shock—I fell absolutely *flat* on my back—I thought it was a dam' pariah dog scratching itself under the floor—I thought it must be an explosion somewhere—' and so on and so forth; the usual earthquake-chatter. Even the butler was included in the conversation.

'I expect you can remember ever so many earthquakes can't you butler?' said Mrs Lackersteen, quite graciously, for her.

'Oh yes, madam, many earthquakes! 1887, 1899, 1906, 1912—many, many I can remember, madam!'

'The 1912 one was a biggish one,' Flory said.

'Oh, sir, but 1906 was bigger! Very bad shock, sir! And big heathen idol in the temple fall down on top of the *thathanabaing,* that is Buddhist bishop, madam, which the Burmese say mean bad omen for failure of paddy crop and foot-and-mouth disease. Also in 1887 my first earthquake I remember, when I was a little *chokra,* and Major Maclagan sahib was lying under the table and promising he sign the teetotal pledge tomorrow morning. He not know it was an earthquake. Also two cows was killed by falling roofs,' etc., etc.

The Europeans stayed in the Club till midnight, and the butler popped into the room as many as half a dozen times, to relate a new anecdote. So far from snubbing him, the Europeans even encouraged him to talk. There is nothing like an earthquake for drawing people together. One more tremor, or perhaps two, and they would have asked the butler to sit down at table with them.

Meanwhile, Flory's proposal went no further. One cannot propose marriage immediately after an earthquake. In any case, he did not see Elizabeth alone for the rest of that evening. But it did not matter, he knew that she was his now. In the morning there would be time enough. On this thought, at peace in his mind, and dog-tired after the long day, he went to bed.

# 16

The vultures in the big pyinkado trees by the cemetery flapped from their dung-whitened branches, steadied themselves on the wing, and climbed by vast spirals into the upper air. It was early, but Flory was out already. He was going down to the Club, to wait until Elizabeth came and then ask her formally to marry him. Some instinct, which he did not understand, prompted him to do it before the other Europeans returned from the jungle.

As he came out of the compound gate he saw that there was a new arrival at Kyauktada. A youth with a long spear like a needle in his hand was cantering across the maidan on a white pony. Some Sikhs, looking like sepoys, ran after him, leading two other ponies, a bay and a chestnut, by the bridle. When he came level with him Flory halted on the road and shouted good morning. He had not recognized the youth, but it is usual in small stations to make strangers welcome. The other saw that he was hailed, wheeled his pony negligently round and brought it to the side of the road. He was a youth of about twenty-five, lank but very straight, and manifestly a cavalry officer. He had one of those rabbit-like faces common among English soldiers, with pale blue eyes and a little triangle of fore-teeth visible between the lips; yet hard, fearless and even brutal in a careless fashion—a rabbit, perhaps, but a tough and martial rabbit. He sat his horse as though he were part of it, and he looked offensively young and fit. His fresh face was tanned to the exact shade that went with his light-coloured eyes, and he was as elegant as a picture with his white buckskin topi and his polo-boots that gleamed like an old meerschaum pipe. Flory felt uncomfortable in his presence from the start.

'How d'you do?' said Flory. 'Have you just arrived?'

'Last night, got in by the late train.' He had a surly, boyish voice. 'I've been sent up here with a company of men to stand by in case your local bad-mashes start any trouble. My name's Verrall—Military Police,' he added, not, however, inquiring Flory's name in return.

'Oh yes. We heard they were sending somebody. Where are you putting up?'

'*Dak* bungalow, for the time being. There was some black beggar staying there when I got in last night—Excise Officer or something. I booted him out. This is a filthy hole, isn't it?' he said with a backward movement of his head, indicating the whole of Kyauktada.

'I suppose it's like the rest of these small stations. Are you staying long?'

'Only a month or so, thank God. Till the rains break. What a rotten maidan you've got here, haven't you? Pity they can't keep this stuff cut,' he added, swishing the dried-up grass with the point of his spear. 'Makes it so hopeless for polo or anything.'

'I'm afraid you won't get any polo here,' Flory said. 'Tennis is the best we can manage. There are only eight of us all told, and most of us spend three-quarters of our time in the jungle.'

'Christ! What a hole!'

After this there was a silence. The tall, bearded Sikhs stood in a group round their horses' heads, eyeing Flory without much favour. It was perfectly clear that Verral was bored with the conversation and wanted to escape. Flory had never in his life felt so completely *de trop*, or so old and shabby. He noticed that Verrall's pony was a beautiful Arab, a mare, with proud neck and arching, plume-like tail; a lovely milk-white thing, worth several thousands of rupees. Verrall had already twitched the bridle to turn away, evidently feeling that he had talked enough for one morning.

'That's a wonderful pony of yours,' Flory said.

'She's not bad, better than these Burma scrubs. I've come out to do a bit of tent-pegging. It's hopeless trying to knock a polo ball about in this muck. Hey, Hira Singh!' he called, and turned his pony away.

The sepoy holding the bay pony handed his bridle to a companion, ran to a spot forty yards away, and fixed a narrow boxwood peg in the ground. Verral took no further notice of Flory. He raised his spear and poised himself as though taking aim at the peg, while the Indians backed their horses out of the way and stood watching critically. With a just perceptible movement Verrall dug his knees into the pony's sides. She bounded forward like a bullet from a catapult. As easily as a centaur the lank, straight youth leaned over in the saddle, lowered his spear and plunged it clean through the peg. One of the Indians muttered gruffly '*Shabash!*' Verrall raised his spear behind him in the orthodox fashion, and then, pulling his horse to a canter, wheeled round and handed the transfixed peg to the sepoy.

Verrall rode twice more at the peg, and hit it each time. It was done with matchless grace and with extraordinary solemnity. The whole group of men, Englishman and Indians, were concentrated upon the business of hitting the peg as though it had been a religious ritual. Flory still stood watching, disregarded–Verrall's face was one of those that are specially constructed for ignoring unwelcome strangers–but from the very fact that he had been snubbed unable to tear himself away. Somehow, Verrall had filled him with a horrible sense of inferiority. He was trying to think of some pretext for renewing the conversation, when he looked up the hillside and saw Elizabeth, in pale blue, coming out of her uncle's gate. She must have seen the third transfixing of the peg. His heart stirred painfully. A thought occurred to him, one of those rash thoughts that usually lead to trouble. He called to Verrall, who was a few yards away from him, and pointed with his stick.

'Do these other two know how to do it?'

Verrall looked over his shoulder with a surly air. He had expected Flory to go away after being ignored.

'What?'

'Can these other two do it?' Flory repeated.

'The chestnut's not bad. Bolts if you let him, though.'

'Let me have a shot at the peg, would you?'

'All right,' said Verrall ungraciously. 'Don't go and cut his mouth to bits.'

A sepoy brought the pony, and Flory pretended to examine the curb-chain. In reality he was temporizing until Elizabeth should be thirty or forty yards away. He made up his mind that he would stick the peg exactly at the moment when she passed (it is easy enough on the small Burma ponies, provided that they will gallop straight), and then ride up to her with it on his point. That was obviously the right move. He did not want her to think that that pink-faced young whelp was the only person who could ride. He was wearing shorts, which are uncomfortable to ride in, but he knew that, like nearly everyone, he looked his best on horseback.

Elizabeth was approaching. Flory stepped into the saddle, took the spear from the Indian and waved it in greeting to Elizabeth. She made no response, however. Probably she was shy in front of Verrall. She was looking away, towards the cemetery, and her cheeks were pink.

'*Chalo*,' said Flory to the Indian, and then dug his knees into the horse's sides.

The very next instant, before the horse had taken to bounds, Flory found himself hurtling through the air, hitting the ground with a crack that wrenched his shoulder almost out of joint, and rolling over and over. Mercifully the spear fell clear of him. He lay supine, with a blurred vision of blue sky and floating vultures. Then his eyes focused on the khaki *pagri* and dark face of a Sikh, bearded to the eyes, bending over him.

'What's happened?' he said in English, and he raised himself painfully on his elbow. The Sikh made some gruff answer and pointed. Flory saw the chestnut pony careering away over the maidan, with the saddle under its belly. The girth had not been tightened, and had slipped round; hence his fall.

When Flory sat up he found that he was in extreme pain. The right shoulder of his shirt was torn open and already soaking with blood, and he could feel more blood oozing from his cheek. The hard earth had grazed him. His hat, too, was gone. With a deadly pang he remembered Elizabeth, and he saw her coming towards him, barely ten yards away, looking straight at him as he sprawled there so ignominiously. My God, my God! he thought, O my God, what a fool I must look! The thought of it even drove away the pain of the fall. He clapped a hand over his birth-mark, though the other cheek was the damaged one.

'Elizabeth! Hullo, Elizabeth! Good morning!'

He had called out eagerly, appealingly, as one does when one is conscious of looking a fool. She did not answer, and what was almost incredible, she walked on without pausing even for an instant, as though she had neither seen nor heard him.

'Elizabeth!' he called again, taken aback; 'did you see my fall? The saddle slipped. The fool of a sepoy hadn't—'

There was no question that she had heard him now. She turned her face full upon him for a moment, and looked at him and through him as though he had not existed. Then she gazed away into the distance beyond the cemetery. It was terrible. He called after her in dismay—

'Elizabeth! I say, Elizabeth!'

She passed on without a word, without a sign, without a look. She was walking sharply down the road, with a click of heels, her back turned upon him.

The sepoys had come round him now, and Verrall, too, had ridden across to where Flory lay. Some of the sepoys had saluted Elizabeth; Verrall had ignored her, perhaps not seeing her. Flory rose stiffly to his feet. He was badly bruised, but no bones were broken. The Indians brought him his hat and stick, but they did not apologize for their carelessness. They looked faintly contemptuous, as though thinking that he had only got what he deserved. It was conceivable that they had loosened the girth on purpose.

'The saddle slipped,' said Flory in the weak, stupid way that one does at such moments.

'Why the devil couldn't you look at it before you got up?' said Verrall briefly. 'You ought to know these beggars aren't to be trusted.'

Having said which he twitched his bridle and rode away, feeling the incident closed. The sepoys followed him without saluting Flory. When Flory reached his gate he looked back and saw that the chestnut pony had already been caught and re-saddled, and Verrall was tent-pegging upon it.

The fall had so shaken him that even now he could hardly collect his thoughts. What could have made her behave like that? She had seen him lying bloody and in pain, and she had walked past him as though he had been a dead dog. How could it have happened? *Had* it happened? It was incredible. Could she be angry with him? Could he have offended her in any way? All the servants were waiting at the compound fence. They had come out to watch the tent-pegging, and every one of them had seen his bitter humiliation. Ko S'la ran part of the way down the hill to meet him, with concerned face.

'The god has hurt himself? Shall I carry the god back to the house?'

'No,' said the god. 'Go and get me some whisky and a clean shirt.'

When they got back to the house Ko S'la made Flory sit down on the bed and peeled off his torn shirt which the blood had stuck to his body. Ko S'la clicked his tongue.

'*Ah ma lay?* These cuts are full of dirt. You ought not to play these children's games on strange ponies, *thakin*. Not at your age. It is too dangerous.'

'The saddle slipped,' Flory said.

'Such games,' pursued Ko S'la, 'are all very well for the young police officer. But you are no longer young, *thakin*. A fall hurts at your age. You should take more care of yourself.'

'Do you take me for an old man?' said Flory angrily. His shoulder was smarting abominably.

'You are thirty-five, *thakin*,' said Ko S'la politely but firmly.

It was all very humiliating. Ma Pu and Ma Yi, temporarily at peace, had brought a pot of some dreadful mess which they declared was good for cuts.

Flory told Ko S'la privately to throw it out of the window and substitute boracic ointment. Then, while he sat in a tepid bath and Ko S'la sponged the dirt out of his grazes, he puzzled helplessly, and, as his head grew clearer, with a deeper and deeper dismay, over what had happened. He had offended her bitterly, that was clear. But, when he had not even seen her since last night, how *could* he have offended her? And there was no even plausible answer.

He explained to Ko S'la several times over that his fall was due to the saddle slipping. But Ko S'la, though sympathetic, clearly did not believe him. To the end of his days, Flory perceived, the fall would be attributed to his own bad horsemanship. On the other hand, a fortnight ago, he had won undeserved renown by putting to flight the harmless buffalo. Fate is even-handed, after a fashion.

# 17

Flory did not see Elizabeth again until he went down to the Club after dinner. He had not, as he might have done, sought her out and demanded an explanation. His face unnerved him when he looked at it in the glass. With the birthmark on one side and the graze on the other it was so woebegone, so hideous, that he dared not show himself by daylight. As he entered the Club lounge he put his hand over his birthmark—pretext, a mosquito bite on the forehead. It would have been more than his nerve was equal to, not to cover his birthmark at such a moment. However, Elizabeth was not there.

Instead, he tumbled into an unexpected quarrel. Ellis and Westfield had just got back from the jungle, and they were sitting drinking, in a sour mood. News had come from Rangoon that the editor of the *Burmese Patriot* had been given only four months' imprisonment for his libel against Mr Macgregor, and Ellis was working himself up into a rage over this light sentence. As soon as Flory came in Ellis began baiting him with remarks about 'that little nigger Very-slimy'. At the moment the very thought of quarrelling made Flory yawn, but he answered incautiously, and there was an argument. It grew heated, and after Ellis had called Flory a nigger's Nancy Boy and Flory had replied in kind, Westfield too lost his temper. He was a good-natured man, but Flory's Bolshie ideas sometimes annoyed him. He could never understand why, when there was so clearly a right and a wrong opinion about everything, Flory always seemed to delight in choosing the wrong one. He told Flory 'not to start talking like a damned Hyde Park agitator', and then read him a snappish little sermon, taking as his text the five chief beatitudes of the pukka sahib, namely:

> Keeping up our prestige,
> The firm hand (without the velvet glove),

We white men must hang together,
Give them an inch and they'll take an ell, and
*Esprit de Corps.*

All the while his anxiety to see Elizabeth was so gnawing at Flory's heart that he could hardly hear what was said to him. Besides, he had heard it all so often, so very often—a hundred times, a thousand times it might be, since his first week in Rangoon, when his burra sahib (an old Scotch gin-soaker and great breeder of racing ponies, afterwards warned off the turf for some dirty business of running the same horse under two different names) saw him take off his topi to pass a native funeral and said to him reprovingly: 'Remember laddie, always remember, we are *sahiblog* and they are dirrt!' It sickened him, now, to have to listen to such trash. So he cut Westfield short by saying blasphemously:

'Oh, shut up! I'm sick of the subject. Veraswami's a damned good fellow—a damned sight better than some white men I can think of. Anyway, I'm going to propose his name for the Club when the general meeting comes. Perhaps he'll liven this bloody place up a bit.'

Whereat the row would have become serious if it had not ended as most rows ended at the Club—with the appearance of the butler, who had heard the raised voices.

'Did master call, sir?'

'No. Go to hell,' said Ellis morosely.

The butler retired, but that was the end of the dispute for the time being. At this moment there were footsteps and voices outside; the Lackersteens were arriving at the Club.

When they entered the lounge, Flory could not even nerve himself to look directly at Elizabeth; but he noticed that all three of them were much more smartly dressed than usual. Mr Lackersteen was even wearing a dinner-jacket—white, because of the season—and was completely sober. The boiled shirt and *piqué* waistcoat seemed to hold him upright and stiffen his moral fibre like a breastplate. Mrs Lackersteen looked handsome and serpentine in a red dress. In some indefinable way all three gave the impression that they were waiting to receive some distinguished guest.

When drinks had been called for, and Mrs Lackersteen had usurped the place under the punkah, Flory took a chair on the outside of the group. He dared not accost Elizabeth yet. Mrs Lackersteen had begun talking in an extraordinary, silly manner about the dear Prince of Wales, and putting on an accent like a temporarily promoted chorus-girl playing the part of a duchess in a musical comedy. The others wondered privately what the devil was the matter with her. Flory had stationed himself almost behind Elizabeth. She was wearing a yellow frock, cut very short as the fashion then was, with champagne-coloured stockings and slippers to match, and she carried a big ostrich-feather fan. She looked so modish, so adult, that he feared her more than he had ever done. It was unbelievable that he had ever kissed her. She was talking easily to all the others at once, and now and again he dared to put a word into the general conversation; but she never answered him directly, and whether or not she meant to ignore him, he could not tell.

'Well,' said Mrs Lackersteen presently, 'and who's for a rubbah?'

She said quite distinctly a 'rubbah'. Her accent was growing more aristocratic with every word she uttered. It was unaccountable. It appeared that Ellis, Westfield and Mr Lackersteen were for a 'rubbah'. Flory refused as soon as he saw that Elizabeth was not playing. Now or never was his chance to get her alone. When they all moved for the card-room, he saw with a mixture of fear and relief that Elizabeth came last. He stopped in the doorway, barring her path. He had turned dreadly pale. She shrank from him a little.

'Excuse me,' they both said simultaneously.

'One moment,' he said, and do what he would his voice trembled. 'May I speak to you? You don't mind—there's something I must say.'

'Will you please let me pass, Mr Flory?'

'Please! Please! We're alone now. You won't refuse just to let me speak?'

'What is it, then?'

'It's only this. Whatever I've done to offend you—please tell me what it is. Tell me and let me put it right. I'd sooner cut my hand off than offend you. Just tell me, don't let me go on not even knowing what it is.'

'I really don't know what you're talking about. "Tell you how you've offended me?" Why should you have *offended* me?'

'But I must have! After the way you behaved!'

'"After the way I behaved?" I don't know what you mean. I don't know why you're talking in this extraordinary way at all.'

'But you won't even speak to me! This morning you cut me absolutely dead.'

'Surely I can do as I like without being questioned?'

'But please, please! Don't you see, you must see, what it's like for me to be snubbed all of a sudden. After all, only last night you—'

She turned pink. 'I think it's absolutely—absolutely caddish of you to mention such things!'

'I know, I know. I know all that. But what else can I do? You walked past me this morning as though I'd been a stone. I know that I've offended you in some way. Can you blame me if I want to know what it is that I've done?'

He was, as usual, making it worse with every word he said. He perceived that whatever he had done, to be made to speak of it seemed to her worse than the thing itself. She was not going to explain. She was going to leave him in the dark—snub him and then pretend that nothing had happened; the natural feminine move. Nevertheless he urged her again:

'Please tell me. I can't let everything end between us like this.'

'"End between us"? There was nothing to end,' she said coldly.

The vulgarity of this remark wounded him, and he said quickly:

'That wasn't like you, Elizabeth! It's not generous to cut a man dead after you've been kind to him, and then refuse even to tell him the reason. You might be straightforward with me. Please tell me what it is that I've done.'

She gave him an oblique, bitter look, bitter not because of what he had done, but because he had made her speak of it. But perhaps she was anxious to end the scene, and she said:

'Well then, if you absolutely force me to speak of it—'

'Yes?'

'I'm told that at the very same time as you were pretending to—well, when you were . . . with me—oh, it's too beastly! I can't speak of it.'

'Go on.'

'I'm told that you're keeping a Burmese woman. And *now,* will you please let me pass?'

With that she sailed—there was no other possible word for it—she sailed past him with a swish of her short skirts, and vanished into the card-room. And he remained looking after her, too appalled to speak, and looking unutterably ridiculous.

It was dreadful. He could not face her after that. He turned to hurry out of the Club, and then dared not even pass the door of the card-room, lest she should see him. He went into the lounge, wondering how to escape, and finally climbed over the veranda rail and dropped on to the small square of lawn that ran down to the Irrawaddy. The sweat was running from his forehead. He could have shouted with anger and distress. The accursed luck of it! To be caught out over a thing like that. 'Keeping a Burmese woman'—and it was not even true! But much use it would ever be to deny it. Ah, what damned, evil chance could have brought it to her ears?

But as a matter of fact, it was no chance. It had a perfectly sound cause, which was also the cause of Mrs Lackersteen's curious behaviour at the Club this evening. On the previous night, just before the earthquake, Mrs Lackersteen had been reading the Civil List. The Civil List (which tells you the exact income of every official in Burma) was a source of inexhaustible interest to her. She was in the middle of adding up the pay and allowances of a Conservator of Forests whom she had once met in Mandalay, when it occurred to her to look up the name of Lieutenant Verrall, who, she had heard from Mr Macgregor, was arriving at Kyauktada tomorrow with a hundred Military Policemen. When she found the name, she saw in front of it two words that startled her almost out of her wits.

The words were 'The Honourable'!

The *Honourable*! Lieutenants the Honourable are rare anywhere, rare as diamonds in the Indian Army, rare as dodos in Burma. And when you are the aunt of the only marriageable young woman within fifty miles, and you hear that a lieutenant the Honourable is arriving no later than tomorrow—well! With dismay Mrs Lackersteen remembered that Elizabeth was out in the garden with Flory—that drunken wretch Flory, whose pay was barely seven hundred rupees a month, and who, it was only too probable, was already proposing to her! She hastened immediately to call Elizabeth inside, but at this moment the earthquake intervened. However, on the way home there was an opportunity to speak. Mrs Lackersteen laid her hand affectionately on Elizabeth's arm and said in the tenderest voice she had ever succeeded in producing:

'Of course you know, Elizabeth dear, that Flory is keeping a Burmese woman?'

For a moment this deadly charge actually failed to explode. Elizabeth was so new to the ways of the country that the remark made no impression on her. It sounded hardly more significant than 'keeping a parrot'.

'Keeping a Burmese woman? What for?'

'What *for*? My dear! what *does* a man keep a woman for?'

And, of course, that was that.

For a long time Flory remained standing by the river bank. The moon was up, mirrored in the water like a broad shield of electron. The coolness of the outer air had changed Flory's mood. He had not even the heart to be angry any longer. For he had perceived, with the deadly self-knowledge and self-loathing that come to one at such a time, that what had happened served him perfectly right. For a moment it seemed to him that an endless procession of Burmese women, a regiment of ghosts, were marching past him in the moonlight. Heavens, what numbers of them! A thousand—no, but a full hundred at the least. 'Eyes right!' he thought despondently. Their heads turned towards him, but they had no faces, only featureless discs. He remembered a blue *longyi* here, a pair of ruby ear-rings there, but hardly a face or a name. The gods are just and of our pleasant vices (pleasant, indeed!) make instruments to plague us. He had dirtied himself beyond redemption, and this was his just punishment.

He made his way slowly through the croton bushes and round the clubhouse. He was too saddened to feel the full pain of the disaster yet. It would begin hurting, as all deep wounds do, long afterwards. As he passed through the gate something stirred the leaves behind him. He started. There was a whisper of harsh Burmese syllables.

'*Pike-san pay-like! Pike-san pay-like!*'

He turned sharply. The '*pike-san pay-like*' ('Give me the money') was repeated. He saw a woman standing under the shadow of the gold mohur tree. It was Ma Hla May. She stepped out into the moonlight warily, with a hostile air, keeping her distance as though afraid that he would strike her. Her face was coated with powder, sickly white in the moon, and it looked as ugly as a skull, and defiant.

She had given him a shock. 'What the devil are you doing here?' he said angrily in English.

'*Pike-san pay-like!*'

'What money? What do you mean? Why are you following me about like this?'

'*Pike-san pay-like!*' she repeated almost in a scream. 'The money you promised me, *thakin*. You said you would give me more money. I want it now, this instant!'

'How can I give it you now? You shall have it next month. I have given you a hundred and fifty rupees already.'

To his alarm she began shrieking '*Pike-san pay-like!*' and a number of similar phrases almost at the top of her voice. She seemed on the verge of hysterics. The volume of noise that she produced was startling.

'Be quiet! They'll hear you in the Club!' he exclaimed, and was instantly sorry for putting the idea into her head.

'Aha! *Now* I know what will frighten you! Give me the money this instant, or I will scream for help and bring them all out here. Quick, now, or I begin screaming!'

'You bitch!' he said, and took a step towards her. She sprang nimbly out of reach, whipped off her slipper, and stood defying him.

'Be quick! Fifty rupees now and the rest tomorrow. Out with it! Or I give a scream they can hear as far as the bazaar!'

Flory swore. This was not the time for such a scene. Finally he took out his pocket-book, found twenty-five rupees in it, and threw them on to the ground. Ma Hla May pounced on the notes and counted them.

'I said fifty rupees, *thakin!*'

'How can I give it you if I haven't got it? Do you think I carry hundreds of rupees about with me?'

'I said fifty rupees!'

'Oh, get out of my way!' he said in English, and pushed past her.

But the wretched woman would not leave him alone. She began to follow him up the road like a disobedient dog, screaming out *'Pike-san pay-like! Pike-san pay-like!'* as though mere noise could bring the money into existence. He hurried, partly to draw her away from the Club, partly in hopes of shaking her off, but she seemed ready to follow him as far as the house if necessary. After a while he could not stand it any longer, and he turned to drive her back.

'Go away this instant! If you follow me any farther you shall never have another anna.'

*'Pike-san pay-like!'*

'You fool,' he said, 'what good is this doing? How can I give you the money when I have not another pice on me?'

'That is a likely story!'

He felt helplessly in his pockets. He was so wearied that he would have given her anything to be rid of her. His fingers encountered his cigarette-case, which was of gold. He took it out.

'Here, if I give you this will you go away? You can pawn it for thirty rupees.'

Ma Hla May seemed to consider, then said sulkily, 'Give it me.'

He threw the cigarette-case on to the grass beside the road. She grabbed it and immediately sprang back clutching it to her *ingyi*, as though afraid that he would take it away again. He turned and made for the house, thanking God to be out of the sound of her voice. The cigarette-case was the same one that she had stolen ten days ago.

At the gate he looked back. Ma Hla May was still standing at the bottom of the hill, a greyish figurine in the moonlight. She must have watched him up the hill like a dog watching a suspicious stranger out of sight. It was queer. The thought crossed his mind, as it had a few days earlier when she sent him the blackmailing letter, that her behaviour had been curious and unlike herself. She was showing a tenacity of which he would never have thought her capable—almost, indeed, as though someone else were egging her on.

# 18

After the row overnight Ellis was looking forward to a week of baiting Flory. He had nicknamed him Nancy—short for nigger's Nancy Boy, but the women did not know that—and was already inventing wild scandals about him. Ellis always invented scandals about anyone with whom he had quarrelled—scandals which grew, by repeated embroideries, into a species of saga. Flory's incautious remark that Dr Veraswami was a 'damned good fellow' had swelled before long into a whole *Daily Worker*-ful of blasphemy and sedition.

'On my honour, Mrs Lackersteen,' said Ellis—Mrs Lackersteen had taken a sudden dislike to Flory after discovering the great secret about Verrall, and she was quite ready to listen to Ellis's tales—'on my honour, if you'd been there last night and heard the things that man Flory was saying—well, it'd have made you shiver in your shoes!'

'Really! You know, I always thought he had such *curious* ideas. What has he been talking about now? Not *Socialism,* I hope?'

'Worse.'

There were long recitals. However, to Ellis's disappointment, Flory had not stayed in Kyauktada to be baited. He had gone back to camp the day after his dismissal by Elizabeth. Elizabeth heard most of the scandalous tales about him. She understood his character perfectly now. She understood why it was that he had so often bored her and irritated her. He was a highbrow—her deadliest word—a highbrow, to be classed with Lenin, A. J. Cook and the dirty little poets in the Montparnasse cafés. She could have forgiven him even his Burmese mistress more easily than that. Flory wrote to her three days later; a weak, stilted letter, which he sent by hand—his camp was a day's march from Kyauktada. Elizabeth did not answer.

It was lucky for Flory that at present he was too busy to have time to think. The whole camp was at sixes and sevens since his long absence. Nearly thirty coolies were missing, the sick elephant was worse than ever, and a vast pile of teak logs which should have been sent off ten days earlier were still waiting because the engine would not work. Flory, a fool about machinery, struggled with the bowels of the engine until he was black with grease and Ko S'la told him sharply that white men ought not to do 'coolie-work'. The engine was finally persuaded to run, or at least to totter. The sick elephant was discovered to be suffering from tapeworms. As for the coolies, they had deserted because their supply of opium had been cut off—they would not stay in the jungle without opium, which they took as a prophylactic against fever. U Po Kyin, willing to do Flory a bad turn, had caused the Excise Officers to make a raid and seize the opium. Flory wrote to Dr Veraswami, asking for his help. The doctor sent back a quantity of opium, illegally procured, medicine for the elephant and a careful letter of instructions. A tapeworm measuring twenty-one feet was extracted. Flory was busy twelve hours a day. In the evening if there was no more to do he would plunge into the jungle and walk and walk until the sweat stung his eyes and his knees were bleeding from the briers. The nights were his bad time. The bitterness of what had happened was sinking into him, as it usually does, by slow degrees.

Meanwhile, several days had passed and Elizabeth had not yet seen Verrall at less than a hundred yards' distance. It had been a great disappointment when he had not appeared at the Club on the evening of his arrival. Mr Lackersteen was really quite angry when he discovered that he had been hounded into his dinner-jacket for nothing. Next morning Mrs Lackersteen made her husband send an officious note to the *dak*bungalow, inviting Verrall to the Club; there was no answer, however. More days passed, and Verrall made no move to join in the local society. He had even neglected his official calls, not even bothering to present himself at Mr Macgregor's office. The *dak*bungalow was at the other end of the town, near the station, and he had made himself quite comfortable there. There is a rule that one must vacate a *dak*bungalow after a stated number of days, but Verrall peaceably ignored it. The Europeans only saw him at morning and evening on the maidan. On the second day after his arrival fifty of his men turned out with sickles and cleared a large patch of the maidan, after which Verrall was to be seen galloping to and fro, practising polo strokes. He took not the smallest notice of any Europeans who passed down the road. Westfield and Ellis were furious, and even Mr Macgregor said that Verrall's behaviour was 'ungracious'. They would all have fallen at the feet of a lieutenant the Honourable if he had shown the smallest courtesy; as it was, everyone except the two women detested him from the start. It is always so with titled people, they are either adored or hated. If they accept one it is charming simplicity, if they ignore one it is loathsome snobbishness; there are no half-measures.

Verrall was the youngest son of a peer, and not at all rich, but by the method of seldom paying a bill until a writ was issued against him, he managed to keep himself in the only things he seriously cared about: clothes and horses. He had come out to India in a British cavalry regiment, and exchanged into the Indian Army because it was cheaper and left him greater freedom for polo. After two years his debts were so enormous that he entered the Burma Military Police, in which it was notoriously possible to save money; however, he detested Burma—it is no country for a horseman—and he had already applied to go back to his regiment. He was the kind of soldier who can get exchanges when he wants them. Meanwhile, he was only to be in Kyauktada for a month, and he had no intention of mixing himself up with all the petty *sahiblog* of the district. He knew the society of those small Burma stations—a nasty, poodle-faking, horseless riffraff. He despised them.

They were not the only people whom Verrall despised, however. His various contempts would take a long time to catalogue in detail. He despised the entire non-military population of India, a few famous polo players excepted. He despised the entire Army as well, except the cavalry. He despised all Indian regiments, infantry and cavalry alike. It was true that he himself belonged to a native regiment, but that was only for his own convenience. He took no interest in Indians, and his Urdu consisted mainly of swear-words, with all the verbs in the third person singular. His Military Policemen he looked on as no better than coolies. 'Christ, what God-forsaken swine!' he was often heard to mutter as he moved down the ranks inspecting, with the old subahdar carrying his sword behind him. Verrall had even been in trouble once for his outspoken opinions on native troops. It was at a review, and Verrall was among the group of officers standing behind the general. An Indian infantry regiment approached for the march-past.

'The — Rifles,' somebody said.

'*And* look at it,' said Verrall in his surly boy's voice.

The white-haired colonel of the — Rifles was standing near. He flushed to the neck, and reported Verrall to the general. Verrall was reprimanded, but the general, a British Army officer himself, did not rub it in very hard. Somehow, nothing very serious ever did happen to Verrall, however offensive he made himself. Up and down India, wherever he was stationed, he left behind him a trail of insulted people, neglected duties and unpaid bills. Yet the disgraces that ought to have fallen on him never did. He bore a charmed life, and it was not only the handle to his name that saved him. There was something in his eye before which duns, burra memsahibs and even colonels quailed.

It was a disconcerting eye, pale blue and a little protuberant, but exceedingly clear. It looked you over, weighed you in the balance and found you wanting, in a single cold scrutiny of perhaps five seconds. If you were the right kind of man—that is, if you were a cavalry officer and a polo player—Verrall took you for granted and even treated you with a surly respect; if you were any other type of man whatever, he despised you so utterly that he could not have hidden it even if he would. It did not even make any difference whether you were rich or poor, for in the social sense he was not more than normally a snob. Of course, like all sons of rich families, he thought poverty disgusting and that poor people are poor because they prefer disgusting habits. But he despised soft living. Spending, or rather owing, fabulous sums on clothes, he yet lived almost as ascetically as a monk. He exercised himself ceaselessly and brutally, rationed his drink and his cigarettes, slept on a camp bed (in silk pyjamas) and bathed in cold water in the bitterest winter. Horsemanship and physical fitness were the only gods he knew. The stamp of hoofs on the maidan, the strong, poised feeling of his body, wedded centaur-like to the saddle, the polo-stick springy in his hand—these were his religion, the breath of his life. The Europeans in Burma—boozing, womanizing, yellow-faced loafers—made him physically sick when he thought of their habits. As for social duties of all descriptions, he called them poodle-faking and ignored them. Women he abhorred. In his view they were a kind of siren whose one aim was to lure men away from polo and enmesh them in tea-fights and tennis-parties. He was not, however, quite proof against women. He was young, and women of nearly all kinds threw themselves at his head; now and again he succumbed. But his lapses soon disgusted him, and he was too callous when the pinch came to have any difficulty about escaping. He had had perhaps a dozen such escapes during his two years in India.

A whole week went by. Elizabeth had not even succeeded in making Verrall's acquaintance. It was so tantalizing! Every day, morning and evening, she and her aunt walked down to the Club and back again, past the maidan; and there was Verrall, hitting the polo-balls the sepoys threw for him, ignoring the two women utterly. So near and yet so far! What made it even worse was that neither woman would have considered it decent to speak of the matter directly. One evening the polo-ball, struck too hard, came swishing through the grass and rolled across the road in front of them. Elizabeth and her aunt stopped involuntarily. But it was only a sepoy who ran to fetch the ball. Verrall had seen the women and kept his distance.

Next morning Mrs Lackersteen paused as they came out of the gate. She had given up riding in her rickshaw lately. At the bottom of the maidan the Military Policemen were drawn up, a dust-coloured rank with bayonets glittering. Verrall was facing them, but not in uniform—he seldom put on his uniform for morning parade, not thinking it necessary with mere Military Policemen. The two women were looking at everything except Verrall, and at the same time, in some manner, were contriving to look at him.

'The wretched thing is,' said Mrs Lackersteen—this was *à propos de bottes,* but the subject needed no introduction—'the wretched thing is that I'm afraid your uncle simply *must* go back to camp before long.'

'Must he really?'

'I'm afraid so. It is so *hateful* in camp at this time of year! Oh, those mosquitoes!'

'Couldn't he stay a bit longer? A week, perhaps?'

'I don't see how he can. He's been nearly a month in headquarters now. The firm would be furious if they heard of it. And of course both of us will have to go with him. *Such* a bore! The mosquitoes—simply terrible!'

Terrible indeed! To have to go away before Elizabeth had so much as said how-do-you-do to Verrall! But they would certainly have to go if Mr Lackersteen went. It would never do to leave him to himself. Satan finds some mischief still, even in the jungle. A ripple like fire ran down the line of sepoys; they were unfixing bayonets before marching away. The dusty rank turned left, saluted, and marched off in columns of fours. The orderlies were coming from the police lines with the ponies and polo-sticks. Mrs Lackersteen took a heroic decision.

'I think,' she said, 'we'll take a short-cut across the maidan. It's *so* much quicker than going right round by the road.'

It *was* quicker by about fifty yards, but no one ever went that way on foot, because of the grass-seeds that got into one's stockings. Mrs Lackersteen plunged boldly into the grass, and then, dropping even the pretence of making for the Club, took a bee-line for Verrall, Elizabeth following. Either woman would have died on the rack rather than admit that she was doing anything but take a short-cut. Verrall saw them coming, swore, and reined in his pony. He could not very well cut them dead now that they were coming openly to accost him. The damned cheek of these women! He rode slowly towards them with a sulky expression on his face, chivvying the polo-ball with small strokes.

'Good morning, Mr Verrall!' Mrs Lackersteen called out in a voice of saccharine, twenty yards away.

'Morning!' he returned surlily, having seen her face and set her down as one of the usual scraggy old boiling-fowls of an Indian station.

The next moment Elizabeth came level with her aunt. She had taken off her spectacles and was swinging her Terai hat on her hand. What did she care for sunstroke? She was perfectly aware of the prettiness of her cropped hair. A puff of wind—oh, those blessed breaths of wind, coming from nowhere in the stifling hot-weather days!—had caught her cotton frock and blown it against her, showing the outline of her body, slender and strong like a tree. Her sudden appearance beside the older, sun-scorched woman was a revelation to Verrall. He started so that the Arab mare felt it and would have reared on her hind legs, and he had to tighten the rein. He had not known until this moment, not having bothered to inquire, that there were any *young* women in Kyauktada.

'My niece,' Mrs Lackersteen said.

He did not answer, but he had thrown away the polo-stick, and he took off his topi. For a moment he and Elizabeth remained gazing at one another. Their fresh faces were unmarred in the pitiless light. The grass-seeds were tickling Elizabeth's shins so that it was agony, and without her spectacles she could only see Verrall and his horse as a whitish blur. But she was happy, happy! Her heart bounded and the blood flowed into her face, dyeing it like a thin wash of aquarelle. The thought, 'A peach, by Christ!' moved almost fiercely through Verrall's mind. The sullen Indians, holding the ponies' heads, gazed curiously at the scene, as though the beauty of the two young people had made its impression even on them.

Mrs Lackersteen broke the silence, which had lasted half a minute.

'You know, Mr Verrall,' she said somewhat archly, 'we think it *rather* unkind of you to have neglected us poor people all this time. When we're so *pining* for a new face at the Club.'

He was still looking at Elizabeth when he answered, but the change in his voice was remarkable.

'I've been meaning to come for some days. Been so fearfully busy—getting my men into their quarters and all that. I'm sorry,' he added—he was not in the habit of apologizing, but really, he had decided, this girl was rather an exceptional bit of stuff—'I'm sorry about not answering your note.'

'Oh, not at all! We *quite* understood. But we do hope we shall see you at the Club this evening! Because, you know,' she concluded even more archly, 'if you disappoint us any longer, we shall begin to think you rather a *naughty* young man!'

'I'm sorry,' he repeated. 'I'll be there this evening.'

There was not much more to be said, and the two women walked on to the Club. But they stayed barely five minutes. The grass-seeds were causing their shins such torment that they were obliged to hurry home and change their stockings at once.

Verrall kept his promise and was at the Club that evening. He arrived a little earlier than the others, and he had made his presence thoroughly felt before being in the place five minutes. As Ellis entered the Club the old butler darted out of the card-room and waylaid him. He was in great distress, the tears rolling down his cheeks.

'Sir! Sir!'

'What the devil's the matter now!' said Ellis.

'Sir! Sir! New master been beating me, sir!'

'What?'

'*Beating* me sir!' His voice rose on the 'beating' with a long tearful wail–'be-e-e-eating!'

'Beating you? Do you good. Who's been beating you?'

'New master, sir. Military Police sahib. Beating me with his foot, sir–*here*!' He rubbed himself behind.

'Hell!' said Ellis.

He went into the lounge. Verrall was reading the *Field,* and invisible except for Palm Beach trouser-ends and two lustrous sooty-brown shoes. He did not trouble to stir at hearing someone else come into the room. Ellis halted.

'Here, you–what's your name–Verrall!'

'What?'

'Have you been kicking our butler?'

Verrall's sulky blue eye appeared round the corner of the *Field,* like the eye of a crustacean peering round a rock.

'What?' he repeated shortly.

'I said, have you been kicking our bloody butler?'

'Yes.'

'Then what the hell do you mean by it?'

'Beggar gave me his lip. I sent him for a whisky and soda, and he brought it warm. I told him to put ice in it, and he wouldn't–talked some bloody rot about saving the last pieces of ice. So I kicked his bottom. Serve him right.'

Ellis turned quite grey. He was furious. The butler was a piece of Club property and not to be kicked by strangers. But what most angered Ellis was the thought that Verrall quite possibly suspected him of being *sorry* for the butler–in fact, of disapproving of kicking *as such.*

'Serve him right? I dare say it bloody well did serve him right. But what in hell's that got to do with it? Who are *you* to come kicking our servants?'

'Bosh, my good chap. Needed kicking. You've let your servants get out of hand here.'

'You damned, insolent young tick, what's it got to do with *you* if he needed kicking? You're not even a member of this Club. It's our job to kick the servants, not yours.'

Verrall lowered the *Field* and brought his other eye into play. His surly voice did not change its tone. He never lost his temper with a European; it was never necessary.

'My good chap, if anyone gives me lip I kick his bottom. Do you want me to kick yours?'

All the fire went out of Ellis suddenly. He was not afraid, he had never been afraid in his life; only, Verrall's eye was too much for him. That eye could make you feel as though you were under Niagara! The oaths wilted on Ellis's lips; his voice almost deserted him. He said querulously and even plaintively:

'But damn it, he was quite right not to give you the last bit of ice. Do you think we only buy ice for you? We can only get the stuff twice a week in this place.'

'Rotten bad management on your part, then,' said Verrall, and retired behind the *Field,* content to let the matter drop.

Ellis was helpless. The calm way in which Verrall went back to his paper, quite genuinely forgetting Ellis's existence, was maddening. Should he not give the young swab a good, rousing kick?

But somehow, the kick was never given. Verrall had earned many kicks in his life, but he had never received one and probably never would. Ellis seeped helplessly back to the card-room, to work off his feelings on the butler, leaving Verrall in possession of the lounge.

As Mr Macgregor entered the Club gate he heard the sound of music. Yellow chinks of lantern-light showed through the creeper that covered the tennis-screen. Mr Macgregor was in a happy mood this evening. He had promised himself a good, long talk with Miss Lackersteen—such an exceptionally intelligent girl, that!—and he had a most interesting anecdote to tell her (as a matter of fact, it had already seen the light in one of those little articles of his in *Blackwood's*) about a dacoity that had happened in Sagaing in 1913. She would love to hear it, he knew. He rounded the tennis-screen expectantly. On the court, in the mingled light of the waning moon and of lanterns slung among the trees, Verrall and Elizabeth were dancing. The *chokras* had brought out chairs and a table for the gramophone, and round these the other Europeans were sitting or standing. As Mr Macgregor halted at the corner of the court, Verrall and Elizabeth circled round and glided past him, barely a yard away. They were dancing very close together, her body bent backwards under his. Neither noticed Mr Macgregor.

Mr Macgregor made his way round the court. A chilly, desolate feeling had taken possession of his entrails. Good-bye, then, to his talk with Miss Lackersteen! It was an effort to screw his face into its usual facetious good-humour as he came up to the table.

'A Terpsichorean evening!' he remarked in a voice that was doleful in spite of himself.

No one answered. They were all watching the pair on the tennis court. Utterly oblivious of the others, Elizabeth and Verrall glided round and round, round and round, their shoes sliding easily on the slippery concrete. Verrall danced as he rode, with matchless grace. The gramophone was playing 'Show Me the Way to Go Home,' which was then going round the world like a pestilence and had got as far as Burma:

'Show me the way to go home,
I'm tired an' I wanna go to bed;
I had a little drink 'bout an hour ago,
An' it's gone right *to* my head!' etc.

The dreary, depressing trash floated out among the shadowy trees and the streaming scents of flowers, over and over again, for Mrs Lackersteen was putting the gramophone needle back to the start when it neared the centre. The moon climbed higher, very yellow, looking, as she rose from the murk of dark clouds at the horizon, like a sick woman creeping out of bed. Verrall and Elizabeth danced on and on, indefatigably, a pale voluptuous shape in the gloom. They moved in perfect unison like some single animal. Mr Macgregor, Ellis, Westfield and Mr Lackersteen stood watching them, their hands in their pockets, finding nothing to say. The mosquitoes came nibbling at their ankles. Someone called for drinks, but the whisky was like ashes in their mouths. The bowels of all four older men were twisted with bitter envy.

Verrall did not ask Mrs Lackersteen for a dance, nor, when he and Elizabeth finally sat down, did he take any notice of the other Europeans. He merely monopolized Elizabeth for half an hour more, and then, with a brief good night to the Lackersteens and not a word to anyone else, left the Club. The long dance with Verrall had left Elizabeth in a kind of dream. He had asked her to come out riding with him! He was going to lend her one of his ponies! She never even noticed that Ellis, angered by her behaviour, was doing his best to be openly rude. It was late when the Lackersteens got home, but there was no sleep yet for Elizabeth or her aunt. They were feverishly at work till midnight, shortening a pair of Mrs Lackersteen's jodhpurs, and letting out the calves, to fit Elizabeth.

'I hope, dear, you *can* ride a horse?' said Mrs Lackersteen.

'Oh, of course! I've ridden ever such a lot, at home.'

She had ridden perhaps a dozen times in all, when she was sixteen. No matter, she would manage somehow! She would have ridden a tiger, if Verrall were to accompany her.

When at last the jodhpurs were finished and Elizabeth had tried them on, Mrs Lackersteen sighed to see her. She looked ravishing in jodhpurs, simply ravishing! And to think that in only a day or two they had got to go back to camp, for weeks, months perhaps, leaving Kyauktada and this most *desirable* young man! The pity of it! As they moved to go upstairs Mrs Lackersteen paused at the door. It had come into her head to make a great and painful sacrifice. She took Elizabeth by the shoulders and kissed her with a more real affection than she had ever shown.

'My dear, it would be such a *shame* for you to go away from Kyauktada just now!'

'It would, rather.'

'Then I'll tell you what, dear. We *won't* go back to that horrid jungle! Your uncle shall go alone. You and I shall stay in Kyauktada.'

# 19

The heat was growing worse and worse. April was nearly over, but there was no hope of rain for another three weeks, five weeks it might be. Even the lovely transient dawns were spoiled by the thought of the long, blinding hours to come, when one's head would ache and the glare would penetrate through every covering and glue up one's eyelids with restless sleep. No one, Oriental or European, could keep awake in the heat of the day without a struggle; at night, on the other hand, with the howling dogs and the pools of sweat that collected and tormented one's prickly heat, no one could sleep. The mosquitoes at the Club were so bad that sticks of incense had to be kept burning in all the corners, and the women sat with their legs in pillowslips. Only Verrall and Elizabeth were indifferent to the heat. They were young and their blood was fresh, and Verrall was too stoical and Elizabeth too happy to pay any attention to the climate.

There was much bickering and scandal-mongering at the Club these days. Verrall had put everyone's nose out of joint. He had taken to coming to the Club for an hour or two in the evenings, but he ignored the other members, refused the drinks they offered him, and answered attempts at conversation with surly monosyllables. He would sit under the punkah in the chair that had once been sacred to Mrs Lackersteen, reading such of the papers as interested him, until Elizabeth came, when he would dance and talk with her for an hour or two and then make off without so much as a good-night to anybody. Meanwhile Mr Lackersteen was alone in his camp, and, according to the rumours which drifted back to Kyauktada, consoling loneliness with quite a miscellany of Burmese women.

Elizabeth and Verrall went out riding together almost every evening now. Verrall's mornings, after parade, were sacred to polo practice, but he had decided that it was worth while giving up the evenings to Elizabeth. She took naturally to riding, just as she had to shooting; she even had the assurance to tell Verrall that she had 'hunted quite a lot' at home. He saw at a glance that she was lying, but at least she did not ride so badly as to be a nuisance to him.

They used to ride up the red road into the jungle, ford the stream by the big pyinkado tree covered with orchids, and then follow the narrow cart-track, where the dust was soft and the horses could gallop. It was stifling hot in the dusty jungle, and there were always mutterings of faraway, rainless thunder. Small martins flitted round the horses, keeping pace with them, to hawk for the flies their hooves turned up. Elizabeth rode the bay pony, Verrall the white. On the way home they would walk their sweat-dark horses abreast, so close sometimes his knee brushed against hers, and talk. Verrall could drop his offensive manner and talk amicably enough when he chose, and he did choose with Elizabeth.

Ah, the joy of those rides together! The joy of being on horseback and in the world of horses—the world of hunting and racing, polo and pigsticking! If Elizabeth had loved Verrall for nothing else, she would have loved him for bringing horses into her life. She tormented him to talk about horses as once she had tormented Flory to talk about shooting. Verrall was no talker, it was true. A few gruff, jerky sentences about polo and pigsticking, and a catalogue of Indian stations and the names of regiments, were the best he could do. And yet somehow the little he said could thrill Elizabeth as all Flory's talk had never done. The mere sight of him on horseback was more evocative than any words. An aura of horsemanship and soldiering surrounded him. In his tanned face and his hard, straight body Elizabeth saw all the romance, the splendid panache of a cavalryman's life. She saw the North-West Frontier and the Cavalry Club—she saw the polo grounds and the parched barrack yards, and the brown squadrons of horsemen galloping with their long lances poised and the trains of their *pagris* streaming; she heard the bugle-calls and the jingle of spurs, and the regimental bands playing outside the messrooms while the officers sat at dinner in their stiff, gorgeous uniforms. How splendid it was, that equestrian world, how splendid! And it was *her* world, she belonged to it, she had been born of it. These days, she lived, thought, dreamed horses, almost like Verrall himself. The time came when she not only *told* her taradiddle about having 'hunted quite a lot', she even came near believing it.

In every possible way they got on so well together. He never bored her and fretted her as Flory had done. (As a matter of fact, she had almost forgotten Flory, these days; when she thought of him, it was for some reason always his birthmark that she remembered.) It was a bond between them that Verrall detested anything 'highbrow' even more than she did. He told her once that he had not read a book since he was eighteen, and that indeed he 'loathed' books; 'except, of course, Jorrocks and all that'. On the evening of their third or fourth ride they were parting at the Lackersteens' gate. Verrall had successfully resisted all Mrs Lackersteen's invitations to meals; he had not yet set foot inside the Lackersteens' house, and he did not intend to do so. As the *syce* was taking Elizabeth's pony, Verrall said:

'I tell you what. Next time we come out you shall ride Belinda. I'll ride the chestnut. I think you've got on well enough not to go and cut Belinda's mouth up.'

Belinda was the Arab mare. Verrall had owned her two years, and till this moment he had never once allowed anyone else to mount her, not even the *syce*. It was the greatest favour that he could imagine. And so perfectly did Elizabeth appreciate Verrall's point of view that she understood the greatness of the favour, and was thankful.

The next evening, as they rode home side by side, Verrall put his arm round Elizabeth's shoulder, lifted her out of the saddle and pulled her against him.

He was very strong. He dropped the bridle, and with his free hand, lifted her face up to meet his; their mouths met. For a moment he held her so, then lowered her to the ground and slipped from his horse. They stood embraced, their thin, drenched shirts pressed together, the two bridles held in the crook of his arm.

It was about the same time that Flory, twenty miles away, decided to come back to Kyauktada. He was standing at the jungle's edge by the bank of a dried-up stream, where he had walked to tire himself, watching some tiny, nameless finches eating the seeds of the tall grasses. The cocks were chrome-yellow, the hens like hen sparrows. Too tiny to bend the stalks, they came whirring towards them, seized them in midflight and bore them to the ground by their own weight. Flory watched the birds incuriously, and almost hated them because they could light no spark of interest in him. In his idleness he flung his *dah* at them, scaring them away. If she were here, if she were here! Everything—birds, trees, flowers, everything—was deadly and meaningless because she was not here. As the days passed the knowledge that he had lost her had grown surer and more actual until it poisoned every moment.

He loitered a little way into the jungle, flicking at creepers with his *dah*. His limbs felt slack and leaden. He noticed a wild vanilla plant trailing over a bush, and bent down to sniff at its slender, fragrant pods. The scent brought him a feeling of staleness and deadly ennui. Alone, alone, in the sea of life enisled! The pain was so great that he struck his fist against a tree, jarring his arm and splitting two knuckles. He must go back to Kyauktada. It was folly, for barely a fortnight had passed since the scene between them, and his only chance was to give her time to forget it. Still, he must go back. He could not stay any longer in this deadly place, alone with his thoughts among the endless, mindless leaves.

A happy thought occurred to him. He could take Elizabeth the leopard-skin that was being cured for her in the jail. It would be a pretext for seeing her, and when one comes bearing gifts one is generally listened to. This time he would not let her cut him short without a word. He would explain, extenuate—make her realize that she had been unjust to him. It was not right that she should condemn him because of Ma Hla May, whom he had turned out of doors for Elizabeth's own sake. Surely she must forgive him when she heard the truth of the story? And this time she *should* hear it; he would force her to listen to him if he had to hold her by the arms while he did it.

He went back the same evening. It was a twenty-mile journey, by rutted cart-tracks, but Flory decided to march by night, giving the reason that it was cooler. The servants almost mutinied at the idea of a night-march, and at the very last moment old Sammy collapsed in a semi-genuine fit and had to be plied with gin before he could start. It was a moonless night. They made their way by the light of lanterns, in which Flo's eyes gleamed like emeralds and the bullocks' eyes like moonstones. When the sun was up the servants halted to gather sticks and cook breakfast, but Flory was in a fever to be at Kyauktada, and he hurried ahead. He had no feeling of tiredness. The thought of the leopard-skin had filled him with extravagant hopes. He crossed the glittering river by sampan and went straight to Dr Veraswami's bungalow, getting there about ten.

The doctor invited him to breakfast, and–having shooed the women into some suitable hiding-place–took him into his own bath-room so that he could wash and shave. At breakfast the doctor was very excited and full of denunciations of 'the crocodile'; for it appeared that the pseudo-rebellion was now on the point of breaking out. It was not till after breakfast that Flory had an opportunity to mention the leopard-skin.

'Oh, by the way, doctor. What about that skin I sent to the jail to be cured? Is it done yet?'

'Ah–' said the doctor in a slightly disconcerted manner, rubbing his nose. He went inside the house–they were breakfasting on the veranda, for the doctor's wife had protested violently against Flory being brought indoors–and came back in a moment with the skin rolled up in a bundle.

'Ass a matter of fact–' he began, unrolling it.

'Oh, doctor!'

The skin had been utterly ruined. It was as stiff as cardboard, with the leather cracked and the fur discoloured and even rubbed off in patches. It also stank abominably. Instead of being cured, it had been converted into a piece of rubbish.

'Oh, doctor! What a mess they've made of it! How the devil did it happen?'

'I am so sorry, my friend! I wass about to apologize. It wass the best we could do. There iss no one at the jail who knows how to cure skins now.'

'But, damn it, that convict used to cure them so beautifully!'

'Ah, yes. But he iss gone from us these three weeks, alas.'

'Gone? I thought he was doing seven years?'

'What? Did you not hear, my friend? I thought you knew who it wass that used to cure the skins. It was Nga Shwe O.'

'Nga Shwe O?'

'The dacoit who escaped with U Po Kyin's assistance.'

'Oh, hell!'

The mishap had daunted him dreadfully. Nevertheless, in the afternoon, having bathed and put on a clean suit, he went up to the Lackersteens' house, at about four. It was very early to call, but he wanted to make sure of catching Elizabeth before she went down to the Club. Mrs Lackersteen, who had been asleep and was not prepared for visitors, received him with an ill grace, not even asking him to sit down.

'I'm afraid Elizabeth isn't down yet. She's dressing to go out riding. Wouldn't it be better if you left a message?'

'I'd like to see her, if you don't mind. I've brought her the skin of that leopard we shot together.'

Mrs Lackersteen left him standing up in the drawing-room, feeling lumpish and abnormally large as one does at such times. However, she fetched Elizabeth, taking the opportunity of whispering to her outside the door: 'Get rid of that dreadful man as soon as you can, dear. I can't bear him about the house at this time of day.'

As Elizabeth entered the room Flory's heart pounded so violently that a reddish mist passed behind his eyes. She was wearing a silk shirt and jodhpurs, and she was a little sunburned. Even in his memory she had never been so beautiful. He quailed; on the instant he was lost—every scrap of his screwed-up courage had fled. Instead of stepping forward to meet her he actually backed away. There was a fearful crash behind him; he had upset an occasional table and sent a bowl of zinnias hurtling across the floor.

'I'm so sorry!' he exclaimed in horror.

'Oh, not at *all*! *Please* don't worry about it!'

She helped him to pick up the table, chattering all the while as gaily and easily as though nothing had happened: 'You *have* been away a long time, Mr Flory! You're quite a *stranger*! We've *so* missed you at the Club!' etc., etc. She was italicizing every other word, with that deadly, glittering brightness that a woman puts on when she is dodging a moral obligation. He was terrified of her. He could not even look her in the face. She took up a box of cigarettes and offered him one, but he refused it. His hand was shaking too much to take it.

'I've brought you that skin,' he said flatly.

He unrolled it on the table they had just picked up. It looked so shabby and miserable that he wished he had never brought it. She came close to him to examine the skin, so close that her flower-like cheek was not a foot from his own, and he could feel the warmth of her body. So great was his fear of her that he stepped hurriedly away. And in the same moment she too stepped back with a wince of disgust, having caught the foul odour of the skin. It shamed him terribly. It was almost as though it had been himself and not the skin that stank.

'Thank you *ever* so much, Mr Flory!' She had put another yard between herself and the skin. 'Such a *lovely* big skin, isn't it?'

'It was, but they've spoiled it, I'm afraid.'

'Oh no! I shall love having it!—Are you back in Kyauktada for long? How dreadfully hot it must have been in camp!'

'Yes, it's been very hot.'

For three minutes they actually talked of the weather. He was helpless. All that he had promised himself to say, all his arguments and pleadings, had withered in his throat. 'You fool, you fool,' he thought, 'what are you doing? Did you come twenty miles for this? Go on, say what you came to say! Seize her in your arms; make her listen, kick her, beat her—anything sooner than let her choke you with this drivel!' But it was hopeless, hopeless. Not a word could his tongue utter except futile trivialities. How could he plead or argue, when that bright easy air of hers, that dragged every word to the level of Club-chatter silenced him before he spoke? Where do they learn it, that dreadful tee-heeing brightness? In these brisk modern girls' schools, no doubt. The piece of carrion on the table made him more ashamed every moment. He stood there almost voiceless, lumpishly ugly with his face yellow and creased after the sleepless night, and his birthmark like a smear of dirt.

She got rid of him after a very few minutes. 'And now, Mr Flory, if you *don't* mind, I ought really—'

He mumbled rather than said, 'Won't you come out with me again some time? Walking, shooting—something?'

'I have so *little* time nowadays! *All* my evenings seem to be full. This evening I'm going out riding. With Mr Verrall,' she added.

It was possible that she added that in order to wound him. This was the first that he had heard of her friendship with Verrall. He could not keep the dread, flat tone of envy out of his voice as he said:

'Do you go out riding much with Verrall?'

'Almost every evening. He's such a wonderful horseman! And he has absolute *strings* of polo ponies!'

'Ah. And of course I have no polo ponies.'

It was the first thing he had said that even approached seriousness, and it did no more than offend her. However, she answered him with the same gay easy air as before, and then showed him out. Mrs Lackersteen came back to the drawing-room, sniffed the air, and immediately ordered the servants to take the reeking leopard-skin outside and burn it.

Flory lounged at his garden gate, pretending to feed the pigeons. He could not deny himself the pain of seeing Elizabeth and Verrall start on their ride. How vulgarly, how cruelly she had behaved to him! It is dreadful when people will not even have the decency to quarrel. Presently Verrall rode up to the Lackersteens' house on the white pony, with a *syce* riding the chestnut, then there was a pause, then they emerged together, Verrall on the chestnut pony, Elizabeth on the white, and trotted quickly up the hill. They were chattering and laughing, her silk-shirted shoulder very close to his. Neither looked towards Flory.

When they had disappeared into the jungle, Flory still loafed in the garden. The glare was waning to yellow. The *mali* was at work grubbing up the English flowers, most of which had died, slain by too much sunshine, and planting balsams, cockscombs, and more zinnias. An hour passed, and a melancholy, earth-coloured Indian loitered up the drive, dressed in a loin-cloth and a salmon-pink *pagri* on which a washing-basket was balanced. He laid down his basket and salaamed to Flory.

'Who are you?'

'Book-wallah, sahib.'

The book-wallah was an itinerant peddler of books who wandered from station to station throughout Upper Burma. His system of exchange was that for any book in his bundle you gave him four annas, and any other book. Not quite *any* book, however, for the book-wallah, though analphabetic, had learned to recognize and refuse a Bible.

'No, sahib,' he would say plaintively, 'no. This book (he would turn it over disapprovingly in his flat brown hands) this book with a black cover and gold letters—this one I cannot take. I know not how it is, but all sahibs are offering me this book, and none are taking it. What can it be that is in this black book? Some evil, undoubtedly.'

'Turn out your trash,' Flory said.

He hunted among them for a good thriller—Edgar Wallace or Agatha Christie or something; anything to still the deadly restlessness that was at his heart. As he bent over the books he saw that both Indians were exclaiming and pointing towards the edge of the jungle.

'Dekko!' said the *mali* in his plum-in-the-mouth voice.

The two ponies were emerging from the jungle. But they were riderless. They came trotting down the hill with the silly guilty air of a horse that has escaped from its master, with the stirrups swinging and clashing under their bellies.

Flory remained unconsciously clasping one of the books against his chest. Verrall and Elizabeth had dismounted. It was not an accident; by no effort of the mind could one imagine Verrall falling off his horse. They had dismounted, and the ponies had escaped.

They had dismounted—for what? Ah, but he knew for what! It was not a question of suspecting; he *knew*. He could see the whole thing happening, in one of those hallucinations that are so perfect in detail, so vilely obscene, that they are past bearing. He threw the book violently down and made for the house, leaving the book-wallah disappointed. The servants heard him moving about indoors, and presently he called for a bottle of whisky. He had a drink and it did him no good. Then he filled a tumbler two-thirds full, added enough water to make it drinkable, and swallowed it. The filthy, nauseous dose was no sooner down his throat than he repeated it. He had done the same thing in camp once, years ago, when he was tortured by toothache and three hundred miles from a dentist. At seven Ko S'la came in as usual to say that the bath-water was hot. Flory was lying in one of the long chairs, with his coat off and his shirt torn open at the throat.

'Your bath, *thakin*,' said Ko S'la.

Flory did not answer, and Ko S'la touched his arm, thinking him asleep. Flory was much too drunk to move. The empty bottle had rolled across the floor, leaving a trail of whisky-drops behind it. Ko S'la called for Ba Pe and picked up the bottle, clicking his tongue.

'Just look at this! He has drunk more than three-quarters of a bottle!'

'What, again? I thought he had given up drinking?'

'It is that accursed woman, I suppose. Now we must carry him carefully. You take his heels, I'll take his head. That's right. Hoist him up!'

They carried Flory into the other room and laid him gently on the bed.

'Is he really going to marry this "Ingaleikma"?' said Ba Pe.

'Heaven knows. She is the mistress of the young police officer at present, so I was told. Their ways are not our ways. I think I know what he will be wanting tonight,' he added as he undid Flory's braces—for Ko S'la had the art, so necessary in a bachelor's servant, of undressing his master without waking him.

The servants were rather more pleased than not to see this return to bachelor habits. Flory woke about midnight, naked in a pool of sweat. His head felt as though some large, sharp-cornered metal object were bumping about inside it. The mosquito net was up, and a young woman was sitting beside the bed fanning him with a wicker fan. She had an agreeable negroid face, bronze-gold in the candlelight. She explained that she was a prostitute, and that Ko S'la had engaged her on his own responsibility for a fee of ten rupees.

Flory's head was splitting. 'For God's sake get me something to drink,' he said feebly to the woman. She brought him some soda-water which Ko S'la had cooled in readiness and soaked a towel and put a wet compress round his forehead. She was a fat, good-tempered creature. She told him that her name was Ma Sein Galay, and that besides plying her other trade she sold paddy baskets in the bazaar near Li Yeik's shop. Flory's head felt better presently, and he asked for a cigarette; whereupon Ma Sein Galay, having fetched the cigarette, said naïvely, 'Shall I take my clothes off now, *thakin?*'

Why not? he thought dimly. He made room for her in the bed. But when he smelled the familiar scent of garlic and coco-nut oil, something painful happened within him, and with his head pillowed on Ma Sein Galay's fat shoulder he actually wept, a thing he had not done since he was fifteen years old.

# 20

Next morning there was great excitement in Kyauktada, for the long-rumoured rebellion had at last broken out. Flory heard only a vague report of it at the time. He had gone back to camp as soon as he felt fit to march after the drunken night, and it was not until several days later that he learned the true history of the rebellion, in a long, indignant letter from Dr Veraswami.

The doctor's epistolary style was queer. His syntax was shaky and he was as free with capital letters as a seventeenth-century divine, while in the use of italics he rivalled Queen Victoria. There were eight pages of his small but sprawling handwriting.

MY DEAR FRIEND [the letter ran],—You will much regret to hear that the *wiles of the crocodile* have matured. The rebellion—the *so-called* rebellion—is all over and finished. And it has been, alas! a more Bloody affair than I had hoped should have been the case.

All has fallen out as I have prophesied to you it would be. On the day when you came back to Kyauktada U Po Kyin's *spies* have informed him that the poor unfortunate men whom he have Deluded are assembling in the jungle near Thongwa. The same night he sets out secretly with U Lugale, the Police Inspector, who is as great a Rogue as he, if that could be, and twelve constables. They make a swift raid upon Thongwa and surprise the rebels, of whom they are only Seven!! in a ruined field hut in the jungle. Also Mr Maxwell, who have heard rumours of the rebellion, came across from his camp bringing his Rifle and was in time to join U Po Kyin and the police in their attack on the hut. The next morning the clerk Ba Sein, who is U Po Kyin's *jackall* and *dirty worker,* have orders to raise the cry of rebellion as Sensationally as possible, which was done, and Mr Macgregor, Mr Westfield and Lieutenant Verrall all rush out to Thongwa carrying fifty sepoys armed with rifles besides Civil Police. But they arrive to find it is all over and U Po Kyin was sitting under a big teak tree in the middle of the village and *putting on airs* and lecturing the villages, whereat they are all bowing very frightened and touching the ground with their foreheads and swearing they will be forever loyal to the Government, and the rebellion is already at an end. The *so-called* weiksa, who is no other than a circus conjurer and the *minion* of U Po Kyin, have vanished for parts unknown, but six rebels have been Caught. So there is an end.

Also I should inform you that there was most regrettably a Death. Mr Maxwell was I think *too anxious* to use his Rifle and when one of the rebels try to run away he fired and shoot him in the abdomen, at which he died. I think the villagers have some *bad feeling* towards Mr Maxwell because of it. But from the point of view legal all is well for Mr Maxwell, because the men were undoubtedly conspiring against the Government.

Ah, but, my Friend, I trust that you understand how disastrous may all this be for me! You will realise, I think, what is its bearing upon the Contest between U Po Kyin and myself, and the supreme *leg-up* it must give to him. It is the *triumph of the crocodile*. U Po Kyin is now the Hero of the district. He is the *pet* of the Europeans. I am told that even Mr Ellis has praised his conduct. If you could witness the abominable Conceitedness and the *lies* he is now telling as to how there were not seven rebels but Two Hundred!! and how he crushed upon them revolver in hand—he who only directing operations from a *safe distance* while the police and Mr Maxwell creep up upon the hut—you would find it veritably Nauseous I assure you. He has had the effrontery to send in an official report of the matter which started, 'By my loyal promptitude and reckless daring', and I hear that positively he had had this Conglomeration of lies written out in readiness days *before the occurrence*. It is Disgusting. And to think that now when he is at the Height of his triumph he will again begin to calumniate me with all the venom at his disposal etc., etc.

The rebels' entire stock of weapons had been captured. The armoury with which, when their followers were assembled, they had proposed to march upon Kyauktada, consisted of the following:

Item, one shotgun with a damaged left barrel, stolen from a Forest Officer three years earlier.

Item, six home-made guns with barrels of zinc piping stolen from the railway. These could be fired, after a fashion, by thrusting a nail through the touch-hole and striking it with a stone.

Item, thirty-nine twelve-bore cartridges.

Item, eleven dummy guns carved out of teakwood.

Item, some large Chinese crackers which were to have been fired *in terrorem*.

Later, two of the rebels were sentenced to fifteen years' transportation, three to three years' imprisonment and twenty-five lashes, and one to two years' imprisonment.

The whole miserable rebellion was so obviously at an end that the Europeans were not considered to be in any danger, and Maxwell had gone back to his camp unguarded. Flory intended to stay in camp until the rains broke, or at least until the general meeting at the Club. He had promised to be in for that, to propose the doctor's election; though now, with his own trouble to think of, the whole business of the intrigue between U Po Kyin and the doctor sickened him.

More weeks crawled by. The heat was dreadful now. The overdue rain seemed to have bred a fever in the air. Flory was out of health, and worked incessantly, worrying over petty jobs that should have been left to the overseer, and making the coolies and even the servants hate him. He drank gin at all hours, but not even drinking could distract him now. The vision of Elizabeth in Verrall's arms haunted him like a neuralgia or an earache. At any moment it would come upon him, vivid and disgusting, scattering his thoughts, wrenching him back from the brink of sleep, turning his food to dust in his mouth. At times he flew into savage rages, and once even struck Ko S'la. What was worse than all was the *detail*–the always filthy detail–in which the imagined scene appeared. The very perfection of the detail seemed to prove that it was true.

Is there anything in the world more graceless, more dishonouring, than to desire a woman whom you will never have? Throughout all these weeks Flory's mind held hardly a thought which was not murderous or obscene. It is the common effect of jealousy. Once he had loved Elizabeth spiritually, sentimentally indeed, desiring her sympathy more than her caresses; now, when he had lost her, he was tormented by the basest physical longing. He did not even idealize her any longer. He saw her now almost as she was–silly, snobbish, heartless–and it made no difference to his longing for her. Does it ever make any difference? At nights when he lay awake, his bed dragged outside the tent for coolness, looking at the velvet dark from which the barking of a *gyi* sometimes sounded, he hated himself for the images that inhabited his mind. It was so base, this envying of the better man who had beaten him. For it was only envy–even jealousy was too good a name for it. What right had he to be jealous? He had offered himself to a girl who was too young and pretty for him, and she had turned him down–rightly. He had got the snub he deserved. Nor was there any appeal from that decision; nothing would ever make him young again, or take away his birthmark and his decade of lonely debaucheries. He could only stand and look on while the better man took her, and envy him, like–but the simile was not even mentionable. Envy is a horrible thing. It is unlike all other kinds of suffering in that there is no disguising it, no elevating it into tragedy. It is more than merely painful, it is disgusting.

But meanwhile, was it true, what he suspected? Had Verrall really become Elizabeth's lover? There is no knowing, but on the whole the chances were against it, for, had it been so, there would have been no concealing it in such a place as Kyauktada. Mrs Lackersteen would probably have guessed it, even if the others had not. One thing was certain, however, and that was that Verrall had as yet made no proposal of marriage. A week went by, two weeks, three weeks; three weeks is a very long time in a small Indian station. Verrall and Elizabeth rode together every evening, danced together every night; yet Verrall had never so much as entered the Lackersteens' house. There was endless scandal about Elizabeth, of course. All the Orientals of the town had taken it for granted that she was Verrall's mistress. U Po Kyin's version (he had a way of being essentially right even when he was wrong in detail) was that Elizabeth had been Flory's concubine and had deserted him for Verrall because Verrall paid her more. Ellis, too, was inventing tales about Elizabeth that made Mr Macgregor squirm. Mrs Lackersteen, as a relative, did not hear these scandals, but she was growing nervous. Every evening when Elizabeth came home from her ride she would meet her hopefully, expecting the 'Oh, aunt! What *do* you think!'–and then the glorious news. But the news never came, and however carefully she studied Elizabeth's face, she could divine nothing.

When three weeks had passed Mrs Lackersteen became fretful and finally half angry. The thought of her husband, alone–or rather, not alone–in his camp, was troubling her. After all, she had sent him back to camp in order to give Elizabeth her chance with Verrall (not that Mrs Lackersteen would have put it so vulgarly as that). One evening she began lecturing and threatening Elizabeth in her oblique way. The conversation consisted of a sighing monologue with very long pauses—for Elizabeth made no answer whatever.

Mrs Lackersteen began with some general remarks, apropos of a photograph in the *Tatler,* about these fast *modern* girls who went about in beach pyjamas and all that and made themselves so dreadfully *cheap* with men. A girl, Mrs Lackersteen said, should *never* make herself too cheap with a man; she should make herself—but the opposite of 'cheap' seemed to be 'expensive', and that did not sound at all right, so Mrs Lackersteen changed her tack. She went on to tell Elizabeth about a letter she had had from home with further news of that poor, *poor* dear girl who was out in Burma for a while and had so foolishly neglected to get married. Her sufferings had been quite heartrending, and it just showed how glad a girl ought to be to marry anyone, literally *anyone*. It appeared that the poor, poor dear girl had lost her job and been practically *starving* for a long time, and now she had actually had to take a job as a common kitchen maid under a horrid, vulgar cook who bullied her most shockingly. And it seemed that the black beetles in the kitchen were simply beyond belief! Didn't Elizabeth think it too absolutely dreadful? *Black beetles!*

Mrs Lackersteen remained silent for some time, to allow the black beetles to sink in, before adding:

'*Such* a pity that Mr Verrall will be leaving us when the rains break. Kyauktada will seem quite *empty* without him!'

'When do the rains break, usually?' said Elizabeth as indifferently as she could manage.

'About the beginning of June, up here. Only a week or two now. . . . My dear, it seems absurd to mention it again, but I cannot get out of my head the thought of that poor, poor dear girl in the kitchen among the *black beetles*!'

Black beetles recurred more than once in Mrs Lackersteen's conversation during the rest of the evening. It was not until the following day that she remarked in the tone of someone dropping an unimportant piece of gossip:

'By the way, I believe Flory is coming back to Kyauktada at the beginning of June. He said he was going to be in for the general meeting at the Club. Perhaps we might invite him to dinner some time.'

It was the first time that either of them had mentioned Flory since the day when he had brought Elizabeth the leopard-skin. After being virtually forgotten for several weeks, he had returned to each woman's mind, a depressing *pis aller*.

Three days later Mrs Lackersteen sent word to her husband to come back to Kyauktada. He had been in camp long enough to earn a short spell in headquarters. He came back, more florid than ever—sunburn, he explained—and having acquired such a trembling of the hands that he could barely light a cigarette. Nevertheless, that evening he celebrated his return by manœuvring Mrs Lackersteen out of the house, coming into Elizabeth's bedroom and making a spirited attempt to rape her.

During all this time, unknown to anyone of importance, further sedition was afoot. The 'weiksa' (now far away, peddling the philosopher's stone to innocent villagers in Martaban) had perhaps done his job a little better than he intended. At any rate, there was a possibility of fresh trouble—some isolated, futile outrage, probably. Even U Po Kyin knew nothing of this yet. But as usual the gods were fighting on his side, for any further rebellion would make the first seem more serious than it had been, and so add to his glory.

# 21

O western wind, when wilt thou blow, that the small rain down can rain? It was the first of June, the day of the general meeting, and there had not been a drop of rain yet. As Flory came up the Club path the sun of afternoon, slanting beneath his hat-brim, was still savage enough to scorch his neck uncomfortably. The *mali* staggered along the path, his breast-muscles slippery with sweat, carrying two kerosene-tins of water on a yoke. He dumped them down, slopping a little water over his lank brown feet, and salaamed to Flory.

'Well, *mali*, is the rain coming?'

The man gestured vaguely towards the west. 'The hills have captured it, sahib.'

Kyauktada was ringed almost round by hills, and these caught the earlier showers, so that sometimes no rain fell till amost the end of June. The earth of the flower-beds, hoed into large untidy lumps, looked grey and hard as concrete. Flory went into the lounge and found Westfield loafing by the veranda, looking out over the river, for the chicks had been rolled up. At the foot of the veranda a *chokra* lay on his back in the sun, pulling the punkah rope with his heel and shading his face with a broad strip of banana leaf.

'Hullo, Flory! You've got thin as a rake.'

'So've you.'

'H'm, yes. Bloody weather. No appetite except for booze. Christ, won't I be glad when I hear the frogs start croaking. Let's have a spot before the others come. Butler!'

'Do you know who's coming to the meeting?' Flory said, when the butler had brought whisky and tepid soda.

'Whole crowd, I believe. Lackersteen got back from camp three days ago. By God, that man's been having the time of his life away from his missus! My inspector was telling me about the goings-on at his camp. Tarts by the score. Must have imported 'em specially from Kyauktada. He'll catch it all right when the old woman sees his Club bill. Eleven bottles of whisky sent out to his camp in a fortnight.'

'Is young Verrall coming?'

'No, he's only a temporary member. Not that he'd trouble to come anyway, young tick. Maxwell won't be here either. Can't leave camp just yet, he says. He sent word Ellis was to speak for him if there's any voting to be done. Don't suppose there'll be anything to vote about, though eh?' he added, looking at Flory obliquely, for both of them remembered their previous quarrel on this subject.

'I suppose it lies with Macgregor.'

'What I mean is; Macgregor'll have dropped that bloody rot about electing a native member, eh? Not the moment for it just now. After the rebellion and all that.'

'What about the rebellion, by the way?' said Flory. He did not want to start wrangling about the doctor's election yet. There was going to be trouble and to spare in a few minutes. 'Any more news—are they going to have another try, do you think?'

'No. All over, I'm afraid. They caved in like the funks they are. The whole district's as quiet as a bloody girls' school. Most disappointing.'

Flory's heart missed a beat. He had heard Elizabeth's voice in the next room. Mr Macgregor came in at this moment, Ellis and Mr Lackersteen following. This made up the full quota, for the women members of the Club had no votes. Mr Macgregor was already dressed in a silk suit, and was carrying the Club account books under his arm. He managed to bring a sub-official air even into such petty business as a Club meeting.

'As we seem to be all here,' he said after the usual greetings, 'shall we—ah—proceed with our labours?'

'Lead on, Macduff,' said Westfield, sitting down.

'Call the butler, someone, for Christ's sake,' said Mr Lackersteen. 'I daren't let my missus hear me calling him.'

'Before we apply ourselves to the agenda,' said Mr Macgregor when he had refused a drink and the others had taken one, 'I expect you will want me to run through the accounts for the half-year?'

They did not want it particularly, but Mr Macgregor, who enjoyed this kind of thing, ran through the accounts with great thoroughness. Flory's thoughts were wandering. There was going to be such a row in a moment—oh, such a devil of a row! They would be furious when they found that he was proposing the doctor after all. And Elizabeth was in the next room. God send she didn't hear the noise of the row when it came. It would make her despise him all the more to see the others baiting him. Would he see her this evening? Would she speak to him? He gazed across the quarter-mile of gleaming river. By the far bank a knot of men, one of them wearing a green *gaungbaung*, were waiting beside a sampan. In the channel, by the nearer bank, a huge, clumsy Indian barge struggled with desperate slowness against the racing current. At each stroke the ten rowers, Dravidian starvelings, ran forward and plunged their long primitive oars, with heart-shaped blades, into the water. They braced their meagre bodies, then tugged, writhed, strained backwards like agonized creatures of black rubber, and the ponderous hull crept onwards a yard or two. Then the rowers sprang foward, panting, to plunge their oars again before the current should check her.

'And now,' said Mr Macgregor more gravely, 'we come to the main point of the agenda. That, of course, is this–ah–distasteful question, which I am afraid must be faced, of electing a native member to this Club. When we discussed the matter before–'

'What the hell!'

It was Ellis who had interrupted. He was so excited that he had sprung to his feet.

'What the hell! Surely we aren't starting *that* over again? Talk about electing a damned nigger to this Club, after everything that's happened! Good God, I thought even Flory had dropped it by this time!'

'Our friend Ellis appears surprised. The matter has been discussed before, I believe.'

'I should think it damned well was discussed before! And we all said what we thought of it. By God–'

'If our friend Ellis will sit down for a few moments–' said Mr Macgregor tolerantly.

Ellis threw himself into his chair again, exclaiming, 'Bloody rubbish!' Beyond the river Flory could see the group of Burmans embarking. They were lifting a long, awkward-shaped bundle into the sampan. Mr Macregor had produced a letter from his file of papers.

'Perhaps I had better explain how this question arose in the first place. The Commissioner tells me that a circular has been sent round by the Government, suggesting that in those Clubs where there are no native members, one at least shall be co-opted; that is, admitted automatically. The circular says–ah yes! here it is: "It is mistaken policy to offer social affronts to native officials of high standing." I may say that I disagree most emphatically. No doubt we all do. We who have to do the actual work of government see things very differently from these–ah–Paget M.P.s who interfere with us from above. The Commissioner quite agrees with me. However–'

'But it's all bloody rot!' broke in Ellis. 'What's it got to do with the Commissioner or anyone else? Surely we can do as we like in our own bloody Club? They've no right to dictate to us when we're off duty.'

'Quite,' said Westfield.

'You anticipate me. I told the Commissioner that I should have to put the matter before the other members. And the course he suggests is this. If the idea finds any support in the Club, he thinks it would be better if we co-opted our native member. On the other hand, if the entire Club is against it, it can be dropped. That is, if opinion is quite unanimous.'

'Well, it damned well is unanimous,' said Ellis.

'D'you mean,' said Westfield, 'that it depends on ourselves whether we have 'em in here or no?'

'I fancy we can take it as meaning that.'

'Well, then, let's say we're against it to a man.'

'And say it bloody firmly, by God. We want to put our foot down on this idea once and for all.'

'Hear, hear!' said Mr Lackersteen gruffly. 'Keep the black swabs out of it. *Esprit de corps* and all that.'

Mr Lackersteen could always be relied upon for sound sentiments in a case like this. In his heart he did not care and never had cared a damn for the British Raj, and he was as happy drinking with an Oriental as with a white man; but he was always ready with a loud 'Hear, hear!' when anyone suggested the bamboo for disrespectful servants or boiling oil for Nationalists. He prided himself that though he might booze a bit and all that, dammit, he *was* loyal. It was his form of respectability. Mr Macgregor was secretly rather relieved by the general agreement. If any Oriental member were co-opted, that member would have to be Dr Veraswami, and he had had the deepest distrust of the doctor ever since Nga Shwe O's suspicious escape from the jail.

'Then I take it that you are all agreed?' he said. 'If so, I will inform the Commissioner. Otherwise, we must begin discussing the candidate for election.'

Flory stood up. He had got to say his say. His heart seemed to have risen into his throat and to be choking him. From what Mr Macgregor had said, it was clear that it was in his power to secure the doctor's election by speaking the word. But oh, what a bore, what a nuisance it was! What an infernal uproar there would be! How he wished he had never given the doctor that promise! No matter, he had given it, and he could not break it. So short a time ago he would have broken it, *en bon pukka sahib,* how easily! But not now. He had got to see this thing through. He turned himself sidelong so that his birthmark was away from the others. Already he could feel his voice going flat and guilty.

'Our friend Flory has something to suggest?'

'Yes. I propose Dr Veraswami as a member of this Club.'

There was such a yell of dismay from three of the others that Mr Macgregor had to rap sharply on the table and remind them that the ladies were in the next room. Ellis took not the smallest notice. He had sprung to his feet again, and the skin round his nose had gone quite grey. He and Flory remained facing one another, as though on the point of blows.

'Now, you damned swab, will you take that back?'

'No, I will not.'

'You oily swine! You nigger's Nancy Boy! You crawling, sneaking,–bloody bastard!'

'Order!' exclaimed Mr Macgregor.

'But look at him, look at him!' cried Ellis almost tearfully. 'Letting us all down for the sake of a pot-bellied nigger! After all we've said to him! When we've only got to hang together and we can keep the stink of garlic out of this Club for ever. My God, wouldn't it make you spew your guts up to see anyone behaving like such a–?'

'Take it back, Flory, old man!' said Westfield. 'Don't be a bloody fool!'

'Downright Bolshevism, dammit!' said Mr Lackersteen.

'Do you think I care what you say? What business is it of yours? It's for Macgregor to decide.'

'Then do you–ah–adhere to your decision?' said Mr Macgregor gloomily.

'Yes.'

Mr Macgregor sighed. 'A pity! Well, in that case I suppose I have no choice–'

'No, no, no!' cried Ellis, dancing about in his rage. 'Don't give in to him! Put it to the vote. And if that son of a bitch doesn't put in a black ball like the rest of us, we'll first turf him out of the Club himself, and then–well! Butler!'

'Sahib!' said the butler, appearing.

'Bring the ballot box and the balls. Now clear out!' he added roughly when the butler had obeyed.

The air had gone very stagnant; for some reason the punkah had stopped working. Mr Macgregor stood up with a disapproving but judicial mien, taking the two drawers of black and white balls out of the ballot box.

'We must proceed in order. Mr Flory proposes Dr Veraswami, the Civil Surgeon, as a member of this Club. Mistaken, in my opinion, greatly mistaken; however–! Before putting the matter to the vote–'

'Oh, why make a song and dance about it?' said Ellis. 'Here's my contribution! And another for Maxwell.' He plumped two black balls into the box. Then one of his sudden spasms of rage seized him, and he took the drawer of white balls and pitched them across the floor. They went flying in all directions. 'There! Now pick one up if you want to use it!'

'You damned fool! What good do you think that does?'

'Sahib!'

They all started and looked round. The *chokra* was goggling at them over the veranda rail, having climbed up from below. With one skinny arm he clung to the rail and with the other gesticulated towards the river.

'Sahib! Sahib!'

'What's up?' said Westfield.

They all moved for the window. The sampan that Flory had seen across the river was lying under the bank at the foot of the lawn, one of the men clinging to a bush to steady it. The Burman in the green *gaungbaung* was climbing out.

'That's one of Maxwell's Forest Rangers!' said Ellis in quite a different voice. 'By God! something's happened!'

The Forest Ranger saw Mr Macgregor, shikoed in a hurried, preoccupied way and turned back to the sampan. Four other men, peasants, climbed out after him, and with difficulty lifted ashore the strange bundle that Flory had seen in the distance. It was six feet long, swathed in cloths, like a mummy. Something happened in everybody's entrails. The Forest Ranger glanced at the veranda, saw that there was no way up, and led the peasants round the path to the front of the Club. They had hoisted the bundle on to their shoulders as funeral bearers hoist a coffin. The butler had flitted into the lounge again, and even his face was pale after its fashion–that is, grey.

'Butler!' said Mr Macgregor sharply.

'Sir!'

'Go quickly and shut the door of the card-room. Keep it shut. Don't let the memsahibs see.'

'Yes, sir!'

The Burmans, with their burden, came heavily down the passage. As they entered the leading man staggered and almost fell; he had trodden on one of the white balls that were scattered about the floor. The Burmans knelt down, lowered their burden to the floor and stood over it with a strange reverent air, slightly bowing, their hands together in a shiko. Westfield had fallen on his knees, and he pulled back the cloth.

'Christ! Just look at him!' he said, but without much surprise. 'Just look at the poor little b—!'

Mr Lackersteen had retreated to the other end of the room, with a bleating noise. From the moment when the bundle was lifted ashore they had all known what it contained. It was the body of Maxwell, cut almost to pieces with *dahs* by two relatives of the man whom he had shot.

# 22

Maxwell's death had caused a profound shock in Kyauktada. It would cause a shock throughout the whole of Burma, and the case—'the Kyauktada case, do you remember?'—would still be talked of years after the wretched youth's name was forgotten. But in a purely personal way no one was much distressed. Maxwell had been almost a nonentity—just a 'good fellow' like any other of the ten thousand *ex colore* good fellows of Burma—and with no close friends. No one among the Europeans genuinely mourned for him. But that is not to say that they were not angry. On the contrary, for the moment they were almost mad with rage. For the unforgivable had happened—*a white man* had been killed. When that happens, a sort of shudder runs through the English of the East. Eight hundred people, possibly, are murdered every year in Burma; they matter nothing; but the murder of *a white man* is a monstrosity, a sacrilege. Poor Maxwell would be avenged, that was certain. But only a servant or two, and the Forest Ranger who had brought in his body and who had been fond of him, shed any tears for his death.

On the other hand, no one was actually pleased, except U Po Kyin.

'This is a positive gift from heaven!' he told Ma Kin. 'I could not have arranged it better myself. The one thing I needed to make them take my rebellion seriously was a little bloodshed. And here it is! I tell you, Ma Kin, every day I grow more certain that some higher power is working on my behalf.'

'Ko Po Kyin, truly you are without shame! I do not know how you dare to say such things. Do you not shudder to have murder upon your soul?'

'What! I? Murder upon my soul? What are you talking about? I have never killed so much as a chicken in my life.'

'But you are profiting by this poor boy's death.'

'Profiting by it! Of course I am profiting by it! And why not, indeed? Am I to blame if somebody else choose to commit murder? The fisherman catches fish, and he is damned for it. But are we damned for eating the fish? Certainly not. Why *not* eat the fish, once it is dead? You should study the Scriptures more carefully, my dear Kin Kin.'

The funeral took place next morning, before breakfast. All the Europeans were present, except Verrall, who was careering about the maidan quite as usual, almost opposite the cemetery. Mr Macgregor read the burial service. The little group of Englishmen stood round the grave, their topis in their hands, sweating into the dark suits that they had dug out from the bottom of their boxes. The harsh morning light beat without mercy upon their faces, yellower than ever against the ugly, shabby clothes. Every face except Elizabeth's looked lined and old. Dr Veraswami and half a dozen other Orientals were present, but they kept themselves decently in the background. There were sixteen gravestones in the little cemetery; assistants of timber firms, officials, soldiers killed in forgotten skirmishes.

'Sacred to the memory of John Henry Spagnall, late of the Indian Imperial Police, who was cut down by cholera while in the unremitting exercise of' etc., etc., etc.

Flory remembered Spagnall dimly. He had died very suddenly in camp after his second go of delirium tremens. In a corner there were some graves of Eurasians, with wooden crosses. The creeping jasmine, with tiny orange-hearted flowers, had overgrown everything. Among the jasmine, large rat-holes led down into the graves.

Mr Macgregor concluded the burial service in a ripe, reverent voice, and led the way out of the cemetery, holding his grey topi–the Eastern equivalent of a top hat–against his stomach. Flory lingered by the gate, hoping that Elizabeth would speak to him, but she passed him without a glance. Everyone had shunned him this morning. He was in disgrace; the murder had made his disloyalty of last night seem somehow horrible. Ellis had caught Westfield by the arm, and they halted at the grave-side, taking out their cigarette-cases. Flory could hear their slangy voices coming across the open grave.

'My God, Westfield, my God, when I think of that poor little b— lying down there–oh, my God, how my blood does boil! I couldn't sleep all night, I was so furious.'

'Pretty bloody, I grant. Never mind, promise you a couple of chaps shall swing for it. Two corpses against their one–best we can do.'

'Two! It ought to be fifty! We've got to raise heaven and hell to get these fellows hanged. Have you got their names yet?'

'Yes, rather!! Whole blooming district knows who did it. We always do know who's done it in these cases. Getting the bloody villagers to talk–that's the only trouble.'

'Well, for God's sake get them to talk this time. Never mind the bloody law. Whack it out of them. Torture them–anything. If you want to bribe any witnesses, I'm good for a couple of hundred chips.'

Westfield sighed. 'Can't do that sort of thing, I'm afraid. Wish we could. My chaps'd know how to put the screw on a witness if you gave 'em the word. Tie 'em down on an ant-hill. Red peppers. But that won't do nowadays. Got to keep our own bloody silly laws. But never mind, those fellows'll swing all right. We've got all the evidence we want.'

'Good! And when you've arrested them, if you aren't sure of getting a conviction, shoot them, jolly well shoot them! Fake up an escape or something. Anything sooner than let those b—s go free.'

'They won't go free, don't you fear. We'll get 'em. Get *somebody,* anyhow. Much better hang wrong fellow than no fellow,' he added, unconsciously quoting.

'That's the stuff! I'll never sleep easy again till I've seen them swinging,' said Ellis as they moved away from the grave. 'Christ! Let's get out of this sun! I'm about perishing with thirst.'

Everyone was perishing, more or less, but it seemed hardly decent to go down to the Club for drinks immediately after the funeral. The Europeans scattered for their houses, while four sweepers with *mamooties* flung the grey, cement-like earth back into the grave, and shaped it into a rough mound.

After breakfast, Ellis was walking down to his office, cane in hand. It was blinding hot. Ellis had bathed and changed back into shirt and shorts, but wearing a thick suit even for an hour had brought on his prickly heat abominably. Westfield had gone out already, in his motor launch, with an Inspector and half a dozen men, to arrest the murderers. He had ordered Verrall to accompany him—not that Verrall was needed, but, as Westfield said, it would do the young swab good to have a spot of work.

Ellis wriggled his shoulders—his prickly heat was almost beyond bearing. The rage was stewing in his body like a bitter juice. He had brooded all night over what had happened. They had killed a white man, killed *a white man,* the bloody sods, the sneaking, cowardly hounds! Oh, the swine, the swine, how they ought to be made to suffer for it! Why did we make these cursed kid-glove laws? Why did we take everything lying down? Just suppose this had happened in a German colony, before the War! The good old Germans! They knew how to treat the niggers. Reprisals! Rhinoceros hide whips! Raid their villages, kill their cattle, burn their crops, decimate them, blow them from the guns.

Ellis gazed into the horrible cascades of light that poured through the gaps in the trees. His greenish eyes were large and mournful. A mild, middle-aged Burman came by, balancing a huge bamboo, which he shifted from one shoulder to the other with a grunt as he passed Ellis. Ellis's grip tightened on his stick. If that swine, now, would only attack you! Or even insult you—anything, so that you had the right to smash him! If only these gutless curs would ever show fight in any conceivable way! Instead of just sneaking past you, keeping within the law so that you never had a chance to get back at them. Ah, for a real rebellion—martial law proclaimed and no quarter given! Lovely, sanguinary images moved through his mind. Shrieking mounds of natives, soldiers slaughtering them. Shoot them, ride them down, horses' hooves trample their guts out, whips cut their faces in slices!

Five High School boys came down the road abreast. Ellis saw them coming, a row of yellow, malicious faces—epicene faces, horribly smooth and young, grinning at him with deliberate insolence. It was in their minds to bait him, as a white man. Probably they had heard of the murder, and—being Nationalists, like all schoolboys—regarded it as a victory. They grinned full in Ellis's face as they passed him. They were trying openly to provoke him, and they knew that the law was on their side. Ellis felt his breast swell. The look of their faces, jeering at him like a row of yellow images, was maddening. He stopped short.

'Here! What are you laughing at, you young ticks?'

The boys turned.

'I said what the bloody hell are you laughing at?'

One of the boys answered, insolently—but perhaps his bad English made him seem more insolent than he intended.

'Not your business.'

There was about a second during which Ellis did not know what he was doing. In that second he had hit out with all his strength, and the cane landed, crack! right across the boy's eyes. The boy recoiled with a shriek, and in the same instant the other four had thrown themselves upon Ellis. But he was too strong for them. He flung them aside and sprang back, lashing out with his stick so furiously that none of them dared come near.

'Keep your distance, you —s! Keep off, or by God I'll smash another of you!'

Though they were four to one he was so formidable that they surged back in fright. The boy who was hurt had fallen on his knees with his arms across his face, and was screaming 'I am blinded! I am blinded!' Suddenly the other four turned and darted for a pile of laterite, used for road-mending, which was twenty yards away. One of Ellis's clerks had appeared on the veranda of the office and was leaping up and down in agitation.

'Come up, sir come up at once. They will murder you!'

Ellis disdained to run, but he moved for the veranda steps. A lump of laterite came sailing through the air and shattered itself against a pillar, whereat the clerk scooted indoors. But Ellis turned on the veranda to face the boys, who were below, each carrying an armful of laterite. He was cackling with delight.

'You damned, dirty little niggers!' he shouted down at them. 'You got a surprise that time, didn't you? Come up on this veranda and fight me, all four of you! You daren't. Four to one and you daren't face me! Do you call yourselves men? You sneaking, mangy little rats!'

He broke into Burmese, calling them the incestuous children of pigs. All the while they were pelting him with lumps of laterite, but their arms were feeble and they threw ineptly. He dodged the stones, and as each one missed him he cackled in triumph. Presently there was a sound of shouts up the road, for the noise had been heard at the police station, and some constables were emerging to see what was the matter. The boys took fright and bolted, leaving Ellis a complete victor.

Ellis had heartily enjoyed the affray, but he was furiously angry as soon as it was over. He wrote a violent note to Mr Macgregor, telling him that he had been wantonly assaulted and demanding vengeance. Two clerks who had witnessed the scene, and a *chaprassi,* were sent along to Mr Macgregor's office to corroborate the story. They lied in perfect unison. 'The boys had attacked Mr Ellis without any provocation whatever, he had defended himself,' etc., etc. Ellis, to do him justice, probably believed this to be a truthful version of the story. Mr Macgregor was somewhat disturbed, and ordered the police to find the four schoolboys and interrogate them. The boys, however, had been expecting something of the kind, and were lying very low; the police searched the bazaar all day without finding them. In the evening the wounded boy was taken to a Burmese doctor, who, by applying some poisonous concoction of crushed leaves to his left eye, succeeded in blinding him.

The Europeans met at the Club as usual that evening, except for Westfield and Verrall, who had not yet returned. Everyone was in a bad mood. Coming on top of the murder, the unprovoked attack on Ellis (for that was the accepted description of it) had scared them as well as angered them. Mrs Lackersteen was twittering to the tune of 'We shall all be murdered in our beds'. Mr Macgregor, to reassure her, told her in cases of riot the European ladies were always locked inside the jail until everything was over; but she did not seem much comforted. Ellis was offensive to Flory, and Elizabeth cut him almost dead. He had come down to the Club in the insane hope of making up their quarrel, and her demeanour made him so miserable that for the greater part of the evening he skulked in the library. It was not till eight o'clock when everyone had swallowed a number of drinks, that the atmosphere grew a little more friendly, and Ellis said:

'What about sending a couple of *chokras* up to our houses and getting our dinners sent down here? We might as well have a few rubbers of bridge. Better than mooning about at home.'

Mrs Lackersteen, who was in dread of going home, jumped at the suggestion. The Europeans occasionally dined at the Club when they wanted to stay late. Two of the *chokras* were sent for, and on being told what was wanted of them, immediately burst into tears. It appeared that if they went up the hill they were certain of encountering Maxwell's ghost. The *mali* was sent instead. As the man set out Flory noticed that it was again the night of the full moon—four weeks to a day since that evening, now unutterably remote, when he had kissed Elizabeth under the frangipani tree.

They had just sat down at the bridge table, and Mrs Lackersteen had just revoked out of pure nervousness, when there was a heavy thump on the roof. Everyone started and look up.

'A coco-nut falling!' said Mr Macgregor.

'There aren't any coco-nut trees here,' said Ellis.

The next moment a number of things happened all together. There was another and much louder bang, one of the petrol lamps broke from its hook and crashed to the ground, narrowly missing Mr Lackersteen, who jumped aside with a yelp, Mrs Lackersteen began screaming, and the butler rushed into the room, bareheaded, his face the colour of bad coffee.

'Sir, sir! Bad men come! Going to murder us all, sir!'

'What? Bad men? What do you mean?'

'Sir, all the villagers are outside! Big stick and *dah* in their hands, and all dancing about! Going to cut master's throat, sir!'

Mrs Lackersteen threw herself backwards in her chair. She was setting up such a din of screams as to drown the butler's voice.

'Oh, be quiet!' said Ellis sharply, turning on her. 'Listen, all of you! Listen to that!'

There was a deep, murmurous, dangerous sound outside, like the humming of an angry giant. Mr Macgregor, who had stood up, stiffened as he heard it, and settled his spectacles pugnaciously on his nose.

'This is some kind of disturbance! Butler, pick that lamp up. Miss Lackersteen, look to your aunt. See if she is hurt. The rest of you come with me!'

They all made for the front door, which someone, presumably the butler, had closed. A fusillade of small pebbles was rattling against it like hail. Mr Lackersteen wavered at the sound and retreated behind the others.

'I say, dammit, bolt that bloody door, someone!' he said.

'No, no!' said Mr Macgregor. 'We must go outside. It's fatal not to face them!'

He opened the door and presented himself boldly at the top of the steps. There were about twenty Burmans·on the path, with *dahs* or sticks in their hands. Outside the fence, stretching up the road in either direction and far out on to the maidan, was an enormous crowd of people. It was like a sea of people, two thousand at the least, black and white in the moon, with here and there a curved *dah* glittering. Ellis had coolly placed himself beside Mr Macgregor, with his hands in his pockets. Mr Lackersteen had disappeared.

Mr Macgregor raised his hand for silence. 'What is the meaning of this?' he shouted sternly.

There were yells, and some lumps of laterite the size of cricket balls came sailing from the road, but fortunately hit no one. One of the men on the path turned and waved his arms to the others, shouting that they were not to begin throwing yet. Then he stepped forward to address the Europeans. He was a strong debonair fellow of about thirty, with down-curving moustaches, wearing a singlet, with his *longyi* kilted to the knee.

'What is the meaning of this?' Mr Macgregor repeated.

The man spoke up with a cheerful grin, and not very insolently.

'We have no quarrel with you, *min gyi*. We have come for the timber merchant, Ellis.' (He pronounced it Ellit.) 'The boy whom he struck this morning has gone blind. You must send Ellit out to us here, so that we can punish him. The rest of you will not be hurt.'

'Just remember that fellow's face,' said Ellis over his shoulder to Flory. 'We'll get him seven years for this afterwards.'

Mr Macgregor had turned temporarily quite purple. His rage was so great that it almost choked him. For several moments he could not speak, and when he did so it was in English.

'Whom do you think you are speaking to? In twenty years I have never heard such insolence! Go away this instant, or I shall call out the Military Police!'

'You'd better be quick, *min gyi*. We know that there is no justice for us in your courts, so we must punish Ellit ourselves. Send him out to us here. Otherwise, all of you will weep for it.'

Mr Macgregor made a furious motion with his fist, as though hammering in a nail. 'Go away, son of a dog!' he cried, using his first oath in many years.

There was a thunderous roar from the road, and such a shower of stones, that everyone was hit, including the Burmans on the path. One stone took Mr Macgregor full in the face, almost knocking him down. The Europeans bolted hastily inside and barred the door. Mr Macgregor's spectacles were smashed and his nose streaming blood. They got back to the lounge to find Mrs Lackersteen looping about in one of the long chairs like a hysterical snake, Mr Lackersteen standing irresolutely in the middle of the room, holding an empty bottle, the butler on his knees in the corner, crossing himself (he was a Roman Catholic), the *chokras* crying, and only Elizabeth calm, though she was very pale.

'What's happened?' she exclaimed.

'We're in the soup, that's what's happened!' said Ellis angrily, feeling at the back of his neck where a stone had hit him. 'The Burmans are all round, shying rocks. But keep calm! They haven't the guts to break the doors in.'

'Call out the police at once!' said Mr Macgregor indistinctly, for he was stanching his nose with his handkerchief.

'Can't!' said Ellis. 'I was looking round while you were talking to them. They've cut us off, rot their damned souls! No one could possibly get to the police lines. Veraswami's compound is full of men.'

'Then we must wait. We can trust them to turn out of their own accord. Calm yourself, my dear Mrs Lackersteen, *please* calm yourself! The danger is very small.'

It did not sound small. There were no gaps in the noise now, and the Burmans seemed to be pouring into the compounds by hundreds. The din swelled suddenly to such a volume that no one could make himself heard except by shouting. All the windows in the lounge had been shut, and some perforated zinc shutters within, which were sometimes used for keeping out insects, pulled to and bolted. There was a series of crashes as the windows were broken, and then a ceaseless thudding of stones from all sides, that shook the thin wooden walls and seemed likely to split them. Ellis opened a shutter and flung a bottle viciously among the crowd, but a dozen stones came hurtling in and he had to close the shutter hurriedly. The Burmans seemed to have no plan beyond flinging stones, yelling and hammering at the walls, but the mere volume of noise was unnerving. The Europeans were half dazed by it at first. None of them thought to blame Ellis, the sole cause of this affair; their common peril seemed, indeed, to draw them closer together for the while. Mr Macgregor, half-blind without his spectacles, stood distractedly in the middle of the room, yielding his right hand to Mrs Lackersteen, who was caressing it, while a weeping *chokra* clung to his left leg. Mr Lackersteen had vanished again. Ellis was stamping furiously up and down, shaking his fist in the direction of the police lines.

'Where are the police, the f— cowardly sods?' he yelled, heedless of the women. 'Why don't they turn out? My God, we won't get another chance like this in a hundred years! If we'd only ten rifles here, how we could slosh these b—s!'

'They'll be here presently!' Mr Macgregor shouted back. 'It will take them some minutes to penetrate that crowd.'

'But why don't they use their rifles, the miserable sons of bitches? They could slaughter them in bloody heaps if they'd only open fire. Oh, God, to think of missing a chance like this!'

A lump of rock burst one of the zinc shutters. Another followed through the hole it had made, stove in a 'Bonzo' picture, bounced off, cut Elizabeth's elbow, and finally landed on the table. There was a roar of triumph from outside, and then a succession of tremendous thumps on the roof. Some children had climbed into the trees and were having the time of their lives sliding down the roof on their bottoms. Mrs Lackersteen outdid all previous efforts with a shriek that rose easily above the din outside.

'Choke that bloody hag, somebody!' cried Ellis. 'Anyone'd think a pig was being killed. We've got to do something. Flory, Macgregor, come here! Think of a way out of this mess, someone!'

Elizabeth had suddenly lost her nerve and begun crying. The blow from the stone had hurt her. To Flory's astonishment, he found her clinging tightly to his arm. Even in that moment it made his heart turn over. He had been watching the scene almost with detachment—dazed by the noise, indeed, but not much frightened. He always found it difficult to believe Orientals could be really dangerous. Only when he felt Elizabeth's hand on his arm did he grasp the seriousness of the situation.

'Oh, Mr Flory, please, please think of something! You can, you can! Anything sooner than let those dreadful men get in here!'

'If only one of us could get to the police lines!' groaned Mr Macgregor. 'A British officer to lead them! At the worst I must try and go myself.'

'Don't be a fool! Only get your throat cut!' yelled Ellis. '*I'll* go if they really look like breaking in. But, oh, to be killed by swine like that! How furious it'd make me! And to think we could murder the whole bloody crowd if only we could get the police here!'

'Couldn't someone get along the river bank?' Flory shouted despairingly.

'Hopeless! Hundreds of them prowling up and down. We're cut off—Burmans on three sides and the river on the other!'

'The river!'

One of those startling ideas that are overlooked simply because they are so obvious had sprung into Flory's mind.

'The river! Of course! We can get to the police lines as easy as winking. Don't you see?'

'How?'

'Why, down the river—in the water! Swim!'

'Oh, good man!' cried Ellis, and smacked Flory on the shoulder. Elizabeth squeezed his arm and actually danced a step or two in glee. 'I'll go if you like!' Ellis shouted, but Flory shook his head. He had already begun slipping his shoes off. There was obviously no time to be lost. The Burmans had behaved like fools hitherto, but there was no saying what might happen if they succeeded in breaking in. The butler, who had got over his first fright, prepared to open the window that gave on the lawn, and glanced obliquely out. There were barely a score of Burmans on the lawn. They had left the back of the Club unguarded, supposing that the river cut off retreat.

'Rush down the lawn like hell!' Ellis shouted in Flory's ear. 'They'll scatter all right when they see you.'

'Order the police to open fire at once!' shouted Mr Macgregor from the other side. 'You have my authority.'

'And tell them to aim low! No firing over their heads. Shoot to kill. In the guts for choice!'

Flory leapt down from the veranda, hurting his feet on the hard earth, and was at the river bank in six paces. As Ellis had said, the Burmans recoiled for a moment when they saw him leaping down. A few stones followed him, but no one pursued—they thought, no doubt, that he was only attempting to escape, and in the clear moonlight they could see that it was not Ellis. In another moment he had pushed his way through the bushes and was in the water.

He sank deep down, and the horrible river ooze received him, sucking him knee-deep so that it was several seconds before he could free himself. When he came to the surface a tepid froth, like the froth on stout, was lapping round his lips, and some spongy thing had floated into his throat and was choking him. It was a sprig of water hyacinth. He managed to spit it out, and found that the swift current had floated him twenty yards already. Burmans were rushing rather aimlessly up and down the bank, yelling. With his eye at the level of the water, Flory could not see the crowd besieging the Club; but he could hear their deep, devilish roaring, which sounded even louder than it had sounded on shore. By the time he was opposite the Military Police lines the bank seemed almost bare of men. He managed to struggle out of the current and flounder through the mud, which sucked off his left sock. A little way down the bank two old men were sitting beside a fence, sharpening fence-posts, as though there had not been a riot within a hundred miles of them. Flory crawled ashore, clambered over the fence and ran heavily across the moonwhite parade-ground, his wet trousers sagging. As far as he could tell in the noise, the lines were quite empty. In some stalls over to the right Verrall's horses were plunging about in a panic. Flory ran out on to the road, and saw what had happened.

The whole body of policemen, military and civil, about a hundred and fifty men in all, had attacked the crowd from the rear, armed only with sticks. They had been utterly engulfed. The crowd was so dense that it was like an enormous swarm of bees seething and rotating. Everywhere one could see policemen wedged helplessly among the hordes of Burmans, struggling furiously but uselessly, and too cramped even to use their sticks. Whole knots of men were tangled Laocoön-like in the folds of unrolled *pagris*. There was a terrific bellowing of oaths in three or four languages, clouds of dust, and a suffocating stench of sweat and marigolds—but no one seemed to have been seriously hurt. Probably the Burmans had not used their *dahs* for fear of provoking rifle-fire. Flory pushed his way into the crowd and was immediately swallowed up like the others. A sea of bodies closed in upon him and flung him from side to side, bumping his ribs and choking him with their animal heat. He struggled onwards with an almost dreamlike feeling, so absurd and unreal was the situation. The whole riot had been ludicrous from the start, and what was most ludicrous of all was that the Burmans, who might have killed him, did not know what to do with him now he was among them. Some yelled insults in his face, some jostled him and stamped on his feet, some even tried to make way for him, as a white man. He was not certain whether he was fighting for his life, or merely pushing his way through the crowd. For quite a long time he was jammed, helpless, with his arms pinned against his sides, then he found himself wrestling with a stumpy Burman much stronger than himself, then a dozen men rolled against him like a wave and drove him deeper into the heart of the crowd. Suddenly he felt an agonizing pain in his right big toe—someone in boots had trodden on it. It was the Military Police subahdar, a Rajput, very fat, moustachioed, with his *pagri* gone. He was grasping a Burman by the throat and trying to hammer his face, while the sweat rolled off his bare, bald crown. Flory threw his arm round the subahdar's neck and managed to tear him away from his adversary and shout in his ear. His Urdu deserted him, and he bellowed in Burmese:

'Why did you not open fire?'

For a long time he could not hear the man's answer. Then he caught it:

'*Hukm ne aya*'—'I have had no order!'

'Idiot!'

At this moment another bunch of men drove against them, and for a minute or two they were pinned and quite unable to move. Flory realized that the subahdar had a whistle in his pocket and was trying to get at it. Finally he got it loose and blew piercing blasts, but there was no hope of rallying any men until they could get into a clear space. It was a fearful labour to struggle out of the crowd—it was like wading neck-deep through a viscous sea. At times the exhaustion of Flory's limbs was so complete that he stood passive, letting the crowd hold him and even drive him backwards. At last, more from the natural eddying of the crowd than by his own effort, he found himself flung out into the open. The subahdar had also emerged, ten or fifteen sepoys, and a Burmese Inspector of Police. Most of the sepoys collapsed on their haunches almost falling with fatigue, and limping, their feet having been trampled on.

'Come on, get up! Run like hell for the lines! Get some rifles and a clip of ammunition each.'

He was too overcome even to speak in Burmese, but the men understood him and lopped heavily towards the police lines. Flory followed them, to get away from the crowd before they turned on him again. When he reached the gate the sepoys were returning with their rifles and already preparing to fire.

'The sahib will give the order!' the subahdar panted.

'Here you!' cried Flory to the Inspector. 'Can you speak Hindustani?'

'Yes, sir.'

'Then tell them to fire high, right over the people's heads. And above all, to fire all together. Make them understand that.'

The fat Inspector, whose Hindustani was even worse than Flory's, explained what was wanted, chiefly by leaping up and down and gesticulating. The sepoys raised their rifles, there was a roar, and a rolling echo from the hillside. For a moment Flory thought that his order had been disregarded, for almost the entire section of the crowd nearest them had fallen like a swath of hay. However, they had only flung themselves down in panic. The sepoys fired a second volley, but it was not needed. The crowd had immediately begun to surge outwards from the Club like a river changing its course. They came pouring down the road, saw the armed men barring their way, and tried to recoil, whereupon there was a fresh battle between those in front and those behind; finally the whole crowd bulged outwards and began to roll slowly up the maidan. Flory and the sepoys moved slowly towards the Club on the heels of the retreating crowd. The policemen who had been engulfed were straggling back by ones and twos. Their *pagris* were gone and their puttees trailing yards behind them, but they had no damage worse than bruises. The Civil Policemen were dragging a very few prisoners among them. When they reached the Club compound the Burmans were still pouring out, an endless line of young men leaping gracefully through a gap in the hedge like a procession of gazelles. It seemed to Flory that it was getting very dark. A small white-clad figure extricated itself from the last of the crowd and tumbled limply into Flory's arms. It was Dr Veraswami, with his tie torn off but his spectacles miraculously unbroken.

'Doctor!'

'Ach, my friend! Ach, how I am exhausted!'

'What are you doing here? Were you right in the middle of that crowd?'

'I was trying to restrain them, my friend. It was hopeless until you came. But there is at least one man who bears the mark of this, I think!'

He held out a small fist for Flory to see the damaged knuckles. But it was certainly quite dark now. At the same moment Flory heard a nasal voice behind him.

'Well, Mr Flory, so it's all over already! A mere flash in the pan as usual. You and I together were a little too much for them—ha, ha!'

It was U Po Kyin. He came towards them with a martial air, carrying a huge stick, and with a revolver thrust into his belt. His dress was a studious *négligé*—singlet and Shan trousers—to give the impression that he had rushed out of his house post-haste. He had been lying low until the danger should be over, and was now hurrying forth to grab a share of any credit that might be going.

'A smart piece of work, sir!' he said enthusiastically. 'Look how they are flying up the hillside! We have routed them most satisfactory.'

'*We!*' panted the doctor indignantly.

'Ah, my dear doctor! I did not perceive that you were there. It is possible that *you* also have been in the fighting? *You*—risking your most valuable life! Who would have believed such a thing?'

'You've taken your time getting here yourself!' said Flory angrily.

'Well, well sir, it is enough that we have dispersed them. Although,' he added with a touch of satisfaction, for he had noticed Flory's tone, 'they are going in the direction of the European houses, you will observe. I fancy that it will occur to them to do a little plundering on their way.'

One had to admire the man's impudence. He tucked his great stick under his arm and strolled beside Flory in an almost patronizing manner, while the doctor dropped behind, abashed in spite of himself. At the Club gate all three men halted. It was now extraordinarily dark, and the moon had vanished. Low overhead, just visible, black clouds were streaming eastward like a pack of hounds. A wind, almost cold, blew down the hillside and swept a cloud of dust and fine water-vapour before it. There was a sudden intensely rich scent of damp. The wind quickened, the trees rustled, then began beating themselves furiously together, the big frangipani tree by the tennis court flinging out a nebula of dimly seen blossom. All three men turned and hurried for shelter, the Orientals to their houses, Flory to the Club. It had begun raining.

## 23

Next day the town was quieter than a cathedral city on Monday morning. It is usually the case after a riot. Except for the handful of prisoners, everyone who could possibly have been concerned in the attack on the Club had a watertight alibi. The Club garden looked as though a herd of bison had stampeded across it, but the houses had not been plundered, and there were no new casualties among the Europeans, except that after everything was over Mr Lackersteen had been found very drunk under the billiard-table, where he had retired with a bottle of whisky. Westfield and Verrall came back early in the morning, bringing Maxwell's murderers under arrest; or at any rate, bringing two people who would presently be hanged for Maxwell's murder. Westfield, when he heard the news of the riot, was gloomy but resigned. *Again* it happened—a veritable riot, and he not there to quell it! It seemed fated that he should never kill a man. Depressing, depressing. Verrall's only comment was that it had been 'damned lip' on the part of Flory (a civilian) to give orders to the Military Police.

Meanwhile, it was raining almost without cease. As soon as he woke up and heard the rain hammering on the roof Flory dressed and hurried out, Flo following. Out of sight of the houses he took off his clothes and let the rain sluice down on his bare body. To his surprise, he found that he was covered with bruises from last night; but the rain had washed away every trace of his prickly heat within three minutes. It is wonderful, the healing power of rain-water. Flory walked down to Dr Veraswami's house, with his shoes squelching and periodical jets of water flowing down his neck from the brim of his Terai hat. The sky was leaden, and innumerable whirling storms chased one another across the maidan like squadrons of cavalry. Burmans passed, under vast wooden hats in spite of which their bodies streamed water like the bronze gods in the fountains. A network of rivulets was already washing the stones of the road bare. The doctor had just got home when Flory arrived, and was shaking a wet umbrella over the veranda rail. He hailed Flory excitedly.

'Come up, Mr Flory, come up at once! You are just apropos. I was on the point of opening a bottle of Old Tommy Gin. Come up and let me drink to your health, ass the saviour of Kyauktada!'

They had a long talk together. The doctor was in a triumphant mood. It appeared that what had happened last night had righted his troubles almost miraculously. U Po Kyin's schemes were undone. The doctor was no longer at his mercy—in fact, it was the other way about. The doctor explained to Flory:

'You see, my friend, this riot—or rather, your most noble behaviour in it—wass quite outside U Po Kyin's programme. He had started the *so-called* rebellion and had the glory of crushing it, and he calculated that any further outbreak would simply mean more glory still. I am told that when he heard of Mr Maxwell's death, hiss joy was positively'—the doctor nipped his thumb and forefinger together—'what iss the word I want?'

'Obscene?'

'Ah yes. Obscene. It iss said that actually he attempted to dance—can you imagine such a disgusting spectacle?—and exclaimed, "Now at least they will take my rebellion seriously!" Such iss his regard for human life. But now hiss triumph iss at an end. The riot hass tripped up in mid-career.'

'How?'

'Because, do you not see, the honours of the riot are not hiss, but yours! And I am known to be your friend. I stand, so to speak, in the reflection of your glory. Are you not the hero of the hour? Did not your European friends receive you with open arms when you returned to the Club last night?'

'They did, I must admit. It was quite a new experience for me. Mrs Lackersteen was all over me. "*Dear* Mr Flory", she calls me now. And she's got her knife properly in Ellis. She hasn't forgotten that he called her a bloody hag and told her to stop squealing like a pig.'

'Ah, Mr Ellis iss sometimes over-emphatic in hiss expressions. I have noticed it.'

'The only fly in the ointment is that I told the police to fire over the crowd's heads instead of straight at them. It seems that's against all the Government regulations. Ellis was a little vexed about it. "Why didn't you plug some of the b—s when you had the chance?" he said. I pointed out that it would have meant hitting the police who were in the middle of the crowd; but as he said, they were only niggers anyway. However, all my sins are forgiven me. And Macgregor quoted something in Latin—Horace, I believe.'

It was half an hour later when Flory walked along to the Club. He had promised to see Mr Macgregor and settle the business of the doctor's election. But there would be no difficulty about it now. The others would eat out of his

hand until the absurd riot was forgotten; he could have gone into the Club and
made a speech in favour of Lenin, and they would have put up with it. The
lovely rain streamed down, drenching him from head to foot, and filling his
nostrils with the scent of earth, forgotten during the bitter months of drought.
He walked up the wrecked garden, where the *mali*, bending down with the rain
splashing on his bare back, was trowelling holes for zinnias. Nearly all the
flowers had been trampled out of existence. Elizabeth was there, on the side
veranda, almost as though she were waiting for him. He took off his hat,
spilling a pool of water from the brim, and went round to join her.

'Good morning!' he said, raising his voice because of the rain that beat
noisily on the low roof.

'Good morning! *Isn't* it coming down? Simply *pelting!*'

'Oh, this isn't real rain. You wait till July. The whole Bay of Bengal is going
to pour itself on us, by instalments.'

It seemed that they must never meet without talking of the weather.
Nevertheless, her face said something very different from the banal words. Her
demeanour had changed utterly since last night. He took courage.

'How is the place where that stone hit you?'

She held her arm out to him and let him take it. Her air was gentle, even
submissive. He realized that his exploit of last night had made him almost a
hero in her eyes. She could not know how small the danger had really been, and
she forgave him everything, even Ma Hla May, because he had shown courage
at the right moment. It was the buffalo and the leopard over again. His heart
thumped in his breast. He slipped his hand down her arm and clasped her
fingers in his own.

'Elizabeth—'

'Someone will see us!' she said, and she withdrew her hand, but not angrily.

'Elizabeth, I've something I want to say to you. Do you remember a letter I
wrote you from the jungle, after our—some weeks ago?'

'Yes.'

'You remember what I said in it?'

'Yes. I'm sorry I didn't answer it. Only—'

'I couldn't expect you to answer it, then. But I just wanted to remind you of
what I said.'

In the letter, of course, he had only said, and feebly enough, that he loved
her—would always love her, no matter what happened. They were standing
face to face, very close together. On an impulse—and it was so swiftly done that
afterwards he had difficulty in believing that it had ever happened—he took her
in his arms and drew her towards him. For a moment she yielded and let him
lift up her face and kiss her; then suddenly she recoiled and shook her head.
Perhaps she was frightened that someone would see them, perhaps it was only
because his moustache was so wet from the rain. Without saying anything
more she broke from him and hurried away into the Club. There was a look of
distress or compunction in her face; but she did not seem angry.

He followed her more slowly into the Club, and ran into Mr Macgregor,
who was in a very good humour. As soon as he saw Flory he boomed genially,

'Aha! The conquering hero comes!' and then, in a more serious vein, offered him fresh congratulations. Flory improved the occasion by saying a few words on behalf of the doctor. He painted quite a lively picture of the doctor's heroism in the riot. 'He was right in the middle of the crowd, fighting like a tiger,' etc., etc. It was not too much exaggerated—for the doctor had certainly risked his life. Mr Macgregor was impressed, and so were the others when they heard of it. At all times the testimony of one European can do an Oriental more good than that of a thousand of his fellow countrymen; and at this moment Flory's opinion carried weight. Practically, the doctor's good name was restored. His election to the Club could be taken as assured.

However, it was not finally agreed upon yet, because Flory was returning to camp. He set out the same evening, marching by night, and he did not see Elizabeth again before leaving. It was quite safe to travel in the jungle now, for the futile rebellion was obviously finished. There is seldom any talk of rebellion after the rains have started—the Burmans are too busy ploughing, and in any case the waterlogged fields are impassable for large bodies of men. Flory was to return to Kyauktada in ten days, when the padre's six-weekly visit fell due. The truth was that he did not care to be in Kyauktada while both Elizabeth and Verrall were there. And yet, it was strange, but all the bitterness—all the obscene, crawling envy that had tormented him before—was gone now that he knew she had forgiven him. It was only Verrall who stood between them now. And even the thought of her in Verrall's arms could hardly move him, because he knew that at the worst the affair must have an end. Verrall, it was quite certain, would never marry Elizabeth; young men of Verrall's stamp do not marry penniless girls met casually at obscure Indian stations. He was only amusing himself with Elizabeth. Presently he would desert her, and she would return to him—to Flory. It was enough—it was far better than he had hoped. There is a humility about genuine love that is rather horrible in some ways.

U Po Kyin was furiously angry. The miserable riot had taken him unawares, so far as anything ever took him unawares, and it was like a handful of grit thrown into the machinery of his plans. The business of disgracing the doctor had got to be begun all over again. Begun it was, sure enough, with such a spate of anonymous letters that Hla Pe had to absent himself from office for two whole days—it was bronchitis this time—to get them written. The doctor was accused of every crime from pederasty to stealing Government postage stamps. The prison warder who had let Nga Shwe O escape had now come up for trial. He was triumphantly acquitted, U Po Kyin having spent as much as two hundred rupees in bribing the witnesses. More letters showered up on Mr Macgregor, proving in detail that Dr Veraswami, the real author of the escape, had tried to shift the blame on to a helpless subordinate. Nevertheless, the results were disappointing. The confidential letter which Mr Macgregor wrote to the Commissioner, reporting on the riot, was steamed open, and its tone was so alarming—Mr Macgregor had spoken of the doctor as 'behaving most creditably' on the night of the riot—that U Po Kyin called a council of war.

'The time has come for a vigorous move,' he said to the others—they were in conclave on the front veranda, before breakfast. Ma Kin was there, and Ba Sein and Hla Pe—the latter a bright-faced, promising boy of eighteen, with the manner of one who will certainly succeed in life.

'We are hammering against a brick wall,' U Po Kyin continued; 'and that wall is Flory. Who could have foreseen that that miserable coward would stand by his friend? However, there it is. So long as Veraswami has his backing, we are helpless.'

'I have been talking to the Club butler, sir,' said Ba Sein. 'He tells me that Mr Ellis and Mr Westfield still do not want the doctor to be elected to the Club. Do you not think they will quarrel with Flory again as soon as this business of the riot is forgotten?'

'Of course they will quarrel, they always quarrel. But in the meantime the harm is done. Just suppose that man *were* elected! I believe I should die of rage if it happened. No, there is only one move left. We must strike at Flory himself!'

'At Flory, sir! But he is a white man!'

'What do I care? I have ruined white men before now. Once let Flory be disgraced, and there is an end of the doctor. And he shall be disgraced! I will shame him so that he will never dare show his face in that Club again!'

'But, sir! A white man! What are we to accuse him of? Who would believe anything against a white man?'

'You have no strategy, Ko Ba Sein. One does not *accuse* a white man; one has got to catch him in the act. Public disgrace, *in flagrante delicto*. I shall know how to set about it. Now be silent while I think.'

There was a pause. U Po Kyin stood gazing out into the rain with his small hands clasped behind him and resting on the natural plateau of his posterior. The other three watched him from the end of the veranda, almost frightened by this talk of attacking a white man, and waiting for some masterstroke to cope with a situation that was beyond them. It was a little like the familiar picture (is it Meissonier's?) of Napoleon at Moscow, poring over his maps while his marshals wait in silence, with their cocked hats in their hands. But of course U Po Kyin was more equal to the situation than Napoleon. His plan was ready within two minutes. When he turned round his vast face was suffused with excessive joy. The doctor had been mistaken when he described U Po Kyin as attempting to dance; U Po Kyin's figure was not designed for dancing; but, had it been so designed, he would have danced at this moment. He beckoned to Ba Sein and whispered in his ear for a few seconds.

'That is the correct move, I think?' he concluded.

A broad, unwilling, incredulous grin stole slowly across Ba Sein's face.

'Fifty rupees ought to cover all the expenses,' added U Po Kyin, beaming.

The plan was unfolded in detail. And when the others had taken it in, all of them, even Ba Sein, who seldom laughed, even Ma Kin, who disapproved from the bottom of her soul, burst into irrepressible peals of laughter. The plan was really too good to be resisted. It was genius.

All the while it was raining, raining. The day after Flory went back to camp it rained for thirty-eight hours at a stretch, sometimes slowing to the pace of

English rain, sometimes pouring down in such cataracts that one thought the whole ocean must by now have been sucked up into the clouds. The rattling on the roof became maddening after a few hours. In the intervals between the rain the sun glared as fiercely as ever, the mud began to crack and steam, and patches of prickly heat sprang out all over one's body. Hordes of flying beetles had emerged from their cocoons as soon as the rain started; there was a plague of loathly creatures known as stink-bugs, which invaded the houses in incredible numbers, littered themselves over the dining-table and made one's food uneatable. Verrall and Elizabeth still went out riding in the evenings, when the rain was not too fierce. To Verrall, all climates were alike, but he did not like to see his ponies plastered with mud. Nearly a week went by. Nothing was changed between them—they were neither less nor more intimate than they had been before. The proposal of marriage, still confidently expected, was still unuttered. Then an alarming thing happened. The news filtered to the Club, through Mr Macgregor, that Verrall was leaving Kyauktada; the Military Police were to be kept at Kyauktada, but another officer was coming in Verrall's place, no one was certain when. Elizabeth was in horrible suspense. Surely, if he was going away, he must say something definite soon? She could not question him—dared not even ask him whether he was really going; she could only wait for him to speak. He said nothing. Then one evening, without warning, he failed to turn up at the Club. And two whole days passed during which Elizabeth did not see him at all.

It was dreadful, but there was nothing that could be done. Verrall and Elizabeth had been inseparable for weeks, and yet in a way they were almost strangers. He had kept himself so aloof from them all—had never even seen the inside of the Lackersteens' house. They did not know him well enough to seek him out at the *dak*bungalow, or write to him; nor did he reappear at morning parade on the maidan. There was nothing to do except wait until he chose to present himself again. And when he did, would he ask her to marry him? Surely, surely he must! Both Elizabeth and her aunt (but neither of them had even spoken of it openly) held it as an article of faith that he must ask her. Elizabeth looked forward to their next meeting with a hope that was almost painful. Please God it would be a week at least before he went! If she rode with him four times more, or three times—even if it were only twice, all might yet be well. Please God he would come back to her soon! It was unthinkable that when he came, it would only be to say good-bye! The two women went down to the Club each evening and sat there until quite late, listening for Verrall's footsteps outside while seeming not to listen; but he never appeared. Ellis, who understood the situation perfectly, watched Elizabeth with spiteful amusement. What made it worst of all was that Mr Lackersteen was now pestering Elizabeth unceasingly. He had become quite reckless. Almost under the eyes of the servants he would waylay her, catch hold of her and begin pinching and fondling her in the most revolting way. Her sole defence was to threaten that she would tell her aunt; happily he was too stupid to realize that she would never dare do it.

On the third morning Elizabeth and her aunt arrived at the Club just in time to escape a violent storm of rain. They had been sitting in the lounge for a few minutes when they heard the sound of someone stamping the water off his shoes in the passage. Each woman's heart stirred, for this might be Verrall. Then a young man entered the lounge, unbuttoning a long raincoat as he came. He was a stout, rollicking, chuckle-headed youth of about twenty-five, with fat fresh cheeks, butter-coloured hair, no forehead, and, as it turned out afterwards, a deafening laugh.

Mrs Lackersteen made some inarticulate sound—it was jerked out of her by her disappointment. The youth, however, hailed them with immediate bonhomie, being one of those who are on terms of slangy intimacy with everyone from the moment of meeting them.

'Hullo, hullo!' he said 'Enter the fairy prince! Hope I don't sort of intrude and all that? Not shoving in on any family gatherings or anything?'

'Not at all!' said Mrs Lackersteen in surprise.

'What I mean to say—thought I'd just pop in at the Club and have a glance round, don't you know. Just to get acclimatized to the local brand of whisky. I only got here last night.'

'Are you *stationed* here?' said Mrs Lackersteen, mystified—for they had not been expecting any newcomers.

'Yes, rather. Pleasure's mine, entirely.'

'But we hadn't heard. . . . Oh, of course! I suppose you're from the Forest Department? In place of poor Mr Maxwell?'

'What? Forest Department? No fear! I'm the new Military Police bloke, you know.'

'The—what?'

'New Military Police bloke. Taking over from dear ole Verrall. The dear ole chap got orders to go back to his regiment. Going off in a fearful hurry. And a nice mess he's left everything in for yours truly, too.'

The Military Policeman was a crass youth, but even he noticed that Elizabeth's face turned suddenly sickly. She found herself quite unable to speak. It was several seconds before Mrs Lackersteen managed to exclaim:

'Mr Verrall—going? Surely he isn't going away *yet*?'

'Going? He's gone!'

'*Gone?*'

'Well, what I mean to say—train's due to start in about half an hour. He'll be along at the station now. I sent a fatigue party to look after him. Got to get his ponies aboard and all that.'

There were probably further explanations, but neither Elizabeth nor her aunt heard a word of them. In any case, without even a good-bye to the Military Policeman, they were out on the front steps within fifteen seconds. Mrs Lackersteen called sharply for the butler.

'Butler! Send my rickshaw round to the front at once! To the station, *jaldi*!' she added as the rickshaw-man appeared, and, having settled herself in the rickshaw, poked him in the back with the ferrule of her umbrella to start him.

Elizabeth had put on her raincoat and Mrs Lackersteen was cowering in the rickshaw behind her umbrella, but neither was much use against the rain. It came driving towards them in such sheets that Elizabeth's frock was soaked before they had reached the gate, and the rickshaw almost overturned in the wind. The rickshaw-wallah put his head down and struggled into it, groaning. Elizabeth was in agony. It was a mistake, *surely* it was a mistake. He had written to her and the letter had gone astray. That was it, that *must* be it! It could not be that he had meant to leave her without even saying good-bye! And if it were so—no, not even then would she give up hope! When he saw her on the platform, for the last time, he could not be so brutal as to forsake her! As they neared the station she fell behind the rickshaw and pinched her cheeks to bring the blood into them. A squad of Military Police sepoys shuffled hurriedly by, their thin uniforms sodden into rags, pushing a handcart among them. Those would be Verrall's fatigue party. Thank God, there was a quarter of an hour yet. The train was not due to leave for another quarter of an hour. Thank God, at least, for this last chance of seeing him!

They arrived on the platform just in time to see the train draw out of the station and gather speed with a series of deafening snorts. The stationmaster, a little round, black man, was standing on the line looking ruefully after the train, and holding his waterproof-covered topi on to his head with one hand, while with the other he fended off two clamorous Indians who were bobbing at him and trying to thrust something upon his attention. Mrs Lackersteen leaned out of the rickshaw and called agitatedly through the rain.

'Stationmaster!'

'Madam!'

'What train is that?'

'That is the Mandalay train, madam.'

'The Mandalay train! It can't be!'

'But I assure you, madam! It is precisely the Mandalay train.' He came towards them, removing his topi.

'But Mr Verrall—the Police officer? Surely he's not on it?'

'Yes, madam, he have departed.' He waved his hand towards the train, now receding rapidly in a cloud of rain and steam.

'But the train wasn't due to start yet!'

'No, madam. Not due to start for another ten minutes.'

'Then why has it gone?'

The stationmaster waved his topi apologetically from side to side. His dark, squabby face looked quite distressed.

'I know, madam, I know! *Most* unprecedented! But the young Military Police officer have positively *commanded* me to start the train! He declare that all is ready and he do not wish to be kept waiting. I point out the irregularity. He say he do not care about irregularity. I expostulate. He insist. And in short—'

He made another gesture. It meant that Verrall was the kind of man who would have his way, even when it came to starting a train ten minutes early. There was a pause. The two Indians, imagining that they saw their chance, suddenly rushed forward, wailing, and offered some grubby notebooks for Mrs Lackersteen's inspection.

'What *do* these men want?' cried Mrs Lackersteen distractedly.

'They are grass-wallahs, madam. They say that Lieutenant Verrall have departed owing them large sums of money. One for hay, the other for corn. Of mine it is no affair.'

There was a hoot from the distant train. It rolled round the bend, like a black-behinded caterpillar that looks over its shoulder as it goes, and vanished. The stationmaster's wet white trousers flapped forlornly about his legs. Whether Verrall had started the train early to escape Elizabeth, or to escape the grass-wallahs, was an interesting question that was never cleared up.

They made their way back along the road, and then struggled up the hill in such a wind that sometimes they were driven several paces backwards. When they gained the veranda they were quite out of breath. The servants took their streaming raincoats, and Elizabeth shook some of the water from her hair. Mrs Lackersteen broke her silence for the first time since they had left the station:

'*Well!* Of all the unmannerly—of the simply *abominable*. . . !'

Elizabeth looked pale and sickly, in spite of the rain and wind that had beaten into her face. But she would betray nothing.

'I think he might have waited to say good-bye to us,' she said coldly.

'Take my word for it, dear, you are thoroughly well rid of him! . . . As I said from the start, a most *odious* young man!'

Some time later, when they were sitting down to breakfast, having bathed and got into dry clothes, and feeling better, she remarked:

'Let me see, what day is this?'

'Saturday, Aunt.'

'Ah, Saturday. Then the dear padre will be arriving this evening. How many shall we be for the service tomorrow? Why, I think we shall *all* be here! How very nice! Mr Flory will be here too. I think he said he was coming back from the jungle tomorrow.' She added almost lovingly, '*Dear* Mr Flory!'

---

# 24

It was nearly six o'clock in the evening, and the absurd bell in the six-foot tin steeple of the church went clank-clank, clank-clank! as old Mattu pulled the rope within. The rays of the setting sun, refracted by distant rainstorms, flooded the maidan with a beautiful, lurid light. It had been raining earlier in the day, and would rain again. The Christian community of Kyauktada, fifteen in number, were gathering at the church door for the evening service.

Flory was already there, and Mr Macgregor, grey topi and all, and Mr Francis and Mr Samuel, frisking about in freshly laundered drill suits—for the six-weekly church service was the great social event of their lives. The padre, a tall man with grey hair and a refined, discoloured face, wearing pince-nez, was standing on the church steps in his cassock and surplice, which he had put on in Mr Macgregor's house. He was smiling in an amiable but rather helpless way at four pink-cheeked Karen Christians who had come to make their bows to him; for he did not speak a word of their language nor they of his. There was one other Oriental Christian, a mournful, dark Indian of uncertain race, who stood humbly in the background. He was always present at the church services, but no one knew who he was or why he was a Christian. Doubtless he had been captured and baptized in infancy by the missionaries, for Indians who are converted when adults almost invariably lapse.

Flory could see Elizabeth coming down the hill, dressed in lilac-colour, with her aunt and uncle. He had seen her that morning at the Club—they had had just a minute alone together before the others came in. He had only asked her one question.

'Has Verrall gone—for good?'

'Yes.'

There had been no need to say any more. He had simply taken her by the arms and drawn her towards him. She came willingly, even gladly—there in the clear daylight, merciless to his disfigured face. For a moment she had clung to him almost like a child. It was a though he had saved her or protected her from something. He raised her face to kiss her, and found with surprise that she was crying. There had been no time to talk then, not even to say, 'Will you marry me?' No matter, after the service there would be time enough. Perhaps at his next visit, only six weeks hence, the padre would marry them.

Ellis and Westfield and the new Military Policeman were approaching from the Club, where they had been having a couple of quick ones to last them through the service. The Forest Officer who had been sent to take Maxwell's place, a sallow, tall man, completely bald except for two whisker-like tufts in front of his ears, was following them. Flory had not time to say more than 'Good evening' to Elizabeth when she arrived. Mattu, seeing that everyone was present, stopped ringing the bell, and the clergyman led the way inside, followed by Mr Macgregor, with his topi against his stomach, and the Lackersteens and the native Christians. Ellis pinched Flory's elbow and whispered boozily in his ear:

'Come on, line up. Time for the snivel-parade. Quick march!'

He and the Military Policeman went in behind the others, arm-in-arm, with a dancing step—the policeman, till they got inside, wagging his fat behind in imitation of a *pwe*-dancer. Flory sat down in the same pew as these two, opposite Elizabeth, on her right. It was the first time that he had ever risked sitting with his birthmark towards her. 'Shut your eyes and count twenty-five'. whispered Ellis as they sat down, drawing a snigger from the policeman. Mrs Lackersteen had already taken her place at the harmonium, which was no bigger than a writing-desk. Mattu stationed himself by the door and began to pull the punkah—it was so arranged that it only flapped over the front pews, where the Europeans sat. Flo came nosing up the aisle, found Flory's pew and settled down underneath it. The service began.

Flory was only attending intermittently. He was dimly aware of standing and kneeling and muttering 'Amen' to interminable prayers, and of Ellis nudging him and whispering blasphemies behind his hymn book. But he was too happy to collect his thoughts. Hell was yielding up Eurydice. The yellow light flooded in through the open door, gilding the broad back of Mr Macgregor's silk coat like cloth-of-gold. Elizabeth, across the narrow aisle, was so close to Flory that he could hear every rustle of her dress and feel, as it seemed to him, the warmth of her body; yet he would not look at her even once, lest the others should notice it. The harmonium quavered bronchitically as Mrs Lackersteen struggled to pump sufficient air into it with the sole pedal that worked. The singing was a queer, ragged noise—an earnest booming from Mr Macgregor, a kind of shamefaced muttering from the other Europeans, and from the back a loud, wordless lowing, for the Karen Christians knew the tunes of the hymns but not the words.

They were kneeling down again. 'More bloody knee-drill,' Ellis whispered. The air darkened, and there was a light patter of rain on the roof; the trees outside rustled, and a cloud of yellow leaves whirled past the window. Flory watched them through the chinks of his fingers. Twenty years ago, on winter Sundays in his pew in the parish church at home, he used to watch the yellow leaves, as at this moment, drifting and fluttering against leaden skies. Was it not possible, now, to begin over again as though those grimy years had never touched him? Through his fingers he glanced sidelong at Elizabeth, kneeling with her head bent and her face hidden in her youthful, mottled hands. When they were married, when they were married! What fun they would have together in this alien yet kindly land! He saw Elizabeth in his camp, greeting him as he came home tired from work and Ko S'la hurried from the tent with a bottle of beer; he saw her walking in the forest with him, watching the hornbills in the peepul trees and picking nameless flowers, and in the marshy grazing-grounds, tramping through the cold-weather mist after snipe and teal. He saw his home as she would remake it. He saw his drawing-room, sluttish and bachelor-like no longer, with new furniture from Rangoon, and a bowl of pink balsams like rosebuds on the table, and books and water-colours and a black piano. Above all the piano! His mind lingered upon the piano—symbol, perhaps because he was unmusical, of civilized and settled life. He was delivered for ever from the sub-life of the past decade—the debaucheries, the lies, the pain of exile and solitude, the dealings with whores and money-lenders and pukka sahibs.

The clergyman stepped to the small wooden lectern that also served as a pulpit, slipped the band from a roll of sermon paper, coughed, and announced a text. 'In the name of the Father, the Son and the Holy Ghost. Amen.'

'Cut it short, for Christ's sake,' murmured Ellis.

Flory did not notice how many minutes passed. The words of the sermon flowed peacefully through his head, an indistinct burbling sound, almost unheard. When they were married, he was still thinking, when they were married—

Hullo! What was happening?

The clergyman had stopped short in the middle of a word. He had taken off his pince-nez and was shaking them with a distressed air at someone in the doorway. There was a fearful, raucous scream.

'*Pike-san pay-like! Pike-san pay-like!*'

Everyone jumped in their seats and turned round. It was Ma Hla May. As they turned she stepped inside the church and shoved old Mattu violently aside. She shook her fist at Flory.

'*Pike-san pay-like! Pike-san pay-like!* Yes, *that's* the one I mean—Flory, Flory! (She pronounced it Porley.) That one sitting in front there, with the black hair! Turn round and face me, you coward! Where is the money you promised me?'

She was shrieking like a maniac. The people gaped at her, too astounded to move or speak. Her face was grey with powder, her greasy hair was tumbling down, her *longyi* was ragged at the bottom. She looked like a screaming hag of the bazaar. Flory's bowels seemed to have turned to ice. Oh God, God! Must they know—must Elizabeth know—that *that* was the woman who had been his mistress? But there was not a hope, not the vestige of a hope, of any mistake. She had screamed his name over and over again. Flo, hearing the familiar voice, wriggled from under the pew, walked down the aisle and wagged her tail at Ma Hla May. The wretched woman was yelling out a detailed account of what Flory had done to her.

'Look at me, you white men, and you women, too, look at me! Look how he has ruined me! Look at these rags I am wearing! And he is sitting there, the liar, the coward, pretending not to see me! He would let me starve at his gate like a pariah dog. Ah, but I will shame you! Turn round and look at me! Look at this body that you have kissed a thousand times—look—look—'

She began actually to tear her clothes open—the last insult of a base-born Burmese woman. The harmonium squeaked as Mrs Lackersteen made a convulsive movement. People had at last found their wits and began to stir. The clergyman, who had been bleating ineffectually, recovered his voice, 'Take that woman outside!' he said sharply.

Flory's face was ghastly. After the first moment he had turned his head away from the door and set his teeth in a desperate effort to look unconcerned. But it was useless, quite useless. His face was as yellow as bone, and the sweat glistened on his forehead. Francis and Samuel, doing perhaps the first useful deed of their lives, suddenly sprang from their pew, grabbed Ma Hla May by the arms and hauled her outside, still screaming.

It seemed very silent in the church when they had finally dragged her out of hearing. The scene had been so violent, so squalid, that everyone was upset by it. Even Ellis looked disgusted. Flory could neither speak nor stir. He sat staring fixedly at the altar, his face rigid and so bloodless that the birth-mark seemed to glow upon it like a streak of blue paint. Elizabeth glanced across the aisle at him, and her revulsion made her almost physically sick. She had not understood a word of what Ma Hla May was saying, but the meaning of the scene was perfectly clear. The thought that he had been the lover of that grey-faced, maniacal creature made her shudder in her bones. But worse than that, worse than anything, was his ugliness at this moment. His face appalled her, it was so ghastly, rigid and old. It was like a skull. Only the birthmark seemed alive in it. She hated him now for his birthmark She had never known till this moment how dishonouring, how unforgivable a thing it was.

Like the crocodile, U Po Kyin had struck at the weakest spot. For, needless to say, this scene was U Po Kyin's doing. He had seen his chance, as usual, and tutored Ma Hla May for her part with considerable care. The clergyman brought his sermon to an end almost at once. As soon as it was over Flory hurried outside, not looking at any of the others. It was getting dark, thank God. At fifty yards from the church he halted, and watched the others making in couples for the Club. It seemed to him that they were hurrying. Ah, they would, of course! There would be something to talk about at the Club tonight! Flo rolled belly-upwards against his ankles, asking for a game. 'Get out, you bloody brute!' he said, and kicked her. Elizabeth had stopped at the church door. Mr Macgregor, happy chance, seemed to be introducing her to the clergyman. In a moment the two men went on in the direction of Mr Macgregor's house, where the clergyman was to stay for the night, and Elizabeth followed the others, thirty yards behind them. Flory ran after her and caught up with her almost at the Club gate.

'Elizabeth!'

She looked round, saw him, turned white, and would have hurried on without a word. But his anxiety was too great, and he caught her by the wrist.

'Elizabeth! I must—I've got to speak to you!'

'Let me go, will you!'

They began to struggle, and then stopped abruptly. Two of the Karens who had come out of the church were standing fifty yards away, gazing at them through the half-darkness with deep interest. Flory began again in a lower tone:

'Elizabeth, I know I've no right to stop you like this. But I must speak to you, I must! Please hear what I've got to say. Please don't run away from me!'

'What are you doing? Why are you holding on to my arm? Let me go this instant!'

'I'll let you go—there, look! But do listen to me, please! Answer me this one thing. After what's happened, can you ever forgive me?'

'Forgive you? What do you mean, *forgive* you?'

'I know I'm disgraced. It was the vilest thing to happen! Only, in a sense it wasn't my fault. You'll see that when you're calmer. Do you think—not now, it was too bad, but later—do you think you can forget it?'

'I really don't know what you're talking about. Forget it? What has it got to do with *me*? I thought it was very disgusting, but it's not *my* business. I can't think why you're questioning me like this at all.'

He almost despaired at that. Her tone and even her words were the very ones she had used in that earlier quarrel of theirs. It was the same move over again. Instead of hearing him out she was going to evade him and put him off—snub him by pretending that he had no claim upon her.

'Elizabeth! Please answer me. Please be fair to me! It's serious this time I don't expect you to take me back all at once. You couldn't, when I'm publicly disgraced like this. But, after all, you virtually promised to marry me—'

'What! Promised to marry you? *When* did I promise to marry you?'

'Not in words, I know. But it was understood between us.'

'Nothing of the kind was understood between us! I think you are behaving in the most horrible way. I'm going along to the Club at once. Good evening!'

'Elizabeth! Elizabeth! Listen. It's not fair to condemn me unheard. You knew before what I'd done, and you knew that I'd lived a different life since I met you. What happened this evening was only an accident. That wretched woman, who, I admit, was once my—well—'

'I won't listen, I won't listen to such things! I'm going!'

He caught her by the wrists again, and this time held her. The Karens had disappeared, fortunately.

'No, no, you shall hear me! I'd rather offend you to the heart than have this uncertainty. It's gone on week after week, month after month, and I've never once been able to speak straight out to you. You don't seem to know or care how much you make me suffer. But this time you've got to answer me.'

She struggled in his grip, and she was surprisingly strong. Her face was more bitterly angry than he had ever seen or imagined it. She hated him so that she would have struck him if her hands were free.

'Let me go! Oh, you beast, you beast, let me go!'

'My God, my God, that we should fight like this! But what else can I do? I can't let you go without even hearing me. Elizabeth, you *must* listen to me!'

'I will not! I will not discuss it! What right have you to question me? Let me go!'

'Forgive me, forgive me! This one question. Will you—not now, but later, when this vile business is forgotten—will you marry me?'

'No, never, never!'

'Don't say it like that! Don't make it final. Say no for the present if you like—but in a month, a year, five years—'

'Haven't I said no? Why must you keep on and on?'

'Elizabeth, listen to me. I've tried again and again to tell you what you mean to me—oh, it's so useless talking about it! But do try and understand. Haven't I told you something of the life we live here? The sort of horrible death-in-life! The decay, the loneliness, the self-pity? Try and realize what it means, and that you're the sole person on earth who could save me from it.'

'Will you let me go? Why do you have to make this dreadful scene?'

'Does it mean nothing to you when I say that I love you? I don't believe you've ever realized what it is that I want from you. If you like, I'd marry you and promise never even touch you with my finger. I wouldn't mind even that, so long as you were with me. But I can't go on with my life alone, always alone. Can't you bring yourself ever to forgive me?'

'Never, never! I wouldn't marry you if you were the last man on earth. I'd as soon marry the—the sweeper!'

She had begun crying now. He saw that she meant what she said. The tears came into his own eyes. He said again:

'For the last time. Remember that it's something to have one person in the world who loves you. Remember that though you'll find men who are richer, and younger, and better in every way than I, you'll never find one who cares for you so much. And though I'm not rich, at least I could make you a home. There's a way of living—civilized, decent—'

'Haven't we said enough?' she said more calmly. 'Will you let me go before somebody comes?'

He relaxed his grip on her wrists. He had lost her, that was certain. Like a hallucination, painfully clear, he saw again their home as he had imagined it; he saw their garden, and Elizabeth feeding Nero and the pigeons on the drive by the sulphur-yellow phloxes that grew as high as her shoulder; and the drawing-room, with the water-colours on the walls, and the balsams in the china bowl mirrored by the table, and the book-shelves, and the black piano. The impossible, mythical piano—symbol of everything that that futile accident had wrecked!

'You should have a piano,' he said despairingly.

'I don't play the piano.'

He let her go. It was no use continuing. She was no sooner free of him than she took to her heels and actually ran into the Club garden, so hateful was his presence to her. Among the trees she stopped to take off her spectacles and remove the signs of tears from her face. Oh, the beast, the beast! He had hurt her wrists abominably. Oh, what an unspeakable beast he was! When she thought of his face as it had looked in church, yellow and glistening with the hideous birthmark upon it, she could have wished him dead. It was not what he had done that horrified her. He might have committed a thousand abominations and she could have forgiven him. But not after that shameful, squalid scene, and the devilish ugliness of his disfigured face in that moment. It was, finally, the birthmark that had damned him.

Her aunt would be furious when she heard that she had refused Flory. And there was her uncle and his leg-pinching—between the two of them, life here would become impossible. Perhaps she would have to go Home unmarried after all. Black beetles! No matter. Anything—spinsterhood, drudgery, anything—sooner than the alternative. Never, never, would she yield to a man who had been so disgraced! Death sooner, far sooner. If there had been mercenary thoughts in her mind an hour ago, she had forgotten them. She did not even remember that Verrall had jilted her and that to have married Flory would have saved her face. She knew only that he was dishonoured and less than a man, and that she hated him as she would have hated a leper or a lunatic. The instinct was deeper than reason or even self-interest, and she could no more have disobeyed it than she could have stopped breathing.

Flory, as he turned up the hill, did not run, but he walked as fast as he could. What he had to do must be done quickly. It was getting very dark. The wretched Flo, who even now had not grasped that anything serious was the matter, trotted close to his heels, whimpering in a self-pitying manner to reproach him for the kick he had given her. As he came up the path a wind blew through the plaintain trees, rattling the tattered leaves and bringing a scent of damp. It was going to rain again. Ko S'la had laid the dinner-table and was removing some flying beetles that had committed suicide against the petrol-lamp. Evidently he had not heard about the scene in church yet.

'The holy one's dinner is ready. Will the holy one dine now?'

'No, not yet. Give me that lamp.'

He took the lamp, went into the bedroom and shut the door, The stale scent of dust and cigarette-smoke met him, and in the white, unsteady glare of the lamp he could see the mildewed books and the lizards on the wall. So he was back again to this—to the old, secret life—after everything, back where he had been before

Was it not possible to endure it! He had endured it before. There were palliatives—books, his garden, drink, work, whoring, shooting, conversations with the doctor.

No, it was not endurable any longer, Since Elizabeth's coming the power to suffer and above all to hope, which he had thought dead in him, had sprung to new life. The half-comfortable lethargy in which he had lived was broken. And if he suffered now, there was far worse to come. In a little while someone else would marry her. How he could picture it—the moment when he heard the news!—'Did you hear the Lackersteen kid's got off at last? Poor old So-and-so—booked for the altar, God help him,' etc., etc. And the casual question—'Oh, really? When is it to be?'—stiffening one's face, pretending to be uninterested. And then her wedding day approaching, her bridal night—ah, not that! Obscene, obscene. Keep your eyes fixed on that. Obscene. He dragged his tin uniform-case from under the bed, took out his automatic pistol, slid a clip of cartridges into the magazine, and pulled one into the breech.

Ko S'la was remembered in his will. There remained Flo. He laid his pistol on the table and went outside. Flo was playing with Ba Shin, Ko S'la's youngest son, under the lee of the cookhouse, where the servants had left the remains of a woodfire. She was dancing round him with her small teeth bared, pretending to bite him, while the tiny boy, his belly red in the glow of the embers, smacked weakly at her, laughing, and yet half frightened.

'Flo! Come here, Flo!'

She heard him and came obediently, and then stopped short at the bedroom door. She seemed to have grasped now that there was something wrong. She backed a little and stood looking timorously up at him, unwilling to enter the bedroom.

'Come in here!'

She wagged her tail, but did not move.

'Come on, Flo! Good old Flo! Come on!'

Flo was suddenly stricken with terror. She whined, her tail went down, and she shrank back. 'Come here, blast you!' he cried, and he took her by the collar and flung her into the room, shutting the door behind her. He went to the table for the pistol.

'No come here! Do as you're told!'

She crouched down and whined for forgiveness. It hurt him to hear it. 'Come on, old girl! Dear old Flo! Master wouldn't hurt you. Come here!' She crawled very slowly towards his feet, flat on her belly, whining, her head down as though afraid to look at him. When she was a yard away he fired, blowing her skull to fragments.

Her shattered brain looked like red velvet. Was that what he would look like? The heart, then, not the head. He could hear the servants running out of their quarters and shouting—they must have heard the sound of the shot. He hurriedly tore open his coat and pressed the muzzle of the pistol against his shirt. A tiny lizard, translucent like a creature of gelatine, was stalking a white moth along the edge of the table. Flory pulled the trigger with his thumb.

As Ko S'la burst into the room, for a moment he saw nothing but the dead body of the dog. Then he saw his master's feet, heels upwards, projecting from beyond the bed. He yelled to the others to keep the children out of the room, and all of them surged back from the doorway with screams. Ko S'la fell on his knees behind Flory's body, at the same moment as Ba Pe came running through the veranda.

'Has he shot himself?'

'I think so. Turn him over on his back. Ah, look at that! Run for the Indian doctor! Run for your life!'

There was a neat hole, no bigger than that made by a pencil passing through a sheet of blotting-paper, in Flory's shirt. He was obviously quite dead. With great difficulty Ko S'la managed to drag him on to the bed, for the other servants refused to touch the body. It was only twenty minutes before the doctor arrived. He had heard only a vague report that Flory was hurt, and had bicycled up the hill at top speed through a storm of rain. He threw his bicycle down in the flower-bed and hurried in through the veranda. He was out of breath, and could not see through his spectacles. He took them off, peering myopically at the bed. 'What iss it, my friend?' he said anxiously. 'Where are you hurt?' Then, coming closer, he saw what was on the bed, and uttered a harsh sound.

'Ach, what is this? What has happened to him?'

The doctor fell on his knees, tore Flory's shirt open and put his ear to his chest. An expression of agony came into his face, and he seized the dead man by the shoulders and shook him as though mere violence could bring him to life. One arm fell limply over the edge of the bed. The doctor lifted it back again, and then, with the dead hand between his own, suddenly burst into tears. Ko S'la was standing at the foot of the bed, his brown face full of lines. The doctor stood up, and then losing control of himself for a moment, leaned against the bedpost and wept noisily and grotesquely his back turned on Ko S'la. His fat shoulders were quivering. Presently he recovered himself and turned round again.

'How did this happen?'

'We heard two shots. He did it himself, that is certain. I do not know why.'

'How did you know that he did it on purpose? How do you know that it was not an accident?'

For answer, Ko S'la pointed silently to Flo's corpse. The doctor thought for a moment, and then, with gentle, practised hands, swathed the dead man in the sheet and knotted it at foot and head. With death, the birthmark had faded immediately, so that it was no more than a faint grey stain.

'Bury the dog at once. I will tell Mr Macgregor that this happened accidentally while he was cleaning his revolver. Be sure that you bury the dog. Your master was my friend. It shall not be written on his tombstone that he committed suicide.'

---

## 25

It was lucky that the padre should have been at Kyauktada, for he was able, before catching the train on the following evening, to read the burial service in due form and even to deliver a short address on the virtues of the dead man. All Englishmen are virtuous when they are dead. 'Accidental death' was the official verdict (Dr Veraswami had proved with all his medico-legal skill that the circumstances pointed to accident) and it was duly inscribed upon the tombstone. Not that anyone believed it, of course. Flory's real epitaph was the remark, very occasionally uttered—for an Englishman who dies in Burma is so soon forgotten—'Flory? Oh yes, he was a dark chap, with a birthmark. He shot himself in Kyauktada in 1926. Over a girl, people said. Bloody fool.' Probably no one, except Elizabeth, was much surprised at what had happened. There is a rather large number of suicides among the Europeans in Burma, and they occasion very little surprise.

Flory's death had several results. The first and most important of them was that Dr Veraswami was ruined, even as he had foreseen. The glory of being a white man's friend—the one thing that had saved him before—had vanished. Flory's standing with the other Europeans had never been good, it is true; but he was after all a white man, and his friendship conferred a certain prestige. Once he was dead, the doctor's ruin was assured. U Po Kyin waited the necessary time, and then struck again, harder than ever. It was barely three months before he had fixed it in the head of every European in Kyauktada that the doctor was an unmitigated scoundrel. No public accusation was ever made against him—U Po Kyin was most careful of that. Even Ellis would have been puzzled to say just what scoundrelism the doctor had been guilty of; but still, it was agreed that he was a scoundrel. By degrees, the general suspicion of him crystallized in a single Burmese phrase—'*shok de*'. Veraswami, it was said, was quite a clever little chap in his way—quite a good doctor for a native—but he was *thoroughly shok de*. *Shok de* means, approximately, untrustworthy, and when a 'native' official comes to be known as *shok de*, there is an end of him.

The dreaded nod and wink passed somewhere in high places, and the doctor was reverted to the rank of Assistant Surgeon and transferred to Mandalay General Hospital. He is still there, and is likely to remain. Mandalay is rather a disagreeable town—it is dusty and intolerably hot, and it is said to have five main products all beginning with P, namely, pagodas, pariahs, pigs, priests and prostitutes—and the routine-work of the hospital is a dreary business. The doctor lives just outside the hospital grounds in a little bake-house of a bungalow with a corrugated iron fence round its tiny compound, and in the evenings he runs a private clinic to supplement his reduced pay. He has joined a second-rate club frequented by Indian pleaders. Its chief glory is a single European member–a Glasgow electrician named Macdougall, sacked from the Irrawaddy Flotilla Company for drunkenness, and now making a precarious living out of a garage. Macdougall is a dull lout, only interested in whisky and magnetos. The doctor, who will never believe that a white man can be a fool, tries almost every night to engage him in what he still calls 'cultured conversation'; but the results are very unsatisfying.

Ko S'la inherited four hundred rupees under Flory's will, and with his family he set up a tea-shop in the bazaar. But the shop failed, as it was bound to do with the two women fighting in it at all hours, and Ko S'la and Ba Pe were obliged to go back to service. Ko S'la was an accomplished servant. Besides the useful arts of pimping, dealing with money-lenders, carrying master to bed when drunk and making pick-me-ups known as prairie oysters on the following morning, he could sew, darn, refill cartridges, attend to a horse, press a suit, and decorate a dinner-table with wonderful, intricate patterns of chopped leaves and dyed rice-grains. He was worth fifty rupees a month. But he and Ba Pe had fallen into lazy ways in Flory's service, and they were sacked from one job after another. They had a bad year of poverty, and little Ba Shin developed a cough, and finally coughed himself to death one stifling hot-weather night. Ko S'la is now a second boy to a Rangoon rice-broker with a neurotic wife who makes unending kit-kit, and Ba Pe is pani-wallah in the same house at sixteen rupees a month. Ma Hla May is in a brothel in Mandalay. Her good looks are all but gone, and her clients pay her only four annas and sometimes kick her and beat her. Perhaps more bitterly than any of the others, she regrets the good time when Flory was alive, and when she had not the wisdom to put aside any of the money she extracted from him.

U Po Kyin realized all his dreams except one. After the doctor's disgrace, it was inevitable that U Po Kyin should be elected to the Club, and elected he was, in spite of bitter protests from Ellis. In the end the other Europeans came to be rather glad that they had elected him, for he was a bearable addition to the Club. He did not come too often, was ingratiating in his manner, stood drinks freely, and developed almost at once into a brilliant bridge-player. A few months later he was transferred from Kyauktada and promoted. For a whole year, before his retirement, he officiated as Deputy Commissioner, and during that year alone he made twenty thousand rupees in bribes. A month after his retirement he was summoned to a durbar in Rangoon, to receive the decoration that had been awarded to him by the Indian Government.

It was an impressive scene, that durbar. On the platform, hung with flags and flowers, sat the Governor, frock-coated, upon a species of throne, with a bevy of aides-de-camp and secretaries behind him. All round the hall, like glittering waxworks, stood the tall, bearded sowars of the Governor's bodyguard, with pennoned lances in their hands. Outside, a band was blaring at intervals. The gallery was gay with the white *ingyis* and pink scarves of Burmese ladies, and in the body of the hall a hundred men or more were waiting to receive their decorations. There were Burmese officials in blazing Mandalay *pasos*, and Indians in cloth-of-gold *pagris*, and British officers in full-dress uniform with clanking sword-scabbards, and old *thugyis* with their grey hair knotted behind their heads and silver-hilted *dahs* slung from their shoulders. In a high, clear voice a secretary was reading out the list of awards, which varied from the C.I.E. to certificates of honour in embossed silver cases. Presently U Po Kyin's turn came and the secretary read from his scroll:

'To U Po Kyin, Deputy Assistant Commissioner, retired, for long and loyal service and especially for his timely aid in crushing a most dangerous rebellion in Kyauktada district'—and so on and so on.

Then two henchmen, placed there for the purpose hoisted U Po Kyin upright, and he waddled to the platform, bowed as low as his belly would permit, and was duly decorated and felicitated, while Ma Kin and other supporters clapped wildly and fluttered their scarves from the gallery.

U Po Kyin had done all that mortal man could do. It was time now to be making ready for the next world—in short, to begin building pagodas. But unfortunately, this was the very point at which his plans went wrong. Only three days after the Governor's durbar, before so much as a brick of those atoning pagodas had been laid, U Po Kyin wa stricken with apoplexy and died without speaking again. There is no armour against fate. Ma Kin was heartbroken at the disaster. Even if she had built the pagodas herself, it would have availed U Po Kyin nothing; no merit can be acquired save by one's own act. She suffers greatly to think of U Po Kyin where he must be now—wandering in God knows what dreadful subterranean hell of fire, and darkness, and serpents, and genii. Or even if he has escaped the worst, his other fear has been realized, and he has returned to the earth in the shape of a rat or a frog. Perhaps at this very moment a snake is devouring him.

As to Elizabeth, things fell out better than she had expected. After Flory's death Mrs Lackersteen, dropping all pretences for once, said openly that there were no men in this dreadful place and the only hope was to go and stay several months in Rangoon or Maymyo. But she could not very well send Elizabeth to Rangoon or Maymyo alone, and to go with her practically meant condemning Mr Lackersteen to death from delirium tremens. Months passed, and the rains reached their climax, and Elizabeth had just made up her mind that she must go home after all, penniless and unmarried, when—Mr Macgregor proposed to her. He had had it in his mind for a long time; indeed, he had only been waiting for a decent interval to elapse after Flory's death.

Elizabeth accepted him gladly. He was rather old, perhaps, but a Deputy Commissioner is not to be despised—certainly he was a far better match than Flory. They are very happy. Mr Macgregor was always a good-hearted man, but he has grown more human and likeable since his marriage. His voice booms less, and he has given up his morning exercises. Elizabeth has grown mature surprisingly quickly, and a certain hardness of manner that always belonged to her has become accentuated. Her servants live in terror of her, though she speaks no Burmese. She has an exhaustive knowledge of the Civil List, gives charming little dinner-parties and knows how to put the wives of subordinate officials in their places—in short, she fills with complete success the position for which Nature had designed her from the first, that of a burra memsahib.

# A CLERGYMAN'S DAUGHTER

# CHAPTER I

## I

As the alarm clock on the chest of drawers exploded like a horrid little bomb of bell metal, Dorothy, wrenched from the depths of some complex, troubling dream, awoke with a start and lay on her back looking into the darkness in extreme exhaustion.

The alarm clock continued its nagging, feminine clamour, which would go on for five minutes or thereabouts if you did not stop it. Dorothy was aching from head to foot, and an insidious and contemptible self-pity, which usually seized upon her when it was time to get up in the morning, caused her to bury her head under the bedclothes and try to shut the hateful noise out of her ears. She struggled against her fatigue, however, and, according to her custom, exhorted herself sharply in the second person plural. Come on, Dorothy, up you get! No snoozing, please! Proverbs vi, 9. Then she remembered that if the noise went on any longer it would wake her father, and with a hurried movement she bounded out of bed, seized the clock from the chest of drawers, and turned off the alarm. It was kept on the chest of drawers precisely in order that she should have to get out of bed to silence it. Still in darkness, she knelt down at her bedside and repeated the Lord's Prayer, but rather distractedly, her feet being troubled by the cold.

It was just half past five, and coldish for an August morning. Dorothy (her name was Dorothy Hare, and she was the only child of the Reverend Charles Hare, Rector of St Athelstan's, Knype Hill, Suffolk) put on her aged flannelette dressing-gown and felt her way downstairs. There was a chill morning smell of dust, damp plaster, and the fried dabs from yesterday's supper, and from either side of the passage on the second floor she could hear the antiphonal snoring of her father and of Ellen, the maid of all work. With care—for the kitchen table had a nasty trick of reaching out of the darkness and banging you on the hip-bone—Dorothy felt her way into the kitchen, lighted the candle on the mantelpiece, and, still aching with fatigue, knelt down and raked the ashes out of the range.

The kitchen fire was a 'beast' to light. The chimney was crooked and therefore perpetually half choked, and the fire, before it would light, expected to be dosed with a cupful of kerosene, like a drunkard's morning nip of gin. Having set the kettle to boil for her father's shaving-water, Dorothy went upstairs and turned on her bath. Ellen was still snoring, with heavy youthful snores. She was a good hard-working servant once she was awake, but she was one of those girls whom the Devil and all his angels cannot get out of bed before seven in the morning.

Dorothy filled the bath as slowly as possible—the splashing always woke her father if she turned on the tap too fast—and stood for a moment regarding the pale, unappetizing pool of water. Her body had gone goose-flesh all over. She detested cold baths; it was for that very reason that she made it a rule to take all her baths cold from April to November. Putting a tentative hand into the water—and it was horribly cold—she drove herself forward with her usual exhortations. Come on, Dorothy! In you go! No funking, please! Then she stepped resolutely into the bath, sat down and let the icy girdle of water slide up her body and immerse her all except her hair, which she had twisted up behind her head. The next moment she came to the surface gasping and wriggling, and had no sooner got her breath back than she remembered her 'memo list', which she had brought down in her dressing-gown pocket and intended to read. She reached out for it, and, leaning over the side of the bath, waist deep in icy water, read through the 'memo list' by the light of the candle on the chair.

It ran:

7 oc. H.C.

Mrs T baby? Must visit.

*Breakfast*. Bacon. *Must* ask father money. (P)

Ask Ellen what stuff kitchen father's tonic NB. to ask about stuff for curtains at Solepipe's.

Visiting call on Mrs P cutting from Daily M angelica tea good for rheumatism Mrs L's cornplaster.

12 oc. Rehearsal Charles I. NB. to order $\frac{1}{2}$lb glue 1 pot aluminium paint.

*Dinner* (crossed out) *Luncheon* . . . ?

Take round Parish Mag NB. Mrs F owes 3/6d.

4.30 pm Mothers' U tea don't forget $2\frac{1}{2}$ yards casement cloth.

Flowers for church NB. 1 tin Brasso.

*Supper*. Scrambled eggs.

Type Father's sermon what about new ribbon typewriter?

NB. to fork between peas bindweed awful.

Dorothy got out of her bath, and as she dried herself with a towel hardly bigger than a table napkin—they could never afford decent-sized towels at the Rectory—her hair came unpinned and fell down over her collar-bones in two heavy strands. It was thick, fine, exceedingly pale hair, and it was perhaps as well that her father had forbidden her to bob it, for it was her only positive beauty. For the rest, she was a girl of middle height, rather thin, but strong and shapely, and her face was her weak point. It was a thin, blonde, unremarkable kind of face, with pale eyes and a nose just a shade too long; if you looked closely you could see crow's feet round the eyes, and the mouth, when it was in repose, looked tired. Not definitely a spinsterish face as yet, but it certainly would be so in a few years' time. Nevertheless, strangers commonly took her to be several years younger than her real age (she was not quite twenty-eight) because of the expression of almost childish earnestness in her eyes. Her left forearm was spotted with tiny red marks like insect bites.

Dorothy put on her nightdress again and cleaned her teeth—plain water, of course; better not to use toothpaste before H.C. After all, either you are fasting or you aren't. The R.C.s are quite right there—and, even as she did so, suddenly faltered and stopped. She put her toothbrush down. A deadly pang, an actual physical pang, had gone through her viscera.

She had remembered, with the ugly shock with which one remembers something disagreeable for the first time in the morning, the bill at Cargill's, the butcher's, which had been owing for seven months. That dreadful bill—it might be nineteen pounds or even twenty, and there was hardly the remotest hope of paying it—was one of the chief torments of her life. At all hours of the night or day it was waiting just round the corner of her consciousness, ready to spring upon her and agonize her; and with it came the memory of a score of lesser bills, mounting up to a figure of which she dared not even think. Almost involuntarily she began to pray, 'Please God, let not Cargill send in his bill again today!' but the next moment she decided that this prayer was worldly and blasphemous, and she asked forgiveness for it. Then she put on her dressing-gown and ran down to the kitchen in hopes of putting the bill out of mind.

The fire had gone out, as usual. Dorothy relaid it, dirtying her hands with coal-dust, dosed it afresh with kerosene and hung about anxiously until the kettle boiled. Father expected his shaving-water to be ready at a quarter past six. Just seven minutes late, Dorothy took the can upstairs and knocked at her father's door.

'Come in, come in!' said a muffled, irritable voice.

The room, heavily curtained, was stuffy, with a masculine smell. The Rector had lighted the candle on his bed-table, and was lying on his side, looking at his gold watch, which he had just drawn from beneath his pillow. His hair was as white and thick as thistledown. One dark bright eye glanced irritably over his shoulder at Dorothy.

'Good morning, father.'

'I do wish, Dorothy,' said the Rector indistinctly—his voice always sounded muffled and senile until he put his false teeth in—'you would make some effort to get Ellen out of bed in the mornings. Or else be a little more punctual yourself.'

'I'm so sorry, Father. The kitchen fire kept going out.'

'Very well! Put it down on the dressing-table. Put it down and draw those curtains.'

It was daylight now, but a dull, clouded morning. Dorothy hastened up to her room and dressed herself with the lightning speed which she found necessary six mornings out of seven. There was only a tiny square of mirror in the room, and even that she did not use. She simply hung her gold cross about her neck—plain gold cross; no crucifixes, please!—twisted her hair into a knot behind, stuck a number of hairpins rather sketchily into it, and threw her clothes (grey jersey, threadbare Irish tweed coat and skirt, stockings not quite matching the coat and skirt, and much-worn brown shoes) on to herself in the space of about three minutes. She had got to 'do out' the dining-room and her father's study before church, besides saying her prayers in preparation for Holy Communion, which took her not less than twenty minutes.

When she wheeled her bicycle out of the front gate the morning was still overcast, and the grass sodden with heavy dew. Through the mist that wreathed the hillside St Athelstan's Church loomed dimly, like a leaden sphinx, its single bell tolling funereally boom! boom! boom! Only one of the bells was now in active use; the other seven had been unswung from their cage and had lain silent these three years past, slowly splintering the floor of the belfry beneath their weight. In the distance, from the mists below, you could hear the offensive clatter of the bell in the R.C. church–a nasty, cheap, tinny little thing which the Rector of St Athelstan's used to compare with a muffin-bell.

Dorothy mounted her bicycle and rode swiftly up the hill, leaning over her handlebars. The bridge of her thin nose was pink in the morning cold. A redshank whistled overhead, invisible against the clouded sky. Early in the morning my song shall rise to Thee! Dorothy propped her bicycle against the lychgate, and, finding her hands still grey with coal-dust, knelt down and scrubbed them clean in the long wet grass between the graves. Then the bell stopped ringing, and she jumped up and hastened into church, just as Proggett, the sexton, in ragged cassock and vast labourer's boots, was clumping up the aisle to take his place at the side altar.

The church was very cold, with a scent of candle-wax and ancient dust. It was a large church, much too large for its congregation, and ruinous and more than half empty. The three narrow islands of pews stretched barely half-way down the nave, and beyond them were great wastes of bare stone floor in which a few worn inscriptions marked the sites of ancient graves. The roof over the chancel was sagging visibly; beside the Church Expenses box two fragments of riddled beam explained mutely that this was due to that mortal foe of Christendom, the death-watch beetle. The light filtered, pale-coloured, through windows of anaemic glass. Through the open south door you could see a ragged cypress and the boughs of a lime-tree, greyish in the sunless air and swaying faintly.

As usual, there was only one other communicant–old Miss Mayfill, of The Grange. The attendance at Holy Communion was so bad that the Rector could not even get any boys to serve him, except on Sunday mornings, when the boys liked showing off in front of the congregation in their cassocks and surplices. Dorothy went into the pew behind Miss Mayfill, and, in penance for some sin of yesterday, pushed away the hassock and knelt on the bare stones. The service was beginning. The Rector, in cassock and short linen surplice, was reciting the prayers in a swift practised voice, clear enough now that his teeth were in, and curiously ungenial. In his fastidious, aged face, pale as a silver coin, there was an expression of aloofness, almost of contempt. 'This is a valid sacrament,' he seemed to be saying, 'and it is my duty to administer it to you. But remember that I am only your priest, not your friend. As a human being I dislike you and despise you.' Proggett, the sexton, a man of forty with curly grey hair and a red, harassed face, stood patiently by, uncomprehending but reverent, fiddling with the little communion bell which was lost in his huge red hands.

Dorothy pressed her fingers against her eyes. She had not yet succeeded in concentrating her thoughts—indeed, the memory of Cargill's bill was still worrying her intermittently. The prayers, which she knew by heart, were flowing through her head unheeded. She raised her eyes for a moment, and they began immediately to stray. First upwards, to the headless roof-angels on whose necks you could still see the sawcuts of the Puritan soldiers, then back again, to Miss Mayfill's black, quasi-pork-pie hat and tremulous jet ear-rings. Miss Mayfill wore a long musty black overcoat, with a little collar of greasy-looking astrakhan, which had been the same ever since Dorothy could remember. It was of some very peculiar stuff, like watered silk but coarser, with rivulets of black piping wandering all over it in no discoverable pattern. It might even have been that legendary and proverbial substance, black bombazine. Miss Mayfill was very old, so old that no one remembered her as anything but an old woman. A faint scent radiated from her—an ethereal scent, analysable as eau-de-Cologne, mothballs, and a sub-flavour of gin.

Dorothy drew a long glass-headed pin from the lapel of her coat, and furtively, under cover of Miss Mayfill's back, pressed the point against her forearm. Her flesh tingled apprehensively. She made it a rule, whenever she caught herself not attending to her prayers, to prick her arm hard enough to make blood come. It was her chosen form of self-discipline, her guard against irreverence and sacrilegious thoughts.

With the pin poised in readiness she managed for several moments to pray more collectedly. Her father had turned one dark eye disapprovingly upon Miss Mayfill, who was crossing herself at intervals, a practice he disliked. A starling chattered outside. With a shock Dorothy discovered that she was looking vaingloriously at the pleats of her father's surplice, which she herself had sewn two years ago. She set her teeth and drove the pin an eighth of an inch into her arm.

They were kneeling again. It was the General Confession. Dorothy recalled her eyes—wandering, alas! yet again, this time to the stained-glass window on her right, designed by Sir Warde Tooke, A.R.A., in 1851 and representing St Athelstan's welcome at the gate of Heaven by Gabriel and a legion of angels all remarkably like one another and the Prince Consort—and pressed the pinpoint against a different part of her arm. She began to meditate conscientiously upon the meaning of each phrase of the prayer, and so brought her mind back to a more attentive state. But even so she was all but obliged to use the pin again when Proggett tinkled the bell in the middle of 'Therefore with Angels and Archangels'—being visited, as always, by a dreadful temptation to begin laughing at that passage. It was because of a story her father had told her once, of how when he was a little boy, and serving the priest at the altar, the communion bell had a screw-on clapper, which had come loose; and so the priest had said: 'Therefore with Angels and Archangels, and with all the company of Heaven, we laud and magnify Thy glorious name; evermore praising Thee, and saying, Screw it up, you little fat-head, screw it up!'

As the Rector finished the consecration Miss Mayfill began to struggle to her feet with extreme difficulty and slowness, like some disjointed wooden creature picking itself up by sections, and disengaging at each movement a powerful whiff of mothballs. There was an extraordinary creaking sound—from her stays, presumably, but it was a noise as of bones grating against one another. You could have imagined that there was only a dry skeleton inside that black overcoat.

Dorothy remained on her feet a moment longer. Miss Mayfill was creeping towards the altar with slow, tottering steps. She could barely walk, but she took bitter offence if you offered to help her. In her ancient, bloodless face her mouth was surprisingly large, loose, and wet. The underlip, pendulous with age, slobbered forward, exposing a strip of gum and a row of false teeth as yellow as the keys of an old piano. On the upper lip was a fringe of dark, dewy moustache. It was not an appetizing mouth; not the kind of mouth that you would like to see drinking out of your cup. Suddenly, spontaneously, as though the Devil himself had put it there, the prayer slipped from Dorothy's lips: O God, let me not have to take the chalice after Miss Mayfill!

The next moment, in self-horror, she grasped the meaning of what she had said, and wished that she had bitten her tongue in two rather than utter that deadly blasphemy upon the altar steps. She drew the pin again from her lapel and drove it into her arm so hard that it was all she could do to suppress a cry of pain. Then she stepped to the altar and knelt down meekly on Miss Mayfill's left, so as to make quite sure of taking the chalice after her.

Kneeling, with head bent and hands clasped against her knees, she set herself swiftly to pray for forgiveness before her father should reach her with the wafer. But the current of her thoughts had been broken. Suddenly it was quite useless attempting to pray; her lips moved, but there was neither heart nor meaning in her prayers. She could hear Proggett's boots shuffling and her father's clear low voice murmuring 'Take and eat', she could see the worn strip of red carpet beneath her knees, she could smell dust and eau-de-Cologne and mothballs; but of the Body and Blood of Christ, of the purpose for which she had come here, she was as though deprived of the power to think. A deadly blankness had descended upon her mind. It seemed to her that actually she *could* not pray. She struggled, collected her thoughts, uttered mechanically the opening phrases of a prayer; but they were useless, meaningless—nothing but the dead shells of words. Her father was holding the wafer before her in his shapely, aged hand. He held it between finger and thumb, fastidiously, somehow distastefully, as though it had been a spoon of medicine. His eye was upon Miss Mayfill, who was doubling herself up like a geometrid caterpillar, with many creakings and crossing herself so elaborately that one might have imagined that she was sketching a series of braid frogs on the front of her coat. For several seconds Dorothy hesitated and did not take the wafer. She dared not take it. Better, far better to step down from the altar than to accept the sacrament with such chaos in her heart!

Then it happened that she glanced sidelong, through the open south door. A momentary spear of sunlight had pierced the clouds. It struck downwards through the leaves of the limes, and a spray of leaves in the doorway gleamed with a transient, matchless green, greener than jade or emerald or Atlantic waters. It was as though some jewel of unimaginable splendour had flashed for an instant, filling the doorway with green light, and then faded. A flood of joy ran through Dorothy's heart. The flash of living colour had brought back to her, by a process deeper than reason, her peace of mind, her love of God, her power to worship. Somehow, because of the greenness of the leaves, it was again possible to pray. O all ye green things upon the earth, praise ye the Lord! She began to pray, ardently, joyfully, thankfully. The wafer melted upon her tongue. She took the chalice from her father, and tasted with repulsion, even with an added joy in this small act of self-abasement, the wet imprint of Miss Mayfill's lips on its silver rim.

## 2

St Athelstan's Church stood at the highest point of Knype Hill, and if you chose to climb the tower you could see ten miles or so across the surrounding country. Not that there was anything worth looking at—only the low, barely undulating East Anglian landscape, intolerably dull in summer, but redeemed in winter by the recurring patterns of the elms, naked and fanshaped against leaden skies.

Immediately below you lay the town, with the High Street running east and west and dividing unequally. The southern section of the town was the ancient, agricultural, and respectable section. On the northern side were the buildings of the Blifil-Gordon sugar-beet refinery, and all round and leading up to them were higgledy-piggledly rows of vile yellow brick cottages, mostly inhabited by the employees of the factory. The factory employees, who made up more than half of the town's two thousand inhabitants, were newcomers, townfolk, and godless almost to a man.

The two pivots, or foci, about which the social life of the town moved were Knype Hill Conservative Club (fully licensed), from whose bow window, any time after the bar was open, the large, rosy-gilled faces of the town's élite were to be seen gazing like chubby goldfish from an aquarium pane; and Ye Olde Tea Shoppe, a little farther down the High Street, the principal rendezvous of the Knype Hill ladies. Not to be present at Ye Olde Tea Shoppe between ten and eleven every morning, to drink your 'morning coffee' and spend your half-hour or so in that agreeable twitter of upper-middle-class voices ('My dear, he had *nine* spades to the ace-queen and he went one no trump, if you please. What, my dear, you don't mean to say you're paying for my coffee *again*? Oh, but my dear, it is simply *too* sweet of you! Now tomorrow I shall *simply insist* upon paying for yours. And just *look* at dear little Toto sitting up and looking such a *clever* little man with his little black nose wiggling, and he would, would he, the darling duck, he would, he would, and his mother would give him a lump of sugar, she would, she would. *There,* Toto!'), was to be definitely out of Knype Hill society. The Rector in his acid way nicknamed these ladies 'the coffee brigade'. Close to the colony of sham-picturesque villas inhabited by the coffee brigade, but cut off from them by its larger grounds, was The Grange, Miss Mayfill's house. It was a curious, machicolated, imitation castle of dark red brick—somebody's Folly, built about 1870—and fortunately almost hidden among dense shrubberies.

The Rectory stood half way up the hill, with its face to the church and its back to the High Street. It was a house of the wrong age, inconveniently large, and faced with chronically peeling yellow plaster. Some earlier Rector had added, at one side, a large greenhouse which Dorothy used as a workroom, but which was constantly out of repair. The front garden was choked with ragged fir-trees and a great spreading ash which shadowed the front rooms and made it impossible to grow any flowers. There was a large vegetable garden at the back. Proggett did the heavy digging of the garden in the spring and autumn, and Dorothy did the sowing, planting, and weeding in such spare time as she could command; in spite of which the vegetable garden was usually an impenetrable jungle of weeds.

Dorothy jumped off her bicycle at the front gate, upon which some officious person had stuck a poster inscribed 'Vote for Blifil-Gordon and Higher Wages!' (There was a by-election going on, and Mr Blifil-Gordon was standing in the Conservative interest.) As Dorothy opened the front door she saw two letters lying on the worn coconut mat. One was from the Rural Dean, and the other was a nasty, thin-looking letter from Catkin & Palm, her father's clerical tailors. It was a bill undoubtedly. The Rector had followed his usual practice of collecting the letters that interested him and leaving the others. Dorothy was just bending down to pick up the letters, when she saw, with a horrid shock of dismay, an unstamped envelope sticking to the letter-flap.

It was a bill—for certain it was a bill! Moreover, as soon as she set eyes on it she 'knew' that it was that horrible bill from Cargill's, the butcher's. A sinking feeling passed through her entrails. For a moment she actually began to pray that it might not be Cargill's bill—that it might only be the bill for three and nine from Solepipe's, the draper's, or the bill from the International or the baker's or the dairy—anything except Cargill's bill! Then, mastering her panic, she took the envelope from the letter-flap and tore it open with a convulsive movement.

'To account rendered: £21 7s. 9d.'

This was written in the innocuous handwriting of Mr Cargill's accountant. But underneath, in thick, accusing-looking letters, was added and heavily underlined: 'Shd. like to bring to your notice that this bill has been owing a *very long time*. The *earliest possible* settlement will oblige, S. Cargill.'

Dorothy had turned a shade paler, and was conscious of not wanting any breakfast. She thrust the bill into her pocket and went into the dining-room. It was a smallish, dark room, badly in need of repapering, and, like every other room in the Rectory, it had the air of having been furnished from the sweepings of an antique shop. The furniture was 'good', but battered beyond repair, and the chairs were so worm-eaten that you could only sit on them in safety if you knew their individual foibles. There were old, dark, defaced steel engravings hanging on the walls, one of them—an engraving of Van Dyck's portrait of Charles I—probably of some value if it had not been ruined by damp.

The Rector was standing before the empty grate, warming himself at an imaginary fire and reading a letter that came from a long blue envelope. He was still wearing his cassock of black watered silk, which set off to perfection his thick white hair and his pale, fine, none too amiable face. As Dorothy came in he laid the letter aside, drew out his gold watch and scrutinized it significantly.

'I'm afraid I'm a bit late, Father.'

'Yes, Dorothy, you are *a bit late,*' said the Rector, repeating her words with delicate but marked emphasis. 'You are twelve minutes late, to be exact. Don't you think, Dorothy, that when I have to get up at a quarter past six to celebrate Holy Communion, and come home exceedingly tired and hungry, it would be better if you could manage to come to breakfast without being *a bit late*?'

It was clear that the Rector was in what Dorothy called, euphemistically, his 'uncomfortable mood'. He had one of those weary, cultivated voices which are never definitely angry and never anywhere near good humour—one of those voices which seem all the while to be saying, 'I really *cannot* see what you are making all this fuss about!' The impression he gave was of suffering perpetually from other people's stupidity and tiresomeness.

'I'm so sorry, Father! I simply had to go and ask after Mrs Tawney.' (Mrs Tawney was the 'Mrs T' of the 'memo list'.) 'Her baby was born last night, and you know she promised me she'd come and be churched after it was born. But of course she won't if she thinks we aren't taking any interest in her. You know what these women are—they seem so to hate being churched. They'll never come unless I coax them into it.'

The Rector did not actually grunt, but he uttered a small dissatisfied sound as he moved towards the breakfast table. It was intended to mean, first, that it was Mrs Tawney's duty to come and be churched without Dorothy's coaxing; secondly, that Dorothy had no business to waste her time visiting all the riff-raff of the town, especially before breakfast. Mrs Tawney was a labourer's wife and lived *in partibus infidelium,* north of the High Street. The Rector laid his hand on the back of his chair, and, without speaking, cast Dorothy a glance which meant: 'Are we ready *now*? Or are there to be any *more* delays?'

'I think everything's here, Father,' said Dorothy. 'Perhaps if you'd just say grace—'

'*Benedictus benedicat,*' said the Rector, lifting the worn silver coverlet off the breakfast dish. The silver coverlet, like the silver-gilt marmalade spoon, was a family heirloom; the knives and forks, and most of the crockery, came from Woolworths. 'Bacon again, I see,' the Rector added, eyeing the three minute rashers that lay curled up on squares of fried bread.

'It's all we've got in the house, I'm afraid,' Dorothy said.

The Rector picked up his fork between finger and thumb, and with a very delicate movement, as though playing at spillikins, turned one of the rashers over.

'I know, of course,' he said, 'that bacon for breakfast is an English institution almost as old as parliamentary government. But still, don't you think we might *occasionally* have a change, Dorothy?'

'Bacon's so cheap now,' said Dorothy regretfully. 'It seems a sin not to buy it. This was only fivepence a pound, and I saw some quite decent-looking bacon as low as threepence.'

'Ah, Danish, I suppose? What a variety of Danish invasions we have had in this country! First with fire and sword, and now with their abominable cheap bacon. Which has been responsible for the more deaths, I wonder?'

Feeling a little better after this witticism, the Rector settled himself in his chair and made a fairly good breakfast off the despised bacon, while Dorothy (she was not having any bacon this morning—a penance she had set herself yesterday for saying 'Damn' and idling for half an hour after lunch) meditated upon a good conversational opening.

There was an unspeakably hateful job in front of her—a demand for money. At the very best of times getting money out of her father was next door to impossible, and it was obvious that this morning he was going to be even more 'difficult' than usual. 'Difficult' was another of her euphemisms. He's had bad news, I suppose, she thought despondently, looking at the blue envelope.

Probably no one who had ever spoken to the Rector for as long as ten minutes would have denied that he was a 'difficult' kind of man. The secret of his almost unfailing ill humour really lay in the fact that he was an anachronism. He ought never to have been born into the modern world; its whole atmosphere disgusted and infuriated him. A couple of centuries earlier, a happy pluralist writing poems or collecting fossils while curates at £40 a year administered his parishes, he would have been perfectly at home. Even now, if he had been a richer man, he might have consoled himself by shutting the twentieth century out of his consciousness. But to live in past ages is very expensive; you can't do it on less than two thousand a year. The Rector, tethered by his poverty to the age of Lenin and the *Daily Mail*, was kept in a state of chronic exasperation which it was only natural that he should work off on the person nearest to him—usually, that is, on Dorothy.

He had been born in 1871, the younger son of the younger son of a baronet, and had gone into the Church for the outmoded reason that the Church is the traditional profession for younger sons. His first cure had been in a large, slummy parish in East London—a nasty, hooliganish place it had been, and he looked back on it with loathing. Even in those days the lower class (as he made a point of calling them) were getting decidedly out of hand. It was a little better when he was curate-in-charge at some remote place in Kent (Dorothy had been born in Kent), where the decently down-trodden villagers still touched their hats to 'parson'. But by that time he had married, and his marriage had been diabolically unhappy; moreover, because clergymen must not quarrel with their wives, its unhappiness had been secret and therefore ten times worse. He had come to Knype Hill in 1908, aged thirty-seven and with a temper incurably soured–a temper which had ended by alienating every man, woman, and child in the parish.

It was not that he was a bad priest, merely *as* a priest. In his purely clerical duties he was scrupulously correct–perhaps a little too correct for a Low Church East Anglian parish. He conducted his services with perfect taste, preached admirable sermons, and got up at uncomfortable hours of the morning to celebrate Holy Communion every Wednesday and Friday. But that a clergyman has any duties outside the four walls of the church was a thing that had never seriously occurred to him. Unable to afford a curate, he left the dirty work of the parish entirely to his wife, and after her death (she died in 1921) to Dorothy. People used to say, spitefully and untruly, that he would have let Dorothy preach his sermons for him if it had been possible. The 'lower classes' had grasped from the first what was his attitude towards them, and if he had been a rich man they would probably have licked his boots, according to their custom; as it was, they merely hated him. Not that he cared whether they hated him or not, for he was largely unaware of their existence. But even with the upper classes he had got on no better. With the County he had quarrelled one by one, and as for the petty gentry of the town, as the grandson of a baronet he despised them, and was at no pains to hide it. In twenty-three years he had succeeded in reducing the congregation of St Athelstan's from six hundred to something under two hundred.

This was not solely due to personal reasons. It was also because the old-fashioned High Anglicanism to which the Rector obstinately clung was of a kind to annoy all parties in the parish about equally. Nowadays, a clergyman who wants to keep his congregation has only two courses open to him. Either it must be Anglo-Catholicism pure and simple–or rather, pure and not simple; or he must be daringly modern and broad-minded and preach comforting sermons proving that there is no Hell and all good religions are the same. The Rector did neither. On the one hand, he had the deepest contempt for the Anglo-Catholic movement. It had passed over his head, leaving him absolutely untouched; 'Roman Fever' was his name for it. On the other hand, he was too 'High' for the older members of his congregation. From time to time he scared them almost out of their wits by the use of the fatal word 'Catholic', not only in its sanctified place in the Creeds, but also from the pulpit. Naturally the congregation dwindled year by year, and it was the Best People who were the first to go. Lord Pockthorne of Pockthorne Court, who owned a fifth of the county, Mr Leavis, the retired leather merchant, Sir Edward Huson of Crabtree Hall, and such of the petty gentry as owned motor-cars, had all deserted St Athelstan's. Most of them drove over on Sunday mornings to Millborough, five miles away. Millborough was a town of five thousand inhabitants, and you had your choice of two churches, St Edmund's and St Wedekind's. St Edmund's was Modernist–text from Blake's 'Jerusalem' blazoned over the altar, and communion wine out of liqueur glasses–and St

Wedekind's was Anglo-Catholic and in a state of perpetual guerrilla warfare with the Bishop. But Mr Cameron, the secretary of the Knype Hill Conservative Club, was a Roman Catholic convert, and his children were in the thick of the Roman Catholic literary movement. They were said to have a parrot which they were teaching to say *'Extra ecclesiam nulla salus'*. In effect, no one of any standing remained true to St Athelstan's, except Miss Mayfill, of The Grange. Most of Miss Mayfill's money was bequeathed to the Church—so she said; meanwhile, she had never been known to put more than sixpence in the collection bag, and she seemed likely to go on living for ever.

The first ten minutes of breakfast passed in complete silence. Dorothy was trying to summon up courage to speak—obviously she had got to start *some* kind of conversation before raising the money-question—but her father was not an easy man with whom to make small talk. At times he would fall into such deep fits of abstraction that you could hardly get him to listen to you; at other times he was all too attentive, listened carefully to what you said and then pointed out, rather wearily, that it was not worth saying. Polite platitudes—the weather, and so forth—generally moved him to sarcasm. Nevertheless, Dorothy decided to try the weather first.

'It's a funny kind of day, isn't it?' she said—aware, even as she made it, of the inanity of this remark.

'*What* is funny?' inquired the Rector.

'Well, I mean, it was so cold and misty this morning, and now the sun's come out and it's turned quite fine.'

'*Is* there anything particularly funny about that?'

That was no good, obviously. He *must* have had bad news, she thought. She tried again.

'I do wish you'd come out and have a look at the things in the back garden some time, Father. The runner beans are doing so splendidly! The pods are going to be over a foot long. I'm going to keep all the best of them for the Harvest Festival, of course. I thought it would look so nice if we decorated the pulpit with festoons of runner beans and a few tomatoes hanging in among them.'

This was a *faux pas*. The Rector looked up from his plate with an expression of profound distaste.

'My dear Dorothy,' he said sharply, '*is* it necessary to begin worrying me about the Harvest Festival already?'

'I'm sorry, Father!' said Dorothy, disconcerted. 'I didn't mean to worry you. I just thought—'

'Do you suppose', proceeded the Rector, 'it is any pleasure to me to have to preach my sermon among festoons of runner beans? I am not a greengrocer. It quite puts me off my breakfast to think of it. When is the wretched thing due to happen?'

'It's September the sixteenth, Father.'

'That's nearly a month hence. For Heaven's sake let me forget it a little longer! I suppose we *must* have this ridiculous business once a year to tickle the vanity of every amateur gardener in the parish. But don't let's think of it more than is absolutely necessary.'

The Rector had, as Dorothy ought to have remembered, a perfect abhorrence of Harvest Festivals. He had even lost a valuable parishioner–a Mr Toagis, a surly retired market gardener–through his dislike, as he said, of seeing his church dressed up to imitate a coster's stall. Mr Toagis, *anima naturaliter Nonconformistica*, had been kept 'Church' solely by the privilege, at Harvest Festival time, of decorating the side altar with a sort of Stonehenge composed of gigantic vegetable marrows. The previous summer he had succeeded in growing a perfect leviathan of a pumpkin, a fiery red thing so enormous that it took two men to lift it. This monstrous object had been placed in the chancel, where it dwarfed the altar and took all the colour out of the east window. In no matter what part of the church you were standing, the pumpkin, as the saying goes, hit you in the eye. Mr Toagis was in raptures. He hung about the church at all hours, unable to tear himself away from his adored pumpkin, and even bringing relays of friends in to admire it. From the expression of his face you would have thought that he was quoting Wordsworth on Westminster Bridge:

> Earth has not any thing to show more fair:
> Dull would he be of soul who could pass by
> A sight so touching in its majesty!

Dorothy even had hopes, after this, of getting him to come to Holy Communion. But when the Rector saw the pumpkin he was seriously angry, and ordered 'that revolting thing' to be removed at once. Mr Toagis had instantly 'gone chapel', and he and his heirs were lost to the Church for ever.

Dorothy decided to make one final attempt at conversation.

'We're getting on with the costumes for *Charles I*,' she said. (The Church School children were rehearsing a play entitled *Charles I* in aid of the organ fund.) 'But I do wish we'd chosen something a bit easier. The armour is a dreadful job to make, and I'm afraid the jackboots are going to be worse. I think next time we must really have a Roman or Greek play. Something where they only have to wear togas.'

This elicited only another muted grunt from the Rector. School plays, pageants, bazaars, jumble sales, and concerts in aid of were not quite so bad in his eyes as Harvest Festivals, but he did not pretend to be interested in them. They were necessary evils, he used to say. At this moment Ellen, the maidservant, pushed open the door and came gauchely into the room with one large, scaly hand holding her sacking apron against her belly. She was a tall, round-shouldered girl with mouse-coloured hair, a plaintive voice, and a bad complexion, and she suffered chronically from eczema. Her eyes flitted apprehensively towards the Rector, but she addressed herself to Dorothy, for she was too much afraid of the Rector to speak to him directly.

'Please, Miss–' she began.

'Yes, Ellen?'

'Please, Miss,' went on Ellen plaintively, 'Mr Porter's in the kitchen, and he says, please could the Rector come round and baptize Mrs Porter's baby?

Because they don't think as it's going to live the day out, and it ain't been baptized yet, Miss.'

Dorothy stood up. 'Sit down,' said the Rector promptly, with his mouth full.

'What do they think is the matter with the baby?' said Dorothy.

'Well, Miss, it's turning quite black. And it's had diarrhoea something cruel.'

The Rector emptied his mouth with an effort. 'Must I have these disgusting details while I am eating my breakfast?' he exclaimed. He turned on Ellen: 'Send Porter about his business and tell him I'll be round at his house at twelve o'clock. I really cannot think why it is that the lower classes always seem to choose mealtimes to come pestering one,' he added, casting another irritated glance at Dorothy as she sat down.

Mr Porter was a labouring man—a bricklayer, to be exact. The Rector's views on baptism were entirely sound. If it had been urgently necessary he would have walked twenty miles through snow to baptize a dying baby. But he did not like to see Dorothy proposing to leave the breakfast table at the call of a common bricklayer.

There was no further conversation during breakfast. Dorothy's heart was sinking lower and lower. The demand for money had got to be made, and yet it was perfectly obvious that it was foredoomed to failure. His breakfast finished, the Rector got up from the table and began to fill his pipe from the tobacco-jar on the mantelpiece. Dorothy uttered a short prayer for courage, and then pinched herself. Go on, Dorothy! Out with it! No funking, please! With an effort she mastered her voice and said:

'Father—'

'What is it?' said the Rector, pausing with the match in his hand.

'Father, I've something I want to ask you. Something important.'

The expression of the Rector's face changed. He had divined instantly what she was going to say; and, curiously enough, he now looked less irritable than before. A stony calm had settled upon his face. He looked like a rather exceptionally aloof and unhelpful sphinx.

'Now, my dear Dorothy, I know very well what you are going to say. I suppose you are going to ask me for money again. Is that it?'

'Yes, Father. Because—'

'Well, I may as well save you the trouble. I have no money at all—absolutely no money at all until next quarter. You have had your allowance, and I can't give you a halfpenny more. It's quite useless to come worrying me now.'

'But, Father—'

Dorothy's heart sank yet lower. What was worst of all when she came to him for money was the terrible, unhelpful calmness of his attitude. He was never so unmoved as when you were reminding him that he was up to his eyes in debt. Apparently he could not understand that tradesmen occasionally want to be paid, and that no house can be kept going without an adequate supply of money. He allowed Dorothy eighteen pounds a month for all the household expenses, including Ellen's wages, and at the same time he was 'dainty' about his food and instantly detected any falling off in its quality. The result was, of course, that the household was perennially in debt. But the Rector paid not the smallest attention to his debts—indeed, he was hardly even aware of them. When he lost money over an investment, he was deeply agitated; but as for a debt to a mere tradesman—well, it was the kind of thing that he simply could not bother his head about.

A peaceful plume of smoke floated upwards from the Rector's pipe. He was gazing with a meditative eye at the steel engraving of Charles I and had probably forgotten already about Dorothy's demand for money. Seeing him so unconcerned, a pang of desperation went through Dorothy, and her courage came back to her. She said more sharply than before:

'Father, please listen to me! I *must* have some money soon! I simply *must*! We can't go on as we're doing. We owe money to nearly every tradesman in the town. It's got so that some mornings I can hardly bear to go down the street and think of all the bills that are owing. Do you know that we owe Cargill nearly twenty-two pounds?'

'What of it?' said the Rector between puffs of smoke.

'But the bill's been mounting up for over seven months! He's sent it in over and over again. We *must* pay it! It's so unfair to him to keep him waiting for his money like that!'

'Nonsense, my dear child! These people expect to be kept waiting for their money. They like it. It brings them more in the end. Goodness knows how much I owe to Catkin & Palm—I should hardly care to inquire. They are dunning me by every post. But you don't hear *me* complaining, do you?'

'But, Father, I can't look at it as you do, I can't! It's so dreadful to be always in debt! Even if it isn't actually wrong, it's so *hateful*. It makes me so ashamed! When I go into Cargill's shop to order the joint, he speaks to me so shortly and makes me wait after the other customers, all because our bill's mounting up the whole time. And yet I daren't stop ordering from him. I believe he'd run us in if I did.'

The Rector frowned. 'What! Do you mean to say the fellow has been impertinent to you?'

'I didn't say he'd been impertinent, Father. But you can't blame him if he's angry when his bill's not paid.'

'I most certainly can blame him! It is simply abominable how these people take it upon themselves to behave nowadays—abominable! But there you are, you see. That is the kind of thing that we are exposed to in this delightful century. That is democracy—*progress*, as they are pleased to call it. Don't order from the fellow again. Tell him at once that you are taking your account elsewhere. That's the only way to treat these people.'

'But, Father, that doesn't settle anything. Really and truly, don't you think we ought to pay him? Surely we can get hold of the money somehow? Couldn't you sell out some shares, or something?'

'My dear child, don't talk to me about selling out shares! I have just had the most disagreeable news from my broker. He tells me that my Sumatra Tin shares have dropped from seven and fourpence to six and a penny. It means a loss of nearly sixty pounds. I am telling him to sell out at once before they drop any further.'

'Then if you sell out you'll have some ready money, won't you? Don't you think it would be better to get out of debt once and for all?'

'Nonsense, nonsense,' said the Rector more calmly, putting his pipe back in his mouth. 'You know nothing whatever about these matters. I shall have to reinvest at once in something more hopeful—it's the only way of getting my money back.'

With one thumb in the belt of his cassock he frowned abstractedly at the steel engraving. His broker had advised United Celanese. Here—in Sumatra Tin, United Celanese, and numberless other remote and dimly imagined companies—was the central cause of the Rector's money troubles. He was an inveterate gambler. Not, of course, that he thought of it as gambling; it was merely a lifelong search for a 'good investment'. On coming of age he had inherited four thousand pounds, which had gradually dwindled, thanks to his 'investments', to about twelve hundred. What was worse, every year he managed to scrape together, out of his miserable income, another fifty pounds which vanished by the same road. It is a curious fact that the lure of a 'good investment' seems to haunt clergymen more persistently than any other class of man. Perhaps it is the modern equivalent of the demons in female shape who used to haunt the anchorites of the Dark Ages.

'I shall buy five hundred United Celanese,' said the Rector finally.

Dorothy began to give up hope. Her father was now thinking of his 'investments' (she new nothing whatever about these 'investments', except that they went wrong with phenomenal regularity), and in another moment the question of the shop-debts would have slipped entirely out of his mind. She made a final effort.

'Father, let's get this settled, please. Do you think you'll be able to let me have some extra money fairly soon? Not this moment, perhaps—but in the next month or two?'

'No, my dear, I don't. About Christmas time, possibly—it's very unlikely even then. But for the present, certainly not. I haven't a halfpenny I can spare.'

'But, Father, it's so horrible to feel we can't pay our debts! It disgraces us so! Last time Mr Welwyn-Foster was here' (Mr Welwyn-Foster was the Rural Dean) 'Mrs Welwyn-Foster was going all round the town asking everyone the most personal questions about us—asking how we spent our time, and how much money we had, and how many tons of coal we used in a year, and everything. She's always trying to pry into our affairs. Suppose she found out that we were badly in debt!'

'Surely it is our own business? I fail entirely to see what it has to do with Mrs Welwyn-Foster or anyone else.'

'But she'd repeat it all over the place—and she'd exaggerate it too! You know what Mrs Welwyn-Foster is. In every parish she goes to she tries to find out something disgraceful about the clergyman, and then she repeats every word of it to the Bishop. I don't want to be uncharitable about her, but really she—'

Realizing that she *did* want to be uncharitable, Dorothy was silent.

'She is a detestable woman,' said the Rector evenly. 'What of it? Who ever heard of a Rural Dean's wife who wasn't detestable?'

'But, Father, I don't seem to be able to get you to see how serious things are! We've simply nothing to live on for the next month. I don't even know where the meat's coming from for today's dinner.'

'Luncheon, Dorothy, luncheon!' said the Rector with a touch of irritation. 'I do wish you would drop that abominable lower-class habit of calling the midday meal *dinner*!'

'For luncheon, then. Where are we to get the meat from? I daren't ask Cargill for another joint.'

'Go to the other butcher—what's his name? Salter—and take no notice of Cargill. He knows he'll be paid sooner or later. Good gracious, I don't know what all this fuss is about! Doesn't everyone owe money to his tradesmen? I distinctly remember'—the Rector straightened his shoulders a little, and, putting his pipe back into his mouth, looked into the distance; his voice became reminiscent and perceptibly more agreeable—'I distinctly remember that when I was up at Oxford, my father had still not paid some of his own Oxford bills of thirty years earlier. Tom' (Tom was the Rector's cousin, the Baronet) 'owed seven thousand before he came into his money. He told me so himself.'

At that, Dorothy's last hope vanished. When her father began to talk about his cousin Tom, and about things that had happened 'when I was up at Oxford', there was nothing more to be done with him. It meant that he had slipped into an imaginary golden past in which such vulgar things as butchers' bills simply did not exist. There were long periods together when he seemed actually to forget that he was only a poverty-stricken country Rector—that he was not a young man of family with estates and reversions at his back. The aristocratic, the expensive attitude was the one that in all circumstances came the most naturally to him. And of course while he lived, not uncomfortably, in the world of his imagination, it was Dorothy who had to fight the tradesmen and make a leg of mutton last from Sunday to Wednesday. But she knew the complete uselessness of arguing with him any longer. It would only end in making him angry. She got up from the table and began to pile the breakfast things on to the tray.

'You're absolutely certain you can't let me have any money, Father?' she said for the last time, at the door, with the tray in her arms.

The Rector, gazing into the middle distance, amid comfortable wreaths of smoke, did not hear her. He was thinking, perhaps, of his golden Oxford days. Dorothy went out of the room distressed almost to the point of tears. The miserable question of the debts was once more shelved, as it had been shelved a thousand times before, with no prospect of final solution.

# 3

On her elderly bicycle with the basketwork carrier on the handle-bars, Dorothy free-wheeled down the hill, doing mental arithmetic with three pounds nineteen and fourpence—her entire stock of money until next quarter-day.

She had been through the list of things that were needed in the kitchen. But indeed, was there anything that was *not* needed in the kitchen? Tea, coffee, soap, matches, candles, sugar, lentils, firewood, soda, lamp oil, boot polish, margarine, baking powder—there seemed to be practically nothing that they were not running short of. And at every moment some fresh item that she had forgotten popped up and dismayed her. The laundry bill, for example, and the fact that the coal was running short, and the question of the fish for Friday. The Rector was 'difficult' about fish. Roughly speaking, he would only eat the more expensive kinds; cod, whiting, sprats, skate, herrings, and kippers he refused.

Meanwhile, she had got to settle about the meat for today's dinner—luncheon. (Dorothy was careful to obey her father and call it *luncheon,* when she remembered it. On the other hand, you could not in honesty call the evening meal anything but 'supper'; so there was no such meal as 'dinner' at the Rectory.) Better make an omelette for luncheon today, Dorothy decided. She dared not go to Cargill again. Though, of course, if they had an omelette for luncheon and then scrambled eggs for supper, her father would probably be sarcastic about it. Last time they had eggs twice in one day, he had inquired coldly, 'Have you started a chicken farm, Dorothy?' And perhaps tomorrow she would get two pounds of sausages at the International, and that staved off the meat-question for one day more.

Thirty-nine further days, with only three pounds nineteen and fourpence to provide for them, loomed up in Dorothy's imagination, sending through her a wave of self-pity which she checked almost instantly. Now then, Dorothy! No snivelling, please! It all comes right somehow if you trust in God. Matthew vi, 25. The Lord will provide. Will He? Dorothy removed her right hand from the handle-bars and felt for the glass-headed pin, but the blasphemous thought faded. At this moment she became aware of the gloomy red face of Proggett, who was hailing her respectfully but urgently from the side of the road.

Dorothy stopped and got off her bicycle.

'Beg pardon, Miss,' said Proggett. 'I been wanting to speak to you,

Miss—*partic'lar*.'

Dorothy sighed inwardly. When Proggett wanted to speak to you *partic'lar*, you could be perfectly certain what was coming; it was some piece of alarming news about the condition of the church. Proggett was a pessimistic, conscientious man, and very loyal churchman, after his fashion. Too dim of intellect to have any definite religious beliefs, he showed his piety by an intense solicitude about the state of the church buildings. He had decided long ago that the Church of Christ meant the actual walls, roof, and tower of St Athelstan's, Knype Hill, and he would poke round the church at all hours of the day, gloomily noting a cracked stone here, a worm-eaten beam there—and afterwards, of course, coming to harass Dorothy with demands for repairs which would cost impossible sums of money.

'What is it, Proggett?' said Dorothy.

'Well, Miss, it's they—'—here a peculiar, imperfect sound, not a word exactly, but the ghost of a word, all but formed itself on Proggett's lips. It seemed to begin with a B. Proggett was one of those men who are for ever on the verge of swearing, but who always recapture the oath as it is escaping between their teeth. 'It's they *bells*, Miss,' he said, getting rid of the B sound with an effort. 'They bells up in the church tower. They're a-splintering through that there belfry floor in a way as it makes you fair shudder to look at 'em. We'll have 'em down atop of us before we know where we are. I was up the belfry 'smorning, and I tell you I come down faster'n I went up, when I saw how that there floor's a-busting underneath 'em.

Proggett came to complain about the condition of the bells not less than once a fortnight. It was now three years that they had been lying on the floor of the belfry, because the cost of either reswinging or removing them was estimated at twenty-five pounds, which might as well have been twenty-five thousand for all the chance there was of paying for it. They were really almost as dangerous as Proggett made out. It was quite certain that, if not this year or next year, at any rate at some time in the near future, they would fall through the belfry floor into the church porch. And, as Proggett was fond of pointing out, it would probably happen on a Sunday morning just as the congregation were coming into church.

Dorothy sighed again. Those wretched bells were never out of mind for long; there were times when the thought of their falling even got into her dreams. There was always some trouble or other at the church. If it was not the belfry, then it was the roof or the walls; or it was a broken pew which the carpenter wanted ten shillings to mend; or it was seven hymn-books needed at one and sixpence each, or the flue of the stove choked up—and the sweep's fee was half a crown—or a smashed window-pane or the choir-boys' cassocks in rags. There was never enough money for anything. The new organ which the Rector had insisted on buying five years earlier—the old one, he said, reminded him of a cow with the asthma—was a burden under which the Church Expenses fund had been staggering ever since.

'I don't know *what* we can do,' said Dorothy finally; 'I really don't. We've simply no money at all. And even if we do make anything out of the schoolchildren's play, it's all got to go to the organ fund. The organ people are really getting quite nasty about their bill. Have you spoken to my father?'

'Yes, Miss. He don't make nothing of it. "Belfry's held up five hundred years," he says; "we can trust it to hold up a few years longer."'

This was quite according to precedent. The fact that the church was visibly collapsing over his head made no impression on the Rector; he simply ignored it, as he ignored anything else that he did not wish to be worried about.

'Well, I don't know *what* we can do,' Dorothy repeated. 'Of course there's the jumble sale coming off the week after next. I'm counting on Miss Mayfill to give us something really *nice* for the jumble sale. I know she could afford to. She's got such lots of furniture and things that she never uses. I was in her house the other day, and I saw a most beautiful Lowestoft china tea service which was put away in a cupboard, and she told me it hadn't been used for over twenty years. Just suppose she gave us that tea service! It would fetch pounds and pounds. We must just pray that the jumble sale will be a success, Proggett. Pray that it'll bring us five pounds at least. I'm sure we shall get the money somehow if we really and truly pray for it.'

'Yes, Miss,' said Proggett respectfully, and shifted his gaze to the far distance.

At this moment a horn hooted and a vast, gleaming blue car came very slowly down the road, making for the High Street. Out of one window Mr Blifil-Gordon, the Proprietor of the sugar-beet refinery, was thrusting a sleek black head which went remarkably ill with his suit of sandy-coloured Harris tweed. As he passed, instead of ignoring Dorothy as usual, he flashed upon her a smile so warm that it was almost amorous. With him were his eldest son Ralph—or, as he and the rest of the family pronounced it, Walph—an epicene youth of twenty, given to the writing of sub-Eliot *vers libre* poems, and Lord Pockthorne's two daughters. They were all smiling, even Lord Pockthorne's daughters. Dorothy was astonished, for it was several years since any of these people had deigned to recognize her in the street.

'Mr Blifil-Gordon is very friendly this morning,' she said.

'Aye, Miss. I'll be bound he is. It's the election coming on next week, that's what 'tis. All honey and butter they are till they've made sure as you'll vote for them; and then they've forgot your very face the day afterwards.'

'Oh, the election!' said Dorothy vaguely. So remote were such things as parliamentary elections from the daily round of parish work that she was virtually unaware of them—hardly, indeed, even knowing the difference between Liberal and Conservative or Socialist and Communist. 'Well, Proggett,' she said, immediately forgetting the election in favour of something more important, 'I'll speak to Father and tell him how serious it is about the bells. I think perhaps the best thing we can do will be to get up a special subscription, just for the bells alone. There's no knowing, we might make five pounds. We might even make ten pounds! Don't you think if I went to Miss Mayfill and asked her to start the subscription with five pounds, she might give it to us?'

'You take my word, Miss, and don't you let Miss Mayfill hear nothing about it. It'd scare the life out of her. If she thought as that tower wasn't safe, we'd never get her inside that church again.'

'Oh dear! I suppose not.'

'No, Miss. We shan't get nothing out of *her*; the old–'

A ghostly B floated once more across Proggett's lips. His mind a little more at rest now that he had delivered his fortnightly report upon the bells, he touched his cap and departed, while Dorothy rode on into the High Street, with the twin problems of the shop-debts and the Church Expenses pursuing one another through her mind like the twin refrains of a villanelle.

The still watery sun, now playing hide-and-seek, April-wise, among woolly islets of cloud, sent an oblique beam down the High Street, gilding the house-fronts of the northern side. It was one of those sleepy, old-fashioned streets that look so ideally peaceful on a casual visit and so very different when you live in them and have an enemy or a creditor behind every window. The only definitely offensive buildings were Ye Olde Tea Shoppe (plaster front with sham beams nailed on to it, bottle-glass windows and revolting curly roof like that of a Chinese joss-house), and the new, Doric-pillared post office. After about two hundred yards the High Street forked, forming a tiny market-place, adorned with a pump, now defunct, and a worm-eaten pair of stocks. On either side of the pump stood the Dog and Bottle, the principal inn of the town, and the Knype Hill Conservative Club. At the end, commanding the street, stood Cargill's dreaded shop.

Dorothy came round the corner to a terrific din of cheering, mingled with the strains of 'Rule Britannia' played on the trombone. The normally sleepy street was black with people, and more people were hurrying from all the side-streets. Evidently a sort of triumphal procession was taking place. Right across the street, from the roof of the Dog and Bottle to the roof of the Conservative Club, hung a line with innumerable blue streamers, and in the middle a vast banner inscribed 'Blifil-Gordon and the Empire!' Towards this, between the lanes of people, the Blifil-Gordon car was moving at a foot-pace, with Mr Blifil-Gordon smiling richly, first to one side, then to the other. In front of the car marched a detachment of the Buffaloes, headed by an earnest-looking little man playing the trombone, and carrying among them another banner inscribed:

Who'll save Britain from the Reds?
BLIFIL-GORDON
Who'll put the Beer back into your Pot?
BLIFIL-GORDON
Blifil-Gordon for ever!

From the window of the Conservative Club floated an enormous Union Jack, above which six scarlet faces were beaming enthusiastically.

Dorothy wheeled her bicycle slowly down the street, too much agitated by the prospect of passing Cargill's shop (she had got to pass it, to get to Solepipe's) to take much notice of the procession. The Blifil-Gordon car had halted for a moment outside Ye Olde Tea Shoppe. Forward, the coffee brigade! Half the ladies of the town seemed to be hurrying forth, with lapdogs or shopping baskets on their arms, to cluster about the car like Bacchantes about the car of the vine-god. After all, an election is practically the only time when you get a chance of exchanging smiles with the County. There were eager feminine cries of 'Good luck, Mr Blifil-Gordon! *Dear* Mr Blifil-Gordon! We *do* hope you'll get in, Mr Blifil-Gordon!' Mr Blifil-Gordon's largesse of smiles was unceasing, but carefully graded. To the populace he gave a diffused, general smile, not resting on individuals; to the coffee ladies and the six scarlet patriots of the Conservative Club he gave one smile each; to the most favoured of all, young Walph gave an occasional wave of the hand and a squeaky 'Cheewio!'

Dorothy's heart tightened. She had seen that Mr Cargill, like the rest of the shopkeepers, was standing on his doorstep. He was a tall, evil-looking man, in blue-striped apron, with a lean, scraped face as purple as one of his own joints of meat that had lain a little too long in the window. So fascinated were Dorothy's eyes by that ominous figure that she did not look where she was going, and bumped into a very large, stout man who was stepping off the pavement backwards.

The stout man turned round. 'Good Heavens! It's Dorothy!' he exclaimed.

'Why, Mr Warburton! How extraordinary! Do you know, I had a feeling I was going to meet you today.'

'By the pricking of your thumbs, I presume?' said Mr Warburton, beaming all over a large, pink, Micawberish face. 'And how are you? But by Jove!' he added, 'What need is there to ask? You look more bewitching than ever.'

He pinched Dorothy's bare elbow—she had changed, after breakfast, into a sleeveless gingham frock. Dorothy stepped hurriedly backwards to get out of his reach—she hated being pinched or otherwise 'mauled about'—and said rather severely:

'*Please* don't pinch my elbow. I don't like it.'

'My dear Dorothy, who could resist an elbow like yours? It's the sort of elbow one pinches automatically. A reflex action, if you understand me.'

'When did you get back to Knype Hill?' said Dorothy, who had put her bicycle between Mr Warburton and herself. 'It's over two months since I've seen you.'

'I got back the day before yesterday. But this is only a flying visit. I'm off again tomorrow. I'm taking the kids to Brittany. The *bastards,* you know.'

Mr Warburton pronounced the word *bastards,* at which Dorothy looked away in discomfort, with a touch of naïve pride. He and his 'bastards' (he had three of them) were one of the chief scandals of Knype Hill. He was a man of independent income, calling himself a painter—he produced about half a dozen mediocre landscapes every year—and he had come to Knype Hill two years earlier and bought one of the new villas behind the Rectory. There he lived, or rather stayed periodically, in open concubinage with a woman whom he called his housekeeper. Four months ago this woman—she was a foreigner, a Spaniard it was said—had created a fresh and worse scandal by abruptly deserting him, and his three children were now parked with some long-suffering relative in London. In appearance he was a fine, imposing-looking man, though entirely bald (he was at great pains to conceal this), and he carried himself with such a rakish air as to give the impression that his fairly sizeable belly was merely a kind of annexe to his chest. His age was forty-eight, and he owned to forty-four. People in the town said that he was a 'proper old rascal'; young girls were afraid of him, not without reason.

Mr Warburton had laid his hand pseudo-paternally on Dorothy's shoulder and was shepherding her through the crowd, talking all the while almost without a pause. The Blifil-Gordon car, having rounded the pump, was now wending its way back, still accompanied by its troupe of middle-aged Bacchantes. Mr Warburton, his attention caught, paused to scrutinize it.

'What is the meaning of these disgusting antics?' he asked.

'Oh, they're—what is it they call it?—electioneering. Trying to get us to vote for them, I suppose.'

'Trying to get us to vote for them! Good God!' murmured Mr Warburton, as he eyed the triumphal cortège. He raised the large, silver-headed cane that he always carried, and pointed, rather expressively, first at one figure in the procession and then at another. 'Look at it! Just look at it! Look at those fawning hags, and that half-witted oaf grinning at us like a monkey that sees a bag of nuts. Did you ever see such a disgusting spectacle?'

'Do be careful!' Dorothy murmured. 'Somebody's sure to hear you.'

'Good!' said Mr Warburton, immediately raising his voice. 'And to think that low-born hound actually has the impertinence to think that he's pleasing us with the sight of his false teeth! And that suit he's wearing is an offence in itself. Is there a Socialist candidate? If so, I shall certainly vote for him.'

Several people on the pavement turned and stared. Dorothy saw little Mr Twiss, the ironmonger, a weazened, leather-coloured old man, peering with veiled malevolence round the corner of the rush baskets that hung in his doorway. He had caught the word Socialist, and was mentally registering Mr Warburton as a Socialist and Dorothy as the friend of Socialists.

'I really *must* be getting on,' said Dorothy hastily, feeling that she had better escape before Mr Warburton said something even more tactless. 'I've got ever such a lot of shopping to do. I'll say good-bye for the present, then.'

'Oh, no, you won't!' said Mr Warburton cheerfully. 'Not a bit of it! I'll come with you.'

As she wheeled her bicycle down the street he marched at her side, still talking, with his large chest well forward and his stick tucked under his arm. He was a difficult man to shake off, and though Dorothy counted him as a friend, she did sometimes wish, he being the town scandal and she the Rector's daughter, that he would not always choose the most public places to talk to her in. At this moment, however, she was rather grateful for his company, which made it appreciably easier to pass Cargill's shop—for Cargill was still on his doorstep and was regarding her with a sidelong, meaning gaze.

'It was a bit of luck my meeting you this morning,' Mr Warburton went on. 'In fact, I was looking for you. Who do you think I've got coming to dinner with me tonight? Bewley—Ronald Bewley. You've heard of him, of course?'

'Ronald Bewley? No, I don't think so. Who is he?'

'Why, dash it! Ronald Bewley, the novelist. Author of *Fishpools and Concubines*. Surely you've read *Fishpools and Concubines*?'

'No, I'm afraid I haven't. In fact, I'd never even heard of it.'

'My dear Dorothy! You *have* been neglecting yourself. You certainly ought to read *Fishpools and Concubines*. It's hot stuff, I assure you—real high-class pornography. Just the kind of thing you need to take the taste of the Girl Guides out of your mouth.'

'I do wish you wouldn't say such things!' said Dorothy, looking away uncomfortably, and then immediately looking back again because she had all but caught Cargill's eye. 'Where does this Mr Bewley live?' she added. 'Not here, surely, does he?'

'No. He's coming over from Ipswich for dinner, and perhaps to stay the night. That's why I was looking for you. I thought you might like to meet him. How about your coming to dinner tonight?'

'I can't possibly come to dinner,' said Dorothy. 'I've got Father's supper to see to, and thousands of other things. I shan't be free till eight o'clock or after.'

'Well, come along after dinner, then. I'd like you to know Bewley. He's an interesting fellow—very *au fait* with all the Bloomsbury scandal, and all that. You'll enjoy meeting him. It'll do you good to escape from the church hencoop for a few hours.'

Dorothy hesitated. She was tempted. To tell the truth, she enjoyed her occasional visits to Mr Warburton's house extremely. But of course they were *very* occasional—once in three or four months at the oftenest; it so obviously *didn't do* to associate too freely with such a man. And even when she did go to his house she was careful to make sure beforehand that there was going to be at least one other visitor.

Two years earlier, when Mr Warburton had first come to Knype Hill (at that time he was posing as a widower with two children; a little later, however, the housekeeper suddenly gave birth to a third child in the middle of the night), Dorothy had met him at a tea-party and afterwards called on him. Mr Warburton had given her a delightful tea, talked amusingly about books, and then, immediately after tea, sat down beside her on the sofa and begun making love to her, violently, outrageously, even brutally. It was practically an assault. Dorothy was horrified almost out of her wits, though not too horrified to resist. She escaped from him and took refuge on the other side of the sofa, white, shaking, and almost in tears. Mr Warburton, on the other hand, was quite unashamed and even seemed rather amused.

'Oh, how could you, how could you?' she sobbed.

'But it appears that I couldn't,' said Mr Warburton.

'Oh, but how could you be such a brute?'

'Oh, *that*? Easily, my child, easily. You will understand that when you get to my age.'

In spite of this bad beginning, a sort of friendship had grown up between the two, even to the extent of Dorothy being 'talked about' in connexion with Mr

Warburton. It did not take much to get you 'talked about' in Knype Hill. She only saw him at long intervals and took the greatest care never to be alone with him, but even so he found opportunities of making casual love to her. But it was done in a gentlemanly fashion; the previous disagreeable incident was not repeated. Afterwards, when he was forgiven, Mr Warburton had explained that he 'always tried it on' with every presentable woman he met.

'Don't you get rather a lot of snubs?' Dorothy could not help asking him.

'Oh, certainly. But I get quite a number of successes as well, you know.'

People wondered sometimes how such a girl as Dorothy could consort, even occasionally, with such a man as Mr Warburton; but the hold that he had over her was the hold that the blasphemer and evil-liver always has over the pious. It is a fact—you have only to look about you to verify it—that the pious and the immoral drift naturally together. The best brothel-scenes in literature have been written, without exception, by pious believers or pious unbelievers. And of course Dorothy, born into the twentieth century, made a point of listening to Mr Warburton's blasphemies as calmly as possible; it is fatal to flatter the wicked by letting them see that you are shocked by them. Besides, she was genuinely fond of him. He teased her and distressed her, and yet she got from him, without being fully aware of it, a species of sympathy and understanding which she could not get elsewhere. For all his vices he was distinctly likeable, and the shoddy brilliance of his conversation—Oscar Wilde seven times watered—which she was too inexperienced to see through, fascinated while it shocked her. Perhaps, too, in this instance, the prospect of meeting the celebrated Mr Bewley had its effect upon her; though certainly *Fishponds and Concubines* sounded like the kind of book that she either didn't read or else set herself heavy penances for reading. In London, no doubt, one would hardly cross the road to see fifty novelists; but these things appeared differently in places like Knype Hill.

'Are you *sure* Mr Bewley is coming?' she said.

'Quite sure. And his wife's coming as well, I believe. Full chaperonage. No Tarquin and Lucrece business this evening.'

'All right,' said Dorothy finally; 'thanks very much. I'll come round—about half past eight, I expect.'

'Good. If you can manage to come while it is still daylight, so much the better. Remember that Mrs Semprill is my next-door neighbour. We can count on her to be on the *qui vive* any time after sundown.'

Mrs Semprill was the town scandalmonger—the most eminent, that is, of the town's many scandalmongers. Having got what he wanted (he was constantly pestering Dorothy to come to his house more often), Mr Warburton said *au revoir* and left Dorothy to do the remainder of her shopping.

In the semi-gloom of Solepipe's shop, she was just moving away from the counter with her two and a half yards of casement cloth, when she was aware of a low, mournful voice at her ear. It was Mrs Semprill. She was a slender woman of forty, with a lank, sallow, distinguished face, which, with her glossy dark hair and air of settled melancholy, gave her something the appearance of a Van Dyck portrait. Entrenched behind a pile of cretonnes near the window, she had been watching Dorothy's conversation with Mr Warburton. Whenever you were doing something that you did not particularly want Mrs Semprill to see you doing, you could trust her to be somewhere in the neighbourhood. She seemed to have the power of materializing like an Arabian jinneeyeh at any place where she was not wanted. No indiscretion, however small, escaped her vigilance. Mr Warburton used to say that she was like the four beasts of the Apocalypse—'They are full of eyes, you remember, and they rest not night nor day.'

'Dorothy *dearest*,' murmured Mrs Semprill in the sorrowful, affectionate voice of someone breaking a piece of bad news as gently as possible. 'I've been so *wanting* to speak to you. I've something simply *dreadful* to tell you—something that will really *horrify* you!'

'What is it?' said Dorothy resignedly, well knowing what was coming—for Mrs Semprill had only one subject of conversation.

They moved out of the shop and began to walk down the street, Dorothy wheeling her bicycle, Mrs Semprill mincing at her side with a delicate birdlike step and bringing her mouth closer and closer to Dorothy's ear as her remarks grew more and more intimate.

'Do you happen to have noticed,' she began, 'that girl who sits at the end of the pew nearest the organ in church? A rather *pretty* girl, with red hair. I've no idea what her name is,' added Mrs Semprill, who knew the surname and all the Christian names of every man, woman, and child in Knype Hill.

'Molly Freeman,' said Dorothy. 'She's the niece of Freeman the greengrocer.'

'Oh, Molly Freeman? Is *that* her name? I'd often wondered. Well—'

The delicate red mouth came closer, the mournful voice sank to a shocked whisper. Mrs Semprill began to pour forth a stream of purulent libel involving Molly Freeman and six young men who worked at the sugar-beet refinery. After a few moments the story became so outrageous that Dorothy, who had turned very pink, hurriedly withdrew her ear from Mrs Semprill's whispering lips. She stopped her bicycle.

'I won't listen to such things!' she said abruptly. 'I *know* that isn't true about Molly Freeman. It *can't* be true! She's such a nice quiet girl—she was one of my very best Girl Guides, and she's always been so good about helping with the church bazaars and everything. I'm perfectly certain she wouldn't do such things as you're saying.'

'But, Dorothy *dearest*! When, as I told you, I actually saw with my own eyes . . .'

'I don't care! It's not fair to say such things about people. Even if they were true it wouldn't be right to repeat them. There's quite enough evil in the world without going about looking for it.'

'*Looking* for it!' sighed Mrs Semprill. 'But, my dear Dorothy, as though one ever wanted or *needed* to look! The trouble is that one can't *help* seeing all the dreadful wickedness that goes on in this town.'

Mrs Semprill was always genuinely astonished if you accused her of *looking* for subjects for scandal. Nothing, she would protest, pained her more than the spectacle of human wickedness; but it was constantly forced upon her unwilling eyes, and only a stern sense of duty impelled her to make it public. Dorothy's remarks, so far from silencing her, merely set her talking about the general corruption of Knype Hill, of which Molly Freeman's misbehaviour was only one example. And so from Molly Freeman and her six young men she proceeded to Dr Gaythorne, the town medical officer, who had got two of the nurses at the Cottage Hospital with child, and then to Mrs Corn, the Town Clerk's wife, found lying in a field dead drunk on eau-de-Cologne, and then to the curate at St Wedekind's in Millborough, who had involved himself in a grave scandal with a choirboy; and so it went on, one thing leading to another. For there was hardly a soul in the town or the surrounding country about whom Mrs Semprill could not disclose some festering secret if you listened to her long enough.

It was noticeable that her stories were not only dirty and libellous, but they had nearly always some monstrous tinge of perversion about them. Compared with the ordinary scandalmongers of a country town, she was Freud to Boccaccio. From hearing her talk you would have gathered the impression that Knype Hill with its thousand inhabitants held more of the refinements of evil than Sodom, Gomorrah, and Buenos Aires put together. Indeed, when you reflected upon the lives led by the inhabitants of this latter-day City of the Plain—from the manager of the local bank squandering his clients' money on the children of his second and bigamous marriage, to the barmaid of the Dog and Bottle serving drinks in the taproom dressed only in high-heeled satin slippers, and from old Miss Channon, the music-teacher, with her secret gin bottle and her anonymous letters, to Maggie White, the baker's daughter, who had borne three children to her own brother—when you considered these people, all, young and old, rich and poor, sunken in monstrous and Babylonian vices, you wondered that fire did not come down from Heaven and consume the town forthwith. But if you listened just a little longer, the catalogue of obscenities became first monstrous and then unbearably dull. For in a town in which *everyone* is either a bigamist, a pederast, or a drug-taker, the worst scandal loses its sting. In fact, Mrs Semprill was something worse than a slanderer; she was a bore.

As to the extent to which her stories were believed, it varied. At times the word would go round that she was a foul-mouthed old cat and everything she said was a pack of lies; at other times one of her accusations would take effect on some unfortunate person, who would need months or even years to live it down. She had certainly been instrumental in breaking off not less than half a dozen engagements and starting innumerable quarrels between husbands and wives.

All this while Dorothy had been making abortive efforts to shake Mrs Semprill off. She had edged her way gradually across the street until she was wheeling her bicycle along the right-hand kerb; but Mrs Semprill had followed, whispering without cease. It was not until they reached the end of the High Street that Dorothy summoned up enough firmness to escape. She halted and put her right foot on the pedal of her bicycle.

'I really can't stop a moment longer,' she said. 'I've got a thousand things to do, and I'm late already.'

'Oh, but, Dorothy dear! I've something else I simply *must* tell you—something most *important!*'

'I'm sorry—I'm in such a terrible hurry. Another time, perhaps.'

'It's about that *dreadful* Mr Warburton,' said Mrs Semprill hastily, lest Dorothy should escape without hearing it. 'He's just come back from London, and do you know—I most *particularly* wanted to tell you this—do you know, he actually—'

But here Dorothy saw that she must make off instantly, at no matter what cost. She could imagine nothing more uncomfortable than to have to discuss Mr Warburton with Mrs Semprill. She mounted her bicycle, and with only a very brief 'Sorry—I really *can't* stop!' began to ride hurriedly away.

'I wanted to tell you—he's taken up with a new woman!' Mrs Semprill cried after her, even forgetting to whisper in her eagerness to pass on this juicy titbit.

But Dorothy rode swiftly round the corner, not looking back, and pretending not to have heard. An unwise thing to do, for it did not pay to cut Mrs Semprill too short. Any unwillingness to listen to her scandals was taken as a sign of depravity, and led to fresh and worse scandals being published about yourself the moment you had left her.

As Dorothy rode homewards she had uncharitable thoughts about Mrs Semprill, for which she duly pinched herself. Also, there was another, rather disturbing idea which had not occurred to her till this moment—that Mrs Semprill would certainly learn of her visit to Mr Warburton's house this evening, and would probably have magnified it into something scandalous by tomorrow. The thought sent a vague premonition of evil through Dorothy's mind as she jumped off her bicycle at the Rectory gate, where Silly Jack, the town idiot, a third-grade moron with a triangular scarlet face like a strawberry, was loitering, vacantly flogging the gatepost with a hazel switch.

## 4

It was a little after eleven. The day, which, like some overripe but hopeful widow playing at seventeen, had been putting on unseasonable April airs, had now remembered that it was August and settled down to be boiling hot.

Dorothy rode into the hamlet of Fennelwick, a mile out of Knype Hill. She had delivered Mrs Lewin's corn-plaster, and was dropping in to give old Mrs Pither that cutting from the *Daily Mail* about angelica tea for rheumatism. The sun, burning in the cloudless sky, scorched her back through her gingham frock, and the dusty road quivered in the heat, and the hot, flat meadows, over which even at this time of year numberless larks chirruped tiresomely, were so green that it hurt your eyes to look at them. It was the kind of day that is called 'glorious' by people who don't have to work.

Dorothy leaned her bicycle against the gate of the Pithers'cottage, and took her handkerchief out of her bag and wiped her hands, which were sweating from the handle-bars. In the harsh sunlight her face looked pinched and colourless. She looked her age, and something over, at that hour of the morning. Throughout her day—and in general it was a seventeen-hour day—she had regular, alternating periods of tiredness and energy; the middle of the morning, when she was doing the first instalment of the day's 'visiting', was one of the tired periods.

'Visiting', because of the distances she had to bicycle from house to house, took up nearly half of Dorothy's day. Every day of her life, except on Sundays, she made from half a dozen to a dozen visits at parishioners' cottages. She penetrated into cramped interiors and sat on lumpy, dust-diffusing chairs gossiping with overworked, blowsy housewives; she spent hurried half-hours giving a hand with the mending and the ironing, and read chapters from the Gospels, and readjusted bandages on 'bad legs', and condoled with sufferers from morning-sickness; she played ride-a-cock-horse with sour-smelling children who grimed the bosom of her dress with their sticky little fingers; she gave advice about ailing aspidistras, and suggested names for babies, and drank 'nice cups of tea' innumerable—for the working women always wanted her to have a 'nice cup of tea', out of the teapot endlessly stewing.

Much of it was profoundly discouraging work. Few, very few, of the women seemed to have even a conception of the Christian life that she was trying to help them to lead. Some of them were shy and suspicious, stood on the defensive, and made excuses when urged to come to Holy Communion; some shammed piety for the sake of the tiny sums they could wheedle out of the church alms box; those who welcomed her coming were for the most part the talkative ones, who wanted an audience for complaints about the 'goings on' of their husbands, or for endless mortuary tales ('And he had to have glass chubes let into his veins,' etc., etc.) about the revolting diseases their relatives had died of. Quite half the women on her list, Dorothy knew, were at heart atheistical in a vague unreasoning way. She came up against it all day long—that vague, blank disbelief so common in illiterate people, against which all argument is powerless. Do what she would, she could never raise the number of regular communicants to more than a dozen or thereabouts. Women would promise to communicate, keep their promise for a month or two, and then fall away. With the younger women it was especially hopeless. They would not even join the local branches of the church leagues that were run for their benefit—Dorothy was honorary secretary of three such leagues, besides being captain of the Girl Guides. The Band of Hope and the Companionship of Marriage languished almost memberless, and the Mothers' Union only kept going because gossip and unlimited strong tea made the weekly sewing-parties acceptable. Yes, it was discouraging work; so discouraging that at times it would have seemed altogether futile if she had not known the sense of futility for what it is—the subtlest weapon of the Devil.

Dorothy knocked at the Pithers' badly fitting door, from beneath which a melancholy smell of boiled cabbage and dish-water was oozing. From long experience she knew and could taste in advance the individual smell of every cottage on her rounds. Some of their smells were peculiar in the extreme. For instance, there was the salty, feral smell that haunted the cottage of old Mr Tombs, an aged retired bookseller who lay in bed all day in a darkened room, with his long, dusty nose and pebble spectacles protruding from what appeared to be a fur rug of vast size and richness.

But if you put your hand on the fur rug it disintegrated, burst and fled in all directions. It was composed entirely of cats—twenty-four cats, to be exact. Mr Tombs 'found they kept him warm', he used to explain. In nearly all the cottages there was a basic smell of old overcoats and dish-water upon which the other, individual smells were superimposed; the cesspool smell, the cabbage smell, the smell of children, the strong, bacon-like reek of corduroys impregnated with the sweat of a decade.

Mrs Pither opened the door, which invariably stuck to the jamb, and then, when you wrenched it open, shook the whole cottage. She was a large, stooping, grey woman with wispy grey hair, a sacking apron, and shuffling carpet slippers.

'Why, if it isn't Miss Dorothy!' she exclaimed in a dreary, lifeless but not unaffectionate voice.

She took Dorothy between her large, gnarled hands, whose knuckles were as shiny as skinned onions from age and ceaseless washing up, and gave her a wet kiss. Then she drew her into the unclean interior of the cottage.

'Pither's away at work, Miss,' she announced as they got inside. 'Up to Dr Gaythorne's he is, a-digging over the doctor's flower-beds for him.'

Mr Pither was a jobbing gardener. He and his wife, both of them over seventy, were one of the few genuinely pious couples on Dorothy's visiting list. Mrs Pither led a dreary, wormlike life of shuffling to and fro, with a perpetual crick in her neck because the door lintels were too low for her, between the well, the sink, the fireplace, and the tiny plot of kitchen garden. The kitchen was decently tidy, but oppressively hot, evil-smelling and saturated with ancient dust. At the end opposite the fireplace Mrs Pither had made a kind of prie-dieu out of a greasy rag mat laid in front of a tiny, defunct harmonium, on top of which were an oleographed crucifixion, 'Watch and Pray' done in beadwork, and a photograph of Mr and Mrs Pither on their wedding day in 1882.

'Poor Pither!' went on Mrs Pither in her depressing voice, 'him a-digging at his age, with his rheumatism *that* bad! Ain't it cruel hard, Miss? And he's had a kind of a pain between his legs, Miss, as he can't seem to account for —terrible bad he's been with it, these last few mornings. Ain't it bitter hard, Miss, the lives us poor working folks has to lead?'

'It's a shame,' said Dorothy. 'But I hope you've been keeping a little better yourself, Mrs Pither?'

'Ah, Miss, there's nothing don't make *me* better. I ain't a case for curing, not in *this* world, I ain't. I shan't never get no better, not in this wicked world down here.'

'Oh, you mustn't say that, Mrs Pither! I hope we shall have you with us for a long time yet.'

'Ah, Miss, you don't know how poorly I've been this last week! I've had the rheumatism a-coming and a-going all down the backs of my poor old legs, till there's some mornings when I don't feel as I can't walk so far as to pull a handful of onions in the garden. Ah, Miss, it's a weary world we lives in, ain't it, Miss? A weary, sinful world.'

'But of course we must never forget, Mrs Pither, that there's a better world coming. This life is only a time of trial—just to strengthen us and teach us to be patient, so that we'll be ready for Heaven when the time comes.'

At this a sudden and remarkable change came over Mrs Pither. It was produced by the word 'Heaven'. Mrs Pither had only two subjects of conversation; one of them was the joys of Heaven, and the other the miseries of her present state. Dorothy's remark seemed to act upon her like a charm. Her dull grey eye was not capable of brightening, but her voice quickened with an almost joyful enthusiasm.

'Ah, Miss, there you said it! That's a true word, Miss! That's what Pither and me keeps a-saying to ourselves. And that's just the one thing as keeps us a-going—just the thought of Heaven and the long, long rest we'll have there. Whatever we've suffered, we gets it all back in Heaven, don't we, Miss? Every little bit of suffering, you gets it back a hundredfold and a thousandfold. That *is* true, ain't it, Miss? There's rest for us all in Heaven—rest and peace and no more rheumatism nor digging nor cooking nor laundering nor nothing. You *do* believe that, don't you, Miss Dorothy?'

'Of course,' said Dorothy.

'Ah, Miss, if you knew how it comforts us—just the thoughts of Heaven! Pither he says to me, when he comes home tired of a night and our rheumatism's bad, "Never you mind, my dear," he says, "we ain't far off Heaven now," he says. "Heaven was made for the likes of us," he says; "just for poor working folks like us, that have been sober and godly and kept our Communions regular." That's the best way, ain't it, Miss Dorothy—poor in this life and rich in the next? Not like some of them rich folks as all their motorcars and their beautiful houses won't save from the worm that dieth not and the fire that's not quenched. Such a beautiful text, that is. Do you think you could say a little prayer with me, Miss Dorothy? I been looking forward all the morning to a little prayer.'

Mrs Pither was always ready for a 'little prayer' at any hour of the night or day. It was her equivalent to a 'nice cup of tea'. They knelt down on the rag mat and said the Lord's Prayer and the Collect for the week; and then Dorothy, at Mrs Pither's request, read the parable of Dives and Lazarus, Mrs Pither coming in from time to time with 'Amen! That's a true word, ain't it, Miss Dorothy? "And he was carried by angels into Abraham's bosom." Beautiful! Oh, I do call that just too beautiful! Amen, Miss Dorothy—Amen!'

Dorothy gave Mrs Pither the cutting from the *Daily Mail* about angelica tea for rheumatism, and then, finding that Mrs Pither had been too 'poorly' to draw the day's supply of water, she drew three bucketfuls for her from the well. It was a very deep well, with such a low parapet that Mrs Pither's final doom would almost certainly be to fall into it and get drowned, and it had not even a winch– you had to haul the bucket up hand over hand. And then they sat down for a few minutes, and Mrs Pither talked some more about Heaven. It was extraordinary how constantly Heaven reigned in her thoughts; and more extraordinary yet was the actuality, the vividness with which she could see it. The golden streets and the gates of orient pearl were as real to her as though they had been actually before her eyes. And her vision extended to the most concrete, the most earthly details. The softness of the beds up there! The deliciousness of the food! The lovely silk clothes that you would put on clean every morning! The surcease from everlasting to everlasting from work of any description! In almost every moment of her life the vision of Heaven supported and consoled her, and her abject complaints about the lives of 'poor working folks' were curiously tempered by a satisfaction in the thought that, after all, it is 'poor working folks' who are the principal inhabitants of Heaven. It was a sort of bargain that she had struck, setting her lifetime of dreary labour against an eternity of bliss. Her faith was almost *too* great, if that is possible. For it was a curious fact, but the certitude with which Mrs Pither looked forward to Heaven–as to some kind of glorified home for incurables–affected Dorothy with strange uneasiness.

Dorothy prepared to depart, while Mrs Pither thanked her, rather too effusively, for her visit, winding up, as usual, with fresh complaints about her rheumatism.

'I'll be sure and take the angelica tea,' she concluded, 'and thank you kindly for telling me of it, Miss. Not as I don't expect as it'll do me much good. Ah, Miss, if you knew how cruel bad my rheumatism's been this last week! All down the backs of my legs, it is, like a regular shooting red-hot poker, and I don't seem to be able to get at them to rub them properly. Would it be asking too much of you, Miss, to give me a bit of a rub-down before you go? I got a bottle of Elliman's under the sink.'

Unseen by Mrs Pither, Dorothy gave herself a severe pinch. She had been expecting this, and–she had done it so many times before–she really did *not* enjoy rubbing Mrs Pither down. She exhorted herself angrily. Come on, Dorothy! No sniffishness, please! John xiii, 14. 'Of course I will, Mrs Pither!' she said instantly.

They went up the narrow, rickety staircase, in which you had to bend almost double at one place to avoid the overhanging ceiling. The bedroom was lighted by a tiny square of window that was jammed in its socket by the creeper outside, and had not been opened in twenty years. There was an enormous double bed that almost filled the room, with sheets perennially damp and a flock mattress as full of hills and valleys as a contour map of Switzerland. With many groans the old woman crept on to the bed and laid herself face down. The room reeked of urine and paregoric. Dorothy took the bottle of Elliman's embrocation and carefully anointed Mrs Pither's large, grey-veined, flaccid legs.

Outside, in the swimming heat, she mounted her bicycle and began to ride swiftly homewards. The sun burned in her face, but the air now seemed sweet and fresh. She was happy, happy! She was always extravagantly happy when her morning's 'visiting' was over; and, curiously enough, she was not aware of the reason for this. In Borlase the dairy-farmer's meadow the red cows were grazing, knee-deep in shining seas of grass. The scent of cows, like a distillation of vanilla and fresh hay, floated into Dorothy's nostrils. Though she had still a morning's work in front of her she could not resist the temptation to loiter for a moment, steadying her bicycle with one hand against the gate of Borlase's meadow, while a cow, with moist shell-pink nose, scratched its chin upon the gatepost and dreamily regarded her.

Dorothy caught sight of a wild rose, flowerless of course, growing beyond the hedge, and climbed over the gate with the intention of discovering whether it were not sweetbriar. She knelt down among the tall weeds beneath the hedge. It was very hot down there, close to the ground. The humming of many unseen insects sounded in her ears, and the hot summery fume from the tangled swathes of vegetation flowed up and enveloped her. Near by, tall stalks of fennel were growing, with trailing fronds of foliage like the tails of sea-green horses. Dorothy pulled a frond of the fennel against her face and breathed in the strong sweet scent. Its richness overwhelmed her, almost dizzied her for a moment. She drank it in, filling her lungs with it. Lovely, lovely scent—scent of summer days, scent of childhood joys, scent of spice-drenched islands in the warm foam of Oriental seas!

Her heart swelled with sudden joy. It was that mystical joy in the beauty of the earth and the very nature of things that she recognized, perhaps mistakenly, as the love of God. As she knelt there in the heat, the sweet odour and the drowsy hum of insects, it seemed to her that she could momentarily hear the mighty anthem of praise that the earth and all created things send up everlastingly to their maker. All vegetation, leaves, flowers, grass, shining, vibrating, crying out in their joy. Larks also chanting, choirs of larks invisible, dripping music from the sky. All the riches of summer, the warmth of the earth, the song of birds, the fume of cows, the droning of countless bees, mingling and ascending like the smoke of ever-burning altars. Therefore with Angels and Archangels! She began to pray, and for a moment she prayed ardently, blissfully, forgetting herself in the joy of her worship. Then, less than a minute later, she discovered that she was kissing the frond of the fennel that was still against her face.

She checked herself instantly, and drew back. What was she doing? Was it God that she was worshipping, or was it only the earth? The joy ebbed out of her heart, to be succeeded by the cold, uncomfortable feeling that she had been betrayed into a half-pagan ecstasy. She admonished herself. None of *that*, Dorothy! No Nature-worship, please! Her father had warned her against Nature-worship. She had heard him preach more than one sermon against it; it was, he said, mere pantheism, and, what seemed to offend him even more, a disgusting modern fad. Dorothy took a thorn of the wild rose, and pricked her arm three times, to remind herself of the Three Persons of the Trinity, before climbing over the gate and remounting her bicycle.

A black, very dusty shovel hat was approaching round the corner of the hedge. It was Father McGuire, the Roman Catholic priest, also bicycling his rounds. He was a very large, rotund man, so large that he dwarfed the bicycle beneath him and seemed to be balanced on top of it like a golf-ball on a tee. His face was rosy, humorous, and a little sly.

Dorothy looked suddenly unhappy. She turned pink, and her hand moved instinctively to the neighbourhood of the gold cross beneath her dress. Father McGuire was riding towards her with an untroubled, faintly amused air. She made an endeavour to smile, and murmured unhappily, 'Good morning.' But he rode on without a sign; his eyes swept easily over her face and then beyond her into vacancy, with an admirable pretence of not having noticed her existence. It was the Cut Direct. Dorothy—by nature, alas! unequal to delivering the Cut Direct—got on to her bicycle and rode away, struggling with the uncharitable thoughts which a meeting with Father McGuire never failed to arouse in her.

Five or six years earlier, when Father McGuire was holding a funeral in St Athelstan's churchyard (there was no Roman Catholic cemetery at Knype Hill), there had been some dispute with the Rector about the propriety of Father McGuire robing in the church, or not robing in the church, and the two priests had wrangled disgracefully over the open grave. Since then they had not been on speaking terms. It was better so, the Rector said.

As to the other ministers of religion in Knype Hill—Mr Ward the Congregationalist minister, Mr Foley the Wesleyan pastor, and the braying bald-headed elder who conducted the orgies at Ebenezer Chapel—the Rector called them a pack of vulgar Dissenters and had forbidden Dorothy on pain of his displeasure to have anything to do with them.

## 5

It was twelve o'clock. In the large, dilapidated conservatory, whose roof-panes, from the action of time and dirt, were dim, green, and iridescent like old Roman glass, they were having a hurried and noisy rehearsal of *Charles I*.

Dorothy was not actually taking part in the rehearsal, but was busy making costumes. She made the costumes, or most of them, for all the plays the schoolchildren acted. The production and stage management were in the hands of Victor Stone—Victor, Dorothy called him—the Church schoolmaster. He was a small-boned, excitable, black-haired youth of twenty-seven, dressed in dark sub-clerical clothes, and at this moment he was gesturing fiercely with a roll of manuscript at six dense-looking children. On a long bench against the wall four more children were alternately practising 'noises off' by clashing fire-irons together, and squabbling over a grimy little bag of Spearmint Bouncers, forty a penny.

It was horribly hot in the conservatory, and there was a powerful smell of glue and the sour sweat of children. Dorothy was kneeling on the floor, with her mouth full of pins and a pair of shears in her hand, rapidly slicing sheets of brown paper into long narrow strips. The glue-pot was bubbling on an oil-stove beside her; behind her, on the rickety, ink-stained work-table, were a tangle of half-finished costumes, more sheets of brown paper, her sewing-machine, bundles of tow, shards of dry glue, wooden swords, and open pots of paint. With half her mind Dorothy was meditating upon the two pairs of seventeenth-century jackboots that had got to be made for Charles I and Oliver Cromwell, and with the other half listening to the angry shouts of Victor, who was working himself up into a rage, as he invariably did at rehearsals. He was a natural actor, and withal thoroughly bored by the drudgery of rehearsing half-witted children. He strode up and down, haranguing the children in a vehement slangy style, and every now and then breaking off to lunge at one or other of them with a wooden sword that he had grabbed from the table.

'Put a bit of life into it, can't you?' he cried, prodding an ox-faced boy of eleven in the belly. 'Don't drone! Say it as if it meant something! You look like a corpse that's been buried and dug up again. What's the good of gurgling it down in your inside like that? Stand up and shout at him. Take off that second murderer expression!'

'Come here, Percy!' cried Dorothy through her pins. 'Quick!'

She was making the armour—the worst job of the lot, except those wretched jackboots—out of glue and brown paper. From long practice Dorothy could make very nearly anything out of glue and brown paper; she could even make a passably good periwig, with a brown paper skull-cap and dyed tow for the hair. Taking the year through, the amount of time she spent in struggling with glue, brown paper, butter muslin, and all the other paraphernalia of amateur theatricals was enormous. So chronic was the need of money for all the church funds that hardly a month ever passed when there was not a school play or a pageant or an exhibition of tableaux vivants on hand—not to mention the bazaars and jumble sales.

As Percy—Percy Jowett, the blacksmith's son, a small curly-headed boy—got down from the bench and stood wriggling unhappily before her, Dorothy seized a sheet of brown paper, measured it against him, snipped out the neckhole and armholes, draped it round his middle and rapidly pinned it into the shape of a rough breastplate. There was a confused din of voices.

VICTOR: Come on, now, come on! Enter Oliver Cromwell—that's you! *No*, not like that! Do you think Oliver Cromwell would come slinking on like a dog that's just had a hiding? Stand up. Stick your chest out. Scowl. That's better. Now go on, *Cromwell*: 'Halt! I hold a pistol in my hand!' Go on.

A GIRL: Please, Miss, Mother said as I was to tell you, Miss—

DOROTHY: Keep still, Percy! For goodness' *sake* keep still!

CROMWELL: 'Alt! I 'old a pistol in my 'and!

A SMALL GIRL ON THE BENCH: Mister! I've dropped my sweetie! [*Snivelling*] I've dropped by swee-e-e-etie!

VICTOR: No, no, *no,* Tommie! No, no, *no*!

THE GIRL: Please, Miss, Mother said as I was to tell you as she couldn't make my knickers like she promised, Miss, because—

DOROTHY: You'll make me swallow a pin if you do that again.

CROMWELL: *H*alt! I *h*old a pistol—

THE SMALL GIRL [*in tears*]: My swee-e-e-e-eetie!

Dorothy seized the glue-brush, and with feverish speed pasted strips of brown paper all over Percy's thorax, up and down, backwards and forwards, one on top of another, pausing only when the paper stuck to her fingers. In five minutes she had made a cuirass of glue and brown paper stout enough, when it was dry, to have defied a real sword-blade. Percy, 'locked up in complete steel' and with the sharp paper edge cutting his chin, looked down at himself with the miserable resigned expression of a dog having its bath. Dorothy took the shears, slit the breastplate up one side, set it on end to dry and started immediately on another child. A fearful clatter broke out as the 'noises off' began practising the sound of pistol-shots and horses galloping. Dorothy's fingers were getting stickier and stickier, but from time to time she washed some of the glue off them in a bucket of hot water that was kept in readiness. In twenty minutes she had partially completed three breastplates. Later on they would have to be finished off, painted over with aluminium paint and laced up the sides; and after that there was the job of making the thigh-pieces, and, worst of all, the helmets to go with them. Victor, gesticulating with his sword and shouting to overcome the din of galloping horses, was personating in turn Oliver Cromwell, Charles I, Roundheads, Cavaliers, peasants, and Court ladies. The children were now growing restive and beginning to yawn, whine, and exchange furtive kicks and pinches. The breastplates finished for the moment, Dorothy swept some of the litter off the table, pulled her sewing-machine into position and set to work on a Cavalier's green velvet doublet—it was butter muslin Twinked green, but it looked all right at a distance.

There was another ten minutes of feverish work. Dorothy broke her thread, all but said 'Damn!' checked herself and hurriedly re-threaded the needle. She was working against time. The play was now a fortnight distant, and there was such a multitude of things yet to be made—helmets, doublets, swords, jackboots (those miserable jackboots had been haunting her like a nightmare for days past), scabbards, ruffles, wigs, spurs, scenery—that her heart sank when she thought of them. The children's parents never helped with the costumes for the school plays; more exactly, they always promised to help and then backed out afterwards. Dorothy's head was aching diabolically, partly from the heat of the conservatory, partly from the strain of simultaneously sewing and trying to visualize patterns for brown paper jackboots. For the moment she had even forgotten the bill for twenty-one pounds seven and ninepence at Cargill's. She could think of nothing save that fearful mountain of unmade clothes that lay ahead of her. It was so throughout the day. One thing loomed up after another—whether it was the costumes for the school play or the collapsing floor of the belfry, or the shop-debts or the bindweed in the peas—and each in its turn so urgent and so harassing that it blotted all the others out of existence.

Victor threw down his wooden sword, took out his watch and looked at it.

'That'll do!' he said in the abrupt, ruthless tone from which he never departed when he was dealing with children. 'We'll go on on Friday. Clear out, the lot of you! I'm sick of the sight of you.'

He watched the children out, and then, having forgotten their existence as soon as they were out of his sight, produced a page of music from his pocket and began to fidget up and down, cocking his eye at two forlorn plants in the corner which trailed their dead brown tendrils over the edges of their pots. Dorothy was still bending over her machine, stitching up the seams of the green velvet doublet.

Victor was a restless, intelligent little creature, and only happy when he was quarrelling with somebody or something. His pale, fine-featured face wore an expression that appeared to be discontent and was really boyish eagerness. People meeting him for the first time usually said that he was wasting his talents in his obscure job as a village schoolmaster; but the truth was that Victor had no very marketable talents except a slight gift for music and a much more pronounced gift for dealing with children. Ineffectual in other ways, he was excellent with children; he had the proper, ruthless attitude towards them. But of course, like everyone else, he despised his own especial talent. His interests were almost purely ecclesiastical. He was what people call a *churchy* young man. It had always been his ambition to enter the Church, and he would actually have done so if he had possessed the kind of brain that is capable of learning Greek and Hebrew. Debarred from the priesthood, he had drifted quite naturally into his position as a Church schoolmaster and organist. It kept him, so to speak, within the Church precincts. Needless to say, he was an Anglo-Catholic of the most truculent *Church Times* breed—more clerical than the clerics, knowledgeable about Church history, expert on vestments, and ready at any moment with a furious tirade against Modernists, Protestants, scientists, Bolshevists, and atheists.

'I was thinking,' said Dorothy as she stopped her machine and snipped off the thread, 'we might make those helmets out of old bowler hats, if we can get hold of enough of them. Cut the brims off, put on paper brims of the right shape and silver them over.'

'Oh Lord, why worry your head about such things?' said Victor, who had lost interest in the play the moment the rehearsal was over.

'It's those wretched jackboots that are worrying me the most,' said Dorothy, taking the doublet on to her knee and looking at it.

'Oh, bother the jackboots! Let's stop thinking about the play for a moment. Look here,' said Victor, unrolling his page of music, 'I want you to speak to your father for me. I wish you'd ask him whether we can't have a procession some time next month.'

'Another procession? What for?'

'Oh, I don't know. You can always find an excuse for a procession. There's the Nativity of the B.V.M. coming off on the eighth—that's good enough for a procession, I should think. We'll do it in style. I've got hold of a splendid rousing hymn that they can all bellow, and perhaps we could borrow their blue banner with the Virgin Mary on it from St Wedekind's in Millborough. If he'll say the word I'll start practising the choir at once.'

'You know he'll only say no,' said Dorothy, threading a needle to sew buttons on the doublet. 'He doesn't really approve of processions. It's much better not to ask him and make him angry.'

'Oh, but dash it all!' protested Victor. 'It's simply months since we've had a procession. I never saw such dead-alive services as we have here. You'd think we were a Baptist chapel or something, from the way we go on.'

Victor chafed ceaselessly against the dull correctness of the Rector's services. His ideal was what he called 'the real Catholic worship'—meaning unlimited incense, gilded images, and more Roman vestments. In his capacity of organist he was for ever pressing for more processions, more voluptuous music, more elaborate chanting in the liturgy, so that it was a continuous pull devil, pull baker between him and the Rector. And on this point Dorothy sided with her father. Having been brought up in the peculiar, frigid *via media* of Anglicanism, she was by nature averse to and half-afraid of anything 'ritualistic'.

'But dash it all!' went on Victor, 'a procession is such fun! Down the aisle, out through the west door and back through the south door, with the choir carrying candles behind and the Boy Scouts in front with the banner. It would look fine.' He sang a stave in a thin but tuneful tenor:

'Hail thee, Festival Day, blest day that art hallowed for ever!'

'If I had *my* way,' he added, 'I'd have a couple of boys swinging jolly good censers of incense at the same time.'

'Yes, but you know how much Father dislikes that kind of thing. Especially when it's anything to do with the Virgin Mary. He says it's all Roman Fever and leads to people crossing themselves and genuflecting at the wrong times and goodness knows what. You remember what happened at Advent.'

The previous year, on his own responsibility, Victor had chosen as one of the hymns for Advent, Number 642, with the refrain 'Hail Mary, hail Mary, hail Mary full of grace!' This piece of popishness had annoyed the Rector extremely. At the close of the first verse he had pointedly laid down his hymn book, turned round in his stall and stood regarding the congregation with an air so stony that some of the choirboys faltered and almost broke down. Afterwards he had said that to hear the rustics bawling "'Ail Mary! 'Ail Mary!" made him think he was in the four-ale bar of the Dog and Bottle.

'But dash it!' said Victor in his aggrieved way, 'your father always puts his foot down when I try and get a bit of life into the service. He won't allow us incense, or decent music, or proper vestments, or anything. And what's the result? We can't get enough people to fill the church a quarter full, even on Easter Sunday. You look round the church on Sunday morning, and it's nothing but the Boy Scouts and the Girl Guides and a few old women.'

'I know. It's dreadful,' admitted Dorothy, sewing on her button. 'It doesn't seem to make any difference what we do—we simply *can't* get the people to come to church. Still,' she added, 'they do come to us to be married and buried. And I don't think the congregation's actually gone down this year. There were nearly two hundred people at Easter Communion.'

'Two hundred! It ought to be two thousand. That's the population of this town. The fact is that three quarters of the people in this place never go near a church in their lives. The Church has absolutely lost its hold over them. They don't know that it exists. And why? That's what I'm getting at. Why?'

'I suppose it's all this Science and Free Thought and all that,' said Dorothy rather sententiously, quoting her father.

This remark deflected Victor from what he had been about to say. He had been on the very point of saying that St Athelstan's congregation had dwindled because of the dullness of the services; but the hated words of Science and Free Thought set him off in another and even more familiar channel.

'Of course it's this so-called Free Thought!' he exclaimed, immediately beginning to fidget up and down again. 'It's these swine of atheists like Bertrand Russell and Julian Huxley and all that crowd. And what's ruined the Church is that instead of jolly well answering them and showing them up for the fools and liars they are, we just sit tight and let them spread their beastly atheist propaganda wherever they choose. It's all the fault of the bishops, of course.' (Like every Anglo-Catholic, Victor had an abysmal contempt for bishops.) 'They're all Modernists and time-servers. By Jove!' he added more cheerfully, halting, 'did you see my letter in the *Church Times* last week?'

'No, I'm afraid I didn't,' said Dorothy, holding another button in position with her thumb. 'What was it about?'

'Oh, Modernist bishops and all that. I got in a good swipe at old Barnes.'

It was very rarely that a week passed when Victor did not write a letter to the *Church Times*. He was in the thick of every controversy and in the forefront of every assault upon Modernists and atheists. He had twice been in combat with Dr Major, had written letters of withering irony about Dean Inge and the Bishop of Birmingham, and had not hesitated to attack even the fiendish Russell himself—but Russell, of course, had not dared to reply. Dorothy, to tell the truth, very seldom read the *Church Times*, and the Rector grew angry if he so much as saw a copy of it in the house. The weekly paper they took in the Rectory was the *High Churchman's Gazette*—a fine old High Tory anachronism with a small and select circulation.

'That swine Russell!' said Victor reminiscently, with his hands deep in his pockets. 'How he does make my blood boil!'

'Isn't that the man who's such a clever mathematician, or something?' said Dorothy, biting off her thread.

'Oh, I dare say he's clever enough in his own line, of course,' admitted Victor grudgingly. 'But what's that got to do with it? Just because a man's clever at figures it doesn't mean to say that—well, anyway! Let's come back to what I was saying. Why is it that we can't get people to come to church in this place? It's because our services are so dreary and godless, that's what it is. People want worship that *is* worship–they want the real Catholic worship of the real Catholic Church we belong to. And they don't get if from us. All they get is the old Protestant mumbo-jumbo, and Protestantism's as dead as a doornail, and everyone knows it.'

'That's not true!' said Dorothy rather sharply as she pressed the third button into place. 'You know we're not Protestants. Father's always saying that the Church of England is the Catholic Church–he's preached I don't know how many sermons about the Apostolic Succession. That's why Lord Pockthorne and the others won't come to church here. Only he won't join in the Anglo-Catholic movement because he thinks they're too fond of ritualism for its own sake. And so do I.'

'Oh, I don't say your father isn't absolutely sound on doctrine–absolutely sound. But if he thinks we're the Catholic Church, why doesn't he hold the service in a proper Catholic way? It's a shame we can't have incense *occasionally*. And his ideas about vestments–if you don't mind my saying it–are simply awful. On Easter Sunday he was wearing a Gothic cope with a modern Italian lace alb. Dash it, it's like wearing a top hat with brown boots.'

'Well, I don't think vestments are so important as you do,' said Dorothy. 'I think it's the spirit of the priest that matters, not the clothes he wears.'

'That's the kind of thing a Primitive Methodist would say!' exclaimed Victor disgustedly. 'Of course vestments are important! Where's the sense of worshipping at all if we can't make a proper job of it? Now, if you want to see what real Catholic worship *can* be like, look at St Wedekind's in Millborough! By Jove, they do things in style there! Images of the Virgin, reservation of the Sacrament–everything. They've had the Kensitites on to them three times, and they simply defy the Bishop.'

'Oh, I hate the way they go on at St Wedekind's!' said Dorothy. 'They're absolutely spiky. You can hardly see what's happening at the altar, there are such clouds of incense. I think people like that ought to turn Roman Catholic and have done with it.'

'My dear Dorothy, you ought to have been a Nonconformist. You really ought. A Plymouth Brother–or a Plymouth Sister or whatever it's called. I think your favourite hymn must be Number 567, "O my God I fear Thee, Thou art very High!"'

'Yours is Number 231, "I nightly pitch my moving tent a day's march nearer Rome!"' retorted Dorothy, winding the thread round the last button.

The argument continued for several minutes while Dorothy adorned a Cavalier's beaver hat (it was an old black felt school hat of her own) with plume and ribbons. She and Victor were never long together without being involved in an argument upon the question of 'ritualism'. In Dorothy's opinion Victor was a kind to 'go over to Rome' if not prevented, and she was very likely right. But Victor was not yet aware of his probable destiny. At present the fevers of the Anglo-Catholic movement, with its ceaseless exciting warfare on three fronts at once–Protestants to right of you, Modernists to the left of you, and, unfortunately, Roman Catholics to rear of you and always ready for a sly kick in the pants—filled his mental horizon. Scoring off Dr Major in the *Church Times* meant more to him than any of the serious business of life. But for all his churchiness he had not an atom of real piety in his constitution. It was essentially as a game that religious controversy appealed to him—the most absorbing game ever invented, because it goes on for ever and because just a little cheating is allowed.

'Thank goodness, that's done!' said Dorothy, twiddling the Cavalier's beaver hat round on her hand and then putting it down. 'Oh dear, what piles of things there are still to do, though! I wish I could get those wretched jackboots off my mind. What's the time, Victor?'

'It's nearly five to one.'

'Oh, good gracious! I must run. I've got three omelettes to make. I daren't trust them to Ellen. And, oh, Victor! Have you got anything you can give us for the jumble sale? If you had an old pair of trousers you could give us, that would be best of all, because we can always sell trousers.'

'Trousers? No. But I tell you what I have got, though. I've got a copy of *The Pilgrim's Progress* and another of Foxe's *Book of Martyrs* that I've been wanting to get rid of for years. Beastly Protestant trash! An old Dissenting aunt of mine gave them to me.—Doesn't it make you sick, all this cadging for pennies? Now, if we only held our services in a proper Catholic way, so that we could get up a proper congregation, don't you see, we shouldn't need—'

'That'll be splendid,' said Dorothy. 'We always have a stall for books—we charge a penny for each book, and nearly all of them get sold. We simply *must* make that jumble sale a success, Victor! I'm counting on Miss Mayfill to give us something really *nice*. What I'm specially hoping is that she might give us that beautiful old Lowestoft china tea service of hers, and we could sell it for five pounds at least. I've been making special prayers all the morning that she'll give it to us.'

'Oh?' said Victor, less enthusiastically than usual. Like Proggett earlier in the morning, he was embarrassed by the word 'prayer'. He was ready to talk all day long about a point of ritual; but the mention of private devotions struck him as slightly indecent. 'Don't forget to ask your father about the procession,' he said, getting back to a more congenial topic.

'All right, I'll ask him. But you know how it'll be. He'll only get annoyed and say it's Roman Fever.'

'Oh, damn Roman Fever!' said Victor, who, unlike Dorothy, did not set himself penances for swearing.

Dorothy hurried to the kitchen, discovered that there were only five eggs to make the omelettes for three people, and decided to make one large omelette and swell it out a bit with the cold boiled potatoes left over from yesterday. With a short prayer for the success of the omelette (for omelettes are so dreadfully apt to get broken when you take them out of the pan), she whipped up the eggs, while Victor made off down the drive, half wistfully and half sulkily humming 'Hail thee, Festival Day', and passing on his way a disgusted-looking manservant carrying the two handleless chamber-pots which were Miss Mayfill's contribution to the jumble sale.

# 6

It was a little after ten o'clock. Various things had happened–nothing, however, of any particular importance; only the usual round of parish jobs that filled up Dorothy's afternoon and evening. Now, as she had arranged earlier in the day, she was at Mr Warburton's house, and was trying to hold her own in one of those meandering arguments in which he delighted to entangle her.

They were talking–but indeed, Mr Warburton never failed to manœuvre the conversation towards this subject–about the question of religious belief.

'My dear Dorothy,' he was saying argumentatively, as he walked up and down with one hand in his coat pocket and the other manipulating a Brazilian cigar. 'My dear Dorothy, you don't seriously mean to tell me that at your age–twenty-seven, I believe–and with your intelligence, you will retain your religious beliefs more or less *in toto*?'

'Of course I do. You know I do.'

'Oh, come, now! The whole bag of tricks? All that nonsense that you learned at your mother's knee–surely you're not going to pretend to me that you still believe in it? But of course you don't! You can't! You're afraid to own up, that's all it is. No need to worry about that here, you know. The Rural Dean's wife isn't listening, and *I* won't give the show away.'

'I don't know what you mean by "all that *nonsense*",' began Dorothy, sitting up straighter in her chair, a little offended.

'Well, let's take an instance. Something particularly hard to swallow–Hell, for instance. Do you believe in Hell? When I say *believe*, mind you, I'm not asking whether you believe it in some milk and water metaphorical way like these Modernist bishops young Victor Stone gets so excited about. I mean do you believe in it literally? Do you believe in Hell as you believe in Australia?'

'Yes, of course I do,' said Dorothy, and she endeavoured to explain to him that the existence of Hell is much more real and permanent than the existence of Australia.

'Hm,' said Mr Warburton, unimpressed. 'Very sound in its way, of course. But what always makes me so suspicious of you religious people is that you're so deucedly cold-blooded about your beliefs. It shows a very poor imagination, to say the least of it. Here am I an infidel and blasphemer and neck deep in at least six out of the Seven Deadly, and obviously doomed to eternal torment. There's no knowing that in an hour's time I mayn't be roasting in the hottest part of Hell. And yet you can sit there talking to me as calmly as though I'd nothing the matter with me. Now, if I'd merely got cancer or leprosy or some other bodily ailment, you'd be quite distressed about it—at least, I like to flatter myself that you would. Whereas, when I'm going to sizzle on the grid throughout eternity, you seem positively unconcerned about it.'

'I never said *you* were going to Hell,' said Dorothy somewhat uncomfortably, and wishing that the conversation would take a different turn. For the truth was, though she was not going to tell him so, that the point Mr Warburton had raised was one with which she herself had had certain difficulties. She did indeed believe in Hell, but she had never been able to persuade herself that anyone actually *went* there. She believed that Hell existed, but that it was empty. Uncertain of the orthodoxy of this belief, she preferred to keep it to herself. 'It's never certain that *anyone* is going to Hell,' she said more firmly, feeling that here at least she was on sure ground.

'What!' said Mr Warburton, halting in mock surprise. 'Surely you don't mean to say that there's hope for me yet?'

'Of course there is. It's only those horrid Predestination people who pretend that you go to Hell whether you repent or not. You don't think the Church of England are Calvinists, do you?'

'I suppose there's always the chance of getting off on a plea of Invincible Ignorance,' said Mr Warburton reflectively; and then, more confidently: 'Do you know, Dorothy, I've a sort of feeling that even now, after knowing me two years, you've still half an idea you can make a convert of me. A lost sheep—brand plucked from the burning, and all that. I believe you still hope against hope that one of these days my eyes will be opened and you'll meet me at Holy Communion at seven o'clock on some damned cold winter morning. Don't you?'

'Well—' said Dorothy, again uncomfortably. She did, in fact, entertain some such hope about Mr Warburton, though he was not exactly a promising case for conversion. It was not in her nature to see a fellow being in a state of unbelief without making some effort to reclaim him. What hours she had spent, at different times, earnestly debating with vague village atheists who could not produce a single intelligible reason for their unbelief! 'Yes,' she admitted finally, not particularly wanting to make the admission, but not wanting to prevaricate.

Mr Warburton laughed delightedly.

'You've a hopeful nature,' he said. 'But you aren't afraid, by any chance, that I might convert *you*? "The dog it was that died", you may remember.'

At this Dorothy merely smiled. 'Don't let him see he's shocking you'—that was always her maxim when she was talking to Mr Warburton. They had been arguing in this manner, without coming to any kind of conclusion, for the past hour, and might have gone on for the rest of the night if Dorothy had been willing to stay; for Mr Warburton delighted in teasing her about her religious beliefs. He had that fatal cleverness that so often goes with unbelief, and in their arguments, though Dorothy was always *right*, she was not always victorious. They were sitting, or rather Dorothy was sitting and Mr Warburton was standing, in a large agreeable room, giving on a moonlit lawn, that Mr Warburton called his 'studio'—not that there was any sign of work ever having been done in it. To Dorothy's great disappointment, the celebrated Mr Bewley had not turned up. (As a matter of fact, neither Mr Bewley, nor his wife, nor his novel entitled *Fishpools and Concubines*, actually existed. Mr Warburton had invented all three of them on the spur of the moment, as a pretext for inviting Dorothy to his house, well knowing that she would never come unchaperoned.) Dorothy had felt rather uneasy on finding that Mr Warburton was alone. It had occurred to her, indeed she had felt perfectly certain, that it would be wiser to go home at once; but she had stayed, chiefly because she was horribly tired and the leather armchair into which Mr Warburton had thrust her the moment she entered the house was too comfortable to leave. Now, however, her conscience was pricking her. It *didn't do* to stay too late at his house—people would talk if they heard of it. Besides, there was a multitude of jobs that she ought to be doing and that she had neglected in order to come here. She was so little used to idleness that even an hour spent in mere talking seemed to her vaguely sinful.

She made an effort, and straightened herself in the too-comfortable chair. 'I think, if you don't mind, it's really time I was getting home,' she said.

'Talking of Invincible Ignorance,' went on Mr Warburton, taking no notice of Dorothy's remark, 'I forget whether I ever told you that once when I was standing outside the World's End pub in Chelsea, waiting for a taxi, a damned ugly little Salvation Army lassie came up to me and said—without any kind of introduction, you know—"What will you say at the Judgement Seat?" I said, "I am reserving my defence." Rather neat, I think, don't you?'

Dorothy did not answer. Her conscience had given her another and harder jab—she had remembered those wretched, unmade jackboots, and the fact that at least one of them had got to be made tonight. She was, however, unbearably tired. She had had an exhausting afternoon, starting off with ten miles or so bicycling to and fro in the sun, delivering the parish magazine, and continuing with the Mothers' Union tea in the hot little wooden-walled room behind the parish hall. The Mothers met every Wednesday afternoon to have tea and do some charitable sewing while Dorothy read aloud to them. (At present she was reading Gene Stratton Porter's *A Girl of the Limberlost*.) It was nearly always upon Dorothy that jobs of that kind devolved, because the phalanx of devoted women (the church fowls, they are called) who do the dirty work of most parishes had dwindled at Knype Hill to four or five at most. The only helper on whom Dorothy could count at all regularly was Miss Foote, a tall, rabbit-faced, dithering virgin of thirty-five, who meant well but made a mess of everything and was in a perpetual state of flurry. Mr Warburton used to say that she reminded him of a comet—'a ridiculous blunt-nosed creature rushing round on an eccentric orbit and always a little behind time'. You could trust Miss Foote with the church decorations, but not with the Mothers or the Sunday School, because, though a regular churchgoer, her orthodoxy was suspect. She had confided to Dorothy that she could worship God best under the blue dome of the sky. After tea Dorothy had dashed up to the church to put fresh flowers on the altar, and then she had typed out her father's sermon—her typewriter was a rickety pre-Boer War 'invisible', on which you couldn't average eight hundred words an hour–and after supper she had weeded the pea rows until the light failed and her back seemed to be breaking. With one thing and another, she was even more tired than usual.

'I really *must* be getting home,' she repeated more firmly. 'I'm sure it's getting fearfully late.'

'Home?' said Mr Warburton. 'Nonsense! The evening's hardly begun.'

He was walking up and down the room again, with his hands in his coat pockets, having thrown away his cigar. The spectre of the unmade jackboots stalked back into Dorothy's mind. She would, she suddenly decided, make two jackboots tonight instead of only one, as a penance for the hour she had wasted. She was just beginning to make a mental sketch of the way she would cut out the pieces of brown paper for the insteps, when she noticed that Mr Warburton had halted behind her chair.

'What time is it, do you know?' she said.

'I dare say it might be half past ten. But people like you and me don't talk of such vulgar subjects as the time.'

'If it's half past ten, then I really must be going,' said Dorothy. 'I've got a whole lot of work to do before I go to bed.'

'Work! At this time of night? Impossible!'

'Yes, I have. I've got to make a pair of jackboots.'

'You've got to make a pair of *what*?' said Mr Warburton.

'Of jackboots. For the play the schoolchildren are acting. We make them out of glue and brown paper.'

'Glue and brown paper! Good God!' murmured Mr Warburton. He went on, chiefly to cover the fact that he was drawing nearer to Dorothy's chair: 'What a life you lead! Messing about with glue and brown paper in the middle of the night! I must say, there are times when I feel just a little glad that I'm not a clergyman's daughter.'

'I think–' began Dorothy.

But at the same moment Mr Warburton, invisible behind her chair, had lowered his hands and taken her gently by the shoulders. Dorothy immediately wriggled herself in an effort to get free of him; but Mr Warburton pressed her back into her place.

'Keep still,' he said peaceably.

'Let me go!' exclaimed Dorothy.

Mr Warburton ran his right hand caressingly down her upper arm. There was something very revealing, very characteristic in the way he did it; it was the lingering, appraising touch of a man to whom a woman's body is valuable precisely in the same way as though it were something to eat.

'You really have extraordinary nice arms,' he said. 'How on earth have you managed to remain unmarried all these years?'

'Let me go at once!' repeated Dorothy, beginning to struggle again.

'But I don't particularly want to let you go,' objected Mr Warburton.

'*Please* don't stroke my arm like that! I don't like it!'

'What a curious child you are! Why don't you like it?'

'I tell you I don't like it!'

'Now don't go and turn round,' said Mr Warburton mildly. 'You don't seem to realize how tactful it was on my part to approach you from behind your back. If you turn round you'll see that I'm old enough to be your father, and hideously bald into the bargain. But if you'll only keep still and not look at me you can imagine I'm Ivor Novello.'

Dorothy caught sight of the hand that was caressing her—a large, pink, very masculine hand, with thick fingers and a fleece of gold hairs upon the back. She turned very pale; the expression of her face altered from mere annoyance to aversion and dread. She made a violent effort, wrenched herself free, and stood up, facing him.

'I *do* wish you wouldn't do that!' she said, half in anger and half in distress.

'What is the matter with you?' said Mr Warburton.

He had stood upright, in his normal pose, entirely unconcerned, and he looked at her with a touch of curiosity. Her face had changed. It was not only that she had turned pale; there was a withdrawn, half-frightened look in her eyes—almost as though, for the moment, she were looking at him with the eyes of a stranger. He perceived that he had wounded her in some way which he did not understand, and which perhaps she did not want him to understand.

'What is the matter with you?' he repeated.

'*Why* must you do that every time you meet me?'

'"Every time I meet you" is an exaggeration,' said Mr Warburton. 'It's really very seldom that I get the opportunity. But if you really and truly don't like it—'

'Of course I don't like it! You know I don't like it!'

'Well, well! Then let's say no more about it,' said Mr Warburton generously. 'Sit down, and we'll change the subject.'

He was totally devoid of shame. It was perhaps his most outstanding characteristic. Having attempted to seduce her, and failed, he was quite willing to go on with the conversation as though nothing whatever had happened.

'I'm going home at once,' said Dorothy. 'I can't stay here any longer.'

'Oh nonsense! Sit down and forget about it. We'll talk of moral theology, or cathedral architecture, or the Girl Guides' cooking classes, or anything you choose. Think how bored I shall be all alone if you go home at this hour.'

But Dorothy persisted, and there was an argument. Even if it had not been his intention to make love to her—and whatever he might promise he would certainly begin again in a few minutes if she did not go—Mr Warburton would have pressed her to stay, for, like all thoroughly idle people, he had a horror of going to bed and no conception of the value of time. He would, if you let him, keep you talking till three or four in the morning. Even when Dorothy finally escaped, he walked beside her down the moonlit drive, still talking voluminously and with such perfect good humour that she found it impossible to be angry with him any longer.

'I'm leaving first thing tomorrow,' he told her as they reached the gate. 'I'm going to take the car to town and pick up the kids—the *bastards,* you know—and we're leaving for France the next day. I'm not certain where we shall go after that; eastern Europe, perhaps. Prague, Vienna, Bucharest.'

'How nice,' said Dorothy.

Mr Warburton, with an adroitness surprising in so large and stout a man, had manœuvred himself between Dorothy and the gate.

'I shall be away six months or more,' he said. 'And of course I needn't ask, before so long a parting, whether you want to kiss me good-bye?'

Before she knew what he was doing he had put his arm about her and drawn her against him. She drew back—too late; he kissed her on the cheek—would have kissed her on the mouth if she had not turned her head away in time. She struggled in his arms, violently and for a moment helplessly.

'Oh, let me go!' she cried. '*Do* let me go!'

'I believe I pointed out before,' said Mr Warburton, holding her easily against him, 'that I don't want to let you go.'

'But we're standing right in front of Mrs Semprill's window! She'll see us absolutely for certain!'

'Oh, good God! So she will!' said Mr Warburton. 'I was forgetting.'

Impressed by this argument, as he would not have been by any other, he let Dorothy go. She promptly put the gate between Mr Warburton and herself. He, meanwhile, was scrutinizing Mrs Semprill's windows.

'I can't see a light anywhere,' he said finally. 'With any luck the blasted hag hasn't seen us.'

'Good-bye,' said Dorothy briefly. 'This time I really *must* go. Remember me to the children.'

With this she made off as fast as she could go without actually running, to get out of his reach before he should attempt to kiss her again.

Even as she did so a sound checked her for an instant—the unmistakable bang of a window shutting, somewhere in Mrs Semprill's house. Could Mrs Semprill have been watching them after all? But (reflected Dorothy) of *course* she had been watching them! What else could you expect? You could hardly imagine Mrs Semprill missing such a scene as that. And if she *had* been watching them, undoubtedly the story would be all over the town tomorrow morning, and it would lose nothing in the telling. But this thought, sinister though it was, did no more than flight momentarily through Dorothy's mind as she hurried down the road.

When she was well out of sight of Mr Warburton's house she stopped, took out her handkerchief and scrubbed the place on her cheek where he had kissed her. She scrubbed it vigorously enough to bring the blood into her cheek. It was not until she had quite rubbed out the imaginary stain which his lips had left there that she walked on again.

What he had done had upset her. Even now her heart was knocking and fluttering uncomfortably. I can't *bear* that kind of thing! she repeated to herself several times over. And unfortunately this was no more than the literal truth; she really could not bear it. To be kissed or fondled by a man—to feel heavy male arms about her and thick male lips bearing down upon her own—was terrifying and repulsive to her. Even in memory or imagination it made her wince. It was her especial secret, the especial, incurable disability that she carried through life.

If only they would leave you *alone*! she thought as she walked onwards a little more slowly. That was how she put it to herself habitually—'If only they would leave you *alone*!' For it was not that in other ways she disliked men. On the contrary, she liked them better than women. Part of Mr Warburton's hold over her was in the fact that he was a man and had the careless good humour and the intellectual largeness that women so seldom have. But why couldn't they leave you *alone*? Why did they always have to kiss you and maul you about? They were dreadful when they kissed you—dreadful and a little disgusting, like some large, furry beast that rubs itself against you, all too friendly and yet liable to turn dangerous at any moment. And beyond their kissing and mauling there lay always the suggestion of those other, monstrous things (*'all that'* was her name for them) of which she could hardly even bear to think.

Of course, she had had her share, and rather more than her share, of casual attention from men. She was just pretty enough, and just plain enough, to be the kind of girl that men habitually pester. For when a man wants a little casual amusement, he usually picks out a girl who is not *too* pretty. Pretty girls (so he reasons) are spoilt and therefore capricious; but plain girls are easy game. And even if you are a clergyman's daughter, even if you live in a town like Knype Hill and spend almost your entire life in parish work, you don't altogether escape pursuit. Dorothy was all too used to it—all too used to the fattish middle-aged men, with their fishily hopeful eyes, who slowed down their cars when you passed them on the road, or who manœuvred an introduction and then began pinching your elbow about ten minutes afterwards. Men of all descriptions. Even a clergyman, on one occasion—a bishop's chaplain, he was. . . .

But the trouble was that it was not better, but oh! infinitely worse when they were the right kind of man and the advances they made you were honourable. Her mind slipped backwards five years, to Francis Moon, curate in those days at St Wedekind's in Millborough. Dear Francis! How gladly would she have married him if only it had not been for *all that*! Over and over again he had asked her to marry him, and of course she had had to say No; and, equally of course, he had never known why. Impossible to tell him why. And then he had gone away, and only a year later had died so irrelevantly of pneumonia. She whispered a prayer for his soul, momentarily forgetting that her father did not really approve of prayers for the dead, and then, with an effort, pushed the memory aside. Ah, better not to think of it again! It hurt her in her breast to think of it.

She could never marry, she had decided long ago upon that. Even when she was a child she had known it. Nothing would ever overcome her horror of *all that*—at the very thought of it something within her seemed to shrink and freeze. And of course, in a sense she did not want to overcome it. For, like all abnormal people, she was not fully aware that she was abnormal.

And yet, though her sexual coldness seemed to her natural and inevitable, she knew well enough how it was that it had begun. She could remember, as clearly as though it were yesterday, certain dreadful scenes between her father and her mother—scenes that she had witnessed when she was no more than nine years old. They had left a deep, secret wound in her mind. And then a little later she had been frightened by some old steel engravings of nymphs pursued by satyrs. To her childish mind there was something inexplicably, horribly sinister in those horned, semi-human creatures that lurked in thickets and behind large trees, ready to come bounding forth in sudden swift pursuit. For a whole year of her childhood she had actually been afraid to walk through woods alone, for fear of satyrs. She had grown out of the fear, of course, but not out of the feeling that was associated with it. The satyr had remained with her as a symbol. Perhaps she would never grow out of it, that special feeling of dread, of hopeless flight from something more than rationally dreadful—the stamp of hooves in the lonely wood, the lean, furry thighs of the satyr. It was a thing not to be altered, not to be argued away. It is, moreover, a thing too common nowadays, among educated women, to occasion any kind of surprise.

Most of Dorothy's agitation had disappeared by the time she reached the Rectory. The thoughts of satyrs and Mr Warburton, of Francis Moon and her foredoomed sterility, which had been going to and fro in her mind, faded out of it and were replaced by the accusing image of a jackboot. She remembered that she had the best part of two hours' work to do before going to bed tonight. The house was in darkness. She went round to the back and slipped in on tiptoe by the scullery door, for fear of waking her father, who was probably asleep already.

As she felt her way through the dark passage to the conservatory, she suddenly decided that she had gone wrong in going to Mr Warburton's house tonight. She would, she resolved, never go there again, even when she was certain that somebody else would be there as well. Moreover, she would do penance tomorrow for having gone there tonight. Having lighted the lamp, before doing anything else she found her 'memo list', which was already written out for tomorrow, and pencilled a capital P against 'breakfast', P stood for penance—no bacon again for breakfast tomorrow. Then she lighted the oilstove under the glue-pot.

The light of the lamp fell yellow upon her sewing-machine and upon the pile of half-finished clothes on the table, reminding her of the yet greater pile of clothes that were not even begun; reminding her, also, that she was dreadfully, overwhelmingly tired. She had forgotten her tiredness at the moment when Mr Warburton laid his hands on her shoulders, but now it had come back upon her with double force. Moreover, there was a somehow exceptional quality about her tiredness tonight. She felt, in an almost literal sense of the words, washed out. As she stood beside the table she had a sudden, very strange feeling as though her mind had been entirely emptied, so that for several seconds she actually forgot what it was that she had come into the conservatory to do.

Then she remembered—the jackboots, of course! Some contemptible little demon whispered in her ear, 'Why not go straight to bed and leave the jackboots till tomorrow?' She uttered a prayer for strength, and pinched herself. Come on, Dorothy! No slacking please! Luke ix, 62. Then, clearing some of the litter off the table, she got out her scissors, a pencil, and four sheets of brown paper, and sat down to cut out those troublesome insteps for the jackboots while the glue was boiling.

When the grandfather clock in her father's study struck midnight she was still at work. She had shaped both jackboots by this time, and was reinforcing them by pasting narrow strips of paper all over them—a long, messy job. Every bone in her body was aching, and her eyes were sticky with sleep. Indeed, it was only rather dimly that she remembered what she was doing. But she worked on, mechanically pasting strip after strip of paper into place, and pinching herself every two minutes to counteract the hypnotic sound of the oilstove singing beneath the glue-pot.

# CHAPTER 2

## I

Out of a black, dreamless sleep, with the sense of being drawn upwards through enormous and gradually lightening abysses, Dorothy awoke to a species of consciousness.

Her eyes were still closed. By degrees, however, their lids became less opaque to the light, and then flickered open of their own accord. She was looking out upon a street—a shabby, lively street of small shops and narrow-faced houses, with streams of men, trams, and cars passing in either direction.

But as yet it could not properly be said that she was *looking*. For the things she saw were not apprehended as men, trams, and cars, nor as anything in particular; they were not even apprehended as things moving; not even as *things*. She merely *saw*, as an animal sees, without speculation and almost without consciousness. The noises of the street—the confused din of voices, the hooting of horns and the scream of the trams grinding on their gritty rails—flowed through her head provoking purely physical responses. She had no words, nor any conception of the purpose of such things as words, nor any consciousness of time or place, or of her own body or even of her own existence.

Nevertheless, by degrees her perceptions became sharper. The stream of moving things began to penetrate beyond her eyes and sort themselves out into separate images in her brain. She began, still wordlessly, to observe the shapes of things. A long-shaped thing swam past, supported on four other, narrower long-shaped things, and drawing after it a square-shaped thing balanced on two circles. Dorothy watched it pass; and suddenly, as though spontaneously, a word flashed into her mind. The word was 'horse'. It faded, but returned presently in the more complex form: '*That is a horse.*' Other words followed—'house', 'street', 'tram', 'car', 'bicycle'—until in a few minutes she had found a name for almost everything within sight. She discovered the words 'man' and 'woman', and, speculating upon these words, discovered that she knew the difference between living and inanimate things, and between human beings and horses, and between men and women.

It was only now, after becoming aware of most of the things about her, that she became aware of *herself*. Hitherto she had been as it were a pair of eyes with a receptive but purely impersonal brain behind them. But now, with a curious little shock, she discovered her separate and unique existence; she could *feel* herself existing; it was as though something within her were exclaiming 'I am I!' Also, in some way she knew that this 'I' had existed and been the same from remote periods in the past, though it was a past of which she had no remembrance.

But it was only for a moment that this discovery occupied her. From the first there was a sense of incompleteness in it, of something vaguely unsatisfactory. And it was this: the 'I am I' which had seemed an answer had itself become a question. It was no longer 'I am I', but *'who* am I'?

*Who was she?* She turned the question over in her mind, and found that she had not the dimmest notion of who she was; except that, watching the people and horses passing, she grasped that she was a human being and not a horse. And that the question altered itself and took this form: 'Am I a man or a woman?' Again neither feeling nor memory gave any clue to the answer. But at that moment, by accident possibly, her finger-tips brushed against her body. She realized more clearly than before that her body existed, and that it was her own—that it was, in fact, herself. She began to explore it with her hands, and her hands encountered breasts. She was a woman, therefore. Only women had breasts. In some way she knew, without knowing how she knew, that all those women who passed had breasts beneath their clothes, though she could not see them.

She now grasped that in order to identify herself she must examine her own body, beginning with her face; and for some moments she actually attempted to look at her own face, before realizing that this was impossible. She looked down, and saw a shabby black satin dress, rather long, a pair of flesh-coloured artificial silk stockings, laddered and dirty, and a pair of very shabby black satin shoes with high heels. None of them was in the least familiar to her. She examined her hands, and they were both strange and unstrange. They were smallish hands, with hard palms, and very dirty. After a moment she realized that it was their dirtiness that made them strange to her. The hands themselves seemed natural and appropriate, though she did not recognize them.

After hesitating a few moments longer, she turned to her left and began to walk slowly along the pavement. A fragment of knowledge had come to her, mysteriously, out of the blank past: the existence of mirrors, their purpose, and the fact that there are often mirrors in shop windows. After a moment she came to a cheap little jeweller's shop in which a strip of mirror, set at an angle, reflected the faces of people passing. Dorothy picked her reflection out from among a dozen others, immediately realizing it to be her own. Yet it could not be said that she had recognized it; she had no memory of ever having seen it till this moment. It showed her a woman's youngish face, thin, very blonde, with

crow's-feet round the eyes, and faintly smudged with dirt. A vulgar black
cloche hat was stuck carelessly on the head, concealing most of the hair. The
face was quite unfamiliar to her, and yet not strange. She had not known till
this moment what face to expect, but now that she had seen it she realized that
it was the face she might have expected. It was appropriate. It corresponded to
something within her.

As she turned away from the jeweller's mirror, she caught sight of the words
'Fry's Chocolate' on a shop window opposite, and discovered that she
understood the purpose of writing, and also, after a momentary effort, that she
was able to read. Her eyes flitted across the street, taking in and deciphering
odd scraps of print; the names of shops, advertisements, newspaper posters.
She spelled out the letters of two red and white posters outside a tobacconist's
shop. One of them read, 'Fresh Rumours about Rector's Daughter', and the
other, 'Rector's Daughter. Now believed in Paris'. Then she looked upwards,
and saw in white lettering on the corner of a house: 'New Kent Road'. The
words arrested her. She grasped that she was standing in the New Kent Road,
and—another fragment of her mysterious knowledge—the New Kent Road was
somewhere in London. So she was in London.

As she made this discovery a peculiar tremor ran through her. Her mind was
now fully awakened; she grasped, as she had not grasped before, the
strangeness of her situation, and it bewildered and frightened her. What could
it all *mean*? What was she doing here? How had she got here? What had
happened to her?

The answer was not long in coming. She thought—and it seemed to her that
she understood perfectly well what the words meant: 'Of course! I've lost my
memory!'

At this moment two youths and a girl who were trudging past, the youths
with clumsy sacking bundles on their backs, stopped and looked curiously at
Dorothy. They hesitated for a moment, then walked on, but halted again by a
lamp-post five yards away. Dorothy saw them looking back at her and talking
among themselves. One of the youths was about twenty, narrow-chested,
black-haired, ruddy-cheeked, good-looking in a nosy cockney way, and
dressed in the wreck of a raffishly smart blue suit and a check cap. The other
was about twenty-six, squat, nimble, and powerful, with a snub nose, a clear
pink skin and huge lips as coarse as sausages, exposing strong yellow teeth. He
was frankly ragged, and he had a mat of orange-coloured hair cropped short
and growing low on his head, which gave him a startling resemblance to an
orang-outang. The girl was a silly-looking, plump creature, dressed in clothes
very like Dorothy's own. Dorothy could hear some of what they were saying:

'That tart looks ill,' said the girl.

The orange-headed one, who was singing 'Sonny Boy' in a good baritone
voice, stopped singing to answer. 'She ain't ill,' he said. 'She's on the beach all
right, though. Same as us.'

'She'd do jest nicely for Nobby, wouldn't she?' said the dark-haired one.

'Oh, *you*!' exclaimed the girl with a shocked-amorous air, pretending to
smack the dark one over the head.

The youths had lowered their bundles and leaned them against the lamp-post. All three of them now came rather hesitantly towards Dorothy, the orange-headed one, whose name seemed to be Nobby, leading the way as their ambassador. He moved with a gambolling, apelike gait, and his grin was so frank and wide that it was impossible not to smile back at him. He addressed Dorothy in a friendly way.

'Hullo, kid!'

'Hullo!'

'You on the beach, kid?'

'On the beach?'

'Well, on the bum?'

'On the bum?'

'Christ! she's batty,' murmured the girl, twitching at the black-haired one's arm as though to pull him away.

'Well, what I mean to say, kid—have you got any money?'

'I don't know.'

At this all three looked at one another in stupefaction. For a moment they probably thought that Dorothy really *was* batty. But simultaneously Dorothy, who had earlier discovered a small pocket in the side of her dress, put her hand into it and felt the outline of a large coin.

'I believe I've got a penny,' she said.

'A penny!' said the dark youth disgustedly, '—lot of good that is to us!'

Dorothy drew it out. It was a half-crown. An astonishing change came over the faces of the three others. Nobby's mouth split open with delight, he gambolled several steps to and fro like some great jubilant ape, and then, halting, took Dorothy confidentially by the arm.

'That's the mulligatawny!' he said. 'We've struck it lucky—and so've you, kid, believe me. You're going to bless the day you set eyes on us lot. We're going to make your fortune for you, we are. Now, see here, kid—are you on to go into cahoots with us three?'

'What?' said Dorothy.

'What I mean to say—how about you chumming in with Flo and Charlie and me? Partners, see? Comrades all, shoulder to shoulder. United we stand, divided we fall. We put up the brains, you put up the money. How about it, kid? Are you on, or are you off?'

'Shut up, Nobby!' interrupted the girl. 'She don't understand a word of what you're saying. Talk to her proper, can't you?'

'That'll do, Flo,' said Nobby equably. 'You keep it shut and leave the talking to me. I got a way with the tarts, I have. Now, you listen to me, kid—what might your name happen to be, kid?'

Dorothy was within an ace of saying 'I don't know,' but she was sufficiently on the alert to stop herself in time. Choosing a feminine name from the half-dozen that sprang immediately into her mind, she answered, 'Ellen.'

'Ellen. That's the mulligatawny. No surnames when you're on the bum. Well now, Ellen dear, you listen to me. Us three are going down hopping, see—'

'Hopping?'

''Opping!' put in the dark youth impatiently, as though disgusted by Dorothy's ignorance. His voice and manner were rather sullen, and his accent much baser than Nobby's. 'Pickin' 'ops—dahn in Kent! C'n understand that, can't yer?'

'Oh, *hops*! For beer?'

'That's the mulligatawny! Coming on fine, she is. Well, kid, 'z I was saying, here's us three going down hopping, and got a job promised us and all—Blessington's farm, Lower Molesworth. Only we're just a bit in the mulligatawny, see? Because we ain't got a brown between us, and we got to do it on the toby—thirty-five miles it is—and got to tap for our tommy and skipper at night as well. And that's a bit of a mulligatawny, with ladies in the party. But now s'pose f'rinstance you was to come along with us, see? We c'd take the twopenny tram far as Bromley, and that's fifteen miles done, and we won't need skipper more'n one night on the way. And you can chum in at our bin—four to a bin's the best picking—and if Blessington's paying twopence a bushel you'll turn your ten bob a week easy. What do you say to it, kid? Your two and a tanner won't do you much good here in Smoke. But you go into partnership with us, and you'll get your kip for a month and something over—and *we'll* get a lift to Bromley and a bit of scran as well.'

About a quarter of his speech was intelligible to Dorothy. She asked rather at random:

'What is *scran*?'

'Scran? Tommy—food. I can see *you* ain't been long on the beach, kid.'

'Oh. . . . Well, you want me to come down hop-picking with you, is that it?'

'That's it, Ellen my dear. Are you on, or are you off?'

'All right,' said Dorothy promptly. 'I'll come.'

She made this decision without any misgiving whatever. It is true that if she had had time to think over her position, she would probably have acted differently; in all probability she would have gone to a police station and asked for assistance. That would have been the sensible course to take. But Nobby and the others had appeared just at the critical moment, and, helpless as she was, it seemed quite natural to throw in her lot with the first human being who presented himself. Moreover, for some reason which she did not understand, it reassured her to hear that they were making for Kent. Kent, it seemed to her, was the very place to which she wanted to go. The others showed no further curiosity, and asked no uncomfortable questions. Nobby simply said, 'O.K. That's the mulligatawny!' and then gently took Dorothy's half-crown out of her hand and slid it into his pocket—in case she should lose it, he explained. The dark youth—apparently his name was Charlie—said in his surly, disagreeable way:

'Come on, less get movin'! It's 'ar-parse two already. We don't want to miss that there — tram. Where d'they start from, Nobby?'

'The Elephant,' said Nobby: 'and we got to catch it before four o'clock, because they don't give no free rides after four.'

'Come on, then, don't less waste no more time. Nice job we'll 'ave of it if we got to 'ike it down to Bromley *and* look for a place to skipper in the — dark. C'm on, Flo.'

'Quick march!' said Nobby, swinging his bundle on to his shoulder.

They set out, without more words said, Dorothy, still bewildered but feeling much better than she had felt half an hour ago, walked beside Flo and Charlie, who talked to one another and took no further notice of her. From the very first they seemed to hold themselves a little aloof from Dorothy—willing enough to share her half-crown, but with no friendly feelings towards her. Nobby marched in front, stepping out briskly in spite of his burden, and singing, with spirited imitations of military music, the well-known military song of which the only recorded words seem to be:

> '"—!" was all the band could play;
> "—! —!" And the same to you!'

## 2

This was the twenty-ninth of August. It was on the night of the twenty-first that Dorothy had fallen asleep in the conservatory; so that there had been an interregnum in her life of not quite eight days.

The thing that had happened to her was commonplace enough—almost every week one reads in the newspapers of a similar case. A man disappears from home, is lost sight of for days or weeks, and presently fetches up at a police station or in a hospital, with no notion of who he is or where he has come from. As a rule it is impossible to tell how he has spent the intervening time; he has been wandering, presumably, in some hypnotic or somnambulistic state in which he has nevertheless been able to pass for normal. In Dorothy's case only one thing is certain, and that is that she had been robbed at some time during her travels; for the clothes she was wearing were not her own, and her gold cross was missing.

At the moment when Nobby accosted her, she was already on the road to recovery; and if she had been properly cared for, her memory might have come back to her within a few days or even hours. A very small thing would have been enough to accomplish it; a chance meeting with a friend, a photograph of her home, a few questions skilfully put. But as it was, the slight mental stimulus that she needed was never given. She was left in the peculiar state in which she had first found herself—a state in which her mind was potentially normal, but not quite strung up to the effort of puzzling out her own identity.

For of course, once she had thrown in her lot with Nobby and the others, all chance of reflection was gone. There was no time to sit down and think the matter over—no time to come to grips with her difficulty and reason her way to its solution. In the strange, dirty sub-world into which she was instantly plunged, even five minutes of consecutive thought would have been impossible. The days passed in ceaseless nightmarish activity. Indeed, it was very like a nightmare; a nightmare not of urgent terrors, but of hunger, squalor, and fatigue, and of alternating heat and cold. Afterwards, when she looked back upon that time, days and nights merged themselves together so that she could never remember with perfect certainty how many of them there had been. She only knew that for some indefinite period she had been perpetually footsore and almost perpetually hungry. Hunger and the soreness of her feet were her clearest memories of that time; and also the cold of the nights, and a peculiar, blowsy, witless feeling that came of sleeplessness and constant exposure to the air.

After getting to Bromley they had 'drummed up' on a horrible, paper-littered rubbish dump, reeking with the refuse of several slaughter-houses, and then passed a shuddering night, with only sacks for cover, in long wet grass on the edge of a recreation ground. In the morning they had started out, on foot, for the hopfields. Even at this early date Dorothy had discovered that the tale Nobby had told her, about the promise of a job, was totally untrue. He had invented it—he confessed this quite light-heartedly—to induce her to come with them. Their only chance of getting a job was to march down into the hop country and apply at every farm till they found one where pickers were still needed.

They had perhaps thirty-five miles to go, as the crow flies, and yet at the end of three days they had barely reached the fringe of the hopfields. The need of getting food, of course, was what slowed their progress. They could have marched the whole distance in two days or even in a day if they had not been obliged to feed themselves. As it was, they had hardly even time to think of whether they were going in the direction of the hopfields or not; it was food that dictated all their movements. Dorothy's half-crown had melted within a few hours, and after that there was nothing for it except to beg. But there came the difficulty. One person can beg his food easily enough on the road, and even two can manage it, but it is a very different matter when there are four people together. In such circumstances one can only keep alive if one hunts for food as persistently and single-mindedly as a wild beast. Food—that was their sole preoccupation during those three days—just food, and the endless difficulty of getting it.

From morning to night they were begging. They wandered enormous distances, zigzagging right across the country, trailing from village to village and from house to house, 'tapping' at every butcher's and every baker's and every likely looking cottage, and hanging hopefully round picnic parties, and waving—always vainly—at passing cars, and accosting old gentlemen with the right kind of face and pitching hard-up stories. Often they went five miles out of their way to get a crust of bread or a handful of scraps of bacon. All of them begged, Dorothy with the others; she had no remembered past, no standards of comparison to make her ashamed of it. And yet with all their efforts they would have gone empty-bellied half the time if they had not stolen as well as begged. At dusk and in the early mornings they pillaged the orchards and the fields, stealing apples, damsons, pears, cobnuts, autumn raspberries, and, above all, potatoes; Nobby counted it a sin to pass a potato field without getting at least a pocketful. It was Nobby who did most of the stealing, while the others kept guard. He was a bold thief; it was his peculiar boast that he would steal anything that was not tied down, and he would have landed them all in prison if they had not restrained him sometimes. Once he even laid hands on a goose, but the goose set up a fearful clamour, and Charlie and Dorothy dragged Nobby off just as the owner came out of doors to see what was the matter.

Each of those first days they walked between twenty and twenty-five miles. They trailed across commons and through buried villages with incredible names, and lost themselves in lanes that led nowhere, and sprawled exhausted in dry ditches smelling of fennel and tansies, and sneaked into private woods and 'drummed up' in thickets where firewood and water were handy, and cooked strange, squalid meals in the two two-pound snuff-tins that were their only cooking pots. Sometimes, when their luck was in, they had excellent stews of cadged bacon and stolen cauliflowers, sometimes great insipid gorges of potatoes roasted in the ashes, sometimes jam made of stolen autumn raspberries which they boiled in one of the snuff-tins and devoured while it was still scalding hot. Tea was the one thing they never ran short of. Even when there was no food at all there was always tea, stewed, dark brown and reviving. It is a thing that can be begged more easily than most. 'Please, ma'am, could you spare me a pinch of tea?' is a plea that seldom fails, even with the case-hardened Kentish housewives.

The days were burning hot, the white roads glared and the passing cars sent stinging dust into their faces. Often families of hop-pickers drove past, cheering, in lorries piled sky-high with furniture, children, dogs, and birdcages. The nights were always cold. There is hardly such a thing as a night in England when it is really warm after midnight. Two large sacks were all the bedding they had between them. Flo and Charlie had one sack, Dorothy had the other, and Nobby slept on the bare ground. The discomfort was almost as bad as the cold. If you lay on your back, your head, with no pillow, lolled backwards so that your neck seemed to be breaking; if you lay on your side, your hip-bone pressing against the earth caused you torments. Even when, towards the small hours, you managed to fall asleep by fits and starts, the cold penetrated into your deepest dreams. Nobby was the only one who could really stand it. He could sleep as peacefully in a nest of sodden grass as in a bed, and his coarse, simian face, with barely a dozen red-gold hairs glittering on the chin like snippings of copper wire, never lost its warm, pink colour. He was one of those red-haired people who seem to glow with an inner radiance that warms not only themselves but the surrounding air.

All this strange, comfortless life Dorothy took utterly for granted—only dimly aware, if at all, that the other, unremembered life that lay behind her had been in some way different from this. After only a couple of days she had ceased to wonder any longer about her queer predicament. She accepted everything—accepted the dirt and hunger and fatigue, the endless trailing to and fro, the hot, dusty days and the sleepless, shivering nights. She was, in any

case, far too tired to think. By the afternoon of the second day they were all
desperately, overwhelmingly tired, except Nobby, whom nothing could tire.
Even the fact that soon after they set out a nail began to work its way through
the sole of his boot hardly seemed to trouble him. There were periods of an
hour at a time when Dorothy seemed almost to be sleeping as she walked. She
had a burden to carry now, for as the two men were already loaded and Flo
steadfastly refused to carry anything, Dorothy had volunteered to carry the
sack that held the stolen potatoes. They generally had ten pounds or so of
potatoes in reserve. Dorothy slung the sack over her shoulder as Nobby and
Charlie did with their bundles, but the string cut into her like a saw and the
sack bumped against her hip and chafed it so that finally it began to bleed. Her
wretched, flimsy shoes had begun to go to pieces from the very beginning. On
the second day the heel of her right shoe came off and left her hobbling; but
Nobby, expert in such matters, advised her to tear the heel off the other shoe
and walk flatfooted. The result was a fiery pain down her shins when she
walked uphill, and a feeling as though the soles of her feet had been hammered
with an iron bar.

But Flo and Charlie were in a much worse case than she. They were not so
much exhausted as amazed and scandalized by the distances they were
expected to walk. Walking twenty miles in a day was a thing they had never
heard of till now. They were cockneys born and bred, and though they had had
several months of destitution in London, neither of them had ever been on the
road before. Charlie, till fairly recently, had been in good employment, and
Flo, too, had had a good home until she had been seduced and turned out of
doors to live on the streets. They had fallen in with Nobby in Trafalgar Square
and agreed to come hop-picking with him, imagining that it would be a bit of a
lark. Of course, having been 'on the beach' a comparatively short time, they
looked down on Nobby and Dorothy. They valued Nobby's knowledge of the
road and his boldness in thieving, but he was their social inferior—that was
their attitude. And as for Dorothy, they scarcely even deigned to look at her
after her half-crown came to an end.

Even on the second day their courage was failing. They lagged behind,
grumbled incessantly, and demanded more than their fair share of food. By
the third day it was almost impossible to keep them on the road at all. They
were pining to be back in London, and had long ceased to care whether they
ever got to the hopfields or not; all they wanted to do was to sprawl in any
comfortable halting place they could find, and, when there was any food left,
devour endless snacks. After every halt there was a tedious argument before
they could be got to their feet again.

'Come on, blokes!' Nobby would say. 'Pack your peter up, Charlie. Time we
was getting off.'

'Oh, — getting off!' Charlie would answer morosely.

'Well, we can't skipper here, can we? We said we was going to hike as far as
Sevenoaks tonight, didn't we?'

'Oh, — Sevenoaks! Sevenoaks or any other bleeding place—it don't make
any bleeding difference to me.'

'But — it! We want to get a job tomorrow, don't we? And we got to get down among the farms 'fore we can start looking for one.'

'Oh, — the farms! I wish I'd never 'eard of a — 'op! I wasn't brought up to this—'iking and skippering like you was. I'm fed up; that's what I am — fed up.'

'If this is bloody 'opping,' Flo would chime in, 'I've 'ad my bloody bellyful of it already.'

Nobby gave Dorothy his private opinion that Flo and Charlie would probably 'jack off' if they got the chance of a lift back to London. But as for Nobby, nothing disheartened him or ruffled his good temper, not even when the nail in his boot was at its worst and his filthy remnant of a sock was dark with blood. By the third day the nail had worn a permanent hole in his foot, and Nobby had to halt once in a mile to hammer it down.

''Scuse me, kid,' he would say; 'got to attend to my bloody hoof again. This nail's a mulligatawny.'

He would search for a round stone, squat in the ditch and carefully hammer the nail down.

'There!' he would say optimistically, feeling the place with his thumb. '*That* b—'s in his grave!'

The epitaph should have been Resurgam, however. The nail invariably worked its way up again within a quarter of an hour.

Nobby had tried to make love to Dorothy, of course, and, when she repulsed him, bore her no grudge. He had that happy temperament that is incapable of taking its own reverses very seriously. He was always debonair, always singing in a lusty baritone voice—his three favourite songs were: 'Sonny Boy', ''Twas Christmas Day in the Workhouse' (to the tune of 'The Church's One Foundation'), and '"—!" was all the band could play', given with lively renderings of military music. He was twenty-six years old and was a widower, and had been successively a seller of newspapers, a petty thief, a Borstal boy, a soldier, a burglar, and a tramp. These facts, however, you had to piece together for yourself, for he was not equal to giving a consecutive account of his life. His conversation was studded with casual picturesque memories—the six months he had served in a line regiment before he was invalided out with a damaged eye, the loathsomeness of the skilly in Holloway, his childhood in the Deptford gutters, the death of his wife, aged eighteen, in childbirth, when he was twenty, the horrible suppleness of the Borstal canes, the dull boom of the nitro-glycerine, blowing in the safe door at Woodward's boot and shoe factory, where Nobby had cleared a hundred and twenty-five pounds and spent it in three weeks.

On the afternoon of the third day they reached the fringe of the hop country, and began to meet discouraged people, mostly tramps, trailing back to London with the news that there was nothing doing—hops were bad and the price was low, and the gypsies and 'home pickers' had collared all the jobs. At this Flo and Charlie gave up hope altogether, but by an adroit mixture of bullying and persuasion Nobby managed to drive them a few miles farther. In a little village called Wale they fell in with an old Irishwoman—Mrs McElligot was her name–who had just been given a job at a neighbouring hopfield, and they swapped some of their stolen apples for a piece of meat she had 'bummed' earlier in the day. She gave them some useful hints about hop-picking and about what farms to try. They were all sprawling on the village green, tired out, opposite a little general shop with some newspaper posters outside.

'You'd best go down'n have a try at Chalmers's,' Mrs McElligot advised them in her base Dublin accent. 'Dat's a bit above five mile from here. I've heard tell as Chalmers wants a dozen pickers still. I daresay he'd give y'a job if you gets dere early enough.'

'Five miles! Cripes! Ain't there none nearer'n that?' grumbled Charlie.

'Well, dere's Norman's. I got a job at Norman's meself–I'm startin' tomorrow morning'. But 'twouldn't be no use for you to try at Norman's. He ain't takin' on none but home pickers, an' dey say as he's goin' to let half his hops blow.'

'What's home pickers?' said Nobby.

'Why, dem as has got homes o' deir own. Eider you got to live in de neighbourhood, or else de farmer's got to give y'a hut to sleep in. Dat's de law nowadays. In de ole days when you come down hoppin', you kipped in a stable an' dere was no questions asked. But dem bloody interferin' gets of a Labour Government brought in a law to say as no pickers was to be taken on widout de farmer had proper accommodation for 'em. So Norman only takes on folks as has got homes o' deir own.'

'Well, you ain't got a home of your own, have you?'

'No bloody fear! But Norman t'inks I have. I kidded'm I was stayin' in a cottage near by. Between you an' me, I'm skipperin' in a cow byre. 'Tain't so bad except for de stink o' de muck, but you got to be out be five in de mornin', else de cowmen 'ud catch you.'

'We ain't got no experience of hopping,' Nobby said. 'I wouldn't know a bloody hop if I saw one. Best to let on you're an old hand when you go up for a job, eh?'

'Hell! Hops don't need no experience. Tear 'em off an' fling 'em into de bin. Dat's all der is to it, wid hops.'

Dorothy was nearly asleep. She heard the others talking desultorily, first about hop-picking, then about some story in the newspapers of a girl who had disappeared from home. Flo and Charlie had been reading the posters on the shop-front opposite; and this had revived them somewhat, because the posters reminded them of London and its joys. The missing girl, in whose fate they seemed to be rather interested, was spoken of as 'The Rector's Daughter'.

'J'a see that one, Flo?' said Charlie, reading a poster aloud with intense relish: '"Secret Love Life of Rector's Daughter. Startling Revelations." Coo! Wish I 'ad a penny to 'ave a read of that!'

'Oh? What's 't all about, then?'

'What? Didn't j'a read about it? Papers 'as bin full of it. Rector's Daughter this and Rector's Daughter that–wasn't 'alf smutty, some of it, too.'

'She's bit of hot stuff, the ole Rector's Daughter,' said Nobby reflectively, lying on his back. 'Wish she was here now! I'd know what to do with her, all right, I would.'

'"Twas a kid run away from home,' put in Mrs McElligot. 'She was carryin' on wid a man twenty year older'n herself, an' now she's disappeared an' dey're searchin' for her high an' low.'

'Jacked off in the middle of the night in a motor-car with no clo'es on 'cep' 'er nightdress,' said Charlie appreciatively. 'The 'ole village sore 'em go.'

'Dere's some t'ink as he's took her abroad an' sold her to one o' dem flash cat-houses in Parrus,' added Mrs McElligot.

'No clo'es on 'cep' 'er nightdress? Dirty tart she must 'a been!'

The conversation might have proceeded to further details, but at this moment Dorothy interrupted it. What they were saying had roused a faint curiosity in her. She realized that she did not know the meaning of the word 'Rector'. She sat up and asked Nobby:

'What is a Rector?'

'Rector? Why, a sky-pilot—parson bloke. Bloke that preaches and gives out the hymns and that in church. We passed one of 'em yesterday—riding a green bicycle and had his collar on back to front. A priest—clergyman. *You* know.'

'Oh. . . . Yes, I think so.'

'Priests! Bloody ole getsies dey are too, some o' dem,' said Mrs McElligot reminiscently.

Dorothy was left not much the wiser. What Nobby had said did enlighten her a little, but only a very little. The whole train of thought connected with 'church' and 'clergyman' was strangely vague and blurred in her mind. It was one of the gaps—there was a number of such gaps—in the mysterious knowledge that she had brought with her out of the past.

That was their third night on the road. When it was dark they slipped into a spinney as usual to 'skipper', and a little after midnight it began to pelt with rain. They spent a miserable hour stumbling to and fro in the darkness, trying to find a place to shelter, and finally found a hay-stack, where they huddled themselves on the lee side till it was light enough to see. Flo blubbered throughout the night in the most intolerable manner, and by the morning she was in a state of semi-collapse. Her silly fat face, washed clean by rain and tears, looked like a bladder of lard, if one can imagine a bladder of lard contorted with self-pity. Nobby rooted about under the hedge until he had collected an armful of partially dry sticks, and then managed to get a fire going and boil some tea as usual. There was no weather so bad that Nobby could not produce a can of tea. He carried, among other things, some pieces of old motor tyre that would make a flare when the wood was wet, and he even possessed the art, known only to a few cognoscenti among tramps, of getting water to boil over a candle.

Everyone's limbs had stiffened after the horrible night, and Flo declared herself unable to walk a step farther. Charlie backed her up. So, as the other two refused to move, Dorothy and Nobby went on to Chalmers's farm, arranging a rendezvous where they should meet when they had tried their luck. They got to Chalmers's, five miles away, found their way through vast orchards to the hop-fields, and were told that the overseer 'would be along presently'. So they waited four hours on the edge of the plantation, with the sun drying their clothes on their backs, watching the hop-pickers at work. It was a scene somehow peaceful and alluring. The hop bines, tall climbing plants like runner beans enormously magnified, grew in green leafy lanes, with the hops dangling from them in pale green bunches like gigantic grapes. When the wind stirred them they shook forth a fresh, bitter scent of sulphur and cool beer. In each lane of bines a family of sunburnt people were shredding the hops into sacking bins, and singing as they worked; and presently a hooter sounded and they knocked off to boil cans of tea over crackling fires of hop bines. Dorothy envied them greatly. How happy they looked, sitting round the fires with their cans of tea and their hunks of bread and bacon, in the smell of hops and wood smoke! She pined for such a job—however, for the present there was nothing doing. At about one o'clock the overseer arrived and told them that he had no jobs for them, so they trailed back to the road, only avenging themselves on Chalmers's farm by stealing a dozen apples as they went.

When they reached their rendezvous, Flo and Charlie had vanished. Of course they searched for them, but, equally of course, they knew very well what had happened. Indeed, it was perfectly obvious. Flo had made eyes at some passing lorry driver, who had given the two of them a lift back to London for the chance of a good cuddle on the way. Worse yet, they had stolen both bundles. Dorothy and Nobby had not a scrap of food left, not a crust of bread nor a potato nor a pinch of tea, no bedding, and not even a snuff-tin in which to cook anything they could cadge or steal—nothing, in fact, except the clothes they stood up in.

The next thirty-six hours were a bad time—a very bad time. How they pined for a job, in their hunger and exhaustion! But the chances of getting one seemed to grow smaller and smaller as they got farther into the hop country. They made interminable marches from farm to farm, getting the same answer everywhere—no pickers needed—and they were so busy marching to and fro that they had not even time to beg, so that they had nothing to eat except stolen apples and damsons that tormented their stomachs with their acid juice and yet left them ravenously hungry. It did not rain that night, but it was much colder than before. Dorothy did not even attempt to sleep, but spent the night in crouching over the fire and keeping it alight. They were hiding in a beech wood, under a squat, ancient tree that kept the wind away but also wetted them periodically with sprinklings of chilly dew. Nobby, stretched on his back, mouth open, one broad cheek faintly illumined by the feeble rays of the fire, slept as peacefully as a child. All night long a vague wonder, born of sleeplessness and intolerable discomfort, kept stirring in Dorothy's mind. Was this the life to which she had been bred—this life of wandering empty-bellied all day and shivering at night under dripping trees? Had it been like this even in the blank past? Where had she come from? Who was she? No answer came, and they were on the road at dawn. By the evening they had tried at eleven farms in all, and Dorothy's legs were giving out, and she was so dizzy with fatigue that she found difficulty in walking straight.

But late in the evening, quite unexpectedly, their luck turned. They tried at a farm named Cairns's, in the village of Clintock, and were taken on immediately, with no questions asked. The overseer merely looked them up and down, said briefly, 'Right you are—you'll do. Start in the morning; bin number 7, set 19,' and did not even bother to ask their names. Hop-picking, it seemed, needed neither character nor experience.

They found their way to the meadow where the pickers' camp was situated. In a dreamlike state, between exhaustion and the joy of having got a job at last, Dorothy found herself walking through a maze of tin-roofed huts and gypsies' caravans with many-coloured washing hanging from the windows. Hordes of children swarmed in the narrow grass alleys between the huts, and ragged, agreeable-looking people were cooking meals over innumerable faggot fires. At the bottom of the field there were some round tin huts, much inferior to the others, set apart for unmarried people. An old man who was toasting cheese at a fire directed Dorothy to one of the women's huts.

Dorothy pushed open the door of the hut. It was about twelve feet across, with unglazed windows which had been boarded up, and it had no furniture whatever. There seemed to be nothing in it but an enormous pile of straw reaching to the roof—in fact, the hut was almost entirely filled with straw. To Dorothy's eyes, already sticky with sleep, the straw looked paradisically comfortable. She began to push her way into it, and was checked by a sharp yelp from beneath her.

''Ere! What yer doing' of? Get off of it! 'Oo asked *you* to walk about on my belly, stoopid?'

Seemingly there were women down among the straw. Dorothy burrowed foward more circumspectly, tripped over something, sank into the straw and in the same instant began to fall asleep. A rough-looking woman, partially undressed, popped up like a mermaid from the strawy sea.

''Ullo, mate!' she said. 'Jest about all in, ain't you, mate?'

'Yes, I'm tired—very tired.'

'Well, you'll bloody freeze in this straw with no bed-clo'es on you. Ain't you got a blanket?'

'No,'

''Alf a mo, then. I got a poke 'ere.'

She dived down into the straw and re-emerged with a hop-poke seven feet long. Dorothy was asleep already. She allowed herself to be woken up, and inserted herself somehow into the sack, which was so long that she could get into it head and all; and then she was half wriggling, half sinking down, deep down, into a nest of straw warmer and drier than she had conceived possible. The straw tickled her nostrils and got into her hair and pricked her even through the sack, but at that moment no imaginable sleeping place—not Cleopatra's couch of swan's-down nor the floating bed of Haroun al Raschid—could have caressed her more voluptuously.

# 3

It was remarkable how easily, once you had got a job, you settled down to the routine of hop-picking. After only a week of it you ranked as an expert picker, and felt as though you had been picking hops all your life.

It was exceedingly easy work. Physically, no doubt, it was exhausting—it kept you on your feet ten or twelve hours a day, and you were dropping with sleep by six in the evening—but it needed no kind of skill. Quite a third of the pickers in the camp were as new to the job as Dorothy herself. Some of them had come down from London with not the dimmest idea of what hops were like, or how you picked them, or why. One man, it was said, on his first morning on the way to the fields, had asked, 'Where are the spades?' He imagined that hops were dug up out of the ground.

Except for Sundays, one day at the hop camp was very like another. At half past five, at a tap on the wall of your hut, you crawled out of your sleeping nest and began searching for your shoes, amid sleepy curses from the women (there were six or seven or possibly even eight of them) who were buried here and there in the straw. In that vast pile of straw any clothes that you were so unwise as to take off always lost themselves immediately. You grabbed an armful of straw and another of dried hop bines, and a faggot from the pile outside, and got the fire going for breakfast. Dorothy always cooked Nobby's breakfast as well as her own, and tapped on the wall of his hut when it was ready, she being better at waking up in the morning than he. It was very cold on those September mornings, the eastern sky was fading slowly from black to cobalt, and the grass was silvery white with dew. Your breakfast was always the same—bacon, tea, and bread fried in the grease of the bacon. While you ate it you cooked another exactly similar meal, to serve for dinner, and then, carrying your dinner-pail, you set out for the fields, a mile-and-a-half walk through the blue, windy dawn, with your nose running so in the cold that you had to stop occasionally and wipe it on your sacking apron.

The hops were divided up into plantations of about an acre, and each set—forty pickers or thereabouts, under a foreman who was often a gypsy—picked one plantation at a time. The bines grew twelve feet high or more, and they were trained up strings and slung over horizontal wires, in rows a yard or two apart; in each row there was a sacking bin like a very deep hammock slung on a heavy wooden frame. As soon as you arrived you swung your bin into position, slit the strings from the next two bines, and tore them down—huge, tapering strands of foliage, like the plaits of Rapunzel's hair, that came tumbling down on top of you, showering you with dew. You dragged them into place over the bin, and then, starting at the thick end of the bine, began tearing off the heavy bunches of hops. At that hour of the morning you could only pick slowly and awkwardly. Your hands were still stiff and the coldness of the dew numbed them, and the hops were wet and slippery. The great difficulty was to pick the hops without picking the leaves and stalks as well; for the measurer was liable to refuse your hops if they had too many leaves among them.

The stems of the bines were covered with minute thorns which within two or three days had torn the skin of your hands to pieces. In the morning it was a torment to begin picking when your fingers were almost too stiff to bend and bleeding in a dozen places; but the pain wore off when the cuts had reopened and the blood was flowing freely. If the hops were good and you picked well, you could strip a bine in ten minutes, and the best bines yielded half a bushel of hops. But the hops varied greatly from one plantation to another. In some they were as large as walnuts, and hung in great leafless bunches which you could rip off with a single twist; in others they were miserable things no bigger than peas, and grew so thinly that you had to pick them one at a time. Some hops were so bad that you could not pick a bushel of them in an hour.

It was slow work in the early morning, before the hops were dry enough to handle. But presently the sun came out, and the lovely, bitter odour began to stream from the warming hops, and people's early-morning surliness wore off, and the work got into its stride. From eight till midday you were picking, picking, picking, in a sort of passion of work—a passionate eagerness, which grew stronger and stronger as the morning advanced, to get each bine done and shift your bin a little farther along the row. At the beginning of each plantation all the bins started abreast, but by degrees the better pickers forged ahead, and some of them had finished their lane of hops when the others were barely half-way along; whereupon, if you were far behind, they were allowed to turn back and finish your row for you, which was called 'stealing your hops'. Dorothy and Nobby were always among the last, there being only two of them—there were four people at most of the bins. And Nobby was a clumsy picker, with his great coarse hands; on the whole, the women picked better than the men.

It was always a neck and neck race between the two bins on either side of Dorothy and Nobby, bin number 6 and bin number 8. Bin number 6 was a family of gypsies—a curly-headed, ear-ringed father, an old dried-up leather-coloured mother, and two strapping sons—and bin number 8 was an old East End costerwoman who wore a broad hat and long black cloak and took snuff out of a papiermâché box with a steamer painted on the lid. She was always helped by relays of daughters and granddaughters who came down from London for two days at a time. There was quite a troop of children working with the set, following the bins with baskets and gathering up the fallen hops while the adults picked. And the old costerwoman's tiny, pale granddaughter Rose, and a little gypsy girl, dark as an Indian, were perpetually slipping off to steal autumn raspberries and make swings out of hop bines; and the constant singing round the bins was pierced by shrill cries from the costerwoman of,

'Go on, Rose, you lazy little cat! Pick them 'ops up! I'll warm your a— for you!' etc., etc.

Quite half the pickers in the set were gypsies–there were not less than two hundred of them in the camp. Diddykies, the other pickers called them. They were not a bad sort of people, friendly enough, and they flattered you grossly when they wanted to get anything out of you; yet they were sly, with the impenetrable slyness of savages. In their oafish, Oriental faces there was a look as of some wild but sluggish animal–a look of dense stupidity existing side by side with untameable cunning. Their talk consisted of about half a dozen remarks which they repeated over and over again without ever growing tired of them. The two young gypsies at bin number 6 would ask Nobby and Dorothy as many as a dozen times a day the same conundrum:

'What is it the cleverest man in England couldn't do?'

'I don't know. What?'

'Tickle a gnat's a— with a telegraph pole.'

At this, never-failing bellows of laughter. They were all abysmally ignorant; they informed you with pride that not one of them could read a single word. The old curly-headed father, who had conceived some dim notion that Dorothy was a 'scholard', once seriously asked her whether he could drive his caravan to New York.

At twelve o'clock a hooter down at the farm signalled to the pickers to knock off work for an hour, and it was generally a little before this that the measurer came round to collect the hops. At a warning shout from the foreman of ''Ops ready, number nineteen!' everyone would hasten to pick up the fallen hops, finish off the tendrils that had been left unpicked here and there, and clear the leaves out of the bin. There was an art in that. It did not pay to pick too 'clean', for leaves and hops alike all went to swell the tally. The old hands, such as the gypsies, were adepts at knowing just how 'dirty' it was safe to pick.

The measurer would come round, carrying a wicker basket which held a bushel, and accompanied by the 'bookie,' who entered the pickings of each bin in a ledger. The 'bookies' were young men, clerks and chartered accountants and the like, who took this job as a paying holiday. The measurer would scoop the hops out of the bin a bushel at a time, intoning as he did so, 'One! Two! Three! Four!' and the pickers would enter the number in their tally books. Each bushel they picked earned them twopence, and naturally there were endless quarrels and accusations of unfairness over the measuring. Hops are spongy things–you can crush a bushel of them into a quart pot if you choose; so after each scoop one of the pickers would lean over into the bin and stir the hops up to make them lie looser, and then the measurer would hoist the end of the bin and shake the hops together again. Some mornings he had orders to 'take them heavy', and would shovel them in so that he got a couple of bushels at each scoop, whereat there were angry yells of, 'Look how the b—'s ramming them down! Why don't you bloody well stamp on them?' etc.; and the old hands would say darkly that they had known measurers to be ducked in cowponds on the last day of picking. From the bins the hops were put into pokes which theoretically held a hundredweight; but it took two men to hoist a full poke when the measurer had been 'taking them heavy'. You had an hour for dinner, and you made a fire of hop bines–this was forbidden, but everyone did it–and heated up your tea and ate your bacon sandwiches. After dinner you were picking again till five or six in the evening, when the measurer came once more to take your hops, after which you were free to go back to the camp.

Looking back, afterwards, upon her interlude of hop-picking, it was always the afternoons that Dorothy remembered. Those long, laborious hours in the strong sunlight, in the sound of forty voices singing, in the smell of hops and wood smoke, had a quality peculiar and unforgettable. As the afternoon wore on you grew almost too tired to stand, and the small green hop lice got into your hair and into your ears and worried you, and your hands, from the sulphurous juice, were as black as a Negro's except where they were bleeding. Yet you were happy, with an unreasonable happiness. The work took hold of you and absorbed you. It was stupid work, mechanical, exhausting, and every day more painful to the hands, and yet you never wearied of it; when the weather was fine and the hops were good you had the feeling that you could go on picking for ever and for ever. It gave you a physical joy, a warm satisfied feeling inside you, to stand there hour after hour, tearing off the heavy clusters and watching the pale green pile grow higher and higher in your bin, every bushel another twopence in your pocket. The sun burned down upon you, baking you brown, and the bitter, never-palling scent, like a wind from oceans of cool beer, flowed into your nostrils and refreshed you. When the sun was shining everybody sang as they worked; the plantations rang with singing. For some reason all the songs were sad that autumn–songs about rejected love and fidelity unrewarded, like gutter versions of *Carmen* and *Manon Lescaut*. There was:

> *There* they *go–in* their joy–
> '*Appy* girl–*lucky* boy–
> But 'ere am *I-I-I*–
> Broken–'*a-a-a*rted!

And there was:

> But I'm dan–cing with tears–in my eyes–
> 'Cos the girl–in my arms–isn't you-o-ou!

And:

> The bells–are ringing–for Sally–
> But no-o-ot–for Sally–and me!

The little gypsy girl used to sing over and over again:

> We're so misable, all so misable,
> Down on Misable Farm!

And though everyone told her that the name of it was Misery Farm, she persisted in calling it Misable Farm. The old costerwoman and her granddaughter Rose had a hop-picking song which went:

> 'Our lousy 'ops!
> Our lousy 'ops!
> When the measurer 'e comes round,
> Pick 'em up, pick 'em up off the ground!
> When 'e comes to measure,
> 'E never knows where to stop;
> Ay, ay, get in the bin
> And take the bloody lot!'

'There they go in their joy', and 'The bells are ringing for Sally', were the especial favourites. The pickers never grew tired of singing them; they must have sung both of them several hundred times over before the season came to an end. As much a part of the atmosphere of the hopfields as the bitter scent and the blowsy sunlight were the tunes of those two songs, ringing through the leafy lanes of the bines.

When you got back to the camp, at half past six or thereabouts, you squatted down by the stream that ran past the huts, and washed your face, probably for the first time that day. It took you twenty minutes or so to get the coal-black filth off your hands. Water and even soap made no impression on it; only two things would remove it—one of them was mud, and the other, curiously enough, was hop juice. Then you cooked your supper, which was usually bread and tea and bacon again, unless Nobby had been along to the village and bought two pennyworth of pieces from the butcher. It was always Nobby who did the shopping. He was the sort of man who knows how to get four pennyworth of meat from the butcher for twopence, and, besides, he was expert in tiny economies. For instance, he always bought a cottage loaf in preference to any of the other shapes, because, as he used to point out, a cottage loaf seems like two loaves when you tear it in half.

Even before you had eaten your supper you were dropping with sleep, but the huge fires that people used to build between the huts were too agreeable to leave. The farm allowed two faggots a day for each hut, but the pickers plundered as many more as they wanted, and also great lumps of elm root which kept smouldering till morning. On some nights the fires were so enormous that twenty people could sit round them in comfort, and there was singing far into the night, and telling of stories and roasting of stolen apples. Youths and girls slipped off to the dark lanes together, and a few bold spirits like Nobby set out with sacks and robbed the neighbouring orchards, and the children played hide-and-seek in the dusk and harried the nightjars which haunted the camp and which, in their cockney ignorance, they imagined to be pheasants. On Saturday nights fifty or sixty of the pickers used to get drunk in the pub and then march down the village street roaring bawdy songs, to the scandal of the inhabitants, who looked on the hopping season as decent provincials in Roman Gaul might have looked on the yearly incursion of the Goths.

When finally you managed to drag yourself away to your nest in the straw, it was none too warm or comfortable. After that first blissful night, Dorothy discovered that straw is wretched stuff to sleep in. It is not only prickly, but, unlike hay, it lets in the draught from every possible direction. However, you had the chance to steal an almost unlimited number of hop-pokes from the fields, and by making herself a sort of cocoon of four hop-pokes, one on top of the other, she managed to keep warm enough to sleep at any rate five hours a night.

# 4

As to what you earned by hop-picking, it was just enough to keep body and soul together, and no more.

The rate of pay at Cairns's was twopence a bushel, and given good hops a practised picker can average three bushels an hour. In theory, therefore, it would have been possible to earn thirty shillings by a sixty-hour week. Actually, no one in the camp came anywhere near this figure. The best pickers of all earned thirteen or fourteen shillings a week, and the worst hardly as much as six shillings. Nobby and Dorothy, pooling their hops and dividing the proceeds, made round about ten shillings a week each.

There were various reasons for this. To begin with, there was the badness of the hops in some of the fields. Again, there were the delays which wasted an hour or two of every day. When one plantation was finished you had to carry your bin to the next, which might be a mile distant; and then perhaps it would turn out that there was some mistake, and the set, struggling under their bins (they weighed a hundredweight), would have to waste another half-hour in traipsing elsewhere. Worst of all, there was the rain. It was a bad September that year, raining one day in three. Sometimes for a whole morning or afternoon you shivered miserably in the shelter of the unstripped bines, with a dripping hop-poke round your shoulders, waiting for the rain to stop. It was impossible to pick when it was raining. The hops were too slippery to handle, and if you did pick them it was worse than useless, for when sodden with water they shrank all to nothing in the bin. Sometimes you were in the fields all day to earn a shilling or less.

This did not matter to the majority of the pickers, for quite half of them were gypsies and accustomed to starvation wages, and most of the others were respectable East Enders, costermongers and small shopkeepers and the like, who came hop-picking for a holiday and were satisfied if they earned enough for their fare both ways and a bit of fun on Saturday nights. The farmers knew this and traded on it. Indeed, were it not that hop-picking is regarded as a holiday, the industry would collapse forthwith, for the price of hops is now so low that no farmer could afford to pay his pickers a living wage.

Twice a week you could 'sub' up to the amount of half your earnings. If you left before the picking was finished (an inconvenient thing for the farmers) they had the right to pay you off at the rate of a penny a bushel instead of twopence—that is, to pocket half of what they owed you. It was also common knowledge that towards the end of the season, when all the pickers had a fair sum owing to them and would not want to sacrifice it by throwing up their jobs, the farmer would reduce the rate of payment from twopence a bushel to a penny halfpenny. Strikes were practically impossible. The pickers had no union, and the foremen of the sets, instead of being paid twopence a bushel like the others, were paid a weekly wage which stopped automatically if there was a strike; so naturally they would raise Heaven and earth to prevent one. Altogether, the farmers had the pickers in a cleft stick; but it was not the farmers who were to blame—the low price of hops was the root of the trouble. Also as Dorothy observed later, very few of the pickers had more than a dim idea of the amount they earned. The system of piecework disguised the low rate of payment.

For the first few days, before they could 'sub', Dorothy and Nobby very nearly starved, and would have starved altogether if the other pickers had not fed them. But everyone was extraordinarily kind. There was a party of people who shared one of the larger huts a little farther up the row, a flower-seller named Jim Burrows and a man named Jim Turle who was vermin man at a large London restaurant, who had married sisters and were close friends, and these people had taken a liking to Dorothy. They saw to it that she and Nobby should not starve. Every evening during the first few days May Turle, aged fifteen, would arrive with a saucepan full of stew, which was presented with studied casualness, lest there should be any hint of charity about it. The formula was always the same:

'Please, Ellen, mother says as she was just going to throw this stew away, and then she thought as p'raps you might like it. She ain't got no use for it, she says, and so you'd be doing her a kindness if you was to take it.'

It was extraordinary what a lot of things the Turles and the Burrowses were 'just going to throw away' during those first few days. On one occasion they even gave Nobby and Dorothy half a pig's head ready stewed; and besides food they gave them several cooking pots and a tin plate which could be used as a frying-pan. Best of all, they asked no uncomfortable questions. They knew well enough that there was some mystery in Dorothy's life—'You could see,' they said, 'as Ellen had *come down in the world*'—but they made it a point of honour not to embarrass her by asking questions about it. It was not until she had been more than a fortnight at the camp that Dorothy was even obliged to put herself to the trouble of inventing a surname.

As soon as Dorothy and Nobby could 'sub', their money troubles were at an end. They lived with surprising ease at the rate of one and sixpence a day for the two of them. Fourpence of this went on tobacco for Nobby, and fourpence-halfpenny on a loaf of bread; and they spent about sevenpence a day on tea, sugar, milk (you could get milk at the farm at a halfpenny a half-pint), and margarine and 'pieces' of bacon. But, of course, you never got through the day without squandering another penny or two. You were everlastingly hungry, everlastingly doing sums in farthings to see whether you could afford a kipper or a doughnut or a pennyworth of potato chips, and, wretched as the pickers' earnings were, half the population of Kent seemed to be in conspiracy to tickle their money out of their pockets. The local shopkeepers, with four hundred hop-pickers quartered upon them, made more during the hop season than all the rest of the year put together, which did not prevent them from looking down on the pickers as cockney dirt. In the afternoon the farm hands would come round the bins selling apples and pears at seven a penny, and London hawkers would come with baskets of doughnuts or water ices or 'halfpenny lollies'. At night the camp was thronged by hawkers who drove down from London with vans of horrifyingly cheap groceries, fish and chips, jellied eels, shrimps, shop-soiled cakes, and gaunt, glassy-eyed rabbits which had lain two years on the ice and were being sold off at ninepence a time.

For the most part it was a filthy diet upon which the hop-pickers lived—inevitably so, for even if you had the money to buy proper food, there was no time to cook it except on Sundays. Probably it was only the abundance of stolen apples that prevented the camp from being ravaged by scurvy. There was constant, systematic thieving of apples; practically everyone in the camp either stole them or shared them. There were even parties of young men (employed, so it was said, by London fruit-costers) who bicycled down from London every week-end for the purpose of raiding the orchards. As for Nobby, he had reduced fruit-stealing to a science. Within a week he had collected a gang of youths who looked up to him as a hero because he was a real burglar and had been in jail four times, and every night they would set out at dusk with sacks and come back with as much as two hundredweight of fruit. There were vast orchards near the hopfields, and the apples, especially the beautiful little Golden Russets, were lying in piles under the trees, rotting, because the farmers could not sell them. It was a sin not to take them, Nobby said. On two occasions he and his gang even stole a chicken. How they managed to do it without waking the neighbourhood was a mystery; but it appeared that Nobby knew some dodge of slipping a sack over a chicken's head, so that it 'ceas'd upon the midnight with no pain'—or at any rate, with no noise.

In this manner a week and then a fortnight went by, and Dorothy was no nearer to solving the problem of her own identity. Indeed, she was further from it than ever, for except at odd moments the subject had almost vanished from her mind. More and more she had come to take her curious situation for granted, to abandon all thoughts of either yesterday or tomorrow. That was the natural effect of life in the hopfields; it narrowed the range of your consciousness to the passing minute. You could not struggle with nebulous mental problems when you were everlastingly sleepy and everlastingly occupied—for when you were not at work in the fields you were either cooking, or fetching things from the village, or coaxing a fire out of wet sticks, or trudging to and fro with cans of water. (There was only one water tap in the camp, and that was two hundred yards from Dorothy's hut, and the unspeakable earth latrine was at the same distance.) It was a life that wore you out, used up every ounce of your energy, and kept you profoundly, unquestionably happy. In the literal sense of the word, it stupefied you. The long days in the fields, the coarse food and insufficient sleep, the smell of hops and wood smoke, lulled you into an almost beastlike heaviness. Your wits seemed to thicken, just as your skin did, in the rain and sunshine and perpetual fresh air.

On Sundays, of course, there was no work in the fields; but Sunday morning was a busy time, for it was then that people cooked their principal meal of the week, and did their laundering and mending. All over the camp, while the jangle of bells from the village church came down the wind, mingling with the thin strains of 'O God our Help' from the ill-attended open-air service held by St Somebody's Mission to Hop-pickers, huge faggot fires were blazing, and water boiling in buckets and tin cans and saucepans and anything else that people could lay their hands on, and ragged washing fluttering from the roofs of all the huts. On the first Sunday Dorothy borrowed a basin from the Turles and washed first her hair, then her underclothes and Nobby's shirt. Her underclothes were in a shocking state. How long she had worn them she did not know, but certainly not less than ten days, and they had been slept in all that while. Her stockings had hardly any feet left to them, and as for her shoes, they only held together because of the mud that caked them.

After she had set the washing to dry she cooked the dinner, and they dined opulently off half a stewed chicken (stolen), boiled potatoes (stolen), stewed apples (stolen), and tea out of real tea-cups with handles on them, borrowed from Mrs Burrows. And after dinner, the whole afternoon, Dorothy sat against the sunny side of the hut, with a dry hop-poke across her knees to hold her dress down, alternately dozing and reawakening. Two-thirds of the people in the camp were doing exactly the same thing; just dozing in the sun, and waking to gaze at nothing, like cows. It was all you felt equal to, after a week of heavy work.

About three o'clock, as she sat there on the verge of sleep, Nobby sauntered by, bare to the waist—his shirt was drying—with a copy of a Sunday newspaper that he had succeeded in borrowing. It was *Pippin's Weekly,* the dirtiest of the five dirty Sunday newspapers. He dropped it in Dorothy's lap as he passed.

'Have a read of that, kid,' he said generously.

Dorothy took *Pippin's Weekly* and laid it across her knees, feeling herself far too sleepy to read. A huge headline stared her in the face: 'PASSION DRAMA IN COUNTRY RECTORY'. And then there were some more headlines, and something in leaded type, and an inset photograph of a girl's face. For the space of five seconds or thereabouts Dorothy was actually gazing at a blackish, smudgy, but quite recognizable portrait of herself.

There was a column or so of print beneath the photograph. As a matter of fact, most of the newspapers had dropped the 'Rector's Daughter' mystery by this time, for it was more than a fortnight old and stale news. But *Pippin's Weekly* cared little whether its news was new so long as it was spicy, and that week's crop of rapes and murders had been a poor one. They were giving the

'Rector's Daughter' one final boost—giving her, in fact, the place of honour at the top left-hand corner of the front page.

Dorothy gazed inertly at the photograph. A girl's face, looking out at her from beds of black unappetizing print—it conveyed absolutely nothing to her mind. She re-read mechanically the words, 'PASSION DRAMA IN COUNTRY RECTORY', without either understanding them or feeling the slightest interest in them. She was, she discovered, totally unequal to the effort of reading; even the effort of looking at the photographs was too much for her. Heavy sleep was weighing down her head. Her eyes, in the act of closing, flitted across the page to a photograph that was either of Lord Snowden or of the man who wouldn't wear a truss, and then, in the same instant, she fell asleep, with *Pippin's Weekly* across her knees.

It was not uncomfortable against the corrugated iron wall of the hut, and she hardly stirred till six o'clock, when Nobby woke her up to tell her that he had got tea ready; whereat Dorothy put *Pippin's Weekly* thriftily away (it would come in for lighting the fire), without looking at it again. So for the moment the chance of solving her problem passed by. And the problem might have remained unsolved even for months longer, had not a disagreeable accident, a week later, frightened her out of the contented and unreflecting state in which she was living.

## 5

The following Sunday night two policemen suddenly descended upon the camp and arrested Nobby and two others for theft.

It happened all in a moment, and Nobby could not have escaped even if he had been warned beforehand, for the countryside was pullulating with special constables. There are vast numbers of special constables in Kent. They are sworn in every autumn—a sort of militia to deal with the marauding tribes of hop-pickers. The farmers had been growing tired of the orchard-robbing, and had decided to make an example, *in terrorem.*

Of course there was a tremendous uproar in the camp. Dorothy came out of her hut to discover what was the matter, and saw a firelit ring of people towards which everyone was running. She ran after them, and a horrid chill went through her, because it seemed to her that she knew already what it was that had happened. She managed to wriggle her way to the front of the crowd, and saw the very thing that she had been fearing.

There stood Nobby, in the grip of an enormous policeman, and another policeman was holding two frightened youths by the arms. One of them, a wretched child hardly sixteen years old, was crying bitterly. Mr Cairns, a stiff-built man with grey whiskers, and two farm hands, were keeping guard over the stolen property that had been dug out of the straw of Nobby's hut. Exhibit A, a pile of apples; Exhibit B, some blood-stained chicken feathers. Nobby caught sight of Dorothy among the crowd, grinned at her with a flash of large teeth, and winked. There was a confused din of shouting:

'Look at the pore little b— crying! Let 'im go! Bloody shame, pore little kid like that! Serve the young bastard right, getting us all into trouble! Let 'im go! Always got to put the blame on us bloody hop-pickers! Can't lose a bloody apple without it's us that's took it. Let 'im go! Shut up, can't you? S'pose they was *your* bloody apples? Wouldn't *you* bloodiwell—' etc., etc., etc. And then: 'Stand back mate! 'Ere comes the kid's mother.'

A huge Toby jug of a woman, with monstrous breasts and her hair coming down her back, forced her way through the ring of people and began roaring first at the policeman and Mr Cairns, then at Nobby, who had led her son astray. Finally the farm hands managed to drag her away. Through the woman's yells Dorothy could hear Mr Cairns gruffly interrogating Nobby:

'Now then, young man, just you own up and tell us who you shared them apples with! We're going to put a stop to this thieving game, once and for all. You own up, and I dessay we'll take it into consideration.'

Nobby answered, as blithely as ever, 'Consideration, your a—!'

'Don't you get giving me any of your lip, young man! Or else you'll catch it all the hotter when you go up before the magistrate.'

'Catch it hotter, your a—!'

Nobby grinned. His own wit filled him with delight. He caught Dorothy's eye and winked at her once again before being led away. And that was the last she ever saw of him.

There was further shouting, and when the prisoners were removed a few dozen men followed them, booing at the policemen and Mr Cairns, but nobody dared to interfere. Dorothy meanwhile had crept away; she did not even stop to find out whether there would be an opportunity of saying good-bye to Nobby—she was too frightened, too anxious to escape. Her knees were trembling uncontrollably. When she got back to the hut, the other women were sitting up, talking excitedly about Nobby's arrest. She burrowed deep into the straw and hid herself, to be out of the sound of their voices. They continued talking half the night, and of course, because Dorothy had supposedly been Nobby's 'tart', they kept condoling with her and plying her with questions. She did not answer them—pretended to be asleep. But there would be, she knew well enough, no sleep for her that night.

The whole thing had frightened and upset her—but it had frightened her more than was reasonable or understandable. For she was in no kind of danger. The farm hands did not know that she had shared the stolen apples—for that matter, nearly everyone in the camp had shared them—and Nobby would never betray her. It was not even that she was greatly concerned for Nobby, who was frankly not troubled by the prospect of a month in jail. It was something that was happening inside her—some change that was taking place in the atmosphere of her mind.

It seemed to her that she was no longer the same person that she had been an hour ago. Within her and without, everything was changed. It was as though a bubble in her brain had burst, setting free thoughts, feelings, fears of which she had forgotten the existence. All the dreamlike apathy of the past three weeks was shattered. For it was precisely as in a dream that she had been living—it is the especial condition of a dream that one accepts everything, questions nothing. Dirt, rags, vagabondage, begging, stealing—all had seemed natural to her. Even the loss of her memory had seemed natural; at least, she had hardly given it a thought till this moment. The question '*Who am I?*' had faded out of her mind till sometimes she had forgotten it for hours together. It was only now that it returned with any real urgency.

For nearly the whole of a miserable night that question went to and fro in her brain. But it was not so much the question itself that troubled her as the knowledge that it was about to be answered. Her memory was coming back to her, that was certain, and some ugly shock was coming with it. She actually feared the moment when she should discover her own identity. Something that she did not want to face was waiting just below the surface of her consciousness.

At half past five she got up and groped for her shoes as usual. She went outside, got the fire going, and stuck the can of water among the hot embers to boil. Just as she did so a memory, seeming irrelevant, flashed across her mind. It was of that halt on the village green at Wale, a fortnight ago—the time when they had met the old Irishwoman, Mrs McElligot. Very vividly she remembered the scene. Herself lying exhausted on the grass, with her arm over her face; and Nobby and Mrs McElligot talking across her supine body; and Charlie, with succulent relish, reading out the poster, 'Secret Love Life of Rector's Daughter'; and herself, mystified but not deeply interested, sitting up and asking, 'What is a Rector?'

At that a deadly chill, like a hand of ice, fastened about her heart. She got up and hurried, almost ran back to the hut, then burrowed down to the place where her sacks lay and felt in the straw beneath them. In that vast mound of straw all your loose possessions got lost and gradually worked their way to the bottom. But after searching for some minutes, and getting herself well cursed by several women who were still half asleep, Dorothy found what she was looking for. It was the copy of *Pippin's Weekly* which Nobby had given her a week ago. She took it outside, knelt down, and spread it out in the light of the fire.

It was on the front page—a photograph, and three big headlines. Yes! There it was!

PASSION DRAMA IN COUNTRY RECTORY
—
PARSON'S DAUGHTER AND ELDERLY SEDUCER
—
WHITE-HAIRED FATHER PROSTRATE WITH GRIEF
(*Pippin's Weekly Special*)

'I would sooner have seen her in her grave!' was the heartbroken cry of the Rev. Charles Hare, Rector of Knype Hill, Suffolk, on learning of his twenty-eight-year-old daughter's elopement with an elderly bachelor named Warburton, described as an artist.

Miss Hare, who left the town on the night of the twenty-first of August, is still missing, and all attempts to trace her have failed. [In leaded type] Rumour, as yet unconfirmed, states that she was recently seen with a male companion in a hotel of evil repute in Vienna.

—

Readers of *Pippin's Weekly* will recall that the elopement took place in dramatic circumstances. A little before midnight on the twenty-first of August, Mrs Evelina Semprill, a widowed lady who inhabits the house next door to Mr Warburton's, happened by chance to look out of her bedroom window and saw Mr Warburton standing at his front gate in conversation with a young woman. As it was a clear moonlight night, Mrs Semprill was able to distinguish this young woman as Miss Hare, the Rector's daughter. The pair remained at the gate for several minutes, and before going indoors they exchanged embraces which Mrs Semprill describes as being of a passionate nature. About half an hour later they reappeared in Mr Warburton's car, which was backed out of the front gate, and drove off in the direction of the Ipswich road. Miss Hare was dressed in scanty attire, and appeared to be under the influence of alcohol.

It is now learned that for some time past Miss Hare had been in the habit of making clandestine visits to Mr Warburton's house. Mrs Semprill, who could only with great difficulty be persuaded to speak upon so painful a subject, has further revealed—

Dorothy crumpled *Pippin's Weekly* violently between her hands and thrust it into the fire, upsetting the can of water. There was a cloud of ashes and sulphurous smoke, and almost in the same instant Dorothy pulled the paper out of the fire unburnt. No use funking it—better to learn the worst. She read on, with a horrible fascination. It was not a nice kind of story to read about yourself. For it was strange, but she had no longer any shadow of doubt that this girl of whom she was reading was herself. She examined the photograph. It was a blurred, nebulous thing, but quite unmistakable. Besides, she had no need of the photograph to remind her. She could remember everything—every circumstance of her life, up to that evening when she had come home tired out from Mr Warburton's house, and, presumably, fallen asleep in the conservatory. It was all so clear in her mind that it was almost incredible that she had ever forgotten it.

She ate no breakfast that day, and did not think to prepare anything for the midday meal; but when the time came, from force of habit, she set out for the hopfields with the other pickers. With difficulty, being alone, she dragged the heavy bin into position, pulled the next bine down and began picking. But after a few minutes she found that it was quite impossible; even the mechanical labour of picking was beyond her. That horrible, lying story in *Pippin's Weekly* had so unstrung her that it was impossible even for an instant to focus her mind upon anything else. Its lickerish phrases were going over and over in her head. 'Embraces of a passionate nature'—'in scanty attire'—'under the influence of alcohol'—as each one came back into her memory it brought with it such a pang that she wanted to cry out as though in physical pain.

After a while she stopped even pretending to pick, let the bine fall across her bin, and sat down against one of the posts that supported the wires. The other pickers observed her plight, and were sympathetic. Ellen was a bit cut up, they said. What else could you expect, after her bloke had been knocked off? (Everyone in the camp, of course, had taken it for granted that Nobby was Dorothy's lover.) They advised her to go down to the farm and report sick.

And towards twelve o'clock, when the measurer was due, everyone in the set came across with a hatful of hops and dropped it into her bin.

When the measurer arrived he found Dorothy still sitting on the ground. Beneath her dirt and sunburn she was very pale; her face looked haggard, and much older than before. Her bin was twenty yards behind the rest of the set, and there were less than three bushels of hops in it.

'What's the game?' he demanded. 'You ill?'

'No.'

'Well, why ain't you bin pickin', then? What you think this is—toff's picnic? You don't come up 'ere to sit about on the ground, you know.'

'You cheese it and don't get nagging of 'er!' shouted the old cockney costerwoman suddenly. 'Can't the pore girl 'ave a bit of rest and peace if she wants it? Ain't 'er bloke in the clink thanks to you and your bloody nosing pals of coppers? She's got enough to worry 'er 'thout being — about by every bloody copper's nark in Kent!'

'That'll be enough from you, Ma!' said the measurer gruffly, but he looked more sympathetic on hearing that it was Dorothy's lover who had been arrested on the previous night. When the costerwoman had got her kettle boiling she called Dorothy to her bin and gave her a cup of strong tea and a hunk of bread and cheese; and after the dinner interval another picker who had no partner was sent up to share Dorothy's bin. He was a small, weazened old tramp named Deafie. Dorothy felt somewhat better after the tea. Encouraged by Deafie's example—for he was an excellent picker—she managed to do her fair share of work during the afternoon.

She had thought things over, and was less distracted than before. The phrases in *Pippin's Weekly* still made her wince with shame, but she was equal now to facing the situation. She understood well enough what had happened to her, and what had led to Mrs Semprill's libel. Mrs Semprill had seen them together at the gate and had seen Mr Warburton kissing her; and after that, when they were both missing from Knype Hill, it was only too natural—natural for Mrs Semprill, that is—to infer that they had eloped together. As for the picturesque details, she had invented them later. Or *had* she invented them? That was the one thing you could never be certain of with Mrs Semprill—whether she told her lies consciously and deliberately *as* lies, or whether, in her strange and disgusting mind, she somehow succeeded in believing them.

Well, anyway, the harm was done—no use worrying about it any longer. Meanwhile, there was the question of getting back to Knype Hill. She would have to send for some clothes, and she would need two pounds for her train fare home. Home! The word sent a pang through her heart. Home, after weeks of dirt and hunger! How she longed for it, now that she remembered it!

But—!

A chilly little doubt raised its head. There was one aspect of the matter that she had not thought of till this moment. *Could* she, after all, go home? Dared she?

Could she face Knype Hill after everything that had happened? That was the question. When you have figured on the front page of *Pippin's Weekly*—'in scanty attire'—'under the influence of alcohol'—ah, don't let's think of it again! But when you have been plastered all over with horrible, dishonouring libels, can you go back to a town of two thousand inhabitants where everybody knows everybody else's private history and talks about it all day long?

She did not know—could not decide. At one moment it seemed to her that the story of her elopement was so palpably absurd that no one could possibly have believed it. Mr Warburton, for instance, could contradict it—most certainly would contradict it, for every possible reason. But the next moment she remembered that Mr Warburton had gone abroad, and unless this affair had got into the continental newspapers, he might not even have heard of it; and then she quailed again. She knew what it means to have to live down a scandal in a small country town. The glances and furtive nudges when you passed! The prying eyes following you down the street from behind curtained windows! The knots of youths on the corners round Blifil-Gordon's factory, lewdly discussing you!

'George! Say, George! J'a see that bit of stuff over there? With fair 'air?'

'What, the skinny one? Yes. 'Oo's she?'

'Rector's daughter, she is. Miss 'Are. But, say! What you think she done two years ago? Done a bunk with a bloke old enough to bin 'er father. Regular properly went on the razzle with 'im in Paris! Never think it to look at 'er, would you?'

'*Go* on!'

'She did! Straight, she did. It was in the papers and all. Only 'e give 'er the chuck three weeks afterwards, and she come back 'ome again as bold as brass. Nerve, eh?'

Yes, it would take some living down. For years, for a decade it might be, they would be talking about her like that. And the worst of it was that the story in *Pippin's Weekly* was probably a mere bowdlerized vestige of what Mrs Semprill had been saying in the town. Naturally, *Pippin's Weekly* had not wanted to commit itself too far. But was there anything that would ever restrain Mrs Semprill? Only the limits of her imagination—and they were almost as wide as the sky.

One thing, however, reassured Dorothy, and that was the thought that her father, at any rate, would do his best to shield her. Of course, there would be others as well. It was not as though she were friendless. The church congregation, at least, knew her and trusted her, and the Mothers' Union and the Girl Guides and the women on her visiting list would never believe such stories about her. But it was her father who mattered most. Almost any situation is bearable if you have a home to go back to and a family who will stand by you. With courage, and her father's support, she might face things out. By the evening she had decided that it would be perfectly all right to go back to Knype Hill, though no doubt it would be disagreeable at first, and when work was over for the day she 'subbed' a shilling, and went down to the general shop in the village and bought a penny packet of notepaper. Back in the camp, sitting on the grass by the fire—no tables or chairs in the camp, of course—she began to write with a stump of pencil:

Dearest Father,—I can't tell you how glad I am, after everything that has happened, to be able to write to you again. And I do hope you have not been too anxious about me or too worried by those horrible stories in the newspapers. I don't know what you must have thought when I suddenly disappeared like that and you didn't hear from me for nearly a month. But you see—'

How strange the pencil felt in her torn and stiffened fingers! She could only write a large, sprawling hand like that of a child. But she wrote a long letter, explaining everything, and asking him to send her some clothes and two pounds for her fare home. Also, she asked him to write to her under an assumed name she gave him—Ellen Millborough, after Millborough in Suffolk. It seemed a queer thing to have to do, to use a false name; dishonest—criminal, almost. But she dared not risk its being known in the village, and perhaps in the camp as well, that she was Dorothy Hare, the notorious 'Rector's Daughter'.

# 6

Once her mind was made up, Dorothy was pining to escape from the hop camp. On the following day she could hardly bring herself to go on with the stupid work of picking, and the discomforts and bad food were intolerable now that she had memories to compare them with. She would have taken to flight immediately if only she had had enough money to get her home. The instant her father's letter with the two pounds arrived, she would say good-bye to the Turles and take the train for home, and breathe a sigh of relief to get there, in spite of the ugly scandals that had got to be faced.

On the third day after writing she went down the village post office and asked for her letter. The postmistress, a woman with the face of a dachshund and a bitter contempt for all hop-pickers, told her frostily that no letter had come. Dorothy was disappointed. A pity—it must have been held up in the post. However, it didn't matter; tomorrow would be soon enough—only another day to wait.

The next evening she went again, quite certain that it would have arrived this time. Still no letter. This time a misgiving assailed her; and on the fifth evening, when there was yet again no letter, the misgiving changed into a horrible panic. She bought another packet of notepaper and wrote an enormous letter, using up the whole four sheets, explaining over and over again what had happened and imploring her father not to leave her in such suspense. Having posted it, she made up her mind that she would let a whole week go by before calling at the post office again.

This was Saturday. By Wednesday her resolve had broken down. When the hooter sounded for the midday interval she left her bin and hurried down to the post office—it was a mile and a half away, and it meant missing her dinner. Having got there she went shame-facedly up to the counter, almost afraid to speak. The dog-faced postmistress was sitting in her brass-barred cage at the end of the counter, ticking figures in a long shaped account book. She gave Dorothy a brief nosy glance and went on with her work, taking no notice of her.

Something painful was happening in Dorothy's diaphragm. She was finding it difficult to breathe, 'Are there any letters for me?' she managed to say at last.

'Name?' said the postmistress, ticking away.

'Ellen Millborough.'

The postmistress turned her long dachshund nose over her shoulder for an instant and glanced at the M partition of the Poste Restante letter-box.

'No,' she said, turning back to her account book.

In some manner Dorothy got herself outside and began to walk back towards the hopfields, then halted. A deadly feeling of emptiness at the pit of her stomach, caused partly by hunger, made her too weak to walk.

Her father's silence could mean only one thing. He believed Mrs Semprill's story—believed that she, Dorothy, had run away from home in disgraceful circumstances and then told lies to excuse herself. He was too angry and too disgusted to write to her. All he wanted was to get rid of her, drop all communication with her; get her out of sight and out of mind, as a mere scandal to be covered up and forgotten.

She could not go home after this. She dared not. Now that she had seen what her father's attitude was, it had opened her eyes to the rashness of the thing she had been contemplating. Of *course* she could not go home! To slink back in disgrace, to bring shame on her father's house by coming there—ah, impossible, utterly impossible! How could she even have thought of it?

What then? There was nothing for it but to go right away—right away to some place that was big enough to hide in. London, perhaps. Somewhere where nobody knew her and the mere sight of her face or mention of her name would not drag into the light a string of dirty memories.

As she stood there the sound of bells floated towards her, from the village church round the bend of the road, where the ringers were amusing themselves by ringing 'Abide with Me', as one picks out a tune with one finger on the piano. But presently 'Abide with Me' gave way to the familiar Sunday-morning jangle. 'Oh do leave my wife alone! She is so drunk she can't get home!'—the same peal that the bells of St Athelstan's had been used to ring three years ago before they were unswung. The sound planted a spear of homesickness in Dorothy's heart, bringing back to her with momentary vividness a medley of remembered things—the smell of the glue-pot in the conservatory when she was making costumes for the school play, and the chatter of starlings outside her bedroom window, interrupting her prayers before Holy Communion, and Mrs Pither's doleful voice chronicling the pains in the backs of her legs, and the worries of the collapsing belfry and the shop-debts and the bindweed in the peas—all the multitudinous, urgent details of a life that had alternated between work and prayer.

Prayer! For a very short time, a minute perhaps, the thought arrested her. Prayer—in those days it had been the very source and centre of her life. In trouble or in happiness, it was to prayer that she had turned. And she realized—the first time that it had crossed her mind—that she had not uttered a prayer since leaving home, not even since her memory had come back to her. Moreover, she was aware that she had no longer the smallest impulse to pray. Mechanically, she began a whispered prayer, and stopped almost instantly; the words were empty and futile. Prayer, which had been the mainstay of her life, had no meaning for her any longer. She recorded this fact as she walked slowly up the road, and she recorded it briefly, almost casually, as though it had been something seen in passing—a flower in the ditch or a bird crossing the road—something noticed and then dismissed. She had not even the time to reflect upon what it might mean. It was shouldered out of her mind by more momentous things.

It was of the future that she had got to be thinking now. She was already fairly clear in her mind as to what she must do. When the hop-picking was at an end she must go up to London, write to her father for money and her clothes—for however angry he might be, she could not believe that he intended to leave her utterly in the lurch—and then start looking for a job. It was the measure of her ignorance that those dreaded words 'looking for a job' sounded hardly at all dreadful in her ears. She knew herself strong and willing—knew that there were plenty of jobs that she was capable of doing. She could be a nursery governess, for instance—no, better, a housemaid or a parlourmaid. There were not many things in a house that she could not do better than most servants; besides, the more menial her job, the easier it would be to keep her past history secret.

At any rate, her father's house was closed to her, that was certain. From now on she had got to fend for herself. On this decision, with only a very dim idea of what it meant, she quickened her pace and got back to the fields in time for the afternoon shift.

The hop-picking season had not much longer to run. In a week or thereabouts Cairns's would be closing down, and the cockneys would take the hoppers' train to London, and the gypsies would catch their horses, pack their caravans, and march northward to Lincolnshire, to scramble for jobs in the potato fields. As for the cockneys, they had had their bellyful of hop-picking by this time. They were pining to be back in dear old London, with Woolworths and the fried-fish shop round the corner, and no more sleeping in straw and frying bacon in tin lids with your eyes weeping from wood smoke. Hopping was a holiday, but the kind of holiday that you were glad to see the last of. You came down cheering, but you went home cheering louder still and swearing that you would never go hopping again—until next August, when you had forgotten the cold nights and the bad pay and the damage to your hands, and remembered only the blowsy afternoons in the sun and the boozing of stone pots of beer round the red camp fires at night.

The mornings were growing bleak and Novemberish; grey skies, the first leaves falling, and finches and starlings already flocking for the winter.

Dorothy had written yet again to her father, asking for money and some clothes; he had left her letter unanswered, nor had anybody else written to her. Indeed, there was no one except her father who knew her present address; but somehow she had hoped that Mr Warburton might write. Her courage almost failed her now, especially at nights in the wretched straw, when she lay awake thinking of the vague and menacing future. She picked her hops with a sort of desperation, a sort of frenzy of energy, more aware each day that every handful of hops meant another fraction of a farthing between herself and starvation. Deafie, her bin-mate, like herself, was picking against time, for it was the last money he would earn till next year's hopping season came round. The figure they aimed at was five shillings a day—thirty bushels—between the two of them, but there was no day when they quite attained it.

Deafie was a queer old man and a poor companion after Nobby, but not a bad sort. He was a ship's steward by profession, but a tramp of many years' standing, as deaf as a post and therefore something of a Mr F.'s aunt in conversation. He was also an exhibitionist, but quite harmless. For hours together he used to sing a little song that went 'With my willy willy—*with* my willy willy', and though he could not hear what he was singing it seemed to cause him some kind of pleasure. He had the hairiest ears Dorothy had ever seen. There were tufts like miniature Dundreary whiskers growing out of each of his ears. Every year Deafie came hop-picking at Cairns's farm, saved up a pound, and then spent a paradisiac week in a lodging-house in Newington Butts before going back to the road. This was the only week in the year when he slept in what could be called, except by courtesy, a bed.

The picking came to an end on 28 September. There were several fields still unpicked, but they were poor hops and at the last moment Mr Cairns decided to 'let them blow'. Set number 19 finished their last field at two in the afternoon, and the little gypsy foreman swarmed up the poles and retrieved the derelict bunches, and the measurer carted the last hops away. As he disappeared there was a sudden shout of 'Put 'em in the bins!' and Dorothy saw six men bearing down upon her with a fiendish expression on their faces, and all the women in the set scattering and running. Before she could collect her wits to escape the men had seized her, laid her at full length in a bin and swung her violently from side to side. Then she was dragged out and kissed by a young gypsy smelling of onions. She struggled at first, but she saw the same thing being done to the other women in the set, so she submitted. It appeared that putting the women in the bins was an invariable custom on the last day of picking. There were great doings in the camp that night, and not much sleep for anybody. Long after midnight Dorothy found herself moving with a ring of people about a mighty fire, one hand clasped by a rosy butcher-boy and the other by a very drunk old woman in a Scotch bonnet out of a cracker, to the tune of 'Auld Lang Syne'.

In the morning they went up to the farm to draw their money, and Dorothy drew one pound and fourpence, and earned another fivepence by adding up their tally books for people who could not read or write. The cockney pickers paid you a penny for this job; the gypsies paid you only in flattery. Then

Dorothy set out for West Ackworth station, four miles away, together with the Turles, Mr Turle carrying the tin trunk, Mrs Turle carrying the baby, the other children carrying various odds and ends, and Dorothy wheeling the perambulator which held the Turles' entire stock of crockery, and which had two circular wheels and two elliptical.

They got to the station about midday, the hoppers' train was due to start at one, and it arrived at two and started at a quarter past three. After a journey of incredible slowness, zigzagging all over Kent to pick up a dozen hop-pickers here and half a dozen there, going back on its tracks over and over again and backing into sidings to let other trains pass—taking, in fact, six hours to do thirty-five miles—it landed them in London a little after nine at night.

# 7

Dorothy slept that night with the Turles. They had grown so fond of her that they would have given her shelter for a week or a fortnight if she had been willing to impose on their hospitality. Their two rooms (they lived in a tenement house not far from Tower Bridge Road) were a tight fit for seven people including children, but they made her a bed of sorts on the floor out of two rag mats, an old cushion and an overcoat.

In the morning she said good-bye to the Turles and thanked them for all their kindness towards her, and then went straight to Bermondsey public baths and washed off the accumulated dirt of five weeks. After that she set out to look for a lodging, having in her possession sixteen and eightpence in cash, and the clothes she stood up in. She had darned and cleaned her clothes as best she could, and being black they did not show the dirt quite as badly as they might have done. From the knees down she was now passably respectable. On the last day of picking a 'home picker' in the next set, named Mrs Killfrew, had presented her with a good pair of shoes that had been her daughter's, and a pair of woollen stockings.

It was not until the evening that Dorothy managed to find herself a room. For something like ten hours she was wandering up and down, from Bermondsey into Southwark, from Southwark into Lambeth, through labyrinthine streets where snotty-nosed children played at hop-scotch on pavements horrible with banana skins and decaying cabbage leaves. At every house she tried it was the same story—the landlady refused point-blank to take her in. One after another a succession of hostile women, standing in their doorways as defensively as though she had been a motor bandit or a government inspector, looked her up and down, said briefly, 'We don't *take* single girls,' and shut the door in her face. She did not know it, of course, but the very look of her was enough to rouse any respectable landlady's suspicions.

Her stained and ragged clothes they might possibly have put up with; but the fact that she had no luggage damned her from the start. A single girl with no luggage is invariably a bad lot—this is the first and greatest of the apophthegms of the London landlady.

At about seven o'clock, too tired to stand on her feet any longer, she ventured into a filthy, flyblown little café near the Old Vic theatre and asked for a cup of tea. The proprietress, getting into conversation with her and learning that she wanted a room, advised her to 'try at Mary's, in Wellings Court, jest orff the Cut'. 'Mary', it appeared, was not particular and would let a room to anybody who could pay. Her proper name was Mrs Sawyer, but the boys all called her Mary.

Dorothy found Wellings Court with some difficulty. You went along Lambeth Cut till you got to a Jew clothes-shop called Knockout Trousers Ltd, then you turned up a narrow alley, and then turned to your left again up another alley so narrow that its grimy plaster walls almost brushed you as you went. In the plaster, persevering boys had cut the word — innumerable times and too deeply to be erased. At the far end of the alley you found yourself in a small court where four tall narrow houses with iron staircases stood facing one another.

Dorothy made inquiries and found 'Mary' in a subterranean den beneath one of the houses. She was a drabby old creature with remarkably thin hair and face so emaciated that it looked like a rouged and powdered skull. Her voice was cracked, shrewish, and nevertheless ineffably dreary. She asked Dorothy no questions, and indeed scarcely even looked at her, but simply demanded ten shillings and then said in her ugly voice:

'Twenty-nine. Third floor. Go up be the back stairs.'

Apparently the back stairs were those inside the house. Dorothy went up the dark, spiral staircase, between sweating walls, in a smell of old overcoats, dishwater and slops. As she reached the second floor there was a loud squeal of laughter, and two rowdy-looking girls came out of one of the rooms and stared at her for a moment. They looked young, their faces being quite hidden under rouge and pink powder, and their lips painted scarlet as geranium petals. But amid the pink powder their china-blue eyes were tired and old; and that was somehow horrible, because it reminded you of a girl's mask with an old woman's face behind it. The taller of the two greeted Dorothy.

''Ullo, dearie!'

'Hullo!'

'You new 'ere? Which room you kipping in?'

'Number twenty-nine.'

'God, ain't that a bloody dungeon to put you in! You going out tonight?'

'No, I don't think so,' said Dorothy, privately a little astonished at the question. 'I'm too tired.'

'Thought you wasn't, when I saw you 'adn't dolled up. But, say! dearie, you ain't on the beach, are you? Not spoiling the ship for a 'aporth of tar? Because f'rinstance if you want the lend of a lipstick, you only got to say the word. We're all chums 'ere, you know.'

'Oh. . . . No, thank you,' said Dorothy, taken aback.

'Oh, well! Time Doris and me was moving. Got a 'portant business engagement in Leicester Square.' Here she nudged the other girl with her hip, and both of them sniggered in a silly mirthless manner. 'But, say!' added the taller girl confidentially, 'ain't it a bloody treat to 'ave a good night's kip all alone once in a way? Wish *I* could. All on your Jack Jones with no bloody great man's feet shoving you about. 'S all right when you can afford it, eh?'

'Yes,' said Dorothy, feeling that this answer was expected of her, and with only a very vague notion of what the other was talking about.

'Well, ta ta, dearie! Sleep tight. And jes' look out for the smash and grab raiders 'bout 'ar-parse one!'

When the two girls had skipped downstairs with another of their meaningless squeals of laughter, Dorothy found her way to room number 29 and opened the door. A cold, evil smell met her. The room measured about eight feet each way, and was very dark. The furniture was simple. In the middle of the room, a narrow iron bedstead with a ragged coverlet and greyish sheets; against the wall, a packing case with a tin basin and an empty whisky bottle intended for water; tacked over the bed, a photograph of Bebe Daniels torn out of *Film Fun*.

The sheets were not only dirty, but damp. Dorothy got into the bed, but she had only undressed to her chemise, or what was left of her chemise, her underclothes by this time being almost entirely in ruins; she could not bring herself to lay her bare body between those nauseous sheets. And once in bed, though she was aching from head to foot with fatigue, she could not sleep. She was unnerved and full of forebodings. The atmosphere of this vile place brought home to her more vividly than before the fact that she was helpless and friendless and had only six shillings between herself and the streets. Moreover, as the night wore on the house grew noisier and noisier. The walls were so thin that you could hear everything that was happening. There were bursts of shrill idiotic laughter, hoarse male voices singing, a gramophone drawling out limericks, noisy kisses, strange deathlike groans, and once or twice the violent rattling of an iron bed. Towards midnight the noises began to form themselves into a rhythm in Dorothy's brain, and she fell lightly and unrestfully asleep. She was woken about a minute later, as it seemed, by her door being flung open, and two dimly seen female shapes rushed in, tore every scrap of clothing from her bed except the sheets, and rushed out again. There was a chronic shortage of blankets at 'Mary's', and the only way of getting enough of them was to rob somebody else's bed. Hence the term 'smash and grab raiders'.

In the morning, half an hour before opening time, Dorothy went to the nearest public library to look at the advertisements in the newspapers. Already a score of vaguely mangy-looking people were prowling up and down, and the number swelled by ones and twos till there were no less than sixty. Presently the doors of the library opened, and in they all surged, racing for a board at the other end of the reading-room where the 'Situations Vacant' columns from various newspapers had been cut out and pinned up. And in the wake of the job-hunters came poor old bundles of rags, men and women both, who had spent the night in the streets and came to the library to sleep. They came shambling in behind the others, flopped down with grunts of relief at the nearest table, and pulled the nearest periodical towards them; it might be the *Free Church Messenger,* it might be the *Vegetarian Sentinel*–it didn't matter what it was, but you couldn't stay in the library unless you pretended to be reading. They opened their papers, and in the same instant fell asleep, with their chins on their breasts. And the attendant walked round prodding them in turn like a stoker poking a succession of fires, and they grunted and woke up as he prodded them, and then fell asleep again the instant he had passed.

Meanwhile a battle was raging round the advertisement board, everybody struggling to get to the front. Two young men in blue overalls came running up behind the others, and one of them put his head down and fought his way through the crowd as though it had been a football scrum. In a moment he was at the board. He turned to his companion: "'Ere we are, Joe–I got it! "Mechanics wanted–Locke's Garage, Camden Town." C'm on out of it!' He fought his way out again, and both of them scooted for the door. They were going to Camden Town as fast as their legs would carry them. And at this moment, in every public library in London, mechanics out of work were reading that identical notice and starting on the race for the job, which in all probability had already been given to someone who could afford to buy a paper for himself and had seen the notice at six in the morning.

Dorothy managed to get to the board at last, and made a note of some of the addresses where 'cook generals' were wanted. There were plenty to choose from–indeed, half the ladies in London seemed to be crying out for strong capable general servants. With a list of twenty addresses in her pocket, and having had a breakfast of bread and margarine and tea which cost her threepence, Dorothy set out to look for a job, not unhopefully.

She was too ignorant as yet to know that her chances of finding work unaided were practically nil; but the next four days gradually enlightened her. During those four days she applied for eighteen jobs, and sent written applications for four others. She trudged enormous distances all through the southern suburbs: Clapham, Brixton, Dulwich, Penge, Sydenham, Beckenham, Norwood–even as far as Croydon on one occasion. She was haled into neat suburban drawing-rooms and interviewed by women of every conceivable type–large, chubby, bullying women, thin, acid, catty women, alert frigid women in gold *pince-nez,* vague rambling women who looked as though they practised vegetarianism or attended spiritualist séances. And one and all, fat or thin, chilly or motherly, they reacted to her in precisely the same way. They simply looked her over, heard her speak, stared inquisitively, asked her a dozen embarrassing and impertinent questions, and then turned her down.

Any experienced person could have told her how it would be. In her circumstances it was not to be expected that anyone would take the risk of employing her. Her ragged clothes and her lack of references were against her, and her educated accent, which she did not know how to disguise, wrecked whatever chances she might have had. The tramps and côckney hop-pickers had not noticed her accent, but the suburban housewives noticed it quickly enough, and it scared them in just the same way as the fact that she had no luggage had scared the landladies. The moment they had heard her speak, and spotted her for a gentlewoman, the game was up. She grew quite used to the startled, mystified look that came over their faces as soon as she opened her mouth—the prying, feminine glance from her face to her damaged hands, and from those to the darns in her skirt. Some of the women asked her outright what a girl of her class was doing seeking work as a servant. They sniffed, no doubt, that she had 'been in trouble'—that is, had an illegitimate baby—and after probing her with their questions they got rid of her as quickly as possible.

As soon as she had an address to give Dorothy had written to her father, and when on the third day no answer came, she wrote again, despairingly this time—it was her fifth letter, and four had gone unanswered—telling him that she must starve if he did not send her money at once. There was just time for her to get an answer before her week at 'Mary's' was up and she was thrown out for not paying her rent.

Meanwhile, she continued the useless search for work, while her money dwindled at the rate of a shilling a day—a sum just sufficient to keep her alive while leaving her chronically hungry. She had almost given up the hope that her father would do anything to help her. And strangely enough her first panic had died down, as she grew hungrier and the chances of getting a job grew remoter, into a species of miserable apathy. She suffered, but she was not greatly afraid. The sub-world into which she was descending seemed less terrible now that it was nearer.

The autumn weather, though fine, was growing colder. Each day the sun, fighting his losing battle against the winter, struggled a little later through the mist to dye the house-fronts with pale aquarelle colours. Dorothy was in the streets all day, or in the public library, only going back to 'Mary's' to sleep, and then taking the precaution of dragging her bed across the door. She had grasped by this time that 'Mary's' was—not actually a brothel, for there is hardly such a thing in London, but a well-known refuge of prostitutes. It was for that reason that you paid ten shillings a week for a kennel not worth five. Old 'Mary' (she was not the proprietress of the house, merely the manageress) had been a prostitute herself in her day, and looked it. Living in such a place damned you even in the eyes of Lambeth Cut. Women sniffed when you passed them, men took an offensive interest in you. The Jew on the corner, the owner of Knockout Trousers Ltd, was the worst of all. He was a solid young man of about thirty, with bulging red cheeks and curly black hair like astrakhan. For twelve hours a day he stood on the pavement roaring with brazen lungs that you couldn't get a cheaper pair of trousers in London, and obstructing the passers-by. You had only to halt for a fraction of a second, and he seized you by the arm and bundled you inside the shop by main force. Once he got you there his manner became positively threatening. If you said anything disparaging about his trousers he offered to fight, and weak-minded people bought pairs of trousers in sheer physical terror. But busy though he was, he kept a sharp eye open for the 'birds', as he called them; and Dorothy appeared to fascinate him beyond all other 'birds'. He had grasped that she was not a prostitute, but living at 'Mary's', she must—so he reasoned—be on the very verge of becoming one. The thought made his mouth water. When he saw her coming down the alley he would post himself at the corner, with his massive chest well displayed and one black lecherous eye turned inquiringly upon her ('Are you ready to begin yet?' his eye seemed to be saying), and, as she passed, give her a discreet pinch on the backside.

On the last morning of her week at 'Mary's', Dorothy went downstairs and looked, with only a faint flicker of hope, at the slate in the hallway where the names of people for whom there were letters were chalked up. There was no letter for 'Ellen Millborough'. That settled it; there was nothing left to do except to walk out into the street. It did not occur to her to do as every other woman in the house would have done—that is, pitch a hard-up tale and try to cadge another night's lodging rent free. She simply walked out of the house, and had not even the nerve to tell 'Mary' that she was going.

She had no plan, absolutely no plan whatever. Except for half an hour at noon when she went out to spend threepence out of her last fourpence on bread and margarine and tea, she passed the entire day in the public library, reading weekly papers. In the morning she read the *Barber's Record,* and in the afternoon *Cage Birds.* They were the only papers she could get hold of, for there were always so many idlers in the library that you had to scramble to get hold of a paper at all. She read them from cover to cover, even the advertisements. She pored for hours together over such technicalities as How to strop French Razors, Why the Electric Hairbrush is Unhygienic, Do Budgies thrive on Rapeseed? It was the only occupation that she felt equal to. She was in a strange lethargic state in which it was easier to interest herself in How to strop French Razors than in her own desperate plight. All fear had left her. Of the future she was utterly unable to think; even so far ahead as tonight she could barely see. There was a night in the streets ahead of her, that was all she knew, and even about that she only vaguely cared. Meanwhile there were *Cage Birds* and the *Barber's Record*; and they were, strangely, absorbingly interesting.

At nine o'clock the attendant came round with a long hooked pole and turned out the gaslights, the library was closed. Dorothy turned to the left, up the Waterloo Road, towards the river. On the iron footbridge she halted for a moment. The night wind was blowing. Deep banks of mist, like dunes, were rising from the river, and, as the wind caught them, swirling north-eastward across the town. A swirl of mist enveloped Dorothy, penetrating her thin clothes and making her shudder with a sudden foretaste of the night's cold. She walked on and arrived, by the process of gravitation that draws all roofless people to the same spot, at Trafalgar Square.

# CHAPTER 3

## I

[SCENE: *Trafalgar Square. Dimly visible through the mist, a dozen people, Dorothy among them, are grouped about one of the benches near the north parapet.*]

CHARLIE [*singing*]: 'Ail Mary, 'ail Mary, 'a-il Ma-ary — [*Big Ben strikes ten.*]

SNOUTER [*mimicking the noise*]: Ding dong, ding dong! Shut your — noise, can't you? Seven more hours of it on this — square before we get the chance of a setdown and a bit of sleep! Cripes!

MR TALLBOYS [*to himself*]: *Non sum qualis eram boni sub regno Edwardi!* In the days of my innocence, before the Devil carried me up into a high place and dropped me into the Sunday newspapers–that is to say when I was Rector of Little Fawley-cum-Dewsbury. . . .

DEAFIE [*singing*]: With my willy willy, *with* my willy willy—

MRS WAYNE: Ah, dearie, as soon as I set eyes on you I knew as you was a lady born and bred. You and me've known what it is to come down in the world, haven't we, dearie? It ain't the same for us as what it is for some of these others here.

CHARLIE [*singing*]: 'Ail Mary, 'ail Mary, 'a-il Ma-ary, full of grace!

MRS BENDIGO: Calls himself a bloody husband, does he? Four pound a week in Covent Garden and 'is wife doing a starry in the bloody Square! Husband!

MR TALLBOYS [*to himself*]: Happy days, happy days! My ivied church under the sheltering hillside–my red-tiled Rectory slumbering among Elizabethan yews! My library, my vinery, my cook, house-parlourmaid and groom-gardener! My cash in the bank, my name in Crockford! My black suit of irreproachable cut, my collar back to front, my watered silk cassock in the church precincts. . . .

MRS WAYNE: Of course the one thing I *do* thank God for, dearie, is that my poor dear mother never lived to see this day. Because if she ever *had* of lived to see the day when her eldest daughter–as was brought up, mind you, with no expense spared and milk straight from the cow. . . .

MRS BENDIGO: *Husband!*

GINGER: Come on, less 'ave a drum of tea while we got the chance. Last we'll get tonight–coffee shop shuts at 'ar-parse ten.

THE KIKE: Oh Jesus! This bloody cold's gonna kill me! I ain't got nothing on under my trousers. Oh Je-e-e-*eeze*!

CHARLIE [*singing*]: 'Ail Mary, 'ail Mary–

SNOUTER: Fourpence! Fourpence for six — hours on the bum! And that there nosing sod with the wooden leg queering our pitch at every boozer between Aldgate and the Mile End Road. With 'is — wooden leg and 'is war medals as 'e bought in Lambeth Cut! Bastard!

DEAFIE [*singing*]: With my willy willy, *with* my willy willy—

MRS BENDIGO: Well, I told the bastard what I thought of 'im, anyway. 'Call yourself a man?' I says. 'I've seen things like you kep' in a bottle at the 'orspital,' I says. . . .

MR TALLBOYS [*to himself*]: Happy days, happy days! Roast beef and bobbing villagers, and the peace of God that passeth all understanding! Sunday mornings in my oaken stall, cool flower scent and frou-frou of surplices mingling in the sweet corpse-laden air! Summer evenings when the late sun slanted through my study window—I pensive, boozed with tea, in fragrant wreaths of Cavendish, thumbing drowsily some half-calf volume—*Poetical Works of William Shenstone, Esq.*, Percy's *Reliques of Ancient English Poetry*, J. Lempriere, D.D., professor of immoral theology . . .

GINGER: Come on, 'oo's for that drum of riddleme-ree? We got the milk and we got the tea. Question is, 'oo's got any bleeding sugar?

DOROTHY: This cold, this cold! It seems to go right through you! Surely it won't be like this all night?

MRS BENDIGO: Oh, cheese it! I 'ate these snivelling tarts.

CHARLIE: Ain't it going to be a proper perisher, too? Look at the perishing river mist creeping up that there column. Freeze the fish-hooks off of ole Nelson before morning.

MRS WAYNE: Of course, at the time that I'm speaking of we still had our little tobacco and sweetstuff business on the corner, you'll understand. . . .

THE KIKE: Oh Je-e-e-*eeze*! Lend's that overcoat of yours, Ginger. I'm bloody freezing!

SNOUTER: — double-crossing bastard! P'raps I won't bash 'is navel in when I get a 'old of 'im!

CHARLIE: Fortunes o' war, boy, fortunes o' war. Perishing Square tonight— rumpsteak and kip on feathers tomorrow. What else d'you expect on perishing Thursday?

MRS BENDIGO: Shove up, Daddy, shove up! Think I want your lousy old 'ed on my shoulder—me a married woman?

MR TALLBOYS [*to himself*]: For preaching, chanting, and intoning I was unrivalled. My 'Lift up your Hearts' was renowned throughout the diocese. All styles I could do you, High Church, Low Church, Broad Church and No Church. Throaty Anglo-Cat Warblings, straight from the shoulder muscular Anglican, or the adenoidal Low Church whine in which still lurk the Houyhnhnm-notes of neighing chapel elders. . . .

DEAFIE [*singing*]: *With* my willy willy—

GINGER: Take your 'ands off that bleeding overcoat, Kikie. You don't get no clo'es of mine while you got the chats on you.

CHARLIE [*singing*]:

> As pants the 'art for cooling streams,
> When 'eated in the chase—

MRS MCELLIGOT [*in her sleep*]: Was 'at you, Michael dear?

MRS BENDIGO: It's my belief as the sneaking bastard 'ad another wife living when 'e married me.

MR TALLBOYS [*from the roof of his mouth, stage curate-wise, reminiscently*]: If any of you know cause of just impediment why these two persons should not be joined together in holy matrimony . . .

THE KIKE: A pal! A bloody pal! And won't lend his bloody overcoat!

MRS WAYNE: Well, now as you've mentioned it, I must admit as I never *was* one to refuse a nice cup of tea. I know that when our poor dear mother was alive, pot after pot we used to . . .

NOSY WATSON [*to himself, angrily*]: Sod! . . . Gee'd into it and then a stretch all round. . . . Never even done the bloody job. . . . Sod!

DEAFIE [*singing*]: *With* my willy willy—

MRS MCELLIGOT [*half asleep*]: *Dear* Michael. . . . He was real loving, Michael was. Ténder an' true. . . . Never looked at another man since dat evenin' when I met'm outside Kronk's slaughter-house an' he gimme de two pound o' sausage as he'd bummed off de International Stores for his own supper. . . .

MRS BENDIGO: Well, I suppose we'll get that bloody tea this time tomorrow.

MR TALLBOYS [*chanting, reminiscently*]: By the waters of Babylon we sat down and wept, when we remembered thee, O Zion! . . .

DOROTHY: Oh, this cold, this cold!

SNOUTER: Well, I don't do no more — starries this side of Christmas. I'll 'ave my kip tomorrow if I 'ave to cut it out of their bowels.

NOSY WATSON: Detective, is he? Smith of the Flying Squad! Flying Judas more likely! All they can bloody do—copping the old offenders what no beak won't give a fair chance.

GINGER: Well, I'm off for the fiddlede-dee. 'Oo's got a couple of clods for the water?

MRS MCELLIGOT [*waking*]: Oh dear, oh dear! If my back ain't fair broke! Oh holy Jesus, if dis bench don't catch you across de kidneys! An' dere was me dreamin' I was warm in kip wid a nice cup a' tea an' two o' buttered toast waitin' by me bedside. Well, dere goes me last wink o' sleep till I gets into Lambeth public lib'ry tomorrow.

DADDY [*his head emerging from within his overcoat like a tortoise's from within its shell*]: Wassat you said, boy? Paying money for water! How long've you bin on the road, you ignorant young scut? Money for bloody water? Bum it, boy, bum it! Don't buy what you can bum and don't bum what you can steal. That's my word—fifty year on the road, man and boy. [*Retires within his coat.*]

MR TALLBOYS [*chanting*]: O all ye works of the Lord—

DEAFIE [*singing*]: *With* my willy willy—

CHARLIE: 'Oo was it copped you, Nosy?

THE KIKE: Oh Je-e-e-*eeze*!

MRS BENDIGO: Shove up, shove up! Seems to me some folks think they've took a mortgage on this bloody seat.

MR TALLBOYS [*chanting*]: O all ye works of the Lord, curse ye the Lord, curse Him and vilify Him for ever!

MRS MCELLIGOT: What I always says is, it's always us poor bloody Catholics dat's down in de bloody dumps.

NOSY WATSON: Smithy. Flying Squad—flying sod! Give us the plans of the house and everything, and then had a van full of coppers waiting and nipped the lot of us. I wrote it up in the Black Maria:

> 'Detective Smith knows how to gee;
> Tell him he's a — from me.'

SNOUTER: 'Ere, what about our — tea? Go on, Kikie, you're a young 'un; shut that — noise and take the drums. Don't you pay nothing. Worm it out of the old tart. Snivel. Do the doleful.

MR TALLBOYS [*chanting*]: O all ye children of men, curse ye the Lord, curse Him and vilify Him for ever!

CHARLIE: What, is Smithy crooked too?

MRS BENDIGO: I tell you what, girls, I tell you what gets *me* down, and that's to think of my bloody husband snoring under four blankets and me freezing in this bloody Square. That's what *I* can't stomach. The unnatural sod!

GINGER [*singing*]: *There* they go—*in* their joy—Don't take that there drum with the cold sausage in it, Kikie.

NOSY WATSON: Crooked? *Crooked?* Why, a corkscrew 'ud look like a bloody bradawl beside of him! There isn't one of them double—sons of whores in the Flying Squad but 'ud sell his grandmother to the knackers for two pound ten and then sit on her gravestone eating potato crisps. The geeing, narking toe rag!

CHARLIE: Perishing tough. 'Ow many convictions you got?

GINGER [*singing*]:

> *There* they go—*in* their joy—
> '*Ap*py girl—*luc*ky boy—

NOSY WATSON: Fourteen. You don't stand no chance with that lot against you.

MRS WAYNE: What, don't he keep you, then?

MRS BENDIGO: No, I'm married to this one, sod 'im!

CHARLIE: I got perishing nine myself.

MR TALLBOYS [*chanting*]: O Ananias, Azarias and Misael, curse ye the Lord, curse Him and vilify Him for ever!

GINGER [*singing*]:

> *There* they go—*in* their joy—
> '*Ap*py girl—*luc*ky boy—
> But 'ere am *I-I-I*—
> Broken—'*a-a-aar*ted!

God, I ain't 'ad a dig in the grave for three days. 'Ow long since you washed your face, Snouter?

MRS MCELLIGOT: Oh dear, oh dear! If dat boy don't come soon wid de tea me insides'll dry up like a bloody kippered herring.

CHARLIE: *You* can't sing, none of you. Ought to 'ear Snouter and me 'long towards Christmas time when we pipe up 'Good King Wenceslas' outside the boozers. 'Ymns, too. Blokes in the bar weep their perishing eyes out to 'ear us. 'Member when we tapped twice at the same 'ouse by mistake, Snouter? Old tart fair tore the innards out of us.

MR TALLBOYS [*marching up and down behind an imaginary drum and singing*]:
>            All things vile and damnable,
>            All creatures great and small—

[*Big Ben strikes half past ten.*]

SNOUTER [*mimicking the clock*]: Ding dong, ding dong! Six and a — half hours of it! Cripes!

GINGER: Kikie and me knocked off four of them safety-razor blades in Woolworth's 's afternoon. I'll 'ave a dig in the bleeding fountains tomorrow if I can bum a bit of soap.

DEAFIE: When I was a stooard in the P. & O., we used to meet them black Indians two days out at sea, in them there great canoes as they call catamarans, catching sea-turtles the size of dinner tables.

MRS WAYNE: Did yoo used to be a clergyman, then, sir?

MR TALLBOYS [*halting*]: After the order of Melchizedec. There is no question of 'used to be', Madam. Once a priest always a priest. *Hoc est corpus* hocus-pocus. Even though unfrocked—un-Crooked, we call it—and dog-collar publicly torn off by the bishop of the diocese.

GINGER [*singing*]: *There* they go—*in* their joy—Thank Christ! 'Ere comes Kikie. Now for the consultation-free!

MRS BENDIGO: Not before it's bloody needed.

CHARLIE: 'Ow come they give you the sack, mate? Usual story? Choirgirls in the family way?

MRS MCELLIGOT: You've took your time, ain't you, young man? But come on, let's have a sup of it before me tongue falls out o' me bloody mouth.

MRS BENDIGO: Shove up, Daddy! You're sitting on my packet of bloody sugar.

MR TALLBOYS: Girls is a euphemism. Only the usual flannel-bloomered hunters of the unmarried clergy. Church hens—altar-dressers and brass-polishers—spinsters growing bony and desperate. There is a demon that enters into them at thirty-five.

THE KIKE: The old bitch wouldn't give me the hot water. Had to tap a toff in the street and pay a penny for it.

SNOUTER: — likely story! Bin swigging it on the way more likely.

DADDY [*emerging from his overcoat*]: Drum o' tea, eh? I could sup a drum o' tea. [*Belches slightly.*]

CHARLIE: When their bubs get like perishing razor stops? *I* know.

NOSY WATSON: Tea—bloody catlap. Better'n that cocoa in the stir, though. Lend's your cup, matie.

GINGER: Jest wait'll I knock a 'ole in this tin of milk. Shy us a money or your life, someone.

MRS BENDIGO: Easy with that bloody sugar! 'Oo paid for it, I sh'd like to know?

MR TALLBOYS: When their bubs get like razor stops. I thank thee for that humour. *Pippin's Weekly* made quite a feature of the case. 'Missing Canon's Sub Rosa Romance. Intimate Revelations.' And also an Open Letter in *John*

*Bull*: 'To a Skunk in Shepherd's Clothing'. A pity—I was marked out for preferment. [*To Dorothy*] Gaiters in the family, if you understand me. You would not think, would you, that the time has been when this unworthy backside dented the plush cushions of a cathedral stall?

CHARLIE: 'Ere comes Florry. Thought she'd be along soon as we got the tea going. Got a nose like a perishing vulture for tea, that girl 'as.

SNOUTER: Ay, always on the tap. [*Singing*]

Tap, tap, tappety tap,
I'm a perfec' devil at that—

MRS MCELLIGOT: De poor kid, she ain't got no sense. Why don't she go up to Piccadilly Circus where she'd get her five bob reg'lar? She won't do herself no good bummin' round de Square wid a set of miserable ole Tobies.

DOROTHY: Is that milk all right?

GINGER: All right? [*Applies his mouth to one of the holes in the tin and blows. A sticky greyish stream dribbles from the other.*]

CHARLIE: What luck, Florry? 'Ow 'bout that perishing toff as I see you get off with just now?

DOROTHY: It's got 'Not fit for babies' on it.

MRS BENDIGO: Well, you ain't a bloody baby, are you? You can drop your Buckingham Palace manners, 'ere, dearie.

FLORRY: Stood me a coffee and a fag—mingy bastard! That tea you got there, Ginger? You always *was* my favourite, Ginger dear.

MRS WAYNE: There's jest thirteen of us.

MR TALLBOYS: As we are not going to have any dinner you need not disturb yourself.

GINGER: What-o, ladies and gents! Tea is served. Cups forward, please!

THE KIKE: Oh Jeez! You ain't filled my bloody cup half full!

MRS MCELLIGOT: Well, here's luck to us all, an' a better bloody kip tomorrow. I'd ha' took shelter in one o' dem dere churches meself, only de b—s won't let you in if so be as dey t'ink you got de chats on you. [*Drinks.*]

MRS WAYNE: Well, I can't say as this is exactly the way as I've been *accustomed* to drinking a cup of tea—but still—[*Drinks.*]

CHARLIE: Perishing good cup of tea. [*Drinks.*]

DEAFIE: And there was flocks of them there green parakeets in the coco-nut palms, too. [*Drinks.*]

MR TALLBOYS:

What potions have I drunk of siren tears,
Distilled from limbecs foul as Hell within!

[*Drinks.*]

SNOUTER: Last we'll get till five in the — morning. [*Drinks.*]

[*Florry produces a broken shop-made cigarette from her stocking, and cadges a match. The men, except Daddy, Deafie, and Mr Tallboys, roll cigarettes from picked-up fag-ends. The red ends glow through the misty twilight, like a crooked constellation, as the smokers sprawl on the bench, the ground, or the slope of the parapet.*]

MRS WAYNE: Well, there now! A nice cup of tea do seem to warm you up, don't it, now? Not but what I don't feel it a bit different, as you might say, not having no nice clean table-cloth like I've been accustomed to, and the beautiful china tea service as our mother used to have; and always, of course, the very best tea as money could buy—real Pekoe Points at two and nine a pound. . . .

GINGER [*singing*]:

> There they go—*in* their joy—
> 'Appy girl—*lucky* boy—

MR TALLBOYS [*singing, to the tune of* 'Deutschland, Deutschland über alles']: Keep the aspidistra flying—

CHARLIE: 'Ow long you two kids been in Smoke?

SNOUTER: I'm going to give them boozers such a doing tomorrow as they won't know if theyr'e on their 'eads or their — 'eels. I'll 'ave my 'alf dollar if I 'ave to 'old them upside down and — shake 'em.

GINGER: Three days. We come down from York—skippering 'alf the way. God, wasn't it jest about bleeding nine carat gold, too!

FLORRY: Got any more tea there, Ginger dear? Well, so long, folks. See you all at Wilkins's tomorrow morning.

MRS BENDIGO: Thieving little tart! Swallers 'er tea and then jacks off without so much as a thank you. Can't waste a bloody moment.

MRS MCELLIGOT: Cold? Ay, I b'lieve you. Skipperin' in de long grass wid no blanket an' de bloody dew fit to drown you, an' den can't get your bloody fire going' in de mornin', an' got to tap de milkman 'fore you can make yourself a drum o' tea. I've had some'v it when me and Michael was on de toby.

MRS BENDIGO: Even go with blackies and Chinamen she will, the dirty little cow.

DOROTHY: How much does she get each time?

SNOUTER: Tanner.

DOROTHY: *Sixpence?*

CHARLIE: Bet your life. Do it for a perishing fag along towards morning.

MRS MCELLIGOT: I never took less'n a shilling, never.

GINGER: Kikie and me skippered in a boneyard one night. Woke up in the morning and found I was lying on a bleeding gravestone.

THE KIKE: She ain't half got the crabs on her, too.

MRS MCELLIGOT: Michael an' me skippered in a pigsty once. We was just a-creepin' in, when, 'Holy Mary!' says Michael, 'dere's a pig in here!' 'Pig be —!' I says, 'he'll keep us warm anyway.' So in we goes, an' dere was an old sow lay on her side snorin' like a traction engine. I creeps up agen her an' puts me arms round her, an' begod she kept me warm all night. I've skippered worse.

DEAFIE [*singing*]: *With* my willy willy—

CHARLIE: Don't ole Deafie keep it up? Sets up a kind of a 'umming inside of 'im, 'e says.

DADDY: When I was a boy we didn't live on this 'ere bread and marg and tea and suchlike trash. Good solid tommy we 'ad in them days. Beef stoo. Black pudden. Bacon dumpling. Pig's 'ead. Fed like a fighting-cock on a tanner a day. And now fifty year I've 'ad of it on the toby. Spud-grabbing, pea-picking, lambing, turnip-topping—everythink. And sleeping in wet straw and not once in a year you don't fill your guts right full: Well—! [*Retires within his coat.*]

MRS MCELLIGOT: But he was real bold, Michael was. He'd go in anywhere. Many's de time we've broke into an empty house an' kipped in de best bed. 'Other people got homes,' he'd say. 'Why shouln't we have'm too!'

GINGER [*singing*]: But I'm dan-cing with tears—in my eyes—

MR TALLBOYS [*to himself*]: *Absumet haeres Caecuba dignior!* To think that there were twenty-one bottles of Clos St Jacques 1911 in my cellar still, that night when the baby was born and I left for London on the milk train! . . .

MRS WAYNE: And as for the *wreaths* we 'as sent us when our mother died—well, you wouldn't believe! 'Uge, they was. . . .

MRS BENDIGO: If I'ad my time over again I'd marry for bloody money.

GINGER [*singing*]:

> But I'm dan-cing with tears—in my eyes—
> 'Cos the girl—in my arms—isn't you-o-ou!

NOSY WATSON: Some of you lot think you got a bloody lot to howl about, don't you? What about a poor sod like me? You wasn't narked into the stir when you was eighteen year old, was you?

THE KIKE: Oh Je-e-ee*eze*!

CHARLIE: Ginger, you can't sing no more'n a perishing tomcat with the guts-ache. Just you listen to me. I'll give y'a treat. [*Singing*]: Jesu, lover *of* my soul—

MR TALLBOYS [*to himself*]: *Et ego* in Crockford. . . . With Bishops and Archbishops and with all the Company of Heaven. . . .

NOSY WATSON: D'you know how I got in the stir the first time? Narked by my own sister—yes, my own bloody sister! My sister's a cow if ever there was one. She got married to a religious maniac—he's so bloody religious that she's got fifteen kids now—well, it was him put her up to narking me. But I got back on 'em, *I* can tell you. First thing, I done when I come out of the stir, I buys a hammer and goes round to my sister's house, and smashed her piano to bloody matchwood. 'There!' I says, 'that's what you get for narking *me*! You nosing mare!' I says.

DOROTHY: This cold, this cold! I don't know whether my feet are there or not.

MRS MCELLIGOT: Bloody tea don't warm you for long, do it? I'm fair froze myself.

MR TALLBOYS [*to himself*]: My curate days, my curate days! My fancywork bazaars and morris-dancers in aid of on the village green, my lectures to the Mothers' Union—missionary work in Western China with fourteen magic lantern slides! My Boys' Cricket Club, teetotallers only, my Confirmation classes—purity lecture once monthly in the Parish Hall—my Boy Scout orgies! The Wolf Cubs will deliver the Grand Howl. Household Hints for the Parish Magazine, 'Discarded fountain-pen fillers can be used as enemas for canaries. . . .'

CHARLIE [*singing*]: Jesu, lover *of* my soul—

GINGER: 'Ere comes the bleeding flattie! Get up off the ground, all of you. [*Daddy emerges from his overcoat.*]

THE POLICEMAN [*shaking the sleepers on the next bench*]: Now then, wake up, wake up! Rouse up, you! Got to go home if you want to sleep. This isn't a common lodging house. Get up, there! [*etc., etc.*]

MRS BENDIGO: It's that nosy young sod as wants promotion. Wouldn't let you bloody breathe if 'e 'ad 'is way.

CHARLIE [*singing*]:

> Jesu, lover *of* my soul,
> Let me *to* Thy bosom fly—

THE POLICEMAN: Now then, *you*! What you think *this* is? Baptist prayer meeting? [*To the Kike*] Up you get, and look sharp about it!

CHARLIE: I can't 'elp it, sergeant. It's my toonful nature. It comes out of me natural-like.

THE POLICEMAN [*shaking Mrs Bendigo*]: Wake up, mother, wake up!

MRS BENDIGO: Mother? *Mother*, is it? Well, if I am a mother, thank God I ain't got a bloody son like you! And I'll tell you another little secret, constable. Next time I want a man's fat 'ands feeling round the back of my neck, I won't ask *you* to do it. I'll 'ave someone with a bit more sex-appeal.

THE POLICEMAN: Now then, now then! No call to get abusive, you know. We got our orders to carry out. [*Exit majestically.*]

SNOUTER [*sotto voce*]: — off, you — son of a —!

CHARLIE [*singing*]:

> While the gathering waters roll,
> While the tempest still is 'igh!

Sung bass in the choir my last two years in Dartmoor, I did.

MRS BENDIGO: I'll bloody mother 'im! [*Shouting after the policeman*] 'I! Why don't you get after them bloody cat burglars 'stead of coming nosing round a respectable married woman?

GINGER: Kip down, blokes. 'E's jacked. [*Daddy retires within his coat.*]

NOSY WATSON: Wassit like in Dartmoor now? D'they give you jam now?

MRS WAYNE: Of course, you can see as they couldn't reely allow people to sleep in the streets—I mean, it wouldn't be quite nice—and then you've got to remember as it'd be encouraging of all the people as haven't got homes of their own—the kind of riff-raff, if you take my meaning. . . .

MR TALLBOYS [*to himself*]: Happy days, happy days! Outings with the Girl Guides in Epping Forest—hired brake and sleek roan horses, and I on the box in my grey flannel suit, speckled straw hat, and discreet layman's necktie. Buns and ginger pop under the green elms. Twenty Girl Guides pious yet susceptible frisking in the breast-high bracken, and I a happy curate sporting among them, *in loco parentis* pinching the girls' backsides. . . .

MRS MCELLIGOT: Well, you may talk about kippin' down, but begod dere won't be much sleep for my poor ole bloody bones tonight. I can't skipper it now de way me and Michael used to.

CHARLIE: Not jam. Gets cheese, though, twice a week.

THE KIKE: Oh Jeez! I can't stand it no longer. I going down to the M.A.B.

[*Dorothy stands up, and then, her knees having stiffened with the cold, almost falls.*]

GINGER: Only send you to the bleeding Labour Home. What you say we all go up to Covent Garden tomorrow morning? Bum a few pears if we get there early enough.

CHARLIE: I've 'ad my perishing bellyful of Dartmoor, b'lieve me. Forty on us went through 'ell for getting off with the ole women down on the allotments. Ole trots seventy years old they was—spud-grabbers. Didn't we cop it just! Bread and water, chained to the wall—perishing near murdered us.

MRS BENDIGO: No fear! Not while my bloody husband's there. One black eye in a week's enough for me, thank you.

MR TALLBOYS [*chanting, reminiscently*]: As for our harps, we hanged them up, upon the willow trees of Babylon! . . .

MRS MCELLIGOT: Hold up, kiddie! Stamp your feet an' get de blood back into 'm. I'll take y'a walk up to Paul's in a coupla minutes.

DEAFIE [*singing*]: *With* my willy willy—
    [*Big Ben strikes eleven.*]

SNOUTER: Six more — hours! Cripes!

[*An hour passes. Big Ben stops striking. The mist thins and the cold increases. A grubby-faced moon is seen sneaking among the clouds of the southern sky. A dozen hardened old men remain on the benches, and still contrive to sleep, doubled up and hidden in their greatcoats. Occasionally they groan in their sleep. The others set out in all directions, intending to walk all night and so keep their blood flowing, but nearly all of them have drifted back to the Square by midnight. A new policeman comes on duty. He strolls through the Square at intervals of half an hour, scrutinizing the faces of the sleepers but letting them alone when he has made sure that they are only asleep and not dead. Round each bench revolves a knot of people who take it in turns to sit down and are driven to their feet by the cold after a few minutes. Ginger and Charlie fill two drums at the fountains and set out in the desperate hope of boiling some tea over the navvies' clinker fire in Chandos Street; but a policeman is warming himself at the fire, and orders them away. The Kike suddenly vanishes, probably to beg a bed at the M.A.B. Towards one o'clock a rumour goes round that a lady is distributing hot coffee, ham sandwiches, and packets of cigarettes under Charing Cross Bridge; there is a rush to the spot, but the rumour turns out to be unfounded. As the Square fills again the ceaseless changing of places upon the benches quickens until it is a game of musical chairs. Sitting down, with one's hands under one's armpits, it is possible to get into a kind of sleep, or doze, for two or three minutes on end. In this state, enormous ages seem to pass. One sinks into a complex, troubling dreams which leave one conscious of one's surroundings and of the bitter cold. The night is growing clearer and colder every minute. There is a chorus of varying sound—groans, curses, bursts of laughter, and singing, and through them all the uncontrollable chattering of teeth.*]

MR TALLBOYS [*chanting*]: I am poured out like water, and all my bones are out of joint! . . .

MRS MCELLIGOT: Ellen an' me bin wanderin' round de City dis two hours. Begod it's like a bloody tomb wid dem great lamps glarin' down on you an' not a soul stirren' excep' de flatties strollin' two an' two.

SNOUTER: Five past — one and I ain't 'ad a bite since dinner! Course it 'ad to 'appen to us on a — night like this!

MR TALLBOYS: A drinking night I should have called it. But every man to his taste. [*Chanting*] 'My strength is dried like a potsherd, and my tongue cleaveth to my gums!' . . .

CHARLIE: Say, what you think? Nosy and me done a smash jest now. Nosy sees a tobacconist's show-case full of them fancy boxes of Gold Flake, and 'e says, 'By cripes I'm going to 'ave some of them fags if they give me a perishing stretch for it!' 'e says. So 'e wraps 'is scarf round 'is 'and, and we waits till there's a perishing great van passing as'll drown the noise, and then Nosy lets fly—biff! We nipped a dozen packets of fags, and then I bet you didn't see our a—s for dust. And when we gets round the corner and opens them, there wasn't no perishing fags inside! Perishing dummy boxes. I 'ad to laugh.

DOROTHY: My knees are giving way. I can't stand up much longer.

MRS BENDIGO: Oh, the sod, the sod! To turn a woman out of doors on a night like bloody this! You wait'll I get 'im drunk o' Saturday night and 'e can't 'it back. I'll mash 'im to bloody shin of beef, I will. 'E'll look like two pennorth of pieces after I've swiped 'im with the bloody flat-iron.

MRS MCELLIGOT: Here, make room'n let de kid sit down. Press up agen ole Daddy, dear. Put his arm round you. He's chatty, but he'll keep you warm.

GINGER [*double marking time*]: Stamp your feet on the ground—only bleeding thing to do. Strike up a song, someone, and less all stamp our bleeding feet in time to it.

DADDY [*waking and emerging*]: Wassat? [*Still half asleep, he lets his head fall back, with mouth open and Adam's apple protruding from his withered throat like the blade of a tomahawk.*]

MRS BENDIGO: There's women what if they'd stood what *I've* stood, they'd ave put spirits of salts in 'is cup of bloody tea.

MR TALLBOYS [*beating an imaginary drum and singing*]: Onward, heathen so-oldiers—

MRS WAYNE: Well, reely now! If any of us'd ever of thought, in the dear old days when we used to sit round our own Silkstone coal fire, with the kettle on the hob and a nice dish of toasted crumpets from the baker's over the way. . . . [*The chattering of her teeth silences her.*]

CHARLIE: No perishing church trap now, matie. I'll give y'a bit of smut—something as we can perishing dance to. You listen t'me.

MRS MCELLIGOT: Don't you get talkin' about crumpets, Missis. Me bloody belly's rubbin' agen me backbone already.

[*Charlie draws himself up, clears his throat, and in an enormous voice roars out a song entitled 'Rollicking Bill the Sailor'. A laugh that is partly a shudder bursts from the people on the bench. They sing the song through again, with increasing volume of noise, stamping and clapping in time. Those sitting down, packed elbow to elbow, sway grotesquely from side to side, working their*] *feet as though stamping on the pedals of a harmonium. Even Mrs Wayne joins in after a moment, laughing in spite of herself. They are all laughing, though with chattering teeth. Mr Tallboys marches up and down behind his vast swag belly, pretending to carry a banner or crozier in front of him. The night is now quite clear, and an icy wind comes shuddering at intervals through the Square. The stamping and clapping rise to a kind of frenzy as the people feel the deadly cold penetrate to their bones. Then the policeman is seen wandering into the Square from the eastern end, and the singing ceases abruptly.]*

CHARLIE: There! You can't say as a bit of music don't warm you up.

MRS BENDIGO: This bloody wind! And I ain't even got any drawers on, the bastard kicked me out in such a 'urry.

MRS MCELLIGOT: Well, glory be to Jesus, 'twon't be long before dat dere church in de Gray's Inn Road opens up for de winter. Dey gives you a roof over your head of a night, 't any rate.

THE POLICEMAN: Now then, now *then*! D'you think this is the time of night to begin singing like a blooming bear garden? I shall have to send you back to your homes if you can't keep quiet.

SNOUTER [*sotto voce*]: You — son of a —!

GINGER: Yes—they lets you kip on the bleeding stone floor with three newspaper posters 'stead of blankets. Might as well be in the Square and 'ave done with it. God, I wish I was in the bleeding spike.

MRS MCELLIGOT: Still, you gets a cup of Horlicks an' two slices. I bin glad to kip dere often enough.

MR TALLBOYS [*chanting*]: I was glad when they said unto me, We will go into the house of the Lord! . . .

DOROTHY [*starting up*]: Oh, this cold, this cold! I don't know whether it's worse when you're sitting down or when you're standing up. Oh, how can you all stand it? Surely you don't have to do this every night of your lives?

MRS WAYNE: You mustn't think, dearie, as there isn't *some* of us wasn't brought up respectable.

CHARLIE [*singing*]: Cheer up, cully, you'll soon be dead! Brrh! Perishing Jesus! Ain't my fish-hooks blue! [*Double marks time and beats his arms against his sides.*]

DOROTHY: Oh, but how can you stand it? How can you go on like this, night after night, year after year? It's not possible that people can live so! It's so absurd that one wouldn't believe it if one didn't know it was true. It's impossible!

SNOUTER: — possible if you ask me.

MR TALLBOYS [*stage curate-wise*]: With God, all things are possible.

[*Dorothy sinks back on to the bench, her knees still being unsteady.*]

CHARLIE: Well, it's jest on 'ar-parse one. Either we got to get moving, or else make a pyramid on that perishing bench. Unless we want to perishing turn up our toes. 'Oo's for a little constitootional up to the Tower of London?

MRS MCELLIGOT: 'Twon't be me dat'll walk another step tonight. Me bloody legs've given out on me.

GINGER: What-o for the pyramid! This is a bit too bleeding nine-day-old for me. Less scrum into that bench—beg pardon, Ma!

DADDY [*sleepily*]: Wassa game? Can't a man get a bit of kip but what you must come worriting 'im and shaking of 'im?

CHARLIE: That's the stuff! Shove in! Shift yourself, Daddy, and make room for my little sit-me-down. Get one atop of each other. That's right. Never mind the chats. Jam all together like pilchards in a perishing tin.

MRS WAYNE: Here! I didn't ask you to sit on my lap, young man!

GINGER: Sit on mine, then, mother—'sall the same. What-o! First bit of stuff I've 'ad my arm round since Easter.

[*They pile themselves in a monstrous shapeless clot, men and women clinging indiscriminately together, like a bunch of toads at spawning time. There is a writhing movement as the heap settles down, and a sour stench of clothes diffuses itself. Only Mr Tallboys remains marching up and down.*]

MR TALLBOYS [*declaiming*]: O ye nights and days, ye light and darkness, ye lightnings and clouds, curse ye the Lord!

[*Deafie, someone having sat on his diaphragm, utters a strange, unreproducible sound.*]

MRS BENDIGO: Get off my bad leg, can't you? What you think I am? Bloody drawing-room sofa?

CHARLIE: Don't ole Daddy stink when you get up agen 'im?

GINGER: Bleeding Bank 'oliday for the chats this'll be.

DOROTHY: Oh, God, God!

MR TALLBOYS [*halting*]: Why call on God, you puling deathbed penitent? Stick to your guns and call on the Devil as I do. Hail to thee, Lucifer, Prince of the Air! [*Singing to the tune of 'Holy, holy holy'*]: Incubi and Succubi, falling down before Thee! . . .

MRS BENDIGO: Oh, shut up, you blarsphemous old sod! 'E's too bloody fat to feel the cold, that's what's wrong with 'im.

CHARLIE: Nice soft be'ind you got, Ma. Keep an eye out for the perishing flattie, Ginger.

MR TALLBOYS: *Malecidite, omnia opera!* The Black Mass! Why not? Once a priest always a priest. Hand me a chunk of toke and I will work the miracle. Sulphur candles, Lord's Prayer backwards, crucifix upside down. [*To Dorothy*] If we had a black he-goat you would come in useful.

[*The animal heat of the piled bodies had already made itself felt. A drowsiness is descending upon everyone.*]

MRS WAYNE: You mustn't think as I'm *accustomed* to sitting on a gentleman's knee, you know . . .

MRS MCELLIGOT [*drowsily*]: It took my sacraments reg'lar till de bloody priest wouldn't give me absolution along o' my Michael. De ole get, de ole getsie! . . .

MR TALLBOYS [*striking an attitude*]: *Per aquam sacratam quam nunc spargo, signumque crucis quod nunc facio . . . .*

GINGER: 'Oo's got a fill of 'ard-up? I've smoked by last bleeding fag-end.

MR TALLBOYS [*as at the altar*]: Dearly beloved brethren we are gathered together in the sight of God for the solemnization of unholy blasphemy. He has afflicted us with dirt and cold, with hunger and solitude, with the pox and the itch, with the headlouse and the crablouse. Our food is damp crusts and slimy meat-scraps handed out in packets from hotel doorways. Our pleasure is stewed tea and sawdust cakes bolted in reeking cellars, bar-rinsing sand spittle of common ale, the embrace of toothless hags. Our destiny is the pauper's grave, twenty-feet deep in deal coffins, the kip-house of underground. It is very meet, right and our bounden duty at all times and in all places to curse Him and revile Him. Therefore with Demons and Archdemons [*etc., etc., etc.*].

MRS MCELLIGOT [*drowsily*]: By holy Jesus, I'm half asleep right now, only some b—'s lyin' across my legs and crushin' 'em.

MR TALLBOYS: Amen. Evil from us deliver, but temptation into not us lead [*etc., etc., etc.*].

[*As he reaches the first word of the prayer he tears the consecrated bread across. The blood runs out of it. There is a rolling sound, as of thunder, and the landscape changes. Dorothy's feet are very cold. Monstrous winged shapes of Demons and Archdemons are dimly visible, moving to and fro. Something, beak or claw, closes upon Dorothy's shoulder, reminding her that her feet and hands are aching with cold.*]

THE POLICEMAN [*shaking Dorothy by the shoulder*]: Wake up, now, wake up, wake up! Haven't you got an overcoat? You're as white as death. Don't you know better than to let yourself sprawl about in the cold like that?

[*Dorothy finds that she is stiff with cold. The sky is now quite clear, with gritty little stars twinkling like electric lamps enormously remote. The pyramid has unrolled itself.*]

MRS MCELLIGOT: De poor kid, she ain't used to roughin' it de way us others are.

GINGER [*beating his arms*]: Brr! Woo! 'Taters in the bleeding mould!

MRS WAYNE: She's a lady born and bred.

THE POLICEMAN: Is that so?—See here, Miss, you best come down to the M.A.B. with me. They'll give you a bed all right. Anyone can see with half an eye as you're a cut above these others here.

MRS BENDIGO: Thank you, constable, *thank* you! 'Ear that, girls? 'A cut above us,' 'e says. Nice, ain't it? [*To the policeman*] Proper bloody Ascot swell yourself, ain't you?

DOROTHY: No, no! Leave me, I'd rather stay here.

THE POLICEMAN: Well, please yourself. You looked real bad just now. I'll be along later and take a look at you. [*Moves off doubtfully.*]

CHARLIE: Wait'll the perisher's round the corner and then pile up agen. Only perishing way we'll keep warm.

MRS MCELLIGOT: Come on, kid. Get underneath an' let'm warm you.

SNOUTER: Ten minutes to — two. Can't last for ever, I s'pose.

MR TALLBOYS [*chanting*]: I am poured out like water, and all my bones are out of joint: My heart also in the midst of my body is like unto melting wax! . . .

[*Once more the people pile themselves on the bench. But the temperature is now not many degrees above freezing-point, and the wind is blowing more cuttingly. The people wriggle their wind-nipped faces into the heap like*] *sucking pigs struggling for their mother's teats. One's interludes of sleep shrink to a few seconds, and one's dreams grow more monstrous, troubling, and undreamlike. There are times when the nine people are talking almost normally, times when they can even laugh at their situation, and times when they press themselves together in a kind of frenzy, with deep groans of pain. Mr Tallboys suddenly becomes exhausted and his monologue degenerates into a stream of nonsense. He drops his vast bulk on top of the others, almost suffocating them. The heap rolls apart. Some remain on the bench, some slide to the ground and collapse against the parapet or against the others' knees. The policeman enters the Square and orders those on the ground to their feet. They get up, and collapse again the moment he is gone. There is no sound from the ten people save of snores that are partly groans. Their heads nod like those of joined porcelain Chinamen as they fall asleep and reawake as rhythmically as the ticking of a clock. Three strikes somewhere. A voice yells like a trumpet from the eastern end of the Square:* 'Boys! Up you get! The noospapers is come!']

CHARLIE [*starting from his sleep*]: The perishing papers! C'm on, Ginger! Run like Hell!

[*They run, or shamble, as fast as they can to the corner of the Square, where three youths are distributing surplus posters given away in charity by the morning newspapers. Charlie and Ginger come back with a thick wad of posters. The five largest men now jam themselves together on the bench, Deafie and the four women sitting across their knees; then, with infinite difficulty (as it has to be done from the inside), they wrap themselves in a monstrous cocoon of paper, several sheets thick, tucking the loose ends into their necks or breasts or between their shoulders and the back of the bench. Finally nothing is uncovered save their heads and the lower part of their legs. For their heads they fashion hoods of paper. The paper constantly comes loose and lets in cold shafts of wind, but it is now possible to sleep for as much as five minutes consecutively. At this time—between three and five in the morning—it is customary with the police not to disturb the Square sleepers. A measure of warmth steals through everyone and extends even to their feet. There is some furtive fondling of the women under cover of the paper. Dorothy is too far gone to care.*

*By a quarter past four the paper is all crumpled and torn to nothing, and it is far too cold to remain sitting down. The people get up, swear, find their legs somewhat rested, and begin to slouch to and fro in couples, frequently halting from mere lassitude. Every belly is now contorted with hunger. Ginger's tin of condensed milk is torn open and the contents devoured, everyone dipping their fingers into it and licking them. Those who have no money at all leave the Square for the Green Park, where they will be undisturbed till seven. Those who can command even a halfpenny make for Wilkins's café not far from the Charing Cross Road. It is known that the café will not open till five o'clock; nevertheless, a crowd is waiting outside the door by twenty to five.*]

MRS MCELLIGOT: Got your halfpenny, dearie? Dey won't let more'n four of us in on one cup o'tea, de stingy ole gets!

MR TALLBOYS [*singing*]: The roseate hu-ues of early da-awn—

GINGER: God, that bit of sleep we 'ad under the newspapers done me some good. [*Singing*] But I'm dan-cing with tears—in my eyes—

CHARLIE: Oh, boys, boys! Look through that perishing window, will you? Look at the 'eat steaming down the window pane! Look at the tea-urns jest on the boil, and them great piles of 'ot toast and 'am sandwiches, and them there sausages sizzling in the pan! Don't it make your belly turn perishing summersaults to see 'em?

DOROTHY: I've got a penny. I can't get a cup of tea for that, can I?

SNOUTER: — lot of sausages we'll get this morning with fourpence between us. 'Alf a cup of tea and a — doughnut more likely. There's a breakfus' for you!

MRS MCELLIGOT: You don't need buy a cup o' tea all to yourself. I got a halfpenny an' so's Daddy, an' we'll put'm to your penny an' have a cup between de t'ree of us. He's got sores on his lip, but Hell! who cares? Drink near de handle an' dere's no harm done.

[*A quarter to five strikes.*]

MRS BENDIGO: I'd bet a dollar my ole man's got a bit of 'addock to 'is breakfast. I 'ope it bloody chokes 'im.

GINGER [*singing*]: But I'm dan-cing with tears—in my eyes—

MR TALLBOYS [*singing*]: Early in the morning my song shall rise to Thee!

MRS MCELLIGOT: You gets a bit o' kip in dis place, dat's one comfort. Dey lets you sleep wid your head on de table till seven o'clock. It's a bloody godsend to us Square Tobies.

CHARLIE [*slavering like a dog*]: Sausages! Perishing sausages! Welsh rabbit! 'Ot dripping toast! And a rump-steak two inches thick with chips and a pint of Ole Burton! Oh, perishing Jesus!

[*He bounds forward, pushes his way through the crowd and rattles the handle of the glass door. The whole crowd of people, about forty strong, surge forward and attempt to storm the door, which is stoutly held within by Mr Wilkins, the proprietor of the café. He menaces them through the glass. Some press their breasts and faces against the window as though warming themselves. With a whoop and a rush Florry and four other girls, comparatively fresh from having spent part of the night in bed, debouch from a neighbouring alley, accompanied by a gang of youths in blue suits. They hurl themselves upon the rear of the crowd with such momentum that the door is almost broken. Mr Wilkins pulls it furiously open and shoves the leaders back. A fume of sausages, kippers, coffee, and hot bread streams into the outer cold.*]

YOUTHS' VOICES FROM THE REAR: Why can't he — open before five? We're starving for our — tea! Ram the — door in! [*etc., etc.*]

MR WILKINS: Get out! Get out, the lot of you! Or by God not one of you comes in this morning!

GIRLS' VOICES FROM THE REAR: Mis-ter Wil-kins! Mis-ter Wil-kins! *Be* a sport and let us in! I'll give y'a kiss all free for nothing. *Be* a sport now! [*etc., etc.*]

MR WILKINS: Get on out of it! We don't open before five, and you know it. [*Slams the door.*]

MRS MCELLIGOT: Oh, holy Jesus, if dis ain't de longest ten minutes o' de whole bloody night! Well, I'll give me poor ole legs a rest, anyway. [*Squats on her heels coal-miner-fashion. Many others do the same.*]

GINGER: 'Oo's got a 'alfpenny? I'm ripe to go fifty-fifty on a doughnut.

YOUTHS' VOICES [*imitating military music, then singing*]:

> '—!' was all the band could play;
> '—! —' And the same to you!

DOROTHY [*to Mrs McElligot*]: Look at us all! Just look at us! What clothes! What faces!

MRS BENDIGO: You're no Greta Garbo yourself, if you don't mind my mentioning it.

MRS WAYNE: Well, now, the time *do* seem to pass slowly when you're waiting for a nice cup of tea, don't it now?

MR TALLBOYS [*chanting*]: For our soul is brought low, even unto the dust: our belly cleaveth unto the ground!

CHARLIE: Kippers! Perishing piles of 'em! I can smell 'em through the perishing glass.

GINGER [*singing*]:

> But I'm dan-cing with tears—in my eyes—
> 'Cos the girl—in my arms—isn't you-o-ou!

[*Much time passes. Five strikes. Intolerable ages seem to pass. Then the door is suddenly wrenched open and the people stampede in to fight for the corner seats. Almost swooning in the hot air, they fling themselves down and sprawl across the tables, drinking in the heat and the smell of food through all their pores.*]

MR WILKINS: Now then, all! You know the rules, I s'pose. No hokey-pokey this morning! Sleep till seven if you like, but if I see any man asleep after that, out he goes on his neck. Get busy with that tea, girls!

A DEAFENING CHORUS OF YELLS: Two teas 'ere! Large tea and a doughnut between us four! Kippers! Mis-ter Wil-kins! 'Ow much them sausages? Two slices! Mis-ter Wil-kins! Got any fag papers? Kipp-*ers*! [*etc., etc.*]

MR WILKINS: Shut up, shut up! Stop that hollering or I don't serve any of you.

MRS MCELLIGOT: D'you feel de blood runnin' back into your toes, dearie?

MRS WAYNE: He do speak rough to you, don't he? Not what I'd call a reely gentlemanly kind of man.

SNOUTER: This is — starvation Corner, this is. Cripes! Couldn't I do a couple of them sausages!

THE TARTS [*in chorus*]: Kippers 'ere! 'Urry up with them kippers! Mis-ter Wil-kins! Kippers all round! *And* a doughnut!

CHARLIE: Not 'alf! Got to fill up on the smell of 'em this morning. Sooner be 'ere than on the perishing Square, *all* the same.

GINGER: 'Ere, Deafie! You've 'ad your 'alf! Gimme me that bleeding cup.

MR TALLBOYS [*chanting*]: Then was our mouth filled with laughter, and our tongue with joy! . . .

MRS MCELLIGOT: Begod I'm half asleep already. It's de heat o' de room as does it.

MR WILKINS: Stop that singing there! You know the rules.

THE TARTS [*in chorus*]: Kipp-*ers*!

SNOUTER: — doughnuts! Cold prog! It turns my belly sick.

DADDY: Even the tea they give you ain't no more than water with a bit of dust in it. [*Belches.*]

CHARLIE: Bes' thing—'ave a bit of shut-eye and forget about it. Dream about perishing cut off the joint and two veg. Less get our 'eads on the table and pack up comfortable.

MRS MCELLIGOT: Lean up agen me shoulder, dearie. I've got more flesh on me bones'n what you have.

GINGER: I'd give a tanner for a bleeding fag, if I 'ad a bleeding tanner.

CHARLIE: Pack up. Get your 'ead agenst mine, Snouter. That's right. Jesus, won't I perishing sleep!

[*A dish of smoking kippers is borne past to the tarts' table.*]

SNOUTER [*drowsily*]: More — kippers. Wonder 'ow many times she's bin on 'er back to pay for that lot.

MRS MCELLIGOT [*half-asleep*]: 'Twas a pity, 'twas a real pity, when Michael went off on his jack an' left me wid de bloody baby an' all. . . .

MRS BENDIGO [*furiously, following the dish of kippers with accusing finger*]: Look at that, girls! Look at that! *Kippers!* Don't it make you bloody wild? *We* don't get kippers for breakfast, do we, girls? Bloody tarts swallering down kippers as fast as they can turn 'em out of the pan, and us 'ere with a cup of tea between four of us and lucky to get that! Kippers!

MR TALLBOYS [*stage curate-wise*]: The wages of sin is kippers.

GINGER: Don't breathe in my face, Deafie. I can't bleeding stand it.

CHARLIE [*in his sleep*]: Charles-Wisdom-drunk-and-incapable-drunk?-yes-six-shillings-move-on-*next*!

DOROTHY [*on Mrs McElligot's bosom*]: Oh, joy, joy!

[*They are asleep.*]

## 2

And so it goes on.

Dorothy endured this life for ten days—to be exact, nine days and ten nights. It was hard to see what else she could do. Her father, seemingly, had abandoned her altogether, and though she had friends in London who would readily have helped her, she did not feel that she could face them after what had happened, or what was supposed to have happened. And she dared not apply to organized charity because it would almost certainly lead to the discovery of her name, and hence, perhaps, to a fresh hullabaloo about the 'Rector's Daughter'.

So she stayed in London, and became one of that curious tribe, rare but never quite extinct—the tribe of women who are penniless and homeless, but who make such desperate efforts to hide it that they very nearly succeed; women who wash their faces at drinking fountains in the cold of the dawn, and carefully uncrumple their clothes after sleepless nights, and carry themselves with an air of reserve and decency, so that only their faces, pale beneath sunburn, tell you for certain that they are destitute. It was not in her to become a hardened beggar like most of the people about her. Her first twenty-four hours on the Square she spent without any food whatever, except for the cup of tea that she had had overnight and a third of a cup more that she had had at Wilkins's café in the morning. But in the evening, made desperate by hunger and the others' example, she walked up to a strange woman, mastered her voice with an effort, and said: 'Please, Madam, could you give me twopence? I have had nothing to eat since yesterday.' The woman stared, but she opened her purse and gave Dorothy threepence. Dorothy did not know it, but her educated accent, which had made it impossible to get work as a servant, was an invaluable asset to her as a beggar.

After that she found that it was really very easy to beg the daily shilling or so that was needed to keep her alive. And yet she never begged—it seemed to her that actually she could not do it—except when hunger was past bearing or when she had got to lay in the precious penny that was the passport to Wilkins's café in the morning. With Nobby, on the way to the hopfields, she had begged without fear or scruple. But it had been different then; she had not known what she was doing. Now, it was only under the spur of actual hunger that she could screw her courage to the point, and ask for a few coppers from some woman whose face looked friendly. It was always women that she begged from, of course. She did once try begging from a man—but only once.

For the rest, she grew used to the life that she was leading—used to the enormous sleepless nights, the cold, the dirt, the boredom, and the horrible communism of the Square. After a day or two she had ceased to feel even a flicker of surprise at her situation. She had come, like everyone about her, to accept this monstrous existence almost as though it were normal. The dazed, witless feeling that she had known on the way to the hopfields had come back upon her more strongly than before. It is the common effect of sleeplessness and still more of exposure. To live continuously in the open air, never going under a roof for more than an hour or two, blurs your perceptions like a strong light glaring in your eyes or a noise drumming in your ears. You act and plan and suffer, and yet all the while it is as though everything were a little out of focus, a little unreal. The world, inner and outer, grows dimmer till it reaches almost the vagueness of a dream.

Meanwhile, the police were getting to know her by sight. On the Square people are perpetually coming and going, more or less unnoticed. They arrive from nowhere with their drums and their bundles, camp for a few days and nights, and then disappear as mysteriously as they come. If you stay for more than a week or thereabouts, the police will mark you down as an habitual beggar, and they will arrest you sooner or later. It is impossible for them to enforce the begging laws at all regularly, but from time to time they make a sudden raid and capture two or three of the people they have had their eye on. And so it happened in Dorothy's case.

One evening she was 'knocked off', in company with Mrs McElligot and another woman whose name she did not know. They had been careless and begged off a nasty old lady with a face like a horse, who had promptly walked up to the nearest policeman and given them in charge.

Dorothy did not mind very much. Everything was dreamlike now—the face of the nasty old lady, eagerly accusing them, and the walk to the station with a young policeman's gentle, almost deferential hand on her arm; and then the white-tiled cell, with the fatherly sergeant handing her a cup of tea through the grille and telling her that the magistrate wouldn't be too hard on her if she pleaded guilty. In the cell next door Mrs McElligot stormed at the sergeant, called him a bloody get, and then spent half the night in bewailing her fate. But Dorothy had no feeling save vague relief at being in so clean and warm a place. She crept immediately on to the plank bed that was fixed like a shelf to the wall, too tired even to pull the blankets about her, and slept for ten hours without stirring. It was only on the following morning that she began to grasp the reality of her situation, as the Black Maria rolled briskly up to Old Street Police Court, to the tune of 'Adeste fideles' shouted by five drunks inside.

# CHAPTER 4

## I

Dorothy had wronged her father in supposing that he was willing to let her starve to death in the street. He had, as a matter of fact, made efforts to get in touch with her, though in a roundabout and not very helpful way.

His first emotion on learning of Dorothy's disappearance had been rage pure and simple. At about eight in the morning, when he was beginning to wonder what had become of his shaving water, Ellen had come into his bedroom and announced in a vaguely panic-stricken tone:

'Please, Sir, Miss Dorothy ain't in the house, Sir. I can't find her nowhere!'

'What?' said the Rector.

'She ain't in the house, Sir! And her bed don't look as if it hadn't been slept in, neither. It's my belief as she's *gorn*, Sir!'

'Gone!' exclaimed the Rector, partly sitting up in bed. 'What do you mean—*gone*?'

'Well, Sir, I believe she's run away from 'ome, Sir!'

'Run away from home! At *this* hour of the morning? And what about my breakfast, pray?'

By the time the Rector got downstairs—unshaven, no hot water having appeared—Ellen had gone down into the town to make fruitless inquiries for Dorothy. An hour passed, and she did not return. Whereupon there occurred a frightful, unprecedented thing–a thing never to be forgotten this side of the grave; the Rector was obliged to prepare his own breakfast–yes, actually to mess about with a vulgar black kettle and rashers of Danish bacon–with his own sacerdotal hands.

After that, of course, his heart was hardened against Dorothy for ever. For the rest of the day he was far too busy raging over unpunctual meals to ask himself *why* she had disappeared and whether any harm had befallen her. The point was that the confounded girl (he said several times 'confounded girl', and came near to saying something stronger) *had* disappeared, and had upset the whole household by doing so. Next day, however, the question became more urgent, because Mrs Semprill was now publishing the story of the elopement far and wide. Of course, the Rector denied it violently, but in his heart he had a sneaking suspicion that it might be true. It was the kind of thing, he now decided, that Dorothy *would* do. A girl who would suddenly walk out of the house without even taking thought for her father's breakfast was capable of anything.

Two days later the newspapers got hold of the story, and a nosy young reporter came down to Knype Hill and began asking questions. The Rector made matters worse by angrily refusing to interview the reporter, so that Mrs Semprill's version was the only one that got into print. For about a week, until the papers got tired of Dorothy's case and dropped her in favour of a plesiosaurus that had been seen at the mouth of the Thames, the Rector enjoyed a horrible notoriety. He could hardly open a newspaper without seeing some flaming headline about 'Rector's Daughter. Further Revelations', or 'Rector's Daughter. Is she in Vienna? Reported seen in Low-class Cabaret'. Finally there came an article in the Sunday *Spyhole,* which began, 'Down in a Suffolk Rectory a broken old man sits staring at the wall', and which was so absolutely unbearable that the Rector consulted his solicitor about an action for libel. However, the solicitor was against it; it might lead to a verdict, he said, but it would certainly lead to further publicity. So the Rector did nothing, and his anger against Dorothy, who had brought this disgrace upon him, hardened beyond possibility of forgiveness.

After this there came three letters from Dorothy, explaining what had happened. Of course the Rector never really believed that Dorothy had lost her memory. It was too thin a story altogether. He believed that she either *had* eloped with Mr Warburton, or had gone off on some similar escapade and had landed herself penniless in Kent; at any rate–this he had settled once and for all, and no argument would ever move him from it–whatever had happened to her was entirely her own fault. The first letter he wrote was not to Dorothy herself but to his cousin Tom, the baronet. For a man of the Rector's upbringing it was second nature, in any serious trouble, to turn to a rich relative for help. He had not exchanged a word with his cousin for the last fifteen years, since they had quarrelled over a little matter of a borrowed fifty pounds; still, he wrote fairly confidently, asking Sir Thomas to get in touch with Dorothy if it could be done, and to find her some kind of job in London. For of course, after what had happened, there could be no question of letting her come back to Knype Hill.

Shortly after this there came two despairing letters from Dorothy, telling him that she was in danger of starvation and imploring him to send her some money. The Rector was disturbed. It occurred to him—it was the first time in his life that he had seriously considered such a thing—that it *is* possible to starve if you have no money. So, after thinking it over for the best part of a week, he sold out ten pounds' worth of shares and sent a cheque for ten pounds to his cousin, to be kept for Dorothy till she appeared. At the same time he sent a cold letter to Dorothy herself, telling her that she had better apply to Sir Thomas Hare. But several more days passed before this letter was posted, because the Rector had qualms about addressing a letter to 'Ellen Millborough'—he dimly imagined that it was against the law to use false names—and, of course, he had delayed far too long. Dorothy was already in the streets when the letter reached 'Mary's'.

Sir Thomas Hare was a widower, a good-hearted, chuckle-headed man of about sixty-five, with an obtuse rosy face and curling moustaches. He dressed by preference in checked overcoats and curly brimmed bowler hats that were at once dashingly smart and four decades out of date. At a first glance he gave the impression of having carefully disguised himself as a cavalry major of the 'nineties, so that you could hardly look at him without thinking of devilled bones with a b and s, and the tinkle of hansom bells, and the *Pink 'Un* in its great 'Pitcher' days, and Lottie Collins and 'Tarara-BOOM-deay'. But his chief characteristic was an abysmal mental vagueness. He was one of those people who say 'Don't you know?' and 'What! What!' and lose themselves in the middle of their sentences. When he was puzzled or in difficulties, his moustaches seemed to bristle forward, giving him the appearance of a well-meaning but exceptionally brainless prawn.

So far as his own inclinations went Sir Thomas was not in the least anxious to help his cousins, for Dorothy herself he had never seen, and the Rector he looked on as a cadging poor relation of the worst possible type. But the fact was that he had had just about as much of this 'Rector's Daughter' business as he could stand. The accursed chance that Dorothy's surname was the same as his own had made his life a misery for the past fortnight, and he foresaw further and worse scandals if she were left at large any longer. So, just before leaving London for the pheasant shooting, he sent for his butler, who was also his confidant and intellectual guide, and held a council of war.

'Look here, Blyth, dammit,' said Sir Thomas prawnishly (Blyth was the butler's name), 'I suppose you've seen all this damn' stuff in the newspapers, hey? This "Rector's Daughter" stuff? About this damned niece of mine.'

Blyth was a small sharp-featured man with a voice that never rose above a whisper. It was as nearly silent as a voice can be while still remaining a voice. Only by watching his lips as well as listening closely could you catch the whole of what he said. In this case his lips signalled something to the effect that Dorothy was Sir Thomas's cousin, not his niece.

'What, my cousin, is she?' said Sir Thomas. 'So she is, by Jove! Well, look here, Blyth, what I mean to say—it's about time we got hold of the damn' girl and locked her up somewhere. See what I mean? Get hold of her before there's any *more* trouble. She's knocking about somewhere in London, I believe. What's the best way of getting on her track? Police? Private detectives and all that? D'you think we could manage it?'

Blyth's lips registered disapproval. It would, he seemed to be saying, be possible to trace Dorothy without calling in the police and having a lot of disagreeable publicity.

'Good man!' said Sir Thomas. 'Get to it, then. Never mind what it costs. I'd give fifty quid not to have that "Rector's Daughter" business over again. And for God's sake, Blyth,' he added confidentially, 'once you've got hold of the damn' girl, don't let her out of your sight. Bring her back to the house and damn' well keep her here. See what I mean? Keep her under lock and key till I get back. Or else God knows what she'll be up to next.'

Sir Thomas, of course, had never seen Dorothy, and it was therefore excusable that he should have formed his conception of her from the newspaper reports.

It took Blyth about a week to track Dorothy down. On the morning after she came out of the police-court cells (they had fined her six shillings, and, in default of payment, detained her for twelve hours: Mrs McElligot, as an old offender, got seven days), Blyth came up to her, lifted his bowler hat a quarter of an inch from his head, and inquired noiselessly whether she were not Miss Dorothy Hare. At the second attempt Dorothy understood what he was saying, and admitted that she *was* Miss Dorothy Hare; whereupon Blyth explained that he was sent by her cousin, who was anxious to help her, and that she was to come home with him immediately.

Dorothy followed him without more words said. It seemed queer that her cousin should take this sudden interest in her, but it was no queerer than the other things that had been happening lately. They took the bus to Hyde Park Corner, Blyth paying the fares, and then walked to a large, expensive-looking house with shuttered windows, on the borderland between Knightsbridge and Mayfair. They went down some steps, and Blyth produced a key and they went in. So, after an absence of something over six weeks, Dorothy returned to respectable society, by the area door.

She spent three days in the empty house before her cousin came home. It was a queer, lonely time. There were several servants in the house, but she saw nobody except Blyth, who brought her her meals and talked to her, noiselessly, with a mixture of deference and disapproval. He could not quite make up his mind whether she was a young lady of family or a rescued Magdalen, and so treated her as something between the two. The house had that hushed, corpse-like air peculiar to houses whose master is away, so that you instinctively went about on tiptoe and kept the blinds over the windows. Dorothy did not even dare to enter any of the main rooms. She spent all the daytime lurking in a dusty, forlorn room at the top of the house which was a sort of museum of bric-à-brac dating from 1880 onwards. Lady Hare, dead these five years, had been an industrious collector of rubbish, and most of it had been stowed away in this room when she died. It was a doubtful point whether the queerest object in the room was a yellowed photograph of Dorothy's father, aged eighteen but with respectable side-whiskers, standing self-consciously beside an 'ordinary' bicycle—this was in 1888; or whether it was a little sandalwood box labelled 'Piece of Bread touched by Cecil Rhodes at the City and South Africa Banquet, June 1897'. The sole books in the room were some grisly school prizes that had been won by Sir Thomas's children—he had three, the youngest being the same age as Dorothy.

It was obvious that the servants had orders not to let her go out of doors. However, her father's cheque for ten pounds had arrived, and with some difficulty she induced Blyth to get it cashed, and, on the third day, went out and bought herself some clothes. She bought herself a ready-made tweed coat and skirt and a jersey to go with them, a hat, and a very cheap frock of artificial printed silk; also a pair of passable brown shoes, three pairs of lisle stockings, a nasty, cheap little handbag, and a pair of grey cotton gloves that would pass for suède at a little distance. That came to eight pounds ten, and she dared not spend more. As for underclothes, nightdresses, and handkerchiefs, they would have to wait. After all, it is the clothes that show that matter.

Sir Thomas arrived on the following day, and never really got over the surprise that Dorothy's appearance gave him. He had been expecting to see some rouged and powdered siren who would plague him with temptations to which alas! he was no longer capable of succumbing; and this countrified, spinsterish girl upset all his calculations. Certain vague ideas that had been floating about his mind, of finding her a job as a manicurist or perhaps as a private secretary to a bookie, floated out of it again. From time to time Dorothy caught him studying her with a puzzled, prawnish eye, obviously wondering how on earth such a girl could ever have figured in an elopement. It was very little use, of course, telling him that she had *not* eloped. She had given him her version of the story, and he had accepted it with a chivalrous 'Of course, m'dear, of course!' and thereafter, in every other sentence, betrayed the fact that he disbelieved her.

So for a couple of days nothing definite was done. Dorothy continued her solitary life in the room upstairs, and Sir Thomas went to his club for most of his meals, and in the evening there were discussions of the most unutterable vagueness. Sir Thomas was genuinely anxious to find Dorothy a job, but he had great difficulty in remembering what he was talking about for more than a few minutes at a time. 'Well, m'dear,' he would start off, 'you'll understand, of course, that I'm very keen to do what I can for you. Naturally, being your uncle and all that—what? What's that? Not your uncle? No, I suppose I'm not, by Jove! Cousin—that's it; cousin. Well, now, m'dear, being your cousin—now, what was I saying?' Then, when Dorothy had guided him back to the subject, he would throw out some such suggestion as, 'Well, now, for instance, m'dear, how would you like to be companion to an old lady? Some dear old girl, don't you know—black mittens and rheumatoid arthritis. Die and leave you ten thousand quid and care of the parrot. What, what?' which did not get them very much further. Dorothy repeated a number of times that she would rather be a housemaid or a parlourmaid, but Sir Thomas would not hear of it. The very idea awakened in him a class-instinct which he was usually too vague-minded to remember. 'What!' he would say. 'A dashed skivvy? Girl of your upbringing? No, m'dear—no, no! Can't do *that* kind of thing, dash it!'

But in the end everything was arranged, and with surprising ease; not by Sir Thomas, who was incapable of arranging anything, but by his solicitor, whom he had suddenly thought of consulting. And the solicitor, without even seeing Dorothy, was able to suggest a job for her. She could, he said, almost certainly find a job as a schoolmistress. Of all jobs, that was the easiest to get.

Sir Thomas came home very pleased with this suggestion, which struck him as highly suitable. (Privately, he thought that Dorothy had just the kind of face that a schoolmistress ought to have.) But Dorothy was momentarily aghast when she heard of it.

'A schoolmistress!' she said. 'But I couldn't possibly! I'm sure no school would give me a job. There isn't a single subject I can teach.'

'What? What's that? Can't teach? Oh, dash it! Of course you can! Where's the difficulty?'

'But I don't know enough! I've never taught anybody anything, except cooking to the Girl Guides. You have to be properly qualified to be a teacher.'

'Oh, nonsense! Teaching's the easiest job in the world. Good thick ruler—rap 'em over the knuckles. They'll be glad enough to get hold of a decently brought up young woman to teach the youngsters their ABC. That's the line for you, m'dear—schoolmistress. You're just cut out for it.'

And sure enough, a schoolmistress Dorothy became. The invisible solicitor had made all the arrangements in less than three days. It appeared that a certain Mrs Creevy, who kept a girls' day school in the suburb of Southbridge, was in need of an assistant, and was quite willing to give Dorothy the job. How it had all been settled so quickly, and what kind of school it could be that would take on a total stranger, and unqualified at that, in the middle of the term, Dorothy could hardly imagine. She did not know, of course, that a bribe of five pounds, miscalled a premium, had changed hands.

So, just ten days after her arrest for begging, Dorothy set out for Ringwood House Academy, Brough Road, Southbridge, with a small trunk decently full of clothes and four pounds ten in her purse—for Sir Thomas had made her a present of ten pounds. When she thought of the ease with which this job had been found for her, and then of the miserable struggles of three weeks ago, the contrast amazed her. It brought home to her, as never before, the mysterious power of money. In fact, it reminded her of a favourite saying of Mr Warburton's, that if you took 1 Corinthians, chapter thirteen, and in every verse wrote 'money' instead of 'charity', the chapter had ten times as much meaning as before.

Southbridge was a repellent suburb ten or a dozen miles from London. Brough Road lay somewhere at the heart of it, amid labyrinths of meanly decent streets, all so indistinguishably alike, with their ranks of semi-detached houses, their privet and laurel hedges and plots of ailing shrubs at the crossroads, that you could lose yourself there almost as easily as in a Brazilian forest. Not only the houses themselves, but even their names were the same over and over again. Reading the names on the gates as you came up Brough Road, you were conscious of being haunted by some half-remembered passage of poetry; and when you paused to identify it, you realized that it was the first two lines of Lycidas.

Ringwood House was a dark-looking, semi-detached house of yellow brick, three storeys high, and its lower windows were hidden from the road by ragged and dusty laurels. Above the laurels, on the front of the house, was a board inscribed in faded gold letters:

RINGWOOD HOUSE ACADEMY FOR GIRLS
Ages 5 to 18
Music and Dancing Taught
Apply within for Prospectus

Edge to edge with this board, on the other half of the house, was another board which read:

RUSHINGTON GRANGE HIGH SCHOOL FOR BOYS
Ages 6 to 16
Book-keeping and Commercial Arithmetic a Speciality
Apply within for Prospectus

The district pullulated with small private schools; there were four of them in Brough Road alone. Mrs Creevy, the Principal of Ringwood House, and Mr Boulger, the Principal of Rushington Grange, were in a state of warfare, though their interests in no way clashed with one another. Nobody knew what the feud was about, not even Mrs Creevy or Mr Boulger themselves; it was a feud that they had inherited from earlier proprietors of the two schools. In the mornings after breakfast they would stalk up and down their respective back gardens, beside the very low wall that separated them, pretending not to see one another and grinning with hatred.

Dorothy's heart sank at the sight of Ringwood House. She had not been expecting anything very magnificent or attractive, but she had expected something a little better than this mean, gloomy house, not one of whose windows was lighted, though it was after 8 o'clock in the evening. She knocked at the door, and it was opened by a woman, tall and gaunt-looking in the dark hallway, whom Dorothy took for a servant, but who was actually Mrs Creevy herself. Without a word, except to inquire Dorothy's name, the woman led the way up some dark stairs to a twilit, fireless drawing-room, where she turned up a pinpoint of gas, revealing a black piano, stuffed horsehair chairs, and a few yellowed, ghostly photos on the walls.

Mrs Creevy was a woman somewhere in her forties, lean, hard, and angular, with abrupt decided movements that indicated a strong will and probably a vicious temper. Though she was not in the least dirty or untidy there was something discoloured about her whole appearance, as though she lived all her life in a bad light; and the expression of her mouth, sullen and ill-shaped with the lower lip turned down, recalled that of a toad. She spoke in a sharp, commanding voice, with a bad accent and occasional vulgar turns of speech. You could tell her at a glance for a person who knew exactly what she wanted, and would grasp it as ruthlessly as any machine; not a bully exactly—you could somehow infer from her appearance that she would not take enough interest in you to want to bully you—but a person who would make use of you and then throw you aside with no more compunction than if you had been a worn-out scrubbing-brush.

Mrs Creevy did not waste any words on greetings. She motioned Dorothy to a chair, with the air rather of commanding than of inviting her to sit down, and then sat down herself, with her hands clasped on her skinny forearms.

'I hope you and me are going to get on well together, Miss Millborough,' she began in her penetrating, subhectoring voice. (On the advice of Sir Thomas's everwise solicitor, Dorothy had stuck to the name of Ellen Millborough.) 'And I hope I'm not going to have the same nasty business with you as I had with my last two assistants. You say you haven't had an experience of teaching before this?'

'Not in a school,' said Dorothy—there had been a tarradiddle in her letter of introduction, to the effect that she had had experience of 'private teaching'.

Mrs Creevy looked Dorothy over as though wondering whether to induct her into the inner secrets of school-teaching, and then appeared to decide against it.

'Well, we shall see,' she said. 'I must say,' she added complainingly, 'it's not easy to get hold of good hardworking assistants nowadays. You give them good wages and good treatment, and you get no thanks for it. The last one I had—the one I've just had to get rid of—Miss Strong, wasn't so bad so far as the teaching part went; in fact, she was a B.A., and I don't know what you could have better than a B.A., unless it's an M.A. You don't happen to be a B.A. or an M.A., do you, Miss Millborough?'

'No, I'm afraid not,' said Dorothy.

'Well, that's a pity. It looks so much better on the prospectus if you've got a few letters after your name. Well! Perhaps it doesn't matter. I don't suppose many of *our* parents'd know what B.A. stands for; and they aren't so keen on showing their ignorance. I suppose you can talk French, of course?'

'Well—I've learnt French.'

'Oh, that's all right, then. Just so as we can put it on the prospectus. Well, now, to come back to what I was saying, Miss Strong was all right as a teacher, but she didn't come up to my ideas on what I call the *moral side*. We're very strong on the moral side at Ringwood House. It's what counts most with the parents, you'll find. And the one before Miss Strong, Miss Brewer—well, she had what I call a weak nature. You don't get on with girls if you've got a weak nature. The end of it all was that one morning one little girl crept up to the desk with a box of matches and set fire to Miss Brewer's skirt. Of course I wasn't going to keep her after that. In fact I had her out of the house the same afternoon—and I didn't give her any refs either, I can tell you!'

'You mean you expelled the girl who did it?' said Dorothy, mystified.

'What? The *girl*? Not likely! You don't suppose I'd go and turn fees away from my door, do you? I mean I got rid of Miss Brewer, not the *girl*. It's no good having teachers who let the girls get saucy with them. We've got twenty-one in the class just at present, and you'll find they need a strong hand to keep them down.'

'You don't teach yourself?' said Dorothy.

'Oh dear, no!' said Mrs Creevy almost contemptuously. 'I've got a lot too much on my hands to waste my time *teaching*. There's the house to look after, and seven of the children stay to dinner—I've only a daily woman at present. Besides, it takes me all my time getting the fees out of the parents. After all, the fees *are* what matter, aren't they?'

'Yes. I suppose so,' said Dorothy.

'Well, we'd better settle about your wages,' continued Mrs Creevy. 'In term time I'll give you your board and lodging and ten shillings a week; in the holidays it'll just be your board and lodging. You can have the use of the copper in the kitchen for your laundering, and I light the geyser for hot baths every Saturday night; or at least *most* Saturday nights. You can't have the use of this room we're in now, because it's my reception-room, and I don't want you to go wasting the gas in your bedroom. But you can have the use of the morning-room whenever you want it.'

'Thank you,' said Dorothy.

'Well, I should think that'll be about all. I expect you're feeling ready for bed. You'll have had your supper long ago, of course?'

This was clearly intended to mean that Dorothy was not going to get any food tonight, so she answered Yes, untruthfully, and the conversation was at an end. That was always Mrs Creevy's way—she never kept you talking an instant longer than was necessary. Her conversation was so very definite, so exactly to the point, that it was not really conversation at all. Rather, it was the skeleton of conversation; like the dialogue in a badly written novel where everyone talks a little too much in character. But indeed, in the proper sense of the word she did not *talk*; she merely said, in her brief shrewish way, whatever it was necessary to say, and then got rid of you as promptly as possible. She now showed Dorothy along the passage to her bedroom, and lighted a gas-jet no bigger than an acorn, revealing a gaunt bedroom with a narrow white-quilted bed, a rickety wardrobe, one chair and a wash-hand-stand with a frigid white china basin and ewer. It was very like the bedrooms in seaside lodging houses, but it lacked the one thing that gives such rooms their air of homeliness and decency—the text over the bed.

'This is your room,' Mrs Creevy said; 'and I just hope you'll keep it a bit tidier than what Miss Strong used to. And don't go burning the gas half the night, please, because I can tell what time you turn it off by the crack under the door.'

With this parting salutation she left Dorothy to herself. The room was dismally cold; indeed, the whole house had a damp, chilly feeling, as though fires were rarely lighted in it. Dorothy got into bed as quickly as possible, feeling bed to be the warmest place. On top of the wardrobe, when she was putting her clothes away, she found a cardboard box containing no less than nine empty whisky bottles—relics, presumably, of Miss Strong's weakness on the *moral side*.

At eight in the morning Dorothy went downstairs and found Mrs Creevy already at breakfast in what she called the 'morning-room'. This was a smallish room adjoining the kitchen, and it had started life as the scullery; but Mrs Creevy had converted it into the 'morning-room' by the simple process of removing the sink and copper into the kitchen. The breakfast table, covered with a cloth of harsh texture, was very large and forbiddingly bare. Up at Mrs Creevy's end were a tray with a very small teapot and two cups, a plate on which were two leathery fried eggs, and a dish of marmalade; in the middle, just within Dorothy's reach if she stretched, was a plate of bread and butter; and beside her plate—as though it were the only thing she could be trusted with—a cruet stand with some dried-up, clotted stuff inside the bottles.

'Good morning, Miss Millborough,' said Mrs Creevy. 'It doesn't matter this morning, as this is the first day, but just remember another time that I want you down here in time to help me get breakfast ready.'

'I'm so sorry,' said Dorothy.

'I hope you're fond of fried eggs for your breakfast?' went on Mrs Creevy. Dorothy hastened to assure her that she was very fond of fried eggs.

'Well, that's a good thing, because you'll always have to have the same as what I have. So I hope you're not going to be what I call *dainty* about your food. I always think,' she added, picking up her knife and fork, 'that a fried egg tastes a lot better if you cut it well up before you eat it.'

She sliced the two eggs into thin strips, and then served them in such a way that Dorothy received about two-thirds of an egg. With some difficulty Dorothy spun out her fraction of egg so as to make half a dozen mouthfuls of it, and then, when she had taken a slice of bread and butter, she could not help glancing hopefully in the direction of the dish of marmalade. But Mrs Creevy was sitting with her lean left arm—not exactly *round* the marmalade, but in a protective position on its left flank, as though she suspected that Dorothy was going to make an attack upon it. Dorothy's nerve failed her, and she had no marmalade that morning—nor, indeed, for many mornings to come.

Mrs Creevy did not speak again during breakfast, but presently the sound of feet on the gravel outside, and of squeaky voices in the schoolroom, announced that the girls were beginning to arrive. They came in by a side-door that was left open for them. Mrs Creevy got up from the table and banged the breakfast things together on the tray. She was one of those women who can never move anything without banging it about; she was as full of thumps and raps as a poltergeist. Dorothy carried the tray into the kitchen, and when she returned Mrs Creevy produced a penny notebook from a drawer in the dresser and laid it open on the table.

'Just take a look at this,' she said. 'Here's a list of the girls' names that I've got ready for you. I shall want you to know the whole lot of them by this evening.' She wetted her thumb and turned over three pages: 'Now, do you see these three lists here?'

'Yes,' said Dorothy.

'Well, you'll just have to learn those three lists by heart, and make sure you know what girls are on which. Because I don't want you to go thinking that all the girls are to be treated alike. They aren't—not by a long way, they aren't. Different girls, different treatment—that's my system. Now, do you see this lot on the first page?'

'Yes,' said Dorothy again.

'Well, the parents of that lot are what I call the *good* payers. You know what I mean by that? They're the ones that pay cash on the nail and no jibbing at an extra half-guinea or so now and again. You're not to smack any of that lot, not on *any* account. This lot over here are the *medium* payers. Their parents do pay up sooner or later, but you don't get the money out of them without you worry them for it night and day. You can smack that lot if they get saucy, but don't go and leave a mark their parents can see. If you'll take *my* advice, the best thing with children is to twist their ears. Have you ever tried that?'

'No,' said Dorothy.

'Well, I find it answers better than anything. It doesn't leave a mark, and the children can't bear it. Now these three over here are the *bad* payers. Their fathers are two terms behind already, and I'm thinking of a solicitor's letter. I don't care *what* you do to that lot—well, short of a police-court case, naturally. Now, shall I take you in and start you with the girls? You'd better bring that book along with you, and just keep your eye on it all the time so as there'll be no mistakes.'

They went into the schoolroom. It was a largish room, with grey-papered walls that were made yet greyer by the dullness of the light, for the heavy laurel bushes outside choked the windows, and no direct ray of the sun ever penetrated into the room. There was a teacher's desk by the empty fireplace, and there were a dozen small double desks, a light blackboard, and, on the mantelpiece, a black clock that looked like a miniature mausoleum; but there were no maps, no pictures, nor even, as far as Dorothy could see, any books. The sole objects in the room that could be called ornamental were two sheets of black paper pinned to the walls, with writing on them in chalk in beautiful copperplate. On one was 'Speech is Silver. Silence is Golden', and on the other

'Punctuality is the Politeness of Princes'.

The girls, twenty-one of them, were already sitting at their desks. They had grown very silent when they heard footsteps approaching, and as Mrs Creevy came in they seemed to shrink down in their places like partridge chicks when a hawk is soaring. For the most part they were dull-looking, lethargic children with bad complexions, and adenoids seemed to be remarkably common among them. The eldest of them might have been fifteen years old, the youngest was hardly more than a baby. The school had no uniform, and one or two of the children were verging on raggedness.

'Stand up, girls,' said Mrs Creevy as she reached the teacher's desk. 'We'll start off with the morning prayer.'

The girls stood up, clasped their hands in front of them, and shut their eyes. They repeated the prayer in unison, in weak piping voices, Mrs Creevy leading them, her sharp eyes darting over them all the while to see that they were attending.

'Almighty and everlasting Father,' they piped, 'we beseech Thee that our studies this day may be graced by Thy divine guidance. Make us to conduct ourselves quietly and obediently; look down upon our school and make it to prosper, so that it may grow in numbers and be a good example to the neighbourhood and not a disgrace like some schools of which Thou knowest, O Lord. Make us, we beseech Thee, O Lord, industrious, punctual, and ladylike, and worthy in all possible respects to walk in Thy ways: for Jesus Christ's sake, our Lord, Amen.'

This prayer was of Mrs Creevy's own composition. When they had finished it, the girls repeated the Lord's Prayer, and then sat down.

'Now, girls,' said Mrs Creevy, 'this is your new teacher, Miss Millborough. As you know, Miss Strong had to leave us all of a sudden after she was taken so bad in the middle of the arithmetic lesson; and I can tell you I've had a hard week of it looking for a new teacher. I had seventy-three applications before I took on Miss Millborough, and I had to refuse them all because their qualifications weren't high enough. Just you remember and tell your parents that, all of you—seventy-three applications! Well, Miss Millborough is going to take you in Latin, French, history, geography, mathematics, English literature and composition, spelling, grammar, handwriting, and freehand drawing; and Mr Booth will take you in chemistry as usual on Thursday afternoons. Now, what's the first lesson on your time-table this morning?'

'History, Ma'am,' piped one or two voices.

'Very well. I expect Miss Millborough'll start off by asking you a few questions about the history you've been learning. So just you do your best, all of you, and let her see that all the trouble we've taken over you hasn't been wasted. You'll find they can be quite a sharp lot of girls when they try, Miss Millborough.'

'I'm sure they are,' said Dorothy.

'Well, I'll be leaving you, then. And just you behave yourselves, girls! Don't you get trying it on with Miss Millborough like you did with Miss Brewer, because I warn you she won't stand it. If I hear any noise coming from this room, there'll be trouble for somebody.'

She gave a glance round which included Dorothy and indeed suggested that Dorothy would probably be the 'somebody' referred to, and departed.

Dorothy faced the class. She was not afraid of them—she was too used to dealing with children ever to be afraid of them—but she did feel a momentary qualm. The sense of being an impostor (what teacher has not felt it at times?) was heavy upon her. It suddenly occurred to her, what she had only been dimly aware of before, that she had taken this teaching job under flagrantly false pretences, without having any kind of qualification for it. The subject she was now supposed to be teaching was history, and, like most 'educated' people, she knew virtually no history. How awful, she thought, if it turned out that these girls knew more history than she did! She said tentatively:

'What period exactly were you doing with Miss Strong?'

Nobody answered. Dorothy saw the older girls exchanging glances, as though asking one another whether it was safe to say anything, and finally deciding not to commit themselves.

'Well, whereabouts had you got to?' she said, wondering whether perhaps the word 'period' was too much for them.

Again no answer.

'Well, now, surely you remember *something* about it? Tell me the names of some of the people you were learning about in your last history lesson.'

More glances were exchanged, and a very plain little girl in the front row, in a brown jumper and skirt, with her hair screwed into two tight pigtails, remarked cloudily, 'It was about the Ancient Britons.' At this two other girls took courage, and answered simultaneously. One of them said, 'Columbus', and the other 'Napoleon'.

Somehow, after that, Dorothy seemed to see her way more clearly. It was obvious that instead of being uncomfortably knowledgeable as she had feared, the class knew as nearly as possible no history at all. With this discovery her stage-fright vanished. She grasped that before she could do anything else with them it was necessary to find out what, if anything, these children knew. So, instead of following the time-table, she spent the rest of the morning in questioning the entire class on each subject in turn; when she had finished with history (and it took about five minutes to get to the bottom of their historical knowledge) she tried them with geography, with English grammar, with French, with arithmetic—with everything, in fact, that they were supposed to have learned. By twelve o'clock she had plumbed, though not actually explored, the frightful abysses of their ignorance.

For they knew nothing, absolutely nothing—nothing, nothing, nothing, like the Dadaists. It was appalling that even children could be so ignorant. There were only two girls in the class who knew whether the earth went round the sun or the sun round the earth, and not a single one of them could tell Dorothy who was the last king before George V, or who wrote *Hamlet*, or what was meant by a vulgar fraction, or which ocean you crossed to get to America, the Atlantic or the Pacific. And the big girls of fifteen were not much better than the tiny infants of eight, except that the former could at least read consecutively and write neat copperplate. That was the one thing that nearly all of the older girls could do—they could write neatly. Mrs Creevy had seen to that. And of course, here and there in the midst of their ignorance, there were small, disconnected islets of knowledge; for example, some odd stanzas from 'pieces of poetry' that they had learned by heart, and a few Ollendorffian French sentences such as *'Passez-moi le beurre, s'il vous plaît'* and *'Le fils du jardinier a perdu son chapeau'*, which they appeared to have learned as a parrot learns 'Pretty Poll'. As for their arithmetic, it was a little better than the other subjects. Most of them knew how to add and subtract, about half of them had some notion of how to multiply, and there were even three or four who had struggled as far as long division. But that was the utmost limit of their knowledge; and beyond, in every direction, lay utter, impenetrable night.

Moreover, not only did they know nothing, but they were so unused to being questioned that it was often difficult to get answers out of them at all. It was obvious that whatever they knew they had learned in an entirely mechanical manner, and they could only gape in a sort of dull bewilderment when asked to think for themselves. However, they did not seem unwilling, and evidently they had made up their minds to be 'good'—children are always 'good' with a new teacher; and Dorothy persisted, and by degrees the children grew, or seemed to grow, a shade less lumpish. She began to pick up, from the answers they gave her, a fairly accurate notion of what Miss Strong's régime had been like.

It appeared that, though theoretically they had learned all the usual school subjects, the only ones that had been at all seriously taught were handwriting and arithmetic. Mrs Creevy was particularly keen on handwriting. And besides this they had spent great quantities of time—an hour or two out of every day, it seemed—in drudging through a dreadul routine called 'copies.' 'Copies' meant copying things out of textbooks or off the blackboard. Miss Strong would write up, for example, some sententious little 'essay' (there was an essay entitled 'Spring' which recurred in all the older girls' books, and which began, 'Now, when girlish April is tripping through the land, when the birds are chanting gaily on the boughs and the dainty flowerets bursting from their buds', etc., etc.), and the girls would make fair copies of it in their copybooks; and the parents, to whom the copybooks were shown from time to time, were no doubt suitably impressed. Dorothy began to grasp that everything that the girls had been taught was in reality aimed at the parents. Hence the 'copies', the insistence on handwriting, and the parroting of ready-made French phrases; they were cheap and easy ways of creating an impression. Meanwhile, the little girls at the bottom of the class seemed barely able to read and write, and one of them—her name was Mavis Williams, and she was a rather sinister-looking child of eleven, with eyes too far apart—could not even count. This child seemed to have done nothing at all during the past term and a half except to write pothooks. She had quite a pile of books filled with pothooks—page after page of pothooks, looping on and on like the mangrove roots in some tropical swamp.

Dorothy tried not to hurt the children's feelings by exclaiming at their ignorance, but in her heart she was amazed and horrified. She had not known that schools of this description still existed in the civilized world. The whole atmosphere of the place was so curiously antiquated—so reminiscent of those dreary little private schools that you read about in Victorian novels. As for the few textbooks that the class possessed, you could hardly look at them without feeling as though you had stepped back into the mid nineteenth century. There were only three textbooks of which each child had a copy. One was a shilling arithmetic, pre Great War but fairly serviceable, and another was a horrid little book called *The Hundred Page History of Britain*—a nasty little duodecimo book with a gritty brown cover, and, for frontispiece, a portrait of Boadicea with a Union Jack draped over the front of her chariot. Dorothy opened this book at random, came to page 91, and read:

After the French Revolution was over, the self-styled Emperor Napoleon Buonaparte attempted to set up his sway, but though he won a few victories against continental troops, he soon found that in the 'thin red line' he had more than met his match. Conclusions were tried upon the field of Waterloo, where 50,000 Britons put to flight 70,000 Frenchmen—for the Prussians, our allies, arrived too late for the battle. With a ringing British cheer our men charged down the slope and the enemy broke and fled. We now come on to the great Reform Bill of 1832, the first of those beneficent reforms which have made British liberty what it is and marked us off from the less fortunate nations [etc., etc.]. . . .

The date of the book was 1888. Dorothy, who had never seen a history book of this description before, examined it with a feeling approaching horror. There was also an extraordinary little 'reader', dated 1863. It consisted mostly of bits out of Fenimore Cooper, Dr Watts, and Lord Tennyson, and at the end there were the queerest little 'Nature Notes' with woodcut illustrations. There would be a woodcut of an elephant, and underneath in small print: 'The elephant is a sagacious beast. He rejoices in the shade of the Palm Trees, and though stronger than six horses he will allow a little child to lead him. His food is Bananas.' And so on to the Whale, the Zebra, and Porcupine, and the Spotted Camelopard. There were also, in the teacher's desk, a copy of *Beautiful Joe,* a forlorn book called *Peeps at Distant Lands,* and a French phrase-book dated 1891. It was called *All you will need on your Parisian Trip,* and the first phrase given was 'Lace my stays, but not too tightly'. In the whole room there was not such a thing as an atlas or a set of geometrical instruments.

At eleven there was a break of ten minutes, and some of the girls played dull little games at noughts and crosses or quarrelled over pencil-cases, and a few who had got over their first shyness clustered round Dorothy's desk and talked to her. They told her some more about Miss Strong and her methods of teaching, and how she used to twist their ears when they made blots on their copybooks. It appeared that Miss Strong had been a very strict teacher except when she was 'taken bad', which happened about twice a week. And when she was taken bad she used to drink some medicine out of a little brown bottle, and after drinking it she would grow quite jolly for a while and talk to them about her brother in Canada. But on her last day—the time when she was taken so bad during the arithmetic lesson—the medicine seemed to make her worse than ever, because she had no sooner drunk it than she began sinking and fell across a desk, and Mrs Creevy had to carry her out of the room.

After the break there was another period of three quarters of an hour, and then school ended for the morning. Dorothy felt stiff and tired after three hours in the chilly but stuffy room, and she would have liked to go out of doors for a breath of fresh air, but Mrs Creevy had told her beforehand that she must come and help get dinner ready. The girls who lived near the school mostly went home for dinner, but there were seven who had dinner in the 'morning-room' at tenpence a time. It was an uncomfortable meal, and passed in almost complete silence, for the girls were frightened to talk under Mrs Creevy's eye. The dinner was stewed scrag end of mutton, and Mrs Creevy showed extraordinary dexterity in serving the pieces of lean to the 'good payers' and the pieces of fat to the 'medium payers'. As for the three 'bad payers', they ate a shamefaced lunch out of paper bags in the school-room.

School began again at two o'clock. Already, after only one morning's teaching, Dorothy went back to her work with secret shrinking and dread. She was beginning to realize what her life would be like, day after day and week after week, in that sunless room, trying to drive the rudiments of knowledge into unwilling brats. But when she had assembled the girls and called their names over, one of them, a little peaky child with mouse-coloured hair, called Laura Firth, came up to her desk and presented her with a pathetic bunch of browny-yellow chrysanthemums, 'from all of us'. The girls had taken a liking to Dorothy, and had subscribed fourpence among themselves, to buy her a bunch of flowers.

Something stirred in Dorothy's heart as she took the ugly flowers. She looked with more seeing eyes than before at the anaemic faces and shabby clothes of the children, and was all of a sudden horribly ashamed to think that in the morning she had looked at them with indifference, almost with dislike. Now, a profound pity took possession of her. The poor children, the poor children! How they had been stunted and maltreated! And with it all they had retained the childish gentleness that could make them squander their few pennies on flowers for their teacher.

She felt quite differently towards her job from that moment onwards. A feeling of loyalty and affection had sprung up in her heart. This school was *her* school; she would work for it and be proud of it, and make every effort to turn it from a place of bondage into a place human and decent. Probably it was very little that she could do. She was so inexperienced and unfitted for her job that she must educate herself before she could even begin to educate anybody else. Still, she would do her best; she would do whatever willingness and energy could do to rescue these children from the horrible darkness in which they had been kept.

# 3

During the next few weeks there were two things that occupied Dorothy to the exclusion of all others. One, getting her class into some kind of order; the other, establishing a concordat with Mrs Creevy.

The second of the two was by a great deal the more difficult. Mrs Creevy's house was as vile a house to live in as one could possibly imagine. It was always more or less cold, there was not a comfortable chair in it from top to bottom, and the food was disgusting. Teaching is harder work than it looks, and a teacher needs good food to keep him going. It was horribly dispiriting to have to work on a diet of tasteless mutton stews, damp boiled potatoes full of little black eyeholes, watery rice puddings, bread and scrape, and weak tea—and never enough even of these. Mrs Creevy, who was mean enough to take a pleasure in skimping even her own food, ate much the same meals as Dorothy, but she always had the lion's share of them. Every morning at breakfast the two fried eggs were sliced up and unequally partitioned, and the dish of marmalade remained for ever sacrosanct. Dorothy grew hungrier and hungrier as the term went on. On the two evenings a week when she managed to get out of doors she dipped into her dwindling store of money and bought slabs of plain chocolate, which she ate in the deepest secrecy—for Mrs Creevy, though she starved Dorothy more or less intentionally, would have been mortally offended if she had known that she bought food for herself.

The worst thing about Dorothy's position was that she had no privacy and very little time that she could call her own. Once school was over for the day her only refuge was the 'morning-room', where she was under Mrs Creevy's eye, and Mrs Creevy's leading idea was that Dorothy must never be left in peace for ten minutes together. She had taken it into her head, or pretended to do so, that Dorothy was an idle person who needed keeping up to the mark. And so it was always, 'Well, Miss Millborough, you don't seem to have very much to do this evening, do you? Aren't there some exercise books that want correcting? Or why don't you get your needle and do a bit of sewing? I'm sure *I* couldn't bear to just sit in my chair doing nothing like you do!' She was for ever finding household jobs for Dorothy to do, even making her scrub the schoolroom floor on Saturday mornings when the girls did not come to school; but this was done out of pure ill nature, for she did not trust Dorothy to do the work properly, and generally did it again after her. One evening Dorothy was unwise enough to bring back a novel from the public library. Mrs Creevy flared up at the very sight of it. 'Well, really, Miss Millborough! I shouldn't have thought you'd have had time to *read*!' she said bitterly. She herself had never read a book right through in her life, and was proud of it.

Moreover, even when Dorothy was not actually under her eye, Mrs Creevy had ways of making her presence felt. She was for ever prowling in the neighbourhood of the schoolroom, so that Dorothy never felt quite safe from her intrusion; and when she thought there was too much noise she would suddenly rap on the wall with her broom-handle in a way that made the children jump and put them off their work. At all hours of the day she was restlessly, noisily active. When she was not cooking meals she was banging about with broom and dustpan, or harrying the charwoman, or pouncing down upon the schoolroom to 'have a look round' in hopes of catching Dorothy or the children up to mischief, or 'doing a bit of gardening'–that is, mutilating with a pair of shears the unhappy little shrubs that grew amid wastes of gravel in the back garden. On only two evenings a week was Dorothy free of her, and that was when Mrs Creevy sallied forth on forays which she called 'going after the girls'; that is to say, canvassing likely parents. These evenings Dorothy usually spent in the public library, for when Mrs Creevy was not at home she expected Dorothy to keep out of the house, to save fire and gaslight. On other evenings Mrs Creevy was busy writing dunning letters to the parents, or letters to the editor of the local paper, haggling over the price of a dozen advertisements, or poking about the girls' desks to see that their exercise books had been properly corrected, or 'doing a bit of sewing'. Whenever occupation failed her for even five minutes she got out her workbox and 'did a bit of sewing'–generally restitching some bloomers of harsh white linen of which she had pairs beyond number. They were the most chilly looking garments that one could possibly imagine; they seemed to carry upon them, as no nun's coif or anchorite's hair shirt could ever have done, the impress of a frozen and awful chastity. The sight of them set you wondering about the late Mr Creevy, even to the point of wondering whether he had ever existed.

Looking with an outsider's eye at Mrs Creevy's manner of life, you would have said that she had no *pleasures* whatever. She never did any of the things that ordinary people do to amuse themselves–never went to the pictures, never looked at a book, never ate sweets, never cooked a special dish for dinner or dressed herself in any kind of finery. Social life meant absolutely nothing to her. She had no friends, was probably incapable of imagining such a thing as friendship, and hardly ever exchanged a word with a fellow being except on business. Of religious belief she had not the smallest vestige. Her attitude towards religion, though she went to the Baptist Chapel every Sunday to impress the parents with her piety, was a mean anti-clericalism founded on the notion that the clergy are 'only after your money'. She seemed a creature utterly joyless, utterly submerged by the dullness of her existence. But in reality it was not so. There were several things from which she derived acute and inexhaustible pleasure.

For instance, there was her avarice over money. It was the leading interest of her life. There are two kinds of avaricious person–the bold, grasping type who will ruin you if he can, but who never looks twice at twopence, and the petty miser who has not the enterprise actually to *make* money, but who will always, as the saying goes, take a farthing from a dunghill with his teeth. Mrs Creevy belonged to the second type. By ceaseless canvassing and impudent bluff she had worked her school up to twenty-one pupils, but she would never get it much further, because she was too mean to spend money on the necessary equipment and to pay proper wages to her assistant. The fees the girls paid, or didn't pay, were five guineas a term with certain extras, so that, starve and sweat her assistant as she might, she could hardly hope to make more than a hundred and fifty pounds a year clear profit. But she was fairly satisfied with that. It meant more to her to save sixpence than to earn a pound. So long as she could think of a way of docking Dorothy's dinner of another potato, or getting her exercise books a halfpenny a dozen cheaper, or shoving an unauthorized half guinea on to one of the 'good payers'' bills, she was happy after her fashion.

And again, in pure, purposeless malignity—in petty acts of spite, even when there was nothing to be gained by them—she had a hobby of which she never wearied. She was one of those people who experience a kind of spiritual orgasm when they manage to do somebody else a bad turn. Her feud with Mr Boulger next door—a one-sided affair, really, for poor Mr Boulger was not up to Mrs Creevy's fighting weight—was conducted ruthlessly, with no quarter given or expected. So keen was Mrs Creevy's pleasure in scoring off Mr Boulger that she was even willing to spend money on it occasionally. A year ago Mr Boulger had written to the landlord (each of them was for ever writing to the landlord, complaining about the other's behaviour), to say that Mrs Creevy's kitchen chimney smoked into his back windows, and would she please have it heightened two feet. The very day the landlord's letter reached her, Mrs Creevy called in the bricklayers and had the chimney lowered two feet. It cost her thirty shillings, but it was worth it. After that there had been the long guerrilla campaign of throwing things over the garden wall during the night, and Mrs Creevy had finally won with a dustbinful of wet ashes thrown on to Mr Boulger's bed of tulips. As it happened, Mrs Creevy won a neat and bloodless victory soon after Dorothy's arrival. Discovering by chance that the roots of Mr Boulger's plum tree had grown under the wall into her own garden, she promptly injected a whole tin of weed-killer into them and killed the tree. This was remarkable as being the only occasion when Dorothy ever heard Mrs Creevy laugh.

But Dorothy was too busy, at first, to pay much attention to Mrs Creevy and her nasty characteristics. She saw quite clearly that Mrs Creevy was an odious woman and that her own position was virtually that of a slave; but it did not greatly worry her. Her work was too absorbing, too all-important. In comparison with it, her own comfort and even her future hardly seemed to matter.

It did not take her more than a couple of days to get her class into running order. It was curious, but though she had no experience of teaching and no preconceived theories about it, yet from the very first day she found herself, as though by instinct, rearranging, scheming, innovating. There was so much that was crying out to be done. The first thing, obviously, was to get rid of the grisly routine of 'copies', and after Dorothy's second day no more 'copies' were done in the class, in spite of a sniff or two from Mrs Creevy. The handwriting lessons, also, were cut down. Dorothy would have liked to do away with handwriting lessons altogether so far as the older girls were concerned—it seemed to her ridiculous that girls of fifteen should waste time in practising copperplate—but Mrs Creevy would not hear of it. She seemed to attach an almost superstitious value to handwriting lessons. And the next thing, of course, was to scrap the repulsive *Hundred Page History* and the preposterous little 'readers'. It would have been worse than useless to ask Mrs Creevy to buy new books for the children, but on her first Saturday afternoon Dorothy begged leave to go up to London, was grudgingly given it, and spent two pounds three shillings out of her precious four pounds ten on a dozen second-hand copies of a cheap school edition of Shakespeare, a big second-hand atlas, some volumes of Hans Andersen's stories for the younger children, a set of geometrical instruments, and two pounds of plasticine. With these, and history books out of the public library, she felt that she could make a start.

She had seen at a glance that what the children most needed, and what they had never had, was individual attention. So she began by dividing them up into three separate classes, and so arranging things that two lots could be working by themselves while she 'went through' something with the third. It was difficult at first, especially with the younger girls, whose attention wandered as soon as they were left to themselves, so that you could never really take your eyes off them. And yet how wonderfully, how unexpectedly, nearly all of them improved during those first few weeks! For the most part they were not really stupid, only dazed by a dull, mechanical rigmarole. For a week, perhaps, they continued unteachable; and then, quite suddenly, their warped little minds seemed to spring up and expand like daisies when you move the garden roller off them.

Quite quickly and easily Dorothy broke them in to the habit of thinking for themselves. She got them to make up essays out of their own heads instead of copying out drivel about the birds chanting on the boughs and the flowerets bursting from their buds. She attacked their arithmetic at the foundations and started the little girls on multiplication and piloted the older ones through long division to fractions; she even got three of them to the point where there was talk of starting on decimals. She taught them the first rudiments of French grammar in place of '*Passez-moi le beurre, s'il vous plaît*' and '*Le fils du jardinier a perdu son chapeau*'. Finding that not a girl in the class knew what any of the countries of the world looked like (though several of them knew that Quito was the capital of Ecuador), she set them to making a large contour-map of Europe in plasticine, on a piece of three-ply wood, copying it in scale from the atlas. The children adored making the map; they were always clamouring to be allowed to go on with it. And she started the whole class, except the six youngest girls and Mavis Williams, the pothook specialist, on reading *Macbeth*. Not a child among them had ever voluntarily read anything in her life before, except perhaps the *Girl's Own Paper*; but they took readily to

Shakespeare, as all children do when he is not made horrible with parsing and analysing.

History was the hardest thing to teach them. Dorothy had not realized till now how hard it is for children who come from poor homes to have even a conception of what history means. Every upper-class person, however ill-informed, grows up with some notion of history; he can visualize a Roman centurion, a medieval knight, an eighteenth-century nobleman; the terms Antiquity, Middle Ages, Renaissance, Industrial Revolution evoke some meaning, even if a confused one, in his mind. But these children came from bookless homes and from parents who would have laughed at the notion that the past has any meaning for the present. They had never heard of Robin Hood, never played at being Cavaliers and Roundheads, never wondered who built the English churches or what Fid. Def. on a penny stands for. There were just two historical characters of whom all of them, almost without exception, had heard, and those were Columbus and Napoleon. Heaven knows why—perhaps Columbus and Napoleon get into the newspapers a little oftener than most historical characters. They seemed to have swelled up in the children's minds, like Tweedledum and Tweedledee, till they blocked out the whole landscape of the past. Asked when motor-cars were invented, one child, aged ten, vaguely hazarded, 'About a thousand years ago, by Columbus.'

Some of the older girls, Dorothy discovered, had been through the *Hundred Page History* as many as four times, from Boadicea to the first Jubilee, and forgotten practically every word of it. Not that that mattered greatly, for most of it was lies. She started the whole class over again at Julius Caesar's invasion, and at first she tried taking history books out of the public library and reading them aloud to the children; but that method failed, because they could understand nothing that was not explained to them in words of one or two syllables. So she did what she could in her own words and with her own inadequate knowledge, making a sort of paraphrase of what she read and delivering it to the children; striving all the while to drive into their dull little minds some picture of the past, and what was always more difficult, some interest in it. But one day a brilliant idea struck her. She bought a roll of cheap plain wallpaper at an upholsterer's shop, and set the children to making an historical chart. They marked the roll of paper into centuries and years, and stuck scraps that they cut out of illustrated papers—pictures of knights in armour and Spanish galleons and printing-presses and railway trains—at the appropriate places. Pinned round the walls of the room, the chart presented, as the scraps grew in number, a sort of panorama of English history. The children were even fonder of the chart than of the contour map. They always, Dorothy found, showed more intelligence when it was a question of *making* something instead of merely learning. There was even talk of making a contour map of the world, four feet by four, in papiermâché, if Dorothy could 'get round' Mrs Creevy to allow the preparation of the papiermâché—a messy process needing buckets of water.

Mrs Creevy watched Dorothy's innovations with a jealous eye, but she did not interfere actively at first. She was not going to show it, of course, but she was secretly amazed and delighted to find that she had got hold of an assistant who was actually willing to work. When she saw Dorothy spending her own money on textbooks for the children, it gave her the same delicious sensation that she would have had in bringing off a successful swindle. She did, however, sniff and grumble at everything that Dorothy did, and she wasted a great deal of time by insisting on what she called 'thorough correction' of the girls' exercise books. But her system of correction, like everything else in the school curriculum, was arranged with one eye on the parents. Periodically the children took their books home for their parents' inspection, and Mrs Creevy would never allow anything disparaging to be written in them. Nothing was to be marked 'bad' or crossed out or too heavily underlined; instead, in the evenings, Dorothy decorated the books, under Mrs Creevy's dictation, with more or less applauding comments in red ink. 'A very creditable performance', and 'Excellent! You are making great strides. Keep it up!' were Mrs Creevy's favourites. All the children in the school, apparently, were for ever 'making great strides'; in what direction they were striding was not stated. The parents, however, seemed willing to swallow an almost unlimited amount of this kind of thing.

There were times, of course, when Dorothy had trouble with the girls themselves. The fact that they were all of different ages made them difficult to deal with, and though they were fond of her and were very 'good' with her at first, they would not have been children at all if they had been invariably 'good'. Sometimes they were lazy and sometimes they succumbed to that most damnable vice of schoolgirls—giggling. For the first few days Dorothy was greatly exercised over little Mavis Williams, who was stupider than one would have believed it possible for any child of eleven to be. Dorothy could do nothing with her at all. At the first attempt to get her to do anything beyond pothooks a look of almost subhuman blankness would come into her wide-set eyes. Sometimes, however, she had talkative fits in which she would ask the most amazing and unanswerable questions. For instance, she would open her 'reader', find one of the illustrations—the sagacious Elephant, perhaps—and ask Dorothy:

'Please, Miss, wass 'at thing there?' (She mispronounced her words in a curious manner.)

'That's an elephant, Mavis.'

'Wass a elephant?'

'An elephant's a kind of wild animal.'

'Wass a animal?'

'Well—a dog's an animal.'

'Wass a dog?'

And so on, more or less indefinitely. About half-way through the fourth morning Mavis held up her hand and said with a sly politeness that ought to have put Dorothy on her guard:

'Please, Miss, may I be 'scused?'

'Yes,' said Dorothy.

One of the bigger girls put up her hand, blushed, and put her hand down again as though too bashful to speak. On being prompted by Dorothy, she said shamefacedly:

'Please, Miss, Miss Strong didn't used to let Mavis go to the lavatory alone. She locks herself in and won't come out, and then Mrs Creevy gets angry, Miss.'

Dorothy dispatched a messenger, but it was too late. Mavis remained *in latebra pudenda* till twelve o'clock. Afterwards, Mrs Creevy explained privately to Dorothy that Mavis was a congenital idiot—or, as she put it, 'not right in the head'. It was totally impossible to teach her anything. Of course, Mrs Creevy didn't 'let on' to Mavis's parents, who believed that their child was only 'backward' and paid their fees regularly. Mavis was quite easy to deal with. You just had to give her a book and a pencil and tell her to draw pictures and be quiet. But Mavis, a child of habit, drew nothing but pothooks —remaining quiet and apparently happy for hours together, with her tongue hanging out, amid festoons of pothooks.

But in spite of these minor difficulties, how well everything went during those first few weeks! How ominously well, indeed! About the tenth of November, after much grumbling about the price of coal, Mrs Creevy started to allow a fire in the schoolroom. The children's wits brightened noticeably when the room was decently warm. And there were happy hours, sometimes, when the fire crackled in the grate, and Mrs Creevy was out of the house, and the children were working quietly and absorbedly at one of the lessons that were their favourites. Best of all was when the two top classes were reading *Macbeth*, the girls squeaking breathlessly through the scenes, and Dorothy pulling them up to make them pronounce the words properly and to tell them who Bellona's bridegroom was and how witches rode on broomsticks; and the girls wanting to know, almost as excitedly as though it had been a detective story, how Birnam Wood could possible come to Dunsinane and Macbeth be killed by a man who was not of woman born. Those are the times that make teaching worth while—the times when the children's enthusiasm leaps up, like an answering flame, to meet your own, and sudden unlooked-for gleams of intelligence reward your earlier drudgery. No job is more fascinating than teaching if you have a free hand at it. Nor did Dorothy know, as yet, that that 'if' is one of the biggest 'ifs' in the world.

Her job suited her, and she was happy in it. She knew the minds of the children intimately by this time, knew their individual peculiarities and the special stimulants that were needed before you could get them to think. She was more fond of them, more interested in their development, more anxious to do her best for them, than she would have conceived possible a short while ago. The complex, never-ended labour of teaching filled her life just as the round of parish jobs had filled it at home. She thought and dreamed of teaching; she took books out of the public library and studied theories of education. She felt that quite willingly she would go on teaching all her life, even at ten shillings a week and her keep, if it could always be like this. It was her vocation, she thought.

Almost any job that fully occupied her would have been a relief after the horrible futility of the time of her destitution. But this was more than a mere job; it was—so it seemed to her—a mission, a life-purpose. Trying to awaken the dulled minds of these children, trying to undo the swindle that had been worked upon them in the name of education—that, surely, was something to which she could give herself heart and soul? So for the time being, in the interest of her work, she disregarded the beastliness of living in Mrs Creevy's house, and quite forgot her strange, anomalous position and the uncertainty of her future.

## 4

But of course, it could not last.

Not many weeks had gone by before the parents began interfering with Dorothy's programme of work. That—trouble with the parents—is part of the regular routine of life in a private school. All parents are tiresome from a teacher's point of view, and the parents of children at fourth-rate private schools are utterly impossible. On the one hand, they have only the dimmest idea of what is meant by education; on the other hand, they look on 'schooling' exactly as they look on a butcher's bill or a grocer's bill, and are perpetually suspicious that they are being cheated. They bombard the teacher with ill-written notes making impossible demands, which they send by hand and which the child reads on the way to school. At the end of the first fortnight Mabel Briggs, one of the most promising girls in the class, brought Dorothy the following note:

> Dear Miss,—Would you please give Mabel a bit more *arithmetic*? I feel that what your giving her is not practcale enough. All these maps and that. She wants practcale work, not all this fancy stuff. So more *arithmetic*, please. And remain,
>
> > Yours Faithfully,
> > Geo. Briggs
>
> P.S. Mabel says your talking of starting her on something called decimals. I don't want her taught decimals, I want her taught *arithmetic*.

So Dorothy stopped Mabel's geography and gave her extra arithmetic instead, whereat Mabel wept. More letters followed. One lady was disturbed to hear that her child was being given Shakespeare to read. 'She had heard', she wrote, 'that this Mr Shakespeare was a writer of stage-plays, and was Miss Millborough quite certain that he wasn't a very *immoral* writer? For her own part she had never so much as been to the pictures in her life, let alone to a stage-play, and she felt that even in *reading* stage-plays there was a very grave danger,' etc., etc. She gave way, however, on being informed that Mr Shakespeare was dead. This seemed to reassure her. Another parent wanted more attention to his child's handwriting, and another thought French was a waste of time; and so it went on, until Dorothy's carefully arranged time-table was almost in ruins. Mrs Creevy gave her clearly to understand that whatever the parents demanded she must do, or pretend to do. In many cases it was next door to impossible, for it disorganized everything to have one child studying, for instance, arithmetic while the rest of the class were doing history or geography. But in private schools the parents' word is law. Such schools exist, like shops, by flattering their customers, and if a parent wanted his child taught nothing but cat's-cradle and the cuneiform alphabet, the teacher would have to agree rather than lose a pupil.

The fact was that the parents were growing perturbed by the tales their children brought home about Dorothy's methods. They saw no sense whatever in these new-fangled ideas of making plasticine maps and reading poetry, and the old mechanical routine which had so horrified Dorothy struck them as eminently sensible. They became more and more restive, and their letters were peppered with the word 'practical', meaning in effect more handwriting lessons and more arithmetic. And even their notion of arithmetic was limited to addition, subtraction, multiplication and 'practice', with long division thrown in as a spectacular *tour de force* of no real value. Very few of them could have worked out a sum in decimals themselves, and they were not particularly anxious for their children to be able to do so either.

However, if this had been all, there would probably never have been any serious trouble. The parents would have nagged at Dorothy, as all parents do; but Dorothy would finally have learned—as, again, all teachers finally learn—that if one showed a certain amount of tact one could safely ignore them. But there was one fact that was absolutely certain to lead to trouble, and that was the fact that the parents of all except three children were Nonconformists, whereas Dorothy was an Anglican. It was true that Dorothy had lost her faith—indeed, for two months past, in the press of varying adventures, had hardly thought either of her faith or of its loss. But that made very little difference; Roman or Anglican, Dissenter, Jew, Turk or infidel, you retain the habits of thought that you have been brought up with. Dorothy, born and bred in the precincts of the Church, had no understanding of the Nonconformist mind. With the best will in the world, she could not help doing things that would cause offence to some of the parents.

Almost at the beginning there was a skirmish over the Scripture lessons—twice a week the children used to read a couple of chapters from the Bible, Old Testament and New Testament alternately—several of the parents writing to say, would Miss Millborough please *not* answer the children when they asked questions about the Virgin Mary; texts about the Virgin Mary were to be passed over in silence, or, if possible, missed out altogether. But it was Shakespeare, that immoral writer, who brought things to a head. The girls had worked their way through *Macbeth*, pining to know how the witches' prophecy was to be fulfilled. They reached the closing scenes. Birnam Wood had come to Dunsinane—that part was settled, anyway; now what about the man who was not of woman born? They came to the fatal passage:

MACBETH:                    Thou losest labour;
  As easy may'st thou the intrenchant air
  With thy keen sword impress, as make me bleed:
  Let fall thy blade on vulnerable crests,
  I bear a charmed life, which must not yield
  To one of woman born.
MACDUFF:                    Despair thy charm,
  And let the Angel whom thou still hast served
  Tell thee, Macduff was from his mother's womb
  Untimely ripp'd.

The girls looked puzzled. There was a momentary silence, and then a chorus of voices round the room:

'Please, Miss, what does that mean?'

Dorothy explained. She explained haltingly and incompletely, with a sudden horrid misgiving—a premonition that this was going to lead to trouble—but still, she did explain. And after that, of course, the fun began.

About half the children in the class went home and asked their parents the meaning of the word 'womb'. There was a sudden commotion, a flying to and fro of messages, an electric thrill of horror through fifteen decent Nonconformist homes. That night the parents must have held some kind of conclave, for the following evening, about the time when school ended, a deputation called upon Mrs Creevy. Dorothy heard them arriving by ones and twos, and guessed what was going to happen. As soon as she had dismissed the children, she heard Mrs Creevy call sharply down the stairs:

'Come up here a minute, Miss Millborough!'

Dorothy went up, trying to control the trembling of her knees. In the gaunt drawing-room Mrs Creevy was standing grimly beside the piano, and six parents were sitting round on horsehair chairs like a circle of inquisitors. There was the Mr Geo. Briggs who had written the letter about Mabel's arithmetic—he was an alert-looking greengrocer with a dried-up, shrewish wife—and there was a large, buffalo-like man with drooping moustaches and a colourless, peculiarly *flat* wife who looked as though she had been flattened out by the pressure of some heavy object—her husband, perhaps. The names of these two Dorothy did not catch. There was also Mrs Williams, the mother of the congenital idiot, a small, dark, very obtuse woman who always agreed with the last speaker, and there was a Mr Poynder, a commerical traveller. He was a youngish to middle-aged man with a grey face, mobile lips, and a bald scalp across which some strips of rather nasty-looking damp hair were carefully plastered. In honour of the parents' visit, a fire composed of three large coals was sulking in the grate.

'Sit down there, Miss Millborough,' said Mrs Creevy, pointing to a hard chair which stood like a stool of repentance in the middle of the ring of parents.

Dorothy sat down.

'And now,' said Mrs Creevy, 'just you listen to what Mr Poynder's got to say to you.'

Mr Poynder had a great deal to say. The other parents had evidently chosen him as their spokesman, and he talked till flecks of yellowish foam appeared at the corners of his mouth. And what was remarkable, he managed to do it all—so nice was his regard for the decencies—without ever once repeating the word that had caused all the trouble.

'I feel that I'm voicing the opinion of all of us,' he said with his facile bagman's eloquence, 'in saying that if Miss Millborough knew that this play—*Macduff*, or whatever its name is—contained such words as—well, such words as we're speaking about, she never ought to have given it to the children to read at all. To my mind it's a disgrace that schoolbooks can be printed with such words in them. I'm sure if any of us had ever known that Shakespeare was that kind of stuff, we'd have put our foot down at the start. It surprises me, I must say. Only the other morning I was reading a piece in my *News Chronicle* about Shakespeare being the father of English Literature; well, if that's Literature, let's have a bit *less* Literature, say I! I think everyone'll agree with me there. And on the other hand, if Miss Millborough didn't know that the word—well, the word I'm referring to—was coming, she just ought to have gone straight on and taken no notice when it did come. There wasn't the slightest need to go explaining it to them. Just tell them to keep quiet and not get asking questions—that's the proper way with children.'

'But the children wouldn't have understood the play if I hadn't explained!' protested Dorothy for the third or fourth time.

'Of course they wouldn't! You don't seem to get my point, Miss Millborough! We don't want them to understand. Do you think we want them to go picking up dirty ideas out of books? Quite enough of that already with all these dirty films and these twopenny girls' papers that they get hold of—all these filthy, dirty love-stories with pictures of—well, I won't go into it. We don't send our children to school to have ideas put into their heads. I'm speaking for all the parents in saying this. We're all of decent God-fearing folk—some of us are Baptists and some of us are Methodists, and there's even one or two Church of England among us; but we can sink our differences when it comes to a case like this—and we try to bring our children up decent and save them from knowing anything about the Facts of Life. If I had my way, no child—at any rate, no girl—would know anything about the Facts of Life till she was twenty-one.'

There was a general nod from the parents, and the buffalo-like man added, 'Yer, yer! I'm with you there, Mr Poynder. Yer, yer!' deep down in his inside.

After dealing with the subject of Shakespeare, Mr Poynder added some remarks about Dorothy's new-fangled methods of teaching, which gave Mr Geo. Briggs the opportunity to rap out from time to time, 'That's it! Practical work—that's what we want—practical work! Not all this messy stuff like po'try and making maps and sticking scraps of paper and such like. Give 'em a good bit of figuring and handwriting and bother the rest. Practical work! You've said it!'

This went on for about twenty minutes. At first Dorothy attempted to argue, but she saw Mrs Creevy angrily shaking her head at her over the buffalo-like man's shoulder, which she rightly took as a signal to be quiet. By the time the parents had finished they had reduced Dorothy very nearly to tears, and after this they made ready to go. But Mrs Creevy stopped them.

'*Just* a minute, ladies and gentlemen,' she said. 'Now that you've all had your say—and I'm sure I'm most glad to give you the opportunity—I'd just like to say a little something on my own account. Just to make things clear, in case any of you might think *I* was to blame for this nasty business that's happened. And *you* stay here too, Miss Millborough!' she added.

She turned on Dorothy, and, in front of the parents, gave her a venomous 'talking to' which lasted upwards of ten minutes. The burden of it all was that Dorothy had brought these dirty books into the house behind her back; that it was monstrous treachery and ingratitude; and that if anything like it happened again, out Dorothy would go with a week's wages in her pocket. She rubbed it in and in and in. Phrases like 'girl that I've taken into my house', 'eating my bread', and even 'living on my charity', recurred over and over again. The parents sat round watching, and in their crass faces—faces not harsh or evil, only blunted by ignorance and mean virtues—you could see a solemn approval, a solemn pleasure in the spectacle of sin rebuked. Dorothy understood this; she understood that it was necessary that Mrs Creevy should give her her 'talking to' in front of the parents, so that they might feel that they were getting their money's worth and be satisfied. But still, as the stream of mean, cruel reprimand went on and on, such anger rose in her heart that she could with pleasure have stood up and struck Mrs Creevy across the face. Again and again she thought, 'I won't stand it, I won't stand it any longer! I'll tell her what I think of her and then walk straight out of the house!' But she did nothing of the kind. She saw with dreadful clarity the helplessness of her position. Whatever happened, whatever insults it meant swallowing, she had got to keep her job. So she sat still, with pink humiliated face, amid the circle of parents, and presently her anger turned to misery, and she realized that she was going to begin crying if she did not struggle to prevent it. But she realized, too, that if she began crying it would be the last straw and the parents would demand her dismissal. To stop herself, she dug her nails so hard into the palms that afterwards she found that she had drawn a few drops of blood.

Presently the 'talking to' wore itself out in assurances from Mrs Creevy that this should never happen again and that the offending Shakespeares should be burnt immediately. The parents were now satisfied. Dorothy had had her lesson and would doubtless profit by it; they did not bear her any malice and were not conscious of having humiliated her. They said good-bye to Mrs Creevy, said good-bye rather more coldly to Dorothy, and departed. Dorothy also rose to go, but Mrs Creevy signed to her to stay where she was.

'Just you wait a minute,' she said ominously as the parents left the room. 'I haven't finished yet, not by a long way I haven't.'

Dorothy sat down again. She felt very weak at the knees, and nearer to tears than ever. Mrs Creevy, having shown the parents out by the front door, came back with a bowl of water and threw it over the fire—for where was the sense of burning good coals after the parents had gone? Dorothy supposed that the 'talking to' was going to begin afresh. However, Mrs Creevy's wrath seemed to have cooled—at any rate, she had laid aside the air of outraged virtue that it had been necessary to put on in front of the parents.

'I just want to have a bit of a talk with you, Miss Millborough,' she said. 'It's about time we got it settled once and for all how this school's going to be run and how it's not going to be run.'

'Yes,' said Dorothy.

'Well, I'll be straight with you. When you came here I could see with half an eye that you didn't know the first thing about school-teaching; but I wouldn't have minded that if you'd just had a bit of common sense like any other girl would have had. Only it seems you hadn't. I let you have your own way for a week or two, and the first thing you do is to go and get all the parents' backs up. Well, I'm not going to have *that* over again. From now on I'm going to have things done *my* way, not *your* way. Do you understand that?'

'Yes,' said Dorothy again.

'You're not to think as I can't do without you, mind,' proceeded Mrs Creevy. 'I can pick up teachers at two a penny any day of the week, M.A.s and B.A.s and all. Only the M.A.s and B.A.s mostly take to drink, or else they—well, no matter what—and I will say for you you don't seem to be given to the drink or anything of that kind. I dare say you and me can get on all right if you'll drop these new-fangled ideas of yours and understand what's meant by practical school-teaching. So just you listen to me.'

Dorothy listened. With admirable clarity, and with a cynicism that was all the more disgusting because it was utterly unconscious, Mrs Creevy explained the technique of the dirty swindle that she called practical school-teaching.

'What you've got to get hold of once and for all,' she began, 'is that there's only one thing that matters in a school, and that's the fees. As for all this stuff about "developing the children's minds", as you call it, it's neither here nor there. It's the fees I'm after, not *developing the children's minds*. After all, it's no more than common sense. It's not to be supposed as anyone'd go to all the trouble of keeping school and having the house turned upside down by a pack of brats, if it wasn't that there's a bit of money to be made out of it. The fees come first, and everything else comes afterwards. Didn't I tell you that the very first day you came here?'

'Yes,' admitted Dorothy humbly.

'Well, then, it's the parents that pay the fees, and it's the parents you've got to think about. Do what the parents want—that's our rule here. I dare say all this messing about with plasticine and paper-scraps that you go in for doesn't do the children any particular harm; but the parents don't want it, and there's an end of it. Well, there's just two subjects that they *do* want their children taught, and that's handwriting and arithmetic. Especially handwriting. That's something they *can* see the sense of. And so handwriting's the thing you've got to keep on and on at. Plenty of nice neat copies that the girls can take home, and that the parents'll show off to the neighbours and give us a bit of a free advert. I want you to give the children two hours a day just at handwriting and nothing else.'

'Two hours a day just at handwriting,' repeated Dorothy obediently.

'Yes. And plenty of arithmetic as well. The parents are very keen on arithmetic: especially money-sums. Keep your eye on the parents all the time. If you meet one of them in the street, get hold of them and start talking to them about their own girl. Make out that she's the best girl in the class and that if she stays just three terms longer she'll be working wonders. You see what I mean? Don't go and tell them there's no room for improvement; because if you tell them *that,* they generally take their girls away. Just three terms longer—that's the thing to tell them. And when you make out the end of term reports, just you bring them to me and let me have a good look at them. I like to do the marking myself.'

Mrs Creevy's eye met Dorothy's. She had perhaps been about to say that she always arranged the marks so that every girl came out somewhere near the top of the class; but she refrained. Dorothy could not answer for a moment. Outwardly she was subdued, and very pale, but in her heart were anger and deadly repulsion against which she had to struggle before she could speak. She had no thought, however, of contradicting Mrs Creevy. The 'talking to' had quite broken her spirit. She mastered her voice, and said:

'I'm to teach nothing but handwriting and arithmetic—is that it?'

'Well, I didn't say that exactly. There's plenty of other subjects that look well on the prospectus. French, for instance—French looks *very* well on the prospectus. But it's not a subject you want to waste much time over. Don't go filling them up with a lot of grammar and syntax and verbs and all that. That kind of stuff doesn't get them anywhere so far as *I* can see. Give them a bit of "Parley vous Francey", and "Passey moi le beurre", and so forth; that's a lot more use than grammar. And then there's Latin—I always put Latin on the prospectus. But I don't suppose you're very great on Latin, are you?'

'No,' admitted Dorothy.

'Well, it doesn't matter. You won't have to teach it. None of *our* parents'd want their children to waste time over Latin. But they like to see it on the prospectus. It looks classy. Of course there's a whole lot of subjects that we can't actually teach, but we have to advertise them all the same. Book-keeping and typing and shorthand, for instance; besides music and dancing. It all looks well on the prospectus.'

'Arithmetic, handwriting, French—is there anything else?' Dorothy said.

'Oh, well, history and geography and English Literature, of course. But just drop that map-making business at once—it's nothing but waste of time. The best geography to teach is lists of capitals. Get them so that they can rattle off the capitals of all the English counties as if it was the multiplication table. Then they've got something to show for what they've learnt, anyway. And as for history, keep on with the *Hundred Page History of Britian.* I won't have them taught out of those big history books you keep bringing home from the library. I opened one of those books the other day, and the first thing I saw was a piece where it said the English had been beaten in some battle or other. There's a nice thing to go teaching children! The parents won't stand for *that* kind of thing, I can tell you!'

'And Literature?' said Dorothy.

'Well, of course they've got to do a bit of reading, and I can't think why you wanted to turn up your nose at those nice little readers of ours. Keep on with the readers. They're a bit old, but they're quite good enough for a pack of children, I should have thought. And I suppose they might as well learn a few pieces of poetry by heart. Some of the parents like to hear their children say a piece of poetry. "The Boy stood on the Burning Deck"—that's a very good piece—and then there's "The Wreck of the Steamer"—now, what was that ship called? "The Wreck of the Steamer Hesperus". A little poetry doesn't hurt now and again. But don't let's have any more *Shakespeare*, please!'

Dorothy got no tea that day. It was now long past tea-time, but when Mrs Creevy had finished her harangue she sent Dorothy away without saying anything about tea. Perhaps this was a little extra punishment for *l'affaire Macbeth*.

Dorothy had not asked permission to go out, but she did not feel that she could stay in the house any longer. She got her hat and coat and set out down the ill-lit road, for the public library. It was late into November. Though the day had been damp the night wind blew sharply, like a threat, through the almost naked trees, making the gas-lamps flicker in spite of their glass chimneys, and stirring the sodden plane leaves that littered the pavement. Dorothy shivered slightly. The raw wind sent through her a bone-deep memory of the cold of Trafalgar Square. And though she did not actually think that if she lost her job it would mean going back to the sub-world from which she had come—indeed, it was not so desperate as that; at the worst her cousin or somebody else would help her—still, Mrs Creevy's 'talking to' had made Trafalgar Square seem suddenly very much nearer. It had driven into her a far deeper understanding than she had had before of the great modern commandment—the eleventh commandment which has wiped out all the others: 'Thou shalt not lose thy job.'

But as to what Mrs Creevy had said about 'practical school-teaching', it had been no more than a realistic facing of the facts. She had merely said aloud what most people in her position think but never say. Her oft-repeated phrase, 'It's the fees I'm after', was a motto that might be—indeed, ought to be—written over the doors of every private school in England.

There are, by the way, vast numbers of private schools in England. Second-rate, third-rate, and fourth-rate (Ringwood House was a specimen of the fourth-rate school), they exist by the dozen and the score in every London suburb and every provincial town. At any given moment there are somewhere in the neighbourhood of ten thousand of them, of which less than a thousand are subject to Government inspection. And though some of them are better than others, and a certain number, probably, are better than the council schools with which they compete, there is the same fundamental evil in all of them; that is, that they have ultimately no purpose except to make money. Often, except that there is nothing illegal about them, they are started in exactly the same spirit as one would start a brothel or a bucket shop. Some snuffy little man of business (it is quite usual for these schools to be owned by people who don't teach themselves) says one morning to his wife:

'Emma, I got a notion! What you say to us two keeping school, eh? There's plenty of cash in a school, you know, and there ain't the same work in it as what there is in a shop or a pub. Besides, you don't risk nothing; no over'ead to worry about, 'cept jest your rent and few desks and a blackboard. But we'll do it in style. Get in one of these Oxford and Cambridge chaps as is out of a job and'll come cheap, and dress 'im up in a gown and—what do they call them little square 'ats with tassels on top? That 'ud fetch the parents, eh? You jest keep your eyes open and see if you can't pick on a good district where there's not too many on the same game already.'

He chooses a situation in one of those middle-class districts where the people are too poor to afford the fees of a decent school and too proud to send their children to the council schools, and 'sets up'. By degrees he works up a connexion in very much the same manner as a milkman or a greengrocer, and if he is astute and tactful and has not too many competitors, he makes his few hundreds a year out of it.

Of course, these schools are not all alike. Not every principal is a grasping low-minded shrew like Mrs Creevy, and there are plenty of schools where the atmosphere is kindly and decent and the teaching is as good as one could reasonably expect for fees of five pounds a term. On the other hand, some of them are crying scandals. Later on, when Dorothy got to know one of the teachers at another private school in Southbridge, she heard tales of schools that were worse by far than Ringwood House. She heard of a cheap boarding-school where travelling actors dumped their children as one dumps luggage in a railway cloakroom, and where the children simply vegetated, doing absolutely nothing, reaching the age of sixteen without learning to read; and another school where the days passed in a perpetual riot, with a broken-down old hack of a master chasing the boys up and down and slashing at them with a cane, and then suddenly collapsing and weeping with his head on a desk, while the boys laughed at him. So long as schools are run primarily for money, things like this will happen. The expensive private schools to which the rich send their children are not, on the surface, so bad as the others, because they can afford a proper staff, and the Public School examination system keeps them up to the mark; but they have the same essential taint.

It was only later, and by degrees, that Dorothy discovered these facts about private schools. At first, she used to suffer from an absurd fear that one day the school inspectors would descend upon Ringwood House, find out what a sham and a swindle it all was, and raise the dust accordingly. Later on, however, she learned that this could never happen. Ringwood House was not 'recognized', and therefore was not liable to be inspected. One day a Government inspector did, indeed, visit the school, but beyond measuring the dimensions of the schoolroom to see whether each girl had her right number of cubic feet of air, he did nothing; he had no power to do more. Only the tiny minority of 'recognized' schools—less than one in ten—are officially tested to decide whether they keep up a reasonable educational standard. As for the others, they are free to teach or not teach exactly as they choose. No one controls or inspects them except the children's parents—the blind leading the blind.

# 5

Next day Dorothy began altering her programme in accordance with Mrs Creevy's orders. The first lesson of the day was handwriting, and the second was geography.

'That'll do, girls,' said Dorothy as the funereal clock struck ten. 'We'll start our geography lesson now.'

The girls flung their desks open and put their hated copybooks away with audible sighs of relief. There were murmurs of 'Oo, jography! Good!' It was one of their favourite lessons. The two girls who were 'monitors' for the week, and whose job it was to clean the blackboard, collect exercise books and so forth (children will fight for the privilege of doing jobs of that kind), leapt from their places to fetch the half-finished contour map that stood against the wall. But Dorothy stopped them.

'Wait a moment. Sit down, you two. We aren't going to go on with the map this morning.'

There was a cry of dismay. 'Oh, Miss! Why can't we, Miss? *Please* let's go on with it!'

'No. I'm afraid we've been wasting a little too much time over the map lately. We're going to start learning some of the capitals of the English counties. I want every girl in the class to know the whole lot of them by the end of the term.'

The children's faces fell. Dorothy saw it, and added with an attempt at brightness—that hollow, undeceiving brightness of a teacher trying to palm off a boring subject as an interesting one:

'Just think how pleased your parents will be when they can ask you the capital of any county in England and you can tell it them!'

The children were not in the least taken in. They writhed at the nauseous prospect.

'Oh, *capitals*! Learning *capitals*! That's just what we used to do with Miss Strong. Please, Miss, *why* can't we go on with the map?'

'Now don't argue. Get your notebooks out and take them down as I give them to you. And afterwards we'll say them all together.'

Reluctantly, the children fished out their notebooks, still groaning. 'Please, Miss, can we go on with the map *next* time?'

'I don't know. We'll see.'

That afternoon the map was removed from the schoolroom, and Mrs Creevy scraped the plasticine off the board and threw it away. It was the same with all the other subjects, one after another. All the changes that Dorothy had made were undone. They went back to the routine of interminable 'copies' and interminable 'practice' sums, to the learning parrot-fashion of *'Passez-moi le beurre'* and *'Le fils du jardinier a perdu son chapeau'*, to the *Hundred Page History* and the insufferable little 'reader'. (Mrs Creevy had impounded the Shakespeares, ostensibly to burn them. The probability was that she had sold them.) Two hours a day were set apart for handwriting lessons. The two depressing pieces of black paper, which Dorothy had taken down from the wall, were replaced, and their proverbs written upon them afresh in neat copperplate. As for the historical chart, Mrs Creevy took it away and burnt it.

When the children saw the hated lessons, from which they had thought to have escaped for ever, coming back upon them one by one, they were first astonished, then miserable, then sulky. But it was far worse for Dorothy than for the children. After only a couple of days the rigmarole through which she was obliged to drive them so nauseated her that she began to doubt whether she could go on with it any longer. Again and again she toyed with the idea of disobeying Mrs Creevy. Why not, she would think, as the children whined and groaned and sweated under their miserable bondage—why not stop it and go back to proper lessons, even if it was only for an hour or two a day? Why not drop the whole pretence of lessons and simply let the children play? It would be so much better for them than this. Let them draw pictures or make something out of plasticine or begin making up a fairy tale—anything *real,* anything that would interest them, instead of this dreadful nonsense. But she dared not. At any moment Mrs Creevy was liable to come in, and if she found the children 'messing about' instead of getting on with their routine work, there would be fearful trouble. So Dorothy hardened her heart, and obeyed Mrs Creevy's instructions to the letter, and things were very much as they had been before Miss Strong was 'taken bad'.

The lessons reached such a pitch of boredom that the brightest spot in the week was Mr Booth's so-called chemistry lecture on Thursday afternoons. Mr Booth was a seedy, tremulous man of about fifty, with long, wet, cowdung-coloured moustaches. He had been a Public School master once upon a time, but nowadays he made just enough for a life of chronic sub-drunkenness by delivering lectures at two and sixpence a time. The lectures were unrelieved drivel. Even in his palmiest days Mr Booth had not been a particularly brilliant lecturer, and now, when he had had his first go of delirium tremens and lived in a daily dread of his second, what chemical knowledge he had ever had was fast deserting him. He would stand dithering in front of the class, saying the same thing over and over again and trying vainly to remember what he was talking about. 'Remember, girls,' he would say in his husky, would-be fatherly voice, 'the number of the elements is ninety-three—ninety-three elements, girls—you all of you know what an element is, don't you?—there are just ninety-three of them—remember that number, girls—ninety-three,' until Dorothy (she had to stay in the schoolroom during the chemistry lectures, because Mrs Creevy considered that it *didn't do* to leave the girls alone with a man) was miserable with vicarious shame. All the lectures started with the ninety-three elements, and never got very much further. There was also talk of 'a very interesting little experiment that I'm going to perform for you next week, girls—very interesting you'll find it—we'll have it next week without fail—a very interesting little experiment', which, needless to say, was never performed. Mr Booth possessed no chemical apparatus, and his hands were far too shaky to have used it even if he had had any. The girls sat through his lectures in a suety stupor of boredom, but even he was a welcome change from handwriting lessons.

The children were never quite the same with Dorothy after the parents' visit. They did not change all in a day, of course. They had grown to be fond of 'old Millie', and they expected that after a day or two of tormenting them with handwriting and 'commercial arithmetic' she would go back to something interesting. But the handwriting and arithmetic went on, and the popularity Dorothy had enjoyed, as a teacher whose lessons weren't boring and who didn't slap you, pinch you, or twist your ears, gradually vanished. Moreover, the story of the row there had been over *Macbeth* was not long in leaking out. The children grasped that old Millie had done something wrong—they didn't exactly know what—and had been given a 'talking to'. It lowered her in their eyes. There is no dealing with children, even with children who are fond of you, unless you can keep your prestige as an adult; let that prestige be once damaged, and even the best-hearted children will despise you.

So they began to be naughty in the normal, traditional way. Before, Dorothy had only had to deal with occasional laziness, outbursts of noise and silly giggling fits; now there were spite and deceitfulness as well. The children revolted ceaselessly against the horrible routine. They forgot the short weeks when old Millie had seemed quite a good sort and school itself had seemed rather fun. Now, school was simply what it had always been, and what indeed you expected it to be—a place where you slacked and yawned and whiled the time away by pinching your neighbour and trying to make the teacher lose her temper, and from which you burst with a yell of relief the instant the last lesson was over. Sometimes they sulked and had fits of crying, sometimes they argued in the maddening persistent way that children have, '*Why* should we do this? *Why* does anyone have to learn to read and write?' over and over again, until Dorothy had to stand over them and silence them with threats of blows. She was growing almost habitually irritable nowadays; it surprised and shocked her, but she could not stop it. Every morning she vowed to herself, 'Today I will *not* lose my temper', and every morning, with depressing regularity, she *did* lose her temper, especially at about half past eleven when the children were at their worst. Nothing in the world is quite so irritating as dealing with mutinous children. Sooner or later, Dorothy knew, she would lose control of herself and begin hitting them. It seemed to her an unforgivable thing to do, to hit a child; but nearly all teachers come to it in the end. It was impossible now to get any child to work except when your eye was upon it. You had only to turn your back for an instant and blotting-paper pellets were flying to and fro. Nevertheless, with ceaseless slave-driving the children's handwriting and 'commercial arithmetic' did certainly show some improvement, and no doubt the parents were satisfied.

The last few weeks of the term were a very bad time. For over a fortnight Dorothy was quite penniless, for Mrs Creevy had told her that she couldn't pay her her term's wages 'till some of the fees came in'. So she was deprived of the secret slabs of chocolate that had kept her going, and she suffered from a perpetual slight hunger that made her languid and spiritless. There were leaden mornings when the minutes dragged like hours, when she struggled with herself to keep her eyes away from the clock, and her heart sickened to think that beyond this lesson there loomed another just like it, and more of them and more, stretching on into what seemed like a dreary eternity. Worse yet were the times when the children were in their noisy mood and it needed a constant exhausting effort of the will to keep them under control at all; and beyond the wall, of course, lurked Mrs Creevy, always listening, always ready to descend upon the schoolroom, wrench the door open, and glare round the room with 'Now then! What's all this noise about, please?' and the sack in her eye.

Dorothy was fully awake, now, to the beastliness of living in Mrs Creevy's house. The filthy food, the cold, and the lack of baths seemed much more important than they had seemed a little while ago. Moreover, she was beginning to appreciate, as she had not done when the joy of her work was fresh upon her, the utter loneliness of her position. Neither her father nor Mr Warburton had written to her, and in two months she had made not a single friend in Southbridge. For anyone so situated, and particularly for a woman, it is all but impossible to make friends. She had no money and no home of her own, and outside the school her sole places of refuge were the public library, on the few evenings when she could get there, and church on Sunday mornings. She went to church regularly, of course—Mrs Creevy had insisted on that. She had settled the question of Dorothy's religious observances at breakfast on her first Sunday morning.

'I've just been wondering what Place of Worship you ought to go to,' she said. 'I suppose you were brought up C. of E., weren't you?'

'Yes,' said Dorothy.

'Hm, well. I can't quite make up my mind where to send you. There's St George's—that's the C. of E.—and there's the Baptist Chapel where I go myself. Most of our parents are Nonconformists, and I don't know as they'd quite approve of a C. of E. teacher. You can't be too careful with the parents. They had a bit of a scare two years ago when it turned out that the teacher I had then was actually a Roman Catholic, if you please! Of course she kept it dark as long as she could, but it came out in the end, and three of the parents took their children away. I got rid of her the same day as I found it out, naturally.'

Dorothy was silent.

'Still,' went on Mrs Creevy, 'we *have* got three C. of E. pupils, and I don't know as the Church connexion mightn't be worked up a bit. So perhaps you'd better risk it and go to St George's. But you want to be a bit careful, you know. I'm told St George's is one of these churches where they go in for a lot of bowing and scraping and crossing yourself and all that. We've got two parents that are Plymouth Brothers, and they'd throw a fit if they heard you'd been seen crossing yourself. So don't go and do *that,* whatever you do.'

'Very well,' said Dorothy.

'And just you keep your eyes well open during the sermon. Have a good look round and see if there's any young girls in the congregation that we could get hold of. If you see any likely looking ones, get on to the parson afterwards and try and find out their names and addresses.'

So Dorothy went to St George's. It was a shade 'Higher' than St Athelstan's had been; chairs, not pews, but no incense, and the vicar (his name was Mr Gore-Williams) wore a plain cassock and surplice except on festival days. As for the services, they were so like those at home that Dorothy could go through them, and utter all the responses at the right moment, in a state of the completest abstraction.

There was never a moment when the power of worship returned to her. Indeed, the whole concept of worship was meaningless to her now; her faith had vanished, utterly and irrevocably. It is a mysterious thing, the loss of faith—as mysterious as faith itself. Like faith, it is ultimately not rooted in logic; it is a change in the climate of the mind. But however little the church services might mean to her, she did not regret the hours she spent in church. On the contrary, she looked forward to her Sunday mornings as blessed interludes of peace; and that not only because Sunday morning meant a respite from Mrs Creevy's prying eye and nagging voice. In another and deeper sense the atmosphere of the church was soothing and reassuring to her. For she perceived that in all that happens in church, however absurd and cowardly its supposed purpose may be, there is something—it is hard to define, but something of decency, of spiritual comeliness—that is not easily found in the world outside. It seemed to her that even though you no longer believe, it is better to go to church than not; better to follow in the ancient ways, than to drift in rootless freedom. She knew very well that she would never again be able to utter a prayer and mean it; but she knew also that for the rest of her life she must continue with the observances to which she had been bred. Just this much remained to her of the faith that had once, like the bones in a living frame, held all her life together.

But as yet she did not think very deeply about the loss of her faith and what it might mean to her in the future. She was too busy merely existing, merely struggling to make her nerves hold out for the rest of that miserable term. For as the term drew to an end, the job of keeping the class in order grew more and more exhausting. The girls behaved atrociously, and they were all the bitterer against Dorothy because they had once been fond of her. She had deceived them, they felt. She had started off by being decent, and now she had turned out to be just a beastly old teacher like the rest of them—a nasty old beast who kept on and on with those awful handwriting lessons and snapped your head off if you so much as made a blot on your book. Dorothy caught them eyeing her face, sometimes, with the aloof, cruel scrutiny of children. They had thought her pretty once, and now they thought her ugly, old, and scraggy. She had grown, indeed, much thinner since she had been at Ringwood House.

They hated her now, as they had hated all their previous teachers.

Sometimes they baited her quite deliberately. The older and more intelligent girls understood the situation well enough—understood that Millie was under old Creevy's thumb and that she got dropped on afterwards when they had been making too much noise; sometimes they made all the noise they dared, just so as to bring old Creevy in and have the pleasure of watching Millie's face while old Creevy told her off. There were times when Dorothy could keep her temper and forgive them all they did, because she realized that it was only a healthy instinct that made them rebel against the loathsome monotony of their work. But there were other times when her nerves were more on edge than usual, and when she looked round at the score of silly little faces, grinning or mutinous, and found it possible to hate them. Children are so blind, so selfish, so merciless. They do not know when they are tormenting you past bearing, and if they did know they would not care. You may do your very best for them, you may keep your temper in situations that would try a saint, and yet if you are forced to bore them and oppress them, they will hate you for it without ever asking themselves whether it is you who are to blame. How true—when you happen not to be a school-teacher yourself—how true those often-quoted lines sound—

> Under a cruel eye outworn
> The little ones spend the day
> in sighing and dismay!

But when you yourself are the cruel eye outworn, you realize that there is another side to the picture.

The last week came, and the dirty farce of 'exams', was carried through. The system, as explained by Mrs Creevy, was quite simple. You coached the children in, for example, a series of sums until you were quite certain that they could get them right, and then set them the same sums as an arithmetic paper before they had time to forget the answers; and so with each subject in turn. The children's papers were, of course, sent home for their parents' inspection. And Dorothy wrote the reports under Mrs Creevy's dictation, and she had to write 'excellent' so many times that—as sometimes happens when you write a word over and over again—she forgot how to spell it and began writing in 'excelent', 'exsellent', 'ecsellent', 'eccelent'.

The last day passed in fearful tumults. Not even Mrs Creevy herself could keep the children in order. By midday Dorothy's nerves were in rags, and Mrs Creevy gave her a 'talking to' in front of the seven children who stayed to dinner. In the afternoon the noise was worse than ever, and at last Dorothy, overcome, appealed to the girls almost tearfully to stop.

'Girls!' she called out, raising her voice to make herself heard through the din. '*Please* stop it, *please*! You're behaving horribly to me. Do you think it's kind to go on like this?'

That was fatal, of course. Never, never, never throw yourself on the mercy of a child! There was an instant's hush, and then one child cried out, loudly and derisively, 'Mill-iee!' The next moment the whole class had taken it up, even the imbecile Mavis, chanting all together 'Mill-iee! Mill-iee! Mill-iee!' At that, something within Dorothy seemed to snap. She paused for an instant, picked out the girl who was making the most noise, walked up to her, and gave her a smack across the ear almost as hard as she could hit. Happily it was only one of the 'medium payers'.

# 6

On the first day of the holidays Dorothy received a letter from Mr Warburton.

My Dear Dorothy [he wrote],—Or should I call you Ellen, as I understand that is your new name? You must, I am afraid, have thought it very heartless of me not to have written sooner, but I assure you that it was not until ten days ago that I even heard anything about our supposed escapade. I have been abroad, first in various parts of France, then in Austria and then in Rome, and, as you know, I avoid my fellow countrymen most strenuously on these trips. They are disgusting enough even at home, but in foreign parts their behaviour makes me so ashamed of them that I generally try to pass myself off as an American.

When I got to Knype Hill your father refused to see me, but I managed to get hold of Victor Stone, who gave me your address and the name you are using. He seemed rather reluctant to do so, and I gathered that even he, like everyone else in this poisonous town, still believes that you have misbehaved yourself in some way. I think the theory that you and I eloped together has been dropped, but you must, they feel, have done *something* scandalous. A young woman has left home suddenly, therefore there must be a man in the case; that is how the provincial mind works, you see. I need not tell you that I have been contradicting the whole story with the utmost vigour. You will be glad to hear that I managed to corner that disgusting hag, Mrs Semprill, and give her a piece of my mind; and I assure you that a piece of *my* mind is distinctly formidable. But the woman is simply sub-human. I could get nothing out of her except hypocritical snivellings about 'poor, *poor* Dorothy'.

I hear that your father misses you very much, and would gladly have you home again if it were not for the scandal. His meals are never punctual nowadays, it seems. He gives it out that you 'went away to recuperate from a slight illness and have now got an excellent post at a girls' school'. You will be surpised to hear of one thing that has happened to him. He has been obliged to pay off all his debts! I am told that the tradesmen rose in a body and held what was practically a creditors' meeting in the Rectory. Not the kind of thing that could have happened at Plumstead Episcopi—but these are democratic days, alas! You, evidently, were the only person who could keep the tradesmen permanently at bay.

And now I must tell you some of my own news, *etc., etc., etc.*

At this point Dorothy tore the letter up in disappointment and even in annoyance. He might have shown a little more sympathy! she thought. It was just like Mr Warburton after getting her into serious trouble—for after all, he was principally to blame for what had happened—to be so flippant and unconcerned about it. But when she had thought it over she acquitted him of heartlessness. He had done what little was possible to help her, and he could not be expected to pity her for troubles of which he had not heard. Besides, his own life had been a series of resounding scandals; probably he could not understand that to a woman a scandal is a serious matter.

At Christmas Dorothy's father also wrote, and what was more, sent her a Christmas present of two pounds. It was evident from the tone of his letter that he had forgiven Dorothy by this time. *What* exactly he had forgiven her was not certain, because it was not certain what exactly she had done; but still, he had forgiven her. The letter started with some perfunctory but quite friendly inquiries. He hoped her new job suited her, he wrote. And were her rooms at the school comfortable and the rest of the staff congenial? He had heard that they did one very well at schools nowadays—very different from what it had been forty years ago. Now, in his day, etc., etc., etc. He had, Dorothy perceived, not the dimmest idea of her present circumstances. At the mention of schools his mind flew to Winchester, his old school; such a place as Ringwood House was beyond his imagining.

The rest of the letter was taken up with grumblings about the way things were going in the parish. The Rector complained of being worried and overworked. The wretched churchwardens kept bothering him with this and that, and he was growing very tired of Proggett's reports about the collapsing belfry, and the daily woman whom he had engaged to help Ellen was a great nuisance and had put her broom-handle through the face of the grandfather clock in his study—and so on, and so forth, for a number of pages. He said several times in a mumbling roundabout way that he wished Dorothy were there to help him; but he did not actually suggest that she should come home. Evidently it was still necessary that she should remain out of sight and out of mind—a skeleton in a distant and well-locked cupboard.

The letter filled Dorothy with sudden painful homesickness. She found herself pining to be back at her parish visiting and her Girl Guides' cooking class, and wondering unhappily how her father had got on without her all this while and whether those two women were looking after him properly. She was fond of her father, in a way that she had never dared to show; for he was not a person to whom you could make any display of affection. It surprised and rather shocked her to realize how little he had been in her thoughts during the past four months. There had been periods of weeks at a time when she had forgotten his existence. But the truth was that the mere business of keeping body and soul together had left her with no leisure for other emotions.

Now, however, school work was over, and she had leisure and to spare, for though Mrs Creevy did her best she could not invent enough household jobs to keep Dorothy busy for more than part of the day. She made it quite plain to Dorothy that during the holidays she was nothing but a useless expense, and she watched her at her meals (obviously feeling it an outrage that she should eat when she wasn't working) in a way that finally became unbearable. So Dorothy kept out of the house as much as possible, and, feeling fairly rich with her wages (four pounds ten, for nine weeks) and her father's two pounds, she took to buying sandwiches at the ham and beef shop in the town and eating her dinner out of doors. Mrs Creevy acquiesced, half sulkily because she liked to have Dorothy in the house to nag at her, and half pleased at the chance of skimping a few more meals.

Dorothy went for long solitary walks, exploring Southbridge and its yet more desolate neighbours, Dorley, Wembridge, and West Holton. Winter had descended, dank and windless, and more gloomy in those colourless labyrinthine suburbs than in the bleakest wilderness. On two or three occasions, though such extravagance would probably mean hungry days later on, Dorothy took a cheap return ticket to Iver Heath or Burnham Beeches. The woods were sodden and wintry, with great beds of drifted beech leaves that glowed like copper in the still, wet air, and the days were so mild that you could sit out of doors and read if you kept your gloves on. On Christmas Eve Mrs Creevy produced some sprigs of holly that she had saved from last year, dusted them, and nailed them up; but she did not, she said, intend to have a Christmas dinner. She didn't hold with all this Christmas nonsense, she said—it was just a lot of humbug got up by the shopkeepers, and such an unnecessary expense; and she hated turkey and Christmas pudding anyway. Dorothy was relieved; a Christmas dinner in that joyless 'morning-room' (she had an awful momentary vision of Mrs Creevy in a paper hat out of a cracker) was something that didn't bear thinking about. She ate her Christmas dinner—a hard-boiled egg, two cheese sandwiches, and a bottle of lemonade—in the woods near Burnham, against a great gnarled beech tree, over a copy of George Gissing's *The Odd Women*.

On days when it was too wet to go for walks she spent most of her time in the public library—becoming, indeed, one of the regular *habituées* of the library, along with the out-of-work men who sat drearily musing over illustrated papers which they did not read, and the elderly discoloured bachelor who lived in 'rooms' on two pounds a week and came to the library to study books on yachting by the hour together. It had been a great relief to her when the term ended, but this feeling soon wore off; indeed, with never a soul to talk to, the days dragged even more heavily than before. There is perhaps no quarter of the inhabited world where one can be quite so completely alone as in the London suburbs. In a big town the throng and bustle give one at least the illusion of companionship, and in the country everyone is interested in everyone else—too much so, indeed. But in places like Southbridge, if you have no family and no home to call your own, you could spend half a lifetime without managing to make a friend. There are women in such places, and especially derelict gentlewomen in ill-paid jobs, who go for years upon end in almost utter solitude. It was not long before Dorothy found herself in a perpetually low-spirited, jaded state in which, try as she would, nothing seemed able to interest her. And it was in the hateful ennui of this time—the corrupting ennui that lies in wait for every modern soul—that she first came to a full understanding of what it meant to have lost her faith.

She tried drugging herself with books, and it succeeded for a week or so. But after a while very nearly all books seemed wearisome and unintelligible; for the mind will not work to any purpose when it is quite alone. In the end she found that she could not cope with anything more difficult than a detective story. She took walks of ten and fifteen miles, trying to tire herself into a better mood; but the mean suburban roads, and the damp, miry paths through the woods, the naked trees, the sodden moss and great spongy fungi, afflicted her with a deadly melancholy. It was human companionship that she needed, and there seemed no way of getting it. At nights when she walked back to the school and looked at the warm-lit windows of the houses, and heard voices laughing and gramophones playing within, her heart swelled with envy. Ah, to be like those people in there—to have at least a home, a family, a few friends who were interested in you! There were days when she pined for the courage to speak to strangers in the street. Days, too, when she contemplated shamming piety in order to scrape acquaintance with the Vicar of St George's and his family, and perhaps get the chance of occupying herself with a little parish work; days, even, when she was so desperate that she thought of joining the Y.W.C.A.

But almost at the end of the holidays, through a chance encounter at the library, she made friends with a little woman named Miss Beaver, who was geography mistress at Toot's Commercial College, another of the private schools in Southbridge. Toot's Commerical College was a much larger and more pretentious school than Ringwood House—it had about a hundred and fifty day-pupils of both sexes and even rose to the dignity of having a dozen boarders—and its curriculum was a somewhat less blatant swindle. It was one of those schools that are aimed at the type of parent who blathers about 'up-to-date business training', and its watch-word was Efficiency; meaning a tremendous parade of hustling, and the banishment of all humane studies. One of its features was a kind of catechism called the Efficiency Ritual, which all the children were required to learn by heart as soon as they joined the school. It had questions and answers such as:

> *Q.* What is the secret of success?
> *A.* The secret of success is efficiency.
> *Q.* What is the test of efficiency?
> *A.* The test of efficiency is success.

And so on and so on. It was said that the spectacle of the whole school, boys and girls together, reciting the Efficiency Ritual under the leadership of the Headmaster—they had this ceremony two mornings a week instead of prayers—was most impressive.

Miss Beaver was a prim little woman with a round body, a thin face, a reddish nose, and the gait of a guinea-hen. After twenty years of slave-driving she had attained to an income of four pounds a week and the privilege of 'living out' instead of having to put the boarders to bed at nights. She lived in 'rooms'—that is, in a bed-sitting room—to which she was sometimes able to invite Dorothy when both of them had a free evening. How Dorothy looked forward to those visits! They were only possible at rare intervals, because Miss Beaver's landlady 'didn't approve of visitors', and even when you got there there was nothing much to do except to help solve the crossword puzzle out of the *Daily Telegraph* and look at the photographs Miss Beaver had taken on her trip (this trip had been the summit and glory of her life) to the Austrian Tyrol in 1913. But still, how much it meant to sit talking to somebody in a friendly way and to drink a cup of tea less wishy-washy than Mrs Creevy's! Miss Beaver had a spirit lamp in a japanned travelling case (it had been with her to the Tyrol in 1913) on which she brewed herself pots of tea as black as coal-tar, swallowing about a bucketful of this stuff during the day. She confided to Dorothy that she always took a Thermos flask to school and had a nice hot cup of tea during the break and another after dinner. Dorothy perceived that by one of two well-beaten roads every third-rate schoolmistress must travel: Miss Strong's road, via whisky to the workhouse; or Miss Beaver's road, via strong tea to a decent death in the Home for Decayed Gentlewomen.

Miss Beaver was in truth a dull little woman. She was a *memento mori*, or rather *memento senescere*, to Dorothy. Her soul seemed to have withered until it was as forlorn as a dried-up cake of soap in a forgotten soap dish. She had come to a point where life in a bed-sitting room under a tyrannous landlady and the 'efficient' thrusting of Commercial Geography down children's retching throats, were almost the only destiny she could imagine. Yet Dorothy grew to be very fond of Miss Beaver, and those occasional hours that they spent together in the bed-sitting room, doing the *Daily Telegraph* crossword over a nice hot cup of tea, were like oases in her life.

She was glad when the Easter term began, for even the daily round of slave-driving was better than the empty solitude of the holidays. Moreover, the girls were much better in hand this term; she never again found it necessary to smack their heads. For she had grasped now that it is easy enough to keep children in order if you are ruthless with them from the start. Last term the girls had behaved badly, because she had started by treating them as human beings, and later on, when the lessons that interested them were discontinued, they had rebelled like human beings. But if you are obliged to teach children rubbish, you mustn't treat them as human beings. You must treat them like animals—driving, not persuading. Before all else, you must teach them that it is more painful to rebel than to obey. Possibly this kind of treatment is not very good for children, but there is no doubt they understand it and respond to it.

She learned the dismal arts of the school-teacher. She learned to glaze her mind against the interminable boring hours, to economize her nervous energy, to be merciless and ever-vigilant, to take a kind of pride and pleasure in seeing a futile rigmarole well done. She had grown, quite suddenly it seemed, much tougher and maturer. Her eyes had lost the half-childish look that they had once had, and her face had grown thinner, making her nose seem longer. At times it was quite definitely a schoolmarm's face; you could imagine *pince-nez* upon it. But she had not become cynical as yet. She still knew that these children were the victims of a dreary swindle, still longed, if it had been possible, to do something better for them. If she harried them and stuffed their heads with rubbish, it was for one reason alone: because whatever happened she had got to keep her job.

There was very little noise in the schoolroom this term. Mrs Creevy, anxious as she always was for a chance of finding fault, seldom had reason to rap on the wall with her broom-handle. One morning at breakfast she looked rather hard at Dorothy, as though weighing a decision, and then pushed the dish of marmalade across the table.

'Have some marmalade if you like, Miss Millborough,' she said, quite graciously for her.

It was the first time that marmalade had crossed Dorothy's lips since she had come to Ringwood House. She flushed slightly. 'So the woman realizes that I have done my best for her,' she could not help thinking.

Thereafter she had marmalade for breakfast every morning. And in other ways Mrs Creevy's manner became—not indeed, genial, for it could never be that, but less brutally offensive. There were even times when she produced a grimace that was intended for a smile; her face, it seemed to Dorothy, *creased* with the effort. About this time her conversation became peppered with references to 'next term'. It was always 'Next term we'll do this', and 'Next term I shall want you to do that', until Dorothy began to feel that she had won Mrs Creevy's confidence and was being treated more like a colleague than a slave. At that a small, unreasonable but very exciting hope took root in her heart. Perhaps Mrs Creevy was going to raise her wages! It was profoundly unlikely, and she tried to break herself of hoping for it, but could not quite succeed. If her wages were raised even half a crown a week, what a difference it would make!

The last day came. With any luck Mrs Creevy might pay her wages tomorrow, Dorothy thought. She wanted the money very badly indeed; she had been penniless for weeks past, and was not only unbearably hungry, but also in need of some new stockings, for she had not a pair that were not darned almost out of existence. The following morning she did the household jobs allotted to her, and then, instead of going out, waited in the 'morning-room' while Mrs Creevy banged about with her broom and pan upstairs. Presently Mrs Creevy came down.

'Ah, so *there* you are, Miss Millborough!' she said in a peculiar meaning tone. 'I had a sort of an idea you wouldn't be in such a hurry to get out of doors this morning. Well, as you *are* here, I suppose I may as well pay you your wages.'

'Thank you,' said Dorothy.

'And after that,' added Mrs Creevy, 'I've got a little something as I want to say to you.'

Dorothy's heart stirred. Did that 'little something' mean the longed-for rise in wages? It was just conceivable. Mrs Creevy produced a worn, bulgy leather purse from a locked drawer in the dresser, opened it and licked her thumb.

'Twelve weeks and five days,' she said. 'Twelve weeks is near enough. No need to be particular to a day. That makes six pounds.'

She counted out five dingy pound notes and two ten-shilling notes; then, examining one of the notes and apparently finding it too clean, she put it back into her purse and fished out another that had been torn in half. She went to the dresser, got a piece of transparent sticky paper and carefully stuck the two halves together. Then she handed it, together with the other six, to Dorothy.

'There you are, Miss Millborough,' she said. 'And now, will you just leave the house *at* once, please? I shan't be wanting you any longer.'

'You won't be—'

Dorothy's entrails seemed to have turned to ice. All the blood drained out of her face. But even now, in her terror and despair, she was not absolutely sure of the meaning of what had been said to her. She still half thought that Mrs Creevy merely meant that she was to stay out of the house for the rest of the day.

'You won't be wanting me any longer?' she repeated faintly.

'No. I'm getting in another teacher at the beginning of next term. And it isn't to be expected as I'd keep you through the holidays all free for nothing, is it?'

'But you don't mean that you want me to *leave*–that you're dismissing me?'

'Of course I do. What else did you think I meant?'

'But you've given me no notice!' said Dorothy.

'Notice!' said Mrs Creevy, getting angry immediately. 'What's it got to do with *you* whether I give you notice or not? You haven't got a written contract, have you?'

'No . . . I suppose not.'

'Well, then! You'd better go upstairs and start packing your box. It's no good your staying any longer, because I haven't got anything in for your dinner.'

Dorothy went upstairs and sat down on the side of the bed. She was trembling uncontrollably, and it was some minutes before she could collect her wits and begin packing. She felt dazed. The disaster that had fallen upon her was so sudden, so apparently causeless, that she had difficulty in believing that it had actually happened. But in truth the reason why Mrs Creevy had sacked her was quite simple and adequate.

Not far from Ringwood House there was a poor, moribund little school called The Gables, with only seven pupils. The teacher was an incompetent old hack called Miss Allcock, who had been at thirty-eight different schools in her life and was not fit to have charge of a tame canary. But Miss Allcock had one outstanding talent; she was very good at double-crossing her employers. In these third-rate and fourth-rate private schools a sort of piracy is constantly going on. Parents are 'got round' and pupils stolen from one school to another. Very often the treachery of the teacher is at the bottom of it. The teacher secretly approaches the parents one by one ('Send your child to me and I'll take her at ten shillings a term cheaper'), and when she has corrupted a sufficient number she suddenly deserts and 'sets up' on her own, or carries the children off to another school. Miss Allcock had succeeded in stealing three out of her employer's seven pupils, and had come to Mrs Creevy with the offer of them. In return, she was to have Dorothy's place and a fifteen-per-cent commission on the pupils she brought.

There were weeks of furtive chaffering before the bargain was clinched, Miss Allcock being finally beaten down from fifteen per cent to twelve and a half. Mrs Creevy privately resolved to sack old Allcock the instant she was certain that the three children she brought with her would stay. Simultaneously, Miss Allcock was planning to begin stealing old Creevy's pupils as soon as she had got a footing in the school.

Having decided to sack Dorothy, it was obviously most important to prevent her from finding it out. For, of course, if she knew what was going to happen, she would begin stealing pupils on her own account, or at any rate wouldn't do a stroke of work for the rest of the term. (Mrs Creevy prided herself on knowing human nature.) Hence the marmalade, the creaky smiles, and the other ruses to allay Dorothy's suspicions. Anyone who knew the ropes would have begun thinking of another job the very moment when the dish of marmalade was pushed across the table.

Just half an hour after her sentence of dismissal, Dorothy, carrying her handbag, opened the front gate. It was the fourth of April, a bright blowy day, too cold to stand about in, with a sky as blue as a hedgesparrow's egg, and one of those spiteful spring winds that come tearing along the pavement in sudden gusts and blow dry, stinging dust into your face. Dorothy shut the gate behind her and began to walk very slowly in the direction of the main-line station.

She had told Mrs Creevy that she would give her an address to which her box could be sent, and Mrs Creevy had instantly exacted five shillings for the carriage. So Dorothy had five pounds fifteen in hand, which might keep her for three weeks with careful economy. What she was going to do, except that she must start by going to London and finding a suitable lodging, she had very little idea. But her first panic had worn off, and she realized that the situation was not altogether desperate. No doubt her father would help her, at any rate for a while, and at the worst, though she hated even the thought of doing it, she could ask her cousin's help a second time. Besides, her chances of finding a job were probably fairly good. She was young, she spoke with a genteel accent, and she was willing to drudge for a servant's wages—qualities that are much sought after by the proprietors of fourth-rate schools. Very likely all would be well. But that there was an evil time ahead of her, a time of job-hunting, of uncertainty and possibly of hunger—that, at any rate, was certain.

# CHAPTER 5

## I

However, it turned out quite otherwise. For Dorothy had not gone five yards from the gate when a telegraph boy came riding up the street in the opposite direction, whistling and looking at the names of the houses. He saw the name Ringwood House, wheeled his bicycle round, propped it against the kerb, and accosted Dorothy.

'Miss Mill-*burrow* live 'ere?' he said, jerking his head in the direction of Ringwood House.

'Yes. I am Miss Millborough.'

'Gotter wait case there's a answer,' said the boy, taking an orange-coloured envelope from his belt.

Dorothy put down her bag. She had once more begun trembling violently. And whether this was from joy or fear she was not certain, for two conflicting thoughts had sprung almost simultaneously into her brain. One, 'This is some kind of good news!' The other, 'Father is seriously ill!' She managed to tear the envelope open, and found a telegram which occupied two pages, and which she had the greatest difficulty in understanding. It ran:

Rejoice in the lord o ye righteous note of exclamation great news note of exclamation your reputation absolutely reestablished stop mrs semprill fallen into the pit that she hath digged stop action for libel stop no one believes her any longer stop your father wishes you return home immediately stop am coming up to town myself comma will pick you up if you like stop arriving shortly after this stop wait for me stop praise him with the loud cymbals note of exclamation much love stop.

No need to look at the signature. It was from Mr Warburton, of course. Dorothy felt weaker and more tremulous than ever. She was dimly aware the telegraph boy was asking her something.

'Any answer?' he said for the third or fourth time.

'Not today, thank you,' said Dorothy vaguely.

The boy remounted his bicycle and rode off, whistling with extra loudness to show Dorothy how much he despised her for not tipping him. But Dorothy was unaware of the telegraph's boy's scorn. The only phrase of the telegram that she had fully understood was 'your father wishes you return home immediately', and the surprise of it had left her in a semi-dazed condition. For some indefinite time she stood on the pavement, until presently a taxi rolled up the street, with Mr Warburton inside it. He saw Dorothy, stopped the taxi, jumped out and came across to meet her, beaming. He seized her both hands.

'Hullo!' he cried, and at once threw his arm pseudo-paternally about her and drew her against him, heedless of who might be looking. 'How are you? But by Jove, how thin you've got! I can feel all your ribs. Where is this school of yours?'

Dorothy, who had not yet managed to get free of his arm, turned partly round and cast a glance towards the dark windows of Ringwood House.

'What! That place? Good God, what a hole! What have you done with your luggage?'

'It's inside. I've left them the money to send it on. I think it'll be all right.'

'Oh, nonsense! Why pay? We'll take it with us. It can go on top of the taxi.'

'No, no! Let them send it. I daren't go back. Mrs Creevy would be horribly angry.'

'Mrs Creevy? Who's Mrs Creevy?'

'The headmistress—at least, she owns the school.'

'What, a dragon, is she? Leave her to me—I'll deal with her. Perseus and the Gorgon, what? You are Andromeda. Hi!' he called to the taxi-driver.

The two of them went up to the front door and Mr Warburton knocked. Somehow, Dorothy never believed that they would succeed in getting her box from Mrs Creevy. In fact, she half expected to see them come out flying for their lives, and Mrs Creevy after them with her broom. However, in a couple of minutes they reappeared, the taxi-driver carrying the box on his shoulder. Mr Warburton handed Dorothy into the taxi and, as they sat down, dropped half a crown into her hand.

'What a woman! What a woman!' he said comprehensively as the taxi bore them away. 'How the devil have you put up with it all this time?'

'What is this?' said Dorothy, looking at the coin.

'Your half-crown that you left to pay for the luggage. Rather a feat getting it out of the old girl, wasn't it?'

'But I left five shillings!' said Dorothy.

'What! The woman told me you only left half a crown. By God, what impudence! We'll go back and have the half-crown out of her. Just to spite her!' He tapped on the glass.

'No, no!' said Dorothy, laying her hand on his arm. 'It doesn't matter in the least. Let's get away from here—right away. I couldn't bear to go back to that place again—*ever*!'

It was quite true. She felt that she would sacrifice not merely half a crown, but all the money in her possession, sooner than set eyes on Ringwood House again. So they drove on, leaving Mrs Creevy victorious. It would be interesting to know whether this was another of the occasions when Mrs Creevy laughed.

Mr Warburton insisted on taking the taxi the whole way into London, and talked so voluminously in the quieter patches of the traffic that Dorothy could hardly get a word in edgeways. It was not till they had reached the inner suburbs that she got from him an explanation of the sudden change in her fortunes.

'Tell me,' she said, 'what is it that's happened? I don't understand. Why is it all right for me to go home all of a sudden? Why don't people believe Mrs Semprill any longer? Surely she hasn't confessed?'

'Confessed? Not she! But her sins have found her out, all the same. It was the kind of thing that you pious people would ascribe to the finger of Providence. Cast thy bread upon the waters, and all that. She got herself into a nasty mess—an action for libel. We've talked of nothing else in Knype Hill for the last fortnight. I though you would have seen something about it in the newspapers.'

'I've hardly looked at a paper for ages. Who brought an action for libel? Not my father, surely?'

'Good gracious, no! Clergymen can't bring actions for libel. It was the bank manager. Do you remember her favourite story about him—how he was keeping a woman on the bank's money, and so forth?'

'Yes, I think so.'

'A few months ago she was foolish enough to put some of it in writing. Some kind friend—some female friend, I presume—took the letter round to the bank manager. He brought an action—Mrs Semprill was ordered to pay a hundred and fifty pounds damages. I don't suppose she paid a halfpenny, but still, that's the end of her career as a scandalmonger. You can go on blackening people's reputations for years, and everyone will believe you, more or less, even when it's perfectly obvious that you're lying. But once you've been proved a liar in open court, you're disqualified, so to speak. Mrs Semprill's done for, so far as Knype Hill goes. She left the town between days—practically did a moonlight flit, in fact. I believe she's inflicting herself on Bury St Edmunds at present.'

'But what has all that got to do with the things she said about you and me?'

'Nothing—nothing whatever. But why worry? The point is that you're reinstated; and all the hags who've been smacking their chops over you for months past are saying, "Poor, poor Dorothy, how *shockingly* that dreadful woman has treated her!"'

'You mean they think that because Mrs Semprill was telling lies in one case she must have been telling lies in another?'

'No doubt that's what they'd say if they were capable of reasoning it out. At any rate, Mrs Semprill's in disgrace, and so all the people she's slandered must be martyrs. Even *my* reputation is practically spotless for the time being.'

'And do you think that's really the end of it? Do you think they honestly believe that it was all an accident—that I only lost my memory and didn't elope with anybody?'

'Oh, well, I wouldn't go as far as that. In these country places there's always a certain amount of suspicion knocking about. Not suspicion of anything in particular, you know; just generalized suspicion. A sort of instinctive rustic dirty-mindedness. I can imagine its being vaguely rumoured in the bar parlour of the Dog and Bottle in ten years' time that you've got some nasty secret in your past, only nobody can remember what. Still, your troubles are over. If I were you I wouldn't give any explanations till you're asked for them. The official theory is that you had a bad attack of flu and went away to recuperate. I should stick to that. You'll find they'll accept it all right. Officially, there's nothing against you.'

Presently they got to London, and Mr Warburton took Dorothy to lunch at a restaurant in Coventry Street, where they had a young chicken, roasted, with asparagus and tiny, pearly-white potatoes that had been ripped untimely from their mother earth, and also treacle tart and a nice warm bottle of Burgundy; but what gave Dorothy the most pleasure of all, after Mrs Creevy's lukewarm water tea, was the black coffee they had afterwards. After lunch they took another taxi to Liverpool Street Station and caught the 2.45. It was a four-hour journey to Knype Hill.

Mr Warburton insisted on travelling first-class, and would not hear of Dorothy paying her own fare; he also, when Dorothy was not looking, tipped the guard to let them have a carriage to themselves. It was one of those bright cold days which are spring or winter according as you are indoors or out. From behind the shut windows of the carriage the too-blue sky looked warm and kind, and all the slummy wilderness through which the train was rattling—the labyrinths of little dingy-coloured houses, the great chaotic factories, the miry canals, and derelict building lots littered with rusty boilers and overgrown by smoke-blackened weeds—all were redeemed and gilded by the sun. Dorothy hardly spoke for the first half-hour of the journey. For the moment she was too happy to talk. She did not even think of anything in particular, but merely sat there luxuriating in the glass-filtered sunlight, in the comfort of the padded seat and the feeling of having escaped from Mrs Creevy's clutches. But she was aware that this mood could not last very much longer. Her contentment, like the warmth of the wine that she had drunk at lunch, was ebbing away, and thoughts either painful or difficult to express were taking shape in her mind. Mr Warburton had been watching her face, more observantly than was usual for him, as though trying to gauge the changes that the past eight months had worked in her.

'You look older,' he said finally.

'I am older,' said Dorothy.

'Yes; but you look—well, more completely grown up. Tougher. Something has changed in your face. You look—if you'll forgive the expression—as though the Girl Guide had been exorcized from you for good and all. I hope seven devils haven't entered into you instead?' Dorothy did not answer, and he added: 'I suppose, as a matter of fact, you must have had the very devil of a time?'

'Oh, beastly! Sometimes too beastly for words. Do you know that sometimes—'

She paused. She had been about to tell him how she had had to beg for her food; how she had slept in the streets; how she had been arrested for begging and spent a night in the police cells; how Mrs Creevy had nagged at her and starved her. But she stopped, because she had suddenly realized that these were not the things that she wanted to talk about. Such things as these, she perceived, are of no real importance; they are mere irrelevant accidents, not essentially different from catching a cold in the head or having to wait two hours at a railway junction. They are disagreeable, but they do not matter. The truism that all real happenings are in the mind struck her more forcibly than ever before, and she said:

'Those things don't really matter. I mean, things like having no money and not having enough to eat. Even when you're practically starving—it doesn't *change* anything inside you.'

'Doesn't it? I'll take your word for it. I should be very sorry to try.'

'Oh, well, it's beastly while it's happening, of course; but it doesn't make any real difference; it's the things that happen inside you that matter.'

'Meaning?' said Mr Warburton.

'Oh—things change in your mind. And then the whole world changes, because you look at it differently.'

She was still looking out of the window. The train had drawn clear of the eastern slums and was running at gathering speed past willow-bordered streams and low-lying meadows upon whose hedges the first buds made a faint soft greenness, like a cloud. In a field near the line a month-old calf, flat as a Noah's Ark animal, was bounding stiff-legged after its mother, and in a cottage garden an old labourer, with slow, rheumatic movements, was turning over the soil beneath a pear tree covered with ghostly bloom. His spade flashed in the sun as the train passed. The depressing hymn-line 'Change and decay in all around I see' moved through Dorothy's mind. It was true what she had said just now. Something had happened in her heart, and the world was a little emptier, a little poorer from that minute. On such a day as this, last spring or any earlier spring, how joyfully, and how unthinkingly, she would have thanked God for the first blue skies and the first flowers of the reviving year! And now, seemingly, there was no God to thank, and nothing—not a flower or a stone or a blade of grass—nothing in the universe would ever be the same again.

'Things change in your mind,' she repeated. 'I've lost my faith,' she added, somewhat abruptly, because she found herself half ashamed to utter the words.

'You've lost your *what*?' said Mr Warburton, less accustomed than she to this kind of phraseology.

'My faith. Oh, you know what I mean! A few months ago, all of a sudden, it seemed as if my whole mind had changed. Everything that I'd believed in till then—everything—seemed suddenly meaningless and almost silly. God—what I'd meant by God—immortal life, Heaven and Hell—everything. It had all gone. And it wasn't that I'd reasoned it out; it just happened to me. It was like when you're a child, and one day, for no particular reason, you stop believing in fairies. I just couldn't go on believing in it any longer.'

'You never did believe in it,' said Mr Warburton unconcernedly.

'But I did, really I did! I know you always thought I didn't—you thought I was just pretending because I was ashamed to own up. But it wasn't that at all. I believed it just as I believe that I'm sitting in this carriage.'

'Of course you didn't, my poor child! How could you, at your age? You were far too intelligent for that. But you'd been brought up in these absurd beliefs, and you'd allowed yourself to go on thinking, in a sort of way, that you could still swallow them. You'd built yourself a life-pattern—if you'll excuse a bit of psychological jargon—that was only possible for a believer, and naturally it was beginning to be a strain on you. In fact, it was obvious all the time what was the matter with you. I should say that in all probability that was why you lost your memory.'

'What do you mean?' she said, rather puzzled by this remark.

He saw that she did not understand, and explained to her that loss of memory is only a device, unconsciously used, to escape from an impossible situation. The mind, he said, will play curious tricks when it is in a tight corner. Dorothy had never heard of anything of this kind before, and she could not at first accept his explanation. Nevertheless she considered it for a moment, and perceived that, even if it were true, it did not alter the fundamental fact.

'I don't see that it makes any difference,' she said finally.

'Doesn't it? I should have said it made a considerable difference.'

'But don't you see, if my faith is gone, what does it matter whether I've only lost it now or whether I'd really lost it years ago? All that matters is that it's gone, and I've got to begin my life all over again.'

'Surely I don't take you to mean,' said Mr Warburton, 'that you actually *regret* losing your faith, as you call it? One might as well regret losing a goitre. Mind you, I'm speaking, as it were, without the book—as a man who never had very much faith to lose. The little I had passed away quite painlessly at the age of nine. But it's hardly the kind of thing I should have thought anyone would *regret* losing. Used you not, if I remember rightly, to do horrible things like getting up at five in the morning to go to Holy Communion on an empty belly? Surely you're not homesick for that kind of thing?'

'I don't believe in it any longer, if that's what you mean. And I see now that a lot of it was rather silly. But that doesn't help. The point is that all the beliefs I had are gone, and I've nothing to put in their place.'

'But good God! why do you want to put anything in their place? You've got rid of a load of superstitious rubbish, and you ought to be glad of it. Surely it doesn't make you any happier to go about quaking in fear of Hell fire?'

'But don't you see—you must see—how different everything is when all of a sudden the whole world is empty?'

'Empty?' exclaimed Mr Warburton. 'What do you mean by saying it's empty? I call that perfectly scandalous in a girl of your age. It's not empty at all, it's a deuced sight too full, that's the trouble with it. We're here today and gone tomorrow, and we've no time to enjoy what we've got.'

'But how *can* one enjoy anything when all the meaning's been taken out of it?'

'Good gracious! What do you want with a meaning? When I eat my dinner I don't do it to the greater glory of God; I do it because I enjoy it. The world's full of amusing things—books, pictures, wine, travel, friends—everything. I've never seen any meaning in it all, and I don't want to see one. Why not take life as you find it?'

'But—'

She broke off, for she saw already that she was wasting words in trying to make herself clear to him. He was quite incapable of understanding her difficulty—incapable of realizing how a mind naturally pious must recoil from a world discovered to be meaningless. Even the loathsome platitudes of the pantheists would be beyond his understanding. Probably the idea that life was essentially futile, if he thought of it at all, struck him as rather amusing than otherwise. And yet with all this he was sufficiently acute. He could see the difficulty of her own particular position, and he adverted to it a moment later.

'Of course,' he said, 'I can see that things are going to be a little awkward for you when you get home. You're going to be, so to speak, a wolf in sheep's clothing. Parish work—Mothers' Meetings, prayers with the dying, and all that—I suppose it might be a little distasteful at times. Are you afraid you won't be able to keep it up—is that the trouble?'

'Oh, no. I wasn't thinking of that. I shall go on with it, just the same as before. It's what I'm most used to. Besides, Father needs my help. He can't afford a curate, and the work's got to be done.'

'Then what's the matter? Is it the hypocrisy that's worrying you? Afraid that the consecrated bread might stick in your throat, and so forth? I shouldn't trouble. Half the parsons' daughters in England are probably in the same difficulty. And quite nine-tenths of the parsons, I should say.'

'It's partly that. I shall have to be always pretending—oh, you can't imagine in what ways! But that's not the worst. Perhaps that part of it doesn't matter, really. Perhaps it's better to be a hypocrite—*that* kind of hypocrite—than some things.'

'Why do you say *that* kind of hypocrite? I hope you don't mean that pretending to believe is the next best thing to believing?'

'Yes . . . I suppose that's what I do mean. Perhaps it's better–less selfish–to pretend one believes even when one doesn't, than to say openly that one's an unbeliever and perhaps help turn other people into unbelievers too.'

'My dear Dorothy,' said Mr Warburton, 'your mind, if you'll excuse my saying so, is in a morbid condition. No, dash it! it's worse than morbid; it's downright septic. You've a sort of mental gangrene hanging over from your Christian upbringing. You tell me that you've got rid of these ridiculous beliefs that were stuffed into you from your cradle upwards, and yet you're taking an attitude to life which is simply meaningless without those beliefs. Do you call that reasonable?'

'I don't know. No perhaps it's not. But I suppose it's what comes naturally to me.'

'What you're trying to do, apparently,' pursued Mr Warburton, 'is to make the worst of both worlds. You stick to the Christian scheme of things, but you leave Paradise out of it. And I suppose, if the truth were known, there are quite a lot of your kind wandering about among the ruins of C. of E. You're practically a sect in yourselves,' he added reflectively: 'the Anglican Atheists. Not a sect I should care to belong to, I must say.'

They talked for a little while longer, but not to much purpose. In reality the whole subject of religious belief and religious doubt was boring and incomprehensible to Mr Warburton. Its only appeal to him was as a pretext for blasphemy. Presently he changed the subject, as though giving up the attempt to understand Dorothy's outlook.

'This is nonsense that we're talking,' he said. 'You've got hold of some very depressing ideas, but you'll grow out of them later on, you know. Christianity isn't really an incurable disease. However, there was something quite different that I was going to say to you. I want you to listen to me for a moment. You're coming home, after being away eight months, to what I expect you realize is a rather uncomfortable situation. You had a hard enough life before–at least, what I should call a hard life–and now that you aren't quite such a good Girl Guide as you used to be, it's going to be a great deal harder. Now, do you think it's absolutely necessary to go back to it?'

'But I don't see what else I can do, unless I could get another job. I've really no alternative.'

Mr Warburton, with his head cocked a little on one side, gave Dorothy a rather curious look.

'As a matter of fact,' he said, in a more serious tone than usual, 'there's at least one other alternative that I could suggest to you.'

'You mean that I could go on being a schoolmistress? Perhaps that's what I ought to do, really. I shall come back to it in the end, in any case.'

'No. I don't think that's what I should advise.'

All this time Mr Warburton, unwilling as ever to expose his baldness, had been wearing his rakish, rather broad-brimmed grey felt hat. Now, however, he took it off and laid it carefully on the empty seat beside him. His naked cranium, with only a wisp or two of golden hair lingering in the neighbourhood of the ears, looked like some monstrous pink pearl. Dorothy watched him with a slight surprise.

'I am taking my hat off,' he said, 'in order to let you see me at my very worst. You will understand why in a moment. Now, let me offer you another alternative besides going back to your Girl Guides and your Mothers' Union, or imprisoning yourself in some dungeon of a girls' school.'

'What do you mean?' said Dorothy.

'I mean, will you—think well before you answer; I admit there are some very obvious objections, but—will you marry me?'

Dorothy's lips parted with surprise. Perhaps she turned a little paler. With a hasty, almost unconscious recoil she moved as far away from him as the back of the seat would allow. But he had made no movement towards her. He said with complete equanimity:

'You know, of course, that Dolores [Dolores was Mr Warburton's ex-mistress] left me a year ago?'

'But I can't, I can't!' exclaimed Dorothy. 'You know I can't! I'm not—like that. I thought you always knew. I shan't ever marry.'

Mr Warburton ignored this remark.

'I grant you,' he said, still with exemplary calmness, 'that I don't exactly come under the heading of eligible young men. I am somewhat older than you. We both seem to be putting our cards on the table today, so I'll let you into a great secret and tell you that my age is forty-nine. And then I've three children and a bad reputation. It's a marriage that your father would—well, regard with disfavour. And my income is only seven hundred a year. But still, don't you think it's worth considering!'

'I can't, you know why I can't!' repeated Dorothy.

She took it for granted that he 'knew why she couldn't', though she had never explained to him, or to anyone else, why it was impossible for her to marry. Very probably, even if she had explained, he would not have understood her. He went on speaking, not appearing to notice what she had said.

'Let me put it to you', he said, 'in the form of a bargain. Of course, I needn't tell you that it's a great deal more than that. I'm not a marrying kind of man, as the saying goes, and I shouldn't ask you to marry me if you hadn't a rather special attraction for me. But let me put the business side of it first. You need a home and a livelihood; I need a wife to keep me in order. I'm sick of these disgusting women I've spent my life with, if you'll forgive my mentioning them, and I'm rather anxious to settle down. A bit late in the day, perhaps, but better late than never. Besides, I need somebody to look after the children; the *bastards,* you know. I don't expect you to find me overwhelmingly attractive,' he added, running a hand reflectively over his bald crown, 'but on the other hand I am very easy to get on with. Immoral people usually are, as a matter of fact. And from your own point of view the scheme would have certain advantages. Why should you spend your life delivering parish magazines and rubbing nastly old women's legs with Elliman's embrocation? You would be happier married, even to a husband with a bald head and a clouded past. You've had a hard, dull life for a girl of your age, and your future isn't exactly rosy. Have you really considered what your future will be like if you don't marry?'

'I don't know. I have to some extent,' she said.

As he had not attempted to lay hands on her or to offer any endearments, she answered his question without repeating her previous refusal. He looked out of the window, and went on in a musing voice, much quieter than his normal tone, so that at first she could barely hear him above the rattle of the train; but presently his voice rose, and took on a note of seriousness that she had never heard in it before, or even imagined that it could hold.

'Consider what your future would be like,' he repeated. 'It's the same future that lies before any woman of your class with no husband and no money. Let us say your father will live another ten years. By the end of that time the last penny of his money will have gone down the sink. The desire to squander it will keep him alive just as long as it lasts, and probably no longer. All that time he will be growing more senile, more tiresome, more impossible to live with; he will tyrannize over you more and more, keep you shorter and shorter of money, make more and more trouble for you with the neighbours and the tradesmen. And you will go on with that slavish, worrying life that you have lived, struggling to make both ends meet, drilling the Girl Guides, reading novels to the Mothers' Union, polishing the altar brasses, cadging money for the organ fund, making brown paper jackboots for the schoolchildren's plays, keeping your end up in the vile little feuds and scandals of the church hen-coop. Year after year, winter and summer, you will bicycle from one reeking cottage to another, to dole out pennies from the poor box and repeat prayers that you don't even believe in any longer. You will sit through interminable church services which in the end will make you physically sick with their sameness and futility. Every year your life will be a little bleaker, a little fuller of those deadly little jobs that are shoved off on to lonely women. And remember that you won't always be twenty-eight. All the while you will be fading, withering, until one morning you will look in the glass and realize that you aren't a girl any longer, only a skinny old maid. You'll fight against it, of course. You'll keep your physical energy and your girlish mannerisms—you'll keep them just a little bit too long. Do you know that type of bright—too bright—spinster who says "topping" and "ripping" and "right-ho", and prides herself on being such a good sport, and she's such a good sport that she makes everyone feel a little unwell? And she's so splendidly hearty at tennis and so handy at amateur theatricals, and she throws herself with a kind of desperation into her Girl Guide work and her parish visiting, and she's the life and soul of Church socials, and always, year after year, she thinks of herself as a young girl still and never realizes that behind her back everyone laughs at her for a poor, disappointed old maid? That's what you'll become, what you must become, however much you foresee it and try to avoid it. There's no other future possible to you unless you marry. Women who don't marry wither up—they wither up like aspidistras in back-parlour windows; and the devilish thing is that they don't even know that they're withering.'

Dorothy sat silent and listening with intent and horrified fascination. She did not even notice that he had stood up, with one hand on the door to steady him against the swaying of the train. She was as though hypnotized, not so much by his voice as by the visions that his words had evoked in her. He had described her life, as it must inevitably be, with such dreadful fidelity that he seemed actually to have carried her ten years onward into the menacing future, and she felt herself no longer a girl full of youth and energy, but a desperate, worn virgin of thirty-eight. As he went on he took her hand, which was lying idle on the arm of the seat; and even that she scarcely noticed.

'After ten years,' he continued, 'your father will die, and he will leave you with not a penny, only debts. You will be nearly forty, with no money, no profession, no chance of marrying; just a derelict parson's daughter like the ten thousand others in England. And after that, what do you suppose will become of you? You will have to find yourself a job—the sort of job that parsons' daughters get. A nursery governess, for instance, or companion to some diseased hag who will occupy herself in thinking of ways to humiliate you. Or you will go back to school-teaching; English mistress in some grisly girls' school, seventy-five pounds a year and your keep, and a fortnight in a seaside boarding-house every August. And all the time withering, drying up, growing more sour and more angular and more friendless. And therefore—'

As he said 'therefore' he pulled Dorothy to her feet. She made no resistance. His voice had put her under a spell. As her mind took in the prospect of that forbidding future, whose emptiness she was far more able to appreciate than he, such a despair had grown in her that if she had spoken at all it would have been to say, 'Yes, I will marry you.' He put his arm very gently about her and drew her a little towards him, and even now she did not attempt to resist. Her eyes, half hypnotized, were fixed upon his. When he put his arm about her it was as though he were protecting her, sheltering her, drawing her away from the brink of grey, deadly poverty and back to the world of friendly and desirable things—to security and ease, to comely houses and good clothes, to books and friends and flowers, to summer days and distant lands. So for nearly a minute the fat, debauched bachelor and the thin, spinsterish girl stood face to face, their eyes meeting, their bodies all but touching, while the train swayed them in its motion, and clouds and telegraph poles and bud-misted hedges and fields green with young wheat raced past unseen.

Mr Warburton tightened his grip and pulled her against him. It broke the spell. The visions that had held her helpless—visions of poverty and of escape from poverty—suddenly vanished and left only a shocked realization of what was happening to her. She was in the arms of a man—a fattish, oldish man! A wave of disgust and deadly fear went through her, and her entrails seemed to shrink and freeze. His thick male body was pressing her backwards and downwards, his large, pink face, smooth, but to her eyes old, was bearing down upon her own. The harsh odour of maleness forced itself into her nostrils. She recoiled. Furry thighs of satyrs! She began to struggle furiously, though indeed he made hardly any effort to retain her, and in a moment she had wrenched herself free and fallen back into her seat, white and trembling. She looked up at him with eyes which, from fear and aversion, were for a moment those of a stranger.

Mr Warburton remained on his feet, regarding her with an expression of resigned, almost amused disappointment. He did not seem in the least distressed. As her calmness returned to her she perceived that all he had said had been no more than a trick to play upon her feelings and cajole her into saying that she would marry him; and what was stranger yet, that he had said it without seriously caring whether she married him or not. He had, in fact, merely been amusing himself. Very probably the whole thing was only another of his periodical attempts to seduce her.

He sat down, but more deliberately than she, taking care of the creases of his trousers as he did so.

'If you want to pull the communication cord,' he said mildly, 'you had better let me make sure that I have five pounds in my pocket-book.'

After that he was quite himself again, or as nearly himself as anyone could possibly be after such a scene, and he went on talking without the smallest symptom of embarrassment. His sense of shame, if he had ever possessed one, had perished many years ago. Perhaps it had been killed by overwork in a lifetime of squalid affairs with women.

For an hour, perhaps, Dorothy was ill at ease, but after that the train reached Ipswich, where it stopped for a quarter of an hour, and there was the diversion of going to the refreshment room for a cup of tea. For the last twenty miles of the journey they talked quite amicably. Mr Warburton did not refer again to his proposal of marriage, but as the train neared Knype Hill he returned, less seriously than before, to the question of Dorothy's future.

'So you really propose', he said 'to go back to your parish work? "The trivial round, the common task?" Mrs Pither's rheumatism and Mrs Lewin's corn-plaster and all the rest of it? The prospect doesn't dismay you?'

'I don't know—sometimes it does. But I expect it'll be all right once I'm back at work. I've got the habit, you see.'

'And you really feel equal to years of calculated hypocrisy? For that's what it amounts to, you know. Not afraid of the cat getting out of the bag? Quite sure you won't find yourself teaching the Sunday School kids to say the Lord's Prayer backwards, or reading Gibbon's fifteenth chapter to the Mothers' Union instead of Gene Stratton Porter?'

'I don't think so. Because, you see, I do feel that that kind of work, even if it means saying prayers that one doesn't believe in, and even if it means teaching children things that one doesn't always think are true—I do feel that in a way it's useful.'

'Useful?' said Mr Warburton distastefully. 'You're a little too fond of that depressing word "useful". Hypertrophy of the sense of duty—that's what's the matter with you. Now, to me, it seems the merest common sense to have a bit of fun while the going's good.'

'That's just hedonism,' Dorothy objected.

'My dear child, can you show me a philosophy of life that isn't hedonism?

Your verminous Christian saints are the biggest hedonists of all. They're out for an eternity of bliss, whereas we poor sinners don't hope for more than a few years of it. Ultimately we're all trying for a bit of fun; but some people take it in such perverted forms. Your notion of fun seems to be massaging Mrs Pither's legs.'

'It's not that exactly, but—oh! somehow I can't explain!'

What she would have said was that though her faith had left her, she had not changed, could not change, did not want to change, the spiritual background of her mind; that her cosmos, though now it seemed to her empty and meaningless, was still in a sense the Christian cosmos; that the Christian way of life was still the way that must come naturally to her. But she could not put this into words, and felt that if she tried to do so he would probably begin making fun of her. So she concluded lamely:

'Somehow I feel that it's better for me to go on as I was before.'

'*Exactly* the same as before? The whole bill of fare? The Girl Guides, the Mothers' Union, the Band of Hope, the Companionship of Marriage, parish visiting and Sunday School teaching, Holy Communion twice a week and here we go round the doxology-bush, chanting Gregorian plain-song? You're quite certain you can manage it?'

Dorothy smiled in spite of herself. 'Not plain-song. Father doesn't like it.'

'And you think that, except for your inner thoughts, your life will be precisely what it was before you lost your faith? There will be *no* change in your habits?'

Dorothy thought. Yes, there *would* be changes in her habits; but most of them would be secret ones. The memory of the disciplinary pin crossed her mind. It had always been a secret from everyone except herself and she decided not to mention it.

'Well,' she said finally, 'perhaps at Holy Communion I shall kneel down on Miss Mayfill's right instead of on her left.'

---

## 2

A week had gone by.

Dorothy rode up the hill from the town and wheeled her bicycle in at the Rectory gate. It was a fine evening, clear and cold, and the sun, unclouded, was sinking in remote, greenish skies. Dorothy noticed that the ash tree by the gate was in bloom, with clotted dark red blossoms that looked like festerings from a wound.

She was rather tired. She had had a busy week of it, what with visiting all the women on her list in turn and trying to get the parish affairs into some kind of order again. Everything was in a fearful mess after her absence. The church was dirty beyond all belief—in fact, Dorothy had had to spend the best part of a day cleaning up with scrubbing-brushes, broom and dustpan, and the beds of 'mouse dirts' that she had found behind the organ made her wince when she thought of them. (The reason why the mice came there was because Georgie Frew, the organ-blower, *would* bring penny packets of biscuits into church and eat them during the sermon.) All the Church associations had been neglected, with the result that the Band of Hope and the Companionship of Marriage had now given up the ghost, Sunday School attendance had dropped by half, and there was internecine warfare going on in the Mothers' Union because of some tactless remark that Miss Foote had made. The belfry was in a worse state than ever. The parish magazine had not been delivered regularly and the money for it had not been collected. None of the accounts of the Church Funds had been properly kept up, and there was nineteen shillings unaccounted for in all, and even the parish registers were in a muddle—and so on and so on, *ad infinitum*. The Rector had let everying slide.

Dorothy had been up to her eyes in work from the moment of reaching home. Indeed, things had slipped back into their old routine with astonishing swiftness. It was as though it had been only yesterday that she had gone away. Now that the scandal had blown over, her return to Knype Hill had aroused very little curiosity. Some of the women on her visiting list, particularly Mrs Pither, were genuinely glad to see her back, and Victor Stone, perhaps, seemed just a little ashamed of having temporarily believed Mrs Semprill's libel; but he soon forgot it in recounting to Dorothy his latest triumph in the *Church Times*. Various of the coffee-ladies, of course, had stopped Dorothy in the street with 'My dear, how *very* nice to see you back again! You *have* been away a long time! And you know, dear, we all thought it such a *shame* when that horrible woman was going round telling those stories about you. But I do hope you'll understand, dear, that whatever anyone else may have thought, I never believed a word of them', etc., etc., etc. But nobody had asked her the uncomfortable questions that she had been fearing. 'I've been teaching in a school near London' had satisfied everyone; they had not even asked her the name of the school. Never, she saw, would she have to confess that she had slept in Trafalgar Square and been arrested for begging. The fact is that people who live in small country towns have only a very dim conception of anything that happens more than ten miles from their own front door. The world outside is a *terra incognita*, inhabited, no doubt, by dragons and anthropophagi, but not particularly interesting.

Even Dorothy's father had greeted her as though she had only been away for the week-end. He was in his study when she arrived, musingly smoking his pipe in front of the grandfather clock, whose glass, smashed by the charwoman's broom-handle four months ago, was still unmended. As Dorothy came into the room he took his pipe out of his mouth and put it away in his pocket with an absent-minded, old-mannish movement. He looked a great deal older, Dorothy thought.

'So here you are at last,' he said. 'Did you have a good journey?'

Dorothy put her arms round his neck and touched his silver-pale cheek with her lips. As she disengaged herself he patted her shoulder with a just perceptible trace more affection than usual.

'What made you take it into your head to run away like that?' he said.

'I told you, Father–I lost my memory.'

'Hm,' said the Rector; and Dorothy saw that he did not believe her, never would believe her, and that on many and many a future occasion, when he was in a less agreeable mood than at present, that escapade would be brought up against her. 'Well,' he added, 'when you've taken your bag upstairs, just bring your typewriter down here, would you? I want you to type out my sermon.'

Not much that was of interest had happened in the town. Ye Olde Tea Shoppe was enlarging its premises, to the further disfigurement of the High Street. Mrs Pither's rheumatism was better (thanks to the angelica tea, no doubt), but Mr Pither had 'been under the doctor' and they were afraid he had stone in the bladder. Mr Blifil-Gordon was now in Parliament, a docile deadhead on the back benches of the Conservative Party. Old Mr Tombs had died just after Christmas, and Miss Foote had taken over seven of his cats and made heroic efforts to find homes for the others. Eva Twiss, the niece of Mr Twiss the ironmonger, had had an illegitimate baby, which had died. Proggett had dug the kitchen garden and sowed a few seeds, and the broad beans and the first peas were just showing. The shop-debts had begun to mount up again after the creditors' meeting, and there was six pounds owing to Cargill. Victor Stone had had a controversy with Professor Coulton in the *Church Times*, about the Holy Inquisition, and utterly routed him. Ellen's eczema had been very bad all the winter. Walph Blifil-Gordon had had two poems accepted by the *London Mercury*.

Dorothy went into the conservatory. She had got a big job on hand–costumes for a pageant that the schoolchildren were going to have on St George's Day, in aid of the organ fund. Not a penny had been paid towards the organ during the past eight months, and it was perhaps as well that the Rector always threw the organ-people's bills away unopened, for their tone was growing more and more sulphurous. Dorothy racked her brains for a way of raising some money, and finally decided on a historical pageant, beginning with Julius Caesar and ending with the Duke of Wellington. They might raise two pounds by a pageant, she thought–with luck and a fine day, they might even raise three pounds!

She looked round the conservatory. She had hardly been in here since coming home, and evidently nothing had been touched during her absence. Her things were lying just as she had left them; but the dust was thick on everything. Her sewing-machine was on the table amid the old familiar litter of scraps of cloth, sheets of brown paper, cotton-reels and pots of paint, and though the needle had rusted, the thread was still in it. And, yes! there were the jackboots that she had been making the night she went away. She picked one of them up and looked at it. Something stirred in her heart. Yes, say what you like, they *were* good jackboots! What a pity they had never been used! However, they would come in useful for the pageant. For Charles II, perhaps–or, no, better not have Charles II; have Oliver Cromwell instead;

because if you had Oliver Cromwell you wouldn't have to make him a wig.

Dorothy lighted the oilstove, found her scissors and two sheets of brown paper, and sat down. There was a mountain of clothes to be made. Better start off with Julius Caesar's breastplate, she thought. It was always that wretched armour that made all the trouble! What did a Roman soldier's armour look like? Dorothy made an effort, and called to mind the statue of some idealized curly-bearded emperor in the Roman Room at the British Museum. You might make a sort of rough breastplate out of glue and brown paper, and glue narrow strips of paper across it to represent the plates of the armour, and then silver them over. No helmet to make, thank goodness! Julius Caesar always wore a laurel wreath—ashamed of his baldness, no doubt, like Mr Warburton. But what about greaves? Did they wear greaves in Julius Caesar's time? And boots? Was a caligum a boot or a sandal?

After a few moments she stopped with the shears resting on her knee. A thought which had been haunting her like some inexorcizable ghost at every unoccupied moment during the past week had returned once more to distract her. It was the thought of what Mr Warburton had said to her in the train—of what her life was going to be like hereafter, unmarried and without money.

It was not that she was in any doubt about the external facts of her future. She could see it all quite clearly before her. Ten years, perhaps, as unsalaried curate, and then back to school-teaching. Not necessarily in quite such a school as Mrs Creevy's—no doubt she could do something rather better for herself than that—but at least in some more or less shabby, more or less prison-like school; or perhaps in some even bleaker, even less human kind of drudgery. Whatever happened, at the very best, she had got to face the destiny that is common to all lonely and penniless women. 'The Old Maids of Old England', as somebody called them. She was twenty-eight—just old enough to enter their ranks.

But it didn't matter, it didn't matter! That was the thing that you could never drive into the heads of the Mr Warburtons of this world, not if you talked to them for a thousand years; that mere outward things like poverty and drudgery, and even loneliness, don't matter in themselves. It is the things that happen in your heart that matter. For just a moment—an evil moment—while Mr Warburton was talking to her in the train, she had known the fear of poverty. But she had mastered it; it was not a thing worth worrying about. It was not because of *that* that she had got to stiffen her courage and remake the whole structure of her mind.

No, it was something far more fundamental; it was the deadly emptiness that she had discovered at the heart of things. She thought of how a year ago she had sat in this chair, with these scissors in her hand, doing precisely what she was doing now; and yet it was as though then and now she had been two different beings. Where had she gone, that well-meaning, ridiculous girl who had prayed ecstatically in summer-scented fields and pricked her arm as a punishment for sacrilegious thoughts? And where is any of ourselves of even a year ago? And yet after all—and here lay the trouble—she *was* the same girl. Beliefs change, thoughts change, but there is some inner part of the soul that does not change. Faith vanishes, but the need for faith remains the same as before.

And given only faith, how can anything else matter? How can anything dismay you if only there is some purpose in the world which you can serve, and which, while serving it, you can understand? Your whole life is illumined by the sense of purpose. There is no weariness in your heart, no doubts, no feeling of futility, no Baudelairean ennui waiting for unguarded hours. Every act is significant, every moment sanctified, woven by faith as into a pattern, a fabric of never-ending joy.

She began to meditate upon the nature of life. You emerged from the womb, you lived sixty or seventy years, and then you died and rotted. And in every detail of your life, if no ultimate purpose redeemed it, there was a quality of greyness, of desolation, that could never be described, but which you could feel like a physical pang at your heart. Life, if the grave really ends it, is monstrous and dreadful. No use trying to argue it away. Think of life as it really is, think of the *details* of life; and then think that there is no meaning in it, no purpose, no goal except the grave. Surely only fools or self-deceivers, or those whose lives are exceptionally fortunate, can face that thought without flinching?

She shifted her position in her chair. But after all there must be *some* meaning, *some* purpose in it all! The world cannot be an accident. Everything that happens must have a cause—ultimately, therefore, a purpose. Since you exist, God must have created you, and since He created you a conscious being, He must be conscious. The greater doesn't come out of the less. He created you, and He will kill you, for His own purpose. But that purpose is inscrutable. It is in the nature of things that you can never discover it, and perhaps even if you did discover it you would be averse to it. Your life and death, it may be, are a single note in the eternal orchestra that plays for His diversion. And suppose you don't like the tune? She thought of that dreadful unfrocked clergyman in Trafalgar Square. Had she dreamed the things he said, or had he really said them? 'Therefore with Demons and Archdemons and with all the company of Hell'. But that was silly, really. For your not liking the tune was also part of the tune.

Her mind struggled with the problem, while perceiving that there was no solution. There was, she saw clearly, no possible substitute for faith; no pagan acceptance of life as sufficient to itself, no pantheistic cheer-up stuff, no pseudo-religion of 'progress' with visions of glittering Utopias and ant-heaps of steel and concrete. It is all or nothing. Either life on earth is a preparation for something greater and more lasting, or it is meaningless, dark, and dreadful.

Dorothy started. A frizzling sound was coming from the glue-pot. She had forgotten to put any water in the saucepan, and the glue was beginning to burn. She took the saucepan, hastened to the scullery sink to replenish it, then brought it back and put it on the oilstove again. I simply *must* get that breastplate done before supper! she thought. After Julius Caesar there was William the Conqueror to be thought of. More armour! And presently she must go along to the kitchen and remind Ellen to boil some potatoes to go with the minced beef for supper; also there was her 'memo list' to be written out for tomorrow. She shaped the two halves of the breastplate, cut out the armholes and neckholes, and then stopped again.

Where had she got to? She had been saying that if death ends all, then there is no hope and no meaning in anything. Well, what then?

The action of going to the scullery and refilling the saucepan had changed the tenor of her thoughts. She perceived, for a moment at least, that she had allowed herself to fall into exaggeration and self-pity. What a fuss about nothing, after all! As though in reality there were not people beyond number in the same case as herself! All over the world, thousands, millions of them; people who had lost their faith without losing their need of faith. 'Half the parsons' daughters in England,' Mr Warburton had said. He was probably right. And not only parsons' daughters; people of every description—people in illness and loneliness and failure, people leading thwarted, discouraging lives—people who needed faith to support them, and who hadn't got it. Perhaps even nuns in convents, scrubbing floors and singing *Ave Marias,* secretly unbelieving.

And how cowardly, after all, to regret a superstition that you had got rid of—to want to believe something that you knew in your bones to be untrue!

And yet—!

Dorothy had put down her scissors. Almost from force of habit, as though her return home, which had not restored her faith, had restored the outward habits of piety, she knelt down beside her chair. She buried her face in her hands. She began to pray.

'Lord, I believe, help Thou my unbelief. Lord, I believe, I believe; help Thou my unbelief.'

It was useless, absolutely useless. Even as she spoke the words she was aware of their uselessness, and was half ashamed of her action. She raised her head. And at that moment there stole into her nostrils a warm, evil smell, forgotten these eight months but unutterably familiar—the smell of glue. The water in the saucepan was bubbling noisily. Dorothy jumped to her feet and felt the handle of the glue-brush. The glue was softening—would be liquid in another five minutes.

The grandfather clock in her father's study struck six. Dorothy started. She realized that she had wasted twenty minutes, and her conscience stabbed her so hard that all the questions that had been worrying her fled out of her mind. What on earth have I been doing all this time? she thought; and at that moment it really seemed to her that she did not know what she had been doing. She admonished herself. Come on, Dorothy! No slacking, please! You've got to get that breastplate done before supper. She sat down, filled her mouth with pins and began pinning the two halves of the breastplate together, to get it into shape before the glue should be ready.

The smell of glue was the answer to her prayer. She did not know this. She did not reflect, consciously, that the solution to her difficulty lay in accepting the fact that there was no solution; that if one gets on with the job that lies to hand, the ultimate purpose of the job fades into insignificance; that faith and no faith are very much the same provided that one is doing what is customary, useful, and acceptable. She could not formulate these thoughts as yet, she could only live them. Much later, perhaps, she would formulate them and draw comfort from them.

There was still a minute or two before the glue would be ready to use. Dorothy finished pinning the breastplate together, and in the same instant began mentally sketching the innumerable costumes that were yet to be made. After William the Conqueror—was it chain mail in William the Conqueror's day?—there were Robin Hood—Lincoln Green and a bow and arrow—and Thomas à Becket in his cope and mitre, and Queen Elizabeth's ruff, and a cocked hat for the Duke of Wellington. And I must go and see about those potatoes at half past six, she thought. And there was her 'memo list' to be written out for tomorrow. Tomorrow was Wednesday—mustn't forget to set the alarm clock for half past five. She took a slip of paper and began writing out the 'memo list':

7 oc. H.C.
Mrs J. baby next month go and see her.
*Breakfast*. Bacon.

She paused to think of fresh items. Mrs J. was Mrs Jowett, the blacksmith's wife; she came sometimes to be churched after her babies were born, but only if you coaxed her tactfully beforehand. And I must take old Mrs Frew some paregoric lozenges, Dorothy thought, and then perhaps she'll speak to Georgie and stop him eating those biscuits during the sermon. She added Mrs Frew to her list. And then what about tomorrow's dinner—luncheon? We simply *must* pay Cargill something! she thought. And tomorrow was the day of the Mothers' Union tea, and they had finished the novel that Miss Foote had been reading to them. The question was, what to get for them next? There didn't seem to be any more books by Gene Stratton Porter, their favourite. What about Warwick Deeping? Too highbrow, perhaps? And I must ask Proggett to get us some young cauliflowers to plant out, she thought finally.

The glue had liquefied. Dorothy took two fresh sheets of brown paper, sliced them into narrow strips, and—rather awkwardly, because of the difficulty of keeping the breastplate convex—pasted the strips horizontally across it, back and front. By degrees it stiffened under her hands. When she had reinforced it all over she set it on end to look at it. It really wasn't half bad! One more coating of paper and it would be almost like real armour. We *must* make that pageant a success! she thought. What a pity we can't borrow a horse from somebody and have Boadicea in her chariot! We might make five pounds if we had a really good chariot, with scythes on the wheels. And what about Hengist and Horsa? Cross-gartering and winged helmets. Dorothy sliced two more sheets of brown paper into strips, and took up the breastplate to give it its final coating. The problem of faith and no faith had vanished utterly from her mind. It was beginning to get dark, but, too busy to stop and light the lamp, she worked on, pasting strip after strip of paper into place, with absorbed, with pious concentration, in the penetrating smell of the glue-pot.

# COMING UP FOR AIR

# COMING UP FOR AIR

'He's dead, but he won't lie down'

*Popular song*

# PART I

## I

The idea really came to me the day I got my new false teeth.

I remember the morning well. At about a quarter to eight I'd nipped out of bed and got into the bathroom just in time to shut the kids out. It was a beastly January morning, with a dirty yellowish-grey sky. Down below, out of the little square of bathroom window, I could see the ten yards by five of grass, with a privet hedge round it and a bare patch in the middle, that we call the back garden. There's the same back garden, some privets, and same grass, behind every house in Ellesmere Road. Only difference—where there are no kids there's no bare patch in the middle.

I was trying to shave with a bluntish razor-blade while the water ran into the bath. My face looked back at me out of the mirror, and underneath, in a tumbler of water on the little shelf over the washbasin, the teeth that belonged in the face. It was the temporary set that Warner, my dentist, had given me to wear while the new ones were being made. I haven't such a bad face, really. It's one of those bricky-red faces that go with butter-coloured hair and pale-blue eyes. I've never gone grey or bald, thank God, and when I've got my teeth in I probably don't look my age, which is forty-five.

Making a mental note to buy razor-blades, I got into the bath and started soaping. I soaped my arms (I've got those kind of pudgy arms that are freckled up to the elbow) and then took the back-brush and soaped my shoulder-blades, which in the ordinary way I can't reach. It's a nuisance, but there are several parts of my body that I can't reach nowadays. The truth is that I'm inclined to be a little bit on the fat side. I don't mean that I'm like something in a side-show at a fair. My weight isn't much over fourteen stone, and last time I measured round my waist it was either forty-eight or forty-nine, I forget which. And I'm not what they call 'disgustingly' fat, I haven't got one of those bellies that sag half-way down to the knees. It's merely that I'm a little bit broad in the beam, with a tendency to be barrel-shaped. Do you know the active, hearty kind of fat man, the athletic bouncing type that's nicknamed Fatty or Tubby and is always the life and soul of the party? I'm that type. 'Fatty' they mostly call me. Fatty Bowling. George Bowling is my real name.

But at that moment I didn't feel like the life and soul of the party. And it struck me that nowadays I nearly always do have a morose kind of feeling in the early mornings, although I sleep well and my digestion's good. I knew what it was, of course—it was those bloody false teeth. The things were magnified by the water in the tumbler, and they were grinning at me like the teeth in a skull. It gives you a rotten feeling to have your gums meet, a sort of pinched-up, withered feeling like when you've bitten into a sour apple. Besides, say what you will, false teeth are a landmark. When your last natural tooth goes, the time when you can kid yourself that you're a Hollywood sheik, is definitely at an end. And I was fat as well as forty-five. As I stood up to soap my crutch I had a look at my figure. It's all rot about fat men being unable to see their feet, but it's a fact that when I stand upright I can only see the front halves of mine. No woman, I thought as I worked the soap round my belly, will ever look twice at me again, unless she's paid to. Not that at that moment I particularly wanted any woman to look twice at me.

But it struck me that this morning there were reasons why I ought to have been in a better mood. To begin with I wasn't working today. The old car, in which I 'cover' my district (I ought to tell you that I'm in the insurance business. The Flying Salamander. Life, fire, burglary, twins, shipwreck—everything), was temporarily in dock, and though I'd got to look in at the London office to drop some papers, I was really taking the day off to go and fetch my new false teeth. And besides, there was another business that had been in and out of my mind for some time past. This was that I had seventeen quid which nobody else had heard about—nobody in the family, that is. It had happened this way. A chap in our firm, Mellors by name, had got hold of a book called *Astrology applied to Horse-racing* which proved that it's all a question of influence of the planets on the colours the jockey is wearing. Well, in some race or other there was a mare called Corsair's Bride, a complete outsider, but her jockey's colour was green, which it seemed was just the colour for the planets that happened to be in the ascendant. Mellors, who was deeply bitten with this astrology business, was putting several quid on the horse and went down on his knees to me to do the same. In the end, chiefly to shut him up, I risked ten bob, though I don't bet as a general rule. Sure enough Corsair's Bride came home in a walk. I forget the exact odds, but my share worked out at seventeen quid. By a kind of instinct—rather queer, and probably indicating another landmark in my life—I just quietly put the money in the bank and said nothing to anybody. I'd never done anything of this kind before. A good husband and father would have spent it on a dress for Hilda (that's my wife) and boots for the kids. But I'd been a good husband and father for fifteen years and I was beginning to get fed up with it.

After I'd soaped myself all over I felt better and lay down in the bath to think about my seventeen quid and what to spend it on. The alternatives, it seemed to me, were either a week-end with a woman or dribbling it quietly away on odds and ends such as cigars and double whiskies. I'd just turned on some more hot water and was thinking about women and cigars when there was a noise like a herd of buffaloes coming down the two steps that lead to the bathroom. It was the kids, of course. Two kids in a house the size of ours is like a quart of beer in a pint mug. There was a frantic stamping outside and then a yell of agony.

'Dadda! I wanna come in!'

'Well, you can't. Clear out!'

'But dadda! I wanna go somewhere!'

'Go somewhere else, then. Hop it. I'm having my bath.'

'Dad-*da*! I wanna *go some–where*!'

No use! I knew the danger signal. The w.c. is in the bathroom–it would be, of course, in a house like ours. I hooked the plug out of the bath and got partially dry as quickly as I could. As I opened the door, little Billy–my youngest, aged seven–shot past me, dodging the smack which I aimed at his head. It was only when I was nearly dressed and looking for a tie that I discovered that my neck was still soapy.

It's a rotten thing to have a soapy neck. It gives you a disgusting sticky feeling, and the queer thing is that, however carefully you sponge it away, when you've once discovered that your neck is soapy you feel sticky for the rest of the day. I went downstairs in a bad temper and ready to make myself disagreeable.

Our dining-room, like the other dining-rooms in Ellesmere Road, is a poky little place, fourteen feet by twelve, or maybe it's twelve by ten, and the Japanese oak sideboard, with the two empty decanters and the silver egg-stand that Hilda's mother gave us for a wedding present, doesn't leave much room. Old Hilda was glooming behind the teapot, in her usual state of alarm and dismay because the *News Chronicle* had announced that the price of butter was going up, or something. She hadn't lighted the gas-fire, and though the windows were shut it was beastly cold. I bent down and put a match to the fire, breathing rather loudly through my nose (bending always makes me puff and blow) as a kind of hint to Hilda. She gave me the little sidelong glance that she always gives me when she thinks I'm doing something extravagant.

Hilda is thirty-nine, and when I first knew her she looked just like a hare. So she does still, but she's got very thin and rather wizened, with a perpetual brooding, worried look in her eyes, and when she's more upset than usual she's got a trick of humping her shoulders and folding her arms across her breast, like an old gypsy woman over her fire. She's one of those people who get their main kick in life out of foreseeing disasters. Only petty disasters, of course. As for wars, earthquakes, plagues, famines, and revolutions, she pays no attention to them. Butter is going up, and the gas-bill is enormous, and the kids' boots are wearing out, and there's another instalment due on the radio–that's Hilda's litany. She gets what I've finally decided is a definite pleasure out of rocking herself to and fro with her arms across her breast, and glooming at me, 'But, George, it's very *serious*! I don't know what we're going to *do*! I don't know where the money's coming from! You don't seem to realize how serious it *is*!' and so on and so forth. It's fixed firmly in her head that we shall end up in the workhouse. The funny thing is that if we ever do get to the workhouse Hilda won't mind it a quarter as much as I shall, in fact she'll probably rather enjoy the feeling of security.

The kids were downstairs already, having washed and dressed at lightning speed, as they always do when there's no chance to keep anyone else out of the bathroom. When I got to the breakfast table they were having an argument which went to the tune of 'Yes, you did!' 'No, I didn't!' 'Yes, you did!' 'No, I didn't!' and looked like going on for the rest of the morning, until I told them to cheese it. There are only the two of them, Billy, aged seven, and Lorna, aged eleven. It's a peculiar feeling that I have towards the kids. A great deal of the time I can hardly stick the sight of them. As for their conversation, it's just unbearable. They're at that dreary bread-and-butter age when a kid's mind revolves round things like rulers, pencil-boxes, and who got top marks in French. At other times, especially when they're asleep, I have quite a different feeling. Sometimes I've stood over their cots, on summer evenings when it's light, and watched them sleeping, with their round faces and their tow-coloured hair, several shades lighter than mine, and it's given me that feeling you read about in the Bible when it says your bowels yearn. At such times I feel that I'm just a kind of dried-up seed-pod that doesn't matter twopence and that my sole importance has been to bring these creatures into the world and feed them while they're growing. But that's only at moments. Most of the time my separate existence looks pretty important to me, I feel that there's life in the old dog yet and plenty of good times ahead, and the notion of myself as a kind of tame dairy-cow for a lot of women and kids to chase up and down doesn't appeal to me.

We didn't talk much at breakfast. Hilda was in her 'I don't know what we're going to *do*!' mood, partly owing to the price of butter and partly because the Christmas holidays were nearly over and there was still five pounds owing on the school fees for last term. I ate my boiled egg and spread a piece of bread with Golden Crown marmalade. Hilda will persist in buying the stuff. It's fivepence-halfpenny a pound, and the label tells you, in the smallest print the law allows, that it contains 'a certain proportion of neutral fruit-juice'. This started me off, in the rather irritating way I have sometimes, talking about neutral fruit-trees, wondering what they looked like and what countries they grew in, until finally Hilda got angry. It's not that she minds me chipping her, it's only that in some obscure way she thinks it's wicked to make jokes about anything you save money on.

I had a look at the paper, but there wasn't much news. Down in Spain and over in China they were murdering one another as usual, a woman's legs had been found in a railway waiting-room, and King Zog's wedding was wavering in the balance. Finally, at about ten o'clock, rather earlier than I'd intended, I started out for town. The kids had gone off to play in the public gardens. It was a beastly raw morning. As I stepped out of the front door a nasty little gust of wind caught the soapy patch on my neck and made me suddenly feel that my clothes didn't fit and that I was sticky all over.

# 2

Do you know the road I live in—Ellesmere Road, West Bletchley? Even if you don't, you know fifty others exactly like it.

You know how these streets fester all over the inner-outer suburbs. Always the same. Long, long rows of little semi-detached houses—the numbers in Ellesmere Road run to 212 and ours is 191—as much alike as council houses and generally uglier. The stucco front, the creosoted gate, the privet hedge, the green front door. The Laurels, the Myrtles, the Hawthorns, Mon Abri, Mon Repos, Belle Vue. At perhaps one house in fifty some anti-social type who'll probably end in the workhouse has painted his front door blue instead of green.

That sticky feeling round my neck had put me into a demoralized kind of mood. It's curious how it gets you down to have a sticky neck. It seems to take all the bounce out of you, like when you suddenly discover in a public place that the sole of one of your shoes is coming off. I had no illusions about myself that morning. It was almost as if I could stand at a distance and watch myself coming down the road, with my fat, red face and my false teeth and my vulgar clothes. A chap like me is incapable of looking like a gentleman. Even if you saw me at two hundred yards' distance you'd know immediately—not, perhaps, that I was in the insurance business, but that I was some kind of tout or salesman. The clothes I was wearing were practically the uniform of the tribe. Grey herring-bone suit, a bit the worse for wear, blue overcoat costing fifty shillings, bowler hat, and no gloves. And I've got the look that's peculiar to people who sell things on commission, a kind of coarse, brazen look. At my best moments, when I've got a new suit or when I'm smoking a cigar, I might pass for a bookie or a publican, and when things are very bad I might be touting vacuum cleaners, but at ordinary times you'd place me correctly. 'Five to ten quid a week', you'd say as soon as you saw me. Economically and socially I'm about at the average level of Ellesmere Road.

I had the street pretty much to myself. The men had bunked to catch the 8.21 and the women were fiddling with the gas-stoves. When you've time to look about you, and when you happen to be in the right mood, it's a thing that makes you laugh inside to walk down these streets in the inner-outer suburbs and to think of the lives that go on there. Because, after all, what *is* a road like Ellesmere Road? Just a prison with the cells all in a row. A line of semi-detached torture-chambers where the poor little five-to-ten-pound-a-weekers quake and shiver, every one of them with the boss twisting his tail and his wife riding him like the nightmare and the kids sucking his blood like leeches. There's a lot of rot talked about the sufferings of the working class. I'm not so sorry for the proles myself. Did you ever know a navvy who lay awake thinking about the sack? The prole suffers physically, but he's a free man when he isn't working. But in every one of those little stucco boxes there's some poor bastard who's *never* free except when he's fast asleep and dreaming that he's got the boss down the bottom of a well and is bunging lumps of coal at him.

Of course, the basic trouble with people like us, I said to myself, is that we all imagine we've got something to lose. To begin with, nine-tenths of the people in Ellesmere Road are under the impression that they own their houses. Ellesmere Road, and the whole quarter surrounding it, until you get to the High Street, is part of a huge racket called the Hesperides Estate, the property of the Cheerful Credit Building Society. Building societies are probably the cleverest racket of modern times. My own line, insurance, is a swindle, I admit, but it's an open swindle with the cards on the table. But the beauty of the building society swindles is that your victims think you're doing them a kindness. You wallop them, and they lick your hand. I sometimes think I'd like to have the Hesperides Estate surmounted by an enormous statue to the god of building societies. It would be a queer sort of god. Among other things it would be bisexual. The top half would be a managing director and the bottom half would be a wife in the family way. In one hand it would carry an enormous key—the key of the workhouse, of course—and in the other—what do they call those things like French horns with presents coming out of them?—a cornucopia, out of which would be pouring portable radios, life-insurance policies, false teeth, aspirins, French letters, and concrete garden rollers.

As a matter of fact, in Ellesmere Road we don't own our houses, even when we've finished paying for them. They're not freehold, only leasehold. They're priced at five-fifty, payable over a period of sixteen years, and they're a class of house, which, if you bought them for cash down, would cost round about three-eighty. That represents a profit of a hundred and seventy for the Cheerful Credit, but needless to say that Cheerful Credit makes a lot more out of it than that. Three-eighty includes the builder's profit, but the Cheerful Credit, under the name of Wilson & Bloom, builds the houses itself and scoops the builder's profit. All it has to pay for is the materials. But it also scoops the profit on the materials, because under the name of Brookes & Scatterby it sells itself the bricks, tiles, doors, window-frames, sand, cement, and, I think, glass. And it wouldn't altogether surprise me to learn that under yet another alias it sells itself the timber to make the doors and window-frames. Also—and this was something which we really might have foreseen, though it gave us all a knock when we discovered it—the Cheerful Credit doesn't always keep to its end of the bargain. When Ellesmere Road was built it gave on some open fields—nothing very wonderful, but good for the kids to play in—known as Platt's Meadows. There was nothing in black and white, but it had always been understood that Platt's Meadows weren't to be built on. However, West Bletchley was a growing suburb, Rothwell's jam factory had opened in '28 and the Anglo-American All-Steel Bicycle factory started in '33, and the population was increasing and rents were going up. I've never seen Sir Herbert Crum or any other of the big noises of the Cheerful Credit in the flesh, but in my mind's eye I could see their mouths watering. Suddenly the builders arrived and houses began to go up on Platt's Meadows. There was a howl of agony from the Hesperides, and a tenants' defence association was set up. No use! Crum's lawyers had knocked the stuffing out of us in five minutes, and Platt's Meadows were built over. But the really subtle swindle, the one that makes me feel old Crum deserved his baronetcy, is the mental one. Merely because of the illusion that we own our houses and have what's called 'a stake in the country', we poor saps in the Hesperides, and in all such places, are turned into Crum's devoted slaves for ever. We're all respectable householders—that's to say Tories, yes-men, and bumsuckers. Daren't kill the goose that lays the gilded eggs! And the fact that actually we aren't householders, that we're all in the middle of paying for our houses and eaten up with the ghastly fear that something might happen before we've made the last payment, merely increases the effect. We're all bought, and what's more we're bought with our own money. Every one of those poor downtrodden bastards, sweating his guts out to pay twice the proper price for a brick doll's house that's called Belle Vue because there's no view and the bell doesn't ring—every one of those poor suckers would die on the field of battle to save his country from Bolshevism.

I turned down Walpole Road and got into the High Street. There's a train to London at 10.14. I was just passing the Sixpenny Bazaar when I remembered the mental note I'd made that morning to buy a packet of razor-blades. When I got to the soap counter the floor-manager, or whatever his proper title is, was cursing the girl in charge there. Generally there aren't many people in the Sixpenny at that hour of the morning. Sometimes if you go in just after opening-time you see all the girls lined up in a row and given their morning curse, just to get them into trim for the day. They say these big chain-stores have chaps with special powers of sarcasm and abuse who are sent from branch to branch to ginger the girls up. The floor-manager was an ugly little devil, under-sized, with very square shoulders and a spiky grey moustache. He'd just pounced on her about something, some mistake in the change evidently, and was going for her with a voice like a circular saw.

'Ho, no! Course you couldn't count it! *Course* you couldn't. Too much trouble, that'd be. Ho, no!'

Before I could stop myself I'd caught the girl's eye. It wasn't so nice for her to have a fat middle-aged bloke with a red face looking on while she took her cursing. I turned away as quickly as I could and pretended to be interested in some stuff at the next counter, curtain rings or something. He was on to her again. He was one of those people who turn away and then suddenly dart back at you, like a dragon-fly.

'*Course* you couldn't count it! Doesn't matter to *you* if we're two bob out. Doesn't matter at all. What's two bob to *you*? Couldn't ask *you* to go to the trouble of counting it properly. Ho, no! Nothing matters 'ere 'cept *your* convenience. You don't think about others, do you?'

This went on for about five minutes in a voice you could hear half across the shop. He kept turning away to make her think he'd finished with her and then darting back to have another go. As I edged a bit farther off I had a glance at them. The girl was a kid about eighteen, rather fat, with a sort of moony face, the kind that would never get the change right anyway. She'd turned pale pink and she was wriggling, actually wriggling with pain. It was just the same as if he'd been cutting into her with a whip. The girls at the other counters were pretending not to hear. He was an ugly, stiff-built little devil, the sort of cock-sparrow type of man that sticks his chest out and puts his hands under his coat-tails—the type that'd be a sergeant-major only they aren't tall enough. Do you notice how often they have under-sized men for these bullying jobs? He was sticking his face, moustaches and all, almost into hers so as to scream at her better. And the girl all pink and wriggling.

Finally he decided that he'd said enough and strutted off like an admiral on the quarter-deck, and I came up to the counter for my razor-blades. He knew I'd heard every word, and so did she, and both of them knew I knew they knew. But the worst of it was that for my benefit she'd got to pretend that nothing had happened and put on the standoffish keep-your-distance attitude that a shopgirl's supposed to keep up with male customers. Had to act the grown-up young lady half a minute after I'd seen her cursed like a skivvy! Her face was still pink and her hands were trembling. I asked her for penny blades and she started fumbling in the threepenny tray. Then the little devil of a floor-manager turned our way and for a moment both of us thought he was coming back to begin again. The girl flinched like a dog that sees the whip. But she was looking at me out of the corner of her eye. I could see that because I'd seen her cursed she hated me like the devil. Queer!

I cleared out with my razor-blades. Why do they stand it? I was thinking. Pure funk, of course. One back-answer and you get the sack. It's the same everywhere. I thought of the lad that sometimes serves me at the chain-store grocery we deal at. A great hefty lump of twenty, with cheeks like roses and enormous fore-arms, ought to be working in a blacksmith's shop. And there he is in his white jacket, bent double across the counter, rubbing his hands together with his 'Yes, sir! Very true, sir! Pleasant weather for the time of the year, sir! What can I have the pleasure of getting you today, sir?' practically asking you to kick his bum. Orders, of course. The customer is always right. The thing you can see in his face is mortal dread that you might report him for impertinence and get him sacked. Besides, how's he to know you aren't one of the narks the company sends round? Fear! We swim in it. It's our element. Everyone that isn't scared stiff of losing his job is scared stiff of war, or Fascism, or Communism, or something. Jews sweating when they think of Hitler. It crossed my mind that that little bastard with the spiky moustache was probably a damn sight more scared for his job than the girl was. Probably got a family to support. And perhaps, who knows, at home he's meek and mild, grows cucumbers in the back garden, lets his wife sit on him and the kids pull his moustache. And by the same token you never read about a Spanish Inquisitor or one of these higher-ups in the Russian Ogpu without being told that in private life he was such a good kind man, best of husbands and fathers, devoted to his tame canary, and so forth.

The girl at the soap counter was looking after me as I went out of the door. She'd have murdered me if she could. How she hated me because of what I'd seen! Much more than she hated the floor-manager.

# 3

There was a bombing plane flying low overhead. For a minute or two it seemed to be keeping pace with the train. Two vulgar kind of blokes in shabby overcoats, obviously commercials of the lowest type, newspaper canvassers probably, were sitting opposite me. One of them was reading the *Mail* and the other was reading the *Express*. I could see by their manner that they'd spotted me for one of their kind. Up at the other end of the carriage two lawyers' clerks with black bags were keeping up a conversation full of legal baloney that was meant to impress the rest of us and show that they didn't belong to the common herd.

I was watching the backs of the houses sliding past. The line from West Bletchley runs most of the way through slums, but it's kind of peaceful, the glimpses you get of little backyards with bits of flowers stuck in boxes and the flat roofs where the women peg out the washing and the bird-cage on the wall. The great black bombing plane swayed a little in the air and zoomed ahead so that I couldn't see it. I was sitting with my back to the engine. One of the commercials cocked his eye at it for just a second. I knew what he was thinking. For that matter it's what everybody else is thinking. You don't have to be a highbrow to think such thoughts nowadays. In two years' time, one year's time, what shall we be doing when we see one of those things? Making a dive for the cellar, wetting our bags with fright.

The commercial bloke put down his *Daily Mail*.

'Templegate's winner come in,' he said.

The lawyers' clerks were sprouting some learned rot about fee-simple and peppercorns. The other commercial felt in his waistcoat pocket and took out a bent Woodbine. He felt in the other pocket and then leaned across to me.

'Got a match, Tubby?'

I felt for my matches. 'Tubby', you notice. That's interesting, really. For about a couple of minutes I stopped thinking about bombs and began thinking about my figure as I'd studied it in my bath that morning.

It's quite true I'm tubby, in fact my upper half is almost exactly the shape of a tub. But what's interesting, I think, is that merely because you happen to be a little bit fat, almost anyone, even a total stranger, will take it for granted to give you a nickname that's an insulting comment on your personal appearance.

Suppose a chap was a hunchback or had a squint or a hare-lip—would you give him a nickname to remind him of it? But every fat man's labelled as a matter of course. I'm the type that people automatically slap on the back and punch in the ribs, and nearly all of them think I like it. I never go into the saloon bar of the Crown at Pudley (I pass that way once a week on business) without that ass Waters, who travels for the Seafoam Soap people but who's more or less a permanency in the saloon bar of the Crown, prodding me in the ribs and singing out 'Here a sheer hulk lies poor Tom Bowling!' which is a joke the bloody fools in the bar never get tired of. Waters has got a finger like a bar of iron. They all think a fat man doesn't have any feelings.

The commercial took another of my matches, to pick his teeth with, and chucked the box back. The train whizzed on to an iron bridge. Down below I got a glimpse of a baker's van and a long string of lorries loaded with cement. The queer thing, I was thinking, is that in a way they're right about fat men. It's a fact that a fat man, particularly a man who's been fat from birth—from childhood, that's to say—isn't quite like other men. He goes through his life on a different plane, a sort of light-comedy plane, though in the case of blokes in side-shows at fairs, or in fact anyone over twenty stone, it isn't so much light comedy as low farce. I've been both fat and thin in my life, and I know the difference fatness makes to your outlook. It kind of prevents you from taking things too hard. I doubt whether a man who's never been anything but fat, a man who's been called Fatty ever since he could walk, even knows of the existence of any really deep emotions. How could he? He's got no experience of such things. He can't ever be present at a tragic scene, because a scene where there's a fat man present isn't tragic, it's comic. Just imagine a fat Hamlet, for instance! Or Oliver Hardy acting Romeo. Funnily enough I'd been thinking something of the kind only a few days earlier when I was reading a novel I'd got out of Boots. *Wasted Passion,* it was called. The chap in the story finds out that his girl has gone off with another chap. He's one of these chaps you read about in novels, that have pale sensitive faces and dark hair and a private income. I remember more or less how the passage went:

David paced up and down the room, his hands pressed to his forehead. The news seemed to have stunned him. For a long time he could not believe it. Sheila untrue to him! It could not be! Suddenly realization rushed over him, and he saw the fact in all its stark horror. It was too much. He flung himself down in a paroxysm of weeping.

Anyway, it went something like that. And even at the time it started me thinking. There you have it, you see. That's how people—some people—are expected to behave. But how about a chap like me? Suppose Hilda went off for a week-end with somebody else—not that I'd care a damn, in fact it would rather please me to find that she'd still got that much kick left in her—but suppose I did care, would I fling myself down in a paroxysm of weeping? Would anyone expect me to? You couldn't, with a figure like mine. It would be downright obscene.

The train was running along an embankment. A little below us you could see the roofs of the houses stretching on and on, the little red roofs where the bombs are going to drop, a bit lighted up at this moment because a ray of sunshine was catching them. Funny how we keep on thinking about bombs. Of course there's no question that it's coming soon. You can tell how close it is by the cheer-up stuff they're talking about it in the newspaper. I was reading a piece in the *News Chronicle* the other day where it said that bombing planes can't do any damage nowadays. The anti-aircraft guns have got so good that the bomber has to stay at twenty thousand feet. The chap thinks, you notice, that if an aeroplane's high enough the bombs don't reach the ground. Or more likely what he really meant was that they'll miss Woolwich Arsenal and only hit places like Ellesmere Road.

But taking it by and large, I thought, it's not so bad to be fat. One thing about a fat man is that he's always popular. There's really no kind of company, from bookies to bishops, where a fat man doesn't fit in and feel at home. As for women, fat men have more luck with them than people seem to think. It's all bunk to imagine, as some people do, that a woman looks on a fat man as just a joke. The truth is that a woman doesn't look on *any* man as a joke if he can kid her that he's in love with her.

Mind you, I haven't always been fat. I've been fat for eight or nine years, and I suppose I've developed most of the characteristics. But it's also a fact that internally, mentally, I'm not altogether fat. No! Don't mistake me. I'm not trying to put myself over as a kind of tender flower, the aching heart behind the smiling face and so forth. You couldn't get on in the insurance business if you were anything like that. I'm vulgar, I'm insensitive, and I fit in with my environment. So long as anywhere in the world things are being sold on commission and livings are picked up by sheer brass and lack of finer feelings, chaps like me will be doing it. In almost all circumstances I'd manage to make a living—always a living and never a fortune—and even in war, revolution, plague, and famine I'd back myself to stay alive longer than most people. I'm that type. But also I've got something else inside me, chiefly a hangover from the past. I'll tell you about that later. I'm fat, but I'm thin inside. Has it ever struck you that there's a thin man inside every fat man, just as they say there's a statue inside every block of stone?

The chap who'd borrowed my matches was having a good pick at his teeth over the *Express*.

'Legs case don't seem to get much forrader,' he said.

'They'll never get 'im,' said the other. ''Ow could you identify a pair of legs? They're all the bleeding same, aren't they?'

'Might trace 'im through the piece of paper 'e wrapped 'em up in,' said the first.

Down below you could see the roofs of the houses stretching on and on, twisting this way and that with the streets, but stretching on and on, like an enormous plain that you could have ridden over. Whichever way you cross London it's twenty miles of houses almost without a break. Christ! how can the bombers miss us when they come? We're just one great big bull's-eye. And no warning, probably. Because who's going to be such a bloody fool as to declare war nowadays? If I was Hitler I'd send my bombers across in the middle of a disarmament conference. Some quiet morning, when the clerks are streaming across London Bridge, and the canary's singing, and the old woman's pegging the bloomers on the line–zoom, whizz, plonk! Houses going up into the air, bloomers soaked with blood, canary singing on above the corpses.

Seems a pity somehow, I thought. I looked at the great sea of roofs stretching on and on. Miles and miles of streets, fried-fish shops, tin chapels, picture houses, little printing-shops up back alleys, factories, blocks of flats, whelk stalls, dairies, power stations–on and on and on. Enormous! And the peacefulness of it! Like a great wilderness with no wild beasts. No guns firing, nobody chucking pineapples, nobody beating anybody else up with a rubber truncheon. If you come to think of it, in the whole of England at this moment there probably isn't a single bedroom window from which anyone's firing a machine-gun.

But how about five years from now? Or two years? Or one year?

# 4

I'd dropped my papers at the office. Warner is one of these cheap American dentists, and he has his consulting-room, or 'parlour' as he likes to call it, half-way up a big block of offices, between a photographer and a rubber-goods wholesaler. I was early for my appointment, but it was time for a bit of grub. I don't know what put it into my head to go into a milk-bar. They're places I generally avoid. We five-to-ten-pound-a-weekers aren't well served in the way of eating-places in London. If your idea of the amount to spend on a meal is one and threepence, it's either Lyons, the Express Dairy, or the A.B.C., or else it's the kind of funeral snack they serve you in the saloon bar, a pint of bitter and a slab of cold pie, so cold that it's colder than the beer. Outside the milk-bar the boys were yelling the first editions of the evening papers.

Behind the bright red counter a girl in a tall white cap was fiddling with an ice-box, and somewhere at the back a radio was playing, plonk-tiddle-tiddle-plonk, a kind of tinny sound. Why the hell am I coming here? I thought to myself as I went in. There's a kind of atmosphere about these places that gets me down. Everything slick and shiny and streamlined; mirrors, enamel, and chromium plate whichever direction you look in. Everything spent on the decorations and nothing on the food. No real food at all. Just lists of stuff with American names, sort of phantom stuff that you can't taste and can hardly believe in the existence of. Everything comes out of a carton or a tin, or it's hauled out of a refrigerator or squirted out of a tap or squeezed out of a tube. No comfort, no privacy. Tall stools to sit on, a kind of narrow ledge to eat off, mirrors all round you. A sort of propaganda floating round, mixed up with the noise of the radio, to the effect that food doesn't matter, comfort doesn't matter, nothing matters except slickness and shininess and streamlining. Everything's streamlined nowadays, even the bullet Hitler's keeping for you. I ordered a large coffee and a couple of frankfurters. The girl in the white cap jerked them at me with about as much interest as you'd throw ants' eggs to a goldfish.

Outside the door a newsboy yelled 'Starnoosstan*nerd*!' I saw the poster flapping against his knees: LEGS. FRESH DISCOVERIES. Just 'legs', you notice. It had got down to that. Two days earlier they'd found a woman's legs in a railway waiting-room, done up in a brown-paper parcel, and what with successive editions of the papers, the whole nation was supposed to be so passionately interested in these blasted legs that they didn't need any further introduction. They were the only legs that were news at the moment. It's queer, I 'thought, as I ate a bit of roll, how dull the murders are getting nowadays. All this cutting people up and leaving bits of them about the countryside. Not a patch on the old domestic poisoning dramas, Crippen, Seddon, Mrs Maybrick; the truth being, I suppose, that you can't do a good murder unless you believe you're going to roast in hell for it.

At this moment I bit into one of my frankfurters, and—Christ!

I can't honestly say that I'd expected the thing to have a pleasant taste. I'd expected it to taste of nothing, like the roll. But this—well, it was quite an experience. Let me try and describe it to you.

The frankfurter had a rubber skin, of course, and my temporary teeth weren't much of a fit. I had to do a kind of sawing movement before I could get my teeth through the skin. And then suddenly—pop! The thing burst in my mouth like a rotten pear. A sort of horrible soft stuff was oozing all over my tongue. But the taste! For a moment I just couldn't believe it. Then I rolled my tongue round it again and had another try. It was *fish*! A sausage, a thing calling itself a frankfurter, filled with fish! I got up and walked straight out without touching my coffee. God knows what that might have tasted of.

Outside the newsboy shoved the *Standard* into my face and yelled, 'Legs! 'Orrible revelations! All the winners! Legs! Legs!' I was still rolling the stuff round my tongue, wondering where I could spit it out. I remembered a bit I'd read in the paper somewhere about these food-factories in Germany where everything's made out of something else. Ersatz, they call it. I remembered reading that *they* were making sausages out of fish, and fish, no doubt, out of something different. It gave me the feeling that I'd bitten into the modern world and discovered what it was really made of. That's the way we're going nowadays. Everything slick and streamlined, everything made out of something else. Celluloid, rubber, chromium-steel everywhere, arc-lamps blazing all night, glass roofs over your head, radios all playing the same tune, no vegetation left, everything cemented over, mock-turtles grazing under the neutral fruit-trees. But when you come down to brass tacks and get your teeth into something solid, a sausage for instance, that's what you get. Rotten fish in a rubber skin. Bombs of filth bursting inside your mouth.

When I'd got the new teeth in I felt a lot better. They sat nice and smooth over the gums, and though very likely it sounds absurd to say that false teeth can make you feel younger, it's a fact that they did so. I tried a smile at myself in a shop window. They weren't half bad. Warner, though cheap, is a bit of an artist and doesn't aim at making you look like a toothpaste advert. He's got huge cabinets full of false teeth—he showed them to me once—all graded according to size and colour, and he picks them out like a jeweller choosing stones for a necklace. Nine people out of ten would have taken my teeth for natural.

I caught a full-length glimpse of myself in another window I was passing, and it struck me that really I wasn't such a bad figure of a man. A bit on the fat side, admittedly, but nothing offensive, only what the tailors call a 'full figure', and some women like a man to have a red face. There's life in the old dog yet, I thought. I remembered my seventeen quid, and definitely made up my mind that I'd spend it on a woman. There was time to have a pint before the pubs shut, just to baptize the teeth, and feeling rich because of my seventeen quid I stopped at a tobacconist's and bought myself a sixpenny cigar of a kind I'm rather partial to. They're eight inches long and guaranteed pure Havana leaf all through. I suppose cabbages grow in Havana the same as anywhere else.

When I came out of the pub I felt quite different.

I'd had a couple of pints, they'd warmed me up inside, and the cigar smoke oozing round my new teeth gave me a fresh, clean, peaceful sort of feeling. All of a sudden I felt kind of thoughtful and philosophic. It was partly because I didn't have any work to do. My mind went back to the thoughts of war I'd been having earlier that morning, when the bomber flew over the train. I felt in a kind of prophetic mood, the mood in which you foresee the end of the world and get a certain kick out of it.

I was walking westward up the Strand, and though it was coldish I went slowly to get the pleasure of my cigar. The usual crowd that you can hardly fight your way through was streaming up the pavement, all of them with that insane fixed expression on their faces that people have in London streets, and there was the usual jam of traffic with the great red buses nosing their way between the cars, and the engines roaring and horns tooting. Enough noise to waken the dead, but not to waken this lot, I thought. I felt as if I was the only person awake in a city of sleep-walkers. That's an illusion, of course. When you walk through a crowd of strangers it's next door to impossible not to imagine that they're all waxworks, but probably they're thinking just the same about you. And this kind of prophetic feeling that keeps coming over me nowadays, the feeling that war's just round the corner and that war's the end of all things, isn't peculiar to me. We've all got it, more or less. I suppose even among the people passing at that moment there must have been chaps who were seeing mental pictures of the shellbursts and the mud. Whatever thought you think there's always a million people thinking it at the same moment. But that was how I felt. We're all on the burning deck and nobody knows it except me. I looked at the dumb-bell faces streaming past. Like turkeys in November, I thought. Not a notion of what's coming to them. It was as if I'd got X-rays in my eyes and could see the skeletons walking.

I looked forward a few years. I saw this street as it'll be in five years' time, say, or three years' time (1941 they say it's booked for), after the fighting's started.

No, not all smashed to pieces. Only a little altered, kind of chipped and dirty-looking, the shop-windows almost empty and so dusty that you can't see into them. Down a side street there's an enormous bomb-crater and a block of buildings burnt out so that it looks like a hollow tooth. Thermite. It's all curiously quiet, and everyone's very thin. A platoon of soldiers comes marching up the street. They're all as thin as rakes and their boots are dragging. The sergeant's got corkscrew moustaches and holds himself like a ramrod, but he's thin too and he's got a cough that almost tears him open. Between his coughs he's trying to bawl at them in the old parade-ground style. 'Nah then, Jones! Lift yer 'ed up! What yer keep starin' at the ground for? All them fag-ends was picked up years ago.' Suddenly a fit of coughing catches him. He tries to stop it, can't, doubles up like a ruler, and almost coughs his guts out. His face turns pink and purple, his moustache goes limp, and the water runs out of his eyes.

I can hear the air-raid sirens blowing and the loud-speakers bellowing that our glorious troops have taken a hundred thousand prisoners. I see a top-floor-back in Birmingham and a child of five howling and howling for a bit of bread. And suddenly the mother can't stand it any longer, and she yells at it, 'Shut your trap, you little bastard!' and then she ups the child's frock and smacks its bottom hard, because there isn't any bread and isn't going to be any bread. I see it all. I see the posters and the food-queues, and the castor oil and the rubber truncheons and the machine-guns squirting out of bedroom windows.

Is it going to happen? No knowing. Some days it's impossible to believe it. Some days I say to myself that it's just a scare got up by the newspapers. Some days I know in my bones there's no escaping it.

When I got down near Charing Cross the boys were yelling a later edition of the evening papers. There was some more drivel about the murder. LEGS. FAMOUS SURGEON'S STATEMENT. Then another poster caught my eye: KING ZOG'S WEDDING POSTPONED. King Zog! What a name! It's next door to impossible to believe a chap with a name like that isn't a jet-black Negro.

But just at that moment a queer thing happened. King Zog's name—but I suppose, as I'd already seen the name several times that day, it was mixed up with some sound in the traffic or the smell of horse-dung or something—had started memories in me.

The past is a curious thing. It's with you all the time. I suppose an hour never passes without your thinking of things that happened ten or twenty years ago, and yet most of the time it's got no reality, it's just a set of facts that you've learned, like a lot of stuff in a history book. Then some chance sight or sound or smell, especially smell, sets you going, and the past doesn't merely come back to you, you're actually *in* the past. It was like that at this moment.

I was back in the parish church at Lower Binfield, and it was thirty-eight years ago. To outward appearances, I suppose, I was still walking down the Strand, fat and forty-five, with false teeth and a bowler hat, but inside me I was Georgie Bowling, aged seven, younger son of Samuel Bowling, corn and seed merchant, of 57 High Street, Lower Binfield. And it was Sunday morning, and I could smell the church. How I could smell it! You know the smell churches have, a peculiar, dank, dusty, decaying, sweetish sort of smell. There's a touch of candle-grease in it, and perhaps a whiff of incense and a suspicion of mice, and on Sunday mornings it's a bit overlaid by yellow soap and serge dresses, but predominantly it's that sweet, dusty, musty smell that's like the smell of death and life mixed up together. It's powdered corpses, really.

In those days I was about four feet high. I was standing on the hassock so as to see over the pew in front, and I could feel Mother's black serge dress under my hand. I could also feel my stockings pulled up over my knees—we used to wear them like that then—and the saw edge of the Eton collar they used to buckle me into on Sunday mornings. And I could hear the organ wheezing and two enormous voices bellowing out the psalm. In our church there were two men who led the singing, in fact they did so much of the singing that nobody else got much of a chance. One was Shooter, the fishmonger, and the other was old Wetherall, the joiner and undertaker. They used to sit opposite one another on either side of the nave, in the pews nearest the pulpit. Shooter was a short fat man with a very pink, smooth face, a big nose, drooping moustache, and a chin that kind of fell away beneath his mouth. Wetherall was quite different. He was a great, gaunt, powerful old devil of about sixty, with a face like a death's-head and stiff grey hair half an inch long all over his head. I've never seen a living man who looked so exactly like a skeleton. You could see every line of the skull in his face, his skin was like parchment, and his great lantern jaw full of yellow teeth worked up and down just like the jaw of a skeleton in an anatomical museum. And yet with all his leanness he looked as strong as iron, as though he'd live to be a hundred and make coffins for everyone in that church before he'd finished. Their voices were quite different, too. Shooter had a kind of desperate, agonized bellow, as though someone had a knife at his throat and he was just letting out his last yell for help. But Wetherall had a tremendous, churning, rumbling noise that happened deep down inside him, like enormous barrels being rolled to and fro underground. However much noise he let out, you always knew he'd got plenty more in reserve. The kids nicknamed him Rumbletummy.

They used to get up a kind of antiphonal effect, especially in the psalms. It was always Wetherall who had the last word. I suppose really they were friends in private life, but in my kid's way I used to imagine that they were deadly enemies and trying to shout one another down. Shooter would roar out 'The Lord is my shepherd', and then Wetherall would come in with 'Therefore can I lack nothing', drowning him completely. You always knew which of the two was master. I used especially to look forward to that psalm that has the bit about Sihon king of the Amorites and Og the king of Bashan (this was what King Zog's name had reminded me of). Shooter would start off with 'Sihon king of the Amorites', then perhaps for half a second you could hear the rest of the congregation singing the 'and', and then Wetherall's enormous bass would come in like a tidal wave and swallow everybody up with 'Og the king of Bashan'. I wish I could make you hear the tremendous, rumbling, subterranean barrel-noise that he could get into that word 'Og'. He even used to clip off the end of the 'and', so that when I was a very small kid I used to think it was Dog the king of Bashan. But later, when I got the names right, I formed a picture in my mind's eye of Sihon and Og. I saw them as a couple of those great Egyptian statues that I'd seen pictures of in the penny encyclopedia, enormous stone statues thirty feet high, sitting on their thrones opposite one another, with their hands on their knees and a faint mysterious smile on their faces.

How it came back to me! That peculiar feeling—it was only a feeling, you couldn't describe it as an activity—that we used to call 'Church'. The sweet corpsy smell, the rustle of Sunday dresses, the wheeze of the organ and the roaring voices, the spot of light from the hole in the window creeping slowly up the nave. In some way the grown-ups could put it across that this extraordinary performance was necessary. You took it for granted, just as you took the Bible, which you got in big doses in those days. There were texts on every wall and you knew whole chapters of the O.T. by heart. Even now my head's stuffed full of bits out of the Bible. And the children of Israel did evil again in the sight of the Lord. And Asher abode in his breeches. Followed them from Dan until thou come unto Beersheba. Smote him under the fifth rib, so that he died. You never understood it, you didn't try to or want to, it was just a kind of medicine, a queer-tasting stuff that you had to swallow and knew to be in some way necessary. An extraordinary rigmarole about people with names like Shimei and Nebuchadnezzar and Ahithophel and Hash-badada; people with long stiff garments and Assyrian beards, riding up and down on camels among temples and cedar trees and doing extraordinary things. Sacrificing burnt offerings, walking about in fiery furnaces, getting nailed on crosses, getting swallowed by whales. And all mixed up with the sweet graveyard smell and the serge dresses and the wheeze of the organ.

That was the world I went back to when I saw the poster about King Zog. For a moment I didn't merely remember it, I was *in* it. Of course such impressions don't last more than a few seconds. A moment later it was as though I'd opened my eyes again, and I was forty-five and there was a traffic jam in the Strand. But it had left a kind of after-effect behind. Sometimes when you come out of a train of thought you feel as if you were coming up from deep water, but this time it was the other way about, it was as though it was back in 1900 that I'd been breathing real air. Even now, with my eyes open, so to speak, all those bloody fools hustling to and fro, and the posters and the petrol-stink and the roar of the engines, seemed to me less real than Sunday morning in Lower Binfield thirty-eight years ago.

I chucked away my cigar and walked on slowly. I could smell the corpse-smell. In a manner of speaking I can smell it now. I'm back in Lower Binfield, and the year's 1900. Beside the horse-trough in the market-place the carrier's horse is having its nose-bag. At the sweet-shop on the corner Mother Wheeler is weighing out a ha'porth of brandy balls. Lady Rampling's carriage is driving by, with the tiger sitting behind in his pipeclayed breeches with his arms folded. Uncle Ezekiel is cursing Joe Chamberlain. The recruiting-sergeant in his scarlet jacket, tight blue overalls, and pillbox hat, is strutting up and down twisting his moustache. The drunks are puking in the yard behind the George. Vicky's at Windsor, God's in heaven, Christ's on the cross, Jonah's in the whale, Shadrach, Meshach, and Abednego are in the fiery furnace, and Sihon king of the Amorites and Og the king of Bashan are sitting on their thrones looking at one another—not doing anything exactly, just existing, keeping their appointed place, like a couple of fire-dogs, or the Lion and the Unicorn.

Is it gone for ever? I'm not certain. But I tell you it was a good world to live in. I belong to it. So do you.

# PART II

## I

The world I momentarily remembered when I saw King Zog's name on the poster was so different from the world I live in now that you might have a bit of difficulty in believing I ever belonged to it.

I suppose by this time you've got a kind of picture of me in your mind—a fat middle-aged bloke with false teeth and a red face—and subconsciously you've been imagining that I was just the same even when I was in my cradle. But forty-five years is a long time, and though some people don't change and develop, others do. I've changed a great deal, and I've had my ups and downs, mostly ups. It may seem queer, but my father would probably be rather proud of me if he could see me now. He'd think it a wonderful thing that a son of his should own a motor-car and live in a house with a bathroom. Even now I'm a little above my origin, and at other times I've touched levels that we should never have dreamed of in those old days before the war.

Before the war! How long shall we go on saying that, I wonder? How long before the answer will be 'Which war?' In my case the never-never land that people are thinking of when they say 'before the war' might almost be before the Boer War. I was born in '93, and I can actually remember the outbreak of the Boer War, because of the first-class row that Father and Uncle Ezekiel had about it. I've several other memories that would date from about a year earlier than that.

The very first thing I remember is the smell of sainfoin chaff. You went up the stone passage that led from the kitchen to the shop, and the smell of sainfoin got stronger all the way. Mother had fixed a wooden gate in the doorway to prevent Joe and myself (Joe was my elder brother) from getting into the shop. I can still remember standing there clutching the bars, and the smell of sainfoin mixed up with the damp plastery smell that belonged to the passage. It wasn't till years later that I somehow managed to crash the gate and get into the shop when nobody was there. A mouse that had been having a go at one of the meal-bins suddenly plopped out and ran between my feet. It was quite white with meal. This must have happened when I was about six.

When you're very young you seem to suddenly become conscious of things that have been under your nose for a long time past. The things round about you swim into your mind one at a time, rather as they do when you're waking from sleep. For instance, it was only when I was nearly four that I suddenly realized that we owned a dog. Nailer, his name was, an old white English terrier of the breed that's gone out nowadays. I met him under the kitchen table and in some way seemed to grasp, having only learnt it that moment, that he belonged to us and that his name was Nailer. In the same way, a bit earlier, I'd discovered that beyond the gate at the end of the passage there was a place where the smell of sainfoin came from. And the shop itself, with the huge scales and the wooden measures and the tin shovel, and the white lettering on the window, and the bullfinch in its cage—which you couldn't see very well even from the pavement, because the window was always dusty—all these things dropped into place in my mind one by one, like bits of a jig-saw puzzle.

Time goes on, you get stronger on your legs, and by degrees you begin to get a grasp of geography. I suppose Lower Binfield was just like any other market town of about two thousand inhabitants. It was in Oxfordshire—I keep saying *was,* you notice, though after all the place still exists—about five miles from the Thames. It lay in a bit of a valley, with a low ripple of hills between itself and the Thames, and higher hills behind. On top of the hills there were woods in sort of dim blue masses among which you could see a great white house with a colonnade. This was Binfield House ('The Hall', everybody called it), and the top of the hill was known as Upper Binfield, though there was no village there and hadn't been for a hundred years or more. I must have been nearly seven before I noticed the existence of Binfield House. When you're very small you don't look into the distance. But by that time I knew every inch of the town, which was shaped roughly like a cross with the market-place in the middle. Our shop was in the High Street a little before you got to the market-place, and on the corner there was Mrs Wheeler's sweet-shop where you spent a halfpenny when you had one. Mother Wheeler was a dirty old witch and people suspected her of sucking the bull's-eyes and putting them back in the bottle, though this was never proved. Farther down there was the barber's shop with the advert for Abdulla cigarettes—the one with the Egyptian soldiers on it, and curiously enough they're using the same advert to this day—and the rich boozy smell of bay rum and latakia. Behind the houses you could see the chimneys of the brewery. In the middle of the market-place there was the stone horse-trough, and on top of the water there was always a fine film of dust and chaff.

Before the war, and especially before the ·Boer War, it was summer all the year round. I'm quite aware that that's a delusion. I'm merely trying to tell you how things come back to me. If I shut my eyes and think of Lower Binfield any time before I was, say, eight, it's always in summer weather that I remember it. Either it's the market-place at dinner-time, with a sort of sleepy dusty hush over everything and the carrier's horse with his nose dug well into his nose-bag, munching away, or it's a hot afternoon in the great green juicy meadows round the town, or it's about dusk in the lane behind the allotments, and there's a smell of pipe-tobacco and night-stocks floating through the hedge.

But in a sense I do remember different seasons, because all my memories are bound up with things to eat, which varied at different times of the year. Especially the things you used to find in the hedges. In July there were dewberries—but they're very rare—and the blackberries were getting red enough to eat. In September there were sloes and hazel-nuts. The best hazel-nuts were always out of reach. Later on there were beech-nuts and crab-apples. Then there were the kind of minor foods that you used to eat when there was nothing better going. Haws—but they're not much good—and hips, which have a nice sharp taste if you clean the hairs out of them. Angelica is good in early summer, especially when you're thirsty, and so are the stems of various grasses. Then there's sorrel, which is good with bread and butter, and pig-nuts, and a kind of wood shamrock which has a sour taste. Even plantain seeds are better than nothing when you're a long way from home and very hungry.

Joe was two years older than myself. When we were very small Mother used to pay Katie Simmons eighteen pence a week to take us out for walks in the afternoons. Katie's father worked in the brewery and had fourteen children, so that the family were always on the lookout for odd jobs. She was only twelve when Joe was seven and I was five, and her mental level wasn't very different from ours. She used to drag me by the arm and call me 'Baby', and she had just enough authority over us to prevent us from being run over by dogcarts or chased by bulls, but so far as conversation went we were almost on equal terms. We used to go for long, trailing kind of walks—always, of course, picking and eating things all the way—down the lane past the allotments, across Roper's Meadows, and down to the Mill Farm, where there was a pool with newts and tiny carp in it (Joe and I used to go fishing there when we were a bit older), and back by the Upper Binfield Road so as to pass the sweet-shop that stood on the edge of the town. This shop was in such a bad position that anyone who took it went bankrupt, and to my own knowledge it was three times a sweet-shop, once a grocer's, and once a bicycle-repair shop, but it had a peculiar fascination for children. Even when we had no money, we'd go that way so as to glue our noses against the window. Katie wasn't in the least above sharing a farthing's worth of sweets and quarrelling over her share. You could buy things worth having for a farthing in those days. Most sweets were four ounces a penny, and there was even some stuff called Paradise Mixture, mostly broken sweets from other bottles, which was six. Then there were Farthing Everlastings, which were a yard long and couldn't be finished inside half an hour. Sugar mice and sugar pigs were eight a penny, and so were liquorice pistols, popcorn was a halfpenny for a large bag, and a prize packet which contained several different kinds of sweets, a gold ring, and sometimes a whistle, was a penny. You don't see prize packets nowadays. A whole lot of the kinds of sweets we had in those days have gone out. There was a kind of flat white sweet with mottoes printed on them, and also a kind of sticky pink stuff in an oval matchwood box with a tiny tin spoon to eat it with, which cost a halfpenny. Both of those have disappeared. So have Caraway Comfits, and so have chocolate pipes and sugar matches, and even Hundreds and Thousands you hardly ever see. Hundreds and Thousands were a great standby when you'd only a farthing. And what about Penny Monsters? Does one ever see a Penny Monster nowadays? It was a huge bottle, holding more than a quart of fizzy lemonade, all for a penny. That's another thing that the war killed stone dead.

It always seems to be summer when I look back. I can feel the grass round me as tall as myself, and the heat coming out of the earth. And the dust in the lane, and the warm greeny light coming through the hazel boughs. I can see the three of us trailing along, eating stuff out of the hedge, with Katie dragging at my arm and saying 'Come on, Baby!' and sometimes yelling ahead to Joe, 'Joe! You come back 'ere this minute! You'll catch it!' Joe was a hefty boy with a big, lumpy sort of head and tremendous calves, the kind of boy who's always doing something dangerous. At seven he'd already got into short trousers, with the thick black stockings drawn up over the knee and the great clumping boots that boys had to wear in those days. I was still in frocks—a kind of holland overall that Mother used to make for me. Katie used to wear a dreadful ragged parody of a grown-up dress that descended from sister to sister in her family. She had a ridiculous great hat with her pigtails hanging down behind it, and a long, draggled skirt which trailed on the ground, and button boots with the heels trodden down. She was a tiny thing, not much taller than Joe, but not bad at 'minding' children. In a family like that a child is 'minding' other children about as soon as it's weaned. At times she'd try to be grown-up and ladylike, and she had a way of cutting you short with a proverb, which to her mind was something unanswerable. If you said 'Don't care', she'd answer immediately:

> 'Don't care was made to care,
> Don't care was hung,
> Don't care was put in a pot
> And boiled till he was done.'

Or if you called her names it would be 'Hard words break no bones', or, when you'd been boasting, 'Pride comes before a fall'. This came very true one day when I was strutting along pretending to be a soldier and fell into a cowpat. Her family lived in a filthy little rat-hole of a place in the slummy street behind the brewery. The place swarmed with children like a kind of vermin. The whole family had managed to dodge going to school, which was fairly easy to do in those days, and started running errands and doing other odd jobs as soon as they could walk. One of the elder brothers got a month for stealing turnips. She stopped taking us out for walks a year later when Joe was eight and getting too tough for a girl to handle. He'd discovered that in Katie's home they slept five in a bed, and used to tease the life out of her about it.

Poor Katie! She had her first baby when she was fifteen. No one knew who was the father, and probably Katie wasn't too certain herself. Most people believe it was one of her brothers. The workhouse people took the baby, and Katie went into service in Walton. Some time afterwards she married a tinker, which even by the standards of her family was a come-down. The last time I saw her was in 1913. I was biking through Walton, and I passed some dreadful wooden shacks beside the railway line, with fences round them made out of barrel-staves, where the gypsies used to camp at certain times of the year, when the police would let them. A wrinkled-up hag of a woman, with her hair coming down and a smoky face, looking at least fifty years old, came out of one of the huts and began shaking out a rag mat. It was Katie, who must have been twenty-seven.

# 2

Thursday was market day. Chaps with round red faces like pumpkins and dirty smocks and huge boots covered with dry cow-dung, carrying long hazel switches, used to drive their brutes into the market-place early in the morning. For hours there'd be a terrific hullabaloo: dogs barking, pigs squealing, chaps in tradesmen's vans who wanted to get through the crush cracking their whips and cursing, and everyone who had anything to do with the cattle shouting and throwing sticks. The big noise was always when they brought a bull to market. Even at that age it struck me that most of the bulls were harmless law-abiding brutes that only wanted to get to their stalls in peace, but a bull wouldn't have been regarded as a bull if half the town hadn't had to turn out and chase it. Sometimes some terrified brute, generally a half-grown heifer, used to break loose and charge down a side street, and then anyone who happened to be in the way would stand in the middle of the road and swing his arms backwards like the sails of a windmill, shouting, 'Woo! Woo!' This was supposed to have a kind of hypnotic effect on an animal and certainly it did frighten them.

Half-way through the morning some of the farmers would come into the shop and run samples of seed through their fingers. Actually Father did very little business with the farmers, because he had no delivery van and couldn't afford to give long credits. Mostly he did a rather petty class of business, poultry food and fodder for the tradesmen's horses and so forth. Old Brewer, of the Mill Farm, who was a stingy old bastard with a grey chin-beard, used to stand there for half an hour, fingering samples of chicken corn and letting them drop into his pocket in an absent-minded manner, after which, of course, he finally used to make off without buying anything. In the evenings the pubs were full of drunken men. In those days beer cost twopence a pint, and unlike the beer nowadays it had some guts in it. All through the Boer War the recruiting sergeant used to be in the four-ale bar of the George every Thursday and Saturday night, dressed up to the nines and very free with his money. Sometimes next morning you'd see him leading off some great sheepish, red-faced lump of a farm lad who'd taken the shilling when he was too drunk to see and found in the morning that it would cost him twenty pounds to get out of it. People used to stand in their doorways and shake their heads when they saw them go past, almost as if it had been a funeral. 'Well now! Listed for a soldier!

Just think of it! A fine young fellow like that!' It just shocked them. Listing for a soldier, in their eyes, was the exact equivalent of a girl's going on the streets. Their attitude to the war, and to the Army, was very curious. They had the good old English notions that the red-coats are the scum of the earth and anyone who joins the Army will die of drink and go straight to hell, but at the same time they were good patriots, stuck Union Jacks in their windows, and held it as an article of faith that the English had never been beaten in battle and never could be. At that time everyone, even the Nonconformists, used to sing sentimental songs about the thin red line and the soldier boy who died on the battlefield far away. These soldier boys always used to die 'when the shot and shell were flying', I remember. It puzzled me as a kid. Shot I could understand, but it produced a queer picture in my mind to think of cockleshells flying through the air. When Mafeking was relieved the people nearly yelled the roof off, and there were at any rate times when they believed the tales about the Boers chucking babies into the air and skewering them on their bayonets. Old Brewer got so fed up with the kids yelling 'Krooger!' after him that towards the end of the war he shaved his beard off. The people's attitude towards the Government was really the same. They were all true-blue Englishmen and swore that Vicky was the best queen that ever lived and foreigners were dirt, but at the same time nobody ever thought of paying a tax, not even a dog-licence, if there was any way of dodging it.

Before and after the war Lower Binfield was a Liberal constituency. During the war there was a by-election which the Conservatives won. I was too young to grasp what it was all about, I only knew that I was a Conservative because I liked the blue streamers better than the red ones, and I chiefly remember it because of a drunken man who fell on his nose on the pavement outside the George. In the general excitement nobody took any notice of him, and he lay there for hours in the hot sun with his blood drying round him, and when it dried it was purple. By the time the 1906 election came along I was old enough to understand it, more or less, and this time I was a Liberal because everybody else was. The people chased the Conservative candidate half a mile and threw him into a pond full of duckweed. People took politics seriously in those days. They used to begin storing up rotten eggs weeks before an election.

Very early in life, when the Boer War broke out, I remember the big row between Father and Uncle Ezekiel. Uncle Ezekiel had a little boot-shop in one of the streets off the High Street, and also did some cobbling. It was a small business and tended to get smaller, which didn't matter greatly because Uncle Ezekiel wasn't married. He was only a half-brother and much older than Father, twenty years older at least, and for the fifteen years or so that I knew him he always looked exactly the same. He was a fine-looking old chap, rather tall, with white hair and the whitest whiskers I ever saw—white as thistledown. He had a way of slapping his leather apron and standing up very straight—a reaction from bending over the last, I suppose—after which he'd bark his opinions straight in your face, ending up with a sort of ghostly cackle. He was a real old nineteenth-century Liberal, the kind that not only used to ask you what Gladstone said in '78 but could tell you the answer, and one of the very few people in Lower Binfield who stuck to the same opinions all through the war. He was always denouncing Joe Chamberlain and some gang of people that he referred to as 'the Park Lane riff-raff'. I can hear him now, having one of his arguments with Father. 'Them and their far-flung Empire! Can't fling it too far for me. He-he-he!' And then Father's voice, a quiet, worried, conscientious kind of voice, coming back at him with the white man's burden and our dooty to the pore blacks whom these here Boars treated something shameful. For a week or so after Uncle Ezekiel gave it out that he was a pro-Boer and a Little Englander they were hardly on speaking terms. They had another row when the atrocity stories started. Father was very worried by the tales he'd heard, and he tackled Uncle Ezekiel about it. Little Englander or no, surely he couldn't think it right for these here Boars to throw babies in the air and catch them on their bayonets, even if they *were* only nigger babies? But Uncle Ezekiel just laughed in his face. Father had got it all wrong! It wasn't the Boars who threw babies in the air, it was the British soldiers! He kept grabbing hold of me—I must have been about five—to illustrate. 'Throw them in the air and skewer them like frogs, I tell you! Same as I might throw this youngster here!' And then he'd swing me up and almost let go of me, and I had a vivid picture of myself flying through the air and landing plonk on the end of a bayonet.

Father was quite different from Uncle Ezekiel. I don't know much about my grandparents, they were dead before I was born, I only know that my grandfather had been a cobbler and late in life he married the widow of a seedsman, which was how we came to have the shop. It was a job that didn't really suit Father, though he knew the business inside out and was everlastingly working. Except on Sunday and very occasionally on week-day evenings I never remember him without meal on the backs of his hands and in the lines of his face and in what was left of his hair. He'd married when he was in his thirties and must have been nearly forty when I first remember him. He was a small man, a sort of grey, quiet little man, always in shirtsleeves and white apron and always dusty-looking because of the meal. He had a round head, a blunt nose, a rather bushy moustache, spectacles, and butter-coloured hair, the same colour as mine, but he'd lost most of it and it was always mealy. My grandfather had bettered himself a good deal by marrying the seedsman's widow, and Father had been educated at Walton Grammar School, where the farmers and the better-off tradesmen sent their sons, whereas Uncle Ezekiel liked to boast that he'd never been to school in his life and had taught himself to read by a tallow candle after working hours. But he was a much quicker-witted man than Father, he could argue with anybody, and he used to quote Carlyle and Spencer by the yard. Father had a slow sort of mind, he'd never taken to 'book-learning', as he called it, and his English wasn't good. On Sunday afternoons, the only time when he really took things easy, he'd settle down by the parlour fireplace to have what he called a 'good read' at the Sunday paper. His favourite paper was *The People*—Mother preferred the *News of the World,* which she considered had more murders in it. I can see them now. A Sunday afternoon—summer, of course, always summer—a smell of roast pork and greens still floating in the air, and Mother on one side of the fireplace, starting off to read the latest murder but gradually falling asleep with her mouth open, and Father on the other, in slippers and spectacles, working his way slowly through the yards of smudgy print. And the soft feeling of summer all round you, the geranium in the window, a starling cooing somewhere, and myself under the table with the *B.O.P.*, making believe that the tablecloth is a tent. Afterwards, at tea, as he chewed his way through the radishes and spring onions, Father would talk in a ruminative kind of way about the stuff he'd been reading, the fires and shipwrecks and scandals in high society, and these here new flying machines and the chap (I notice that to this day he turns up in the Sunday papers about once in three years) who was swallowed by a whale in the Red Sea and taken out three days later, alive but bleached white by the whale's gastric juice. Father was always a bit sceptical of this story, and of the new flying machines, otherwise he believed everything he read. Until 1909 no one in Lower Binfield believed that human beings would ever learn to fly. The official doctrine was that if God had meant us to fly He'd have given us wings. Uncle Ezekiel couldn't help retorting that if God had meant us to ride He'd have given us wheels, but even he didn't believe in the new flying machines.

It was only on Sunday afternoons, and perhaps on the one evening a week when he looked in at the George for a half-pint, that Father turned his mind to such things. At other times he was always more or less overwhelmed by business. There wasn't really such a lot to do, but he seemed to be always busy, either in the loft behind the yard, struggling about with sacks and bales, or in the kind of dusty little cubby-hole behind the counter in the shop, adding figures up in a notebook with a stump of pencil. He was a very honest man and a very obliging man, very anxious to provide good stuff and swindle nobody, which even in those days wasn't the best way to get on in business. He would have been just the man for some small official job, a postmaster, for instance, or station-master of a country station. But he hadn't either the cheek and enterprise to borrow money and expand the business, or the imagination to think of new selling-lines. It was characteristic of him that the only streak of imagination he ever showed, the invention of a new seed mixture for cage-birds (Bowling's Mixture it was called, and it was famous over a radius of nearly five miles) was really due to Uncle Ezekiel. Uncle Ezekiel was a bit of a bird-fancier and had quantities of goldfinches in his dark little shop. It was his theory that cage-birds lose their colour because of lack of variation in their diet. In the yard behind the shop Father had a tiny plot of ground in which he used to grow about twenty kinds of weed under wire-netting, and he used to dry them and mix their seeds with ordinary canary seed. Jackie, the bullfinch who hung in the shop-window, was supposed to be an advertisement for Bowling's Mixture. Certainly, unlike most bullfinches in cages, Jackie never turned black.

Mother was fat ever since I remember her. No doubt it's from her that I inherit my pituitary deficiency, or whatever it is that makes you get fat.

She was a largish woman, a bit taller than Father, with hair a good deal fairer than his and a tendency to wear black dresses. But except on Sundays I never remember her without an apron. It would be an exaggeration, but not a very big one, to say that I never remember her when she wasn't cooking. When you look back over a long period you seem to see human beings always fixed in some special place and some characteristic attitude. It seems to you that they were always doing exactly the same thing. Well, just as when I think of Father I remember him always behind the counter, with his hair all mealy, adding up figures with a stump of pencil which he moistens between his lips, and just as I remember Uncle Ezekiel, with his ghostly white whiskers, straightening himself out and slapping his leather apron, so when I think of Mother I remember her at the kitchen table, with her forearms covered with flour, rolling out a lump of dough.

You know the kind of kitchen people had in those days. A huge place, rather dark and low, with a great beam across the ceiling and a stone floor and cellars underneath. Everything enormous, or so it seemed to me when I was a kid. A vast stone sink which didn't have a tap but an iron pump, a dresser covering one wall and going right up to the ceiling, a gigantic range which burned half a ton a month and took God knows how long to blacklead. Mother at the table rolling out a huge flap of dough. And myself crawling round, messing about with bundles of firewood and lumps of coal and tin beetle-traps (we had them in all the dark corners and they used to be baited with beer) and now and again coming up to the table to try and cadge a bit of food. Mother 'didn't hold with' eating between meals. You generally got the same answer: 'Get along with you, now! I'm not going to have you spoiling your dinner. Your eye's bigger than your belly.' Very occasionally, however, she'd cut you off a thin strip of candied peel.

I used to like to watch Mother rolling pastry. There's always a fascination in watching anybody do a job which he really understands. Watch a woman—a woman who really knows how to cook, I mean—rolling dough. She's got a peculiar, solemn, indrawn air, a satisfied kind of air, like a priestess celebrating a sacred rite. And in her own mind, of course, that's exactly what she is. Mother had thick, pink, strong forearms which were generally mottled with flour. When she was cooking, all her movements were wonderfully precise and firm. In her hands egg-whisks and mincers and rolling-pins did exactly what they were meant to do. When you saw her cooking you knew that she was in a world where she belonged, among things she really understood. Except through the Sunday papers and an occasional bit of gossip the outside world didn't really exist for her. Although she read more easily than Father, and unlike him used to read novelettes as well as newspapers, she was unbelievably ignorant. I realized this even by the time I was ten years old. She certainly couldn't have told you whether Ireland was east or west of England, and I doubt whether any time up to the outbreak of the Great War she could have told you who was Prime Minister. Moreover she hadn't the smallest wish to know such things. Later on when I read books about Eastern countries where they practise polygamy, and the secret harems where the women are locked up with black eunuchs mounting guard over them, I used to think how shocked Mother would have been if she'd heard of it. I can almost hear her

voice–'Well, now! Shutting their wives up like that! The *idea*!' Not that she'd
have known what a eunuch was. But in reality she lived her life in a space that
must have been as small and almost as private as the average zenana. Even in
our own house there were parts where she never set foot. She never went into
the loft behind the yard and very seldom into the shop. I don't think I ever
remember her serving a customer. She wouldn't have known where any of the
things were kept, and until they were milled into flour she probably didn't
know the difference between wheat and oats. Why should she? The shop was
Father's business, it was 'the man's work', and even about the money side of it
she hadn't very much curiosity. Her job, 'the woman's work', was to look after
the house and the meals and the laundry and the children. She'd have had a fit
if she'd seen Father or anyone else of the male sex trying to sew on a button for
himself.

So far as the meals and so forth went, ours was one of those houses where
everything goes like clockwork. Or no, not like clockwork, which suggests
something mechanical. It was more like some kind of natural process. You
knew that breakfast would be on the table tomorrow morning in much the
same way as you knew the sun would rise. All through her life Mother went to
bed at nine and got up at five, and she'd have thought it vaguely wicked–sort of
decadent and foreign and aristocratic–to keep later hours. Although she didn't
mind paying Katie Simmons to take Joe and me out for walks, she would never
tolerate the idea of having a woman in to help with the housework. It was her
firm belief that a hired woman always sweeps the dirt under the dresser. Our
meals were always ready on the tick. Enormous meals–boiled beef and
dumplings, roast beef and Yorkshire, boiled mutton and capers, pig's head,
apple pie, spotted dog, and jam roly-poly–with grace before and after. The old
ideas about bringing up children still held good, though they were going out
fast. In theory children were still thrashed and put to bed on bread and water,
and certainly you were liable to be sent away from table if you made too much
noise eating, or choked, or refused something that was 'good for you', or
'answered back'. In practice there wasn't much discipline in our family, and of
the two Mother was the firmer. Father, though he was always quoting 'Spare
the rod and spoil the child', was really much too weak with us, especially with
Joe, who was a hard case from the start. He was always 'going to' give Joe a
good hiding, and he used to tell us stories, which I now believe were lies, about
the frightful thrashings his own father used to give him with a leather strap,
but nothing ever came of it. By the time Joe was twelve he was too strong for
Mother to get him across her knee, and after that there was no doing anything
with him.

At that time it was still thought proper for parents to say 'don't' to their
children all day long. You'd often hear a man boasting that he'd 'thrash the life
out of' his son if he caught him smoking, or stealing apples, or robbing a bird's
nest. In some families these thrashings actually took place. Old Lovegrove, the
saddler, caught his two sons, great lumps aged sixteen and fifteen, smoking in
the garden shed and walloped them so that you could hear it all over the town.
Lovegrove was a very heavy smoker. The thrashings never seemed to have any

effect, all boys stole apples, robbed birds' nests, and learned to smoke sooner or later, but the idea was still knocking around that children should be treated rough. Practically everything worth doing was forbidden, in theory anyway. According to Mother, everything that a boy ever wants to do was 'dangerous'. Swimming was dangerous, climbing trees was dangerous, and so were sliding, snowballing, hanging on behind carts, using catapults and squailers, and even fishing. All animals were dangerous, except Nailer, the two cats, and Jackie the bullfinch. Every animal had its special recognized methods of attacking you. Horses bit, bats got into your hair, earwigs got into your ears, swans broke your leg with a blow of their wings, bulls tossed you, and snakes 'stung'. All snakes stung, according to Mother, and when I quoted the penny encyclopedia to the effect that they didn't sting but bit, she only told me not to answer back. Lizards, slow-worms, toads, frogs, and newts also stung. All insects stung, except flies and blackbeetles. Practically all kinds of food, except the food you had at meals, were either poisonous or 'bad for you'. Raw potatoes were deadly poison, and so were mushrooms unless you bought them at the greengrocer's. Raw gooseberries gave you colic and raw raspberries gave you a skin-rash. If you had a bath after a meal you died of cramp, if you cut yourself between the thumb and forefinger you got lockjaw, and if you washed your hands in the water eggs were boiled in you got warts. Nearly everything in the shop was poisonous, which was why Mother had put the gate in the doorway. Cowcake was poisonous, and so was chicken corn, and so were mustard seed and Karswood poultry spice. Sweets were bad for you and eating between meals was bad for you, though curiously enought there were certain kinds of eating between meals that Mother always allowed. When she was making plum jam she used to let us eat the syrupy stuff that was skimmed off the top, and we used to gorge ourselves with it till we were sick. Although nearly everying in the world was either dangerous or poisonous, there were certain things that had mysterious virtues. Raw onions were a cure for almost everything. A stocking tied round your neck was a cure for a sore throat. Sulphur in a dog's drinking water acted as a tonic, and old Nailer's bowl behind the back door always had a lump of sulphur in it which stayed there year after year, never dissolving.

We used to have tea at six. By four Mother had generally finished the housework, and between four and six she used to have a quiet cup of tea and 'read her paper', as she called it. As a matter of fact she didn't often read the newspaper except on Sundays. The week-day papers only had the day's news, and it was only occasionally that there was a murder. But the editors of the Sunday papers had grasped that people don't really mind whether their murders are up to date and when there was no new murder on hand they'd hash up an old one, sometimes going as far back as Dr Palmer and Mrs Manning. I think Mother thought of the world outside Lower Binfield chiefly as a place where murders were committed. Murders had a terrible fascination for her, because, as she often said, she just didn't know how people could *be* so wicked. Cutting their wives' throats, burying their fathers under cement floors, throwing babies down wells! How anyone could *do* such things! The Jack the Ripper scare had happened about the time when Father and Mother

were married, and the big wooden shutters we used to draw over the shop
windows every night dated from then. Shutters for shop windows were going
out, most of the shops in the High Street didn't have them, but Mother felt
safe behind them. All along, she said, she'd had a dreadful feeling that Jack the
Ripper was hiding in Lower Binfield. The Crippen case—but that was years
later, when I was almost grown up—upset her badly. I can hear her voice now.
'Cutting his poor wife up and burying her in the coal cellar! The *idea*! What I'd
do to that man if I got hold of him!' And curiously enough, when she thought
of the dreadful wickedness of that little American doctor who dismembered his
wife (and made a very neat job of it by taking all the bones out and chucking the
head into the sea, if I remember rightly) the tears actually came into her eyes.

But what she mostly read on week-days was *Hilda's Home Companion*. In
those days it was part of the regular furnishing of any home like ours, and as a
matter of fact it still exists, though it's been a bit crowded out by the more
streamlined women's papers that have come up since the war. I had a look at a
copy only the other day. It's changed, but less than most things. There are still
the same enormous serial stories that go on for six months (and it all comes
right in the end with orange blossoms to follow), and the same Household
Hints, and the same ads for sewing-machines and remedies for bad legs. It's
chiefly the print and the illustrations that have changed. In those days the
heroine had to look like an egg-timer and now she has to look like a cylinder.
Mother was a slow reader and believed in getting her threepennyworth out of
*Hilda's Home Companion*. Sitting in the old yellow armchair beside the hearth,
with her feet on the iron fender and the little pot of strong tea stewing on the
hob, she'd work her way steadily from cover to cover, right through the serial,
the two short stories, the Household Hints, the ads for Zam-Buk, and the
answers to correspondents. *Hilda's Home Companion* generally lasted her the
week out, and some weeks she didn't even finish it. Sometimes the heat of the
fire, or the buzzing of the bluebottles on summer afternoons, would send her
off into a doze, and at about a quarter to six she'd wake up with a tremendous
start, glance at the clock on the mantelpiece, and then get into a stew because
tea was going to be late. But tea was never late.

In those days—till 1909, to be exact—Father could still afford an errand boy,
and he used to leave the shop to him and come in to tea with the backs of his
hands all mealy. Then Mother would stop cutting slices of bread for a moment
and say, 'If you'll give us grace, Father', and Father, while we all bent our
heads on our chests, would mumble reverently, 'Fwat we bout to
receive—Lord make us truly thankful—Amen.' Later on, when Joe was a bit
older, it would be '*You* give us grace today, Joe', and Joe would pipe it out.
Mother never said grace: it had to be someone of the male sex.

There were always bluebottles buzzing on summer afternoons. Ours wasn't
a sanitary house, precious few houses in Lower Binfield were. I suppose the
town must have contained five hundred houses and there certainly can't have
been more than ten with bathrooms or fifty with what we should now describe
as a w.c. In summer our backyard always smelt of dustbins. And all houses had
insects in them. We had blackbeetles in the wainscoting and crickets

somewhere behind the kitchen range, besides, of course, the meal-worms in the shop. In those days even a house-proud woman like Mother didn't see anything to object to in blackbeetles. They were as much a part of the kitchen as the dresser or the rolling-pin. But there were insects and insects. The houses in the bad street behind the brewery, where Katie Simmons lived, were overrun by bugs. Mother or any of the shopkeepers' wives would have died of shame if they'd had bugs in the house. In fact it was considered proper to say that you didn't even know a bug by sight.

The great blue flies used to come sailing into the larder and sit longingly on the wire covers over the meat. 'Drat the flies!' people used to say, but the flies were an act of God and apart from meat-covers and fly-papers you couldn't do much about them. I said a little while back that the first thing I remember is the smell of sainfoin, but the smell of dustbins is also a pretty early memory. When I think of Mother's kitchen, with the stone floor and the beetle-traps and the steel fender and the blackleaded range, I always seem to hear the bluebottles buzzing and smell the dustbin, and also old Nailer, who carried a pretty powerful smell of dog. And God knows there are worse smells and sounds. Which would you sooner listen to, a bluebottle or a bombing plane?

## 3

Joe started going to Walton Grammar School two years before I did. Neither of us went there till we were nine. It meant a four-mile bike ride morning and evening, and Mother was scared of allowing us among the traffic, which by that time included a very few motor-cars.

For several years we went to the dame-school kept by old Mrs Howlett. Most of the shopkeepers' children went there, to save them from the shame and come-down of going to the board school, though everyone knew that Mother Howlett was an old imposter and worse than useless as a teacher. She was over seventy, she was very deaf, she could hardly see through her spectacles, and all she owned in the way of equipment was a cane, a blackboard, a few dog-eared grammar books, and a couple of dozen smelly slates. She could just manage the girls, but the boys simply laughed at her and played truant as often as they felt like it. Once there was a frightful scandal because a boy put his hand up a girl's dress, a thing I didn't understand at the time. Mother Howlett succeeded in hushing it up. When you did something particularly bad her formula was 'I'll tell your father', and on very rare occasions she did so. But we were quite sharp enough to see that she daren't do it too often, and even when she let out at you with the cane she was so old and clumsy that it was easy to dodge.

Joe was only eight when he got in with a tough gang of boys who called themselves the Black Hand. The leader was Sid Lovegrove, the saddler's younger son, who was about thirteen, and there were two other shopkeepers' sons, an errand boy from the brewery, and two farm lads who sometimes managed to cut work and go off with the gang for a couple of hours. The farm lads were great lumps bursting out of corduroy breeches, with very broad accents and rather looked down on by the rest of the gang, but they were tolerated because they knew twice as much about animals as any of the others. One of them, nicknamed Ginger, would even catch a rabbit in his hands occasionally. If he saw one lying in the grass he used to fling himself on it like a spread-eagle. There was a big social distinction between the shopkeepers' sons and the sons of labourers and farm-hands, but the local boys didn't usually pay much attention to it till they were about sixteen. The gang had a secret password and an 'ordeal' which included cutting your finger and eating an earthworm, and they gave themselves out to be frightful desperadoes. Certainly they managed to make a nuisance of themselves, broke windows, chased cows, tore the knockers off doors, and stole fruit by the hundredweight. Sometimes in winter they managed to borrow a couple of ferrets and go ratting, when the farmers would let them. They all had catapults and squailers, and they were always saving up to buy a saloon pistol, which in those days cost five shillings, but the savings never amounted to more than about threepence. In summer they used to go fishing and bird-nesting. When Joe was at Mrs Howlett's he used to cut school at least once a week, and even at the Grammar School he managed it about once a fortnight. There was a boy at the Grammar School, an auctioneer's son, who could copy any handwriting and for a penny he'd forge a letter from your mother saying you'd been ill yesterday. Of course I was wild to join the Black Hand, but Joe always choked me off and said they didn't want any blasted kids hanging round.

It was the thought of going fishing that really appealed to me. At eight years old I hadn't yet been fishing, except with a penny net, with which you can sometimes catch a stickleback. Mother was always terrified of letting us go anywhere near water. She 'forbade' fishing, in the way in which parents in those days 'forbade' almost everything, and I hadn't yet grasped that grown-ups can't see round corners. But the thought of fishing sent me wild with excitement. Many a time I'd been past the pool at the Mill Farm and watched the small carp basking on the surface, and sometimes under the willow tree at the corner a great diamond-shaped carp that to my eyes looked enormous—six inches long, I suppose—would suddenly rise to the surface, gulp down a grub, and sink again. I'd spent hours gluing my nose against the window of Wallace's in the High Street, where fishing tackle and guns and bicycles were sold. I used to lie awake on summer mornings thinking of the tales Joe had told me about fishing, how you mixed bread paste, how your float gives a bob and plunges under and you feel the rod bending and the fish tugging at the line. Is it any use talking about it, I wonder—the sort of fairy light that fish and fishing tackle have in a kid's eyes? Some kids feel the same about guns and shooting, some feel it about motor-bikes or aeroplanes or horses. It's not a thing that you can explain or rationalize, it's merely magic. One morning—it was in June and I must have been eight—I knew that Joe was going to cut school and go out fishing, and I made up my mind to follow. In some way Joe guessed what I was thinking about, and he started on me while we were dressing.

'Now then, young George! Don't you get thinking you're coming with the gang today. You stay back home.'

'No, I didn't. I didn't think nothing about it.'

'Yes, you did! You thought you were coming with the gang.'

'No, I didn't!'

'Yes, you did!'

'No, I didn't!'

'Yes, you did! You stay back home. We don't want any bloody kids along.'

Joe had just learned the word 'bloody' and was always using it. Father overheard him once and swore that he'd thrash the life out of Joe, but as usual he didn't do so. After breakfast Joe started off on his bike, with his satchel and his Grammar School cap, five minutes early as he always did when he meant to cut school, and when it was time for me to leave for Mother Howlett's I sneaked off and hid in the lane behind the allotments. I knew the gang were going to the pond at the Mill Farm, and I was going to follow them if they murdered me for it. Probably they'd give me a hiding, and probably I wouldn't get home to dinner, and then Mother would know that I'd cut school and I'd get another hiding, but I didn't care. I was just desperate to go fishing with the gang. I was cunning, too. I allowed Joe plenty of time to make a circuit round and get to the Mill Farm by road, and then I followed down the lane and skirted round the meadows on the far side of the hedge, so as to get almost to the pond before the gang saw me. It was a wonderful June morning. The buttercups were up to my knees. There was a breath of wind just stirring the tops of the elms, and the great green clouds of leaves were sort of soft and rich like silk. And it was nine in the morning and I was eight years old, and all round me it was early summer, with great tangled hedges where the wild roses were still in bloom, and bits of soft white cloud drifting overhead, and in the distance the low hills and the dim blue masses of the woods round Upper Binfield. And I didn't give a damn for any of it. All I was thinking of was the green pool and the carp and the gang with their hooks and lines and bread paste. It was as though they were in paradise and I'd got to join them. Presently I managed to sneak up on them—four of them, Joe and Sid Lovegrove and the errand boy and another shopkeeper's son, Harry Barnes I think his name was.

Joe turned and saw me. 'Christ!' he said. 'It's the kid.' He walked up to me like a tom-cat that's going to start a fight. 'Now then, you! What'd I tell you? You get back 'ome double quick.'

Both Joe and I were inclined to drop our aitches if we were at all excited. I backed away from him.

'I'm not going back 'ome.'

'Yes you are.'

'Clip his ear, Joe,' said Sid. 'We don't want no kids along.'

'*Are* you going back 'ome?' said Joe.

'No.'

'Righto, my boy! Right-*ho*!'

Then he started on me. The next minute he was chasing me round, catching me one clip after another. But I didn't run away from the pool, I ran in circles. Presently he'd caught me and got me down, and then he knelt on my upper arms and began screwing my ears, which was his favourite torture and one I couldn't stand. I was blubbing by this time, but still I wouldn't give in and promise to go home. I wanted to stay and go fishing with the gang. And suddenly the others swung round in my favour and told Joe to get up off my chest and let me stay if I wanted to. So I stayed after all.

The others had some hooks and lines and floats and a lump of bread paste in a rag, and we all cut ourselves willow switches from the tree at the corner of the pool. The farmhouse was only about two hundred yards away, and you had to keep out of sight because old Brewer was very down on fishing. Not that it made any difference to him, he only used the pool for watering his cattle, but he hated boys. The others were still jealous of me and kept telling me to get out of the light and reminding me that I was only a kid and knew nothing about fishing. They said that I was making such a noise I'd scare all the fish away, though actually I was making about half as much noise as anyone else there. Finally they wouldn't let me sit beside them and sent me to another part of the pool where the water was shallower and there wasn't so much shade. They said a kid like me was sure to keep splashing the water and frighten the fish away. It was a rotten part of the pool, a part where no fish would ordinarily come. I knew that. I seemed to know by a kind of instinct the places where a fish would lie. Still, I was fishing at last. I was sitting on the grass bank with the rod in my hands, with the flies buzzing round, and the smell of wild peppermint fit to knock you down, watching the red float on the green water, and I was happy as a tinker although the tear-marks mixed up with dirt were still all over my face.

Lord knows how long we sat there. The morning stretched out and out, and the sun got higher and higher, and nobody had a bite. It was a hot still day, too clear for fishing. The floats lay on the water with never a quiver. You could see deep down into the water as though you were looking into a kind of dark green glass. Out in the middle of the pool you could see the fish lying just under the surface, sunning themselves, and sometimes in the weeds near the side a newt would come gliding upwards and rest there with his fingers on the weeds and his nose just out of the water. But the fish weren't biting. The others kept shouting that they'd got a nibble, but it was always a lie. And the time stretched out and out and it got hotter and hotter, and the flies ate you alive, and the wild peppermint under the bank smelt like Mother Wheeler's sweet-shop. I was getting hungrier and hungrier, all the more because I didn't know for certain where my dinner was coming from. But I sat as still as a mouse and never took my eyes off the float. The others had given me a lump of bait about the size of a marble, telling me that would have to do for me, but for a long time I didn't even dare to re-bait my hook, because every time I pulled my line up they swore I was making enough noise to frighten every fish within five miles.

I suppose we must have been there about two hours when suddenly my float gave a quiver. I knew it was a fish. It must have been a fish that was just passing accidentally and saw my bait. There's no mistaking the movement your float gives when it's a real bite. It's quite different from the way it moves when you twitch your line accidentally. The next moment it gave a sharp bob and almost went under. I couldn't hold myself in any longer. I yelled to the others:

'I've got a bite!'

'Rats!' yelled Sid Lovegrove instantly.

But the next moment there wasn't any doubt about it. The float dived straight down, I could still see it under the water, kind of dim red, and I felt the rod tighten in my hand. Christ, that feeling! The line jerking and straining and a fish on the other end of it! The others saw my rod bending, and the next moment they'd all flung their rods down and rushed round to me. I gave a terrific haul and the fish—a great huge silvery fish—came flying up through the air. The same moment all of us gave a yell of agony. The fish had slipped off the hook and fallen into the wild peppermint under the bank. But he'd fallen into shallow water where he couldn't turn over, and for perhaps a second he lay there on his side helpless. Joe flung himself into the water, splashing us all over, and grabbed him in both hands. 'I got 'im!' he yelled. The next moment he'd flung the fish on to the grass and we were all kneeling round it. How we gloated! The poor dying brute flapped up and down and his scales glistened all the colours of the rainbow. It was a huge carp, seven inches long at least, and must have weighed a quarter of a pound. How we shouted to see him! But the next moment it was as though a shadow had fallen across us. We looked up, and there was old Brewer standing over us, with his tall billycock hat—one of those hats they used to wear that were a cross between a top hat and a bowler—and his cowhide gaiters and a thick hazel stick in his hand.

We suddenly cowered like partridges when there's a hawk overhead. He looked from one to other of us. He had a wicked old mouth with no teeth in it, and since he'd shaved his beard off his chin looked like a nutcracker.

'What are you boys doing here?' he said.

There wasn't much doubt about what we were doing. Nobody answered.

'I'll learn 'ee come fishing in my pool!' he suddenly roared, and the next moment he was on us, whacking out in all directions.

The Black Hand broke and fled. We left all the rods behind and also the fish. Old Brewer chased us half across the meadow. His legs were stiff and he couldn't move fast, but he got in some good swipes before we were out of his reach. We left him in the middle of the field, yelling after us that he knew all our names and was going to tell our fathers. I'd been at the back and most of the wallops had landed on me. I had some nasty red weals on the calves of my legs when we got to the other side of the hedge.

I spent the rest of the day with the gang. They hadn't made up their mind whether I was really a member yet, but for the time being they tolerated me. The errand boy, who'd had the morning off on some lying pretext or other, had to go back to the brewery. The rest of us went for a long, meandering, scrounging kind of walk, the sort of walk that boys go for when they're away

from home all day, and especially when they're away without permission. It
was the first real boy's walk I'd had, quite different from the walks we used to
go with Katie Simmons. We had our dinner in a dry ditch on the edge of the
town, full of rusty cans and wild fennel. The others gave me bits of their
dinner, and Sid Lovegrove had a penny, so someone fetched a Penny Monster
which we had between us. It was very hot, and the fennel smelt very strong,
and the gas of the Penny Monster made us belch. Afterwards we wandered up
the dusty white road to Upper Binfield, the first time I'd been that way, I
believe, and into the beech woods with the carpets of dead leaves and the great
smooth trunks that soar up into the sky so that the birds in the upper branches
look like dots. You could go wherever you liked in the woods in those days.
Binfield House, was shut up, they didn't preserve the pheasants any longer,
and at the worst you'd only meet a carter with a load of wood. There was a tree
that had been sawn down, and the rings of the trunk looked like a target, and
we had shots at it with stones. Then the others had shots at birds with their
catapults, and Sid Lovegrove swore he'd hit a chaffinch and it had stuck in a
fork in the tree. Joe said he was lying, and they argued and almost fought.
Then we went down into a chalk hollow full of beds of dead leaves and shouted
to hear the echo. Someone shouted a dirty word, and then we said over all the
dirty words we knew, and the others jeered at me because I only knew three.
Sid Lovegrove said he knew how babies were born and it was just the same as
rabbits except that the baby came out of the woman's navel. Harry Barnes
started to carve the word—on a beech tree, but got fed up with it after the first
two letters. Then we went round by the lodge of Binfield House. There was a
rumour that somewhere in the grounds there was a pond with enormous fish in
it, but no one ever dared go inside because old Hodges, the lodge-keeper who
acted as a kind of caretaker, was 'down' on boys. He was digging in his
vegetable garden by the lodge when we passed. We cheeked him over the fence
until he chased us off, and then we went down to the Walton Road and cheeked
the carters, keeping on the other side of the hedge so that they couldn't reach
us with their whips. Beside the Walton Road there was a place that had been a
quarry and then a rubbish dump, and finally had got overgrown with
blackberry bushes. There were great mounds of rusty old tin cans and bicycle
frames and saucepans with holes in them and broken bottles with weeds
growing all over them, and we spent nearly an hour and got ourselves filthy
from head to foot routing out iron fence posts, because Harry Barnes swore
that the blacksmith in Lower Binfield would pay sixpence a hundredweight for
old iron. Then Joe found a late thrush's nest with half-fledged chicks in it in a
blackberry bush. After a lot of argument about what to do with them we took
the chicks out, had shots at them with stones, and finally stamped on them.
There were four of them, and we each had one to stamp on. It was getting on
towards tea-time now. We knew that old Brewer would be as good as his word
and there was a hiding ahead of us, but we were getting too hungry to stay out
much longer. Finally we trailed home, with one more row on the way, because
when we were passing the allotments we saw a rat and chased it with sticks, and
old Bennet the station-master, who worked at his allotment every night and

was very proud of it, came after us in a tearing rage because we'd trampled on his onion-bed.

I'd walked ten miles and I wasn't tired. All day I'd trailed after the gang and tried to do everything they did, and they'd called me 'the kid' and snubbed me as much as they could, but I'd more or less kept my end up. I had a wonderful feeling inside me, a feeling you can't know about unless you've had it—but if you're a man you'll have had it some time. I knew that I wasn't a kid any longer, I was a boy at last. And it's a wonderful thing to be a boy, to go roaming where grown-ups can't catch you, and to chase rats and kill birds and shy stones and cheek carters and shout dirty words. It's a kind of strong, rank feeling, a feeling of knowing everything and fearing nothing, and it's all bound up with breaking rules and killing things. The white dusty roads, the hot sweaty feeling of one's clothes, the smell of fennel and wild peppermint, the dirty words, the sour stink of the rubbish dump, the taste of fizzy lemonade and the gas that made one belch, the stamping on the young birds the feel of the fish straining on the line—it was all part of it. Thank God I'm a man, because no woman ever has that feeling.

Sure enough, old Brewer had sent round and told everybody. Father looked very glum, fetched a strap out of the shop, and said he was going to 'thrash the life out of' Joe. But Joe struggled and yelled and kicked, and in the end Father didn't get in more than a couple of whacks at him. However, he got a caning from the headmaster of the Grammar School next day. I tried to struggle too, but I was small enough for Mother to get me across her knee, and she gave me what-for with the strap. So I'd had three hidings that day, one from Joe, one from old Brewer, and one from Mother. Next day the gang decided that I wasn't really a member yet and that I'd got to go through the 'ordeal' (a word they'd got out of the Red Indian stories) after all. They were very strict in insisting that you had to bite the worm before you swallowed it. Moreover, because I was the youngest and they were jealous of me for being the only one to catch anything, they all made out afterwards that the fish I'd caught wasn't really a big one. In a general way the tendency of fish, when people talk about them, is to get bigger and bigger, but this one got smaller and smaller, until to hear the others talk you'd have thought it was no bigger than a minnow.

But it didn't matter. I'd been fishing. I'd seen the float dive under the water and felt the fish tugging at the line, and however many lies they told they couldn't take that away from me.

# 4

For the next seven years, from when I was eight to when I was fifteen, what I chiefly remember is fishing.

Don't think that I did nothing else. It's only that when you look back over a long period of time, certain things seem to swell up till they overshadow everything else. I left Mother Howlett's and went to the Grammar School, with a leather satchel and a black cap with yellow stripes, and got my first bicycle and a long time afterwards my first long trousers. My first bike was a fixed-wheel—free-wheel bikes were very expensive then. When you went downhill you put your feet up on the front rests and let the pedals go whizzing round. That was one of the characteristic sights of the early nineteen-hundreds—a boy sailing downhill with his head back and his feet up in the air. I went to the Grammar School in fear and trembling, because of the frightful tales Joe had told me about old Whiskers (his name was Wicksey) the headmaster, who was certainly a dreadful-looking little man, with a face just like a wolf, and at the end of the big schoolroom he had a glass case with canes in it, which he'd sometimes take out and swish through the air in a terrifying manner. But to my surprise I did rather well at school. It had never occurred to me that I might be cleverer than Joe, who was two years older than me and had bullied me ever since he could walk. Actually Joe was an utter dunce, got the cane about once a week, and stayed somewhere near the bottom of the school till he was sixteen. My second term I took a prize in arithmetic and another in some queer stuff that was mostly concerned with pressed flowers and went by the name of Science, and by the time I was fourteen Whiskers was talking about scholarships and Reading University. Father, who had ambitions for Joe and me in those days, was very anxious that I should go to 'college'. There was an idea floating round that I was to be a schoolteacher and Joe was to be an auctioneer.

But I haven't many memories connected with school. When I've mixed with chaps from the upper classes, as I did during the war, I've been struck by the fact that they never really get over that frightful drilling they go through at public schools. Either it flattens them out into half-wits or they spend the rest of their lives kicking against it. It wasn't so with boys of our class, the sons of shopkeepers and farmers. You went to the Grammar School and you stayed there till you were sixteen, just to show that you weren't a prole, but school was chiefly a place that you wanted to get away from. You'd no sentiment of loyalty, no goofy feeling about the old grey stones (and they *were* old, right enough, the school had been founded by Cardinal Wolsey), and there was no Old Boy's tie and not even a school song. You had your half-holidays to yourself, because games weren't compulsory and as often as not you cut them. We played football in braces, and though it was considered proper to play cricket in a belt, you wore your ordinary shirt and trousers. The only game I really cared about was the stump cricket we used to play in the gravel yard during the break, with a bat made out of a bit of packing case and a compo ball.

But I remember the smell of the big schoolroom, a smell of ink and dust and boots, and the stone in the yard that had been a mounting block and was used for sharpening knives on, and the little baker's shop opposite where they sold a kind of Chelsea bun, twice the size of the Chelsea buns you get nowadays, which were called Lardy Busters and cost a halfpenny. I did all the things you do at school. I carved my name on a desk and got the cane for it—you were always caned for it if you were caught, but it was the etiquette that you had to carve your name. And I got inky fingers and bit my nails and made darts out of penholders and played conkers and passed round dirty stories and learned to masturbate and cheeked old Blowers, the English master, and bullied the life out of little Willy Simeon, the undertaker's son, who was half-witted and believed everything you told him. Our favourite trick was to send him to shops to buy things that didn't exist. All the old gags—the ha'porth of penny stamps, the rubber hammer, the left-handed screwdriver, the pot of striped paint—poor Willy fell for all of them. We had grand sport one afternoon, putting him in a tub and telling him to lift himself up by the handles. He ended up in an asylum, poor Willy. But it was in the holidays that one really lived.

There were good things to do in those days. In winter we used to borrow a couple of ferrets—Mother would never let Joe and me keep them at home, 'nasty smelly things' she called them—and go round the farms and ask leave to do a bit of ratting. Sometimes they let us, sometimes they told us to hook it and said we were more trouble than the rats. Later in winter we'd follow the threshing machine and help kill the rats when they threshed the stacks. One winter, 1908 it must have been, the Thames flooded and then froze and there was skating for weeks on end, and Harry Barnes broke his collar-bone on the ice. In early spring we went after squirrels with squailers, and later on we went birdnesting. We had a theory that birds can't count and it's all right if you leave one egg, but we were cruel little beasts and sometimes we'd just knock the nest down and trample on the eggs or chicks. There was another game we had when the toads were spawning. We used to catch toads, ram the nozzle of a bicycle pump up their backsides, and blow them up till they burst. That's what boys are like, I don't know why. In summer we used to bike over the Burford Weir and bathe. Wally Lovegrove, Sid's young cousin, was drowned in 1906. He got tangled in the weeds at the bottom, and when the drag-hooks brought his body to the surface his face was jet black.

But fishing was the real thing. We went many a time to old Brewer's pool, and took tiny carp and tench out of it, and once a whopping eel, and there were other cow-ponds that had fish in them and were within walking distance on Saturday afternoons. But after we got bicycles we started fishing in the

Thames below Burford Weir. It seemed more grown-up than fishing in cow-ponds. There were no farmers chasing you away, and there are thumping fish in the Thames—though, so far as I know, nobody's ever been known to catch one.

It's queer, the feeling I had for fishing—and still have, really. I can't call myself a fisherman. I've never in my life caught a fish two feet long, and it's thirty years now since I've had a rod in my hands. And yet when I look back the whole of my boyhood from eight to fifteen seems to have revolved round the days when we went fishing. Every detail has stuck clear in my memory. I can remember individual days and individual fish, there isn't a cow-pond or a backwater that I can't see a picture of if I shut my eyes and think. I could write a book on the technique of fishing. When we were kids we didn't have much in the way of tackle, it cost too much and most of our threepence a week (which was the usual pocket-money in those days) went on sweets and Lardy Busters. Very small kids generally fish with a bent pin, which is too blunt to be much use, but you can make a pretty good hook (though of course it's got no barb) by bending a needle in a candle flame with a pair of pliers. The farm lads knew how to plait horsehair so that it was almost as good as gut, and you can take a small fish on a single horsehair. Later we got to having two-shilling fishing-rods and even reels of sorts. God, what hours I've spent gazing into Wallace's window! Even the .410 guns and saloon pistols didn't thrill me so much as the fishing tackle. And the copy of Gamage's catalogue that I picked up somewhere, on a rubbish dump I think, and studied as though it had been the Bible! Even now I could give you all the details about gut-substitute and gimp and Limerick hooks and priests and disgorgers and Nottingham reels and God knows how many other technicalities.

Then there were the kinds of bait we used to use. In our shop there were always plenty of mealworms, which were good but not very good. Gentles were better. You had to beg them off old Gravitt, the butcher, and the gang used to draw lots or do enamena-mina-mo to decide who should go and ask, because Gravitt wasn't usually too pleasant about it. He was a big, rough-faced old devil with a voice like a mastiff, and when he barked, as he generally did when speaking to boys, all the knives and steels on his blue apron would give a jingle. You'd go in with an empty treacle-tin in your hand, hang round till any customers had disappeared and then say very humbly:

'Please, Mr Gravitt, y'got any gentles today?'

Generally he'd roar out: 'What! Gentles! Gentles in my shop! Ain't seen such a thing in years. Think I got blow-flies in my shop?'

He had, of course. They were everywhere. He used to deal with them with a strip of leather on the end of a stick, with which he could reach out to enormous distances and smack a fly into paste. Sometimes you had to go away without any gentles, but as a rule he'd shout after you just as you were going:

''Ere! Go round the backyard an' 'ave a look. P'raps you might find one or two if you looked careful.'

You used to find them in little clusters everywhere. Gravitt's backyard smelt like a battlefield. Butchers didn't have refrigerators in those days. Gentles live longer if you keep them in sawdust.

Wasp grubs are good, though it's hard to make them stick on the hook, unless you bake them first. When someone found a wasps' nest we'd go out at night and pour turnpentine down it and plug up the hole with mud. Next day the wasps would all be dead and you could dig out the nest and take the grubs. Once something went wrong, the turps missed the hole or something, and when we took the plug out the wasps, which had been shut up all night, came out all together with a zoom. We weren't very badly stung, but it was a pity there was no one standing by with a stopwatch. Grasshoppers are about the best bait there is, especially for chub. You stick them on the hook without any shot and just flick them to and fro on the surface–'dapping', they call it. But you can never get more than two or three grasshoppers at a time. Greenbottle flies, which are also damned difficult to catch, are the best bait for dace, especially on clear days. You want to put them on the hook alive, so that they wriggle. A chub will even take a wasp, but it's a ticklish job to put a live wasp on the hook.

God knows how many other baits there were. Bread paste you make by squeezing water through white bread in a rag. Then there are cheese paste and honey paste and paste with aniseed in it. Boiled wheat isn't bad for roach. Redworms are good for gudgeon. You find them in very old manure heaps. And you also find another kind of worm called a brandling, which is striped and smells like an earwig, and which is very good bait for perch. Ordinary earthworms are good for perch. You have to put them in moss to keep them fresh and lively. If you try to keep them in earth they die. Those brown flies you find on cowdung are pretty good for roach. You can take a chub on a cherry, so they say, and I've seen a roach taken with a currant out of a bun.

In those days, from the sixteenth of June (when the coarse-fishing season starts) till midwinter I wasn't often without a tin of worms or gentles in my pocket. I had some fights with Mother about it, but in the end she gave in, fishing came off the list of forbidden things and Father even gave me a two-shilling fishing-rod for Christmas in 1903. Joe was barely fifteen when he started going after girls, and from then on he seldom came out fishing, which he said was a kid's game. But there were about half a dozen others who were as mad on fishing as I was. Christ, those fishing days! The hot sticky afternoons in the schoolroom when I've sprawled across my desk, with old Blowers's voice grating away about predicates and subjunctives and relative clauses, and all that's in my mind is the backwater near Burford Weir and the green pool under the willows with the dace gliding to and fro. And then the terrific rush on bicycles after tea, to Chamford Hill and down to the river to get in an hour's fishing before dark. The still summer evening, the faint splash of the weir, the rings on the water where the fish are rising, the midges eating you alive, the shoals of dace swarming round your hook and never biting. And the kind of passion with which you'd watch the black backs of the fish swarming round, hoping and praying (yes, literally praying) that one of them would change his mind and grab your bait before it got too dark. And then it was always 'Let's have five minutes more', and then 'Just five minutes more', until in the end you had to walk your bike into the town because Towler, the copper, was prowling round and you could be 'had up' for riding without a light. And the times in the summer holidays when we went out to make a day of it with boiled eggs and bread and butter and a bottle of lemonade, and fished and bathed and then fished again and did occasionally catch something. At night you'd come home with filthy hands so hungry that you'd eaten what was left of your bread paste, with three or four smelly dace wrapped up in your handerchief. Mother always refused to cook the fish I brought home. She would never allow that river fish were edible, except trout and salmon. 'Nasty muddy things', she called them. The fish I remember best of all are the ones I didn't catch. Especially the monstrous fish you always used to see when you went for a walk along the towpath on Sunday afternoons and hadn't a rod with you. There was no fishing on Sundays, even the Thames Conservancy Board didn't allow it. On Sundays you had to go for what was called a 'nice walk' in your thick black suit and the Eton collar that sawed your head off. It was on a Sunday that I saw a pike a yard long asleep in shallow water by the bank and nearly got him with a stone. And sometimes in the green pools on the edge of the reeds you'd see a huge Thames trout go sailing past. The trout grow to vast sizes in the Thames, but they're practically never caught. They say that one of the real Thames fishermen, the old bottle-nosed blokes that you see muffled up in overcoats on camp-stools with twenty-foot roach-poles at all seasons of the year, will willingly give up a year of his life to catching a Thames trout. I don't blame them, I see their point entirely, and still better I saw it then.

Of course other things were happening. I grew three inches in a year, got my long trousers, won some prizes at school, went to Confirmation classes, told dirty stories, took to reading, and had crazes for white mice, fretwork, and postage stamps. But it's always fishing that I remember. Summer days, and the flat water-meadows and the blue hills in the distance, and the willows up the backwater and the pools underneath like a kind of deep green glass. Summer evenings, the fish breaking the water, the nightjars hawking round your head, the smell of nightstocks and latakia. Don't mistake what I'm talking about. It's not that I'm trying to put across any of that poetry of childhood stuff. I know that's all baloney. Old Porteous (a friend of mine, a retired schoolmaster, I'll tell you about him later) is great on the poetry of childhood. Sometimes he reads me stuff about it out of books. Wordsworth. Lucy Gray. There was a time when meadow, grove, and all that. Needless to say he's got no kids of his own. The truth is that kids aren't in any way poetic, they're merely savage little animals, except that no animal is a quarter as selfish. A boy isn't interested in meadows, groves, and so forth. He never looks at a landscape, doesn't give a damn for flowers, and unless they affect him in some way, such as being good to eat, he doesn't know one plant from another. Killing things—that's about as near to poetry as a boy gets. And yet all the while there's that peculiar intensity, the power of longing for things as you can't long when you're grown up, and the feeling that time stretches out and out in front of you and that whatever you're doing you could go on for ever.

I was rather an ugly little boy, with butter-coloured hair which was always cropped short except for a quiff in front. I don't idealize my childhood, and unlike many people I've no wish to be young again. Most of the things I used to care for would leave me something more than cold. I don't care if I never see a cricket ball again, and I wouldn't give you threepence for a hundredweight of sweets. But I've still got, I've always had, that peculiar feeling for fishing. You'll think it damned silly, no doubt, but I've actually half a wish to go fishing even now, when I'm fat and forty-five and got two kids and a house in the suburbs. Why? Because in a manner of speaking I *am* sentimental about my childhood—not my own particular childhood, but the civilization which I grew up in and which is now, I suppose, just about at its last kick. And fishing is somehow typical of that civilization. As soon as you think of fishing you think of things that don't belong to the modern world. The very idea of sitting all day under a willow tree beside a quiet pool—and being able to find a quiet pool to sit beside—belongs to the time before the war, before the radio, before aeroplanes, before Hitler. There's a kind of peacefulness even in the names of English coarse fish. Roach, rudd, dace, bleak, barbel, bream, gudgeon, pike, chub, carp, tench. They're solid kind of names. The people who made them up hadn't heard of machine-guns, they didn't live in terror of the sack or spend their time eating aspirins, going to the pictures, and wondering how to keep out of the concentration camp.

Does anyone go fishing nowadays, I wonder? Anywhere within a hundred miles of London there are no fish left to catch. A few dismal fishing-clubs plant themselves in rows along the banks of canals, and millionaires go trout-fishing in private waters round Scotch hotels, a sort of snobbish game of catching hand-reared fish with artificial flies. But who fishes in mill-streams or moats or cow-ponds any longer? Where are the English coarse fish now? When I was a kid every pond and stream had fish in it. Now all the ponds are drained, and when the streams aren't poisoned with chemicals from factories they're full of rusty tins and motor-bike tyres.

My best fishing-memory is about some fish that I never caught. That's usual enough, I suppose.

When I was about fourteen Father did a good turn of some kind to old Hodges, the caretaker at Binfield House. I forget what it was—gave him some medicine that cured his fowls of the worms, or something. Hodges was a crabby old devil, but he didn't forget a good turn. One day a little while afterwards when he'd been down to the shop to buy chicken-corn he met me outside the door and stopped me in his surly way. He had a face like something carved out of a bit of root, and only two teeth, which were dark brown and very long.

'Hey, young 'un! Fisherman, ain't you?'

'Yes.'

'Thought you was. You listen, then. If so be you wanted to, you could bring your line and have a try in that they pool up ahind the Hall. There's plenty bream and jack in there. But don't you tell no one as I told you. And don't you go for to bring any of them other young whelps, or I'll beat the skin off their backs.'

Having said this he hobbled off with his sack of corn over his shoulder, as though feeling that he'd said too much already. The next Saturday afternoon I biked up to Binfield House with my pockets full of worms and gentles, and looked for old Hodges at the lodge. At that time Binfield House had already been empty for ten or twenty years. Mr Farrel, the owner, couldn't afford to live in it and either couldn't or wouldn't let it. He lived in London on the rent of his farms and let the house and grounds go to the devil. All the fences were green and rotting, the park was a mass of nettles, the plantations were like a jungle, and even the gardens had gone back to meadow, with only a few old gnarled rose-bushes to show you where the beds had been. But it was a very beautiful house, especially from a distance. It was a great white place with colonnades and long-shaped windows, which had been built, I suppose, about Queen Anne's time by someone who'd travelled in Italy. If I went there now I'd probably get a certain kick out of wandering round the general desolation and thinking about the life that used to go on there, and the people who built such places because they imagined that the good days would last for ever. As a boy I didn't give either the house or the grounds a second look. I dug out old Hodges, who'd just finished his dinner and was a bit surly, and got him to show me the way down to the pool. It was several hundred yards behind the house and completely hidden in the beech woods, but it was a good-sized pool, almost a lake, about a hundred and fifty yards across. It was astonishing, and even at that age it astonished me, that there, a dozen miles from Reading and not fifty from London, you could have such solitude. You felt as much alone as if you'd been on the banks of the Amazon. The pool was ringed completely round by the enormous beech trees, which in one place came down to the edge and were reflected in the water. On the other side there was a patch of grass where there was a hollow with beds of wild peppermint, and up at one end of the pool an old wooden boathouse was rotting among the bulrushes.

The pool was swarming with bream, small ones, about four to six inches long. Every now and again you'd see one of them turn half over and gleam reddy brown under the water. There were pike there too, and they must have been big ones. You never saw them, but sometimes one that was basking among the weeds would turn over and plunge with a splash that was like a brick being bunged into the water. It was no use trying to catch them, though of course I always tried every time I went there. I tried them with dace and minnows I'd caught in the Thames and kept alive in a jam-jar, and even with a spinner made out of a bit of tin. But they were gorged with fish and wouldn't bite, and in any case they'd have broken any tackle I possessed. I never came back from the pool without at least a dozen small bream. Sometimes in the summer holidays I went there for a whole day, with my fishing-rod and a copy of *Chums* or the *Union Jack* or something, and a hunk of bread and cheese which Mother had wrapped up for me. And I've fished for hours and then lain in the grass hollow and read the *Union Jack*, and then the smell of my bread paste and the plop of a fish jumping somewhere would send me wild again, and I'd go back to the water and have another go, and so on all through a summer's day. And the best of all was to be alone, utterly alone, though the road wasn't a quarter of a mile away. I was just old enough to know that it's good to be alone occasionally. With the trees all round you it was as though the pool belonged to you, and nothing ever stirred except the fish ringing the water and the pigeons passing overhead. And yet, in the two years or so that I went fishing there, how many times did I really go, I wonder? Not more than a dozen. It was a three-mile bike ride from home and took up a whole afternoon at least. And sometimes other things turned up, and sometimes when I'd meant to go it rained. You know the way things happen.

One afternoon the fish weren't biting and I began to explore at the end of the pool farthest from Binfield House. There was a bit of an overflow of water and the ground was boggy, and you had to fight your way through a sort of jungle of blackberry bushes and rotten boughs that had fallen off the trees. I struggled through it for about fifty yards, and then suddenly there was a clearing and I came to another pool which I had never known existed. It was a small pool not more than twenty yards wide, and rather dark because of the boughs that overhung it. But it was very clear water and immensely deep. I could see ten or fifteen feet down into it. I hung about for a bit, enjoying the dampness and the rotten boggy smell, the way a boy does. And then I saw something that almost made me jump out of my skin.

It was an enormous fish. I don't exaggerate when I say it was enormous. It was almost the length of my arm. It glided across the pool, deep under water, and then became a shadow and disappeared into the darker water on the other side. I felt as if a sword had gone through me. It was far the biggest fish I'd ever seen, dead or alive. I stood there without breathing, and in a moment another huge thick shape glided through the water, and then another and then two more close together. The pool was full of them. They were carp, I suppose. Just possibly they were bream or tench, but more probably carp. Bream or tench wouldn't grow so huge. I knew what had happened. At some time this pool had been connected with the other, and then the stream had dried up and the woods had closed round the small pool and it had just been forgotten. It's a thing that happens occasionally. A pool gets forgotten somehow, nobody fishes in it for years and decades and the fish grow to monstrous sizes. The brutes that I was watching might be a hundred years old. And not a soul in the world knew about them except me. Very likely it was twenty years since anyone had so much as looked at the pool, and probably even old Hodges and Mr Farrel's bailiff had forgotten its existence.

Well, you can imagine what I felt. After a bit I couldn't even bear the tantalization of watching. I hurried back to the other pool and got my fishing things together. It was no use trying for those colossal brutes with the tackle I had. They'd snap it as if it had been a hair. And I couldn't go on fishing any longer for the tiny bream. The sight of the big carp had given me a feeling in my stomach almost as if I was going to be sick. I got on to my bike and whizzed down the hill and home. It was a wonderful secret for a boy to have. There was the dark pool hidden away in the woods and the monstrous fish sailing round it—fish that had never been fished for and would grab the first bait you offered them. It was only a question of getting hold of a line strong enough to hold them. Already I'd made all the arrangements. I'd buy the tackle that would hold them if I had to steal the money out of the till. Somehow, God knew how, I'd get hold of half a crown and buy a length of silk salmon line and some thick gut or gimp and Number 5 hooks, and come back with cheese and gentles and paste and mealworms and brandlings and grasshoppers and every mortal bait a carp might look at. The very next Saturday afternoon I'd come back and try for them.

**But as it happened I never went back. One never does go back.** I never stole the money out of the till or bought the bit of salmon line or had a try for those carp. Almost immediately afterwards something turned up to prevent me, but if it hadn't been that it would have been something else. It's the way things happen.

I know, of course, that you think I'm exaggerating about the size of those fish. You think, probably, that they were just medium-sized fish (a foot long, say) and that they've swollen gradually in my memory. But it isn't so. People tell lies about the fish they've caught and still more about the fish that are hooked and get away, but I never caught any of these or even tried to catch them, and I've no motive for lying. I tell you they were enormous.

## 5

Fishing!

Here I'll make a confession, or rather two. The first is that when I look back through my life I can't honestly say that anything I've ever done has given me quite such a kick as fishing. Everything else has been a bit of a flop in comparison, even women. I don't set up to be one of those men that don't care about women. I've spent plenty of time chasing them, and I would even now if I had the chance. Still, if you gave me the choice of having any woman you care to name, but I mean *any* woman, or catching a ten-pound carp, the carp would win every time. And the other confession is that after I was sixteen I never fished again.

Why? Because that's how things happen. Because in this life we lead—I don't mean human life in general, I mean life in this particular age and this particular country—we don't do the things we want to do. It isn't because we're always working. Even a farm-hand or a Jew tailor isn't always working. It's because there's some devil in us that drives us to and fro on everlasting idiocies. There's time for everything except the things worth doing. Think of something you really care about. Then add hour to hour and calculate the fraction of your life that you've actually spent in doing it. And then calculate the time you've spent on things like shaving, riding to and fro on buses, waiting in railway, junctions, swapping dirty stories, and reading the newspapers.

After I was sixteen I didn't go fishing again. There never seemed to be time. I was at work, I was chasing girls, I was wearing my first button boots and my first high collars (and for the collars of 1909 you needed a neck like a giraffe), I was doing correspondence courses in salesmanship and accountancy and 'improving my mind'. The great fish were gliding round in the pool behind Binfield House. Nobody knew about them except me. They were stored away in my mind; some day, some bank holiday perhaps, I'd go back and catch them. But I never went back. There was time for everything except that. Curiously enough, the only time between then and now when I did very nearly go fishing was during the war.

It was in the autumn of 1916, just before I was wounded. We'd come out of trenches to a village behind the line, and though it was only September we were covered with mud from head to foot. As usual we didn't know for certain how long we were going to stay there or where we were going afterwards. Luckily the C.O. was a bit off-colour, a touch of bronchitis or something, and so didn't bother about driving us through the usual parades, kit-inspections, football matches, and so forth which were supposed to keep up the spirits of the troops when they were out of the line. We spent the first day sprawling about on piles of chaff in the barns where we were billeted and scraping the mud off our putties, and in the evening some of the chaps started queueing up for a couple of wretched worn-out whores who were established in a house at the end of the village. In the morning, although it was against orders to leave the village, I managed to sneak off and wander round the ghastly desolation that had once been fields. It was a damp, wintry kind of morning. All round, of course, were the awful muck and litter of war, the sort of filthy sordid mess that's actually worse than a battlefield of corpses. Trees with boughs torn off them, old shell-holes that had partly filled up again, tin cans, turds, mud, weeds, clumps of rusty barbed wire with weeds growing through them. You know the feeling you had when you came out of the line. A stiffened feeling in all your joints, and inside you a kind of emptiness, a feeling that you'd never again have any interest in anything. It was partly fear and exhaustion but mainly boredom. At that time no one saw any reason why the war shouldn't go on for ever. Today or tomorrow or the day after you were going back to the line, and maybe next week a shell would blow you to potted meat, but that wasn't so bad as the ghastly boredom of the war stretching out for ever.

I was wandering up the side of a hedge when I ran into a chap in our company whose surname I don't remember but who was nicknamed Nobby. He was a dark, slouching, gypsy-looking chap, a chap who even in uniform always gave the impression that he was carrying a couple of stolen rabbits. By trade he was a coster and he was a real Cockney, but one of those Cockneys that make part of their living by hop-picking, bird-catching, poaching, and fruit-stealing in Kent and Essex. He was a great expert on dogs, ferrets, cage-birds, fighting-cocks, and that kind of thing. As soon as he saw me he beckoned to me with his head. He had a sly, vicious way of talking:

''Ere, George!' (The chaps still called me George—I hadn't got fat in those days.) 'George! Ja see that clump of poplars acrost the field?'

'Yes.'

'Well, there's a pool on t'other side of it, and it's full of bleeding great fish.'

'Fish? Garn!'

'I tell you it's bleeding full of 'em. Perch, they are. As good fish as ever I got my thumbs on. Com'n see f'yerself, then.'

We trudged over the mud together. Sure enough, Nobby was right. On the other side of the poplars there was a dirty-looking pool with sandy banks. Obviously it had been a quarry and had got filled up with water. And it was swarming with perch. You could see their dark blue stripy backs gliding everywhere just under water, and some of them must have weighed a pound. I suppose in two years of war they hadn't been disturbed and had had time to multiply. Probably you can't imagine what the sight of those perch had done to me. It was as though they'd suddenly brought me to life. Of course there was only one thought in both our minds—how to get hold of a rod and line.

'Christ!' I said. 'We'll have some of those.'

'You bet we f— well will. C'mon back to the village and let's get 'old of some tackle.'

'O.K. You want to watch out, though. If the sergeant gets to know we'll cop it.'

'Oh, f— the sergeant. They can 'ang, drore, and quarter me if they want to. I'm going to 'ave some of them bleeding fish.'

You can't know how wild we were to catch those fish. Or perhaps you can, if you've ever been at war. You know the frantic boredom of war and the way you'll clutch at almost any kind of amusement. I've seen two chaps in a dugout fight like devils over half a threepenny magazine. But there was more to it than that. It was the thought of escaping, for perhaps a whole day, right out of the atmosphere of war. To be sitting under the poplar trees, fishing for perch, away from the Company, away from the noise and the stink and the uniforms and the officers and the saluting and the sergeant's voice! Fishing is the opposite of war. But it wasn't at all certain that we could bring it off. That was the thought that sent us into a kind of fever. If the sergeant found out he'd stop us as sure as fate, and so would any of the officers, and the worst of all was that there was no knowing how long we were going to stay at the village. We might stay there a week, we might march off in two hours. Meanwhile we'd no fishing tackle of any kind, not even a pin or a bit of string. We had to start from scratch. And the pool was swarming with fish! The first thing was a rod. A willow wand is best, but of course there wasn't a willow tree anywhere this side of the horizon. Nobby shinned up one of the poplars and cut off a small bough which wasn't actually good but was better than nothing. He trimmed it down with his jack-knife till it looked something like a fishing-rod, and then we hid it in the weeds near the bank and managed to sneak back into the village without being seen.

The next thing was a needle to make a hook. Nobody had a needle. One chap had some darning needles, but they were too thick and had blunt ends. We daren't let anyone know what we wanted it for, for fear the sergeant should hear about it. At last we thought of the whores at the end of the village. They were pretty sure to have a needle. When we got there—you had to go round to the back door through a mucky courtyard—the house was shut up and the whores were having a sleep which they'd no doubt earned. We stamped and yelled and banged on the door until after about ten minutes a fat ugly woman in a wrapper came down and screamed at us in French. Nobby shouted at her:

'Needle! Needle! You got a needle!'

Of course she didn't know what he was talking about. Then Nobby tried pidgin English, which he expected her as a foreigner to understand:

'Wantee needle! Sewee clothee! Likee thisee!'

He made gestures which were supposed to represent sewing. The whore misunderstood him and opened the door a bit wider to let us in. Finally we made her understand and got a needle from her. By this time it was dinner time.

After dinner the sergeant came round the barn where we were billeted looking for men for a fatigue. We managed to dodge him just in time by getting under a pile of chaff. When he was gone we got a candle alight, made the needle red-hot, and managed to bend it into a kind of hook. We didn't have any tools except jack-knives, and we burned our fingers badly. The next thing was a line. Nobody had any string except thick stuff, but at last we came across a fellow who had a reel of sewing thread. He didn't want to part with it and we had to give him a whole packet of fags for it. The thread was much too thin, but Nobby cut it into three lengths, tied them to a nail in the wall, and carefully plaited them. Meanwhile after searching all over the village I'd managed to find a cork, and I cut it in half and stuck a match through it to make a float. By this time it was evening and getting on towards dark.

We'd got the essentials now, but we could do with some gut. There didn't seem much hope of getting any until we thought of the hospital orderly. Surgical gut wasn't part of his equipment, but it was just possible that he might have some. Sure enough, when we asked him, we found he'd a whole hank of medical gut in his haversack. It had taken his fancy in some hospital or other and he'd pinched it. We swapped another packet of fags for ten lengths of gut. It was rotten brittle stuff, in pieces about six inches long. After dark Nobby soaked them till they were pliable and tied them end to end. So now we'd got everything—hook, rod, line, float, and gut. We could dig up worms anywhere. And the pool was swarming with fish! Huge great stripy perch crying out to be caught! We lay down to kip in such a fever that we didn't even take our boots off. Tomorrow! If we could just have tomorrow! If the war would forget about us for just a day! We made up our minds that as soon as roll-call was over we'd hook it and stay away all day, even if they gave us Field Punishment No. 1 for it when we came back.

Well, I expect you can guess the rest. At roll-call orders were to pack all kits and be ready to march in twenty minutes. We marched nine miles down the road and then got on to lorries and were off to another part of the line. As for the pool under the poplar trees, I never saw or heard of it again. I expect it got poisoned with mustard gas later on.

Since then I've never fished. I never seemed to get the chance. There was the rest of the war, and then like everyone else I was fighting for a job, and then I'd got a job and the job had got me. I was a promising young fellow in an insurance office—one of those keen young businessmen with firm jaws and good prospects that you used to read about in the Clark's College adverts—and then I was the usual down-trodden five-to-ten-pounds-a-weeker in a semi-detached villa in the inner-outer suburbs. Such people don't go fishing, any more than stockbrokers go out picking primroses. It wouldn't be suitable. Other recreations are provided for them.

Of course I have my fortnight's holiday every summer. You know the kind of holiday. Margate, Yarmouth, Eastbourne, Hastings, Bournemouth, Brighton. There's a slight variation according to whether or not we're flush that year. With a woman like Hilda along, the chief feature of a holiday is endless mental arithmetic to decide how much the boarding-house keeper is swindling you. That and telling the kids, No, they can't have a new sandbucket. A few years back we were at Bournemouth. One fine afternoon we loitered down the pier, which must be about half a mile long, and all the way along it chaps were fishing with stumpy sea-rods with little bells on the end and their lines stretching fifty yards out to sea. It's a dull kind of fishing, and they weren't catching anything. Still, they were fishing. The kids soon got bored and clamoured to go back to the beach, and Hilda saw a chap sticking a lobworm on his hook and said it made her feel sick, but I kept loitering up and down for a little while longer. And suddenly there was a tremendous ringing from a bell and a chap was winding in his line. Everyone stopped to watch. And sure enough, in it came, the wet line and the lump of lead and on the end a great flat-fish (a flounder, I think) dangling and wriggling. The chap dumped it on to the planks of the pier, and it flapped up and down, all wet and gleaming, with its grey warty back and its white belly and the fresh salty smell of the sea. And something kind of moved inside me.

As we moved off I said casually, just to test Hilda's reaction:

'I've half a mind to do a bit of fishing myself while we're here.'

'What! *You* go fishing, George? But you don't even know how, do you?'

'Oh, I used to be a great fisherman,' I told her.

She was vaguely against it, as usual, but didn't have many ideas one way or the other, except that if I went fishing she wasn't coming with me to watch me put those nasty squashy things on the hook. Then suddenly she got on to the fact that if I was to go fishing the set-out that I'd need, rod and reel and so forth, would cost round about a quid. The rod alone would cost ten bob. Instantly she flew into a temper. You haven't seen old Hilda when there's talk of wasting ten bob. She burst out at me:

'The *idea* of wasting all that money on a thing like that! Absurd! And how they *dare* charge ten shillings for one of those silly little fishing-rods! It's disgraceful. And fancy you going fishing at your age! A great big grown-up man like you. Don't be such a *baby*, George.'

Then the kids got on to it. Lorna sidled up to me and asked in that silly pert way she has, 'Are you a baby, Daddy?' and little Billy, who at that time didn't speak quite plain, announced to the world in general, 'Farver's a baby.' Then suddenly they were both dancing round me, rattling their sandbuckets and chanting:

'Farver's a baby! Farver's a baby!'

Unnatural little bastards!

---

# 6

---

And besides fishing there was reading.

I've exaggerated if I've given the impression that fishing was the *only* thing I cared about. Fishing certainly came first, but reading was a good second. I must have been either ten or eleven when I started reading—reading voluntarily, I mean. At that age it's like discovering a new world. I'm a considerable reader even now, in fact there aren't many weeks in which I don't get through a couple of novels. I'm what you might call the typical Boots Library subscriber, I always fall for the best-seller of the moment (*The Good Companions, Bengal Lancer, Hatter's Castle*—I fell for every one of them), and I've been a member of the Left Book Club for a year or more. And in 1918, when I was twenty-five, I had a sort of debauch of reading that made a certain difference to my outlook. But nothing is ever like those first years when you suddenly discover that you can open a penny weekly paper and plunge straight into thieves' kitchens and Chinese opium dens and Polynesian islands and the forests of Brazil.

It was from when I was eleven to when I was about sixteen that I got my biggest kick out of reading. At first it was always the boys' penny weeklies—little thin papers with vile print and an illustration in three colours on the cover—and a bit later it was books. *Sherlock Holmes, Dr Nikola, The Iron Pirate, Dracula, Raffles*. And Nat Gould and Ranger Gull and a chap whose name I forget who wrote boxing stories almost as rapidly as Nat Gould wrote racing ones. I suppose if my parents had been a little better educated I'd have had 'good' books shoved down my throat, Dickens and Thackeray and so forth, and in fact they did drive us through *Quentin Durward* at school and Uncle Ezekiel sometimes tried to incite me to read Ruskin and Carlyle. But there were practically no books in our house. Father had never read a book in his life, except the Bible and Smiles's *Self Help*, and I didn't of my own accord read a 'good' book till much later. I'm not sorry it happened that way. I read the things I wanted to read, and I got more out of them than I ever got out of the stuff they taught me at school.

The old penny dreadfuls were already going out when I was a kid, and I can barely remember them, but there was a regular line of boys' weeklies, some of which still exist. The Buffalo Bill stories have gone out, I think, and Nat Gould probably isn't read any longer, but Nick Carter and Sexton Blake seem to be still the same as ever. The *Gem* and the *Magnet,* if I'm remembering rightly, started about 1905. The *B.O.P.* was still rather pi in those days, but *Chums,* which I think must have started about 1903, was splendid. Then there was an encyclopedia—I don't remember its exact name—which was issued in penny numbers. It never seemed quite worth buying, but a boy at school used to give away back numbers sometimes. If I now know the length of the Mississippi or the difference between an octopus and a cuttle-fish or the exact composition of bell-metal, that's where I learned it from.

Joe never read. He was one of those boys who can go through years of schooling and at the end of it are unable to read ten lines consecutively. The sight of print made him feel sick. I've seen him pick up one of my numbers of *Chums,* read a paragraph or two and then turn away with just the same movement of disgust as a horse when it smells stale hay. He tried to kick me out of reading, but Mother and Father, who had decided that I was 'the clever one', backed me up. They were rather proud that I showed a taste for 'book-learning', as they called it. But it was typical of both of them that they were vaguely upset by my reading things like *Chums* and the *Union Jack,* thought that I ought to read something 'improving' but didn't know enough about books to be sure which books were 'improving'. Finally Mother got hold of a second-hand copy of Foxe's *Book of Martyrs,* which I didn't read, though the illustrations weren't half bad.

All through the winter of 1905 I spent a penny on *Chums* every week. I was following up their serial story, 'Donovan the Dauntless'. Donovan the Dauntless was an explorer who was employed by an American millionaire to fetch incredible things from various corners of the earth. Sometimes it was diamonds the size of golf balls from the craters of volcanoes in Africa, sometimes it was petrified mammoths' tusks from the frozen forests of Siberia, sometimes it was buried Inca treasures from the lost cities of Peru. Donovan went on a new journey every week, and he always made good. My favourite place for reading was the loft behind the yard. Except when Father was getting out fresh sacks of grain it was the quietest place in the house. There were huge piles of sacks to lie on, and a sort of plastery smell mixed up with the smell of sainfoin, and bunches of cobwebs in all the corners, and just over the place where I used to lie there was a hole in the ceiling and a lath sticking out of the plaster. I can feel the feeling of it now. A winter day, just warm enough to lie still. I'm lying on my belly with *Chums* open in front of me. A mouse runs up the side of a sack like a clockwork toy, then suddenly stops dead and watches me with his little eyes like tiny jet beads. I'm twelve years old, but I'm Donovan the Dauntless. Two thousand miles up the Amazon I've just pitched my tent, and the roots of the mysterious orchid that blooms once in a hundred years are safe in the tin box under my camp bed. In the forests all round Hopi-Hopi Indians, who paint their teeth scarlet and skin white men alive, are beating their war-drums. I'm watching the mouse and the mouse is watching me, and I can smell the dust and sainfoin and the cool plastery smell, and I'm up the Amazon, and it's bliss, pure bliss.

# 7

That's all, really.

I've tried to tell you something about the world before the war, the world I got a sniff of when I saw King Zog's name on the poster, and the chances are that I've told you nothing. Either you remember before the war and don't need to be told about it, or you don't remember, and it's no use telling you. So far I've only spoken about the things that happened to me before I was sixteen. Up to that time things had gone pretty well with the family. It was a bit before my sixteenth birthday that I began to get glimpses of what people call 'real life', meaning unpleasantness.

About three days after I'd seen the big carp at Binfield House, Father came in to tea looking very worried and even more grey and mealy than usual. He ate his way solemnly through his tea and didn't talk much. In those days he had a rather preoccupied way of eating, and his moustache used to work up and down with a sidelong movement, because he hadn't many back teeth left. I was just getting up from table when he called me back.

'Wait a minute, George, my boy. I got suthing to say to you. Sit down jest a minute. Mother, you heard what I got to say last night.'

Mother, behind the huge brown teapot, folded her hands in her lap and looked solemn. Father went on, speaking very seriously but rather spoiling the effect by trying to deal with a crumb that lodged somewhere in what was left of his back teeth:

'George, my boy, I got suthing to say to you. I been thinking it over, and it's about time you left school. 'Fraid you'll have to get to work now and start earning a bit to bring home to your mother. I wrote to Mr Wicksey last night and told him as I should have to take you away.'

Of course this was quite according to precedent—his writing to Mr Wicksey before telling me, I mean. Parents in those days, as a matter of course, always arranged everything over their children's heads.

Father went on to make some rather mumbling and worried explanations. He'd 'had bad times lately', things had 'been a bit difficult', and the upshot was that Joe and I would have to start earning our living. At that time I didn't either know or greatly care whether the business was really in a bad way or not. I hadn't even enough commercial instinct to see the reason why things were 'difficult'. The fact was that Father had been hit by competition. Sarazins', the big retail seedsmen who had branches all over the home counties, had stuck a tentacle into Lower Binfield. Six months earlier they'd taken the lease of a shop in the market-place and dolled it up until what with bright green paint, gilt lettering, gardening tools painted red and green, and huge advertisements for sweet peas, it hit you in the eye at a hundred yards' distance. Sarazins', besides selling flower seeds, described themselves as 'universal poultry and livestock providers', and apart from wheat and oats and so forth they went in for patent poultry mixtures, bird-seed done up in fancy packets, dog-biscuits of all shapes and colours, medicines, embrocations, and conditioning powders, and branched off into such things as rat-traps, dog-chains, incubators, sanitary eggs, bird-nesting, bulbs, weed-killer, insecticide, and even, in some branches, into what they called a 'livestock department', meaning rabbits and day-old chicks. Father, with his dusty old shop and his refusal to stock new lines, couldn't compete with that kind of thing and didn't want to. The tradesmen with their van-horses, and such of the farmers as dealt with the retail seedsmen, fought shy of Sarazins', but in six months they'd gathered in the petty gentry of the neighbourhood, who in those days had carriages or dogcarts and therefore horses. This meant a big loss of trade for Father and the other corn merchant, Winkle. I didn't grasp any of this at the time. I had a boy's attitude towards it all. I'd never taken any interest in the business. I'd never or hardly ever served in the shop, and when, as occasionally happened, Father wanted me to run an errand or give a hand with something, such as hoisting sacks of grain up to the loft or down again, I'd always dodged it whenever possible. Boys in our class aren't such complete babies as public schoolboys, they know that work is work and sixpence is sixpence, but it seems natural for a boy to regard his father's business as a bore. Up till that time fishing-rods, bicycles, fizzy lemonade, and so forth had seemed to me a good deal more real than anything that happened in the grown-up world.

Father had already spoken to old Grimmett, the grocer, who wanted a smart lad and was willing to take me into the shop immediately. Meanwhile Father was going to get rid of the errand boy, and Joe was to come home and help with the shop till he got a regular job. Joe had left school some time back and had been more or less loafing ever since. Father had sometimes talked of 'getting him into' the accounts department at the brewery, and earlier had even had thoughts of making him into an auctioneer. Both were completely hopeless because Joe, at seventeen, wrote a hand like a ploughboy and couldn't repeat the multiplication table. At present he was supposed to be 'learning the trade' at a big bicycle shop on the outskirts of Walton. Tinkering with bicycles suited Joe, who, like most half-wits, had a slight mechanical turn, but he was quite incapable of working steadily and spent all his time loafing about in greasy overalls, smoking Woodbines, getting into fights, drinking (he's started that already), getting 'talked of' with one girl after another, and sticking Father for money. Father was worried, puzzled, and vaguely resentful. I can see him yet, with the meal on his bald head, and the bit of grey hair over his ears, and his spectacles and his grey moustache. He couldn't understand what was happening to him. For years his profits had gone up, slowly and steadily, ten pounds this year, twenty pounds that year, and now suddenly they'd gone down with a bump. He couldn't understand it. He'd inherited the business from his father, he'd done an honest trade, worked hard, sold sound goods, swindled nobody—and his profits were going down. He said a number of times, between sucking at his teeth to get the crumb out, that times were very bad, trade seemed very slack, he couldn't think what had come over people, it wasn't as if the horses didn't have to eat. Perhaps it was these here motors, he decided finally. 'Nasty smelly things!' Mother put in. She was a little worried, and knew that she ought to be more so. Once or twice while Father was talking there was a far-away look in her eyes and I could see her lips moving. She was trying to decide whether it should be a round of beef and carrots tomorrow or another leg of mutton. Except when there was something in her own line that needed foresight, such as buying linen or saucepans, she wasn't really capable of thinking beyond tomorrow's meals. The shop was giving trouble and Father was worried—that was about as far as she saw into it. None of us had any grasp of what was happening. Father had had a bad year and lost money, but was he really frightened by the future? I don't think so. This was 1909, remember. He didn't know what was happening to him, he wasn't capable of foreseeing that these Sarazin people would systematically under-sell him, ruin him, and eat him up. How could he? Things hadn't happened like that when he was a young man. All he knew was that times were bad, trade was very 'slack', very 'slow' (he kept repeating these phrases), but probably things would 'look up presently'.

It would be nice if I could tell you that I was a great help to my father in his time of trouble, suddenly proved myself a man, and developed qualities which no one had suspected in me—and so on and so forth, like the stuff you used to read in the uplift novels of thirty years ago. Or alternatively I'd like to be able to record that I bitterly resented having to leave school, my eager young mind, yearning for knowledge and refinement, recoiled from the soulless mechanical job into which they were thrusting me—and so on and so forth, like the stuff you read in the uplift novels today. Both would be complete bunkum. The truth is that I was pleased and excited at the idea of going to work, especially when I grasped that Old Grimmett was going to pay me real wages, twelve shillings a week, of which I could keep four for myself. The big carp at Binfield House, which had filled my mind for three days past, faded right out of it. I'd no objection to leaving school a few terms early. It generally happened the same way with boys at our school. A boy was always 'going to' go to Reading University, or study to be an engineer, or 'go into business' in London, or run away to sea—and then suddenly, at two days' notice, he'd disappear from school, and a fortnight later you'd meet him on a bicycle, delivering vegetables. Within five minutes of Father telling me that I should have to leave school I was wondering about the new suit I should wear to go to work in. I instantly started demanding a 'grown-up suit', with a kind of coat that was fashionable at that time, a 'cutaway', I think it was called. Of course both Mother and Father were scandalized and said they'd 'never heard of such a thing'. For some reason that I've never fully fathomed, parents in those days always tried to prevent their children wearing grown-up clothes as long as possible. In every family there was a stand-up fight before a boy had his first tall collars or a girl put her hair up.

So the conversation veered away from Father's business troubles and degenerated into a long, nagging kind of argument, with Father gradually getting angry and repeating over and over–dropping an aitch now and again, as he was apt to do when he got angry–'Well, you can't 'ave it. Make up your mind to that–you can't 'ave it.' So I didn't have my 'cutaway', but went to work for the first time in a ready-made black suit and a broad collar in which I looked an overgrown lout. Any distress I felt over the whole business really arose from that. Joe was even more selfish about it. He was furious at having to leave the bicycle shop, and for the short time that he remained at home he merely loafed about, made a nuisance of himself and was no help to Father whatever.

I worked in old Grimmett's shop for nearly six years. Grimmett was a fine, upstanding, white-whiskered old chap, like a rather stouter version of Uncle Ezekiel, and like Uncle Ezekiel a good Liberal. But he was less of a firebrand and more respected in the town. He'd trimmed his sails during the Boer War, he was a bitter enemy of trade unions and once sacked an assistant for possessing a photograph of Keir Hardie, and he was 'chapel'–in fact he was a big noise, literally, in the Baptist Chapel, known locally as the Tin Tab–whereas my family were 'church' and Uncle Ezekiel was an infidel at that. Old Grimmett was a town councillor and an official at the local Liberal Party. With his white whiskers, his canting talk about liberty of conscience and the Grand Old Man, his thumping bank balance, and the extempore prayers you could sometimes hear him letting loose when you passed the Tin Tab, he was a little like a legendary Nonconformist grocer in the story–you've heard it, I expect:

'James!'
'Yessir?'
'Have you sanded the sugar?'
'Yessir!'
'Have you watered the treacle?'
'Yessir!'
'Then come up to prayers.'

God knows how often I heard that story whispered in the shop. We did actually start the day with a prayer before we put up the shutters. Not that old Grimmett sanded the sugar. He knew that that doesn't pay. But he was a sharp man in business, he did all the high-class grocery trade of Lower Binfield and the country round, and he had three assistants in the shop besides the errand boy, the van-man, and his own daughter (he was a widower) who acted as cashier. I was the errand boy for my first six months. Then one of the assistants left to 'set up' in Reading and I moved into the shop and wore my first white apron. I learned to tie a parcel, pack a bag of currants, grind coffee, work the bacon-slicer, carve ham, put an edge on a knife, sweep the floor, dust eggs without breaking them, pass off an inferior article as a good one, clean a window, judge a pound of cheese by eye, open a packing-case, whack a slab of butter into shape, and–what was a good deal the hardest–remember where the stock was kept. I haven't such detailed memories of grocering as I have of fishing, but I remember a good deal. To this day I know the trick of snapping a bit of string in my fingers. If you put me in front of a bacon-slicer I could work it better than I can a typewriter. I could spin you some pretty fair technicalities about grades of China tea and what margarine is made of and the average weight of eggs and the price of paper bags per thousand.

Well, for more than five years that was me—an alert young chap with a round, pink, snubby kind of face and butter-coloured hair (no longer cut short but carefully greased and slicked back in what people used to call a 'smarm'), hustling about behind the counter in a white apron with a pencil behind my ear, tying up bags of coffee like lightning and jockeying the customer along with 'Yes, ma'am! Certainly, ma'am! *And* the next order, ma'am!' in a voice with just a trace of a Cockney accent. Old Grimmett worked us pretty hard, it was an eleven-hour day except on Thursdays and Sundays, and Christmas week was a nightmare. Yet it's a good time to look back on. Don't think that I had no ambitions. I knew I wasn't going to remain a grocer's assistant for ever, I was merely 'learning the trade'. Some time, somehow or other, there'd be enough money for me to 'set up' on my own. That was how people felt in those days. This was before the war, remember, and before the slumps and before the dole. The world was big enough for everyone. Anyone could 'set up in trade', there was always room for another shop. And time was slipping on. 1909, 1910, 1911. King Edward died and the papers came out with a black border round the edge. Two cinemas opened in Walton. The cars got commoner on the roads and cross-country motor-buses began to run. An aeroplane—a flimsy, rickety-looking thing with a chap sitting in the middle on a kind of chair—flew over Lower Binfield and the whole town rushed out of their houses to yell at it. People began to say rather vaguely that this here German Emperor was getting too big for his boots and 'it' (meaning war with Germany) was 'coming some time'. My wages went gradually up, until finally, just before the war, they were twenty-eight shillings a week. I paid Mother ten shillings a week for my board, and later, when times got worse, fifteen shillings, and even that left me feeling richer than I've felt since. I grew another inch, my moustache began to sprout, I wore button boots and collars three inches high. In church on Sundays, in my natty dark grey suit, with my bowler hat and black dogskin gloves on the pew beside me, I looked the perfect gent, so that Mother could hardly contain her pride in me. In between work and 'walking out' on Thursdays, and thinking about clothes and girls, I had fits of ambition and saw myself developing into a Big Business Man like Lever or William Whiteley. Between sixteen and eighteen I made serious efforts to 'improve my mind' and train myself for a business career. I cured myself of dropping aitches and got rid of most of my Cockney accent. (In the Thames Valley the country accents were going out. Except for the farm lads, nearly everyone who was born later than 1890 talked Cockney.) I did a correspondence course with Littleburns' Commercial Academy, learnt book-keeping and business English, read solemnly through a book of frightful blah called *The Art of Salesmanship,* and improved my arithmetic and even my handwriting. When I was as old as seventeen I've sat up late at night with my tongue hanging out of my mouth, practising copperplate by the little oil-lamp on the bedroom table. At times I read enormously, generally crime and adventure stories, and sometimes paper-covered books which were furtively passed round by the chaps at the shop and described as 'hot'. (They were translations of Maupassant and Paul de Kock.) But when I was eighteen I suddenly turned highbrow, got a ticket for the County Library, and began to stodge through books by Marie Corelli and Hall Caine and Anthony Hope. It was at about that time that I joined the Lower Binfield Reading Circle, which was run by the vicar and met one evening a week all through the winter for what was called 'literary discussion'. Under pressure from the vicar I read bits of *Sesame and Lilies* and even had a go at Browning.

And time was slipping away. 1910, 1911, 1912. And Father's business was going down—not slumping suddenly into the gutter, but it was going down. Neither Father nor Mother was ever quite the same after Joe ran away from home. This happened not long after I went to work at Grimmett's.

Joe, at eighteen, had grown into an ugly ruffian. He was a hefty chap, much bigger than the rest of the family, with tremendous shoulders, a big head, and a sulky, lowering kind of face on which he already had a respectable moustache. When he wasn't in the tap-room of the George he was loafing in the shop doorway, with his hands dug deep into his pockets, scowling at the people who passed, except when they happened to be girls, as though he'd like to knock them down. If anyone came into the shop he'd move aside just enough to let them pass, and, without taking his hands out of his pockets, yell over his shoulders 'Da-ad! Shop!' This was as near as he ever got to helping. Father and Mother said despairingly that they 'didn't know what to do with him', and he was costing the devil of a lot with his drinking and endless smoking. Late one night he walked out of the house and was never heard of again. He'd prised open the till and taken all the money that was in it, luckily not much, about eight pounds. That was enough to get him a steerage passage to America. He'd always wanted to go to America, and I think he probably did so, though we never knew for certain. It made a bit of a scandal in the town. The official theory was that Joe had bolted because he'd put a girl in the family way. There was a girl named Sally Chivers who lived in the same street as the Simmonses and was going to have a baby, and Joe had certainly been with her, but so had about a dozen others, and nobody knew whose baby it was. Mother and Father accepted the baby theory and even, in private, used it to excuse their 'poor boy' for stealing the eight pounds and running away. They weren't capable of grasping that Joe had cleared out because he couldn't stand a decent respectable life in a little country town and wanted a life of loafing, fights, and women. We never heard of him again. Perhaps he went utterly to the bad, perhaps he was killed in the war, perhaps he merely didn't bother to write. Luckily the baby was born dead, so there were no complications. As for the fact that Joe had stolen the eight pounds, Mother and Father managed to keep it a secret till they died. In their eyes it was a much worse disgrace than Sally Chivers's baby.

The trouble over Joe aged Father a great deal. To lose Joe was merely to cut a loss, but it hurt him and made him ashamed. From that time forward his moustache was much greyer and he seemed to have grown a lot smaller. Perhaps my memory of him as a little grey man, with a round, lined, anxious face and dusty spectacles, really dates from that time. By slow degrees he was getting more and more involved in money worries and less and less interested in other things. He talked less about politics and the Sunday papers, and more about the badness of trade. Mother seemed to have shrunk a little, too. In my childhood I'd known her as something vast and overflowing, with her yellow hair and her beaming face and her enormous bosom, a sort of great opulent creature like the figure-head of a battleship. Now she'd got smaller and more anxious and older than her years. She was less lordly in the kitchen, went in more for neck of mutton, worried over the price of coal, and began to use margarine, a thing which in the old days she'd never have allowed into the house. After Joe had gone Father had to hire an errand boy again, but from then on he employed very young boys whom he only kept for a year or two and who couldn't lift heavy weights. I sometimes lent him a hand when I was at home. I was too selfish to do it regularly. I can still see him working his way slowly across the yard, bent double and almost hidden under an enormous sack, like a snail under its shell. The huge, monstrous sack, weighing a hundred and fifty pounds, I suppose, pressing his neck and shoulders almost to the ground, and the anxious, spectacled face looking up from underneath it. In 1911 he ruptured himself and had to spend weeks in hospital and hire a temporary manager for the shop, which ate another hole in his capital. A small shopkeeper going down the hill is a dreadful thing to watch, but it isn't sudden and obvious like the fate of a working man who gets the sack and promptly finds himself on the dole. It's just a gradual chipping away of trade, with little ups and downs, a few shillings to the bad here, a few sixpences to the good there. Somebody who's dealt with you for years suddenly deserts and goes to Sarazins'. Somebody else buys a dozen hens and gives you a weekly order for corn. You can still keep going. You're still 'your own master', always a little more worried and a little shabbier, with your capital shrinking all the time. You can go on like that for years, for a lifetime if you're lucky. Uncle Ezekiel died in 1911, leaving £120 which must have made a lot of difference to Father. It wasn't till 1913 that he had to mortgage his life-insurance policy. That I didn't hear about at the time, or I'd have understood what it meant. As it was I don't think I ever got further than realizing that Father 'wasn't doing well', trade was 'slack', there'd be a bit longer to wait before I had the money to 'set up'. Like Father himself, I looked on the shop as something permanent, and I was a bit inclined to be angry with him for not managing things better. I wasn't capable of seeing, and neither was he nor anyone else, that he was being slowly ruined, that his business would never pick up again and if he lived to be seventy he'd certainly end in the workhouse. Many a time I've passed Sarazins' shop in the market-place and merely thought how much I preferred their slick window-front to Father's dusty old shop, with the 'S. Bowling' which you could hardly read, the chipped white lettering, and the faded packets of bird-seed. It didn't occur to me that Sarazins' were tapeworms who were eating him alive. Sometimes I used to repeat to him some of the stuff I'd been reading in my correspondence-course textbooks, about salesmanship and modern methods. He never paid much attention. He'd inherited an old-established business, he'd always worked hard, done a fair trade, and supplied sound goods, and things would look up presently. It's a fact that very few shopkeepers in those days actually ended in the workhouse. With any luck you died with a few pounds still your own. It was a race between death and bankruptcy, and, thank God, death got Father first, and Mother too.

1911, 1912, 1913. I tell you it was a good time to be alive. It was late in 1912, through the vicar's Reading Circle, that I first met Elsie Waters. Till then, although, like all the rest of the boys in the town, I'd gone out looking for girls and occasionally managed to connect up with this girl or that and 'walk out' a few Sunday afternoons, I'd never really had a girl of my own. It's a queer business, that chasing of girls when you're about sixteen. At some recognized part of the town the boys stroll up and down in pairs, watching the girls, and the girls stroll up and down in pairs, pretending not to notice the boys, and presently some kind of contact is established and instead of twos they're trailing along in fours, all four utterly speechless. The chief feature of those walks—and it was worse the second time, when you went out with the girl alone—was the ghastly failure to make any kind of conversation. But Elsie Waters seemed different. The truth was that I was growing up.

I don't want to tell the story of myself and Elsie Waters, even if there was any story to tell. It's merely that she's part of the picture, part of 'before the war'. Before the war it was always summer—a delusion, as I've remarked before, but that's how I remember it. The white dusty road stretching out between the chestnut trees, the smell of night-stocks, the green pools under the willows, the splash of Burford Weir—that's what I see when I shut my eyes and think of 'before the war', and towards the end Elsie Waters is part of it.

I don't know whether Elsie would be considered pretty now. She was then. She was tall for a girl, about as tall as I am, with pale gold, heavy kind of hair which she wore somehow plaited and coiled round her head, and a delicate, curiously gentle face. She was one of those girls that always look their best in black, especially the very plain black dresses they made them wear in the drapery—she worked at Lilywhite's, the drapers, though she came originally from London. I suppose she would have been two years older than I was.

I'm grateful to Elsie, because she was the first person who taught me to care about a woman. I don't mean women in general, I mean an individual woman. I'd met her at the Reading Circle and hardly noticed her, and then one day I went into Lilywhite's during working hours, a thing I wouldn't normally have been able to do, but as it happened we'd run out of butter muslin and old Grimmett sent me to buy some. You know the atmosphere of a draper's shop. It's something peculiarly feminine. There's a hushed feeling, a subdued light, a cool smell of cloth, and a faint whirring from the wooden balls of change rolling to and fro. Elsie was leaning against the counter, cutting off a length of cloth with the big scissors. There was something about her black dress and the curve of her breast against the counter—I can't describe it, something curiously soft, curiously feminine. As soon as you saw her you knew that you could take her in your arms and do what you wanted with her. She was really deeply feminine, very gentle, very submissive, the kind that would always do what a man told her, though she wasn't either small or weak. She wasn't even stupid, only rather silent and, at times, dreadfully refined. But in those days I was rather refined myself.

We were living together for about a year. Of course in a town like Lower Binfield you could only live together in a figurative sense. Officially we were 'walking out', which was a recognized custom and not quite the same as being engaged. There was a road that branched off from the road to Upper Binfield and ran along under the edge of the hills. There was a long stretch of it, nearly a mile, that was quite straight and fringed with enormous horse-chestnut trees, and on the grass at the side there was a footpath under the boughs that was known as Lovers' Lane. We used to go there on the May evenings, when the chestnuts were in blossom. Then the short nights came on, and it was light for hours after we'd left the shop. You know the feeling of a June evening. The kind of blue twilight that goes on and on, and the air brushing against your face like silk. Sometimes on Sunday afternoons we went over Chamford Hill and down to the water-meadows along the Thames. 1913! My God! 1913! The stillness, the green water, the rushing of the weir! It'll never come again. I don't mean that 1913 will never come again. I mean the feeling inside you, the feeling of not being in a hurry and not being frightened, the feeling you've either had and don't need to be told about, or haven't had and won't ever have the chance to learn.

It wasn't till late summer that we began what's called living together. I'd been too shy and clumsy to begin, and too ignorant to realize that there'd been others before me. One Sunday afternoon we went into the beech woods round Upper Binfield. Up there you could always be alone. I wanted her very badly, and I knew quite well that she was only waiting for me to begin. Something, I don't know what, put it into my head to go into the grounds of Binfield House. Old Hodges, who was past seventy and getting very crusty, was capable of turning us out, but he'd probably be asleep on a Sunday afternoon. We slipped through a gap in the fence and down the footpath between the beeches to the big pool. It was four years or more since I'd been that way. Nothing had changed. Still the utter solitude, the hidden feeling with the great trees all round you, the old boat-house rotting among the bulrushes. We lay down in the little grass hollow beside the wild peppermint, and we were as much alone as if we'd been in Central Africa. I'd kissed her God knows how many times, and then I'd got up and was wandering about again. I wanted her very badly, and wanted to take the plunge, only I was half-frightened. And curiously enough there was another thought in my mind at the same time. It suddenly struck me that for years I'd meant to come back here and had never come. Now I was so near, it seemed a pity not to go down to the other pool and have a look at the big carp. I felt I'd kick myself afterwards if I missed the chance, in fact I couldn't think why I hadn't been back before. The carp were stored away in my mind, nobody knew about them except me, I was going to catch them some time. Practically they were *my* carp. I actually started wandering along the bank in that direction, and then when I'd gone about ten yards I turned back. It meant crashing your way through a kind of jungle of brambles and rotten brushwood, and I was dressed up in my Sunday best. Dark-grey suit, bowler hat, button boots, and a collar that almost cut my ears off. That was how people dressed for Sunday afternoon walks in those days. And I wanted Elsie very badly. I went back and stood over her for a moment. She was lying on the grass with her arm over her face, and she didn't stir when she heard me come. In her black dress she looked—I don't know how, kind of soft, kind of yielding, as though her body was a kind of malleable stuff that you could do what you liked with. She was mine and I could have her, this minute if I wanted to. Suddenly I stopped being frightened, I chucked my hat on to the grass (it bounced, I remember), knelt down, and took hold of her. I can smell the wild peppermint yet. It was my first time, but it wasn't hers, and we didn't make such a mess of it as you might expect. So that was that. The big carp faded out of my mind again, and in fact for years afterwards I hardly thought about them.

1913. 1914. The spring of 1914. First the blackthorn, then the hawthorn, then the chestnuts in blossom. Sunday afternoons along the towpath, and the wind rippling the beds of rushes so that they swayed all together in great thick masses and looked somehow like a woman's hair. The endless June evenings, the path under the chestnut trees, an owl hooting somewhere and Elsie's body against me. It was a hot July that year. How we sweated in the shop, and how the cheese and the ground coffee smelt! And then the cool of the evening outside, the smell of night-stocks and pipe-tobacco in the lane behind the allotments, the soft dust underfoot, and the nightjars hawking after the cockchafers.

Christ! What's the use of saying that one oughtn't to be sentimental about 'before the war'? I *am* sentimental about it. So are you if you remember it. It's quite true that if you look back on any special period of time you tend to remember the pleasant bits. That's true even of the war. But it's also true that people then had something that we haven't got now.

What? It was simply that they didn't think of the future as something to be terrified of. It isn't that life was softer then than now. Actually it was harsher. People on the whole worked harder, lived less comfortably, and died more painfully. The farm hands worked frightful hours for fourteen shillings a week and ended up as worn-out cripples with a five-shilling old-age pension and an occasional half-crown from the parish. And what was called 'respectable' poverty was even worse. When little Watson, a small draper at the other end of the High Street, 'failed' after years of struggling, his personal assets were £2 9s. 6d., and he died almost immediately of what was called 'gastric trouble', but the doctor let it out that it was starvation. Yet he'd clung to his frock coat to the last. Old Crimp, the watchmaker's assistant, a skilled workman who'd been at the job, man and boy, for fifty years, got cataract and had to go into the workhouse. His grandchildren were howling in the street when they took him away. His wife went out charing, and by desperate efforts managed to send him a shilling a week for pocket-money. You saw ghastly things happening sometimes. Small businesses sliding down the hill, solid tradesmen turning gradually into broken-down bankrupts, people dying by inches of cancer and liver disease, drunken husbands signing the pledge every Monday and breaking it every Saturday, girls ruined for life by an illegitimate baby. The houses had no bathrooms, you broke the ice in your basin on winter mornings, the back streets stank like the devil in hot weather, and the churchyard was bang in the middle of the town, so that you never went a day without remembering how you'd got to end. And yet what was it that people had in those days? A feeling of security, even when they weren't secure. More exactly, it was a feeling of continuity. All of them knew they'd got to die, and I suppose a few of them knew they were going to go bankrupt, but what they didn't know was that the order of things could change. Whatever might happen to themselves, things would go on as they'd known them. I don't believe it made very much difference that what's called religious belief was still prevalent in those days. It's true that nearly everyone went to church, at any rate in the country—Elsie and I still went to church as a matter of course, even when we were living in what the vicar would have called sin—and if you asked people whether they believed in a life after death they generally answered that they did. But I've never met anyone who gave me the impression of really believing in a future life. I think that, at most, people believe in that kind of thing in the same way as kids believe in Father Christmas. But it's precisely in a settled period, a period when civilization seems to stand on its four legs like an elephant, that such things as a future life don't matter. It's easy enough to die if the things you care about are going to survive. You've had your life, you're getting tired, it's time to go underground—that's how people used to see it. Individually they were finished, but their way of life would continue. Their good and evil would remain good and evil. They didn't feel the ground they stood on shifting under their feet.

Father was failing, and he didn't know it. It was merely that times were very bad, trade seemed to dwindle and dwindle, his bills were harder and harder to meet. Thank God, he never even knew that he was ruined, never actually went bankrupt, because he died very suddenly (it was influenza that turned into pneumonia) at the beginning of 1915. To the end he believed that with thrift, hard work, and fair dealing a man can't go wrong. There must have been plenty of small shopkeepers who carried that belief not merely on to bankrupt deathbeds but even into the workhouse. Even Lovegrove the saddler, with cars and motor-vans staring him in the face, didn't realize that he was as out of date as the rhinoceros. And Mother too—Mother never lived to know that the life she'd been brought up to, the life of a decent God-fearing shopkeeper's daughter and a decent God-fearing shopkeeper's wife in the reign of good Queen Vic, was finished for ever. Times were difficult and trade was bad, Father was worried and this and that was 'aggravating', but you carried on much the same as usual. The old English order of life couldn't change. For ever and ever decent God-fearing women would cook Yorkshire pudding and apple dumplings on enormous coal ranges, wear woollen underclothes and sleep on feathers, make plum jam in July and pickles in October, and read *Hilda's Home Companion* in the afternoons, with the flies buzzing round, in a sort of cosy little underworld of stewed tea, bad legs, and happy endings. I don't say that either Father or Mother was quite the same to the end. They were a bit shaken, and sometimes a little dispirited. But at least they never lived to know that everything they'd believed in was just so much junk. They lived at the end of an epoch, when everything was dissolving into a sort of ghastly flux, and they didn't know it. They thought it was eternity. You couldn't blame them. That was what it felt like.

Then came the end of July, and even Lower Binfield grasped that things were happening. For days there was tremendous vague excitement and endless leading articles in the papers, which Father actually brought in from the shop to read aloud to Mother. And then suddenly the posters everywhere:

GERMAN ULTIMATUM. FRANCE
MOBILIZING

For several days (four days, wasn't it? I forget the exact dates) there was a strange stifled feeling, a kind of waiting hush, Like the moment before a thunderstorm breaks, as though the whole of England was silent and listening. It was very hot, I remember. In the shop it was as though we couldn't work, though already everyone in the neighbourhood who had five bob to spare was rushing in to buy quantities of tinned stuff and flour and oatmeal. It was as if we were too feverish to work, we only sweated and waited. In the evenings people went down to the railway station and fought like devils over the evening papers which arrived on the London train. And then one afternoon a boy came rushing down the High Street with an armful of papers, and people were coming into their doorways to shout across the street. Everyone was shouting 'We've come in! We've come in!' The boy grabbed a poster from his bundle and stuck it on the shop-front opposite:

## ENGLAND DECLARES WAR ON
GERMANY

We rushed out on to the pavement, all three assistants, and cheered. Everybody was cheering. Yes, cheering. But old Grimmett, though he'd already done pretty well out of the war-scare, still held on to a little of his Liberal principles, 'didn't hold' with the war, and said it would be a bad business.

Two months later I was in the Army. Seven months later I was in France.

# 8

I wasn't wounded till late in 1916.

We'd just come out of the trenches and were marching over a bit of road a mile or so back which was supposed to be safe, but which the Germans must have got the range of some time earlier. Suddenly they started putting a few shells over—it was heavy H.E. stuff, and they were only firing about one a minute. There was the usual zwee-e-e-e! and then BOOM! in a field somewhere over to the right. I think it was the third shell that got me. I knew as soon as I heard it coming that it had my name written on it. They say you always know. It didn't say what an ordinary shell says. It said 'I'm after you, you b—, *you, you* b—, YOU!'—all this in the space of about three seconds. And the last YOU was the explosion.

I felt as if an enormous hand made of air were sweeping me along. And presently I came down with a sort of burst, shattered feeling among a lot of old tin cans, splinters of wood, rusty barbed wire, turds, empty cartridge cases, and other muck in the ditch at the side of the road. When they'd hauled me out and cleaned some of the dirt off me they found that I wasn't very badly hurt. It was only a lot of small shell-splinters that had lodged in one side of my bottom and down the backs of my legs. But luckily I'd broken a rib in falling, which made it just bad enough to get me back to England. I spent that winter in a hospital camp on the downs near Eastbourne.

Do you remember those war-time hospital camps? The long rows of wooden huts like chicken-houses stuck right on top of those beastly icy downs—the 'south coast', people used to call it, which made me wonder what the north coast could be like—where the wind seems to blow at you from all directions at once. And the droves of blokes in their pale-blue flannel suits and red ties, wandering up and down looking for a place out of the wind and never finding one. Sometimes the kids from the slap-up boys' schools in Eastbourne used to be led round in crocodiles to hand out fags and peppermint creams to the 'wounded Tommies', as they called us. A pink-faced kid of about eight would walk up to a knot of wounded men sitting on the grass, split open a packet of Woodbines and solemnly hand one fag to each man, just like feeding the monkeys at the zoo. Anyone who was strong enough used to wander for miles over the downs in hopes of meeting girls. There were never enough girls to go round. In the valley below the camp there was a bit of a spinney, and long before dusk you'd see a couple glued against every tree, and sometimes, if it happened to be a thick tree, one on each side of it. My chief memory of that time is sitting against a gorse-bush in the freezing wind, with my fingers so cold I couldn't bend them and the taste of a peppermint cream in my mouth. That's a typical soldier's memory. But I was getting away from a Tommy's life, all the same. The C.O. had sent my name in for a commission a little before I was wounded. By this time they were desperate for officers and anyone who wasn't actually illiterate could have a commission if he wanted one. I went straight from the hospital to an officers' training camp near Colchester.

It's very strange, the things the war did to people. It was less than three years since I'd been a spry young shop-assistant, bending over the counter in my white apron with 'Yes, madam! Certainly, madam! *And* the next order, madam?' with a grocer's life ahead of me and about as much notion of becoming an Army officer as of getting a knighthood. And here I was already, swaggering about in a gorblimey hat and a yellow collar and more or less keeping my end up among a crowd of other temporary gents and some who weren't even temporary. And—this is really the point—not feeling it in any way strange. Nothing seemed strange in those days.

It was like an enormous machine that had got hold of you. You'd no sense of acting of your own free will, and at the same time no notion of trying to resist. If people didn't have some such feeling as that, no war could last three months. The armies would just pack up and go home. Why had I joined the Army? Or the million other idiots who joined up before conscription came in? Partly for a lark and partly because of England my England and Britons never never and all that stuff. But how long did that last? Most of the chaps I knew had forgotten all about it long before they got as far as France. The men in the trenches weren't patriotic, didn't hate the Kaiser, didn't care a damn about gallant little Belgium and the Germans raping nuns on tables (it was always 'on tables', as though that made it worse) in the streets of Brussels. On the other hand it didn't occur to them to try and escape. The machine had got hold of you and it could do what it liked with you. It lifted you up and dumped you down among places and things you'd never dreamed of, and if it had dumped you down on the surface of the moon it wouldn't have seemed particularly strange. The day I joined the Army the old life was finished. It was as though it didn't concern me any longer. I wonder if you'd believe that from that day forward I only once went back to Lower Binfield, and that was to Mother's funeral? It sounds incredible now, but it seemed natural enough at the time. Partly, I admit, it was on account of Elsie, whom, of course, I'd stopped writing to after two or three months. No doubt she'd picked up with someone else, but I didn't want to meet her. Otherwise, perhaps, when I got a bit of leave I'd have gone down and seen Mother, who'd had fits when I joined the Army but would have been proud of a son in uniform.

Father died in 1915. I was in France at the time. I don't exaggerate when I say that Father's death hurts me more now than it did then. At the time it was just a bit of bad news which I accepted almost without interest, in the sort of empty-headed apathetic way in which one accepted everything in the trenches. I remember crawling into the doorway of the dugout to get enough light to read the letter, and I remember Mother's tear-stains on the letter, and the aching feeling in my knees and the smell of mud. Father's life-insurance policy had been mortgaged for most of its value, but there was a little money in the bank and Sarazins' were going to buy up the stock and even pay some tiny amount for the good-will. Anyway, Mother had a bit over two hundred pounds, besides the furniture. She went for the time being to lodge with her cousin, the wife of a small-holder who was doing pretty well out of the war, near Doxley, a few miles the other side of Walton. It was only 'for the time being'. There was a temporary feeling about everything. In the old days, which as a matter of fact were barely a year old, the whole thing would have been an appalling disaster. With Father dead, the shop sold and Mother with two hundred pounds in the world, you'd have seen stretching out in front of you a kind of fifteen-act tragedy, the last act being a pauper's funeral. But now the war and the feeling of not being one's own master overshadowed everything. People hardly thought in terms of things like bankruptcy and the workhouse any longer. This was the case even with Mother, who, God knows, had only very dim notions about the war. Besides, she was already dying, though neither of us knew it.

She came across to see me in the hospital at Eastbourne. It was over two years since I'd seen her, and her appearance gave me a bit of a shock. She seemed to have faded and somehow to have shrunken. Partly it was because by this time I was grown-up, I'd travelled, and everything looked smaller to me, but there was no question that she'd got thinner, and also yellower. She talked in the old rambling way about Aunt Martha (that was the cousin she was staying with), and the changes in Lower Binfield since the war, and all the boys who'd 'gone' (meaning joined the Army), and her indigestion which was 'aggravating', and poor Father's tombstone and what a lovely corpse he made. It was the old talk, the talk I'd listened to for years, and yet somehow it was like a ghost talking. It didn't concern me any longer. I'd known her as a great splendid protecting kind of creature, a bit like a ship's figure-head and a bit like a broody hen, and after all she was only a little old woman in a black dress. Everything was changing and fading. That was the last time I saw her alive. I got the wire saying she was seriously ill when I was at the training school at Colchester, and put in for a week's urgent leave immediately. But it was too late. She was dead by the time I got to Doxley. What she and everyone else had imagined to be indigestion was some kind of internal growth, and a sudden chill on the stomach put the final touch. The doctor tried to cheer me up by telling me that the growth was 'benevolent', which struck me as a queer thing to call it, seeing that it had killed her.

Well, we buried her next to Father, and that was my last glimpse of Lower Binfield. It had changed a lot, even in three years. Some of the shops were shut, some had different names over them. Nearly all the men I'd known as boys were gone, and some of them were dead. Sid Lovegrove was dead, killed on the Somme. Ginger Watson, the farm lad who'd belonged to the Black Hand years ago, the one who used to catch rabbits alive, was dead in Egypt. One of the chaps who'd worked with me at Grimmett's had lost both legs. Old Lovegrove had shut up his shop and was living in a cottage near Walton on a tiny annuity.

Old Grimmett, on the other hand, was doing well out of the war and had turned patriotic and was a member of the local board which tried conscientious objectors. The thing which more than anything else gave the town an empty, forlorn kind of look was that there were practically no horses left. Every horse worth taking had been commandeered long ago. The station fly still existed, but the brute that pulled it wouldn't have been able to stand up if it hadn't been for the shafts. For the hour or so that I was there before the funeral I wandered round the town, saying how d'you do to people and showing off my uniform. Luckily I didn't run into Elsie. I saw all the changes, and yet it was as though I didn't see them. My mind was on other things, chiefly the pleasure of being seen in my second-loot's uniform, with my black armlet (a thing which looks rather smart on khaki) and my new whipcord breeches. I distinctly remember that I was still thinking about those whipcord breeches when we stood at the graveside. And then they chucked some earth on to the coffin and I suddenly realized what it means for your mother to be lying with seven feet of earth on top of her, and something kind of twitched behind my eyes and nose, but even then the whipcord breeches weren't altogether out of my mind.

Don't think I didn't feel for Mother's death. I did. I wasn't in the trenches any longer, I could feel sorry for a death. But the thing I didn't care a damn about, didn't even grasp to be happening, was the passing-away of the old life I'd known. After the funeral, Aunt Martha, who was rather proud of having a 'real officer' for a nephew and would have made a splash of the funeral if I'd let her, went back to Doxley on the bus and I took the fly down to the station, to get the train to London and then to Colchester. We drove past the shop. No one had taken it since Father died. It was shut up and the window-pane was black with dust, and they'd burned the 'S. Bowling' off the signboard with a plumber's blowflame. Well, there was the house where I'd been a child and a boy and a young man, where I'd crawled about the kitchen floor and smelt the sainfoin and read 'Donovan the Dauntless', where I'd done my homework for the Grammar School, mixed bread paste, mended bicycle punctures, and tried on my first high collar. It had been as permanent to me as the Pyramids, and now it would be just an accident if I ever set foot in it again. Father, Mother, Joe, the errand boys, old Nailer the terrier, Spot, the one that came after Nailer, Jackie the bullfinch, the cats, the mice in the loft—all gone, nothing left but dust. And I didn't care a damn. I was sorry Mother was dead, I was even sorry Father was dead, but all the time my mind was on other things. I was a bit proud of being seen riding in a cab, a thing I hadn't yet got used to, and I was thinking of the sit of my new whipcord breeches, and my nice smooth officer's putties, so different from the gritty stuff the Tommies had to wear, and of the other chaps at Colchester and the sixty quid Mother had left and the beanos we'd have with it. Also I was thanking God that I hadn't happened to run into Elsie.

The war did extraordinary things to people. And what was more extraordinary than the way it killed people was the way it sometimes didn't kill them. It was like a great flood rushing you along to death, and suddenly it would shoot you up some backwater where you'd find yourself doing incredible and pointless things and drawing extra pay for them. There were labour battalions making roads across the desert that didn't lead anywhere, there were chaps marooned on oceanic islands to look out for German cruisers which had been sunk years earlier, there were Ministries of this and that with armies of clerks and typists which went on existing years after their function had ended, by a kind of inertia. People were shoved into meaningless jobs and then forgotten by the authorities for years on end. This was what happened to myself, or very likely I wouldn't be here. The whole sequence of events is rather interesting.

A little while after I was gazetted there was a call for officers of the A.S.C. As soon as the O.C. of the training camp heard that I knew something about the grocery trade (I didn't let on that I'd actually been behind the counter) he told me to send my name in. That went through all right, and I was just about to leave for another training-school for A.S.C. officers somewhere in the Midlands when there was a demand for a young officer, with knowledge of the grocery trade, to act as some kind of secretary to Sir Joseph Cheam, who was a big noise in the A.S.C. God knows why they picked me out, but at any rate they did so. I've since thought that they probably mixed my name up with somebody else's. Three days later I was saluting in Sir Joseph's office. He was a lean, upright, rather handsome old boy with grizzled hair and a grave-looking nose which immediately impressed me. He looked the perfect professional soldier, the K.C.M.G., D.S.O. with bar type, and might have been twin brother to the chap in the De Reszke advert, though in private life he was chairman of one of the big chain groceries and famous all over the world for something called the Cheam Wage-Cut System. He stopped writing as I came in and looked me over.

'You a gentleman?'

'No, sir.'

'Good. Then perhaps we'll get some work done.'

In about three minutes he'd wormed out of me that I had no secretarial experience, didn't know shorthand, couldn't use a typewriter, and had worked in a grocery at twenty-eight shillings a week. However, he said that I'd do, there were too many gentlemen in this damned Army and he'd been looking for somebody who could count beyond ten. I liked him and looked forward to working for him, but just at this moment the mysterious powers that seemed to be running the war drove us apart again. Something called the West Coast Defence Force was being formed, or rather was being talked about, and there was some vague idea of establishing dumps of rations and other stores at various points along the coast. Sir Joseph was supposed to be responsible for the dumps in the south-west corner of England. The day after I joined his office he sent me down to check over the stores at a place called Twelve Mile Dump, on the North Cornish Coast. Or rather my job was to find out whether any stores existed. Nobody seemed certain about this. I'd just got there and discovered that the stores consisted of eleven tins of bully beef when a wire arrived from the War Office telling me to take charge of the stores at Twelve

Mile Dump and remain there till further notice. I wired back 'No stores at
Twelve Mile Dump.' Too late. Next day came the official letter informing me
that I was O.C. Twelve Mile Dump. And that's really the end of the story. I
remained O.C. Twelve Mile Dump for the rest of the war.

God knows what it was all about. It's no use asking me what the West Coast
Defence Force was or what it was supposed to do. Even at that time nobody
pretended to know. In any case it didn't exist. It was just a scheme that had
floated through somebody's mind–following on some vague rumour of a
German invasion via Ireland, I suppose–and the food dumps which were
supposed to exist all along the coast were also imaginary. The whole thing had
existed for about three days, like a sort of bubble, and then had been forgotten,
and I'd been forgotten with it. My eleven tins of bully beef had been left
behind by some officers who had been there earlier on some other mysterious
mission. They'd also left behind a very deaf old man called Private Lidgebird.
What Lidgebird was supposed to be doing there I never discovered. I wonder
whether you'll believe that I remained guarding those eleven tins of bully beef
from half-way through 1917 to the beginning of 1919? Probably you won't, but
it's the truth. And at the time even that didn't seem particularly strange. By
1918 one had simply got out of the habit of expecting things to happen in a
reasonable manner.

Once a month they sent me an enormous official form calling upon me to
state the number and condition of pick-axes, entrenching tools, coils of barbed
wire, blankets, waterproof groundsheets, first-aid outfits, sheets of corrugated
iron, and tins of plum and apple jam under my care. I just entered 'nil' against
everything and sent the form back. Nothing ever happened. Up in London
someone was quietly filing the forms, and sending out more forms, and filing
those, and so on. It was the way things were happening. The mysterious
higher-ups who were running the war had forgotten my existence. I didn't jog
their memory. I was up a backwater that didn't lead anywhere, and after two
years in France I wasn't so burning with patriotism that I wanted to get out of
it.

It was a lonely part of the coast where you never saw a soul except a few
yokels who'd barely heard there was a war on. A quarter of a mile away, down a
little hill, the sea boomed and surged over enormous flats of sand. Nine months
of the year it rained, and the other three a raging wind blew off the Atlantic.
There was nothing there except Private Lidgebird, myself, two Army
huts–one of them a decentish two-roomed hut which I inhabited–and the
eleven tins of bully beef. Lidgebird was a surly old devil and I could never get
much out of him except the fact that he'd been a market gardener before he
joined the Army. It was interesting to see how rapidly he was reverting to type.
Even before I got to Twelve Mile Dump he'd dug a patch round one of the
huts and started planting spuds, in the autumn he dug another patch till he'd
got about half an acre under cultivation, at the beginning of 1918 he started
keeping hens which had got to quite a number by the end of the summer, and
towards the end of the year he suddenly produced a pig from God knows
where. I don't think it crossed his mind to wonder what the devil we were

doing there, or what the West Coast Defence Force was and whether it actually existed. It wouldn't surprise me to hear that he's there still, raising pigs and potatoes on the spot where Twelve Mile Dump used to be. I hope he is. Good luck to him.

Meanwhile I was doing something I'd never before had the chance to do as a full-time job—reading.

The officers who'd been there before had left a few books behind, mostly sevenpenny editions and nearly all of them the kind of tripe that people were reading in those days. Ian Hay and Sapper and the Craig Kennedy stories and so forth. But at some time or other somebody had been there who knew what books are worth reading and what are not. I myself, at the time, didn't know anything of the kind. The only books I'd ever voluntarily read were detective stories and once in a way a smutty sex book. God knows I don't set up to be a highbrow even now, but if you'd asked me *then* for the name of a 'good' book I'd have answered *The Woman Thou Gavest Me,* or (in memory of the vicar) *Sesame and Lilies*. In any case a 'good' book was a book one didn't have any intention of reading. But there I was, in a job where there was less than nothing to do, with the sea booming on the beach and the rain streaming down the window-panes—and a whole row of books staring me in the face on the temporary shelf someone had rigged up against the wall of the hut. Naturally I started to read them from end to end, with, at the beginning, about as much attempt to discriminate as a pig working its way through a pail of garbage.

But in among them there were three or four books that were different from the others. No, you've got it wrong! Don't run away with the idea that I suddenly discovered Marcel Proust or Henry James or somebody. I wouldn't have read them even if I had. These books I'm speaking of weren't in the least highbrow. But now and again it so happens that you strike a book which is exactly at the mental level you've reached at the moment, so much so that it seems to have been written especially for you. One of them was H. G. Wells's *The History of Mr Polly,* in a cheap shilling edition which was falling to pieces. I wonder if you can imagine the effect it had upon me, to be brought up as I'd been brought up, the son of a shopkeeper in a country town, and then to come across a book like that? Another was Compton Mackenzie's *Sinister Street*. It had been the scandal of the season a few years back, and I'd even heard vague rumours of it in Lower Binfield. Another was Conrad's *Victory,* parts of which bored me. But books like that started you thinking. And there was a back number of some magazine with a blue cover which had a short story of D. H. Lawrence's in it. I don't remember the name of it. It was a story about a German conscript who shoves his sergeant-major over the edge of a fortification and then does a bunk and gets caught in his girl's bedroom. It puzzled me a lot. I couldn't make out what it was all about, and yet it left me with a vague feeling that I'd like to read some others like it.

Well, for several months I had an appetite for books that was almost like physical thirst. It was the first real go-in at reading that I'd had since my Dick Donovan days. At the beginning I had no idea how to set about getting hold of books. I thought the only way was to buy them. That's interesting, I think. It shows you the difference upbringing makes. I suppose the children of the middle classes, the £500 a year middle classes, know all about Mudie's and the Times Book Club when they're in their cradles. A bit later I learned of the existence of lending libraries and took out a subscription at Mudie's and another at a library in Bristol. And what I read during the next year or so! Wells, Conrad, Kipling, Galsworthy, Barry Pain, W. W. Jacobs, Pett Ridge, Oliver Onions, Compton Mackenzie, H. Seton Merriman, Maurice Baring, Stephen McKenna, May Sinclair, Arnold Bennett, Anthony Hope, Elinor Glyn, O. Henry, Stephen Leacock, and even Silas Hocking and Jean Stratton Porter. How many of the names in that list are known to you, I wonder? Half the books that people took seriously in those days are forgotten now. But at the beginning I swallowed them all down like a whale that's got in among a shoal of shrimps. I just revelled in them. After a bit, of course, I grew more highbrow and began to distinguish between tripe and not-tripe. I got hold of Lawrence's *Sons and Lovers* and sort of half-enjoyed it, and I got a lot of kick out of Oscar Wilde's *Dorian Gray* and Stevenson's *New Arabian Nights*. Wells was the author who made the biggest impression on me. I read George Moore's *Esther Waters* and liked it, and I tried several of Hardy's novels and always got stuck about half-way through. I even had a go at Ibsen, who left me with a vague impression that in Norway it's always raining.

It was queer, really. Even at the time it struck me as queer. I was a second-loot with hardly any Cockney accent left, I could already distinguish between Arnold Bennett and Elinor Glyn, and yet it was only four years since I'd been slicing cheese behind the counter in my white apron and looking forward to the days when I'd be a master-grocer. If I tot up the account, I suppose I must admit that the war did me good as well as harm. At any rate that year of reading novels was the only real education, in the sense of book-learning, that I've ever had. It did certain things to my mind. It gave me an attitude, a kind of questioning attitude, which I probably wouldn't have had if I'd gone through life in a normal sensible way. But—I wonder if you can understand this—the thing that really changed me, really made an impression on me, wasn't so much the books I read as the rotten meaninglessness of the life I was leading.

It really was unspeakably meaningless, that time in 1918. Here I was, sitting beside the stove in an Army hut, reading novels, and a few hundred miles away in France the guns were roaring and droves of wretched children, wetting their bags with fright, were being driven into the machine-gun barrage like you'd shoot small coke into a furnace. I was one of the lucky ones. The higher-ups had taken their eye off me, and here I was in a snug little bolt-hole, drawing pay for a job that didn't exist. At times I got into a panic and made sure they'd remember about me and dig me out, but it never happened. The official forms, on gritty grey paper, came in once a month, and I filled them up and sent them back, and more forms came in, and I filled them up and sent them back, and so it went on. The whole thing had about as much sense in it as a lunatic's dream. The effect of all this, plus the books I was reading, was to leave me with a feeling of disbelief in everything.

I wasn't the only one. The war was full of loose ends and forgotten corners.

By this time literally millions of people were stuck up backwaters of one kind and another. Whole armies were rotting away on fronts that people had forgotten the names of. There were huge Ministries with hordes of clerks and typists all drawing two pounds a week and upwards for piling up mounds of paper. Moreover they knew perfectly well that all they were doing was to pile up mounds of paper. Nobody believed the atrocity stories and the gallant little Belgium stuff any longer. The soldiers thought the Germans were good fellows and hated the French like poison. Every junior officer looked on the General Staff as mental defectives. A sort of wave of disbelief was moving across England, and it even got as far as Twelve Mile Dump. It would be an exaggeration to say that the war turned people into highbrows, but it did turn them into nihilists for the time being. People who in a normal way would have gone through life with about as much tendency to think for themselves as a suet pudding were turned into Bolshies just by the war. What should I be now if it hadn't been for the war? I don't know, but something different from what I am. If the war didn't happen to kill you it was bound to start you thinking. After that unspeakable idiotic mess you couldn't go on regarding society as something eternal and unquestionable, like a pyramid. You knew it was just a balls-up.

# 9

The war had jerked me out of the old life I'd known, but in the queer period that came afterwards I forgot it almost completely.

I know that in a sense one never forgets anything. You remember that piece of orange-peel you saw in the gutter thirteen years ago, and that coloured poster of Torquay that you once got a glimpse of in a railway waiting-room. But I'm speaking of a different kind of memory. In a sense I remembered the old life in Lower Binfield. I remembered my fishing-rod and the smell of sainfoin and Mother behind the brown teapot and Jackie the bullfinch and the horse-trough in the market-place. But none of it was alive in my mind any longer. It was something far away, something that I'd finished with. It would never have occurred to me that some day I might want to go back to it.

It was a queer time, those years just after the war, almost queerer than the war itself, though people don't remember it so vividly. In a rather different form the sense of disbelieving in everything was stronger than ever. Millions of men had suddenly been kicked out of the Army to find that the country they'd fought for didn't want them, and Lloyd George and his pals were giving the works to any illusions that still existed. Bands of ex-service men marched up and down rattling collection boxes, masked women were singing in the streets, and chaps in officers' tunics were grinding barrel-organs. Everybody in

England seemed to be scrambling for jobs, myself included. But I came off luckier than most. I got a small wound-gratuity, and what with that and the bit of money I'd put aside during the last year of war (not having had much opportunity to spend it), I came out of the Army with no less than three hundred and fifty quid. It's rather interesting, I think, to notice my reaction. Here I was, with quite enough money to do the thing I'd been brought up to do and the thing I'd dreamed of for years—that is, start a shop. I had plenty of capital. If you bide your time and keep your eyes open you can run across quite nice little businesses for three hundred and fifty quid. And yet, if you'll believe me, the idea never occurred to me. I not only didn't make any move towards starting a shop, but it wasn't till years later, about 1925 in fact, that it even crossed my mind that I might have done so. The fact was that I'd passed right out of the shopkeeping orbit. That was what the Army did to you. It turned you into an imitation gentleman and gave you a fixed idea that there'd always be a bit of money coming from somewhere. If you'd suggested to me then, in 1919, that I ought to start a shop—a tobacco and sweet shop, say, or a general store in some god-forsaken village—I'd just have laughed. I'd worn pips on my shoulder, and my social standards had risen. At the same time I didn't share the delusion, which was pretty common among ex-officers, that I could spend the rest of my life drinking pink gin. I knew I'd got to have a job. And the job, of course, would be 'in business'—just what kind of job I didn't know, but something high-up and important, something with a car and a telephone and if possible a secretary with a permanent wave. During the last year or so of war a lot of us had had visions like that. The chap who'd been a shop walker saw himself as a travelling salesman, and the chap who'd been a travelling salesman saw himself as a managing director. It was the effect of Army life, the effect of wearing pips and having a cheque-book and calling the evening meal dinner. All the while there'd been an idea floating round—and this applied to the men in the ranks as well as the officers—that when we came out of the Army there'd be jobs waiting for us that would bring in at least as much as our Army pay. Of course, if ideas like that didn't circulate, no war would ever be fought.

Well, I didn't get that job. It seemed that nobody was anxious to pay me £2,000 a year for sitting among streamlined office furniture and dictating letters to a platinum blonde. I was discovering what three-quarters of the blokes who'd been officers were discovering—that from a financial point of view we'd been better off in the Army than we were ever likely to be again. We'd suddenly changed from gentlemen holding His Majesty's commission into miserable out-of-works whom nobody wanted. My ideas soon sank from two thousand a year to three or four pounds a week. But even jobs of the three or four pounds a week kind didn't seem to exist. Every mortal job was filled already, either by men who'd been a few years too old to fight, or by boys who'd been a few months too young. The poor bastards who'd happened to be born between 1890 and 1900 were left out in the cold. And still it never occurred to me to go back to the grocering business. Probably I could have got a job as a grocer's assistant; old Grimmett, if he was still alive and in business (I wasn't in touch with Lower Binfield and didn't know), would have given me good refs. But I'd passed into a different orbit. Even if my social ideas hadn't risen, I could hardly have imagined, after what I'd seen and learned, going back to the old safe existence behind the counter. I wanted to be travelling about and pulling down the big dough. Chiefly I wanted to be a travelling salesman, which I knew would suit me.

But there were no jobs for travelling salesmen—that's to say, jobs with a salary attached. What there were, however, were on-commission jobs. That racket was just beginning on a big scale. It's a beautifully simple method of increasing your sales and advertising your stuff without taking any risks, and it always flourishes when times are bad. They keep you on a string by hinting that perhaps there'll be a salaried job going in three months' time, and when you get fed up there's always some other poor devil ready to take over. Naturally it wasn't long before I had an on-commission job, in fact I had quite a number in rapid succession. Thank God, I never came down to peddling vacuum-cleaners, or dictionaries. But I travelled in cutlery, in soap-powder, in a line of patent corkscrews, tin-openers, and similar gadgets, and finally in a line of office accessories—paper-clips, carbon paper, typewriter ribbons, and so forth. I didn't do so badly either. I'm the type that *can* sell things on commission. I've got the temperament and I've got the manner. But I never came anywhere near making a decent living. You can't, in jobs like that—and, of course, you aren't meant to.

I had about a year of it altogether. It was a queer time. The cross-country journeys, the godless places you fetched up in, suburbs of Midland towns that you'd never hear of in a hundred normal lifetimes. The ghastly bed-and-breakfast houses where the sheets always smell faintly of slops and the fried egg at breakfast has a yolk paler than a lemon. And the other poor devils of salesmen that you're always meeting, middle-aged fathers of families in moth-eaten overcoats and bowler hats, who honestly believe that sooner or later trade will turn the corner and they'll jack their earnings up to five quid a week. And the traipsing from shop to shop, and the arguments with shopkeepers who don't want to listen, and the standing back and making yourself small when a customer comes in. Don't think that it worried me particularly. To some chaps that kind of life is torture. There are chaps who can't even walk into a shop and open their bag of samples without screwing themselves up as though they were going over the top. But I'm not like that. I'm tough, I can talk people into buying things they don't want, and even if they slam the door in my face it doesn't bother me. Selling things on commission is actually what I like doing, provided I can see my way to making a bit of dough out of it. I don't know whether I learned much in that year, but I unlearned a good deal. It knocked the Army nonsense out of me, and it drove into the back of my head the notions that I'd picked up during the idle year when I was reading novels. I don't think I read a single book, barring detective stories, all the time I was on the road. I wasn't a highbrow any longer. I was down among the realities of modern life. And what are the realities of modern life? Well, the chief one is an everlasting, frantic struggle to sell things. With most people it takes the form of selling themselves—that's to say, getting a job and keeping it. I suppose there hasn't

been a single month since the war, in any trade you care to name, in which
there weren't more men than jobs. It's brought a peculiar, ghastly feeling into
life. It's like on a sinking ship when there are nineteen survivors and fourteen
lifebelts. But is there anything particularly modern in that, you say? Has it
anything to do with the war? Well, it feels as if it had. That feeling that you've
got to be everlastingly fighting and hustling, that you'll never get anything
unless you grab it from somebody else, that there's always somebody after
your job, the next month or the month after they'll be reducing staff and
it's you that'll get the bird—*that*, I swear, didn't exist in the old life before the
war.

But meanwhile I wasn't badly off. I was earning a bit and I'd still got plenty
of money in the bank, nearly two hundred quid, and I wasn't frightened for the
future. I knew that sooner or later I'd get a regular job. And sure enough, after
about a year, by a stroke of luck it happened. I say by a stroke of luck, but the
fact is that I was bound to fall on my feet. I'm not the type that starves. I'm
about as likely to end up in the workhouse as to end up in the House of Lords.
I'm the middling type, the type that gravitates by a kind of natural law towards
the five-pound-a-week level. So long as there are any jobs at all I'll back myself
to get one.

It happened when I was peddling paper-clips and typewriter ribbons. I'd
just dodged into a huge block of offices in Fleet Street, a building which
canvassers weren't allowed into, as a matter of fact, but I'd managed to give the
lift attendant the impression that my bag of samples was merely an attaché
case. I was walking along one of the corridors looking for the offices of a small
toothpaste firm that I'd been recommended to try, when I saw that some very
big bug was coming down the corridor in the other direction. I knew
immediately that it was a big bug. You know how it is with these big business
men, they seem to take up more room and walk more loudly than any ordinary
person, and they give off a kind of wave of money that you can feel fifty yards
away. When he got nearly up to me I saw that it was Sir Joseph Cheam. He was
in civvies, of course, but I had no difficulty in recognizing him. I suppose he'd
been there for some business conference or other. A couple of clerks, or
secretaries, or something, were following after him, not actually holding up his
train, because he wasn't wearing one, but you somehow felt that that was what
they were doing. Of course I dodged aside instantly. But curiously enough he
recognized me, though he hadn't seen me for years. To my surprise he stopped
and spoke to me.

'Hullo, you! I've seen you somewhere before. What's your name? It's on the
tip of my tongue.'

'Bowling, sir. Used to be in the A.S.C.'

'Of course. The boy that said he wasn't a gentleman. What are you doing
here?'

I might have told him I was selling typewriter ribbons, and there perhaps
the whole thing would have ended. But I had one of those sudden inspirations
that you get occasionally—a feeling that I might make something out of this if I
handled it properly. I said instead:

'Well, sir, as a matter of fact I'm looking for a job.'

'A job, eh? Hm. Not so easy, nowadays.'

He looked me up and down for a second. The two train-bearers had kind of wafted themselves a little distance away. I saw his rather good-looking old face, with the heavy grey eyebrows and the intelligent nose, looking me over and realized that he'd decided to help me. It's queer, the power of these rich men. He'd been marching past me in his power and glory, with his underlings after him, and then on some whim or other he'd turned aside like an emperor suddenly chucking a coin to a beggar.

'So you want a job? What can you do?'

Again the inspiration. No use, with a bloke like this, cracking up your own merits. Stick to the truth. I said: 'Nothing, sir. But I want a job as a travelling salesman.'

'Salesman? Hm. Not sure that I've got anything for you at present. Let's see.'

He pursed his lips up. For a moment, half a minute perhaps, he was thinking quite deeply. It was curious. Even at the time I realized that it was curious. This important old bloke, who was probably worth at least half a million, was actually taking thought on my behalf. I'd deflected him from his path and wasted at least three minutes of his time, all because of a chance remark I'd happened to make years earlier. I'd stuck in his memory and therefore he was willing to take the tiny bit of trouble that was needed to find me a job. I dare say the same day he gave twenty clerks the sack. Finally he said:

'How'd you like to go into an insurance firm? Always fairly safe, you know. People have got to have insurance, same as they've got to eat.'

Of course I jumped at the idea of going into an insurance firm. Sir Joseph was 'interested' in the Flying Salamander. God knows how many companies he was 'interested' in. One of the underlings wafted himself forward with a scribbling-pad, and there and then, with the gold stylo out of his waistcoat pocket, Sir Joseph scribbled me a note to some higher-up in the Flying Salamander. Then I thanked him, and he marched on, and I sneaked off in the other direction, and we never saw one another again.

Well, I got the job, and, as I said earlier, the job got me. I've been with the Flying Salamander close on eighteen years. I started off in the office, but now I'm what's known as an Inspector, or, when there's reason to sound particularly impressive, a Representative. A couple of days a week I'm working in the district office, and the rest of the time I'm travelling around, interviewing clients whose names have been sent in by the local agents, making assessments of shops and other property, and now and again snapping up a few orders on my own account. I earn round about seven quid a week. And properly speaking that's the end of my story.

When I look back I realize that my active life, if I ever had one, ended when I was sixteen. Everything that really matters to me had happened before that date. But in a manner of speaking things were still happening–the war, for instance–up to the time when I got the job with the Flying Salamander. After that–well, they say that happy people have no histories, and neither do the blokes who work in insurance offices. From that day forward there was nothing in my life that you could properly describe as an event, except that about two and a half years later, at the beginning of '23, I got married.

## 10

I was living in a boarding-house in Ealing. The years were rolling on, or crawling on. Lower Binfield had passed almost out of my memory. I was the usual young city worker who scoots for the 8.15 and intrigues for the other fellow's job. I was fairly well thought of in the firm and pretty satisfied with life. The post-war success dope had caught me, more or less. You remember the line of talk. Pep, punch, grit, sand. Get on or get out. There's plenty of room at the top. You can't keep a good man down. And the ads in the magazines about the chap that the boss clapped on the shoulder, and the keen-jawed executive who's pulling down the big dough and attributes his success to so and so's correspondence course. It's funny how we all swallowed it, even blokes like me to whom it hadn't the smallest application. Because I'm neither a go-getter nor a down-and-out, and I'm by nature incapable of being either. But it was the spirit of the time. Get on! Make good! If you see a man down, jump on his guts before he gets up again. Of course this was in the early twenties, when some of the effects of the war had worn off and the slump hadn't yet arrived to knock the stuffing out of us.

I had an 'A' subscription at Boots and went to half-crown dances and belonged to a local tennis club. You know those tennis clubs in the genteel suburbs—little wooden pavilions and high wire-netting enclosures where young chaps in rather badly cut white flannels prance up and down, shouting 'Fifteen forty!' and 'Vantage all!' in voices which are a tolerable imitation of the Upper Crust. I'd learned to play tennis, didn't dance too badly, and got on well with the girls. At nearly thirty I wasn't a bad-looking chap, with my red face and butter-coloured hair, and in those days it was still a point in your favour to have fought in the war. I never, then or at any other time, succeeded in looking like a gentleman, but on the other hand you probably wouldn't have taken me for the son of a small shopkeeper in a country town. I could keep my end up in the rather mixed society of a place like Ealing, where the office-employee class overlaps with the middling-professional class. It was at the tennis club that I first met Hilda.

At that time Hilda was twenty-four. She was a small, slim, rather timid girl, with dark hair, beautiful movements, and—because of having very large eyes—a distinct resemblance to a hare. She was one of those people who never say much, but remain on the edge of any conversation that's going on, and give the impression that they're listening. If she said anything at all, it was usually 'Oh, yes, I think so too', agreeing with whoever had spoken last. At tennis she hopped about very gracefully, and didn't play badly, but somehow had a helpless, childish air. Her surname was Vincent.

If you're married, there'll have been times when you've said to yourself 'Why the hell did I do it?' and God knows I've said it often enough about Hilda. And once again, looking at it across fifteen years, why *did* I marry Hilda?

Partly, of course, because she was young and in a way very pretty. Beyond that I can only say that because she came of totally different origins from myself it was very difficult for me to get any grasp of what she was really like. I had to marry her first and find out about her afterwards, whereas if I'd married say, Elsie Waters, I'd have known what I was marrying. Hilda belonged to a class I only knew by hearsay, the poverty-stricken officer class. For generations past her family had been soldiers, sailors, clergymen, Anglo-Indian officials, and that kind of thing. They'd never had any money, but on the other hand none of them had ever done anything that I should recognize as work. Say what you will, there's a kind of snob-appeal in that, if you belong as I do to the God-fearing shopkeeper class, the low church, and high-tea class. It wouldn't make any impression on me now, but it did then. Don't mistake what I'm saying. I don't mean that I married Hilda *because* she belonged to the class I'd once served across the counter, with some notion of jockeying myself up in the social scale. It was merely that I couldn't understand her and therefore was capable of being goofy about her. And one thing I certainly didn't grasp was that the girls in these penniless middle-class families will marry anything in trousers, just to get away from home.

It wasn't long before Hilda took me home to see her family. I hadn't known till then that there was a considerable Anglo-Indian colony in Ealing. Talk about discovering a new world! It was quite a revelation to me.

Do you know these Anglo-Indian families? It's almost impossible, when you get inside these people's houses, to remember that out in the street it's England and the twentieth century. As soon as you set foot inside the front door you're in India in the eighties. You know the kind of atmosphere. The carved teak furniture, the brass trays, the dusty tiger-skulls on the wall, the Trichinopoly cigars, the red-hot pickles, the yellow photographs of chaps in sun-helmets, the Hindustani words that you're expected to know the meaning of, the everlasting anecdotes about tiger-shoots and what Smith said to Jones in Poona in '87. It's a sort of little world of their own that they've created, like a kind of cyst. To me, of course, it was all quite new and in some ways rather interesting. Old Vincent, Hilda's father, had been not only in India but also in some even more outlandish place, Borneo or Sarawak, I forget which. He was the usual type, completely bald, almost invisible behind his moustache, and full of stories about cobras and cummerbunds and what the district collector said in '93. Hilda's mother was so colourless that she was just like one of the faded photos on the wall. There was also a son, Harold, who had some official job in Ceylon and was home on leave at the time when I first met Hilda. They had a little dark house in one of those buried back-streets that exist in Ealing.

It smelt perpetually of Trichinopoly cigars and it was so full of spears, blow-pipes, brass ornaments, and the heads of wild animals that you could hardly move about in it.

Old Vincent had retired in 1910, and since then he and his wife had shown about as much activity, mental or physical, as a couple of shellfish. But at the time I was vaguely impressed by a family which had had majors, colonels, and once even an admiral in it. My attitude towards the Vincents, and theirs towards me, is an interesting illustration of what fools people can be when they get outside their own line. Put me among business people—whether they're company directors or commercial travellers—and I'm a fairly good judge of character. But I had no experience whatever of the officer-rentier-clergyman class, and I was inclined to kow-tow to these decayed throw-outs. I looked on them as my social and intellectual superiors, while they on the other hand mistook me for a rising young businessman who before long would be pulling down the big dough. To people of that kind, 'business', whether it's marine insurance or selling peanuts, is just a dark mystery. All they know is that it's something rather vulgar out of which you can make money. Old Vincent used to talk impressively about my being 'in business'—once, I remember, he had a slip of the tongue and said 'in trade'—and obviously didn't grasp the difference between being in business as an employee and being there on your own account. He had some vague notion that as I was 'in' the Flying Salamander I should sooner or later rise to the top of it, by a process of promotion. I think it's possible that he also had pictures of himself touching me for fivers at some future date. Harold certainly had. I could see it in his eye. In fact, even with my income being what it is, I'd probably be lending money to Harold at this moment if he were alive. Luckily he died a few years after we were married, of enteric or something, and both the old Vincents are dead too.

Well, Hilda and I were married, and right from the start it was a flop. Why did you marry her? you say. But why did you marry yours? These things happen to us. I wonder whether you'll believe that during the first two or three years I had serious thoughts of killing Hilda. Of course in practice one never does these things, they're only a kind of fantasy that one enjoys thinking about. Besides, chaps who murder their wives always get copped. However cleverly you've faked the alibi, they know perfectly well that it's you who did it, and they'll pin it on to you somehow. When a woman's bumped off, her husband is always the first suspect—which gives you a little side-glimpse of what people really think about marriage.

One gets used to everything in time. After a year or two I stopped wanting to kill her and started wondering about her. Just wondering. For hours, sometimes, on Sunday afternoons or in the evening when I've come home from work, I've lain on my bed with all my clothes on except my shoes, wondering about women. Why they're like that, how they get like that, whether they're doing it on purpose. It seems to be a most frightful thing, the suddenness with which some women go to pieces after they're married. It's as if they were strung up to do just that one thing, and the instant they've done it they wither off like a flower that's set its seed. What really gets me down is the dreary attitude towards life that it implies. If marriage was just an open swindle—if the woman trapped you into it and then turned round and said, 'Now, you bastard, I've caught you and you're going to work for me while I have a good time!'—I wouldn't mind so much. But not a bit of it. They don't want to have a good time, they merely want to slump into middle age as quickly as possible. After the frightful battle of getting her man to the altar, the woman kind of relaxes, and all her youth, looks, energy, and joy of life just vanish overnight. It was like that with Hilda. Here was this pretty, delicate girl, who'd seemed to me—and in fact when I first knew her she *was*—a finer type of animal than myself, and within only about three years she'd settled down into a depressed, lifeless, middle-aged frump. I'm not denying that I was part of the reason. But whoever she'd married it would have been much the same.

What Hilda lacks—I discovered this about a week after we were married—is any kind of joy in life, any kind of interest in things for their own sake. The idea of doing things because you enjoy them is something she can hardly understand. It was through Hilda that I first got a notion of what these decayed middle-class families are really like. The essential fact about them is that all their vitality has been drained away by lack of money. In families like that, which live on tiny pensions and annuities—that's to say on incomes which never get bigger and generally get smaller—there's more sense of poverty, more crust-wiping, and looking twice at sixpence, than you'd find in any farm-labourer's family, let alone a family like mine. Hilda's often told me that almost the first thing she can remember is a ghastly feeling that there was never enough money for anything. Of course, in that kind of family, the lack of money is always at its worst when the kids are at the school-age. Consequently they grow up, especially the girls, with a fixed idea not only that one always *is* hard-up but that it's one's duty to be miserable about it.

At the beginning we lived in a poky little maisonette and had a job to get by on my wages. Later, when I was transferred to the West Bletchley branch, things were better, but Hilda's attitude didn't change. Always that ghastly glooming about money! The milk bill! The coal bill! The rent! The school fees! We've lived all our life together to the tune of 'Next week we'll be in the workhouse.' It's not that Hilda's mean, in the ordinary sense of the word, and still less that she's selfish. Even when there happens to be a bit of spare cash knocking about I can hardly persuade her to buy herself any decent clothes. But she's got this feeling that you *ought* to be perpetually working yourself up into a stew about lack of money. Just working up an atmosphere of misery from a sense of duty. I'm not like that. I've got more the prole's attitude towards money. Life's here to be lived, and if we're going to be in the soup next week—well, next week is a long way off. What really shocks her is the fact that I refuse to worry. She's always going for me about it. 'But, George! You don't seem to *realize*! We've simply got no money at all! It's very *serious*!' She loves getting into a panic because something or other is 'serious'. And of late she's got that trick, when she's glooming about something, of kind of hunching her shoulders and folding her arms across her breast. If you made a list of Hilda's remarks throughout the day, you'd find three bracketed together at the top–'We can't afford it', 'It's a great saving', and 'I don't know where the money's to come from'. She does everything for negative reasons. When she makes a cake she's not thinking about the cake, only about how to save butter and eggs. When I'm in bed with her all she thinks about is how not to have a baby. If she goes to the pictures she's all the time writhing with indignation about the price of the seats. Her methods of housekeeping, with all the emphasis on 'using things up' and 'making things do', would have given Mother convulsions. On the other hand, Hilda isn't in the least a snob. She's never looked down on me because I'm not a gentleman. On the contrary, from her point of view I'm much too lordly in my habits. We never have a meal in a tea-shop without a frightful row in whispers because I'm tipping the waitress too much. And it's a curious thing that in the last few years she's become much more definitely lower-middle-class, in outlook and even in appearance, than I am. Of course all this 'saving' business has never led to anything. It never does. We live just about as well or as badly as the other people in Ellesmere Road. But the everlasting stew about the gas bill and the milk bill and the awful price of butter and the kids' boots and school-fees goes on and on. It's a kind of game with Hilda.

We moved to West Bletchley in '29 and started buying the house in Ellesmere Road the next year, a little before Billy was born. After I was made an Inspector I was more away from home and had more opportunities with other women. Of course I was unfaithful–I won't say all the time, but as often as I got the chance. Curiously enough, Hilda was jealous. In a way, considering how little that kind of thing means to her, I wouldn't have expected her to mind. And like all jealous women she'll sometimes show a cunning you wouldn't think her capable of. Sometimes the way she's caught me out would have made me believe in telepathy, if it wasn't that she's often been equally suspicious when I didn't happen to be guilty. I'm more or less permanently under suspicion, though, God knows, in the last few years–the last five years, anyway–I've been innocent enough. You have to be, when you're as fat as I am.

Taking it by and large, I suppose Hilda and I don't get on worse than about half the couples in Ellesmere Road. There've been times when I've thought of separation or divorce, but in our walk of life you don't do those things. You can't afford to. And then time goes on, and you kind of give up struggling. When you've lived with a woman for fifteen years, it's difficult to imagine life without her. She's part of the order of things. I dare say you might find things to object to in the sun and the moon, but do you really want to change them? Besides, there were the kids. Kids are a 'link', as they say. Or a 'tie'. Not to say a ball and fetter.

Of late years Hilda has made two great friends called Mrs Wheeler and Miss Minns. Mrs Wheeler is a widow, and I gather she's got very bitter ideas about the male sex. I can feel her kind of quivering with disapproval if I so much as come into the room. She's a faded little woman and gives you a curious impression that she's the same colour all over, a kind of greyish dust-colour, but she's full of energy. She's a bad influence on Hilda, because she's got the same passion for 'saving' and 'making things do', though in a slightly different form. With her it takes the form of thinking that you can have a good time without paying for it. She's for ever nosing out bargains and amusements that don't cost money. With people like that it doesn't matter a damn whether they want a thing or not, it's merely a question of whether they can get it on the cheap. When the big shops have their remnant sales Mrs Wheeler's always at the head of the queue, and it's her greatest pride, after a day's hard fighting round the counter, to come out without having bought anything. Miss Minns is quite a different sort. She's really a sad case, poor Miss Minns. She's a tall thin woman of about thirty-eight, with black patent-leather hair and a very *good*, trusting kind of face. She lives on some kind of tiny fixed income, an annuity or something, and I fancy she's a left-over from the old society of West Bletchley, when it was a little country town, before the suburb grew up. It's written all over her that her father was a clergyman and sat on her pretty heavily while he lived. They're a special by-product of the middle classes, these women who turn into withered hags before they even manage to escape from home. Poor old Miss Minns, for all her wrinkles, still looks exactly like a child. It's still a tremendous adventure to her not to go to church. She's always burbling about 'modern progress' and 'the woman's movement', and she's got a vague yearning to do something she calls 'developing her mind', only she doesn't quite know how to start. I think in the beginning she cottoned on to Hilda and Mrs Wheeler out of pure loneliness, but now they take her with them wherever they go.

And the times they've had together, those three! Sometimes I've almost envied them. Mrs Wheeler is the leading spirit. You couldn't name a kind of idiocy that she hasn't dragged them into at one time or another. Anything from theosophy to cat's-cradle, provided you can do it on the cheap. For months they went in for the food-crank business. Mrs Wheeler had picked up a second-hand copy of some book called *Radiant Energy* which proved t':at you should live on lettuces and other things that don't cost money. Of course this appealed to Hilda, who immediately began starving herself. She'd have tried it on me and the kids as well, only I put my foot down. Then they had a go at faith-healing. Then they thought of tackling Pelmanism, but after a lot of correspondence they found that they couldn't get the booklets free, which had been Mrs Wheeler's idea. Then it was hay-box cookery. Then it was some filthy stuff called bee wine, which was supposed to cost nothing at all because you made it out of water. They dropped that after they'd read an article in the paper saying that bee wine gives you cancer. Then they nearly joined one of those women's clubs which go for conducted tours round factories, but after a lot of arithmetic Mrs Wheeler decided that the free teas the factories gave you didn't quite equal the subscription. Then Mrs Wheeler scraped acquaintance with somebody who gave away free tickets for plays produced by some stage society or other. I've known the three of them sit for hours listening to some highbrow play of which they didn't even pretend to understand a word—couldn't even tell you the name of the play afterwards—but they felt that they were getting something for nothing. Once they even took up spiritualism.

Mrs Wheeler had run across some down-and-out medium who was so desperate that he'd give séances for eighteenpence, so that the three of them could have a glimpse beyond the veil for a tanner a time. I saw him once when he came to give a séance at our house. He was a seedy-looking old devil and obviously in mortal terror of D.T.s. He was so shaky that when he was taking his overcoat off in the hall he had a sort of spasm and a hank of butter-muslin dropped out of his trouser-leg. I managed to shove it back to him before the women saw. Butter-muslin is what they make the ectoplasm with, so I'm told. I suppose he was going on to another seance afterwards. You don't get manifestations for eighteen pence. Mrs Wheeler's biggest find of the last few years is the Left Book Club. I think it was in '36 that the news of the Left Book Club got to West Bletchley. I joined it soon afterwards, and it's almost the only time I can remember spending money without Hilda protesting. She can see some sense in buying a book when you're getting it for a third of its proper price. These women's attitude is curious, really. Miss Minns certainly had a try at reading one or two of the books, but this wouldn't even have occurred to the other two. They've never had any direct connexion with the Left Book Club or any notion what it's all about—in fact I believe at the beginning Mrs Wheeler thought it had something to do with books which had been left in railway carriages and were being sold off cheap. But they do know that it means seven and sixpenny books for half a crown, and so they're always saying that it's 'such a good idea'. Now and again the local Left Book Club branch holds meetings and gets people down to speak, and Mrs Wheeler always takes the others along. She's a great one for public meetings of any kind, always provided that it's indoors and admission free. The three of them sit there like lumps of pudding. They don't know what the meeting's about and they don't care, but they've got a vague feeling, especially Miss Minns, that they're improving their minds, and it isn't costing them anything.

Well, that's Hilda. You see what she's like. Take it by and large, I suppose she's no worse than I am. Sometimes when we were first married I felt I'd like to strangle her, but later I got so that I didn't care. And then I got fat and settled down. It must have been in 1930 that I got fat. It happened so suddenly that it was as if a cannon ball had hit me and got stuck inside. You know how it is. One night you go to bed, still feeling more or less young, with an eye for the girls and so forth, and next morning you wake up in the full consciousness that you're just a poor old fatty with nothing ahead of you this side the grave except sweating your guts out to buy boots for the kids.

And now it's '38, and in every shipyard in the world they're riveting up the battleships for another war, and a name I chanced to see on a poster had stirred up in me a whole lot of stuff which ought to have been buried God knows how many years ago.

# PART III

## I

When I came home that evening I was still in doubt as to what I'd spend my seventeen quid on.

Hilda said she was going to the Left Book Club meeting. It seemed that there was a chap coming down from London to lecture, though needless to say Hilda didn't know what the lecture was going to be about. I told her I'd go with her. In a general way I'm not much of a one for lectures, but the visions of war I'd had that morning, starting with the bomber flying over the train, had put me into a kind of thoughtful mood. After the usual argument we got the kids to bed early and cleared off in time for the lecture, which was billed for eight o'clock.

It was a misty kind of evening, and the hall was cold and not too well lighted. It's a little wooden hall with a tin roof, the property of some Nonconformist sect or other, and you can hire it for ten bob. The usual crowd of fifteen or sixteen people had rolled up. On the front of the platform there was a yellow placard announcing that the lecture was on 'The Menace of Fascism'. This didn't altogether surprise me. Mr Witchett, who acts as chairman of these meetings and who in private life is something in an architect's office, was taking the lecturer round, introducing him to everyone as Mr So-and-so (I forget his name) 'the well-known anti-Fascist', very much as you might call somebody 'the well-known pianist'. The lecturer was a little chap of about forty, in a dark suit, with a bald head which he'd tried rather unsuccessfully to cover up with wisps of hair.

Meetings of this kind never start on time. There's always a period of hanging about on the pretence that perhaps a few more people are going to turn up. It was about twenty-five past eight when Witchett tapped on the table and did his stuff. Witchett's a mild-looking chap, with a pink, baby's bottom kind of face that's always covered in smiles. I believe he's secretary of the local Liberal Party, and he's also on the Parish Council and acts as M.C. at the magic lantern lectures for the Mothers' Union. He's what you might call a born chairman. When he tells you how delighted we all are to have Mr So-and-so on the platform tonight, you can see that he believes it. I never look at him without thinking that he's probably a virgin. The little lecturer took out a wad of notes, chiefly newspaper cuttings, and pinned them down with his glass of water. Then he gave a quick lick at his lips and began to shoot.

Do you ever go to lectures, public meetings, and what-not?

When I go to one myself, there's always a moment during the evening when I find myself thinking the same thought. Why the hell are we doing this? Why is it that people will turn out on a winter night for this kind of thing? I looked round the hall. I was sitting in the back row. I don't ever remember going to any kind of public meeting when I didn't sit in the back row if I could manage it. Hilda and the others had planked themselves in front, as usual. It was rather a gloomy little hall. You know the kind of place. Pitch-pine walls, corrugated iron roof, and enough draughts to make you want to keep your overcoat on. The little knot of us were sitting in the light round the platform, with about thirty rows of empty chairs behind us. And the seats of all the chairs were dusty. On the platform behind the lecturer there was a huge square thing draped in dust-cloths which might have been an enormous coffin under a pall. Actually it was a piano.

At the beginning I wasn't exactly listening. The lecturer was rather a mean-looking little chap, but a good speaker. White face, very mobile mouth, and the rather grating voice that they get from constant speaking. Of course he was pitching into Hitler and the Nazis. I wasn't particularly keen to hear what he was saying—get the same stuff in the *News Chronicle* every morning—but his voice came across to me as a kind of burr-burr-burr, with now and again a phrase that struck out and caught my attention.

'Bestial atrocities. . . . Hideous outbursts of sadism. . . . Rubber truncheons. . . . Concentration camps. . . . Iniquitous persecution of the Jews. . . . Back to the Dark Ages. . . . European civilization. . . . Act before it is too late. . . . Indignation of all decent peoples. . . . Alliance of the democratic nations. . . . Firm stand. . . . Defence of democracy. . . . Democracy. . . . Fascism. . . . Democracy. . . . Fascism. . . . Democracy. . . .'

You know the line of talk. These chaps can churn it out by the hour. Just like a gramophone. Turn the handle, press the button, and it starts. Democracy, Fascism, Democracy. But somehow it interested me to watch him. A rather mean little man, with a white face and a bald head, standing on a platform, shooting out slogans. What's he doing? Quite deliberately, and quite openly, he's stirring up hatred. Doing his damnedest to make you hate certain foreigners called Fascists. It's a queer thing, I thought, to be known as 'Mr So-and-so, the well-known anti-Fascist'. A queer trade, anti-Fascism. This fellow, I suppose, makes his living by writing books against Hitler. But what did he do before Hitler came along? And what what'll he do if Hitler ever disappears? Same question applies to doctors, detectives, rat-catchers, and so forth, of course. But the grating voice went on and on, and another thought struck me. He *means* it. Not faking at all—feels every word he's saying. He's trying to work up hatred in the audience, but that's nothing to the hatred he feels himself. Every slogan's gospel truth to him. If you cut him open all you'd find inside would be Democracy-Fascism-Democracy. Interesting to know a chap like that in private life. But does he have a private life? Or does he only go round from platform to platform, working up hatred? Perhaps even his dreams are slogans.

As well as I could from the back row I had a look at the audience. I suppose, if you come to think of it, we people who'll turn out on winter nights to sit in draughty halls listening to Left Book Club lectures (and I consider that I'm entitled to the 'we', seeing that I'd done it myself on this occasion) have a certain significance. We're the West Bletchley revolutionaries. Doesn't look hopeful at first sight. It struck me as I looked round the audience that only about half a dozen of them had really grasped what the lecturer was talking about, though by this time he'd been pitching into Hitler and the Nazis for over half an hour. It's always like that with meetings of this kind. Invariably half the people come away without a notion of what it's all about. In his chair beside the table Witchett was watching the lecturer with a delighted smile, and his face looked a little like a pink geranium. You could hear in advance the speech he'd make as soon as the lecturer sat down—same speech as he makes at the end of the magic lantern lecture in aid of trousers for the Melanesians: 'Express our thanks—voicing the opinion of all of us—most interesting—give us all a lot to think about—most stimulating evening!' In the front row Miss Minns was sitting very upright, with her head cocked a little on one side, like a bird. The lecturer had taken a sheet of paper from under the tumbler and was reading out statistics about the German suicide-rate. You could see by the look of Miss Minns's long thin neck that she wasn't feeling happy. Was this improving her mind, or wasn't it? If only she could make out what it was all about! The other two were sitting there like lumps of pudding. Next to them a little woman with red hair was knitting a jumper. One plain, two purl, drop one, and knit two together. The lecturer was describing how the Nazis chop people's heads off for treason and sometimes the executioner makes a bosh shot. There was one other woman in the audience, a girl with dark hair, one of the teachers at the Council School. Unlike the other she was really listening, sitting forward with her big round eyes fixed on the lecturer and her mouth a little bit open, drinking it all in.

Just behind her two old blokes from the local Labour Party were sitting. One had grey hair cropped very short, the other had a bald head and a droopy moustache. Both wearing their overcoats. You know the type. Been in the Labour Party since the year dot. Lives given up to the movement. Twenty years of being blacklisted by employers, and another ten of badgering the Council to do something about the slums. Suddenly everything's changed, the old Labour Party stuff doesn't matter any longer. Find themselves pitchforked into foreign politics—Hitler, Stalin, bombs, machine-guns, rubber trun-cheons, Rome-Berlin axis, Popular Front, anti-Comintern pact. Can't make head or tail of it. Immediately in front of me the local Communist Party branch were sitting. All three of them very young. One of them's got money and is something in the Hesperides Estate Company, in fact I believe he's old Crum's nephew. Another's a clerk at one of the banks. He cashes cheques for me occasionally. A nice boy, with a round, very young, eager face, blue eyes like a

baby, and hair so fair that you'd think he peroxided it. He only looks about
seventeen, though I suppose he's twenty. He was wearing a cheap blue suit and
a bright blue tie that went with his hair. Next to these three another
Communist was sitting. But this one, it seems, is a different kind of
Communist and not-quite, because he's what they call a Trotskyist. The
others have got a down on him. He's even younger, a very thin, very dark,
nervous-looking boy. Clever face. Jew, of course. These four were taking the
lecture quite differently from the others. You knew they'd be on their feet the
moment question-time started. You could see them kind of twitching already.
And the little Trotskyist working himself from side to side on his bum in his
anxiety to get in ahead of the others.

I'd stopped listening to the actual words of the lecture. But there are more
ways than one of listening. I shut my eyes for a moment. The effect of that was
curious. I seemed to see the fellow much better when I could only hear his
voice.

It was a voice that sounded as if it could go on for a fortnight without
stopping. It's a ghastly thing, really, to have a sort of human barrel-organ
shooting propaganda at you by the hour. The same thing over and over again.
Hate, hate, hate. Let's all get together and have a good hate. Over and over. It
gives you the feeling that something has got inside your skull and is
hammering down on your brain. But for a moment, with my eyes shut, I
managed to turn the tables on him. I got inside *his* skull. It was a peculiar
sensation. For about a second I was inside him, you might almost say I *was*
him. At any rate, I felt what he was feeling.

I saw the vision that he was seeing. And it wasn't at all the kind of vision that
can be talked about. What he's *saying* is merely that Hitler's after us and we
must all get together and have a good hate. Doesn't go into details. Leaves it all
respectable. But what he's *seeing* is something quite different. It's a picture of
himself smashing people's faces in with a spanner. Fascist faces, of course. I
*know* that's what he was seeing. It was what I saw myself for the second or two
that I was inside him. Smash! Right in the middle! The bones cave in like an
eggshell and what was a face a minute ago is just a great big blob of strawberry
jam. Smash! There goes another! That's what's in his mind, waking and
sleeping, and the more he thinks of it the more he likes it. And it's all O.K.
because the smashed faces belong to Fascists. You could hear all that in the
tone of his voice.

But why? Likeliest explanation, because he's scared. Every thinking person
nowadays is stiff with fright. This is merely a chap who's got sufficient
foresight to be a little more frightened than the others. Hitler's after us! Quick!
Let's all grab a spanner and get together, and perhaps if we smash in enough
faces they won't smash ours. Gang up, choose your Leader. Hitler's black and
Stalin's white. But it might just as well be the other way about, because in the
little chap's mind both Hitler and Stalin are the same. Both mean spanners and
smashed faces.

War! I started thinking about it again. It's coming soon, that's certain. But
who's afraid of war? That's to say, who's afraid of the bombs and the machine-

guns? 'You are', you say. Yes, I am, and so's anybody who's ever seen them. But it isn't the war that matters, it's the after-war. The world we're going down into, the kind of hate-world, slogan-world. The coloured shirts, the barbed wire, the rubber truncheons. The secret cells where the electric light burns night and day, and the detectives watching you while you sleep. And the processions and the posters with enormous faces, and the crowds of a million people all cheering for the Leader till they deafen themselves into thinking that they really worship him, and all the time, underneath, they hate him so that they want to puke. It's all going to happen. Or isn't it? Some days I know it's impossible, other days I know it's inevitable. That night, at any rate, I knew it was going to happen. It was all in the sound of the little lecturer's voice.

So perhaps after all there *is* a significance in this mingy little crowd that'll turn out on a winter night to listen to a lecture of this kind. Or at any rate in the five or six who can grasp what it's all about. They're simply the outposts of an enormous army. They're the long-sighted ones, the first rats to spot that the ship is sinking. Quick, quick! The Fascists are coming! Spanners ready, boys! Smash others or they'll smash you. So terrified of the future that we're jumping straight into it like a rabbit diving down a boa-constrictor's throat.

And what'll happen to chaps like me when we get Fascism in England? The truth is it probably won't make the slightest difference. As for the lecturer and those four Communists in the audience, yes, it'll make plenty of difference to them. They'll be smashing faces, or having their own smashed, according to who's winning. But the ordinary middling chaps like me will be carrying on just as usual. And yet it frightens me—I tell you it frightens me. I'd just started to wonder why when the lecturer stopped and sat down.

There was the usual hollow little sound of clapping that you get when there are only about fifteen people in the audience, and then old Witchett said his piece, and before you could say Jack Robinson the four Communists were on their feet together. They had a good dog-fight that went on for about ten minutes, full of a lot of stuff that nobody else understood, such as dialectical materialism and the destiny of the proletariat and what Lenin said in 1918. Then the lecturer, who'd had a drink of water, stood up and gave a summing-up that made the Trotskyist wriggle about on his chair but pleased the other three, and the dog-fight went on unofficially for a bit longer. Nobody else did any talking. Hilda and the others had cleared off the moment the lecture ended. Probably they were afraid there was going to be a collection to pay for the hire of the hall. The little woman with red hair was staying to finish her row. You could hear her counting her stitches in a whisper while the others argued. And Witchett sat and beamed at whoever happened to be speaking, and you could see him thinking how interesting it all was and making mental notes, and the girl with black hair looked from one to the other with her mouth a little open, and the old Labour man, looking rather like a seal with his droopy moustache and his overcoat up to his ears, sat looking up at them, wondering what the hell it was all about. And finally I got up and began to put on my overcoat.

The dog-fight had turned into a private row between the little Trotskyist and the boy with fair hair. They were arguing about whether you ought to join the Army if war broke out. As I edged my way along the row of chairs to get out, the fair-haired one appealed to me.

'Mr Bowling! Look here. If war broke out and we had the chance to smash Fascism once and for all, wouldn't you fight? If you were young, I mean.'

I suppose he thinks I'm about sixty.

'You bet I wouldn't,' I said. 'I had enough to go on with last time.'

'But to smash Fascism!'

'Oh, b— Fascism! There's been enough smashing done already, if you ask me.'

The little Trotskyist chips in with social-patriotism and betrayal of the workers, but the others cut him short:

'But you're thinking of 1914. That was just an ordinary imperialist war. This time it's different. Look here. When you hear about what's going on in Germany, and the concentration camps and the Nazis beating people up with rubber truncheons and making the Jews spit in each other's faces—doesn't it make your blood boil?'

They're always going on about your blood boiling. Just the same phrase during the war, I remember.

'I went off the boil in 1916,' I told him. 'And so'll you when you know what a trench smells like.'

And then all of a sudden I seemed to see him. It was as if I hadn't properly seen him till that moment.

A very young eager face, might have belonged to a good-looking schoolboy, with blue eyes and tow-coloured hair, gazing into mine, and for a moment actually he'd got tears in his eyes! Felt as strongly as all that about the German Jews! But as a matter of fact I knew just what he felt. He's a hefty lad, probably plays rugger for the bank. Got brains, too. And here he is, a bank clerk in a godless suburb, sitting behind the frosted window, entering figures in a ledger, counting piles of notes, bumsucking to the manager. Feels his life rotting away. And all the while, over in Europe, the big stuff's happening. Shells bursting over the trenches and waves of infantry charging through the drifts of smoke. Probably some of his pals are fighting in Spain. Of course he's spoiling for a war. How can you blame him? For a moment I had a peculiar feeling that he was my son, which in point of years he might have been. And I thought of that sweltering hot day in August when the newsboy stuck up the poster ENGLAND DECLARES WAR ON GERMANY, and we all rushed out on to the pavement in our white aprons and cheered.

'Listen son,' I said, 'you've got it all wrong. In 1914 *we* thought it was going to be a glorious business. Well, it wasn't. It was just a bloody mess. If it comes again, you keep out of it. Why should you get your body plugged full of lead? Keep it for some girl. You think war's all heroism and V.C. charges, but I tell you it isn't like that. You don't have bayonet-charges nowadays, and when you do it isn't like you imagine. You don't feel like a hero. All you know is that you've had no sleep for three days, and stink like a polecat, you're pissing your bags with fright, and your hands are so cold you can't hold your rifle. But that doesn't matter a damn, either. It's the things that happen afterwards.'

Makes no impression of course. They just think you're out of date. Might as well stand at the door of a knocking-shop handing out tracts.

The people were beginning to clear off. Witchett was taking the lecturer home. The three Communists and the little Jew went up the road together, and they were going at it again with proletarian solidarity and dialectic of the dialectic and what Trotsky said in 1917. They're all the same, really. It was a damp, still, very black night. The lamps seemed to hang in the darkness like stars and didn't light the road. In the distance you could hear the trams booming along the High Street. I wanted a drink, but it was nearly ten and the nearest pub was half a mile away. Besides, I wanted somebody to talk to, the way you can't talk in a pub. It was funny how my brain had been on the go all day. Partly the result of not working, of course, and partly of the new false teeth, which had kind of freshened me up. All day I'd been brooding on the future and the past. I wanted to talk about the bad time that's either coming or isn't coming, the slogans and the coloured shirts and the streamlined men from eastern Europe who are going to knock old England cock-eyed. Hopeless trying to talk to Hilda. Suddenly it occurred to me to go and look up old Porteous, who's a pal of mine and keeps late hours.

Porteous is a retired public-school master. He lives in rooms, which luckily are in the lower half of the house, in the old part of the town, near the church. He's a bachelor, of course. You can't imagine that kind married. Lives all alone with his books and his pipe and has a woman in to do for him. He's a learned kind of chap, with his Greek and Latin and poetry and all that. I suppose that if the local Left Book Club branch represents Progress, old Porteous stands for Culture. Neither of them cuts much ice in West Bletchley.

The light was burning in the little room where old Porteous sits reading till all hours of the night. As I tapped on the front door he came strolling out as usual, with his pipe between his teeth and his fingers in a book to keep the place. He's rather a striking looking chap, very tall, with curly grey hair and a thin, dreamy kind of face that's a bit discoloured but might almost belong to a boy, though he must be nearly sixty. It's funny how some of these public-school and university chaps manage to look like boys till their dying day. It's something in their movements. Old Porteous has got a way of strolling up and down, with that handsome head of his, with the grey curls, held a little back that makes you feel that all the while he's dreaming about some poem or other and isn't conscious of what's going on round him. You can't look at him without seeing the way he's lived written all over him. Public School, Oxford, and then back to his old school as a master. Whole life lived in an atmosphere of Latin, Greek, and cricket. He's got all the mannerisms. Always wears an old Harris tweed jacket and old grey flannel bags which he likes you to call 'disgraceful', smokes a pipe and looks down on cigarettes, and though he sits up half the night I bet he has a cold bath every morning. I suppose from his point of view I'm a bit of a bounder. I haven't been to a public school, I don't know any Latin and don't even want to. He tells me sometimes that it's a pity I'm 'insensible to beauty', which I suppose is a polite way of saying that I've got no education. All the same I like him. He's very hospitable in the right kind of way, always ready to have you in and talk at all hours, and always got drinks handy. When you live in a house like ours, more or less infested by women and kids, it does you good to get out of it sometimes into a bachelor atmosphere, a kind of book-pipe-fire atmosphere. And the classy Oxford feeling of nothing mattering except books and poetry and Greek statues, and nothing worth mentioning having happened since the Goths sacked Rome—sometimes that's a comfort too.

He shoved me into the old leather armchair by the fire and dished out whisky and soda. I've never seen his sitting-room when it wasn't dim with pipe-smoke. The ceiling is almost black. It's a smallish room and, except for the door and the window and the space over the fireplace, the walls are covered with books from the floor right up to the ceiling. On the mantelpiece there are all the things you'd expect. A row of old briar pipes, all filthy, a few Greek silver coins, a tobacco jar with the arms of old Porteous's college on it, and a little earthenware lamp which he told me he dug up on some mountain in Sicily. Over the mantelpiece there are photos of Greek statues. There's a big one in the middle, of a woman with wings and no head who looks as if she was stepping out to catch a bus. I remember how shocked old Porteous was when the first time I saw it, not knowing any better, I asked him why they didn't stick a head on it.

Porteous started refilling his pipe from the jar on the mantelpiece.

'That intolerable woman upstairs has purchased a wireless set,' he said. 'I had been hoping to live the rest of my life out of the sound of those things. I suppose there is nothing one can do? Do you happen to know the legal position?'

I told him there was nothing one could do. I rather like the Oxfordy way he says 'intolerable', and it tickles me, in 1938, to find someone objecting to having a radio in the house. Porteous was strolling up and down in his usual dreamy way, with his hands in his coat pockets and his pipe between his teeth, and almost instantly he'd begun talking about some law against musical instruments that was passed in Athens in the time of Pericles. It's always that way with old Porteous. All his talk is about things that happened centuries ago. Whatever you start off with it always comes back to statues and poetry and the Greeks and Romans. If you mention the *Queen Mary* he'd start telling you about Phoenician triremes. He never reads a modern book, refuses to know their names, never looks at any newspaper except *The Times,* and takes a pride in telling you that he's never been to the pictures. Except for a few poets like Keats and Wordsworth he thinks the modern world—and from his point of view the modern world is the last two thousand years—just oughtn't to have happened.

I'm part of the modern world myself, but I like to hear him talk. He'll stroll round the shelves and haul out first one book and then another, and now and again he'll read you a piece between little puffs of smoke, generally having to translate it from the Latin or something as he goes. It's all kind of peaceful, kind of mellow. All a little like a school-master, and yet it soothes you, somehow. While you listen you aren't in the same world as trams and gas bills and insurance companies. It's all temples and olive trees, and peacocks and elephants, and chaps in the arena with their nets and tridents, and winged lions and eunuchs and galleys and catapults, and generals in brass armour galloping their horses over the soldiers' shields. It's funny that he ever cottoned on to a chap like me. But it's one of the advantages of being fat that you can fit into almost any society. Besides we meet on common ground when it comes to dirty stories. They're the one modern thing he cares about, though, as he's always reminding me, they aren't modern. He's rather old-maidish about it, always tells a story in a veiled kind of way. Sometimes he'll pick out some Latin poet and translate a smutty rhyme, leaving a lot to your imagination, or he'll drop hints about the private lives of the Roman emperors and the things that went on in the temples of Ashtaroth. They seem to have been a bad lot, those Greeks and Romans. Old Porteous has got photographs of wall-paintings somewhere in Italy that would make your hair curl.

When I'm fed up with business and home life it's often done me a lot of good to go and have a talk with Porteous. But tonight it didn't seem to. My mind was still running on the same lines as it had been all day. Just as I'd done with the Left Book Club lecturer, I didn't exactly listen to what Porteous was saying, only to the sound of his voice. But whereas the lecturer's voice had got under my skin, old Porteous's didn't. It was too peaceful, too Oxfordy. Finally, when he was in the middle of saying something, I chipped in and said:

'Tell me, Porteous, what do you think of Hitler?'

Old Porteous was leaning in his lanky, graceful kind of way with his elbows on the mantelpiece and a foot on the fender. He was so surprised that he almost took his pipe out of his mouth.

'Hitler? This German person? My dear fellow! I *don't* think of him.'

'But the trouble is he's going to bloody well make us think about him before he's finished.'

Old Porteous shies a bit at the world 'bloody', which he doesn't like, though of course it's part of his pose never to be shocked. He begins walking up and down again, puffing out smoke.

'I see no reason for paying any attention to him. A mere adventurer. These people come and go. Ephemeral, purely ephemeral.'

I'm not certain what the word 'ephemeral' means, but I stick to my point:

'I think you've got it wrong. Old Hitler's something different. So's Joe Stalin. They aren't like these chaps in the old days who crucified people and chopped their heads off and so forth, just for the fun of it. They're after something quite new—something that's never been heard of before.'

'My dear fellow! There is nothing new under the sun.'

Of course that's a favourite saying of old Porteous's. He won't hear of the existence of anything new. As soon as you tell him about anything that's happening nowadays he says that exactly the same thing happened in the reign of King So-and-so. Even if you bring up things like aeroplanes he tells you that they probably had them in Crete, or Mycenae, or wherever it was. I tried to explain to him what I'd felt while the little bloke was lecturing and the kind of vision I'd had of the bad time that's coming, but he wouldn't listen. Merely repeated that there's nothing new under the sun. Finally he hauls a book out of the shelves and reads me a passage about some Greek tyrant back in the B.C.S who certainly might have been Hitler's twin brother.

The argument went on for a bit. All day I'd been wanting to talk to somebody about this business. It's funny. I'm not a fool, but I'm not a highbrow either, and God knows at normal times I don't have many interests that you wouldn't expect a middle-aged seven-pound-a-weeker with two kids to have. And yet I've enough sense to see that the old life we're used to is being sawn off at the roots. I can feel it happening. I can see the war that's coming and I can see the after-war, the food-queues and the secret police and the loudspeakers telling you what to think. And I'm not even exceptional in this. There are millions of others like me. Ordinary chaps that I meet everywhere, chaps I run across in pubs, bus drivers, and travelling salesmen for hardware firms, have got a feeling that the world's gone wrong. They can feel things cracking and collapsing under their feet. And yet here's this learned chap, who's lived all his life with books and soaked himself in history till it's running out of his pores, and he can't even see that things are changing. Doesn't think Hitler matters. Refuses to believe there's another war coming. In any case, as he didn't fight in the last war, it doesn't enter much into his thoughts—he thinks it was a poor show compared with the siege of Troy. Doesn't see why one should bother about the slogans and the loudspeakers and the coloured shirts. What intelligent person would pay any attention to such things? he always says. Hitler and Stalin will pass away, but something which old Porteous calls 'the eternal verities' won't pass away. This, of course, is simply another way of saying that things will always go on exactly as he's known them. For ever and ever, cultivated Oxford blokes will stroll up and down studies full of books, quoting Latin tags and smoking good tobacco out of jars with coats of arms on them. Really it was no use talking to him. I'd have got more change out of the lad with tow-coloured hair. By degrees the conversation twisted off, as it always does, to things that happened B.C. Then it worked round to poetry. Finally old Porteous drags another book out of the shelves and begins reading Keat's 'Ode to a Nightingale' (or maybe it was a skylark—I forget).

So far as I'm concerned a little poetry goes a long way. But it's a curious fact that I rather like hearing old Porteous reading it aloud. There's no question that he reads well. He's got the habit, of course—used to reading to classes of boys. He'll lean up against something in his lounging way, with his pipe between his teeth and little jets of smoke coming out, and his voice goes kind of solemn and rises and falls with the line. You can see that it moves him in some way. I don't know what poetry is or what it's supposed to do. I imagine it has a kind of nervous effect on some people like music has on others. When he's reading I don't actually listen, that's to say I don't take in the words, but sometimes the sound of it brings a kind of peaceful feeling into my mind. On the whole I like it. But somehow tonight it didn't work. It was as if a cold draught had blown into the room. I just felt that this was all bunk. Poetry! What is it? Just a voice, a bit of an eddy in the air. And Gosh! what use would that be against machine-guns?

I watched him leaning up against the bookshelf. Funny, these public-school chaps. Schoolboys all their days. Whole life revolving round the old school and their bits of Latin and Greek and poetry. And suddenly I remembered that almost the first time I was here with Porteous he'd read me the very same poem. Read it in just the same way, and his voice quivered when he got to the same bit—the bit about magic casements, or something. And a curious thought struck me. *He's dead.* He's a ghost. All people like that are dead.

It struck me that perhaps a lot of the people you see walking about are dead. We say that a man's dead when his heart stops and not before. It seems a bit arbitrary. After all, parts of your body don't stop working—hair goes on growing for years, for instance. Perhaps a man really dies when his brain stops, when he loses the power to take in a new idea. Old Porteous is like that. Wonderfully learned, wonderfully good taste—but he's not capable of change. Just says the same things and thinks the same thoughts over and over again. There are a lot of people like that. Dead minds, stopped inside. Just keep moving backwards and forwards on the same little track, getting fainter all the time, like ghosts.

Old Porteous's mind, I thought, probably stopped working at about the time of the Russo-Japanese War. And it's a ghastly thing that nearly all the decent people, the people who *don't* want to go round smashing faces in with spanners, are like that. They're decent, but their minds have stopped. They can't defend themselves against what's coming to them, because they can't see it, even when it's under their noses. They think that England will never change and that England's the whole world. Can't grasp that it's just a left-over, a tiny corner that the bombs happen to have missed. But what about the new kind of men from eastern Europe, the streamlined men who think in slogans and talk in bullets? They're on our track. Not long before they catch up with us. No Marquess of Queensbury rules for those boys. And all the decent people are paralysed. Dead men and live gorillas. Doesn't seem to be anything between.

I cleared out about half an hour later, having completely failed to convince old Porteous that Hitler matters. I was still thinking the same thoughts as I walked home through the shivery streets. The trams had stopped running. The house was all dark and Hilda was asleep. I dropped my false teeth into the glass of water in the bathroom, got into my pyjamas, and prised Hilda over to the other side of the bed. She rolled over without waking, and the kind of hump between her shoulders was towards me. It's funny, the tremendous gloom that sometimes gets hold of you late at night. At that moment the destiny of Europe seemed to me more important than the rent and the kids' school-bills and the work I'd have to do tomorrow. For anyone who has to earn his living such thoughts are just plain foolishness. But they didn't move out of my mind. Still the vision of the coloured shirts and the machine-guns rattling. The last thing I remember wondering before I fell asleep was why the hell a chap like me should care.

# 2

The primroses had started. I suppose it was some time in March.

I'd driven through Westerham and was making for Pudley. I'd got to do an assessment of an ironmonger's shop, and then, if I could get hold of him, to interview a life-insurance case who was wavering in the balance. His name had been sent in by our local agent, but at the last moment he'd taken fright and begun to doubt whether he could afford it. I'm pretty good at talking people round. It's being fat that does it. It puts people in a cheery kind of mood, makes 'em feel that signing a cheque is almost a pleasure. Of course there are different ways of tackling different people. With some it's better to lay all the stress on the bonuses, others you can scare in a subtle way with hints about what'll happen to their wives if they die uninsured.

The old car switchbacked up and down the curly little hills. And by God, what a day! You know the kind of day that generally comes some time in March when winter suddenly seems to give up fighting. For days past we'd been having the kind of beastly weather that people call 'bright' weather, when the sky's a cold hard blue and the wind scrapes you like a blunt razor-blade. Then suddenly the wind had dropped and the sun got a chance. You know the kind of day. Pale yellow sunshine, not a leaf stirring, a touch of mist in the far distance where you could see the sheep scattered over the hillsides like lumps of chalk. And down in the valleys fires were burning, and the smoke twisted slowly upwards and melted into the mist. I'd got the road to myself. It was so warm you could almost have taken your clothes off.

I got to a spot where the grass beside the road was smothered in primroses. A patch of clayey soil, perhaps. Twenty yards farther on I slowed down and stopped. The weather was too good to miss. I felt I'd got to get out and have a smell at the spring air, and perhaps even pick a few primroses if there was nobody coming. I even had some vague notion of picking a bunch of them to take home to Hilda.

I switched the engine off and got out. I never like leaving the old car running in neutral, I'm always half afraid she'll shake her mudguards off or something. She's a 1927 model, and she's done a biggish mileage. When you lift the bonnet and look at the engine it reminds you of the old Austrian Empire, all tied together with bits of string but somehow keeps plugging along. You wouldn't believe any machine could vibrate in so many directions at once. It's like the motion of the earth, which has twenty-two different kinds of wobble, or so I remember reading. If you look at her from behind when she's running in neutral it's for all the world like watching one of those Hawaiian girls dancing the hula-hula.

There was a five-barred gate beside the road. I strolled over and leaned across it. Not a soul in sight. I hitched my hat back a bit to get the kind of balmy feeling of the air against my forehead. The grass under the hedge was full of primroses. Just inside the gate a tramp or somebody had left the remains of a fire. A little pile of white embers and a wisp of smoke still oozing out of them. Farther along there was a little bit of a pool, covered over with duck-weed. The field was winter wheat. It sloped up sharply, and then there was a fall of chalk and a little beech spinney. A kind of mist of young leaves on the trees. And utter stillness everywhere. Not even enough wind to stir the ashes of the fire. A lark singing somewhere, otherwise not a sound, not even an aeroplane.

I stayed there for a bit, leaning over the gate. I was alone, quite alone. I was looking at the field, and the field was looking at me. I felt—I wonder whether you'll understand.

What I felt was something that's so unusual nowadays that to say it sounds like foolishness. I felt *happy*. I felt that though I shan't live for ever, I'd be quite ready to. If you like you can say that that was merely because it was the first day of spring. Seasonal effect on the sex-glands, or something. But there was more to it than that. Curiously enough, the thing that had suddenly convinced me that life was worth living, more than the primroses or the young buds on the hedge, was that bit of fire near the gate. You know the look of a wood fire on a still day. The sticks that have gone all to white ash and still keep the shape of sticks, and under the ash the kind of vivid red that you can see into. It's curious that a red ember looks more alive, gives you more of a feeling of life than any living thing. There's something about it, a kind of intensity, a vibration—I can't think of the exact words. But it lets you know that you're alive yourself. It's the spot on the picture that makes you notice everything else.

I bent down to pick a primrose. Couldn't reach it—too much belly. I squatted down on my haunches and picked a little bunch of them. Lucky there was no one to see me. The leaves were kind of crinkly and shaped like rabbits' ears. I stood up and put my bunch of primroses on the gatepost. Then on an impulse I slid my false teeth out of my mouth and had a look at them.

If I'd had a mirror I'd have looked at the whole of myself, though, as a matter of fact, I knew what I looked like already. A fat man of forty-five, in a grey herring-bone suit a bit the worse for wear and a bowler hat. Wife, two kids, and a house in the suburbs written all over me. Red face and boiled blue eyes. I know, you don't have to tell me. But the thing that struck me, as I gave my dental plate the once-over before slipping it back into my mouth, was that *it doesn't matter*. Even false teeth don't matter. I'm fat—yes. I look like a bookie's unsuccessful brother—yes. No woman will ever go to bed with me again unless she's paid to. I know all that. But I tell you I don't care. I don't want the women, I don't even want to be young again. I only want to be alive. And I was alive that moment when I stood looking at the primroses and the red embers under the hedge. It's a feeling inside you, a kind of peaceful feeling, and yet it's like a flame.

Farther down the hedge the pool was covered with duck-weed, so like a carpet that if you didn't know what duck-weed was you might think it was solid and step on it. I wondered why it is that we're all such bloody fools. Why don't people, instead of the idiocies they do spend their time on, just walk round *looking* at things? That pool, for instance—all the stuff that's in it. Newts, water-snails, water-beetles, caddis-flies, leeches, and God knows how many other things that you can only see with a microscope. The mystery of their lives, down there under water. You could spend a lifetime watching them, ten lifetimes, and still you wouldn't have got to the end even of that one pool. And all the while the sort of feeling of wonder, the peculiar flame inside you. It's the only thing worth having, and we don't want it.

But I do want it. At least I thought so at that moment. And don't mistake what I'm saying. To begin with, unlike most Cockneys, I'm not soppy about 'the country'. I was brought up a damn sight too near to it for that. I don't want to stop people living in towns, or in suburbs for that matter. Let 'em live where they like. And I'm not suggesting that the whole of humanity could spend the whole of their lives wandering round picking primroses and so forth. I know perfectly well that we've got to work. It's only because chaps are coughing their lungs out in mines and girls are hammering at typewriters that anyone ever has time to pick a flower. Besides, if you hadn't a full belly and a warm house you wouldn't want to pick flowers. But that's not the point. Here's this feeling that I get inside me—not often, I admit, but now and again. I know it's a good feeling to have. What's more, so does everybody else, or nearly everybody. It's just round the corner all the time, and we all know it's there. Stop firing that machine-gun! Stop chasing whatever you're chasing! Calm down, get your breath back, let a bit of peace seep into your bones. No use. We don't do it. Just keep on with the same bloody fooleries.

And the next war coming over the horizon, 1941, they say. Three more circles of the sun, and then we whizz straight into it. The bombs diving down on you like black cigars, and the streamlined bullets streaming from the Bren machine-guns. Not that that worries me particularly. I'm too old to fight. There'll be air-raids, of course, but they won't hit everybody. Besides, even if that kind of danger exists, it doesn't really enter into one's thoughts beforehand. As I've said several times already, I'm not frightened of the war, only the after-war. And even that isn't likely to affect me personally. Because who'd bother about a chap like me? I'm too fat to be a political suspect. No one would bump me off or cosh me with a rubber truncheon. I'm the ordinary middling kind that moves on when the policeman tells him. As for Hilda and the kids, they'd probably never notice the difference. And yet it frightens me. The barbed wire! The slogans! The enormous faces! The cork-lined cellars where the executioner plugs you from behind! For that matter it frightens other chaps who are intellectually a good deal dumber than I am. But why! Because it means good-bye to this thing I've been telling you about, this special feeling inside you. Call it peace, if you like. But when I say peace I don't mean absence of war, I mean peace, a feeling in your guts. And it's gone for ever if the rubber truncheon boys get hold of us.

I picked up my bunch of primroses and had a smell at them. I was thinking of Lower Binfield. It was funny how for two months past it had been in and out of my mind all the time, after twenty years during which I'd practically forgotten it. And just at this moment there was the zoom of a car coming up the road.

It brought me up with a kind of jolt. I suddenly realized what I was doing—wandering round picking primroses when I ought to have been going through the inventory at that ironmonger's shop in Pudley. What was more, it suddenly struck me what I'd look like if those people in the car saw me. A fat man in a bowler hat holding a bunch of primroses! It wouldn't look right at all. Fat men mustn't pick primroses, at any rate in public. I just had time to chuck them over the hedge before the car came in sight. It was a good job I'd done so. The car was full of young fools of about twenty. How they'd have sniggered if they'd seen me! They were all looking at me—you know how people look at you when they're in a car coming towards you—and the thought struck me that even now they might somehow guess what I'd been doing. Better let 'em think it was something else. Why should a chap get out of his car at the side of a country road? Obvious! As the car went past I pretended to be doing up a fly-button.

I cranked up the car (the self-starter doesn't work any longer) and got in. Curiously enough, in the very moment when I was doing up the fly-button, when my mind was about three-quarters full of those young fools in the other car, a wonderful idea had occurred to me.

I'd go back to Lower Binfield!

Why not? I thought as I jammed her into top gear. Why shouldn't I? What was to stop me? And why the hell hadn't I thought of it before? A quiet holiday in Lower Binfield—just the thing I wanted.

Don't imagine that I had any ideas of going back to *live* in Lower Binfield. I wasn't planning to desert Hilda and the kids and start life under a different name. That kind of thing only happens in books. But what was to stop me slipping down to Lower Binfield and having a week there all by myself, on the Q.T.?

I seemed to have it all planned out in my mind already. It was all right as far as the money went. There was still twelve quid left in that secret pile of mine, and you can have a very comfortable week on twelve quid. I get a fortnight's holiday a year, generally in August or September. But if I made up some suitable story—relative dying of incurable disease, or something—I could probably get the firm to give me my holiday in two separate halves. Then I could have a week all to myself before Hilda knew what was happening. A week in Lower Binfield, with no Hilda, no kids, no Flying Salamander, no Ellesmere Road, no rumpus about the hire-purchase payments, no noise of traffic driving you silly—just a week of loafing round and listening to the quietness?

But why did I want to go back to Lower Binfield? you say. Why Lower Binfield in particular? What did I mean to do when I got there?

I didn't mean to do anything. That was part of the point. I wanted peace and quiet. Peace! We had it once, in Lower Binfield. I've told you something about our old life there, before the war. I'm not pretending it was perfect. I dare say it was a dull, sluggish, vegetable kind of life. You can say we were like turnips, if you like. But turnips don't live in terror of the boss, they don't lie awake at night thinking about the next slump and the next war. We had peace inside us. Of course I knew that even in Lower Binfield life would have changed. But the place itself wouldn't have. There'd still be the beech woods round Binfield House, and the towpath down by Burford Weir, and the horse-trough in the market-place. I wanted to get back there, just for a week, and let the feeling of it soak into me. It was a bit like one of these Eastern sages retiring into a desert. And I should think, the way things are going, there'll be a good many people retiring into the desert during the next few years. It'll be like the time in ancient Rome that old Porteous was telling me about, when there were so many hermits that there was a waiting list for every cave.

But it wasn't that I wanted to watch my navel. I only wanted to get my nerve back before the bad times begin. Because does anyone who isn't dead from the neck up doubt that there's a bad time coming? We don't even know what it'll be, and yet we know it's coming. Perhaps a war, perhaps a slump—no knowing, except that it'll be something bad. Wherever we're going, we're going downwards. Into the grave, into the cesspool—no knowing. And you can't face that kind of thing unless you've got the right feeling inside you. There's something that's gone out of us in these twenty years since the war. It's a kind of vital juice that we've squirted away until there's nothing left. All this rushing to and fro! Everlasting scramble for a bit of cash. Everlasting din of buses, bombs, radios, telephone bells. Nerves worn all to bits, empty places in our bones where the marrow ought to be.

I shoved my foot down on the accelerator. The very thought of going back to Lower Binfield had done me good already. You know the feeling I had. Coming up for air! Like the big sea-turtles when they come paddling up to the surface, stick their noses out and fill their lungs with a great gulp before they sink down again among the seaweed and the octopuses. We're all stifling at the bottom of a dustbin, but I'd found the way to the top. Back to Lower Binfield! I kept my foot on the accelerator until the old car worked up to her maximum speed of nearly forty miles an hour. She was rattling like a tin tray full of crockery, and under cover of the noise I nearly started singing.

Of course the fly in the milk-jug was Hilda. That thought pulled me up a bit. I slowed down to about twenty to think it over.

There wasn't much doubt Hilda would find out sooner or later. As to getting only a week's holiday in August, I might be able to pass that off all right. I could tell her the firm were only giving me a week this year. Probably she wouldn't ask too many questions about that, because she'd jump at the chance of cutting down the holiday expenses. The kids, in any case, always stay at the seaside for a month. Where the difficulty came in was finding an alibi for that week in May. I couldn't just clear off without notice. Best thing, I thought, would be to tell her a good while ahead that I was being sent on some special job to Nottingham, or Derby, or Bristol, or some other place a good long way away. If I told her about it two months ahead it would look as if I hadn't anything to hide.

But of course she'd find out sooner or later. Trust Hilda! She'd start off by pretending to believe it, and then, in that quiet, obstinate way she has, she'd nose out the fact that I'd never been to Nottingham or Derby or Bristol or wherever it might be. It's astonishing how she does it. Such perseverance! She lies low till she's found out all the weak points in your alibi, and then suddenly, when you've put your foot in it by some careless remark, she starts on you. Suddenly comes out with the whole dossier of the case. 'Where did you spend Saturday night? That's a lie! You've been off with a woman. Look at these hairs I found when I was brushing your waistcoat. Look at them! Is my hair that colour?' And then the fun begins. Lord knows how many times it's happened. Sometimes she's been right about the woman and sometimes she's been wrong, but the after-effects are always the same. Nagging for weeks on end! Never a meal without a row—and the kids can't make out what it's all about. The one completely hopeless thing would be to tell her just where I'd spent that week, and why. If I explained till the Day of Judgment she'd never believe that.

But, hell! I thought, why bother? It was a long way off. You know how different these things seem before and after. I shoved my foot down on the accelerator again. I'd had another idea, almost bigger than the first. I wouldn't go in May. I'd go in the second half of June, when the coarse-fishing season had started, and I'd go fishing!

Why not, after all? I wanted peace, and fishing is peace. And then the biggest idea of all came into my head and very nearly made me swing the car off the road.

I'd go and catch those big carp in the pool at Binfield House!

And once again, why not? Isn't it queer how we go through life, always thinking that the things we want to do are the things that can't be done? Why shouldn't I catch those carp? And yet, as soon as the idea's mentioned, doesn't it sound to you like something impossible, something that just couldn't happen? It seemed so to me, even at that moment. It seemed to me a kind of dope-dream, like the ones you have of sleeping with film stars or winning the heavyweight championship. And yet it wasn't in the least impossible, it wasn't even improbable. Fishing can be rented. Whoever owned Binfield House now would probably let the pool if they got enough for it. And Gosh! I'd be glad to pay five pounds for a day's fishing in that pool. For that matter it was quite likely that the house was still empty and nobody even knew that the pool existed.

I thought of it in the dark place among the trees, waiting for me all those years. And the huge black fish still gliding round it. Jesus! If they were that size thirty years ago, what would they be like now?

# 3

It was June the seventeenth, Friday, the second day of the coarse-fishing season.

I hadn't had any difficulty in fixing things with the firm. As for Hilda, I'd fitted her up with a story that was all shipshape and watertight. I'd fixed on Birmingham for my alibi, and at the last moment I'd even told her the name of the hotel I was going to stay at, Rowbottom's Family and Commercial. I happened to know the address because I'd stayed there some years earlier. At the same time I didn't want her writing to me at Birmingham, which she might do if I was away as long as a week. After thinking it over I took young Saunders, who travels for Glisso Floor Polish, partly into my confidence. He'd happened to mention that he'd be passing through Birmingham on the eighteenth of June, and I got him to promise that he'd stop on his way and post a letter from me to Hilda, addressed from Rowbottom's. This was to tell her that I might be called away and she'd better not write. Saunders understood, or thought he did. He gave me a wink and said I was wonderful for my age. So that settled Hilda. She hadn't asked any questions, and even if she turned suspicious later, an alibi like that would take some breaking.

I drove through Westerham. It was a wonderful June morning. A faint breeze blowing, and the elm tops swaying in the sun, little white clouds streaming across the sky like a flock of sheep, and the shadows chasing each other across the fields. Outside Westerham a Walls' Ice Cream lad, with cheeks like apples, came tearing towards me on his bike, whistling so that it went through your head. It suddenly reminded me of the time when I'd been an errand boy myself (though in those days we didn't have free-wheel bikes) and I very nearly stopped him and took one. They'd cut the hay in places, but they hadn't got it in yet. It lay drying in long shiny rows, and the smell of it drifted across the road and got mixed up with the petrol.

I drove along at a gentle fifteen. The morning had a kind of peaceful, dreamy feeling. The ducks floated about on the ponds as if they felt too satisfied to eat. In Nettlefield, the village beyond Westerham, a little man in a white apron, with grey hair and a huge grey moustache, darted across the green, planted himself in the middle of the road and began doing physical jerks to attract my attention. My car's known all along this road, of course. I pulled up. It's only Mr Weaver, who keeps the village general shop. No, he doesn't want to insure his life, nor his shop either. He's merely run out of change and wants to know whether I've got a quid's worth of 'large silver'. They never have any change in

Nettlefield, not even at the pub.

I drove on. The wheat would have been as tall as your waist. It went undulating up and down the hills like a great green carpet, with the wind rippling it a little, kind of thick and silky-looking. It's like a woman, I thought. It makes you want to lie on it. And a bit ahead of me I saw the sign-post where the road forks right for Pudley and left for Oxford.

I was still on my usual beat, inside the boundary of my own 'district', as the firm calls it. The natural thing, as I was going westward, would have been to leave London along the Uxbridge Road. But by a kind of instinct I'd followed my usual route. The fact was I was feeling guilty about the whole business. I wanted to get well away before I headed for Oxfordshire. And in spite of the fact that I'd fixed things so neatly with Hilda and the firm, in spite of the twelve quid in my pocket-book and the suitcase in the back of the car, as I got nearer the crossroads I actually felt a temptation—I knew I wasn't going to succumb to it, and yet it was a temptation—to chuck the whole thing up. I had a sort of feeling that so long as I was driving along my normal beat I was still inside the law. It's not too late, I thought. There's still time to do the respectable thing. I could run into Pudley, for instance, see the manager of Barclay's Bank (he's our agent at Pudley) and find out if any new business had come in. For that matter I could even turn round, go back to Hilda, and make a clean breast of the plot.

I slowed down as I got to the corner. Should I or shouldn't I? For about a second I was really tempted. But no! I tooted the klaxon and swung the car westward, on to the Oxford road.

Well, I'd done it. I was on the forbidden ground. It was true that five miles farther on, if I wanted to, I could turn to the left again and get back to Westerham. But for the moment I was headed westward. Strictly speaking I was in flight. And what was curious, I was no sooner on the Oxford road than I felt perfectly certain that *they* knew all about it. When I say *they* I mean all the people who wouldn't approve of a trip of this kind and who'd have stopped me if they could—which, I suppose, would include pretty well everybody.

What was more, I actually had a feeling that they were after me already. The whole lot of them! All the people who couldn't understand why a middle-aged man with false teeth should sneak away for a quiet week in the place where he spent his boyhood. And all the mean-minded bastards who *could* understand only too well, and who'd raise heaven and earth to prevent it. They were all on my track. It was as if a huge army were streaming up the road behind me. I seemed to see them in my mind's eye. Hilda was in front, of course, with the kids tagging after her, and Mrs Wheeler driving her forward with a grim, vindictive expression, and Miss Minns rushing along in the rear, with her pince-nez slipping down and a look of distress on her face, like the hen that gets left behind when the others have got hold of the bacon rind. And Sir Herbert Crum and the higher-ups of the Flying Salamander in their Rolls-Royces and Hispano-Suizas. And all the chaps at the office, and all the poor down-trodden pen-pushers from Ellesmere Road and from all such other roads, some of them wheeling prams and mowing-machines and concrete garden-rollers, some of them chugging along in little Austin Sevens. And all the soul-savers and Nosey Parkers, the people whom you've never seen but who rule your destiny all the same, the Home Secretary, Scotland Yard, the Temperance League, the Bank of England, Lord Beaverbrook, Hitler and Stalin on a tandem bicycle, the bench of Bishops, Mussolini, the Pope—they were all of them after me. I could almost hear them shouting:

'There's a chap who thinks he's going to escape! There's a chap who says he won't be streamlined! He's going back to Lower Binfield! After him! Stop him!'

It's queer. The impression was so strong that I actually took a peep through the little window at the back of the car to make sure I wasn't being followed. Guilty conscience, I suppose. But there was nobody. Only the dusty white road and the long line of the elms dwindling out behind me.

I trod on the gas and the old car rattled into the thirties. A few minutes later I was past the Westerham turning. So that was that. I'd burnt my boats. This was the idea which, in a dim sort of way, had begun to form itself in my mind the day I got my new false teeth.

# PART IV

## I

I came towards Lower Binfield over Chamford Hill. There are four roads into Lower Binfield, and it would have been more direct to go through Walton. But I'd wanted to come over Chamford Hill, the way we used to go when we biked home from fishing in the Thames. When you get just past the crown of the hill the trees open out and you can see Lower Binfield lying in the valley below you.

It's a queer experience to go over a bit of country you haven't seen in twenty years. You remember it in great detail, and you remember it all wrong. All the distances are different, and the landmarks seem to have moved about. You keep feeling, surely this hill used to be a lot steeper—surely that turning was on the other side of the road? And on the other hand you'll have memories which are perfectly accurate, but which only belong to one particular occasion. You'll remember, for instance, a corner of a field, on a wet day in winter, with the grass so green that it's almost blue, and a rotten gatepost covered with lichen and a cow standing in the grass and looking at you. And you'll go back after twenty years and be surprised because the cow isn't standing in the same place and looking at you with the same expression.

As I drove up Chamford Hill I realized that the picture I'd had of it in my mind was almost entirely imaginary. But it was a fact that certain things had changed. The road was tarmac, whereas in the old days it used to be macadam (I remember the bumpy feeling of it under the bike), and it seemed to have got a lot wider. And there were far less trees. In the old days there used to be huge beeches growing in the hedgerows, and in places their boughs met across the road and made a kind of arch. Now they were all gone. I'd nearly got to the top of the hill when I came on something which was certainly new. To the right of the road there was a whole lot of fake-picturesque houses, with overhanging eaves and rose pergolas and what-not. You know the kind of houses that are just a little too high-class to stand in a row, and so they're dotted about in a kind of colony, with private roads leading up to them. And at the entrance to one of the private roads there was a huge white board which said:

## THE KENNELS

### PEDIGREE SEALYHAM PUPS

#### DOGS BOARDED

Surely *that* usen't to be there?

I thought for a moment. Yes, I remembered! Where those houses stood there used to be a little oak plantation, and the trees grew too close together, so that they were very tall and thin, and in spring the ground underneath them used to be smothered in anemones. Certainly there were never any houses as far out of the town as this.

I got to the top of the hill. Another minute and Lower Binfield would be in sight. Lower Binfield! Why should I pretend I wasn't excited? At the very thought of seeing it again an extraordinary feeling that started in my guts crept upwards and did something to my heart. Five seconds more and I'd be seeing it. Yes, here we are! I declutched, trod on the foot-brake, and—Jesus!

Oh, yes, I know *you* knew what was coming. But *I* didn't. You can say I was a bloody fool not to expect it, and so I was. But it hadn't even occurred to me.

The first question was, where *was* Lower Binfield?

I don't mean that it had been demolished. It had merely been swallowed. The thing I was looking down at was a good-sized manufacturing town. I remember—Gosh, how I remember! and in this case I don't think my memory is far out—what Lower Binfield used to look like from the top of Chamford Hill. I suppose the High Street was about a quarter of a mile long, and except for a few outlying houses the town was roughly the shape of a cross. The chief landmarks were the church tower and the chimney of the brewery. At this moment I couldn't distinguish either of them. All I could see was an enormous river of brand-new houses which flowed along the valley in both directions and half-way up the hills on either side. Over to the right there were what looked like several acres of bright red roofs all exactly alike. A big Council housing estate, by the look of it.

But where was Lower Binfield? Where was the town I used to know? It might have been anywhere. All I knew was that it was buried somewhere in the middle of that sea of bricks. Of the five or six factory chimneys that I could see, I couldn't even make a guess at which belonged to the brewery. Towards the eastern end of the town there were two enormous factories of glass and concrete. That accounts for the growth of the town, I thought, as I began to take it in. It occurred to me that the population of this place (it used to be about two thousand in the old days) must be a good twenty-five thousand. The only thing that hadn't changed, seemingly, was Binfield House. It wasn't much more than a dot at that distance, but you could see it on the hillside opposite, with the beech trees round it, and the town hadn't climbed that high. As I looked a fleet of black bombing planes came over the hill and zoomed across the town.

I shoved the clutch in and started slowly down the hill. The houses had climbed half-way up it. You know those very cheap small houses which run up a hillside in one continuous row, with the roofs rising one above the other like a flight of steps, all exactly the same. But a little before I got to the houses I stopped again. On the left of the road there was something else that was quite new. The cemetery. I stopped opposite the lych-gate to have a look at it.

It was enormous, twenty acres, I should think. There's always a kind of jumped-up unhomelike look about a new cemetery, with its raw gravel paths and its rough green sods, and the machine-made marble angels that look like something off a wedding-cake. But what chiefly struck me at the moment was that in the old days this place hadn't existed. There was no separate cemetery then, only the churchyard. I could vaguely remember the farmer these fields used to belong to–Blackett, his name was, and he was a dairy-farmer. And somehow the raw look of the place brought it home to me how things have changed. It wasn't only that the town had grown so vast that they needed twenty acres to dump their corpses in. It was their putting the cemetery out here, on the edge of the town. Have you noticed that they always do that nowadays? Every new town puts its cemetery on the outskirts. Shove it away–keep it out of sight! Can't bear to be reminded of death. Even the tombstones tell you the same story. They never say that the chap underneath them 'died', it's always 'passed away' or 'fell asleep'. It wasn't so in the old days. We had our churchyard plumb in the middle of the town, you passed it every day, you saw the spot where your grandfather was lying and where some day you were going to lie yourself. We didn't mind looking at the dead. In hot weather, I admit, we also had to smell them, because some of the family vaults weren't too well sealed.

I let the car run down the hill slowly. Queer! You can't imagine how queer! All the way down the hill I was seeing ghosts, chiefly the ghosts of hedges and trees and cows. It was as if I was looking at two worlds at once, a kind of thin bubble of the thing that used to be, with the thing that actually existed shining through it. There's the field where the bull chased Ginger Rodgers! And there's the place where the horse-mushrooms used to grow! But there weren't any fields or any bulls or any mushrooms. It was houses, houses everywhere, little raw red houses with their grubby window-curtains and their scraps of back-garden that hadn't anything in them except a patch of rank grass or a few larkspurs struggling among the weeds. And blokes walking up and down, and women shaking out mats, and snotty-nosed kids playing along the pavement. All strangers! They'd all come crowding in while my back was turned. And yet it was they who'd have looked on me as a stranger, they didn't know anything about the old Lower Binfield, they'd never heard of Shooter and Wetherall, or Mr Grimmett and Uncle Ezekiel, and cared less, you bet.

It's funny how quickly one adjusts. I suppose it was five minutes since I'd halted at the top of the hill, actually a bit out of breath at the thought of seeing Lower Binfield again. And already I'd got used to the idea that Lower Binfield had been swallowed up and buried like the lost cities of Peru. I braced up and faced it. After all, what else do you expect? Towns have got to grow, people have got to live somewhere. Besides, the old town hadn't been annihilated. Somewhere or other it still existed, though it had houses round it instead of fields. In a few minutes I'd be seeing it again, the church and the brewery chimney and Father's shop-window and the horse-trough in the market-place. I got to the bottom of the hill, and the road forked. I took the left-hand turning, and a minute later I was lost.

I could remember nothing. I couldn't even remember whether it was hereabouts that the town used to begin. All I knew was that in the old days this street hadn't existed. For hundreds of yards I was running along it—a rather mean, shabby kind of street, with the houses giving straight on the pavement and here and there a corner grocery or a dingy little pub—and wondering where the hell it led to. Finally I pulled up beside a woman in a dirty apron and no hat who was walking down the pavement. I stuck my head out of the window.

'Beg pardon—can you tell me the way to the market-place?'

She 'couldn't tell'. Answered in an accent you could cut with a spade. Lancashire. There's lots of them in the south of England now. Overflow from the distressed areas. Then I saw a bloke in overalls with a bag of tools coming along and tried again. This time I got the answer in Cockney, but he had to think for a moment.

'Market-place? Market-place? Lessee, now. Oh—you mean the *Ole* Market?'

I supposed I did mean the Old Market.

'Oh, well—you take the right 'and turning—'

It was a long way. Miles, it seemed to me, though really it wasn't a mile. Houses, shops, cinemas, chapels, football grounds—new, all new. Again I had that feeling of a kind of enemy invasion having happened behind my back. All these people flooding in from Lancashire and the London suburbs, planting themselves down in this beastly chaos, not even bothering to know the chief landmarks of the town by name. But I grasped presently why what we used to call the market-place was now known as the Old Market. There was a big square, though you couldn't properly call it a square, because it was no particular shape, in the middle of the new town, with traffic-lights and a huge bronze statue of a lion worrying an eagle—the war-memorial, I suppose. And the newness of everything! The raw, mean look! Do you know the look of these new towns that have suddenly swelled up like balloons in the last few years, Hayes, Slough, Dagenham, and so forth? The kind of chilliness, the bright red brick everywhere, the temporary-looking shop-windows full of cut-price chocolates and radio parts. It was just like that. But suddenly I swung into a street with older houses. Gosh! The High Street!

After all my memory hadn't played tricks on me. I knew every inch of it now. Another couple of hundred yards and I'd be in the market-place. The old shop was down the other end of the High Street. I'd go there after lunch—I was going to put up at the George. And every inch a memory! I knew all the shops, though all the names had changed, and the stuff they dealt in had mostly changed as well. There's Lovegrove's! And there's Todd's! And a big dark shop with beams and dormer windows. Used to be Lilywhite's the draper's, where Elsie used to work. And Grimmett's! Still a grocer's apparently. Now for the horse-trough in the market-place. There was another car ahead of me and I couldn't see.

It turned aside as we got into the market-place. The horse-trough was gone. There was an A.A. man on traffic-duty where it used to stand. He gave a glance at the car, saw that it hadn't the A.A. sign, and decided not to salute.

I turned the corner and ran down to the George. The horse-trough being gone had thrown me out to such an extent that I hadn't even looked to see whether the brewery chimney was still standing. The George had altered too, all except the name. The front had been dolled up till it looked like one of those riverside hotels, and the sign was different. It was curious that although till that moment I hadn't thought of it once in twenty years, I suddenly found that I could remember every detail of the old sign, which had swung there ever since I could remember. It was a crude kind of picture, with St George on a very thin horse trampling on a very fat dragon, and in the corner, though it was cracked and faded, you could read the little signature, 'Wm. Sandford, Painter & Carpenter'. The new sign was kind of artistic-looking. You could see it had been painted by a real artist. St George looked a regular pansy. The cobbled yard, where the farmers' traps used to stand and the drunks used to puke on Saturday nights, had been enlarged to about three times its size and concreted over, with garages all round it. I backed the car into one of the garages and got out.

One thing I've noticed about the human mind is that it goes in jerks. There's no emotion that stays by you for any length of time. During the last quarter of an hour I'd had what you could fairly describe as a shock. I'd felt it almost like a sock in the guts when I stopped at the top of Chamford Hill and suddenly realized that Lower Binfield had vanished, and there'd been another little stab when I saw the horse-trough was gone. I'd driven through the streets with a gloomy, Ichabod kind of feeling. But as I stepped out of the car and hitched my trilby hat on to my head I suddenly felt that it didn't matter a damn. It was such a lovely sunny day, and the hotel yard had a kind of summery look, with its flowers in green tubs and what-not. Besides, I was hungry and looking forward to a spot of lunch.

I strolled into the hotel with a consequential kind of air, with the boots, who'd already nipped out to meet me, following with the suitcase. I felt pretty prosperous, and probably I looked it. A solid business man, you'd have said, at any rate if you hadn't seen the car. I was glad I'd come in my new suit–blue flannel with a thin white stripe, which suits my style. It has what the tailor calls a 'reducing effect'. I believe that day I could have passed for a stockbroker. And say what you like it's a very pleasant thing, on a June day when the sun's shining on the pink geraniums in the window-boxes, to walk into a nice country hotel with roast lamb and mint sauce ahead of you. Not that it's any treat to me to stay in hotels, Lord knows I see all too much of them–but ninety-nine times out of a hundred it's those godless 'family and commercial' hotels, like Rowbottom's, where I was supposed to be staying at present, the kind of places where you pay five bob for bed and breakfast, and the sheets are always damp and the bath taps never work. The George had got so smart I wouldn't have known it. In the old days it had hardly been a hotel, only a pub, though it had a room or two to let and used to do a farmers' lunch (roast beef and Yorkshire, suet dumpling and Stilton cheese) on market days. It all seemed different except for the public bar, which I got a glimpse of as I went past, and which looked the same as ever. I went up a passage with a soft carpet, and hunting prints and copper warming-pans and such-like junk hanging on the walls. And dimly I could remember the passage as it used to be, the hollowed-out flags underfoot, and the smell of plaster mixed up with the smell of beer. A smart-looking young woman, with frizzed hair and a black dress, who I suppose was the clerk or something, took my name at the office.

'You wish for a room, sir? Certainly, sir. What name shall I put down, sir?'

I paused. After all, this was my big moment. She'd be pretty sure to know the name. It isn't common, and there are a lot of us in the churchyard. We were one of the old Lower Binfield families, the Bowlings of Lower Binfield. And though in a way it's painful to be recognized, I'd been rather looking forward to it.

'Bowling,' I said very distinctly. 'Mr George Bowling.'

'Bowling, sir. B-O-A—oh! B-O-W? Yes, sir. And you are coming from London, sir?'

No response. Nothing registered. She'd never heard of me. Never heard of George Bowling, son of Samuel Bowling—Samuel Bowling who, damn it! had had his half-pint in this same pub every Saturday for over thirty years.

## 2

The dining-room had changed, too.

I could remember the old room, though I'd never had a meal there, with its brown mantelpiece and its bronzy-yellow wallpaper—I never knew whether it was meant to be that colour, or had just got like that from age and smoke—and the oil-painting, also by Wm. Sandford, Painter & Carpenter, of the battle of Tel-el-Kebir. Now they'd got the place up in a kind of medieval style. Brick fireplace with inglenooks, a huge beam across the ceiling, oak panelling on the walls, and every bit of it a fake that you could have spotted fifty yards away. The beam was genuine oak, came out of some old sailing-ship, probably, but it didn't hold anything up, and I had my suspicions of the panels as soon as I set eyes on them. As I sat down at my table, and the slick young waiter came towards me fiddling with his napkin, I tapped the wall behind me. Yes! Thought so! Not even wood. They fake it up with some kind of composition and then paint it over.

But the lunch wasn't bad. I had my lamb and mint sauce, and I had a bottle of some white wine or other with a French name which made me belch a bit but made me feel happy. There was one other person lunching there, a woman of about thirty with fair hair, looked like a widow. I wondered whether she was staying at the George, and made vague plans to get off with her. It's funny how your feelings get mixed up. Half the time I was seeing ghosts. The past was sticking out into the present. Market day, and the great solid farmers throwing their legs under the long table, with their hobnails grating on the stone floor, and working their way through a quantity of beef and dumpling you wouldn't believe the human frame could hold. And then the little tables with their shiny white cloths and wine-glasses and folded napkins, and the faked-up decorations and the general expensiveness would blot it out again. And I'd think, 'I've got twelve quid and a new suit. I'm little Georgie Bowling, and who'd have believed I'd ever come back to Lower Binfield in my own motor-car?' And then the wine would send a kind of warm feeling upwards from my stomach, and I'd run an eye over the woman with fair hair and mentally take her clothes off.

It was the same in the afternoon as I lay about in the lounge—fake-medieval again, but it had streamlined leather armchairs and glass-topped tables—with some brandy and a cigar. I was seeing ghosts, but on the whole I was enjoying it. As a matter of fact I was a tiny bit boozed and hoping that the woman with fair hair would come in so that I could scrape acquaintance. She never showed up, however. It wasn't till nearly tea-time that I went out.

I strolled up to the market-place and turned to the left. The shop! It was funny. Twenty-one years ago, the day of Mother's funeral, I'd passed it in the station fly, and seen it all shut up and dusty, with the sign burnt off with a plumber's blowflame, and I hadn't cared a damn. And now, when I was so much further away from it, when there were actually details about the inside of the house that I couldn't remember, the thought of seeing it again did things to my heart and guts. I passed the barber's shop. Still a barber's, though the name was different. A warm, soapy, almondy smell came out of the door. Not quite so good as the old smell of bay rum and latakia. The shop—our shop—was twenty yards farther down. Ah!

An arty-looking sign—painted by the same chap as did the one at the George, I shouldn't wonder—hanging out over the pavement:

## WENDY'S TEASHOP

### MORNING COFFEE

### HOME-MADE CAKES

A tea-shop!
I suppose if it had been a butcher's or an ironmonger's, or anything else except a seedsman's, it would have given me the same kind of jolt. It's absurd that because you happen to have been born in a certain house you should feel that you've got rights over it for the rest of your life, but so you do. The place lived up to its name, all right. Blue curtains in the window, and a cake or two standing about, the kind of cake that's covered with chocolate and has just one walnut stuck somewhere on the top. I went in. I didn't really want any tea, but I had to see the inside.

They'd evidently turned both the shop and what used to be the parlour into tea-rooms. As for the yard at the back where the dustbin used to stand and Father's little patch of weeds used to grow, they'd paved it all over and dolled it up with rustic tables and hydrangeas and things. I went through into the parlour. More ghosts! The piano and the texts on the wall, and the two lumpy old red armchairs where Father and Mother used to sit on opposite sides of the fireplace, reading the *People* and the *News of the World* on Sunday afternoons! They'd got the place up in an even more antique style than the George, with gateleg tables and a hammered-iron chandelier and pewter plates hanging on the wall and what-not. Do you notice how dark they always manage to make it in these arty tea-rooms? It's part of the antiqueness, I suppose. And instead of an ordinary waitress there was a young woman in a kind of print wrapper who met me with a sour expression. I asked her for tea, and she was ten minutes getting it. You know the kind of tea—China tea, so weak that you could think it's water till you put the milk in. I was sitting almost exactly where Father's armchair used to stand. I could almost hear his voice, reading out a 'piece', as he used to call it, from the *People*, about the new flying machines, or the chap who was swallowed by a whale, or something. It gave me a most peculiar feeling that I was there on false pretences and they could kick me out if they discovered who I was, and yet simultaneously I had a kind of longing to tell somebody that I'd been born here, that I belonged to this house, or rather (what I really felt) that the house belonged to me. There was nobody else having tea. The girl in the print wrapper was hanging about by the window, and I could see that if I hadn't been there she'd have been picking her teeth. I bit into one of the slices of cake she'd brought me. Home-made cakes! You bet they were. Home-made with margarine and egg-substitute. But in the end I had to speak. I said:

'Have you been in Lower Binfield long?'

She started, looked surprised, and didn't answer. I tried again:

'I used to live in Lower Binfield myself, a good while ago.'

Again no answer, or only something that I couldn't hear. She gave me a kind of frigid look and then gazed out of the window again. I saw how it was. Too much of a lady to go in for back-chat with customers. Besides, she probably thought I was trying to get off with her. What was the good of telling her I'd been born in the house? Even if she believed it, it wouldn't interest her. She'd never heard of Samuel Bowling, Corn & Seed Merchant. I paid the bill and cleared out.

I wandered up to the church. One thing that I'd been half afraid of, and half looking forward to, was being recognized by people I used to know. But I needn't have worried, there wasn't a face I knew anywhere in the streets. It seemed as if the whole town had got a new population.

When I got to the church I saw why they'd had to have a new cemetery. The churchyard was full to the brim, and half the graves had names on them that I didn't know. But the names I did know were easy enough to find. I wandered round among the graves. The sexton had just scythed the grass and there was a smell of summer even there. They were all alone, all the older folks I'd known.

Gravitt the butcher, and Winkle the other seedsman, and Trew, who used to keep the George, and Mrs Wheeler from the sweet-shop—they were all lying there. Shooter and Wetherall were opposite one another on either side of the path, just as if they were still singing at each other across the aisle. So Wetherall hadn't got his hundred after all. Born in '43 and 'departed his life' in 1928. But he'd beaten Shooter, as usual. Shooter died in '26. What a time old Wetherall must have had those last two years when there was nobody to sing against him! And old Grimmett under a huge marble thing shaped rather like a veal-and-ham pie, with an iron railing round it, and in the corner a whole batch of Simmonses under cheap little crosses. All gone to dust. Old Hodges with his tobacco-coloured teeth, and Lovegrove with his big brown beard, and Lady Rampling with the coachman and the tiger, and Harry Barnes's aunt who had a glass eye, and Brewer of the Mill Farm with his wicked old face like something carved out of a nut—nothing left of any of them except a slab of stone and God knows what underneath.

I found Mother's grave, and Father's beside it. Both of them in pretty good repair. The sexton had kept the grass clipped. Uncle Ezekiel's was a little way away. They'd levelled a lot of the older graves, and the old wooden head-pieces, the ones that used to look like the end of a bedstead, had all been cleared away. What do you feel when you see your parents' graves after twenty years? I don't know what you ought to feel, but I'll tell you what I did feel, and that was nothing. Father and Mother have never faded out of my mind. It's as if they existed somewhere or other in a kind of eternity, Mother behind the brown teapot, Father with his bald head a little mealy, and his spectacles and his grey moustache, fixed for ever like people in a picture, and yet in some way alive. Those boxes of bones lying in the ground there didn't seem to have anything to do with them. Merely, as I stood there, I began to wonder what you feel like when you're underground, whether you care much and how soon you cease to care, when suddenly a heavy shadow swept across me and gave me a bit of a start.

I looked over my shoulder. It was only a bombing plane which had flown between me and the sun. The place seemed to be creeping with them.

I strolled into the church. For almost the first time since I got back to Lower Binfield I didn't have the ghostly feeling, or rather I had it in a different form. Because nothing had changed. Nothing, except that all the people were gone. Even the hassocks looked the same. The same dusty, sweetish corpse-smell. And by God! the same hole in the window, though, as it was evening and the sun was round the other side, the spot of light wasn't creeping up the aisle. They'd still got pews—hadn't changed over to chairs. There was our pew, and there was the one in front where Wetherall used to bellow against Shooter. Sihon king of the Amorites and Og the king of Bashan! And the worn stones in the aisle where you could still half-read the epitaphs of the blokes who lay beneath them. I squatted down to have a look at the one opposite our pew. I still knew the readable bits of it by heart. Even the pattern they made seemed to have stuck in my memory. Lord knows how often I'd read them during the sermon.

Here ............................................................................fon,    Gent.,
of this parif h.................................................................. his juft &
    upright ....................................................................................
    ................................................................................................
To his ....................................................manifold private bene
volences he added a diligent ....................................................
    ................................................................................................
    .......................................................................... beloved wife
Amelia, by..............................................................iffue feven
daughters ....................................................................................

I remembered how the long S's used to puzzle me as a kid. Used to wonder whether in the old days they pronounced their S's as F's, and if so, why.

There was a step behind me. I looked up. A chap in a cassock was standing over me. It was the vicar.

But I mean *the* vicar! It was old Betterton, who'd been vicar in the old days—not, as a matter of fact, ever since I could remember, but since 1904 or thereabouts. I recognized him at once, though his hair was quite white.

He didn't recognize me. I was only a fat tripper in a blue suit doing a bit of sightseeing. He said good evening and promptly started on the usual line of talk—was I interested in architecture, remarkable old building this, foundations go back to Saxon times and so on and so forth. And soon he was doddering round, showing me the sights, such as they were—Norman arch leading into the vestry, brass effigy of Sir Roderick Bone who was killed at the Battle of Newbury. And I followed him with the kind of whipped-dog air that middle-aged businessmen always have when they're being shown round a church or a picture-gallery. But did I tell him that I knew it all already? Did I tell him that I was Georgie Bowling, son of Samuel Bowling—he'd have remembered my father even if he didn't remember me—and that I'd not only listened to his sermons for ten years and gone to his Confirmation classes, but even belonged to the Lower Binfield Reading Circle and had a go at *Sesame and Lilies* just to please him? No, I didn't. I merely followed him round, making the kind of mumble that you make when somebody tells you that this or that is five hundred years old and you can't think what the hell to say except that it doesn't look it. From the moment that I set eyes on him I'd decided to let him think I was a stranger. As soon as I decently could I dropped sixpence in the Church Expenses box and bunked.

But why? Why not make contact, now that at last I'd found somebody I knew?

Because the change in his appearance after twenty years had actually frightened me. I suppose you think I mean that he looked older. But he didn't! He looked *younger*. And it suddenly taught me something about the passage of time.

I suppose old Betterton would be about sixty-five now, so that when I last saw him he'd have been about forty-five—my own present age. His hair was white now, and the day he buried Mother it was a kind of streaky grey, like a shaving-brush. And yet as soon as I saw him the first thing that struck me was that he looked younger. I'd thought of him as an old, old man, and after all he wasn't so very old. As a boy, it occurred to me, all people over forty had seemed to me just worn-out old wrecks, so old that there was hardly any difference between them. A man of forty-five had seemed to me older than this old dodderer of sixty-five seemed now. And Christ! I was forty-five myself. It frightened me.

So that's what I look like to chaps of twenty, I thought as I made off between the graves. Just a poor old hulk. Finished. It was curious. As a rule I don't care a damn about my age. Why should I? I'm fat, but I'm strong and healthy. I can do everything I want to do. A rose smells the same to me now as it did when I was twenty. Ah, but do I smell the same to the rose? Like an answer a girl, might have been eighteen, came up the churchyard lane. She had to pass within a yard or two of me. I saw the look she gave me, just a tiny momentary look. No, not frightened, not hostile. Only kind of wild, remote, like a wild animal when you catch its eye. She'd been born and grown up in those twenty years while I was away from Lower Binfield. All my memories would have been meaningless to her. Living in a different world from me, like an animal.

I went back to the George. I wanted a drink, but the bar didn't open for another half-hour. I hung about for a bit, reading a *Sporting and Dramatic* of the year before, and presently the fair-haired dame, the one I thought might be a widow, came in. I had a sudden desperate yearning to get off with her. Wanted to show myself that there's life in the old dog yet, even if the old dog does have to wear false teeth. After all, I thought, if she's thirty and I'm forty-five, that's fair enough. I was standing in front of the empty fireplace, making believe to warm my bum, the way you do on a summer day. In my blue suit I didn't look so bad. A bit fat, no doubt, but *distingué*. A man of the world. I could pass for a stockbroker. I put on my toniest accent and said casually:

'Wonderful June weather we're having.'

It was a pretty harmless remark, wasn't it? Not in the same class as 'Haven't I met you somewhere before?'

But it wasn't a success. She didn't answer, merely lowered for about half a second the paper she was reading and gave me a look that would have cracked a window. It was awful. She had one of those blue eyes that go into you like a bullet. In that split second I saw how hopelessly I'd got her wrong. She wasn't the kind of widow with dyed hair who likes being taken out to dance-halls. She was upper-middle-class, probably an admiral's daughter, and been to one of those good schools where they play hockey. And I'd got myself wrong too. New suit or no new suit, I *couldn't* pass for a stockbroker. Merely looked like a commercial traveller who'd happened to get hold of a bit of dough. I sneaked off to the private bar to have a pint or two before dinner.

The beer wasn't the same. I remember the old beer, the good Thames Valley beer that used to have a bit of taste in it because it was made out of chalky water. I asked the barmaid:

'Have Bessemers' still got the brewery?'

'Bessemers? Oo, *no*, sir! They've gorn. Oo, years ago—long before we come 'ere.'

She was a friendly sort, what I call the elder-sister type of barmaid, thirty-fivish, with a mild kind of face and the fat arms they develop from working the beer-handle. She told me the name of the combine that had taken over the brewery. I could have guessed it from the taste, as a matter of fact. The different bars ran round in a circle with compartments in between. Across in the public bar two chaps were playing a game of darts, and in the Jug and Bottle there was a chap I couldn't see who occasionally put in a remark in a sepulchral kind of voice. The barmaid leaned her fat elbows on the bar and had a talk with me. I ran over the names of the people I used to know, and there wasn't a single one of them that she'd heard of. She said she'd only been in Lower Binfield five years. She hadn't even heard of old Trew, who used to have the George in the old days.

'I used to live in Lower Binfield myself,' I told her. 'A good while back, it was, before the war.'

'Before the war? Well, now! You don't look that old.'

'See some changes, I dessay,' said the chap in the Jug and Bottle.

'The town's grown,' I said. 'It's the factories, I suppose.'

'Well, of course they mostly work at the factories. There's the gramophone works, and then there's Truefitt Stockings. But of course they're making bombs nowadays.'

I didn't altogether see why it was of course, but she began telling me about a young fellow who worked at Truefitt's factory and sometimes came to the George, and he'd told her that they were making bombs as well as stockings, the two, for some reason I didn't understand, being easy to combine. And then she told me about the big military aerodrome near Walton—that accounted for the bombing planes I kept seeing—and the next moment we'd started talking about the war, as usual. Funny. It was exactly to escape the thought of war that I'd come here. But how can you, anyway? It's in the air you breathe.

I said it was coming in 1941. The chap in the Jug and Bottle said he reckoned it was a bad job. The barmaid said it gave her the creeps. She said:

'It doesn't seem to do much good, does it, after all said and done? And sometimes I lie awake at night and hear one of those great things going overhead, and think to myself, "Well, now, suppose that was to drop a bomb right down on top of me!" And all this A.R.P., and Miss Todgers, she's the Air Warden, telling you it'll be all right if you keep your head and stuff the windows up with newspaper, and they say they're going to dig a shelter under the Town Hall. But the way I look at it is, how could you put a gas-mask on a baby?'

The chap in the Jug and Bottle said he'd read in the paper that you ought to get into a hot bath till it was all over. The chaps in the public bar overheard this and there was a bit of a by-play on the subject of how many people could get into the same bath, and both of them asked the barmaid if they could share her bath with her. She told them not to get saucy, and then she went up the other end of the bar and hauled them out a couple more pints of old and mild. I took a suck at my beer. It was poor stuff. Bitter, they call it. And it was bitter, right enough, too bitter, a kind of sulphurous taste. Chemicals. They say no English hops ever go into beer nowadays, they're all made into chemicals. Chemicals, on the other hand, are made into beer. I found myself thinking about Uncle Ezekiel, what he'd have said to beer like this, and what he'd have said about A.R.P. and the buckets of sand you're supposed to put the thermite bombs out with. As the barmaid came back to my side of the bar I said:

'By the way, who's got the Hall nowadays?'

We always used to call it the Hall, though its name was Binfield House. For a moment she didn't seem to understand.

'The Hall, sir?'

''E means Binfield 'Ouse,' said the chap in the Jug and Bottle.

'Oh, Binfield House! Oo, I thought you meant the Memorial Hall. It's Dr Merrall's got Binfield House now.'

'Dr Merrall?'

'Yes, sir. He's got more than sixty patients up there, they say.'

'Patients? Have they turned it into a hospital, or something?'

'Well—it's not what you'd call an ordinary hospital. More of a sanatorium. It's mental patients, reely. What they call a Mental Home.'

A loony-bin!

But after all, what else could you expect?

# 3

I crawled out of bed with a bad taste in my mouth and my bones creaking.

The fact was that, what with a bottle of wine at lunch and another at dinner, and several pints in between, besides a brandy or two, I'd had a bit too much to drink the day before. For several minutes I stood in the middle of the carpet, gazing at nothing in particular and too done-in to make a move. You know that god-awful feeling you get sometimes in the early morning. It's a feeling chiefly in your legs, but it says to you clearer than any words could do, 'Why the hell do you go on with it? Chuck it up, old chap! Stick your head in the gas oven!'

Then I shoved my teeth in and went to the window. A lovely June day, again, and the sun was just beginning to slant over the roofs and hit the house-fronts on the other side of the street. The pink geraniums in the window-boxes didn't look half bad. Although it was only about half past eight and this was only a side-street off the market-place there was quite a crowd of people coming and going. A stream of clerkly-looking chaps in dark suits with dispatch-cases were hurrying along, all in the same direction, just as if this had been a London suburb and they were scooting for the Tube, and the school-kids were straggling up towards the market-place in twos and threes. I had the same feeling that I'd had the day before when I saw the jungle of red houses that had swallowed Chamford Hill. Bloody interlopers! Twenty thousand gate-crashers who didn't even know my name. And here was all this new life swarming to and fro, and here was I, a poor old fatty with false teeth, watching them from a window and mumbling stuff that nobody wanted to listen to about things that happened thirty and forty years ago. Christ! I thought, I was wrong to think that I was seeing ghosts. I'm the ghost myself. I'm dead and they're alive.

But after breakfast—haddock, grilled kidneys, toast and marmalade, and a pot of coffee—I felt better. The frozen dame wasn't breakfasting in the dining-room, there was a nice summery feeling in the air, and I couldn't get rid of the feeling that in that blue flannel suit of mine I looked just a little bit *distingué*. By God! I thought, if I'm a ghost, I'll *be* a ghost! I'll walk. I'll haunt the old places. And maybe I can work a bit of black magic on some of these bastards who've stolen my home town from me.

I started out, but I'd got no farther than the market-place when I was pulled up by something I hadn't expected to see. A procession of about fifty school-kids was marching down the street in column of fours—quite military, they looked—with a grim-looking woman marching alongside of them like a sergeant-major. The leading four were carrying a banner with a red, white, and blue border and BRITONS PREPARE on it in huge letters. The barber on the corner had come out on to his doorstep to have a look at them. I spoke to him. He was a chap with shiny black hair and a dull kind of face.

'What are those kids doing?'

'It's this here air-raid practice,' he said vaguely. 'This here A.R.P. Kind of practising, like. That's Miss Todgers, that is.'

I might have guessed it was Miss Todgers. You could see it in her eye. You know the kind of tough old devil with grey hair and a kippered face that's always put in charge of Girl Guide detachments, Y.W.C.A. hostels, and what-not. She had on a coat and skirt that somehow looked like a uniform and gave you a strong impression that she was wearing a Sam Browne belt, though actually she wasn't. I knew her type. Been in the W.A.A.C.s in the war, and never had a day's fun since. This A.R.P. was jam to her. As the kids swung past I heard her letting out at them with the real sergeant-major yell, 'Monica! Lift your feet up!' and I saw that the rear four had another banner with a red, white, and blue border, and in the middle

WE ARE READY. ARE YOU?

'What do they want to march them up and down for?' I said to the barber.

'I dunno. I s'pose it's kind of propaganda, like.'

I knew, of course. Get the kids war-minded. Give us all the feeling that there's no way out of it, the bombers are coming as sure as Christmas, so down to the cellar you go and don't argue. Two of the great black planes from Walton were zooming over the eastern end of the town. Christ! I thought, when it starts it won't surprise us any more than a shower of rain. Already we're listening for the first bomb. The barber went on to tell me that thanks to Miss Todgers's efforts the school-kids had been served with their gas-masks already.

Well, I started to explore the town. Two days I spent just wandering round the old landmarks, such of them as I could identify. And all that time I never ran across a soul that knew me. I was a ghost, and if I wasn't actually invisible, I felt like it.

It was queer, queerer than I can tell you. Did you ever read a story of H.G. Wells's about a chap who was in two places at once—that's to say, he was really in his own home, but he had a kind of hallucination that he was at the bottom of the sea? He'd been walking round his room, but instead of the tables and chairs he'd see the wavy waterweed and the great crabs and cuttlefish reaching out to get him. Well, it was just like that. For hours on end I'd be walking through a world that wasn't there. I'd count my paces as I went down the pavement and think, 'Yes, here's where so-and-so's field begins. The hedge runs across the street and slap through that house. That petrol pump is really an elm tree. And here's the edge of the allotments. And this street (it was a dismal little row of semi-detached houses called Cumberledge Road, I remember) is the lane where we used to go with Katie Simmons, and the nut-bushes grew on both sides.' No doubt I got the distances wrong, but the general directions were right. I don't believe anyone who hadn't happened to be born here would have believed that these streets were fields as little as twenty years ago. It was as though the countryside had been buried by a kind of volcanic eruption from the outer suburbs. Nearly the whole of what used to be old Brewer's land had been swallowed up in the Council housing estate. The Mill Farm had vanished, the cow-pond where I caught my first fish had been drained and filled up and built over, so that I couldn't even say exactly where it used to stand. It was all houses, houses, little red cubes of houses all alike, with privet hedges and asphalt paths leading up to the front door. Beyond the Council Estate the town thinned out a bit, but the jerry-builders were doing their best. And there were little knots of houses dumped here and there, wherever anybody had been able to buy a plot of land, and the makeshift roads leading up to the houses, and empty lots with builders' boards, and bits of ruined fields covered with thistles and tin cans.

In the centre of the old town, on the other hand, things hadn't changed much, so far as buildings went. A lot of the shops were still doing the same line of trade, although the names were different. Lillywhite's was still a draper's, but it didn't look too prosperous. What used to be Gravitt's, the butcher's, was now a shop that sold radio parts. Mother Wheeler's little window had been bricked over. Grimmett's was still a grocer's, but it had been taken over by the International. It gives you an idea of the power of these big combines that they could even swallow up a cute old skinflint like Grimmett. But from what I know of him—not to mention that slap-up tombstone in the churchyard—I bet he got out while the going was good and had ten to fifteen thousand quid to take to heaven with him. The only shop that was still in the same hands was Sarazins', the people who'd ruined Father. They'd swollen to enormous dimensions, and they had another huge branch in the new part of the town. But they'd turned into a kind of general store and sold furniture, drugs, hardware, and ironmongery as well as the old garden stuff.

For the best part of two days I was wandering round, not actually groaning and rattling a chain, but sometimes feeling that I'd like to. Also I was drinking more than was good for me. Almost as soon as I got to Lower Binfield I'd started on the booze, and after that the pubs never seemed to open quite early enough. My tongue was always hanging out of my mouth for the last half-hour before opening time.

Mind you, I wasn't in the same mood all the time. Sometimes it seemed to me that it didn't matter a damn if Lower Binfield had been obliterated. After all, what had I come here for, except to get away from the family? There was no reason why I shouldn't do all the things I wanted to do, even go fishing if I felt like it. On the Saturday afternoon I even went to the fishing-tackle shop in the High Street and bought a split-cane rod (I'd always pined for a split-cane rod as a boy—it's a little bit dearer than a green-heart) and hooks and gut and so forth. The atmosphere of the shop cheered me up. Whatever else changes, fishing-tackle doesn't—because, of course, fish don't change either. And the shopman didn't see anything funny in a fat middle-aged man buying a fishing-rod. On the contrary, we had a little talk about the fishing in the Thames and the big chub somebody had landed the year before last on a paste made of brown bread, honey, and minced boiled rabbit. I even—though I didn't tell him what I wanted them for, and hardly even admitted it to myself—bought the strongest salmon trace he'd got, and some No. 5 roach-hooks, with an eye to those big carp at Binfield House, in case they still existed.

Most of Sunday morning I was kind of debating it in my mind—should I go fishing, or shouldn't I? One moment I'd think, why the hell not, and the next moment it would seem to me that it was just one of those things that you dream about and don't ever do. But in the afternoon I got the car out and drove down to Burford Weir. I thought I'd just have a look at the river, and tomorrow, if the weather was right, maybe I'd take my new fishing-rod and put on the old coat and grey flannel bags I had in my suitcase, and have a good day's fishing. Three or four days, if I felt like it.

I drove over Chamford Hill. Down at the bottom the road turns off and runs parallel to the towpath. I got out of the car and walked. Ah! A knot of little red and white bungalows had sprung up beside the road. Might have expected it, of course. And there seemed to be a lot of cars standing about. As I got nearer the river I came into the sound—yes, plonk-tiddle-tiddle-plonk!—yes, the sound of gramphones.

I rounded the bend and came in sight of the towpath. Christ! Another jolt. The place was black with people. And where the water-meadows used to be—tea-houses, penny-in-the-slot machines, sweet kiosks, and chaps selling Walls' Ice-Cream. Might as well have been at Margate. I remember the old towpath. You could walk along it for miles, and except for the chaps at the lock gates, and now and again a bargeman mooching along behind his horse, you'd meet never a soul. When we went fishing we always had the place to ourselves. Often I've sat there a whole afternoon, and a heron might be standing in the shallow water fifty yards up the bank, and for three or four hours on end there wouldn't be anyone passing to scare him away. But where had I got the idea that grown-up men don't go fishing? Up and down the bank, as far as I could see in both directions, there was a continuous chain of men fishing, one every five yards. I wondered how the hell they could all have got there until it struck me that they must be some fishing-club or other. And the river was crammed with boats—rowing-boats, canoes, punts, motor-launches, full of young fools with next to nothing on, all of them screaming and shouting and most of them with a gramphone aboard as well. The floats of the poor devils who were trying to fish rocked up and down on the wash of the motor-boats.

I walked a little way. Dirty, choppy water, in spite of the fine day. Nobody was catching anything, not even minnows. I wondered whether they expected to. A crowd like that would be enough to scare every fish in creation. But actually, as I watched the floats rocking up and down among the ice-cream tubs and the paper bags, I doubted whether there were any fish to catch. Are there still fish in the Thames? I suppose there must be. And yet I'll swear the Thames water isn't the same as it used to be. Its colour is quite different. Of course you think that's merely my imagination, but I can tell you it isn't so. I know the water has changed. I remember the Thames water as it used to be, a kind of luminous green that you could see deep into, and the shoals of dace cruising round the reeds. You couldn't see three inches into the water now. It's all brown and dirty, with a film of oil in it from the motor-boats, not to mention the fag-ends and the paper bags.

After a bit I turned back. Couldn't stand the noise of the gramophones any longer. Of course it's Sunday, I thought. Mightn't be so bad on a week-day. But after all, I knew I'd never come back. God rot them, let 'em keep their bloody river. Wherever I go fishing it won't be in the Thames.

The crowds swarmed past me. Crowds of bloody aliens, and nearly all of them young. Boys and girls larking along in couples. A troop of girls came past, wearing bell-bottomed trousers and white caps like the ones they wear in the American Navy, with slogans printed on them. One of them, seventeen she might have been, had PLEASE KISS ME. I wouldn't have minded. On an impulse I suddenly turned aside and weighed myself on one of the penny-in-the-slot machines. There was a clicking noise somewhere inside it—you know those machines that tell your fortune as well as your weight—and a typewritten card came sliding out.

'*You are the possessor of exceptional gifts,*' I read, '*but owing to excessive modesty you have never received your reward. Those about you underrate your abilities. You are too fond of standing aside and allowing others to take the credit for what you have done yourself. You are sensitive, affectionate, and always loyal to your friends. You are deeply attractive to the opposite sex. Your worst fault is generosity. Persevere, for you will rise high!*

'*Weight: 14 stone 11 pounds.*'

I'd put on four pounds in the last three days, I noticed. Must have been the booze.

# 4

I drove back to the George, dumped the car in the garage, and had a late cup of tea. As it was Sunday the bar wouldn't open for another hour or two. In the cool of the evening I went out and strolled up in the directon of the church.

I was just crossing the market-place when I noticed a woman walking a little way ahead of me. As soon as I set eyes on her I had a most peculiar feeling that I'd seen her somewhere before. You know that feeling. I couldn't see her face, of course, and so far as her back view went there was nothing I could identify, and yet I could have sworn I knew her.

She went up the High Street and turned down one of the side-streets to the right, the one where Uncle Ezekiel used to have his shop. I followed. I don't quite know why—partly curiosity, perhaps, and partly as a kind of precaution. My first thought had been that here at last was one of the people I'd known in the old days in Lower Binfield, but almost at the same moment it struck me that it was just as likely that she was someone from West Bletchley. In that case I'd have to watch my step, because if she found out I was here she'd probably split to Hilda. So I followed cautiously, keeping at a safe distance and examining her back view as well as I could. There was nothing striking about it. She was a tallish, fattish woman, might have been forty or fifty, in a rather shabby black dress. She'd no hat on, as though she'd just slipped out of her house for a moment, and the way she walked gave you the impression that her shoes were down at heel. All in all, she looked a bit of a slut. And yet there was nothing to identify, only that vague something which I knew I'd seen before. It was something in her movements, perhaps. Presently she got to a little sweet and paper shop, the kind of little shop that always keeps open on a Sunday. The woman who kept it was standing in the doorway, doing something to a stand of postcards. My woman stopped to pass the time of day.

I stopped too, as soon as I could find a shop window which I could pretend to be looking into. It was a plumber's and decorator's, full of samples of wallpaper and bathroom fittings and things. By this time I wasn't fifteen yards away from the other two. I could hear their voices cooing away in one of those meaningless conversations that women have when they're just passing the time of day. 'Yes, that's jest about it That's jest where it is. I said to him myself, I said, "Well, what else do you expect?" I said. It don't seem right, do it? But what's the use, you might as well talk to a stone. It's a shame!' and so on and so forth. I was getting warmer. Obviously my woman was a small shopkeeper's wife, like the other. I was just wondering whether she mightn't be one of the people I'd known in Lower Binfield after all, when she turned almost towards me and I saw three-quarters of her face. And Jesus Christ! It was Elsie!

Yes, it was Elsie. No chance of mistake. Elsie! That fat hag!

It gave me such a shock—not, mind you, seeing Elsie, but seeing what she'd grown to be like—that for a moment things swam in front of my eyes. The brass taps and ballstops and porcelain sinks and things seemed to fade away into the distance, so that I both saw them and didn't see them. Also for a moment I was in a deadly funk that she might recognize me. But she'd looked bang in my face and hadn't made any sign. A moment more, and she turned and went on. Again I followed. It was dangerous, she might spot I was following her, and that might start her wondering who I was, but I just had to have another look at her. The fact was that she exercised a kind of horrible fascination on me. In a manner of speaking I'd been watching her before, but I watched her with quite different eyes now.

It was horrible, and yet I got a kind of scientific kick out of studying her back view. It's frightening, the things that twenty-four years can do to a woman. Only twenty-four years, and the girl I'd known, with her milky-white skin and red mouth and kind of dull-gold hair, had turned into this great round-shouldered hag, shambling along on twisted heels. It made me feel downright glad I'm a man. No man ever goes to pieces quite so completely as that. I'm fat, I grant you. I'm the wrong shape, if you like. But at least I'm *a* shape. Elsie wasn't even particularly fat, she was merely shapeless. Ghastly things had happened to her hips. As for her waist, it had vanished. She was just a kind of soft lumpy cylinder, like a bag of meal.

I followed her a long way, out of the old town and through a lot of mean little streets I didn't know. Finally she turned in at the doorway of another shop. By the way she went in, it was obviously her own. I stopped for a moment outside the window. 'G. Cookson, Confectioner and Tobacconist.' So Elsie was Mrs Cookson. It was a mangy little shop, much like the other one where she'd stopped before, but smaller and a lot more flyblown. Didn't seem to sell anything except tobacco and the cheapest kinds of sweets. I wondered what I could buy that would take a minute or two. Then I saw a rack of cheap pipes in the window, and I went in. I had to brace my nerve up a little before I did it, because there'd need to be some hard lying if by any chance she recognized me.

She'd disappeared into the room behind the shop, but she came back as I tapped on the counter. So we were face to face. Ah! no sign. Didn't recognize me. Just looked at me the way they do. You know the way small shopkeepers look at their customers—utter lack of interest.

It was the first time I'd seen her full face, and though I half expected what I saw, it gave me almost as big a shock as that first moment when I'd recognized her. I suppose when you look at the face of someone young, even of a child, you ought to be able to foresee what it'll look like when it's old. It's all a question of the shape of the bones. But if it had ever occurred to me, when I was twenty and she was twenty-two, to wonder what Elsie would look like at forty-seven, it wouldn't have crossed my mind that she could ever look like *that*. The whole face had kind of sagged, as if it had somehow been drawn downwards. Do you know that type of middle-aged woman that has a face just like a bulldog? Great underhung jaw, mouth turned down at the corners, eyes sunken, with pouches underneath. Exactly like a bulldog. And yet it was the same face, I'd have known it in a million. Her hair wasn't completely grey, it was a kind of dirty colour, and there was much less of it than there used to be. She didn't know me from Adam. I was just a customer, a stranger, an uninteresting fat man. It's queer what an inch or two of fat can do. I wondered whether I'd changed even more than she had, or whether it was merely that she wasn't expecting to see me, or whether—what was the likeliest of all—she's simply forgotten my existence.

'Devening,' she said, in that listless way they have.

'I want a pipe,' I said flatly. 'A briar pipe.'

'A pipe. Now jest lemme see. I know we gossome pipes somewhere. Now where did I—ah! 'Ere we are.'

She took a cardboard box full of pipes from somewhere under the counter. How bad her accent had got! Or maybe I was just imagining that, because my own standards had changed? But no, she used to be so 'superior', all the girls at Lilywhite's were so 'superior', and she'd been a member of the vicar's Reading Circle. I swear she never used to drop her aitches. It's queer how these women go to pieces once they're married. I fiddled among the pipes for a moment and pretended to look them over. Finally I said I'd like one with an amber mouthpiece.

'Amber? I don't know as we got any—' she turned towards the back of the shop and called: 'Ge-orge!'

So the other bloke's name was George too. A noise that sounded something like 'Ur!' came from the back of the shop.

'Ge-orge! Where ju put that other box of pipes?'

George came in. He was a small stoutish chap, in shirtsleeves, with a bald head and a big gingery-coloured soupstrainer moustache. His jaw was working in a ruminative kind of way. Obviously he'd been interrupted in the middle of his tea. The two of them started poking round in search of the other box of pipes. It was about five minutes before they ran it to earth behind some bottles of sweets. It's wonderful, the amount of litter they manage to accumulate in these frowsy little shops where the whole stock is worth about fifty quid.

I watched old Elsie poking about among the litter and mumbling to herself. Do you know the kind of shuffling, round-shouldered movements of an old woman who's lost something? No use trying to describe to you what I felt. A kind of cold, deadly desolate feeling. You can't conceive it unless you've had it. All I can say is, if there was a girl you used to care about twenty-five years ago, go and have a look at her now. Then perhaps you'll know what I felt.

But as a matter of fact, the thought that was chiefly in my mind was how differently things turn out from what you expect. The times I'd had with Elsie! The July nights under the chestnut trees! Wouldn't you think it would leave some kind of after-effect behind? Who'd have thought the time would ever come when there would be just no feeling whatever between us? Here was I and here was she, our bodies might be a yard apart, and we were just as much strangers as though we'd never met. As for her, she didn't even recognize me.

If I told her who I was, very likely she wouldn't remember. And if she did remember, what would she feel? Just nothing. Probably wouldn't even be angry because I'd done the dirty on her. It was as if the whole thing had never happened.

And on the other hand, who'd ever have foreseen that Elsie would end up like this? She'd seemed the kind of girl who's bound to go to the devil. I know there'd been at least one other man before I had met her, and it's safe to bet there were others between me and the second George. It wouldn't surprise me to learn that she'd had a dozen altogether. I treated her badly, there's no question about that, and many a time it had given me a bad half-hour. She'll end up on the streets, I used to think, or stick her head in the gas oven. And sometimes I felt I'd been a bit of a bastard, but other times I reflected (what was true enough) that if it hadn't been me it would have been somebody else. But you see the way things happen, the kind of dull pointless way. How many women really end up on the streets? A damn sight more end up at the mangle. She hadn't gone to the bad, or to the good either. Just ended up like everybody else, a fat old woman muddling about a frowsy little shop, with a gingery-moustached George to call her own. Probably got a string of kids as well. Mrs George Cookson. Lived respected and died lamented—and might die this side of the bankruptcy-court, if she was lucky.

They'd found the box of pipes. Of course there weren't any with amber mouthpieces among them.

'I don't know as we got any amber ones just at present, sir. Not amber. We gossome nice vulcanite ones.'

'I wanted an amber one,' I said.

'We gossome nice pipes 'ere.' She held one out. 'That's a nice pipe, now. 'Alf a crown, that one is.'

I took it. Our fingers touched. No kick, no reaction. The body doesn't remember. And I suppose you think I bought the pipe, just for old sake's sake, to put half a crown in Elsie's pocket. But not a bit of it. I didn't want the thing. I don't smoke a pipe. I'd merely been making a pretext to come into the shop. I turned it over in my fingers and then put it down on the counter.

'Doesn't matter, I'll leave it,' I said. 'Give me a small Players'.'

Had to buy something, after all that fuss. George the second, or maybe the third or fourth, routed out a packet of Players', still munching away beneath his moustache. I could see he was sulky because I'd dragged him away from his tea for nothing. But it seemed too damn silly to waste half a crown. I cleared out and that was the last I ever saw of Elsie.

I went back to the George and had dinner. Afterwards I went out with some vague idea of going to the pictures, if they were open, but instead I landed up in one of the big noisy pubs in the new part of the town. There I ran into a couple of chaps from Staffordshire who were travelling in hardware, and we got talking about the state of trade, and playing darts and drinking Guinness. By closing time they were both so boozed that I had to take them home in a taxi, and I was a bit under the weather myself, and the next morning I woke up with a worse head than ever.

# 5

But I had to see the pool at Binfield House.

I felt really bad that morning. The fact was that ever since I struck Lower Binfield I'd been drinking almost continuously from every opening time to every closing time. The reason, though it hadn't occurred to me till this minute, was that really there'd been nothing else to do. That was all my trip had amounted to so far – three days on the booze.

The same as the other morning, I crawled over to the window and watched the bowler hats and school caps hustling to and fro. My enemies, I thought. The conquering army that's sacked the town and covered the ruins with fagends and paper bags. I wondered why I cared. You think, I dare say, that if it had given me a jolt to find Lower Binfield swollen into a kind of Dagenham, it was merely because I don't like to see the earth getting fuller and country turning into town. But it isn't that at all. I don't mind towns growing, so long as they do grow and don't merely spread like gravy over a tablecloth. I know that people have got to have somewhere to live, and that if a factory isn't in one place it'll be in another. As for the picturesqueness, the sham countrified stuff, the oak panels and pewter dishes and copper warming-pans and what-not, it merely gives me the sick. Whatever we were in the old days, we weren't picturesque. Mother would never have seen any sense in the antiques that Wendy had filled our house with. She didn't like gateleg tables – she said they 'caught your legs'. As for pewter, she wouldn't have it in the house. 'Nasty greasy stuff', she called it. And yet, say what you like, there was something that we had in those days and haven't got now, something that you probably can't have in a streamlined milk-bar with the radio playing. I'd come back to look for it, and I hadn't found it. And yet somehow I half believe in it even now, when I hadn't yet got my teeth in and my belly was crying out for an aspirin and a cup of tea.

And that started me thinking again about the pool at Binfield House. After seeing what they'd done to the town, I'd had a feeling you could only describe as fear about going to see whether the pool still existed. And yet it might, there was no knowing. The town was smothered under red brick, our house was full of Wendy and her junk, the Thames was poisoned with motor-oil and paper bags. But maybe the pool was still there, with the great black fish still cruising round it. Maybe, even, it was still hidden in the woods and from that day to this no one had discovered it existed. It was quite possible. It was a very thick bit of wood, full of brambles and rotten brushwood (the beech trees gave way

to oaks round about there, which made the undergrowth thicker), the kind of
place most people don't care to penetrate. Queerer things have happened.

I didn't start out till late afternoon. It must have been about half past four
when I took the car out and drove on to the Upper Binfield road. Half-way up
the hill the houses thinned out and stopped and the beech trees began. The
road forks about there and I took the right-hand fork, meaning to make a
detour round and come back to Binfield House on the road. But presently I
stopped to have a look at the copse I was driving through. The beech trees
seemed just the same. Lord, how they were the same! I backed the car on to a
bit of grass beside the road, under a fall of chalk, and got out and walked. Just
the same. The same stillness, the same great beds of rustling leaves that seem
to go on from year to year without rotting. Not a creature stirring except the
small birds in the tree-tops which you couldn't see. It wasn't easy to believe
that that great noisy mess of a town was barely three miles away. I began to
make my way through the little copse, in the direction of Binfield House. I
could vaguely remember how the paths went. And Lord! Yes! The same chalk
hollow where the Black Hand went and had catapult shots, and Sid Lovegrove
told us how babies were born, the day I caught my first fish, pretty near forty
years ago!

As the trees thinned out again you could see the other road and the wall of
Binfield House. The old rotting wooden fence was gone, of course, and they'd
put up a high brick wall with spikes on top, such as you'd expect to see round a
loony-bin. I'd puzzled for some time about how to get into Binfield House
until finally it had struck me that I'd only to tell them my wife was mad and I
was looking for somewhere to put her. After that they'd be quite ready to show
me round the grounds. In my new suit I probably looked prosperous enough
to have a wife in a private asylum. It wasn't till I was actually at the gate that it
occurred to me to wonder whether the pool was still inside the grounds.

The old grounds of Binfield House had covered fifty acres, I suppose, and
the grounds of the loony-bin weren't likely to be more than five or ten. They
wouldn't want a great pool of water for the loonies to drown themselves in.
The lodge, where old Hodges used to live, was the same as ever, but the yellow
brick wall and the huge iron gates were new. From the glimpse I got through
the gates I wouldn't have known the place. Gravel walks, flower-beds, lawns,
and a few aimless-looking types wandering about—loonies, I suppose. I
strolled up the road to the right. The pool—the big pool, the one where I used
to fish—was a couple of hundred yards behind the house. It might have been a
hundred yards before I got to the corner of the wall. So the pool was outside
the grounds. The trees seemed to have got much thinner. I could hear
children's voices. And Gosh! there was the pool.

I stood for a moment, wondering what had happened to it. Then I saw what
it was—all the trees were gone from round its edge. It looked all bare and
different, in fact it looked extraordinarily like the Round Pond in Kensington
Gardens. Kids wre playing all round the edge, sailing boats and paddling, and
a few rather older kids were rushing about in those little canoes which you
work by turning a handle. Over to the left, where the old rotting boat-house

used to stand among the reeds, there was a sort of pavilion and a sweet kiosk, and a huge white notice saying ˙UPPER BINFIELD MODEL YACHT CLUB.

I looked over to the right. It was all houses, houses, houses. One might as well have been in the outer suburbs. All the woods that used to grow beyond the pool, and grew so thick that they were like a kind of tropical jungle, had been shaved flat. Only a few clumps of trees still standing round the houses. There were arty-looking houses, another of those sham-Tudor colonies like the one I'd seen the first day at the top of Chamford Hill, only more so. What a fool I'd been to imagine that these woods were still the same! I saw how it was. There was just the one tiny bit of copse, half a dozen acres perhaps, that hadn't been cut down, and it was pure chance that I'd walked through it on my way here. Upper Binfield, which had been merely a name in the old days, had grown into a decent-sized town. In fact it was merely an outlying chunk of Lower Binfield.

I wandered up to the edge of the pool. The kids were splashing about and making the devil of a noise. There seemed to be swarms of them. The water looked kind of dead. No fish in it now. There was a chap standing watching the kids. He was an oldish chap with a bald head and a few tufts of white hair, and pince-nez and very sunburnt face. There was something vaguely queer about his appearance. He was wearing shorts and sandals and one of those celanese shirts open at the neck, I noticed, but what really struck me was the look in his eye. He had very blue eyes that kind of twinkled at you from behind his spectacles. I could see that he was one of those old men who've never grown up. They're always either health-food cranks or else they have something to do with the Boy Scouts—in either case they're great ones for Nature and the open air. He was looking at me as if he'd like to speak.

'Upper Binfield's grown a great deal,' I said.

He twinkled at me.

'Grown! My dear sir, we never allow Upper Binfield to grow. We pride ourselves on being rather exceptional people up here, you know. Just a little colony of us all by ourselves. No interlopers—te-hee!'

'I mean compared with before the war,' I said. 'I used to live here as a boy.'

'Oh-ah. No doubt. That was before my time, of course. But the Upper Binfield Estate is something rather special in the way of building estates, you know. Quite a little world of its own. All designed by young Edward Watkin, the architect. You've heard of him, of course. We live in the midst of Nature up here. No connexion with the town down there'—he waved a hand in the direction of Lower Binfield—'the dark satanic mills—te-hee!'

He had a benevolent old chuckle, and a way of wrinkling his face up, like a rabbit. Immediately, as though I'd asked him, he began telling me all about the Upper Binfield Estate and young Edward Watkin, the architect, who had such a feeling for the Tudor, and was such a wonderful fellow at finding genuine Elizabethan beams in old farmhouses and buying them at ridiculous prices. And such an interesting young fellow, quite the life and soul of the nudist parties. He repeated a number of times that they were very exceptional people in Upper Binfield, quite different from Lower Binfield, they were determined to enrich the countryside instead of defiling it (I'm using his own phrase), and there weren't any public houses on the estate.

'They talk of their Garden Cities. But we call Upper Binfield the Woodland City—te-hee! Nature!' He waved a hand at what was left of the trees. 'The primeval forest brooding round us. Our young people grow up amid surroundings of natural beauty. We are nearly all of us enlightened people, of course. Would you credit that three-quarters of us up here are vegetarians? The local butchers don't like us at all—te-hee! And some quite eminent people live here. Miss Helena Thurloe, the novelist—you've heard of her, of course. And Professor Woad, the psychic research worker. Such a poetic character! He goes wandering out into the woods and the family can't find him at mealtimes. He says he's walking among the fairies. Do you believe in fairies? I admit—te-hee!—I am just a wee bit sceptical. But his photographs are most convincing.'

I began to wonder whether he was someone who'd escaped from Binfield House. But no, he was sane enough, after a fashion. I knew the type. Vegetarianism, simple life, poetry, nature-worship, roll in the dew before breakfast. I'd met a few of them years ago in Ealing. He began to show me round the estate. There was nothing left of the woods. It was all houses, houses—and what houses! Do you know these faked-up Tudor houses with the curly roofs and the buttresses that don't buttress anything, and the rock-gardens with concrete bird-baths and those red plaster elves you can buy at the florists'? You could see in your mind's eye the awful gang of food-cranks and spook-hunters and simple-lifers with £1,000 a year that lived there. Even the pavements were crazy. I didn't let him take me far. Some of the houses made me wish I'd got a hand-grenade in my pocket. I tried to damp him down by asking whether people didn't object to living so near the lunatic asylum, but it didn't have much effect. Finally I stopped and said:

'There used to be another pool, besides the big one. It can't be far from here.'

'Another pool? Oh, surely not. I don't think there was ever another pool.'

'They may have drained it off,' I said. 'It was a pretty deep pool. It would leave a big pit behind.'

For the first time he looked a bit uneasy. He rubbed his nose.

'Oh-ah. Of course, you must understand our life up here is in some ways primitive. The simple life, you know. We prefer it so. But being so far from the town has its inconveniences, of course. Some of our sanitary arrangements are not altogether satisfactory. The dust-cart only calls once a month, I believe.'

'You mean they've turned the pool into a rubbish-dump?'

'Well, there *is* something in the nature of a—' he shied at the word rubbish-dump. 'We have to dispose of tins and so forth, of course. Over there, behind that clump of trees.'

We went across there. They'd left a few trees to hid it. But yes, there it was. It was my pool, all right. They'd drained the water off. It made a great round hole, like an enormous well, twenty or thirty feet deep. Already it was half full of tin cans.

I stood looking at the tin cans.

'It's a pity they drained it,' I said. 'There used to be some big fish in that pool.'

'Fish? Oh, I never heard anything about that. Of course we could hardly have a pool of water here among the houses. The mosquitoes, you know. But it was before my time.'

'I suppose these houses have been built a good long time?' I said.

'Oh—ten or fifteen years, I think.'

'I used to know this place before the war.' I said. 'It was all woods then. There weren't any houses except Binfield House. But that little bit of copse over there hasn't changed. I walked through it on my way here.'

'Ah, that! That is sacrosanct. We have decided never to build in it. It is sacred to the young people. Nature, you know.' He twinkled at me, a kind of roguish look, as if he was letting me into a little secret: 'We call it the Pixy Glen.'

The Pixy Glen. I got rid of him, went back to the car and drove down to Lower Binfield. The Pixy Glen. And they'd filled my pool up with tin cans. God rot them and bust them! Say what you like—call it silly, childish, anything—but doesn't it make you puke sometimes to see what they're doing to England, with their bird-baths and their plaster gnomes, and their pixies and tin cans, where the beech woods used to be?

Sentimental, you say? Anti-social? Oughtn't to prefer trees to men? I say it depends what trees and what men. Not that there's anything one can do about it, except to wish them the pox in their guts.

One thing, I thought as I drove down the hill, I'm finished with this notion of getting back into the past. What's the good of trying to revisit the scenes of your boyhood? They don't exist. Coming up for air! But there isn't any air. The dustbin that we're in reaches up to the stratosphere. All the same, I didn't particularly care. After all, I thought, I've still got three days left. I'd have a bit of peace and quiet, and stop bothering about what they'd done to Lower Binfield. As for my idea of going fishing—that was off, of course. Fishing, indeed! At my age! Really, Hilda was right.

I dumped the car in the garage of the George and walked into the lounge. It was six o'clock. Somebody had switched on the wireless and the news-broadcast was beginning. I came through the door just in time to hear the last few words of an S.O.S. And it gave me a bit of a jolt, I admit. For the words I heard were:

'—where his wife, Hilda Bowling, is seriously ill.'

The next instant the plummy voice went on: 'Here is another S.O.S. Will Percival Chute, who was last heard of—', but I didn't wait to hear any more. I just walked straight on. What made me feel rather proud, when I thought it over afterwards, was that when I heard those words come out of the loudspeaker I never turned an eyelash. Not even a pause in my step to let anyone know that I was George Bowling, whose wife Hilda Bowling was seriously ill. The landlord's wife was in the lounge, and she knew my name was Bowling, at any rate she'd seen it in the register. Otherwise there was nobody there except a couple of chaps who were staying at the George and who didn't know me from Adam. But I kept my head. Not a sign to anyone. I merely walked on into the private bar, which had just opened, and ordered my pint as usual.

I had to think it over. By the time I'd drunk about half the pint I began to get the bearings of the situation. In the first place, Hilda *wasn't* ill, seriously or otherwise. I knew that. She'd been perfectly well when I came away, and it wasn't the time of the year for 'flu or anything of that kind. She was shamming. Why?

Obviously it was just another of her dodges. I saw how it was. She'd got wind somehow—trust Hilda!—that I wasn't really at Birmingham, and this was just her way of getting me home. Couldn't bear to think of me any longer with that other woman. Because of course she'd take it for granted that I was with a woman. Can't imagine any other motive. And naturally she assumed that I'd come rushing home as soon as I heard she was ill.

But that's just where you've got it wrong, I thought to myself as I finished off the pint. I'm too cute to be caught that way. I remembered the dodges she'd pulled before, and the extraordinary trouble she'll take to catch me out. I've even known her, when I'd been on some journey she was suspicious about, check it all up with a Bradshaw and a road-map, just to see whether I was telling the truth about my movements. And then there was that time when she followed me all the way to Colchester and suddenly burst in on me at the Temperance Hotel. And that time, unfortunately, she happened to be right—at least, she wasn't, but there were circumstances which made it look as if she was. I hadn't the slightest belief that she was ill. In fact, I knew she wasn't, although I couldn't say exactly how.

I had another pint and things looked better. Of course there was a row coming when I got home, but there'd have been a row anyway. I've got three good days ahead of me, I thought. Curiously enough, now that the things I'd come to look for had turned out not to exist, the idea of having a bit of holiday appealed to me all the more. Being away from home—that was the great thing. Peace perfect peace with loved ones far away, as the hymn puts it. And suddenly I decided that I *would* have a woman if I felt like it. It would serve Hilda right for being so dirty-minded, and besides, where's the sense of being suspected if it isn't true?

But as the second pint worked inside me, the thing began to amuse me. I hadn't fallen for it, but it was damned ingenious all the same. I wondered how she'd managed about the S.O.S. I've no idea what the procedure is. Do you have to have a doctor's certificate, or do you just send your name in? I felt pretty sure it was the Wheeler woman who'd put her up to it. It seemed to me to have the Wheeler touch.

But all the same, the cheek of it! The lengths that women will go! Sometimes you can't help kind of admiring them

# 6

After breakfast I strolled out into the market-place. It was a lovely morning, kind of cool and still, with a pale yellow light like white wine playing over everything. The fresh smell of the morning was mixed up with the smell of my cigar. But there was a zooming noise from behind the houses, and suddenly a fleet of great black bombers came whizzing over. I looked up at them. They seemed to be bang overhead.

The next moment I heard something. And at the same moment, if you'd happened to be there, you'd have seen an interesting instance of what I believe is called conditioned reflex. Because what I'd heard—there wasn't any question of mistake—was the whistle of a bomb. I hadn't heard such a thing for twenty years, but I didn't need to be told what it was. And without taking any kind of thought I did the right thing. I flung myself on my face.

After all I'm glad you didn't see me. I don't suppose I looked dignified. I was flattened out on the pavement like a rat when it squeezes under a door. Nobody else had been half as prompt. I'd acted so quickly that in the split second while the bomb was whistling down I even had time to be afraid that it was all a mistake and I'd made a fool of myself for nothing.

But the next moment—ah!

BOOM–BRRRRR!

A noise like the Day of Judgment, and then a noise like a ton of coal falling on to a sheet of tin. That was falling bricks. I seemed to kind of melt into the pavement. 'It's started,' I thought. 'I knew it! Old Hitler didn't wait. Just sent his bombers across without warning.'

And yet here's a peculiar thing. Even in the echo of that awful, deafening crash, which seemed to freeze me up from top to toe, I had time to think that there's something grand about the bursting of a big projectile. What does it sound like? It's hard to say, because what you hear is mixed up with what you're frightened of. Mainly it gives you a vision of bursting metal. You seem to see great sheets of iron bursting open. But the peculiar thing is the feeling it gives you of being suddenly shoved up against reality. It's like being woken up by somebody shying a bucket of water over you. You're suddenly dragged out of your dreams by a clang of bursting metal, and it's terrible, and it's real.

There was a sound of screams and yells, and also of car brakes being suddenly jammed on. The second bomb which I was waiting for didn't fall. I raised my head a little. On every side people seemed to be rushing round and screaming. A car was skidding diagonally across the road, I could hear a woman's voice shrieking, 'The Germans! The Germans!' To the right I had a vague impression of a man's round white face, rather like a wrinkled paper bag, looking down at me. He was kind of dithering:

'What is it? What's happened? What are they doing?'

'It's started,' I said. 'That was a bomb. Lie down.'

But still the second bomb didn't fall. Another quarter of a minute or so, and I raised my head again. Some of the people were still rushing about, others were standing as if they'd been glued to the ground. From somewhere behind the houses a huge haze of dust had risen up, and through it a black jet of smoke was streaming upwards. And then I saw an extraordinary sight. At the other end of the market-place the High Street rises a little. And down this little hill a herd of pigs was galloping, a sort of huge flood of pig-faces. The next moment, of course, I saw what it was. It wasn't pigs at all, it was only the schoolchildren in their gas-masks. I suppose they were bolting for some cellar where they'd been told to take cover in case of air-raids. At the back of them I could even make out a taller pig who was probably Miss Todgers. But I tell you for a moment they looked exactly like a herd of pigs.

I picked myself up and walked across the market-place. People were calming down already, and quite a little crowd had begun to flock towards the place where the bomb had dropped.

Oh, yes, you're right, of course. It wasn't a German aeroplane after all. The war hadn't broken out. It was only an accident. The planes were flying over to do a bit of bombing practice—at any rate they were carrying bombs—and somebody had put his hands on the lever by mistake. I expect he got a good ticking off for it. By the time that the postmaster had rung up London to ask whether there was a war on, and been told that there wasn't, everyone had grasped that it was an accident. But there'd been a space of time, something between a minute and five minutes, when several thousand people believed we were at war. A good job it didn't last any longer. Another quarter of an hour and we'd have been lynching our first spy.

I followed the crowd. The bomb had dropped in a little side-street off the High Street, the one where Uncle Ezekiel used to have his shop. It wasn't fifty yards from where the shop used to be. As I came round the corner I could hear voices murmuring 'Oo-oo!'—a kind of awed noise, as if they were frightened and getting a big kick out of it. Luckily I got there a few minutes before the ambulance and the fire-engine, and in spite of the fifty people or so that had already collected I saw everything.

At first sight it looked as if the sky had been raining bricks and vegetables. There were cabbage leaves everywhere. The bomb had blown a greengrocer's shop out of existence. The house to the right of it had part of its roof blown off, and the roof beams were on fire, and all the houses round had been more or less damaged and had their windows smashed. But what everyone was looking at was the house on the left. Its wall, the one that joined the greengrocer's shop, was ripped off as neatly as if someone had done it with a knife. And what was extraordinary was that in the upstairs rooms nothing had been touched. It was just like looking into a doll's house. Chests-of-drawers, bedroom chairs, faded

wallpaper, a bed not yet made, and a jerry under the bed—all exactly as it had
been lived in, except that one wall was gone. But the lower rooms had caught
the force of the explosion. There was a frightful smashed-up mess of bricks,
plaster, chair-legs, bits of a varnished dresser, rags of tablecloth, piles of
broken plates, and chunks of a scullery sink. A jar of marmalade had rolled
across the floor, leaving a long streak of marmalade behind, and running side
by side with it there was a ribbon of blood. But in among the broken crockery
there was lying a leg. Just a leg, with the trouser still on it and a black boot with
a Wood-Milne rubber heel. This was what people were oo-ing and ah-ing at.

I had a good look at it and took it in. The blood was beginning to get mixed
up with the marmalade. When the fire-engine arrived I cleared off to the
George to pack my bag.

This finishes me with Lower Binfield, I thought. I'm going home. But as a
matter of fact I didn't shake the dust off my shoes and leave immediately. One
never does. When anything like that happens, people always stand about and
discuss it for hours. There wasn't much work done in the old part of Lower
Binfield that day, everyone was too busy talking about the bomb, what it
sounded like and what they thought when they heard it. The barmaid at the
George said it fair gave her the shudders. She said she'd never sleep sound in
her bed again, and what did you expect, it just showed that with these here
bombs you never knew. A woman had bitten off part of her tongue owing to the
jump the explosion gave her. It turned out that whereas at our end of the town
everyone had imagined it was a German air-raid, everyone at the other end had
taken it for granted that it was an explosion at the stocking factory. Afterwards
(I got this out of the newspaper) the Air Ministry sent a chap to inspect the
damage, and issued a report saying that the effects of the bomb were
'disappointing'. As a matter of fact it only killed three people, the greengrocer,
Perrott his name was, and an old couple who lived next door. The woman
wasn't much smashed about, and they identified the old man by his boots, but
they never found a trace of Perrott. Not even a trouser-button to read the
burial service over.

In the afternoon I paid my bill and hooked it. I didn't have much more than
three quid left after I'd paid the bill. They know how to cut it out of you these
dolled-up country hotels, and what with drinks and other odds and ends I'd
been shying money about pretty freely. I left my new rod and the rest of the
fishing tackle in my bedroom. Let 'em keep it. No use to me. It was merely a
quid that I'd chucked down the drain to teach myself a lesson. And I'd learnt
the lesson all right. Fat men of forty-five can't go fishing. That kind of thing
doesn't happen any longer, it's just a dream, there'll be no more fishing this
side of the grave.

It's funny how things sink into you by degrees. What had I really felt when
the bomb exploded? At the actual moment, of course, it scared the wits out of
me, and when I saw the smashed-up house and the old man's leg I'd had the
kind of mild kick that you get from seeing a street-accident. Disgusting, of
course. Quite enough to make me fed-up with this so-called holiday. But it
hadn't really made much impression.

But as I got clear of the outskirts of Lower Binfield and turned the car eastward, it all came back to me. You know how it is when you're in a car alone. There's something either in the hedges flying past you, or in the throb of the engine, that gets your thoughts running in a certain rhythm. You have the same feeling sometimes when you're in the train. It's a feeling of being able to see things in better perspective than usual. All kinds of things that I'd been doubtful about I felt certain about now. To begin with, I'd come to Lower Binfield with a question in my mind. What's ahead of us? Is the game really up? Can we get back to the life we used to live, or is it gone for ever? Well, I'd had my answer. The old life's finished, and to go back to Lower Binfield, you can't put Jonah back into the whale. I *knew*, though I don't expect you to follow my train of thought. And it was a queer thing I'd done coming here. All those years Lower Binfield had been tucked away somewhere or other in my mind, a sort of quiet corner that I could step back into when I felt like it, and finally I'd stepped back into it and found that it didn't exist. I'd chucked a pineapple into my dreams, and lest there should be any mistake the Royal Air Force had followed up with five hundred pounds of T.N.T.

War is coming. 1941, they say. And there'll be plenty of broken crockery, and little houses ripped open like packing-cases, and the guts of the chartered accountant's clerk plastered over the piano that he's buying on the never-never. But what does that kind of thing matter, anyway? I'll tell you what my stay in Lower Binfield had taught me, and it was this. *It's all going to happen.* All the things you've got at the back of your mind, the things you're terrified of, the things that you tell yourself are just a nightmare or only happen in foreign countries. The bombs, the food-queues, the rubber truncheons, the barbed wire, the coloured shirts, the slogans, the enormous faces, the machine-guns squirting out of bedroom windows. It's all going to happen. I know it—at any rate, I knew it then. There's no escape. Fight against it if you like, or look the other way and pretend not to notice, or grab your spanner and rush out to do a bit of face-smashing along with the others. But there's no way out. It's just something that's got to happen.

I trod on the gas, and the old car whizzed up and down the little hills, and the cows and elm trees and fields of wheat rushed past till the engine was pretty nearly red-hot. I felt in much the same mood as I'd felt that day in January when I was coming down the Strand, the day I got my new false teeth. It was as though the power of prophecy had been given me. It seemed to me that I could see the whole of England, and all the people in it, and all the things that'll happen to all of them. Sometimes, of course, even then, I had a doubt or two. The world is very large, that's a thing you notice when you're driving about in a car, and in a way it's reassuring. Think of the enormous stretches of land you pass over when you cross a corner of a single English county. It's like Siberia. And the fields and beech spinneys and farmhouses and churches, and the villages with their little grocers' shops and the parish hall and the ducks walking across the green. Surely it's too big to be changed? Bound to remain more or less the same. And presently I struck into outer London and followed the Uxbridge Road as far as Southall. Miles and miles of ugly houses, with people living dull decent lives inside them. And beyond it London stretching on and on, streets, squares, back-alleys, tenements, blocks of flats, pubs, fried-fish shops, picture-houses, on and on for twenty miles, and all the eight million people with their little private lives which they don't want to have altered. The bombs aren't made that could smash it out of existence. And the chaos of it! The privateness of all those lives! John Smith cutting out the football coupons, Bill Williams swapping stories in the barber's. Mrs Jones coming home with the supper beer. Eight million of them! Surely they'll manage somehow, bombs or no bombs, to keep on with the life that they've been used to?

Illusion! Baloney! It doesn't matter how many of them there are, they're all for it. The bad times are coming, and the streamlined men are coming too. What's coming afterwards I don't know, it hardly even interests me. I only know that if there's anything you care a curse about, better say good-bye to it now, because everything you've ever known is going down, down, into the muck, with the machine-guns rattling all the time.

But when I got back to the suburb my mood suddenly changed.

It suddenly struck me—and it hadn't even crossed my mind till that moment—that Hilda might really be ill after all.

That's the effect of environment, you see. In Lower Binfield I'd taken it absolutely for granted that she wasn't ill and was merely shamming in order to get me home. It had seemed natural at the time, I don't know why. But as I drove into West Bletchley and the Hesperides Estate closed round me like a kind of red-brick prison, which is what it is, the ordinary habits of thought came back. I had this kind of Monday morning feeling when everything seems bleak and sensible. I saw what bloody rot it was, this business that I'd wasted the last five days on. Sneaking off to Lower Binfield to try and recover the past, and then, in the car coming home, thinking a lot of prophetic baloney about the future. The future! What's the future got to do with chaps like you and me? Holding down our jobs—that's our future. As for Hilda, even when the bombs are dropping she'll be still thinking about the price of butter.

And suddenly I saw what a fool I'd been to think she'd do a thing like that. Of course the S.O.S. wasn't a fake! As though she'd have the imagination! It was just the plain cold truth. She wasn't shamming at all, she was really ill. And Gosh! at this moment she might be lying somewhere in ghastly pain, or even dead, for all I knew. The thought sent a most horrible pang of fright through me, a sort of dreadful cold feeling in my guts. I whizzed down Ellesmere Road at nearly forty miles an hour, and instead of taking the car to the lock-up garage as usual I stopped outside the house and jumped out.

So I'm fond of Hilda after all, you say! I don't know exactly what you mean by fond. Are you fond of your own face? Probably not, but you can't imagine yourself without it. It's part of you. Well, that's how I felt about Hilda. When things are going well I can't stick the sight of her, but the thought that she might be dead or even in pain sent the shivers through me.

I fumbled with the key, got the door open, and the familiar smell of old mackintoshes hit me.

'Hilda!' I yelled. 'Hilda!'

No answer. For a moment I was yelling 'Hilda! Hilda!' into utter silence, and some cold sweat started out on my backbone. Maybe they carted her away to hospital already–maybe there was a corpse lying upstairs in the empty house.

I started to dash up the stairs, but at the same moment the two kids, in their pyjamas, came out of their rooms on either side of the landing. It was eight or nine o'clock, I suppose–at any rate the light was just beginning to fail. Lorna hung over the banisters.

'Oo, Daddy! Oo, it's Daddy! Why have you come back today? Mummy said you weren't coming till Friday.'

'Where's your mother?' I said.

'Mummy's out. She went out with Mrs Wheeler. Why have you come home today, Daddy?'

'Then your mother hasn't been ill?'

'No. Who said she'd been ill? Daddy! Have you been in Birmingham?'

'Yes. Get back to bed, now. You'll be catching cold.'

'But where's our presents, Daddy?'

'What presents?'

'The presents you've bought us from Birmingham.'

'You'll see them in the morning,' I said.

'Oo, Daddy! Can't we see them tonight?'

'No. Dry up. Get back to bed or I'll wallop the pair of you.'

So she wasn't ill after all. She *had* been shamming. And really I hardly knew whether to be glad or sorry. I turned back to the front door, which I'd left open, and there, as large as life, was Hilda coming up the garden path.

I looked at her as she came towards me in the last of the evening light. It was queer to think that less than three minutes earlier I'd been in the devil of a stew, with actual cold sweat on my backbone, at the thought that she might be dead. Well, she wasn't dead, she was just as usual. Old Hilda with her thin shoulders and her anxious face, and the gas bill and the school-fees, and the mackintoshy smell and the office on Monday–all the bedrock facts that you invariably come back to, the eternal verities as old Porteous calls them. I could see that Hilda wasn't in too good a temper. She darted me a little quick look, like she does sometimes when she's got something on her mind, the kind of look some little thin animal, a weasel for instance, might give you. She didn't seem surprised to see me back, however.

'Oh, so you're back already, are you?' she said.

It seemed pretty obvious that I was back, and I didn't answer. She didn't make any move to kiss me.

'There's nothing for your supper,' she went on promptly. That's Hilda all over. Always manages to say something depressing the instant you set foot inside the house. 'I wasn't expecting you. You'll just have to have bread and cheese–but I don't think we've got any cheese.'

I followed her indoors, into the smell of mackintoshes. We went into the sitting-room. I shut the door and switched on the light. I meant to get my say in first, and I knew it would make things better if I took a strong line from the start.

'Now', I said, 'what the bloody hell do you mean by playing that trick on me?'

She'd just laid her bag down on top of the radio, and for a moment she looked genuinely surprised.

'What trick? What do you mean?'

'Sending out that S.O.S.!'

'What S.O.S.? What are you *talking* about, George?'

'Are you trying to tell me you didn't get them to send out an S.O.S. saying you were seriously ill?'

'Of course I didn't! How could I? I wasn't ill. What would I do a thing like that for?'

I began to explain, but almost before I began I saw what had happened. It was all a mistake. I'd only heard the last few words of the S.O.S. and obviously it was some other Hilda Bowling. I suppose there'd be scores of Hilda Bowlings if you looked the name up in the directory. It just was the kind of dull stupid mistake that's always happening. Hilda hadn't even showed that little bit of imagination I'd credited her with. The sole interest in the whole affair had been the five minutes or so when I thought she was dead, and found that I cared after all. But that was over and done with. While I explained she was watching me, and I could see in her eye that there was trouble of some kind coming. And then she began questioning me in what I call her third-degree voice, which isn't, as you might expect, angry and nagging, but quiet and kind of watchful.

'So you heard this S.O.S. in the hotel at Birmingham?'

'Yes. Last night, on the National Broadcast.'

'When did you leave Birmingham, then?'

'This morning, of course.' (I'd planned out the journey in my mind, just in case there should be any need to lie my way out of it. Left at ten, lunch at Coventry, tea at Bedford—I'd got it all mapped out.)

'So you thought last night I was seriously ill, and you didn't even leave till this morning?'

'But I tell you I didn't think you were ill. Haven't I explained? I thought it was just another of your tricks. It sounded a damn sight more likely.'

'Then I'm rather surprised you left at all!' she said with so much vinegar in her voice that I knew there was something more coming. But she went on more quietly: 'So you left this morning, did you?'

'Yes. I left about ten. I had lunch at Coventry—'

'Then how do you account for *this*?' she suddenly shot out at me, and in the same instant she ripped her bag open, took out a piece of paper, and held it out as if it had been a forged cheque, or something.

I felt as if someone had hit me a sock in the wind. I might have known it! She'd caught me after all. And there was the evidence, the dossier of the case. I didn't even know what it was, except that it was something that proved I'd been off with a woman. All the stuffing went out of me. A moment earlier I'd been kind of bullying her, making out to be angry because I'd been dragged back from Birmingham for nothing, and now she'd suddenly turned the tables on me. You don't have to tell me what I look like at that moment. I know. Guilt written all over me in big letters—I know. And I wasn't even guilty! But it's a matter of habit. I'm used to being in the wrong. For a hundred quid I couldn't have kept the guilt out of my voice as I answered:

'What do you mean? What's that thing you've got there?'

'You read it and you'll see what it is.'

I took it. It was a letter from what seemed to be a firm of solicitors, and it was addressed from the same street as Rowbottom's Hotel, I noticed.

'Dear Madam,' I read, 'With reference to your letter of the 18th inst., we think there must be some mistake. Rowbottom's Hotel was closed down two years ago and has been converted into a block of offices. No one answering the description of your husband has been here. Possibly—'

I didn't read any further. Of course I saw it all in a flash. I'd been a little bit too clever and put my foot in it. There was just one faint ray of hope—young Saunders might have forgotten to post the letter I'd addressed from Rowbottom's, in which case it was just possible I could brazen it out. But Hilda soon put the lid on that idea.

'Well, George, you see what the letter says? The day you left here I wrote to Rowbottom's Hotel—oh, just a little note, asking them whether you'd arrived there. And you see the answer I got! There isn't even any such place as Rowbottom's Hotel! And the same day, the very same post, I got your letter saying you were at the hotel. You got someone to post it for you, I suppose. *That* was your business in Birmingham!'

'But look here, Hilda! You've got all this wrong. It isn't what you think at all. You don't understand.'

'Oh, yes, I do, George. I understand *perfectly*.'

'But look here, Hilda—'

Wasn't any use, of course. It was a fair cop. I couldn't even meet her eye. I turned and tried to make for the door.

'I'll have to take the car round to the garage,' I said.

'Oh, no George! You don't get out of it like that. You'll stay here and listen to what I've got to say, please.'

'But, damn it! I've got to switch the lights on, haven't I? It's past lighting-up time. You don't want us to get fined?'

At that she let me go, and I went out and switched the car lights on, but when I came back she was still standing there like a figure of doom, with the two letters, mine and the solicitor's on the table in front of her. I'd got a little of my nerve back, and I had another try:

'Listen, Hilda. You've got hold of the wrong end of the stick about this business. I can explain the whole thing.'

'I'm sure *you* could explain anything, George. The question is whether I'd believe you.'

'But you're just jumping to conclusions! What made you write to these hotel people, anyway?'

'It was Mrs Wheeler's idea. And a very good idea too, as it turned out.'

'Oh, Mrs Wheeler, was it? So you don't mind letting that blasted woman into our private affairs?'

'She didn't need any letting in. It was she who warned me what you were up to this week. Something seemed to tell her, she said. And she was right, you see. She knows all about you, George. She used to have a husband *just* like you.'

'But, Hilda—'

I looked at her. Her face had gone a kind of white under the surface, the way it does when she thinks of me with another woman. A woman. If only it had been true!

And Gosh! what I could see ahead of me! You know what it's like. The weeks on end of ghastly nagging and sulking, and the catty remarks after you think peace has been signed, and the meals always late, and the kids wanting to know what it's all about. But what really got me down was the kind of mental squalor, the kind of mental atmosphere in which the real reason why I'd gone to Lower Binfield wouldn't even be conceivable. That was what chiefly struck me at the moment. If I spent a week explaining to Hilda *why* I'd been to Lower Binfield, she'd never understand. And who *would* understand, here in Ellesmere Road? Gosh! did I even understand myself? The whole thing seemed to be fading out of my mind. Why had I gone to Lower Binfield? *Had* I gone there? In this atmosphere it just seemed meaningless. Nothing's real in Ellesmere Road except gas bills, school-fees, boiled cabbage, and the office on Monday.

One more try:

'But look here, Hilda! I know what you think. But you're absolutely wrong. I swear to you you're wrong.'

'Oh, no, George. If I was wrong why did you have to tell all those lies?'

No getting away from that, of course.

I took a pace or two up and down. The smell of old mackintoshes was very strong. Why had I run away like that? Why had I bothered about the future and the past, seeing that the future and the past don't matter? Whatever motives I might have had, I could hardly remember them now. The old life in Lower Binfield, the war and the after-war, Hitler, Stalin, bombs, machine-guns, food-queues, rubber truncheons—it was fading out, all fading out. Nothing remained except a vulgar low-down row in a smell of old mackintoshes.

One last try:

'Hilda! Just listen to me a minute. Look here, you don't know where I've been all this week, do you?'

'I don't want to know where you've been. I know *what* you've been doing. That's quite enough for me.'

'But dash it—'

Quite useless, of course. She'd found me guilty and now she was going to tell me what she thought of me. That might take a couple of hours. And after that there was further trouble looming up, because presently it would occur to her to wonder where I'd got the money for this trip, and then she'd discover that I'd been holding out on her about the seventeen quid. Really there was no reason why this row shouldn't go on till three in the morning. No use playing injured innocence any longer. All I wanted was the line of least resistance. And in my mind I ran over the three possibilities, which were:

A. To tell her what I'd really been doing and somehow make her believe me.

B. To pull the old gag about losing my memory.

C. To let her go on thinking it was a woman, and take my medicine.

But, damn it! I knew which it would have to be.

# KEEP THE ASPIDISTRA FLYING

# KEEP THE ASPIDISTRA FLYING

Though I speak with the tongues of men and of angels, and
have not money, I am become as a sounding brass, or a
tinkling cymbal. And though I have the gift of prophecy,
and understand all mysteries, and all knowledge; and though
I have all faith, so that I could remove mountains, and have
not money, I am nothing. And though I bestow all my
goods to feed the poor, and though I give my body to be
burned, and have not money, it profiteth me nothing.
Money suffereth long, and is kind; money envieth not;
money vaunteth not itself, is not puffed up, doth not behave
unseemly, seeketh not her own, is not easily provoked,
thinketh no evil; rejoiceth not in iniquity, but rejoiceth in
the truth; beareth all things, believeth all things, hopeth all
things, endureth all things. . . . And now abideth faith,
hope, money, these three; but the greatest of these is
money.

*1 Corinthians xiii (adapted)*

# I

The clock struck half past two. In the little office at the back of Mr McKechnie's bookshop, Gordon—Gordon Comstock, last member of the Comstock family, aged twenty-nine and rather moth-eaten already—lounged across the table, pushing a four-penny packet of Player's Weights open and shut with his thumb.

The ding-dong of another, remoter clock—from the Prince of Wales, the other side of the street—rippled the stagnant air. Gordon made an effort, sat upright, and stowed his packet of cigarettes away in his inside pocket. He was perishing for a smoke. However, there were only four cigarettes left. Today was Wednesday and he had no money coming to him till Friday. It would be too bloody to be without tobacco tonight as well as all tomorrow.

Bored in advance by tomorrow's tobaccoless hours, he got up and moved towards the door—a small frail figure, with delicate bones and fretful movements. His coat was out at elbow in the right sleeve and its middle button was missing; his ready-made flannel trousers were stained and shapeless. Even from above you could see that his shoes needed resoling.

The money clinked in his trouser pocket as he got up. He knew the precise sum that was there. Fivepence halfpenny—twopence halfpenny and a Joey. He paused, took out the miserable little threepenny-bit, and looked at it. Beastly, useless thing! And bloody fool to have taken it! It had happened yesterday, when he was buying cigarettes. 'Don't mind a threepenny-bit, do you, sir?' the little bitch of a shop-girl had chirped. And of course he had let her give it him. 'Oh no, not at all!' he had said—fool, bloody fool!

His heart sickened to think that he had only fivepence halfpenny in the world, threepence of which couldn't even be spent. Because how can you buy anything with a threepenny-bit? It isn't a coin, it's the answer to a riddle. You look such a fool when you take it out of your pocket, unless it's in among a whole handful of other coins. 'How much?' you say. 'Threepence,' the shop-girl says. And then you feel all round your pocket and fish out that absurd little thing, all by itself, sticking on the end of your finger like a tiddley-wink. The shop-girl sniffs. She spots immediately that it's your last threepence in the world. You see her glance quickly at it—she's wondering whether there's a piece of Christmas pudding still sticking to it. And you stalk out with your nose in the air, and can't ever go to that shop again. No! We won't spend our Joey. Twopence halfpenny left—twopence halfpenny to last till Friday.

This was the lonely after-dinner hour, when few or no customers were to be expected. He was alone with seven thousand books. The small dark room, smelling of dust and decayed paper, that gave on the office, was filled to the brim with books, mostly aged and unsaleable. On the top shelves near the ceiling the quarto volumes of extinct encyclopedias slumbered on their sides in piles like the tiered coffins in common graves. Gordon pushed aside the blue, dust-sodden curtains that served as a doorway to the next room. This, better lighted than the other, contained the lending library. It was one of those 'twopenny no-deposit' libraries beloved of book-pinchers. No books in it except novels, of course. And *what* novels! But that too was a matter of course.

Eight hundred strong, the novels lined the room on three sides ceiling-high, row upon row of gaudy oblong backs, as though the walls had been built of many-coloured bricks laid upright. They were arranged alphabetically. Arlen, Burroughs, Deeping, Dell, Frankau, Galsworthy, Gibbs, Priestley, Sapper, Walpole. Gordon eyed them with inert hatred. At this moment he hated all books, and novels most of all. Horrible to think of all that soggy, half-baked trash massed together in one place. Pudding, suet pudding. Eight hundred slabs of pudding, walling him in—a vault of puddingstone. The thought was oppressive. He moved on through the open doorway into the front part of the shop. In doing so, he smoothed his hair. It was an habitual movement. After all, there might be girls outside the glass door. Gordon was not impressive to look at. He was just five feet seven inches high, and because his hair was usually too long he gave the impression that his head was a little too big for his body. He was never quite unconscious of his small stature. When he knew that anyone was looking at him he carried himself very upright, throwing a chest, with a you-be-damned air which occasionally deceived simple people.

However, there was nobody outside. The front room, unlike the rest of the shop, was smart and expensive-looking, and it contained about two thousand books, exclusive of those in the window. On the right there was a glass show-case in which children's books were kept. Gordon averted his eyes from a beastly Rackhamesque dust-jacket; elvish children tripping Wendily through a bluebell glade. He gazed out through the glass door. A foul day, and the wind rising. The sky was leaden, the cobbles of the street were slimy. It was St Andrew's day, the thirtieth of November. McKechnie's stood on a corner, on a sort of shapeless square where four streets converged. To the left, just within sight from the door, stood a great elm-tree, leafless now, its multitudinous twigs making sepia-coloured lace against the sky. Opposite, next to the Prince of Wales, were tall hoardings covered with ads for patent foods and patent medicines. A gallery of monstrous doll-faces—pink vacuous faces, full of goofy optimism. Q. T. Sauce, Truweet Breakfast Crisps ('Kiddies clamour for their Breakfast Crisps'), Kangaroo Burgundy, Vitamalt Chocolate, Bovex. Of them all, the Bovex one oppressed Gordon the most. A spectacled rat-faced clerk, with patent-leather hair, sitting at a café table grinning over a white mug of Bovex. 'Corner Table enjoys his meal with Bovex', the legend ran.

Gordon shortened the focus of his eyes. From the dust-dulled pane the reflection of his own face looked back at him. Not a good face. Not thirty yet, but moth-eaten already. Very pale, with bitter, ineradicable lines. What people call a 'good' forehead—high, that is—but a small pointed chin, so that the face as a whole was pear-shaped rather than oval. Hair mouse-coloured and unkempt, mouth unamiable, eyes hazel inclining to green. He lengthened the focus of his eyes again. He hated mirrors nowadays. Outside, all was bleak and wintry. A tram, like a raucous swan of steel, glided groaning over the cobbles, and in its wake the wind swept a debris of trampled leaves. The twigs of the elm-tree were swirling, straining eastward. The poster that advertised Q.T. Sauce was torn at the edge; a ribbon of paper fluttered fitfully like a tiny pennant. In the side street too, to the right, the naked poplars that lined the pavement bowed sharply as the wind caught them. A nasty raw wind. There was a threatening note in it as it swept over; the first growl of winter's anger. Two lines of a poem struggled for birth in Gordon's mind:

Sharply the something wind—for instance, threatening wind? No, better, menacing wind. The menacing wind blows over—no, sweeps over, say.

The something poplars—yielding poplars? No, better, bending poplars. Assonance between bending and menacing? No matter. The bending poplars, newly bare. Good.

> Sharply the menacing wind sweeps over
> The bending poplars, newly bare.

Good. 'Bare' is a sod to rhyme; however, there's always 'air', which every poet since Chaucer has been struggling to find rhymes for. But the impulse died away in Gordon's mind. He turned the money over in his pocket. Twopence halfpenny and a Joey—twopence halfpenny. His mind was sticky with boredom. He couldn't cope with rhymes and adjectives. You can't, with only twopence halfpenny in your pocket.

His eyes refocused themselves upon the posters opposite. He had his private reasons for hating them. Mechanically he re-read their slogans. 'Kangaroo Burgundy—the wine for Britons.' 'Asthma was choking her!' 'Q.T. Sauce Keeps Hubby Smiling.' 'Hike all day on a Slab of Vitamalt!' 'Curve Cut—the Smoke for Outdoor Men.' 'Kiddies clamour for their Breakfast Crisps.' 'Corner Table enjoys his meal with Bovex.'

Ha! A customer—potential, at any rate. Gordon stiffened himself. Standing by the door, you could get an oblique view out of the front window without being seen yourself. He looked the potential customer over.

A decentish middle-aged man, black suit, bowler hat, umbrella, and dispatch-case—provincial solicitor or Town Clerk—keeking at the window with large pale-coloured eyes. He wore a guilty look. Gordon followed the direction of his eyes. Ah! So that was it! He had nosed out those D.H. Lawrence first editions in the far corner. Pining for a bit of smut, of course. He had heard of Lady Chatterley afar off. A bad face he had, Gordon thought. Pale, heavy, downy, with bad contours. Welsh, by the look of him—Nonconformist, anyway. He had the regular Dissenting pouches round the corners of his mouth. At home, president of the local Purity League or Seaside Vigilance Committee (rubber-soled slippers and electric torch, spotting kissing couples along the beach parade), and now up in town on the razzle. Gordon wished he would come in. Sell him a copy of *Women in Love*. How it would disappoint him!

But no! The Welsh solicitor had funked it. He tucked his umbrella under his arm and moved off with righteously turned backside. But doubtless tonight, when darkness hid his blushes, he'd slink into one of the rubber-shops and buy *High Jinks in a Parisian Convent*, by Sadie Blackeyes.

Gordon turned away from the door and back to the book-shelves. In the shelves to your left as you came out of the library the new and nearly-new books were kept—a patch of bright colour that was meant to catch the eye of anyone glancing through the glass door. Their sleek unspotted backs seemed to yearn at you from the shelves. 'Buy me, buy me!' they seemed to be saying. Novels fresh from the press—still unravished brides, pining for the paperknife to deflower them—and review copies, like youthful widows, blooming still though virgin no longer, and here and there, in sets of half a dozen, those pathetic spinster-things, 'remainders', still guarding hopefully their long preserv'd virginity. Gordon turned his eyes away from the 'remainders'. They called up evil memories. The single wretched little book that he himself had published, two years ago, had sold exactly a hundred and fifty-three copies and then been 'remaindered'; and even as a 'remainder' it hadn't sold. He passed the new books by and paused in front of the shelves which ran at right angles to them and which contained more second-hand books.

Over to the right were shelves of poetry. Those in front of him were prose, a miscellaneous lot. Upwards and downwards they were graded, from clean and expensive at eye-level to cheap and dingy at top and bottom. In all book-shops there goes on a savage Darwinian struggle in which the works of living men gravitate to eye-level and the works of dead men go up or down—down to Gehenna or up to the throne, but always away from any position where they will be noticed. Down in the bottom shelves the 'classics', the extinct monsters of the Victorian age, were quietly rotting. Scott, Carlyle, Meredith, Ruskin, Pater, Stevenson—you could hardly read the names upon their broad dowdy backs. In the top shelves, almost out of sight, slept the pudgy biographies of dukes. Below those, saleable still and therefore placed within reach, was 'religious' literature—all sects and all creeds, lumped indiscriminately together. *The World Beyond*, by the author of *Spirit Hands Have Touched me*. Dean Farrar's *Life of Christ*. *Jesus the First Rotarian*. Father Hilaire Chestnut's latest book of R.C. propaganda. Religion always sells provided it is soppy enough. Below, exactly at eye-level, was the contemporary stuff. Priestley's latest. Dinky little books of reprinted 'middles'. Cheer-up 'humour' from Herbert and Knox and Milne. Some highbrow stuff as well. A novel or two by Hemingway and Virginia Woolf. Smart pseudo-Strachey predigested biographies. Snooty, refined books on safe painters and safe poets by those moneyed young beasts who glide so gracefully from Eton to Cambridge and from Cambridge to the literary reviews.

Dull-eyed, he gazed at the wall of books. He hated the whole lot of them, old and new, highbrow and lowbrow, snooty and chirpy. The mere sight of them brought home to him his own sterility. For here was he, supposedly a 'writer', and he couldn't even 'write'! It wasn't merely a question of not getting published; it was that he produced nothing, or next to nothing. And all that tripe cluttering the shelves—well, at any rate it existed; it was an achievement of sorts. Even the Dells and Deepings do at least turn out their yearly acre of print. But it was the snooty 'cultured' kind of books that he hated the worst. Books of criticism and belles-lettres. The kind of thing that those moneyed young beasts from Cambridge write almost in their sleep—and that Gordon himself might have written if he had had a little more money. Money and culture! In a country like England you can no more be cultured without money than you can join the Cavalry Club. With the same instinct that makes a child waggle a loose tooth, he took out a snooty-looking volume—*Some Aspects of the Italian Baroque*—opened it, read a paragraph, and shoved it back with mingled loathing and envy. That devastating omniscience! That noxious, horn-spectacled refinement! And the money that such refinement means! For after all, what is there behind it, except money? Money for the right kind of education, money for influential friends, money for leisure and peace of mind, money for trips to Italy. Money writes books, money sells them. Give me not righteousness, O Lord, give me money, only money.

He jingled the coins in his pocket. He was nearly thirty and had accomplished nothing; only his miserable book of poems that had fallen flatter than any pancake. And ever since, for two whole years, he had been struggling in the labyrinth of a dreadful book that never got any further, and which, as he knew in his moments of clarity, never would get any further. It was the lack of money, simply the lack of money, that robbed him of the power to 'write'. He clung to that as to an article of faith. Money, money, all is money! Could you write even a penny novelette without money to put heart in you? Invention, energy, wit, style, charm—they've all got to be paid for in hard cash.

Nevertheless, as he looked along the shelves he felt himself a little comforted. So many of the books were faded and unreadable. After all, we're all in the same boat. *Memento mori*. For you and for me and for the snooty young men from Cambridge, the same oblivion waits—though doubtless it'll wait rather longer for those snooty young men from Cambridge. He looked at the time-dulled 'classics' near his feet. Dead, all dead. Carlyle and Ruskin and Meredith and Stevenson—all are dead, God rot them. He glanced over their faded titles. *Collected Letters of Robert Louis Stevenson*. Ha, ha! That's good. *Collected Letters of Robert Louis Stevenson*! Its top edge was black with dust. Dust thou art, to dust returnest. Gordon kicked Stevenson's buckram backside. Art there, old false-penny? You're cold meat, if ever Scotchman was.

Ping! The shop bell. Gordon turned round. Two customers, for the library.

A dejected, round-shouldered, lower-class woman, looking like a draggled duck nosing among garbage, seeped in, fumbling with a rush basket. In her wake hopped a plump little sparrow of a woman, red-cheeked, middle-middle class, carrying under her arm a copy of *The Forsyte Saga*—title outwards, so that passers-by could spot her for a high-brow.

Gordon had taken off his sour expression. He greeted them with the homey, family-doctor geniality reserved for library-subscribers.

'Good afternoon, Mrs Weaver. Good afternoon, Mrs Penn. What terrible weather!'

'Shocking!' said Mrs Penn.

He stood aside to let them pass. Mrs Weaver upset her rush basket and spilled on to the floor a much-thumbed copy of Ethel M. Dell's *Silver Wedding*. Mrs Penn's bright bird-eye lighted upon it. Behind Mrs Weaver's back she smiled up to Gordon, archly, as highbrow to highbrow. Dell! The lowness of it! The books these lower classes read! Understandingly, he smiled back. They passed into the library, highbrow to highbrow smiling.

Mrs Penn laid *The Forsyte Saga* on the table and turned her sparrow-bosom upon Gordon. She was always very affable to Gordon. She addressed him as Mister Comstock, shopwalker though he was, and held literary conversations with him. There was the free-masonry of highbrows between them.

'I hope you enjoyed *The Forsyte Saga*, Mrs Penn?'

'What a perfectly *marvellous* achievement that book is, Mr Comstock! Do you know that that makes the fourth time I've read it? An epic, a real epic!'

Mrs Weaver nosed among the books, too dim-witted to grasp that they were in alphabetical order.

'I don't know what to 'ave this week, that I don't,' she mumbled through untidy lips. 'My daughter she keeps on at me to 'ave a try at Deeping. She's great on Deeping, my daughter is. But my son-in-law, now, 'e's more for Burroughs. I don't know, I'm sure.'

A spasm passed over Mrs Penn's face at the mention of Burroughs. She turned her back markedly on Mrs Weaver.

'What I feel, Mr Comstock, is that there's something so *big* about Galsworthy. He's so broad, so universal, and yet at the same time so thoroughly English in spirit, so *human*. His books are real *human* documents.'

'And Priestley, too,' said Gordon. 'I think Priestley's such an awfully fine writer, don't you?'

'Oh, he is! So big, so broad, so human! And so essentially English!'

Mrs Weaver pursed her lips. Behind them were three isolated yellow teeth.

'I think p'raps I can do better'n 'ave another Dell,' she said. 'You 'ave got some more Dells, 'aven't you? I *do* enjoy a good read of Dell, I must say. I says to my daughter, I says, "You can keep your Deepings and your Burroughses. Give me Dell," I says.'

Ding Dong Dell! Dukes and dogwhips! Mrs Penn's eye signalled highbrow irony. Gordon returned her signal. Keep in with Mrs Penn! A good, steady customer.

'Oh, certainly, Mrs Weaver. We've got a whole shelf by Ethel M. Dell. Would you like *The Desire of his Life*? Or perhaps you've read that. Then what about *The Alter of Honour*?'

'I wonder whether you have Hugh Walpole's latest book?' said Mrs Penn. 'I feel in the mood this week for something epic, something *big*. Now Walpole, you know, I consider a really *great* writer, I put him second only to Galsworthy. There's something so *big* about him. And yet he's so human with it.'

'And so essentially English,' said Gordon.

'Oh, of course! So essentially English!'

'I b'lieve I'll jest 'ave *The Way of an Eagle* over again,' said Mrs Weaver finally. 'You don't never seem to get tired of *The Way of an Eagle*, do you, now?'

'It's certainly astonishingly popular,' said Gordon, diplomatically, his eye on Mrs Penn.

'Oh, as*ton*ishingly!' echoed Mrs Penn, ironically, her eye on Gordon.

He took their twopences and sent them happy away, Mrs Penn with Walpole's *Rogue Herries* and Mrs Weaver with *The Way of an Eagle*.

Soon he had wandered back to the other room and towards the shelves of poetry. A melancholy fascination, those shelves had for him. His own wretched book was there—skied, of course, high up among the unsaleable. *Mice*, by Gordon Comstock; a sneaky little foolscap octavo, price three and sixpence but now reduced to a bob. Of the thirteen B.F.s who had reviewed it (and *The Times Lit. Supp.* had declared that it showed 'exceptional promise') not one had seen the none too subtle joke of that title. And in the two years he had been at McKechnie's bookshop, not a single customer, not a single one, had ever taken *Mice* out of its shelf.

There were fifteen or twenty shelves of poetry. Gordon regarded them sourly. Dud stuff, for the most part. A little above eye-level, already on their way to heaven and oblivion, were the poets of yesteryear, the stars of his earlier youth. Yeats, Davies, Housman, Thomas, De la Mare, Hardy. Dead stars. Below them, exactly at eye-level, were the squibs of the passing minute. Eliot, Pound, Auden, Campbell, Day Lewis, Spender. Very damp squibs, that lot. Dead stars above, damp squibs below. Shall we ever again get a writer worth reading? But Lawrence was all right, and Joyce even better before he went off his coconut. And if we did get a writer worth reading, should we know him when we saw him, so choked as we are with trash?

Ping! Shop bell. Gordon turned. Another customer.

A youth of twenty, cherry-lipped, with gilded hair, tripped Nancifully in. Moneyed, obviously. He had the golden aura of money. He had been in the shop before. Gordon assumed the gentlemanly-servile mien reserved for new customers. He repeated the usual formula:

'Good afternoon. Can I do anything for you? Are you looking for any particular book?'

'Oh, no, not weally.' An R-less Nancy voice. 'May I just *bwowse*? I simply couldn't wesist your fwont window. I have such a tewwible weakness for bookshops! So I just floated in—tee-hee!'

Float out again, then, Nancy. Gordon smiled a cultured smile, as booklover to booklover.

'Oh, please do. We like people to look round. Are you interested in poetry, by any chance?'

'Oh, of course! I *adore* poetwy!'

Of course! Mangy little snob. There was a sub-artistic look about his clothes. Gordon slid a 'slim' red volume from the poetry shelves.

'These are just out. They might interest you, perhaps. They're translations—something rather out of the common. Translations from the Bulgarian.'

Very subtle, that. Now leave him to himself. That's the proper way with customers. Don't hustle them; let them browse for twenty minutes or so; then they get ashamed and buy something. Gordon moved to the door, discreetly, keeping out of Nancy's way; yet casually, one hand in his pocket, with the insouciant air proper to a gentleman.

Outside, the slimy street looked grey and drear. From somewhere round the corner came the clatter of hooves, a cold hollow sound. Caught by the wind, the dark columns of smoke from the chimneys veered over and rolled flatly down the sloping roofs. Ah!

> Sharply the menacing wind sweeps over
> The bending poplars, newly bare,
> And the dark ribbons of the chimneys
> Veer downward tumty tumty (something like 'murky') air.

Good. But the impulse faded. His eye fell again upon the ad-posters across the street.

He almost wanted to laugh at them, they were so feeble, so dead-alive, so unappetizing. As though anybody could be tempted by *those*! Like succubi with pimply backsides. But they depressed him all the same. The money-stink, everywhere the money-stink. He stole a glance at the Nancy, who had drifted away from the poetry shelves and taken out a large expensive book on the Russian ballet. He was holding it delicately between his pink non-prehensile paws, as a squirrel holds a nut, studying the photographs. Gordon knew his type. The moneyed 'artistic' young man. Not an artist himself, exactly, but a hanger-on of the arts; frequenter of studios, retailer of scandal. A nice-looking boy, though, for all his Nancitude. The skin at the back of his neck was as silky-smooth as the inside of a shell. You can't have a skin like that under five hundred a year. A sort of charm he had, a glamour, like all moneyed people. Money and charm; who shall separate them?

Gordon thought of Ravelston, his charming, rich friend, editor of *Antichrist*, of whom he was extravagantly fond, and whom he did not see so often as once in a fortnight; and of Rosemary, his girl, who loved him—adored him, so she said—and who, all the same, had never slept with him. Money, once again; all is money. All human relationships must be purchased with money. If you have no money, men won't care for you, women won't love you; won't, that is, care for you or love you the last little bit that matters. And how right they are, after all! For, moneyless, you are unlovable. Though I speak with the tongues of men and of angels. But then, if I haven't money, I *don't* speak with the tongues of men and of angels.

He looked again at the ad-posters. He really hated them this time. That Vitamalt one, for instance! 'Hike all day on a slab of Vitamalt!' A youthful couple, boy and girl, in clean-minded hiking kit, their hair picturesquely tousled by the wind, climbing a stile against a Sussex landscape. That girl's face! The awful bright tomboy cheeriness of it! The kind of girl who goes in for

Plenty of Clean Fun. Windswept. Tight khaki shorts but that doesn't mean you can pinch her backside. And next to them—Corner Table. 'Corner Table enjoys his meal with Bovex'. Gordon examined the thing with the intimacy of hatred. The idiotic grinning face, like the face of a self-satisfied rat, the slick black hair, the silly spectacles. Corner Table, heir of the ages; victor of Waterloo, Corner Table, Modern man as his master want him to be. A docile little porker, sitting in the money-sty, drinking Bovex.

Faces passed, wind-yellowed. A tram boomed across the square, and the clock over the Prince of Wales struck three. A couple of old creatures, a tramp or a beggar and his wife, in long greasy overcoats that reached almost to the ground, were shuffling towards the shop. Book-pinchers, by the look of them. Better keep an eye on the boxes outside. The old man halted on the kerb a few yards away while his wife came to the door. She pushed it open and looked up at Gordon, between grey strings of hair, with a sort of hopeful malevolence.

'Ju buy books?' she demanded hoarsely.

'Sometimes. It depends what books they are.'

'I gossome *lovely* books 'ere.'

She came in, shutting the door with a clang. The Nancy glanced over his shoulder distastefully and moved a step or two away, into the corner. The old woman had produced a greasy little sack from under her overcoat. She moved confidentially nearer to Gordon. She smelt of very, very old breadcrusts.

'Will you 'ave 'em?' she said, clasping the neck of the sack. 'Only 'alf a crown the lot.'

'What are they? Let me see them, please.'

'*Lovely* books, they are,' she breathed, bending over to open the sack and emitting a sudden very powerful whiff of breadcrusts.

''Ere!' she said, and thrust an armful of filthy-looking books almost into Gordon's face.

They were an 1884 edition of Charlotte M. Yonge's novels, and had the appearance of having been slept on for many years. Gordon stepped back, suddenly revolted.

'We can't possibly buy those,' he said shortly.

'Can't buy 'em? *Why* can't yer buy 'em?'

'Because they're no use to us. We can't sell that kind of thing.'

'Wotcher make me take 'em out o' me bag for, then?' demanded the old woman ferociously.

Gordon made a detour round her, to avoid the smell, and held the door open, silently. No use arguing. You had people of this type coming into the shop all day long. The old woman made off, mumbling, with malevolence in the hump of her shoulders, and joined her husband. He paused on the kerb to cough, so fruitily that you could hear him through the door. A clot of phlegm, like a little white tongue, came slowly out between his lips and was ejected into the gutter. Then the two old creatures shuffled away, beetle-like in the long greasy overcoats that hid everything except their feet.

Gordon watched them go. They were just by-products. The throw-outs of the money-god. All over London, by tens of thousands, draggled old beasts of that description; creeping like unclean beetles to the grave.

He gazed out at the graceless street. At this moment it seemed to him that in a street like this, in a town like this, every life that is lived must be meaningless and intolerable. The sense of disintegration, of decay, that is endemic in our time, was strong upon him. Somehow it was mixed up with the ad-posters opposite. He looked now with more seeing eyes at those grinning yard-wide faces. After all, there was more there than mere silliness, greed, and vulgarity. Corner Table grins at you, seemingly optimistic, with a flash of false teeth. But what is behind the grin? Desolation, emptiness, prophecies of doom. For can you not see, if you know how to look, that behind that slick self-satisfaction, that tittering fat-bellied triviality, there is nothing but a frightful emptiness, a secret despair? The great death-wish of the modern world. Suicide pacts. Heads stuck in gas-ovens in lonely maisonettes. French letters and Amen Pills. And the reverberations of future wars. Enemy aeroplanes flying over London; the deep threatening hum of the propellers, the shattering thunder of the bombs. It is all written in Corner Table's face.

More customers coming. Gordon stood back, gentlemanly-servile.

The door-bell clanged. Two upper-middle-class ladies sailed noisily in. One pink and fruity, thirty-fivish, with voluptuous bosom burgeoning from her coat of squirrel-skin, emitting a super-feminine scent of Parma violets: the other middle-aged, tough, and curried—India, presumably. Close behind them a dark, grubby, shy young man slipped through the doorway as apologetically as a cat. He was one of the shop's best customers—a flitting, solitary creature who was almost too shy to speak and who by some strange manipulation kept himself always a day away from a shave.

Gordon repeated his formula:

'Good afternoon. Can I do anything for you? Are you looking for any particular book?'

Fruity-face overwhelmed him with a smile, but curry-face decided to treat the question as an impertinence. Ignoring Gordon, she drew fruity-face across to the shelves next to the new books where the dog-books and cat-books were kept. The two of them immediately began taking books out of the shelves and talking loudly. Curry-face had the voice of a drill-sergeant. She was no doubt a colonel's wife, or widow. The Nancy, still deep in the big book on the Russian ballet, edged delicately away. His face said that he would leave the shop if his privacy were disturbed again. The shy young man had already found his way to the poetry shelves. The two ladies were fairly frequent visitors to the shop. They always wanted to see books about cats and dogs, but never actually bought anything. There were two whole shelves of dog-books and cat-books. 'Ladies' Corner,' old McKechnie called it.

Another customer arrived, for the library. An ugly girl of twenty, hatless, in a white overall, with a sallow, blithering, honest face and powerful spectacles that distorted her eyes. She was an assistant at a chemist's shop. Gordon put on his homey library manner. She smiled at him, and with a gait as clumsy as a bear's followed him into the library.

'What kind of book would you like this time, Miss Weeks?'

'Well'–she clutched the front of her overall. Her distorted, black-treacle eyes beamed trustfully into his. 'Well, what I'd *really* like's a good hot-stuff love story. You know–something *modern.*'

'Something modern? Something by Barbara Bedworthy for instance? Have you read *Almost a Virgin?*'

'Oh no, not her. She's too Deep. I can't bear Deep books. But I want something–well, *you* know–*modern.* Sex-problems and divorce and all that. *You* know.'

'Modern, but not Deep,' said Gordon, as lowbrow to lowbrow.

He ranged among the hot-stuff modern love-stories. There were not less than three hundred of them in the library. From the front room came the voices of the two upper-middle-class ladies, the one fruity, the other curried, disputing about dogs. They had taken out one of the dog-books and were examining the photographs. Fruity-voice enthused over the photograph of a Peke, the ickle angel pet, wiv his gweat big Soulful eyes and his ickle black nosie–oh, so ducky-duck! But curry-voice–yes, undoubtedly a colonel's widow–said Pekes were soppy. Give her dogs with guts–dogs that would fight, she said; she hated these soppy lapdogs, she said. 'You have no Soul, Bedelia, no Soul,' said fruity-voice plaintively. The door-bell pinged again. Gordon handed the chemist's girl *Seven Scarlet Nights* and booked it on her ticket. She took a shabby leather purse out of her overall pocket and paid him twopence.

He went back to the front room. The Nancy had put his book back in the wrong shelf and vanished. A lean, straight-nosed, brisk woman, with sensible clothes and gold-rimmed pince-nez–schoolmarm possibly, feminist certainly–came in and demanded Mrs Wharton-Beverley's history of the suffrage movement. With secret joy Gordon told her that they hadn't got it. She stabbed his male incompetence with gimlet eyes and went out again. The thin young man stood apologetically in the corner, his face buried in D.H.Lawrence's Collected Poems, like some long-legged bird with its head buried under its wing.

Gordon waited by the door. Outside, a shabby-genteel old man with a strawberry nose and a khaki muffler round his throat was picking over the books in the sixpenny box. The two upper-middle-class ladies suddenly departed, leaving a litter of open books on the table. Fruity-face cast reluctant backward glances at the dog-books, but curry-face drew her away, resolute not to buy anything. Gordon held the door open. The two ladies sailed noisily out, ignoring him.

He watched their fur-coated upper-middle-class backs go down the street. The old strawberry-nosed man was talking to himself as he pawed over the books. A bit wrong in the head, presumably. He would pinch something if he wasn't watched. The wind blew colder, drying the slime of the street. Time to light up presently. Caught by a swirl of air, the torn strip of paper on the Q.T.Sauce advertisement fluttered sharply, like a piece of washing on the line. Ah!

> Sharply the menacing wind sweeps over
> The bending poplars, newly bare,

> And the dark ribbons of the chimneys
> Veer downward; flicked by whips of air
> Torn posters flutter.

Not bad, not bad at all. But he had no wish to go on—could not go on, indeed. He fingered the money in his pocket, not chinking it, lest the shy young man should hear. Twopence-halfpenny. No tobacco all tomorrow. His bones ached.

A light sprang up in the Prince of Wales. They would be swabbing out the bar. The old strawberry-nosed man was reading an Edgar Wallace out of the twopenny box. A tram boomed in the distance. In the room upstairs Mr McKechnie, who seldom came down to the shop, drowsed by the gas-fire, white-haired and white-bearded, with snuff-box handy, over his calf-bound folio of Middleton's *Travels in the Levant*.

The thin young man suddenly realized that he was alone and looked up guiltily. He was a *habitué* of bookshops, yet never stayed longer than ten minutes in any one shop. A passionate hunger for books, and the fear of being a nuisance, were constantly at war in him. After ten minutes in any shop he would grow uneasy, feel himself *de trop*, and take to flight, having bought something out of sheer nervousness. Without speaking he held out the copy of Lawrence's poems and awkwardly extracted three florins from his pocket. In handing them to Gordon he dropped one. Both dived for it simultaneously; their heads bumped against one another. The young man stood back, blushing sallowly.

'I'll wrap it up for you,' said Gordon.

But the shy young man shook his head—he stammered so badly that he never spoke when it was avoidable. He clutched his book to him and slipped out with the air of having committed some disgraceful action.

Gordon was alone. He wandered back to the door. The strawberry-nosed man glanced over his shoulder, caught Gordon's eye, and moved off, foiled. He had been on the point of slipping Edgar Wallace into his pocket. The clock over the Prince of Wales struck a quarter past three.

Ding Dong! A quarter past three. Light up at half past. Four and three-quarter hours till closing time. Five and a quarter hours till supper. Twopence halfpenny in pocket. No tobacco tomorrow.

Suddenly a ravishing, irresistible desire to smoke came over Gordon. He had made up his mind not to smoke this afternoon. He had only four cigarettes left. They must be saved for tonight, when he intended to 'write'; for he could no more 'write' without tobacco than without air. Nevertheless, he had got to have a smoke. He took out his packet of Player's Weights and extracted one of the dwarfish cigarettes. It was sheer stupid indulgence; it meant half an hour off tonight's 'writing' time. But there was no resisting it. With a sort of shameful joy he sucked the soothing smoke into his lungs.

The reflection of his own face looked back at him from the greyish pane. Gordon Comstock, author of *Mice; en l'an trentiesme de son eage*, and moth-eaten already. Only twenty-six teeth left. However, Villon at the same age was poxed on his own showing. Let's be thankful for small mercies.

He watched the ribbon of torn paper whirling, fluttering on the Q. T. Sauce advertisement. Our civilization is dying. It *must* be dying. But it isn't going to die in its bed. Presently the aeroplanes are coming. Zoom–whizz–crash! The whole western world going up in a roar of high explosives.

He looked at the darkening street, at the greyish reflection of his face in the pane, at the shabby figures shuffling past. Almost involuntarily he repeated:

> 'C'est l'Ennui–l'œil chargé d'un pleur involontaire,
> Il rêve d'échafauds en fumant son houka!'

Money, money! Corner Table! The humming of the aeroplanes and the crash of the bombs.

Gordon squinted up at the leaden sky. Those aeroplanes are coming. In imagination he saw them coming now; squadron after squadron, innumerable, darkening the sky like clouds of gnats. With his tongue not quite against his teeth he made a buzzing, bluebottle-on-the-window-pane sound to represent the humming of the aeroplanes. It was a sound which, at that moment, he ardently desired to hear.

# 2

Gordon walked homeward against the rattling wind, which blew his hair backward and gave him more of a 'good' forehead than ever. His manner conveyed to the passers-by–at least, he hoped it did–that if he wore no overcoat it was from pure caprice. His overcoat was up the spout for fifteen shillings, as a matter of fact.

Willowbed Road, NW, was not definitely slummy, only dingy and depressing. There were real slums hardly five minutes' walk away. Tenement houses where families slept five in a bed, and, when one of them died, slept every night with the corpse until it was buried; alley-ways where girls of fifteen were deflowered by boys of sixteen against leprous plaster walls. But Willowbed Road itself contrived to keep up a kind of mingy, lower-middle-class decency. There was even a dentist's brass plate on one of the houses. In quite two-thirds of them, amid the lace curtains of the parlour window, there was a green card with 'Apartments' on it in silver lettering, above the peeping foliage of an aspidistra.

Mrs Wisbeach, Gordon's landlady, specialized in 'single gentlemen'. Bed-sitting-rooms, with gaslight laid on and find your own heating, baths extra (there was a geyser), and meals in the tomb-dark dining-room with the phalanx of clotted sauce-bottles in the middle of the table. Gordon, who came home for his midday dinner, paid twenty-seven and six a week.

The gaslight shone yellow through the frosted transom above the door of

Number 31. Gordon took out his key and fished about in the keyhole—in that kind of house the key never quite fits the lock. The darkish little hallway—in reality it was only a passage—smelt of dishwater, cabbage, rag mats, and bedroom slops. Gordon glanced at the japanned tray on the hall-stand. No letters, of course. He had told himself not to hope for a letter, and nevertheless had continued to hope. A stale feeling, not quite a pain, settled upon his breast. Rosemary might have written! It was four days now since she had written. Moreover, there were a couple of poems that he had sent out to magazines and had not yet had returned to him. The one thing that made the evening bearable was to find a letter waiting for him when he got home. But he received very few letters—four or five in a week at the very most.

On the left of the hall was the never-used parlour, then came the staircase, and beyond that the passage ran down to the kitchen and to the unapproachable lair inhabited by Mrs Wisbeach herself. As Gordon came in, the door at the end of the passage opened a foot or so. Mrs Wisbeach's face emerged, inspected him briefly but suspiciously, and disappeared again. It was quite impossible to get in or out of the house, at any time before eleven at night, without being scrutinized in this manner. Just what Mrs Wisbeach suspected you of it was hard to say; smuggling women into the house, possibly. She was one of those malignant respectable women who keep lodging-houses. Age about forty-five, stout but active, with a pink, fine-featured, horribly observant face, beautifully grey hair, and a permanent grievance.

Gordon halted at the foot of the narrow stairs. Above, a coarse rich voice was singing, 'Who's afraid of the Big Bad Wolf?' A very fat man of thirty-eight or nine came round the angle of the stairs, with the light dancing step peculiar to fat men, dressed in a smart grey suit, yellow shoes, a rakish trilby hat, and a belted blue overcoat of startling vulgarity. This was Flaxman, the first-floor lodger and travelling representative of the Queen of Sheba Toilet Requisites Co. He saluted Gordon with a lemon-coloured glove as he came down.

'Hullo, chappie!' he said blithely. (Flaxman called everyone 'chappie'.) 'How's life with you?'

'Bloody,' said Gordon shortly.

Flaxman had reached the bottom of the stairs. He threw a roly-poly arm affectionately round Gordon's shoulders.

'Cheer up, old man, cheer up! You look like a bloody funeral. I'm off down to the Crichton. Come on down and have a quick one.'

'I can't. I've got to work.'

'Oh, hell! Be matey, can't you? What's the good of mooning about up here? Come on down to the Cri and we'll pinch the barmaid's bum.'

Gordon wriggled free of Flaxman's arm. Like all small frail people, he hated being touched. Flaxman merely grinned, with the typical fat man's good humour. He was really horribly fat. He filled his trousers as though he had been melted and then poured into them. But of course, like other fat people, he never admitted to being fat. No fat person ever uses the word 'fat' if there is any way of avoiding it. 'Stout' is the word they use—or, better still, 'robust'. A fat man is never so happy as when he is describing himself as 'robust'.

Flaxman, at his first meeting with Gordon, had been on the point of calling himself 'robust', but something in Gordon's greenish eye had deterred him. He compromised on 'stout' instead.

'I do admit, chappie,' he said, 'to being—well, just a wee bit on the stout side. Nothing unwholesome, you know.' He patted the vague frontier between his belly and his chest. 'Good firm flesh. I'm pretty nippy on my feet, as a matter of fact. But—well, I suppose you might call me *stout*.'

'Like Cortez,' Gordon suggested.

'Cortez? Cortez? Was that the chappie who was always wandering about in the mountains in Mexico?'

'That's the fellow. He was stout, but he had eagle eyes.'

'Ah? Now that's funny. Because the wife said something rather like that to me once. "George," she said, "you've got the most wonderful eyes in the world. You've got eyes just like an eagle," she said. That would be before she married me, you'll understand.'

Flaxman was living apart from his wife at the moment. A little while back the Queen of Sheba Toilet Requisites Co. had unexpectedly paid out a bonus of thirty pounds to all its travellers, and at the same time Flaxman and two others had been sent across to Paris to press the new Sexapeal Naturetint lipstick on various French firms. Flaxman had not thought it necessary to mention the thirty pounds to his wife. He had had the time of his life on that Paris trip, of course. Even now, three months afterwards, his mouth watered when he spoke of it. He used to entertain Gordon with luscious descriptions. Ten days in Paris with thirty quid that wifie hadn't heard about! Oh boy! But unfortunately there had been a leakage somewhere; Flaxman had got home to find retribution awaiting him. His wife had broken his head with a cut-glass whisky decanter, a wedding present which they had had for fourteen years, and then fled to her mother's house, taking the children with her. Hence Flaxman's exile in Willowbed Road. But he wasn't letting it worry him. It would blow over, no doubt; it had happened several times before.

Gordon made another attempt to get past Flaxman and escape up the stairs. The dreadful thing was that in his heart he was pining to go with him. He needed a drink so badly—the mere mention of the Crichton Arms had made him feel thirsty. But it was impossible, of course; he had no money. Flaxman put an arm across the stairs, barring his way. He was genuinely fond of Gordon. He considered him 'clever'—'cleverness', to him, being a kind of amiable lunacy. Moreover, he detested being alone, even for so short a time as it would take him to walk to the pub.

'Come on, chappie!' he urged. 'You want a Guinness to buck you up, that's what you want. You haven't seen the new girl they've got in the saloon bar yet. Oh, boy! There's a peach for you!'

'So that's why you're all dolled up, is it?' said Gordon, looking coldly at Flaxman's yellow gloves.

'You bet it is, chappie! Coo, what a peach! Ash blonde she is. And she knows a thing or two, that girlie does. I gave her a stick of our Sexapeal Naturetint last night. You ought to have seen her wag her little bottom at me as she went past my table. Does she give me the palpitations? Does she? Oh, boy!'

Flaxman wriggled lasciviously. His tongue appeared between his lips. Then, suddenly pretending that Gordon was the ash-blonde barmaid, he seized him by the waist and gave him a tender squeeze. Gordon shoved him away. For a moment the desire to go down to the Crichton Arms was so ravishing that it almost overcame him. Oh, for a pint of beer! He seemed almost to feel it going down his throat. If only he had had any money! Even sevenpence for a pint. But what was the use? Twopence halfpenny in pocket. You can't let other people buy your drinks for you.

'Oh, leave me alone, for God's sake!' he said irritably, stepping out of Flaxman's reach, and went up the stairs without looking back.

Flaxman settled his hat on his head and made for the front door, mildly offended. Gordon reflected dully that it was always like this nowadays. He was for ever snubbing friendly advances. Of course it was money that was at the bottom of it, always money. You can't be friendly, you can't even be civil, when you have no money in your pocket. A spasm of self-pity went through him. His heart yearned for the saloon bar at the Crichton; the lovely smell of beer, the warmth and bright lights, the cheery voices, the clatter of glasses on the beer-wet bar. Money, money! He went on, up the dark evil-smelling stairs. The thought of his cold lonely bedroom at the top of the house was like a doom before him.

On the second floor lived Lorenheim, a dark, meagre, lizard-like creature of uncertain age and race, who made about thirty-five shillings a week by touting vacuum-cleaners. Gordon always went very hurriedly past Lorenheim's door. Lorenheim was one of those people who have not a single friend in the world and who are devoured by a lust for company. His loneliness was so deadly that if you so much as slowed your pace outside his door he was liable to pounce out upon you and half drag, half wheedle you in to listen to interminable paranoiac tales of girls he had seduced and employers he had scored off. And his room was more cold and squalid than even a lodging-house bedroom has any right to be. There were always half-eaten bits of bread and margarine lying about everywhere. The only other lodger in the house was an engineer of some kind, employed on nightwork. Gordon only saw him occasionally—a massive man with a grim, discoloured face, who wore a bowler hat indoors and out.

In the familiar darkness of his room, Gordon felt for the gas-jet and lighted it. The room was medium-sized, not big enough to be curtained into two, but too big to be sufficiently warmed by one defective oil lamp. It had the sort of furniture you expect in a top floor back. White-quilted single-bed; brown lino floor-covering; wash-hand-stand with jug and basin of that cheap white ware which you can never see without thinking of chamberpots. On the window-sill there was a sickly aspidistra in a green-glazed pot.

Up against this, under the window, there was a kitchen table with an inkstained green cloth. This was Gordon's 'writing' table. It was only after a bitter struggle that he had induced Mrs Wisbeach to give him a kitchen table instead of the bamboo 'occasional' table—a mere stand for the **aspidistra**—which she considered proper for a top floor back. And even now there was endless nagging because Gordon would never allow his table to be 'tidied up'. The table was in a permanent mess. It was almost covered with a muddle of papers, perhaps two hundred sheets of sermon paper, grimy and dog-eared, and all written on and crossed out and written on again—a sort of sordid labyrinth of papers to which only Gordon possessed the key. There was a film of dust over everything, and there were several foul little trays containing tobacco ash and the twisted stubs of cigarettes. Except for a few books on the mantelpiece, this table, with its mess of papers, was the sole mark Gordon's personality had left on the room.

It was beastly cold. Gordon thought he would light the oil lamp. He lifted it—it felt very light; the spare oil can also was empty—no oil till Friday. He applied a match; a dull yellow flame crept unwillingly round the wick. It might burn for a couple of hours, with any luck. As Gordon threw away the match his eye fell upon the aspidistra in its grass-green pot. It was a peculiarly mangy specimen. It had only seven leaves and never seemed to put forth any new ones. Gordon had a sort of secret feud with the aspidistra. Many a time he had furtively attempted to kill it—starving it of water, grinding hot cigarette-ends against its stem, even mixing salt with its earth. But the beastly things are practically immortal. In almost any circumstances they can preserve a wilting, diseased existence. Gordon stood up and deliberately wiped his kerosiny fingers on the aspidistra leaves.

At this moment Mrs Wisbeach's voice rang shrewishly up the stairs:

'Mister Com-stock!'

Gordon went to the door. 'Yes?' he called down.

'Your supper's been waiting for you this ten minutes. Why can't you come down and have it, 'stead of keeping me waiting for the washing up?'

Gordon went down. The dining-room was on the first floor, at the back, opposite Flaxman's room. It was a cold, close-smelling room, twilit even at midday. There were more aspidistras in it than Gordon had ever accurately counted. They were all over the place—on the sideboard, on the floor, on 'occasional' tables; in the window there was a sort of florist's stand of them, blocking out the light. In the half-darkness, with aspidistras all about you, you had the feeling of being in some sunless aquarium amid the dreary foliage of water-flowers. Gordon's supper was set out, waiting for him, in the circle of white light that the cracked gas-jet cast upon the table cloth. He sat down with his back to the fireplace (there was an aspidistra in the grate instead of a fire) and ate his plate of cold beef and his two slices of crumbly white bread, with Canadian butter, mousetrap cheese and Pan Yan pickle, and drank a glass of cold but musty water.

When he went back to his room the oil lamp had got going, more or less. It was hot enough to boil a kettle by, he thought. And now for the great event of the evening—his illicit cup of tea. He made himself a cup of tea almost every night, in the deadliest secrecy. Mrs Wisbeach refused to give her lodgers tea with their supper, because she 'couldn't be bothered with hotting up extra water', but at the same time making tea in your bedroom was strictly forbidden. Gordon looked with disgust at the muddled papers on the table. He told himself defiantly that he wasn't going to do any work tonight. He would have a cup of tea and smoke up his remaining cigarettes, and read *King Lear* or *Sherlock Holmes*. His books were on the mantelpiece beside the alarm clock—Shakespeare in the Everyman edition, *Sherlock Holmes*, Villon's poems, *Roderick Random, Les Fleurs du Mal*, a pile of French novels. But he read nothing nowadays, except Shakespeare and *Sherlock Holmes*. Meanwhile, that cup of tea.

Gordon went to the door, pushed it ajar, and listened. No sound of Mrs Wisbeach. You had to be very careful; she was quite capable of sneaking upstairs and catching you in the act. This tea-making was the major household offence, next to bringing a woman in. Quietly he bolted the door, dragged his cheap suitcase from under the bed, and unlocked it. From it he extracted a sixpenny Woolworth's kettle, a packet of Lyons' tea, a tin of condensed milk, a tea-pot, and a cup. They were all packed in newspaper to prevent them from chinking.

He had his regular procedure for making tea. First he half filled the kettle with water from the jug and set it on the oil stove. Then he knelt down and spread out a piece of newspaper. Yesterday's tea-leaves were still in the pot, of course. He shook them out on to the newspaper, cleaned out the pot with his thumb and folded the leaves into a bundle. Presently he would smuggle them downstairs. That was always the most risky part—getting rid of the used tea-leaves. It was like the difficulty murderers have in disposing of the body. As for the cup, he always washed it in his hand basin in the morning. A squalid business. It sickened him, sometimes. It was queer how furtively you had to live in Mrs Wisbeach's house. You had the feeling that she was always watching you; and indeed, she was given to tiptoeing up and downstairs at all hours, in hope of catching the lodgers up to mischief. It was one of those houses where you cannot even go to the w.c. in peace because of the feeling that somebody is listening to you.

Gordon unbolted the door again and listened intently. No one stirring. Ah! A clatter of crockery far below. Mrs Wisbeach was washing up the supper things. Probably safe to go down, then.

He tiptoed down, clutching the damp bundle of tea-leaves against his breast. The w.c. was on the second floor. At the angle of the stairs he halted, listened a moment longer. Ah! Another clatter of crockery.

All clear! Gordon Comstock, poet ('of exceptional promise', *The Times Lit. Supp.* had said), hurriedly slipped into the w.c., flung his tea-leaves down the waste-pipe, and pulled the plug. Then he hurried back to his room, rebolted the door, and, with precautions against noise, brewed himself a fresh pot of tea.

The room was passably warm by now. The tea and a cigarette worked their short-lived magic. He began to feel a little less bored and angry. Should he do a spot of work after all? He ought to work, of course. He always hated himself afterwards when he had wasted a whole evening. Half unwillingly, he shoved his chair up to the table. It needed an effort even to disturb that frightful jungle of papers. He pulled a few grimy sheets towards him, spread them out, and looked at them. God, what a mess! Written on, scored out, written over, scored out again, till they were like poor old hacked cancer-patients after twenty operations. But the handwriting, where it was not crossed out, was delicate and 'scholarly'. With pain and trouble Gordon had acquired that 'scholarly' hand, so different from the beastly copper-plate they had taught him at school.

Perhaps he *would* work; for a little while, anyway. He rummaged in the litter of papers. Where was that passage he had been working on yesterday? The poem was an immensely long one—that is, it was going to be immensely long when it was finished—two thousand lines or so, in rhyme royal, describing a day in London. *London Pleasures*, its name was. It was a huge, ambitious project—the kind of thing that should only be undertaken by people with endless leisure. Gordon had not grasped that fact when he began the poem; he grasped it now, however. How light-heartedly he had begun it, two years ago! When he had chucked up everything and descended into the slime of poverty, the conception of this poem had been at least a part of his motive. He had felt so certain, then, that he was equal to it. But somehow, almost from the start, *London Pleasures* had gone wrong. It was too big for him, that was the truth. It had never really progressed, it had simply fallen apart into a series of fragments. And out of two years' work that was all that he had to show—just fragments, incomplete in themselves and impossible to join together. On every one of those sheets of paper there was some hacked scrap of verse which had been written and rewritten and rewritten over intervals of months. There were not five hundred lines that you could say were definitely finished. And he had lost the power to add to it any longer; he could only tinker with this passage or that, groping now here, now there, in its confusion. It was no longer a thing that he created, it was merely a nightmare with which he struggled.

For the rest, in two whole years he had produced nothing except a handful of short poems—perhaps a score in all. It was so rarely that he could attain the peace of mind in which poetry, or prose for that matter, has got to be written. The times when he 'could not' work grew commoner and commoner. Of all types of human being, only the artist takes it upon him to say that he 'cannot' work. But it is quite true; there *are* times when one cannot work. Money again, always money! Lack of money means discomfort, means squalid worries, means shortage of tobacco, means ever-present conciousness of failure—above all, it means loneliness. How can you be anything but lonely on two quid a week? And in loneliness no decent book was ever written. It was quite certain that *London Pleasures* would never be the poem he had conceived—it was quite certain, indeed, that it would never even be finished. And in the moments when he faced facts Gordon himself was aware of this.

Yet all the same, and all the more for that very reason, he went on with it. It was something to cling to. It was a way of hitting back at his poverty and his loneliness. And after all, there were times when the mood of creation returned, or seemed to return. It returned tonight, for just a little while—just as long as it takes to smoke two cigarettes. With smoke tickling his lungs, he abstracted himself from the mean and actual world. He drove his mind into the abyss where poetry is written. The gas-jet sang soothing overhead. Words became vivid and momentous things. A couplet, written a year ago and left as unfinished, caught his eye with a note of doubt. He repeated it to himself, over and over. It was wrong, somehow. It had seemed all right, a year ago; now, on the other hand, it seemed subtly vulgar. He rummaged among the sheets of foolscap till he found one that had nothing written on the back, turned it over, wrote the couplet out anew, wrote a dozen different versions of it, repeated each of them over and over to himself. Finally there was none that satisfied him. The couplet would have to go. It was cheap and vulgar. He found the original sheet of paper and scored the couplet out with thick lines. And in doing this there was a sense of achievement, of time not wasted, as though the destruction of much labour were in some way an act of creation.

Suddenly a double knock deep below made the whole house rattle. Gordon started. His mind fled upwards from the abyss. The post! *London Pleasures* was forgotten.

His heart fluttered. Perhaps Rosemary *had* written. Besides, there were those two poems he had sent to the magazines. One of them, indeed, he had almost given up as lost; he had sent it to an American paper, the *Californian Review*, months ago. Probably they wouldn't even bother to send it back. But the other was with an English paper, the *Primrose Quarterly*. He had wild hopes of that one. The *Primrose Quarterly* was one of those poisonous literary papers in which the fashionable Nancy Boy and the professional Roman Catholic walk *bras dessus, bras dessous*. It was also by a long way the most influential literary paper in England. You were a made man once you had had a poem in it. In his heart Gordon knew that the *Primrose Quarterly* would never print his poems. He wasn't up to their standard. Still, miracles sometimes happen; or, if not miracles, accidents. After all, they'd had his poem six weeks. Would they keep it six weeks if they didn't mean to accept it? He tried to quell the insane hope. But at the worst there was a chance that Rosemary had written. It was four whole days since she had written. She wouldn't do it, perhaps, if she knew how it disappointed him. Her letters—long, ill-spelt letters, full of absurd jokes and protestations of love for him—meant far more to him than she could ever understand. They were a reminder that there was still somebody in the world who cared for him. They even made up for the times when some beast had sent back one of his poems; and, as a matter of fact, the magazines always did send back his poems, except *Antichrist*, whose editor, Ravelston, was his personal friend.

There was a shuffling below. It was always some minutes before Mrs Wisbeach brought the letters upstairs. She liked to paw them about, feel them to see how thick they were, read their postmarks, hold them up to the light and speculate on their contents, before yielding them to their rightful owners. She exercised a sort of *droit du seigneur* over letters. Coming to her house, they were, she felt, at least partially hers. If you had gone to the front door and collected your own letters she would have resented it bitterly. On the other hand, she also resented the labour of carrying them upstairs. You would hear her footsteps very slowly ascending, and then, if there was a letter for you, there would be loud aggrieved breathing on the landing—this to let you know that you had put Mrs Wisbeach out of breath by dragging her up all those stairs. Finally, with a little impatient grunt, the letters would be shoved under your door.

Mrs Wisbeach was coming up the stairs. Gordon listened. The footsteps paused on the first floor. A letter for Flaxman. They ascended, paused again on the second floor. A letter for the engineer. Gordon's heart beat painfully. A letter, please God, a letter! More footsteps. Ascending or descending? They were coming nearer, surely! Ah, no, no! The sound grew fainter. She was going down again. The footsteps died away. No letters.

He took up his pen again. It was a quite futile gesture. She hadn't written after all! The little beast! He had not the smallest intention of doing any more work. Indeed, he could not. The disappointment had taken all the heart out of him. Only five minutes ago his poem had still seemed to him a living thing; now he knew it unmistakably for the worthless tripe that it was. With a kind of nervous disgust he bundled the scattered sheets together, stacked them in an untidy heap, and dumped them on the other side of the table, under the aspidistra. He could not even bear to look at them any longer.

He got up. It was too early to go to bed; at least, he was not in the mood for it. He pined for a bit of amusement—something cheap and easy. A seat in the pictures, cigarettes, beer. Useless! No money to pay for any of them. He would read *King Lear* and forget this filthy century. Finally, however, it was *The Adventures of Sherlock Holmes* that he took from the mantelpiece. *Sherlock Holmes* was his favourite of all books, because he knew it by heart. The oil in the lamp was giving out and it was getting beastly cold. Gordon dragged the quilt from his bed, wrapped it round his legs, and sat down to read. His right elbow on the table, his hands under his coat to keep them warm, he read through 'The Adventure of the Speckled Band.' The little gas-mantle sighed above, the circular flame of the oil lamp burned low, a thin bracket of fire, giving out no more heat than a candle.

Down in Mrs Wisbeach's lair the clock struck half past ten. You could always hear it striking at night. Ping-ping, ping-ping—a note of doom! The ticking of the alarm clock on the mantelpiece became audible to Gordon again, bringing with it the consciousness of the sinister passage of time. He looked about him. Another evening wasted. Hours, days, years slipping by. Night after night, always the same. The lonely room, the womanless bed; dust, cigarette ash, the aspidistra leaves. And he was thirty, nearly. In sheer self-punishment he dragged forth a wad of *London Pleasures*, spread out the grimy sheets, and looked at them as one looks at a skull for a *memento mori*. *London Pleasures*, by Gordon Comstock, author of *Mice*. His *magnum opus*. The fruit (fruit, indeed!) of two years' work—that labyrinthine mess of words! And tonight's achievement—two lines crossed out; two lines backward instead of forward.

The lamp made a sound like a tiny hiccup and went out. With an effort Gordon stood up and flung the quilt back on to his bed. Better get to bed, perhaps, before it got any colder. He wandered over towards the bed. But wait. Work tomorrow. Wind the clock, set the alarm. Nothing accomplished, nothing done, has earned a night's repose.

It was some time before he could find the energy to undress. For a quarter of an hour, perhaps, he lay on the bed fully dressed, his hands under his head. There was a crack on the ceiling that resembled the map of Australia. Gordon contrived to work off his shoes and socks without sitting up. He held up one foot and looked at it. A smallish, delicate foot. Ineffectual, like his hands. Also, it was very dirty. It was nearly ten days since he had a bath. Becoming ashamed of the dirtiness of his feet, he sagged into a sitting position and undressed himself, throwing his clothes on to the floor. Then he turned out the gas and slid between the sheets, shuddering, for he was naked. He always slept naked. His last suit of pyjamas had gone west more than a year ago.

The clock downstairs struck eleven. As the first coldness of the sheets wore off, Gordon's mind went back to the poem he had begun that afternoon. He repeated in a whisper the single stanza that was finished:

> Sharply the menacing wind sweeps over
> The bending poplars, newly bare,
> And dark ribbons of the chimneys
> Veer downward; flicked by whips of air,
> Torn posters flutter.

The octosyllables flicked to and fro. Click-click, click-click! The awful, mechanical emptiness of it appalled him. It was like some futile little machine ticking over. Rhyme to rhyme, click-click, click-click. Like the nodding of a clock-work doll. Poetry! The last futility. He lay awake, aware of his own futility, of his thirty years, of the blind alley into which he had led his life.

The clock struck twelve. Gordon had stretched his legs out straight. The bed had grown warm and comfortable. The upturned beam of a car, somewhere in the street parallel to Willowbed Road, penetrated the blind and threw into silhouette a leaf of the aspidistra, shaped like Agamemnon's sword.

# 3

'Gordon Comstock' was a pretty bloody name, but then Gordon came from a pretty bloody family. The 'Gordon' part of it was Scotch, of course. The prevalence of such names nowadays is merely a part of the Scotchification of England that has been going on these last fifty years. 'Gordon', 'Colin', 'Malcolm', 'Donald'—these are the gifts of Scotland to the world, along with golf, whisky, porridge, and the works of Barrie and Stevenson.

The Comstocks belonged to the most dismal of all classes, the middle-middle class, the landless gentry. In their miserable poverty they had not even the snobbish consolation of regarding themselves as an 'old' family fallen on evil days, for they were not an 'old' family at all, merely one of those families which rose on the wave of Victorian prosperity and then sank again faster than the wave itself. They had had at most fifty years of comparative wealth, corresponding with the lifetime of Gordon's grandfather, Samuel Comstock–Gran'pa Comstock, as Gordon was taught to call him, though the old man died four years before he was born.

Gran'pa Comstock was one of those people who even from the grave exert a powerful influence. In life he was a tough old scoundrel. He plundered the proletariat and the foreigner of fifty thousand pounds, he built himself a red brick mansion as durable as a pyramid, and he begot twelve children, of whom eleven survived. Finally he died quite suddenly, of a cerebral haemorrhage. In Kensal Green his children placed over him a monolith with the following inscription:

IN EVER LOVING MEMORY OF
SAMUEL EZEKIEL COMSTOCK,
A FAITHFUL HUSBAND, A TENDER FATHER AND
AN UPRIGHT AND GODLY MAN,
WHO WAS BORN ON 9 JULY 1828, AND
DEPARTED THIS LIFE 5 SEPTEMBER 1901,
THIS STONE IS ERECTED BY
HIS SORROWING CHILDREN.
HE SLEEPS IN THE ARMS OF JESUS.

No need to repeat the blasphemous comments which everyone who had known Gran'pa Comstock made on that last sentence. But it is worth pointing out that the chunk of granite on which it was inscribed weighed close on five tons and was quite certainly put there with the intention, though not the conscious intention, of making sure that Gran'pa Comstock shouldn't get up from underneath it. If you want to know what a dead man's relatives really think of him, a good rough test is the weight of his tombstone.

The Comstocks, as Gordon knew them, were a peculiarly dull, shabby, dead-alive, ineffectual family. They lacked vitality to an extent that was surprising. That was Gran'pa Comstock's doing, of course. By the time when he died all his children were grown up and some of them were middle-aged, and he had long ago succeeded in crushing out of them any spirit they might ever have possessed. He had lain upon them as a garden roller lies upon daisies, and there was no chance of their flattened personalities ever expanding again. One and all they turned out listless, gutless, unsuccessful sort of people. None of the boys had proper professions, because Gran'pa Comstock had been at the greatest pains to drive all of them into professions for which they were totally unsuited. Only one of them–John, Gordon's father–had even braved Gran'pa Comstock to the extent of getting married during the latter's lifetime. It was impossible to imagine any of them making any sort of mark in the world, or creating anything, or destroying anything, or being happy, or vividly unhappy, or fully alive, or even earning a decent income. They just drifted along in an atmosphere of semi-genteel failure. They were one of those depressing families, so common among the middle-middle classes, in which *nothing ever happens.*

From his earliest childhood Gordon's relatives had depressed him horribly. When he was a little boy he still had great numbers of uncles and aunts living. They were all more or less alike—grey, shabby, joyless people, all rather sickly in health and all perpetually harassed by money-worries which fizzled along without ever reaching the sensational explosion of bankruptcy. It was noticeable even then that they had lost all impulse to reproduce themselves. Really vital people, whether they have money or whether they haven't, multiply almost as automatically as animals. Gran'pa Comstock, for instance, himself one of a litter of twelve, had produced eleven progeny. Yet all those eleven produced only two progeny between them, and those two—Gordon and his sister Julia—had produced, by 1934, not even one. Gordon, last of the Comstocks, was born in 1905, an unintended child; and thereafter, in thirty long, long years, there was not a single birth in the family, only deaths. And not only in the matter of marrying and begetting, but in every possible way, *nothing ever happened* in the Comstock family. Every one of them seemed doomed, as though by a curse, to a dismal, shabby, hole-and-corner existence. None of them ever *did* anything. They were the kind of people who in every conceivable activity, even if it is only getting on to a bus, are automatically elbowed away from the heart of things. All of them, of course, were hopeless fools about money. Gran'pa Comstock had finally divided his money among them more or less equally, so that each received, after the sale of the red-brick mansion, round about five thousand pounds. And no sooner was Gran'pa Comstock underground than they began to fritter their money away. None of them had the guts to lose it in sensational ways such as squandering it on women or at the races; they simply dribbled it away and dribbled it away, the women in silly investments and the men in futile little business ventures that petered out after a year or two, leaving a net loss. More than half of them went unmarried to their graves. Some of the women did make rather undesirable middle-aged marriages after their father was dead, but the men, because of their incapacity to earn a proper living, were the kind who 'can't afford' to marry. None of them, except Gordon's Aunt Angela, ever had so much as a home to call their own; they were the kind of people who live in godless 'rooms' and tomb-like boarding-houses. And year after year they died off and died off, of dingy but expensive little diseases that swallowed up the last penny of their capital. One of the women, Gordon's Aunt Charlotte, wandered off into the Mental Home at Clapham in 1916. The Mental Homes of England, how chock-a-block they stand! And it is above all derelict spinsters of the middle-classes who keep them going. By 1934 only three of that generation survived; Aunt Charlotte already mentioned, and Aunt Angela, who by some happy chance had been induced to buy a house and a tiny annuity in 1912, and Uncle Walter, who dingily existed on the few hundred pounds that were left out of his five thousand and by running short-lived 'agencies' for this and that.

Gordon grew up in the atmosphere of cut-down clothes and stewed neck of mutton. His father, like the other Comstocks, was a depressed and therefore depressing person, but he had some brains and a slight literary turn. And seeing that his mind was of the literary type and he had a shrinking horror of anything to do with figures, it had seemed only natural to Gran'pa Comstock to make him into a chartered accountant. So he practised, ineffectually, as a chartered accountant, and was always buying his way into partnerships which were dissolved after a year or two, and his income fluctuated, sometimes rising to five hundred a year and sometimes falling to two hundred, but always with a tendency to decrease. He died in 1922, aged only fifty-six, but worn out—he had suffered from a kidney disease for a long time past.

Since the Comstocks were genteel as well as shabby, it was considered necessary to waste huge sums on Gordon's 'education'. What a fearful thing it is, this incubus of 'education'! It means that in order to send his son to the right kind of school (that is, a public school or an imitation of one) a middle-class man is obliged to live for years on end in a style that would be scorned by a jobbing plumber. Gordon was sent to wretched, pretentious schools whose fees were round about £120 a year. Even these fees, of course, meant fearful sacrifices at home. Meanwhile Julia, who was five years older than he, received as nearly as possible no education at all. She was, indeed, sent to one or two poor, dingy little boarding schools, but she was 'taken away' for good when she was sixteen. Gordon was 'the boy' and Julia was 'the girl', and it seemed natural to everyone that 'the girl' should be sacrificed to 'the boy'. Moreover, it had early been decided in the family that Gordon was 'clever'. Gordon, with his wonderful 'cleverness', was to win scholarships, make a brilliant success in life, and retrieve the family fortunes—that was the theory, and no one believed in it more firmly than Julia. Julia was a tall, ungainly girl, much taller than Gordon, with a thin face and a neck just a little too long—one of those girls who even at their most youthful remind one irresistibly of a goose. But her nature was simple and affectionate. She was a self-effacing, home-keeping, ironing, darning, and mending kind of girl, a natural spinster-soul. Even at sixteen she had 'old maid' written all over her. She idolized Gordon. All through his childhood she watched over him, nursed him, spoiled him, went in rags so that he might have the right clothes to go to school in, saved up her wretched pocket-money to buy him Christmas presents and birthday presents. And of course he repaid her, as soon as he was old enough, by despising her because she was not pretty and not 'clever'.

Even at the third-rate schools to which Gordon was sent nearly all the boys were richer than himself. They soon found out his poverty, of course, and gave him hell because of it. Probably the greatest cruelty one can inflict on a child is to send it to school among children richer than itself. A child conscious of poverty will suffer snobbish agonies such as a grown-up person can scarcely imagine. In those days, especially at his preparatory school, Gordon's life had been one long conspiracy to keep his end up and pretend that his parents were richer than they were. Ah, the humiliations of those days! That awful business, for instance, at the beginning of each term, when you had to 'give in' to the headmaster, publicly, the money you had brought back with you; and the contemptuous, cruel sniggers from the other boys when you didn't 'give in' ten bob or more. And the time when the others found out that Gordon was wearing a ready-made suit which had cost thirty-five shillings! The times that Gordon dreaded most of all were when his parents came down to see him. Gordon, in those days still a believer, used actually to pray that his parents wouldn't come down to school. His father, especially, was the kind of father you couldn't help being ashamed of; a cadaverous, despondent man, with a bad stoop, his clothes dismally shabby and hopelessly out of date. He carried about with him an atmosphere of failure, worry, and boredom. And he had such a dreadful habit, when he was saying good-bye, of tipping Gordon half a crown right in front of the other boys, so that everyone could see that it was only half a crown and not, as it ought to have been, ten bob! Even twenty years afterwards the memory of that school made Gordon shudder.

The first effect of all this was to give him a crawling reverence for money. In those days he actually hated his poverty-stricken relatives—his father and mother, Julia, everybody. He hated them for their dingy homes, their dowdiness, their joyless attitude to life, their endless worrying and groaning over threepences and sixpences. By far the commonest phrase in the Comstock household was, 'We can't afford it.' In those days he longed for money as only a child can long. Why *shouldn't* one have decent clothes and plenty of sweets and go to the pictures as often as one wanted to? He blamed his parents for their poverty as though they had been poor on purpose. Why couldn't they be like other boys' parents? They *preferred* being poor, it seemed to him. That is how a child's mind works.

But as he grew older he grew—not less unreasonable, exactly, but unreasonable in a different way. By this time he had found his feet at school and was less violently oppressed. He never was very successful at school—he did no work and won no scholarships—but he managed to develop his brain along the lines that suited it. He read the books which the headmaster denounced from the pulpit, and developed unorthodox opinions about the C. of E., patriotism, and the Old Boys' tie. Also he began writing poetry. He even, after a year or two, began to send poems to the *Athenaeum*, the *New Age*, and the *Weekly Westminster*; but they were invariably rejected. Of course there were other boys of similar type with whom he associated. Every public school has its small self-conscious intelligentsia. And at that moment, in the years just after the War, England was so full of revolutionary opinion that even the public schools were infected by it. The young, even those who had been too young to fight, were in a bad temper with their elders, as well they might be; practically everyone with any brains at all was for the moment a revolutionary. Meanwhile the old—those over sixty, say—were running in circles like hens, squawking about 'subversive ideas'. Gordon and his friends had quite an exciting time with their 'subversive ideas'. For a whole year they ran an unofficial monthly paper called the *Bolshevik*, duplicated with a jellygraph. It advocated Socialism, free love, the dismemberment of the British Empire, the abolition of the Army and Navy, and so on and so forth. It was great fun. Every intelligent boy of sixteen is a Socialist. At that age one does not see the hook sticking out of the rather stodgy bait.

In a crude, boyish way, he had begun to get the hang of this money-business. At an earlier age than most people he grasped that *all* modern commerce is a swindle. Curiously enough, it was the advertisements in the Underground stations that first brought it home to him. He little knew, as the biographers say, that he himself would one day have a job in an advertising firm. But there was more to it than the mere fact that business is a swindle. What he realized, and more clearly as time went on, was that money-worship has been elevated into a religion. Perhaps it is the only real religion—the only really *felt* religion—that is left to us. Money is what God used to be. Good and evil have no meaning any longer except failure and success. Hence the profoundly significant phrase, to *make good*. The decalogue has been reduced to two commandments. One for the employers—the elect, the money-priesthood as it were—'Thou shalt make money'; the other for the employed—the slaves and underlings—'Thou shalt not lose thy job.' It was about this time that he came across *The Ragged Trousered Philanthropists* and read about the starving carpenter who pawns everything but sticks to his aspidistra. The aspidistra became a sort of symbol for Gordon after that. The aspidistra, flower of England! It ought to be on our coat of arms instead of the lion and the unicorn. There will be no revolution in England while there are aspidistras in the windows.

He did not hate and despise his relatives now—or not so much, at any rate. They still depressed him greatly—those poor old withering aunts and uncles, of whom two or three had already died, his father, worn out and spiritless, his mother, faded, nervy, and 'delicate' (her lungs were none too strong), Julia, already, at one-and-twenty, a dutiful, resigned drudge who worked twelve hours a day and never had a decent frock. But he grasped now what was the matter with them. It was not *merely* the lack of money. It was rather that, having no money, they still lived mentally in the money-world—the world in which money is virtue and poverty is crime. It was not poverty but the down-dragging of *respectable* poverty that had done for them. They had accepted the money-code, and by that code they were failures. They had never had the sense to lash out and just *live*, money or no money, as the lower classes do. How right the lower classes are! Hats off to the factory lad who with fourpence in the world puts his girl in the family way! At least he's got blood and not money in his veins.

Gordon thought it all out, in the naïve selfish manner of a boy. There are two ways to live, he decided. You can be rich, or you can deliberately refuse to be rich. You can possess money, or you can despise money; the one fatal thing is to worship money and fail to get it. He took it for granted that he himself would never be able to make money. It hardly even occurred to him that he might have talents which could be turned to account. That was what his schoolmasters had done for him; they had rubbed it into him that he was a seditious little nuisance and not likely to 'succeed' in life. He accepted this. Very well, then, he would refuse the whole business of 'succeeding'; he would make it his especial purpose *not* to 'succeed'. Better to reign in hell than serve in heaven; better to serve in hell than serve in heaven, for that matter. Already, at sixteen, he knew which side he was on. He was *against* the money-god and all his swinish priesthood. He had declared war on money; but secretly, of course.

It was when he was seventeen that his father died, leaving about two hundred pounds. Julia had been at work for some years now. During 1918 and 1919 she had worked in a Government office, and after that she took a course of cookery and got a job in a nasty, ladylike little teashop near Earl's Court Underground Station. She worked a seventy-two hour week and was given her lunch and tea and twenty-five shillings; out of this she contributed twelve shillings a week, often more, to the household expenses. Obviously the best thing to do, now that Mr Comstock was dead, would have been to take Gordon away from school, find him a job, and let Julia have the two hundred pounds to set up a teashop of her own. But here the habitual Comstock folly about money stepped in. Neither Julia nor her mother would hear of Gordon leaving school. With the strange idealistic snobbishness of the middle classes, they were willing to go to the workhouse sooner than let Gordon leave school before the statutory age of eighteen. The two hundred pounds, or more than half of it, must be used in completing Gordon's 'education'. Gordon let them do it. He had declared war on money but that did not prevent him from being damnably selfish. Of course he dreaded this business of going to work. What boy wouldn't dread it? Pen-pushing in some filthy office—God! His uncles and aunts were already talking dismally about 'getting Gordon settled in life'. They saw everything in terms of 'good' jobs. Young Smith had got such a 'good' job in a bank, and young Jones had got such a 'good' job in an insurance office. It made him sick to hear them. They seemed to want to see every young man in England nailed down in the coffin of a 'good' job.

Meanwhile, money had got to be earned. Before her marriage Gordon's mother had been a music teacher, and even since then she had taken pupils, sporadically, when the family were in lower water than usual. She now decided that she would start giving lessons again. It was fairly easy to get pupils in the suburbs—they were living in Acton—and with the music fees and Julia's contribution they could probably 'manage' for the next year or two. But the state of Mrs Comstock's lungs was now something more than 'delicate'. The doctor who had attended her husband before his death had put his stethoscope to her chest and looked serious. He had told her to take care of herself, keep warm, eat nourishing food, and, above all, avoid fatigue. The fidgeting, tiring job of giving piano lessons was, of course, the worst possible thing for her. Gordon knew nothing of this. Julia knew, however. It was a secret between the two women, carefully kept from Gordon.

A year went by. Gordon spent it rather miserably, more and more embarrassed by his shabby clothes and lack of pocket-money, which made girls an object of terror to him. However, the *New Age* accepted one of his poems that year. Meanwhile, his mother sat on comfortless piano stools in draughty drawing-rooms, giving lessons at two shillings an hour. And then Gordon left school, and fat interfering Uncle Walter, who had business connexions in a small way, came forward and said that a friend of a friend of his could get Gordon ever such a 'good' job in the accounts department of a red lead firm. It was really a splendid job–a wonderful opening for a young man. If Gordon buckled to work in the right spirit he might be a Big Pot one of these days. Gordon's soul squirmed. Suddenly, as weak people do, he stiffened, and, to the horror of the whole family, refused even to try for the job.

There were fearful rows, of course. They could not understand him. It seemed to them a kind of blasphemy to refuse such a 'good' job when you got the chance of it. He kept reiterating that he didn't want *that kind* of job. Then what *did* he want? they all demanded. He wanted to 'write', he told them sullenly. But how could he possibly make a living by 'writing'? they demanded again. And of course he couldn't answer. At the back of his mind was the idea that he could somehow live by writing poetry; but that was too absurd even to be mentioned. But at any rate, he wasn't going into business, into the money-world. He would have a job, but not a 'good' job. None of them had the vaguest idea what he meant. His mother wept, even Julia 'went for' him, and all round him there were uncles and aunts (he still had six or seven of them left) feebly volleying and incompetently thundering. And after three days a dreadful thing happened. In the middle of supper his mother was seized by a violent fit of coughing, put her hand to her breast, fell forward, and began bleeding at the mouth.

Gordon was terrified. His mother did not die, as it happened, but she looked deathly as they carried her upstairs. Gordon rushed for the doctor. For several days his mother lay at death's door. It was the draughty drawing-rooms and the trudging to and fro in all weathers that had done it. Gordon hung helplessly about the house, a dreadful feeling of guilt mingling with his misery. He did not exactly know but he half divined, that his mother had killed herself in order to pay his school fees. After this he could not go on opposing her any longer. He went to Uncle Walter and told him that he would take that job in the red lead firm, if they would give it him. So Uncle Walter spoke to his friend, and the friend spoke to his friend, and Gordon was sent for and interviewed by an old gentleman with badly fitting false teeth, and finally was given a job, on probation. He started on twenty-five bob a week. And with this firm he remained six years.

They moved away from Acton and took a flat in a desolate red block of flats somewhere in the Paddington district. Mrs Comstock had brought her piano, and when she had got some of her strength back she gave occasional lessons. Gordon's wages were gradually raised, and the three of them 'managed', more or less. It was Julia and Mrs Comstock who did most of the 'managing'. Gordon still had a boy's selfishness about money. At the office he got on not absolutely badly. It was said of him that he was worth his wages but wasn't the type that Makes Good. In a way the utter contempt that he had for his work made things easier for him. He could put up with this meaningless office-life, because he never for an instant thought of it as permanent. Somehow, sometime, God knew how or when, he was going to break free of it. After all, there was always his 'writing'. Some day, perhaps, he might be able to make a living of sorts by 'writing'; and you'd feel you were free of the money-stink if you were a 'writer', would you not? The types he saw all round him, especially the older men, made him squirm. That was what it meant to worship the money-god! To settle down, to Make Good, to sell your soul for a villa and an aspidistra! To turn into the typical little bowler-hatted sneak—Strube's 'little man'—the little docile cit who slips home by the six-fifteen to a supper of cottage pie and stewed tinned pears, half an hour's listening-in to the B.B.C. Symphony Concert, and then perhaps a spot of licit sexual intercourse if his wife 'feels in the mood'! What a fate! No, it isn't like that that one was meant to live. One's got to get right out of it, out of the money-stink. It was a kind of plot that he was nursing. He was as though dedicated to this war against money. But it was still a secret. The people at the office never suspected him of unorthodox ideas. They never even found out that he wrote poetry—not that there was much to find out, for in six years he had less than twenty poems printed in the magazines. To look at, he was just the same as any other City clerk—just a soldier in the strap-hanging army that sways eastward at morning, westward at night in the carriages of the Underground.

He was twenty-four when his mother died. The family was breaking up. Only four of the older generation of Comstocks were left now—Aunt Angela, Aunt Charlotte, Uncle Walter, and another uncle who died a year later. Gordon and Julia gave up the flat. Gordon took a furnished room in Doughty Street (he felt vaguely literary, living in Bloomsbury), and Julia moved to Earl's Court, to be near the shop. Julia was nearly thirty now, and looked much older. She was thinner than ever, though healthy enough, and there was grey in her hair. She still worked twelve hours a day, and in six years her wages had only risen by ten shillings a week. The horribly ladylike lady who kept the teashop was a semi-friend as well as an employer, and thus could sweat and bully Julia to the tune of 'dearest' and 'darling'. Four months after his mother's death Gordon suddenly walked out of his job. He gave the firm no reasons. They imagined that he was going to 'better himself', and—luckily, as it turned out—gave him quite good references. He had not even thought of looking for another job. He wanted to burn his boats. From now on he would breathe free air, free of the money-stink. He had not consciously waited for his mother to die before doing this; still, it was his mother's death that had nerved him to it.

Of course there was another and more desolating row in what was left of the family. They thought Gordon must have gone mad. Over and over again he tried, quite vainly, to explain to them why he would not yield himself to the servitude of a 'good' job. 'But what are you going to live on? What are you going to live on?' was what they all wailed at him. He refused to think seriously about it. Of course, he still harboured the notion that he could make a living of sorts by 'writing'. By this time he had got to know Ravelston, editor of *Antichrist*, and Ravelston, besides printing his poems, managed to get him books to review occasionally. His literary prospects were not so bleak as they had been six years ago. But still, it was not the desire to 'write' that was his real motive. To get out of the money-world—that was what he wanted. Vaguely he looked forward to some kind of moneyless, anchorite existence. He had a feeling that if you genuinely despise money you can keep going somehow, like the birds of the air. He forgot that the birds of the air don't pay room-rent. The poet starving in a garret—but starving, somehow, not uncomfortably—that was his vision of himself.

The next seven months were devastating. They scared him and almost broke his spirit. He learned what it means to live for weeks on end on bread and margarine, to try to 'write' when you are half starved, to pawn your clothes, to sneak trembling up the stairs when you owe three weeks' rent and your landlady is listening for you. Moreover, in those seven months he wrote pratically nothing. The first effect of poverty is that it kills thought. He grasped, as though it were a new discovery, that you do not escape from money merely by being moneyless. On the contrary, you are the hopeless slave of money until you have enough of it to live on—a 'competence', as the beastly middle-class phrase goes. Finally he was turned out of his room, after a vulgar row. He was three days and four nights in the street. It was bloody. Three mornings, on the advice of another man he met on the Embankment, he spent in Billingsgate, helping to shove fish-barrows up the twisty little hills from Billingsgate into Eastcheap. 'Twopence an up' was what you got, and the work knocked hell out of your thigh muscles. There were crowds of people on the same job, and you had to wait your turn; you were lucky if you made eighteen-pence between four in the morning and nine. After three days of it Gordon gave up. What was the use? He was beaten. There was nothing for it but to go back to his family, borrow some money, and find another job.

But now, of course, there was no job to be had. For months he lived by cadging on the family. Julia kept him going till the last penny of her tiny savings was gone. It was abominable. Here was the outcome of all his fine attitudes! He had renounced ambition, made war on money, and all it led to was cadging from his sister! And Julia, he knew, felt his failure far more than she felt the loss of her savings. She had had such hopes of Gordon. He alone of all the Comstocks had had it in him to 'succeed'. Even now she believed that somehow, some day, he was going to retrieve the family fortunes. He was so 'clever'—surely he could make money if he tried! For two whole months Gordon stayed with Aunt Angela in her little house at Highgate—poor, faded, mummified Aunt Angela, who even for herself had barely enough to eat. All this time he searched desperately for work. Uncle Walter could not help him. His influence in the business world, never large, was now practically nil. At last, however, in a quite unexpected way, the luck turned. A friend of a friend of Julia's employer's brother managed to get Gordon a job in the accounts department of the New Albion Publicity Company.

The New Albion was one of those publicity firms which have sprung up everywhere since the War—the fungi, as you might say, that sprout from a decaying capitalism. It was a smallish rising firm and took every class of publicity it could get. It designed a certain number of large-scale posters for oatmeal stout, self-raising flour, and so forth, but its main line was millinery and cosmetic advertisements in the women's illustrated papers, besides minor ads in twopenny weeklies, such as Whiterose Pills for Female Disorders, Your Horoscope Cast by Professor Raratongo, The Seven Secrets of Venus, New

Hope for the Ruptured, Earn Five Pounds a Week in your Spare Time, and Cyprolax Hair Lotion Banishes all Unpleasant Intruders. There was a large staff of commercial artists, of course. It was here that Gordon first made the acquaintance of Rosemary. She was in the 'studio' and helped to design fashion plates. It was a long time before he actually spoke to her. At first he knew her merely as a remote personage, small, dark, with swift movements, distinctly attractive but rather intimidating. When they passed one another in the corridors she eyed him ironically, as though she knew all about him and considered him a bit of a joke; nevertheless she seemed to look at him a little oftener than was necessary. He had nothing to do with her side of the business. He was in the accounts department, a mere clerk on three quid a week.

The interesting thing about the New Albion was that it was so completely modern in spirit. There was hardly a soul in the firm who was not perfectly well aware that publicity—advertising—is the dirtiest ramp that capitalism has yet produced. In the red lead firm there had still lingered certain notions of commercial honour and usefulness. But such things would have been laughed at in the New Albion. Most of the employees were the hard-boiled, Americanized, go-getting type to whom nothing in the world is sacred, except money. They had their cynical code worked out. The public are swine; advertising is the rattling of a stick inside a swill-bucket. And yet beneath their cynicism there was the final naïveté, the blind worship of the money-god. Gordon studied them unobtrusively. As before, he did his work passably well and his fellow-employees looked down on him. Nothing had changed in his inner mind. He still despised and repudiated the money-code. Somehow, sooner or later, he was going to escape from it; even now, after his first fiasco, he still plotted to escape. He was *in* the money world, but not *of* it. As for the types about him, the little bowler-hatted worms who never turned, and the go-getters, the American business-college gutter-crawlers, they rather amused him than not. He liked studying their slavish keep-your-job mentality. He was the chiel amang them takin' notes.

One day a curious thing happened. Somebody chanced to see a poem of Gordon's in a magazine, and put it about that they 'had a poet in the office'. Of course Gordon was laughed at, not ill-naturedly, by the other clerks. They nicknamed him 'the bard' from that day forth. But though amused, they were also faintly contemptuous. It confirmed all their ideas about Gordon. A fellow who wrote poetry wasn't exactly the type to Make Good. But the thing had an unexpected sequel. About the time when the clerks grew tired of chaffing Gordon, Mr Erskine, the managing director, who had hitherto taken only the minimum notice of him, sent for him and interviewed him.

Mr Erskine was a large, slow-moving man with a broad, healthy, expressionless face. From his appearance and the slowness of his speech you would have guessed with confidence that he had something to do with either agriculture or cattle-breeding. His wits were as slow as his movements, and he was the kind of man who never hears of anything until everybody else has stopped talking about it. How such a man came to be in charge of an advertising agency, only the strange gods of capitalism know. But he was quite a likeable person. He had not that sniffish, buttoned-up spirit that usually goes with an ability to make money. And in a way his fat-wittedness stood him in good stead. Being insensible to popular prejudice, he could assess people on their merits; consequently, he was rather good at choosing talented employees. The news that Gordon had written poems, so far from shocking him, vaguely impressed him. They wanted literary talents in the New Albion. Having sent for Gordon, he studied him in a somnolent, sidelong way and asked him a number of inconclusive questions. He never listened to Gordon's answers, but punctuated his questions with a noise that sounded like 'Hm, hm, hm.' Wrote poetry, did he? Oh yes? Hm. And had it printed in the papers? Hm, hm. Suppose they paid you for that kind of thing? Not much, eh? No, suppose not. Hm, hm. Poetry? Hm. A bit difficult, that must be. Getting the lines the same length, and all that. Hm, hm. Write anything else? Stories, and so forth? Hm. Oh yes? Very interesting. Hm!

Then, without further questions, he promoted Gordon to a special post as secretary—in effect, apprentice—to Mr Clew, the New Albion's head copywriter. Like every other advertising agency, the New Albion was constantly in search of copywriters with a touch of imagination. It is a curious fact, but it is much easier to find competent draughtsmen than to find people who can think of slogans like 'Q. T. Sauce keeps Hubby Smiling' and 'Kiddies clamour for their Breakfast Crisps'. Gordon's wages were not raised for the moment, but the firm had their eye on him. With luck he might be a full-fledged copywriter in a year's time. It was an unmistakable chance to Make Good.

For six months he was working with Mr Clew. Mr Clew was a harassed man of about forty, with wiry hair into which he often plunged his fingers. He worked in a stuffy little office whose walls were entirely papered with his past triumphs in the form of posters. He took Gordon under his wing in a friendly way, showed him the ropes, and was even ready to listen to his suggestions. At that time they were working on a line of magazine ads for April Dew, the great new deodorant which the Queen of Sheba Toilet Requisites Co. (this was Flaxman's firm, curiously enough) were putting on the market. Gordon started on the job with secret loathing. But now there was a quite unexpected development. It was that Gordon showed, almost from the start, a remarkable talent for copywriting. He could compose an ad as though he had been born to it. The vivid phrase that sticks and rankles, the neat little para. that packs a world of lies into a hundred words—they came to him almost unsought. He had always had a gift for words, but this was the first time he had used it successfully. Mr Clew thought him very promising. Gordon watched his own development, first with surprise, then with amusement, and finally with a kind of horror. *This*, then, was what he was coming to! Writing lies to tickle the money out of fools' pockets! There was a beastly irony, too, in the fact that he, who wanted to be a 'writer', should score his sole success in writing ads for deodorants. However, that was less unusual than he imagined. Most copywriters, they say, are novelists *manqués*; or is it the other way about?

The Queen of Sheba were very pleased with their ads. Mr Erskine also was pleased. Gordon's wages were raised by ten shillings a week. And it was now that Gordon grew frightened. Money was getting him after all. He was sliding down, down, into the money-sty. A little more and he would be stuck in it for life. It is queer how these things happen. You set your face against success, you swear never to Make Good—you honestly believe that you couldn't Make Good even if you wanted to; and then something happens along, some mere chance, and you find yourself Making Good almost automatically. He saw that now or never was the time to escape. He had got to get out of it—out of the money-world, irrevocably, before he was too far involved.

But this time he wasn't going to be starved into submission. He went to Ravelston and asked his help. He told him that he wanted some kind of job; not a 'good' job, but a job that would keep his body without wholly buying his soul. Ravelston understood perfectly. The distinction between a job and a 'good' job did not have to be explained to him; nor did he point out to Gordon the folly of what he was doing. That was the great thing about Ravelston. He could always see another person's point of view. It was having money that did it, no doubt; for the rich can afford to be intelligent. Moreover, being rich himself, he could find jobs for other people. After only a fortnight he told Gordon of something that might suit him. A Mr McKechnie, a rather dilapidated second-hand bookseller with whom Ravelston dealt occasionally, was looking for an assistant. He did not want a trained assistant who would expect full wages; he wanted somebody who looked like a gentleman and could talk about books—somebody to impress the more bookish customers. It was the very reverse of a 'good' job. The hours were long, the pay was wretched—two pounds a week—and there was no chance of advancement. It was a blind-alley job. And, of course, a blind-alley job was the very thing Gordon was looking for. He went and saw Mr McKechnie, a sleepy, benign old Scotchman with a red nose and a white beard stained by snuff, and was taken on without demur. At this time, too, his volume of poems, *Mice*, was going to press. The seventh publisher to whom he had sent it had accepted it. Gordon did not know that this was Ravelston's doing. Ravelston was a personal friend of the publisher. He was always arranging this kind of thing, stealthily, for obscure poets. Gordon thought the future was opening before him. He was a made man—or, by Smilesian, aspidistral standards, *un*made.

He gave a month's notice at the office. It was a painful business altogether. Julia, of course, was more distressed than ever at this second abandonment of a 'good' job. By this time Gordon had got to know Rosemary. She did not try to prevent him from throwing up his job. It was against her code to interfere—'You've got to live your own life,' was always her attitude. But she did not in the least understand why he was doing it. The thing that most upset him, curiously enough, was his interview with Mr Erskine. Mr Erskine was genuinely kind. He did not want Gordon to leave the firm, and said so frankly. With a sort of elephantine politeness he refrained from calling Gordon a young fool. He did, however, ask him why he was leaving. Somehow, Gordon could not bring himself to avoid answering or to say—the only thing Mr Erskine would have understood—that he was going after a better-paid job. He blurted out shamefacedly that he 'didn't think business suited him' and that he 'wanted to go in for writing'. Mr Erskine was noncommittal. Writing, eh? Hm. Much money in that sort of thing nowadays? Not much, eh? Hm. No, suppose not. Hm. Gordon, feeling and looking ridiculous, mumbled that he had 'got a book just coming out'. A book of poems, he added with difficulty in pronouncing the word. Mr Erskine regarded him sidelong before remarking:

'Poetry, eh? Hm. Poetry? Make a living out of that sort of thing, do you think?'

'Well—not a living, exactly. But it would help.'

'Hm—well! You know best, I expect. If you want a job any time, come back to us. I dare say we could find room for you. We can do with your sort here. Don't forget.'

Gordon left with a hateful feeling of having behaved perversely and ungratefully. But he had got to do it; he had got to get out of the money-world. It was queer. All over England young men were eating their hearts out for lack of jobs, and here was he, Gordon, to whom the very word 'job' was faintly nauseous, having jobs thrust unwanted upon him. It was an example of the fact that you can get anything in this world if you genuinely don't want it. Moreover, Mr Erskine's words stuck in his mind. Probably he had meant what he said. Probably there *would* be a job waiting for Gordon if he chose to go back. So his boats were only half burned. The New Albion was a doom before him as well as behind.

But how happy had he been, just at first, in Mr McKechnie's bookshop! For a little while—a very little while—he had the illusion of being really out of the money-world. Of course the book-trade was a swindle, like all other trades; but how different a swindle! Here was no hustling and Making Good, no gutter-crawling. No go-getter could put up for ten minutes with the stagnant air of the book-trade. As for the work, it was very simple. It was mainly a question of being in the shop ten hours a day. Mr McKechnie wasn't a bad old stick. He was a Scotchman, of course, but Scottish is as Scottish does. At any rate he was reasonably free from avarice—his most distinctive trait seemed to be laziness. He was also a teetotaller and belonged to some Nonconformist sect or other, but this did not affect Gordon. Gordon had been at the shop about a month when *Mice* was published. No less than thirteen papers reviewed it! And *The Times Lit. Supp.* said that it showed 'exceptional promise'. It was not till months later that he realized what a hopeless failure *Mice* had really been.

And it was only now, when he was down to two quid a week and had practically cut himself off from the prospect of earning more, that he grasped the real nature of the battle he was fighting. The devil of it is that the glow of renunciation never lasts. Life on two quid a week ceases to be a heroic gesture and becomes a dingy habit. Failure is as great a swindle as success. He had thrown up his 'good' job and renounced 'good' jobs for ever. Well, that was necessary. He did not want to go back on it. But it was no use pretending that because his poverty was self-imposed he had escaped the ills that poverty drags in its train. It was not a question of hardship. You don't suffer real physical hardship on two quid a week, and if you did it wouldn't matter. It is in the brain and the soul that lack of money damages you. Mental deadness, spiritual squalor–they seem to descend upon you inescapably when your income drops below a certain point. Faith, hope, money–only a saint could have the first two without having the third.

He was growing more mature. Twenty-seven, twenty-eight, twenty-nine. He had reached the age when the future ceases to be a rosy blur and becomes actual and menacing. The spectacle of his surviving relatives depressed him more and more. As he grew older he felt himself more akin to them. That was the way he was going! A few years more, and he would be like that, just like that! He felt this even with Julia, whom he saw oftener than his uncle and aunt. In spite of various resolves never to do it again, he still borrowed money off Julia periodically. Julia's hair was greying fast; there was a deep line scored down each of her thin red cheeks. She had settled her life into a routine in which she was not unhappy. There was her work at the shop, her 'sewing' at nights in her Earl's Court bed-sitting-room (second floor, back, nine bob a week unfurnished), her occasional forgatherings with spinster friends as lonely as herself. It was the typical submerged life of the penniless unmarried woman; she accepted it, hardly realizing that her destiny could ever have been different. Yet in her way she suffered, more for Gordon than for herself. The gradual decay of the family, the way they had died off and died off and left nothing behind, was a sort of tragedy in her mind. Money, money! 'None of us ever seems to make any money!' was her perpetual lament. And of them all, Gordon alone had had the chance to make money; and Gordon had chosen not to. He was sinking effortless into the same rut of poverty as the others. After the first row was over, she was too decent to 'go for' him again because he had thrown up his job at the New Albion. But his motives were quite meaningless to her. In her wordless feminine way she knew that the sin against money is the ultimate sin.

And as for Aunt Angela and Uncle Walter–oh dear, oh dear! What a couple! It made Gordon feel ten years older every time he looked at them.

Uncle Walter, for example. Uncle Walter was very depressing. He was sixty-seven, and what with his various 'agencies' and the dwindling remnants of his patrimony his income might have been nearly three pounds a week. He had a tiny little cabin of an office off Cursitor Street, and he lived in a very cheap boarding-house in Holland Park. That was quite according to precedent; all the Comstock men drifted naturally into boarding-houses. When you looked at poor old uncle, with his large tremulous belly, his bronchitic voice, his broad, pale, timidly pompous face, rather like Sargent's portrait of Henry James, his entirely hairless head, his pale, pouchy eyes, and his ever-drooping moustache, to which he tried vainly to give an upward twirl–when you looked at him, you found it totally impossible to believe that he had ever been young. Was it conceivable that such a being had ever felt life tingle in his veins? Had he ever climbed a tree, taken a header off a spring-board, or been in love? Had he ever had a brain in working order? Even back in the early nineties, when he was arithmetically young, had he ever made any kind of stab at life? A few furtive half-hearted frolics, perhaps. A few whiskies in dull bars, a visit or two to the Empire promenade, a little whoring on the Q.T.; the sort of dingy, drabby fornications that you can imagine happening between Egyptian mummies after the museum is closed for the night. And after that the long, long quiet years of business failure, loneliness, and stagnation in godless boarding-houses.

And yet uncle in his old age was probably not unhappy. He had one hobby of never-failing interest, and that was his diseases. He suffered, by his own account, from every disease in the medical dictionary, and was never weary of talking about them. Indeed, it seemed to Gordon that none of the people in his uncle's boarding-house—he had been there occasionally—ever did talk about anything except their diseases. All over the darkish drawing-room, ageing, discoloured people sat about in couples, discussing symptoms. Their conversation was like the dripping of stalactite to stalagmite. Drip, drip. 'How is your lumbago?' says stalactite to stalagmite. 'I find my Kruschen Salts are doing me good,' says stalagmite to stalactite. Drip, drip, drip.

And then there was Aunt Angela, aged sixty-nine. Gordon tried not even to think of Aunt Angela oftener than he could help.

Poor, dear, good, kind, depressing Aunt Angela!

Poor, shrivelled, parchment-yellow, skin-and-bone Aunt Angela! There in her miserable little semi-detached house in Highgate—Briarbrae, its name was—there in her palace in the northern mountains, there dwelleth she, Angela the Ever-virgin, of whom no man either living or among the shades can say truly that upon her lips he hath pressed the dear caresses of a lover. All alone she dwelleth, and all day long she fareth to and fro, and in her hand is the feather-mop fashioned from the tail feathers of the contumacious turkey, and with it she polisheth the dark-leaved aspidistras and flicketh the hated dust from the resplendent never-to-be-used Crown Derby china tea-service. And ever and anon she comforteth her dear heart with draughts of the dark brown tea, both Flowery Orange and Pekoe Points, which the small-bearded sons of Coromandel have ferried to her across the wine-dark sea. Poor, dear, good, kind, but on the whole unloveable Aunt Angela! Her annuity was ninety-eight pounds a year (thirty-eight bob a week, but she retained a middle-class habit of thinking of her income as a yearly and not weekly thing), and out of that, twelve and sixpence a week went on house rates. She would probably have starved occasionally if Julia had not smuggled her packets of cakes and bread and butter from the shop—always, of course, presented as 'Just a few little things that it seemed a pity to throw away', with the solemn pretence that Aunt Angela didn't really need them.

Yet she too had her pleasures, poor old aunty. She had become a great novel-reader in her old age, the public library being only ten minutes' walk from Briarbrae. During his lifetime, on some whim or other, Gran'pa Comstock had forbidden his daughters to read novels. Consequently, having only begun to read novels in 1902, Aunt Angela was always a couple of decades behind the current mode in fiction. But she plodded along in the rear, faint yet pursuing. In the nineteen-hundreds she was still reading Rhoda Broughton and Mrs Henry Wood. In the War years she discovered Hall Caine and Mrs Humphry

Ward. In the nineteen-twenties she was reading Silas Hocking and H. Seton Merriman, and by the nineteen-thirties she had almost, but not quite, caught up with W. B. Maxwell and William J. Locke. Further she would never get. As for the post-War novelists, she had heard of them afar off, with their immorality and their blasphemies and their devastating 'cleverness'. But she would never live to read them. Walpole we know, and Hichens we read, but Hemingway, who are you?

Well, this was 1934, and that was what was left of the Comstock family. Uncle Walter, with his 'agencies' and his diseases. Aunt Angela, dusting the Crown Derby china tea-service in Briarbrae. Aunt Charlotte, still preserving a vague vegetable existence in the Mental Home. Julia, working a seventy-two-hour week and doing her 'sewing' at nights by the tiny gas-fire in her bed-sitting-room. Gordon, nearly thirty, earning two quid a week in a fool's job, and struggling, as the sole demonstrable object of his existence, with a dreadful book that never got any further.

Possibly there were some other, more distantly related Comstocks, for Gran'pa Comstock had been one of a family of twelve. But if any survived they had grown rich and lost touch with their poor relations; for money is thicker than blood. As for Gordon's branch of the family, the combined income of the five of them, allowing for the lump sum that had been paid down when Aunt Charlotte entered the Mental Home, might have been six hundred a year. Their combined ages were two hundred and sixty-three years. None of them had ever been out of England, fought in a war, been in prison, ridden a horse, travelled in an aeroplane, got married, or given birth to a child. There seemed no reason why they should not continue in the same style until they died. Year in, year out, *nothing ever happened* in the Comstock family.

<hr>

# 4

Sharply the menacing wind sweeps over
The bending poplars, newly bare.

As a matter of fact, though, there was not a breath of wind that afternoon. It was almost as mild as spring. Gordon repeated to himself the poem he had begun yesterday, in a cadenced whisper, simply for the pleasure of the sound of it. He was pleased with the poem at this moment. It was a good poem—or would be when it was finished, anyway. He had forgotten that last night it had almost made him sick.

The plane trees brooded motionless, dimmed by faint wreaths of mist. A tram boomed in the valley far below. Gordon walked up Malkin Hill, rustling instep-deep through the dry, drifted leaves. All down the pavement they were strewn, crinkly and golden, like the rustling flakes of some American breakfast cereal; as though the queen of Brobdingnag had upset her packet of Truweet Breakfast Crisps down the hillside.

Jolly, the windless winter days! Best time of all the year—or so Gordon thought at this moment. He was as happy as you can be when you haven't smoked all day and have only three-halfpence and a Joey in the world. This was Thursday, early-closing day and Gordon's afternoon off. He was going to the house of Paul Doring, the critic, who lived in Coleridge Grove and gave literary tea-parties.

It had taken him an hour or more to get himself ready. Social life is so complicated when your income is two quid a week. He had had a painful shave in cold water immediately after dinner. He had put on his best suit—three years old but just passable when he remembered to press the trousers under his mattress. He had turned his collar inside out and tied his tie so that the torn place didn't show. With the point of a match he had scraped enough blacking from the tin to polish his shoes. He had even borrowed a needle from Lorenheim and darned his socks—a tedious job, but better than inking the places where your ankle shows through. Also he had procured an empty Gold Flake packet and put into it a single cigarette extracted from the penny-in-the-slot-machine. That was just for the look of the thing. You can't, of course, go to other people's houses with *no* cigarettes. But if you have even one it's all right, because when people see one cigarette in a packet they assume that the packet has been full. It is fairly easy to pass the thing off as an accident.

'Have a cigarette?' you say casually to someone.

'Oh—thanks.'

You push the packet open and then register surprise. 'Hell! I'm down to my last. And I could have sworn I had a full packet.'

'Oh, I won't take your last. Have one of *mine*,' says the other.

'Oh—thanks.'

And after that, of course, your host and hostess press cigarettes upon you. But you must have *one* cigarette, just for honour's sake.

*Sharply the menacing wind sweeps over*. He would finish that poem presently. He could finish it whenever he chose. It was queer, how the mere prospect of going to a literary tea-party bucked him up. When your income is two quid a week you at least aren't jaded by too much human contact. Even to see the inside of somebody else's house is a kind of treat. A padded armchair under your bum, and tea and cigarettes and the smell of women—you learn to appreciate such things when you are starved of them. In practice, though, Doring's parties never in the least resembled what Gordon looked forward to. Those wonderful, witty, erudite conversations that he imagined beforehand—they never happened or began to happen. Indeed there was never anything that could properly be called conversation at all; only the stupid clacking that goes on at parties everywhere, in Hampstead or Hong Kong. No one really worth meeting ever came to Doring's parties. Doring was such a very mangy lion himself that his followers were hardly even worthy to be called jackals. Quite half of them were those hen-witted middle-aged women who have lately escaped from good Christian homes and are trying to be literary.

The star exhibits were troops of bright young things who dropped in for half an hour, formed circles of their own, and talked sniggeringly about the other bright young things to whom they referred by nicknames. For the most part Gordon found himself hanging about on the edges of conversations. Doring was kind in a slapdash way and introduced him to everybody as 'Gordon Comstock—*you* know; the poet. He wrote that dashed clever book of poems called *Mice. You* know.' But Gordon had never yet encountered anybody who *did* know. The bright young things summed him up at a glance and ignored him. He was thirtyish, moth-eaten, and obviously penniless. And yet, in spite of the invariable disappointment, how eagerly he looked forward to those literary tea-parties! They were a break in his loneliness, anyway. That is the devilish thing about poverty, the ever-recurrent thing—loneliness. Day after day with never an intelligent person to talk to; night after night back to your godless room, always alone. Perhaps it sounds rather fun if you are rich and sought-after; but how different it is when you do it from necessity!

*Sharply the menacing wind sweeps over.* A stream of cars hummed easily up the hill. Gordon eyed them without envy. Who wants a car, anyway? The pink doll-faces of upper-class women gazed at him through the car window. Bloody nit-witted lapdogs. Pampered bitches dozing on their chains. Better the lone wolf than the cringing dogs. He thought of the Tube stations at early morning. The black hordes of clerks scurrying underground like ants into a hole; swarms of little ant-like men, each with dispatch-case in right hand, newspaper in left hand, and the fear of the sack like a maggot in his heart. How it eats at them, that secret fear! Especially on winter days, when they hear the menace of the wind. Winter, the sack, the workhouse, the Embankment benches! Ah!

> Sharply the menacing wind sweeps over
> The bending poplars, newly bare,
> And the dark ribbons of the chimneys
> Veer downward; flicked by whips of air,
> Torn posters flutter; Coldly sound
> The boom of trams and the rattle of hooves,
> And the clerks who hurry to the station
> Look, shuddering, over the eastern rooves,
> Thinking—

What do they think? Winter's coming. Is my job safe? The sack means the workhouse. Circumcise ye your foreskins, saith the Lord. Suck the blacking off the boss's boots. Yes!

> Thinking each one, 'Here comes the winter!
> Please God I keep my job this year!'
> And bleakly, as the cold strikes through
> Their entrails like an icy spear,
> They think—

'Think' again. No matter. What do they think? Money, money! Rent, rates, taxes, school bills, season tickets, boots for the children. And the life insurance policy and the skivvy's wages. And, my God, suppose the wife gets in the family way again! And did I laugh loud enough when the boss made that joke yesterday? And the next instalment on the vacuum cleaner.

Neatly, taking a pleasure in his neatness, with the sensation of dropping piece after piece of a jigsaw puzzle into place, he fashioned another stanza:

> They think of rent, rates, season tickets,
> Insurance, coal, the skivvy's wages,
> Boots, school bills, and the next instalment
> Upon the two twin beds from Drage's.

Not bad, not bad at all. Finish it presently. Four or five more stanzas. Ravelston would print it.

A starling sat in the naked boughs of a plane tree, crooning self-pitifully as starlings do on warm winter days when they believe spring is in the air. At the foot of the tree a huge sandy cat sat motionless, mouth open, gazing upwards with rapt desire, plainly expecting that the starling would drop into its mouth. Gordon repeated to himself the four finished stanzas of his poem. It was *good*. Why had he thought last night that it was mechanical, weak, and empty? He was a poet. He walked more upright, arrogantly almost, with the pride of a poet. Gordon Comstock, author of *Mice*. 'Of exceptional promise,' *The Times Lit. Supp.* had said. Author also of *London Pleasures*. For that too would be finished quite soon. He knew now that he could finish it when he chose. Why had he ever despaired of it? Three months it might take; soon enough to come out in the summer. In his mind's eye he saw the 'slim' white buckram shape of *London Pleasures*; the excellent paper, the wide margins, the good Caslon type, the refined dust-jacket. and the reviews in all the best papers. 'An outstanding achievement'—*The Times Lit. Supp.* 'A welcome relief from the Sitwell school'—*Scrutiny*.

Coleridge Grove was a damp, shadowy, secluded road, a blind alley and therefore void of traffic. Literary associations of the wrong kind (Coleridge was rumoured to have lived there for six weeks in the summer of 1821) hung heavy upon it. You could not look at its antique decaying houses, standing back from the road in dank gardens under heavy trees, without feeling an atmosphere of outmoded 'culture' envelop you. In some of those houses, undoubtedly, Browning Societies still flourished, and ladies in art serge sat at the feet of extinct poets talking about Swinburne and Walter Pater. In spring the gardens were sprinkled with purple and yellow crocuses, and later with harebells, springing up in little Wendy rings among the anaemic grass; and even the trees, it seemed to Gordon, played up to their environment and twisted themselves into whimsy Rackhamesque attitudes. It was queer that a prosperous hack critic like Paul Doring should live in such a place. For Doring was an astonishingly bad critic. He reviewed novels for the *Sunday Post* and discovered the great English novel with Walpolean regularity once a fortnight. You would have expected him to live in a flat on Hyde Park Corner. Perhaps it was a kind of penance that he had imposed upon himself, as though by living in the refined discomfort of Coleridge Grove he propitiated the injured gods of literature.

Gordon came round the corner, turning over in his mind a line from *London*

*Pleasures.* And then suddenly he stopped short. There was something wrong about the look of the Dorings' gate. What was it? Ah, of course! There were no cars waiting outside.

He paused, walked on a step or two, and stopped again, like a dog that smells danger. It was all wrong. There *ought* to be some cars. There were always quite a lot of people at the Dorings' parties, and half of them came in cars. Why had nobody else arrived? Could he be too early? But no! They had said half past three and it was at least twenty to four.

He hastened towards the gate. Already he felt practically sure that the party *had* been put off. A chill like the shadow of a cloud had fallen across him. Suppose the Dorings weren't at home! Suppose the party had been put off! And this thought, though it dismayed him, did not strike him as in the least improbable. It was his special bugbear, the especial childish dread he carried about with him, to be invited to people's houses and then find them not at home. Even when there was no doubt about the invitation he always half expected that there would be some hitch or other. He was never quite certain of his welcome. He took it for granted that people would snub him and forget about him. Why not, indeed? He had no money. When you have no money your life is one long series of snubs.

He swung the iron gate open. It creaked with a lonely sound. The dank mossy path was bordered with chunks of some Rackhamesque pinkish stone. Gordon inspected the house-front narrowly. He was so used to this kind of thing. He had developed a sort of Sherlock Holmes technique for finding out whether a house was inhabited or not. Ah! Not much doubt about it this time. The house had a deserted look. No smoke coming from the chimneys, no windows lighted. It must be getting darkish indoors—surely they would have lighted the lamps? And there was not a single footmark on the steps; that settled it. Nevertheless with a sort of desperate hope he tugged at the bell. An old-fashioned wire bell, of course. In Coleridge Grove it would have been considered low and unliterary to have an electric bell.

Clang, clang, clang! went the bell.

Gordon's last hope vanished. No mistaking the hollow clangour of a bell echoing through an empty house. He seized the handle again and gave it a wrench that almost broke the wire. A frightful, clamorous peal answered him. But it was useless, quite useless. Not a foot stirred within. Even the servants were out. At this moment he became aware of a lace cap, some dark hair, and a pair of youthful eyes regarding him furtively from the basement of the house next door. It was a servant-girl who had come out to see what all the noise was about. She caught his eye and gazed into the middle distance. He looked a fool and knew it. One always does look a fool when one rings the bell of an empty house. And suddenly it came to him that that girl knew all about him—knew that the party had been put off and that everyone except Gordon had been told of it—knew that it was because he had no money that he wasn't worth the trouble of telling. *She* knew. Servants always know.

He turned and made for the gate. Under the servant's eye he had to stroll casually away, as though this were a small disappointment that scarcely mattered. But he was trembling so with anger that it was difficult to control his movements. The sods! The bloody sods! To have played a trick like that on him! To have invited him, and then changed the day and not even bothered to tell him! There might be other explanations—he just refused to think of them. The sods, the bloody sods! His eye fell upon one of the Rackhamesque chunks of stone. How he'd love to pick that thing up and bash it through the window! He grasped the rusty gate-bar so hard that he hurt his hand and almost tore it. The physical pain did him good. It counteracted the agony at his heart. It was not merely that he had been cheated of an evening spent in human company, though that was much. It was the feeling of helplessness, of insignificance, of being set aside, ignored—a creature not worth worrying about. They'd changed the day and hadn't even bothered to tell him. Told everybody else, but not him. That's how people treat you when you've no money! Just wantonly, cold-bloodedly insult you. It was likely enough, indeed, that the Dorings' had honestly forgotten, meaning no harm; it was even possible that he himself had mistaken the date. But no! He wouldn't think of it. The Dorings' had done it on purpose. Of *course* they had done it on purpose! Just hadn't troubled to tell him, because he had no money and consequently didn't matter. The sods!

He walked rapidly away. There was a sharp pain in his breast. Human contact, human voices! But what was the good of wishing? He'd have to spend the evening alone, as usual. His friends were so few and lived so far away. Rosemary would still be at work; besides, she lived at the back of beyond, in West Kensington, in a women's hostel guarded by female dragons. Ravelston lived nearer, in the Regent's Park district. But Ravelston was a rich man and had many engagements; the chances were always against his being at home. Gordon could not even ring him up, because he hadn't the necessary two pennies; only three halfpence and the Joey. Besides, how could he go and see Ravelston when he had no money? Ravelston would be sure to say 'Let's go to a pub,' or something! He couldn't let Ravelston pay for his drinks. His friendship with Ravelston was only possible on the understanding that he paid his share of everything.

He took out his single cigarette and lighted it. It gave him no pleasure to smoke, walking fast; it was a mere reckless gesture. He did not take much notice of where he was going. All he wanted was to tire himself, to walk and walk till the stupid physical fatigue had obliterated the Dorings' snub. He moved roughly southward—through the wastes of Camden Town, down Tottenham Court Road. It had been dark for some time now. He crossed Oxford Street, threaded through Covent Garden, found himself in the Strand, and crossed the river by Waterloo Bridge. With night the cold had descended. As he walked his anger grew less violent, but his mood could not fundamentally improve. There was a thought that kept haunting him—a thought from which he fled, but which was not to be escaped. It was the thought of his poems. His empty, silly, futile poems! How could he ever have believed in them? To think that actually he had imagined, so short a time ago, that even *London Pleasures* might one day come to something! It made him sick to think of his poems now. It was like remembering last night's debauch. He knew in his bones that he was no good and his poems were no good. *London Pleasures* would never be finished. If he lived to be a thousand he would never write a line worth reading. Over and over, in self-hatred, he repeated those four stanzas of the poem he had been making up. Christ, what tripe! Rhyme to rhyme—tinkle, tinkle, tinkle! Hollow as an empty biscuit tin. *That* was the kind of muck he had wasted his life on.

He had walked a long way, five or seven miles perhaps. His feet were hot and swollen from the pavements. He was somewhere in Lambeth, in a slummy quarter where the narrow, puddled street plunged into blackness at fifty yards' distance. The few lamps, mist-ringed, hung like isolated stars, illumining nothing save themselves. He was getting devilishly hungry. The coffee-shops tempted him with their steamy windows and their chalked signs: 'Good Cup of Tea, 2d. No Urns Used.' But it was no use, he couldn't spend his Joey. He went under some echoing railway arches and up the alley on to Hungerford Bridge. On the miry water, lit by the glare of skysigns, the muck of East London was racing inland. Corks, lemons, barrel-staves, a dead dog, hunks of bread. Gordon walked along the Embankment to Westminster. The wind made the plane trees rattle. *Sharply the menacing wind sweeps over.* He winced. That tripe again! Even now, though it was December, a few poor draggled old wrecks were settling down on the benches, tucking themselves up in sort of parcels of newspaper. Gordon looked at them callously. On the bum, they called it. He would come to it himself some day. Better so, perhaps? He never felt any pity for the genuine poor. It is the black-coated poor, the middle-middle class, who need pitying.

He walked up to Trafalgar Square. Hours and hours to kill. The National Gallery? Ah, shut long ago, of course. It would be. It was a quarter past seven. Three, four, five hours before he could sleep. He walked seven times round the square, slowly. Four times clockwise, three times widdershins. His feet were sore and most of the benches were empty, but he would not sit down. If he halted for an instant the longing for tobacco would come upon him. In the Charing Cross Road the teashops called like sirens. Once the glass door of a Lyons swung open, letting out a wave of hot cake-scented air. It almost overcame him. After all, why *not* go in? You could sit there for nearly an hour. A cup of tea twopence, two buns a penny each. He had fourpence halfpenny, counting the Joey. But no! That bloody Joey! The girl at the cash desk would titter. In a vivid vision he saw the girl at the cash desk, as she handled his threepenny-bit, grin sidelong at the girl behind the cake-counter. They'd *know* it was your last threepence. No use. Shove on. Keep moving.

In the deadly glare of the Neon lights the pavements were densely crowded. Gordon threaded his way, a small shabby figure, with pale face and unkempt hair. The crowd slid past him; he avoided and was avoided. There is something horrible about London at night; the coldness, the anonymity, the aloofness. Seven million people, sliding to and fro, avoiding contact, barely aware of one another's existence, like fish in an aquarium tank. The street swarmed with pretty girls. By scores they streamed past him, their faces averted or unseeing; cold nymph-creatures, dreading the eyes of the male. It was queer how many of them seemed to be alone, or with another girl. Far more women alone than women with men, he noted. That too was money. How many girls alive wouldn't be manless sooner than take a man who's moneyless?

The pubs were open, oozing sour whiffs of beer. People were trickling by ones and twos into the picture-houses. Gordon halted outside a great garish picture-house, under the weary eye of the commissionaire, to examine the photographs. Greta Garbo in *The Painted Veil*. He yearned to go inside, not for Greta's sake, but just for the warmth and the softness of the velvet seat. He hated the pictures, of course, seldom went there even when he could afford it. Why encourage the art that is destined to replace literature? But still, there is a kind of soggy attraction about it. To sit on the padded seat in the warm smoke-scented darkness, letting the flickering drivel on the screen gradually overwhelm you—feeling the waves of its silliness lap you round till you seem to drown, intoxicated, in a viscous sea—after all, it's the kind of drug we need. The right drug for friendless people. As he approached the Palace Theatre a tart on sentry-go under the porch marked him down, stepped forward, and stood in his path. A short, stocky Italian girl, very young, with big black eyes. She looked agreeable, and, what tarts so seldom are, merry. For a moment he checked his step, even allowing himself to catch her eye. She looked up at him, ready to break out into a broad-lipped smile. Why not stop and talk to her? She looked as though she might understand him. But no! No money! He looked away and side-stepped her with the cold haste of a man whom poverty makes virtuous. How furious she'd be if he stopped and then she found he had no money! He pressed on. Even to talk costs money.

Up Tottenham Court Road and Camden Road it was a dreary drudge. He walked slower, dragging his feet a little. He had done ten miles over pavements. More girls streamed past, unseeing. Girls alone, girls with youths, girls with other girls, girls alone. Their cruel youthful eyes went over him and through him as though he had not existed. He was too tired to resent it. His shoulders surrendered to their weariness; he slouched, not trying any longer to preserve his upright carriage and his you-be-damned air. They flee from me that someone did me seek. How could you blame them? He was thirty, moth-eaten, and without charm. Why should any girl ever look at him again?

He reflected that he must go home at once if he wanted any food—for Ma Wisbeach refused to serve meals after nine o'clock. But the thought of his cold womanless bedroom sickened him. To climb the stairs, light the gas, flop down at the table with hours to kill and nothing to do, nothing to read, nothing to smoke—no, *not* endurable. In Camden Town the pubs were full and noisy, though this was only Thursday. Three women, red-armed, squat as the beer mugs in their hands, stood outside a pub door, talking. From within came hoarse voices, fag-smoke, the fume of beer. Gordon thought of the Crichton Arms. Flaxman might be there. Why not risk it? A half of bitter, threepence halfpenny. He had fourpence halfpenny counting the Joey. After all, a Joey *is* legal tender.

He felt dreadfully thirsty already. It had been a mistake to let himself think of beer. As he approached the Crichton, he heard voices singing. The great garish pub seemed to be more brightly lighted than usual. There was a concert of something going on inside. Twenty ripe male voices were chanting in unison:

> 'Fo—or *ree's* a jorrigoo' fellow,
> For *ree's* a jorrigoo' fellow,
> For *ree's* a jorrigoo' fe—ELL—OW—
> And toori oori us!'

At least, that was what it sounded like. Gordon drew nearer, pierced by a ravishing thirst. The voices were so soggy, so infinitely beery. When you heard them you saw the scarlet faces of prosperous plumbers. There was a private room behind the bar where the Buffaloes held their secret conclaves. Doubtless it was they who were singing. They were giving some kind of commemorative booze to their president, secretary, Grand Herbivore, or whatever he is called. Gordon hesitated outside the Saloon bar. Better to go to the public bar, perhaps. Draught beer in the public, bottled beer in the saloon. He went round to the other side of the pub. The beer-choked voices followed him:

> 'With a toori oori ay.
> An' a toori oori ay!'
>
> 'Fo—or *ree's* a jorrigoo' fellow,
> For *ree's* a jorrigoo' fellow—'

He felt quite faint for a moment. But it was fatigue and hunger as well as thirst. He could picture the cosy room where those Buffaloes were singing; the roaring fire, the big shiny table, the bovine photographs on the wall. Could picture also, as the singing ceased, twenty scarlet faces disappearing into pots of beer. He put his hand into his pocket and made sure that the threepenny-bit was still there. After all, why not? In the public bar, who would comment? Slap the Joey down on the bar and pass it off as a joke. 'Been saving that up from the Christmas pudding—ha, ha!' Laughter all round. Already he seemed to have the metallic taste of draught beer on his tongue.

He fingered the tiny disc, irresolute. The Buffaloes had tuned up again:

> 'With a toori oori ay,
> An' a toori oori ay!'
>
> 'Fo—or *ree's* a jorrigoo' fellow—'

Gordon moved back to the saloon bar. The window was frosted, and also steamy from the heat in side. Still, there were chinks where you could see through. He peeped in. Yes, Flaxman was there.

The saloon bar was crowded. Like all rooms seen from the outside, it looked ineffably cosy. The fire that blazed in the grate danced, mirrored, in the brass spittoons. Gordon thought he could almost smell the beer through the glass.

Flaxman was propping up the bar with two fish-faced pals who looked like insurance-touts of the better type. One elbow on the bar, his foot on the rail, a beer-streaked glass in the other hand, he was swapping backchat with the blonde cutie barmaid. She was standing on a chair behind the bar, ranging the bottled beer and talking saucily over her shoulder. You couldn't hear what they were saying, but you could guess. Flaxman let fall some memorable witticism. The fish-faced men bellowed with obscene laughter. And the blonde cutie, tittering down at him, half shocked and half delighted, wriggled her neat little bum.

Gordon's heart sickened. To be in there, just to be in there! In the warmth and light, with people to talk to, with beer and cigarettes and a girl to flirt with! After all, why *not* go in? You could borrow a bob off Flaxman. Flaxman would lend it to you all right. He pictured Flaxman's careless assent–'What ho, chappie! How's life? What? A bob? Sure! Take two. Catch, chappie!'–and the florin flicked along the beer-wet bar. Flaxman was a decent sort, in his way.

Gordon put his hand against the swing door. He even pushed it open a few inches. The warm fog of smoke and beer slipped through the crack. A familiar, reviving smell; nevertheless as he smelled it his nerve failed him. No! Impossible to go in. He turned away. He couldn't go shoving in that saloon bar with only fourpence halfpenny in his pocket. Never let other people buy your drinks for you! The first commandment of the moneyless. He made off, down the dark pavement.

> 'For *ree's* a jorrigoo' fe—ELL—OW—
> And toori oori us!

> 'With a toori oori ay!
> An' a—'

The voices, diminishing with distance, rolled after him, bearing faint tidings of beer. Gordon took the threepenny-bit from his pocket and sent it skimming away into the darkness.

He was going home, if you could call it 'going'. At any rate he was gravitating in that direction. He did not want to go home, but he had got to sit down. His legs ached and his feet were bruised, and that vile bedroom was the sole place in London where he had purchased the right to sit down. He slipped in quietly, but, as usual, not quite so quietly that Mrs Wisbeach failed to hear him. She gave him a brief nosy glance round the corner of her door. It would be a little after nine. She might get him a meal if he asked her. But she would grizzle and make a favour of it, and he would go to bed hungry sooner than face that.

He started up the stairs. He was half way up the first flight when a double knock behind made him jump. The post! Perhaps a letter from Rosemary!

Forced from outside, the letter flap lifted, and with an effort, like a heron regurgitating a flatfish, vomited a bunch of letters on to the mat. Gordon's heart bounded. There were six or seven of them. Surely among all that lot there must be one for himself! Mrs Wisbeach, as usual, had darted from her lair at the sound of the postman's knock. As a matter of fact, in two years

Gordon had never once succeeded in getting hold of a letter before Mrs Wisbeach laid hands on it. She gathered the letters jealously to her breast, and then, holding them up one at a time, scanned their addresses. From her manner you could gather that she suspected each one of them of containing a writ, an improper love letter, or an ad for Amen Pills.

'One for you, Mr Comstock,' she said sourly, handing him a letter.

His heart shrank and paused in its beat. A long-shaped envelope. Not from Rosemary, therefore. Ah! It was addressed in his own handwriting. From the editor of a paper, then. He had two poems 'out' at present. One with the *Californian Review*, the other with the *Primrose Quarterly*. But this wasn't an American stamp. And the *Primrose* had had his poem at least six weeks! Good God, supposing they'd accepted it!

He had forgotten Rosemary's existence. He said 'Thanks!', stuck the letter in his pocket, and started up the stairs with outward calm, but no sooner was he out of Mrs Wisbeach's sight that he bounded up three steps at a time. He had got to be alone to open that letter. Even before he reached the door he was feeling for his matchbox, but his fingers were trembling so that in lighting the gas he chipped the mantle. He sat down, took the letter from his pocket, and then quailed. For a moment he could not nerve himself to open it. He held it up to the light and felt it to see how thick it was. His poem had been two sheets. Then, calling himself a fool, he ripped the envelope open. Out tumbled his own poem, and with it a neat—oh, so neat!—little printed slip of imitation parchment:

> The Editor regrets that he is unable to make use of the enclosed contribution.

The slip was decorated with a design of funereal laurel leaves.

Gordon gazed at the thing with wordless hatred. Perhaps no snub in the world is so deadly as this, because none is so unanswerable. Suddenly he loathed his own poem and was acutely ashamed of it. He felt it the weakest, silliest poem ever written. Without looking at it again he tore it into small bits and flung them into the wastepaper basket. He would put that poem out of his mind for ever. The rejection slip, however, he did not tear up yet. He fingered it, feeling its loathly sleekness. Such an elegant little thing, printed in admirable type. You could tell at a glance that it came from a 'good' magazine—a snooty highbrow magazine with the money of a publishing house behind it. Money, money! Money and culture! It was a stupid thing that he had done. Fancy sending a poem to a paper like the *Primrose*! As though they'd accept poems from people like *him*. The mere fact that the poem wasn't typed would tell them what kind of person he was. He might as well have dropped a card on Buckingham Palace. He thought of the people who wrote for the *Primrose*; a coterie of moneyed highbrows—those sleek, refined young animals who suck in money and culture with their mother's milk. The idea of trying to horn in among that pansy crowd! But he cursed them all the same. The sods! The bloody sods! 'The Editor regrets!' Why be so bloody mealy-mouthed about it? Why not say outright, 'We don't want your bloody poems. We only take poems from chaps we were at Cambridge with. You proletarians keep your distance'? The bloody, hypocritical sods!

At last he crumpled up the rejection slip, threw it away, and stood up. Better get to bed while he had the energy to undress. Bed was the only place that was warm. But wait. Wind the clock, set the alarm. He went through the familiar action with a sense of deadly staleness. His eye fell upon the aspidistra. Two years he had inhabited this vile room; two mortal years in which nothing had been accomplished. Seven hundred wasted days, all ending in the lonely bed. Snubs, failures, insults, all of them unavenged. Money, money, all is money! Because he had no money the Dorings' snubbed him, because he had no money the *Primrose* had turned down his poem, because he had no money Rosemary wouldn't sleep with him. Social failure, artistic failure, sexual failure—they are all the same. And lack of money is at the bottom of them all.

He must hit back at somebody or something. He could not go to bed with that rejection slip as the last thing in his mind. He thought of Rosemary. It was five days now since she had written. If there had been a letter from her this evening even that rap over the knuckles from the *Primrose Quarterly* would have mattered less. She declared that she loved him, and she wouldn't sleep with him, wouldn't even write to him! She was the same as all the others. She despised him and forgot about him because he had no money and therefore didn't matter. He would write her an enormous letter, telling her what it felt like to be ignored and insulted, making her see how cruelly she had treated him.

He found a clean sheet of paper and wrote in the top right-hand corner: '31 Willowbed Road, NW, 1 December, 9.30 p.m.'

But having written that much, he found that he could write no more. He was in the defeated mood when even the writing of a letter is too great an effort. Besides, what was the use? She would never understand. No woman ever understands. But he must write something. Something to wound her—that was what he most wanted, at this moment. He meditated for a long time, and at last wrote, exactly in the middle of the sheet:

You have broken my heart.

No address, no signature. Rather neat it looked, all by itself, there in the middle of the sheet, in his small 'scholarly' handwriting. Almost like a little poem in itself. This thought cheered him up a little.

He stuck the letter in an envelope and went out and posted it at the post office on the corner, spending his last three halfpence on a penny stamp and a halfpenny stamp out of the slot machine.

# 5

'We're printing that poem of yours in next month's *Antichrist*,' said Ravelston from his first-floor window.

Gordon, on the pavement below, affected to have forgotten the poem Ravelston was speaking about; he remembered it intimately, of course, as he remembered all his poems.

'Which poem?' he said.

'The one about the dying prostitute. We thought it was rather successful.'

Gordon laughed a laugh of gratified conceit, and managed to pass it off as a laugh of sardonic amusement.

'Aha! A dying prostitute! That's rather what you might call one of my subjects. I'll do you one about an aspidistra next time.'

Ravelston's over-sensitive, boyish face, framed by nice dark-brown hair, drew back a little from the window.

'It's intolerably cold,' he said. 'You'd better come up and have some food, or something.'

'No, you come down. I've had dinner. Let's go to a pub and have some beer.'

'All right then. Half a minute while I get my shoes on.'

They had been talking for some minutes, Gordon on the pavement, Ravelston leaning out of the window above. Gordon had announced his arrival not by knocking at the door but by throwing a pebble against the window pane. He never, if he could help it, set foot inside Ravelston's flat. There was something in the atmosphere of the flat that upset him and made him feel mean, dirty, and out of place. It was so overwhelmingly, though unconsciously, upper-class. Only in the street or in a pub could he feel himself approximately Ravelston's equal. It would have astonished Ravelston to learn that his four-roomed flat, which he thought of as a poky little place, had this effect upon Gordon. To Ravelston, living in the wilds of Regent's Park was practically the same thing as living in the slums; he had chosen to live there, *en bon socialiste*, precisely as your social snob will live in a mews in Mayfair for the sake of the 'W1' on his notepaper. It was part of a lifelong attempt to escape from his own class and become, as it were, an honorary member of the proletariat. Like all such attempts, it was foredoomed to failure. No rich man ever succeeds in disguising himself as a poor man; for money, like murder, will out.

On the street door there was a brass plate inscribed:

P. W. H. RAVELSTON
ANTICHRIST

Ravelston lived on the first floor, and the editorial offices of *Antichrist* were downstairs. *Antichrist* was a middle- to high-brow monthly, Socialist in a vehement but ill-defined way. In general, it gave the impression of being edited by an ardent Nonconformist who had transferred his allegiance from God to Marx, and in doing so had got mixed up with a gang of *vers libre* poets. This was not really Ravelston's character; merely he was softer-hearted than an editor ought to be, and consequently was at the mercy of his contributors. Practically anything got printed in *Antichrist* if Ravelston suspected that its author was starving.

Ravelston appeared a moment later, hatless and pulling on a pair of gauntlet gloves. You could tell him at a glance for a rich young man. He wore the uniform of the moneyed intelligentsia; an old tweed coat—but it was one of those coats which have been made by a good tailor and grow more aristocratic as they grow older—very loose grey flannel bags, a grey pullover, much-worn brown shoes. He made a point of going everywhere, even to fashionable houses and expensive restaurants, in these clothes, just to show his contempt for upper-class conventions; he did not fully realize that it is only the upper classes who can do these things. Though he was a year older than Gordon he looked much younger. He was very tall, with a lean, wide-shouldered body and the typical lounging grace of the upper-class youth. But there was something curiously apologetic in his movements and in the expression of his face. He seemed always in the act of stepping out of somebody else's way. When expressing an opinion he would rub his nose with the back of his left forefinger. The truth was that in every moment of his life he was apologizing, tacitly, for the largeness of his income. You could make him uncomfortable as easily by reminding him that he was rich as you could make Gordon by reminding him that he was poor.

'You've had dinner, I gather?' said Ravelston, in his rather Bloomsbury voice.

'Yes, ages ago. Haven't you?'

'Oh, yes, certainly. Oh, quite!'

It was twenty past eight and Gordon had had no food since midday. Neither had Ravelston. Gordon did not know that Ravelston was hungry, but Ravelston knew that Gordon was hungry, and Gordon knew that Ravelston knew it. Nevertheless, each saw good reason for pretending not to be hungry. They seldom or never had meals together. Gordon would not let Ravelston buy his meals for him, and for himself he could not afford to go to restaurants, not even to a Lyons or an A.B.C. This was Monday and he had five and ninepence left. He might afford a couple of pints at a pub, but not a proper meal. When he and Ravelston met it was always agreed, with silent manoeuvrings, that they should do nothing that involved spending money, beyond the shilling or so one spends in a pub. In this way the fiction was kept up that there was no serious difference in their incomes.

Gordon sidled closer to Ravelston as they started down the pavement. He would have taken his arm, only of course one can't do that kind of thing. Beside Ravelston's taller, comelier figure he looked frail, fretful, and miserably shabby. He adored Ravelston and was never quite at ease in his presence. Ravelston had not merely a charm of manner, but also a kind of fundamental decency, a graceful attitude to life, which Gordon scarcely encountered elsewhere. Undoubtedly it was bound up with the fact that Ravelston was rich. For money buys all virtues. Money suffereth long and is kind, is not puffed up, doth not behave unseemly, seeketh not her own. But in some ways Ravelston was not even like a moneyed person. The fatty degeneration of the spirit which goes with wealth had missed him, or he had escaped it by a conscious effort. Indeed his whole life was a struggle to escape it. It was for this reason that he gave up his time and a large part of his income to editing an unpopular Socialist monthly. And apart from *Antichrist*, money flowed from him in all directions. A tribe of cadgers ranging from poets to pavement-artists browsed upon him unceasingly. For himself he lived upon eight hundred a year or thereabouts. Even of this income he was acutely ashamed. It was not, he realized, exactly a proletarian income; but he had never learned to get along on less. Eight hundred a year was a minimum living wage to him, as two pounds a week was to Gordon.

'How is your work getting on?' said Ravelston presently.

'Oh, as usual. It's a drowsy kind of job. Swapping back-chat with old hens about Hugh Walpole. I don't object to it.'

'I meant your own work—your writing. Is *London Pleasures* getting on all right?'

'Oh, Christ! Don't speak of it. It's turning my hair grey.'

'Isn't it going forward at all?'

'My books don't go forward. They go backward.'

Ravelston sighed. As editor of *Antichrist*, he was used to encouraging despondent poets that it had become a second nature to him. He did not need telling why Gordon 'couldn't' write, and why all poets nowadays 'can't' write, and why when they do write it is something as arid as the rattling of a pea inside a big drum. He said with sympathetic gloom:

'Of course I admit this isn't a hopeful age to write poetry in.'

'You bet it isn't.'

Gordon kicked his heel against the pavement. He wished that *London Pleasures* had not been mentioned. It brought back to him the memory of his mean, cold bedroom and the grimy papers littered under the aspidistra. He said abruptly:

'This writing business! What b—s it all is! Sitting in a corner torturing a nerve which won't even respond any longer. And who wants poetry nowadays? Training performing fleas would be more useful by comparison.'

'Still, you oughtn't to let yourself be discouraged. After all, you do produce something, which is more than one can say for a lot of poets nowadays. There was *Mice*, for instance.'

'Oh, *Mice*! It makes me spew to think of it.'

He thought with loathing of that sneaky little foolscap octavo. Those forty or fifty drab, dead little poems, each like a little abortion in its labelled jar. 'Exceptional promise', *The Times Lit. Supp.* had said. A hundred and fifty-three copies sold and the rest remaindered. He had one of those movements of contempt and even horror which every artist has at times when he thinks of his own work.

'It's dead,' he said. 'Dead as a blasted foetus in a bottle.'

'Oh, well, I suppose that happens to most books. You can't expect an enormous sale for poetry nowadays. There's too much competition.'

'I didn't mean that. I meant the poems themselves are dead. There's no life in them. Everything I write is like that. Lifeless, gutless. Not necessarily ugly or vulgar; but dead—just dead.' The word 'dead' re-echoed in his mind, setting up its own train of thought. He added: 'My poems are dead because I'm dead. You're dead. We're all dead. Dead people in a dead world.'

Ravelston murmured agreement, with a curious air of guilt. And now they were off upon their favourite subject—Gordon's favourite subject, anyway; the futility, the bloodiness, the deathliness of modern life. They never met without talking for at least half an hour in this vein. But it always made Ravelston feel rather uncomfortable. In a way, of course, he knew—it was precisely this that *Antichrist* existed to point out—that life under a decaying capitalism is deathly and meaningless. But this knowledge was only theoretical. You can't really *feel* that kind of thing when your income is eight hundred a year. Most of the time, when he wasn't thinking of coal-miners, Chinese junk-coolies, and the unemployed in Middlesbrough, he felt that life was pretty good fun. Moreover, he had the naïve belief that in a little while Socialism is going to put things right. Gordon always seemed to him to exaggerate. So there was subtle disagreement between them, which Ravelston was too good-mannered to press home.

But with Gordon it was different. Gordon's income was two pounds a week. Therefore the hatred of modern life, the desire to see our money-civilization blown to hell by bombs, was a thing he genuinely felt. They were walking southward, down a darkish, meanly decent residential street with a few shuttered shops. From a hoarding on the blank end of a house the yard-wide face of Corner Table simpered, pallid in the lamplight. Gordon caught a glimpse of a withering aspidistra in a lower window. London! Mile after mile of mean lonely houses, let off in flats and single rooms; not homes, not communities, just clusters of meaningless lives drifting in a sort of drowsy chaos to the grave! He saw men as corpses walking. The thought that he was merely objectifying his own inner misery hardly troubled him. His mind went back to Wednesday afternoon, when he had desired to hear the enemy aeroplanes zooming over London. He caught Ravelston's arm and paused to gesticulate at the Corner Table poster.

'Look at that bloody thing up there! Look at it, just look at it! Doesn't it make you spew?'

'It's aesthetically offensive, I grant. But I don't see that it matters very greatly.'

'Of course it matters—having the town plastered with things like that.'

'Oh, well, it's merely a temporary phenomenon. Capitalism in its last phase. I doubt whether it's worth worrying about.'

'But there's more in it than that. Just look at that fellow's face gaping down at us! You can see our whole civilization written there. The imbecility, the emptiness, the desolation! You can't look at it without thinking of French letters and machine guns. Do you know that the other day I was actually wishing war would break out? I was longing for it—praying for it, almost.'

'Of course, the trouble is, you see, that about half the young men in Europe are wishing the same thing.'

'Let's hope they are. Then perhaps it'll happen.'

'My dear old chap, no! Once is enough, surely.'

Gordon walked on, fretfully. 'This life we live nowadays! It's not life, it's stagnation, death-in-life. Look at all these bloody houses, and the meaningless people inside them! Sometimes I think we're all corpses. Just rotting upright.'

'But where you make your mistake, don't you see, is in talking as if all this was incurable. This is only something that's got to happen before the proletariat take over.'

'Oh, Socialism! Don't talk to me about Socialism.'

'You ought to read Marx, Gordon, you really ought. Then you'd realize that this is only a phase. It can't go on for ever.'

'Can't it? It *feels* as if it was going on for ever.'

'It's merely that we're at a bad moment. We've got to die before we can be reborn, if you take my meaning.'

'We're dying right enough. I don't see much signs of our being reborn.'

Ravelston rubbed his nose. 'Oh, well, we must have faith, I suppose. And hope.'

'We must have money you mean,' said Gordon gloomily.

'Money?'

'It's the price of optimism. Give me five quid a week and *I'd* be a Socialist, I dare say.'

Ravelston looked away, discomforted. This money-business! Everywhere it came up against you! Gordon wished he had not said it. Money is the one thing you must never mention when you are with people richer than yourself. Or if you do, then it must be money in the abstract, money with a big 'M', not the actual concrete money that's in your pocket and isn't in mine. But the accursed subject drew him like a magnet. Sooner or later, especially when he had a few drinks inside him, he invariably began talking with self-pitiful detail about the bloodiness of life on two quid a week. Sometimes, from sheer nervous impulse to say the wrong thing, he would come out with some squalid confession—as, for instance, that he had been without tobacco for two days, or that his underclothes were in holes and his overcoat up the spout. But nothing of that sort should happen tonight, he resolved. They veered swiftly away from the subject of money and began talking in a more general way about Socialism. Ravelston had been trying for years to convert Gordon to Socialism, without even succeeding in interesting him in it. Presently they passed a low-looking pub on a corner in a side-street. A sour cloud of beer seemed to hang about it. The smell revolted Ravelston. He would have quickened his pace to get away from it. But Gordon paused, his nostrils tickled.

'Christ! I could do with a drink,' he said.

'So could I,' said Ravelston gallantly.

Gordon shoved open the door of the public bar, Ravelston following. Ravelston persuaded himself that he was fond of pubs, especially low-class pubs. Pubs are genuinely proletarian. In a pub you can meet the working class on equal terms—or that's the theory, anyway. But in practice Ravelston never went into a pub unless he was with somebody like Gordon, and he always felt like a fish out of water when he got there. A foul yet coldish air enveloped them. It was a filthy, smoky room, low-ceilinged, with a sawdusted floor and plain deal tables ringed by generations of beer-pots. In one corner four monstrous women with breasts the size of melons were sitting drinking porter and talking with bitter intensity about someone called Mrs Croop. The landlady, a tall grim woman with a black fringe, looking like the madame of a brothel, stood behind the bar, her powerful forearms folded, watching a game of darts which was going on between four labourers and a postman. You had to duck under the darts as you crossed the room. there was a moment's hush and people glanced inquisitively at Ravelston. He was so obviously a gentleman. They didn't see his type very often in the public bar.

Ravelston pretended not to notice that they were staring at him. He lounged towards the bar, pulling off a glove to feel for the money in his pocket. 'What's yours?' he said casually.

But Gordon had already shoved his way ahead and was tapping a shilling on the bar. Always pay for the first round of drinks! It was his point of honour. Ravelston made for the only vacant table. A navvy leaning on the bar turned on his elbow and gave him a long, insolent stare 'A — toff!' he was thinking. Gordon came back balancing two pint glasses of the dark common ale. They were thick cheap glasses, thick as jam jars almost, and dim and greasy. A thin yellow froth was subsiding on the beer. The air was thick with gunpowdery tobacco-smoke. Ravelston caught sight of a well-filled spittoon near the bar and averted his eyes. It crossed his mind that this beer had been sucked up from some beetle-ridden cellar through yards of slimy tube, and that the glasses had never been washed in their lives, only rinsed in beery water. Gordon was very hungry. He could have done with some bread and cheese, but to order any would have been to betray the fact that he had had no dinner. He took a deep pull at his beer and lighted a cigarette, which made him forget his hunger a little. Ravelston also swallowed a mouthful or so and set his glass gingerly down. It was typical London beer, sickly and yet leaving a chemical after-taste. Ravelston thought of the wines of Burgundy. They went on arguing about Socialism.

'You know, Gordon, it's really time you started reading Marx,' said Ravelston, less apologetically than usual, because the vile taste of the beer had annoyed him.

'I'd sooner read Mrs Humphry Ward,' said Gordon.

'But don't you see, your attitude is so unreasonable. You're always tirading against Capitalism, and yet you won't accept the only possible alternative. One can't put things right in a hole-and-corner way. One's got to accept either

Capitalism or Socialism. There's no way out of it.'

'I tell you I can't be bothered with Socialism. The very thought of it makes me yawn.'

'But what's your objection to Socialism, anyway?'

'There's only one objection to Socialism, and that is that nobody wants it.'

'Oh, surely it's rather absurd to say that!'

'That's to say, nobody who could see what Socialism would really mean.'

'But what *would* Socialism mean, according to your idea of it?'

'Oh! Some kind of Aldous Huxley *Brave New World*: only not so amusing. Four hours a day in a model factory, tightening up bolt number 6003. Rations served out in grease-proof paper at the communal kitchen. Community-hikes from Marx Hostel to Lenin Hostel and back. Free abortion-clinics on all the corners. All very well in its way, of course. Only we don't want it.'

Ravelston sighed. Once a month, in *Antichrist*, he repudiated this version of Socialism. 'Well, what *do* we want, then?'

'God knows. All we know is what we don't want. That's what's wrong with us nowadays. We're stuck, like Buridan's donkey. Only there are three alternatives instead of two, and all three of them make us spew. Socialism's only one of them.'

'And what are the other two?'

'Oh, I suppose suicide and the Catholic Church.'

Ravelston smiled, anticlerically shocked. 'The Catholic Church! Do you consider that an alternative?'

'Well, it's a standing temptation to the intelligentsia, isn't it?'

'Not what *I* should call the intelligentsia. Though there was Eliot, of course,' Ravelston admitted.

'And there'll be plenty more, you bet. I dare say it's fairly cosy under Mother Church's wing. A bit insanitary, of course—but you'd feel safe there, anyway.'

Ravelston rubbed his nose reflectively. 'It seems to me that's only another form of suicide.'

'In a way. But so's Socialism. At least it's a counsel of despair. But I couldn't commit suicide, real suicide. It's too meek and mild. I'm not going to give up my share of earth to anyone else. I'd want to do in a few of my enemies first.'

Ravelston smiled again. 'And who are your enemies?'

'Oh, anyone with over five hundred a year.'

A momentary uncomfortable silence fell. Ravelston's income, after payment of income tax, was probably two thousand a year. This was the kind of thing Gordon was always saying. To cover the awkwardness of the moment, Ravelston took up his glass, steeled himself against the nauseous taste, and swallowed about two-thirds of his beer—enough at any rate, to give the impression that he had finished it.

'Drink up!' he said with would-be heartiness. 'It's time we had the other half of that.'

Gordon emptied his glass and let Ravelston take it. He did not mind letting Ravelston pay for the drinks now. He had paid the first round and honour was satisfied. Ravelston walked self-consciously to the bar. People began staring at him again as soon as he stood up. The navvy, still leaning against the bar over his untouched pot of beer, gazed at him with quiet insolence. Ravelston resolved that he would drink no more of this filthy common ale.

'Two double whiskies, would you, please?' he said apologetically.

The grim landlady stared. 'What?' she said.

'Two double whiskies, please.'

'No whisky 'ere. We don't sell spirits. Beer 'ouse, we are.'

The navvy smiled flickering under his moustache. '— ignorant toff!' he was thinking. 'Asking for a whisky in a — beer 'ouse!' Ravelston's pale face flushed slightly. He had not known till this moment that some of the poorer pubs cannot afford a spirit licence.

'Bass, then, would you? Two pint bottles of Bass.'

There were no pint bottles. they had to have four half pints. It was a very poor house. Gordon took a deep, satisfying swallow of Bass. More alcoholic than the draught beer, it fizzed and prickled in his throat, and because he was hungry it went a little to his head. He felt at once more philosophic and more self-pitiful. He had made up his mind not to begin belly-aching about his poverty; but now he was going to begin after all. He said abruptly:

'This is all b—s that we've been talking.'

'What's all b—s?'

'All this about Socialism and Capitalism and the state of the modern world and God knows what. I don't give a — for the state of the modern world. If the whole of England was starving except myself and the people I care about, I wouldn't give a damn.'

'Don't you exaggerate just a little?'

'No. All this talk we make—we're only objectifying our own feelings. It's all dictated by what we've got in our pockets. I go up and down London saying it's a city of the dead, and our civilization's dying, and I wish war would break out, and God knows what; and all it means is that my wages are two quid a week and I wish they were five.'

Ravelston, once again reminded obliquely of his income, stroked his nose slowly with the knuckle of his left forefinger.

'Of course, I'm with you up to a point. After all, it's only what Marx said. Every ideology is a reflection of economic circumstances.'

'Ah, but you only understand it out of Marx! You don't know what it means to have to crawl along on two quid a week. It isn't a question of hardship—it's nothing so decent as hardship. It's the bloody, sneaking, squalid meaness of it. Living alone for weeks on end because when you've no money you've no friends. Calling yourself a writer and never even producing anything because you're always too washed out to write. It's a sort of filthy sub-world one lives in. A sort of spiritual sewer.'

He had started now. They were never together long without Gordon beginning to talk in this strain. It was the vilest manners. It embarrassed Ravelston horribly. And yet somehow Gordon could not help it. He had got to retail his troubles to somebody, and Ravelston was the only person who

understood. Poverty, like every other dirty wound, has got to be exposed
occasionally. He began to talk in obscene detail of his life in Willowbed Road.
He dilated on the smell of slops and cabbage, the clotted sauce-bottles in the
dining-room, the vile food, the aspidistras. He described his furtive cups of tea
and his trick of throwing used tea-leaves down the w.c. Ravelston, guilty and
miserable, sat staring at his glass and revolving it slowly between his hands.
Against his right breast he could feel, a square accusing shape, the pocket-book
in which, as he knew, eight pound notes and two ten-bob notes nestled against
his fat green cheque-book. How awful these details of poverty are! Not that
what Gordon was describing was real poverty. It was at worst the fringe of
poverty. But what of the real poor? What of the unemployed in
Middlesbrough, seven in a room on twenty-five bob a week? When there are
people living like that, how dare one walk the world with pound notes and
cheque-books in one's pocket?

'It's bloody,' he murmured several times, impotently. In his heart he
wondered—it was his invariable reaction—whether Gordon would accept a
tenner if you offered to lend it to him.

They had another drink, which Ravelston again paid for, and went out into
the street. It was almost time to part. Gordon never spent more than an hour or
two with Ravelston. One's contacts with rich people, like one's visits to high
altitudes, must always be brief. It was a moonless, starless night, with a damp
wind blowing. The night air, the beer, and the watery radiance of the lamps
induced in Gordon a sort of dismal clarity. He perceived that it is quite
impossible to explain to any rich person, even to anyone so decent as
Ravelston, the essential bloodiness of poverty. For this reason it became all the
more important to explain it. He said suddenly:

'Have you read Chaucer's *Man of Lawe's Tale*?'

'The *Man of Lawe's Tale*? Not that I remember. What's it about?'

'I forget. I was thinking of the first six stanzas. Where he talks about
poverty. The way it gives everyone the right to stamp on you! The way
everyone *wants* to stamp on you! It makes people *hate* you, to know that you've
no money. They insult you just for the pleasure of insulting you and knowing
that you can't hit back.'

Ravelston was pained. 'Oh, no, surely not! People aren't so bad as all that.'

'Ah, but you don't know the things that happen!'

Gordon did not want to be told that 'people aren't so bad'. He clung with a
sort of painful joy to the notion that because he was poor everyone must *want*
to insult him. It fitted in with his philosophy of life. And suddenly, with the
feeling that he could not stop himself, he was talking of the thing that had been
rankling in his mind for two days past—the snub he had had from the Dorings
on Thursday. He poured the whole story out quite shamelessly. Ravelston was
amazed. He could not understand what Gordon was making such a fuss about.
To be disappointed at missing a beastly literary tea-party seemed to him
absurd. He would not have gone to a literary tea-party if you had paid him.
Like all rich people, he spent far more time in avoiding human society than in
seeking it. He interrupted Gordon:

'Really, you know, you ought not to take offence so easily. After all, a thing like that doesn't really matter.'

'It isn't the thing itself that matters, it's the spirit behind it. The way they snub you as a matter of course, just because you've got no money.'

'But quite possibly it was all a mistake, or something. Why should anyone want to snub you?'

' "If thou be poure, thy brother hateth thee," ' quoted Gordon perversely.

Ravelston, deferential even to the opinions of the dead, rubbed his nose. 'Does Chaucer say that? Then I'm afraid I disagree with Chaucer. People don't hate you, exactly.'

'They do. And they're quite right to hate you. You *are* hateful. It's like those ads for Listerine. "Why is he always alone? Halitosis is ruining his career." Poverty is spiritual halitosis.'

Ravelston sighed. Undoubtedly Gordon was perverse. They walked on, arguing, Gordon vehemently, Ravelston deprecatingly. Ravelston was helpless against Gordon in an argument of this kind. He felt that Gordon exaggerated, and yet he never liked to contradict him. How could he? He was rich and Gordon was poor. And how can you argue about poverty with someone who is genuinely poor?

'And then the way women treat you when you've no money!' Gordon went on. 'That's another thing about this accursed money business—women!'

Ravelston nodded rather gloomily. This sounded to him more reasonable than what Gordon had been saying before. He thought of Hermione Slater, his own girl. They had been lovers two years but had never bothered to get married. It was 'too much fag', Hermione always said. She was rich, of course, or rather her people were. He thought of her shoulders, wide, smooth, and young, that seemed to rise out of her clothes like a mermaid rising from the sea; and her skin and hair, which were somehow warm and sleepy, like a wheatfield in the sun. Hermione always yawned at the mention of Socialism, and refused even to read *Antichrist*. 'Don't talk to me about the lower classes,' she used to say. 'I hate them. They *smell*.' And Ravelston adored her.

'Of course women *are* a difficulty,' he admitted.

'They're more than a difficulty, they're a bloody curse. That is, if you've got no money. A woman hates the sight of you if you've got no money.'

'I think that's putting it a little too strongly. Things aren't so crude as all that.'

Gordon did not listen. 'What rot it is to talk about Socialism or any other ism when women are what they are! The only thing a woman ever wants is money; money for a house of her own and two babies and Drage furniture and an aspidistra. The only sin they can imagine is not wanting to grab money. No woman ever judges a man by anything except his income. Of course she doesn't put it to herself like that. She says he's *such a nice man*—meaning that he's got plenty of money. And if you haven't got money you aren't *nice*. You're dishonoured, somehow. You've sinned. Sinned against the aspidistra.'

'You talk a great deal about aspidistras,' said Ravelston.

'They're a dashed important subject,' said Gordon.

Ravelston rubbed his nose and looked away uncomfortably.

'Look here, Gordon, you don't mind my asking—have you got a girl of your own?'

'Oh, Christ! don't speak of her!'

He began, nevertheless, to talk about Rosemary. Ravelston had never met Rosemary. At this moment Gordon could not even remember what Rosemary was like. He could not remember how fond he was of her and she of him, how happy they always were together on the rare occasions when they could meet, how patiently she put up with his almost intolerable ways. He remembered nothing save that she would not sleep with him and that it was now a week since she had even written. In the dank night air, with beer inside him, he felt himself a forlorn, neglected creature. Rosemary was 'cruel' to him—that was how he saw it. Perversely, for the mere pleasure of tormenting himself and making Ravelston uncomfortable, be began to invent an imaginary character for Rosemary. He built up a picture of her as a callous creature who was amused by him and yet half despised him, who played with him and kept him at arm's length, and who would nevertheless fall into his arms if only he had a little more money. And Ravelston, who had never met Rosemary, did not altogether disbelieve him. He broke in:

'But I say, Gordon, look here. This girl, Miss—Miss Waterlow, did you say her name was?—Rosemary; doesn't she care for you at all, really?'

Gordon's conscience pricked him, though not very deeply. He could not say that Rosemary did not care for him.

'Oh, yes, she does care for me. In her own way, I dare say she cares for me quite a lot. But not enough, don't you see. She can't, while I've got no money. It's all money.'

'But surely money isn't so important as all that? After all, there *are* other things.'

'What other things? Don't you see that a man's whole personality is bound up with his income? His personality *is* his income. How can you be attractive to a girl when you've got no money? You can't wear decent clothes, you can't take her out to dinner or to the theatre or away for week-ends, you can't carry a cheery, interesting atmosphere about with you. And it's rot to say that kind of thing doesn't matter. It does. If you haven't got money there isn't even anywhere where you can meet. Rosemary and I never meet except in the streets or in picture galleries. She lives in some foul women's hostel, and my bitch of a landlady won't allow women in the house. Wandering up and down beastly wet streets—that's what Rosemary associates me with. Don't you see how it takes the gilt off everything?'

Ravelston was distressed. It must be pretty bloody when you haven't even the money to take your girl out. He tried to nerve himself to say something, and failed. With guilt, and also with desire, he thought of Hermione's body, naked like a ripe warm fruit. With any luck she would have dropped in at the flat this evening. Probably she was waiting for him now. He thought of the unemployed in Middlesbrough. Sexual starvation is awful among the unemployed. They were nearing the flat. He glanced up at the windows. Yes, they were lighted up. Hermione must be there. She had her own latchkey.

As they approached the flat Gordon edged closer to Ravelston. Now the evening was ending, and he must part from Ravelston, whom he adored, and go back to his foul lonely bedroom. And all evenings ended in this way; the return through the dark streets to the lonely room, the womanless bed. And Ravelston would say 'Come up, won't you?' and Gordon, in duty bound, would say, 'No.' Never stay too long with those you love—another commandment of the moneyless.

They halted at the foot of the steps. Ravelston laid his gloved hand on one of the iron spearheads of the railing.

'Come up, won't you?' he said without conviction.

'No, thanks. It's time I was getting back.'

Ravelston's fingers tightened round the spearhead. He pulled as though to go up, but did not go. Uncomfortably, looking over Gordon's head into the distance, he said:

'I say, Gordon, look here. You won't be offended if I say something?'

'What?'

'I say, you know, I hate that business about you and your girl. Not being able to take her out, and all that. It's bloody, that kind of thing.'

'Oh, it's nothing really.'

As soon as he heard Ravelston say that it was 'bloody', he knew that he had been exaggerating. He wished that he had not talked in that silly self-pitiful way. One says these things, with the feeling that one cannot help saying them, and afterwards one is sorry.

'I dare say I exaggerate,' he said.

'I say, Gordon, look here. Let me lend you ten quid. Take the girl out to dinner a few times. Or away for the week-end, or something. It might make all the difference. I hate to think—'

Gordon frowned bitterly, almost fiercely. He had stepped a pace back, as though from a threat or an insult. The terrible thing was that the temptation to say 'Yes' had almost overwhelmed him. There was so much that ten quid would do! He had a fleeting vision of Rosemary and himself at a restaurant table—a bowl of grapes and peaches, a bowing hovering waiter, a wine bottle dark and dusty in its wicker cradle.

'No fear!' he said.

'I do wish you would. I tell you I'd *like* to lend it you.'

'Thanks. But I prefer to keep my friends.'

'Isn't that rather—well, rather a bourgeois kind of thing to say?'

'Do you think it would be *borrowing* if I took ten quid off you? I couldn't pay it back in ten years.'

'Oh, well! It wouldn't matter so very much.' Ravelston looked away. Out it had got to come—the disgraceful, hateful admission that he found himself forced so curiously often to make! 'You know, I've got quite a lot of money.'

'I know you have. That's exactly why I won't borrow off you.'

'You know, Gordon, sometimes you're just a little bit—well, pigheaded.'

'I dare say. I can't help it.'

'Oh, well! Good night, then.'

'Good night.'

Ten minutes later Ravelston rode southwards in a taxi, with Hermione. She had been waiting for him, asleep or half asleep in one of the monstrous armchairs in front of the sitting-room fire. Whenever there was nothing particular to do, Hermione always fell asleep as promptly as an animal, and the more she slept the healthier she became. As he came across to her she woke and stretched herself with voluptuous, sleepy writhings, half smiling, half yawning up at him, one cheek and bare arm rosy in the firelight. Presently she mastered her yawns to greet him:

'Hullo, Philip! Where have you been all this time? I've been waiting ages.'

'Oh, I've been out with a fellow. Gordon Comstock. I don't expect you know him. The poet.'

'Poet! How much did he borrow off you?'

'Nothing. He's not that kind of person. He's rather a fool about money, as a matter of fact. But he's very gifted in his way.'

'You and your poets! You look tired, Philip. What time did you have dinner?'

'Well—as a matter of fact I didn't have any dinner.'

'Didn't have any dinner! Why?'

'Oh, well, you see—I don't know if you'll understand. It was a kind of accident. It was like this.'

He explained. Hermione burst out laughing and dragged herself into a more upright position.

'Philip! You *are* a silly old ass! Going without your dinner, just so as not to hurt that little beast's feelings! You must have some food at once. And of course your char's gone home. Why don't you keep some proper servants, Philip? I hate this hole-and-corner way you live. We'll go out and have supper at Modigliani's.'

'But it's after ten. They'll be shut.'

'Nonsense! They're open till two. I'll ring up for a taxi. I'm not going to have you starving yourself.'

In the taxi she lay against him, still half asleep, her head pillowed on his breast. He thought of the unemployed in Middlesbrough, seven in a room on twenty-five bob a week. But the girl's body was heavy against him, and Middlesbrough was very far away. Also he was damnably hungry. He thought of his favourite corner table at Modigliani's, and of that vile pub with its hard benches, stale beer-stink, and brass spittoons. Hermione was sleepily lecturing him.

'Philip, why do you have to live in such a dreadful way?'

'But I don't live in a dreadful way.'

'Yes, you do. Pretending you're poor when you're not, and living in that poky flat with no servants, and going about with all these beastly people.'

'What beastly people?'

'Oh, people like this poet friend of yours. All those people who write for your paper. They only do it to cadge from you. Of course I know you're a

Socialist. So am I. I mean we're all Socialists nowadays. But I don't see why you have to give all your money away and make friends with the lower classes. You can be a Socialist *and* have a good time, that's what I say.'

'Hermione, dear, please don't call them the lower classes!'

'Why not? They *are* the lower classes, aren't they?'

'It's such a hateful expression. Call them the working class, can't you?'

'The working class, if you like, then. But they smell just the same.'

'You oughtn't to say that kind of thing,' he protested weakly.

'Do you know, Philip, sometimes I think you *like* the lower classes.'

'Of course I like them.'

'How disgusting. How absolutely disgusting.'

She lay quiet, content to argue no longer, her arms round him, like a sleepy siren. The woman-scent breathed out of her, a powerful wordless propaganda against all altruism and all justice. Outside Modigliani's they had paid off the taxi and were moving for the door when a big, lank wreck of a man seemed to spring up from the paving-stones in front of them. He stood across their path like some fawning beast, with dreadful eagerness and yet timorously, as though afraid that Ravelston would strike him. His face came close up to Ravelston's—a dreadful face, fish-white and scrubby-bearded to the eyes. The words 'A cup of tea, guv'nor!' were breathed through carious teeth. Ravelston shrank from him in disgust. He could not help it. His hand moved automatically to his pocket. But in the same instant Hermione caught him by the arm and hauled him inside the restaurant.

'You'd give away every penny you've got if I let you,' she said.

They went to their favourite table in the corner. Hermione played with some grapes, But Ravelston was very hungry. He ordered the grilled rumpsteak he had been thinking of, and half a bottle of Beaujolais. The fat, white-haired Italian waiter, an old friend of Ravelston's, brought the smoking steak. Ravelston cut it open. Lovely, its red-blue heart! In Middlesbrough the unemployed huddle in frowzy beds, bread and marg and milkless tea in their bellies. He settled down to his steak with all the shameful joy of a dog with a stolen leg of mutton.

Gordon walked rapidly homewards. It was cold. The fifth of December—real winter now. Circumcise ye your foreskins, saith the Lord. The damp wind blew spitefully through the naked trees. *Sharply the menacing wind sweeps over.* The poem he had begun on Wednesday, of which six stanzas were now finished, came back to his mind. He did not dislike it at this moment. It was queer how talking with Ravelston always bucked him up. The mere contact with Ravelston seemed to reassure him somehow. Even when their talk had been unsatisfactory, he came away with the feeling that, after all, he wasn't quite a failure. Half aloud he repeated the six finished stanzas. They were not bad, not bad at all.

But intermittently he was going over in his mind the things he had said to Ravelston. He stuck to everything he had said. The humiliation of poverty! That's what they can't understand and won't understand. Not hardship—you don't suffer hardship on two quid a week, and if you did it wouldn't matter—but just humiliation, the awful, bloody humiliation. The way it gives everyone the right to stamp on you. The way everyone *wants* to stamp on you. Ravelston wouldn't believe it. He had too much decency, that was why. He thought you could be poor and still be treated like a human being. But Gordon knew better. He went into the house repeating to himself that he knew better.

There was a letter waiting for him on the hall tray. His heart jumped. All letters excited him nowadays. He went up the stairs three at a time, shut himself in and lit the gas. The letter was from Doring.

DEAR COMSTOCK,—What a pity you didn't turn up on Saturday. There were some people I wanted you to meet. We did tell you it was Saturday and not Thursday this time, didn't we? My wife says she's certain she told you. Anyway, we're having another party on the twenty-third, a sort of before-Christmas party, about the same time. Won't you come then? Don't forget the date this time.

Yours<br>PAUL DORING

A painful convulsion happened below Gordon's ribs. So Doring was pretending that it was all a mistake—was pretending not to have insulted him! True, he could not actually have gone there on Saturday, because on Saturday he had to be at the shop; still, it was the intention that counted.

His heart sickened as he re-read the words 'some people I wanted you to meet'. Just like his bloody luck! He thought of the people he might have met—editors of highbrow magazines, for instance. They might have given him books to review or asked to see his poems or Lord knew what. For a moment he was dreadfully tempted to believe that Doring had spoken the truth. Perhaps after all they *had* told him it was Saturday and not Thursday. Perhaps if he searched his memory he might remember about it—might even find the letter itself lying among his muddle of papers. But no! He wouldn't think of it. He fought down the temptation. The Dorings *had* insulted him on purpose. He was poor, therefore they had insulted him. If you are poor, people will insult you. It was his creed. Stick to it!

He went across to the table, tearing Doring's letter into small bits. The aspidistra stood in its pot, dull green, ailing, pathetic in its sickly ugliness. As he sat down, he pulled it towards him and looked at it meditatively. There was the intimacy of hatred between the aspidistra and him. 'I'll beat you yet, you b—,' he whispered to the dusty leaves.

Then he rummaged among his papers until he found a clean sheet, took his pen and wrote in his small, neat hand, right in the middle of the sheet:

DEAR DORING,—With reference to your letter: Go and — yourself.

Yours truly<br>GORDON COMSTOCK

He stuck it into an envelope, addressed it, and at once went out to get stamps from the slot machine. Post it tonight: these things look different in the morning. He dropped it into the pillar-box. So there was another friend gone west.

# 6

This woman business! What a bore it is! What a pity we can't cut it right out, or at least be like the animals—minutes of ferocious lust and months of icy chastity. Take a cock pheasant, for example. He jumps up on the hens' backs without so much as a with your leave or by your leave. And no sooner it is over than the whole subject is out of his mind. He hardly even notices his hens any longer; he ignores them, or simply pecks them if they come too near his food. He is not called upon to support his offspring, either. Lucky pheasant! How different from the lord of creation, always on the hop between his memory and his conscience!

Tonight Gordon wasn't even pretending to do any work. He had gone out again immediately after supper. He walked southward, rather slowly, thinking about women. It was a mild, misty night, more like autumn than winter. This was Tuesday and he had four and fourpence left. He could go down to the Crichton if he chose. Doubtless Flaxman and his pals were already boozing there. But the Crichton, which had seemed like paradise when he had no money, bored and disgusted him when it was in his power to go there. He hated the stale, beery place, and the sights, sounds, smells, all so blatantly and offensively male. There were no women there; only the barmaid with her lewd smile which seemed to promise everything and promised nothing.

Women, women! The mist that hung motionless in the air turned the passers-by into ghosts at twenty yards' distance; but in the little pools of li₌ht about the lamp-posts there were glimpses of girls' faces. He thought of Rosemary, of women in general, and of Rosemary again. All afternoon he had been thinking of her. It was with a kind of resentment that he thought of her small, strong body, which he had never yet seen naked. How damned unfair it is that we are filled to the brim with these tormenting desires and then forbidden to satisfy them! Why should one, merely because one has no money, be deprived of *that*? It seems so natural, so necessary, so much a part of the inalienable rights of a human being. As he walked down the dark street, through the cold yet languorous air, there was a strangely hopeful feeling in his breast. He half believed that somewhere ahead in the darkness a woman's body was waiting for him. But also he knew that no woman was waiting, not even Rosemary. It was eight days now since she had even written to him. The little beast! Eight whole days without writing! When she knew how much her letters meant to him! How manifest it was that she didn't care for him any longer, that he was merely a nuisance to her with his poverty and his shabbiness and his everlasting pestering of her to say she loved him! Very likely she would never write again. She was sick of him—sick of him because he had no money. What else could you expect? He had no hold over her. No money, therefore no hold. In the last resort, what holds a woman to any man, except money?

A girl came down the pavement alone. He passed her in the light of the lamp-post. A working-class girl, eighteen years old it might be, hatless, with wildrose face. She turned her head quickly when she saw him looking at her. She dreaded to meet his eyes. Beneath the thin silky raincoat she was wearing, belted at the waist, her youthful flanks showed supple and trim. He could have turned and followed her, almost. But what was the use? She'd run away or call a policeman. My golden locks time hath to silver turned, he thought. He was thirty and moth-eaten. What woman worth having would ever look at him again?

This woman business! Perhaps you'd feel differently about it if you were married? But he had taken an oath against marriage long ago. Marriage is only a trap set for you by the money-god. You grab the bait; snap goes the trap; and there you are, chained by the leg to some 'good' job till they cart you to Kensal Green. And what a life! Licit sexual intercourse in the shade of the aspidistra. Pram-pushing and sneaky adulteries. And the wife finding you out and breaking the cut-glass whisky decanter over your head.

Nevertheless he perceived that in a way it is necessary to marry. If marriage is bad, the alternative is worse. For a moment he wished that he were married; he pined for the difficulty of it, the reality, the pain. And marriage must be indissoluble, for better for worse, for richer for poorer, till death do you part. The old Christian ideal—marriage tempered by adultery. Commit adultery if you must, but at any rate have the decency to *call* it adultery. None of that American soul-mate slop. Have your fun and then sneak home, juice of the forbidden fruit dripping from your whiskers, and take the consequences. Cut-glass whisky decanters broken over your head, nagging, burnt meals, children crying, clash and thunder of embattled mothers-in-law. Better that, perhaps, than horrible freedom? You'd know, at least, that it was real life that you were living.

But anyway, how can you marry on two quid a week? Money, money, always money! The devil of it is, that outside marriage, no decent relationship with a woman is possible. His mind moved backwards, over his ten years of adult life. The faces of women flowed through his memory. Ten or a dozen of them there had been. Tarts, also. *Comme au long d'un cadavre un cadavre étendu.* And even when they were not tarts it had been squalid, always squalid. Always it had started in a sort of cold-blooded wilfulness and ended in some mean, callous desertion. That, too, was money. Without money, you can't be straightforward in your dealings with women. For without money, you can't pick and choose, you've got to take what women you can get; and then, necessarily, you've got to break free of them. Constancy, like all other virtues, has got to be paid for in money. And the mere fact that he had rebelled against the money code and wouldn't settle down in the prison of a 'good' job—a thing no woman will ever understand—had brought a quality of impermanence, of deception, into all his affairs with women. Abjuring money, he ought to have abjured women to. Serve the money-god, or do without women—those are the only alternatives. And both were equally impossible.

From the side-street just ahead, a shade of white light cut through the mist, and there was a bellowing of street hawkers. It was Luton Road, where they have the open-air market two evenings a week. Gordon turned to his left, into the market. He often came this way. The street was so crowded that you could only with difficulty thread your way down the cabbage-littered alley between the stalls. In the glare of hanging electric bulbs, the stuff on the stalls glowed with fine lurid colours—hacked, crimson chunks of meat, piles of oranges and green and white broccoli, stiff, glassy-eyed rabbits, live eels looping in enamel troughs, plucked fowls hanging in rows, sticking out their naked breasts like guardsmen naked on parade. Gordon's spirits revived a little. He liked the noise, the bustle, the vitality. Whenever you see a street-market you know there's hope for England yet. But even here he felt his solitude. Girls were thronging everywhere, in knots of four or five, prowling desirously about the stalls of cheap underwear and swapping backchat and screams of laughter with the youths who followed them. None had eyes for Gordon. He walked among them as though invisible, save that their bodies avoided him when he passed them. Ah, look there! Involuntarily he paused. Over a pile of art-silk undies on a stall, three girls were bending, intent, their faces close together—three youthful faces, flower-like in the harsh light, clustering side by side like a truss of blossom on a Sweet William or phlox. His heart stirred. No eyes for him, of course! One girl looked up. Ah! Hurriedly, with an offended air, she looked away again. A delicate flush like a wash of aquarelle flooded her face. The hard, sexual stare in his eyes had frightened her. They flee from me that sometime did me seek! He walked on. If only Rosemary were here! He forgave her now for not writing to him. He could forgive her anything, if only she were here. He knew how much she meant to him, because she alone of all women was willing to save him from the humiliation of his loneliness.

At this moment he looked up, and saw something that made his heart jump. He changed the focus of his eyes abruptly. For a moment he thought he was imagining it. But no! It *was* Rosemary!

She was coming down the alley between the stalls, twenty or thirty yards away. It was as though his desire had called her into being. She had not seen him yet. She came towards him, a small debonair figure, picking her way nimbly through the crowd and the muck underfoot, her face scarcely visible because of a flat black hat which she wore cocked down over her eyes like a Harrow boy's straw hat. He started towards her and called her name.

'Rosemary! Hi, Rosemary!'

A blue-aproned man thumbing codfish on a stall turned to stare at him. Rosemary did not hear him because of the din. He called again.

'Rosemary! I say, Rosemary!'

They were only a few yards apart now. She started and looked up.

'Gordon! What are you doing here?'

'What are *you* doing here?'

'I was coming to see you.'

'But how did you know I was here?'

'I didn't. I always come this way. I get out of the tube at Camden Town.'

Rosemary sometimes came to see Gordon at Willowbed Road. Mrs Wisbeach would inform him sourly that 'there was a young woman to see him', and he would come downstairs and they would go out for a walk in the streets. Rosemary was never allowed indoors, not even into the hall. That was a rule of the house. You would have thought 'young women' were plague-rats by the way Mrs Wisbeach spoke of them. Gordon took Rosemary by the upper arm and made to pull her against him.

'Rosemary! Oh, what a joy to see you again! I was so vilely lonely. Why didn't you come before?'

She shook off his hand and stepped back out of his reach. Under her slanting hat-brim she gave him a glance that was intended to be angry.

'Let me go, now! I'm very angry with you. I very nearly didn't come after that beastly letter you sent me.'

'What beastly letter?'

'You know very well.'

'No, I don't. Oh, well, let's get out of this. Somewhere where we can talk. This way.'

He took her arm, but she shook him off again, continuing however, to walk at his side. Her steps were quicker and shorter than his. And walking beside him she had the appearance of something extremely small, nimble, and young, as though he had had some lively little animal, a squirrel for instance, frisking at his side. In reality she was not very much smaller than Gordon, and only a few months younger. But no one would ever have described Rosemary as a spinster of nearly thirty, which in fact she was. She was a strong, agile girl, with stiff black hair, a small triangular face, and very pronounced eyebrows. It was one of those small, peaky faces, full of character, which one sees in sixteenth-century portraits. The first time you saw her take her hat off you got a surprise, for on her crown three white hairs glittered among the black ones like silver wires. It was typical of Rosemary that she never bothered to pull the white hairs out. She still thought of herself as a very young girl, and so did everybody else. Yet if you looked closely the marks of time were plain enough on her face.

Gordon walked more boldly with Rosemary at his side. He was proud of her. People were looking at her, and therefore at him as well. He was no longer invisible to women. As always, Rosemary was rather nicely dressed. It was a mystery how she did it on four pounds a week. He liked particularly the hat she was wearing—one of those flat felt hats which were then coming into fashion and which caricatured a clergyman's shovel hat. There was something essentially frivolous about it. In some way difficult to be described, the angle at which it was cocked forward harmonized appealingly with the curve of Rosemary's behind.

'I like your hat,' he said.

In spite of herself, a small smile flickered at the corner of her mouth.

'It *is* rather nice,' she said, giving the hat a little pat with her hand.

She was still pretending to be angry, however. She took care that their bodies should not touch. As soon as they had reached the end of the stalls and were in the main street she stopped and faced him sombrely.

'What do you mean by writing me letters like that?' she said.

'Letters like what?'

'Saying I'd broken your heart.'

'So you have.'

'It looks like it, doesn't it!'

'I don't know. It certainly feels like it.'

The words were spoken half jokingly, and yet they made her look more closely at him—at his pale, wasted face, his uncut hair, his general down-at-heel, neglected appearance. Her heart softened instantly, and yet she frowned. Why *won't* he take care of himself? was the thought in her mind. They had moved closer together. He took her by the shoulders. She let him do it, and, putting her small arms round him, squeezed him very hard, partly in affection, partly in exasperation.

'Gordon, you *are* a miserable creature!' she said.

'Why am I a miserable creature?'

'Why can't you look after yourself properly? You're a perfect scarecrow. Look at these awful old clothes you're wearing!'

'They're suited to my station. One can't dress decently on two quid a week, you know.'

'But surely there's no need to go about looking like a rag-bag? Look at this button on your coat, broken in half!'

She fingered the broken button, then suddenly lifted his discoloured Woolworth's tie aside. In some feminine way she had divined that he had no buttons on his shirt.

'Yes, *again*! Not a single button. You are awful, Gordon!'

'I tell you I can't be bothered with things like that. I've got a soul above buttons.'

'But why not give them to *me* and let me sew them on for you? And, oh, Gordon! You haven't even shaved today. How absolutely beastly of you. You might at least take the trouble to shave every morning.'

'I can't afford to shave every morning,' he said perversely.

'What *do* you mean, Gordon? It doesn't cost money to shave, does it?'

'Yes, it does. Everything costs money. Cleanness, decency, energy, self-respect—everything. It's all money. Haven't I told you that a million times?'

She squeezed his ribs again—she was surprisingly strong—and frowned up at him, studying his face as a mother looks at some peevish child of which she is unreasonably fond.

'*What* a fool I am!' she said.

'In what way a fool?'

'Because I'm so fond of you.'

'Are you fond of me?'

'Of course I am. You know I am. I adore you. It's idiotic of me.'

'Then come somewhere where it's dark. I want to kiss you.'

'Fancy being kissed by a man who hasn't even shaved!'

'Well, that'll be a new experience for you.'

'No, it won't, Gordon. Not after knowing *you* for two years.'

'Oh, well, come on, anyway.'

They found an almost dark alley between the backs of houses. All their lovemaking was done in such places. The only place where they could ever be private was the streets. He pressed her shoulders against the rough damp bricks of the wall. She turned her face readily up to his and clung to him with a sort of eager violent affection, like a child. And yet all the while, though they were body to body, it was as though there were a shield between them. She kissed him as a child might have done, because she knew that he expected to be kissed. It was always like this. Only at very rare moments could he awake in her the beginnings of physical desire; and these she seemed afterwards to forget, so that he always had to begin at the beginning over again. There was something defensive in the feeling of her small, shapely body. She longed to know the meaning of physical love, but also she dreaded it. It would destroy her youth, the youthful, sexless world in which she chose to live.

He parted his mouth from hers in order to speak to her.

'Do you love me?' he said.

'Of course, silly. Why do you always ask me that?'

'I like to hear you say it. Somehow I never feel sure of you till I've heard you say it.'

'But why?'

'Oh, well, you might have changed your mind. After all, I'm not exactly the answer to a maiden's prayer. I'm thirty, and moth-eaten at that.'

'Don't be so absurd, Gordon! Anyone would think you were a hundred, to hear you talk. You know I'm the same age as you are.'

'Yes, but not moth-eaten.'

She rubbed her cheek against his, feeling the roughness of his day-old beard. Their bellies were close together. He thought of the two years he had wanted her and never had her. With his lips almost against her ear he murmured:

'Are you *ever* going to sleep with me?'

'Yes, some day I will. Not now. Some day.'

'It's always "some day". It's been "some day" for two years now.'

'I know. But I can't help it.'

He pressed her back against the wall, pulled off the absurd flat hat, and buried his face in her hair. It was tormenting to be so close to her and all for nothing. He put a hand under her chin and lifted her small face up to his, trying to distinguish her features in the almost complete darkness.

'Say you will, Rosemary, There's a dear! Do!'

'You know I'm going to *some* time.'

'Yes, but not *some* time—now. I don't mean this moment, but soon. When we get an opportunity. Say you will!'

'I can't. I can't promise.'

'Say "yes," Rosemary. *please* do!'

'No.'

Still stroking her invisible face, he quoted:

> 'Veuillez le dire donc selon
> Que vous estes benigne et doulche,
> Car ce doulx mot n'est pas si long
> Qu'il vous face mal en la bouche.'

'What does that mean?'

He translated it.

'I can't, Gordon. I just can't.'

'Say "yes," Rosemary, there's a dear. Surely it's as easy to say "yes" as "no"?'

'No, it isn't. It's easy enough for you. You're a man. It's different for a woman.'

'Say "yes," Rosemary! "Yes"– it's such an easy word. Go on, now; say it. "Yes!" '

'Anyone would think you were teaching a parrot to talk, Gordon.'

'Oh, damn! Don't make jokes about it.'

It was not much use arguing. Presently they came out into the street and walked on, southward. Somehow, from Rosemary's swift, neat movements, from her general air of a girl who knows how to look after herself and who yet treats life mainly as a joke, you could make a good guess at her upbringing and her mental background. She was the youngest child of one of those huge-hungry families which still exist here and there in the middle classes. There had been fourteen children all told–the father was a country solicitor. Some of Rosemary's sisters were married, some of them were schoolmistresses or running typing bureaux; the brothers were farming in Canada, on tea-plantations in Ceylon, in obscure regiments of the Indian Army. Like all women who have had an eventful girlhood, Rosemary wanted to remain a girl. That was why, sexually, she was so immature. She had kept late into life the high-spirited sexless atmosphere of a big family. Also she had absorbed into her very bones the code of fair play and live-and-let-live. She was profoundly magnanimous, quite incapable of spiritual bullying. From Gordon, whom she adored, she put up with almost anything. It was the measure of her magnanimity that never once, in the two years that she had known him, had she blamed him for not attempting to earn a proper living.

Gordon was aware of all this. But at the moment he was thinking of other things. In the pallid circles of light about the lamp-posts, beside Rosemary's smaller, trimmer figure, he felt graceless, shabby, and dirty. He wished very much that he had shaved that morning. Furtively he put a hand into his pocket and felt his money, half afraid–it was a recurrent fear with him–that he might have dropped a coin. However, he could feel the milled edge of a florin, his principal coin at the moment. Four and fourpence left. He couldn't possibly take her out to supper, he reflected. They'd have to trail dismally up and down the streets, as usual, or at best go to a Lyons for a coffee. Bloody! How can you have any fun when you've got no money? He said broodingly:

'Of course it all comes back to money.'

This remark came out of the blue. She looked up at him in surprise.

'What do you mean, it all comes back to money?'

'I mean the way nothing ever goes right in my life. It's always money, money, money that's at the bottom of everything. And especially between me and you. That's why you don't really love me. There's a sort of film of money between us. I can feel it every time I kiss you.'

'Money! What *has* money got to do with it, Gordon?'

'Money's got to do with everything. If I had more money you'd love me more.'

'Of course, I wouldn't! Why should I?'

'You couldn't help it. Don't you see that if I had more money I'd be more worth loving? Look at me now! Look at my face, look at these clothes I'm wearing, look at everything else about me. Do you suppose I'd be like that if I had two thousand a year? If I had more money I should be a different person.'

'If you were a different person I shouldn't love you.'

'That's nonsense, too. But look at it like this. If we were married would you sleep with me?'

'What questions you do ask! Of course I would. Otherwise, where would be the sense of being married?'

'Well then, suppose I was decently well off, *would* you marry me?'

'What's the good of talking about it, Gordon? You know we can't afford to marry.'

'Yes, but *if* we could. Would you?'

'I don't know. Yes, I would, I dare say.'

'There you are, then! That's what I said—money!'

'No, Gordon, no! That's not fair! You're twisting my words round.'

'No, I'm not. You've got this money-business at the bottom of your heart. Every woman's got it. You wish I was in a *good* job now, don't you?'

'Not in the way you mean it. I'd like you to be earning more money—yes.'

'And you think I ought to have stayed on at the New Albion, don't you? You'd like me to go back there now and write slogans for Q.T. Sauce and Truweet Breakfast Crisps. Wouldn't you?'

'No, I wouldn't. I *never* said that.'

'You thought it, though. It's what any woman would think.'

He was being horribly unfair, and he knew it. The one thing Rosemary had never said, the thing she was probably quite incapable of saying, was that he ought to go back to the New Albion. But for the moment he did not even want to be fair. His sexual disappointment still pricked him. With a sort of melancholy triumph he reflected that, after all, he was right. It was money that stood between them. Money, money, all is money! He broke into a half-serious tirade:

'Women! What nonsense they make of all our ideas! Because one can't keep free of women, and every woman makes one pay the same price. "Chuck away your decency and make more money"—that's what women say. "Chuck away your decency, suck the blacking off the boss's boots, and buy me a better fur coat than the woman next door." Every man you can see has got some blasted woman hanging round his neck like a mermaid, dragging him down and down—down to some beastly little semi-detached villa in Putney, with hire-purchase furniture and a portable radio and an aspidistra in the window. It's women who make all progress impossible. Not that I believe in progress,' he added rather unsatisfactorily.

'What absolute *nonsense* you do talk, Gordon! As though women were to blame for everything!'

'They are to blame, finally. Because it's the women who really believe in the money-code. The men obey it; they have to, but they don't believe in it. It's the women who keep it going. The women and their Putney villas and their fur coats and their babies and their aspidistras.'

'It is *not* the women, Gordon! Women didn't invent money, did they?'

'It doesn't matter who invented it, the point is that it's women who worship it. A woman's got a sort of mystical feeling towards money. Good and evil in a women's mind mean simply money and no money. Look at you and me. You won't sleep with me, simply and solely because I've got no money. Yes, that *is* the reason. (He squeezed her arm to silence her.) You admitted it only a minute ago. And if I had a decent income you'd go to bed with me tomorrow. It's not because you're mercenary. You don't want me to *pay* you for sleeping with me. It's not so crude as that. But you've got that deep-down mystical feeling that somehow a man without money isn't worthy of you. He's a weakling, a sort of half-man—that's how you feel. Hercules, god of strength and god of money—you'll find that in Lemprière. It's women who keep all mythologies going. Women!'

'Women!' echoed Rosemary on a different note. 'I hate the way men are always talking about *women*. "Women do this," and "*Women* do that"—as though all women were exactly the same!'

'Of course all women are the same! What does any woman want except a safe income and two babies and a semi-detached villa in Putney with an aspidistra in the window?'

'Oh, you and your aspidistras!'

'On the contrary, *your* aspidistras. You're the sex that cultivates them.'

She squeezed his arm and burst out laughing. She was really extraordinarily good-natured. Besides, what he was saying was such palpable nonsense that it did not even exasperate her. Gordon's diatribes against women were in reality a kind of perverse joke; indeed, the whole sex-war is at bottom only a joke. For the same reason it is great fun to pose as a feminist or an anti-feminist according to your sex. As they walked on they began a violent argument upon the eternal and idiotic question of Man versus Woman. The moves in this argument—for they had it as often as they met—were always very much the same. Men are brutes and women are soulless, and women have always been kept in subjection and they jolly well ought to be kept in subjection, and look at Patient Griselda and look at Lady Astor, and what about polygamy and Hindu widows, and what about Mother Pankhurst's piping days when every decent woman wore mousetraps on her garters and couldn't look at a man without feeling her right hand itch for a castrating knife? Gordon and Rosemary never grew tired of this kind of thing. Each laughed with delight at the other's absurdities. There was a merry war between them. Even as they disputed, arm in arm, they pressed their bodies delightedly together. They were very happy. Indeed, they adored one another. Each was to the other a standing joke and an object infinitely precious. Presently a red and blue haze of Neon lights appeared in the distance. They had reached the beginning of the Tottenham Court Road. Gordon put his arm round her waist and turned her to the right, down a darkish side-street. They were so happy together that they had got to kiss. They stood clasped together under the lamp-post, still laughing, two enemies breast to breast. She rubbed her cheek against his.

'Gordon, you are such a dear old ass! I can't help loving you, scrubby jaw and all.'

'Do you really?'

'Really and truly.'

Her arms still round him, she leaned a little backwards, pressing her belly against his with a sort of innocent voluptuousness.

'Life *is* worth living, isn't it , Gordon?'

'Sometimes.'

'If only we could meet a bit oftener! Sometimes I don't see you for weeks.'

'I know. It's bloody. If you knew how I hate my evenings alone!'

'One never seems to have time for anything. I don't even leave that beastly office till nearly seven. What do you do with yourself on Sundays, Gordon?'

'Oh, God! Moon about and look miserable, like everyone else.'

'Why not let's go out for a walk in the country sometimes. Then we would have all day together. Next Sunday, for instance?'

The words chilled him. They brought back the thought of money, which he had succeeded in putting out of his mind for half an hour past. A trip into the country would cost money, far more than he could possibly afford. He said in a non-committal tone that transferred the whole thing to the realm of abstraction:

'Of course, it's not too bad in Richmond Park on Sundays. Or even Hampstead Heath. Especially if you go in the mornings before the crowds get there.'

'Oh, but do let's go right out into the country! Somewhere in Surrey, for instance, or to Burnham Beeches. It's so lovely at this time of year, with all the dead leaves on the ground, and you can walk all day and hardly meet a soul. We'll walk for miles and miles and have dinner at a pub. It would be such fun. Do let's!'

Blast! The money-business was coming back. A trip even as far as Burnham Beeches would cost all of ten bob. He did some hurried arithmetic. Five bob he might manage, and Julia would 'lend' him five; *give* him five, that was. At the same moment he remembered his oath, constantly renewed and always broken, not to 'borrow' money off Julia. He said in the same casual tone as before:

'It *would* be rather fun. I should think we might manage it. I'll let you know later in the week, anyway.'

They came out of the side-street, still arm in arm. There was a pub on the corner. Rosemary stood on tiptoe, and, clinging to Gordon's arm to support herself, managed to look over the frosted lower half of the window.

'Look, Gordon, there's a clock in there. It's nearly half past nine. Aren't you getting frightfully hungry?'

'No,' he said instantly and untruthfully.

'I am. I'm simply starving. Let's go and have something to eat somewhere.'

Money again! One moment more, and he must confess that he had only four and fourpence in the world—four and fourpence to last till Friday.

'I couldn't eat anything,' he said. 'I might manage a drink, I dare say. Let's go and have some coffee or something. I expect we'll find a Lyons open.'

'Oh, don't let's go to a Lyons! I know such a nice little Italian restaurant, only just down the road. We'll have Spaghetti Napolitaine and a bottle of red wine. I adore spaghetti. Do let's!'

His heart sank. It was no good. He would have to own up. Supper at the Italian Restaurant could not possibly cost less than five bob for the two of them. He said almost sullenly:

'It's about time I was getting home, as a matter of fact.'

'Oh, Gordon! Already? Why?'

'Oh, well! If you *must* know, I've only got four and fourpence in the world. And it's got to last till Friday.'

Rosemary stopped short. She was so angry that she pinched his arm with all her strength, meaning to hurt him and punish him.

'Gordon, you *are* an ass! You're a perfect idiot! You're the most unspeakable idiot I've ever seen!'

'Why am I an idiot?'

'Because what does it matter whether you've got any money! I'm asking *you* to have supper with *me.*'

He freed his arm from hers and stood away from her. He did not want to look her in the face.

'What! Do you think I'd go to a restaurant and let you pay for my food?'

'But why not?'

'Because one can't do that sort of thing. It isn't done.'

'It "isn't done"! You'll be saying it's "not cricket" in another moment. *What* "isn't done"?'

'Letting you pay for my meals. A man pays for a woman, a woman doesn't pay for a man.'

'Oh, Gordon! Are we living in the reign of Queen Victoria?'

'Yes, we are, as far as that kind of thing's concerned. Ideas don't change so quickly.'

'But *my* ideas have changed.'

'No, they haven't. You think they have, but they haven't. You've been brought up as a woman, and you can't help behaving like a woman, however much you don't want to.'

'But what do you mean by *behaving like a woman*, anyway?'

'I tell you every woman's the same when it comes to a thing like this. A woman despises a man who's dependent on her and sponges on her. She may say she doesn't, she may *think* she doesn't, but she does. She can't help it. If I let you pay for my meals *you'd* despise me.'

He had turned away. He knew how abominably he was behaving. But somehow he had got to say these things. The feeling that people—even Rosemary—*must* despise him for his poverty was too strong to be overcome. Only by rigid, jealous independence could he keep his self-respect. Rosemary was really distressed this time. She caught his arm and pulled him round, making him face her. With an insistent gesture, angrily and yet demanding to be loved, she pressed her breast against him.

'Gordon! I won't let you say such things. How can you say I'd ever despise you?'

'I tell you you couldn't help it if I let myself sponge on you.'

'Sponge on me! What expressions you do use! How is it sponging on me to let me pay for your supper just for once!'

He could feel the small breasts, firm and round, just beneath his own. She looked up at him, frowning and yet not far from tears. She thought him perverse, unreasonable, cruel. But her physical nearness distracted him. At this moment all he could remember was that in two years she had never yielded to him. She had starved him of the one thing that mattered. What was the good of pretending that she loved him when in the last essential she recoiled? He added with a kind of deadly joy:

'In a way you do despise me. Oh, yes, I know you're fond of me. But after all, you can't take me quite seriously. I'm a kind of joke to you. You're fond of me, and yet I'm not quite your equal—that's how you feel.'

It was what he had said before, but with this difference, that now he meant it, or said it as if he meant it. She cried out with tears in her voice:

'I don't, Gordon, I don't! You *know* I don't!'

'You do. That's why you won't sleep with me. Didn't I tell you that before?'

She looked up at him an instant longer, and then buried her face in his breast as suddenly as though ducking from a blow. It was because she had burst into tears. She wept against his breast, angry with him, hating him, and yet clinging to him like a child. It was the childish way in which she clung to him, as a mere male breast to weep on, that hurt him most. With a sort of self-hatred he remembered the other women who in just the same way had cried against his breast. It seemed the only thing he could do with women, to make them cry. With his arm round her shoulders he caressed her clumsily, trying to console her.

'You've gone and made me cry!' she whimpered in self-contempt.

'I'm sorry! Rosemary, dear one! Don't cry, *please* don't cry.'

'Gordon, dearest! *Why* do you have to be so beastly to me?'

'I'm sorry, I'm sorry! Sometimes I can't help it.'

'But why? Why?'

She had got over her crying. Rather more composed, she drew away from him and felt for something to wipe her eyes. Neither of them had a handkerchief. Impatiently, she wrung the tears out of her eyes with her knuckles.

'How silly we always are! Now, Gordon, *be* nice for once. Come along to the restaurant and have some supper and let me pay for it.'

'No.'

'Just this once. Never mind about the old money-business. Do it just to please me.'

'I tell you I can't do that kind of thing. I've got to keep my end up.'

'But what do you mean, keep your end up?'

'I've made a war on money, and I've got to keep the rules. The first rule is never to take charity.'

'Charity! Oh, Gordon, I *do* think you're silly!'

She squeezed his ribs again. It was a sign of peace. She did not understand him, probably never would understand him; yet she accepted him as he was, hardly even protesting against his unreasonableness. As she put her face up to be kissed he noticed that her lips were salt. A tear had trickled here. He strained her against him. The hard defensive feeling had gone out of her body. She shut her eyes and sank against him and into him as though her bones had grown weak, and her lips parted and her small tongue sought for his. It was very seldom that she did that. And suddenly, as he felt her body yielding, he seemed to know with certainty that their struggle was ended. She was his now when he chose to take her, and yet perhaps she did not fully understand what it was that she was offering; it was simply an instinctive movement of generosity, a desire to reassure him—to smooth away that hateful feeling of being unloveable and unloved. She said nothing of this in words. It was the feeling of her body that seemed to say it. But even if this had been the time and the place he could not have taken her. At this moment he loved her but did not desire her. His desire could only return at some future time when there was no quarrel fresh in his mind and no consciousness of four and fourpence in his pocket to daunt him.

Presently they separated their mouths, though still clinging closely together.

'How stupid it is, the way we quarrel, isn't it Gordon? When we meet so seldom.'

'I know. It's all my fault. I can't help it. Things rub me up. It's money at the bottom of it, always money.'

'Oh, money! You let it worry you too much, Gordon.'

'Impossible. It's the only thing worth worrying about.'

'But, anyway, we *will* go out into the country next Sunday, won't we? To Burnham Beeches or somewhere. It would be so nice if we could.'

'Yes, I'd love to. We'll go early and be out all day. I'll raise the train fares somehow.'

'But you'll let me pay my own fare, won't you?'

'No, I'd rather I paid them, but we'll go, anyway.'

'And you really won't let me pay for your supper—just this once, just to show you trust me?'

'No, I can't. I'm sorry. I've told you why.'

'Oh, dear! I suppose we shall have to say good night. It's getting late.'

They stayed talking a long time, however, so long that Rosemary got no supper after all. She had to be back at her lodgings by eleven, or the she-dragons were angry. Gordon went to the top of the Tottenham Court Road and took the tram. It was a penny cheaper than taking the bus. On the wooden seat upstairs he was wedged against a small dirty Scotchman who read the football finals and oozed beer. Gordon was very happy. Rosemary was going to be his mistress. *Sharply the menacing wind sweeps over.* To the music of the tram's booming he whispered the seven completed stanzas of his poem. Nine stanzas there would be in all. It was *good*. He believed in it and in himself. He was a poet. Gordon Comstock, author of *Mice*. Even in *London Pleasures* he once again believed.

He thought of Sunday. They were to meet at nine o'clock at Paddington Station. Ten bob or so it would cost; he would raise the money if he had to pawn his shirt. And she was going to become his mistress; this very Sunday, perhaps, if the right chance offered itself. Nothing had been said. Only, somehow, it was agreed between them.

Please God it kept fine on Sunday! It was deep winter now. What luck if it turned out one of those splendid windless days—one of those days that might almost be summer, when you can lie for hours on the dead bracken and never feel cold! But you don't get many days like that; a dozen at most in every winter. As likely as not it would rain. He wondered whether they would get a chance to do it after all. They had nowhere to go, except the open air. There are so many pairs of lovers in London with 'nowhere to go'; only the streets and the parks, where there is no privacy and it is always cold. It is not easy to make love in a cold climate when you have no money. The 'never the time and the place' motif is not made enough of in novels.

---

# 7

The plumes of the chimneys floated perpendicular against skies of smoky rose.

Gordon caught the 27 bus at ten past eight. The streets were still locked in their Sunday sleep. On the doorsteps the milk bottles waited ungathered like little white sentinels. Gordon had fourteen shillings in his hand—thirteen and nine, rather, because the bus fare was threepence. Nine bob he had set aside from his wages—God knew what that was going to mean, later in the week!—and five he had borrowed from Julia.

He had gone round to Julia's place on Thursday night. Julia's room in Earl's Court, though only a second-floor back, was not just a vulgar bedroom like Gordon's. It was a bed-sitting with the accent on the sitting. Julia would have died of starvation sooner than put up with such squalor as Gordon lived in. Indeed every one of her scraps of furniture, collected over intervals of years, represented a period of semi-starvation. There was a divan bed that could very nearly be mistaken for a sofa, and a little round fumed oak table, and two 'antique' hardwood chairs, and an ornamental footstool and a chintz-covered armchair—Drage's: thirteen monthly payments—in front of the tiny gas-fire; and there were various brackets with framed photos of father and mother and Gordon and Aunt Angela, and a birchwood calendar—somebody's Christmas present—with 'It's a long lane that has no turning' done on it in pokerwork. Julia depressed Gordon horribly. He was always telling himself that he ought to go and see her oftener; but in practice he never went near her except to 'borrow' money.

When Gordon had given three knocks—three knocks for second floor—Julia took him up to her room and knelt down in front of the gas-fire.

'I'll light the fire again,' she said. 'You'd like a cup of tea, wouldn't you?'

He noted the 'again'. The room was beastly cold—no fire had been lighted in it this evening. Julia always 'saved gas' when she was alone. He looked at her long narrow back as she knelt down. How grey her hair was getting! Whole locks of it were quite grey. A little more, and it would be 'grey hair' *tout court*.

'You like your tea strong, don't you?' breathed Julia, hovering over the tea-caddy with tender, goose-like movements.

Gordon drank his cup of tea standing up, his eye on the birchwood calendar. Out with it! Get it over! Yet his heart almost failed him. The meanness of this hateful cadging! What would it all tot up to, the money he had 'borrowed' from her in all these years?

'I say, Julia, I'm damned sorry—I hate asking you; but look here—'

'Yes, Gordon?' she said quietly. She knew what was coming.

'Look here, Julia, I'm damned sorry, but could you lend me five bob?'

'Yes, Gordon, I expect so.'

She sought out the small, worn black leather purse that was hidden at the bottom of her linen drawer. He knew what she was thinking. It meant less for Christmas presents. That was the great event of her life nowadays—Christmas and the giving of presents: hunting through the glittering streets, late at night after the teashop was shut, from one bargain counter to another, picking out the trash that women are so curiously fond of. Handkerchief sachets, letter racks, teapots, manicure sets, birchwood calendars with mottoes in pokerwork. All through the year she was scraping from her wretched wages for 'So-and-so's Christmas present', or 'So-and-so's birthday present'. And had she not, last Christmas, because Gordon was 'fond of poetry', given him the *Selected Poems* of John Drinkwater in green morocco, which he had sold for half a crown? Poor Julia! Gordon made off with his five bob as soon as he decently could. Why is it that one can't borrow from a rich friend and can from a half-starved relative? But one's family, of course, 'don't count'.

On the top of the bus he did mental arithmetic. Thirteen and nine in hand. Two day-returns to Slough, five bob. Bus fares, say two bob more, seven bob. Bread and cheese and beer at a pub, say a bob each, nine bob. Tea, eightpence each, twelve bob. A bob for cigarettes, thirteen bob. That left ninepence for emergencies. They would manage all right. And how about the rest of the week? Not a penny for tobacco! But he refused to let it worry him. Today would be worth it, anyway.

Rosemary met him on time. It was one of her virtues that she was never late, and even at this hour of the morning she was bright and debonair. She was rather nicely dressed, as usual. She was wearing her mock-shovel hat again, because he had said he liked it. They had the station practically to themselves. The huge grey place, littered and deserted, had a blowsy, unwashed air, as though it were still sleeping off a Saturday night debauch. A yawning porter in need of a shave told them the best way to get to Burnham Beeches, and presently they were in a third-class smoker, rolling westward, and the mean wilderness of London was opening out and giving way to narrow sooty fields dotted with ads for Carter's Little Liver Pills. The day was very still and warm. Gordon's prayer had come true. It was one of those windless days which you can hardly tell from summer. You could feel the sun behind the mist; it would break through presently, with any luck. Gordon and Rosemary were profoundly and rather absurdly happy. There was a sense of wild adventure in getting out of London, with the long day in 'the country' stretching out ahead of them. It was months since Rosemary and a year since Gordon had set foot in 'the country'. They sat close together with the *Sunday Times* open across their knees; they did not read it, however, but watched the fields and cows and houses and the empty goods trucks and great sleeping factories rolling past. Both of them enjoyed the railway journey so much that they wished it had been longer.

At Slough they got out and travelled to Farnham Common in an absurd chocolate-coloured bus with no top. Slough was still half asleep. Rosemary remembered the way now that they had got to Farnham Common. You walked down a rutted road and came out on to stretches of fine, wet, tussocky grass dotted with little naked birches. The beech woods were beyond. Not a bough or a blade was stirring. The trees stood like ghosts in the still, misty air. Both Rosemary and Gordon exclaimed at the loveliness of everything. The dew, the stillness, the satiny stems of the birches, the softness of the turf under your feet! Nevertheless, at first they felt shrunken and out of place, as Londoners do when they get outside London. Gordon felt as though he had been living underground for a long time past. He felt etiolated and unkempt. He slipped behind Rosemary as they walked, so that she should not see his lined, colourless face. Also, they were out of breath before they had walked far, because they were only used to London walking, and for the first half hour they scarcely talked. They plunged into the woods and started westward, with not much idea of where they were making for—anywhere, so long as it was away from London. All round them the beech-trees soared, curiously phallic with their smooth skin-like bark and their flutings at the base. Nothing grew at their roots, but the dried leaves were strewn so thickly that in the distance the slopes looked like folds of copper-coloured silk. Not a soul seemed to be awake. Presently Gordon came level with Rosemary. They walked on hand in hand, swishing through the dry coppery leaves that had drifted into the ruts. Sometimes they came out on to stretches of road where they passed huge desolate houses—opulent country houses, once, in the carriage days, but now deserted and unsaleable. Down the road the mist-dimmed hedges wore that strange purplish brown, the colour of brown madder, that naked brushwood takes on in winter. There were a few birds about—jays, sometimes, passing between the trees with dipping flight, and pheasants that loitered across the road with long tails trailing, almost as tame as hens, as though knowing they were safe on Sunday. But in half an hour Gordon and Rosemary had not passed a human being. Sleep lay upon the countryside. It was hard to believe that they were only twenty miles out of London.

Presently they had walked themselves into trim. They had got their second wind and the blood glowed in their veins. It was one of those days when you feel you could walk a hundred miles if necessary. Suddenly, as they came out on to the road again, the dew all down the hedge glittered with a diamond flash. The sun had pierced the clouds. The light came slanting and yellow across the fields, and delicate unexpected colours sprang out in everything, as though some giant's child had been let loose with a new paintbox. Rosemary caught Gordon's arm and pulled him against her.

'Oh, Gordon, what a *lovely* day!'

'Lovely.'

'And, oh, look, look! Look at all the rabbits in that field!'

Sure enough, at the other end of the field, innumerable rabbits were browsing, almost like a flock of sheep. Suddenly there was a flurry under the hedge. A rabbit had been lying there. It leapt from its nest in the grass with a flirt of dew and dashed away down the field, its white tail lifted. Rosemary threw herself into Gordon's arms. It was astonishingly warm, as warm as summer. They pressed their bodies together in a sort of sexless rapture, like children. Here in the open air he could see the marks of time quite clearly upon her face. She was nearly thirty, and looked it, and he was nearly thirty, and looked more; and it mattered nothing. He pulled off the absurd flat hat. The three white hairs gleamed on her crown. At the moment he did not wish them away. They were part of her and therefore lovable.

'What fun to be here alone with you! I'm so glad we came!'

'And, oh, Gordon, to think we've got all day together! And it might so easily have rained. How lucky we are!'

'Yes. We'll burn a sacrifice to the immortal gods, presently.'

They were extravagantly happy. As they walked on they fell into absurd enthusiasms over everything they saw: over a jay's feather that they picked up, blue as lapis lazuli; over a stagnant pool like a jet mirror, with boughs reflected deep down in it; over the fungi that sprouted from the trees like monstrous horizontal ears. They discussed for a long time what would be the best epithet to describe a beech-tree. Both agreed that beeches look more like sentient creatures than other trees. It is because of the smoothness of their bark, probably, and the curious limb-like way in which the boughs sprout from the trunk. Gordon said that the little knobs on the bark were like the nipples of breasts and that the sinuous upper boughs, with their smooth sooty skin, were like the writhing trunks of elephants. They argued about similes and metaphors. From time to time they quarrelled vigorously, according to their custom. Gordon began to tease her by finding ugly similes for everything they passed. He said that the russet foliage of the hornbeams was like the hair of Burne-Jones maidens, and that the smooth tentacles of the ivy that wound about the trees were like the clinging arms of Dickens heroines. Once he insisted upon destroying some mauve toadstools because he said they reminded him of a Rackham illustration and he suspected fairies of dancing round them. Rosemary called him a soulless pig. She waded through a bed of drifted beech leaves that rustled about her, knee-deep, like a weightless red-gold sea.

'Oh, Gordon, these leaves! Look at them with the sun on them! They're like gold. They really are like gold.'

'Fairy gold. You'll be going all Barrie in another moment. As a matter of fact, if you want an exact simile, they're just the colour of tomato soup.'

'Don't be a pig, Gordon! Listen how they rustle. "Thick as autumnal leaves that strow the brooks in Vallombrosa." '

'Or like one of those American breakfast cereals. Truweet Breakfast Crisps. "Kiddies clamour for their Breakfast Crisps." '

'You are a beast!'

She laughed. They walked on hand in hand, swishing ankle-deep through the leaves and declaiming:

> 'Thick as the Breakfast Crisps that strow the plates
> In Welwyn Garden City!'

It was great fun. Presently they came out of the wooded area. There were plenty of people abroad now, but not many cars if you kept away from the main roads. Sometimes they heard church bells ringing and made detours to avoid the churchgoers. They began to pass through straggling villages on whose outskirts pseudo-Tudor villas stood sniffishly apart, amid their garages, their laurel shrubberies and their raw-looking lawns. And Gordon had some fun railing against the villas and the godless civilization of which they were part—a civilization of stockbrokers and their lip-sticked wives, of golf, whisky, ouija-boards, and Aberdeen terriers called Jock. So they walked another four miles or so, talking and frequently quarrelling. A few gauzy clouds were drifting across the sky, but there was hardly a breath of wind.

They were growing rather footsore and more and more hungry. Of its own accord the conversation began to turn upon food. Neither of them had a watch, but when they passed through a village they saw that the pubs were open, so that it must be after twelve o'clock. They hesitated outside a rather low-looking pub called the Bird in Hand. Gordon was for going in; privately he reflected that in a pub like that your bread and cheese and beer would cost you a bob at the very most. But Rosemary said that it was a nasty-looking place, which indeed it was, and they went on, hoping to find a pleasanter pub at the other end of the village. They had visions of a cosy bar-parlour, with an oak settle and perhaps a stuffed pike in a glass case on the wall.

But there were no more pubs in the village, and presently they were in open country again, with no houses in sight and not even any signposts. Gordon and Rosemary began to be alarmed. At two the pubs would shut, and then there would be no food to be had, except perhaps a packet of biscuits from some village sweetshop. At this thought a ravening hunger took possession of them. They toiled exhaustedly up an enormous hill, hoping to find a village on the other side. There was no village, but far below a dark green river wound, with what seemed quite like a large town scattered along its edge and a grey bridge crossing it. They did not even know what river it was—it was the Thames, of course.

'Thank God!' said Gordon. 'There must be plenty of pubs down there. We'd better take the first one we can find.'

'Yes, do let's. I'm starving.'

But when they neared the town it seemed strangely quiet. Gordon wondered whether the people were all at church or eating their Sunday dinners, until he realized that the place was quite deserted. It was Crickham-on-Thames, one of those riverside towns which live for the boating season and go into hibernation for the rest of the year. It straggled along the bank for a mile or more, and it consisted entirely of boat-houses and bungalows, all of them shut up and empty. There were no signs of life anywhere. At last, however, they came upon a fat, aloof, red-nosed man, with a ragged moustache, sitting on a camp-stool beside a jar of beer on the towpath. He was fishing with a twenty-foot roach pole, while on the smooth green water two swans circled about his float, trying to steal his bait as often as he pulled it up.

'Can you tell us where we can get something to eat?' said Gordon.

The fat man seemed to have been expecting this question and to derive a sort of private pleasure from it. He answered without looking at Gordon.

'*You* won't get nothing to eat. Not here you won't,' he said.

'But dash it! Do you mean to say there isn't a pub in the whole place? We've walked all the way from Farnham Common.'

The fat man sniffed and seemed to reflect, still keeping his eye on the float.

'I dessay you might try the Ravenscroft Hotel,' he said. 'About half a mile along, that is. I dessay they'd give you something; that is, they would if they was open.'

'But *are* they open?'

'They might be and they might not,' said the fat man comfortably.

'And can you tell us what time it is?' said Rosemary.

'It's jest gone ten parse one.'

The two swans followed Gordon and Rosemary a little way along the towpath, evidently expecting to be fed. There did not seem much hope that the Ravenscroft Hotel would be open. The whole place had that desolate flyblown air of pleasure resorts in the off-season. The woodwork of the bungalows was cracking, the white paint was peeling off, the dusty windows showed bare interiors. Even the slot machines that were dotted along the bank were out of order. There seemed to be another bridge at the other end of the town. Gordon swore heartily.

'What bloody fools we were not to go in that pub when we had the chance!'

'Oh, dear! I'm simply *starving*. Had we better turn back, do you think?'

'It's no use, there were no pubs the way we came. We must keep on. I suppose the Ravenscroft Hotel's on the other side of that bridge. If that's a main road there's just a chance it'll be open. Otherwise we're sunk.'

They dragged their way as far as the bridge. They were thoroughly footsore now. But behold! here at last was what they wanted, for just beyond the bridge, down a sort of private road, stood a biggish, smartish hotel, its back lawns running down to the river. It was obviously open. Gordon and Rosemary started eagerly towards it, and then paused, daunted.

'It looks frightfully expensive,' said Rosemary.

It did look expensive. It was a vulgar pretentious place, all gilt and white paint—one of those hotels which have overcharging and bad service written on every brick. Beside the drive, commanding the road, a snobbish board announced in gilt lettering:

THE RAVENSCROFT HOTEL

OPEN TO NON-RESIDENTS

LUNCHEONS–TEAS–DINNERS

DANCE HALL AND TENNIS COURTS

PARTIES CATERED FOR

Two gleaming two-seater cars were parked in the drive. Gordon quailed. The money in his pocket seemed to shrink to nothing, this was the very opposite to the cosy pub they had been looking for. But he was very hungry. Rosemary tweaked at his arm.

'It looks a beastly place. I vote we go on.'

'But we've got to get some food. It's our last chance. We shan't find another pub.'

'The food's always so disgusting in these places. Beastly cold beef that tastes as if it had been saved up from last year. And they charge you the earth for it.'

'Oh, well, we'll just order bread and cheese and beer. It always costs about the same.'

'But they hate you doing that. They'll try to bully us into having a proper lunch, you'll see. We must be firm and just say bread and cheese.'

'All right, we'll be firm. Come on.'

They went in, resolved to be firm. But there was an expensive smell in the draughty hallway—a smell of chintz, dead flowers, Thames water, and the rinsings of wine bottles. It was the characteristic smell of a riverside hotel. Gordon's heart sank lower. He knew the type of place this was. It was one of those desolate hotels which exist all along the motor roads and are frequented by stockbrokers airing their whores on Sunday afternoons. In such places you are insulted and overcharged almost as a matter of course. Rosemary shrank nearer to him. She too was intimidated. They saw a door marked 'Saloon' and pushed it open, thinking it must be the bar. It was not a bar, however, but a large, smart, chilly room with corduroy-upholstered chairs and settees. You could have mistaken it for an ordinary drawing-room except that all the ashtrays advertised White Horse whisky. And round one of the tables the people from the cars outside—two blond, flat-headed, fattish men, over-youthfully dressed, and two disagreeable elegant young women—were sitting, having evidently just finished lunch. A waiter, bending over their table, was serving them with liqueurs.

Gordon and Rosemary had halted in the doorway. The people at the table were already eyeing them with offensive upper-middle-class eyes. Gordon and Rosemary looked tired and dirty, and they knew it. The notion of ordering bread and cheese and beer had almost vanished from their minds. In such a place as this you couldn't possibly say 'Bread and cheese and beer'; 'Lunch' was the only thing you could say. There was nothing for it but 'Lunch' or flight. The waiter was almost openly contemptuous. He had summed them up at a glance as having no money; but also he had divined that it was in their minds to fly and was determined to stop them before they could escape.

'Sare?' he demanded, lifting his tray off the table.

Now for it! Say 'Bread and cheese and beer', and damn the consequences! Alas! his courage was gone. 'Lunch' it would have to be. With a seeming-careless gesture he thrust his hand into his pocket. He was feeling his money to make sure that it was still there. Seven and elevenpence left, he knew. The waiter's eye followed the movement; Gordon had a hateful feeling that the man could actually see through the cloth and count the money in his pocket. In a tone as lordly as he could make it, he remarked:

'Can we have some lunch, please?'

'Luncheon, sare? Yes, sare. Zees way.'

The waiter was a black-haired young man with a very smooth, well-featured, sallow face. His dress clothes were excellently cut and yet unclean-looking, as though he seldom took them off. He looked like a Russian prince; probably he was an Englishman and had assumed a foreign accent because this was proper in a waiter. Defeated, Rosemary and Gordon followed him to the dining-room, which was at the back, giving on to the lawn. It was exactly like an aquarium. It was built entirely of greenish glass, and it was so damp and chilly that you could almost have fancied yourself under water. You could both see and smell the river outside. In the middle of each of the small round tables there was a bowl of paper flowers, but at one side, to complete the aquarium effect, there was a whole florist's stand of evergreens, palms, and aspidistras and so forth, like dreary water-plants. In summer such a room might be pleasant enough; at present, when the sun had gone behind a cloud, it was merely dank and miserable. Rosemary was almost as much afraid of the waiter as Gordon was. As they sat down and he turned away for a moment she made a face at his back.

'I'm going to pay for my own lunch,' she whispered to Gordon, across the table.

'No, you're not.'

'What a horrible place! The food's sure to be filthy. I do wish we hadn't come.'

'Sh!'

The waiter had come back with a flyblown printed menu. He handed it to Gordon and stood over him with the menacing air of a waiter who knows that you have not much money in your pocket. Gordon's heart pounded. If it was a table d'hôte lunch at three and sixpence or even half a crown, they were sunk. He set his teeth and looked at the menu. Thank God! It was à la carte. The cheapest thing on the list was cold beef and salad for one and sixpence. He said, or rather mumbled:

'We'll have some cold beef, please.'

The waiter's delicate eyebrows lifted. He feigned surprise.

'*Only* ze cold beef, sare?'

'Yes that'll do to go on with, anyway.'

'But you will not have *anysing* else, sare?'

'Oh, well. Bring us some bread, of course. And butter.'

'But no soup to start wiz, sare?'

'No. No soup.'

'Nor any fish, sare? Only ze cold beef?'

'Do we want any fish, Rosemary? I don't think we do. No. No fish.'

'Nor any sweet to follow, sare? *Only* ze cold beef?'

Gordon had difficulty in controlling his features. He thought he had never hated anyone so much as he hated this waiter.

'We'll tell you afterwards if we want anything else,' he said.

'And you will drink sare?'

Gordon had meant to ask for beer, but he hadn't the courage now. He had got to win back his prestige after this affair of the cold beef.

'Bring me the wine list,' he said flatly.

Another flyblown list was produced. All the wines looked impossibly expensive. However, at the very top of the list there was some nameless table claret at two and nine a bottle. Gordon made hurried calculations. He could just manage two and nine. He indicated the wine with his thumbnail.

'Bring us a bottle of this,' he said.

The waiter's eyebrows rose again. He essayed a stroke of irony.

'You will have ze *whole* bottle, sare? You would not prefare ze half bottle?'

'A whole bottle,' said Gordon coldly.

All in a single delicate movement of contempt the waiter inclined his head, shrugged his left shoulder, and turned away. Gordon could not stand it. He caught Rosemary's eye across the table. Somehow or other they had got to put that waiter in his place! In a moment the waiter came back, carrying the bottle of cheap wine by the neck, and half concealing it behind his coat tails, as though it were something a little indecent or unclean. Gordon had thought of a way to avenge himself. As the waiter displayed the bottle he put out a hand, felt it, and frowned.

'That's not the way to serve red wine,' he said.

Just for a moment the waiter was taken aback. 'Sare?' he said.

'It's stone cold. Take the bottle away and warm it.'

'Very good, sare.'

But it was not really a victory. The waiter did not look abashed. Was the wine worth warming? his raised eyebrow said. He bore the bottle away with easy disdain, making it quite clear to Rosemary and Gordon that it was bad enough to order the cheapest wine on the list without making this fuss about it afterwards.

The beef and salad were corpse-cold and did not seem like real food at all. They tasted like water. The rolls, also, though stale, were damp. The reedy Thames water seemed to have got into everything. It was no surprise that when the wine was opened it tasted like mud. But it was alcoholic, that was the great thing. It was quite a surprise to find how stimulating it was, once you had got it past your gullet and into your stomach. After drinking a glass and a half Gordon felt very much better. The waiter stood by the door, ironically patient, his napkin over his arm, trying to make Gordon and Rosemary uncomfortable by his presence. At first he succeeded, but Gordon's back was towards him, and he disregarded him and presently almost forgot him. By degrees their courage returned. They began to talk more easily and in louder voices.

'Look,' said Gordon. 'Those swans have followed us all the way up here.'

Sure enough, there were the two swans sailing vaguely to and fro over the dark green water. And at this moment the sun burst out again and the dreary aquarium of a dining-room was flooded with pleasant greenish light. Gordon and Rosemary felt suddenly warm and happy. They began chattering about nothing, almost as though the waiter had not been there, and Gordon took up the bottle and poured out two more glasses of wine. Over their glasses their eyes met. She was looking at him with a sort of yielding irony. 'I'm your mistress,' her eyes said; 'what a joke!' Their knees were touching under the small table; momentarily she squeezed his knee between her own. Something leapt inside him; a warm wave of sensuality and tenderness crept up his body. He had remembered! She was his girl, his mistress. Presently, when they were alone, in some hidden place in the warm, windless air, he would have her naked body all for his own at last. True, all the morning he had known this, but somehow the knowledge had been unreal. It was only now that he grasped it. Without words said, with a sort of bodily certainty, he knew that within an hour she would be in his arms, naked. As they sat there in the warm light, their knees touching, their eyes meeting, they felt as though already everything had been accomplished. There was deep intimacy between them. They could have sat there for hours, just looking at one another and talking of trivial things that had meanings for them and for nobody else. They did sit there for twenty minutes or more. Gordon had forgotten the waiter—had even forgotten, momentarily, the disaster of being let in for this wretched lunch that was going to strip him of every penny he had. But presently the sun went in, the room grew grey again, and they realized that it was time to go.

'The bill,' said Gordon, turning half round.

The waiter made a final effort to be offensive.

'Ze bill, sare? But you do not wish any coffee, sare?'

'No, no coffee. The bill.'

The waiter retired and came back with a folded slip on a salver. Gordon opened it. Six and threepence—and he had exactly seven and elevenpence in

the world! Of course he had known approximately what the bill must be, and
yet it was a shock now that it came. He stood up, felt in his pocket, and took out
all his money. The sallow young waiter, his salver on his arm, eyed the handful
of money; plainly he divined that it was all Gordon had. Rosemary also had got
up and come round the table. She pinched Gordon's elbow; this was a signal
that she would like to pay her share. Gordon pretended not to notice. He paid
the six and threepence, and, as he turned away, dropped another shilling on to
the salver. The waiter balanced it for a moment on his hand, flicked it over, and
then slipped it into his waistcoat pocket with the air of covering up something
unmentionable.

As they went down the passage, Gordon felt dismayed, helpless—dazed,
almost. All his money gone at a single swoop! It was a ghastly thing to happen.
If only they had not come to this accursed place! The whole day was ruined
now—and all for the sake of a couple of plates of cold beef and a bottle of muddy
wine! Presently there would be tea to think about, and he had only six
cigarettes left, and there were the bus fares back to Slough and God knew what
else; and he had just eightpence to pay for the lot! They got outside the hotel
feeling as if they had been kicked out and the door slammed behind them. All
the warm intimacy of a moment ago was gone. Everything seemed different
now that they were outside. Their blood seemed to grow suddenly cooler in the
open air. Rosemary walked ahead of him, rather nervous, not speaking. She
was half frightened now by the thing she had resolved to do. He watched her
strong delicate limbs moving. There was her body that he had wanted so long;
but now when the time had come it only daunted him. He wanted her to be his,
he wanted to *have had* her, but he wished it were over and done with. It was an
effort—a thing he had got to screw himself up to. It was strange that that beastly
business of the hotel bill could have upset him so completely. The easy
carefree mood of the morning was shattered; in its place there had come back
the hateful, harassing, familiar thing—worry about money. In a minute he
would have to own up that he had only eightpence left; he would have to
borrow money off her to get them home; it would be squalid and shameful.
Only the wine inside him kept up his courage. The warmth of the wine, and the
hateful feeling of having only eightpence left, warred together in his body,
neither getting the better of the other.

They walked rather slowly, but soon they were away from the river and on
higher ground again. Each searched desperately for something to say and
could think of nothing. He came level with her, took her hand, and wound her
fingers within his own. Like that they felt better. But his heart beat painfully,
his entrails were constricted. He wondered whether she felt the same.

'There doesn't seem to be a soul about,' she said at last.

'It's Sunday afternoon. They're all asleep under the aspidistra, after roast
beef and Yorkshire.'

There was another silence. They walked on fifty yards or so. With difficulty
mastering his voice, he managed to say:

'It's extraordinarily warm. We might sit down for a bit if we can find a
place.'

'Yes, all right. If you like.'

Presently they came to a small copse on the left of the road. It looked dead and empty, nothing growing under the naked trees. But at the corner of the copse, on the far side, there was a great tangled patch of sloe or blackthorn bushes. He put his arm round her without saying anything and turned her in that direction. There was a gap in the hedge with some barbed wire strung across it. He held the wire up for her and she slipped nimbly under it. His heart leapt again. How supple and strong she was! But as he climbed over the wire to follow her, the eightpence—a sixpence and two pennies—clinked in his pocket, daunting him anew.

When they got to the bushes they found a natural alcove. On three sides were beds of thorns, leafless but impenetrable, and on the other side you looked downhill over a sweep of naked ploughed fields. At the bottom of the hill stood a low-roofed cottage, tiny as a child's toy, its chimneys smokeless. Not a creature was stirring anywhere. You could not have been more alone than in such a place. The grass was the fine mossy stuff that grows under trees.

'We ought to have brought a mackintosh,' he said. He had knelt down.

'It doesn't matter. The ground's fairly dry.'

He pulled her to the ground beside him, kissed her, pulled off the flat felt hat, lay upon her breast to breast, kissed her face all over. She lay under him, yielding rather than responding. She did not resist when his hand sought her breasts. But in her heart she was still frightened. She would do it—oh, yes! she would keep her implied promise, she would not draw back; but all the same she was frightened. And at heart he too was half reluctant. It dismayed him to find how little, at this moment, he really wanted her. The money-business still unnerved him. How can you make love when you have only eightpence in your pocket and are thinking about it all the time? Yet in a way he wanted her. Indeed, he could not do without her. His life would be a different thing when once they were really lovers. For a long time he lay on her breast, her head turned sideways, his face against her neck and hair, attempting nothing further.

Then the sun came out again. It was getting low in the sky now. The warm light poured over them as though a membrane across the sky had broken. It had been a little cold on the grass, really, with the sun behind the clouds; but now once again it was almost as warm as summer. Both of them sat up to exclaim at it.

'Oh, Gordon, look! Look how the sun's lighting everything up!'

As the clouds melted away a widening yellow beam slid swiftly across the valley, gilding everything in its path. Grass that had been dull green shone suddenly emerald. The empty cottage below sprang out into warm colours, purply-blue of tiles, cherry-red of brick. Only the fact that no birds were singing reminded you that it was winter. Gordon put his arm round Rosemary and pulled her hard against him. They sat cheek to cheek, looking down the hill. He turned her round and kissed her.

'You do like me, don't you?'

'Adore you, silly.'

'And you're going to be nice to me, aren't you?'

'Nice to you?'

'Let me do what I want with you?'

'Yes, I expect so.'

'Anything?'

'Yes, all right. Anything.'

He pressed her back upon the grass. It was quite different now. The warmth of the sun seemed to have got into their bones. 'Take your clothes off, there's a dear,' he whispered. She did it readily enough. She had no shame before him. Besides, it was so warm and the place was so solitary that it did not matter how many clothes you took off. They spread her clothes out and made a sort of bed for her to lie on. Naked, she lay back, her hands behind her head, her eyes shut, smiling slightly, as though she had considered everything and were at peace in her mind. For a long time he knelt and gazed at her body. Its beauty startled him. She looked much younger naked than with her clothes on. Her face, thrown back, with eyes shut, looked almost childish. He moved closer to her. Once again the coins clinked in his pocket. Only eightpence left! Trouble coming presently. But he wouldn't think of it now. Get on with it, that's the great thing, get on with it and damn the future! He put an arm beneath her and laid his body to hers.

'May I?—now?'

'Yes. All right.'

'You're not frightened?'

'No.'

'I'll be as gentle as I can with you.'

'It doesn't matter.'

A moment later:

'Oh, Gordon, no! No, no, no!'

'What? What is it?'

'No, Gordon, no! You mustn't! *No!*'

She put her hands against him and pushed him violently back. Her face looked remote, frightened, almost hostile. It was terrible to feel her push him away at such a moment. It was as though cold water had been dashed all over him. He fell back from her, dismayed, hurriedly rearranging his clothes.

'What is it? What's the matter?'

'Oh, Gordon! I thought you—oh, dear!'

She threw her arm over her face and rolled over on her side, away from him, suddenly ashamed.

'What is it?' he repeated.

'How could you be so *thoughtless*?'

'What do you mean—thoughtless?'

'Oh! you know what I mean!'

His heart shrank. He did know what she meant; but he had never thought of it till this moment. And of course—oh, yes!—he ought to have thought of it. He stood up and turned away from her. Suddenly he knew that he could go no further with this business. In a wet field on a Sunday afternoon—and in midwinter at that! Impossible! It seemed so right, so natural only a minute ago; now it seemed merely squalid and ugly.

'I didn't expect *this*,' he said bitterly.

'But I couldn't help it, Gordon! You ought to have–you know.'

'You don't think I go in for that kind of thing, do you?'

'But what else can we do? I can't have a baby, can I?'

'You must take your chance.'

'Oh, Gordon, how impossible you are!'

She lay looking up at him, her face full of distress, too overcome for the moment even to remember that she was naked. His disappointment had turned to anger. There you are, you see! Money again! Even the most secret action of your life you don't escape it; you've still got to spoil everything with filthy cold-blooded precautions for money's sake. Money, money, always money! Even in the bridal bed, the finger of the money-god intruding! In the heights or in the depths, he is there. He walked a pace or two up and down, his hands in his pockets.

'Money again, you see!' he said. 'Even at a moment like this it's got the power to stand over us and bully us. Even when we're alone and miles from anywhere, with not a soul to see us.'

'What's *money* got to do with it?'

'I tell you it'd never enter your head to worry about a baby if it wasn't for the money. You'd *want* the baby if it wasn't for that. You say you "can't" have a baby. What do you mean, you "can't" have a baby? You mean you daren't; because you'd lose your job and I've got no money and all of us would starve. This birth-control business! It's just another way they've found out of bullying us. And you want to acquiesce in it, apparently.'

'But what am I to do, Gordon? What am I to do?'

At this moment the sun disappeared behind the clouds. It became perceptibly colder. After all, the scene was grotesque–the naked woman lying in the grass, the dressed man standing moodily by with his hands in his pockets. She'd catch her death of cold in another moment, lying there like that. The whole thing was absurd and indecent.

'But what else am I to do?' she repeated.

'I should think you might start by putting your clothes on,' he said coldly.

He had only said it to avenge his irritation; but its result was to make her so painfully and obviously embarrassed that he had to turn his back on her. She had dressed herself in a very few moments. As she knelt lacing up her shoes he heard her sniff once or twice. She was on the point of crying and was struggling to restrain herself. He felt horribly ashamed. He would have liked to throw himself on his knees beside her, put his arms round her, and ask her pardon. But he could do nothing of the kind; the scene had left him lumpish and awkward. It was with difficulty that he could command his voice even for the most banal remark.

'Are you ready?' he said flatly.

'Yes.'

They went back to the road, climbed through the wire, and started down the hill without another word. Fresh clouds were rolling across the sun. It was getting much colder. Another hour and the early dusk would have fallen. They reached the bottom of the hill and came in sight of the Ravenscroft Hotel, scene of their disaster.

'Where are we going?' said Rosemary in a small sulky voice.

'Back to Slough, I suppose. We must cross the bridge and have a look at the signposts.'

They scarcely spoke again till they had gone several miles. Rosemary was embarrassed and miserable. A number of times she edged closer to him, meaning to take his arm, but he edged away from her; and so they walked abreast with almost the width of the road between them. She imagined that she had offended him mortally. She supposed that it was because of his disappointment—because she had pushed him away at the critical moment—that he was angry with her; she would have apologized if he had given her a quarter of a chance. But as a matter of fact he was scarcely thinking of this any longer. His mind had turned away from that side of things. It was the money-business that was troubling him now—the fact that he had only eightpence in his pocket. In a very little while he would have to confess it. There would be the bus fares from Farnham to Slough, and tea in Slough, and cigarettes, and more bus fares and perhaps another meal when they got back to London; and just eightpence to cover the lot! He would have to borrow from Rosemary after all. And that was so damned humiliating. It is hateful to have to borrow money off someone you have just been quarrelling with. What nonsense it made of all his fine attitudes! There was he, lecturing her, putting on superior airs, pretending to be shocked because she took contraception for granted; and the next moment turning round and asking her for money! But there you are, you see, that's what money can do. There is no attitude that money or the lack of it cannot puncture.

By half past four it was almost completely dark. They tramped along misty roads where there was no illumination save the cracks of cottage windows and the yellow beam of an occasional car. It was getting beastly cold, too, but they had walked four miles and the exercise had warmed them. It was impossible to go on being unsociable any longer. They began to talk more easily and by degrees they edged closer together. Rosemary took Gordon's arm. Presently she stopped him and swung him round to face her.

'Gordon, *why* are you so beastly to me?'

'How am I beastly to you?'

'Coming all this way without speaking a word!'

'Oh, well!'

'Are you still angry with me because of what happened just now?'

'No. I was never angry with you. *You're* not to blame.'

She looked up at him, trying to divine the expression of his face in the almost pitch darkness. He drew her against him, and, as she seemed to expect it, tilted her face back and kissed her. She clung to him eagerly; her body melted against his. She had been waiting for this, it seemed.

'Gordon, you do love me, don't you?'

'Of course I do.'

'Things went wrong somehow. I couldn't help it. I got frightened suddenly.'

'It doesn't matter. Another time it'll be all right.'

She was lying limp against him, her head on his breast. He could feel her heart beating. It seemed to flutter violently, as though she were taking some decision.

'I don't care,' she said indistinctly, her face buried in his coat.

'Don't care about what?'

'The baby. I'll risk it. You can do what you like with me.'

At these surrendering words a weak desire raised itself in him and died away at once. He knew why she had said it. It was not because, at this moment, she really wanted to be made love to. It was from a mere generous impulse to let him know that she loved him and would take a dreaded risk rather than disappoint him.

'Now?' he said.

'Yes, if you like.'

He considered. He so wanted to be sure that she was his! But the cold night air flowed over them. Behind the hedges the long grass would be wet and chill. This was not the time or the place. Besides, that business of the eightpence had usurped his mind. He was not in the mood any longer.

'I can't,' he said finally.

'You can't! But, Gordon! I thought–'

'I know. But it's all different now.'

'You're still upset?'

'Yes. In a way.'

'Why?'

He pushed her a little away from him. As well have the explanation now as later. Nevertheless he was so ashamed that he mumbled rather than said:

'I've got a beastly thing to say to you. It's been worrying me all the way along.'

'What is it?'

'It's this. Can you lend me some money? I'm absolutely cleaned out. I had just enough money for today, but that beastly hotel bill upset everything. I've only eightpence left.'

Rosemary was amazed. She broke right out of his arms in her amazement.

'Only eightpence left! What *are* you talking about? What does it matter if you've only eightpence left?'

'Don't I tell you I shall have to borrow money off you in another minute? You'll have to pay for your own bus fares, and my bus fares, and your tea and Lord knows what. And I asked you to come out with me! You're supposed to be my guest. It's bloody.'

'Your *guest*! Oh, Gordon. Is *that* what's been worrying you all this time?'

'Yes.'

'Gordon, you *are* a baby! How can you let yourself be worried by a thing like that? As though I minded lending you money! Aren't I always telling you I want to pay my share when we go out together?'

'Yes, and you know how I hate your paying. We had that out the other night.'

'Oh, how absurd, how absurd you are! Do you think there's anything to be ashamed of in having no money?'

'Of course there is! It's the only thing in the world there *is* to be ashamed of.'

'But what's it got to do with you and me making love, anyway? I don't understand you. First you want to and then you don't want to. What's money got to do with it?'

'Everything.'

He wound her arm in his and started down the road. She would never understand. Nevertheless he had got to explain.

'Don't you understand that one isn't a full human being—that one doesn't *feel* a human being—unless one's got money in one's pocket?'

'No. I think that's just silly.'

'It isn't that I don't want to make love to you. I do. But I tell you I can't make love to you when I've only eightpence in my pocket. At least when you know I've only eightpence. I just can't do it. It's physically impossible.'

'But why? Why?'

'You'll find it in Lemprière,' he said obscurely.

That settled it. They talked no more about it. For the second time he had behaved grossly badly and yet he had made her feel as if it were she who was in the wrong. They walked on. She did not understand him; on the other hand, she forgave him everything. Presently they reached Farnham Common, and, after a wait at the cross road, got a bus to Slough. In the darkness, as the bus loomed near, Rosemary found Gordon's hand and slipped half a crown into it, so that he might pay the fares and not be shamed in public by letting a woman pay for him.

For his own part Gordon would sooner have walked to Slough and saved the bus fares, but he knew Rosemary would refuse. In Slough, also, he was for taking the train straight back to London, but Rosemary said indignantly that she wasn't going to go without her tea, so they went to a large, dreary, draughty hotel near the station. Tea, with little wilting sandwiches and rock cakes like balls of putty, was two shillings a head. It was torment to Gordon to let her pay for his food. He sulked, ate nothing, and, after a whispered argument, insisted on contributing his eightpence towards the cost of the tea.

It was seven o'clock when they took the train back to London. The train was full of tired hikers in khaki shorts. Rosemary and Gordon did not talk much. They sat close together, Rosemary with her arm twined through his, playing with his hand, Gordon looking out of the window. People in the carriage eyed them, wondering what they had quarrelled about. Gordon watched the lamp-starred darkness streaming past. So the day to which he had looked forward was ended. And now back to Willowbed Road, with a penniless week ahead. For a whole week, unless some miracle happened, he wouldn't even be able to buy himself a cigarette. What a bloody fool he had been! Rosemary was not angry with him. By the pressure of her hand she tried to make it clear to him that she loved him. His pale discontented face, turned half away from her, his shabby coat, and his unkempt mouse-coloured hair that wanted cutting more than ever, filled her with profound pity. She felt more tenderly towards him than she would have done if everything had gone well, because in her feminine way she grasped that he was unhappy and that life was difficult for him.

'See me home, will you?' she said as they got out at Paddington.

'If you don't mind walking. I haven't got the fare.'

'But let *me* pay the fare. Oh, dear! I suppose you won't. But how are you going to get home yourself?'

'Oh, I'll walk. I know the way. It's not very far.'

'I hate to think of you walking all that way. You look so tired. Be a dear and let me pay your fare home. *Do!*'

'No. You've paid quite enough for me already.'

'Oh, dear! You are so silly!'

They halted at the entrance to the Underground. He took her hand. 'I suppose we must say good-bye for the present,' he said.

'Good-bye, Gordon dear. Thanks ever so much for taking me out. It was such fun this morning.'

'Ah, this morning! It was different then.' His mind went back to the morning hours, when they had been alone on the road together and there was still money in his pocket. Compunction seized him. On the whole he had behaved badly. He pressed her hand a little tighter. 'You're not angry with me, are you?'

'No, silly, of course not.'

'I didn't mean to be beastly to you. It was the money. It's always the money.'

'Never mind, it'll be better next time. We'll go to some better place. We'll go down to Brighton for the week-end, or something.'

'Perhaps, when I've got the money. You will write soon, won't you?'

'Yes.'

'Your letters are the only things that keep me going. Tell me when you'll write, so that I can have your letter to look forward to.'

'I'll write tomorrow night and post it on Tuesday. Then you'll get it last post on Tuesday night.'

'Then good-bye, Rosemary dear.'

'Good-bye, Gordon darling.'

He left her at the booking-office. When he had gone twenty yards he felt a hand laid on his arm. He turned sharply. It was Rosemary. She thrust a packet of twenty Gold Flake, which she had bought at the tobacco kiosk, into his coat pocket and ran back to the Underground before he could protest.

He trailed homeward through the wastes of Marylebone and Regent's Park. It was the fag-end of the day. The streets were dark and desolate, with that strange listless feeling of Sunday night when people are more tired after a day of idleness than after a day of work. It was vilely cold, too. The wind had risen when the night fell. *Sharply the menacing wind sweeps over.* Gordon was footsore, having walked a dozen or fifteen miles, and also hungry. He had had little food all day. In the morning he had hurried off without a proper breakfast, and the lunch at the Ravenscroft Hotel wasn't the kind of meal that did you much good; since then he had had no solid food. However, there was no hope of getting anything when he got home. He had told Mother Wisbeach that he would be away all day.

When he reached the Hampstead Road he had to wait on the kerb to let a stream of cars go past. Even here everything seemed dark and gloomy, in spite of the glaring lamps and the cold glitter of the jewellers' windows. The raw wind pierced his thin clothes, making him shiver. *Sharply the menacing wind sweeps over The bending poplars, newly bare.* He had finished that poem, all except the last two lines. He thought again of those hours this morning—the empty misty roads, the feeling of freedom and adventure, of having the whole day and the whole country before you in which to wander at will. It was having money that did it, of course. Seven and elevenpence he had had in his pocket this morning. It had been a brief victory over the money-god; a morning's apostasy, a holiday in the groves of Ashtaroth. But such things never last. Your money goes and your freedom with it. Circumcise ye your foreskins, saith the Lord. And back we creep, duly snivelling.

Another shoal of cars swam past. One in particular caught his eye, a long slender thing, elegant as a swallow, all gleaming blue and silver; a thousand guineas it would have cost, he thought. A blue-clad chauffeur sat at the wheel, upright, immobile, like some scornful statue. At the back, in the pink-lit interior, four elegant young people, two youths, and two girls, were smoking cigarettes and laughing. He had a glimpse of sleek bunny-faces; faces of ravishing pinkness and smoothness, lit by that peculiar inner glow that can never be counterfeited, the soft warm radiance of money.

He crossed the road. No food tonight. However, there was still oil in the lamp, thank God; he would have a secret cup of tea when he got back. At this moment he saw himself and his life without saving disguises. Every night the same—back to the cold lonely bedroom and the grimy littered sheets of the poem that never got any further. It was a blind alley. He would never finish *London Pleasures,* he would never marry Rosemary, he would never set his life in order. He would only drift and sink, drift and sink, like the others of his family; but worse than them—down, down into some dreadful sub-world that as yet he could only dimly imagine. It was what he had chosen when he declared war on money. Serve the money-god or go under; there is no other rule.

Something deep below made the stone street shiver. The tube-train, sliding through middle earth. He had a vision of London, of the western world; he saw a thousand million slaves toiling and grovelling about the throne of money. The earth is ploughed, ships sail, miners sweat in dripping tunnels underground, clerks hurry for the eight-fifteen with the fear of the boss eating at their vitals. And even in bed with their wives they tremble and obey. Obey whom? The money-priesthood, the pink-faced masters of the world. The Upper Crust. A welter of sleek young rabbits in thousand guinea motor cars, of golfing stockbrokers and cosmopolitan financiers, of Chancery lawyers and fashionable Nancy boys, of bankers, newspaper peers, novelists of all four sexes, American pugilists, lady aviators, film stars, bishops, titled poets, and Chicago gorillas.

When he had gone another fifty yards the rhyme for the final stanza of his poem occurred to him. He walked homeward, repeating the poem to himself:

> Sharply the menacing wind sweeps over
> The bending poplars, newly bare,
> And the dark ribbons of the chimneys
> Veer downward; flicked by whips of air,
>
> Torn posters flutter; coldly sound
> The boom of trams and the rattle of hooves,
> And the clerks who hurry to the station
> Look, shuddering, over the eastern rooves,
>
> Thinking, each one, 'Here comes the winter!
> Please God I keep my job this year!'
> And bleakly, as the cold strikes through
> Their entrails like an icy spear,
>
> They think of rent, rates, season tickets,
> Insurance, coal, the skivvy's wages,
> Boots, school-bills, and the next instalment
> Upon the two twin beds from Drage's.
>
> For if in careless summer days
> In groves of Ashtaroth we whored,
> Repentant now, when winds blow cold,
> We kneel before our rightful lord;
>
> The lord of all, the money-god,
> Who rules us blood and hand and brain,
> Who gives the roof that stops the wind,
> And, giving, takes away again;
>
> Who spies with jealous, watchful care,
> Our thoughts, our dreams, our secret ways,
> Who picks our words and cuts our clothes,
> And maps the pattern of our days;
>
> Who chills our anger, curbs our hope,
> And buys our lives and pays with toys,
> Who claims as tribute broken faith,
> Accepted insults, muted joys;
>
> Who binds with chains the poet's wit,
> The navvy's strength, the soldier's pride,
> And lays the sleek, estranging shield
> Between the lover and his bride.

# 8

As the clock struck one Gordon slammed the shop door to and hurried, almost ran, to the branch of the Westminster Bank down the street.

With a half-conscious gesture of caution he was clutching the lapel of his coat, holding it tight against him. In there, stowed away in his right-hand inner pocket, was an object whose very existence he partly doubted. It was a stout blue envelope with an American stamp; in the envelope was a cheque for fifty dollars; and the cheque was made out to 'Gordon Comstock'!

He could feel the square shape of the envelope outlined against his body as clearly as though it had been red hot. All the morning he had felt it there, whether he touched it or whether he did not; he seemed to have developed a special patch of sensitiveness in the skin below his right breast. As often as once in ten minutes he had taken the cheque out of its envelope and anxiously examined it. After all, cheques are tricky things. It would be frightful if there turned out to be some hitch about the date or the signature. Besides, he might lose it—it might even vanish of its own accord like fairy gold.

The cheque had come from the *Californian Review*, that American magazine to which, weeks or months ago, he had despairingly sent a poem. He had almost forgotten about the poem, it had been so long away, until this morning their letter had come sailing out of the blue. And what a letter! No English editor ever writes letters like that. They were 'very favorably impressed' by his poem. They would 'endeavor' to include it in their next number. Would he 'favor' them by showing them some more of his work? (Would he? Oh, boy!—as Flaxman would say.) And the cheque had come with it. It seemed the most monstrous folly, in this year of blight 1934, that anyone should pay fifty dollars for a poem. However, there it was; and there was the cheque, which looked perfectly genuine however often he inspected it.

He would have no peace of mind till the cheque was cashed—for quite possibly the bank would refuse it—but already a stream of visions was flowing through his mind. Visions of girls' faces, visions of cobwebby claret bottles and quart pots of beer, visions of a new suit and his overcoat out of pawn, visions of a week-end at Brighton with Rosemary, visions of the crisp, crackling five pound note which he was going to give to Julia. Above all, of course, that fiver for Julia. It was almost the first thing he had thought of when the cheque came. Whatever else he did with the money, he must give Julia half of it. It was only the barest justice, considering how much he had 'borrowed' from her in all these years. All the morning the thought of Julia and the money he owed her had been cropping up in his mind at odd moments. It was a vaguely distasteful thought, however. He would forget about it for half an hour at a time, would plan a dozen ways of spending his ten pounds to the uttermost farthing, and then suddenly he would remember about Julia. Good old Julia! Julia should have her share. A fiver at the very least. Even that was not a tenth of what he owed her. For the twentieth time, with a faint malaise, he registered the thought: five quid for Julia.

The bank made no trouble about the cheque. Gordon had no banking account, but they knew him well, for Mr McKechnie banked there. They had cashed editors' cheques for Gordon before. There was only a minute's consultation, and then the cashier came back.

'Notes, Mr Comstock?'

'One five pound, and the rest pounds, please.'

The flimsy luscious fiver and the five clean pound notes slid rustling under the brass rail. And after them the cashier pushed a little pile of half-crowns and pennies. In lordly style Gordon shot the coins into his pocket without even counting them. That was a bit of backsheesh. He had only expected ten pounds for fifty dollars. The dollar must be above par. The five pound note, however, he carefully folded up and stowed away in the American envelope. That was Julia's fiver. It was sacrosanct. He would post it to her presently.

He did not go home for dinner. Why chew leathery beef in the aspidistral dining-room when he had ten quid in pocket—five quid, rather? (He kept forgetting that half the money was already mortgaged to Julia.) For the moment he did not bother to post Julia's five pounds. This evening would be soon enough. Besides, he rather enjoyed the feeling of it in his pocket. It was queer how different you felt with all that money in your pocket. Not opulent, merely, but reassured, revivified, reborn. He felt a different person from what he had been yesterday. He *was* a different person. He was no longer the downtrodden wretch who made secret cups of tea over the oil stove at 31 Willowbed Road. He was Gordon Comstock, the poet, famous on both sides of the Atlantic. Publications: *Mice* (1932), *London Pleasures* (1935). He thought with perfect confidence of *London Pleasures* now. In three months it should see the light. Demy octavo, white buckram covers. There was nothing that he did not feel equal to now that his luck had turned.

He strolled into the Prince of Wales for a bite of food. A cut off the joint and two veg., one and twopence, a pint of pale ale ninepence, twenty Gold Flakes a shilling. Even after that extravagance he still had well over ten pounds in hand—or rather, well over five pounds. Beer-warmed, he sat and meditated on the things you can do with five pounds. A new suit, a week-end in the country, a day-trip to Paris, five rousing drunks, ten dinners in Soho restaurants. At this point it occurred to him that he and Rosemary and Ravelston must certainly have dinner together tonight. Just to celebrate his stroke of luck; after all, it isn't every day that ten pounds—five pounds—drops out of the sky into your lap. The thought of the three of them together, with good food and wine and money no object took hold of him as something not to be resisted. He had just a tiny twinge of caution. Mustn't spend *all* his money, of course. Still, he could afford a quid—two quid. In a couple of minutes he had got Ravelston on the pub phone.

'Is that you, Ravelston? I say, Ravelston! Look here, you've got to have dinner with me tonight.'

From the other end of the line Ravelston faintly demurred. 'No, dash it! You have dinner with *me*.' But Gordon overbore him. Nonsense! Ravelston had got to have dinner with *him* tonight. Unwillingly, Ravelston assented. All right, yes, thanks; he'd like it very much. There was a sort of apologetic misery in his voice. He guessed what had happened. Gordon had got hold of money from somewhere and was squandering it immediately; as usual, Ravelston felt he hadn't the right to interfere. Where should they go? Gordon was demanding. Ravelston began to speak in praise of those jolly little Soho restaurants where you get such a wonderful dinner for half a crown. But the Soho restaurants sounded beastly as soon as Ravelston mentioned them. Gordon wouldn't hear of it. Nonsense! They must go somewhere decent. Let's do it all regardless, was his private thought; might as well spend two quid—three quid, even. Where did Ravelston generally go? Modigliani's, admitted Ravelston. But Modigliani's was very—but no! not even over the phone could Ravelston frame that hateful word 'expensive'. How remind Gordon of his poverty? Gordon mightn't care for Modigliani's, he euphemistically said. But Gordon was satisfied. Modigliani's? Right you are—half past eight. Good! After all, if he spent even three quid on the dinner he'd still have two quid to buy himself a new pair of shoes and a vest and a 'pair of pants.

He had fixed it up with Rosemary in another five minutes. The New Albion did not like their employees being rung up on the phone, but it did not matter once in a way. Since that disastrous Sunday journey, five days ago, he had heard from her once but had not seen her. She answered eagerly when she heard whose voice it was. Would she have dinner with him tonight? Of course! What fun! And so in ten minutes the whole thing was settled. He had always wanted Rosemary and Ravelston to meet, but somehow had never been able to contrive it. These things are so much easier when you've got a little money to spend.

The taxi bore him westward through the darkling streets. A three-mile journey—still, he could afford it. Why spoil the ship for a ha'porth of tar? He had dropped that notion of spending only two pounds tonight. He would spend three pounds, three pounds ten—four pounds if he felt like it. Slap up and regardless—that was the idea. And, oh! by the way! Julia's fiver. He hadn't sent it yet. No matter. Send it first thing in the morning. Good old Julia! She should have her fiver.

How voluptuous were the taxi cushions under his bum! He lolled this way and that. He had been drinking, of course—had had two quick ones, or possibly three, before coming away. The taxi-driver was a stout philosophic man with a weatherbeaten face and a knowing eye. He and Gordon understood one another. They had palled up in the bar where Gordon was having his quick ones. As they neared the West End the taximan drew up, unbidden, at a discreet pub on a corner. He knew what was in Gordon's mind. Gordon could do with a quick one. So could the taximan. But the drinks were on Gordon—that too was understood.

'You anticipated my thoughts,' said Gordon, climbing out.

'Yes, sir.'

'I could just about do with a quick one.'

'Thought you might, sir.'

'And could you manage one yourself, do you think?'

'Where there's a will there's a way,' said the taximan.

'Come inside,' said Gordon.

They leaned matily on the brass-edged bar, elbow to elbow, lighting two of the taximan's cigarettes. Gordon felt witty and expansive. He would have liked to tell the taximan the history of his life. The white-aproned barman hastened towards them.

'Yes sir?' said the barman.

'Gin,' said Gordon.

'Make it two,' said the taximan.

More matily than ever, they clinked glasses.

'Many happy returns,' said Gordon.

'Your birthday today, sir?'

'Only metaphorically. My re-birthday, so to speak.'

'I never had much education,' said the taximan.

'I was speaking in parables,' said Gordon.

'English is good enough for me,' said the taximan.

'It was the tongue of Shakespeare,' said Gordon.

'Literary gentleman, are you, sir, by any chance?'

'Do I look as moth-eaten as all that?'

'Not moth-eaten, sir. Only intellectual-like.'

'You're quite right. A poet.'

'Poet! It takes all sorts to make a world, don't it now?' said the taximan.

'And a bloody good world it is,' said Gordon.

His thoughts moved lyrically tonight. They had another gin and presently went back to the taxi all but arm in arm, after yet another gin. That made five gins Gordon had had this evening. There was an ethereal feeling in his veins; the gin seemed to be flowing there, mingled with his blood. He lay back in the corner of the seat, watching the great blazing skysigns swim across the bluish dark. The evil red and blue of the Neon lights pleased him at this moment. How smoothly the taxi glided! More like a gondola than a car. It was having money that did that. Money greased the wheels. He thought of the evening ahead of him; good food, good wine, good talk—above all, no worrying about money. No damned niggling with sixpences and 'We can't afford this' and 'We can't afford that!' Rosemary and Ravelston would try to stop him being extravagant. But he would shut them up. He'd spend every penny he had if he felt like it. Ten whole quid to bust! At least, five quid. The thought of Julia passed flickeringly through his mind and disappeared again.

He was quite sober when they got to Modigliani's. The monstrous commissionaire, like a great glittering waxwork with the minimum of joints,

stepped stiffly forward to open the taxi door. His grim eye looked askance at
Gordon's clothes. Not that you were expected to 'dress' at Modigliani's. They
were tremendously Bohemian at Modigliani's, of course; but there are ways
and ways of being Bohemian, and Gordon's way was the wrong way. Gordon
did not care. He bade the taximan an affectionate farewell, and tipped him half
a crown over his fare, whereat the commissionaire's eye looked a little less
grim. At this moment Ravelston emerged from the doorway. The
commissionaire knew Ravelston, of course. He lounged out on to the
pavement, a tall distinguished figure, aristocratically shabby, his eye rather
moody. He was worrying already about the money this dinner was going to
cost Gordon.

'Ah, there you are, Gordon!'

'Hullo, Ravelston! Where's Rosemary?'

'Perhaps she's waiting inside. I don't know her by sight, you know. But I
say, Gordon, look here! Before we go in, I wanted—'

'Ah, look, there she is!'

She was coming towards them, swift and debonair. She threaded her way
through the crowd with the air of some neat little destroyer gliding between
large clumsy cargo-boats. And she was nicely dressed, as usual. The sub-
shovel hat was cocked at its most provocative angle. Gordon's heart stirred.
There was a girl for you! He was proud that Ravelston should see her. She was
very gay tonight. It was written all over her that she was not going to remind
herself or Gordon of their last disastrous encounter. Perhaps she laughed and
talked just a little too vivaciously as Gordon introduced them and they went
inside. But Ravelston had taken a liking to her immediately. Indeed, everyone
who met her did take a liking to Rosemary. The inside of the restaurant
overawed Gordon for a moment. It was so horribly, artistically smart. Dark
gate-leg tables, pewter candlesticks, pictures by modern French painters on
the walls. One, a street scene, looked like a Utrillo. Gordon stiffened his
shoulders. Damn it, what was there to be afraid of? The five pound note was
tucked away in its envelope in his pocket. It was Julia's five pounds, of course;
he wasn't going to spend it. Still, its presence gave him moral support. It was a
kind of talisman. They were making for the corner table—Ravelston's favourite
table—at the far end. Ravelston took Gordon by the arm and drew him a little
back, out of Rosemary's hearing.

'Gordon, look here!'

'What?'

'Look here, you're going to have dinner with *me* tonight.'

'Bosh! This is on me.'

'I do wish you would. I hate to see you spending all that money.'

'We won't talk about money tonight,' said Gordon.

'Fifty-fifty, then,' pleaded Ravelston.

'It's on me,' said Gordon firmly.

Ravelston subsided. The fat, white-haired Italian waiter was bowing and
smiling beside the corner table. But it was at Ravelston, not at Gordon, that he
smiled. Gordon sat down with the feeling that he must assert himself quickly.

He waved away the menu which the waiter had produced.

'We must settle what we're going to drink first,' he said.

'Beer for me,' said Ravelston, with a sort of gloomy haste. 'Beer's the only drink I care about.'

'Me too,' echoed Rosemary.

'Oh, rot! We've got to have some wine. What do you like, red or white? Give me the wine list,' he said to the waiter.

'Then let's have a plain Bordeaux. Médoc or St Julien or something,' said Ravelston.

'I adore St Julien,' said Rosemary, who thought she remembered that St Julien was always the cheapest wine on the list.

Inwardly, Gordon damned their eyes. There you are, you see! They were in league against him already. They were trying to prevent him from spending his money. There was going to be that deadly, hateful atmosphere of 'You can't afford it' hanging over everything. It made him all the more anxious to be extravagant. A moment ago he would have compromised on Burgundy. Now he decided that they must have something really expensive–something fizzy, something with a kick in it. Champagne? No, they'd never let him have champagne. Ah!

'Have you got any Asti?' he said to the waiter.

The waiter suddenly beamed, thinking of his corkage. He had grasped now that Gordon and not Ravelston was the host. He answered in the peculiar mixture of French and English which he affected.

'Asti, sir? Yes, sir. Very nice Asti! Asti Spumanti. *Très fin! Très vif!*'

Ravelston's worried eye sought Gordon's across the table. You can't afford it! his eye pleaded.

'Is that one of those fizzy wines?' said Rosemary.

'Very fizzy, madame. Very lively wine. *Très vif!* Pop!' His fat hands made a gesture, picturing cascades of foam.

'Asti,' said Gordon, before Rosemary could stop him.

Ravelston looked miserable. He knew that Asti would cost Gordon ten or fifteen shillings a bottle. Gordon pretended not to notice. He began talking about Stendhal–association with Duchesse de Sanseverina and her *'force vin d'Asti'*. Along came the Asti in a pail of ice–a mistake, that, as Ravelston could have told Gordon. Out came the cork. Pop! The wild wine foamed into the wide flat glasses. Mysteriously the atmosphere of the table changed. Something had happened to all three of them. Even before it was drunk the wine had worked its magic. Rosemary had lost her nervousness, Ravelston his worried preoccupation with the expense, Gordon his defiant resolve to be extravagant. They were eating anchovies and bread and butter, fried sole, roast pheasant with bread sauce and chipped potatoes; but principally they were drinking and talking. And how brilliantly they were talking–or so it seemed to them, anyway! They talked about the bloodiness of modern life and the bloodiness of modern books. What else is there to talk about nowadays? As usual (but, oh! how differently, now that there was money in his pocket and he didn't really believe what he was saying) Gordon descanted on the deadness, the dreadfulness of the age we live in. French letters and machine-guns! The movies and the *Daily Mail*! It was a bone-deep truth when he walked the streets with a couple of coppers in his pocket; but it was a joke at this moment. It was great fun—it *is* fun when you have good food and good wine inside you—to demonstrate that we live in a dead and rotting world. He was being witty at the expense of the modern literature; they were all being witty. With the fine scorn of the unpublished Gordon knocked down reputation after reputation. Shaw, Yeats, Eliot, Joyce, Huxley, Lewis, Hemingway—each with a careless phrase or two was shovelled into the dustbin. What fun it all was, if only it could last! And of course, at this particular moment, Gordon believed that it *could* last. Of the first bottle of Asti, Gordon drank three glasses, Ravelston two, and Rosemary one. Gordon became aware that a girl at the table opposite was watching him. A tall elegant girl with a shell-pink skin and wonderful, almond-shaped eyes. Rich, obviously; one of the moneyed intelligentsia. She thought him interesting—was wondering who he was. Gordon found himself manufacturing special witticisms for her benefit. And he *was* being witty, there was no doubt about that. That too was money. Money greasing the wheels—wheels of thought as well as wheels of taxis.

But somehow the second bottle of Asti was not such a success as the first. To begin with there was uncomfortableness over its ordering. Gordon beckoned to the waiter.

'Have you got another bottle of this?'

The waiter beamed fatly. 'Yes, sir! *Mais certainement, monsieur!*'

Rosemary frowned and tapped Gordon's foot under the table. 'No, Gordon, *no*! You're not to.'

'Not to what?'

'Order another bottle. We don't want it.'

'Oh, bosh! Get another bottle, waiter.'

'Yes, sir.'

Ravelston rubbed his nose. With eyes too guilty to meet Gordon's he looked at his wine glass. 'Look here, Gordon. Let *me* stand this bottle. I'd like to.'

'Bosh!' repeated Gordon.

'Get half a bottle, then,' said Rosemary.

'A whole bottle, waiter,' said Gordon.

After that nothing was the same. They still talked, laughed, argued, but things were not the same. The elegant girl at the table opposite had ceased watching Gordon. Somehow, Gordon wasn't being witty any longer. It is almost always a mistake to order a second bottle. It is like bathing for a second time on a summer day. However warm the day is, however much you have enjoyed your first bathe, you are always sorry for it if you go in a second time. The magic had departed from the wine. It seemed to foam and sparkle less, it was merely a clogging sourish liquid which you gulped down half in disgust and half in hopes of getting drunk quicker. Gordon was now definitely though secretly drunk. One half of him was drunk and the other half sober. He was beginning to have that peculiar blurred feeling, as though your features had swollen and your fingers grown thicker, which you have in the second stage of drunkenness. But the sober half of him was still in command to outward appearance, anyway. The conversation grew more and more tedious. Gordon and Ravelston talked in the detached uncomfortable manner of people who have had a little scene and are not going to admit it. They talked about Shakespeare. The conversation tailed off into a long discussion about the meaning of Hamlet. It was very dull. Rosemary stifled a yawn. While Gordon's sober half talked, his drunken half stood aside and listened. Drunken half was very angry. They'd spoiled his evening, damn them! with their arguing about that second bottle. All he wanted now was to be properly drunk and have done with it. Of the six glasses in the second bottle he drank four–for Rosemary refused more wine. But you couldn't do much on this weak stuff. Drunken half clamoured for more drink, and more, and more. Beer by the quart and the bucket! A real good rousing drink! And by God! he was going to have it later on. He thought of the five pound note stowed away in his inner pocket. He still had that to blow, anyway.

The musical clock that was concealed somewhere in Modigliani's interior struck ten.

'Shall we shove off?' said Gordon.

Ravelston's eyes looked pleadingly, guiltily across the table. Let me share the bill! his eyes said. Gordon ignored him.

'I vote we go to the Café Imperial,' he said.

The bill failed to sober him. A little over two quid for the dinner, thirty bob for the wine. He did not let the others see the bill, of course, but they saw him paying. He threw four pound notes on to the waiter's salver and said casually, 'Keep the change.' That left him with about ten bob besides the fiver. Ravelston was helping Rosemary on with her coat; as she saw Gordon throw notes to the waiter her lips parted in dismay. She had had no idea that the dinner was going to cost anything like four pounds. It horrified her to see him throwing money about like that. Ravelston looked gloomy and disapproving. Gordon damned their eyes again. Why did they have to keep on worrying? He could afford it, couldn't he? He still had that fiver. But by God, it wouldn't be his fault if he got home with a penny left!

But outwardly he was quite sober, and much more subdued than he had been half an hour ago. 'We'd better have a taxi to the Café Imperial,' he said.

'Oh, let's walk!' said Rosemary. 'It's only a step.'

'No, we'll have a taxi.'

They got into the taxi and were driven away, Gordon sitting next to Rosemary. He had half a mind to put his arm round her, in spite of Ravelston's presence. But at that moment a swirl of cold night air came in at the window and blew against Gordon's forehead. It gave him a shock. It was like one of those moments in the night when suddenly from deep sleep you are broad awake and full of some dreadful realization–as that you are doomed to die, for instance, or that your life is a failure. For perhaps a minute he was cold sober. He knew all about himself and the awful folly he was committing–knew that he had squandered five pounds on utter foolishness and was now going to squander the other five that belonged to Julia. He had a fleeting but terribly vivid vision of Julia, with her thin face and her greying hair, in the cold of her dismal bed-sitting room. Poor, good Julia! Julia who had been sacrificed to him all her life, from whom he had borrowed pound after pound after pound; and now he hadn't even the decency to keep her five intact! He recoiled from the thought; he fled back into his drunkenness as into a refuge. Quick, quick, we're getting sober! Booze, more booze! Recapture that first fine careless rapture! Outside, the multi-coloured window of an Italian grocery, still open, swam towards them. He tapped sharply on the glass. The taxi drew up. Gordon began to climb out across Rosemary's knees.

'Where are you going, Gordon?'

'To recapture that first fine careless rapture,' said Gordon, on the pavement.

'What?'

'It's time we laid in some more booze. The pubs'll be shutting in half an hour.'

'No, Gordon, no! You're not to get anything more to drink. You've had quite enough already.'

'Wait!'

He came out of the shop nursing a litre bottle of Chianti. The grocer had taken the cork out for him and put it in loosely again. The others had grasped now that he was drunk—that he must have been drinking before he met them. It made them both embarrassed. They went into the Café Imperial, but the chief thought in both their minds was to get Gordon away and to bed as quickly as possible. Rosemary whispered behind Gordon's back,'*Please* don't let him drink any more!' Ravelston nodded gloomily. Gordon was marching ahead of them to a vacant table, not in the least troubled by the stares everyone was casting at the wine-bottle which he carried on his arm. They sat down and ordered coffee, and with some difficulty Ravelston restrained Gordon from ordering brandy as well. All of them were ill at ease. It was horrible in the great garish café, stuffily hot and deafeningly noisy with the jabber of several hundred voices, the clatter of plates and glasses, and the intermittent squalling of the band. All three of them wanted to get away. Ravelston was still worrying about the expense, Rosemary was worried because Gordon was drunk, Gordon was restless and thirsty. He had wanted to come here, but he was no sooner here than he wanted to escape. Drunken half was clamouring for a bit of fun. And drunken half wasn't going to be kept in check much longer. Beer, beer! cried drunken half. Gordon hated this stuffy place. He had visions of a pub taproom with great oozy barrels and quart pots topped with foam. He kept an eye on the clock. It was nearly half past ten and the pubs even in Westminster would shut at eleven. Mustn't miss his beer! The bottle of wine was for afterwards, when the pubs were shut. Rosemary was sitting opposite him, talking to Ravelston, uncomfortably but with a sufficient pretence that she was enjoying herself and there was nothing the matter. They were still talking in a rather futile way about Shakespeare. Gordon hated Shakespeare. As he watched Rosemary talking there came over him a violent, perverse desire for her. She was leaning forward, her elbows on the table; he could see her small breasts clearly through her dress. It came to him with a kind of shock, a catch of breath, which once again almost sobered him, that he had seen her naked. She was his girl! He could have her whenever he wanted her! And by God, he was going to have her tonight! Why not? It was a fitting end to the evening. They could find a place easily enough; there are plenty of hotels round Shaftesbury Avenue where they don't ask questions if you can pay the bill. He still had his fiver. He felt her foot under the table, meaning to imprint a delicate caress upòn it, and only succeeded in treading on her toe. She drew her foot away from him.

'Let's get out of this,' he said abruptly, and at once stood up.

'Oh, let's!' said Rosemary with relief.

They were in Regent Street again. Down on the left Piccadilly Circus blazed, a horrible pool of light. Rosemary's eyes turned towards the bus stop opposite.

'It's half past ten,' she said doubtfully. 'I've got to be back by eleven.'

'Oh, rot! Let's look for a decent pub. I mustn't miss my beer.'

'Oh, no, Gordon! No more pubs tonight. I couldn't drink any more. Nor ought you.'

'It doesn't matter. Come this way.'

He took her by the arm and began to lead her down towards the bottom of Regent Street, holding her rather tight as though afraid she would escape. For the moment he had forgotten about Ravelston. Ravelston followed, wondering whether he ought to leave them to themselves or whether he ought to stay and keep an eye on Gordon. Rosemary hung back, not liking the way Gordon was pulling at her arm.

'Where are you taking me, Gordon?'

'Round the corner, where it's dark. I want to kiss you.'

'I don't think I want to be kissed.'

'Of course you do.'

'No!'

'Yes!'

She let him take her. Ravelston waited on the corner by the Regent Palace, uncertain what to do. Gordon and Rosemary disappeared round the corner and were almost immediately in darker, narrower streets. The appalling faces of tarts, like skulls coated with pink powder, peered meaningly from several doorways. Rosemary shrank from them. Gordon was rather amused.

'They think you're one of them,' he explained to her.

He stood his bottle on the pavement, carefully, against the wall, then suddenly seized her and twisted her backwards. He wanted her badly, and he did not want to waste time over preliminaries. He began to kiss her face all over, clumsily but very hard. She let him do it for a moment, but it frightened her; his face, so close to hers, looked pale, strange, and distracted. He smelt very strongly of wine. She struggled, turning her face away so that he was only kissing her hair and neck.

'Gordon, you mustn't!'

'Why mustn't I?'

'What are you doing?'

'What do you suppose I'm doing?'

He shoved her back against the wall, and with the careful, preoccupied movements of a drunken man, tried to undo the front of her dress. It was of a kind that did not undo, as it happened. This time she was angry. She struggled violently, fending his hand aside.

'Gordon, stop that at once!'

'Why?'

'If you do it again I'll smack your face.'

'Smack my face! Don't you come the Girl Guide with me.'

'Let me go, will you!'

'Think of last Sunday,' he said lewdly.

'Gordon, if you go on I'll hit you, honestly I will.'

'Not you.'

He thrust his hand right into the front of her dress. The movement was curiously brutal, as though she had been a stranger to him. She grasped that from the expression of his face. She was not Rosemary to him any longer, she was just a girl, a girl's body. That was the thing that upset her. She struggled and managed to free herself from him. He came after her again and clutched her arm. She smacked his face as hard as she could and dodged neatly out of his reach.

'What did you do that for?' he said, feeling his cheek but not hurt by the blow.

'I'm not going to stand that sort of thing. I'm going home. You'll be different tomorrow.'

'Rot! You come along with me. You're going to bed with me.'

'Good night!' she said, and fled up the dark side street.

For a moment he thought of following her, but found his legs too heavy. It did not seem worth while, anyway. He wandered back to where Ravelston was still waiting, looking moody and alone, partly because he was worried about Gordon and partly because he was trying not to notice two hopeful tarts who were on patrol just behind him. Gordon looked properly drunk, Ravelston thought. His hair was tumbling down over his forehead, one side of his face was very pale and on the other there was a red smudge where Rosemary had slapped him. Ravelston thought this must be the flush of drunkenness.

'What have you done with Rosemary?' he said.

'She's gone,' said Gordon, with a wave of his hand which was meant to explain everything. 'But the night's still young.'

'Look here, Gordon, it's time you were in bed.'

'In bed, yes. But not alone.'

He stood on the kerb gazing out into the hideous midnight-noon. For a moment he felt quite deathly. His face was burning. His whole body had a dreadful, swollen, fiery feeling. His head in particular seemed on the point of bursting. Somehow the baleful light was bound up with his sensations. He watched the skysigns flicking on and off, glaring red and blue, arrowing up and down—the awful, sinister glitter of a doomed civilization, like the still blazing lights of a sinking ship. He caught Ravelston's arm and made a gesture that comprehended the whole of Piccadilly Circus.

'The lights down in hell will look just like that.'

'I shouldn't wonder.'

Ravelston was looking out for a disengaged taxi. He must get Gordon home to bed without further delay. Gordon wondered whether he was in joy or in agony. That burning, bursting feeling was dreadful. The sober half of him was not dead yet. Sober half still knew with ice-cold clarity what he had done and what he was doing. He had committed follies for which tomorrow he would feel like killing himself. He had squandered five pounds in senseless extravagance, he had robbed Julia, he had insulted Rosemary. And tomorrow—oh, tomorrow, we'll be sober! Go home, go home! cried sober half—to you! said drunken half contemptuously. Drunken half was still clamouring for a bit of fun. And drunken half was the stronger. A fiery clock somewhere opposite caught his eye. Twenty to eleven. Quick, before the pubs are shut! *Haro! la gorge m'ard!* Once again his thoughts moved lyrically. He felt a hard round shape under his arm, discovered that it was the Chianti bottle, and tweaked out the cork. Ravelston was waving to a taxi-driver without managing to catch his eye. He heard a shocked squeal from the tarts behind. Turning, he saw with horror that Gordon had up-ended the bottle and was drinking from it.

'Hi! Gordon!'

He sprang towards him and forced his arm down. A gout of wine went down Gordon's collar.

'For God's sake be careful! You don't want the police to get hold of you, do you?'

'I want a drink,' complained Gordon.

'But dash it! You can't start drinking here.'

'Take me to a pub,' said Gordon.

Ravelston rubbed his nose helplessly. 'Oh, God! I suppose that's better than drinking on the pavement. Come on, we'll go to a pub. You shall have your drink there.'

Gordon recorked his bottle carefully. Ravelston shepherded him across the circus, Gordon clinging to his arm, but not for support, for his legs were still quite steady. They halted on the island, then managed to find a gap in the traffic and went down the Haymarket.

In the pub the air seemed wet with beer. It was all a mist of beer shot through with the sickly tang of whisky. Along the bar a press of men seethed, downing with Faustlike eagerness their last drinks before eleven should sound its knell. Gordon slid easily through the crowd. He was not in a mood to worry about a few jostlings and elbowings. In a moment he had fetched up at the bar between a stout commercial traveller drinking Guinness and a tall, lean, decayed major type of man with droopy moustaches, whose entire conversation seemed to consist of 'What ho!' and 'What, what!' Gordon threw half a crown on to the beer-wet bar.

'A quart of bitter, please!'

'No quart pots here!' cried the harassed barmaid, measuring pegs of whisky with one eye on the clock.

'Quart pots on the the top shelf, Effie!' shouted the landlord over his shoulder, from the other side of the bar.

The barmaid hauled the beer-handle three times hurriedly. The monstrous glass pot was set before him. He lifted it. What a weight! A pint of pure water weighs a pound and a quarter. Down with it! Swish–gurgle! A long, long sup of beer flowed gratefully down his gullet. He paused for breath, and felt a little sickish. Come on, now for another. Swish–gurgle! It almost choked him this time. But stick it out, stick it out! Through the cascade of beer that poured down his throat and seemed to drown his ears he heard the landlord's shout: 'Last orders, gentlemen, please!' For a moment he removed his face from the pot, gasped, and got his breath back. Now for the last. Swish–gurgle! A-a-ah! Gordon set down the pot. Emptied in three gulps–not bad. He clattered it on the bar.

'Hi! Give me the other half of that–quick!'

'What ho!' said the major.

'Coming it a bit, aren't you?' said the commercial traveller.

Ravelston, farther down the bar and hemmed in by several men, saw what Gordon was doing. He called to him, 'Hi, Gordon!', frowned and shook his head, too shy to say in front of everybody, 'Don't drink any more.' Gordon settled himself on his legs. He was still steady, but consciously steady. His head seemed to have swollen to an immense size, his whole body had the same horrible, swollen, fiery feeling as before. Languidly he lifted the refilled beer-pot. He did not want it now. Its smell nauseated him. It was just a hateful, pale yellow, sickly-tasting liquid. Like urine, almost! That bucketful of stuff to be forced down into his bursting guts–horrible! But come on, no flinching! What else are we here for? Down with it! Here she is so near my nose. So tip her up and down she goes. Swish–gurgle!

In the same moment something dreadful happened. His gullet had shut up of its own accord, or the beer had missed his mouth. It was pouring all over him, a tidal wave of beer. He was drowning in beer like lay-brother Peter in the *Ingoldsby Legends*. Help! He tried to shout, choked, and let fall the beer-pot. There was a flurry all round him. People were leaping aside to avoid the jet of beer. Crash! went the pot. Gordon stood rocking. Men, bottles, mirrors were going round and round. He was falling, losing consciousness. But dimly visible before him was a black upright shape, sole point of stability in a reeling world–the beer-handle. He clutched it, swung, held tight. Ravelston started towards him.

The barmaid leaned indignantly over the bar. The roundabout world slowed down and stopped. Gordon's brain was quite clear.

'Here! What are you hanging on to the beer-handle for?'

'All over my bloody trousers!' cried the commercial traveller.

'What am I hanging on to the beer-handle for?'

'*Yes!* What are you hanging on to the beer-handle for?'

Gordon swung himself sideways. The elongated face of the major peered down at him, with wet moustaches drooping.

'She says, "What am I hanging on to the beer-handle for?"'

'What ho! What?'

Ravelston had forced his way between several men and reached him. He put a strong arm round Gordon's waist and hoisted him to his feet.

'Stand up, for God's sake! You're drunk.'

'Drunk?' said Gordon.

Everyone was laughing at them. Ravelston's pale face flushed.

'Two and three those mugs cost,' said the barmaid bitterly.

'And what about my bloody trousers?' said the commercial traveller.

'I'll pay for the mug,' said Ravelston. He did so. 'Now come on out of it. You're drunk.'

He began to shepherd Gordon towards the door, one arm round his shoulder, the other holding the Chianti bottle, which he had taken from him earlier. Gordon freed himself. He could walk with perfect steadiness. He said in a dignified manner:

'Drunk did you say I was?'

Ravelston took his arm again. 'Yes, I'm afraid you are. Decidedly.'

'Swan swam across the sea, well swam swan,' said Gordon.

'Gordon, you *are* drunk. The sooner you're in bed the better.'

'First cast out the beam that is in thine own eye before thou castest out the mote that is in thy brother's,' said Gordon.

Ravelston had got him out on to the pavement by this time. 'We'd better get hold of a taxi,' he said, looking up and down the street.

There seemed to be no taxis about, however. The people were streaming noisily out of the pub, which was on the point of closing. Gordon felt better in the open air. His brain had never been clearer. The red satanic gleam of a Neon light, somewhere in the distance, put a new and brilliant idea into his head. He plucked at Ravelston's arm.

'Ravelston! I say, Ravelston!'

'What?'

'Let's pick up a couple of tarts.'

In spite of Gordon's drunken state, Ravelston was scandalized. 'My dear old chap! You can't do that kind of thing.'

'Don't be so damned upper-class. Why not?'

'But how could you, dash it! After you've just said good night to Rosemary—a really charming girl like that!'

'At night all cats are grey,' said Gordon, with the feeling that he voiced a profound and cynical wisdom.

Ravelston decided to ignore this remark. 'We'd better walk up to Piccadilly Circus,' he said. 'There'll be plenty of taxis there.'

The theatres were emptying. Crowds of people and streams of cars flowed to and fro in the frightful corpse-light. Gordon's brain was marvellously clear. He knew what folly and evil he had committed and was about to commit. And yet after all it hardly seemed to matter. He saw as something far, far away, like something seen through the wrong end of the telescope, his thirty years, his wasted life, the blank future, Julia's five pounds, Rosemary. He said with a sort of philosophic interest:

'Look at the Neon lights! Look at those awful blue ones over the rubber shop. When I see those lights I know that I'm a damned soul.'

'Quite,' said Ravelston, who was not listening. 'Ah, there's a taxi!' He signalled. 'Damn! He didn't see me. Wait here a second.'

He left Gordon by the Tube station and hurried across the street. For a little while Gordon's mind receded into blankness. Then he was aware of two hard yet youthful faces, like the faces of young predatory animals, that had come close up to his own. They had blackened eye-brows and hats that were like vulgarer versions of Rosemary's. He was exchanging badinage with them. This seemed to him to have been going on for several minutes.

'Hullo, Dora! Hullo, Barbara! (He knew their names, it seemed.) And how are you? And how's old England's winding-sheet?'

'Oo—haven't you got a cheek, just!'

'And what are you up to at this time of night?'

'Oo—jes' strolling around.'

'Like a lion, seeking whom he may devour?'

'Oo—you haven't half got a cheek! Hasn't he got a cheek, Barbara? You *have* got a cheek!'

Ravelston had caught the taxi and brought it round to where Gordon was standing. He stepped out, saw Gordon between the two girls, and stood aghast.

'Gordon! Oh, my God! What the devil have you been doing?'

'Let me introduce you. Dora and Barbara,' said Gordon.

For a moment Ravelston looked almost angry. As a matter of fact, Ravelston was incapable of being properly angry. Upset, pained, embarrassed—yes; but not angry. He stepped forward with a miserable effort not to notice the two girls' existence. Once he noticed them the game was up. He took Gordon by the arm and would have bundled him into the taxi.

'Come on, Gordon, for God's sake! Here's the taxi. We'll go straight home and put you to bed.'

Dora caught Gordon's other arm and hauled him out of reach as though he had been a stolen handbag.

'What bloody business is it of yours?' she cried ferociously.

'You don't want to insult these two ladies, I hope?' said Gordon.

Ravelston faltered, stepped back, rubbed his nose. It was a moment to be firm; but Ravelston had never in his life been firm. He looked from Dora to Gordon, from Gordon to Barbara. That was fatal. Once he had looked them in the face he was lost. Oh, God! What could he do? They were human beings—he couldn't insult them. The same instinct that sent his hand into his pocket at the very sight of a beggar made him helpless at this moment. The poor, wretched girls! He hadn't the heart to send them packing into the night. Suddenly he realized that he would have to go through with this abominable adventure into which Gordon had led him. For the first time in his life he was let in for going home with a tart.

'But dash it all!' he said feebly.

'*Allons-y,*' said Gordon.

The taximan had taken his direction at a nod from Dora. Gordon slumped into the corner seat and seemed immediately to sink into some immense abyss from which he rose again more gradually and with only partial consciousness of what he had been doing. He was gliding smoothly through darkness starred with lights. Or were the lights moving and he stationary? It was like being on the ocean bottom, among the luminous, gliding fishes. The fancy returned to him that he was a damned soul in hell. The landscape in hell would be just like this. Ravines of cold evil-coloured fire, with darkness all above. But in hell there would be torment. Was this torment? He strove to classify his sensations. The momentary lapse into unconsciousness had left him weak, sick, shaken; his forehead seemed to be splitting. He put out a hand. It encountered a knee, a garter, and a small soft hand which sought mechanically for his. He became aware that Ravelston, sitting opposite, was tapping his toe urgently and nervously.

'Gordon! Gordon! Wake up!'

'What?'

'Gordon! Oh, damn! *Causons en français. Qu'est-ce que tu as fait? Crois-tu que je veux coucher avec une sale*—oh, damnation!'

'Oo-parley-voo francey!' squealed the girls.

Gordon was mildly amused. Do Ravelston good, he thought. A parlour Socialist going home with a tart! The first genuinely proletarian action of his life. As though aware of this thought, Ravelston subsided into his corner in silent misery, sitting as far away from Barbara as possible. The taxi drew up at a hotel in a side-street; a dreadful, shoddy, low place it was. The 'hotel' sign over the door looked skew-eyed. The windows were almost dark, but the sound of singing, boozy and dreary, trickled from within. Gordon staggered out of the taxi and felt for Dora's arm. Give us a hand, Dora. Mind the step. What ho!

A smallish, darkish, smelly hallway, lino-carpeted, mean, uncared-for, and somehow impermanent. From a room somewhere on the left the singing swelled, mournful as a church organ. A cross-eyed, evil-looking chambermaid appeared from nowhere. She and Dora seemed to know one another. What a mug! No competition there. From the room on the left a single voice took up the song with would-be facetious emphasis:

> 'The man that kisses a pretty girl
> And goes and tells his mother,
> Ought to have his lips cut off,
> Ought to—'

It tailed away, full of the ineffable, undisguisable sadness of debauchery. A very young voice it sounded. The voice of some poor boy who in his heart only wanted to be at home with his mother and sisters, playing hunt-the-slipper. There was a party of young fools in there, on the razzle with whisky and girls. The tune reminded Gordon. He turned to Ravelston as he came in, Barbara following.

'Where's my Chianti?' he said.

Ravelston gave him the bottle. His face looked pale, harassed, hunted, almost. With guilty restless movements he kept himself apart from Barbara. He could not touch her or even look at her, and yet to escape was beyond him. His eyes sought Gordon's. 'For the love of God can't we get out of it somehow?' they signalled. Gordon frowned at him. Stick it out! No flinching! He took Dora's arm again. Come on, Dora! Now for those stairs. Ah! Wait a moment.

Her arm round his waist, supporting him, Dora drew him aside. Down the darkish, smelly stairs a young woman came mincingly, buttoning on a glove; after her a bald, middle-aged man in evening clothes, black overcoat, and white silk muffler, his opera hat in his hand. He walked past them with small mean mouth tightened, pretending not to see them. A family man, by the guilty look in his eye. Gordon watched the gaslight gleam on the back of his bald head. His predecessor. In the same bed, probably. The mantle of Elisha. Now then, Dora, up we go! Ah, these stairs! *Difficilis ascensus Averni.* That's right, here we are! 'Mind the step,' said Dora. They were on the landing. Black and white lino like a chessboard. White-painted doors. A smell of slops and a fainter smell of stale linen.

We this way, you that. At the other door Ravelston halted, his fingers on the handle. He could not—no, he *could* not do it. He could not enter that dreadful room. For the last time his eyes, like those of a dog about to be whipped, turned upon Gordon. 'Must I, must I?' his eyes said. Gordon eyed him sternly. Stick it out, Regulus! March to your doom! *Atqui sciebat quae sibi Barbara.* It is a far, far more proletarian thing that you do. And then with startling suddenness Ravelston's face cleared. An expression of relief, almost of joy, stole over it. A wonderful thought had occurred to him. After all, you could always pay the girl without actually doing anything! Thank God! He set his shoulders, plucked up courage, went in. The door shut.

So here we are. A mean, dreadful room. Lino on the floor, gas-fire, huge double bed with sheets vaguely dingy. Over the bed a framed coloured picture from *La Vie Parisienne.* A mistake, that. Sometimes the originals don't compare so well. And, by Jove! on the bamboo table by the window, positively an aspidistra! Hast thou found me, O mine enemy? But come here, Dora. Let's have a look at you.

He seemed to be lying on the bed. He could not see very well. Her youthful, rapacious face, with blackened eyebrows, leaned over him as he sprawled there.

'How about my present?' she demanded, half wheedling, half menacing.

Never mind that now. To work! Come here. Not a bad mouth. Come here. Come closer. Ah!

No. No use. Impossible. The will but not the way. The spirit is willing but the flesh is weak. Try again. No. The booze, it must be. See Macbeth. One last try. No, no use. Not this evening, I'm afraid.

All right, Dora, don't you worry. You'll get your two quid all right. We aren't paying by results.

He made a clumsy gesture. 'Here, give us that bottle. That bottle off the dressing-table.'

Dora brought it. Ah, that's better. That at least doesn't fail. With hands that had swollen to monstrous size he up-ended the Chianti bottle. The wine flowed down his throat, bitter and choking, and some of it went up his nose. It overwhelmed him. He was slipping, sliding, falling off the bed. His head met the floor. His legs were still on the bed. For a while he lay in this position. Is this the way to live? Down below the youthful voices were still mournfully singing:

> 'For tonight we'll merry be,
> For tonight we'll merry be,
> For tonight we'll merry be-e-e—
> Tomorrow we'll be so-ober!'

# 9

And, by Jove, tomorrow we *were* sober!

Gordon emerged from some long, sickly dream to the consciousness that the books in the lending library were the wrong way up. They were all lying on their sides. Moreover, for some reason their backs had turned white—white and shiny, like porcelain.

He opened his eyes a little wider and moved an arm. Small rivulets of pain, seemingly touched off by the movement, shot through his body at unexpected places—down the calves of his legs, for instance, and up both sides of his head. He perceived that he was lying on his side, with a hard smooth pillow under his cheek and a coarse blanket scratching his chin and pushing its hairs into his mouth. Apart from the minor pains that stabbed him every time he moved, there was a large, dull sort of pain which was not localized but which seemed to hover all over him.

Suddenly he flung off the blanket and sat up. He was in a police cell. At this moment a frightful spasm of nausea overcame him. Dimly perceiving a w.c. in the corner, he crept towards it and was violently sick, three or four times.

After that, for several minutes, he was in agonizing pain. He could scarcely stand on his feet, his head throbbed as though it were going to burst, and the light seemed like some scalding white liquid pouring into his brain through the sockets of his eyes. He sat on the bed holding his head between his hands. Presently, when some of the throbbing had died down, he had another look about him. The cell measured about twelve feet long by six wide and was very high. The walls were all of white porcelain bricks, horribly white and clean. He wondered dully how they cleaned as high up as the ceiling. Perhaps with a hose, he reflected. At one end there was a little barred window, very high up, and at the other end, over the door, an electric bulb let into the wall and protected by a stout grating. The thing he was sitting on was not actually a bed, but a shelf with one blanket and a canvas pillow. The door was of steel, painted green. In the door there was a little round hole with a flap on the outside.

Having seen this much he lay down and pulled the blanket over him again. He had no further curiosity about his surroundings. As to what had happened last night, he remembered everything—at least, he remembered everything up to the time when he had gone with Dora into the room with the aspidistra. God knew what had happened after that. There had been some kind of bust-up and he had landed in the clink. He had no notion of what he had done; it might be murder for all he knew. In any case he did not care. He turned his face to the wall and pulled the blanket over his head to shut out the light.

After a long time the spyhole in the door was pushed aside. Gordon managed to turn his head round. His neck-muscles seemed to creak. Through the spyhole he could see a blue eye and a semi-circle of pink chubby cheek.

' 'Ja do with a cup of tea?' a voice said.

Gordon sat up and instantly felt very sick again. He took his head between his hands and groaned. The thought of a cup of hot tea appealed to him, but he knew it would make him sick if it had sugar in it.

'Please,' he said.

The police constable opened a partition in the top half of the door and passed in a thick white mug of tea. It had sugar in it. The constable was a solid rosy young man of about twenty-five, with a kind face, white eyelashes, and a tremendous chest. It reminded Gordon of the chest of a carthorse. He spoke with a good accent but with vulgar turns of speech. For a minute or so he stood regarding Gordon.

'You weren't half bad last night,' he said finally.

'I'm bad now.'

'You was worse last night, though. What you go and hit the sergeant for?'

'Did I hit the sergeant?'

'Did you? Coo! He wasn't half wild. He turns to me and he says—holding his ear he was, like this—he says, "Now, if that man wasn't too drunk to stand, I'd knock his block off." It's all gone down on your charge sheet. Drunk and disorderly. You'd only ha' bin drunk and incapable if you hadn't of hit the sergeant.'

'Do you know what I shall get for this?'

'Five quid or fourteen days. You'll go up before Mr Croom. Lucky for you it wasn't Mr Walker. He'd give you a month without the option, Mr Walker would. Very severe on the drunks he is. Teetotaller.'

Gordon had drunk some of the tea. It was nauseatingly sweet but its warmth made him feel stronger. He gulped it down. At this moment a nasty, snarling sort of voice—the sergeant whom Gordon had hit, no doubt—yelped from somewhere outside:

'Take that man out and get him washed. Black Maria leaves at half past nine.'

The constable hastened to open the cell door. As soon as Gordon stepped outside he felt worse then ever. This was partly because it was much colder in the passage than in the cell. He walked a step or two, and then suddenly his head was going round and round. 'I'm going to be sick!' he cried. He was falling—he flung out a hand and stopped himself against the wall. The constable's strong arm went round him. Across the arm, as over a rail, Gordon sagged, doubled up and limp. A jet of vomit burst from him. It was the tea, of course. There was a gutter running along the stone floor. At the end of the passage the moustachio'd sergeant, in tunic without a belt, stood with his hand on his hip, looking on disgustedly.

'Dirty little tyke,' he muttered, and turned away.

'Come on, old chap,' said the constable. 'You'll be better in half a mo'.'

He half led, half dragged Gordon to a big stone sink at the end of the passage and helped him to strip to the waist. His gentleness was astonishing. He handled Gordon almost like a nurse handling a child. Gordon had recovered enough strength to sluice himself with the ice-cold water and rinse his mouth out. The constable gave him a torn towel to dry himself with and then led him back to the cell.

'Now you sit quiet till the Black Maria comes. And take my tip—when you go up to the court, you plead guilty and say you won't do it again. Mr Croom won't be hard on you.'

'Where are my collar and tie?' said Gordon.

'We took 'em away last night. You'll get 'em back before you go up to court. We had a bloke hung himself with his tie, once.'

Gordon sat down on the bed. For a little while he occupied himself by calculating the number of porcelain bricks in the walls, then sat with his elbows on his knees, his head between his hands. He was still aching all over; he felt weak, cold, jaded, and, above all, bored. He wished that boring business of going up to the court could be avoided somehow. The thought of being put into some jolting vehicle and taken across London to hang about in chilly cells and passages, and of having to answer questions and be lectured by magistrates, bored him indescribably. All he wanted was to be left alone. But presently there was the sound of several voices farther down the passage, and then of feet approaching. The partition in the door was opened.

'Couple of visitors for you,' the constable said.

Gordon was bored by the very thought of visitors. Unwillingly he looked up, and saw Flaxman and Ravelston looking in upon him. How they had got there together was a mystery, but Gordon felt not the faintest curiosity about it. They bored him. He wished they would go away.

'Hullo, chappie!' said Flaxman.

'*You* here?' said Gordon with a sort of weary offensiveness.

Ravelston looked miserable. He had been up since the very early morning, looking for Gordon. This was the first time he had seen the interior of a police cell. His face shrank with disgust as he looked at the chilly white-tiled place with its shameless w.c. in the corner. But Flaxman was more accustomed to this kind of thing. He cocked a practised eye at Gordon.

'I've seen 'em worse,' he said cheerfully. 'Give him a prairie oyster and he'd

buck up something wonderful. D'you know what your eyes look like, chappie?'
he added to Gordon. 'They look as if they'd been taken out and poached.'

'I was drunk last night,' said Gordon, his head between his hands.

'I gathered something of the kind, old chappie.'

'Look here, Gordon,' said Ravelston, 'we came to bail you out, but it seems
we're too late. They're taking you up to court in a few minutes' time. This is a
bloody show. It's a pity you didn't give them a false name when they brought
you here last night.'

'Did I tell them my name?'

'You told them everything. I wish to God I hadn't let you out of my sight.
You slipped out of that house somehow and into the street.'

'Wandering up and down Shaftesbury Avenue, drinking out of a bottle,'
said Flaxman appreciatively. 'But you oughtn't to have hit the sergeant, old
chappie! That was a bit of bloody foolishness. And I don't mind telling you
Mother Wisbeach is on your track. When your pal here came round this
morning and told her you'd been for a night on the tiles, she took on as if you'd
done a bloody murder.'

'And look here, Gordon,' said Ravelston.

There was the familiar note of discomfort in his face. It was something about
money, as usual. Gordon looked up. Ravelston was gazing into the distance.

'Look here.'

'What?'

'About your fine. You'd better leave that to me. I'll pay it.'

'No, you won't.'

'My dear old chap! They'll send you to jail if I don't.'

'Oh, hell! I don't care.'

He did not care. At this moment he did not care if they sent him to prison for
a year. Of course he couldn't pay his fine himself. He knew without even
needing to look that he had no money left. He would have given it all to Dora,
or more probably she would have pinched it. He lay down on the bed again and
turned his back on the others. In the sulky, sluggish state that he was in, his
sole desire was to get rid of them. They made a few more attempts to talk to
him, but he would not answer, and presently they went away. Flaxman's voice
boomed cheerfully down the passage. He was giving Ravelston minute
instructions as to how to make a prairie oyster.

The rest of that day was very beastly. Beastly was the ride in the Black
Maria, which, inside, was like nothing so much as a miniature public lavatory,
with tiny cubicles down each side, into which you were locked and in which
you had barely room to sit down. Beastlier yet was the long wait in one of the
cells adjoining the magistrate's court. This cell was an exact replica of the cell
at the police station, even to having precisely the same number of porcelain
bricks. But it differed from the police station cell in being repulsively dirty. It
was cold, but the air was so fetid as to be almost unbreathable. Prisoners were
coming and going all the time. They would be thrust into the cell, taken out
after an hour or two to go up to the court, and then perhaps brought back again
to wait while the magistrate decided upon their sentence or fresh witnesses

were sent for. There were always five or six men in the cell, and there was nothing to sit on except the plank bed. And the worst was that nearly all of them used the w.c.—there, publicly, in the tiny cell. They could not help it. There was nowhere else to go. And the plug of the beastly thing did not even pull properly.

Until the afternoon Gordon felt sick and weak. He had had no chance to shave, and his face was hatefully scrubby. At first he merely sat on the corner of the plank bed, at the end nearest the door, as far away from the w.c. as he could get, and took no notice of the other prisoners. They bored and disgusted him; later, as his headache wore off, he observed them with a faint interest. There was a professional burglar, a lean worried-looking man with grey hair, who was in a terrible stew about what would happen to his wife and kids if he were sent to jail. He had been arrested for 'loitering with intent to enter'—a vague offence for which you generally get convicted if there are previous convictions against you. He kept walking up and down, flicking the fingers of his right hand with a curious nervous gesture, and exclaiming against the unfairness of it. There was also a deaf mute who stank like a ferret, and a small middle-aged Jew with a fur-collared overcoat, who had been buyer to a large firm of kosher butchers. He had bolted with twenty-seven pounds, gone to Aberdeen, of all places, and spent the money on tarts. He too had a grievance, for he said his case ought to have been tried in the rabbi's court instead of being turned over to the police. There was also a publican who had embezzled his Christmas club money. He was a big, hearty, prosperous-looking man of about thirty-five, with a loud red face and a loud blue overcoat—the sort of man who, if he were not a publican, would be a bookie. His relatives had paid back the embezzled money, all except twelve pounds, but the club members had decided to prosecute. There was something in this man's eyes that troubled Gordon. He carried everything off with a swagger, but all the while there was that blank, staring look in his eyes; he would fall into a kind of reverie at every gap in the conversation. It was somehow rather dreadful to see him. There he was, still in his smart clothes, with the splendour of a publican's life only a month or two behind him; and now he was ruined, probably for ever. Like all London publicans he was in the claw of the brewer, he would be sold up and his furniture and fittings seized, and when he came out of jail he would never have a pub or a job again.

The morning wore on with dismal slowness. You were allowed to smoke—matches were forbidden, but the constable on duty outside would give you a light through the trap in the door. Nobody had any cigarettes except the publican, who had his pockets full of them and distributed them freely. Prisoners came and went. A ragged dirty man who claimed to be a coster 'up' for obstruction was put into the cell for half an hour. He talked a great deal, but the others were deeply suspicious of him; when he was taken out again they all declared he was a 'split'. The police, it was said, often put a 'split' into the cells, disguised as a prisoner, to pick up information. Once there was great excitement when the constable whispered through the trap that a murderer, or would-be murderer, was being put into the cell next door. He was a youth of eighteen who had stabbed his 'tart' in the belly, and she was not expected to live. Once the trap opened and the tired, pale face of a clergyman looked in. He saw the burglar, said wearily, '*You* here again, Jones?' and went away again. Dinner, so-called, was served out at about twelve o'clock. All you got was a cup of tea and two slices of bread and marg. You could have food sent in, though, if you could pay for it. The publican had a good dinner sent in in covered dishes; but he had no appetite for it, and gave most of it away. Ravelston was still hanging about the court, waiting for Gordon's case to come on, but he did not know the ropes well enough to have food sent in to Gordon. Presently the burglar and the publican were taken away, sentenced, and brought back to wait till the Black Maria should take them off to jail. They each got nine months. The publican questioned the burglar about what prison was like. There was a conversation of unspeakable obscenity about the lack of women there.

Gordon's case came on at half past two, and it was over so quickly that it seemed preposterous to have waited all that time for it. Afterwards he could remember nothing about the court except the coat of arms over the magistrate's chair. The magistrate was dealing with the drunks at the rate of two a minute. To the tune of 'John-Smith-drunk-and-incapable-drunk?-yes-six-shillings-move-on-*next*!' they filed past the railings of the dock, precisely like a crowd taking tickets at a booking-office. Gordon's case, however, took two minutes instead of thirty seconds, because he had been disorderly and the sergeant had to testify that Gordon had struck him on the ear and called him a—bastard. There was also a mild sensation in the court because Gordon, when questioned at the police station, had described himself as a poet. He must have been very drunk to say a thing like that. The magistrate looked at him suspiciously.

'I see you call yourself a *poet*. *Are* you a poet?'

'I write poetry,' said Gordon sulkily.

'Hm! Well, it doesn't seem to teach you to behave yourself, does it? You will pay five pounds or go to prison for fourteen days. *Next!*'

And that was all. Nevertheless, somewhere at the back of the court a bored reporter had pricked up his ears.

On the other side of the court there was a room where a police sergeant sat with a large ledger, entering up the drunks' fines and taking payment. Those who could not pay were taken back to the cells. Gordon had expected this to happen to himself. He was quite resigned to going to prison. But when he emerged from the court it was to find that Ravelston was waiting there and had already paid his fine for him. Gordon did not protest. He allowed Ravelston to pack him into a taxi and take him back to the flat in Regent's Park. As soon as they got there Gordon had a hot bath; he needed one, after the beastly contaminating grime of the last twelve hours. Ravelston lent him a razor, lent him a clean shirt and pyjamas and socks and underclothes, even went out of doors and bought him a toothbrush. He was strangely solicitous about Gordon. He could not rid himself of a guilty feeling that what had happened last night was mainly his own fault; he ought to have put his foot down and taken Gordon home as soon as he showed signs of being drunk. Gordon scarcely noticed what was being done for him. Even the fact the Ravelston had paid his fine failed to trouble him. For the rest of that afternoon he lay in one of the armchairs in front of the fire, reading a detective story. About the future he refused to think. He grew sleepy very early. At eight o'clock he went to bed in the spare bedroom and slept like a log for nine hours.

It was not till next morning that he began to think seriously about his situation. He woke in the wide caressing bed, softer and warmer than any bed he had ever slept in, and began to grope about for his matches. Then he remembered that in places like this you didn't need matches to get a light, and felt for the electric switch that hung on a cord at the bedhead. Soft light flooded the room. There was a syphon of soda water on the bed-table. Gordon discovered that even after thirty-six hours there was still a vile taste in his mouth. He had a drink and looked about him.

It was a queer feeling, lying there in somebody else's pyjamas in somebody else's bed. He felt that he had no business there—that this wasn't the sort of place where he belonged. There was a sense of guilt in lying here in luxury when he was ruined and hadn't a penny in the world. For he was ruined right enough, there was no doubt about that. He seemed to know with perfect certainty that his job was lost. God knew what was going to happen next. The memory of that stupid dull debauch rolled back upon him with beastly vividness. He could recall everything, from his first pink gin before he started out to Dora's peach-coloured garters. He squirmed when he thought of Dora. *Why* does one do these things? Money again, always money! The rich don't behave like that. The rich are graceful even in their vices. But if you have no money you don't even know how to spend it when you get it. You just splurge it frantically away, like a sailor in a bawdy-house his first night ashore.

He had been in the clink, twelve hours. He thought of the cold faecal stench of that cell at the police court. A foretaste of future days. And everyone would know that he had been in the clink. With luck it might be kept from Aunt Angela and Uncle Walter, but Julia and Rosemary probably knew already. With Rosemary it didn't matter so much, but Julia would be ashamed and miserable. He thought of Julia. Her long thin back as she bent over the tea-caddy; her good, goose-like, defeated face. She had never lived. From childhood she had been sacrificed to him—to Gordon, to 'the boy'. It might be a hundred quid he had 'borrowed' from her in all these years; and then even five quid he couldn't spare her. Five quid he had set aside for her, and then spent it on a tart!

He turned out the light and lay on his back, wide awake. At this moment he saw himself with frightful clarity. He took a sort of inventory of himself and his possessions. Gordon Comstock, last of the Comstocks, thirty years old, with twenty-six teeth left; with no money and no job; in borrowed pyjamas in a borrowed bed; with nothing before him except cadging and destitution, and nothing behind him except squalid fooleries. His total wealth a puny body and two cardboard suitcases full of worn-out clothes.

At seven Ravelston was awakened by a tap on his door. He rolled over and said sleepily, 'Hullo?' Gordon came in, a dishevelled figure almost lost in the borrowed silk pyjamas. Ravelston roused himself, yawning. Theoretically he got up at the proletarian hour of seven. Actually he seldom stirred until Mrs Beaver, the charwoman, arrived at eight. Gordon pushed the hair out of his eyes and sat down on the foot of Ravelston's bed.

'I say, Ravelston, this is bloody. I've been thinking things over. There's going to be hell to pay.'

'What?'

'I shall lose my job. McKechnie can't keep me on after I've been in the clink. Besides, I ought to have been at work yesterday. Probably the shop wasn't opened all day.'

Ravelston yawned. 'It'll be all right, I think. That fat chap—what's his name? Flaxman—rang McKechnie up and told him you were down with flu. He made it pretty convincing. He said your temperature was a hundred and three. Of course your landlady knows. But I don't suppose she'd tell McKechnie.'

'But suppose it's got into the papers!'

'Oh, lord! I suppose that might happen. The char brings the papers up at eight. But do they report drunk cases? Surely not?'

Mrs Beaver brought the *Telegraph* and the *Herald*. Ravelston sent her out for the *Mail* and the *Express*. They searched hurriedly through the police-court news. Thank God! it hadn't 'got into the papers' after all. There was no reason why it should, as a matter of fact. It was not as if Gordon had been a racing motorist or a professional footballer. Feeling better, Gordon managed to eat some breakfast, and after breakfast Ravelston went out. It was agreed that he should go up to the shop, see Mr McKechnie, give him further details of Gordon's illness, and find out how the land lay. It seemed quite natural to Ravelston to waste several days in getting Gordon out of his scrape. All the morning Gordon hung about the flat, restless and out of sorts, smoking cigarettes in an endless chain. Now that he was alone, hope had deserted him. He knew by profound instinct that Mr McKechnie would have heard about his arrest. It wasn't the kind of thing you could keep dark. He had lost his job, and that was all about it.

He lounged across to the window and looked out. A desolate day; the whitey-grey sky looked as if it could never be blue again; the naked trees wept slowly into the gutters. Down a neighbouring street the cry of the coal-man echoed mournfully. Only a fortnight to Christmas now. Jolly to be out of work at this time of year! But the thought, instead of frightening him, merely bored him. The peculiar lethargic feeling, the stuffy heaviness behind the eyes, that one has after a fit of drunkenness, seemed to have settled upon him permanently. The prospect of searching for another job bored him even more than the prospect of poverty. Besides, he would never find another job. There are no jobs to be had nowadays. He was going down, down into the sub-world of the unemployed—down, down into God knew what workhouse depths of dirt and hunger and futility. And chiefly he was anxious to get it over with as little fuss and effort as possible.

Ravelston came back at about one o'clock. He pulled his gloves off and threw them into a chair. He looked tired and depressed. Gordon saw at a glance that the game was up.

'He's heard, of course?' he said.

'Everything, I'm afraid.'

'How? I suppose that cow of a Wisbeach woman went and sneaked to him?'

'No. It was in the paper after all. The local paper. He got it out of that.'

'Oh, hell! I'd forgotten that.'

Ravelston produced from his coat pocket a folded copy of a bi-weekly paper. It was one that they took in at the shop because Mr McKechnie advertised in it—Gordon had forgotten that. He opened it. Gosh! What a splash! It was all over the middle page.

BOOKSELLER'S ASSISTANT FINED
MAGISTRATE'S SEVERE STRICTURE
'DISGRACEFUL FRACAS'

There were nearly two columns of it. Gordon had never been so famous before and never would be again. They must have been very hard up for a bit of news. But these local papers have a curious notion of patriotism. They are so avid for local news that a bicycle-accident in the Harrow Road will occupy more space than a European crisis, and such items of news as 'Hampstead Man on Murder Charge' or 'Dismembered Baby in Cellar in Camberwell' are displayed with positive pride.

Ravelston described his interview with Mr McKechnie. Mr McKechnie, it seemed, was torn between his rage against Gordon and his desire not to offend such a good customer as Ravelston. But of course, after such a thing like that, you could hardly expect him to take Gordon back. These scandals were bad for trade, and besides, he was justly angry at the lies Flaxman had told him over the phone. But he was angriest of all at the thought of *his* assistant being drunk and disorderly. Ravelston said that the drunkenness seemed to anger him in a way that was peculiar. He gave the impression that he would almost have preferred Gordon to pinch money out of the till. Of course, he was a teetotaller himself. Gordon had sometimes wondered whether he wasn't also a secret drinker, in the traditional Scottish style. His nose was certainly very red. But perhaps it was snuff that did it. Anyway, that was that. Gordon was in the soup, full fathom five.

'I suppose the Wisbeach will stick to my clothes and things,' he said. 'I'm not going round there to fetch them. Besides, I owe her a week's rent.'

'Oh, don't worry about that. I'll see to your rent and everything.'

'My dear chap, I can't let you pay my rent!'

'Oh, dash it!' Ravelston's face grew faintly pink. He looked miserably into the distance, and then said what he had to say all in a sudden burst: 'Look here, Gordon, we must get this settled. You've just got to stay here till this business has blown over. I'll see you through about money and all that. You needn't think you're being a nuisance, because you're not. And anyway, it's only till you get another job.'

Gordon moved moodily away from him, his hands in his pockets. He had foreseen all this, of course. He knew that he ought to refuse, he *wanted* to refuse, and yet he had not quite the courage.

'I'm not going to sponge on you like that,' he said sulkily.

'Don't use such expressions, for God's sake! Besides, where could you go if you didn't stay here?'

'I don't know—into the gutter, I suppose. It's where I belong. The sooner I get there the better.'

'Rot! You're going to stay here till you've found another job.'

'But there isn't a job in the world. It might be a year before I found a job. I don't *want* a job.'

'You mustn't talk like that. You'll find a job right enough. Something's bound to turn up. And for God's sake don't talk about *sponging* on me. It's only an arrangement between friends. If you really want to, you can pay it all back when you've got the money.'

'Yes—*when*!'

But in the end he let himself be persuaded. He had known that he would let himself be persuaded. He stayed on at the flat, and allowed Ravelston to go round to Willowbed Road and pay his rent and recover his two cardboard suitcases; he even allowed Ravelston to 'lend' him a further two pounds for current expenses. His heart sickened while he did it. He was living on Ravelston—sponging on Ravelston. How could there ever be a real friendship between them again? Besides, in his heart he didn't want to be helped. He only wanted to be left alone. He was headed for the gutter; better to reach the gutter quickly and get it over. Yet for the time being he stayed, simply because he lacked the courage to do otherwise.

But as for this business of getting a job, it was hopeless from the start. Even Ravelston, though rich, could not manufacture jobs out of nothing. Gordon knew beforehand that there were no jobs going begging in the book trade. During the next three days he wore his shoes out traipsing from bookseller to bookseller. At shop after shop he set his teeth, marched in, demanded to see the manager, and three minutes later marched out again with his nose in the air. The answer was always the same—no jobs vacant. A few booksellers were taking on an extra man for the Christmas rush, but Gordon was not the type they were looking for. He was neither smart nor servile; he wore shabby clothes and spoke with the accent of a gentleman. Besides, a few questions always brought it out that he had been sacked from his last job for drunkenness. After only three days he gave it up. He knew it was no use. It was only to please Ravelston that he had even been pretending to look for work.

In the evening he trailed back to the flat, footsore and with his nerves on edge from a series of snubs. He was making all his journeys on foot, to economize Ravelston's two pounds. When he got back Ravelston had just come up from the office and was sitting in one of the armchairs in front of the fire, with some long galley-proofs over his knee. He looked up as Gordon came in.

'Any luck?' he said as usual.

Gordon did not answer. If he had answered it would have been with a stream of obscenities. Without even looking at Ravelston he went straight into his bedroom, kicked off his shoes, and flung himself on the bed. He hated himself at this moment. Why had he come back? What right had he to come back and sponge on Ravelston when he hadn't even the intention of looking for a job any longer? He ought to have stayed out in the streets, slept in Trafalgar Square, begged—anything. But he hadn't the guts to face the streets as yet. The prospect of warmth and shelter had tugged him back. He lay with his hands beneath his head, in a mixture of apathy and self-hatred. After about half an hour he heard the door-bell ring and Ravelston get up to answer it. It was that bitch Hermione Slater, presumably. Ravelston had introduced Gordon to Hermione a couple of days ago, and she had treated him like dirt. But a moment later there was a knock at the bedroom door.

'What is it?' said Gordon.

'Somebody's come to see you,' said Ravelston.

'To see *me*?'

'Yes. Come on into the other room.'

Gordon swore and rolled sluggishly off the bed. When he got to the other room he found that the visitor was Rosemary. He had been half expecting her, of course, but it wearied him to see her. He knew why she had come; to sympathize with him, to pity him, to reproach him—it was all the same. In his despondent, bored mood he did not want to make the effort of talking to her. All he wanted was to be left alone. But Ravelston was glad to see her. He had taken a liking to her in their single meeting and thought she might cheer Gordon up. He made a transparent pretext to go downstairs to the office, leaving the two of them together.

They were alone, but Gordon made no move to embrace her. He was standing in front of the fire, round-shouldered, his hands in his coat pockets, his feet thrust into a pair of Ravelston's slippers which were much too big for him. She came rather hesitantly towards him, not yet taking off her hat or her coat with the lamb-skin collar. It hurt her to see him. In less than a week his appearance had deteriorated strangely. Already he had that unmistakable, seedy, lounging look of a man who is out of work. His face seemed to have grown thinner, and there were rings round his eyes. Also it was obvious that he had not shaved that day.

She laid her hand on his arm, rather awkwardly, as a woman does when it is she who has to make the first embrace.

'Gordon—'

'Well?'

He said it almost sulkily. The next moment she was in his arms. But it was she who had made the first movement, not he. Her head was on his breast, and behold! she was struggling with all her might against the tears that almost overwhelmed her. It bored Gordon dreadfully. He seemed so often to reduce her to tears! And he didn't want to be cried over; he only wanted to be left alone—alone to sulk and despair. As he held her there, one hand mechanically caressing her shoulder, his main feeling was boredom. She had made things more difficult for him by coming here. Ahead of him were dirt, cold, hunger, the streets, the workhouse, and the jail. It was against *that* that he had got to steel himself. And he could steel himself, if only she would leave him alone and not come plaguing him with these irrelevant emotions.

He pushed her a little way from him. She had recovered herself quickly, as she always did.

'Gordon, my dear one! Oh, I'm so sorry, so sorry!'

'Sorry about what?'

'You losing your job and everything. You look so unhappy.'

'I'm not unhappy. Don't pity me, for God's sake.'

He disengaged himself from her arms. She pulled her hat off and threw it into a chair. She had come here with something definite to say. It was something she had refrained from saying all these years—something that it had seemed to her a point of chivalry not to say. But now it had got to be said, and she would come straight out with it. It was not in her nature to beat about the bush.

'Gordon, will you do something to please me?'

'What?'

'Will you go back to the New Albion?'

So that was it! Of course he had foreseen it. She was going to start nagging at him like all the others. She was going to add herself to the band of people who worried him and badgered him to 'get on'. But what else could you expect? It was what any woman would say. The marvel was that she had never said it before. Go back to the New Albion! It had been the sole significant action of his life, leaving the New Albion. It was his religion, you might say, to keep out of that filthy money-world. Yet at this moment he could not remember with any clarity the motives for which he had left the New Albion. All he knew was that he would never go back, not if the skies fell, and that the argument he foresaw bored him in advance.

He shrugged his shoulders and looked away. 'The New Albion wouldn't take me back,' he said shortly.

'Yes, they would. You remember what Mr Erskine said. It's not so long ago—only two years. And they're always on the look-out for good copywriters. Everyone at the office says so. I'm sure they'd give you a job if you went and asked them. And they'd pay you at least four pounds a week.'

'Four pounds a week! Splendid! I could afford to keep an aspidistra on that, couldn't I?'

'No, Gordon, don't joke about it now.'

'I'm not joking. I'm serious.'

'You mean you won't go back to them—not even if they offered you a job?'

'Not in a thousand years. Not if they paid me fifty pounds a week.'

'But why? Why?'

'I've told you why,' he said wearily.

She looked at him helplessly. After all, it was no use. There was this money-business standing in the way—these meaningless scruples which she had never understood but which she had accepted merely because they were his. She felt all the impotence, the resentment of a woman who sees an abstract idea triumphing over common sense. How maddening it was, that he should let himself be pushed into the gutter by a thing like that! She said almost angrily:

'I don't understand you, Gordon, I really don't. Here you are out of work, you may be starving in a little while for all you know; and yet when there's a good job which you can have almost for the asking, you won't take it.'

'No, you're quite right. I won't.'

'But you must have *some* kind of job, mustn't you?'

'A job, but not a *good* job. I've explained that God knows how often. I dare say I'll get a job of sorts sooner or later. The same kind of job as I had before.'

'But I don't believe you're even *trying* to get a job, are you?'

'Yes, I am. I've been out all today seeing booksellers.'

'And you didn't even shave this morning!' she said, changing her ground with feminine swiftness.

He felt his chin. 'I don't believe I did, as a matter of fact.'

'And then you expect people to give you a job! Oh, Gordon!'

'Oh, well, what does it matter? It's too much fag to shave every day.'

'You're letting yourself go to pieces,' she said bitterly. 'You don't seem to *want* to make any effort. You want to sink—just *sink*!'

'I don't know—perhaps. I'd sooner sink than rise.'

There were further arguments. It was the first time she had ever spoken to him like this. Once again the tears came into her eyes, and once again she fought them back. She had come here swearing to herself that she would not cry. The dreadful thing was that her tears, instead of distressing him, merely bored him. It was as though he *could* not care, and yet at his very centre there was an inner heart that cared because he could not care. If only she would leave him alone! Alone, alone! Free from the nagging consciousness of his failure; free to sink, as she had said, down, down into quiet worlds where money and effort and moral obligation did not exist. Finally he got away from her and went back to the spare bedroom. It was definitely a quarrel—the first really deadly quarrel they had ever had. Whether it was to be final he did not know. Nor did he care, at this moment. He locked the door behind him and lay on the bed smoking a cigarette. He must get out of this place, and quickly! Tomorrow morning he would clear out. No more sponging on Ravelston! No more blackmail to the gods of decency! Down, down, into the mud—down to the streets, the workhouse, and the jail. It was only there that he could be at peace.

Ravelston came upstairs to find Rosemary alone and on the point of departure. She said good-bye and then suddenly turned to him and laid her hand on his arm. She felt that she knew him well enough now to take him into her confidence.

'Mr Ravelston, please—*will* you try and persuade Gordon to get a job?'

'I'll do what I can. Of course it's always difficult. But I expect we'll find him a job of sorts before long.'

'It's so dreadful to see him like this! He goes absolutely to pieces. And all the time, you see, there's a job he could quite easily get if he wanted it—a really *good* job. It's not that he can't, it's simply that he won't.'

She explained about the New Albion. Ravelston rubbed his nose.

'Yes. As a matter of fact I've heard all about that. We talked it over when he left the New Albion.'

'But you don't think he was right to leave them?' she said, promptly divining that Ravelston *did* think Gordon right.

'Well—I grant you it wasn't very wise. But there's a certain amount of truth in what he says. Capitalism's corrupt and we ought to keep outside it—that's his idea. It's not practicable, but in a way it's sound.'

'Oh, I dare say it's all right as a theory! But when he's out of work and when he could get this job if he chose to ask for it—*surely* you don't think he's right to refuse?'

'Not from a common-sense point of view. But in principle—well, yes.'

'Oh, in principle! We can't afford principles, people like us. *That's* what Gordon doesn't seem to understand.'

Gordon did not leave the flat next morning. One resolves to do these things, one *wants* to do them; but when the time comes, in the cold morning light, they somehow don't get done. He would stay just one day more he told himself; and then again it was 'just one day more', until five whole days had passed since Rosemary's visit, and he was still lurking there, living on Ravelston, with not even a flicker of a job in sight. He still made some pretence of searching for work, but he only did it to save his face. He would go out and loaf for hours in public libraries, and then come home to lie on the bed in the spare bedroom, dressed except for his shoes, smoking endless cigarettes. And for all that inertia and the fear of the streets still held him there, those five days were awful, damnable, unspeakable. There is nothing more dreadful in the world than to live in somebody else's house, eating his bread and doing nothing in return for it. And perhaps it is worst of all when your benefactor won't for a moment admit that he is your benefactor. Nothing could have exceeded Ravelston's delicacy. He would have perished rather than admit that Gordon was sponging on him. He had paid Gordon's fine, he had paid his arrears of rent, he had kept him for a week, and he had 'lent' him two pounds on top of that; but it was nothing, it was a mere arrangement between friends, Gordon would do the same for him another time. From time to time Gordon made feeble efforts to escape, which always ended in the same way.

'Look here, Ravelston, I can't stay here any longer. You've kept me long enough. I'm going to clear out tomorrow morning.'

'But my dear old chap! Do be sensible. You haven't—' But no! Not even now, when Gordon was openly on the rocks, could Ravelston say, 'You haven't got any money.' One can't say things like that. He compromised: 'Where are you going to live, anyway?'

'God knows—I don't care. There are common lodging-houses and places. I've got a few bob left.'

'Don't be such an ass. You'd much better stay here till you've found a job.'

'But it might be months, I tell you. I can't live on you like this.'

'Rot, my dear chap! I like having you here.'

But of course, in his inmost heart, he didn't really like having Gordon there.

How should he? It was an impossible situation. There was a tension between them all the time. It is always so when one person is living on another. However delicately disguised, charity is still horrible; there is a malaise, almost a secret hatred, between the giver and the receiver. Gordon knew that his friendship with Ravelston would never be the same again. Whatever happened afterwards, the memory of this evil time would be between them. The feeling of his dependent position, of being in the way, unwanted, a nuisance, was with him night and day. At meals he would scarcely eat, he would not smoke Ravelston's cigarettes, but bought himself cigarettes out of his few remaining shillings. He would not even light the gas-fire in his bedroom. He would have made himself invisible if he could. Every day, of course, people were coming and going at the flat and at the office. All of them saw Gordon and grasped his status. Another of Ravelston's pet scroungers, they all said. He even detected a gleam of professional jealousy in one or two of the hangers-on of *Antichrist*. Three times during that week Hermione Slater came. After his first encounter with her he fled from the flat as soon as she appeared; on one occasion, when she came at night, he had to stay out of doors till after midnight. Mrs Beaver, the charwoman, had also 'seen through' Gordon. She knew his type. He was another of those good-for-nothing young 'writing gentlemen' who sponged on poor Mr Ravelston. So in none too subtle ways she made things uncomfortable for Gordon. Her favourite trick was to rout him out with broom and pan—'Now, Mr Comstock, I've got to do this room out, *if* you please'—from whichever room he had settled down in.

But in the end, unexpectedly and through no effort of his own, Gordon did get a job. One morning a letter came for Ravelston from Mr McKechnie. Mr McKechnie had relented—not to the extent of taking Gordon back, of course, but to the extent of helping him find another job. He said that a Mr Cheeseman, a bookseller in Lambeth, was looking for an assistant. From what he said it was evident that Gordon could get the job if he applied for it; it was equally evident that there was some snag about the job. Gordon had vaguely heard of Mr Cheeseman—in the book trade everybody knows everybody else. In his heart the news bored him. He didn't really want this job. He didn't want ever to work again; all he wanted was to sink, sink, effortless, down into the mud. But he couldn't disappoint Ravelston after all Ravelston had done for him. So the same morning he went down to Lambeth to inquire about the job.

The shop was in the desolate stretch of road south of Waterloo Bridge. It was a poky, mean-looking shop, and the name over it, in faded gilt, was not Cheeseman but Eldridge. In the window, however, there were some valuable calf folios, and some sixteenth-century maps which Gordon thought must be worth money. Evidently Mr Cheeseman specialized in 'rare' books. Gordon plucked up his courage and went in.

As the door-bell ping'd, a tiny, evil-looking creature, with a sharp nose and heavy black eyebrows, emerged from the office behind the shop. He looked up at Gordon with a kind of nosy malice. When he spoke it was in an extraordinary clipped manner, as though he were biting each word in half before it escaped from him. 'Ot c'n I do f'yer!'—that approximately was what it sounded like. Gordon explained why he had come. Mr Cheeseman shot a meaning glance at him and answered in the same clipped manner as before:

'Oh, eh? Comstock, eh? Come 'is way. Got mi office back here. Bin 'specting you.'

Gordon followed him. Mr Cheeseman was a rather sinister little man, almost small enough to be called a dwarf, with very black hair, and slightly deformed. As a rule a dwarf, when malformed, has a full-sized torso and practically no legs. With Mr Cheeseman it was the other way about. His legs were normal length, but the top half of his body was so short that his buttocks seemed to sprout almost immediately below his shoulder blades. This gave him, in walking, a resemblance to a pair of scissors. He had the powerful bony shoulders of the dwarf, the large ugly hands, and the sharp nosing movements of the head. His clothes had that peculiar hardened, shiny texture of clothes that are very old and very dirty. They were just going into the office when the door-bell ping'd again, and a customer came in, holding out a book from the sixpenny box outside and half a crown. Mr Cheeseman did not take the change out of the till—apparently there was no till—but produced a very greasy wash-leather purse from some secret place under his waistcoat. He handled the purse, which was almost lost in his big hands, in a peculiarly secretive way, as though to hide it from sight.

'I like keep mi money i' mi pocket,' he explained, with an upward glance, as they went into the office.

It was apparent that Mr Cheeseman clipped his words from a notion that words cost money and ought not to be wasted. In the office they had a talk, and Mr Cheeseman extorted from Gordon the confession that he had been sacked for drunkenness. As a matter of fact he knew all about this already. He had heard about Gordon from Mr McKechnie, whom he had met at an auction a few days earlier. He had pricked up his ears when he heard the story, for he was on the look-out for an assistant, and clearly an assistant who had been sacked for drunkenness would come at reduced wages. Gordon saw that his drunkenness was going to be used as a weapon against him. Yet Mr Cheeseman did not seem absolutely unfriendly. He seemed to be the kind of person who will cheat you if he can, and bully you if you give him the chance, but who will also regard you with a contemptuous good-humour. He took Gordon into his confidence, talked of conditions in the trade, and boasted with much chuckling of his own astuteness. He had a peculiar chuckle, his mouth curving upwards at the corners and his large nose seeming about to disappear into it.

Recently, he told Gordon, he had had an idea for a profitable side-line. He was going to start a twopenny library; but it would have to be quite separate from the shop, because anything so low-class would frighten away the book-lovers who came to the shop in search of 'rare' books. He had taken premises a little distance away, and in the lunch-hour he took Gordon to see them. They were farther down the dreary street, between a flyblown ham-and-beef shop and a smartish undertaker. The ads in the undertaker's window caught Gordon's eye. It seems you can get underground for as little as two pounds ten nowadays. You can even get buried on the hire-purchase. There was also an ad for cremations—'Reverent, Sanitary, and Inexpensive.'

The premises consisted of a single narrow room—a mere pipe of a room with a window as wide as itself, furnished with a cheap desk, one chair, and a card index. The new-painted shelves were ready and empty. This was not, Gordon saw at a glance, going to be the kind of library that he had presided over at McKechnie's. McKechnie's library had been comparatively highbrow. It had dredged no deeper than Dell, and it even had books by Lawrence and Huxley. But this was one of those cheap and evil little libraries ('mushroom libraries', they are called) which are springing up all over London and are deliberately aimed at the uneducated. In libraries like these there is not a single book that is ever mentioned in the reviews or that any civilized person has ever heard of. The books are published by special low-class firms and turned out by wretched hacks at the rate of four a year, as mechanically as sausages and with much less skill. In effect they are merely fourpenny novelettes disguised as novels, and they only cost the library-proprietor one and eightpence a volume. Mr Cheeseman explained that he had not ordered the books yet. He spoke of 'ordering the books' as one might speak of ordering a ton of coals. He was going to start with five hundred assorted titles, he said. The shelves were already marked off into sections—'Sex', 'Crime', 'Wild West', and so forth.

He offered Gordon the job. It was very simple. All you had to do was to remain there ten hours a day, hand out the book, take the money, and choke off the more obvious book-pinchers. The pay, he added with a measuring, side-long glance, was thirty shillings a week.

Gordon accepted promptly. Mr Cheeseman was perhaps faintly disap-pointed. He had expected an argument, and would have enjoyed crushing Gordon by reminding him that beggars can't be choosers. But Gordon was satisfied. The job would do. There was no *trouble* about a job like this; no room for ambition, no effort, no hope. Ten bob less—ten bob nearer the mud. It was what he wanted.

He 'borrowed' another two pounds from Ravelston and took a furnished bed-sitting room, eight bob a week, in a filthy alley parallel to Lambeth Cut. Mr Cheeseman ordered the five hundred assorted titles, and Gordon started work on the twentieth of December. This, as it happened, was his thirtieth birthday.

# 10

Under ground, under ground! Down in the safe soft womb of earth, where there is no getting of jobs or losing of jobs, no relatives or friends to plague you, no hope, fear, ambition, honour, duty–no *duns* of any kind. That was where he wished to be.

Yet it was not death, actual physical death, that he wished for. It was a queer feeling that he had. It had been with him ever since that morning when he had woken up in the police cell. The evil, mutinous mood that comes after drunkenness seemed to have set into a habit. That drunken night had marked a period in his life. It had dragged him downward with strange suddenness. Before, he had fought against the money-code, and yet he had clung to his wretched remnant of decency. But now it was precisely from decency that he wanted to escape. He wanted to go down, deep down, into some world where decency no longer mattered; to cut the strings of his self-respect, to submerge himself–to *sink*, as Rosemary had said. It was all bound up in his mind with the thought of being *under ground*. He liked to think about the lost people, the under-ground people: tramps, beggars, criminals, prostitutes. It is a good world that they inhabit, down there in their frowzy kips and spikes. He liked to think that beneath the world of money there is that great sluttish underworld where failure and success have no meaning; a sort of kingdom of ghosts where all are equal. That was where he wished to be, down in the ghost-kingdom, *below* ambition. It comforted him somehow to think of the smoke-dim slums of South London sprawling on and on, a huge graceless wilderness where you could lose yourself for ever.

And in a way this job was what he wanted; at any rate, it was something near what he wanted. Down there in Lambeth, in winter, in the murky streets where the sepia-shadowed faces of tea-drunkards drifted through the mist, you had a *submerged* feeling. Down here you had no contact with money or with culture. No highbrow customers to whom you had to act the highbrow; no one who was capable of asking you, in that prying way that prosperous people have, 'What are you, with your brains and education, doing in a job like this?' You were just part of the slum, and, like all slum-dwellers, taken for granted. The youths and girls and draggled middle-aged women who came to the library scarcely even spotted the fact that Gordon was an educated man. He was just 'the bloke at the library', and practically one of themselves.

The job itself, of course, was of inconceivable futility. You just sat there, ten hours a day, six hours on Thursdays, handing out books, registering them, and receiving twopences. Between whiles there was nothing to do except read. There was nothing worth watching in the desolate street outside. The principal event of the day was when the hearse drove up to the undertaker's establishment next door. This had a faint interest for Gordon, because the dye was wearing off one of the horses and it was assuming by degrees a curious purplish-brown shade. Much of the time, when no customers came, he spent reading the yellow-jacketed trash that the library contained. Books of that type you could read at the rate of one an hour. And they were the kind of books that suited him nowadays. It is real 'escape literature', that stuff in the twopenny libraries. Nothing has ever been devised that puts less strain on the intelligence; even a film, by comparison, demands a certain effort. And so when a customer demanded a book of this category or that, whether it was 'Sex' or 'Crime' or 'Wild West' or '*Ro*mance' (always with the accent on the *o*). Gordon was ready with expert advice.

Mr Cheeseman was not a bad person to work for, so long as you understood that if you worked till the Day of Judgement you would never get a rise of wages. Needless to say, he suspected Gordon of pinching the till-money. After a week or two he devised a new system of booking, by which he could tell how many books had been taken out and check this with the day's takings. But it was still (he reflected) in Gordon's power to issue books and make no record of them; and so the possibility that Gordon might be cheating him of sixpence or even a shilling a day continued to trouble him, like the pea under the princess's mattress. Yet he was not absolutely unlikeable, in his sinister, dwarfish way. In the evenings, after he had shut the shop, when he came along to the library to collect the day's takings, he would stay talking to Gordon for a while and recounting with nosy chuckles any particularly astute swindles that he had worked lately. From these conversations Gordon pieced together Mr Cheeseman's history. He had been brought up in the old-clothes trade, which was his spiritual vocation, so to speak, and had inherited the bookshop from an uncle three years ago. At that time it was one of those dreadful bookshops in which there are not even any shelves, in which the books lie about in monstrous dusty piles with no attempt at classification. It was frequented to some extent by book-collectors, because there was occasionally a valuable book among the piles of rubbish, but mainly it kept going by selling second-hand paper-covered thrillers at twopence each. Over this dustheap Mr Cheeseman had presided, at first, with intense disgust. He loathed books and had not yet grasped that there was money to be made out of them. He was still keeping his old-clothes shop going by means of a deputy, and intended to return to it as soon as he could get a good offer for the bookshop. But presently it was borne in upon him that books, properly handled, are worth money. As soon as he had made this discovery he developed as astonishing flair for book-dealing. Within two years he had worked his shop up till it was one of the best 'rare' bookshops of its size in London. To him a book was as purely an article of merchandise as a pair of second-hand trousers. He had never in his life *read* a book himself, nor could he conceive why anyone should want to do so. His attitude towards the collectors who pored so lovingly over his rare editions was that of a sexually cold prostitute towards her clientele. Yet he seemed to know by the mere feel of a book whether it was valuable or not. His head was a perfect mine of auction-records and first-edition dates, and he had a marvellous nose for a bargain. His favourite way of acquiring stock was to buy up the libraries of people who had just died, especially clergymen. Whenever a clergyman died Mr Cheeseman was on the spot with the promptness of a vulture. Clergymen, he explained to Gordon, so often have good libraries and ignorant widows. He lived over the shop, was unmarried, of course, and had no amusements and seemingly no friends. Gordon used sometimes to wonder what Mr Cheeseman did with himself in the evenings, when he was not out snooping after bargains. He had a mental picture of Mr Cheeseman sitting in a double-locked room with the shutters over the windows, counting piles of half-crowns and bundles of pound notes which he stowed carefully away in cigarette-tins.

Mr Cheeseman bullied Gordon and was on the look-out for an excuse to dock his wages; yet he did not bear him any particular ill-will. Sometimes in the evening when he came to the library he would produce a greasy packet of Smith's Potato Crisps from his pocket, and, holding it out, say in his clipped style:

'Hassome chips?'

The packet was always grasped so firmly in his large hand that it was impossible to extract more than two or three chips. But he meant it as a friendly gesture.

As for the place where Gordon lived, in Brewer's Yard, parallel to Lambeth Cut on the south side, it was a filthy kip. His bed-sitting room was eight shillings a week and was just under the roof. With its sloping ceiling—it was a room shaped like a wedge of cheese—and its skylight window, it was the nearest thing to the proverbial poet's garret that he had ever lived in. There was a large, low, broken-backed bed with a ragged patchwork quilt and sheets that were changed once fortnightly; a deal table ringed by dynasties of teapots; a rickety kitchen chair; a tin basin for washing in; a gas-ring in the fender. The bare floorboards had never been stained but were dark with dirt. In the cracks in the pink wallpaper dwelt multitudes of bugs; however, this was winter and they were torpid unless you over-warmed the room. You were expected to make your own bed. Mrs Meakin, the landlady, theoretically 'did out' the rooms daily, but four days out of five she found the stairs too much for her. Nearly all the lodgers cooked their own squalid meals in their bedrooms. There was no gas-stove, of course; just the gas-ring in the fender, and, down two flights of stairs, a large evil-smelling sink which was common to the whole house.

In the garret adjoining Gordon's there lived a tall handsome old woman who was not quite right in the head and whose face was often as black as a Negro's from dirt. Gordon could never make out where the dirt came from. It looked like coal dust. The children of the neighbourhood used to shout 'Blackie!' after her as she stalked along the pavement like a tragedy queen, talking to herself. On the floor below there was a woman with a baby which cried, cried everlastingly; also a young couple who used to have frightful quarrels and frightful reconciliations which you could hear all over the house. On the ground floor a house-painter, his wife, and five children existed on the dole and an occasional odd job. Mrs Meakin, the landlady, inhabited some burrow or other in the basement. Gordon liked this house. It was all so different from Mrs Wisbeach's. There was no mingy lower-middle-class decency here, no feeling of being spied upon and disapproved of. So long as you paid your rent you could do almost exactly as you liked; come home drunk and crawl up the stairs, bring women in at all hours, lie in bed all day if you wanted to. Mother Meakin was not the type to interfere. She was a dishevelled, jelly-soft old creature with a figure like a cottage loaf. People said that in her youth she had been no better than she ought, and probably it was true. She had a loving manner towards anything in trousers. Yet it seemed that traces of respectability lingered in her breast. On the day when Gordon installed himself he heard her puffing and struggling up the stairs, evidently bearing some burden. She knocked softly on the door with her knee, or the place where her knee ought to have been, and he let her in.

''Ere y'are, then,' she wheezed kindly as she came in with her arms full. 'I knew as 'ow you'd like this. I likes all my lodgers to feel comfortable-like. Lemme put it on the table for you. There! That makes the room like a bit more 'ome-like, don't it now?'

It was an aspidistra. It gave him a bit of a twinge to see it. Even here, in this final refuge! Hast thou found me, O mine enemy? But it was a poor weedy specimen—indeed, it was obviously dying.

In this place he could have been happy if only people would let him alone. It was a place where you *could* be happy, in a sluttish way. To spend your days in meaningless mechanical work, work that could be slovened through in a sort of coma; to come home and light the fire when you had any coal (there were sixpenny bags at the grocer's) and get the stuffy little attic warm; to sit over a squalid meal of bacon, bread-and-marg and tea, cooked over the gas-ring; to lie on the frowzy bed, reading a thriller or doing the Brain Brighteners in *Tit Bits* until the small hours; it was the kind of life he wanted. All his habits had deteriorated rapidly. He never shaved more than three times a week nowadays, and only washed the parts that showed. There were good public baths near by, but he hardly went to them as often as once in a month. He never made his bed properly, but just turned back the sheets, and never washed his few crocks till all of them had been used twice over. There was a film of dust on everything. In the fender there was always a greasy frying-pan and a couple of plates coated with the remnants of fried eggs. One night the bugs came out of one of the cracks and marched across the ceiling two by two. He lay on his bed, his hands under his head, watching them with interest. Without regret, almost intentionally, he was letting himself go to pieces. At the bottom of all his feelings there was sulkiness a *je m'en fous* in the face of the world. Life had beaten him; but you can still beat life by turning your face away. Better to sink than rise. Down, down into the ghost-kingdom, the shadowy world where shame, effort, decency do not exist!

To sink! How easy it ought to be, since there are so few competitors! But the strange thing is that often it is harder to sink than to rise. There is always something that drags one upwards. After all, one is never quite alone; there are always friends, lovers, relatives. Everyone Gordon knew seemed to be writing him letters, pitying him or bullying him. Aunt Angela had written, Uncle Walter had written, Rosemary had written over and over again, Ravelston had written, Julia had written. Even Flaxman had sent a line to wish him luck. Flaxman's wife had forgiven him, and he was back at Peckham, in aspidistral bliss. Gordon hated getting letters nowadays. They were a link with that other world from which he was trying to escape.

Even Ravelston had turned against him. That was after he had been to see Gordon in his new lodgings. Until this visit he had not realized what kind of neighbourhood Gordon was living in. As his taxi drew up at the corner, in the Waterloo Road, a horde of ragged shock-haired boys came swooping from nowhere, to fight round the taxi door like fish at a bait. Three of them clung to the handle and hauled the door open simultaneously. Their servile, dirty little faces, wild with hope, made him feel sick. He flung some pennies among them and fled up the alley without looking at them again. The narrow pavements were smeared with a quantity of dogs' excrement that was surprising, seeing that there were no dogs in sight. Down in the basement Mother Meakin was boiling a haddock, and you could smell it half-way up the stairs. In the attic Ravelston sat on the rickety chair, with the ceiling sloping just behind his head. The fire was out and there was no light in the room except four candles guttering in a saucer beside the aspidistra. Gordon lay on the ragged bed, fully dressed but with no shoes on. He had scarcely stirred when Ravelston came in. He just lay there, flat on his back, sometimes smiling a little, as though there were some private joke between himself and the ceiling. The room had already the stuffy sweetish smell of rooms that have been lived in a long time and never cleaned. There were dirty crocks lying about in the fender.

'Would you like a cup of tea?' Gordon said, without stirring.

'No thanks awfully—no,' said Ravelston, a little too hastily.

He had seen the brown-stained cups in the fender and the repulsive common sink downstairs. Gordon knew quite well why Ravelston refused the tea. The whole atmosphere of this place had given Ravelston a kind of shock. That awful mixed smell of slops and haddock on the stairs! He looked at Gordon, supine on the ragged bed. And, dash it, Gordon was a gentleman! At another time he would have repudiated that thought; but in this atmosphere pious humbug was impossible. All the class-instincts which he believed himself not to possess rose in revolt. It was dreadful to think of anyone with brains and refinement living in a place like this. He wanted to tell Gordon to get out of it, pull himself together, earn a decent income, and live like a gentleman. But of course he didn't say so. You can't say things like that. Gordon was aware of what was going on inside Ravelston's head. It amused him, rather. He felt no gratitude towards Ravelston for coming here and seeing him; on the other hand, he was not ashamed of his surroundings as he would once have been. There was a faint, amused malice in the way he spoke.

'You think I'm a B.F., of course,' he remarked to the ceiling.

'No, I don't. Why should I?'

'Yes, you do. You think I'm a B.F. to stay in this filthy place instead of getting a proper job. You think I ought to try for that job at the New Albion.'

'No, dash it! I never thought that. I see your point absolutely. I told you that before. I think you're perfectly right in principle.'

'And you think principles are all right so long as one doesn't go putting them into practice.'

'No. But the question always is, when *is* one putting them into practice?'

'It's quite simple. I've made war on money. This is where it's led me.'

Ravelston rubbed his nose, then shifted uneasily on his chair.

'The mistake you make, don't you see, is in thinking one can live in a corrupt society without being corrupt oneself. After all, what do you achieve by refusing to make money? You're trying to behave as though one could stand right outside our economic system. But one can't. One's got to change the system, or one changes nothing. One can't put things right in a hole-and-corner way, if you take my meaning.'

Gordon waved a foot at the buggy ceiling.

'Of course this *is* a hole-and-corner, I admit.'

'I didn't mean that,' said Ravelston, pained.

'But let's face facts. You think I ought to be looking about for a *good* job, don't you?'

'It depends on the job. I think you're quite right not to sell yourself to that advertising agency. But it does seem rather a pity that you should stay in that wretched job you're in at present. After all, you *have* got talents. You ought to be using them somehow.'

'There are my poems,' said Gordon, smiling at his private joke.

Ravelston looked abashed. This remark silenced him. Of course, there *were* Gordon's poems. There was *London Pleasures*, for instance. Ravelston knew, and Gordon knew, and each knew that the other knew, that *London Pleasures* would never be finished. Never again, probably, would Gordon write a line of poetry; never, at least, while he remained in this vile place, this blind-alley job and this defeated mood. He had finished with all that. But this could not be said, as yet. The pretence was still kept up that Gordon was a struggling poet—the conventional poet-in-garret.

It was not long before Ravelston rose to go. This smelly place oppressed him, and it was increasingly obvious that Gordon did not want him here. He moved hesitantly towards the door, pulling on his gloves, then came back again, pulling off his left glove and flicking it against his leg.

'Look here, Gordon, you won't mind my saying it—this is a filthy place, you know. This house, this street—everything.'

'I know. It's a pigsty. It suits me.'

'But do you *have* to live in a place like this?'

'My dear chap, you know what my wages are. Thirty bob a week.'

'Yes, but—! Surely there *are* better places? What rent are you paying?'

'Eight bob.'

'Eight bob? You could get a fairly decent unfurnished room for that. Something a bit better than this, anyway. Look here, why don't you take an unfurnished place and let me lend you ten quid for furniture?'

'"Lend" me ten quid! After all you've "lent" me already? *Give* me ten quid, you mean.'

Ravelston gazed unhappily at the wall. Dash it, what a thing to say! He said flatly:

'All right, if you like to put it like that. *Give* you ten quid.'

'But as it happens, you see, I don't want it.'

'But dash it all! You might as well have a decent place to live in.'

'But I don't want a decent place. I want an indecent place. This one, for instance.'

'But why? Why?'

'It's suited to my station,' said Gordon, turning his face to the wall.

A few days later Ravelston wrote him a long, diffident sort of letter. It reiterated most of what he had said in their conversation. Its general effect was that Ravelston saw Gordon's point entirely, that there was a lot of truth in what Gordon said, that Gordon was absolutely right in principle, but–! It was the obvious, the inevitable 'but'. Gordon did not answer. It was several months before he saw Ravelston again. Ravelston made various attempts to get in touch with him. It was a curious fact–rather a shameful fact from a Socialist's point of view–that the thought of Gordon, who had brains and was of gentle birth, lurking in that vile place and that almost menial job, worried him more than the thought of ten thousand unemployed in Middlesbrough. Several times, in hope of cheering Gordon up, he wrote asking him to send contributions to *Antichrist*. Gordon never answered. The friendship was at an end, it seemed to him. The evil time when he had lived on Ravelston had spoiled everything. Charity kills friendship.

And then there were Julia and Rosemary. They differed from Ravelston in this, that they had no shyness about speaking their minds. They did not say euphemistically that Gordon was 'right in principle'; they knew that to refuse a 'good' job can never be right. Over and over again they besought him to go back to the New Albion. The worst was that he had both of them in pursuit of him together. Before this business they had never met, but now Rosemary had got to know Julia somehow. They were in feminine league against him. They used to get together and talk about the 'maddening' way in which Gordon was behaving. It was the only thing they had in common, their feminine rage against his 'maddening' behaviour. Simultaneously and one after the other, by letter and by word of mouth, they harried him. It was unbearable.

Thank God, neither of them had seen his room at Mother Meakin's yet. Rosemary might have endured it, but the sight of that filthy attic would have been almost the death of Julia. They had been round to see him at the library, Rosemary a number of times, Julia once, when she could make a pretext to get away from the teashop. Even that was bad enough. It dismayed them to see what a mean, dreary little place the library was. The job at McKechnie's, though wretchedly paid, had not been the kind of job that you need actually be ashamed of. It brought Gordon into touch with cultivated people; seeing that he was a 'writer' himself, it might conceivably 'lead to something'. But here, in a street that was almost a slum, serving out yellow-jacketed trash at thirty bob a week—what hope was there in a job like that? It was just a derelict's job, a blind-alley job. Evening after evening, walking up and down the dreary misty street after the library was shut, Gordon and Rosemary argued about it. She kept on and on at him. *Would* he go back to the New Albion? *Why* wouldn't he go back to the New Albion? He always told her that the New Albion wouldn't take him back. After all, he hadn't applied for the job and there was no knowing whether he could get it; he preferred to keep it uncertain. There was something about him now that dismayed and frightened her. He seemed to have changed and deteriorated so suddenly. She divined, though he did not speak to her about it, that desire of his to escape from all effort and all decency, to sink down, down into the ultimate mud. It was not only from money but from life itself that he was turning away. They did not argue now as they had argued in the old days before Gordon had lost his job. In those days she had not paid much attention to his preposterous theories. His tirades against the money-morality had been a kind of joke between them. And it had hardly seemed to matter that time was passing and that Gordon's chance of earning a decent living was infinitely remote. She had still thought of herself as a young girl and of the future as limitless. She had watched him fling away two years of his life—two years of *her* life, for that matter; and she would have felt it ungenerous to protest.

But now she was growing frightened. Time's winged chariot was hurrying near. When Gordon lost his job she had suddenly realized, with the sense of making a startling discovery, that after all she was no longer very young. Gordon's thirtieth birthday was past; her own was not far distant. And what lay ahead of them? Gordon was sinking effortless into grey, deadly failure. He seemed to *want* to sink. What hope was there that they could ever get married now? Gordon knew that she was right. The situation was impossible. And so the thought, unspoken as yet, grew gradually in both their minds that they would have to part—for good.

One night they were to meet under the railway arches. It was a horrible January night; no mist, for once, only a vile wind that screeched round corners and flung dust and torn paper into your face. He waited for her, a small slouching figure, shabby almost to raggedness, his hair blown about by the wind. She was punctual, as usual. She ran towards him, pulled his face down, and kissed his cold cheek.

'Gordon, dear, how cold you are! Why did you come out without an overcoat?'

'My overcoat's up the spout. I thought you knew.'

'Oh, dear! Yes.'

She looked up at him, a small frown between her black brows. He looked so haggard, so despondent, there in the ill-lit archway, his face full of shadows. She wound her arm through his and pulled him out into the light.

'Let's keep walking. It's too cold to stand about. I've got something serious I want to say to you.'

'What?'

'I expect you'll be very angry with me.'

'What is it?'

'This afternoon I went and saw Mr Erskine. I asked leave to speak to him for a few minutes.'

He knew what was coming. He tried to free his arm from hers, but she held on to it.

'Well?' he said sulkily.

'I spoke to him about you. I asked him if he'd take you back. Of course he said trade was bad and they couldn't afford to take on new staff and all that. But I reminded him of what he'd said to you, and he said, Yes, he'd always thought you were very promising. And in the end he said he'd be quite ready to find a job for you if you'd come back. So you see I *was* right. They *will* give you the job.'

He did not answer. She squeezed his arm. 'So *now* what do you think about it?' she said.

'You know what I think,' he said coldly.

Secretly he was alarmed and angry. This was what he had been fearing. He had known all along that she would do it sooner or later. It made the issue more definite and his own blame clearer. He slouched on, his hands still in his coat pockets, letting her cling to his arm but not looking towards her.

'You're angry with me?' she said.

'No, I'm not. But I don't see why you had to do it—behind my back.'

That wounded her. She had had to plead very hard before she had managed to extort that promise from Mr Erskine. And it had needed all her courage to beard the managing director in his den. She had been in deadly fear that she might be sacked for doing it. But she wasn't going to tell Gordon anything of that.

'I don't think you ought to say *behind your back*. After all, I was only trying to help you.'

'How does it help me to get the offer of a job I wouldn't touch with a stick?'

'You mean you won't go back, even now?'

'Never.'

'Why?'

'*Must* we go into it again?' he said wearily.

She squeezed his arm with all her strength and pulled him round, making him face her. There was a kind of desperation in the way she clung to him. She had made her last effort and it had failed. It was as though she could feel him receding, fading away from her like a ghost.

'You'll break my heart if you go on like this,' she said.

'I wish you wouldn't trouble about me. It would be so much simpler if you didn't.'

'But why do you have to throw your life away?'

'I tell you I can't help it. I've got to stick to my guns.'

'You know what this will mean?'

With a chill at his heart, and yet with a feeling of resignation, even of relief, he said: 'You mean we shall have to part—not see each other again?'

They had walked on, and now they emerged into the Westminster Bridge Road. The wind met them with a scream, whirling at them a cloud of dust that made both of them duck their heads. They halted again. Her small face was full of lines, and the cold wind and the cold lamplight did not improve it.

'You want to get rid of me,' he said.

'No. No. It's not exactly that.'

'But you feel we ought to part.'

'How can we go on like this?' she said desolately.

'It's difficult, I admit.'

'It's all so miserable, so hopeless! What can it ever lead to?'

'So you don't love me after all?' he said.

'I do, I do! You know I do.'

'In a way, perhaps. But not enough to go on loving me when it's certain I'll never have the money to keep you. You'll have me as a husband, but not as a lover. It's still a question of money, you see.'

'It is *not* money, Gordon! It's *not* that.'

'Yes, it's just money. There's been money between us from the start. Money, always money!'

The scene continued, but not for very much longer. Both of them were shivering with cold. There is no emotion that matters greatly when one is standing at a street corner in a biting wind. When finally they parted it was with no irrevocable farewell. She simply said, 'I must get back,' kissed him, and ran across the road to the tram-stop. Mainly with relief he watched her go. He could not stop now to ask himself whether he loved her. Simply he wanted to get away—away from the windy street, away from scenes and emotional demands, back in the frowzy solitude of his attic. If there were tears in his eyes it was only from the cold of the wind.

With Julia it was almost worse. She asked him to go and see her one evening. This was after she had heard, from Rosemary, of Mr Erksine's offer of a job. The dreadul thing with Julia was that she understood nothing, absolutely nothing, of his motives. All she understood was that a 'good' job had been offered him and that he had refused it. She implored him almost on her knees not to throw this chance away. And when he told her that his mind was made up, she wept, actually wept. That was dreadful. The poor goose-like girl, with streaks of grey in her hair, weeping without grace or dignity in her little Drage-furnished bed-sitting room! This was the death of all her hopes. She had watched the family go down and down, moneyless and childless, into grey obscurity. Gordon alone had had it in him to succeed; and he, from mad perverseness, would not. He knew what she was thinking; he had to induce in himself a kind of brutality to stand firm. It was only because of Rosemary and Julia that he cared. Ravelston did not matter, because Ravelston understood. Aunt Angela and Uncle Walter, of course, were bleating weakly at him in long, fatuous letters. But them he disregarded.

In desperation Julia asked him, what did he mean to *do* now that he had

flung away his last chance of succeeding in life. He answered simply, 'My
poems.' He had said the same to Rosemary and to Ravelston. With Ravelston
the answer had sufficed. Rosemary had no longer any belief in his poems, but
she would not say so. As for Julia, his poems had never at any time meant
anything to her. 'I don't see much sense in writing if you can't make money out
of it,' was what she had always said. And he himself did not believe in his
poems any longer. But he still struggled to 'write', at least at times. Soon after
he changed his lodgings he had copied out on to clean sheets the completed
portions of *London Pleasures*—not quite four hundred lines, he discovered.
Even the labour of copying it out was a deadly bore. Yet he still worked on it
occasionally; cutting out a line here, altering another there, not making or even
expecting to make any progress. Before long the pages were as they had been
before, a scrawled, grimy labyrinth of words. He used to carry the wad of
grimy manuscript about with him in his pocket. The feeling of it there upheld
him a little; after all it was a kind of achievement, demonstrable to himself
though to nobody else. There it was, sole product of two years—of a thousand
hours' work, it might be. He had no feeling for it any longer as a poem. The
whole concept of poetry was meaningless to him now. It was only that if
*London Pleasures* were ever finished it would be something snatched from fate,
a thing created *outside* the money-world. But he knew, far more clearly than
before, that it never would be finished. How was it possible that any creative
impulse should remain to him, in the life he was living now? As time went on,
even the desire to finish *London Pleasures* vanished. He still carried the
manuscript about in his pocket; but it was only a gesture, a symbol of his
private war. He had finished for ever with that futile dream of being a 'writer'.
After all, was not that too a species of ambition? He wanted to get away from all
that, *below* all that. Down, down! Into the ghost-kingdom, out of the reach of
hope, out of the reach of fear! Under ground, under ground! That was where
he wished to be.

Yet in a way it was not so easy. One night about nine he was lying on his bed,
with the ragged counterpane over his feet, his hands under his head to keep
them warm. The fire was out. The dust was thick on everything. The
aspidistra had died a week ago and was withering upright in its pot. He slid a
shoeless foot from under the counterpane, held it up, and looked at it. His sock
was full of holes—there were more holes than sock. So here he lay, Gordon
Comstock, in a slum attic on a ragged bed, with his feet sticking out of his
socks, with one and fourpence in the world, with three decades behind him and
nothing, nothing accomplished! Surely *now* he was past redemption? Surely,
try as they would, they couldn't prise him out of a hole like this? He had
wanted to reach the mud—well, this was the mud, wasn't it?

Yet he knew that it was not so. That other world, the world of money and
success, is always so strangely near. You don't escape it merely by taking
refuge in dirt and misery. He had been frightened as well as angry when
Rosemary told him about Mr Erskine's offer. It brought the danger so close to
him. A letter, a telephone message, and from this squalor he could step straight
back into the money-world—back to four quid a week, back to effort and

decency and slavery. Going to the devil isn't so easy as it sounds. Sometimes your salvation hunts you down like the Hound of Heaven.

For a while he lay in an almost mindless state, gazing at the ceiling. The utter futility of just lying there, dirty and cold, comforted him a little. But presently he was roused by a light tap at the door. He did not stir. It was Mother Meakin, presumably, though it did not sound like her knock.

'Come in,' he said.

The door opened. It was Rosemary.

She stepped in, and then stopped as the dusty sweetish smell of the room caught her. Even in the bad light of the lamp she could see the state of filth the room was in—the litter of food and papers on the table, the grate full of cold ashes, the foul crocks in the fender, the dead aspidistra. As she came slowly towards the bed she pulled her hat off and threw it on to the chair.

'*What* a place for you to live in!' she said.

'So you've come back?' he said.

'Yes.'

He turned a little away from her, his arm over his face. 'Come back to lecture me some more, I suppose?'

'No.'

'Then why?'

'Because–'

She had knelt down beside the bed. She pulled his arm away, put her face forward to kiss him, then drew back, surprised, and began to stroke the hair over his temple with the tips of her fingers.

'Oh, Gordon!'

'What?'

'You've got grey in your hair!'

'Have I? Where?'

'Here—over the temple. There's quite a little patch of it. It must have happened all of a sudden.'

'"My golden locks time hath to silver turned,"' he said indifferently.

'So we're both going grey,' she said.

She bent her head to show him the three white hairs on her crown. Then she wriggled herself on to the bed beside him, put an arm under him, pulled him towards her, covered his face with kisses. He let her do it. He did not want this to happen—it was the very thing that he least wanted. But she had wriggled herself beneath him; they were breast to breast. Her body seemed to melt into his. By the expression of her face he knew what had brought her here. After all, she was virgin. She did not know what she was doing. It was magnanimity, pure magnanimity, that moved her. His wretchedness had drawn her back to him. Simply because he was penniless and a failure she had got to yield to him, even if it was only once.

'I had to come back,' she said.

'Why?'

'I couldn't bear to think of you here alone. It seemed so awful, leaving you like that.'

'You did quite right to leave me. You'd much better not have come back. You know we can't ever get married.'

'I don't care. That isn't how one behaves to people one loves. I don't care whether you marry me or not. I love you.'

'This isn't wise,' he said.

'I don't care. I wish I'd done it years ago.'

'We'd much better not.'

'Yes.'

'No.'

'Yes!'

After all, she was too much for him. He had wanted her so long, and he could not stop to weigh the consequences. So it was done at last, without much pleasure, on Mother Meakin's dingy bed. Presently Rosemary got up and rearranged her clothes. The room, though stuffy, was dreadfully cold. They were both shivering a little. She pulled the coverlet further over Gordon. He lay without stirring, his back turned to her, his face hidden against his arm. She knelt down beside the bed, took his other hand, and laid it for a moment against her cheek. He scarcely noticed her. Then she shut the door quietly behind her and tiptoed down the bare, evil-smelling stairs. She felt dismayed, disappointed, and very cold.

# I I

Spring, spring! Bytuene Mershe ant Averil, when spray biginneth to spring! When shaws be sheene and swards full fayre, and leaves both large and longe! When the hounds of spring are on winter's traces, in the spring time, the only pretty ring time, when the birds do sing, hey-ding-a-ding ding, cuckoo, jug-jug, pu-wee, ta-witta-woo! And so on and so on and so on. See almost any poet between the Bronze Age and 1805.

But how absurd that even now, in the era of central heating and tinned peaches, a thousand so-called poets are still writing in the same strain! For what difference does spring or winter or any other time of year make to the average civilized person nowadays? In a town like London the most striking seasonal change, apart from the mere change of temperature, is in the things you see lying about on the pavement. In late winter is is mainly cabbage leaves. In July you tread on cherry stones, in November on burnt-out fireworks. Towards Christmas the orange peel grows thicker. It was a different matter in the Middle Ages. There was some sense in writing poems about spring when spring meant fresh meat and green vegetables after months of frowsting in some windowless hut on a diet of salt fish and mouldy bread.

If it was spring Gordon failed to notice it. March in Lambeth did not remind you of Persephone. The days grew longer, there were vile dusty winds and sometimes in the sky patches of harsh blue appeared. Probably there were a few sooty buds on the trees if you cared to look for them. The aspidistra, it turned out, had not died after all; the withered leaves had dropped off it, but it was putting forth a couple of dull green shoots near its base.

Gordon had been three months at the library now. The stupid slovenly routine did not irk him. The library had swelled to a thousand 'assorted titles' and was bringing Mr Cheeseman a pound a week clear profit, so Mr Cheeseman was happy after his fashion. He was, nevertheless, nurturing a secret grudge against Gordon. Gordon had been sold to him, so to speak, as a drunkard. He had expected Gordon to get drunk and miss a day's work at least once, thus giving a sufficient pretext for docking his wages; but Gordon had failed to get drunk. Queerly enough, he had no impulse to drink nowadays. He would have gone without beer even if he could have afforded it. Tea seemed a better poison. All his desires and discontents had dwindled. He was better off on thirty bob a week than he had been previously on two pounds. The thirty bob covered, without too much stretching, his rent, cigarettes, a washing bill of about a shilling a week, a little fuel, and his meals, which consisted almost entirely of bacon, bread-and-marg, and tea, and cost about two bob a day, gas included. Sometimes he even had sixpence over for a seat at a cheap but lousy picture-house near the Westminster Bridge Road. He still carried the grimy manuscript of *London Pleasures* to and fro in his pocket, but it was from mere force of habit; he had dropped even the pretence of working. All his evenings were spent in the same way. There in the remote frowzy attic, by the fire if there was any coal left, in bed if there wasn't, with teapot and cigarettes handy, reading, always reading. He read nothing nowadays except twopenny weekly papers. *Tit Bits, Answers, Peg's Paper, The Gem, The Magnet, Home Notes, The Girl's Own Paper*—they were all the same. He used to get them a dozen at a time from the shop. Mr Cheeseman had great dusty stacks of them, left over from his uncle's day and used for wrapping paper. Some of them were as much as twenty years old.

He had not seen Rosemary for weeks past. She had written a number of times and then, for some reason, abruptly stopped writing. Ravelston had written once, asking him to contribute an article on twopenny libraries to *Antichrist*. Julia had sent a desolate little letter, giving family news. Aunt Angela had had bad colds all the winter, and Uncle Walter was complaining of bladder trouble. Gordon did not answer any of their letters. He would have forgotten their existence if he could. They and their affection were only an encumbrance. He would not be free, free to sink down into the ultimate mud, till he had cut his links with all of them, even with Rosemary.

One afternoon he was choosing a book for a tow-headed factory girl, when someone he only saw out of the corner of his eye came into the library and hesitated just inside the door.

'What kind of book did you want?' he asked the factory girl.

'Oo—jest a kind of a *romance*, please.'

Gordon selected a *romance*. As he turned, his heart bounded violently. The person who had just come in was Rosemary. She did not make any sign, but stood waiting, pale, and worried-looking, with something ominous in her appearance.

He sat down to enter the book on the girl's ticket, but his hands had begun trembling so that he could hardly do it. He pressed the rubber stamp in the wrong place. The girl trailed out, peeping into the book as she went. Rosemary was watching Gordon's face. It was a long time since she had seen him by daylight, and she was struck by the change in him. He was shabby to the point of raggedness, his face had grown much thinner and had the dingy, greyish pallor of people who live on bread and margarine. He looked much older—thirty-five at the least. But Rosemary herself did not look quite as usual. She had lost her gay trim bearing, and her clothes had the appearance of having been thrown on in a hurry. It was obvious that there was something wrong.

He shut the door after the factory girl. 'I wasn't expecting you,' he began.

'I had to come. I got away from the studio at lunch time. I told them I was ill.'

'You don't look well. Here, you'd better sit down.'

There was only one chair in the library. He brought it out from behind the desk and was moving towards her, rather vaguely, to offer some kind of caress. Rosemary did not sit down, but laid her small hand, from which she had removed the glove, on the top rung of the chair-back. By the pressure of her fingers he could see how agitated she was.

'Gordon, I've a most awful thing to tell you. It's happened after all.'

'What's happened?'

'I'm going to have a baby.'

'A baby? Oh, Christ!'

He stopped short. For a moment he felt as though someone had struck him a violent blow under the ribs. He asked the usual fatuous question:

'Are you sure?'

'Absolutely. It's been weeks now. If you knew the time I've had! I kept hoping and hoping—I took some pills—oh, it was too beastly!'

'A baby! Oh, God, what fools we were! As though we couldn't have foreseen it!'

'I know. I suppose it was my fault. I—'

'Damn! Here comes somebody.'

The door-bell ping'd. A fat, freckled woman with an ugly under-lip came in at a rolling gait and demanded 'Something with a murder in it.' Rosemary had sat down and was twisting her glove round and round her fingers. The fat woman was exacting. Each book that Gordon offered her she refused on the ground that she had 'had it already' or that it 'looked dry'. The deadly news that Rosemary had brought had unnerved Gordon. His heart pounding, his entrails constricted, he had to pull out book after book and assure the fat woman that this was the very book she was looking for. At last, after nearly ten minutes, he managed to fob her off with something which she said grudgingly she 'didn't think she'd had before'.

He turned back to Rosemary. 'Well, what the devil are we going to do about it?' he said as soon as the door had shut.

'I don't see what I can do. If I have this baby I'll lose my job, of course. But it isn't only that I'm worrying about. It's my people finding out. My mother—oh, dear! It simply doesn't bear thinking of.'

'Ah, your people! I hadn't thought of them. One's people! What a cursed incubus they are!'

'*My* people are all right. They've always been good to me. But it's different with a thing like this.'

He took a pace or two up and down. Though the news had scared him he had not really grasped it as yet. The thought of a baby, his baby, growing in her womb had awoken in him no emotion except dismay. He did not think of the baby as a living creature; it was a disaster pure and simple. And already he saw where it was going to lead.

'We shall have to get married, I suppose,' he said flatly.

'Well, shall we? That's what I came here to ask you.'

'But I suppose you want me to marry you, don't you?'

'Not unless *you* want to. I'm not going to tie you down. I know it's against your ideas to marry. You must decide for yourself.'

'But we've no alternative—if you're really going to have this baby.'

'Not necessarily. That's what you've got to decide. Because after all there *is* another way.'

'What way?'

'Oh, *you* know. A girl at the studio gave me an address. A friend of hers had it done for only five pounds.'

That pulled him up. For the first time he grasped, with the only kind of knowledge that matters, what they were really talking about. The words 'a baby' took on a new significance. They did not mean any longer a mere abstract disaster, they meant a bud of flesh, a bit of himself, down there in her belly, alive and growing. His eyes met hers. They had a strange moment of sympathy such as they had never had before. For a moment he did feel that in some mysterious way they were one flesh. Though they were feet apart he felt as though they were joined together—as though some invisible living cord stretched from her entrails to his. He knew then that it was a dreadul thing they were contemplating—a blasphemy, if that word had any meaning. Yet if it had been put otherwise he might not have recoiled from it. It was the squalid detail of the five pounds that brought it home.

'No fear!' he said. 'Whatever happens we're not going to do *that*. It's disgusting.'

'I know it is. But I can't have the baby without being married.'

'No! If that's the alternative I'll marry you. I'd sooner cut my right hand off than do a thing like that.'

Ping! went the door-bell. Two ugly louts in cheap bright blue suits, and a girl with a fit of the giggles, came in. One of the youths asked with a sort of sheepish boldness for 'something with a kick in it—something smutty'. Silently, Gordon indicated the shelves where the 'sex' books were kept. There were hundreds of them in the library. They had titles like *Secrets of Paris* and *The Man She Trusted*; on their tattered yellow jackets were pictures of half-naked girls lying on divans with men in dinner-jackets standing over them. The stories inside, however, were painfully harmless. The two youths and the girl ranged among them, sniggering over the pictures on their covers, the girl letting out little squeals and pretending to be shocked. They disgusted Gordon so much that he turned his back on them till they had chosen their books.

When they had gone he came back to Rosemary's chair. He stood behind her, took hold of her small firm shoulders, then slid a hand inside her coat and felt the warmth of her breast. He liked the strong springy feeling of her body; he liked to think that down there, a guarded seed, his baby was growing. She put a hand up and caressed the hand that was on her breast, but did not speak. She was waiting for him to decide.

'If I marry you I shall have to turn respectable,' he said musingly.

'Could you?' she said with a touch of her old manner.

'I mean I shall have to get a proper job—go back to the New Albion. I suppose they'd take me back.'

He felt her grow very still and knew that she had been waiting for this. Yet she was determined to play fair. She was not going to bully him or cajole him.

'I never said I wanted you to do that. I want you to marry me—yes, because of the baby. But it doesn't follow you've got to keep me.'

'There's no sense in marrying if I can't keep you. Suppose I married you when I was like I am at present—no money and no proper job? What would you do then?'

'I don't know. I'd go on working as long as I could. And afterwards, when the baby got too obvious—well, I suppose I'd have to go home to father and mother.'

'That would be jolly for you, wouldn't it? But you were so anxious for me to go back to the New Albion before. You haven't changed your mind?'

'I've thought things over. I know you'd hate to be tied to a regular job. I don't blame you. You've got your own life to live.'

He thought it over a little while longer. 'It comes down to this. Either I marry you and go back to the New Albion, or you go to one of those filthy doctors and get yourself messed about for five pounds.'

At this she twisted herself out of his grasp and stood up facing him. His blunt words had upset her. They had made the issue clearer and uglier than before.

'Oh, why did you say that?'

'Well, those *are* the alternatives.'

'I'd never thought of it like that. I came here meaning to be fair. And now it sounds as if I was trying to bully you into it—trying to play on your feelings by threatening to get rid of the baby. A sort of beastly blackmail.'

'I didn't mean that. I was only stating facts.'

Her face was full of lines, the black brows drawn together. But she had sworn to herself that she would not make a scene. He could guess what this meant to her. He had never met her people, but he could imagine them. He had some notion of what it might mean to go back to a country town with an illegitimate baby; or, what was almost as bad, with a husband who couldn't keep you. But she was going to play fair. No blackmail! She drew a sharp inward breath, taking a decision.

'All right, then, I'm not going to hold *that* over your head. It's too mean. Marry me or don't marry me, just as you like. But I'll have the baby, anyway.'

'You'd do that? Really?'

'Yes, I think so.'

He took her in his arms. Her coat had come open, her body was warm against him. He thought he would be a thousand kinds of fool if he let her go. Yet the alternative was impossible, and he did not see it any less clearly because he held her in his arms.

'Of course, you'd like me to go back to the New Albion,' he said.

'No, I wouldn't. Not if you don't want to.'

'Yes, you would. After all, it's natural. You want to see me earning a decent income again. In a *good* job, with four pounds a week and an aspidistra in the window. Wouldn't you, now? Own up.'

'All right, then—yes, I would. But it's only something I'd *like* to see happening; I'm not going to *make* you do it. I'd just hate you to do it if you didn't really want to. I want you to feel free.'

'Really and truly free?'

'Yes.'

'You know what that means? Supposing I decided to leave you and the baby in the lurch?'

'Well—if you really wanted to. You're free—quite free.'

After a little while she went away. Later in the evening or tomorrow he would let her know what he decided. Of course it was not absolutely certain that the New Albion would give him a job even if he asked them; but presumably they would, considering what Mr Erskine had said. Gordon tried to think and could not. There seemed to be more customers than usual this afternoon. It maddened him to have to bounce out of his chair every time he had sat down and deal with some fresh influx of fools demanding crime-stories and sex-stories and *romances*. Suddenly, about six o'clock, he turned out the lights, locked up the library, and went out. He had got to be alone. The library was not due to shut for two hours yet. God knew what Mr Cheeseman would say when he found out. He might even give Gordon the sack. Gordon did not care.

He turned westward, up Lambeth Cut. It was a dull sort of evening, not cold. There was muck underfoot, white lights, and hawkers screaming. He had got to think this thing out, and he could think better walking. But it was so hard, so hard! Back to the New Albion, or leave Rosemary in the lurch; there was no other alternative. It was no use thinking, for instance, that he might find some 'good' job which would offend his sense of decency a bit less. There aren't so many 'good' jobs waiting for moth-eaten people of thirty. The New Albion was the only chance he had or ever would have.

At the corner, on the Westminster Bridge Road, he paused a moment. There were some posters opposite, livid in the lamplight. A monstrous one, ten feet high at least, advertised Bovex. The Bovex people had dropped Corner Table and got on to a new tack. They were running a series of four-line poems—Bovex Ballads, they were called. There was a picture of a horribly eupeptic family, with grinning ham-pink faces, sitting at breakfast; underneath, in blatant lettering:

> Why should *you* be thin and white?
> And have that washed-out feeling?
> Just take hot Bovex every night—
> Invigorating—healing!

Gordon gazed at the thing. He drank in its puling silliness. God, what trash! 'Invigorating—healing!' The weak incompetence of it! It hadn't even the vigorous badness of the slogans that really stick. Just soppy, lifeless drivel. It would have been almost pathetic in its feebleness if one hadn't reflected that all over London and all over every town in England that poster was plastered, rotting the minds of men. He looked up and down the graceless street. Yes, war is coming soon. You can't doubt it when you see the Bovex ads. The electric drills in our streets presage the rattle of the machine-guns. Only a little while before the aeroplanes come. Zoom—bang! A few tons of T.N.T. to send our civilization back to hell where it belongs.

He crossed the road and walked on, southward. A curious thought had struck him. He did not any longer want that war to happen. It was the first time in months—years, perhaps—that he had thought of it and not wanted it.

If he went back to the New Albion, in a month's time he might be writing Bovex Ballads himself. To go back to *that*! Any 'good' job was bad enough; but to be mixed up in *that*! Christ! Of course he oughtn't to go back. It was just a question of having the guts to stand firm. But what about Rosemary? He thought of the kind of life she would live at home, in her parents' house, with a baby and no money; and of the news running through that monstrous family that Rosemary had married some awful rotter who couldn't even keep her. She would have the whole lot of them nagging at her together. Besides, there was the baby to think about. The money-god is so cunning. If he only baited his traps with yachts and race-horses, tarts and champagne, how easy it would be to dodge them. It is when he gets at you through your sense of decency that he finds you helpless.

The Bovex Ballad jungled in Gordon's head. He ought to stand firm. He had made war on money—he ought to stick it out. After all, hitherto he *had* stuck it out, after a fashion. He looked back over his life. No use deceiving himself. It had been a dreadful life—lonely, squalid, futile. He had lived thirty years and achieved nothing except misery. But that was what he had chosen. It was what he *wanted*, even now. He wanted to sink down, down into the muck where money does not rule. But this baby-business had upset everything. It was a pretty banal predicament, after all. Private vices, public virtues—the dilemma is as old as the world.

He looked up and saw that he was passing a public library. A thought struck him. That baby. What did it mean, anyway, having a baby? What was it that was actually happening to Rosemary at this moment? He had only vague and general ideas of what pregnancy meant. No doubt they would have books in there that would tell him about it. He went in. The lending library was on the left. It was there that you had to ask for works of reference.

The woman at the desk was a university graduate, young, colourless, spectacled, and intensely disagreeable. She had a fixed suspicion that no one—at least, no male person—ever consulted works of reference except in search of pornography. As soon as you approached she pierced you through and through with a flash of her pince-nez and let you know that your dirty secret was no secret from *her*. After all, all works of reference are pornographical, except perhaps Whitaker's *Almanack*. You can put even the Oxford Dictionary to evil purposes by looking up words like — and —.

Gordon knew her type at a glance, but he was too preoccupied to care.

'Have you any book on gynaecology?' he said.

'Any *what*?' demanded the young woman with a pince-nez flash of unmistakable triumph. As usual! Another male in search of dirt!

'Well, any books on midwifery? About babies being born, and so forth.'

'We don't issue books of that description to the general public,' said the young woman frostily.

'I'm sorry—there's a point I particularly want to look up.'

'Are you a medical student?'

'No.'

'Then I don't *quite* see what you want with books on midwifery.'

Curse the woman! Gordon thought. At another time he would have been afraid of her; at present, however, she merely bored him.

'If you want to know, my wife's going to have a baby. We neither of us know much about it. I want to see whether I can find out anything useful.'

The young woman did not believe him. He looked too shabby and worn, she decided, to be a newly married man. However, it was her job to lend out books, and she seldom actually refused them, except to children. You always got your book in the end, after you had been made to feel yourself a dirty swine. With an aseptic air she led Gordon to a small table in the middle of the library and presented him with two fat books in brown covers. Thereafter she left him alone, but kept an eye on him from whatever part of the library she happened to be in. He could feel her pince-nez probing the back of his neck at long range, trying to decide from his demeanour whether he was really searching for information or merely picking out the dirty bits.

He opened one of the books and searched inexpertly through it. There were acres of close-printed text full of Latin words. That was no use. He wanted something simple—pictures, for choice. How long had this thing been going on? Six weeks—nine weeks, perhaps. Ah! This must be it.

He came on a print of a nine weeks' foetus. It gave him a shock to see it, for he had not expected it to look in the least like that. It was a deformed, gnomelike thing, a sort of clumsy caricature of a human being, with a huge domed head as big as the rest of its body. In the middle of the great blank expanse of head there was a tiny button of an ear. The thing was in profile; its boneless arm was bent, and one hand, crude as a seal's flipper, covered its face—fortunately, perhaps. Below were little skinny legs, twisted like a monkey's with the toes turned in. It was a monstrous thing, and yet strangely human. It surprised him that they should begin looking human so soon. He had pictured something much more rudimentary; a mere blob of nucleus, like a bubble of frog-spawn. But it must be very tiny, of course. He looked at the dimensions marked below. Length 30 millimetres. About the size of a large gooseberry.

But perhaps it had not been going on quite so long as that. He turned back a page or two and found a print of a six weeks' foetus. A really dreadful thing this time—a thing he could hardly even bear to look at. Strange that our beginnings and endings are so ugly—the unborn as ugly as the dead. This thing looked as if it were dead already. Its huge head, as though too heavy to hold upright, was bent over at right angles at the place where its neck ought to have been. There was nothing you could call a face, only a wrinkle representing the eye—or was it the mouth? It had no human resemblance this time; it was more like a dead puppy-dog. Its short thick arms were very doglike, the hands being mere stumpy paws. 15·5 millimetres long—no bigger than a hazel nut.

He pored for a long time over the two pictures. Their ugliness made them more credible and therefore more moving. His baby had seemed real to him from the moment when Rosemary spoke of abortion; but it had been a reality without visual shape—something that happened in the dark and was only important after it had happened. But here was the actual process taking place. Here was the poor ugly thing, no bigger than a gooseberry, that he had created by his heedless act. Its future, its continued existence perhaps, depended on him. Besides, it was a bit of himself—it *was* himself. Dare one dodge such a responsibility as that?

But what about the alternative? He got up, handed over his books to the disagreeable young woman, and went out; then, on an impulse, turned back and went into the other part of the library, where the periodicals were kept. The usual crowd of mangy-looking people were dozing over the papers. There was one table set apart for women's papers. He picked up one of them at random and bore it off to another table.

It was an American paper of the more domestic kind, mainly adverts with a few stories lurking apologetically among them. And *what* adverts! Quickly he flicked over the shiny pages. Lingerie, jewellery, cosmetics, fur coats, silk stockings flicked up and down like the figures in a child's peepshow. Page after page, advert after advert. Lipsticks, undies, tinned food, patent medicines, slimming cures, face-creams. A sort of cross-section of the money-world. A panorama of ignorance, greed, vulgarity, snobbishness, whoredom, and disease.

And *that* was the world they wanted him to re-enter. *That* was the business in which he had a chance of Making Good. He flicked over the pages more slowly. Flick, flick. Adorable—until she smiles. The food that is shot out of a gun. Do you let foot-fag affect your personality? Get back that peach-bloom on a Beautyrest Mattress. Only a *penetrating* face-cream will reach that under-surface dirt. Pink toothbrush is *her* trouble. How to alkalize your stomach almost instantly. Roughage for husky kids. Are you one of the four out of five? The world-famed Culturequick Scrapbook. Only a drummer and yet he quoted Dante.

Christ, what muck!

But of course it was an American paper. The Americans always go one better on any kinds of beastliness, whether it is ice-cream soda, racketeering, or theosophy. He went over to the women's table and picked up another paper. An English one this time. Perhaps the ads in an English paper wouldn't be quite so bad—a little less brutally offensive?

He opened the paper. Flick, flick. Britons never shall be slaves!

Flick, flick. Get that waist-line back to normal! She *said* 'Thanks awfully for the lift,' but she *thought*, 'Poor boy, why doesn't somebody tell him?' How a woman of thirty-two stole her young man from a girl of twenty. Prompt relief for feeble kidneys. Silkyseam—the smooth-sliding bathroom tissue. Asthma was choking her! Are *you* ashamed of your undies? Kiddies clamour for their Breakfast Crisps. Now I'm a schoolgirl complexion all over. Hike all day on a slab of Vitamalt!

To be mixed up in *that*! To be in it and of it—part and parcel of it! God, God, God!

Presently he went out. The dreadful thing was that he knew already what he was going to do. His mind was made up—had been made up for a long time past. When this problem appeared it had brought its solution with it; all his hesitation had been a kind of make-believe. He felt as though some force outside himself were pushing him. There was a telephone booth near by. Rosemary's hostel was on the phone—she ought to be at home by now. He went into the booth, feeling in his pocket. Yes, exactly two pennies. He dropped them into the slot, swung the dial.

A refaned, adenoidal feminine voice answered him: 'Who's thyah, please?'

He pressed Button A. So the die was cast.

'Is Miss Waterlow in?'

'Who's *thyah*, please?'

'Say it's Mr Comstock. She'll know. Is she at home?'

'Ay'll see. Hold the lane, please.'

A pause.

'Hullo! Is that you, Gordon?'

'Hullo! Hullo! Is that you, Rosemary? I just wanted to tell you. I've thought it over—I've made up my mind.'

'Oh!' There was another pause. With difficulty mastering her voice, she added: 'Well, what did you decide?'

'It's all right. I'll take the job—if they'll give it me, that is.'

'Oh, Gordon, I'm so glad! You're not angry with me? You don't feel I've sort of bullied you into it?'

'No, it's all right. It's the only thing I can do. I've thought everything out. I'll go up to the office and see them tomorrow.'

'I *am* so glad!'

'Of course, I'm assuming they'll give me the job. But I suppose they will, after what old Erskine said.'

'I'm sure they will. But, Gordon, there's just one thing. You will go there nicely dressed, won't you? It might make a lot of difference.'

'I know. I'll have to get my best suit out of pawn. Ravelston will lend me the money.'

'Never mind about Ravelston. I'll lend you the money. I've got four pounds put away. I'll run out and wire it you before the post-office shuts. I expect you'll want some new shoes and a new tie as well. And, oh, Gordon!'

'What?'

'Wear a hat when you go up to the office, won't you? It looks better, wearing a hat.'

'A hat! God! I haven't worn a hat for two years. Must I?'

'Well—it does look more business-like, doesn't it?'

'Oh, all right. A bowler hat, even, if you think I ought.'

'I think a soft hat would do. But get your hair cut, won't you, there's a dear?'

'Yes, don't you worry. I'll be a smart young business man. Well groomed, and all that.'

'Thanks ever so, Gordon dear. I must run out and wire that money. Good night and good luck.'

'Good night.'

He came out of the booth. So that was that. He had torn it now, right enough.

He walked rapidly away. What had he done? Chucked up the sponge! Broken all his oaths! His long and lonely war had ended in ignominious defeat. Circumcise ye your foreskins, saith the Lord. He was coming back to the fold, repentant. He seemed to be walking faster than usual. There was a peculiar sensation, an actual physical sensation, in his heart, in his limbs, all over him. What was it? Shame, misery, despair? Rage at being back in the clutch of money? Boredom when he thought of the deadly future? He dragged the sensation forth, faced it, examined it. It was relief.

Yes, that was the truth of it. Now that the thing was done he felt nothing but relief; relief that now at last he had finished with dirt, cold, hunger, and loneliness and could get back to decent, fully human life. His resolutions, now that he had broken them, seemed nothing but a frightful weight that he had cast off. Moreover, he was aware that he was only fulfilling his destiny. In some corner of his mind he had always known that this would happen. He thought of the day when he had given them notice at the New Albion; and Mr Erskine's kind, red, beefish face, gently counselling him not to chuck up a 'good' job for nothing. How bitterly he had sworn, then, that he was done with 'good' jobs for ever! Yet it was foredoomed that he should come back, and he had known it even then. And it was not merely because of Rosemary and the baby that he had done it. That was the obvious cause, the precipitating cause, but even without it the end would have been the same; if there had been no baby to think about, something else would have forced his hand. For it was what, in his secret heart, he had desired.

After all he did not lack vitality, and that moneyless existence to which he had condemned himself had thrust him ruthlessly out of the stream of life. He looked back over the last two frightful years. He had blasphemed against money, rebelled against money, tried to live like an anchorite outside the money-world; and it had brought him not only misery, but also a frightful emptiness, an inescapable sense of futility. To abjure money is to abjure life. Be not righteous over much; why shouldst thou die before thy time? Now he was back in the money-world, or soon would be. Tomorrow he would go up to the New Albion, in his best suit and overcoat (he must remember to get his overcoat out of pawn at the same time as his suit), in homburg hat of the correct gutter-crawling pattern, neatly shaved and with his hair cut short. He would be as though born anew. The sluttish poet of today would be hardly recognizable in the natty young business man of tomorrow. They would take him back, right enough; he had the talent they needed. He would buckle to work, sell his soul, and hold down his job.

And what about the future? Perhaps it would turn out that these last two years had not left much mark upon him. They were merely a gap, a small setback in his career. Quite quickly, now that he had taken the first step, he would develop the cynical, blinkered business mentality. He would forget his fine disgusts, cease to rage against the tyranny of money—cease to be aware of it, even—cease to squirm at the ads for Bovex and Breakfast Crisps. He would sell his soul so utterly that he would forget it had ever been his. He would get married, settle down, prosper moderately, push a pram, have a villa and a radio and an aspidistra. He would be a law-abiding little cit like any other law-abiding little cit—a soldier in the strap-hanging army. Probably it was better so.

He slowed his pace a little. He was thirty and there was grey in his hair, yet he had a queer feeling that he had only just grown up. It occurred to him that he was merely repeating the destiny of every human being. Everyone rebels against the money-code, and everyone sooner or later surrenders. He had kept up his rebellion a little longer than most, that was all. And he had made such a wretched failure of it! He wondered whether every anchorite in his dismal cell pines secretly to be back in the world of men. Perhaps there were a few who did not. Somebody or other had said that the modern world is only habitable by saints and scoundrels. He, Gordon, wasn't a saint. Better, then, to be an unpretending scoundrel along with the others. It was what he had secretly pined for; now that he had acknowledged his desire and surrendered to it, he was at peace.

He was making roughly in the direction of home. He looked up at the houses he was passing. It was a street he did not know. Oldish houses, mean-looking and rather dark, let off in flatlets and single rooms for the most part. Railed areas, smoke-grimed bricks, whited steps, dingy lace curtains. 'Apartments' cards in half the windows, aspidistras in nearly all. A typical lower-middle-class street. But not, on the whole, the kind of street that he wanted to see blown to hell by bombs.

He wondered about the people in houses like those. They would be, for example, small clerks, shop-assistants, commercial travellers, insurance touts, tram conductors. Did *they* know that they were only puppets dancing when money pulled the strings? You bet they didn't. And if they did, what would they care? They were too busy being born, being married, begetting, working, dying. It mightn't be a bad thing, if you could manage it, to feel yourself one of them, one of the ruck of men. Our civilization is founded on greed and fear, but in the lives of common men the greed and fear are mysteriously transmuted into something nobler. The lower-middle-class people in there, behind their lace curtains, with their children and their scraps of furniture and their aspidistras–they lived by the money-code, sure enough, and yet they contrived to keep their decency. The money-code as they interpreted it was not merely cynical and hoggish. They had their standards, their inviolable points of honour. They 'kept themselves respectable'–kept the aspidistra flying. Besides, they were *alive*. They were bound up in the bundle of life. They begot children, which is what the saints and the soul-savers never by any chance do.

The aspidistra is the tree of life, he thought suddenly.

He was aware of a lumpish weight in his inner pocket. It was the manuscript of *London Pleasures*. He took it out and had a look at it under a street lamp. A great wad of paper, soiled and tattered, with that peculiar, nasty, grimed-at-the-edges look of papers which have been a long time in one's pocket. About four hundred lines in all. The sole fruit of his exile, a two years' foetus which would never be born. Well, he had finished with all that. Poetry! *Poetry*, indeed! In 1935.

What should he do with the manuscript? Best thing, shove it down the w.c. But he was a long way from home and had not the necessary penny. He halted by the iron grating of a drain. In the window of the nearest house an aspidistra, a striped one, peeped between the yellow lace curtains.

He unrolled a page of *London Pleasures*. In the middle of the labyrinthine scrawlings a line caught his eye. Momentary regret stabbed him. After all, parts of it weren't half bad! If only it could ever be finished! It seemed such a shame to shy it away after all the work he had done on it. Save it, perhaps? Keep it by him and finish it secretly in his spare time? Even now it might come to something.

No, no! Keep your parole. Either surrender or don't surrender.

He doubled up the manuscript and stuffed it between the bars of the drain. It fell with a plop into the water below.

*Vicisti, O aspidistra!*

# 12

Ravelston wanted to say good-bye outside the registry office, but they would not hear of it, and insisted on dragging him off to have lunch with them. Not at Modigliani's, however. They went to one of those jolly little Soho restaurants where you can get such a wonderful four-course lunch for half a crown. They had garlic sausage with bread and butter, fried plaice, entrecôte aux pommes frites, and a rather watery caramel pudding; also a bottle of Médoc Supérieur, three and sixpence the bottle.

Only Ravelston was at the wedding. The other witness was a poor meek creature with no teeth, a professional witness whom they picked up outside the registry office and tipped half a crown. Julia hadn't been able to get away from the teashop, and Gordon and Rosemary had only got the day off from the office by pretexts carefully manœuvred a long time ahead. Nobody knew they were getting married, except Ravelston and Julia. Rosemary was going to go on working at the studio for another month or two. She had preferred to keep her marriage a secret until it was over, chiefly for the sake of her innumerable brothers and sisters, none of whom could afford wedding presents. Gordon, left to himself, would have done it in a more regular manner. He had even wanted to be married in church. But Rosemary had put her foot down to that idea.

Gordon had been back at the office two months now. Four ten a week he was getting. It would be a tight pinch when Rosemary stopped working, but there was hope of a rise next year. They would have to get some money out of Rosemary's parents, of course, when the baby was due to arrive. Mr Clew had left the New Albion a year ago, and his place had been taken by a Mr Warner, a Canadian who had been five years with a New York publicity firm. Mr Warner was a live wire but quite a likeable person. He and Gordon had a big job on hand at the moment. The Queen of Sheba Toilet Requisites Co. were sweeping the country with a monster campaign for their deodorant, April Dew. They had decided that B.O. and halitosis were worked out, or nearly, and had been racking their brains for a long time past to think of some new way of scaring the public. Then some bright spark suggested, What about smelling feet? That field had never been exploited and had immense possibilities. The Queen of Sheba had turned the idea over to the New Albion. What they asked for was a really telling slogan; something in the class of 'Night-starvation'—something that would rankle in the public consciousness like a poisoned arrow. Mr Warner had thought it over for three days and then emerged with the unforgettable phrase 'P.P.' 'P.P.' stood for Pedic Perspiration. It was a real flash of genius, that. It was so simple and so arresting. Once you knew what they stood for, you couldn't possibly see those letters 'P.P.' without a guilty tremor. Gordon had searched for the word 'pedic' in the Oxford Dictionary and found that it did not exist. But Mr Warner has said, Hell! what did it matter, anyway? It would put the wind up them just the same. The Queen of Sheba had jumped at the idea, of course.

They were putting every penny they could spare into the campaign. On every hoarding in the British Isles huge accusing posters were hammering 'P.P.' into the public mind. All the posters were identically the same. They wasted no words, but just demanded with sinister simplicity:

'P.P.'

WHAT ABOUT

YOU?

Just that—no pictures, no explanations. There was no longer any need to say what 'P.P.' stood for; everyone in England knew it by this time. Mr Warner, with Gordon to help him, was designing the smaller ads for the newspapers and magazines. It was Mr Warner who supplied the bold sweeping ideas, sketched the general lay-out of the ads, and decided what pictures would be needed; but it was Gordon who wrote most of the letterpress—wrote the harrowing little stories, each a realistic novel in a hundred words, about despairing virgins of thirty, and lonely bachelors whose girls had unaccountably thrown them over, and overworked wives who could not afford to change their stockings once a week and who saw their husbands subsiding into the clutches of 'the other woman'. He did it very well; he did it far better than he had ever done anything else in his life. Mr Warner gave golden reports of him. There was no doubt about Gordon's literary ability. He could use words with the economy that is only learned by years of effort. So perhaps his long agonizing struggles to be a 'writer' had not been wasted after all.

They said good-bye to Ravelston outside the restaurant. The taxi bore them away. Ravelston had insisted on paying for the taxi from the registry office, so they felt they could afford another taxi. Warmed with wine, they lolled together, in the dusty May sunshine that filtered through the taxi window. Rosemary's head on Gordon's shoulder, their hands together in her lap. He played with the very slender wedding ring on Rosemary's ring finger. Rolled gold, five and sixpence. It looked all right, however.

'I must remember to take if off before I go to the studio tomorrow,' said Rosemary reflectively.

'To think we're really married! Till death do us part. We've done it now, right enough.'

'Terrifying, isn't it?'

'I expect we'll settle down all right, though. With a house of our own and a pram and an aspidistra.'

He lifted her face up to kiss her. She had a touch of make-up on today, the first he had ever seen on her, and not too skilfully applied. Neither of their faces stood the spring sunshine very well. There were fine lines on Rosemary's, deep seams on Gordon's. Rosemary looked twenty-eight, perhaps; Gordon looked at least thirty-five. But Rosemary had pulled the three white hairs out of her crown yesterday.

'Do you love me?' he said.

'Adore you, silly.'

'I believe you do. It's queer. I'm thirty and moth-eaten.'

'I don't care.'

They began to kiss, then drew hurriedly apart as they saw two scrawny upper-middle-class women, in a car that was moving parallel to their own, observing them with catty interest.

The flat off the Edgware Road wasn't too bad. It was a dull quarter and rather a slummy street, but it was convenient for the centre of London; also it was quiet, being a blind alley. From the back window (it was a top floor) you could see the roof of Paddington Station. Twenty-one and six a week, unfurnished. One bed, one reception, kitchenette, bath (with geyser), and w.c. They had got their furniture already, most of it on the never-never. Ravelston had given them a complete set of crockery for a wedding present—a very kindly thought, that. Julia had given them a rather dreadful 'occasional' table, veneered walnut with a scalloped edge. Gordon had begged and implored her not to give them anything. Poor Julia! Christmas had left her utterly broke, as usual, and Aunt Angela's birthday had been in March. But it would have seemed to Julia a kind of crime against nature to let a wedding go by without giving a present. God knew what sacrifices she had made to scrape together thirty bob for that 'occasional' table. They were still very short of linen and cutlery. Things would have to be bought piecemeal, when they had a few bob to spare.

They ran up the last flight of stairs in their excitement to get to the flat. It was all ready to inhabit. They had spent their evenings for weeks past getting the stuff in. It seeemed to them a tremendous adventure to have this place of their own. Neither of them had ever owned furniture before; they had been living in furnished rooms ever since their childhood. As soon as they got inside they made a careful tour of the flat, checking, examining, and admiring everything as though they did not know by heart already every item that was there. They fell into absurd raptures over each separate stick of furniture. The double bed with the clean sheet ready turned down over the pink eiderdown! The linen and towels stowed away in the chest of drawers! The gateleg table, the four hard chairs, the two armchairs, the divan, the bookcase, the red Indian rug, the copper coal-scuttle which they had picked up cheap in the Caledonian market! And it was all their own, every bit of it was their own—at least, so long as they didn't get behind with the instalments! They went into the kitchenette. Everything was ready, down to the minutest detail. Gas stove, meat safe, enamel-topped table, plate rack, saucepans, kettle, sink basket, mops, dish-cloths—even a tin of Panshine, a packet of soapflakes, and a pound of washing soda in a jam-jar. It was all ready for use, ready for life. You could have cooked a meal in it here and now. They stood hand in hand by the enamel-topped table, admiring the view of Paddington Station.

'Oh, Gordon, what fun it all is! To have a place that's really our own and no landladies interfering!'

'What I like best of all is to think of having breakfast together. You opposite me on the other side of the table, pouring out coffee. How queer it is! We've known each other all these years and we've never once had breakfast together.'

'Let's cook something now. I'm dying to use those saucepans.'

She made some coffee and brought it into the front room on the red lacquered tray which they had bought in Selfridge's Bargain Basement. Gordon wandered over to the 'occasional' table by the window. Far below the mean street was drowned in a haze of sunlight, as though a glassy yellow sea had flooded it fathoms deep. He laid his coffee cup down on the 'occasional' table.

'This is where we'll put the aspidistra,' he said.

'Put the *what*?'

'The aspidistra.'

She laughed. He saw that she thought he was joking, and added: 'We must remember to go out and order it before all the florists are shut.'

'Gordon! You don't mean that? You aren't *really* thinking of having an aspidistra?'

'Yes, I am. We won't let ours get dusty, either. They say an old toothbrush is the best thing to clean them with.'

She had come over to his side, and she pinched his arm.

'You aren't serious, by any chance, are you?'

'Why shouldn't I be?'

'An aspidistra! To think of having one of those awful depressing things in here! Besides, where could we put it? I'm not going to have it in this room, and in the bedroom it would be worse. Fancy having an aspidistra in one's bedroom!'

'We don't want one in the bedroom. This is the place for an aspidistra. In the front window, where the people opposite can see it.'

'Gordon, you *are* joking—you must be joking!'

'No, I'm not. I tell you we've got to have an aspidistra.'

'But why?'

'It's the proper thing to have. It's the first thing one buys after one's married. In fact, it's practically part of the wedding ceremony.'

'Don't be so absurd! I simply couldn't bear to have one of those things in here. You shall have a geranium if you really must. But not an aspidistra.'

'A geranium's no good. It's an aspidistra we want.'

'Well, we're not going to have one, that's flat.'

'Yes, we are. Didn't you promise to obey me just now?'

'No, I did not. We weren't married in church.'

'Oh, well, it's implied in the marriage service. "Love, honour, and obey" and all that.'

'No, it isn't. Anyway we aren't going to have that aspidistra.'

'Yes, we are.'

'We are *not*, Gordon!'

'Yes.'

'No!'

'Yes!'

'*No!*'

She did not understand him. She thought he was merely being perverse. They grew heated, and, according to their habit, quarrelled violently. It was their first quarrel as man and wife. Half an hour later they went out to the florist's to order the aspidistra.

But when they were half-way down the first flight of stairs Rosemary stopped short and clutched the banister. Her lips parted; she looked very queer for a moment. She pressed a hand against her middle.

'Oh, Gordon!'

'What?'

'I felt it move!'

'Felt what move?'

'The baby. I felt it move inside me.'

'You did?'

A strange, almost terrible feeling, a sort of warm convulsion, stirred in his entrails. For a moment he felt as though he were sexually joined to her, but joined in some subtle way that he had never imagined. He had paused a step or two below her. He fell on his knees, pressed his ear to her belly, and listened.

'I can't hear anything,' he said at last.

'Of course not, silly! Not for months yet.'

'But I shall be able to hear it later on, shan't I?'

'I think so. *You* can hear it at seven months, *I* can feel it at four. I think that's how it is.'

'But it really did move? You're sure? You really felt it move?'

'Oh, yes. It moved.'

For a long time he remained kneeling there, his head pressed against the softness of her belly. She clasped her hands behind his head and pulled it closer. He could hear nothing, only the blood drumming in his own ear. But she could not have been mistaken. Somewhere in there, in the safe, warm, cushioned darkness, it was alive and stirring.

Well, once again things were happening in the Comstock family.

# NINETEEN EIGHTY-FOUR

# PART I

## I

It was a bright cold day in April, and the clocks were striking thirteen. Winston Smith, his chin nuzzled into his breast in an effort to escape the vile wind, slipped quickly through the glass doors of Victory Mansions, though not quickly enough to prevent a swirl of gritty dust from entering along with him.

The hallway smelt of boiled cabbage and old rag mats. At one end of it a coloured poster, too large for indoor display, had been tacked to the wall. It depicted simply an enormous face, more than a metre wide: the face of a man of about forty-five, with a heavy black moustache and ruggedly handsome features. Winston made for the stairs. It was no use trying the lift. Even at the best of times it was seldom working, and at present the electric current was cut off during daylight hours. It was part of the economy drive in preparation for Hate Week. The flat was seven flights up, and Winston, who was thirty-nine and had a varicose ulcer above his right ankle, went slowly, resting several times on the way. On each landing, opposite the lift-shaft, the poster with the enormous face gazed from the wall. It was one of those pictures which are so contrived that the eyes follow you about when you move. BIG BROTHER IS WATCHING YOU, the caption beneath it ran.

Inside the flat a fruity voice was reading out a list of figures which had something to do with the production of pig-iron. The voice came from an oblong metal plaque like a dulled mirror which formed part of the surface of the right-hand wall. Winston turned a switch and the voice sank somewhat, though the words were still distinguishable. The instrument (the telescreen, it was called) could be dimmed, but there was no way of shutting it off completely. He moved over to the window: a smallish, frail figure, the meagreness of his body merely emphasized by the blue overalls which were the uniform of the Party. His hair was very fair, his face naturally sanguine, his skin roughened by coarse soap and blunt razor blades and the cold of the winter that had just ended.

Outside, even through the shut window-pane, the world looked cold. Down in the street little eddies of wind were whirling dust and torn paper into spirals, and though the sun was shining and the sky a harsh blue, there seemed to be no colour in anything, except the posters that were plastered everywhere. The black-moustachio'd face gazed down from every commanding corner. There was one on the house-front immediately opposite. BIG BROTHER IS WATCHING YOU, the caption said, while the dark eyes looked deep into Winston's own. Down at street level another poster, torn at one corner, flapped fitfully in the wind, alternately covering and uncovering the single word INGSOC. In the far distance a helicopter skimmed down between the roofs, hovered for an instant like a bluebottle, and darted away again with a curving flight. It was the police patrol, snooping into people's windows. The patrols did not matter, however. Only the Thought Police mattered.

Behind Winston's back the voice from the telescreen was still babbling away about pig-iron and the overfulfilment of the Ninth Three-Year Plan. The telescreen received and transmitted simultaneously. Any sound that Winston made, above the level of a very low whisper, would be picked up by it; moreover, so long as he remained within the field of vision which the metal plaque commanded, he could be seen as well as heard. There was of course no way of knowing whether you were being watched at any given moment. How often, or on what system, the Thought Police plugged in on any individual wire was guesswork. It was even conceivable that they watched everybody all the time. But at any rate they could plug in your wire whenever they wanted to. You had to live – did live, from habit that became instinct – in the assumption that every sound you made was overheard, and, except in darkness, every movement scrutinized.

Winston kept his back turned to the telescreen. It was safer; though, as he well knew, even a back can be revealing. A kilometre away the Ministry of Truth, his place of work, towered vast and white above the grimy landscape. This, he thought with a sort of vague distaste – this was London, chief city of Airstrip One, itself the third most populous of the provinces of Oceania. He tried to squeeze out some childhood memory that should tell him whether London had always been quite like this. Were there always these vistas of rotting nineteenth-century houses, their sides shored up with baulks of timber, their windows patched with cardboard and their roofs with corrugated iron, their crazy garden walls sagging in all directions? And the bombed sites where the plaster dust swirled in the air and the willow-herb straggled over the heaps of rubble; and the places where the bombs had cleared a larger patch and there had sprung up sordid colonies of wooden dwellings like chicken-houses? But it was no use, he could not remember: nothing remained of his childhood except a series of bright-lit tableaux, occurring against no background and mostly unintelligible.

The Ministry of Truth–Minitrue, in Newspeak*–was startlingly different from any other object in sight. It was an enormous pyramidal structure of glittering white concrete, soaring up, terrace after terrace, 300 metres into the air. From where Winston stood it was just possible to read, picked out on its white face in elegant lettering, the three slogans of the Party:

* Newspeak was the official language of Oceania. For an account of its structure and etymology see Appendix.

WAR IS PEACE
FREEDOM IS SLAVERY
IGNORANCE IS STRENGTH

The Ministry of Truth contained, it was said, three thousand rooms above ground level, and corresponding ramifications below. Scattered about London there were just three other buildings of similar appearance and size. So completely did they dwarf the surrounding architecture that from the roof of Victory Mansions you could see all four of them simultaneously. They were the homes of the four Ministries between which the entire apparatus of government was divided. The Ministry of Truth, which concerned itself with news, entertainment, education, and the fine arts. The Ministry of Peace, which concerned itself with war. The Ministry of Love, which maintained law and order. And the Ministry of Plenty, which was responsible for economic affairs. Their names, in Newspeak: Minitrue, Minipax, Miniluv, and Miniplenty.

The Ministry of Love was the really frightening one. There were no windows in it at all. Winston had never been inside the Ministry of Love, nor within half a kilometre of it. It was a place impossible to enter except on official business, and then only by penetrating through a maze of barbed-wire entanglements, steel doors, and hidden machine-gun nests. Even the streets leading up to its outer barriers were roamed by gorilla-faced guards in black uniforms, armed with jointed truncheons.

Winston turned round abruptly. He had set his features into the expression of quiet optimism which it was advisable to wear when facing the telescreen. He crossed the room into the tiny kitchen. By leaving the Ministry at this time of day he had sacrificed his lunch in the canteen, and he was aware that there was no food in the kitchen except a hunk of dark-coloured bread which had got to be saved for tomorrow's breakfast. He took down from the shelf a bottle of colourless liquid with a plain white label marked VICTORY GIN. It gave off a sickly, oily smell, as of Chinese rice-spirit. Winston poured out nearly a teacupful, nerved himself for a shock, and gulped it down like a dose of medicine.

Instantly his face turned scarlet and the water ran out of his eyes. The stuff was like nitric acid, and moreover, in swallowing it one had the sensation of being hit on the back of the head with a rubber club. The next moment, however, the burning in his belly died down and the world began to look more cheerful. He took a cigarette from a crumpled packet marked VICTORY CIGARETTES and incautiously held it upright, whereupon the tobacco fell out on to the floor. With the next he was more successful. He went back to the living-room and sat down at a small table that stood to the left of the telescreen. From the table drawer he took out a penholder, a bottle of ink, and a thick, quarto-sized blank book with a red back and a marbled cover.

For some reason the telescreen in the living-room was in an unusual position. Instead of being placed, as was normal, in the end wall, where it could command the whole room, it was in the longer wall, opposite the window. To one side of it there was a shallow alcove in which Winston was now sitting, and which, when the flats were built, had probably been intended to hold bookshelves. By sitting in the alcove, and keeping well back, Winston was able to remain outside the range of the telescreen, so far as sight went. He could be heard, of course, but so long as he stayed in his present position he could not be seen. It was partly the unusual geography of the room that had suggested to him the thing that he was now about to do.

But it had also been suggested by the book that he had just taken out of the drawer. It was a peculiarly beautiful book. Its smooth creamy paper, a little yellowed by age, was of a kind that had not been manufactured for at least forty years past. He could guess, however, that the book was much older than that. He had seen it lying in the window of a frowsy little junk-shop in a slummy quarter of the town (just what quarter he did not now remember) and had been stricken immediately by an overwhelming desire to possess it. Party members were supposed not to go into ordinary shops ('dealing on the free market', it was called), but the rule was not strictly kept, because there were various things, such as shoelaces and razor blades, which it was impossible to get hold of in any other way. He had given a quick glance up and down the street and then had slipped inside and bought the book for two dollars fifty. At the time he was not conscious of wanting it for any particular purpose. He had carried it guiltily home in his brief-case. Even with nothing written in it, it was a compromising possession.

The thing that he was about to do was to open a diary. This was not illegal (nothing was illegal, since there were no longer any laws), but if detected it was reasonably certain that it would be punished by death, or at least by twenty-five years in a forced-labour camp. Winston fitted a nib into the penholder and sucked it to get the grease off. The pen was an archaic instrument, seldom used even for signatures, and he had procured one, furtively and with some difficulty, simply because of a feeling that the beautiful creamy paper deserved to be written on with a real nib instead of being scratched with an ink-pencil. Actually he was not used to writing by hand. Apart from very short notes, it was usual to dictate everything into the speakwrite, which was of course impossible for his present purpose. He dipped the pen into the ink and then faltered for just a second. A tremor had gone through his bowels. To mark the paper was the decisive act. In small clumsy letters he wrote:

April 4th, 1984.

He sat back. A sense of complete helplessness had descended upon him. To begin with, he did not know with any certainty that this *was* 1984. It must be round about that date, since he was fairly sure that his age was thirty-nine, and he believed that he had been born in 1944 or 1945; but it was never possible nowadays to pin down any date within a year or two.

For whom, it suddenly occurred to him to wonder, was he writing this diary? For the future, for the unborn. His mind hovered for a moment round the doubtful date on the page, and then fetched up with a bump against the Newspeak word *doublethink*. For the first time the magnitude of what he had undertaken came home to him. How could you communicate with the future? It was of its nature impossible. Either the future would resemble the present, in which case it would not listen to him: or it would be different from it, and his predicament would be meaningless.

For some time he sat gazing stupidly at the paper. The telescreen had changed over to strident military music. It was curious that he seemed not merely to have lost the power of expressing himself, but even to have forgotten what it was that he had originally intended to say. For weeks past he had been making ready for this moment, and it had never crossed his mind that anything would be needed except courage. The actual writing would be easy. All he had to do was to transfer to paper the interminable restless monologue that had been running inside his head, literally for years. At this moment, however, even the monologue had dried up. Moreover his varicose ulcer had begun itching unbearably. He dared not scratch it, because if he did so it always became inflamed. The seconds were ticking by. He was conscious of nothing except the blankness of the page in front of him, the itching of the skin above his ankle, the blaring of the music, and a slight booziness caused by the gin.

Suddenly he began writing in sheer panic, only imperfectly aware of what he was setting down. His small but childish handwriting straggled up and down the page, shedding first its capital letters and finally even its full stops:

April 4th, 1984. Last night to the flicks. All war films. One very good one of a ship full of refugees being bombed somewhere in the Mediterranean. Audience much amused by shots of a great huge fat man trying to swim away with a helicopter after him, first you saw him wallowing along in the water like a porpoise, then you saw him through the helicopters gunsights, then he was full of holes and the sea round him turned pink and he sank as suddenly as though the holes had let in the water. audience shouting with laughter when he sank. then you saw a lifeboat full of children with a helicopter hovering over it. there was a middle-aged woman might have been a jewess sitting up in the bow with a little boy about three years old in her arms. little boy screaming with fright and hiding his head between her breasts as if he was trying to burrow right into her and the woman putting her arms round him and comforting him although she was blue with fright herself, all the time covering him up as much as possible as if she thought her arms could keep the bullets off him. then the helicopter planted a 20 kilo bomb in among them terrific flash and the boat went all to matchwood. then there was a wonderful shot of a child's arm going up up up right up into the air a helicopter with a camera in its nose must have followed it up and there was a lot of applause from the party seats but a woman down in the prole part of the house suddenly started kicking up a fuss and shouting they didnt oughter of showed it not in front of kids they didnt it aint right not in front of kids it aint until the police turned her turned her out i dont suppose anything happened to her nobody cares what the proles say typical prole reaction they never—

Winston stopped writing, partly because he was suffering from cramp. He did not know what had made him pour out this stream of rubbish. But the curious thing was that while he was doing so a totally different memory had clarified itself in his mind, to the point where he almost felt equal to writing it down. It was, he now realized, because of this other incident that he had suddenly decided to come home and begin the diary today.

It had happened that morning at the Ministry, if anything so nebulous could be said to happen.

It was nearly eleven hundred, and in the Records Department, where Winston worked, they were dragging the chairs out of the cubicles and grouping them in the centre of the hall opposite the big telescreen, in preparation for the Two Minutes Hate. Winston was just taking his place in one of the middle rows when two people whom he knew by sight, but had never spoken to, came unexpectedly into the room. One of them was a girl whom he often passed in the corridors. He did not know her name, but he knew that she worked in the Fiction Department. Presumably – since he had sometimes seen her with oily hands and carrying a spanner – she had some mechanical job on one of the novel-writing machines. She was a bold-looking girl, of about twenty-seven, with thick dark hair, a freckled face, and swift, athletic movements. A narrow scarlet sash, emblem of the Junior Anti-Sex League, was wound several times round the waist of her overalls, just tightly enough to bring out the shapeliness of her hips. Winston had disliked her from the very first moment of seeing her. He knew the reason. It was because of the atmosphere of hockey-fields and cold baths and community hikes and general clean-mindedness which she managed to carry about with her. He disliked nearly all women, and especially the young and pretty ones. It was always the women, and above all the young ones, who were the most bigoted adherents of the Party, the swallowers of slogans, the amateur spies and nosers-out of unorthodoxy. But this particular girl gave him the impression of being more dangerous than most. Once when they passed in the corridor she had given him a quick sidelong glance which seemed to pierce right into him and for a moment had filled him with black terror. The idea had even crossed his mind that she might be an agent of the Thought Police. That, it was true, was very unlikely. Still, he continued to feel a peculiar uneasiness, which had fear mixed up in it as well as hostility, whenever she was anywhere near him.

The other person was a man named O'Brien, a member of the Inner Party and holder of some post so important and remote that Winston had only a dim idea of its nature. A momentary hush passed over the group of people round the chairs as they saw the black overalls of an Inner Party member approaching. O'Brien was a large, burly man with a thick neck and a coarse, humorous, brutal face. In spite of his formidable appearance he had a certain charm of manner. He had a trick of resettling his spectacles on his nose which was curiously disarming – in some indefinable way, curiously civilized. It was a gesture which, if anyone had still thought in such terms, might have recalled an eighteenth-century nobleman offering his snuffbox. Winston had seen O'Brien perhaps a dozen times in almost as many years. He felt deeply drawn to him, and not solely because he was intrigued by the contrast between O'Brien's urbane manner and his prize-fighter's physique. Much more it was because of a secretly held belief – or perhaps not even a belief, merely a hope – that O'Brien's political orthodoxy was not perfect. Something in his face suggested it irresistibly. And again, perhaps it was not even unorthodoxy that was written in his face, but simply intelligence. But at any rate he had the appearance of being a person that you could talk to if somehow you could cheat the telescreen and get him alone. Winston had never made the smallest effort to verify this guess: indeed, there was no way of doing so. At this moment

O'Brien glanced at his wrist-watch, saw that it was nearly eleven hundred, and evidently decided to stay in the Records Department until the Two Minutes Hate was over. He took a chair in the same row as Winston, a couple of places away. A small, sandy-haired woman who worked in the next cubicle to Winston was between them. The girl with dark hair was sitting immediately behind.

The next moment a hideous, grinding speech, as of some monstrous machine running without oil, burst from the big telescreen at the end of the room. It was a noise that set one's teeth on edge and bristled the hair at the back of one's neck. The Hate had started.

As usual, the face of Emmanuel Goldstein, the Enemy of the People, had flashed on to the screen. There were hisses here and there among the audience. The little sandy-haired woman gave a squeak of mingled fear and disgust. Goldstein was the renegade and backslider who once, long ago (how long ago, nobody quite remembered), had been one of the leading figures of the Party, almost on a level with Big Brother himself, and then had engaged in counter-revolutionary activities, had been condemned to death, and had mysteriously escaped and disappeared. The programmes of the Two Minutes Hate varied from day to day, but there was none in which Goldstein was not the principal figure. He was the primal traitor, the earliest defiler of the Party's purity. All subsequent crimes against the Party, all treacheries, acts of sabotage, heresies, deviations, sprang directly out of his teaching. Somewhere or other he was still alive and hatching his conspiracies: perhaps somewhere beyond the sea, under the protection of his foreign paymasters, perhaps even—so it was occasionally rumoured – in some hiding-place in Oceania itself.

Winston's diaphragm was constricted. He could never see the face of Goldstein without a painful mixture of emotions. It was a lean Jewish face, with a great fuzzy aureole of white hair and a small goatee beard – a clever face, and yet somehow inherently despicable, with a kind of senile silliness in the long thin nose, near the end of which a pair of spectacles was perched. It resembled the face of a sheep, and the voice, too, had a sheep-like quality. Goldstein was delivering his usual venomous attack upon the doctrines of the Party – an attack so exaggerated and perverse that a child should have been able to see through it, and yet just plausible enough to fill one with an alarmed feeling that other people, less level-headed than oneself, might be taken in by it. He was abusing Big Brother, he was denouncing the dictatorship of the Party, he was demanding the immediate conclusion of peace with Eurasia, he was advocating freedom of speech, freedom of the Press, freedom of assembly, freedom of thought, he was crying hysterically that the revolution had been betrayed – and all this in rapid polysyllabic speech which was a sort of parody of the habitual style of the orators of the Party, and even contained Newspeak words: more Newspeak words, indeed, than any Party member would normally use in real life. And all the while, lest one should be in any doubt as to the reality which Goldstein's specious claptrap covered, behind his head on the telescreen there marched the endless columns of the Eurasian army – row after row of solid-looking men with expressionless Asiatic faces, who swam up to the surface of the screen and vanished, to be replaced by others exactly similar. The dull rhythmic tramp of the soldiers' boots formed the background to Goldstein's bleating voice.

Before the Hate had proceeded for thirty seconds, uncontrollable exclamations of rage were breaking out from half the people in the room. The self-satisfied sheep-like face on the screen, and the terrifying power of the Eurasian army behind it, were too much to be borne: besides, the sight or even the thought of Goldstein produced fear and anger automatically. He was an object of hatred more constant than either Eurasia or Eastasia, since when Oceania was at war with one of these Powers it was generally at peace with the other. But what was strange was that although Goldstein was hated and despised by everybody, although every day and a thousand times a day, on platforms, on the telescreen, in newspapers, in books, his theories were refuted, smashed, ridiculed, held up to the general gaze for the pitiful rubbish that they were – in spite of all this, his influence never seemed to grow less. Always there were fresh dupes waiting to be seduced by him. A day never passed when spies and saboteurs acting under his directions were not unmasked by the Thought Police. He was the commander of a vast shadowy army, an underground network of conspirators dedicated to the overthrow of the State. The Brotherhood, its name was supposed to be. There were also whispered stories of a terrible book, a compendium of all the heresies, of which Goldstein was the author and which circulated clandestinely here and there. It was a book without a title. People referred to it, if at all, simply as *the book*. But one knew of such things only through vague rumours. Neither the Brotherhood nor *the book* was a subject that any ordinary Party member would mention if there was a way of avoiding it.

In its second minute the Hate rose to a frenzy. People were leaping up and down in their places and shouting at the tops of their voices in an effort to drown the maddening bleating voice that came from the screen. The little sandy-haired woman had turned bright pink, and her mouth was opening and shutting like that of a landed fish. Even O'Brien's heavy face was flushed. He was sitting very straight in his chair, his powerful chest swelling and quivering as though he were standing up to the assault of a wave. The dark-haired girl behind Winston had begun crying out 'Swine! Swine! Swine!' and suddenly she picked up a heavy Newspeak dictionary and flung it at the screen. It struck Goldstein's nose and bounced off; the voice continued inexorably. In a lucid moment Winston found that he was shouting with the others and kicking his heel violently against the rung of his chair. The horrible thing about the Two Minutes Hate was not that one was obliged to act a part, but, on the contrary, that it was impossible to avoid joining in. Within thirty seconds any pretence was always unnecessary. A hideous ecstasy of fear and vindictiveness, a desire to kill, to torture, to smash faces in with a sledge-hammer, seemed to flow through the whole group of people like an electric current, turning one even against one's will into a grimacing, screaming lunatic. And yet the rage that one felt was an abstract, undirected emotion which could be switched from one object to another like the flame of a blowlamp. Thus, at one moment Winston's hatred was not turned against Goldstein at all, but, on the contrary, against Big Brother, the Party, and the Thought Police; and at such moments his heart went out to the lonely, derided heretic on the screen, sole guardian of truth and sanity in a world of lies. And yet the very next instant he was at one with the people about him, and all that was said of Goldstein seemed to him to be true. At those moments his secret loathing of Big Brother changed into adoration, and Big Brother seemed to tower up, an invincible, fearless protector, standing like a rock against the hordes of Asia, and Goldstein, in spite of his isolation, his helplessness, and the doubt that hung about his very existence, seemed like some sinister enchanter, capable by the mere power of his voice of wrecking the structure of civilization.

It was even possible, at moments, to switch one's hatred this way or that by a voluntary act. Suddenly, by the sort of violent effort with which one wrenches one's head away from the pillow in a nightmare, Winston succeeded in transferring his hatred from the face on the screen to the dark-haired girl behind him. Vivid, beautiful hallucinations flashed through his mind. He would flog her to death with a rubber truncheon. He would tie her naked to a stake and shoot her full of arrows like Saint Sebastian. He would ravish her and cut her throat at the moment of climax. Better than before, moreover, he realized *why* it was that he hated her. He hated her because she was young and pretty and sexless, because he wanted to go to bed with her and would never do so, because round her sweet supple waist, which seemed to ask you to encircle it with your arm, there was only the odious scarlet sash, aggressive symbol of chastity.

The Hate rose to its climax. The voice of Goldstein had become an actual sheep's bleat, and for an instant the face changed into that of a sheep. Then the sheep-face melted into the figure of a Eurasian soldier who seemed to be advancing, huge and terrible, his sub-machine gun roaring, and seeming to spring out of the surface of the screen, so that some of the people in the front row actually flinched backwards in their seats. But in the same moment, drawing a deep sigh of relief from everybody, the hostile figure melted into the face of Big Brother, black-haired, black-moustachio'd, full of power and mysterious calm, and so vast that it almost filled up the screen. Nobody heard what Big Brother was saying. It was merely a few words of encouragement, the sort of words that are uttered in the din of battle, not distinguishable individually but restoring confidence by the fact of being spoken. Then the face of Big Brother faded away again, and instead the three slogans of the Party stood out in bold capitals:

WAR IS PEACE
FREEDOM IS SLAVERY
IGNORANCE IS STRENGTH

But the face of Big Brother seemed to persist for several seconds on the screen, as though the impact that it had made on everyone's eyeballs was too vivid to wear off immediately. The little sandy-haired woman had flung herself forward over the back of the chair in front of her. With a tremulous murmur that sounded like 'My Saviour!' she extended her arms towards the screen. Then she buried her face in her hands. It was apparent that she was uttering a prayer.

At this moment the entire group of people broke into a deep, slow, rhythmical chant of 'B-B! . . . B-B! . . . B-B!' – over and over again, very slowly, with a long pause between the first 'B' and the second – a heavy, murmurous sound, somehow curiously savage, in the background of which one seemed to hear the stamp of naked feet and the throbbing of tom-toms. For perhaps as much as thirty seconds they kept it up. It was a refrain that was often heard in moments of overwhelming emotion. Partly it was a sort of hymn to the wisdom and majesty of Big Brother, but still more it was an act of self-hypnosis, a deliberate drowning of consciousness by means of rhythmic noise. Winston's entrails seemed to grow cold. In the Two Minutes Hate he could not help sharing in the general delirium, but this sub-human chanting of 'B-B! . . . B-B!' always filled him with horror. Of course he chanted with the rest: it was impossible to do otherwise. To dissemble your feelings, to control your face, to do what everyone else was doing, was an instinctive reaction. But there was a space of a couple of seconds during which the expression in his eyes might conceivably have betrayed him. And it was exactly at this moment that the significant thing happened – if, indeed, it did happen.

Momentarily he caught O'Brien's eye. O'Brien had stood up. He had taken off his spectacles and was in the act of resettling them on his nose with his characteristic gesture. But there was a fraction of a second when their eyes met, and for as long as it took to happen Winston knew–yes, he *knew*!–that O'Brien was thinking the same thing as himself. An unmistakable message had passed. It was as though their two minds had opened and the thoughts were flowing from one into the other through their eyes. 'I am with you,' O'Brien seemed to be saying to him. 'I know precisely what you are feeling. I know all about your contempt, your hatred, your disgust. But don't worry, I am on your side!' And then the flash of intelligence was gone, and O'Brien's face was as inscrutable as everybody else's.

That was all, and he was already uncertain whether it had happened. Such incidents never had any sequel. All that they did was to keep alive in him the belief, or hope, that others besides himself were the enemies of the Party. Perhaps the rumours of vast underground conspiracies were true after all–perhaps the Brotherhood really existed! It was impossible, in spite of the endless arrests and confessions and executions, to be sure that the Brotherhood was not simply a myth. Some days he believed in it, some days not. There was no evidence, only fleeting glimpses that might mean anything or nothing: snatches of overheard conversation, faint scribbles on lavatory walls–once, even, when two strangers met, a small movement of the hand which had looked as though it might be a signal of recognition. It was all guesswork: very likely he had imagined everything. He had gone back to his cubicle without looking at O'Brien again. The idea of following up their momentary contact hardly crossed his mind. It would have been inconceivably dangerous even if he had known how to set about doing it. For a second, two seconds, they had exchanged an equivocal glance, and that was the end of the story. But even that was a memorable event, in the locked loneliness in which one had to live.

Winston roused himself and sat up straighter. He let out a belch. The gin was rising from his stomach.

His eyes re-focused on the page. He discovered that while he sat helplessly musing he had also been writing, as though by automatic action. And it was no longer the same cramped, awkward handwriting as before. His pen had slid voluptuously over the smooth paper, printing in large neat capitals—

DOWN WITH BIG BROTHER

DOWN WITH BIG BROTHER

DOWN WITH BIG BROTHER

DOWN WITH BIG BROTHER

DOWN WITH BIG BROTHER

over and over again, filling half a page.

He could not help feeling a twinge of panic. It was absurd, since the writing of those particular words was not more dangerous than the initial act of opening the diary; but for a moment he was tempted to tear out the spoiled pages and abandon the enterprise altogether.

He did not do so, however, because he knew that it was useless. Whether he wrote DOWN WITH BIG BROTHER, or whether he refrained from writing it, made no difference. Whether he went on with the diary, or whether he did not go on with it, made no difference. The Thought Police would get him just the same. He had committed—would still have committed, even if he had never set pen to paper—the essential crime that contained all others in itself. Thoughtcrime, they called it. Thoughtcrime was not a thing that could be concealed for ever. You might dodge successfully for a while, even for years, but sooner or later they were bound to get you.

It was always at night—the arrests invariably happened at night. The sudden jerk out of sleep, the rough hand shaking your shoulder, the lights glaring in your eyes, the ring of hard faces round the bed. In the vast majority of cases there was no trial, no report of the arrest. People simply disappeared, always during the night. Your name was removed from the registers, every record of everything you had ever done was wiped out, your one-time existence was denied and then forgotten. You were abolished, annihilated: *vaporized* was the usual word.

For a moment he was seized by a kind of hysteria. He began writing in a hurried untidy scrawl:

theyll shoot me i dont care theyll shoot me in the back of the neck i dont care down with big brother they always shoot you in the back of the neck i dont care down with big brother—

He sat back in his chair, slightly ashamed of himself, and laid down the pen. The next moment he started violently. There was a knocking at the door

Already! He sat as still as a mouse, in the futile hope that whoever it was might go away after a single attempt. But no, the knocking was repeated. The worst thing of all would be to delay. His heart was thumping like a drum, but his face, from long habit, was probably expressionless. He got up and moved heavily towards the door.

## 2

As he put his hand to the door-knob Winston saw that he had left the diary open on the table. DOWN WITH BIG BROTHER was written over it, in letters almost big enough to be legible across the room. It was an inconceivably stupid thing to have done. But, he realized, even in his panic he had not wanted to smudge the creamy paper by shutting the book while the ink was wet.

He drew in his breath and opened the door. Instantly a warm wave of relief flowed through him. A colourless, crushed-looking woman, with wispy hair and a lined face, was standing outside.

'Oh, comrade,' she began in a dreary, whining sort of voice, 'I thought I heard you come in. Do you think you could come across and have a look at our kitchen sink? It's got blocked up and—'

It was Mrs Parsons, the wife of a neighbour on the same floor. ('Mrs' was a word somewhat discountenanced by the Party—you were supposed to call everyone 'comrade'—but with some women one used it instinctively.) She was a woman of about thirty, but looking much older. One had the impression that there was dust in the creases of her face. Winston followed her down the passage. These amateur repair jobs were an almost daily irritation. Victory Mansions were old flats, built in 1930 or thereabouts, and were falling to pieces. The plaster flaked constantly from ceilings and walls, the pipes burst in every hard frost, the roof leaked whenever there was snow, the heating system was usually running at half steam when it was not closed down altogether from motives of economy. Repairs, except what you could do for yourself, had to be sanctioned by remote committees which were liable to hold up even the mending of a window-pane for two years.

'Of course it's only because Tom isn't home,' said Mrs Parsons vaguely.

The Parsons' flat was bigger than Winston's, and dingy in a different way. Everything had a battered, trampled-on look, as though the place had just been visited by some large violent animal. Games impedimenta—hockey-sticks, boxing-gloves, a burst football, a pair of sweaty shorts turned inside out—lay all over the floor, and on the table there was a litter of dirty dishes and dogeared exercise-books. On the walls were scarlet banners of the Youth League and the Spies, and a full-sized poster of Big Brother. There was the usual boiled-cabbage smell, common to the whole building, but it was shot through by a sharper reek of sweat, which—one knew this at the first sniff, though it was hard to say how—was the sweat of some person not present at the moment. In another room someone with a comb and a piece of toilet paper was trying to keep tune with the military music which was still issuing from the telescreen.

'It's the children,' said Mrs Parsons, casting a half-apprehensive glance at the door. 'They haven't been out today. And of course—'

She had a habit of breaking off her sentences in the middle. The kitchen sink was full nearly to the brim with filthy greenish water which smelt worse than ever of cabbage. Winston knelt down and examined the angle-joint of the pipe. He hated using his hands, and he hated bending down, which was always liable to start him coughing. Mrs Parsons looked on helplessly.

'Of course if Tom was home he'd put it right in a moment,' she said. 'He loves anything like that. He's ever so good with his hands, Tom is.'

Parsons was Winston's fellow employee at the Ministry of Truth. He was a fattish but active man of paralysing stupidity, a mass of imbecile enthusiasms—one of those completely unquestioning, devoted drudges on whom, more even than on the Thought Police, the stability of the Party depended. At thirty-five he had just been unwillingly evicted from the Youth League, and before graduating into the Youth League he had managed to stay on in the Spies for a year beyond the statutory age. At the Ministry he was employed in some subordinate post for which intelligence was not required, but on the other hand he was a leading figure on the Sports Committee and all the other committees engaged in organizing community hikes, spontaneous demonstrations, savings campaigns, and voluntary activities generally. He would inform you with quiet pride, between whiffs of his pipe, that he had put in an appearance at the Community Centre every evening for the past four years. An overpowering smell of sweat, a sort of unconscious testimony to the strenuousness of his life, followed him about wherever he went, and even remained behind him after he had gone.

'Have you got a spanner?' said Winston, fiddling with the nut on the angle-joint.

'A spanner,' said Mrs Parsons, immediately becoming invertebrate. 'I don't know, I'm sure. Perhaps the children—'

There was a trampling of boots and another blast on the comb as the children charged into the living-room. Mrs Parsons brought the spanner. Winston let out the water and disgustedly removed the clot of human hair that had blocked up the pipe. He cleaned his fingers as best he could in the cold water from the tap and went back into the other room.

'Up with your hands!' yelled a savage voice.

A handsome, tough-looking boy of nine had popped up from behind the table and was menacing him with a toy automatic pistol, while his small sister, about two years younger, made the same gesture with a fragment of wood. Both of them were dressed in the blue shorts, grey shirts, and red neckerchiefs which were the uniform of the Spies. Winston raised his hands above his head, but with an uneasy feeling, so vicious was the boy's demeanour, that it was not altogether a game.

'You're a traitor!' yelled the boy. 'You're a thought-criminal! You're a Eurasian spy! I'll shoot you, I'll vaporize you, I'll send you to the salt mines!'

Suddenly they were both leaping round him, shouting 'Traitor!' and 'Thought-criminal!' the little girl imitating her brother in every movement. It was somehow slightly frightening, like the gambolling of tiger cubs which will soon grow up into man-eaters. There was a sort of calculating ferocity in the boy's eye, a quite evident desire to hit or kick Winston and a consciousness of being very nearly big enough to do so. It was a good job it was not a real pistol he was holding, Winston thought.

Mrs Parsons' eyes flitted nervously from Winston to the children, and back again. In the better light of the living-room he noticed with interest that there actually *was* dust in the creases of her face.

'They do get so noisy,' she said. 'They're disappointed because they couldn't go to see the hanging, that's what it is. I'm too busy to take them, and Tom won't be back from work in time.'

'Why can't we go and see the hanging?' roared the boy in his huge voice.

'Want to see the hanging! Want to see the hanging!' chanted the little girl, still capering round.

Some Eurasian prisoners, guilty of war crimes, were to be hanged in the Park that evening, Winston remembered. This happened about once a month, and was a popular spectacle. Children always clamoured to be taken to see it. He took his leave of Mrs Parsons and made for the door. But he had not gone six steps down the passage when something hit the back of his neck an agonizingly painful blow. It was as though a red-hot wire had been jabbed into him. He spun round just in time to see Mrs Parsons dragging her son back into the doorway while the boy pocketed a catapult.

'Goldstein!' bellowed the boy as the door closed on him. But what most struck Winston was the look of helpless fright on the woman's greyish face.

Back in the flat he stepped quickly past the telescreen and sat down at the table again, still rubbing his neck. The music from the telescreen had stopped. Instead, a clipped military voice was reading out, with a sort of brutal relish, a description of the armaments of the new Floating Fortress which had just been anchored between Iceland and the Faroe Islands.

With those children, he thought, that wretched woman must lead a life of terror. Another year, two years, and they would be watching her night and day for symptoms of unorthodoxy. Nearly all children nowadays were horrible. What was worst of all was that by means of such organizations as the Spies they were systematically turned into ungovernable little savages, and yet this produced in them no tendency whatever to rebel against the discipline of the Party. On the contrary, they adored the Party and everything connected with it. The songs, the processions, the banners, the hiking, the drilling with dummy rifles, the yelling of slogans, the worship of Big Brother—it was all a sort of glorious game to them. All their ferocity was turned outwards, against the enemies of the State, against foreigners, traitors, saboteurs, thought-criminals. It was almost normal for people over thirty to be frightened of their own children. And with good reason, for hardly a week passed in which *The*

*Times* did not carry a paragraph describing how some eavesdropping little sneak—'child hero' was the phrase generally used—had overheard some compromising remark and denounced its parents to the Thought Police.

The sting of the catapult bullet had worn off. He picked up his pen half-heartedly, wondering whether he could find something more to write in the diary. Suddenly he began thinking of O'Brien again.

Years ago—how long was it? Seven years it must be—he had dreamed that he was walking through a pitch-dark room. And someone sitting to one side of him had said as he passed: 'We shall meet in the place where there is no darkness.' It was said very quietly, almost casually—a statement, not a command. He had walked on without pausing. What was curious was that at the time, in the dream, the words had not made much impression on him. It was only later and by degrees that they had seemed to take on significance. He could not now remember whether it was before or after having the dream that he had seen O'Brien for the first time; nor could he remember when he had first identified the voice as O'Brien's. But at any rate the identification existed. It was O'Brien who had spoken to him out of the dark.

Winston had never been able to feel sure—even after this morning's flash of the eyes it was still impossible to be sure—whether O'Brien was a friend or an enemy. Nor did it even seem to matter greatly. There was a link of understanding between them, more important than affection or partisanship. 'We shall meet in the place where there is no darkness,' he had said. Winston did not know what it meant, only that in some way or another it would come true.

The voice from the telescreen paused. A trumpet call, clear and beautiful, floated into the stagnant air. The voice continued raspingly:

'Attention! Your attention, please! A newsflash has this moment arrived from the Malabar front. Our forces in South India have won a glorious victory. I am authorized to say that the action we are now reporting may well bring the war within measurable distance of its end. Here is the newsflash—'

Bad news coming, thought Winston. And sure enough, following on a gory description of the annihilation of a Eurasian army, with stupendous figures of killed and prisoners, came the announcement that, as from next week, the chocolate ration would be reduced from thirty grammes to twenty.

Winston belched again. The gin was wearing off, leaving a deflated feeling. The telescreen—perhaps to celebrate the victory, perhaps to drown the memory of the lost chocolate—crashed into 'Oceania, 'tis for thee'. You were supposed to stand to attention. However, in his present position he was invisible.

'Oceania, 'tis for thee' gave way to lighter music. Winston walked over to the window, keeping his back to the telescreen. The day was still cold and clear. Somewhere far away a rocket bomb exploded with a dull, reverberating roar. About twenty or thirty of them a week were falling on London at present.

Down in the street the wind flapped the torn poster to and fro, and the word INGSOC fitfully appeared and vanished. Ingsoc. The sacred principles of Ingsoc. Newspeak, doublethink, the mutability of the past. He felt as though he were wandering in the forests of the sea bottom, lost in a monstrous world where he himself was the monster. He was alone. The past was dead, the future was unimaginable. What certainty had he that a single human creature now living was on his side? And what way of knowing that the dominion of the Party would not endure *for ever*? Like an answer, the three slogans on the white face of the Ministry of Truth came back to him:

WAR IS PEACE

FREEDOM IS SLAVERY

IGNORANCE IS STRENGTH

He took a twenty-five cent piece out of his pocket. There, too, in tiny clear lettering, the same slogans were inscribed, and on the other face of the coin the head of Big Brother. Even from the coin the eyes pursued you. On coins, on stamps, on the covers of books, on banners, on posters, and on the wrappings of a cigarette packet—everywhere. Always the eyes watching you and the voice enveloping you. Asleep or awake, working or eating, indoors or out of doors, in the bath or in bed—no escape. Nothing was your own except the few cubic centimetres inside your skull.

The sun had shifted round, and the myriad windows of the Ministry of Truth, with the light no longer shining on them, looked grim as the loopholes of a fortress. His heart quailed before the enormous pyramidal shape. It was too strong, it could not be stormed. A thousand rocket bombs would not batter it down. He wondered again for whom he was writing the diary. For the future, for the past—for an age that might be imaginary. And in front of him there lay not death but annihilation. The diary would be reduced to ashes and himself to vapour. Only the Thought Police would read what he had written, before they wiped it out of existence and out of memory. How could you make appeal to the future when not a trace of you, not even an anonymous word scribbled on a piece of paper, could physically survive?

The telescreen struck fourteen. He must leave in ten minutes. He had to be back at work by fourteen-thirty.

Curiously, the chiming of the hour seemed to have put new heart into him. He was a lonely ghost uttering a truth that nobody would ever hear. But so long as he uttered it, in some obscure way the continuity was not broken. It was not by making yourself heard but by staying sane that you carried on the human heritage. He went back to the table, dipped his pen, and wrote:

To the future or to the past, to a time when thought is free, when men are different from one another and do not live alone—to a time when truth exists and what is done cannot be undone:

From the age of uniformity, from the age of solitude, from the age of Big Brother, from the age of doublethink—greetings!

He was already dead, he reflected. It seemed to him that it was only now, when he had begun to be able to formulate his thoughts, that he had taken the decisive step. The consequences of every act are included in the act itself. He wrote:

*Thoughtcrime does not entail death: thoughtcrime IS death.*

Now he had recognized himself as a dead man it became important to stay alive as long as possible. Two fingers of his right hand were inkstained. It was exactly the kind of detail that might betray you. Some nosing zealot in the Ministry (a woman, probably: someone like the little sandy-haired woman or the dark-haired girl from the Fiction Department) might start wondering why he had been writing during the lunch interval, why he had used an old-fashioned pen, *what* he had been writing—and then drop a hint in the appropriate quarter. He went to the bathroom and carefully scrubbed the ink away with the gritty dark-brown soap which rasped your skin like sandpaper and was therefore well adapted for this purpose.

He put the diary away in the drawer. It was quite useless to think of hiding it, but he could at least make sure whether or not its existence had been discovered. A hair laid across the page-ends was too obvious. With the tip of his finger he picked up an identifiable grain of whitish dust and deposited it on the corner of the cover, where it was bound to be shaken off if the book was moved.

## 3

Winston was dreaming of his mother.

He must, he thought, have been ten or eleven years old when his mother had disappeared. She was a tall, statuesque, rather silent woman with slow movements and magnificent fair hair. His father he remembered more vaguely as dark and thin, dressed always in neat dark clothes (Winston remembered especially the very thin soles of his father's shoes) and wearing spectacles. The two of them must evidently have been swallowed up in one of the first great purges of the 'fifties.

At this moment his mother was sitting in some place deep down beneath him, with his young sister in her arms. He did not remember his sister at all, except as a tiny, feeble baby, always silent, with large, watchful eyes. Both of them were looking up at him. They were down in some subterranean place—the bottom of a well, for instance, or a very deep grave—but it was a place which, already far below him, was itself moving downwards. They were in the saloon of a sinking ship, looking up at him through the darkening water. There was still air in the saloon, they could still see him and he them, but all the while they were sinking down, down into the green waters which in another moment must hide them from sight for ever. He was out in the light and air while they were being sucked down to death, and they were down there *because* he was up here. He knew it and they knew it, and he could see the knowledge in their faces. There was no repoach either in their faces or in their hearts, only the knowledge that they must die in order that he might remain alive, and this was part of the unavoidable order of things.

He could not remember what had happened, but he knew in his dream that in some way the lives of his mother and his sister had been sacrificed to his own. It was one of those dreams which, while retaining the characteristic dream scenery, are a continuation of one's intellectual life, and in which one becomes aware of facts and ideas which still seem new and valuable after one is awake. The thing that now suddenly struck Winston was that his mother's death, nearly thirty years ago, had been tragic and sorrowful in a way that was no longer possible. Tragedy, he perceived, belonged to the ancient time, to a time when there was still privacy, love, and friendship, and when the members of a family stood by one another without needing to know the reason. His mother's memory tore at his heart because she had died loving him, when he was too young and selfish to love her in return, and because somehow, he did not remember how, she had sacrificed herself to a conception of loyalty that was private and unalterable. Such things, he saw, could not happen today. Today there were fear, hatred, and pain, but no dignity of emotion, no deep or complex sorrows. All this he seemed to see in the large eyes of his mother and his sister, looking up at him through the green water, hundreds of fathoms down and still sinking.

Suddenly he was standing on short springy turf, on a summer evening when the slanting rays of the sun gilded the ground. The landscape that he was looking at recurred so often in his dreams that he was never fully certain whether or not he had seen it in the real world. In his waking thoughts he called it the Golden Country. It was an old, rabbit-bitten pasture, with a foot-track wandering across it and a molehill here and there. In the ragged hedge on the opposite side of the field the boughs of the elm trees were swaying very faintly in the breeze, their leaves just stirring in dense masses like women's hair. Somewhere near at hand, though out of sight, there was a clear, slow-moving stream where dace were swimming in the pools under the willow trees.

The girl with dark hair was coming towards them across the field. With what seemed a single movement she tore off her clothes and flung them disdainfully aside. Her body was white and smooth, but it aroused no desire in him, indeed he barely looked at it. What overwhelmed him in that instant was admiration for the gesture with which she had thrown her clothes aside. With its grace and carelessness it seemed to annihilate a whole culture, a whole system of thought, as though Big Brother and the Party and the Thought Police could all be swept into nothingness by a single splendid movement of the arm. That too was a gesture belonging to the ancient time. Winston woke up with the world 'Shakespeare' on his lips.

The telescreen was giving forth an ear-splitting whistle which continued on the same note for thirty seconds. It was nought seven fifteen, getting-up time for office workers. Winston wrenched his body out of bed—naked, for a member of the Outer Party received only 3,000 clothing coupons annually, and a suit of pyjamas was 600—and seized a dingy singlet and a pair of shorts that were lying across a chair. The Physical Jerks would begin in three minutes. The next moment he was doubled up by a violent coughing fit which nearly always attacked him soon after waking up. It emptied his lungs so completely that he could only begin breathing again by lying on his back and taking a series of deep gasps. His veins had swelled with the effort of the cough, and the varicose ulcer had started itching.

'Thirty to forty group!' yapped a piercing female voice. 'Thirty to forty group! Take your places, please. Thirties to forties!'

Winston sprang to attention in front of the telescreen, upon which the image of a youngish woman, scrawny but muscular, dressed in tunic and gym-shoes, had already appeared.

'Arms bending and stretching!' she rapped out. 'Take your time by me. *One*, two, three, four! *One*, two, three, four! Come on, comrades, put a bit of life into it! *One*, two, three, four! *One*, two, three, four! . . .'

The pain of the coughing fit had not quite driven out of Winston's mind the impression made by his dream, and the rhythmic movements of the exercise restored it somewhat. As he mechanically shot his arms back and forth, wearing on his face the look of grim enjoyment which was considered proper during the Physical Jerks, he was struggling to think his way backward into the dim period of his early childhood. It was extraordinarily difficult. Beyond the late 'fifties everying faded. When there were no external records that you could refer to, even the outline of your own life lost its sharpness. You remembered huge events which had quite probably not happened, you remembered the detail of incidents without being able to recapture their atmosphere, and there were long blank periods to which you could assign nothing. Everything had been different then. Even the names of countries, and their shapes on the map, had been different. Airstrip One, for instance, had not been so called in those days: it had been called England or Britain, though London, he felt fairly certain, had always been called London.

Winston could not definitely remember a time when his country had not been at war, but it was evident that there had been a fairly long interval of peace during his childhood, because one of his early memories was of an air raid which appeared to take everyone by surprise. Perhaps it was the time when the atomic bomb had fallen on Colchester. He did not remember the raid itself, but he did remember his father's hand clutching his own as they hurried down, down, down into some place deep in the earth, round and round a spiral staircase which rang under his feet and which finally so wearied his legs that he began whimpering and they had to stop and rest. His mother, in her slow, dreamy way, was following a long way behind them. She was carrying his baby sister—or perhaps it was only a bundle of blankets that she was carrying: he was not certain whether his sister had been born then. Finally they had emerged into a noisy, crowded place which he had realized to be a Tube station.

There were people sitting all over the stone-flagged floor, and other people, packed tightly together, were sitting on metal bunks, one above the other. Winston and his mother and father found themselves a place on the floor, and near them an old man and an old woman were sitting side by side on a bunk.

The old man had on a decent dark suit and a black cloth cap pushed back from very white hair: his face was scarlet and his eyes were blue and full of tears. He reeked of gin. It seemed to breathe out of his skin in place of sweat, and one could have fancied that the tears welling from his eyes were pure gin. But though slightly drunk he was also suffering under some grief that was genuine and unbearable. In his childish way Winston grasped that some terrible thing, something that was beyond forgiveness and could never be remedied, had just happened. It also seemed to him that he knew what it was. Someone whom the old man loved—a little granddaughter, perhaps—had been killed. Every few minutes the old man kept repeating:

'We didn't ought to 'ave trusted 'em. I said so, Ma, didn't I? That's what comes of trusting 'em. I said so all along. We didn't ought to 'ave trusted the buggers.'

But which buggers they didn't ought to have trusted Winston could not now remember.

Since about that time, war had been literally continuous, though strictly speaking it had not always been the same war. For several months during his childhood there had been confused street fighting in London itself, some of which he remembered vividly. But to trace out the history of the whole period, to say who was fighting whom at any given moment, would have been utterly impossible, since no written record, and no spoken word, ever made mention of any other alignment than the existing one. At this moment, for example, in 1984 (if it was 1984), Oceania was at war with Eurasia and in alliance with Eastasia. In no public or private utterance was it ever admitted that the three powers had at any time been grouped along different lines. Actually, as Winston well knew, it was only four years since Oceania had been at war with Eastasia and in alliance with Eurasia. But that was merely a piece of furtive knowledge which he happened to possess because his memory was not satisfactorily under control. Officially the change of partners had never happened. Oceania was at war with Eurasia: therefore Oceania had always been at war with Eurasia. The enemy of the moment always represented absolute evil, and it followed that any past or future agreement with him was impossible.

The frightening thing, he reflected for the ten thousandth time as he forced his shoulders painfully backward (with hands on hips, they were gyrating their bodies from the waist, an exercise that was supposed to be good for the back muscles)—the frightening thing was that it might all be true. If the Party could thrust its hand into the past and say of this or that event, *it never happened*—that, surely, was more terrifying than mere torture and death?

The Party said that Oceania had never been in alliance with Eurasia. He, Winston Smith, knew that Oceania had been in alliance with Eurasia as short a time as four years ago. But where did that knowledge exist? Only in his own consciousness, which in any case must soon be annihilated. And if all others accepted the lie which the Party imposed—if all records told the same tale—then the lie passed into history and became truth. 'Who controls the past,' ran the Party slogan, 'controls the future: who controls the present controls the past.'

And yet the past, though of its nature alterable, never had been altered. Whatever was true now was true from everlasting to everlasting. It was quite simple. All that was needed was an unending series of victories over your own memory. 'Reality control', they called it: in Newspeak, 'doublethink'.

'Stand easy!' barked the instructress, a little more genially.

Winston sank his arms to his sides and slowly refilled his lungs with air. His mind slid away into the labyrinthine world of double-think. To know and not to know, to be conscious of complete truthfulness while telling carefully constructed lies, to hold simultaneously two opinions which cancelled out, knowing them to be contradictory and believing in both of them; to use logic against logic, to repudiate morality while laying claim to it, to believe that democracy was impossible and that the Party was the guardian of democracy; to forget whatever it was necessary to forget, then to draw it back into memory again at the moment when it was needed, and then promptly to forget it again: and above all, to apply the same process to the process itself. That was the ultimate subtlety: consciously to induce unconsciousness, and then, once again, to become unconscious of the act of hypnosis you had just performed. Even to understand the world 'doublethink' involved the use of doublethink.

The instructress had called them to attention again. 'And now let's see which of us can touch our toes!' she said enthusiastically. 'Right over from the hips, please, comrades. *One*-two! *One*-two! . . .'

Winston loathed this exercise, which sent shooting pains all the way from his heels to his buttocks and often ended by bringing on another coughing fit. The half-pleasant quality went out of his meditations. The past, he reflected, had not merely been altered, it had been actually destroyed. For how could you establish even the most obvious fact when there existed no record outside your own memory? He tried to remember in what year he had first heard mention of Big Brother. He thought it must have been at some time in the 'sixties, but it was impossible to be certain. In the Party histories, of course, Big Brother figured as the leader and guardian of the Revolution since its very earliest days. His exploits had been gradually pushed backwards in time until already they extended into the fabulous world of the 'forties and the 'thirties, when the capitalists in their strange cylindrical hats still rode through the streets of London in great gleaming motor-cars or horse carriages with glass sides. There was no knowing how much of this legend was true and how much invented. Winston could not even remember at what date the Party itself had come into existence. He did not believe he had ever heard the word Ingsoc before 1960, but it was possible that in its Oldspeak form—'English Socialism', that is to say—it had been current earlier. Everything melted into mist. Sometimes, indeed, you could put your finger on a definite lie. It was not true, for example, as was claimed in the Party history books, that the Party had invented aeroplanes. He remembered aeroplanes since his earliest childhood. But you could prove nothing. There was never any evidence. Just once in his whole life he had held in his hands unmistakable documentary proof of the falsification of an historical fact And on that occasion—

'Smith!' screamed the shrewish voice from the telescreen. '6079 Smith W.!

Yes, *you*! Bend lower, please! You can do better than that. You're not trying. Lower, please! *That's* better, comrade. Now stand at ease, the whole squad, and watch me.'

A sudden hot sweat had broken out all over Winston's body. His face remained completely inscrutable. Never show dismay! Never show resentment! A single flicker of the eyes could give you away. He stood watching while the instructress raised her arms above her head and–one could not say gracefully, but with remarkable neatness and efficiency–bent over and tucked the first joint of her fingers under her toes.

'*There,* comrades! *That's* how I want to see you doing it. Watch me again. I'm thirty-nine and I've had four children. Now look.' She bent over again. 'You see *my* knees aren't bent. You can all do it if you want to,' she added as she straightened herself up. 'Anyone under forty-five is perfectly capable of touching his toes. We don't all have the privilege of fighting in the front line, but at least we can all keep fit. Remember our boys on the Malabar front! And the sailors in the Floating Fortresses! Just think what *they* have to put up with. Now try again. That's better, comrade, that's *much* better,' she added encouragingly as Winston, with a violent lunge, succeeded in touching his toes with knees unbent, for the first time in several years.

# 4

With the deep, unconscious sigh which not even the nearness of the telescreen could prevent him from uttering when his day's work started, Winston pulled the speakwrite towards him, blew the dust from its mouthpiece, and put on his spectacles. Then he unrolled and clipped together four small cylinders of paper which had already flopped out of the pneumatic tube on the right-hand side of his desk.

In the walls of the cubicle there were three orifices. To the right of the speakwrite, a small pneumatic tube for written messages; to the left, a larger one of newspapers; and in the side wall, within easy reach of Winston's arm, a large oblong slit protected by a wire grating. This last was for the disposal of waste paper. Similar slits existed in thousands or tens of thousands throughout the building, not only in every room but at short intervals in every corridor. For some reason they were nicknamed memory holes. When one knew that any document was due for destruction, or even when one saw a scrap of waste paper lying about, it was an automatic action to lift the flap of the nearest memory hole and drop it in, whereupon it would be whirled away on a current of warm air to the enormous furnaces which were hidden somewhere in the recesses of the building.

Winston examined the four slips of paper which he had unrolled. Each contained a message of only one or two lines, in the abbreviated jargon–not actually Newspeak, but consisting largely of Newspeak words–which was used in the Ministry for internal purposes. They ran:

times 17.3.84 bb speech malreported africa rectify

times 19.12.83 forecasts 3 yp 4th quarter 83 misprints verify current issue

times 14.2.84 miniplenty malquoted chocolate rectify

times 3.12.83 reporting bb dayorder doubleplusungood refs unpersons rewrite fullwise upsub antefiling

With a faint feeling of satisfaction Winston laid the fourth message aside. It was an intricate and responsible job and had better be dealt with last. The other three were routine matters, though the second one one would probably mean some tedious wading through lists of figures.

Winston dialled 'back numbers' on the telescreen and called for the appropriate issues of *The Times*, which slid out of the pneumatic tube after only a few minutes' delay. The message he had received referred to articles or news-items which for one reason or another it was thought necessary to alter, or, as the official phrase had it, to rectify. For example, it appeared from *The Times* of the seventeenth of March that Big Brother, in his speech of the previous day, had predicted that the South Indian front would remain quiet but that a Eurasian offensive would shortly be launched in North Africa. As it happened, the Eurasian Higher Command had launched its offensive in South India and left North Africa alone. It was therefore necessary to rewrite a paragraph of Big Brother's speech, in such a way as to make him predict the thing that had actually happened. Or again, *The Times* of the nineteenth of December had published the official forecasts of the output of various classes of consumption goods in the fourth quarter of 1983, which was also the sixth quarter of the Ninth Three-Year Plan. Today's issue contained a statement of the actual output, from which it appeared that the forecasts were in every instance grossly wrong. Winston's job was to rectify the original figures by making them agree with the later ones. As for the third message, it referred to a very simple error which could be set right in a couple of minutes. As short a time ago as February, the Ministry of Plenty had issued a promise (a 'categorical pledge' were the official words) that there would be no reduction of the chocolate ration during 1984. Actually, as Winston was aware, the chocolate ration was to be reduced from thirty grammes to twenty at the end of the present week. All that was needed was to substitute for the original promise a warning that it would probably be necessary to reduce the ration at some time in April.

As soon as Winston had dealt with each of the messages, he clipped his speakwritten corrections to the appropriate copy of *The Times* and pushed them into the pneumatic tube. Then, with a movement which was as nearly as possible unconscious, he crumpled up the original message and any notes that he himself had made, and dropped them into the memory hole to be devoured by the flames.

What happened in the unseen labyrinth to which the pneumatic tubes led, he did not know in detail, but he did know in general terms. As soon as all the corrections which happened to be necessary in any particular number of *The Times* had been assembled and collated, that number would be reprinted, the original copy destroyed, and the corrected copy placed on the files in its stead. This process of continuous alteration was applied not only to newspapers, but to books, periodicals, pamphlets, posters, leaflets, films, sound-tracks, cartoons, photographs—to every kind of literature or documentation which might conceivably hold any political or ideological significance. Day by day and almost minute by minute the past was brought up to date. In this way every prediction made by the Party could be shown by documentary evidence to have been correct; nor was any item of news, or any expression of opinion, which conflicted with the needs of the moment, ever allowed to remain on record. All history was a palimpsest, scraped clean and reinscribed exactly as often as was necessary. In no case would it have been possible, once the deed was done, to prove that any falsification had taken place. The largest section of the Records Department, far larger than the one on which Winston worked, consisted simply of persons whose duty it was to track down and collect all copies of books, newspapers, and other documents which had been superseded and were due for destruction. A number of *The Times* which might, because of changes in political alignment, or mistaken prophecies uttered by Big Brother, have been rewritten a dozen times still stood on the files bearing its original date, and no other copy existed to contradict it. Books, also, were recalled and rewitten again and again, and were invariably reissued without any admission that any alteration had been made. Even the written instructions which Winston received, and which he invariably got rid of as soon as he had dealt with them, never stated or implied that an act of forgery was to be committed: always the reference was to slips, errors, misprints, or misquotations which it was necessary to put right in the interests of accuracy.

But actually, he thought as he readjusted the Ministry of Plenty's figures, it was not even forgery. It was merely the substitution of one piece of nonsense for another. Most of the material that you were dealing with had no connexion with anything in the real world, not even the kind of connexion that is contained in a direct lie. Statistics were just as much a fantasy in their original version as in their rectified version. A great deal of the time you were expected to make them up out of your head. For example, the Ministry of Plenty's forecast had estimated the output of boots for the quarter at 145 million pairs. The actual output was given as sixty-two millions. Winston, however, in rewriting the forecast, marked the figure down to fifty-seven millions, so as to allow for the usual claim that the quota had been overfulfilled. In any case, sixty-two millions was no nearer the truth than fifty-seven millions, or than 145 millions. Very likely no boots had been produced at all. Likelier still, nobody knew how many had been produced, much less cared. All one knew was that every quarter astronomical numbers of boots were produced on paper, while perhaps half the population of Oceania went barefoot. And so it was with every class of recorded fact, great or small. Everything faded away into a shadow-world in which, finally, even the date of the year had become uncertain.

Winston glanced across the hall. In the corresponding cubicle on the other side a small, precise-looking, dark-chinned man named Tillotson was working steadily away, with a folded newspaper on his knee and his mouth very close to the mouthpiece of the speakwrite. He had the air of trying to keep what he was saying a secret between himself and the telescreen. He looked up, and his spectacles darted a hostile flash in Winston's direction.

Winston hardly knew Tillotson, and had no idea what work he was employed on. People in the Records Department did not readily talk about their jobs. In the long, windowless hall, with its double row of cubicles and its endless rustle of papers and hum of voices murmuring into speakwrites, there were quite a dozen people whom Winston did not even know by name, though he daily saw them hurrying to and fro in the corridors or gesticulating in the Two Minutes Hate. He knew that in the cubicle next to him the little woman with sandy hair toiled day in day out, simply at tracking down and deleting from the Press the names of people who had been vaporized and were therefore considered never to have existed. There was a certain fitness in this, since her own husband had been vaporized a couple of years earlier. And a few cubicles away a mild, ineffectual, dreamy creature named Ampleforth, with very hairy ears and a surprising talent for juggling with rhymes and metres, was engaged in producing garbled versions—definitive texts, they were called—of poems which had become ideologically offensive, but which for one reason or another were to be retained in the anthologies. And this hall, with its fifty workers or thereabouts, was only one sub-section, a single cell, as it were, in the huge complexity of the Records Department. Beyond, above, below, were other swarms of workers engaged in an unimaginable multitude of jobs. There were the huge printing-shops with their sub-editors, their typography experts, and their elaborately equipped studios for the faking of photographs. There was the tele-programmes section with its engineers, its producers, and its teams of actors specially chosen for their skill in imitating voices. There were the armies of reference clerks whose job was simply to draw up lists of books and periodicals which were due for recall. There were the vast repositories where the corrected documents were stored, and the hidden furnaces where the original copies were destroyed. And somewhere or other, quite anonymous, there were the directing brains who co-ordinated the whole effort and laid down the lines of policy which made it necessary that this fragment of the past should be preserved, that one falsified, and the other rubbed out of existence.

And the Records Department, after all, was itself only a single branch of the Ministry of Truth, whose primary job was not to reconstruct the past but to supply the citizens of Oceania with newspapers, films, textbooks, telescreen programmes, plays, novels—with every conceivable kind of information, instruction, or entertainment, from a statue to a slogan, from a lyric poem to a biological treatise, and from a child's spelling-book to a Newspeak dictionary. And the Ministry had not only to supply the multifarious needs of the Party, but also to repeat the whole operation at a lower level for the benefit of the proletariat. There was a whole chain of separate departments dealing with proletarian literature, music, drama, and entertainment generally. Here were produced rubbishy newspapers containing almost nothing except sport, crime, and astrology, sensational five-cent novelettes, films oozing with sex, and sentimental songs which were composed entirely by mechanical means on a special kind of kaleidoscope known as a versificator. There was even a whole sub-section—*Pornosec,* it was called in Newspeak—engaged in producing the lowest kind of pornography, which was sent out in sealed packets and which no Party member, other than those who worked on it, was permitted to look at.

Three messages had slid out of the pneumatic tube while Winston was working; but they were simple matters, and he had disposed of them before the Two Minutes Hate interrupted him. When the Hate was over he returned to his cubicle, took the Newspeak dictionary from the shelf, pushed the speakwrite to one side, cleaned his spectacles, and settled down to his main job of the morning.

Winston's greatest pleasure in life was in his work. Most of it was a tedious routine, but included in it there were also jobs so difficult and intricate that you could lose yourself in them as in the depths of a mathematical problem—delicate pieces of forgery in which you had nothing to guide you except your knowledge of the principles of Ingsoc and your estimate of what the Party wanted you to say. Winston was good at this kind of thing. On occasion he had even been entrusted with the rectification of *The Times* leading articles, which were written entirely in Newspeak. He unrolled the message that he had set aside earlier. It ran:

times 3.12.83 reporting bb dayorder doubleplusungood refs unpersons rewrite fullwise upsub antefiling

In Oldspeak (or standard English) this might be rendered:

The reporting of Big Brother's Order for the Day in *The Times* of December 3rd 1983 is extremely unsatisfactory and makes references to non-existent persons. Rewrite it in full and submit your draft to higher authority before filing.

Winston read through the offending article. Big Brother's Order for the Day, it seemed, had been chiefly devoted to praising the work of an organization known as FFCC, which supplied cigarettes and other comforts to the sailors in the Floating Fortresses. A certain Comrade Withers, a prominent member of the Inner Party, had been singled out for special mention and awarded a decoration, the Order of Conspicuous Merit, Second Class.

Three months later FFCC had suddenly been dissolved with no reasons given. One could assume that Withers and his associates were now in disgrace, but there had been no report of the matter in the Press or on the telescreen. That was to be expected, since it was unusual for political offenders to be put on trial or even publicly denounced. The great purges involving thousands of people, with public trials of traitors and thought-criminals who made abject confession of their crimes and were afterwards executed, were special showpieces not occurring oftener than once in a couple of years. More commonly, people who had incurred the displeasure of the Party simply disappeared and were never heard of again. One never had the smallest clue as to what had happened to them. In some cases they might not even be dead. Perhaps thirty people personally known to Winston, not counting his parents, had disappeared at one time or another.

Winston stroked his nose gently with a paper-clip. In the cubicle across the way Comrade Tillotson was still crouching secretively over his speakwrite. He raised his head for a moment: again the hostile spectacle-flash. Winston wondered whether Comrade Tillotson was engaged on the same job as himself. It was perfectly possible. So tricky a piece of work would never be entrusted to a single person: on the other hand, to turn it over to a committee would be to admit openly that an act of fabrication was taking place. Very likely as many as a dozen people were now working away on rival versions of what Big Brother had actually said. And presently some master brain in the Inner Party would select this version or that, would re-edit it and set in motion the complex processes of cross-referencing that would be required, and then the chosen lie would pass into the permanent records and become truth.

Winston did not know why Withers had been disgraced. Perhaps it was for corruption or incompetence. Perhaps Big Brother was merely getting rid of a too-popular subordinate. Perhaps Withers or someone close to him had been suspected of heretical tendencies. Or perhaps—what was likeliest of all—the thing had simply happened because purges and vaporizations were a necessary part of the mechanics of government. The only real clue lay in the words 'refs unpersons', which indicated that Withers was already dead. You could not invariably assume this to be the case when people were arrested. Sometimes they were released and allowed to remain at liberty for as much as a year or two years before being executed. Very occasionally some person whom you had believed dead long since would make a ghostly reappearance at some public trial where he would implicate hundreds of others by his testimony before vanishing, this time for ever. Withers, however, was already an *unperson*. He did not exist: he had never existed. Winston decided that it would not be enough simply to reverse the tendency of Big Brother's speech. It was better to make it deal with something totally unconnected with its original subject.

He might turn the speech into the usual denunciation of traitors and thought-criminals, but that was a little too obvious; while to invent a victory at the front, or some triumph of over-production in the Ninth Three-Year Plan, might complicate the records too much. What was needed was a piece of pure fantasy. Suddenly there sprang into his mind, ready made as it were, the image of a certain Comrade Ogilvy, who had recently died in battle, in heroic circumstances. There were occasions when Big Brother devoted his Order for the Day to commemorating some humble, rank-and-file Party member whose life and death he held up as an example worthy to be followed. Today he should commemorate Comrade Ogilvy. It was true that there was no such person as Comrade Ogilvy, but a few lines of print and a couple of faked photographs would soon bring him into existence.

Winston thought for a moment, then pulled the speakwrite towards him and began dictating in Big Brother's familiar style: a style at once military and pedantic, and, because of a trick of asking questions and then promptly answering them ('What lessons do we learn from this fact, comrades? The lesson—which is also one of the fundamental principles of Ingsoc—that,' etc., etc.), easy to imitate.

At the age of three Comrade Ogilvy had refused all toys except a drum, a sub-machine gun, and a model helicopter. At six—a year early, by a special relaxation of the rules—he had joined the Spies; at nine he had been a troop leader. At eleven he had denounced his uncle to the Thought Police after overhearing a conversation which appeared to him to have criminal tendencies. At seventeen he had been a district organizer of the Junior Anti-Sex League. At nineteen he had designed a hand-grenade which had been adopted by the Ministry of Peace and which, at its first trial, had killed thirty-one Eurasian prisoners in one burst. At twenty-three he had perished in action. Pursued by enemy jet planes while flying over the Indian Ocean with important despatches, he had weighted his body with his machine-gun and leapt out of the helicopter into deep water, despatches and all—an end, said Big Brother, which it was impossible to contemplate without feelings of envy. Big Brother added a few remarks on the purity and singlemindedness of Comrade Ogilvy's life. He was a total abstainer and a non-smoker, had no recreations except a daily hour in the gymnasium, and had taken a vow of celibacy, believing marriage and the care of a family to be incompatible with a twenty-four-hour-a-day devotion to duty. He had no subjects of conversation except the principles of Ingsoc, and no aim in life except the defeat of the Eurasian enemy and the hunting-down of spies, saboteurs, thought-criminals, and traitors generally.

Winston debated with himself whether to award Comrade Ogilvy the Order of Conspicuous Merit: in the end he decided against it because of the unnecessary cross-referencing that it would entail.

Once again he glanced at his rival in the opposite cubicle. Something seemed to tell him with certainty that Tillotson was busy on the same job as himself. There was no way of knowing whose job would finally be adopted, but he felt a profound conviction that it would be his own. Comrade Ogilvy, unimagined an hour ago, was now a fact. It struck him as curious that you could create dead men but not living ones. Comrade Ogilvy, who had never existed in the present, now existed in the past, and when once the act of forgery was forgotten, he would exist just as authentically, and upon the same evidence, as Charlemagne or Julius Caesar.

# 5

In the low-ceilinged canteen, deep underground, the lunch queue jerked slowly forward. The room was already very full and deafeningly noisy. From the grille at the counter the steam of stew came pouring forth, with a sour metallic smell which did not quite overcome the fumes of Victory Gin. On the far side of the room there was a small bar, a mere hole in the wall, where gin could be bought at ten cents the large nip.

'Just the man I was looking for,' said a voice at Winston's back.

He turned round. It was his friend Syme, who worked in the Research Department. Perhaps 'friend' was not exactly the right word. You did not have friends nowadays, you had comrades: but there were some comrades whose society was pleasanter than that of others. Syme was a philologist, a specialist in Newspeak. Indeed, he was one of the enormous team of experts now engaged in compiling the Eleventh Edition of the Newspeak Dictionary. He was a tiny creature, smaller than Winston, with dark hair and large, protuberant eyes, at once mournful and derisive, which seemed to search your face closely while he was speaking to you.

'I wanted to ask you whether you'd got any razor blades,' he said.

'Not one!' said Winston with a sort of guilty haste. 'I've tried all over the place. They don't exist any longer.'

Everyone kept asking you for razor blades. Actually he had two unused ones which he was hoarding up. There had been a famine of them for months past. At any given moment there was some necessary article which the Party shops were unable to supply. Sometimes it was buttons, sometimes it was darning wool, sometimes it was shoelaces; at present it was razor blades. You could only get hold of them, if at all, by scrounging more or less furtively on the 'free' market.

'I've been using the same blade for six weeks,' he added untruthfully.

The queue gave another jerk forward. As they halted he turned and faced Syme again. Each of them took a greasy metal tray from a pile at the edge of the counter.

'Did you go and see the prisoners hanged yesterday?' said Syme.

'I was working,' said Winston indifferently. 'I shall see it on the flicks, I suppose.'

'A very inadequate substitute,' said Syme.

His mocking eyes roved over Winston's face. 'I know you,' the eyes seemed to say, 'I see through you. I know very well why you didn't go to see those prisoners hanged.' In an intellectual way, Syme was venomously orthodox. He would talk with a disagreeable gloating satisfaction of helicopter raids on enemy villages, the trials and confessions of thought-criminals, the executions in the cellars of the Ministry of Love. Talking to him was largely a matter of getting him away from such subjects and entangling him, if possible, in the technicalities of Newspeak, on which he was authoritative and interesting. Winston turned his head a little aside to avoid the scrutiny of the large dark eyes.

'It was a good hanging,' said Syme reminiscently. 'I think it spoils it when they tie their feet together. I like to see them kicking. And above all, at the end, the tongue sticking right out, and blue—a quite bright blue. That's the detail that appeals to me.'

'Nex', please!' yelled the white-aproned prole with the ladle.

Winston and Syme pushed their trays beneath the grille. On to each was dumped swiftly the regulation lunch—a metal pannikin of pinkish-grey stew, a hunk of bread, a cube of cheese, a mug of milkless Victory Coffee, and one saccharine tablet.

'There's a table over there, under that telescreen,' said Syme. 'Let's pick up a gin on the way.'

The gin was served out to them in handleless china mugs. They threaded their way across the crowded room and unpacked their trays on to the metal-topped table, on one corner of which someone had left a pool of stew, a filthy liquid mess that had the appearance of vomit. Winston took up his mug of gin, paused for an instant to collect his nerve, and gulped the oily-tasting stuff down. When he had winked the tears out of his eyes he suddenly discovered that he was hungry. He began swallowing spoonfuls of the stew, which, in among its general sloppiness, had cubes of spongy pinkish stuff which was probably a preparation of meat. Neither of them spoke again till they had emptied their pannikins. From the table at Winston's left, a little behind his back, someone was talking rapidly and continuously, a harsh gabble almost like the quacking of a duck, which pierced the general uproar of the room.

'How is the Dictionary getting on?' said Winston, raising his voice to overcome the noise.

'Slowly,' said Syme. 'I'm on the adjectives. It's fascinating.'

He had brightened up immediately at the mention of Newspeak. He pushed his pannikin aside, took up his hunk of bread in one delicate hand and his cheese in the other, and leaned across the table so as to be able to speak without shouting.

'The Eleventh Edition is the definitive edition,' he said. 'We're getting the language into its final shape—the shape it's going to have when nobody speaks anything else. When we've finished with it, people like you will have to learn it all over again. You think, I dare say, that our chief job is inventing new words. But not a bit of it! We're destroying words—scores of them, hundreds of them, every day. We're cutting the language down to the bone. The Eleventh Edition won't contain a single word that will become obsolete before the year 2050.'

He bit hungrily into his bread and swallowed a couple of mouthfuls, then continued speaking, with a sort of pedant's passion. His thin dark face had become animated, his eyes had lost their mocking expression and grown almost dreamy.

'It's a beautiful thing, the destruction of words. Of course the great wastage is in the verbs and adjectives, but there are hundreds of nouns that can be got rid of as well. It isn't only the synonyms; there are also the antonyms. After all, what justification is there for a word which is simply the opposite of some other word? A word contains its opposite in itself. Take "good", for instance. If you have a word like "good", what need is there for a word like "bad"? "Ungood" will do just as well—better, because it's an exact opposite, which the other is not. Or again, if you want a stronger version of "good", what sense is there in having a whole string of vague useless words like "excellent" and "splendid" and all the rest of them? "Plusgood" covers the meaning; or "doubleplus-good" if you want something stronger still. Of course we use those forms already, but in the final version of Newspeak there'll be nothing else. In the end the whole notion of goodness and badness will be covered by only six words—in reality, only one word. Don't you see the beauty of that, Winston? It was B.B.'s idea originally, of course,' he added as an afterthought.

A sort of vapid eagerness flitted across Winston's face at the mention of Big Brother. Nevertheless Syme immediately detected a certain lack of enthusiasm.

'You haven't a real appreciation of Newspeak, Winston,' he said almost sadly. 'Even when you write it you're still thinking in Oldspeak. I've read some of those pieces that you write in *The Times* occasionally. They're good enough, but they're translations. In your heart you'd prefer to stick to Oldspeak, with all its vagueness and its useless shades of meaning. You don't grasp the beauty of the destruction of words. Do you know that Newspeak is the only language in the world whose vocabulary gets smaller every year?'

Winston did know that, of course. He smiled, sympathetically he hoped, not trusting himself to speak. Syme bit off another fragment of the dark-coloured bread, chewed it briefly, and went on:

'Don't you see that the whole aim of Newspeak is to narrow the range of thought? In the end we shall make thoughtcrime literally impossible, because there will be no words in which to express it. Every concept that can ever be needed, will be expressed by exactly *one* word, with its meaning rigidly defined and all its subsidiary meanings rubbed out and forgotten. Already, in the Eleventh Edition, we're not far from that point. But the process will still be continuing long after you and I are dead. Every year fewer and fewer words, and the range of consciousness always a little smaller. Even now, of course, there's no reason or excuse for committing thoughtcrime. It's merely a question of self-discipline, reality-control. But in the end there won't be any need even for that. The Revolution will be complete when the language is perfect. Newspeak is Ingsoc and Ingsoc is Newspeak,' he added with a sort of mystical satisfaction. 'Has it ever occurred to you, Winston, that by the year 2050, at the very latest, not a single human being will be alive who could understand such a conversation as we are having now?'

'Except–' began Winston doubtfully, and then stopped.

It had been on the tip of his tongue to say 'Except the proles', but he checked himself, not feeling fully certain that this remark was not in some way unorthodox. Syme, however, had divined what he was about to say.

'The proles are not human beings,' he said carelessly. 'By 2050–earlier, probably–all real knowledge of Oldspeak will have disappeared. The whole literature of the past will have been destroyed. Chaucer, Shakespeare, Milton, Byron–they'll exist only in Newspeak versions, not merely changed into something different, but actually changed into something contradictory of what they used to be. Even the literature of the Party will change. Even the slogans will change. How could you have a slogan like "freedom is slavery" when the concept of freedom has been abolished? The whole climate of thought will be different. In fact there will *be* no thought, as we understand it now. Orthodoxy means not thinking–not needing to think. Orthodoxy is unconsciousness.'

One of these days, thought Winston with sudden deep conviction, Syme will be vaporized. He is too intelligent. He sees too clearly and speaks too plainly. The Party does not like such people. One day he will disappear. It is written in his face.

Winston had finished his bread and cheese. He turned a little sideways in his chair to drink his mug of coffee. At the table on his left the man with the strident voice was still talking remorselessly away. A young woman who was perhaps his secretary, and who was sitting with her back to Winston, was listening to him and seemed to be eagerly agreeing with everything that he said. From time to time Winston caught some such remarks as 'I think you're *so* right, I do *so* agree with you', uttered in a youthful and rather silly feminine voice. But the other voice never stopped for an instant, even when the girl was speaking. Winston knew the man by sight, though he knew no more about him than that he held some important post in the Fiction Department. He was a man of about thirty, with a muscular throat and a large, mobile mouth. His head was thrown back a little, and because of the angle at which he was sitting, his spectacles caught the light and presented to Winston two blank discs instead of eyes. What was slightly horrible, was that from the stream of sound that poured out of his mouth it was almost impossible to distinguish a single word. Just once Winston caught a phrase–'complete and final elimination of Goldsteinism'–jerked out very rapidly and, as it seemed, all in one piece, like a line of type cast solid. For the rest it was just a noise, a quack-quack-quacking. And yet, though you could not actually hear what the man was saying, you could not be in any doubt about its general nature. He might be denouncing Goldstein and demanding sterner measures against thought-criminals and saboteurs, he might be fulminating against the atrocities of the Eurasian army, he might be praising Big Brother or the heroes on the Malabar front–it made no difference. Whatever it was, you could be certain that every word of it was pure orthodoxy, pure Ingsoc. As he watched the eyeless face with the jaw moving rapidly up and down, Winston had a curious feeling that this was not a real human being but some kind of dummy. It was not the man's brain that was speaking, it was his larynx. The stuff that was coming out of him consisted of words, but it was not speech in the true sense: it was a noise uttered in unconsciousness, like the quacking of a duck.

Syme had fallen silent for a moment, and with the handle of his spoon was tracing patterns in the puddle of stew. The voice from the other table quacked rapidly on, easily audible in spite of the surrounding din.

'There is a word in Newspeak,' said Syme, 'I don't know whether you know it: *duckspeak*, to quack like a duck. It is one of those interesting words that have two contradictory meanings. Applied to an opponent, it is abuse; applied to someone you agree with, it is praise.'

Unquestionably Syme will be vaporized, Winston thought again. He thought it with a kind of sadness, although well knowing that Syme despised him and slightly disliked him, and was fully capable of denouncing him as a thought-criminal if he saw any reason for doing so. There was something subtly wrong with Syme. There was something that he lacked: discretion, aloofness, a sort of saving stupidity. You could not say that he was unorthodox. He believed in the principles of Ingsoc, he venerated Big Brother, he rejoiced over victories, he hated heretics, not merely with sincerity but with a sort of restless zeal, an up-to-dateness of information, which the ordinary Party member did not approach. Yet a faint air of disreputability always clung to him. He said things that would have been better unsaid, he had read too many books, he frequented the Chestnut Tree Café, haunt of painters and musicians. There was no law, not even an unwritten law, against frequenting the Chestnut Tree Café, yet the place was somehow ill-omened. The old, discredited leaders of the Party had been used to gather there before they were finally purged. Goldstein himself, it was said, had sometimes been seen there, years and decades ago. Syme's fate was not difficult to foresee. And yet it was a fact that if Syme grasped, even for three seconds, the nature of his, Winston's, secret opinions, he would betray him instantly to the Thought Police. So would anybody else, for that matter: but Syme more than most. Zeal was not enough. Orthodoxy was unconsciousness.

Syme looked up. 'Here comes Parsons,' he said.

Something in the tone of his voice seemed to add, 'that bloody fool'. Parsons, Winston's fellow tenant at Victory Mansions, was in fact threading his way across the room—a tubby, middle-sized man with fair hair and a froglike face. At thirty-five he was already putting on rolls of fat at neck and waistline, but his movements were brisk and boyish. His whole appearance was that of a little boy grown large, so much so that although he was wearing the regulation overalls, it was almost impossible not to think of him as being dressed in the blue shorts, grey shirt, and red neckerchief of the Spies. In visualizing him one saw always a picture of dimpled knees and sleeves rolled back from pudgy forearms. Parsons did, indeed, invariably revert to shorts when a community hike or any other physical activity gave him an excuse for doing so. He greeted them both with a cheery 'Hullo, hullo!' and sat down at the table, giving off an intense smell of sweat. Beads of moisture stood out all over his pink face. His powers of sweating were extraordinary. At the

Community Centre you could always tell when he had been playing table-tennis by the dampness of the bat handle. Syme had produced a strip of paper on which there was a long column of words, and was studying it with an ink-pencil between his fingers.

'Look at him working away in the lunch hour,' said Parsons, nudging Winston. 'Keenness, eh? What's that you've got there, old boy? Something a bit too brainy for me, I expect. Smith, old boy, I'll tell you why I'm chasing you. It's that sub you forgot to give me.'

'Which sub is that?' said Winston, automatically feeling for money. About a quarter of one's salary had to be earmarked for voluntary subscriptions, which were so numerous that it was difficult to keep track of them.

'For Hate Week. You know—the house-by-house fund. I'm treasurer for our block. We're making an all-out effort—going to put on a tremendous show. I tell you, it won't be my fault if old Victory Mansions doesn't have the biggest outfit of flags in the whole street. Two dollars you promised me.'

Winston found and handed over two creased and filthy notes, which Parsons entered in a small notebook, in the neat handwriting of the illiterate.

'By the way, old boy,' he said. 'I hear that little beggar of mine let fly at you with his catapult yesterday. I gave him a good dressing-down for it. In fact I told him I'd take the catapult away if he does it again.'

'I think he was a little upset at not going to the execution,' said Winston.

'Ah, well—what I mean to say, shows the right spirit, doesn't it? Mischievous little beggars they are, both of them, but talk about keenness! All they think about is the Spies, and the war, of course. D'you know what that little girl of mine did last Saturday, when her troop was on a hike out Berkhamsted way? She got two other girls to go with her, slipped off from the hike, and spent the whole afternoon following a strange man. They kept on his tail for two hours, right through the woods, and then, when they got into Amersham, handed him over to the patrols.'

'What did they do that for?' said Winston, somewhat taken aback. Parson went on triumphantly:

'My kid made sure he was some kind of enemy agent—might have been dropped by parachute, for instance. But here's the point, old boy. What do you think put her on to him in the first place? She spotted he was wearing a funny kind of shoes—said she'd never seen anyone wearing shoes like that before. So the chances were he was a foreigner. Pretty smart for a nipper of seven, eh?'

'What happened to the man?' said Winston.

'Ah, that I couldn't say, of course. But I wouldn't be altogether surprised if—' Parsons made the motion of aiming a rifle, and clicked his tongue for the explosion.

'Good,' said Syme abstractedly, without looking up from his strip of paper.

'Of course we can't afford to take chances,' agreed Winston dutifully.

'What I mean to say, there is a war on,' said Parsons.

As though in confirmation of this, a trumpet call floated from the telescreen just above their heads. However, it was not the proclamation of a military victory this time, but merely an announcement from the Ministry of Plenty.

'Comrades!' cried an eager youthful voice. 'Attention, comrades! We have glorious news for you. We have won the battle for production! Returns now completed of the output of all classes of consumption goods show that the standard of living has risen by no less than 20 per cent over the past year. All over Oceania this morning there were irrepressible spontaneous de-monstrations when workers marched out of factories and offices and paraded through the streets with banners voicing their gratitude to Big Brother for the new, happy life which his wise leadership has bestowed upon us. Here are some of the completed figures. Foodstuffs–'

The phrase 'our new, happy life' recurred several times. It had been a favourite of late with the Ministry of Plenty. Parsons, his attention caught by the trumpet call, sat listening with a sort of gaping solemnity, a sort of edified boredom. He could not follow the figures, but he was aware that they were in some way a cause for satisfaction. He had lugged out a huge and filthy pipe which was already half full of charred tobacco. With the tobacco ration at 100 grammes a week it was seldom possible to fill a pipe up to the top. Winston was smoking a Victory Cigarette which he held carefully horizontal. The new ration did not start till tomorrow and he had only four cigarettes left. For the moment he had shut his ears to the remoter noises and was listening to the stuff that streamed out of the telescreen. It appeared that there had even been demonstrations to thank Big Brother for raising the chocolate ration to twenty grammes a week. And only yesterday, he reflected, it had been announced that the ration was to be *reduced* to twenty grammes a week. Was it possible that they could swallow that, after only twenty-four hours? Yes, they swallowed it. Parsons swallowed it easily, with the stupidity of an animal. The eyeless creature at the other table swallowed it fanatically, passionately, with a furious desire to track down, denounce, and vaporize anyone who should suggest that last week the ration had been thirty grammes. Syme, too–in some more complex way, involving doublethink, Syme swallowed it. Was he, then, *alone* in the possession of a memory?

The fabulous statistics continued to pour out of the telescreen. As compared with last year there was more food, more clothes, more houses, more furniture, more cooking-pots, more fuel, more ships, more helicopters, more books, more babies–more of everything except disease, crime, and insanity. Year by year and minute by minute, everybody and everything was whizzing rapidly upwards. As Syme had done earlier Winston had taken up his spoon and was dabbling in the pale-coloured gravy that dribbled across the table, drawing a long streak of it out into a pattern. He meditated resentfully on the physical texture of life. Had it always been like this? Had food always tasted like this? He looked round the canteen. A low-ceilinged, crowded room, its walls grimy from the contact of innumerable bodies; battered metal tables and chairs, placed so close together that you sat with elbows touching; bent spoons, dented trays, coarse white mugs; all surfaces greasy, grime in every crack; and a sourish, composite smell of bad gin and bad coffee and metallic stew and dirty clothes. Always in your stomach and in your skin there was a sort of protest, a feeling that you had been cheated of something that you had a right to. It was true that he had no memories of anything greatly different. In any time that he could accurately remember, there had never been quite enough to eat, one had never had socks or underclothes that were not full of holes, furniture had always been battered and rickety, rooms underheated, tube trains crowded, houses falling to pieces, bread dark-coloured, tea a rarity, coffee filthy-tasting, cigarettes insufficient—nothing cheap and plentiful except synthetic gin. And though, of course, it grew worse as one's body aged, was it not a sign that this was *not* the natural order of things, if one's heart sickened at the discomfort and dirt and scarcity, the interminable winters, the stickiness of one's socks, the lifts that never worked, the cold water, the gritty soap, the cigarettes that came to pieces, the food with its strange evil taste? Why should one feel it to be intolerable unless one had some kind of ancestral memory that things had once been different?

He looked round the canteen again. Nearly everyone was ugly, and would still have been ugly even if dressed otherwise than in the uniform blue overalls. On the far side of the room, sitting at a table alone, a small, curiously beetle-like man was drinking a cup of coffee, his little eyes darting suspicious glances from side to side. How easy it was, thought Winston, if you did not look about you, to believe that the physical type set up by the Party as an ideal—tall muscular youths and deep-bosomed maidens, blond-haired, vital, sunburnt, carefree—existed and even predominated. Actually, so far as he could judge, the majority of people in Airstrip One were small, dark, and ill-favoured. It was curious how that beetle-like type proliferated in the Ministries: little dumpy men, growing stout very early in life, with short legs, swift scuttling movements, and fat inscrutable faces with very small eyes. It was the type that seemed to flourish best under the dominion of the Party.

The announcement from the Ministry of Plenty ended on another trumpet call and gave way to tinny music. Parsons, stirred to vague enthusiasm by the bombardment of figures, took his pipe out of his mouth.

'The Ministry of Plenty's certainly done a good job this year,' he said with a knowing shake of his head. 'By the way, Smith old boy, I suppose you haven't got any razor blades you can let me have?'

'Not one,' said Winston. 'I've been using the same blade for six weeks myself.'

'Ah, well—just thought I'd ask you, old boy.'

'Sorry,' said Winston.

The quacking voice from the next table, temporarily silenced during the Ministry's announcement, had started up again, as loud as ever. For some reason Winston suddenly found himself thinking of Mrs Parsons, with her wispy hair and the dust in the creases of her face. Within two years those children would be denouncing her to the Thought Police. Mrs Parsons would be vaporized. Syme would be vaporized. Winston would be vaporized. O'Brien would be vaporized. Parsons, on the other hand, would never be vaporized. The eyeless creature with the quacking voice would never be vaporized. The little beetle-like men who scuttled so nimbly through the labyrinthine corridors of Ministries—they, too, would never be vaporized. And the girl with dark hair, the girl from the Fiction Department—she would never be vaporized either. It seemed to him that he knew instinctively who would survive and who would perish: though just what it was that made for survival, it was not easy to say.

At this moment he was dragged out of his reverie with a violent jerk. The girl at the next table had turned partly round and was looking at him. It was the girl with dark hair. She was looking at him in a sidelong way, but with curious intensity. The instant that she caught his eye she looked away again.

The sweat started out on Winston's backbone. A horrible pang of terror went through him. It was gone almost at once, but it left a sort of nagging uneasiness behind. Why was she watching him? Why did she keep following him about? Unfortunately he could not remember whether she had already been at that table when he arrived, or had come there afterwards. But yesterday, at any rate, during the Two Minutes Hate, she had sat immediately behind him when there was no apparent need to do so. Quite likely her real object had been to listen to him and make sure whether he was shouting loudly enough.

His earlier thought returned to him: probably she was not actually a member of the Thought Police, but then it was precisely the amateur spy who was the greatest danger of all. He did not know how long she had been looking at him, but perhaps for as much as five minutes, and it was possible that his features had not been perfectly under control. It was terribly dangerous to let your thoughts wander when you were in any public place or within range of a telescreen. The smallest thing could give you away. A nervous tic, an unconscious look of anxiety, a habit of muttering to yourself—anything that carried with it the suggestion of abnormality, of having something to hide. In any case, to wear an improper expression on your face (to look incredulous when a victory was announced, for example) was itself a punishable offence. There was even a word for it in Newspeak: *facecrime*, it was called.

The girl had turned her back on him again. Perhaps after all she was not really following him about; perhaps it was coincidence that she had sat so close to him two days running. His cigarette had gone out, and he laid it carefully on the edge of the table. He would finish smoking it after work, if he could keep the tobacco in it. Quite likely the person at the next table was a spy of the Thought Police, and quite likely he would be in the cellars of the Ministry of Love within three days, but a cigarette end must not be wasted. Syme had folded up his strip of paper and stowed it away in his pocket. Parsons had begun talking again.

'Did I ever tell you, old boy,' he said, chuckling round the stem of his pipe, 'about the time when those two nippers of mine set fire to the old market-woman's skirt because they saw her wrapping up sausages in a poster of B.B.? Sneaked up behind her and set fire to it with a box of matches. Burned her quite badly, I believe. Little beggars, eh? But keen as mustard! That's a first-rate training they give them in the Spies nowadays—better than in my day, even. What d'you think's the latest thing they've served them out with? Ear trumpets for listening through keyholes! My little girl brought one home the other night—tried it out on our sitting-room door, and reckoned she could hear twice as much as with her ear to the hole. Of course it's only a toy, mind you. Still, gives 'em the right idea, eh?'

At this moment the telescreen let out a piercing whistle. It was the signal to return to work. All three men sprang to their feet to join in the struggle round the lifts, and the remaining tobacco fell out of Winston's cigarette.

# 6

Winston was writing in his diary:

It was three years ago. It was on a dark evening, in a narrow side-street near one of the big railway stations. She was standing near a doorway in the wall, under a street lamp that hardly gave any light. She had a young face, painted very thick. It was really the paint that appealed to me, the whiteness of it, like a mask, and the bright red lips. Party women never paint their faces. There was nobody else in the street, and no telescreens. She said two dollars. I—

For the moment it was too difficult to go on. He shut his eyes and pressed his fingers against them, trying to squeeze out the vision that kept recurring. He had an almost overwhelming temptation to shout a string of filthy words at the top of his voice. Or to bang his head against the wall, to kick over the table, and hurl the inkpot through the window—to do any violent or noisy or painful thing that might black out the memory that was tormenting him.

Your worst enemy, he reflected, was your own nervous system. At any moment the tension inside you was liable to translate itself into some visible symptom. He thought of a man whom he had passed in the street a few weeks back: a quite ordinary-looking man, a Party member, aged thirty-five to forty, tallish and thin, carrying a brief-case. They were a few metres apart when the left side of the man's face was suddenly contorted by a sort of spasm. It happened again just as they were passing one another: it was only a twitch, a quiver, rapid as the clicking of a camera shutter, but obviously habitual. He remembered thinking at the time: That poor devil is done for. And what was frightening was that the action was quite possibly unconscious. The most deadly danger of all was talking in your sleep. There was no way of guarding against that, so far as he could see.

He drew his breath and went on writing:

I went with her through the doorway and across a backyard into a basement kitchen. There was a bed against the wall, and a lamp on the table, turned down very low. She—

His teeth were set on edge. He would have liked to spit. Simultaneously with the woman in the basement kitchen he thought of Katharine, his wife. Winston was married—had been married, at any rate: probably he still was married, so far as he knew his wife was not dead. He seemed to breathe again the warm stuffy odour of the basement kitchen, an odour compounded of bugs and dirty clothes and villainous cheap scent, but nevertheless alluring, because no woman of the Party ever used scent, or could be imagined as doing so. Only the proles used scent. In his mind the smell of it was inextricably mixed up with fornication.

When he had gone with that woman it had been his first lapse in two years or thereabouts. Consorting with prostitutes was forbidden, of course, but it was one of those rules that you could occasionally nerve yourself to break. It was dangerous, but it was not a life-and-death matter. To be caught with a prostitute might mean five years in a forced-labour camp: not more, if you had committed no other offence. And it was easy enough, provided that you could avoid being caught in the act. The poorer quarters swarmed with women who were ready to sell themselves. Some could even be purchased for a bottle of gin, which the proles were not supposed to drink. Tacitly the Party was even inclined to encourage prostitution, as an outlet for instincts which could not be altogether suppressed. Mere debauchery did not matter very much, so long as it was furtive and joyless and only involved the women of a submerged and despised class. The unforgivable crime was promiscuity between Party members. But—though this was one of the crimes that the accused in the great purges invariably confessed to—it was difficult to imagine any such thing actually happening.

The aim of the Party was not merely to prevent men and women from forming loyalties which it might not be able to control. Its real, undeclared purpose was to remove all pleasure from the sexual act. Not love so much as eroticism was the enemy, inside marriage as well as outside it. All marriages between Party members had to be approved by a committee appointed for the purpose, and—though the principle was never clearly stated—permission was always refused if the couple concerned gave the impression of being physically attracted to one another. The only recognized purpose of marriage was to beget children for the service of the Party. Sexual intercourse was to be looked on as a slightly disgusting minor operation, like having an enema. This again was never put into plain words, but in an indirect way it was rubbed into every Party member from childhood onwards. There were even organizations such as the Junior Anti-Sex League, which advocated complete celibacy for both sexes. All children were to be begotten by artificial insemination (*artsem,* it was called in Newspeak) and brought up in public institutions. This, Winston was aware, was not meant altogether seriously, but somehow it fitted in with the general ideology of the Party. The Party was trying to kill the sex instinct, or, if it could not be killed, then to distort it and dirty it. He did not know why this was so, but it seemed natural that it should be so. And as far as the women were concerned, the Party's efforts were largely successful.

He thought again of Katharine. It must be nine, ten—nearly eleven years since they had parted. It was curious how seldom he thought of her. For days at a time he was capable of forgetting that he had ever been married. They had only been together for about fifteen months. The Party did not permit divorce, but it rather encouraged separation in cases where there were no children.

Katharine was a tall, fair-haired girl, very straight, with splendid movements. She had a bold, aquiline face, a face that one might have called noble until one discovered that there was as nearly as possible nothing behind it. Very early in her married life he had decided—though perhaps it was only that he knew her more intimately than he knew most people—that she had without exception the most stupid, vulgar, empty mind that he had ever encountered. She had not a thought in her head that was not a slogan, and there was no imbecility, absolutely none that she was not capable of swallowing if the Party handed it out to her. 'The human sound-track' he nicknamed her in his own mind. Yet he could have endured living with her if it had not been for just one thing—sex.

As soon as he touched her she seemed to wince and stiffen. To embrace her was like embracing a jointed wooden image. And what was strange was that even when she was clasping him against her he had the feeling that she was simultaneously pushing him away with all her strength. The rigidity of her muscles managed to convey that impression. She would lie there with shut eyes, neither resisting nor co-operating but *submitting*. It was extraordinarily embarrassing, and, after a while, horrible. But even then he could have borne living with her if it had been agreed that they should remain celibate. But curiously enough it was Katharine who refused this. They must, she said, produce a child if they could. So the performance continued to happen, once a week quite regularly, whenever it was not impossible. She even used to remind him of it in the morning, as something which had to be done that evening and which must not be forgotten. She had two names for it. One was 'making a baby', and the other was 'our duty to the Party' (yes, she had actually used that phrase). Quite soon he grew to have a feeling of positive dread when the appointed day came round. But luckily no child appeared, and in the end she agreed to give up trying, and soon afterwards they parted.

Winston sighed inaudibly. He picked up his pen again and wrote:

She threw herself down on the bed, and at once, without any kind of preliminary, in the most coarse, horrible way you can imagine, pulled up her skirt. I—

He saw himself standing there in the dim lamplight, with the smell of bugs and cheap scent in his nostrils, and in his heart a feeling of defeat and resentment which even at that moment was mixed up with the thought of Katharine's white body, frozen for ever by the hypnotic power of the Party. Why did it always have to be like this? Why could he not have a woman of his own instead of these filthy scuffles at intervals of years? But a real love affair was an almost unthinkable event. The women of the Party were all alike. Chastity was as deep ingrained in them as Party loyalty. By careful early conditioning, by games and cold water, by the rubbish that was dinned into them at school and in the Spies and the Youth League, by lectures, parades, songs, slogans, and martial music, the natural feeling had been driven out of them. His reason told him that there must be exceptions, but his heart did not believe it. They were all impregnable, as the Party intended that they should be. And what he wanted, more even than to be loved, was to break down that wall of virtue, even if it were only once in his whole life. The sexual act, successfully performed, was rebellion. Desire was thoughtcrime. Even to have awakened Katharine, if he could have achieved it, would have been like a seduction, although she was his wife.

But the rest of the story had got to be written down. He wrote:

I turned up the lamp. When I saw her in the light—

After the darkness the feeble light of the paraffin lamp had seemed very bright. For the first time he could see the woman properly. He had taken a step towards her and then halted, full of lust and terror. He was painfully conscious of the risk he had taken in coming here. It was perfectly possible that the patrols would catch him on the way out: for that matter they might be waiting outside the door at this moment. If he went away without even doing what he had come here to do—!

It had got to be written down, it had got to be confessed. What he had suddenly seen in the lamplight was that the woman was *old*. The paint was plastered so thick on her face that it looked as though it might crack like a cardboard mask. There were streaks of white in her hair; but the truly dreadful detail was that her mouth had fallen a little open, revealing nothing except a cavernous blackness. She had no teeth at all.

He wrote hurriedly, in scrabbling handwriting:

When I saw her in the light she was quite an old woman, fifty years old at least. But I went ahead and did it just the same.

He pressed his fingers against his eyelids again. He had written it down at last, but it made no difference. The therapy had not worked. The urge to shout filthy words at the top of his voice was as strong as ever.

## 7

If there is hope, *wrote Winston,* it lies in the proles.

If there was hope, it *must* lie in the proles, because only there, in those swarming disregarded masses, 85 per cent of the population of Oceania, could the force to destroy the Party ever be generated. The Party could not be overthrown from within. Its enemies, if it had any enemies, had no way of coming together or even of identifying one another. Even if the legendary Brotherhood existed, as just possibly it might, it was inconceivable that its members could ever assemble in larger numbers than twos and threes. Rebellion meant a look in the eyes, an inflexion of the voice; at the most, an occasional whispered word. But the proles, if only they could somehow become conscious of their own strength, would have no need to conspire. They needed only to rise up and shake themselves like a horse shaking off flies. If they chose they could blow the Party to pieces tomorrow morning. Surely sooner or later it must occur to them to do it? And yet—!

He remembered how once he had been walking down a crowded street when a tremendous shout of hundreds of voices—women's voices—had burst from a side-street a little way ahead. It was a great formidable cry of anger and despair, a deep, loud 'Oh-o-o-o-oh!' that went humming on like the reverberation of a bell. His heart had leapt. It's started! he had thought. A riot! The proles are breaking loose at last! When he had reached the spot it was to see a mob of two or three hundred women crowding round the stalls of a street market, with faces as tragic as though they had been the doomed passengers on a sinking ship. But at this moment the general despair broke down into a multitude of individual quarrels. It appeared that one of the stalls had been selling tin saucepans. They were wretched, flimsy things, but cooking-pots of any kind were always difficult to get. Now the supply had unexpectedly given out. The successful women, bumped and jostled by the rest, were trying to make off with their saucepans while dozens of others clamoured round the stall, accusing the stall-keeper of favouritism and of having more saucepans somewhere in reserve. There was a fresh outburst of yells. Two bloated women, one of them with her hair coming down, had got hold of the same saucepan and were trying to tear it out of one another's hands. For a moment they were both tugging, and then the handle came off. Winston watched them disgustedly. And yet, just for a moment, what almost frightening power had sounded in that cry from only a few hundred throats! Why was it that they could never shout like that about anything that mattered?

He wrote:

Until they become conscious they will never rebel, and until after they have rebelled they cannot become conscious.

That, he reflected, might almost have been a transcription from one of the Party textbooks. The Party claimed, of course, to have liberated the proles from bondage. Before the Revolution they had been hideously oppressed by the capitalists, they had been starved and flogged, women had been forced to work in the coal mines (women still did work in the coal mines, as a matter of fact), children had been sold into the factories at the age of six. But simultaneously, true to the principles of doublethink, the Party taught that the proles were natural inferiors who must be kept in subjection, like animals, by the application of a few simple rules. In reality very little was known about the proles. It was not necessary to know much. So long as they continued to work and breed, their other activities were without importance. Left to themselves, like cattle turned loose upon the plains of Argentina, they had reverted to a style of life that appeared to be natural to them, a sort of ancestral pattern. They were born, they grew up in the gutters, they went to work at twelve, they passed through a brief blossoming-period of beauty and sexual desire, they married at twenty, they were middle-aged at thirty, they died, for the most part, at sixty. Heavy physical work, the care of home and children, petty quarrels with neighbours, films, football, beer, and, above all, gambling, filled up the horizon of minds. To keep them in control was not difficult. A few agents of the Thought Police moved always among them, spreading false rumours and marking down and eliminating the few individuals who were judged capable of becoming dangerous; but no attempt was made to indoctrinate them with the ideology of the Party. It was not desirable that the proles should have strong political feelings. All that was required of them was a primitive patriotism which could be appealed to whenever it was necessary to make them accept longer working-hours or shorter rations. And even when they became discontented, as they sometimes did, their discontent led nowhere, because being without general ideas, they could only focus it on petty specific grievances. The larger evils invariably escaped their notice. The great majority of proles did not even have telescreens in their homes. Even the civil police interfered with them very little. There was a vast amount of criminality in London, a whole world-within-a-world of thieves, bandits, prostitutes, drug-peddlers, and racketeers of every description; but since it all happened among the proles themselves, it was of no importance. In all questions of morals they were allowed to follow their ancestral code. The sexual puritanism of the Party was not imposed upon them. Promiscuity went unpunished, divorce was permitted. For that matter, even religious worship would have been permitted if the proles had shown any sign of needing or wanting it. They were beneath suspicion. As the Party slogan put it: 'Proles and animals are free.'

Winston reached down and cautiously scratched his varicose ulcer. It had begun itching again. The thing you invariably came back to was the impossibility of knowing what life before the Revolution had really been like. He took out of the drawer a copy of a children's history textbook which he had borrowed from Mrs Parsons, and began copying a passage into the diary:

In the old days (it ran), before the glorious Revolution, London was not the beautiful city that we know today. It was a dark, dirty, miserable place where hardly anybody had enough to eat and where hundreds and thousands of poor people had no boots on their feet and not even a roof to sleep under. Children no older than you are had to work twelve hours a day for cruel masters, who flogged them with whips if they worked too slowly and fed them on nothing but stale breadcrusts and water. But in among all this terrible poverty there were just a few great big beautiful houses that were lived in by rich men who had as many as thirty servants to look after them. These rich men were called capitalists. They were fat, ugly men with wicked faces, like the one in the picture on the opposite page. You see that he is dressed in a long black coat which was called a frock coat, and a queer, shiny hat shaped like a stovepipe, which was called a top hat. This was the uniform of the capitalists, and no one else was allowed to wear it. The capitalists owned everything in the world, and everyone else was their slave. They owned all the land, all the houses, all the factories, and all the money. If anyone disobeyed them they could throw them into prison, or they could take his job away and starve him to death. When any ordinary person spoke to a capitalist he had to cringe and bow to him, and take off his cap and address him as 'Sir'. The chief of all the capitalists was called the King, and—

But he knew the rest of the catalogue. There would be mention of the bishops in their lawn sleeves, the judges in their ermine robes, the pillory, the stocks, the treadmill, the cat-o'-nine tails, the Lord Mayor's Banquet, and the practice of kissing the Pope's toe. There was also something called the *jus primae noctis,* which would probably not be mentioned in a textbook for children. It was the law by which every capitalist had the right to sleep with any woman working in one of his factories.

How could you tell how much of it was lies? It *might* be true that the average human being was better off now than he had been before the Revolution. The only evidence to the contrary was the mute protest in your own bones, the instinctive feeling that the conditions you lived in were intolerable and that at some other time they must have been different. It struck him that the truly characteristic thing about modern life was not its cruelty and insecurity, but simply its bareness, its dinginess, its listlessness. Life, if you looked about you, bore no resemblance not only to the lies that streamed out of the telescreens, but even to the ideals that the Party was trying to achieve. Great areas of it, even for a Party member, were neutral and non-political, a matter of slogging through dreary jobs, fighting for a place on the Tube, darning a worn-out sock, cadging a saccharine tablet, saving a cigarette end. The ideal set up by the Party was something huge, terrible, and glittering—a world of steel and concrete, of monstrous machines and terrifying weapons—a nation of warriors and fanatics, marching forward in perfect unity, all thinking the same thoughts and shouting the same slogans, perpetually working, fighting, triumphing, persecuting—three hundred million people all with the same face. The reality was decaying, dingy cities where under-fed people shuffled to and fro in leaky shoes, in patched-up nineteenth-century houses that smelt always of cabbage and bad lavatories. He seemed to see a vision of London, vast and ruinous, city of a million dustbins, and mixed up with it was a picture of Mrs Parsons, a woman with lined face and wispy hair, fiddling helplessly with a blocked waste-pipe.

He reached down and scratched his ankle again. Day and night the telescreens bruised your ears with statistics proving that people today had more food, more clothes, better houses, better recreations—that they lived longer, worked shorter hours, were bigger, healthier, stronger, happier, more intelligent, better educated, than the people of fifty years ago. Not a word of it could ever be proved or disproved. The Party claimed, for example, that to-day 40 per cent of adult proles were literate: before the Revolution, it was said, the number had only been 15 per cent. The Party claimed that the infant mortality rate was now only 160 per thousand, whereas before the Revolution it had been 300—and so it went on. It was like a single equation with two unknowns. It might very well be that literally every word in the history books, even the things that one accepted without question, was pure fantasy. For all he knew there might never have been any such law as the *jus primae noctis,* or any such creature as a capitalist, or any such garment as a top hat.

Everything faded into mist. The past was erased, the erasure was forgotten, the lie became truth. Just once in his life he had possessed—*after* the event: that was what counted—concrete, unmistakable evidence of an act of falsification. He had held it between his fingers for as long as thirty seconds. In 1973, it must have been—at any rate, it was at about the time when he and Katharine had parted. But the really relevant date was seven or eight years earlier.

The story really began in the middle 'sixties, the period of the great purges in which the original leaders of the Revolution were wiped out once and for all. By 1970 none of them was left, except Big Brother himself. All the rest had by that time been exposed as traitors and counter-revolutionaries. Goldstein had fled and was hiding no one knew where, and of the others, a few had simply disappeared, while the majority had been executed after spectacular public trials at which they made confession of their crimes. Among the last survivors were three men named Jones, Aaronson, and Rutherford. It must have been in 1965 that these three had been arrested. As often happened, they had vanished for a year or more, so that one did not know whether they were alive or dead, and then had suddenly been brought forth to incriminate themselves in the usual way. They had confessed to intelligence with the enemy (at that date, too, the enemy was Eurasia), embezzlement of public funds, the murder of various trusted Party members, intrigues against the leadership of Big Brother which had started long before the Revolution happened, and acts of sabotage causing the death of hundreds of thousands of people. After confessing to these things they had been pardoned, reinstated in the Party, and given posts which were in fact sinecures but which sounded important. All three had written long, abject articles in *The Times,* analysing the reasons for their defection and promising to make amends.

Some time after their release Winston had actually seen all three of them in the Chestnut Tree Café. He remembered the sort of terrified fascination with which he had watched them out of the corner of his eye. They were men far older than himself, relics of the ancient world, almost the last great figures left over from the heroic early days of the Party. The glamour of the underground struggle and the civil war still faintly clung to them. He had the feeling, though already at that time facts and dates were growing blurry, that he had known their names years earlier than he had known that of Big Brother. But also they were outlaws, enemies, untouchables, doomed with absolute certainty to extinction within a year or two. No one who had once fallen into the hands of the Thought Police ever escaped in the end. They were corpses waiting to be sent back to the grave.

There was no one at any of the tables nearest to them. It was not wise even to be seen in the neighbourhood of such people. They were sitting in silence before glasses of the gin flavoured with cloves which was the speciality of the café. Of the three, it was Rutherford whose appearance had most impressed Winston. Rutherford had once been a famous caricaturist, whose brutal cartoons had helped to inflame popular opinion before and during the Revolution. Even now, at long intervals, his cartoons were appearing in *The Times*. They were simply an imitation of his earlier manner, and curiously lifeless and unconvincing. Always they were a rehashing of the ancient themes—slum tenements, starving children, street battles, capitalists in top hats—even on the barricades the capitalists still seemed to cling to their top hats—an endless, hopeless effort to get back into the past. He was a monstrous man, with a mane of greasy grey hair, his face pouched and seamed, with thick negroid lips. At one time he must have been immensely strong; now his great body was sagging, sloping, bulging, falling away in every direction. He seemed to be breaking up before one's eyes, like a mountain crumbling.

It was the lonely hour of fifteen. Winston could not now remember how he had come to be in the café at such a time. The place was almost empty. A tinny music was trickling from the telescreens. The three men sat in their corner almost motionless, never speaking. Uncommanded, the waiter brought fresh glasses of gin. There was a chessboard on the table beside them, with the pieces set out but no game started. And then, for perhaps half a minute in all, something happened to the telescreens. The tune that they were playing changed, and the tone of the music changed too. There came into it—but it was something hard to describe. It was a peculiar, cracked, braying, jeering note: in his mind Winston called it a yellow note. And then a voice from the telescreen was singing:

> Under the spreading chestnut tree
> I sold you and you sold me:
> There lie they, and here lie we
> Under the spreading chestnut tree.

The three men never stirred. But when Winston glanced again at Rutherford's ruinous face, he saw that his eyes were full of tears. And for the first time he noticed, with a kind of inward shudder, and yet not knowing *at what* he shuddered, that both Aaronson and Rutherford had broken noses.

A little later all three were re-arrested. It appeared that they had engaged in fresh conspiracies from the very moment of their release. At their second trial they confessed to all their old crimes over again, with a whole string of new ones. They were executed, and their fate was recorded in the Party histories, a warning to posterity. About five years after this, in 1973, Winston was unrolling a wad of documents which had just flopped out of the pneumatic tube on to his desk when he came on a fragment of paper which had evidently been slipped in among the others and then forgotten. The instant he had flattened it out he saw its significance. It was a half-page torn out of *The Times* of about ten years earlier—the top half of the page, so that it included the date—and it contained a photograph of the delegates at some Party function in New York. Prominent in the middle of the group were Jones, Aaronson, and Rutherford. There was no mistaking them; in any case their names were in the caption at the bottom.

The point was that at both trials all three men had confessed that on that date they had been on Eurasian soil. They had flown from a secret airfield in Canada to a rendezvous somewhere in Siberia, and had conferred with members of the Eurasian General Staff, to whom they had betrayed important military secrets. The date had stuck in Winston's memory because it chanced to be midsummer day; but the whole story must be on record in countless other places as well. There was only one possible conclusion: the confessions were lies.

Of course, this was not in itself a discovery. Even at that time Winston had not imagined that the people who were wiped out in the purges had actually committed the crimes that they were accused of. But this was concrete evidence; it was a fragment of the abolished past, like a fossil bone which turns up in the wrong stratum and destroys a geological theory. It was enough to blow the Party to atoms, if in some way it could have been published to the world and its significance made known.

He had gone straight on working. As soon as he saw what the photograph was, and what it meant, he had covered it up with another sheet of paper, Luckily, when he unrolled it, it had been upside-down from the point of view of the telescreen.

He took his scribbling pad on his knee and pushed back his chair, so as to get as far away from the telescreen as possible. To keep your face expressionless was not difficult, and even your breathing could be controlled, with an effort: but you could not control the beating of your heart, and the telescreen was quite delicate enough to pick it up. He let what he judged to be ten minutes go by, tormented all the while by the fear that some accident—a sudden draught blowing across his desk, for instance—would betray him. Then, without uncovering it again, he dropped the photograph into the memory hole, along with some other waste papers. Within another minute, perhaps, it would have crumbled into ashes.

That was ten—eleven years ago. Today, probably, he would have kept that photograph. It was curious that the fact of having held it in his fingers seemed to him to make a difference even now, when the photograph itself, as well as the event it recorded, was only memory. Was the Party's hold upon the past less strong, he wondered, because a piece of evidence which existed no longer *had once* existed?

But today, supposing that it could be somehow resurrected from its ashes, the photograph might not even be evidence. Already, at the time when he made his discovery, Oceania was no longer at war with Eurasia, and it must have been to the agents of Eastasia that the three dead men had betrayed their country. Since then there had been other charges—two, three, he could not remember how many. Very likely the confessions had been rewritten and rewritten until the original facts and dates no longer had the smallest significance. The past not only changed, but changed continuously. What most afflicted him with the sense of nightmare was that he had never clearly understood *why* the huge imposture was undertaken. The immediate advantages of falsifying the past were obvious, but the ultimate motive was mysterious. He took up his pen again and wrote:

I understand HOW: I do not understand WHY.

He wondered, as he had many times wondered before, whether he himself was a lunatic. Perhaps a lunatic was simply a minority of one. At one time it had been a sign of madness to believe that the earth goes round the sun: today, to believe that the past is unalterable. He might be *alone* in holding that belief, and if alone, then a lunatic. But the thought of being a lunatic did not greatly trouble him: the horror was that he might also be wrong.

He picked up the children's history book and looked at the portrait of Big Brother which formed its frontispiece. The hypnotic eyes gazed into his own. It was as though some huge force were pressing down upon you—something that penetrated inside your skull, battering against your brain, frightening you out of your beliefs, persuading you, almost, to deny the evidence of your senses. In the end the Party would announce that two and two made five, and you would have to believe it. It was inevitable that they should make that claim sooner or later: the logic of their position demanded it. Not merely the validity of experience, but the very existence of external reality, was tacitly denied by their philosophy. The heresy of heresies was common sense. And what was terrifying was not that they would kill you for thinking otherwise, but that they might be right. For, after all, how do we know that two and two make four? Or that the force of gravity works? Or that the past is unchangeable? If both the past and the external world exist only in the mind, and if the mind itself is controllable—what then?

But no! His courage seemed suddenly to stiffen of its own accord. The face of O'Brien, not called up by any obvious association, had floated into his mind. He knew, with more certainty than before, that O'Brien was on his side. He was writing the diary for O'Brien—*to* O'Brien: it was like an interminable letter which no one would ever read, but which was addressed to a particular person and took its colour from that fact.

The Party told you to reject the evidence of your eyes and ears. It was their final, most essential command. His heart sank as he thought of the enormous power arrayed against him, the ease with which any Party intellectual would overthrow him in debate, the subtle arguments which he would not be able to understand, much less answer. And yet he was in the right! They were wrong and he was right. The obvious, the silly, and the true had got to be defended. Truisms are true, hold on to that! The solid world exists, its laws do not change. Stones are hard, water is wet, objects unsupported fall towards the earth's centre. With the feeling that he was speaking to O'Brien, and also that he was setting forth an important axiom, he wrote:

Freedom is the freedom to say that two plus two make four. If that is granted, all else follows.

# 8

From somewhere at the bottom of a passage the smell of roasting coffee—real coffee, not Victory Coffee—came floating out into the street. Winston paused involuntarily. For perhaps two seconds he was back in the half-forgotten world of his childhood. Then a door banged, seeming to cut off the smell as abruptly as though it had been a sound.

He had walked several kilometres over pavements, and his varicose ulcer was throbbing. This was the second time in three weeks that he had missed an evening at the Community Centre: a rash act, since you could be certain that the number of your attendances at the Centre was carefully checked. In principle a Party member had no spare time, and was never alone except in bed. It was assumed that when he was not working, eating, or sleeping he would be taking part in some kind of communal recreation: to do anything that suggested a taste for solitude, even to go for a walk by yourself, was always slightly dangerous. There was a word for it in Newspeak: *ownlife,* it was called, meaning individualism and eccentricity. But this evening as he came out of the Ministry the balminess of the April air had tempted him. The sky was a warmer blue than he had seen it that year, and suddenly the long, noisy evening at the Centre, the boring, exhausting games, the lectures, the creaking camaraderie oiled by gin, had seemed intolerable. On impulse he had turned away from the bus-stop and wandered off into the labyrinth of London, first south, then east, then north again, losing himself among unknown streets and hardly bothering in which direction he was going.

'If there is hope,' he had written in the diary, 'it lies in the proles.' The words kept coming back to him, statement of a mystical truth and a palpable absurdity. He was somewhere in the vague, brown-coloured slums to the north and east of what had once been Saint Pancras Station. He was walking up a cobbled street of little two-storey houses with battered doorways which gave straight on the pavement and which were somehow curiously suggestive of ratholes. There were puddles of filthy water here and there among the cobbles. In and out of the dark doorways, and down narrow alley-ways that branched off on either side, people swarmed in astonishing numbers—girls in full bloom, with crudely lipsticked mouths, and youths who chased the girls, and swollen waddling women who showed you what the girls would be like in ten years' time, and old bent creatures shuffling along on splayed feet, and ragged barefooted children who played in the puddles and then scattered at angry yells from their mothers. Perhaps a quarter of the windows in the street were broken and boarded up. Most of the people paid no attention to Winston; a few eyed him with a sort of guarded curiosity. Two monstrous women with brick-red forearms folded across their aprons were talking outside a doorway. Winston caught scraps of conversation as he approached.

' "Yes," I says to 'er, "that's all very well," I says. "But if you'd of been in my place you'd of done the same as what I done. It's easy to criticize," I says, "but you ain't got the same problems as what I got." ' 'Ah,' said the other, 'that's jest it. That's jest where it is.'

The strident voices stopped abruptly. The women studied him in hostile silence as he went past. But it was not hostility, exactly; merely a kind of wariness, a momentary stiffening, as at the passing of some unfamiliar animal. The blue overalls of the Party could not be a common sight in a street like this. Indeed, it was unwise to be seen in such places, unless you had definite business there. The patrols might stop you if you happened to run into them. 'May I see your papers, comrade? What are you doing here? What time did you leave work? Is this your usual way home?'—and so on and so forth. Not that there was any rule against walking home by an unusual route: but it was enough to draw attention to you if the Thought Police heard about it.

Suddenly the whole street was in commotion. There were yells of warning from all sides. People were shooting into the doorways like rabbits. A young woman leapt out of a doorway a little ahead of Winston, grabbed up a tiny child playing in a puddle, whipped her apron round it, and leapt back again, all in one movement. At the same instant a man in a concertina-like black suit, who had emerged from a side alley, ran towards Winston, pointing excitedly to the sky.

'Steamer!' he yelled. 'Look out, guv'nor! Bang over'ead! Lay down quick!'

'Steamer' was a nickname which, for some reason, the proles applied to rocket bombs. Winston promptly flung himself on his face. The proles were nearly always right when they gave you a warning of this kind. They seemed to possess some kind of instinct which told them several seconds in advance when a rocket was coming, although the rockets supposedly travelled faster than sound. Winston clasped his forearms above his head. There was a roar that seemed to make the pavement heave; a shower of light objects pattered on to his back. When he stood up he found that he was covered with fragments of glass from the nearest window.

He walked on. The bomb had demolished a group of houses 200 metres up the street. A black plume of smoke hung in the sky, and below it a cloud of plaster dust in which a crowd was already forming round the ruins. There was a little pile of plaster lying on the pavement ahead of him, and in the middle of it he could see a bright red streak. When he got up to it he saw that it was a human hand severed at the wrist. Apart from the bloody stump, the hand was so completely whitened as to resemble a plaster cast.

He kicked the thing into the gutter, and then, to avoid the crowd, turned down a side-street to the right. Within three or four minutes he was out of the area which the bomb had affected, and the sordid swarming life of the streets was going on as though nothing had happened. It was nearly twenty hours, and the drinking-shops which the proles frequented ('pubs', they called them) were choked with customers. From their grimy swing doors, endlessly opening and shutting, there came forth a smell of urine, sawdust, and sour beer. In an angle formed by a projecting housefront three men were standing very close together, the middle one of them holding a folded-up newspaper which the other two were studying over his shoulder. Even before he was near enough to make out the expression on their faces, Winston could see absorption in every line of their bodies. It was obviously some serious piece of news that they were reading. He was a few paces away from them when suddenly the group broke up and two of the men were in violent altercation. For a moment they seemed almost on the point of blows.

'Can't you bleeding well listen to what I say? I tell you no number ending in seven ain't won for over fourteen months!'

'Yes, it 'as, then!'

'No, it 'as not! Back 'ome I got the 'ole lot of 'em for over two years wrote down on a piece of paper. I takes 'em down reg'lar as the clock. An' I tell you, no number ending in seven—'

'Yes, a seven *'as* won! I could pretty near tell you the bleeding number. Four oh seven, it ended in. It were in February—second week in February.'

'February your grandmother! I got it all down in black and white. An' I tell you, no number—'

'Oh, pack it in!' said the third man.

They were talking about the Lottery. Winston looked back when he had gone thirty metres. They were still arguing, with vivid, passionate faces. The Lottery, with its weekly pay-out of enormous prizes, was the one public event to which the proles paid serious attention. It was probable that there were some millions of proles for whom the Lottery was the principal if not the only reason for remaining alive. It was their delight, their folly, their anodyne, their intellectual stimulant. Where the Lottery was concerned, even people who could barely read and write seemed capable of intricate calculations and staggering feats of memory. There was a whole tribe of men who made a living simply by selling systems, forecasts, and lucky amulets. Winston had nothing to do with the running of the Lottery, which was managed by the Ministry of Plenty, but he was aware (indeed everyone in the Party was aware) that the prizes were largely imaginary. Only small sums were actually paid out, the winners of the big prizes being non-existent persons. In the absence of any real inter-communication between one part of Oceania and another, this was not difficult to arrange.

But if there was hope, it lay in the proles. You had to cling on to that. When you put it in words it sounded reasonable: it was when you looked at the human beings passing you on the pavement that it became an act of faith. The street into which he had turned ran downhill. He had a feeling that he had been in this neighbourhood before, and that there was a main thoroughfare not far away. From somewhere ahead there came a din of shouting voices. The street took a sharp turn and then ended in a flight of steps which led down into a sunken alley where a few stall-keepers were selling tired-looking vegetables. At this moment Winston remembered where he was. The alley led out into the main street, and down the next turning, not five minutes away, was the junk shop where he had bought the blank book which was now his diary. And in a small stationer's shop not far away he had bought his penholder and his bottle of ink.

He paused for a moment at the top of the steps. On the opposite side of the alley there was a dingy little pub whose windows appeared to be frosted over but in reality were merely coated with dust. A very old man, bent but active, with white moustaches that bristled forward like those of a prawn, pushed open the swing door and went in. As Winston stood watching, it occurred to him that the old man, who must be eighty at the least, had already been middle-aged when the Revolution happened. He and a few others like him were the last links that now existed with the vanished world of capitalism. In the Party itself there were not many people left whose ideas had been formed before the Revolution. The older generation had mostly been wiped out in the great purges of the 'fifties and 'sixties, and the few who survived had long ago been terrified into complete intellectual surrender. If there was any one still alive who could give you a truthful account of conditions in the early part of the century, it could only be a prole. Suddenly the passage from the history book that he had copied into his diary came back into Winston's mind, and a lunatic impulse took hold of him. He would go into the pub, he would scrape acquaintance with that old man and question him. He would say to him: 'Tell me about your life when you were a boy. What was it like in those days? Were things better than they are now, or were they worse?'

Hurriedly, lest he should have time to become frightened, he descended the steps and crossed the narrow street. It was madness of course. As usual, there was no definite rule against talking to proles and frequenting their pubs, but it was far too unusual an action to pass unnoticed. If the patrols appeared he might plead an attack of faintness, but it was not likely that they would believe him. He pushed open the door, and a hideous cheesy smell of sour beer hit him in the face. As he entered the din of voices dropped to about half its volume. Behind his back he could feel everyone eyeing his blue overalls. A game of darts which was going on at the other end of the room interrupted itself for perhaps as much as thirty seconds. The old man whom he had followed was standing at the bar, having some kind of altercation with the barman, a large, stout, hook-nosed young man with enormous forearms. A knot of others, standing round with glasses in their hands, were watching the scene.

'I arst you civil enough, didn't I?' said the old man, straightening his shoulders pugnaciously. 'You telling me you ain't got a pint mug in the 'ole bleeding boozer?'

'And what in hell's name *is* a pint?' said the barman, leaning forward with the tips of his fingers on the counter.

''Ark at 'im! Calls 'isself a barman and don't know what a pint is! Why, a pint's the 'alf of a quart, and there's four quarts to the gallon. 'Ave to teach you the A, B, C next.'

'Never heard of 'em,' said the barman shortly. 'Litre and half litre–that's all we serve. There's the glasses on the shelf in front of you.'

'I likes a pint,' persisted the old man. 'You could 'a drawed me off a pint easy enough. We didn't 'ave these bleeding litres when I was a young man.'

'When you were a young man we were all living in the treetops,' said the barman, with a glance at the other customers.

There was a shout of laughter, and the uneasiness caused by Winston's entry seemed to disappear. The old man's white-stubbled face had flushed pink. He turned away, muttering to himself, and bumped into Winston. Winston caught him gently by the arm.

'May I offer you a drink?' he said.

'You're a gent,' said the other, straightening his shoulders again. He appeared not to have noticed Winston's blue overalls. 'Pint!' he added aggressively to the barman. 'Pint of wallop.'

The barman swished two half-litres of dark-brown beer into thick glasses which he had rinsed in a bucket under the counter. Beer was the only drink you could get in prole pubs. The proles were supposed not to drink gin, though in practice they could get hold of it easily enough. The game of darts was in full swing again, and the knot of men at the bar had begun talking about lottery tickets. Winston's presence was forgotten for a moment. There was a deal table under the window where he and the old man could talk without fear of being overheard. It was horribly dangerous, but at any rate there was no telescreen in the room, a point he had made sure of as soon as he came in.

''E could 'a drawed me off a pint,' grumbled the old man as he settled down behind his glass. 'A 'alf litre ain't enough. It don't satisfy. And a 'ole litre's too much. It starts my bladder running. Let alone the price.'

'You must have seen great changes since you were a young man,' said Winston tentatively.

The old man's pale blue eyes moved from the dart board to the bar, and from the bar to the door of the Gents, as though it were in the bar-room that he expected the changes to have occurred.

'The beer was better,' he said finally. 'And cheaper! When I was a young man, mild beer—wallop we used to call it—was fourpence a pint. That was before the war, of course.'

'Which war was that?' said Winston.

'It's all wars,' said the old man vaguely. He took up his glass, and his shoulders straightened again. ''Ere's wishing you the very best of 'ealth!'

In his lean throat the sharp-pointed Adam's apple made a surprisingly rapid up-and-down movement, and the beer vanished. Winston went to the bar and came back with two more half-litres. The old man appeared to have forgotten his prejudice against drinking a full litre.

'You are very much older than I am,' said Winston. 'You must have been a grown man before I was born. You can remember what it was like in the old days, before the Revolution. People of my age don't really know anything about those times. We can only read about them in books, and what it says in the books may not be true. I should like your opinion on that. The history books say that life before the Revolution was completely different from what it is now. There was the most terrible oppression, injustice, poverty—worse than anything we can imagine. Here in London, the great mass of the people never had enough to eat from birth to death. Half of them hadn't even boots on their feet. They worked twelve hours a day, they left school at nine, they slept ten in a room. And at the same time there were a very few people, only a few thousands—the capitalists, they were called—who were rich and powerful. They owned everything that there was to own. They lived in great gorgeous houses with thirty servants, they rode about in motor-cars and four-horse carriages, they drank champagne, they wore top hats—'

The old man brightened suddenly.

'Top 'ats!' he said. 'Funny you should mention 'em. The same thing come into my 'ead only yesterday, I dono why. I was jest thinking, I ain't seen a top 'at in years. Gorn right out, they 'ave. The last time I wore one was at my sister-in-law's funeral. And that was—well, I couldn't give you the date, but it must 'a been fifty years ago. Of course it was only 'ired for the occasion, you understand.'

'It isn't very important about the top hats,' said Winston patiently. 'The point is, these capitalists—they and a few lawyers and priests and so forth who lived on them—were the lords of the earth. Everything existed for their benefit. You—the ordinary people, the workers—were their slaves. They could do what they liked with you. They could ship you off to Canada like cattle. They could sleep with your daughters if they chose. They could order you to be flogged with something called a cat-o'-nine tails. You had to take your cap off when you passed them. Every capitalist went about with a gang of lackeys who—'

The old man brightened again.

'Lackeys!' he said. 'Now there's a word I ain't 'eard since ever so long. Lackeys! That reg'lar takes me back, that does. I recollect—oh, donkey's years ago—I used to sometimes go to 'Yde Park of a Sunday afternoon to 'ear the blokes making speeches. Salvation Army, Roman Catholics, Jews, Indians—all sorts there was. And there was one bloke—well, I couldn't give you 'is name, but a real powerful speaker, 'e was. 'E didn't 'alf give it 'em! "Lackeys!" 'e says, "lackeys of the bourgeoisie! Flunkies of the ruling class!" Parasites—that was another of them. And 'yenas—'e definitely called 'em 'yenas. Of course 'e was referring to the Labour Party, you understand.'

Winston had the feeling that they were talking at cross-purposes.

'What I really wanted to know was this,' he said. 'Do you feel that you have more freedom now than you had in those days? Are you treated more like a human being? In the old days, the rich people, the people at the top—'

'The 'Ouse of Lords,' put in the old man reminiscently.

'The House of Lords, if you like. What I am asking is, were these people able to treat you as an inferior, simply because they were rich and you were poor? Is it a fact, for instance, that you had to call them "Sir" and take off your cap when you passed them?'

The old man appeared to think deeply. He drank off about a quarter of his beer before answering.

'Yes,' he said. 'They liked you to touch your cap to 'em. It showed respect, like. I didn't agree with it, myself, but I done it often enough. Had to, as you might say.'

'And was it usual—I'm only quoting what I've read in history books—was it usual for these people and their servants to push you off the pavement into the gutter?'

'One of 'em pushed me once,' said the old man. 'I recollect it as if it was yesterday. It was Boat Race night—terribly rowdy they used to get on Boat Race night—and I bumps into a young bloke on Shaftesbury Avenue. Quite the gent, 'e was—dress shirt, top 'at, black overcoat. 'E was kind of zigzagging across the pavement, and I bumps into 'im accidental-like. 'E says, "Why can't you look where you're going?" 'e says. I say, "Ju think you've bought the bleeding pavement?" 'E says, "I'll twist your bloody 'ead off if you get fresh with me." I says, "You're drunk. I'll give you in charge in 'alf a minute," I says. An' if you'll believe me, 'e puts 'is 'and on my chest and gives me a shove as pretty near sent me under the wheels of a bus. Well, I was young in them days, and I was going to 'ave fetched 'im one, only—'

A sense of helplessness took hold of Winston. The old man's memory was nothing but a rubbish-heap of details. One could question him all day without getting any real information. The Party histories might still be true, after a fashion: they might even be completely true. He made a last attempt.

'Perhaps I have not made myself clear,' he said. 'What I'm trying to say is this. You have been alive a very long time; you lived half your life before the Revolution. In 1925, for instance, you were already grown up. Would you say, from what you can remember, that life in 1925 was better than it is now, or worse? If you could choose, would you prefer to live then or now?'

The old man looked meditatively at the dart board. He finished up his beer, more slowly than before. When he spoke it was with a tolerant, philosophic air, as though the beer had mellowed him.

'I know what you expect me to say,' he said. 'You expect me to say as I'd sooner be young again. Most people'd say they'd sooner be young, if you arst 'em. You got your 'ealth and strength when you're young. When you get to my time of life you ain't never well. I suffer something wicked from my feet, and my bladder's jest terrible. Six and seven times a night it 'as me out of bed. On the other 'and, there's great advantages in being a old man. You ain't got the same worries. No truck with women, and that's a great thing. I ain't 'ad a woman for near on thirty year, if you'd credit it. Nor wanted to, what's more.'

Winston sat back against the window-sill. It was no use going on. He was about to buy some more beer when the old man suddenly got up and shuffled rapidly into the stinking urinal at the side of the room. The extra half-litre was already working on him. Winston sat for a minute or two gazing at his empty glass, and hardly noticed when his feet carried him out into the street again. Within twenty years at the most, he reflected, the huge and simple question, 'Was life better before the Revolution than it is now?' would have ceased once and for all to be answerable. But in effect it was unanswerable even now, since the few scattered survivors from the ancient world were incapable of comparing one age with another. They remembered a million useless things, a quarrel with a workmate, a hunt for a lost bicycle pump, the expression on a long-dead sister's face, the swirls of dust on a windy morning seventy years ago: but all the relevant facts were outside the range of their vision. They were like the ant, which can see small objects but not large ones. And when memory failed and written records were falsified—when that happened, the claim of the Party to have improved the conditions of human life had got to be accepted, because there did not exist, and never again could exist, any standard against which it could be tested.

At this moment his train of thought stopped abruptly. He halted and looked up. He was in a narrow street, with a few dark little shops interspersed among dwelling-houses. Immediately above his head there hung three discoloured metal balls which looked as if they had once been gilded. He seemed to know the place. Of course! He was standing outside the junk-shop where he had bought the diary.

A twinge of fear went through him. It had been a sufficiently rash act to buy the book in the beginning, and he had sworn never to come near the place again. And yet the instant that he allowed his thoughts to wander, his feet had brought him back here of their own accord. It was precisely against suicidal impulses of this kind that he had hoped to guard himself by opening the diary. At the same time he noticed that although it was nearly twenty-one hours the shop was still open. With the feeling that he would be less conspicuous inside than hanging about on the pavement, he stepped through the doorway. If questioned, he could plausibly say that he was trying to buy razor blades.

The proprietor had just lighted a hanging oil lamp which gave off an unclean but friendly smell. He was a man of perhaps sixty, frail and bowed, with a long, benevolent nose, and mild eyes distorted by thick spectacles. His hair was almost white, but his eyebrows were bushy and still black. His spectacles, his gentle, fussy movements, and the fact that he was wearing an aged jacket of black velvet, gave him a vague air of intellectuality, as though he had been some kind of literary man, or perhaps a musician. His voice was soft, as though faded, and his accent less debased than that of the majority of proles.

'I recognized you on the pavement,' he said immediately. 'You're the gentleman that bought the young lady's keepsake album. That was a beautiful bit of paper, that was. Cream-laid, it used to be called. There's been no paper like that made for—oh, I dare say fifty years.' He peered at Winston over the top of his spectacles. 'Is there anything special I can do for you? Or did you just want to look round?'

'I was passing,' said Winston vaguely. 'I just looked in. I don't want anything in particular.'

'It's just as well,' said the other, 'because I don't suppose I could have satisfied you.' He made an apologetic gesture with his soft-palmed hand. 'You see how it is; an empty shop, you might say. Between you and me, the antique trade's just about finished. No demand any longer, and no stock either. Furniture, china, glass—it's all been broken up by degrees. And of course the metal stuff's mostly been melted down. I haven't seen a brass candlestick in years.'

The tiny interior of the shop was in fact uncomfortably full, but there was almost nothing in it of the slightest value. The floorspace was very restricted, because all round the walls were stacked innumerable dusty picture-frames. In the window there were trays of nuts and bolts, worn-out chisels, penknives with broken blades, tarnished watches that did not even pretend to be in going order, and other miscellaneous rubbish. Only on a small table in the corner was there a litter of odds and ends—lacquered snuffboxes, agate brooches, and the like—which looked as though they might include something interesting. As Winston wandered towards the table his eye was caught by a round, smooth thing that gleamed softly in the lamplight, and he picked it up.

It was a heavy lump of glass, curved on one side, flat on the other, making almost a hemisphere. There was a peculiar softness, as of rainwater, in both the colour and the texture of the glass. At the heart of it, magnified by the curved surface, there was a strange, pink, convoluted object that recalled a rose or a sea anemone.

'What is it?' said Winston, fascinated.

'That's coral, that is,' said the old man. 'It must have come from the Indian Ocean. They used to kind of embed it in the glass. That wasn't made less than a hundred years ago. More, by the look of it.'

'It's a beautiful thing,' said Winston.

'It is a beautiful thing,' said the other appreciatively. 'But there's not many that'd say so nowadays.' He coughed. 'Now, if it so happened that you wanted to buy it, that'd cost you four dollars. I can remember when a thing like that would have fetched eight pounds, and eight pounds was—well, I can't work it out, but it was a lot of money. But who cares about genuine antiques nowadays—even the few that's left?'

Winston immediately paid over the four dollars and slid the coveted thing into his pocket. What appealed to him about it was not so much its beauty as the air it seemed to possess of belonging to an age quite different from the present one. The soft, rainwatery glass was not like any glass that he had ever seen. The thing was doubly attractive because of its apparent uselessness, though he could guess that it must once have been intended as a paperweight. It was very heavy in his pocket, but fortunately it did not make much of a bulge. It was a queer thing, even a compromising thing, for a Party member to have in his possession. Anything old, and for that matter anything beautiful, was always vaguely suspect. The old man had grown noticeably more cheerful after receiving the four dollars. Winston realized that he would have accepted three or even two.

'There's another room upstairs that you might care to take a look at,' he said. 'There's not much in it. Just a few pieces. We'll do with a light if we're going upstairs.'

He lit another lamp, and, with bowed back, led the way slowly up the steep and worn stairs and along a tiny passage, into a room which did not give on the street but looked out on a cobbled yard and a forest of chimney-pots. Winston noticed that the furniture was still arranged as though the room were meant to be lived in. There was a strip of carpet on the floor, a picture or two on the walls, and a deep, slatternly armchair drawn up to the fireplace. An old-fashioned glass clock with a twelve-hour face was ticking away on the mantelpiece. Under the window, and occupying nearly a quarter of the room, was an enormous bed with the mattress still on it.

'We lived here till my wife died,' said the old man half apologetically. 'I'm selling the furniture off by little and little. Now that's a beautiful mahogany bed, or at least it would be if you could get the bugs out of it. But I dare say you'd find it a little bit cumbersome.'

He was holding the lamp high up, so as to illumine the whole room, and in the warm dim light the place looked curiously inviting. The thought flitted through Winston's mind that it would probably be quite easy to rent the room for a few dollars a week, if he dared to take the risk. It was a wild, impossible notion, to be abandoned as soon as thought of; but the room had awakened in him a sort of nostalgia, a sort of ancestral memory. It seemed to him that he knew exactly what it felt like to sit in a room like this, in an armchair beside an open fire with your feet in the fender and a kettle on the hob; utterly alone, utterly secure, with nobody watching you, no voice pursuing you, no sound except the singing of the kettle and the friendly ticking of the clock.

'There's no telescreen!' he could not help murmuring.

'Ah,' said the old man, 'I never had one of those things. Too expensive. And I never seemed to feel the need of it, somehow. Now that's a nice gateleg table in the corner there. Though of course you'd have to put new hinges on it if you wanted to use the flaps.'

There was a small bookcase in the other corner, and Winston had already gravitated towards it. It contained nothing but rubbish. The hunting-down and destruction of books had been done with the same thoroughness in the prole quarters as everywhere else. It was very unlikely that there existed anywhere in Oceania a copy of a book printed earlier than 1960. The old man, still carrying the lamp, was standing in front of a picture in a rosewood frame which hung on the other side of the fireplace, opposite the bed.

'Now, if you happen to be interested in old prints at all–' he began delicately.

Winston came across to examine the picture. It was a steel engraving of an oval building with rectangular windows, and a small tower in front. There was a railing running round the building, and at the rear end there was what appeared to be a statue. Winston gazed at it for some moments. It seemed vaguely familiar, though he did not remember the statue.

'The frame's fixed to the wall,' said the old man, 'but I could unscrew it for you, I dare say.'

'I know that building,' said Winston finally. 'It's a ruin now. It's in the middle of the street outside the Palace of Justice.'

'That's right. Outside the Law Courts. It was bombed in–oh, many years ago. It was a church at one time. St Clement Danes, its name was.' He smiled apologetically, as though conscious of saying something slightly ridiculous, and added: 'Oranges and lemons, say the bells of St Clement's!'

'What's that?' said Winston.

'Oh–"Oranges and lemons, say the bells of St Clement's." That was a rhyme we had when I was a little boy. How it goes on I don't remember, but I do know it ended up, "Here comes a candle to light you to bed, Here comes a chopper to chop off your head." It was a kind of a dance. They held out their arms for you to pass under, and when they came to "Here comes a chopper to chop off your head" they brought their arms down and caught you. It was just names of churches. All the London churches were in it–all the principal ones, that is.'

Winston wondered vaguely to what century the church belonged. It was always difficult to determine the age of a London building. Anything large and impressive, if it was reasonably new in appearance, was automatically claimed as having been built since the Revolution, while anything that was obviously of earlier date was ascribed to some dim period called the Middle Ages. The centuries of capitalism were held to have produced nothing of any value. One could not learn history from architecture any more than one could learn it from books. Statues, inscriptions, memorial stones, the names of streets–anything that might throw light upon the past had been systematically altered.

'I never knew it had been a church,' he said.

'There's a lot of them left, really,' said the old man, 'though they've been put to other uses. Now, how did that rhyme go? Ah! I've got it!

> "Oranges and lemons, say the bells of St Clement's,
> You owe me three farthings, say the bells of St Martin's—"

there, now, that's as far as I can get. A farthing, that was a small copper coin, looked something like a cent.'

'Where was St Martin's?' said Winston.

'St Martin's? That's still standing. It's in Victory Square, alongside the picture gallery. A building with a kind of a triangular porch and pillars in front, and a big flight of steps.'

Winston knew the place well. It was a museum used for propaganda displays of various kinds—scale models of rocket bombs and Floating Fortresses, wax-work tableaux illustrating enemy atrocities, and the like.

'St Martin's-in-the-Fields it used to be called,' supplemented the old man, 'though I don't recollect any fields anywhere in those parts.'

Winston did not buy the picture. It would have been an even more incongruous possession than the glass paperweight, and impossible to carry home, unless it were taken out of its frame. But he lingered for some minutes more, talking to the old man, whose name, he discovered, was not Weeks—as one might have gathered from the inscription over the shop-front—but Charrington. Mr Charrington, it seemed, was a widower aged sixty-three and had inhabited this shop for thirty years. Throughout that time he had been intending to alter the name over the window, but had never quite got to the point of doing it. All the while that they were talking the half-remembered rhyme kept running through Winston's head. Oranges and lemons say the bells of St Clement's, You owe me three farthings, say the bells of St Martin's! It was curious, but when you said it to yourself you had the illusion of actually hearing bells, the bells of a lost London that still existed somewhere or other, disguised and forgotten. From one ghostly steeple after another he seemed to hear them pealing forth. Yet so far as he could remember he had never in real life heard church bells ringing.

He got away from Mr Charrington and went down the stairs alone, so as not to let the old man see him reconnoitring the street before stepping out of the door. He had already made up his mind that after a suitable interval—a month, say—he would take the risk of visiting the shop again. It was perhaps not more dangerous than shirking an evening at the Centre. The serious piece of folly had been to come back here in the first place, after buying the diary and without knowing whether the proprietor of the shop could be trusted. However—!

Yes, he thought again, he would come back. He would buy further scraps of beautiful rubbish. He would buy the engraving of St Clement Danes, take it out of its frame, and carry it home concealed under the jacket of his overalls. He would drag the rest of that poem out of Mr Charrington's memory. Even the lunatic project of renting the room upstairs flashed momentarily through his mind again. For perhaps five seconds exaltation made him careless, and he stepped out on to the pavement without so much as a preliminary glance through the window. He had even started humming to an improvised tune—

> Oranges and lemons, say the bells of St Clement's,
> You owe me three farthings, say the—

Suddenly his heart seemed to turn to ice and his bowels to water. A figure in blue overalls was coming down the pavement, not ten metres away. It was the girl from the Fiction Department, the girl with dark hair. The light was failing, but there was no difficulty in recognizing her. She looked him straight in the face, then walked quickly on as though she had not seen him.

For a few seconds Winston was too paralysed to move. Then he turned to the right and walked heavily away, not noticing for the moment that he was going in the wrong direction. At any rate, one question was settled. There was no doubting any longer that the girl was spying on him. She must have followed him here, because it was not credible that by pure chance she should have happened to be walking on the same evening up the same obscure back-street, kilometres distant from any quarter where Party members lived. It was too great a coincidence. Whether she was really an agent of the Thought Police, or simply an amateur spy actuated by officiousness, hardly mattered. It was enough that she was watching him. Probably she had seen him go into the pub as well.

It was an effort to walk. The lump of glass in his pocket banged against his thigh at each step, and he was half minded to take it out and throw it away. The worst thing was the pain in his belly. For a couple of minutes he had the feeling that he would die if he did not reach a lavatory soon. But there would be no public lavatories in a quarter like this. Then the spasm passed, leaving a dull ache behind.

The street was a blind alley. Winston halted, stood for several seconds wondering vaguely what to do, then turned round and began to retrace his steps. As he turned it occurred to him that the girl had only passed him three minutes ago and that by running he could probably catch up with her. He could keep on her track till they were in some quiet place, and then smash her skull in with a cobblestone. The piece of glass in his pocket would be heavy enough for the job. But he abandoned the idea immediately, because even the thought of making any physical effort was unbearable. He could not run, he could not strike a blow. Besides, she was young and lusty and would defend herself. He thought also of hurrying to the Community Centre and staying there till the place closed, so as to establish a partial alibi for the evening. But that too was impossible. A deadly lassitude had taken hold of him. All he wanted was to get home quickly and then sit down and be quiet.

It was after twenty-two hours when he got back to the flat. The lights would be switched off at the main at twenty-three thirty. He went into the kitchen and swallowed nearly a teacupful of Victory Gin. Then he went to the table in the alcove, sat down, and took the diary out of the drawer. But he did not open it at once. From the telescreen a brassy female voice was squalling a patriotic song. He sat staring at the marbled cover of the book, trying without success to shut the voice out of his consciousness.

It was at night that they came for you, always at night. The proper thing was to kill yourself before they got you. Undoubtedly some people did so. Many of the disappearances were actually suicides. But it needed desperate courage to kill yourself in a world where firearms, or any quick and certain poison, were completely unprocurable. He thought with a kind of astonishment of the biological uselessness of pain and fear, the treachery of the human body which always freezes into inertia at exactly the moment when a special effort is needed. He might have silenced the dark-haired girl if only he had acted quickly enough: but precisely because of the extremity of his danger he had lost the power to act. It struck him that in moments of crisis one is never fighting against an external enemy, but always against one's own body. Even now, in spite of the gin, the dull ache in his belly made consecutive thought impossible. And it is the same, he perceived, in all seemingly heroic or tragic situations. On the battlefield, in the torture chamber, on a sinking ship, the issues that you are fighting for are always forgotten, because the body swells up until it fills the universe, and even when you are not paralysed by fright or screaming with pain, life is a moment-to-moment struggle against hunger or cold or sleeplessness, against a sour stomach or an aching tooth.

He opened the diary. It was important to write something down. The woman on the telescreen had started a new song. Her voice seemed to stick into his brain like jagged splinters of glass. He tried to think of O'Brien, for whom, or to whom, the diary was written, but instead he began thinking of the things that would happen to him after the Thought Police took him away. It would not matter if they killed you at once. To be killed was what you expected. But before death (nobody spoke of such things, yet everybody knew of them) there was the routine of confession that had to be gone through: the grovelling on the floor and screaming for mercy, the crack of broken bones, the smashed teeth, and bloody clots of hair. Why did you have to endure it, since the end was always the same? Why was it not possible to cut a few days or weeks out of your life? Nobody ever escaped detection, and nobody ever failed to confess. When once you had succumbed to thoughtcrime it was certain that by a given date you would be dead. Why then did that horror, which altered nothing, have to lie embedded in future time?

He tried with a little more success than before to summon up the image of O'Brien. 'We shall meet in the place where there is no darkness,' O'Brien had said to him. He knew what it meant, or thought he knew. The place where there is no darkness was the imagined future, which one would never see, but which, by foreknowledge, one could mystically share in. But with the voice from the telescreen nagging at his ears he could not follow the train of thought further. He put a cigarette in his mouth. Half the tobacco promptly fell out on to his tongue, a bitter dust which was difficult to spit out again. The face of Big Brother swam into his mind, displacing that of O'Brien. Just as he had done a few days earlier, he slid a coin out of his pocket and looked at it. The face gazed up at him, heavy, calm, protecting: but what kind of smile was hidden beneath the dark moustache? Like a leaden knell the words came back at him:

WAR IS PEACE
FREEDOM IS SLAVERY
IGNORANCE IS STRENGTH

# PART II

## I

It was the middle of the morning, and Winston had left the cubicle to go to the lavatory.

A solitary figure was coming towards him from the other end of the long, brightly lit corridor. It was the girl with dark hair. Four days had gone past since the evening when he had run into her outside the junk-shop. As she came nearer he saw that her right arm was in a sling, not noticeable at a distance because it was of the same colour as her overalls. Probably she had crushed her hand while swinging round one of the big kaleidoscopes on which the plots of novels were 'roughed in'. It was a common accident in the Fiction Department.

They were perhaps four metres apart when the girl stumbled and fell almost flat on her face. A sharp cry of pain was wrung out of her. She must have fallen right on the injured arm. Winston stopped short. The girl had risen to her knees. Her face had turned a milky yellow colour against which her mouth stood out redder than ever. Her eyes were fixed on his, with an appealing expression that looked more like fear than pain.

A curious emotion stirred in Winston's heart. In front of him was an enemy who was trying to kill him: in front of him, also, was a human creature, in pain and perhaps with a broken bone. Already he had instinctively started forward to help her. In the moment when he had seen her fall on the bandaged arm, it had been as though he felt the pain in his own body.

'You're hurt?' he said.

'It's nothing. My arm. It'll be all right in a second.'

She spoke as though her heart were fluttering. She had certainly turned very pale.

'You haven't broken anything?'

'No, I'm all right. It hurt for a moment, that's all.'

She held out her free hand to him, and he helped her up. She had regained some of her colour, and appeared very much better.

'It's nothing,' she repeated shortly. 'I only gave my wrist a bit of a bang. Thanks, comrade!'

And with that she walked on in the direction in which she had been going, as briskly as though it had really been nothing. The whole incident could not have taken as much as half a minute. Not to let one's feelings appear in one's face was a habit that had acquired the status of an instinct, and in any case they had been standing straight in front of a telescreen when the thing happened. Nevertheless it had been very difficult not to betray a momentary surprise, for in the two or three seconds while he was helping her up the girl had slipped something into his hand. There was no question that she had done it intentionally. It was something small and flat. As he passed through the lavatory door he transferred it to his pocket and felt it with the tips of his fingers. It was a scrap of paper folded into a square.

While he stood at the urinal he managed, with a little more fingering, to get it unfolded. Obviously there must be a message of some kind written on it. For a moment he was tempted to take it into one of the water-closets and read it at once. But that would be shocking folly, as he well knew. There was no place where you could be more certain that the telescreens were watched continuously.

He went back to his cubicle, sat down, threw the fragment of paper casually among the other papers on the desk, put on his spectacles and hitched the speakwrite towards him. 'Five minutes,' he told himself, 'five minutes at the very least!' His heart bumped in his breast with frightening loudness. Fortunately the piece of work he was engaged on was mere routine, the rectification of a long list of figures, not needing close attention.

Whatever was written on the paper, it must have some kind of political meaning. So far as he could see there were two possibilities. One, much the more likely, was that the girl was an agent of the Thought Police, just as he had feared. He did not know why the Thought Police should choose to deliver their messages in such a fashion, but perhaps they had their reasons. The thing that was written on the paper might be a threat, a summons, an order to commit suicide, a trap of some description. But there was another, wilder possibility that kept raising its head, though he tried vainly to suppress it. This was, that the message did not come from the Thought Police at all, but from some kind of underground organization. Perhaps the Brotherhood existed after all! Perhaps the girl was part of it! No doubt the idea was absurd, but it had sprung into his mind in the very instant of feeling the scrap of paper in his hand. It was not till a couple of minutes later that the other, more probable explanation had occurred to him. And even now, though his intellect told him that the message probably meant death—still, that was not what he believed, and the unreasonable hope persisted, and his heart banged, and it was with difficulty that he kept his voice from trembling as he murmured his figures into the speakwrite.

He rolled up the completed bundle of work and slid it into the pneumatic tube. Eight minutes had gone by. He readjusted his spectacles on his nose, sighed, and drew the next batch of work towards him, with the scrap of paper on top of it. He flattened it out. On it was written, in a large unformed handwriting:

I love you.

For several seconds he was too stunned even to throw the incriminating thing into the memory hole. When he did so, although he knew very well the danger of showing too much interest, he could not resist reading it once again, just to make sure that the words were really there.

For the rest of the morning it was very difficult to work. What was even worse than having to focus his mind on a series of niggling jobs was the need to conceal his agitation from the telescreen. He felt as though a fire were burning in his belly. Lunch in the hot, crowded, noise-filled canteen was torment. He had hoped to be alone for a little while during the lunch hour, but as bad luck would have it the imbecile Parsons flopped down beside him, the tang of his sweat almost defeating the tinny smell of stew, and kept up a stream of talk about the preparations for Hate Week. He was particularly enthusiastic about a papier mâché model of Big Brother's head, two metres wide, which was being made for the occasion by his daughter's troop of Spies. The irritating thing was that in the racket of voices Winston could hardly hear what Parsons was saying, and was constantly having to ask for some fatuous remark to be repeated. Just once he caught a glimpse of the girl, at a table with two other girls at the far end of the room. She appeared not to have seen him, and he did not look in that direction again.

The afternoon was more bearable. Immediately after lunch there arrived a delicate, difficult piece of work which would take several hours and necessitated putting everything else aside. It consisted in falsifying a series of production reports of two years ago, in such a way as to cast discredit on a prominent member of the Inner Party, who was now under a cloud. This was the kind of thing that Winston was good at, and for more than two hours he succeeded in shutting the girl out of his mind altogether. Then the memory of her face came back, and with it a raging, intolerable desire to be alone. Until he could be alone it was impossible to think this new development out. Tonight was one of his nights at the Community Centre. He wolfed another tasteless meal in the canteen, hurried off to the Centre, took part in the solemn foolery of a 'discussion group', played two games of table tennis, swallowed several glasses of gin, and sat for half an hour through a lecture entitled 'Ingsoc in relation to chess'. His soul writhed with boredom, but for once he had had no impulse to shirk his evening at the Centre. At the sight of the words *I love you* the desire to stay alive had welled up in him, and the taking of minor risks suddenly seemed stupid. It was not till twenty-three hours, when he was home and in bed—in the darkness, where you were safe even from the telescreen so long as you kept silent—that he was able to think continuously.

It was a physical problem that had to be solved: how to get in touch with the girl and arrange a meeting. He did not consider any longer the possibility that she might be laying some kind of trap for him. He knew that it was not so, because of her unmistakable agitation when she handed him the note. Obviously she had been frightened out of her wits, as well she might be. Nor did the idea of refusing her advances even cross his mind. Only five nights ago he had contemplated smashing her skull in with a cobblestone, but that was of no importance. He thought of her naked, youthful body, as he had seen it in his dream. He had imagined her a fool like all the rest of them, her head stuffed with lies and hatred, her belly full of ice. A kind of fever seized him at the thought that he might lose her, the white youthful body might slip away from him! What he feared more than anything else was that she would simply change her mind if he did not get in touch with her quickly. But the physical difficulty of meeting was enormous. It was like trying to make a move at chess when you were already mated. Whichever way you turned, the telescreen faced you. Actually, all the possible ways of communicating with her had occurred to him within five minutes of reading the note; but now, with time to think, he went over them one by one, as though laying out a row of instruments on a table.

Obviously the kind of encounter that had happened this morning could not be repeated. If she had worked in the Records Department it might have been comparatively simple, but he had only a very dim idea whereabouts in the building the Fiction Department lay, and he had no pretext for going there. If he had known where she lived, and at what time she left work, he could have contrived to meet her somewhere on her way home; but to try to follow her home was not safe, because it would mean loitering about outside the Ministry, which was bound to be noticed. As for sending a letter through the mails, it was out of the question. By a routine that was not even secret, all letters were opened in transit. Actually, few people ever wrote letters. For the messages that it was occasionally necessary to send, there were printed postcards with long lists of phrases, and you struck out the ones that were inapplicable. In any case he did not know the girl's name, let alone her address. Finally he decided that the safest place was the canteen. If he could get her at a table by herself, somewhere in the middle of the room, not too near the telescreens, and with a sufficient buzz of conversation all round—if these conditions endured for, say, thirty seconds, it might be possible to exchange a few words.

For a week after this, life was like a restless dream. On the next day she did not appear in the canteen until he was leaving it, the whistle having already blown. Presumably she had been changed on to a later shift. They passed each other without a glance. On the day after that she was in the canteen at the usual time, but with three other girls and immediately under a telescreen. Then for three dreadful days she did not appear at all. His whole mind and body seemed to be afflicted with an unbearable sensitivity, a sort of transparency, which made every movement, every sound, every contact, every word that he had to speak or listen to, an agony. Even in sleep he could not altogether escape from her image. He did not touch the diary during those days. If there was any relief, it was in his work, in which he could sometimes forget himself for ten minutes at a stretch. He had absolutely no clue as to what had happened to her. There was no enquiry he could make. She might have been vaporized, she might have committed suicide, she might have been transferred to the other end of Oceania: worst and likeliest of all, she might simply have changed her mind and decided to avoid him.

The next day she reappeared. Her arm was out of the sling and she had a band of sticking-plaster round her wrist. The relief of seeing her was so great that he could not resist staring directly at her for several seconds. On the following day he very nearly succeeded in speaking to her. When he came into the canteen she was sitting at a table well out from the wall, and was quite alone. It was early, and the place was not very full. The queue edged forward till Winston was almost at the counter, then was held up for two minutes because someone in front was complaining that he had not received his tablet of saccharine. But the girl was still alone when Winston secured his tray and began to make for her table. He walked casually towards her, his eyes searching for a place at some table beyond her. She was perhaps three metres away from him. Another two seconds would do it. Then a voice behind him called, 'Smith!' He pretended not to hear. 'Smith!' repeated the voice, more loudly. It was no use. He turned round. A blond-headed, silly-faced young man named Wilsher, whom he barely knew, was inviting him with a smile to a vacant place at his table. It was not safe to refuse. After having been recognized, he could not go and sit at a table with an unattended girl. It was too noticeable. He sat down with a friendly smile. The silly blond face beamed into his. Winston had a hallucination of himself smashing a pick-axe right into the middle of it. The girl's table filled up a few minutes later.

But she must have seen him coming towards her, and perhaps she would take the hint. Next day he took care to arrive early. Sure enough, she was at a table in about the same place, and again alone. The person immediately ahead of him in the queue was a small, swiftly moving, beetle-like man with a flat face and tiny, suspicious eyes. As Winston turned away from the counter with his tray, he saw that the little man was making straight for the girl's table. His hopes sank again. There was a vacant place at a table farther away, but something in the little man's appearance suggested that he would be sufficiently attentive to his own comfort to choose the emptiest table. With ice at his heart Winston followed. It was no use unless he could get the girl alone. At this moment there was a tremendous crash. The little man was sprawling on all fours, his tray had gone flying, two streams of soup and coffee were flowing across the floor. He started to his feet with a malignant glance at Winston, whom he evidently suspected of having tripped him up. But it was all right. Five seconds later, with a thundering heart, Winston was sitting at the girl's table.

He did not look at her. He unpacked his tray and promptly began eating. It was all-important to speak at once, before anyone else came, but now a terrible fear had taken possession of him. A week had gone by since she had first approached him. She would have changed her mind, she must have changed her mind! It was impossible that this affair should end successfully; such things did not happen in real life. He might have flinched altogether from speaking if at this moment he had not seen Ampleforth, the hairy-eared poet, wandering limply round the room with a tray, looking for a place to sit down. In his vague way Ampleforth was attached to Winston, and would certainly sit down at his table if he caught sight of him. There was perhaps a minute in which to act. Both Winston and the girl were eating steadily. The stuff they were eating was a thin stew, actually a soup, of haricot beans. In a low murmur Winston began speaking. Neither of them looked up; steadily they spooned the watery stuff into their mouths, and between spoonfuls exchanged the few necessary words in low expressionless voices.

'What time do you leave work?'

'Eighteen thirty.'

'Where can we meet?'

'Victory Square, near the monument.'

'It's full of telescreens.'

'It doesn't matter if there's a crowd.'

'Any signal?'

'No. Don't come up to me until you see me among a lot of people. And don't look at me. Just keep somewhere near me.'

'What time?'

'Nineteen hours.'

'All right.'

Ampleforth failed to see Winston and sat down at another table. They did not speak again, and, so far as it was possible for two people sitting on opposite sides of the same table, they did not look at one another. The girl finished her lunch quickly and made off, while Winston stayed to smoke a cigarette.

Winston was in Victory Square before the appointed time. He wandered round the base of the enormous fluted column, at the top of which Big Brother's statue gazed southward towards the skies where he had vanquished the Eurasian aeroplanes (the Eastasian aeroplanes, it had been, a few years ago) in the Battle of Airstrip One. In the street in front of it there was a statue of a man on horseback which was supposed to represent Oliver Cromwell. At five minutes past the hour the girl had still not appeared. Again the terrible fear seized upon Winston. She was not coming, she had changed her mind! He walked slowly up to the north side of the square and got a sort of pale-coloured pleasure from identifying St Martin's Church, whose bells, when it had bells, had chimed 'You owe me three farthings.' Then he saw the girl standing at the base of the monument, reading or pretending to read a poster which ran spirally up the column. It was not safe to go near her until some more people had accumulated. There were telescreens all round the pediment. But at this moment there was a din of shouting and a zoom of heavy vehicles from somewhere to the left. Suddenly everyone seemed to be running across the square. The girl nipped nimbly round the lions at the base of the monument and joined in the rush. Winston followed. As he ran, he gathered from some shouted remarks that a convoy of Eurasian prisoners was passing.

Already a dense mass of people was blocking the south side of the square. Winston, at normal times the kind of person who gravitates to the outer edge of any kind of scrimmage, shoved, butted, squirmed his way forward into the heart of the crowd. Soon he was within arm's length of the girl, but the way was blocked by an enormous prole and an almost equally enormous woman, presumably his wife, who seemed to form an impenetrable wall of flesh. Winston wriggled himself sideways, and with a violent lunge managed to drive his shoulder between them. For a moment it felt as though his entrails were being ground to pulp between the two muscular hips, then he had broken through, sweating a little. He was next to the girl. They were shoulder to shoulder, both staring fixedly in front of them.

A long line of trucks, with wooden-faced guards armed with sub-machine guns standing upright in each corner, was passing slowly down the street. In the trucks little yellow men in shabby greenish uniforms were squatting, jammed close together. Their sad, Mongolian faces gazed out over the sides of the trucks utterly incurious. Occasionally when a truck jolted there was a clank-clank of metal: all the prisoners were wearing leg-irons. Truck-load after truck-load of the sad faces passed. Winston knew they were there but he saw them only intermittently. The girl's shoulder, and her arm right down to the elbow, were pressed against his. Her cheek was almost near enough for him to feel its warmth. She had immediately taken charge of the situation, just as she had done in the canteen. She began speaking in the same expressionless voice as before, with lips barely moving, a mere murmur easily drowned by the din of voices and the rumbling of the trucks.

'Can you hear me?'

'Yes.'

'Can you get Sunday afternoon off?'

'Yes.'

'Then listen carefully. You'll have to remember this. Go to Paddington Station—'

With a sort of military precision that astonished him, she outlined the route that he was to follow. A half-hour railway journey; turn left outside the station; two kilometres along the road: a gate with the top bar missing; a path across a field; a grass-grown lane; a track between bushes; a dead tree with moss on it. It was as though she had a map inside her head. 'Can you remember all that?' she murmured finally.

'Yes.'

'You turn left, then right, then left again. And the gate's got no top bar.'

'Yes. What time?'

'About fifteen. You may have to wait. I'll get there by another way. Are you sure you remember everything?'

'Yes.'

'Then get away from me as quick as you can.'

She need not have told him that. But for the moment they could not extricate themselves from the crowd. The trucks were still filing past, the people still insatiably gaping. At the start there had been a few boos and hisses, but it came only from the Party members among the crowd, and had soon stopped. The prevailing emotion was simply curiosity. Foreigners, whether from Eurasia or from Eastasia, were a kind of strange animal. One literally never saw them except in the guise of prisoners, and even as prisoners one never got more than a momentary glimpse of them. Nor did one know what became of them, apart from the few who were hanged as war-criminals: the others simply vanished, presumably into forced-labour camps. The round

Mongol faces had given way to faces of a more European type, dirty, bearded, and exhausted. From over scrubby cheekbones eyes looked into Winston's, sometimes with strange intensity, and flashed away again. The convoy was drawing to an end. In the last truck he could see an aged man, his face a mass of grizzled hair, standing upright with wrists crossed in front of him, as though he were used to having them bound together. It was almost time for Winston and the girl to part. But at the last moment, while the crowd still hemmed them in, her hand felt for his and gave it a fleeting squeeze.

It could not have been ten seconds, and yet it seemed a long time that their hands were clasped together. He had time to learn every detail of her hand. He explored the long fingers, the shapely nails, the work-hardened palm with its row of callouses, the smooth flesh under the wrist. Merely from feeling it he would have known it by sight. In the same instant it occurred to him that he did not know what colour the girl's eyes were. They were probably brown, but people with dark hair sometimes had blue eyes. To turn his head and look at her would have been inconceivable folly. With hands locked together, invisible among the press of bodies, they stared steadily in front of them, and instead of the eyes of the girl, the eyes of the aged prisoner gazed mournfully at Winston out of nests of hair.

## 2

Winston picked his way up the lane through dappled light and shade, stepping out into pools of gold wherever the boughs parted. Under the trees to the left of him the ground was misty with bluebells. The air seemed to kiss one's skin. It was the second of May. From somewhere deeper in the heart of the wood came the droning of ring-doves.

He was a bit early. There had been no difficulties about the journey, and the girl was so evidently experienced that he was less frightened than he would normally have been. Presumably she could be trusted to find a safe place. In general you could not assume that you were much safer in the country than in London. There were no telescreens, of course, but there was always the danger of concealed microphones by which your voice might be picked up and recognized; besides, it was not easy to make a journey by yourself without attracting attention. For distances of less than 100 kilometres it was not necessary to get your passport endorsed, but sometimes there were patrols hanging about the railway stations, who examined the papers of any Party member they found there and asked awkward questions. However, no patrols had appeared, and on the walk from the station he had made sure by cautious backward glances that he was not being followed. The train was full of proles, in holiday mood because of the summery weather. The wooden-seated carriage in which he travelled was filled to overflowing by a single enormous family, ranging from a toothless great-grandmother to a month-old baby, going out to spend an afternoon with 'in-laws' in the country, and, as they freely explained to Winston, to get hold of a little black-market butter.

The lane widened, and in a minute he came to the footpath she had told him of, a mere cattle-track which plunged between the bushes. He had no watch, but it could not be fifteen yet. The bluebells were so thick underfoot that it was impossible not to tread on them. He knelt down and began picking some, partly to pass the time away, but also from a vague idea that he would like to have a bunch of flowers to offer to the girl when they met. He had got together a big bunch and was smelling their faint sickly scent when a sound at his back froze him, the unmistakable crackle of a foot on twigs. He went on picking bluebells. It was the best thing to do. It might be the girl, or he might have been followed after all. A hand fell lightly on his shoulder.

He looked up. It was the girl. She shook her head, evidently as a warning that he must keep silent, then parted the bushes and quickly led the way along the narrow track into the wood. Obviously she had been that way before, for she dodged the boggy bits as though by habit. Winston followed, still clasping his bunch of flowers. His first feeling was relief, but as he watched the strong slender body moving in front of him, with the scarlet sash that was just tight enough to bring out the curve of her hips, the sense of his own inferiority was heavy upon him. Even now it seemed quite likely that when she turned round and looked at him she would draw back after all. The sweetness of the air and the greenness of the leaves daunted him. Already on the walk from the station the May sunshine had made him feel dirty and etiolated, a creature of indoors, with the sooty dust of London in the pores of his skin. It occurred to him that till now she had probably never seen him in broad daylight in the open. They came to the fallen tree that she had spoken of. The girl hopped over and forced apart the bushes, in which there did not seem to be an opening. When Winston followed her, he found that they were in a natural clearing, a tiny grassy knoll surrounded by tall saplings that shut it in completely. The girl stopped and turned.

'Here we are,' she said.

He was facing her at several paces' distance. As yet he did not dare move nearer to her.

'I didn't want to say anything in the lane,' she went on, 'in case there's a mike hidden there. I don't suppose there is, but there could be. There's always the chance of one of those swine recognizing your voice. We're all right here.'

He still had not the courage to approach her. 'We're all right here?' he repeated stupidly

'Yes. Look at the trees.' They were small ashes, which at some time had been cut down and had sprouted up again into a forest of poles, none of them thicker than one's wrist. 'There's nothing big enough to hide a mike in. Besides, I've been here before.'

They were only making conversation. He had managed to move closer to her now. She stood before him very upright, with a smile on her face that looked faintly ironical, as though she were wondering why he was so slow to act. The bluebells had cascaded on to the ground. They seemed to have fallen of their own accord. He took her hand.

'Would you believe,' he said, 'that till this moment I didn't know what colour your eyes were?' They were brown, he noted, a rather light shade of brown, with dark lashes. 'Now that you've seen what I'm really like, can you still bear to look at me?'

'Yes, easily.'

'I'm thirty-nine years old. I've got a wife that I can't get rid of. I've got varicose veins. I've got five false teeth.'

'I couldn't care less,' said the girl.

The next moment, it was hard to say by whose act, she was in his arms. At the beginning he had no feeling except sheer incredulity. The youthful body was strained against his own, the mass of dark hair was against his face, and yes! actually she had turned her face up and he was kissing the wide red mouth. She had clasped her arms about his neck, she was calling him darling, precious one, loved one. He had pulled her down on to the ground, she was utterly unresisting, he could do what he liked with her. But the truth was that he had no physical sensation, except that of mere contact. All he felt was incredulity and pride. He was glad that this was happening, but he had no physical desire. It was too soon, her youth and prettiness had frightened him, he was too much used to living without women—he did not know the reason. The girl picked herself up and pulled a bluebell out of her hair. She sat against him, putting her arm round his waist.

'Never mind, dear. There's no hurry. We've got the whole afternoon. Isn't this a splendid hideout? I found it when I got lost once on a community hike. If anyone was coming you could hear them a hundred metres away.'

'What is your name?' said Winston.

'Julia. I know yours. It's Winston—Winston Smith.'

'How did you find that out?'

'I expect I'm better at finding things out than you are, dear. Tell me, what did you think of me before that day I gave you the note?'

He did not feel any temptation to tell lies to her. It was even a sort of love-offering to start off by telling the worst.

'I hated the sight of you,' he said. 'I wanted to rape you and then murder you afterwards. Two weeks ago I thought seriously of smashing your head in with a cobblestone. If you really want to know, I imagined that you had something to do with the Thought Police.'

The girl laughed delightedly, evidently taking this as a tribute to the excellence of her disguise.

'Not the Thought Police! You didn't honestly think that?'

'Well, perhaps not exactly that. But from your general appearance—merely because you're young and fresh and healthy, you understand—I thought that probably—'

'You thought I was a good Party member. Pure in word and deed. Banners, processions, slogans, games, community hikes—all that stuff. And you thought that if I had a quarter of a chance I'd denounce you as a thought-criminal and get you killed off?'

'Yes, something of that kind. A great many young girls are like that, you know.'

'It's this bloody thing that does it,' she said, ripping off the scarlet sash of the Junior Anti-Sex League and flinging it on to a bough. Then, as though touching her waist had reminded her of something, she felt in the pocket of her overalls and produced a small slab of chocolate. She broke it in half and gave one of the pieces to Winston. Even before he had taken it he knew by the smell that it was very unusual chocolate. It was dark and shiny, and was wrapped in silver paper. Chocolate normally was dull-brown crumbly stuff that tasted, as nearly as one could describe it, like the smoke of a rubbish fire. But at some time or another he had tasted chocolate like the piece she had given him. The first whiff of its scent had stirred up some memory which he could not pin down, but which was powerful and troubling.

'Where did you get this stuff?' he said.

'Black market,' she said indifferently. 'Actually I am that sort of girl, to look at. I'm good at games. I was a troop-leader in the Spies. I do voluntary work three evenings a week for the Junior Anti-Sex League. Hours and hours I've spent pasting their bloody rot all over London. I always carry one end of a banner in the processions. I always look cheerful and I never shirk anything. Always yell with the crowd, that's what I say. It's the only way to be safe.'

The first fragment of chocolate had melted on Winston's tongue. The taste was delightful. But there was still that memory moving round the edges of his consciousness, something strongly felt but not reducible to definite shape, like an object seen out of the corner of one's eye. He pushed it away from him, aware only that it was the memory of some action which he would have liked to undo but could not.

'You are very young,' he said. 'You are ten or fifteen years younger than I am. What could you see to attract you in a man like me?'

'It was something in your face. I thought I'd take a chance. I'm good at spotting people who don't belong. As soon as I saw you I knew you were against *them*.'

*Them*, it appeared, meant the Party, and above all the Inner Party, about whom she talked with an open jeering hatred which made Winston feel uneasy, although he knew that they were safe here if they could be safe anywhere. A thing that astonished him about her was the coarseness of her language. Party members were supposed not to swear, and Winston himself very seldom did swear, aloud, at any rate. Julia, however, seemed unable to mention the Party, and especially the Inner Party, without using the kind of words that you saw chalked up in dripping alley-ways. He did not dislike it. It was merely one symptom of her revolt against the Party and all its ways, and somehow it seemed natural and healthy, like the sneeze of a horse that smells bad hay. They had left the clearing and were wandering again through the chequered shade, with their arms round each other's waists whenever it was wide enough to walk two abreast. He noticed how much softer her waist seemed to feel now that the sash was gone. They did not speak above a whisper. Outside the clearing, Julia said, it was better to go quietly. Presently they had reached the edge of the little wood. She stopped him.

'Don't go out into the open. There might be someone watching. We're all right if we keep behind the boughs.'

They were standing in the shade of hazel bushes. The sunlight, filtering through innumerable leaves, was still hot on their faces. Winston looked out into the field beyond, and underwent a curious, slow shock of recognition. He knew it by sight. An old, close-bitten pasture, with a footpath wandering across it and a molehill here and there. In the ragged hedge on the opposite side the boughs of the elm trees swayed just perceptibly in the breeze, and their leaves stirred faintly in dense masses like women's hair. Surely somewhere near by, but out of sight, there must be a stream with green pools where dace were swimming?

'Isn't there a stream somewhere near here?' he whispered.

'That's right, there is a stream. It's at the edge of the next field, actually. There are fish in it, great big ones. You can watch them lying in the pools under the willow trees, waving their tails.'

'It's the Golden Country—almost,' he murmured.

'The Golden Country?'

'It's nothing, really. A landscape I've seen sometimes in a dream.'

'Look!' whispered Julia.

A thrush had alighted on a bough not five metres away, almost at the level of their faces. Perhaps it had not seen them. It was in the sun, they in the shade. It spread out its wings, fitted them carefully into place again, ducked its head for a moment, as though making a sort of obeisance to the sun, and then began to pour forth a torrent of song. In the afternoon hush the volume of sound was startling. Winston and Julia clung together, fascinated. The music went on and on, minute after minute, with astonishing variations, never once repeating itself, almost as though the bird were deliberately showing off its virtuosity. Sometimes it stopped for a few seconds, spread out and resettled its wings, then swelled its speckled breast and again burst into song. Winston watched it with a sort of vague reverence. For whom, for what, was that bird singing? No mate, no rival was watching it. What made it sit at the edge of the lonely wood and pour its music into nothingness? He wondered whether after all there was a microphone hidden somewhere near. He and Julia had only spoken in low whispers, and it would not pick up what they had said, but it would pick up the thrush. Perhaps at the other end of the instrument some small, beetle-like man was listening intently—listening to *that*. But by degrees the flood of music drove all speculations out of his mind. It was as though it were a kind of liquid stuff that poured all over him and got mixed up with the sunlight that filtered through the leaves. He stopped thinking and merely felt. The girl's waist in the bend of his arm was soft and warm. He pulled her round so that they were breast to breast; her body seemed to melt into his. Wherever his hands moved it was all as yielding as water. Their mouths clung together; it was quite different from the hard kisses they had exchanged earlier. When they moved their faces apart again both of them sighed deeply. The bird took fright and fled with a clatter of wings.

Winston put his lips against her ear. '*Now*,' he whispered.

'Not here,' she whispered back. 'Come back to the hideout. It's safer.'

Quickly, with an occasional crackle of twigs, they threaded their way back to the clearing. When they were once inside the ring of saplings she turned and faced him. They were both breathing fast, but the smile had reappeared round the corners of her mouth. She stood looking at him for an instant, then felt at the zipper of her overalls. And, yes! it was almost as in his dream. Almost as swiftly as he had imagined it, she had torn her clothes off, and when she flung them aside it was with that same magnificent gesture by which a whole civilization seemed to be annihilated. Her body gleamed white in the sun. But for a moment he did not look at her body; his eyes were anchored by the freckled face with its faint, bold smile. He knelt down before her and took her hands in his.

'Have you done this before?'

'Of course. Hundreds of times—well, scores of times anyway.'

'With Party members?'

'Yes, always with Party members.'

'With members of the Inner Party?'

'Not with those swine, no. But there's plenty that *would* if they got half a chance. They're not so holy as they make out.'

His heart leapt. Scores of times she had done it: he wished it had been hundreds—thousands. Anything that hinted at corruption always filled him with a wild hope. Who knew, perhaps the Party was rotten under the surface, its cult of strenuousness and self-denial simply a sham concealing iniquity. If he could have infected the whole lot of them with leprosy or syphilis, how gladly he would have done so! Anything to rot, to weaken, to undermine! He pulled her down so that they were kneeling face to face.

'Listen. The more men you've had, the more I love you. Do you understand that?'

'Yes, perfectly.'

'I hate purity, I hate goodness! I don't want any virtue to exist anywhere. I want everyone to be corrupt to the bones.'

'Well then, I ought to suit you, dear. I'm corrupt to the bones.'

'You like doing this? I don't mean simply me: I mean the thing in itself?'

'I adore it.'

That was above all what he wanted to hear. Not merely the love of one person but the animal instinct, the simple undifferentiated desire: that was the force that would tear the Party to pieces. He pressed her down upon the grass, among the fallen bluebells. This time there was no difficulty. Presently the rising and falling of their breasts slowed to normal speed, and in a sort of pleasant helplessness they fell apart. The sun seemed to have grown hotter. They were both sleepy. He reached out for the discarded overalls and pulled them partly over her. Almost immediately they fell asleep and slept for about half an hour.

Winston woke first. He sat up and watched the freckled face, still peacefully asleep, pillowed on the palm of her hand. Except for her mouth, you could not call her beautiful. There was a line or two round the eyes, if you looked closely. The short dark hair was extraordinarily thick and soft. It occurred to him that he still did not know her surname or where she lived.

The young, strong body, now helpless in sleep, awoke in him a pitying, protecting feeling. But the mindless tenderness that he had felt under the hazel tree, while the thrush was singing, had not quite come back. He pulled the overalls aside and studied her smooth white flank. In the old days, he thought, a man looked at a girl's body and saw that it was desirable, and that was the end of the story. But you could not have pure love or pure lust nowadays. No emotion was pure, because everything was mixed up with fear and hatred. Their embrace had been a battle, the climax a victory. It was a blow struck against the Party. It was a political act.

## 3

'We can come here once again,' said Julia. 'It's generally safe to use any hide-out twice. But not for another month or two, of course.'

As soon as she woke up her demeanour had changed. She became alert and business-like, put her clothes on, knotted the scarlet sash about her waist, and began arranging the details of the journey home. It seemed natural to leave this to her. She obviously had a practical cunning which Winston lacked, and she seemed also to have an exhaustive knowledge of the countryside round London, stored away from innumerable community hikes. The route she gave him was quite different from the one by which he had come, and brought him out at a different railway station. 'Never go home the same way as you went out,' she said, as though enunciating an important general principle. She would leave first, and Winston was to wait half an hour before following her.

She had named a place where they could meet after work, four evenings hence. It was a street in one of the poorer quarters, where there was an open market which was generally crowded and noisy. She would be hanging about among the stalls, pretending to be in search of shoelaces or sewing-thread. If she judged that the coast was clear she would blow her nose when he approached: otherwise he was to walk past her without recognition. But with luck, in the middle of the crowd, it would be safe to talk for a quarter of an hour and arrange another meeting.

'And now I must go,' she said as soon as he had mastered his instructions. 'I'm due back at nineteen-thirty. I've got to put in two hours for the Junior Anti-Sex League, handing out leaflets, or something. Isn't it bloody? Give me a brush-down, would you? Have I got any twigs in my hair? Are you sure?

Then good-bye, my love, good-bye!'

She flung herself into his arms, kissed him almost violently, and a moment later pushed her way through the saplings and disappeared into the wood with very little noise. Even now he had not found out her surname or her address. However, it made no difference, for it was inconceivable that they could ever meet indoors or exchange any kind of written communication.

As it happened, they never went back to the clearing in the wood. During the month of May there was only one further occasion on which they actually succeeded in making love. That was in another hiding-place known to Julia, the belfry of a ruinous church in an almost-deserted stretch of country where an atomic bomb had fallen thirty years earlier. It was a good hiding-place when once you got there, but the getting there was very dangerous. For the rest they could meet only in the streets, in a different place every evening and never for more than half an hour at a time. In the street it was usually possible to talk, after a fashion. As they drifted down the crowded pavements, not quite abreast and never looking at one another, they carried on a curious, intermittent conversation which flicked on and off like the beams of a lighthouse, suddenly nipped into silence by the approach of a Party uniform or the proximity of a telescreen, then taken up again minutes later in the middle of a sentence, then abruptly cut short as they parted at the agreed spot, then continued almost without introduction on the following day. Julia appeared to be quite used to this kind of conversation, which she called 'talking by instalments'. She was also surprisingly adept at speaking without moving her lips. Just once in almost a month of nightly meetings they managed to exchange a kiss. They were passing in silence down a side-street (Julia would never speak when they were away from the main streets) when there was a deafening roar, the earth heaved, and the air darkened, and Winston found himself lying on his side, bruised and terrified. A rocket bomb must have dropped quite near at hand. Suddenly he became aware of Julia's face a few centimetres from his own, deathly white, as white as chalk. Even her lips were white. She was dead! He clasped her against him and found that he was kissing a live warm face. But there was some powdery stuff that got in the way of his lips. Both of their faces were thickly coated with plaster.

There were evenings when they reached their rendezvous and then had to walk past one another without a sign, because a patrol had just come round the corner or a helicopter was hovering overhead. Even if it had been less dangerous, it would still have been difficult to find time to meet. Winston's working week was sixty hours, Julia's was even longer, and their free days varied according to the pressure of work and did not often coincide. Julia, in any case, seldom had an evening completely free. She spent an astonishing amount of time in attending lectures and demonstrations, distributing literature for the Junior Anti-Sex League, preparing banners for Hate Week, making collections for the savings campaign, and such-like activities. It paid, she said; it was camouflage. If you kept the small rules, you could break the big ones. She even induced Winston to mortgage yet another of his evenings by enrolling himself for the part-time munition work which was done voluntarily by zealous Party members. So, one evening every week, Winston spent four hours of paralysing boredom, screwing together small bits of metal which were probably parts of bomb fuses, in a draughty, ill-lit workshop where the knocking of hammers mingled drearily with the music of the telescreens.

When they met in the church tower the gaps in their fragmentary conversation were filled up. It was a blazing afternoon. The air in the little square chamber above the bells was hot and stagnant, and smelt overpoweringly of pigeon-dung. They sat talking for hours on the dusty, twig-littered floor, one or other of them getting up from time to time to cast a glance through the arrowslits and make sure that no one was coming.

Julia was twenty-six years old. She lived in a hostel with thirty other girls ('Always in the stink of women! How I hate women!' she said parenthetically), and she worked, as he had guessed, on the novel-writing machines in the Fiction Department. She enjoyed her work, which consisted chiefly in running and servicing a powerful but tricky electric motor. She was 'not clever', but was fond of using her hands and felt at home with machinery. She could describe the whole process of composing a novel, from the general directive issued by the Planning Committee down to the final touching-up by the Rewrite Squad. But she was not interested in the finished product. She 'didn't much care for reading,' she said. Books were just a commodity that had to be produced, like jam or bootlaces.

She had no memories of anything before the early 'sixties, and the only person she had ever known who talked frequently of the days before the Revolution was a grandfather who had disappeared when she was eight. At school she had been captain of the hockey team and had won the gymnastics trophy two years running. She had been a troop-leader in the Spies and a branch secretary in the Youth League before joining the Junior Anti-Sex League. She had always borne an excellent character. She had even (an infallible mark of good reputation) been picked out to work in Pornosec, the sub-section of the Fiction Department which turned out cheap pornography for distribution among the proles. It was nicknamed Muck House by the people who worked in it, she remarked. There she had remained for a year, helping to produce booklets in sealed packets with titles like *Spanking Stories* or *One Night in a Girls' School*, to be bought furtively by proletarian youths who were under the impression that they were buying something illegal.

'What are these books like?' said Winston curiously.

'Oh, ghastly rubbish. They're boring, really. They only have six plots, but they swap them round a bit. Of course I was only on the kaleidoscopes. I was never in the Rewrite Squad. I'm not literary, dear—not even enough for that.'

He learned with astonishment that all the workers in Pornosec, except the heads of the departments, were girls. The theory was that men, whose sex instincts were less controllable then those of women, were in greater danger of being corrupted by the filth they handled.

'They don't even like having married women there,' she added. 'Girls are always supposed to be so pure. Here's one who isn't, anyway.'

She had had her first love-affair when she was sixteen, with a Party member of sixty who later committed suicide to avoid arrest. 'And a good job too,' said Julia, 'otherwise they'd have had my name out of him when he confessed.' Since then there had been various others. Life as she saw it was quite simple. You wanted a good time; 'they', meaning the Party, wanted to stop you having it; you broke the rules as best you could. She seemed to think it just as natural that 'they' should want to rob you of your pleasures as that you should want to avoid being caught. She hated the Party, and said so in the crudest words, but she made no general criticism of it. Except where it touched upon her own life she had no interest in Party doctrine. He noticed that she never used Newspeak words except the ones that had passed into everyday use. She had never heard of the Brotherhood, and refused to believe in its existence. Any kind of organized revolt against the Party, which was bound to be a failure, struck her as stupid. The clever thing was to break the rules and stay alive all the same. He wondered vaguely how many others like her there might be in the younger generation—people who had grown up in the world of the Revolution, knowing nothing else, accepting the Party as something unalterable, like the sky, not rebelling against its authority but simply evading it, as a rabbit dodges a dog.

They did not discuss the possibility of getting married. It was too remote to be worth thinking about. No imaginable committee would ever sanction such a marriage even if Katharine, Winston's wife, could somehow have been got rid of. It was hopeless even as a daydream.

'What was she like, your wife?' said Julia.

'She was—do you know the Newspeak word *goodthinkful*? Meaning naturally orthodox, incapable of thinking a bad thought?'

'No, I didn't know the word, but I know the kind of person, right enough.'

He began telling her the story of his married life, but curiously enough she appeared to know the essential parts of it already. She described to him, almost as though she had seen or felt it, the stiffening of Katharine's body as soon as he touched her, the way in which she still seemed to be pushing him from her with all her strength, even when her arms were clasped tightly round him. With Julia he felt no difficulty in talking about such things: Katharine, in any case, had long ceased to be a painful memory and became merely a distasteful one.

'I could have stood it if it hadn't been for one thing,' he said. He told her about the frigid little ceremony that Katharine had forced him to go through on the same night every week. 'She hated it, but nothing would make her stop doing it. She used to call it—but you'll never guess.'

'Our duty to the Party,' said Julia promptly.

'How did you know that?'

'I've been at school too, dear. Sex talks once a month for the over-sixteens. And in the Youth Movement. They rub it into you for years. I dare say it works in a lot of cases. But of course you can never tell; people are such hypocrites.'

She began to enlarge upon the subject. With Julia, everything came back to her own sexuality. As soon as this was touched upon in any way she was capable of great acuteness. Unlike Winston, she had grasped the inner meaning of the Party's sexual puritanism. It was not merely that the sex instinct created a world of its own which was outside the Party's control and which therefore had to be destroyed if possible. What was more important was that sexual privation induced hysteria, which was desirable because it could be transformed into war-fever and leader-worship. The way she put it was:

'When you make love you're using up energy; and afterwards you feel happy and don't give a damn for anything. They can't bear you to feel like that. They want you to be bursting with energy all the time. All this marching up and down and cheering and waving flags is simply sex gone sour. If you're happy inside yourself, why should you get excited about Big Brother and the Three-Year Plans and the Two Minutes Hate and all the rest of their bloody rot?'

That was very true, he thought. There was a direct intimate connexion between chastity and political orthodoxy. For how could the fear, the hatred, and the lunatic credulity which the Party needed in its members be kept at the right pitch, except by bottling down some powerful instinct and using it as a driving force? The sex impulse was dangerous to the Party, and the Party had turned it to account. They had played a similar trick with the instinct of parenthood. The family could not actually be abolished, and, indeed, people were encouraged to be fond of their children in almost the old-fashioned way. The children, on the other hand, were systematically turned against their parents and taught to spy on them and report their deviations. The family had become in effect an extension of the Thought Police. It was a device by means of which everyone could be surrounded night and day by informers who knew him intimately.

Abruptly his mind went back to Katharine. Katharine would un-questionably have denounced him to the Thought Police if she had not happened to be too stupid to detect the unorthodoxy of his opinions. But what really recalled her to him at this moment was the stifling heat of the afternoon, which had brought the sweat out on his forehead. He began telling Julia of something that had happened, or rather had failed to happen, on another sweltering summer afternoon, eleven years ago.

It was three or four months after they were married. They had lost their way on a community hike somewhere in Kent. They had only lagged behind the others for a couple of minutes, but they took a wrong turning, and presently found themselves pulled up short by the edge of an old chalk quarry. It was a sheer drop of ten or twenty metres, with boulders at the bottom. There was nobody of whom they could ask the way. As soon as she realized that they were lost Katharine became very uneasy. To be away from the noisy mob of hikers even for a moment gave her a feeling of wrong-doing. She wanted to hurry back by the way they had come and start searching in the other direction. But at this moment Winston noticed some tufts of loosestrife growing in the cracks of the cliff beneath them. One tuft was of two colours, magenta and brick-red, apparently growing on the same root. He had never seen anything of the kind before, and he called to Katharine to come and look at it.

'Look, Katharine! Look at those flowers. That clump down near the bottom. Do you see they're two different colours?'

She had already turned to go, but she did rather fretfully come back for a moment. She even leaned out over the cliff face to see where he was pointing. He was standing a little behind her, and he put his hand on her waist to steady her. At this moment it suddenly occurred to him how completely alone they were. There was not a human creature anywhere, not a leaf stirring, not even a bird awake. In a place like this the danger that there would be a hidden microphone was very small, and even if there was a microphone it would only pick up sounds. It was the hottest sleepiest hour of the afternoon. The sun blazed down upon them, the sweat tickled his face. And the thought struck him . . .

'Why didn't you give her a good shove?' said Julia. 'I would have.'

'Yes, dear, you would have. I would, if I'd been the same person then as I am now. Or perhaps I would–I'm not certain.'

'Are you sorry you didn't?'

'Yes. On the whole I'm sorry I didn't.'

They were sitting side by side on the dusty floor. He pulled her closer against him. Her head rested on his shoulder, the pleasant smell of her hair conquering the pigeon dung. She was very young, he thought, she still expected something from life, she did not understand that to push an inconvenient person over a cliff solves nothing.

'Actually it would have made no difference,' he said.

'Then why are you sorry you didn't do it?'

'Only because I prefer a positive to a negative. In this game that we're playing, we can't win. Some kinds of failure are better than other kinds, that's all.'

He felt her shoulders give a wriggle of dissent. She always contradicted him when he said anything of this kind. She would not accept it as a law of nature that the individual is always defeated. In a way she realized that she herself was doomed, that sooner or later the Thought Police would catch her and kill her, but with another part of her mind she believed that it was somehow possible to construct a secret world in which you could live as you chose. All you needed was luck and cunning and boldness. She did not understand that there was no such thing as happiness, that the only victory lay in the far future, long after you were dead, that from the moment of declaring war on the Party it was better to think of yourself as a corpse.

'We are the dead,' he said.

'We're not dead yet,' said Julia prosaically.

'Not physically. Six months, a year–five years, conceivably. I am afraid of death. You are young, so presumably you're more afraid of it than I am. Obviously we shall put it off as long as we can. But it makes very little difference. So long as human beings stay human, death and life are the same thing.'

'Oh, rubbish! Which would you sooner sleep with, me or a skeleton? Don't you enjoy being alive? Don't you like feeling: This is me, this is my hand, this is my leg, I'm real, I'm solid, I'm alive! Don't you like *this*?'

She twisted herself round and pressed her bosom against him. He could feel her breasts, ripe yet firm, through her overalls. Her body seemed to be pouring some of its youth and vigour into his.

'Yes, I like that,' he said.

'Then stop talking about dying. And now listen, dear, we've got to fix up about the next time we meet. We may as well go back to the place in the wood. We've given it a good long rest. But you must get there by a different way this time. I've got it all planned out. You take the train—but look, I'll draw it out for you.'

And in her practical way she scraped together a small square of dust, and with a twig from a pigeon's nest began drawing a map on the floor.

# 4

Winston looked round the shabby little room above Mr Charrington's shop. Beside the window the enormous bed was made up, with ragged blankets and a coverless bolster. The old-fashioned clock with the twelve-hour face was ticking away on the mantelpiece. In the corner, on the gateleg table, the glass paperweight which he had bought on his last visit gleamed softly out of the half-darkness.

In the fender was a battered tin oilstove, a saucepan, and two cups, provided by Mr Charrington. Winston lit the burner and set a pan of water to boil. He had brought an envelope full of Victory Coffee and some saccharine tablets. The clock's hands said seven-twenty: it was nineteen-twenty really. She was coming at nineteen-thirty.

Folly, folly, his heart kept saying: conscious, gratuitous, suicidal folly. Of all the crimes that a Party member could commit, this one was the least possible to conceal. Actually the idea had first floated into his head in the form of a vision, of the glass paperweight mirrored by the surface of the gateleg table. As he had foreseen, Mr Charrington had made no difficulty about letting the room. He was obviously glad of the few dollars that it would bring him. Nor did he seem shocked or become offensively knowing when it was made clear that Winston wanted the room for the purpose of a love-affair. Instead he looked into the middle distance and spoke in generalities, with so delicate an air as to give the impression that he had become partly invisible. Privacy, he said, was a very valuable thing. Everyone wanted a place where they could be alone occasionally. And when they had such a place, it was only common courtesy in anyone else who knew of it to keep his knowledge to himself. He even, seeming almost to fade out of existence as he did so, added that there were two entries to the house, one of them through the back yard, which gave on an alley.

Under the window somebody was singing. Winston peeped out, secure in the protection of the muslin curtain. The June sun was still high in the sky, and in the sun-filled court below, a monstrous woman, solid as a Norman pillar, with brawny red forearms and a sacking apron strapped about her middle, was stumping to and fro between a washtub and a clothes line, pegging out a series of square white things which Winston recognized as babies' diapers. Whenever her mouth was not corked with clothes pegs she was singing in a powerful contralto:

> It was only an 'opeless fancy,
> It passed like an Ipril dye,
> But a look an' a word an' the dreams they stirred!
> They 'ave stolen my 'eart awye!

The tune had been haunting London for weeks past. It was one of countless similar songs published for the benefit of the proles by a sub-section of the Music Department. The words of these songs were composed without any human intervention whatever on an instrument known as a versificator. But the woman sang so tunefully as to turn the dreadful rubbish into an almost pleasant sound. He could hear the woman singing and the scrape of her shoes on the flagstones, and the cries of the children in the street, and somewhere in the far distance a faint roar of traffic, and yet the room seemed curiously silent, thanks to the absence of a telescreen.

Folly, folly, folly! he thought again. It was inconceivable that they could frequent this place for more than a few weeks without being caught. But the temptation of having a hiding-place that was truly their own, indoors and near at hand, had been too much for both of them. For some time after their visit to the church belfry it had been impossible to arrange meetings. Working hours had been drastically increased in anticipation of Hate Week. It was more than a month distant, but the enormous, complex preparations that it entailed were throwing extra work on to everybody. Finally both of them managed to secure a free afternoon on the same day. They had agreed to go back to the clearing in the wood. On the evening beforehand they met briefly in the street. As usual, Winston hardly looked at Julia as they drifted towards one another in the crowd, but from the short glance he gave her it seemed to him that she was paler than usual.

'It's all off,' she murmured as soon as she judged it safe to speak. 'Tomorrow, I mean.'

'What?'

'Tomorrow afternoon. I can't come.'

'Why not?'

'Oh, the usual reason. It's started early this time.'

For a moment he was violently angry. During the month that he had known her the nature of his desire for her had changed. At the beginning there had been little true sensuality in it. Their first love-making had been simply an act of the will. But after the second time it was different. The smell of her hair, the taste of her mouth, the feeling of her skin seemed to have got inside him, or into the air all round him. She had become a physical necessity, something that he not only wanted but felt that he had a right to. When she said that she could not come, he had the feeling that she was cheating him. But just at this moment the crowd pressed them together and their hands accidentally met. She gave the tips of his fingers a quick squeeze that seemed to invite not desire but affection. It struck him that when one lived with a woman this particular disappointment must be a normal, recurring event; and a deep tenderness, such as he had not felt for her before, suddenly took hold of him. He wished that they were a married couple of ten years' standing. He wished that he were walking through the streets with her just as they were doing now but openly and without fear, talking of trivialities and buying odds and ends for the household. He wished above all that they had some place where they could be alone together without feeling the obligation to make love every time they met. It was not actually at that moment, but at some time on the following day, that the idea of renting Mr Charrington's room had occurred to him. When he suggested it to Julia she had agreed with unexpected readiness. Both of them knew that it was lunacy. It was as though they were intentionally stepping nearer to their graves. As he sat waiting on the edge of the bed he thought again of the cellars of the Ministry of Love. It was curious how that predestined horror moved in and out of one's consciousness. There it lay, fixed in future times, preceding death as surely as 99 precedes 100. One could not avoid it, but one could perhaps postpone it: and yet instead, every now and again, by a conscious, wilful act, one chose to shorten the interval before it happened.

At this moment there was a quick step on the stairs. Julia burst into the room. She was carrying a tool-bag of coarse brown canvas, such as he had sometimes seen her carrying to and fro at the Ministry. He started forward to take her in his arms, but she disengaged herself rather hurriedly, partly because she was still holding the tool-bag.

'Half a second,' she said. 'Just let me show you what I've brought. Did you bring some of that filthy Victory Coffee? I thought you would. You can chuck it away again, because we shan't be needing it. Look here.'

She fell on her knees, threw open the bag, and tumbled out some spanners and a screwdriver that filled the top part of it. Underneath were a number of neat paper packets. The first packet that she passed to Winston had a strange and yet vaguely familiar feeling. It was filled with some kind of heavy, sand-like stuff which yielded wherever you touched it.

'It isn't sugar?' he said.

'Real sugar. Not saccharine, sugar. And here's a loaf of bread—proper white bread, not our bloody stuff—and a little pot of jam. And here's a tin of milk—but look! This is the one I'm really proud of. I had to wrap a bit of sacking round it, because—'

But she did not need to tell him why she had wrapped it up. The smell was already filling the room, a rich hot smell which seemed like an emanation from his early childhood, but which one did occasionally meet with even now, blowing down a passage-way before a door slammed, or diffusing itself mysteriously in a crowded street, sniffed for an instant and then lost again.

'It's coffee,' he murmured, 'real coffee.'

'It's Inner Party coffee. There's a whole kilo here,' she said.

'How did you manage to get hold of all these things?'

'It's all Inner Party stuff. There's nothing those swine don't have, nothing. But of course waiters and servants and people pinch things, and—look, I got a little packet of tea as well.'

Winston had squatted down beside her. He tore open a corner of the packet.

'It's real tea. Not blackberry leaves.'

'There's been a lot of tea about lately. They've captured India, or something,' she said vaguely. 'But listen, dear. I want you to turn your back on me for three minutes. Go and sit on the other side of the bed. Don't go too near the window. And don't turn round till I tell you.'

Winston gazed abstractedly through the muslin curtain. Down in the yard the red-armed woman was still marching to and fro between the washtub and the line. She took two more pegs out of her mouth and sang with deep feeling:

> They sye that time 'eals all things,
> They sye you can always forget;
> But the smiles an' the tears acrorss the years
> They twist my 'eart-strings yet!

She knew the whole drivelling song by heart, it seemed. Her voice floated upward with the sweet summer air, very tuneful, charged with a sort of happy melancholy. One had the feeling that she would have been perfectly content, if the June evening had been endless and the supply of clothes inexhaustible, to remain there for a thousand years, pegging out diapers and singing rubbish. It struck him as a curious fact that he had never heard a member of the Party singing alone and spontaneously. It would even have seemed slightly unorthodox, a dangerous eccentricity, like talking to oneself. Perhaps it was only when people were somewhere near the starvation level that they had anything to sing about.

'You can turn round now,' said Julia.

He turned round, and for a second almost failed to recognize her. What he had actually expected was to see her naked. But she was not naked. The transformation that had happened was much more surprising than that. She had painted her face.

She must have slipped into some shop in the proletarian quarters and bought herself a complete set of make-up materials. Her lips were deeply reddened, her cheeks rouged, her nose powdered; there was even a touch of something under the eyes to make them brighter. It was not very skilfully done, but Winston's standards in such matters were not high. He had never before seen or imagined a woman of the Party with cosmetics on her face. The improvement in her appearance was startling. With just a few dabs of colour in the right places she had become not only very much prettier, but, above all, far more feminine. Her short hair and boyish overalls merely added to the effect. As he took her in his arms a wave of synthetic violets flooded his nostrils. He remembered the half-darkness of a basement kitchen, and a woman's cavernous mouth. It was the very same scent that she had used; but at the moment it did not seem to matter.

'Scent too!' he said.

'Yes, dear, scent too. And do you know what I'm going to do next? I'm going to get hold of a real woman's frock from somewhere and wear it instead of these bloody trousers. I'll wear silk stockings and high-heeled shoes! In this room I'm going to be a woman, not a Party comrade.'

They flung their clothes off and climbed into the huge mahogany bed. It was the first time that he had stripped himself naked in her presence. Until now he had been too much ashamed of his pale and meagre body, with the varicose veins standing out on his calves and the discoloured patch over his ankle. There were no sheets, but the blanket they lay on was threadbare and smooth, and the size and springiness of the bed astonished both of them. 'It's sure to be full of bugs, but who cares?' said Julia. One never saw a double bed nowadays, except in the homes of the proles. Winston had occasionally slept in one in his boyhood: Julia had never been in one before, so far as she could remember.

Presently they fell asleep for a little while. When Winston woke up the hands of the clock had crept round to nearly nine. He did not stir, because Julia was sleeping with her head in the crook of his arm. Most of her make-up had transferred itself to his own face or the bolster, but a light stain of rouge still brought out the beauty of her cheekbone. A yellow ray from the sinking sun fell across the foot of the bed and lighted up the fireplace, where the water in the pan was boiling fast. Down in the yard the woman had stopped singing, but the faint shouts of children floated in from the street. He wondered vaguely whether in the abolished past it had been a normal experience to lie in bed like this, in the cool of a summer evening, a man and a woman with no clothes on, making love when they chose, talking of what they chose, not feeling any compulsion to get up, simply lying there and listening to peaceful sounds outside. Surely there could never have been a time when that seemed ordinary? Julia woke up, rubbed her eyes, and raised herself on her elbow to look at the oilstove.

'Half that water's boiled away,' she said. 'I'll get up and make some coffee in another moment. We've got an hour. What time do they cut the lights off at your flats?'

'Twenty-three thirty.'

'It's twenty-three at the hostel. But you have to get in earlier than that, because—Hi! Get out, you filthy brute!'

She suddenly twisted herself over in the bed, seized a shoe from the floor, and sent it hurtling into the corner with a boyish jerk of her arm, exactly as he had seen her fling the dictionary at Goldstein, that morning during the Two Minutes Hate.

'What was it?' he said in surprise.

'A rat. I saw him stick his beastly nose out of the wainscoting. There's a hole down there. I gave him a good fright, anyway.'

'Rats!' murmured Winston. 'In this room!'

'They're all over the place,' said Julia indifferently as she lay down again. 'We've even got them in the kitchen at the hostel. Some parts of London are swarming with them. Did you know they attack children? Yes, they do. In some of these streets a woman daren't leave a baby alone for two minutes. It's the great huge brown ones that do it. And the nasty thing is that the brutes always—'

'*Don't go on!*' said Winston, with his eyes tightly shut.

'Dearest! You've gone quite pale. What's the matter? Do they make you feel sick?'

'Of all horrors in the world—a rat!'

She pressed herself against him and wound her limbs round him, as though to reassure him with the warmth of her body. He did not reopen his eyes immediately. For several moments he had had the feeling of being back in a nightmare which had recurred from time to time throughout his life. It was always very much the same. He was standing in front of a wall of darkness, and on the other side of it there was something unendurable, something too dreadful to be faced. In the dream his deepest feeling was always one of self-deception, because he did in fact know what was behind the wall of darkness. With a deadly effort, like wrenching a piece out of his own brain, he could even have dragged the thing into the open. He always woke up without discovering what it was: but somehow it was connected with what Julia had been saying when he cut her short.

'I'm sorry,' he said; 'it's nothing, I don't like rats, that's all.'

'Don't worry, dear, we're not going to have the filthy brutes in here. I'll stuff the hole with a bit of sacking before we go. And next time we come here I'll bring some plaster and bung it up properly.'

Already the black instant of panic was half-forgotten. Feeling slightly ashamed of himself, he sat up against the bedhead. Julia got out of bed, pulled on her overalls, and made the coffee. The smell that rose from the saucepan was so powerful and exciting that they shut the window lest anybody outside should notice it and become inquisitive. What was even better than the taste of the coffee was the silky texture given to it by the sugar, a thing Winston had almost forgotten after years of saccharine. With one hand in her pocket and a piece of bread and jam in the other, Julia wandered about the room, glancing indifferently at the bookcase, pointing out the best way of repairing the gateleg table, plumping herself down in the ragged armchair to see if it was comfortable, and examining the absurd twelve-hour clock with a sort of tolerant amusement. She brought the glass paperweight over to the bed to have a look at it in a better light. He took it out of her hand, fascinated, as always, by the soft, rainwatery appearance of the glass.

'What is it, do you think?' said Julia.

'I don't think it's anything—I mean, I don't think it was ever put to any use. That's what I like about it. It's a little chunk of history that they've forgotten to alter. It's a message from a hundred years ago, if one knew how to read it.'

'And that picture over there'—she nodded at the engraving on the opposite wall—'would that be a hundred years old?'

'More. Two hundred, I dare say. One can't tell. It's impossible to discover the age of anything nowadays.'

She went over to look at it. 'Here's where that brute stuck his nose out,' she said, kicking the wainscoting immediately below the picture. 'What is this place? I've seen it before somewhere.'

'It's a church, or at least it used to be. St Clement Danes its name was.' The fragment of rhyme that Mr Charrington had taught him came back into his head, and he added half-nostalgically: ' "Oranges and lemons, say the bells of St Clement's!" '

To his astonishment she capped the line:

> 'You owe me three farthings, say the bells of St Martin's,
> When will you pay me? say the bells of Old Bailey—'

'I can't remember how it goes on after that. But anyway I remember it ends up, "Here comes a candle to light you to bed, here comes a chopper to chop off your head!" '

It was like the two halves of a countersign. But there must be another line after 'the bells of Old Bailey'. Perhaps it could be dug out of Mr Charrington's memory, if he were suitably prompted.

'Who taught you that?' he said.

'My grandfather. He used to say it to me when I was a little girl. He was vaporized when I was eight—at any rate, he disappeared. I wonder what a lemon was,' she added inconsequently. 'I've seen oranges. They're a kind of round yellow fruit with a thick skin.'

'I can remember lemons,' said Winston. 'They were quite common in the 'fifties. They were so sour that it set your teeth on edge even to smell them.'

'I bet that picture's got bugs behind it,' said Julia. 'I'll take it down and give it a good clean some day. I suppose it's almost time we were leaving. I must start washing this paint off. What a bore! I'll get the lipstick off your face afterwards.'

Winston did not get up for a few minutes more. The room was darkening. He turned over towards the light and lay gazing into the glass paperweight. The inexhaustibly interesting thing was not the fragment of coral but the interior of the glass itself. There was such a depth of it, and yet it was almost as transparent as air. It was as though the surface of the glass had been the arch of the sky, enclosing a tiny world with its atmosphere complete. He had the feeling that he could get inside it, and that in fact he was inside it, along with the mahogany bed and the gateleg table, and the clock and the steel engraving and the paperweight itself. The paperweight was the room he was in, and the coral was Julia's life and his own, fixed in a sort of eternity at the heart of the crystal.

# 5

Syme had vanished. A morning came, and he was missing from work: a few thoughtless people commented on his absence. On the next day nobody mentioned him. On the third day Winston went into the vestibule of the Records Department to look at the notice-board. One of the notices carried a printed list of the members of the Chess Committee, of whom Syme had been one. It looked almost exactly as it had looked before—nothing had been crossed out—but it was one name shorter. It was enough. Syme had ceased to exist: he had never existed.

The weather was baking hot. In the labyrinthine Ministry the windowless, air-conditioned rooms kept their normal temperature, but outside the pavements scorched one's feet and the stench of the Tubes at the rush hours was a horror. The preparations for Hate Week were in full swing, and the staffs of all the Ministries were working overtime. Processions, meetings, military parades, lectures, waxwork displays, film shows, telescreen programmes all had to be organized; stands had to be erected, effigies built, slogans coined, songs written, rumours circulated, photographs faked. Julia's unit in the Fiction Department had been taken off the production of novels and was rushing out a series of atrocity pamphlets. Winston, in addition to his regular work, spent long periods every day in going through back files of *The Times* and altering and embellishing news items which were to be quoted in speeches. Late at night, when crowds of rowdy proles roamed the streets, the town had a curiously febrile air. The rocket bombs crashed oftener than ever, and sometimes in the far distance there were enormous explosions which no one could explain and about which there were wild rumours.

The new tune which was to be the theme-song of Hate Week (the Hate Song, it was called) had already been composed and was being endlessly plugged on the telescreens. It had a savage, barking rhythm which could not exactly be called music, but resembled the beating of a drum. Roared out by hundreds of voices to the tramp of marching feet, it was terrifying. The proles had taken a fancy to it, and in the midnight streets it competed with the still-popular 'It was only a hopeless fancy'. The Parsons children played it at all hours of the night and day, unbearably, on a comb and a piece of toilet paper. Winston's evenings were fuller than ever. Squads of volunteers, organized by Parsons, were preparing the street for Hate Week, stitching banners, painting posters, erecting flagstaffs on the roofs, and perilously slinging wires across the street for the reception of streamers. Parsons boasted that Victory Mansions alone would display four hundred metres of bunting. He was in his native element and as happy as a lark. The heat and the manual work had even given him a pretext for reverting to shorts and an open shirt in the evenings. He was everywhere at once, pushing, pulling, sawing, hammering, improvising, jollying everyone along with comradely exhortations and giving out from every fold of his body what seemed an inexhaustible supply of acrid-smelling sweat.

A new poster had suddenly appeared all over London. It had no caption, and represented simply the monstrous figure of a Eurasian soldier, three or four metres high, striding forward with expressionless Mongolian face and enormous boots, a sub-machine gun pointed from his hip. From whatever angle you looked at the poster, the muzzle of the gun, magnified by the foreshortening, seemed to be pointed straight at you. The thing had been plastered on every blank space on every wall, even outnumbering the portraits of Big Brother. The proles, normally apathetic about the war, were being lashed into one of their periodical frenzies of patriotism. As though to harmonize with the general mood, the rocket bombs had been killing larger numbers of people than usual. One fell on a crowded film theatre in Stepney, burying several hundred victims among the ruins. The whole population of the neighbourhood turned out for a long, trailing funeral which went on for hours and was in effect an indignation meeting. Another bomb fell on a piece of waste ground which was used as a playground, and several dozen children were blown to pieces. There were further angry demonstrations, Goldstein was burned in effigy, hundreds of copies of the poster of the Eurasian soldier were torn down and added to the flames, and a number of shops were looted in the turmoil; then a rumour flew round that spies were directing the rocket bombs by means of wireless waves, and an old couple who were suspected of being of foreign extraction had their house set on fire and perished of suffocation.

In the room over Mr Charrington's shop, when they could get there, Julia and Winston lay side by side on a stripped bed under the open window, naked for the sake of coolness. The rat had never come back, but the bugs had multiplied hideously in the heat. It did not seem to matter. Dirty or clean, the room was paradise. As soon as they arrived they would sprinkle everything with pepper bought on the black market, tear off their clothes, and make love with sweating bodies, then fall asleep and wake to find that the bugs had rallied and were massing for the counter-attack.

Four, five, six—seven times they met during the month of June. Winston had dropped his habit of drinking gin at all hours. He seemed to have lost the need for it. He had grown fatter, his varicose ulcer had subsided, leaving only a brown stain on the skin above his ankle, his fits of coughing in the early morning had stopped. The process of life had ceased to be intolerable, he had no longer any impulse to make faces at the telescreen or shout curses at the top of his voice. Now that they had a secure hiding-place, almost a home, it did not even seem a hardship that they could only meet infrequently and for a couple of hours at a time. What mattered was that the room over the junk-shop should exist. To know that it was there, inviolate, was almost the same as being in it. The room was a world, a pocket of the past where extinct animals could walk. Mr Charrington, thought Winston, was another extinct animal. He usually stopped to talk with Mr Charrington for a few minutes on his way upstairs. The old man seemed seldom or never to go out of doors, and on the other hand to have almost no customers. He led a ghostlike existence between the tiny, dark shop, and an even tinier back kitchen where he prepared his meals and which contained, among other things, an unbelievably ancient gramophone with an enormous horn. He seemed glad of the opportunity to talk. Wandering about among his worthless stock, with his long nose and thick spectacles and his bowed shoulders in the velvet jacket, he had always vaguely the air of being a collector rather than a tradesman. With a sort of faded enthusiasm he would finger this scrap of rubbish or that—a china bottle-stopper, the painted lid of a broken snuffbox, a pinchbeck locket containing a strand of some long-dead baby's hair—never asking that Winston should buy it, merely that he should admire it. To talk to him was like listening to the tinkling of a worn-out musical-box. He had dragged out from the corners of his memory some more fragments of forgotten rhymes. There was one about four and twenty blackbirds, and another about a cow with a crumpled horn, and another about the death of poor Cock Robin. 'It just occurred to me you might be interested,' he would say with a deprecating little laugh whenever he produced a new fragment. But he could never recall more than a few lines of any one rhyme.

Both of them knew—in a way, it was never out of their minds—that what was now happening could not last long. There were times when the fact of impending death seemed as palpable as the bed they lay on, and they would cling together with a sort of despairing sensuality, like a damned soul grasping at his last morsel of pleasure when the clock is within five minutes of striking. But there were also times when they had the illusion not only of safety but of permanence. So long as they were actually in this room, they both felt, no harm could come to them. Getting there was difficult and dangerous, but the room itself was sanctuary. It was as when Winston had gazed into the heart of the paperweight, with the feeling that it would be possible to get inside that glassy world, and that once inside it time could be arrested. Often they gave themselves up to daydreams of escape. Their luck would hold indefinitely, and they would carry on their intrigue, just like this, for the remainder of their natural lives. Or Katharine would die, and by subtle manœuvrings Winston and Julia would succeed in getting married. Or they would commit suicide together. Or they would disappear, alter themselves out of recognition, learn to speak with proletarian accents, get jobs in a factory and live out their lives undetected in a back-street. It was all nonsense, as they both knew. In reality there was no escape. Even the one plan that was practicable, suicide, they had no intention of carrying out. To hang on from day to day and from week to week, spinning out a present that had no future, seemed an unconquerable instinct, just as one's lungs will always draw the next breath so long as there is air available.

Sometimes, too, they talked of engaging in active rebellion against the Party, but with no notion of how to take the first step. Even if the fabulous Brotherhood was a reality, there still remained the difficulty of finding one's way into it. He told her of the strange intimacy that existed, or seemed to exist, between himself and O'Brien, and of the impulse he sometimes felt, simply to walk into O'Brien's presence, announce that he was the enemy of the Party, and demand his help. Curiously enough, this did not strike her as an impossibly rash thing to do. She was used to judging people by their faces, and it seemed natural to her that Winston should believe O'Brien to be trustworthy on the strength of a single flash of the eyes. Moreover she took it for granted that everyone, or nearly everyone, secretly hated the Party and would break the rules if he thought it safe to do so. But she refused to believe that widespread, organized opposition existed or could exist. The tales about Goldstein and his underground army, she said, were simply a lot of rubbish which the Party had invented for its own purposes and which you had to pretend to believe in. Times beyond number, at Party rallies and spontaneous demonstrations, she had shouted at the top of her voice for the execution of people whose names she had never heard and in whose supposed crimes she had not the faintest belief. When public trials were happening she had taken her place in the detachments from the Youth League who surrounded the courts from morning to night, chanting at intervals 'Death to the traitors!' During the Two Minutes Hate she always excelled all others in shouting insults at Goldstein. Yet she had only the dimmest idea of who Goldstein was and what doctrines he was supposed to represent. She had grown up since the Revolution and was too young to remember the ideological battles of the 'fifties and 'sixties. Such a thing as an independent political movement was outside her imagination: and in any case the Party was invincible. It would always exist, and it would always be the same. You could only rebel against it by secret disobedience or, at most, by isolated acts of violence such as killing somebody or blowing something up.

In some ways she was far more acute than Winston, and far less susceptible to Party propaganda. Once when he happened in some connexion to mention the war against Eurasia, she startled him by saying casually that in her opinion the war was not happening. The rocket bombs which fell daily on London were probably fired by the Government of Oceania itself, 'just to keep people frightened'. This was an idea that had literally never occurred to him. She also stirred a sort of envy in him by telling him that during the Two Minutes Hate her great difficulty was to avoid bursting out laughing. But she only questioned the teachings of the Party when they in some way touched upon her own life. Often she was ready to accept the official mythology, simply because the difference between truth and falsehood did not seem important to her. She believed, for instance, having learnt it at school, that the Party had invented aeroplanes. (In his own schooldays, Winston remembered, in the late 'fifties, it was only the helicopter that the Party claimed to have invented; a dozen years later, when Julia was at school, it was already claiming the aeroplane; one generation more, and it would be claiming the steam engine.) And when he told her that aeroplanes had been in existence before he was born, and long before the Revolution, the fact struck her as totally uninteresting. After all, what did it matter who had invented aeroplanes? It was rather more of a shock to him when he discovered from some chance remarks that she did not remember that Oceania, four years ago, had been at war with Eastasia and at peace with Eurasia. It was true that she regarded the whole war as a sham: but apparently she had not even noticed that the name of the enemy had changed. 'I thought we'd always been at war with Eurasia,' she said vaguely. It frightened him a little. The invention of aeroplanes dated from long before her birth, but the switchover in the war had happened only four years ago, well after she was grown up. He argued with her about it for perhaps a quarter of an hour. In the end he succeeded in forcing her memory back until she did dimly recall that at one time Eastasia and not Eurasia had been the enemy. But the issue still struck her as unimportant. 'Who cares?' she said impatiently. 'It's always one bloody war after another, and one knows the news is all lies anyway.'

Sometimes he talked to her of the Records Department and the impudent forgeries that he committed there. Such things did not appear to horrify her. She did not feel the abyss opening beneath her feet at the thought of lies becoming truths. He told her the story of Jones, Aaronson, and Rutherford and the momentous slip of paper which he had once held between his fingers. It did not make much impression on her. At first, indeed, she failed to grasp the point of the story.

'Were they friends of yours?' she said.

'No, I never knew them. They were Inner Party members. Besides, they were far older men than I was. They belonged to the old days, before the Revolution. I barely knew them by sight.'

'Then what was there to worry about? People are being killed off all the time, aren't they?'

He tried to make her understand. 'This was an exceptional case. It wasn't just a question of somebody being killed. Do you realize that the past, starting from yesterday, has been actually abolished? If it survives anywhere, it's in a few solid objects with no words attached to them, like that lump of glass there. Already we know almost literally nothing about the Revolution and the years before the Revolution. Every record has been destroyed or falsified, every book has been rewritten, every picture has been repainted, every statue and street and building has been renamed, every date has been altered. And that process is continuing day by day and minute by minute. History has stopped. Nothing exists except an endless present in which the Party is always right. I *know*, of course, that the past is falsified, but it would never be possible for me to prove it, even when I did the falsification myself. After the thing is done, no evidence ever remains. The only evidence is inside my own mind, and I don't know with any certainty that any other human being shares my memories. Just in that one instance, in my whole life, I did possess actual concrete evidence *after* the event—years after it.'

'And what good was that?'

'It was no good, because I threw it away a few minutes later. But if the same thing happened today, I should keep it.'

'Well, I wouldn't!' said Julia. 'I'm quite ready to take risks, but only for something worth while, not for bits of old newspaper. What could you have done with it even if you had kept it?'

'Not much, perhaps. But it was evidence. It might have planted a few doubts here and there, supposing that I'd dared to show it to anybody. I don't imagine that we can alter anything in our own lifetime. But one can imagine little knots of resistance springing up here and there—small groups of people banding themselves together, and gradually growing, and even leaving a few records behind, so that the next generation can carry on where we leave off.'

'I'm not interested in the next generation, dear. I'm interested in *us*.'

'You're only a rebel from the waist downwards,' he told her.

She thought this brilliantly witty and flung her arms round him in delight.

In the ramifications of Party doctrine she had not the faintest interest. Whenever he began to talk of the principles of Ingsoc, doublethink, the mutability of the past, and the denial of objective reality, and to use Newspeak words, she became bored and confused and said that she never paid any attention to that kind of thing. One knew that it was all rubbish, so why let oneself be worried by it? She knew when to cheer and when to boo, and that was all one needed. If he persisted in talking of such subjects, she had a disconcerting habit of falling asleep. She was one of those people who can go to sleep at any hour and in any position. Talking to her, he realized how easy it was to present an appearance of orthodoxy while having no grasp whatever of what orthodoxy meant. In a way, the world-view of the Party imposed itself most successfully on people incapable of understanding it. They could be made to accept the most flagrant violations of reality, because they never fully grasped the enormity of what was demanded of them, and were not sufficiently interested in public events to notice what was happening. By lack of understanding they remained sane. They simply swallowed everything, and what they swallowed did them no harm, because it left no residue behind, just as a grain of corn will pass undigested through the body of a bird.

## 6

It had happened at last. The expected message had come. All his life, it seemed to him, he had been waiting for this to happen.

He was walking down the long corridor at the Ministry and he was almost at the spot where Julia had slipped the note into his hand when he became aware that someone larger than himself was walking just behind him. The person, whoever it was, gave a small cough, evidently as a prelude to speaking. Winston stopped abruptly and turned. It was O'Brien.

At last they were face to face, and it seemed that his only impulse was to run away. His heart bounded violently. He would have been incapable of speaking. O'Brien, however, had continued forward in the same movement, laying a friendly hand for a moment on Winston's arm, so that the two of them were walking side by side. He began speaking with the peculiar grave courtesy that differentiated him from the majority of Inner Party members.

'I had been hoping for an opportunity of talking to you,' he said. 'I was reading one of your Newspeak articles in *The Times* the other day. You take a scholarly interest in Newspeak, I believe?'

Winston had recovered part of his self-possession. 'Hardly scholarly,' he said. 'I'm only an amateur. It's not my subject. I have never had anything to do with the actual construction of the language.'

'But you write it very elegantly,' said O'Brien. 'That is not only my own opinion. I was talking recently to a friend of yours who is certainly an expert. His name has slipped my memory for the moment.'

Again Winston's heart stirred painfully. It was inconceivable that this was anything other than a reference to Syme. But Syme was not only dead, he was abolished, an *unperson*. Any identifiable reference to him would have been mortally dangerous. O'Brien's remark must obviously have been intended as a signal, a codeword. By sharing a small act of thoughtcrime he had turned the two of them into accomplices. They had continued to stroll slowly down the corridor, but now O'Brien halted. With the curious, disarming friendliness that he always managed to put into the gesture he resettled his spectacles on his nose. Then he went on:

'What I had really intended to say was that in your article I noticed you had used two words which have become obsolete. But thcy have only become so very recently. Have you seen the tenth edition of the Newspeak Dictionary?'

'No,' said Winston. 'I didn't think it had been issued yet. We are still using the ninth in the Records Department.'

'The tenth edition is not due to appear for some months, I believe. But a few advance copies have been circulated. I have one myself. It might interest you to look at it, perhaps?'

'Very much so,' said Winston, immediately seeing where this tended.

'Some of the new developments are most ingenious. The reduction in the number of verbs—that is the point that will appeal to you, I think. Let me see, shall I send a messenger to you with the dictionary? But I am afraid I invariably forget anything of that kind. Perhaps you could pick it up at my flat at some time that suited you? Wait. Let me give you my address.'

They were standing in front of a telescreen. Somewhat absentmindedly O'Brien felt two of his pockets and then produced a small leather-covered notebook and a gold ink-pencil. Immediately beneath the telescreen, in such a position that anyone who was watching at the other end of the instrument could read what he was writing, he scribbled an address, tore out the page and handed it to Winston.

'I am usually at home in the evening,' he said. 'If not, my servant will give you the dictionary.'

He was gone, leaving Winston holding the scrap of paper, which this time there was no need to conceal. Nevertheless he carefully memorized what was written on it, and some hours later dropped it into the memory hole along with a mass of other papers.

They had been talking to one another for a couple of minutes at the most. There was only one meaning that the episode could possibly have. It had been contrived as a way of letting Winston know O'Brien's address. This was necessary, because except by direct enquiry it was never possible to discover where anyone lived. There were no directories of any kind. 'If you ever want to see me, this is where I can be found,' was what O'Brien had been saying to him. Perhaps there would even be a message concealed somewhere in the dictionary. But at any rate, one thing was certain. The conspiracy that he had dreamed of did exist, and he had reached the outer edges of it.

He knew that sooner or later he would obey O'Brien's summons. Perhaps tomorrow, perhaps after a long delay—he was not certain. What was happening was only the working-out of a process that had started years ago. The first step had been a secret, involuntary thought, the second had been the opening of the diary. He had moved from thoughts to words, and now from words to actions. The last step was something that would happen in the Ministry of Love. He had accepted it. The end was contained in the beginning. But it was frightening: or, more exactly, it was like a foretaste of death, like being a little less alive. Even while he was speaking to O'Brien, when the meaning of the words had sunk in, a chilly shuddering feeling had taken possession of his body. He had the sensation of stepping into the dampness of a grave, and it was not much better because he had always known that the grave was there and waiting for him.

# 7

Winston had woken up with his eyes full of tears. Julia rolled sleepily against him, murmuring something that might have been 'What's the matter?'

'I dreamt—' he began, and stopped short. It was too complex to be put into words. There was the dream itself, and there was a memory connected with it that had swum into his mind in the few seconds after waking.

He lay back with his eyes shut, still sodden in the atmosphere of the dream. It was a vast, luminous dream in which his whole life seemed to stretch out before him like a landscape on a summer evening after rain. It had all occurred inside the glass paperweight, but the surface of the glass was the dome of the sky, and inside the dome everything was flooded with clear soft light in which one could see into interminable distances. The dream had also been comprehended by—indeed, in some sense it had consisted in—a gesture of the arm made by his mother, and made again thirty years later by the Jewish woman he had seen on the news film, trying to shelter the small boy from the bullets, before the helicopters blew them both to pieces.

'Do you know,' he said, 'that until this moment I believed I had murdered my mother?'

'Why did you murder her?' said Julia, almost asleep.

'I didn't murder her. Not physically.'

In the dream he had remembered his last glimpse of his mother, and within a few moments of waking the cluster of small events surrounding it had all come back. It was a memory that he must have deliberately pushed out of his consciousness over many years. He was not certain of the date, but he could not have been less than ten years old, possibly twelve, when it had happened.

His father had disappeared some time earlier; how much earlier he could not remember. He remembered better the rackety, uneasy circumstances of the time: the periodical panics about air-raids and the sheltering in Tube stations, the piles of rubble everywhere, the unintelligible proclamations posted at street corners, the gangs of youths in shirts all the same colour, the enormous queues outside the bakeries, the intermittent machine-gun fire in the distance—above all, the fact that there was never enough to eat. He remembered long afternoons spent with other boys in scrounging round dustbins and rubbish heaps, picking out the ribs of cabbage leaves, potato peelings, sometimes even scraps of stale breadcrust from which they carefully scraped away the cinders; and also in waiting for the passing of trucks which travelled over a certain route and were known to carry cattle feed, and which, when they jolted over the bad patches in the road, sometimes spilt a few fragments of oil-cake.

When his father disappeared, his mother did not show any surprise or any violent grief, but a sudden change came over her. She seemed to have become completely spiritless. It was evident even to Winston that she was waiting for something that she knew must happen. She did everything that was needed—cooked, washed, mended, made the bed, swept the floor, dusted the mantelpiece—always very slowly and with a curious lack of superfluous motion, like an artist's lay-figure moving of its own accord. Her large shapely body seemed to relapse naturally into stillness. For hours at a time she would sit almost immobile on the bed, nursing his young sister, a tiny, ailing, very silent child of two or three, with a face made simian by thinness. Very occasionally she would take Winston in her arms and press him against her for a long time without saying anything. He was aware, in spite of his youthfulness and selfishness, that this was somehow connected with the never-mentioned thing that was about to happen.

He remembered the room where they lived, a dark, close-smelling room that seemed half filled by a bed with a white counterpane. There was a gas ring in the fender, and a shelf where food was kept, and on the landing outside there was a brown earthenware sink, common to several rooms. He remembered his mother's statuesque body bending over the gas ring to stir at something in a saucepan. Above all he remembered his continuous hunger, and the fierce sordid battles at meal-times. He would ask his mother naggingly, over and over again, why there was not more food, he would shout and storm at her (he even remembered the tones of his voice, which was beginning to break prematurely and sometimes boomed in a peculiar way), or he would attempt a snivelling note of pathos in his efforts to get more than his share. His mother was quite ready to give him more than his share. She took it for granted that he, 'the boy', should have the biggest portion; but however much she gave him he invariably demanded more. At every meal she would beseech him not to be selfish and to remember that his little sister was sick and also needed food, but it was no use. He would cry out with rage when she stopped ladling, he would try to wrench the saucepan and spoon out of her hands, he would grab bits from his sister's plate. He knew that he was starving the other two, but he could not help it; he even felt that he had a right to do it. The clamorous hunger in his belly seemed to justify him. Between meals, if his mother did not stand guard, he was constantly pilfering at the wretched store of food on the shelf.

One day a chocolate-ration was issued. There had been no such issue for weeks or months past. He remembered quite clearly that precious little morsel of chocolate. It was a two-ounce slab (they still talked about ounces in those days) between the three of them. It was obvious that it ought to be divided into three equal parts. Suddenly, as though he were listening to somebody else, Winston heard himself demanding in a loud booming voice that he should be given the whole piece. His mother told him not to be greedy. There was a long, nagging argument that went round and round, with shouts, whines, tears, remonstrances, bargainings. His tiny sister, clinging to her mother with both hands, exactly like a baby monkey, sat looking over her shoulder at him with large, mournful eyes. In the end his mother broke off three-quarters of the chocolate and gave it to Winston, giving the other quarter to his sister. The little girl took hold of it and looked at it duly, perhaps not knowing what it was. Winston stood watching her for a moment. Then with a sudden swift spring he had snatched the piece of chocolate out of his sister's hand and was fleeing for the door.

'Winston, Winston!' his mother called after him. 'Come back! Give your sister back her chocolate!'

He stopped, but he did not come back. His mother's anxious eyes were fixed on his face. Even now he was thinking about the thing, he did not know what it was that was on the point of happening. His sister, conscious of having been robbed of something, had set up a feeble wail. His mother drew her arm round the child and pressed its face against her breast. Something in the gesture told him that his sister was dying. He turned and fled down the stairs, with the chocolate growing sticky in his hand.

He never saw his mother again. After he had devoured the chocolate he felt somewhat ashamed of himself and hung about in the streets for several hours, until hunger drove him home. When he came back his mother had disappeared. This was already becoming normal at that time. Nothing was gone from the room except his mother and his sister. They had not taken any clothes, not even his mother's overcoat. To this day he did not know with any certainty that his mother was dead. It was perfectly possible that she had merely been sent to a forced-labour camp. As for his sister, she might have been removed, like Winston himself, to one of the colonies for homeless children (Reclamation Centres, they were called) which had grown up as a result of the civil war; or she might have been sent to the labour camp along with his mother, or simply left somewhere or other to die.

The dream was still vivid in his mind, especially the enveloping protecting gesture of the arm in which its whole meaning seemed to be contained. His mind went back to another dream of two months ago. Exactly as his mother had sat on the dingy white-quilted bed, with the child clinging to her, so she had sat in the sunken ship, far underneath him, and drowning deeper every minute, but still looking up at him through the darkening water.

He told Julia the story of his mother's disappearance. Without opening her eyes she rolled over and settled herself into a more comfortable position.

'I expect you were a beastly little swine in those days,' she said indistinctly. 'All children are swine.'

'Yes. But the real point of the story—'

From her breathing it was evident that she was going off to sleep again. He would have liked to continue talking about his mother. He did not suppose, from what he could remember of her, that she had been an unusual woman, still less an intelligent one; and yet she had possessed a kind of nobility, a kind of purity, simply because the standards that she obeyed were private ones. Her feelings were her own, and could not be altered from outside. It would not have occurred to her that an action which is ineffectual thereby becomes meaningless. If you loved someone, you loved him, and when you had nothing else to give, you still gave him love. When the last of the chocolate was gone, his mother had clasped the child in her arms. It was no use, it changed nothing, it did not produce more chocolate, it did not avert the child's death or her own; but it seemed natural to her to do it. The refugee woman in the boat had also covered the little boy with her arm, which was no more use against the bullets than a sheet of paper. The terrible thing that the Party had done was to persuade you that mere impulses, mere feelings, were of no account, while at the same time robbing you of all power over the material world. When once you were in the grip of the Party, what you felt or did not feel, what you did or refrained from doing, made literally no difference. Whatever happened you vanished, and neither you nor your actions were ever heard of again. You were lifted clean out of the stream of history. And yet to the people of only two generations ago this would not have seemed all-important, because they were not attempting to alter history. They were governed by private loyalties which they did not question. What mattered were individual relationships, and a completely helpless gesture, an embrace, a tear, a word spoken to a dying man, could have value in itself. The proles, it suddenly occurred to him, had remained in this condition. They were not loyal to a party or a country or an idea, they were loyal to one another. For the first time in his life he did not despise the proles or think of them merely as an inert force which would one day spring to life and regenerate the world. The proles had stayed human. They had not become hardened inside. They had held on to the primitive emotions which he himself had to relearn by conscious effort. And in thinking this he remembered, without apparent relevance, how a few weeks ago he had seen a severed hand lying on the pavement and had kicked it into the gutter as though it had been a cabbage-stalk.

'The proles are human beings,' he said aloud. 'We are not human.'

'Why not?' said Julia, who had woken up again.

He thought for a little while. 'Has it ever occurred to you,' he said, 'that the best thing for us to do would be simply to walk out of here before it's too late, and never see each other again?'

'Yes, dear, it has occurred to me, several times. But I'm not going to do it, all the same.'

'We've been lucky,' he said, 'but it can't last much longer. You're young. You look normal and innocent. If you keep clear of people like me, you might stay alive for another fifty years.'

'No. I've thought it all out. What you do, I'm going to do. And don't be too downhearted. I'm rather good at staying alive.'

'We may be together for another six months—a year—there's no knowing. At the end we're certain to be apart. Do you realize how utterly alone we shall be? When once they get hold of us there will be nothing, literally nothing, that either of us can do for the other. If I confess, they'll shoot you, and if I refuse to confess, they'll shoot you just the same. Nothing that I can do or say, or stop myself from saying, will put off your death for as much as five minutes. Neither of us will even know whether the other is alive or dead. We shall be utterly without power of any kind. The one thing that matters is that we shouldn't betray one another, although even that can't make the slightest difference.'

'If you mean confessing,' she said, 'we shall do that, right enough. Everybody always confesses. You can't help it. They torture you.'

'I don't mean confessing. Confession is not betrayal. What you say or do doesn't matter: only feelings matter. If they could make me stop loving you—that would be the real betrayal.'

She thought it over. 'They can't do that,' she said finally. 'It's the one thing they can't do. They can make you say anything—*anything*—but they can't make you believe it. They can't get inside you.'

'No,' he said a little more hopefully, 'no; that's quite true. They can't get inside you. If you can *feel* that staying human is worth while, even when it can't have any result whatever, you've beaten them.'

He thought of the telescreen with its never-sleeping ear. They could spy upon you night and day, but if you kept your head you could still outwit them. With all their cleverness they had never mastered the secret of finding out what another human being was thinking. Perhaps that was less true when you were actually in their hands. One did not know what happened inside the Ministry of Love, but it was possible to guess: tortures, drugs, delicate instruments that registered your nervous reactions, gradual wearing-down by sleeplessness and solitude and persistent questioning. Facts, at any rate, could not be kept hidden. They could be tracked down by enquiry, they could be squeezed out of you by torture. But if the object was not to stay alive but to stay human, what difference did it ultimately make? They could not alter your feelings: for that matter you could not alter them yourself, even if you wanted to. They could lay bare in the utmost detail everything that you had done or said or thought; but the inner heart, whose workings were mysterious even to yourself, remained impregnable.

# 8

They had done it, they had done it at last!

The room they were standing in was long-shaped and softly lit. The telescreen was dimmed to a low murmur; the richness of the dark-blue carpet gave one the impression of treading on velvet. At the far end of the room O'Brien was sitting at a table under a green-shaded lamp, with a mass of papers on either side of him. He had not bothered to look up when the servant showed Julia and Winston in.

Winston's heart was thumping so hard that he doubted whether he would be able to speak. They had done it, they had done it at last, was all he could think. It had been a rash act to come here at all, and sheer folly to arrive together; though it was true that they had come by different routes and only met on O'Brien's doorstep. But merely to walk into such a place needed an effort of the nerve. It was only on very rare occasions that one saw inside the dwelling-places of the Inner Party, or even penetrated into the quarter of the town where they lived. The whole atmosphere of the huge block of flats, the richness and spaciousness of everything, the unfamiliar smells of good food and tobacco, the silent and incredibly rapid lifts sliding up and down, the white-jacketed servants hurrying to and fro—everything was intimidating. Although he had a good pretext for coming here, he was haunted at every step by the fear that a black-uniformed guard would suddenly appear from round the corner, demand his papers, and order him to get out. O'Brien's servant, however, had admitted the two of them without demur. He was a small, dark-haired man in a white jacket, with a diamond-shaped, completely expressionless face which might have been that of a Chinese. The passage down which he led them was softly carpeted, with cream-papered walls and white wainscoting, all exquisitely clean. That too was intimidating. Winston could not remember ever to have seen a passageway whose walls were not grimy from the contact of human bodies.

O'Brien had a slip of paper between his fingers and seemed to be studying it intently. His heavy face, bent down so that one could see the line of the nose, looked both formidable and intelligent. For perhaps twenty seconds he sat without stirring. Then he pulled the speakwrite towards him and rapped out a message in the hybrid jargon of the Ministries:

'Items one comma five comma seven approved fullwise stop suggestion contained item six doubleplus ridiculous verging crimethink cancel stop unproceed constructionwise antegetting plusfull estimates. machinery overheads stop end message.'

He rose deliberately from his chair and came towards them across the soundless carpet. A little of the official atmosphere seemed to have fallen away from him with the Newspeak words, but his expression was grimmer than usual, as though he were not pleased at being disturbed. The terror that Winston already felt was suddenly shot through by a streak of ordinary embarrassment. It seemed to him quite possible that he had simply made a stupid mistake. For what evidence had he in reality that O'Brien was any kind of political conspirator? Nothing but a flash of the eyes and a single equivocal remark: beyond that, only his own secret imaginings, founded on a dream. He could not even fall back on the pretence that he had come to borrow the dictionary, because in that case Julia's presence was impossible to explain. As O'Brien passed the telescreen a thought seemed to strike him. He stopped, turned aside and pressed a switch on the wall. There was a sharp snap. The voice had stopped.

Julia uttered a tiny sound, a sort of squeak of surprise. Even in the midst of his panic, Winston was too much taken aback to be able to hold his tongue.

'You can turn it off!' he said.

'Yes,' said O'Brien, 'we can turn it off. We have that privilege.'

He was opposite them now. His solid form towered over the pair of them, and the expression on his face was still indecipherable. He was waiting, somewhat sternly, for Winston to speak, but about what? Even now it was quite conceivable that he was simply a busy man wondering irritably why he had been interrupted. Nobody spoke. After the stopping of the telescreen the room seemed deadly silent. The seconds marched past, enormous. With difficulty Winston continued to keep his eyes fixed on O'Brien's. Then suddenly the grim face broke down into what might have been the beginnings of a smile. With his characteristic gesture O'Brien resettled his spectacles on his nose.

'Shall I say it, or will you?' he said.

'I will say it,' said Winston promptly. 'That thing is really turned off?'

'Yes, everything is turned off. We are alone.'

'We have come here because—'

He paused, realizing for the first time the vagueness of his own motives. Since he did not in fact know what kind of help he expected from O'Brien, it was not easy to say why he had come here. He went on, conscious that what he was saying must sound both feeble and pretentious:

'We believe that there is some kind of conspiracy, some kind of secret organization working against the Party, and that you are involved in it. We want to join it and work for it. We are enemies of the Party. We disbelieve in the principles of Ingsoc. We are thought-criminals. We are also adulterers. I tell you this because we want to put ourselves at your mercy. If you want us to incriminate ourselves in any other way, we are ready.'

He stopped and glanced over his shoulder, with the feeling that the door had opened. Sure enough, the little yellow-faced servant had come in without knocking. Winston saw that he was carrying a tray with a decanter and glasses.

'Martin is one of us,' said O'Brien impassively. 'Bring the drinks over here, Martin. Put them on the round table. Have we enough chairs? Then we may as well sit down and talk in comfort. Bring a chair for yourself, Martin. This is business. You can stop being a servant for the next ten minutes.'

The little man sat down, quite at his ease, and yet still with a servant-like air, the air of a valet enjoying a privilege. Winston regarded him out of the corner of his eye. It struck him that the man's whole life was playing a part, and that he felt it to be dangerous to drop his assumed personality even for a moment. O'Brien took the decanter by the neck and filled up the glasses with a dark-red liquid. It aroused in Winston dim memories of something seen long ago on a wall or a hoarding—a vast bottle composed of electric lights which seemed to move up and down and pour its contents into a glass. Seen from the top the stuff looked almost black, but in the decanter it gleamed like a ruby. It had a sour-sweet smell. He saw Julia pick up her glass and sniff at it with frank curiosity.

'It is called wine,' said O'Brien with a faint smile. 'You will have read about it in books, no doubt. Not much of it gets to the Outer Party, I am afraid.' His face grew solemn again, and he raised his glass: 'I think it is fitting that we should begin by drinking a health. To our Leader: To Emmanuel Goldstein.'

Winston took up his glass with a certain eagerness. Wine was a thing he had read and dreamed about. Like the glass paperweight or Mr Charrington's half-remembered rhymes, it belonged to the vanished, romantic past, the olden time as he liked to call it in his secret thoughts. For some reason he had always thought of wine as having an intensely sweet taste, like that of blackberry jam and an immediate intoxicating effect. Actually, when he came to swallow it, the stuff was distinctly disappointing. The truth was that after years of gin-drinking he could barely taste it. He set down the empty glass.

'Then there is such a person as Goldstein?' he said.

'Yes, there is such a person, and he is alive. Where, I do not know.'

'And the conspiracy—the organization? It is real? It is not simply an invention of the Thought Police?'

'No, it is real. The Brotherhood, we call it. You will never learn much more about the Brotherhood than that it exists and that you belong to it. I will come back to that presently.' He looked at his wrist-watch. 'It is unwise even for members of the Inner Party to turn off the telescreen for more than half an hour. You ought not to have come here together, and you will have to leave separately. You, Comrade'—he bowed his head to Julia—'will leave first. We have about twenty minutes at our disposal. You will understand that I must start by asking you certain questions. In general terms, what are you prepared to do?'

'Anything that we are capable of,' said Winston.

O'Brien had turned himself a little in his chair so that he was facing Winston. He almost ignored Julia, seeming to take it for granted that Winston could speak for her. For a moment the lids flitted down over his eyes. He began asking his questions in a low, expressionless voice, as though this were a routine, a sort of catechism, most of whose answers were known to him already.

'You are prepared to give your lives?'

'Yes.'

'You are prepared to commit murder?'

'Yes.'

'To commit acts of sabotage which may cause the death of hundreds of innocent people?'

'Yes.'

'To betray your country to foreign powers?'

'Yes.'

'You are prepared to cheat, to forge, to blackmail, to corrupt the minds of children, to distribute habit-forming drugs, to encourage prostitution, to disseminate venereal diseases—to do anything which is likely to cause demoralization and weaken the power of the Party?'

'Yes.'

'If, for example, it would somehow serve our interests to throw sulphuric acid in a child's face—are you prepared to do that?'

'Yes.'

'You are prepared to lose your identity and live out the rest of your life as a waiter or a dock-worker?'

'Yes.'

'You are prepared to commit suicide, if and when we order you to do so?'

'Yes.'

'You are prepared, the two of you, to separate and never see one another again?'

'No!' broke in Julia.

It appeared to Winston that a long time passed before he answered. For a moment he seemed even to have been deprived of the power of speech. His tongue worked soundlessly, forming the opening syllables first of one word, then of the other, over and over again. Until he had said it, he did not know which word he was going to say. 'No,' he said finally.

'You did well to tell me,' said O'Brien. 'It is necessary for us to know everything.'

He turned himself toward Julia and added in a voice with somewhat more expression in it:

'Do you understand that even if he survives, it may be as a different person? We may be obliged to give him a new identity. His face, his movements, the shape of his hands, the colour of his hair—even his voice would be different. And you yourself might have become a different person. Our surgeons can alter people beyond recognition. Sometimes it is necessary. Sometimes we even amputate a limb.'

Winston could not help snatching another sidelong glance at Martin's Mongolian face. There were no scars that he could see. Julia had turned a shade paler, so that her freckles were showing, but she faced O'Brien boldly. She murmured something that seemed to be assent.

'Good. Then that is settled.'

There was a silver box of cigarettes on the table. With a rather absent-minded air O'Brien pushed them towards the others, took one himself, then stood up and began to pace slowly to and fro, as though he could think better standing. They were very good cigarettes, very thick and well packed, with an unfamiliar silkiness in the paper. O'Brien looked at his wrist-watch again.

'You had better go back to your pantry, Martin,' he said. 'I shall switch on in a quarter of an hour. Take a good look at these comrades' faces before you go. You will be seeing them again. I may not.'

Exactly as they had done at the front door, the little man's dark eyes flickered over their faces. There was not a trace of friendliness in his manner. He was memorizing their appearance, but he felt no interest in them, or appeared to feel none. It occurred to Winston that a synthetic face was perhaps incapable of changing its expression. Without speaking or giving any kind of salutation, Martin went out, closing the door silently behind him. O'Brien was strolling up and down, one hand in the pocket of his black overalls, the other holding his cigarette.

'You understand,' he said, 'that you will be fighting in the dark. You will always be in the dark. You will receive orders and you will obey them, without knowing why. Later I shall send you a book from which you will learn the true nature of the society we live in, and the strategy by which we shall destroy it. When you have read the book, you will be full members of the Brotherhood. But between the general aims that we are fighting for, and the immediate tasks of the moment, you will never know anything. I tell you that the Brotherhood exists, but I cannot tell you whether it numbers a hundred members, or ten million. From your personal knowledge you will never be able to say that it numbers even as many as a dozen. You will have three or four contacts, who will be renewed from time to time as they disappear. As this was your first contact, it will be preserved. When you receive orders, they will come from me. If we find it necessary to communicate with you, it will be through Martin. When you are finally caught, you will confess. That is unavoidable. But you will have very little to confess, other than your own actions. You will not be able to betray more than a handful of unimportant people. Probably you will not even betray me. By that time I may be dead, or I shall have become a different person, with a different face.'

He continued to move to and fro over the soft carpet. In spite of the bulkiness of his body there was a remarkable grace in his movements. It came out even in the gesture with which he thrust a hand into his pocket, or manipulated a cigarette. More even than of strength, he gave an impression of confidence and of an understanding tinged by irony. However much in earnest he might be, he had nothing of the single-mindedness that belongs to a fanatic.

When he spoke of murder, suicide, venereal disease, amputated limbs, and altered faces, it was with a faint air of persiflage. 'This is unavoidable,' his voice seemed to say; 'this is what we have got to do, unflinchingly. But this is not what we shall be doing when life is worth living again.' A wave of admiration, almost of worship, flowed out from Winston towards O'Brien. For the moment he had forgotten the shadowy figure of Goldstein. When you looked at O'Brien's powerful shoulders and his blunt-featured face, so ugly and yet so civilized, it was impossible to believe that he could be defeated. There was no stratagem that he was not equal to, no danger that he could not foresee. Even Julia seemed to be impressed. She had let her cigarette go out and was listening intently. O'Brien went on:

'You will have heard rumours of the existence of the Brotherhood. No doubt you have formed your own picture of it. You have imagined, probably, a huge underworld of conspirators, meeting secretly in cellars, scribbling messages on walls, recognizing one another by code words or by special movements of the hand. Nothing of the kind exists. The members of the Brotherhood have no way of recognizing one another, and it is impossible for any one member to be aware of the identity of more than a few others. Goldstein himself, if he fell into the hands of the Thought Police, could not give them a complete list of members, or any information that would lead them to a complete list. No such list exists. The Brotherhood cannot be wiped out because it is not an organization in the ordinary sense. Nothing holds it together except an idea which is indestructible. You will never have anything to sustain you, except the idea. You will get no comradeship and no encouragement. When finally you are caught, you will get no help. We never help our members. At most, when it is absolutely necessary that someone should be silenced, we are occasionally able to smuggle a razor blade into a prisoner's cell. You will have to get used to living without results and without hope. You will work for a while, you will be caught, you will confess, and then you will die. Those are the only results that you will ever see. There is no possibility that any perceptible change will happen within our own lifetime. We are the dead. Our only true life is in the future. We shall take part in it as handfuls of dust and splinters of bone. But how far away that future may be, there is no knowing. It might be a thousand years. At present nothing is possible except to extend the area of sanity little by little. We cannot act collectively. We can only spread our knowledge outwards from individual to individual, generation after generation. In the face of the Thought Police, there is no other way.'

He halted and looked for the third time at his wrist-watch.

'It is almost time for you to leave, comrade,' he said to Julia. 'Wait. The decanter is still half full.'

He filled the glasses and raised his own glass by the stem.

'What shall it be this time?' he said, still with the same faint suggestion of irony. 'To the confusion of the Thought Police? To the death of Big Brother? To humanity? To the future?'

'To the past,' said Winston.

'The past is more important,' agreed O'Brien gravely.

They emptied their glasses, and a moment later Julia stood up to go. O'Brien took a small box from the top of a cabinet and handed her a flat white tablet which he told her to place on her tongue. It was important, he said, not to go out smelling of wine: the lift attendants were very observant. As soon as the door had shut behind her he appeared to forget her existence. He took another pace or two up and down, then stopped.

'There are details to be settled,' he said. 'I assume that you have a hiding-place of some kind?'

Winston explained about the room over Mr Charrington's shop.

'That will do for the moment. Later we will arrange something else for you. It is important to change one's hiding-place frequently. Meanwhile I shall send you a copy of *the book*'—even O'Brien, Winston noticed, seemed to pronounce the words as though they were in italic—'Goldstein's book, you understand, as soon as possible. It may be some days before I can get hold of one. There are not many in existence, as you can imagine. The Thought Police hunt them down and destroy them almost as fast as we can produce them. It makes very little difference. The book is indestructible. If the last copy were gone, we could reproduce it almost word for word. Do you carry a brief-case to work with you?' he added.

'As a rule, yes.'

'What is it like?'

'Black, very shabby. With two straps.'

'Black, two straps, very shabby—good. One day in the fairly near future—I cannot give a date—one of the messages among your morning's work will contain a misprinted word, and you will have to ask for a repeat. On the following day you will go to work without your brief-case. At some time during the day, in the street, a man will touch you on the arm and say "I think you have dropped your brief-case." The one he gives you will contain a copy of Goldstein's book. You will return it within fourteen days.'

They were silent for a moment.

'There are a couple of minutes before you need go,' said O'Brien. 'We shall meet again—if we do meet again—'

Winston looked up at him. 'In the place where there is no darkness?' he said hesitantly.

O'Brien nodded without appearance of surprise. 'In the place where there is no darkness,' he said, as though he had recognized the allusion. 'And in the meantime, is there anything that you wish to say before you leave? Any message? Any question?'

Winston thought. There did not seem to be any further question that he wanted to ask: still less did he feel any impulse to utter high-sounding generalities. Instead of anything directly connected with O'Brien or the Brotherhood, there came into his mind a sort of composite picture of the dark bedroom where his mother had spent her last days, and the little room over Mr Charrington's shop, and the glass paperweight, and the steel engraving in its rosewood frame. Almost at random he said:

'Did you ever happen to hear an old rhyme that begins "Oranges and lemons, say the bells of St Clement's"?'

Again O'Brien nodded. With a sort of grave courtesy he completed the stanza:

> Oranges and lemons, say the bells of St Clement's,
> You owe me three farthings, say the bells of St Martin's,
> When will you pay me? say the bells of Old Bailey,
> When I grow rich, say the bells of Shoreditch.'

'You knew the last line!' said Winston.

'Yes, I knew the last line. And now, I am afraid, it is time for you to go. But wait. You had better let me give you one of these tablets.'

As Winston stood up O'Brien held out a hand. His powerful grip crushed the bones of Winston's palm. At the door Winston looked back, but O'Brien seemed already to be in process of putting him out of mind. He was waiting with his hand on the switch that controlled the telescreen. Beyond him Winston could see the writing-table with its green-shaded lamp and the speakwrite and the wire baskets deep-laden with papers. The incident was closed. Within thirty seconds, it occurred to him, O'Brien would be back at his interrupted and important work on behalf of the Party.

———

# 9

———

Winston was gelatinous with fatigue. Gelatinous was the right word. It had come into his head spontaneously. His body seemed to have not only the weakness of a jelly, but its translucency. He felt that if he held up his hand he would be able to see the light through it. All the blood and lymph had been drained out of him by an enormous debauch of work, leaving only a frail structure of nerves, bones, and skin. All sensations seemed to be magnified. His overalls fretted his shoulders, the pavement tickled his feet, even the opening and closing of a hand was an effort that made his joints creak.

He had worked more than ninety hours in five days. So had everyone else in the Ministry. Now it was all over, and he had literally nothing to do, no Party work of any description, until tomorrow morning. He could spend six hours in the hiding-place and another nine in his own bed. Slowly, in mild afternoon sunshine, he walked up a dingy street in the direction of Mr Charrington's shop, keeping one eye open for the patrols, but irrationally convinced that this afternoon there was no danger of anyone interfering with him. The heavy brief-case that he was carrying bumped against his knee at each step, sending a tingling sensation up and down the skin of his leg. Inside it was *the book,* which he had now had in his possession for six days and had not yet opened, nor even looked at.

On the sixth day of Hate Week, after the processions, the speeches, the shouting, the singing, the banners, the posters, the films, the waxworks, the rolling of drums and squealing of trumpets, the tramp of marching feet, the grinding of the caterpillars of tanks, the roar of massed planes, the booming of guns—after six days of this, when the great orgasm was quivering to its climax and the general hatred of Eurasia had boiled up into such delirium that if the crowd could have got their hands on the 2,000 Eurasian war-criminals who were to be publicly hanged on the last day of the proceedings, they would unquestionably have torn them to pieces—at just this moment it had been announced that Oceania was not after all at war with Eurasia. Oceania was at war with Eastasia. Eurasia was an ally.

There was, of course, no admission that any change had taken place. Merely it became known, with extreme suddenness and everywhere at once, that Eastasia and not Eurasia was the enemy. Winston was taking part in a demonstration in one of the central London squares at the moment when it happened. It was night, and the white faces and the scarlet banners were luridly floodlit. The square was packed with several thousand people, including a block of about a thousand schoolchildren in the uniform of the Spies. On a scarlet-draped platform an orator of the Inner Party, a small lean man with disproportionately long arms and a large bald skull over which a few lank locks straggled, was haranguing the crowd. A little Rumpelstiltskin figure, contorted with hatred, he gripped the neck of the microphone with one hand while the other, enormous at the end of a bony arm, clawed the air menacingly above his head. His voice, made metallic by the amplifiers, boomed forth an endless catalogue of atrocities, massacres, deportations, lootings, rapings, torture of prisoners, bombing of civilians, lying propaganda, unjust aggressions, broken treaties. It was almost impossible to listen to him without being first convinced and then maddened. At every few moments the fury of the crowd boiled over and the voice of the speaker was drowned by a wild beast-like roaring that rose uncontrollably from thousands of throats. The most savage yells of all came from the schoolchildren. The speech had been proceeding for perhaps twenty minutes when a messenger hurried on to the platform and a scrap of paper was slipped into the speaker's hand. He unrolled and read it without pausing in his speech. Nothing altered in his voice or manner, or in the content of what he was saying, but suddenly the names were different. Without words said, a wave of understanding rippled through the crowd. Oceania was at war with Eastasia! The next moment there was a tremendous commotion. The banners and posters with which the square was decorated were all wrong! Quite half of them had the wrong faces on them. It was sabotage! The agents of Goldstein had been at work! There was a riotous interlude while posters were ripped from the walls, banners torn to shreds and trampled underfoot. The Spies performed prodigies of activity in clambering over the rooftops and cutting the streamers that fluttered from the chimneys. But within two or three minutes it was all over. The orator, still gripping the neck of the microphone, his shoulders hunched forward, his free hand clawing at the air, had gone straight on with his speech. One minute more, and the feral roars of rage were again bursting from the crowd. The Hate continued exactly as before, except that the target had been changed.

The thing that impressed Winston in looking back was that the speaker had switched from one line to the other actually in mid-sentence, not only without a pause, but without even breaking the syntax. But at the moment he had other things to preoccupy him. It was during the moment of disorder while the posters were being torn down that a man whose face he did not see had tapped him on the shoulder and said, 'Excuse me, I think you've dropped your brief-case.' He took the brief-case abstractedly, without speaking. He knew that it would be days before he had an opportunity to look inside it. The instant that the demonstration was over he went straight to the Ministry of Truth, though the time was now nearly twenty-three hours. The entire staff of the Ministry had done likewise. The orders already issuing from the telescreens, recalling them to their posts, were hardly necessary.

Oceania was at war with Eastasia: Oceania had always been at war with Eastasia. A large part of the political literature of five years was now completely obsolete. Reports and records of all kinds, newspapers, books, pamphlets, films, sound tracks, photographs—all had to be rectified at lightning speed. Although no directive was ever issued, it was known that the chiefs of the Department intended that within one week no reference to the war with Eurasia, or the alliance with Eastasia, should remain in existence anywhere. The work was overwhelming, all the more so because the processes that it involved could not be called by their true names. Everyone in the Records Department worked eighteen hours in the twenty-four, with two three-hour snatches of sleep. Mattresses were brought up from the cellars and pitched all over the corridors: meals consisted of sandwiches and Victory Coffee wheeled round on trolleys by attendants from the canteen. Each time that Winston broke off for one of his spells of sleep he tried to leave his desk clear of work, and each time that he crawled back sticky-eyed and aching, it was to find that another shower of paper cylinders had covered the desk like a snowdrift, half-burying the speakwrite and overflowing on to the floor, so that the first job was always to stack them into a neat enough pile to give him room to work. What was worst of all was that the work was by no means purely mechanical. Often it was enough merely to substitute one name for another, but any detailed report of events demanded care and imagination. Even the geographical knowledge that one needed in transferring the war from one part of the world to another was considerable.

By the third day his eyes ached unbearably and his spectacles needed wiping every few minutes. It was like struggling with some crushing physical task, something which one had the right to refuse and which one was nevertheless neurotically anxious to accomplish. In so far as he had time to remember it, he was not troubled by the fact that every word he murmured into the speakwrite, every stroke of his ink-pencil, was a deliberate lie. He was as anxious as anyone else in the Department that the forgery should be perfect. On the morning of the sixth day the dribble of cylinders slowed down. For as much as half an hour nothing came out of the tube; then one more cylinder, then nothing.

Everywhere at about the same time the work was easing off. A deep and as it were secret sigh went through the Department. A mighty deed, which could never be mentioned, had been achieved. It was now impossible for any human being to prove by documentary evidence that the war with Eurasia had ever happened. At twelve hundred it was unexpectedly announced that all workers in the Ministry were free till tomorrow morning. Winston, still carrying the brief-case containing *the book,* which had remained between his feet while he worked and under his body while he slept, went home, shaved himself, and almost fell asleep in his bath, although the water was barely more than tepid.

With a sort of voluptuous creaking in his joints he climbed the stair above Mr Charrington's shop. He was tired, but not sleepy any longer. He opened the window, lit the dirty little oilstove and put on a pan of water for coffee. Julia would arrive presently: meanwhile there was *the book*. He sat down in the sluttish armchair and undid the straps of the brief-case.

A heavy black volume, amateurishly bound, with no name or title on the cover. The print also looked slightly irregular. The pages were worn at the edges, and fell apart, easily, as though the book had passed through many hands. The inscription on the title-page ran:

### THE THEORY AND PRACTICE OF OLIGARCHICAL COLLECTIVISM

BY

EMMANUEL GOLDSTEIN

Winston began reading:

### CHAPTER I
### IGNORANCE IS STRENGTH

Throughout recorded time, and probably since the end of the Neolithic Age, there have been three kinds of people in the world, the High, the Middle, and the Low. They have been subdivided in many ways, they have borne countless different names, and their relative numbers, as well as their attitude towards one another, have varied from age to age: but the essential structure of society has never altered. Even after enormous upheavals and seemingly irrevocable changes, the same pattern has always reasserted itself, just as a gyroscope will always return to equilibrium, however far it is pushed one way or the other.

The aims of these groups are entirely irreconcilable. . . .

Winston stopped reading, chiefly in order to appreciate the fact that he *was* reading, in comfort and safety. He was alone: no telescreen, no ear at the keyhole, no nervous impulse to glance over his shoulder or cover the page with his hand. The sweet summer air played against his cheek. From somewhere far away there floated the faint shouts of children: in the room itself there was no sound except the insect voice of the clock. He settled deeper into the arm-chair and put his feet up on the fender. It was bliss, it was eternity. Suddenly, as one sometimes does with a book of which one knows that one will ultimately read and re-read every word, he opened it at a different place and found himself at Chapter III. He went on reading:

## CHAPTER III
## WAR IS PEACE

The splitting up of the world into three great super-states was an event which could be and indeed was foreseen before the middle of the twentieth century. With the absorption of Europe by Russia and of the British Empire by the United States, two of the three existing powers, Eurasia and Oceania, were already effectively in being. The third, Eastasia, only emerged as a distinct unit after another decade of confused fighting. The frontiers between the three super-states are in some places arbitrary, and in others they fluctuate according to the fortunes of war, but in general they follow geographical lines. Eurasia comprises the whole of the northern part of the European and Asiatic land-mass, from Portugal to the Bering Strait. Oceania comprises the Americas, the Atlantic islands including the British Isles, Australasia, and the southern portion of Africa. Eastasia, smaller than the others and with a less definite western frontier, comprises China and the countries to the south of it, the Japanese islands and a large but fluctuating portion of Manchuria, Mongolia, and Tibet.

In one combination or another, these three super-states are permanently at war, and have been so for the past twenty-five years. War, however, is no longer the desperate, annihilating struggle that it was in the early decades of the twentieth century. It is a warfare of limited aims between combatants who are unable to destroy one another, have no material cause for fighting and are not divided by any genuine ideological difference. This is not to say that either the conduct of war, or the prevailing attitude towards it, has become less bloodthirsty or more chivalrous. On the contrary, war hysteria is continuous and universal in all countries, and such acts as raping, looting, the slaughter of children, the reduction of whole populations to slavery, and reprisals against prisoners which extend even to boiling and burying alive, are looked upon as normal, and, when they are committed by one's own side and not by the enemy, meritorious. But in a physical sense war involves very small numbers of people, mostly highly-trained specialists, and causes comparatively few casualties. The fighting, when there is any, takes place on the vague frontiers whose whereabouts the average man can only guess at, or around the Floating Fortresses which guard strategic spots on the sea lanes. In the centres of civilization war means no more than a continuous shortage of consumption goods, and the occasional crash of a rocket bomb which may cause a few scores of deaths. War has in fact changed its character. More exactly, the reasons for which war is waged have changed in their order of importance. Motives which were already present to some small extent in the great wars of the early twentieth century have now become dominant and are consciously recognized and acted upon.

To understand the nature of the present war—for in spite of the regrouping which occurs every few years, it is always the same war—one must realize in the first place that it is impossible for it to be decisive. None of the three super-states could be definitively conquered even by the other two in combination. They are too evenly matched, and their natural defences are too formidable. Eurasia is protected by its vast land spaces, Oceania by the width of the Atlantic and the Pacific, Eastasia by the fecundity and industriousness of its inhabitants. Secondly, there is no longer, in a material sense, anything to fight about. With the establishment of self-contained economies, in which production and consumption are geared to one another, the scramble for markets which was a main cause of previous wars has come to an end, while the competition for raw materials is no longer a matter of life and death. In any case each of the three super-states is so vast that it can obtain almost all the materials that it needs within its own boundaries. In so far as the war has a direct economic purpose, it is a war for labour power. Between the frontiers of the super-states, and not permanently in the possession of any of them, there lies a rough quadrilateral with its corners at Tangier, Brazzaville, Darwin, and Hong Kong, containing within it about a fifth of the population of the earth. It is for the possession of these thickly-populated regions, and of the northern ice-cap, that the three powers are constantly struggling. In practice no one power ever controls the whole of the disputed area. Portions of it are constantly changing hands, and it is the chance of seizing this or that fragment by a sudden stroke of treachery that dictates the endless changes of alignment.

All of the disputed territories contain valuable minerals, and some of them yield important vegetable products such as rubber which in colder climates it is necessary to synthesize by comparatively expensive methods. But above all they contain a bottomless reserve of cheap labour. Whichever power controls equatorial Africa, or the countries of the Middle East, or Southern India, or the Indonesian Archipelago, disposes also of the bodies of scores or hundreds of millions of ill-paid and hard-working coolies. The inhabitants of these areas, reduced more or less openly to the status of slaves, pass continually from conqueror to conqueror, and are expended like so much coal or oil in the race to turn out more armaments, to capture more territory, to control more labour power, to turn out more armaments, to capture more territory, and so on indefinitely. It should be noted that the fighting never really moves beyond the edges of the disputed areas. The frontiers of Eurasia flow back and forth between the basin of the Congo and the northern shore of the Mediterranean; the islands of the Indian Ocean and the Pacific are constantly being captured and recaptured by Oceania or by Eastasia; in Mongolia the dividing line between Eurasia and Eastasia is never stable; round the Pole all three powers lay claim to enormous territories which in fact are largely uninhabited and unexplored: but the balance of power always remains roughly even, and the territory which forms the heartland of each super-state always remains inviolate. Moreover, the labour of the exploited peoples round the Equator is not really necessary to the world's economy. They add nothing to the wealth of the world, since whatever they produce is used for purposes of war, and the object of waging a war is always to be in a better position in which to wage another war. By their labour the slave populations allow the tempo of continuous warfare to be speeded up. But if they did not exist, the structure of world society, and the process by which it maintains itself, would not be essentially different.

The primary aim of modern warfare (in accordance with the principles of *doublethink,* this aim is simultaneously recognized and not recognized by the directing brains of the Inner Party) is to use up the products of the machine without raising the general standard of living. Even since the end of the nineteenth century, the problem of what to do with the surplus of consumption goods has been latent in industrial society. At present, when few human beings even have enough to eat, this problem is obviously not urgent, and it might not have become so, even if no artificial processes of destruction had been at work. The world of today is a bare, hungry, dilapidated place compared with the world that existed before 1914, and still more so if compared with the imaginary future to which the people of that period looked forward. In the early twentieth century, the vision of a future society unbelievably rich, leisured, orderly, and efficient—a glittering antiseptic world of glass and steel and snow-white concrete—was part of the consciousness of nearly every literate person. Science and technology were developing at a prodigious speed, and it seemed natural to assume that they would go on developing. This failed to happen, partly because of the impoverishment caused by a long series of wars and revolutions, partly because scientific and technical progress depended on the empirical habit of thought, which could not survive in a strictly regimented society. As a whole the world is more primitive today than it was fifty years ago. Certain backward areas have advanced, and various devices, always in some way connected with warfare and police espionage, have been developed, but experiment and invention have largely stopped, and the ravages of the atomic war of the nineteen-fifties have never been fully repaired. Nevertheless the dangers inherent in the machine are still there. From the moment when the machine first made its appearance it was clear to all thinking people that the need for human drudgery, and therefore to a great extent for human inequality, had disappeared. If the machine were used deliberately for that end, hunger, overwork, dirt, illiteracy, and disease could be eliminated within a few generations. And in fact, without being used for any such purpose, but by a sort of automatic process—by producing wealth which it was sometimes impossible not to distribute—the machine did raise the living standards of the average human being very greatly over a period of about fifty years at the end of the nineteenth and the beginning of the twentieth centuries.

But it was also clear that an all-round increase in wealth threatened the destruction—indeed, in some sense was the destruction—of a hierarchical society. In a world in which everyone worked short hours, had enough to eat, lived in a house with a bathroom and a refrigerator, and possessed a motor-car or even an aeroplane, the most obvious and perhaps the most important form of inequality would already have disappeared. If it once became general, wealth would confer no distinction. It was possible, no doubt, to imagine a society in which *wealth,* in the sense of personal possessions and luxuries, should be evenly distributed, while *power* remained in the hands of a small privileged caste. But in practice such a society could not long remain stable. For if leisure and security were enjoyed by all alike, the great mass of human beings who are normally stupefied by poverty would become literate and would learn to think for themselves; and when once they had done this, they would sooner or later realize that the privileged minority had no function, and they would sweep it away. In the long run, a hierarchical society was only possible on a basis of poverty and ignorance. To return to the agricultural past, as some thinkers about the beginning of the twentieth century dreamed of doing, was not a practicable solution. It conflicted with the tendency towards mechanization which had become quasi-instinctive throughout almost the whole world, and moreover, any country which remained industrially backward was helpless in a military sense and was bound to be dominated, directly or indirectly, by its more advanced rivals.

Nor was it a satisfactory solution to keep the masses in poverty by restricting the output of goods. This happened to a great extent during the final phase of capitalism, roughly between 1920 and 1940. The economy of many countries was allowed to stagnate, land went out of cultivation, capital equipment was not added to, great blocks of the population were prevented from working and kept half alive by State charity. But this, too, entailed military weakness, and since the privations it inflicted were obviously unnecessary, it made opposition inevitable. The problem was how to keep the wheels of industry turning without increasing the real wealth of the world. Goods must be produced, but they must not be distributed. And in practice the only way of achieving this was by continuous warfare.

The essential act of war is destruction, not necessarily of human lives, but of the products of human labour. War is a way of shattering to pieces, or pouring into the stratosphere, or sinking in the depths of the sea, materials which might otherwise be used to make the masses too comfortable, and hence, in the long run, too intelligent. Even when weapons of war are not actually destroyed, their manufacture is still a convenient way of expending labour power without producing anything that can be consumed. A Floating Fortress, for example, has locked up in it the labour that would build several hundred cargo-ships. Ultimately it is scrapped as obsolete, never having brought any material benefit to anybody, and with further enormous labours another Floating Fortress is built. In principle the war effort is always so planned as to eat up any surplus that might exist after meeting the bare needs of the population. In practice the needs of the population are always under-estimated, with the result that there is a chronic shortage of half the necessities of life; but this is looked on as an advantage. It is deliberate policy to keep even the favoured groups somewhere near the brink of hardship, because a general state of scarcity increases the importance of small privileges and thus magnifies the distinction between one group and another. By the standards of the early twentieth century, even a member of the Inner Party lives an austere, laborious kind of life. Nevertheless, the few luxuries that he does enjoy—his large, well-appointed flat, the better texture of his clothes, the better quality of his food and drink and tobacco, his two or three servants, his private motor-car or helicopter—set him in a different world from a member of the Outer Party, and the members of the Outer Party have a similar advantage in comparison with the submerged masses whom we call 'the proles'. The social atmosphere is that of a besieged city, where the possession of a lump of horseflesh makes the difference between wealth and poverty. And at the same time the consciousness of being at war, and therefore in danger, makes the handing-over of all power to a small caste seem the natural, unavoidable condition of survival.

War, it will be seen, not only accomplishes the necessary destruction, but accomplishes it in a psychologically acceptable way. In principle it would be quite simple to waste the surplus labour of the world by building temples and pyramids, by digging holes and filling them up again, or even by producing vast quantities of goods and then setting fire to them. But this would provide only the economic and not the emotional basis for a hierarchical society. What is concerned here is not the morale of the masses, whose attitude is unimportant so long as they are kept steadily at work, but the morale of the Party itself. Even the humblest Party member is expected to be competent, industrious, and even intelligent within narrow limits, but it is also necessary that he should be a credulous and ignorant fanatic whose prevailing moods are fear, hatred, adulation, and orgiastic triumph. In other words it is necessary that he should have the mentality appropriate to a state of war. It does not matter whether the war is actually happening, and, since no decisive victory is possible, it does not matter whether the war is going well or badly. All that is needed is that a state of war should exist. The splitting of the intelligence which the Party requires of its members, and which is more easily achieved in an atmosphere of war, is now almost universal, but the higher up the ranks one goes, the more marked it becomes. It is precisely in the Inner Party that war hysteria and hatred of the enemy are strongest. In his capacity as an administrator, it is often necessary for a member of the Inner Party to know that this or that item of war news is untruthful, and he may often be aware that the entire war is spurious and is either not happening or is being waged for purposes quite other than the declared ones: but such knowledge is easily neutralized by the technique of *doublethink*. Meanwhile no Inner Party member wavers for an instant in his mystical belief that the war *is* real, and that it is bound to end victoriously, with Oceania the undisputed master of the entire world.

All members of the Inner Party believe in this coming conquest as an article of faith. It is to be achieved either by gradually acquiring more and more territory and so building up an overwhelming preponderance of power, or by the discovery of some new and unanswerable weapon. The search for new weapons continues unceasingly, and is one of the very few remaining activities in which the inventive or speculative type of mind can find any outlet. In Oceania at the present day, Science, in the old sense, has almost ceased to exist. In Newspeak there is no word for 'Science'. The empirical method of thought, on which all the scientific achievements of the past were founded, is opposed to the most fundamental principles of Ingsoc. And even technological progress only happens when its products can in some way be used for the diminution of human liberty. In all the useful arts the world is either standing still or going backwards. The fields are cultivated with horse-ploughs while books are written by machinery. But in matters of vital importance–meaning, in effect, war and police espionage–the empirical approach is still encouraged, or at least tolerated. The two aims of the Party are to conquer the whole surface of the earth and to extinguish once and for all the possibility of independent thought. There are therefore two great problems which the Party is concerned to solve. One is how to discover, against his will, what another human being is thinking, and the other is how to kill several hundred million people in a few seconds without giving warning beforehand. In so far as scientific research still continues, this is its subject-matter. The scientist of today is either a mixture of psychologist and inquisitor, studying with real ordinary minuteness the meaning of facial expressions, gestures, and tones of voice, and testing the truth-producing effects of drugs, shock therapy, hypnosis, and physical torture; or he is chemist, physicist, or biologist concerned only with such branches of his special subject as are relevant to the taking of life. In the vast laboratories of the Ministry of Peace, and in the experimental stations hidden in the Brazilian forests, or in the Australian desert, or on lost islands of the Antarctic, the teams of experts are indefatigably at work. Some are concerned simply with planning the logistics of future wars; others devise larger and larger rocket bombs, more and more powerful explosives, and more and more impenetrable armour-plating; others search for new and deadlier gases, or for soluble poisons capable of being produced in such quantities as to destroy the vegetation of whole continents, or for breeds of disease germs immunized against all possible antibodies; others strive to produce a vehicle that shall bore its way under the soil like a submarine under the water, or an aeroplane as independent of its base as a sailing-ship; others explore even remoter possibilities such as focusing the sun's rays through lenses suspended thousands of kilometres away in space, or producing artificial earthquakes and tidal waves by tapping the heat at the earth's centre.

But none of these projects ever comes anywhere near realization, and none of the three super-states ever gains a significant lead on the others. What is more remarkable is that all three powers already possess, in the atomic bomb, a weapon far more powerful than any that their present researches are likely to discover. Although the Party, according to its habit, claims the invention for itself, atomic bombs first appeared as early as the nineteen-forties, and were first used on a large scale about ten years later. At that time some hundreds of bombs were dropped on industrial centres, chiefly in European Russia, Western Europe, and North America. The effect was to convince the ruling groups of all countries that a few more atomic bombs would mean the end of organized society, and hence of their own power. Thereafter, although no formal agreement was ever made or hinted at, no more bombs were dropped. All three powers merely continue to produce atomic bombs and store them up against the decisive opportunity which they all believe will come sooner or later. And meanwhile the art of war has remained almost stationary for thirty or forty years. Helicopters are more used than they were formerly, bombing planes have been largely superseded by self-propelled projectiles, and the fragile movable battleship has given way to the almost unsinkable Floating Fortress; but otherwise there has been little development. The tank, the submarine, the torpedo, the machine gun, even the rifle and the hand grenade are still in use. And in spite of the endless slaughters reported in the Press and on the telescreens, the desperate battles of earlier wars, in which hundreds of thousands or even millions of men were often killed in a few weeks, have never been repeated.

None of the three super-states ever attempts any manœuvre which involves the risk of serious defeat. When any large operation is undertaken, it is usually a surprise attack against an ally. The strategy that all three powers are following, or pretend to themselves that they are following, is the same. The plan is, by a combination of fighting, bargaining, and well-timed strokes of treachery, to acquire a ring of bases completely encircling one or other of the rival states, and then to sign a pact of friendship with that rival and remain on peaceful terms for so many years as to lull suspicion to sleep. During this time rockets loaded with atomic bombs can be assembled at all the strategic spots; finally they will all be fired simultaneously, with effects so devastating as to make retaliation impossible. It will then be time to sign a pact of friendship with the remaining world-power, in preparation for another attack. This scheme, it is hardly necessary to say, is a mere daydream, impossible of realization. Moreover, no fighting ever occurs except in the disputed areas round the Equator and the Pole; no invasion of enemy territory is ever undertaken. This explains the fact that in some places the frontiers between the super-states are arbitrary. Eurasia, for example, could easily conquer the British Isles, which are geographically part of Europe, or on the other hand it would be possible for Oceania to push its frontiers to the Rhine or even to the Vistula. But this would violate the principle, followed on all sides though never formulated, of cultural integrity. If Oceania were to conquer the areas that used once to be known as France and Germany, it would be necessary either to exterminate the inhabitants, a task of great physical difficulty, or to assimilate a population of about a hundred million people, who, so far as technical development goes, are roughly on the Oceanic level. The problem is the same for all three super-states. It is absolutely necessary to their structure that there should be no contact with foreigners, except, to a limited extent, with war prisoners and coloured slaves. Even the official ally of the moment is always regarded with the darkest suspicion. War prisoners apart, the average citizen of Oceania never sets eyes on a citizen of either Eurasia or Eastasia, and he is forbidden the knowledge of foreign languages. If he were allowed contact with foreigners he would discover that they are creatures similar to himself and that most of what he has been told about them is lies. The sealed world in which he lives would be broken, and the fear, hatred, and self-righteousness on which his morale depends might evaporate. It is therefore realized on all sides that however often Persia, or Egypt, or Java, or Ceylon may change hands, the main frontiers must never be crossed by anything except bombs.

Under this lies a fact never mentioned aloud, but tacitly understood and acted upon: namely, that the conditions of life in all three superstates are very much the same. In Oceania the prevailing philosophy is called Ingsoc, in Eurasia it is called Neo-Bolshevism, and in Eastasia it is called by a Chinese name usually translated as Death-Worship, but perhaps better rendered as Obliteration of the Self. The citizen of Oceania is not allowed to know anything of the tenets of the other two philosophies, but he is taught to execrate them as barbarous outrages upon morality and common sense. Actually the three philosophies are barely distinguishable, and the social systems which they support are not distinguishable at all. Everywhere there is the same pyramidal structure, the same worship of a semi-divine leader, the same economy existing by and for continuous warfare. It follows that the three super-states not only cannot conquer one another, but would gain no advantage by doing so. On the contrary, so long as they remain in conflict they prop one another up, like three sheaves of corn. And, as usual, the ruling groups of all three powers are simultaneously aware and unaware of what they are doing. Their lives are dedicated to world conquest, but they also know that it is necessary that the war should continue everlastingly and without victory. Meanwhile the fact that there *is* no danger of conquest makes possible the denial of reality which is the special feature of Ingsoc and its rival systems of thought. Here it is necessary to repeat what has been said earlier, that by becoming continuous war has fundamentally changed its character.

In past ages, a war, almost by definition, was something that sooner or later came to an end, usually in unmistakable victory or defeat. In the past, also, war was one of the main instruments by which human societies were kept in touch with physical reality. All rulers in all ages have tried to impose a false view of the world upon their followers, but they could not afford to encourage any illusion that tended to impair military efficiency. So long as defeat meant the loss of independence, or some other result generally held to be undesirable, the precautions against defeat had to be serious. Physical facts could not be ignored. In philosophy, or religion, or ethics, or politics, two and two might make five, but when one was designing a gun or an aeroplane they had to make four. Inefficient nations were always conquered sooner or later, and the struggle for efficiency was inimical to illusions. Moreover, to be efficient it was necessary to be able to learn from the past, which meant having a fairly accurate idea of what had happened in the past. Newspapers and history books were, of course, always coloured and biased, but falsification of the kind that is practised today would have been impossible. War was a sure safeguard of sanity, and so far as the ruling classes were concerned it was probably the most important of all safeguards. While wars could be won or lost, no ruling class could be completely irresponsible.

But when war becomes literally continuous, it also ceases to be dangerous. When war is continuous there is no such thing as military necessity. Technical progress can cease and the most palpable facts can be denied or disregarded. As we have seen, researches that could be called scientific are still carried out for the purposes of war, but they are essentially a kind of daydreaming, and their failure to show results is not important. Efficiency, even military efficiency, is no longer needed. Nothing is efficient in Oceania except the Thought Police. Since each of the three super-states is unconquerable, each is in effect a separate universe within which almost any perversion of thought can be safely practised. Reality only exerts its pressure through the needs of everyday life—the need to eat and drink, to get shelter and clothing, to avoid swallowing poison or stepping out of top-storey windows, and the like. Between life and death, and between physical pleasure and physical pain, there is still a distinction, but that is all. Cut off from contact with the outer world, and with the past, the citizen of Oceania is like a man in interstellar space, who has no way of knowing which direction is up and which is down. The rulers of such a state are absolute, as the Pharaohs or the Caesars could not be. They are obliged to prevent their followers from starving to death in numbers large enough to be inconvenient, and they are obliged to remain at the same low level of military technique as their rivals; but once that minimum is achieved, they can twist reality into whatever shape they choose.

The war, therefore, if we judge it by the standards of previous wars, is merely an imposture. It is like the battles between certain ruminant animals whose horns are set at such an angle that they are incapable of hurting one another. But though it is unreal it is not meaningless. It eats up the surplus of consumable goods, and it helps to preserve the special mental atmosphere that a hierarchical society needs. War, it will be seen, is now a purely internal affair. In the past, the ruling groups of all countries, although they might recognize their common interest and therefore limit the destructiveness of war, did fight against one another, and the victor always plundered the vanquished. In our own day they are not fighting against one another at all. The war is waged by each ruling group against its own subjects, and the object of the war is not to make or prevent conquests of territory, but to keep the structure of society intact. The very word 'war', therefore, has become misleading. It would probably be accurate to say that by becoming continuous war has ceased to exist. The peculiar pressure that it exerted on human beings between the Neolithic Age and the early twentieth century has disappeared and been replaced by something quite different. The effect would be much the same if the three super-states, instead of fighting one another, should agree to live in perpetual peace, each inviolate within its own boundaries. For in that case each would still be a self-contained universe, freed for ever from the sobering influence of external danger. A peace that was truly permanent would be the same as a permanent war. This—although the vast majority of Party members understand it only in a shallower sense—is the inner meaning of the Party slogan: *War is Peace.*

Winston stopped reading for a moment. Somewhere in remote distance a rocket bomb thundered. The blissful feeling of being alone with the forbidden book, in a room with no telescreen, had not worn off. Solitude and safety were physical sensations, mixed up somehow with the tiredness of his body, the softness of the chair, the touch of the faint breeze from the window that played upon his cheek. The book fascinated him, or more exactly it reassured him. In a sense it told him nothing that was new, but that was part of the attraction. It said what he would have said, if it had been possible for him to set his scattered thoughts in order. It was the product of a mind similar to his own, but enormously more powerful, more systematic, less fear-ridden. The best books, he perceived, are those that tell you what you know already. He had just turned back to Chapter I when he heard Julia's footstep on the stair and started out of his chair to meet her. She dumped her brown tool-bag on the floor and flung herself into his arms. It was more than a week since they had seen one another.

'I've got *the book*,' he said as they disentangled themselves.

'Oh, you've got it? Good,' she said without much interest, and almost immediately knelt down beside the oilstove to make the coffee.

They did not return to the subject until they had been in bed for half an hour. The evening was just cool enough to make it worth while to pull up the counterpane. From below came the familiar sound of singing and the scrape of boots on the flagstones. The brawny red-armed woman whom Winston had seen there on his first visit was almost a fixture in the yard. There seemed to be no hour of daylight when she was not marching to and fro between the washtub and the line, alternately gagging herself with clothes pegs and breaking forth into lusty song. Julia had settled down on her side and seemed to be already on the point of falling asleep. He reached out for the book, which was lying on the floor, and sat up against the bedhead.

'We must read it,' he said. 'You too. All members of the Brotherhood have to read it.'

'You read it,' she said with her eyes shut. 'Read it aloud. That's the best way. Then you can explain it to me as you go.'   The clock's hands said six, meaning eighteen. They had three or four hours ahead of them. He propped the book against his knees and began reading:

CHAPTER I
IGNORANCE IS STRENGTH

Throughout recorded time, and probably since the end of the Neolithic Age, there have been three kinds of people in the world, the High, the Middle, and the Low. They have been subdivided in many ways, they have borne countless different names, and their relative numbers, as well as their attitude towards one another, have varied from age to age: but the essential structure of society has never altered. Even after enormous upheavals and seemingly irrevocable changes, the same pattern has always reasserted itself, just as a gyroscope will always return to equilibrium, however far it is pushed one way or the other.

'Julia, are you awake?' said Winston.
'Yes, my love, I'm listening. Go on. It's marvellous.'
He continued reading:

The aims of these three groups are entirely irreconcilable. The aim of the High is to remain where they are. The aim of the Middle is to change places with the High. The aim of the Low, when they have an aim—for it is an abiding characteristic of the Low that they are too much crushed by drudgery to be more than intermittently conscious of anything outside their daily lives—is to abolish all distinctions and create a society in which all men shall be equal. Thus throughout history a struggle which is the same in its main outlines recurs over and over again. For long periods the High seem to be securely in power, but sooner or later there always comes a moment when they lose either their belief in themselves or their capacity to govern efficiently, or both. They are then overthrown by the Middle, who enlist the Low on their side by pretending to them that they are fighting for liberty and justice. As soon as they have reached their objective, the Middle thrust the Low back into their old position of servitude, and themselves become the High. Presently a new Middle group splits off from one of the other groups, or from both of them, and the struggle begins over again. Of the three groups, only the Low -   never even temporarily successful in achieving their aims. It would be an exaggeration to say that throughout history there has been no progress of a material kind. Even today, in a period of decline, the average human being is physically better off than he was a few centuries ago. But no advance in wealth, no softening of manners, no reform or revolution has ever brought human equality a millimetre nearer. From the point of view of the Low, no historic change has ever meant much more than a change in the name of their masters.

By the late nineteenth century the recurrence of this pattern had become obvious to many observers. There then rose schools of thinkers who interpreted history as a cyclical process and claimed to show that inequality was the unalterable law of human life. This doctrine, of course, had always had its adherents, but in the manner in which it was now put forward there was a significant change. In the past the need for a hierarchical form of society had been the doctrine specifically of the High. It had been preached by kings and aristocrats and by the priests, lawyers, and the like who were parasitical upon them, and it had generally been softened by promises of compensation in an imaginary world beyond the grave. The Middle, so long as it was struggling for power, had always made use of such terms as freedom, justice, and fraternity. Now, however, the concept of human brotherhood began to be assailed by people who were not yet in positions of command, but merely hoped to be so before long. In the past the Middle had made revolutions under the banner of equality, and then had established a fresh tyranny as soon as the old one was overthrown. The new Middle groups in effect proclaimed their tyranny beforehand. Socialism, a theory which appeared in the early nineteenth century and was the last link in a chain of thought stretching back to the slave rebellions of antiquity, was still deeply infected by the Utopianism of past ages. But in each variant of Socialism that appeared from about 1900 onwards the aim of establishing liberty and equality was more and more openly abandoned. The new movements which appeared in the middle years of the century, Ingsoc in Oceania, Neo-Bolshevism in Eurasia, Death-Worship, as it is commonly called, in Eastasia, had the conscious aim of perpetuating *un*freedom and *in*equality. These new movements, of course, grew out of the old ones and tended to keep their names and pay lip-service to their ideology. But the purpose of all of them was to arrest progress and freeze history at a chosen moment. The familiar pendulum swing was to happen once more, and then stop. As usual, the High were to be turned out by the Middle, who would then become the High; but this time, by conscious strategy, the High would be able to maintain their position permanently.

The new doctrines arose partly because of the accumulation of historical knowledge, and the growth of the historical sense, which had hardly existed before the nineteenth century. The cyclical movement of history was now intelligible, or appeared to be so; and if it was intelligible, then it was alterable. But the principal, underlying cause was that, as early as the beginning of the twentieth century, human equality had become technically possible. It was still true that men were not equal in their native talents and that functions had to be specialized in ways that favoured some individuals against others; but there was no longer any real need for class distinctions or for large differences of wealth. In earlier ages, class distinctions had been not only inevitable but desirable. Inequality was the price of civilization. With the development of machine production, however, the case was altered. Even if it was still necessary for human beings to do different kinds of work, it was no longer necessary for them to live at different social or economic levels. Therefore, from the point of view of the new groups who were on the point of seizing power, human equality was no longer an ideal to be striven after, but a danger to be averted. In more primitive ages, when a just and peaceful society was in fact not possible, it had been fairly easy to believe it. The idea of an earthly paradise in which men should live together in a state of brotherhood, without laws and without brute labour, had haunted the human imagination for thousands of years. And this vision had had a certain hold even on the group who actually profited by each historical change. The heirs of the French, English, and American revolutions had partly believed in their own phrases about the rights of man, freedom of speech, equality before the law, and the like, and have even allowed their conduct to be influenced by them to some extent. But by the fourth decade of the twentieth century all the main currents of political thought were authoritarian. The earthly paradise had been discredited at exactly the moment when it became realizable. Every new political theory, by whatever name it called itself, led back to hierarchy and regimentation. And in the general hardening of outlook that set in round about 1930, practices which had been long abandoned, in some cases for hundreds of years—imprisonment without trial, the use of war prisoners as slaves, public executions, torture to extract confessions, the use of hostages, and the deportation of whole populations—not only became common again, but were tolerated and even defended by people who considered themselves enlightened and progressive.

It was only after a decade of national wars, civil wars, revolutions, and counter-revolutions in all parts of the world that Ingsoc and its rivals emerged as fully worked-out political theories. But they had been foreshadowed by the various systems, generally called totalitarian, which had appeared earlier in the century, and the main outlines of the world which would emerge from the prevailing chaos had long been obvious. What kind of people would control this world had been equally obvious. The new aristocracy was made up for the most part of bureaucrats, scientists, technicians, trade-union organizers, publicity experts, sociologists, teachers, journalists, and professional politicians. These people, whose origins lay in the salaried middle class and the upper grades of the working class, had been shaped and brought together by the barren world of monopoly industry and centralized government. As compared with their opposite numbers in past ages, they were less avaricious, less tempted by luxury, hungrier for pure power, and, above all, more conscious of what they were doing and more intent on crushing opposition. This last difference was cardinal. By comparison with that existing today, all the tyrannies of the past were half-hearted and inefficient. The ruling groups were always infected to some extent by liberal ideas, and were content to leave loose ends everywhere, to regard only the overt act and to be uninterested in what their subjects were thinking. Even the Catholic Church of the Middle Ages was tolerant by modern standards. Part of the reason for this was that in the past no government had the power to keep its citizens under constant surveillance. The invention of print, however, made it easier to manipulate public opinion, and the film and the radio carried the process further. With the development of television, and the technical advance which made it possible to receive and transmit simultaneously on the same instrument, private life came to an end. Every citizen, or at least every citizen important enough to be worth watching, could be kept for twenty-four hours a day under the eyes of the police and in the sound of official propaganda, with all other channels of communication closed. The possibility of enforcing not only complete obedience to the will of the State, but complete uniformity of opinion on all subjects, now existed for the first time.

After the revolutionary period of the 'fifties and 'sixties, society regrouped itself, as always, into High, Middle, and Low. But the new High group, unlike all its forerunners, did not act upon instinct but knew what was needed to safeguard its position. It had long been realized that the only secure basis for oligarchy is collectivism. Wealth and privilege are most easily defended when they are possessed jointly. The so-called 'abolition of private property' which took place in the middle years of the century meant, in effect, the concentration of property in far fewer hands than before: but with this difference, that the new owners were a group instead of a mass of individuals. Individually, no member of the Party owns anything, except petty personal belongings. Collectively, the Party owns everything in Oceania, because it controls everything, and disposes of the products as it thinks fit. In the years following the Revolution it was able to step into this commanding position almost unopposed, because the whole process was represented as an act of collectivization. It had always been assumed that if the capitalist class were expropriated, Socialism must follow: and unquestionably the capitalists had been expropriated. Factories, mines, land, houses, transport—everything had been taken away from them: and since these things were no longer private property, it followed that they must be public property. Ingsoc, which grew out of the earlier Socialist movement and inherited its phraseology, has in fact carried out the main item in the Socialist programme; with the result, foreseen and intended beforehand, that economic inequality has been made permanent.

But the problems of perpetuating a hierarchical society go deeper than this. There are only four ways in which a ruling group can fall from power. Either it is conquered from without, or it governs so inefficiently that the masses are stirred to revolt, or it allows a strong and discontented Middle group to come into being, or it loses its own self-confidence and willingness to govern. These causes do not operate singly, and as a rule all four of them are present in some degree. A ruling class which could guard against all of them would remain in power permanently. Ultimately the determining factor is the mental attitude of the ruling class itself.

After the middle of the present century, the first danger had in reality disappeared. Each of the three powers which now divide the world is in fact unconquerable, and could only become conquerable through slow demographic changes which a government with wide powers can easily avert. The second danger, also, is only a theoretical one. The masses never revolt of their own accord, and they never revolt merely because they are oppressed. Indeed, so long as they are not permitted to have standards of comparison, they never even become aware that they are oppressed. The recurrent economic crises of past times were totally unnecessary and are not now permitted to happen, but other and equally large dislocations can and do happen without having political results, because there is no way in which discontent can become articulate. As for the problem of over-production, which has been latent in our society since the development of machine technique, it is solved by the device of continuous warfare (see Chapter III), which is also useful in keying up public morale to the necessary pitch. From the point of view of our present rulers, therefore, the only genuine dangers are the splitting-off of a new group of able, under-employed, power-hungry people, and the growth of liberalism and scepticism in their own ranks. The problem, that is to say, is educational. It is a problem of continuously moulding the consciousness both of the directing group and of the larger executive group that lies immediately below it. The consciousness of the masses needs only to be influenced in a negative way.

Given this background, one could infer, if one did not know it already, the general structure of Oceanic society. At the apex of the pyramid comes Big Brother. Big Brother is infallible and all-powerful. Every success, every achievement, every victory, every scientific discovery, all knowledge, all wisdom, all happiness, all virtue, are held to issue directly from his leadership and inspiration. Nobody has ever seen Big Brother. He is a face on the hoardings, a voice on the telescreen. We may be reasonably sure that he will never die, and there is already considerable uncertainty as to when he was born. Big Brother is the guise in which the Party chooses to exhibit itself to the world. His function is to act as a focusing point for love, fear, and reverence, emotions which are more easily felt towards an individual than towards an organization. Below Big Brother comes the Inner Party, its numbers limited to six millions, or something less than 2 per cent of the population of Oceania. Below the Inner Party comes the Outer Party, which, if the Inner Party is described as the brain of the State, may be justly likened to the hands. Below that come the dumb masses whom we habitually refer to as 'the proles', numbering perhaps 85 per cent of the population. In the terms of our earlier classification, the proles are the Low: for the slave population of the equatorial lands, who pass constantly from conqueror to conqueror, are not a permanent or necessary part of the structure.

In principle, membership of these three groups is not hereditary. The child of Inner Party parents is in theory not born into the Inner Party. Admission to either branch of the Party is by examination, taken at the age of sixteen. Nor is there any racial discrimination, or any marked domination of one province by another. Jews, Negroes, South Americans of pure Indian blood are to be found in the highest ranks of the Party, and the administrators of any area are always drawn from the inhabitants of that area. In no part of Oceania do the inhabitants have the feeling that they are a colonial population ruled from a distant capital. Oceania has no capital, and its titular head is a person whose whereabouts nobody knows. Except that English is its chief *lingua franca* and Newspeak its official language, it is not centralized in any way. Its rulers are not held together by blood-ties but by adherence to a common doctrine. It is true that our society is stratified, and very rigidly stratified, on what at first sight appear to be hereditary lines. There is far less to-and-fro movement between the different groups than happened under capitalism or even in the pre-industrial age. Between the two branches of the Party there is a certain amount of interchange, but only so much as will ensure that weaklings are excluded from the Inner Party and that ambitious members of the Outer Party are made harmless by allowing them to rise. Proletarians, in practice, are not allowed to graduate into the Party. The most gifted among them, who might possibly become nuclei of discontent, are simply marked down by the Thought Police and eliminated. But this state of affairs is not necessarily permanent, nor is it a matter of principle. The Party is not a class in the old sense of the word. It does not aim at transmitting power to its own children, as such; and if there were no other way of keeping the ablest people at the top, it would be perfectly prepared to recruit an entire new generation from the ranks of the proletariat. In the crucial years, the fact that the Party was not a hereditary body did a great deal to neutralize opposition. The older kind of Socialist, who had been trained to fight against something called 'class privilege', assumed that what is not hereditary cannot be permanent. He did not see that the continuity of an oligarchy need not be physical, nor did he pause to reflect that hereditary aristocracies have always been shortlived, whereas adoptive organizations such as the Catholic Church have sometimes lasted for hundreds of thousands of years. The essence of oligarchical rule is not father-to-son inheritance, but the persistence of a certain world-view and a certain way of life, imposed by the dead upon the living. A ruling group is a ruling group so long as it can nominate its successors. The Party is not concerned with perpetuating its blood but with perpetuating itself. *Who* wields power is not important, provided that the hierarchical structure remains always the same.

All the beliefs, habits, tastes, emotions, mental attitudes that characterize our time are really designed to sustain the mystique of the Party and prevent the true nature of present-day society from being perceived. Physical rebellion, or any preliminary move towards rebellion, is at present not possible. From the proletarians nothing is to be feared. Left to themselves, they will continue from generation to generation and from century to century, working, breeding, and dying, not only without any impulse to rebel, but without the power of grasping that the world could be other than it is. They could only become dangerous if the advance of industrial technique made it necessary to educate them more highly; but, since military and commercial rivalry are no longer important, the level of popular education is actually declining. What opinions the masses hold, or do not hold, is looked on as a matter of indifference. They can be granted intellectual liberty because they have no intellect. In a Party member, on the other hand, not even the smallest deviation of opinion on the most unimportant subject can be tolerated.

A Party member lives from birth to death under the eye of the Thought Police. Even when he is alone he can never be sure that he is alone. Wherever he may be, asleep or awake, working or resting, in his bath or in bed, he can be inspected without warning and without knowing that he is being inspected. Nothing that he does is indifferent. His friendships, his relaxations, his behaviour towards his wife and children, the expression of his face when he is alone, the words he mutters in sleep, even the characteristic movements of his body, are all jealously scrutinized. Not only any actual misdemeanour, but any eccentricity, however small, any change of habits, any nervous mannerism that could possibly be the symptom of an inner struggle, is certain to be detected. He has no freedom of choice in any direction whatever. On the other hand his actions are not regulated by law or by any clearly formulated code of behaviour. In Oceania there is no law. Thoughts and actions which, when detected, mean certain death are not formally forbidden, and the endless purges, arrests, tortures, imprisonments, and vaporizations are not inflicted as punishment for crimes which have actually been committed, but are merely the wiping-out of persons who might perhaps commit a crime at some time in the future. A Party member is required to have not only the right opinions, but the right instincts. Many of the beliefs and attitudes demanded of him are never plainly stated, and could not be stated without laying bare the contradictions inherent in Ingsoc. If he is a person naturally orthodox (in Newspeak a *goodthinker*), he will in all circumstances know, without taking thought, what is the true belief or the desirable emotion. But in any case an elaborate mental training, undergone in childhood and grouping itself round the Newspeak words *crimestop*, *blackwhite*, and *doublethink*, makes him unwilling and unable to think too deeply on any subject whatever.

A Party member is expected to have no private emotions and no respites from enthusiasm. He is supposed to live in a continuous frenzy of hatred of foreign enemies and internal traitors, triumph over victories, and self-abasement before the power and wisdom of the Party. The discontents produced by his bare, unsatisfying life are deliberately turned outwards and dissipated by such devices as the Two Minutes Hate, and the speculations which might possibly induce a sceptical or rebellious attitude are killed in advance by his early acquired inner discipline. The first and simplest stage in the discipline, which can be taught even to young children, is called, in Newspeak, *crimestop*. *Crimestop* means the faculty of stopping short, as though by instinct, at the threshold of any dangerous thought. It includes the power of not grasping analogies, of failing to perceive logical errors, of misunderstanding the simplest arguments if they are inimical to Ingsoc, and of being bored or repelled by any train of thought which is capable of leading in a heretical direction. *Crimestop*, in short, means protective stupidity. But stupidity is not enough. On the contrary, orthodoxy in the full sense demands a control over one's own mental processes as complete as that of a contortionist over his body. Oceanic society rests ultimately on the belief that Big Brother is omnipotent and that the Party is infallible. But since in reality Big Brother is not omnipotent and the Party is not infallible, there is need for an unwearying, moment-to-moment flexibility in the treatment of facts. The key-word here is *blackwhite*. Like so many Newspeak words, this word has two mutually contradictory meanings. Applied to an opponent, it means the habit of impudently claiming that black is white, in contradiction of the plain facts. Applied to a Party member, it means a loyal willingness to say that black is white when Party discipline demands this. But it means also the ability to *believe* that black is white, and more, to *know* that black is white, and to forget that one has ever believed the contrary. This demands a continuous alteration of the past, made possible by the system of thought which really embraces all the rest, and which is known in Newspeak as *doublethink*.

The alteration of the past is necessary for two reasons, one of which is subsidiary and, so to speak, precautionary. The subsidiary reason is that the Party member, like the proletarian, tolerates present-day conditions partly because he has no standards of comparison. He must be cut off from the past, just as he must be cut off from foreign countries, because it is necessary for him to believe that he is better off than his ancestors and that the average level of material comfort is constantly rising. But by far the more important reason for the readjustment of the past is the need to safeguard the infallibility of the Party. It is not merely that speeches, statistics, and records of every kind must be constantly brought up to date in order to show that the predictions of the Party were in all cases right. It is also that no change in doctrine or in political alignment can ever be admitted. For to change one's mind, or even one's policy, is a confession of weakness. If, for example, Eurasia or Eastasia (whichever it may be) is the enemy today, then that country must always have been the enemy. And if the facts say otherwise then the facts must be altered. Thus history is continuously rewritten. This day-to-day falsification of the past, carried out by the Ministry of Truth, is as necessary to the stability of the régime as the work of repression and espionage carried out by the Ministry of Love.

The mutability of the past is the central tenet of Ingsoc. Past events, it is argued have no objective existence, but survive only in written records and in human memories. The past is whatever the records and the memories agree upon. And since the Party is in full control of all records and in equally full control of the minds of its members, it follows that the past is whatever the Party chooses to make it. It also follows that though the past is alterable, it never has been altered in any specific instance. For when it has been re-created in whatever shape is needed at the moment, then this new version *is* the past, and no different past can ever have existed. This holds good even when, as often happens, the same event has to be altered out of recognition several times in the course of a year. At all times the Party is in possession of absolute truth, and clearly the absolute can never have been different from what it is now. It will be seen that the control of the past depends above all on the training of memory. To make sure that all written records agree with the orthodoxy of the moment is merely a mechanical act. But it is also necessary to *remember* that events happened in the desired manner. And if it is necessary to rearrange one's memories or to tamper with written records, then it is necessary to *forget* that one had done so. The trick of doing this can be learned like any other mental technique. It *is* learned by the majority of Party members, and certainly by all who are intelligent as well as orthodox. In Oldspeak it is called, quite frankly, 'reality control'. In Newspeak it is called *doublethink,* though *doublethink* comprises much else as well.

*Doublethink* means the power of holding two contradictory beliefs in one's mind simultaneously, and accepting both of them. The Party intellectual knows in which direction his memories must be altered; he therefore knows that he is playing tricks with reality; but by the exercise of *doublethink* he also satisfies himself that reality is not violated. The process has to be conscious, or it would not be carried out with sufficient precision, but it also has to be unconscious, or it would bring with it a feeling of falsity and hence of guilt. *Doublethink* lies at the very heart of Ingsoc, since the essential act of the Party is to use conscious deception while retaining the firmness of purpose that goes with complete honesty. To tell deliberate lies while genuinely believing in them, to forget any fact that has become inconvenient, and then, when it becomes necessary again, to draw it back from oblivion for just so long as it is needed, to deny the existence of objective reality and all the while to take account of the reality which one denies—all this is indispensably necessary. Even in using the word *doublethink* it is necessary to exercise *doublethink.* For by using the word one admits that one is tampering with reality; by a fresh act of *doublethink* one erases this knowledge: and s⌃ on indefinitely, with the lie always one leap ahead of the truth. Ultimately it is by means of *doublethink* that the Party has been able—and may, for all we know, continue to be able for thousands of years—to arrest the course of history.

All past oligarchies have fallen from power either because they ossified or because they grew soft. Either they became stupid and arrogant, failed to adjust themselves to changing circumstances, and were overthrown; or they became liberal and cowardly, made concessions when they should have used force, and once again were overthrown. They fell, that is to say, either through consciousness or through unconsciousness. It is the achievement of the Party to have produced a system of thought in which both conditions can exist simultaneously. And upon no other intellectual basis could the dominion of the Party be made permanent. If one is to rule, and to continue ruling, one must be able to dislocate the sense of reality. For the secret of rulership is to combine a belief in one's own infallibility with the power to learn from past mistakes.

It need hardly be said that the subtlest practitioners of *doublethink* are those who invented *doublethink* and know that it is a vast system of mental cheating. In our society, those who have the best knowledge of what is happening are also those who are furthest from seeing the world as it is. In general, the greater the understanding, the greater the delusion: the more intelligent, the less sane. One clear illustration of this is the fact that war hysteria increases in intensity as one rises in the social scale. Those whose attitude towards the war is most nearly rational are the subject peoples of the disputed territories. To these people the war is simply a continuous calamity which sweeps to and fro over their bodies like a tidal wave. Which side is winning is a matter of complete indifference to them. They are aware that a change of overlordship means simply that they will be doing the same work as before for new masters who treat them in the same manner as the old ones. The slightly more favoured workers whom we call 'the proles' are only intermittently conscious of the war. When it is necessary they can be prodded into frenzies of fear and hatred, but when left to themselves they are capable of forgetting for long periods that the war is happening. It is in the ranks of the Party, and above all of the Inner Party, that the true war enthusiasm is found. World-conquest is believed in most firmly by those who know it to be impossible. This peculiar linking-together of opposites—knowledge with ignorance, cynicism with fanaticism—is one of the chief distinguishing marks of Oceanic society. The official ideology abounds with contradictions even when there is no practical reason for them. Thus, the Party rejects and vilifies every principle for which the Socialist movement originally stood, and it chooses to do this in the name of Socialism. It preaches a contempt for the working class unexampled for centuries past, and it dresses its members in a uniform which was at one time peculiar to manual workers and was adopted for that reason. It systematically undermines the solidarity of the family, and it calls its leader by a name which is a direct appeal to the sentiment of family loyalty. Even the names of the four Ministries by which we are governed exhibit a sort of impudence in their deliberate reversal of the facts. The Ministry of Peace concerns itself with war, the Ministry of Truth with lies, the Ministry of Love with torture, and the Ministry of Plenty with starvation. These contradictions are not accidental, nor do they result from ordinary hypocrisy: they are deliberate exercises in *doublethink*. For it is only by reconciling contradictions that power can be retained indefinitely. In no other way could the ancient cycle be broken. If human equality is to be for ever averted—if the High, as we have called them, are to keep their places permanently—then the prevailing mental condition must be controlled insanity.

But there is one question which until this moment we have almost ignored. It is: *why* should human equality be averted? Supposing that the mechanics of the process have been rightly described, what is the motive for this huge, accurately planned effort to freeze history at a particular moment of time?

Here we reach the central secret. As we have seen, the mystique of the Party, and above all of the Inner Party, depends upon *doublethink*. But deeper than this lies the original motive, the never-questioned instinct that first led to the seizure of power and brought *doublethink*, the Thought Police, continuous warfare, and all the other necessary paraphernalia into existence afterwards. This motive really consists. . . .


Winston became aware of silence, as one becomes aware of a new sound. It seemed to him that Julia had been very still for some time past. She was lying on her side, naked from the waist upwards, with her cheek pillowed on her hand and one dark lock tumbling across her eyes. Her breast rose and fell slowly and regularly.

'Julia.'

No answer.

'Julia, are you awake?'

No answer. She was asleep. He shut the book, put it carefully on the floor, lay down, and pulled the coverlet over both of them.

He had still, he reflected, not learned the ultimate secret. He understood *how*; he did not understand *why*. Chapter I, like Chapter III, had not actually told him anything that he did not know, it had merely systematized the knowledge that he possessed already. But after reading it he knew better than before that he was not mad. Being in a minority, even a minority of one, did not make you mad. There was truth and there was untruth, and if you clung to the truth even against the whole world, you were not mad. A yellow beam from the sinking sun slanted in through the window and fell across the pillow. He shut his eyes. The sun on his face and the girl's smooth body touching his own gave him a strong, sleepy, confident feeling. He was safe, everything was all right.

He fell asleep murmuring 'Sanity is not statistical,' with the feeling that this remark contained in it a profound wisdom.

*

When he woke it was with the sensation of having slept for a long time, but a glance at the old-fashioned clock told him that it was only twenty-thirty. He lay dozing for a little while; then the usual deep-lunged singing struck up from the yard below:

> 'It was only an 'opeless fancy,
> It passed like an Ipril dye,
> But a look an' a word an' the dreams they stirred
> They 'ave stolen my 'eart awye!'

The drivelling song seemed to have kept its popularity. You still heard it all over the place. It had outlived the Hate Song. Julia woke at the sound, stretched herself luxuriously, and got out of bed.

'I'm hungry,' she said. 'Let's make some more coffee. Damn! The stove's gone out and the water's cold.' She picked the stove up and shook it. 'There's no oil in it.'

'We can get some from old Charrington, I expect.'

'The funny thing is I made sure it was full. I'm going to put my clothes on,' she added. 'It seems to have got colder.'

Winston also got up and dressed himself. The indefatigable voice sang on:

> 'They sye that time 'eals all things,
> They sye you can always forget;
> But the smiles an' the tears acrorss the years
> They twist my 'eart-strings yet!'

As he fastened the belt of his overalls he strolled across to the window. The sun must have gone down behind the houses; it was not shining into the yard any longer. The flagstones were wet as though they had just been washed, and he had the feeling that the sky had been washed too, so fresh and pale was the blue between the chimney-pots. Tirelessly the woman marched to and fro, corking and uncorking herself, singing and falling silent, and pegging out more diapers, and more and yet more. He wondered whether she took in washing for a living, or was merely the slave of twenty or thirty grand-children. Julia had come across to his side; together they gazed down with a sort of fascination at the sturdy figure below. As he looked at the woman in her characteristic attitude, her thick arms reaching up for the line, her powerful mare-like buttocks protruded, it struck him for the first time that she was beautiful. It had never before occurred to him that the body of a woman of fifty, blown up to monstrous dimensions by childbearing, then hardened, roughened by work till it was coarse in the grain like an over-ripe turnip, could be beautiful. But it was so, and after all, he thought, why not? The solid, contourless body, like a block of granite, and the rasping red skin, bore the same relation to the body of a girl as the rose-hip to the rose. Why should the fruit be held inferior to the flower?

'She's beautiful,' he murmured.

'She's a metre across the hips, easily,' said Julia.

'That is her style of beauty,' said Winston.

He held Julia's supple waist easily encircled by his arm. From the hip to the knee her flank was against his. Out of their bodies no child would ever come. That was the one thing they could never do. Only by word of mouth, from mind to mind, could they pass on the secret. The woman down there had no mind, she had only strong arms, a warm heart, and a fertile belly. He wondered how many children she had given birth to. It might easily be fifteen. She had had her momentary flowering, a year, perhaps, of wild-rose beauty, and then she had suddenly swollen like a fertilized fruit and grown hard and red and coarse, and then her life had been laundering, scrubbing, darning, cooking, sweeping, polishing, mending, scrubbing, laundering, first for children, then for grand-children, over thirty unbroken years. At the end of it she was still singing. The mystical reverence that he felt for her was somehow mixed up with the aspect of the pale, cloudless sky, stretching away behind the chimney-pots into interminable distance. It was curious to think that the sky was the same for everybody, in Eurasia or Eastasia as well as here. And the people under the sky were also very much the same—everywhere, all over the world, hundreds of thousands of millions of people just like this, people ignorant of one another's existence, held apart by walls of hatred and lies, and yet almost exactly the same—people who had never learned to think but who were storing up in their hearts and bellies and muscles the power that would one day overturn the world. If there was hope , it lay in the proles! Without having read to the end of *the book*, he knew that that must be Goldstein's final message. The future belonged to the proles. And could he be sure that when their time came the world they constructed would not be just as alien to him, Winston Smith, as the world of the Party? Yes, because at the least it would be a world of sanity. Where there is equality there can be sanity. Sooner of later it would happen, strength would change into consciousness. The proles were immortal, you could not doubt it when you looked at that valiant figure in the yard. In the end their awakening would come. And until that happened, though it might be a thousand years, they would stay alive against all the odds, like birds, passing on from body to body the vitality which the Party did not share and could not kill.

'Do you remember,' he said, 'the thrush that sang to us, that first day, at the edge of the wood?'

'He wasn't singing to us,' said Julia. 'He was singing to please himself. Not even that. He was just singing.'

The birds sang, the proles sang, the Party did not sing. All round the world, in London and New York, in Africa and Brazil, and in the mysterious, forbidden lands beyond the frontiers, in the streets of Paris and Berlin, in the villages of the endless Russian plain, in the bazaars of China and Japan—everywhere stood the same solid unconquerable figure, made monstrous by work and child bearing, toiling from birth to death and still singing. Out of those mighty loins a race of conscious beings must one day come. You were the dead; theirs was the future. But you could share in that future if you kept alive the mind as they kept alive the body, and passed on the secret doctrine that two plus two make four.

'We are the dead,' he said.

'We are the dead,' echoed Julia dutifully.

'You are the dead,' said an iron voice behind them.

They sprang apart. Winston's entrails seemed to have turned into ice. He could see the white all round the irises of Julia's eyes. Her face had turned a milky yellow. The smear of rouge that was still on each cheekbone stood out sharply, almost as though unconnected with the skin beneath.

'You are the dead,' repeated the iron voice.

'It was behind the picture,' breathed Julia.

'It was behind the picture,' said the voice. 'Remain exactly where you are. Make no movement until you are ordered.'

It was starting, it was starting at last! They could do nothing except stand gazing into one another's eyes. To run for life, to get out of the house before it was too late—no such thought occurred to them. Unthinkable to disobey the iron voice from the wall. There was a snap as though a catch had been turned back, and a crash of breaking glass. The picture had fallen to the floor, uncovering the telescreen behind it.

'Now they can see us,' said Julia.

'Now we can see you,' said the voice. 'Stand out in the middle of the room. Stand back to back. Clasp your hands behind your heads. Do not touch one another.'

They were not touching, but it seemed to him that he could feel Julia's body shaking. Or perhaps it was merely the shaking of his own. He could just stop his teeth from chattering, but his knees were beyond his control. There was a sound of trampling boots below, inside the house and outside. The yard seemed to be full of men. Something was being dragged across the stones. The woman's singing had stopped abruptly. There was a long, rolling, clang, as though the washtub had been flung across the yard, and then a confusion of angry shouts which ended in a yell of pain.

'The house is surrounded,' said Winston.

'The house is surrounded,' said the voice.

He heard Julia snap her teeth together. 'I suppose we may as well say good-bye,' she said.

'You may as well say good-bye,' said the voice. And then another quite different voice, a thin, cultivated voice which Winston had the impression of having heard before, struck in: 'And by the way, while we are on the subject, "Here comes a candle to light you to bed, here comes a chopper to chop off your head"!'

Something crashed on to the bed behind Winston's back. The head of a ladder had been thrust through the window and had burst in the frames. Some one was climbing through the window. There was a stampede of boots up the stairs. The room was full of solid men in black uniforms, with iron-shod boots on their feet and truncheons in their hands.

Winston was not trembling any longer. Even his eyes he barely moved. One thing alone mattered: to keep still, to keep still and not give them an excuse to hit you! A man with a smooth prize-fighter's jowl in which the mouth was only a slit paused opposite him balancing his truncheon meditatively between thumb and forefinger. Winston met his eyes. The feeling of nakedness, with one's hands behind one's head and one's face and body all exposed, was almost unbearable. The man protruded the tip of a white tongue, licked the place where his lips should have been, and then passed on. There was another crash. Someone had picked up the glass paperweight from the table and smashed it to pieces on the hearth-stone.

The fragment of coral, a tiny crinkle of pink like a sugar rosebud from a cake, rolled across the mat. How small, thought Winston, how small it always was! There was a gasp and a thump behind him, and he received a violent kick on the ankle which nearly flung him off his balance. One of the men had smashed his fist into Julia's solar plexus, doubling her up like a pocket ruler. She was thrashing about on the floor, fighting for breath. Winston dared not turn his head even by a millimetre, but sometimes her livid, gasping face came within the angle of his vision. Even in his terror it was as though he could feel the pain in his own body, the deadly pain which nevertheless was less urgent than the struggle to get back her breath. He knew what it was like: the terrible, agonizing pain which was there all the while but could not be suffered yet, because before all else it was necessary to be able to breathe. Then two of the men hoisted her up by knees and shoulders, and carried her out of the room like a sack. Winston had a glimpse of her face, upside down, yellow and contorted, with the eyes shut, and still with a smear of rouge on either cheek; and that was the last he saw of her.

He stood dead still. No one had hit him yet. Thoughts which came of their own accord but seemed totally uninteresting began to flit through his mind. He wondered whether they had got Mr Charrington. He wondered what they had done to the woman in the yard. He noticed that he badly wanted to urinate, and felt a faint surprise, because he had done so only two or three hours ago. He noticed that the clock on the mantelpiece said nine, meaning twenty-one. But the light seemed too strong. Would not the light be fading at twenty-one hours on an August evening? He wondered whether after all he and Julia had mistaken the time—had slept the clock round and thought it was twenty-thirty when really it was nought eight-thirty on the following morning. But he did not pursue the thought further. It was not interesting.

There was another, lighter step in the passage. Mr Charrington came into the room. The demeanour of the black-uniformed men suddenly became more subdued. Something had also changed in Mr Charrington's appearance. His eye fell on the fragments of the glass paperweight.

'Pick up those pieces,' he said sharply.

A man stooped to obey. The Cockney accent had disappeared: Winston suddenly realized whose voice it was that he had heard a few moments ago on the telescreen. Mr Charrington was still wearing his old velvet jacket, but his hair, which had been almost white, had turned black. Also he was not wearing his spectacles. He gave Winston a single sharp glance, as though verifying his identity, and then paid no more attention to him. He was still recognizable, but he was not the same person any longer. His body had straightened, and seemed to have grown bigger. His face had undergone only tiny changes that had nevertheless worked a complete transformation. The black eyebrows were less bushy, the wrinkles were gone, the whole lines of the face seemed to have altered; even the nose seemed shorter. It was the alert, cold face of a man of about five-and-thirty. It occurred to Winston that for the first time in his life he was looking, with knowledge, at a member of the Thought Police.

# PART III

## I

He did not know where he was. Presumably he was in the Ministry of Love; but there was no way of making certain.

He was in a high-ceilinged windowless cell with walls of glittering white porcelain. Concealed lamps flooded it with cold light, and there was a low, steady humming sound which he supposed had something to do with the air supply. A bench, or shelf, just wide enough to sit on ran round the wall, broken only by the door and, at the end opposite the door, a lavatory pan with no wooden seat. There were four telescreens, one in each wall.

There was a dull aching in his belly. It had been there ever since they had bundled him into the closed van and driven him away. But he was also hungry, with a gnawing, unwholesome kind of hunger. It might be twenty-four hours since he had eaten, it might be thirty-six. He still did not know, probably never would know, whether it had been morning or evening when they arrested him. Since he was arrested he had not been fed.

He sat as still as he could on the narrow bench, with his hands crossed on his knees. He had already learned to sit still. If you made unexpected movements they yelled at you from the telescreen. But the craving for food was growing upon him. What he longed for above all was a piece of bread. He had an idea that there were a few breadcrumbs in the pocket of his overalls. It was even possible—he thought this because from time to time something seemed to tickle his leg—that there might be a sizeable bit of crust there. In the end the temptation to find out overcame his fear; he slipped a hand into his pocket.

'Smith!' yelled a voice from the telescreen. '6079 Smith W.! Hands out of pockets in the cells!'

He sat still again, his hands crossed on his knee. Before being brought here he had been taken to another place which must have been an ordinary prison or a temporary lock-up used by the patrols. He did not know how long he had been there; some hours at any rate; with no clocks and no daylight it was hard to gauge the time. It was a noisy, evil-smelling place. They had put him into a cell similar to the one he was now in, but filthily dirty and at all times crowded by ten or fifteen people. The majority of them were common criminals, but there were a few political prisoners among them. He had sat silent against the wall, jostled by dirty bodies, too preoccupied by fear and the pain in his belly to take much interest in his surroundings, but still noticing the astonishing difference in demeanour between the Party prisoners and the others. The Party prisoners were always silent and terrified, but the ordinary criminals seemed to care nothing for anybody. They yelled insults at the guards, fought back fiercely when their belongings were impounded, wrote obscene words on the floor, ate smuggled food which they produced from mysterious hiding-places in their clothes, and even shouted down the telescreen when it tried to restore order. On the other hand some of them seemed to be on good terms with the guards, called them by nicknames, and tried to wheedle cigarettes through the spyhole in the door. The guards, too, treated the common criminals with a certain forbearance, even when they had to handle them roughly. There was much talk about forced-labour camps to which most of the prisoners expected to be sent. It was 'all right' in the camps, he gathered, so long as you had good contacts and knew the ropes. There was bribery, favouritism, and racketeering of every kind, there was homosexuality and prostitution, there was even illicit alcohol distilled from potatoes. The positions of trust were given only to the common criminals, especially the gangsters and the murderers, who formed a sort of aristocracy. All the dirty jobs were done by the politicals.

There was a constant come-and-go of prisoners of every description: drug-peddlers, thieves, bandits, black-marketeers, drunks, prostitutes. Some of the drunks were so violent that the other prisoners had to combine to suppress them. An enormous wreck of a woman, aged about sixty, with great tumbling breasts and thick coils of white hair which had come down in her struggles, was carried in, kicking and shouting, by four guards, who had hold of her one at each corner. They wrenched off the boots with which she had been trying to kick them, and dumped her down across Winston's lap, almost breaking his thigh-bones. The woman hoisted herself upright and followed them out with a yell of 'F— bastards!' Then, noticing that she was sitting on some thing uneven, she slid off Winston's knees on to the bench.

'Beg pardon, dearie,' she said. 'I wouldn't 'a sat on you, only the buggers put me there. They dono 'ow to treat a lady, do they?' She paused, patted her breast, and belched. 'Pardon,' she said, 'I ain't meself, quite.'

She leant forward and vomited copiously on the floor.

'Thass better,' she said, leaning back with closed eyes. 'Never keep it down, thass what I say. Get it up while it's fresh on your stomach, like.'

She revived, turned to have another look at Winston, and seemed immediately to take a fancy to him. She put a vast arm round his shoulder and drew him towards her, breathing beer and vomit into his face.

'Wass your name, dearie?' she said.

'Smith,' said Winston.

'Smith? said the woman. 'Thass funny. My name's Smith too. Why,' she added sentimentally, 'I might be your mother!'

She might, thought Winston, be his mother. She was about the right age and physique, and it was probable that people changed somewhat after twenty years in a forced-labour camp.

No one else had spoken to him. To a surprising extent the ordinary criminals ignored the Party prisoners. 'The pol*its*,' they called them, with a sort of uninterested contempt. The Party prisoners seemed terrified of speaking to anybody, and above all of speaking to one another. Only once, when two Party members, both women, were pressed close together on the bench, he overheard amid the din of voices a few hurriedly whispered words; and in particular a reference to something called 'room one-oh-one', which he did not understand.

It might be two or three hours ago that they had brought him here. The dull pain in his belly never went away, but sometimes it grew better and sometimes worse, and his thoughts expanded or contracted accordingly. When it grew worse he thought only of the pain itself, and of his desire for food. When it grew better, panic took hold of him. There were moments when he foresaw the things that would happen to him with such actuality that his heart galloped and his breath stopped. He felt the smash of truncheons on his elbows and iron-shod boots on his shins; he saw himself grovelling on the floor, screaming for mercy through broken teeth. He hardly thought of Julia. He could not fix his mind on her. He loved her and would not betray her; but that was only a fact, known as he knew the rules of arithmetic. He felt no love for her, and he hardly even wondered what was happening to her. He thought oftener of O'Brien, with a flickering hope. O'Brien must know that he had been arrested. The Brotherhood, he had said, never tried to save its members. But there was the razor blade; they would send the razor blade if they could. There would be perhaps five seconds before the guard could rush into the cell. The blade would bite into him with a sort of burning coldness, and even the fingers that held it would be cut to the bone. Everthing came back to his sick body, which shrank trembling from the smallest pain. He was not certain that he would use the razor blade even if he got the chance. It was more natural to exist from moment to moment, accepting another ten minutes' life even with the certainty that there was torture at the end of it.

Sometimes he tried to calculate the number of porcelain bricks in the walls of the cell. It should have been easy, but he always lost count at some point or another. More often he wondered where he was, and what time of day it was. At one moment he felt certain that it was broad daylight outside, and at the next equally certain that it was pitch darkness. In this place, he knew instinctively, the lights would never be turned out. It was the place with no darkness: he saw now why O'Brien had seemed to recognize the allusion. In the Ministry of Love there were no windows. His cell might be at the heart of the building or against its outer wall; it might be ten floors below ground, or thirty above it. He moved himself mentally from place to place, and tried to determine by the feeling of his body whether he was perched high in the air or buried deep underground.

There was a sound of marching boots outside. The steel door opened with a clang. A young officer, a trim black-uniformed figure who seemed to glitter all over with polished leather, and whose pale, straight-featured face was like a wax mask, stepped smartly through the doorway. He motioned to the guards outside to bring in the prisoner they were leadingl The poet Ampleforth shambled into the cell. The door clanged shut again.   Ampleforth made one or two uncertain movements from side to side, as though having some idea that there was another door to go out of, and then began to wander up and down the cell. He had not yet noticed Winston's presence. His troubled eyes were gazing at the wall about a metre above the level of Winston's head. He was shoeless; large, dirty toes were sticking out of the holes in his socks. He was also several days away from a shave. A scrubby beard covered his face to the cheekbones, giving him an air of ruffianism that went oddly with his large weak frame and nervous movements.

Winston roused himself a little from his lethargy. He must speak to Ampleforth, and risk the yell from the telescreen. It was even conceivable that Ampleforth was the bearer of the razor blade.

'Ampleforth,' he said.

There was no yell from the telescreen. Ampleforth paused, mildly startled. His eyes focused themselves slowly on Winston.

'Ah, Smith!' he said. 'You too!'

'What are you in for?'

'To tell you the truth—' He sat down awkwardly on the bench opposite Winston. 'There is only one offence, is there not?' he said.

'And you have committed it?'

'Apparently I have.'

He put a hand to his forehead and pressed his temples for a moment, as though trying to remember something.

'These things happen,' he began vaguely. 'I have been able to recall one instance—a possible instance. It was an indiscretion, undoubtedly. We were producing a definitive edition of the poems of Kipling. I allowed the word "God" to remain at the end of a line. I could not help it!' he added almost indignantly raising his face to look at Winston. 'It was impossible to change the line. The rhyme was "rod". Do you realize that there are only twelve rhymes to "rod" in the entire language? For days I had racked my brains. There *was* no other rhyme.'

The expression on his face changed. The annoyance passed out of it and for a moment he looked almost pleased. A sort of intellectual warmth, the joy of the pedant who had found out some useless fact, shone through the dirt and scrubby hair.

'Has it ever occurred to you,' he said, 'that the whole history of English poetry has been determined by the fact that the English language lacks rhymes?'

No, that particular thought had never occurred to Winston. Nor, in the circumstances, did it strike him as very important or interesting.

'Do you know what time of day it is?' he said.

Ampleforth looked startled again. 'I had hardly thought about it. They arrested me—it could be two days ago—perhaps three.' His eyes flitted round the walls, as though he half expected to find a window somewhere. 'There is no difference between night and day in this place. I do not see how one can calculate the time.'

They talked desultorily for some minutes, then, without apparent reason, a yell from the telescreen bade them be silent. Winston sat quietly, his hands crossed. Ampleforth, too large to sit in comfort on the narrow bench, fidgeted from side to side, clasping his lank hands first round one knee, then round the other. The telescreen barked at him to keep still. Time passed. Twenty minutes, an hour—it was difficult to judge. Once more there was a sound of boots outside. Winston's entrails contracted. Soon, very soon, perhaps in five minutes, perhaps now, the tramp of boots would mean that his own turn had come.

The door opened. The cold-faced young officer stepped into the cell. With a brief movement of the hand he indicated Ampleforth.

'Room 101,' he said.

Ampleforth marched clumsily out between the guards, his face vaguely perturbed, but uncomprehending.

What seemed like a long time passed. The pain in Winston's belly had revived. His mind sagged round and round on the same track, like a ball falling again and again into the same series of slots. He had only six thoughts. The pain in his belly; a piece of bread; the blood and the screaming; O'Brien; Julia; the razor blade. There was another spasm in his entrails; the heavy boots were approaching. As the door opened, the wave of air that it created brought in a powerful smell of cold sweat. Parsons walked into the cell. He was wearing khaki shorts and a sports-shirt.

This time Winston was startled into self-forgetfulness.

'*You* here!' he said.

Parsons gave Winston a glance in which there was neither interest nor surprise, but only misery. He began walking jerkily up and down, evidently unable to keep still. Each time he straightened his pudgy knees it was apparent that they were trembling. His eyes had a wide-open, staring look, as though he could not prevent himself from gazing at something in the middle distance.

'What are you in for?' said Winston.

'Thoughtcrime!' said Parsons, almost blubbering. The tone of his voice implied at once a complete admission of his guilt and a sort of incredulous horror that such a word could be applied to himself. He paused opposite Winston and began eagerly appealing to him: 'You don't think they'll shoot me, do you, old chap? They don't shoot you if you haven't actually done anything—only thoughts, which you can't help? I know they give you a fair hearing. Oh, I trust them for that! They'll know my record, won't they? *You* know what kind of a chap I was. Not a bad chap in my way. Not brainy, of course, but keen. I tried to do my best for the Party, didn't I? I'll get off with five years, don't you think? Or even ten years? A chap like me could make himself pretty useful in a labour-camp. They wouldn't shoot me for going off the rails just once?'

'Are you guilty?' said Winston.

'Of course I'm guilty!' cried Parsons with a servile glance at the telescreen. 'You don't think the Party would arrest an innocent man, do you?' His frog-like face grew calmer, and even took on a slightly sanctimonious expression. 'Thoughtcrime is a dreadful thing, old man,' he said sententiously. 'It's insidious. It can get hold of you without your even knowing it. Do you know how it got hold of me? In my sleep! Yes, that's a fact. There I was, working away, trying to do my bit—never knew I had any bad stuff in my mind at all. And then I started talking in my sleep. Do you know what they heard me saying?'

He sank his voice, like someone who is obliged for medical reasons to utter an obscenity.

' "Down with Big Brother!" Yes, I said that! Said it over and over again, it seems. Between you and me, old man, I'm glad they got me before it went any further. Do you know what I'm going to say to them when I go up before the tribunal? "Thank you," I'm going to say, "thank you for saving me before it was too late." '

'Who denounced you?' said Winston.

'It was my little daughter,' said Parsons with a sort of doleful pride. 'She listened at the keyhole. Heard what I was saying, and nipped off to the patrols the very next day. Pretty smart for a nipper of seven, eh! I don't bear her any grudge for it. In fact I'm proud of her. It shows I brought her up in the right spirit, anyway.'

He made a few more jerky movements up and down, several times, casting a longing glance at the lavatory pan. Then he suddenly ripped down his shorts.

'Excuse me, old man,' he said. 'I can't help it. It's the waiting.'

He plumped his large posterior into the lavatory pan. Winston covered his face with his hands.

'Smith!' yelled the voice from the telescreen. '6079 Smith W.! Uncover your face. No faces covered in the cells.'

Winston uncovered his face. Parsons used the lavatory, loudly and abundantly. It then turned out that the plug was defective and the cell stank abominably for hours afterwards.

Parsons was removed. More prisoners came and went, mysteriously. One, a woman, was consigned to 'Room 101', and, Winston noticed, seemed to shrivel and turn a different colour when she heard the words. A time came when, if it had been morning when he was brought here, it would be afternoon; or if it had been afternoon, then it would be midnight. There were six prisoners in the cell, men and women. All sat very still. Opposite Winston there sat a man with a chinless, toothy face exactly like that of some large, harmless rodent. His fat, mottled cheeks were so pouched at the bottom that it was difficult not to believe that he had little stores of food tucked away there. His pale-grey eyes flitted timorously from face to face and turned quickly away again when he caught anyone's eye.

The door opened, and another prisoner was brought in whose appearance sent a momentary chill through Winston. He was a commonplace, mean-looking man who might have been an engineer or technician of some kind. But what was startling was the emaciation of his face. It was like a skull. Because of its thinness the mouth and eyes looked disproportionately large, and the eyes seemed filled with a murderous, unappeasable hatred of somebody or something.

The man sat down on the bench at a little distance from Winston. Winston did not look at him again, but the tormented, skull-like face was as vivid in his mind as though it had been straight in front of his eyes. Suddenly he realized what was the matter. The man was dying of starvation. The same thought seemed to occur almost simultaneously to everyone in the cell. There was a very faint stirring all the way round the bench. The eyes of the chinless man kept flitting towards the skull-faced man, then turning guiltily away, then being dragged back by an irresistible attraction. Presently he began to fidget on his seat. At last he stood up, waddled clumsily across the cell, dug down into the pocket of his overalls, and, with an abashed air, held out a grimy piece of bread to the skull-faced man.

There was a furious, deafening roar from the telescreen. The chinless man jumped in his tracks. The skull-faced man had quickly thrust his hands behind his back, as though demonstrating to all the world that he refused the gift.

'Bumstead!' roared the voice. '2713 Bumstead J.! Let fall that piece of bread!'

The chinless man dropped the piece of bread on the floor..

'Remain standing where you are,' said the voice. 'Face the door. Make no movement.'

The chinless man obeyed. His large pouchy cheeks were quivering uncontrollably. The door clanged open. As the young officer entered and stepped aside, there emerged from behind him a short stumpy guard with enormous arms and shoulders. He took his stand opposite the chinless man, and then, at a signal from the officer, let free a frightful blow, with all the weight of his body behind it, full in the chinless man's mouth. The force of it seemed almost to knock him clear of the floor. His body was flung across the cell and fetched up against the base of the lavatory seat. For a moment he lay as though stunned, with dark blood oozing from his mouth and nose. A very faint whimpering or squeaking, which seemed unconscious, came out of him. Then he rolled over and raised himself unsteadily on hands and knees. Amid a stream of blood and saliva, the two halves of a dental plate fell out of his mouth.

The prisoners sat very still, their hands crossed on their knees. The chinless man climbed back into his place. Down one side of his face the flesh was darkening. His mouth had swollen into a shapeless cherry-coloured mass with a black hole in the middle of it. From time to time a little blood dripped on to the breast of his overalls. His grey eyes still flitted from face to face, more guiltily than ever, as though he were trying to discover how much the others despised him for his humiliation.

The door opened. With a small gesture the officer indicated the skull-faced man.

'Room 101,' he said.

There was a gasp and a flurry at Winston's side. The man had actually flung himself on his knees on the floor, with his hands clasped together.

'Comrade! Officer!' he cried. 'You don't have to take me to that place! Haven't I told you everything already? What else is it you want to know? There's nothing I wouldn't confess, nothing! Just tell me what it is and I'll confess it straight off. Write it down and I'll sign it—anything! Not room 101!'

'Room 101,' said the officer.

The man's face, already very pale, turned a colour Winston would not have believed possible. It was definitely, unmistakably, a shade of green.

'Do anything to me!' he yelled. 'You've been starving me for weeks. Finish it off and let me die. Shoot me. Hang me. Sentence me to twenty-five years. Is there somebody else you want me to give away? Just say who it is and I'll tell you anything you want. I don't care who it is or what you do to them. I've got a wife and three children. The biggest of them isn't six years old. You can take the whole lot of them and cut their throats in front of my eyes, and I'll stand by and watch it. But not room101!'

'Room 101,' said the officer.

The man looked frantically round at the other prisoners, as though with some idea that he could put another victim in his own place. His eyes settled on the smashed face of the chinless man. He flung out a lean arm.

'That's the one you ought to be taking, not me!' he shouted. 'You didn't hear what he was saying after they bashed his face. Give me a chance and I'll tell you every word of it. *He's* the one that's against the Party, not me.' The guards stepped forward. The man's voice rose to a shriek. 'You didn't hear him!' he repeated. 'Something went wrong with the telescreen. *He's* the one you want. Take him, not me!'

The two sturdy guards had stooped to take him by the arms. But just at this moment he flung himself across the floor of the cell and grabbed one of the iron legs that supported the bench. He had set up a wordless howling, like an animal. The guards took hold of him to wrench him loose, but he clung on with astonishing strength. For perhaps twenty seconds they were hauling at him. The prisoners sat quiet, their hands crossed on their knees, looking straight in front of them. The howling stopped; the man had no breath left for anything except hanging on. Then there was a different kind of cry. A kick from a guard's boot had broken the fingers of one of his hands. They dragged him to his feet.

'Room 101,' said the officer.

The man was led out, walking unsteadily, with head sunken, nursing his crushed hand, all the fight gone out of him.

A long time passed. If it had been midnight when the skull-faced man was taken away, it was morning: if morning, it was afternoon. Winston was alone, and had been alone for hours. The pain of sitting on the narrow bench was such that often he got up and walked about, unreproved by the telescreen. The piece of bread still lay where the chinless man had dropped it. At the beginning it needed a hard effort not to look at it, but presently hunger gave way to thirst. His mouth was sticky and evil-tasting. The humming sound and the unvarying white light induced a sort of faintness, an empty feeling inside his head. He would get up because the ache in his bones was no longer bearable, and then would sit down again almost at once because he was too dizzy to make sure of staying on his feet. Whenever his physical sensations were a little under control the terror returned. Sometimes with a fading hope he thought of O'Brien and the razor blade. It was thinkable that the razor blade might arrive concealed in his food, if he were ever fed. More dimly he thought of Julia. Somewhere or other she was suffering perhaps far worse than he. She might be screaming with pain at this moment. He thought: 'If I could save Julia by doubling my own pain, would I do it? Yes, I would.' But that was merely an intellectual decision, taken because he knew that he ought to take it. He did not feel it. In this place you could not feel anything, except pain and the foreknowledge of pain. Besides, was it possible, when you were actually suffering it, to wish for any reason whatever that your own pain should increase? But that question was not answerable yet.

The boots were approaching again. The door opened. O'Brien came in.

Winston started to his feet. The shock of the sight had driven all caution out of him. For the first time in many years he forgot the presence of the telescreen.

'They've got you too!' he cried.

'They got me a long time ago,' said O'Brien with a mild, almost regretful irony. He stepped aside. From behind him there emerged a broad-chested guard with a long black truncheon in his hand.

'You knew this, Winston,' said O'Brien. 'Don't deceive yourself. You did know it—you have always known it.'

Yes, he saw now, he had always known it. But there was no time to think of that. All he had eyes for was the truncheon in the guard's hand. It might fall anywhere: on the crown, on the tip of the ear, on the upper arm, on the elbow—

The elbow! He had slumped to his knees, almost paralysed, clasping the stricken elbow with his other hand. Everything had exploded into yellow light. Inconceivable, inconceivable that one blow could cause such pain! The light cleared and he could see the other two looking down at him. The guard was laughing at his contortions. One question at any rate was answered. Never, for any reason on earth, could you wish for an increase of pain. Of pain you could wish only one thing: that it should stop. Nothing in the world was so bad as physical pain. In the face of pain there are no heroes, no heroes, he thought over and over as he writhed on the floor, clutching uselessly at his disabled left arm.

# 2

He was lying on something that felt like a camp bed, except that it was higher off the ground and that he was fixed down in some way so that he could not move. Light that seemed stronger than usual was falling on his face. O'Brien was standing at his side, looking down at him intently. At the other side of him stood a man in a white coat, holding a hypodermic syringe.

Even after his eyes were open he took in his surroundings only gradually. He had the impression of swimming up into this room from some quite different world, a sort of under-water world far beneath it. How long he had been down there he did not know. Since the moment when they arrested him he had not seen darkness or daylight. Besides, his memories were not continuous. There had been times when consciousness, even the sort of consciousness that one has in sleep, had stopped dead and started again after a blank interval. But whether the intervals were of days or weeks or only seconds, there was no way of knowing.

With that first blow on the elbow the nightmare had started. Later he was to realize that all that then happened was merely a preliminary, a routine interrogation to which nearly all prisoners were subjected. There was a long range of crimes—espionage, sabotage, and the like—to which everyone had to confess as a matter of course. The confession was a formality, though the torture was real. How many times he had been beaten, how long the beatings had continued, he could not remember. Always there were five or six men in black uniforms at him simultaneously. Sometimes it was fists, sometimes it was truncheons, sometimes it was steel rods, sometimes it was boots. There were times when he rolled about the floor, as shameless as an animal, writhing his body this way and that in an endless, hopeless effort to dodge the kicks, and simply inviting more and yet more kicks, in his ribs, in his belly, on his elbows, on his shins, in his groin, in his testicles, on the bone at the base of his spine. There were times when it went on and on until the cruel, wicked, unforgivable thing seemed to him not that the guards continued to beat him but that he could not force himself into losing consciousness. There were times when his nerve so forsook him that he began shouting for mercy even before the beating began, when the mere sight of a fist drawn back for a blow was enough to make him pour forth a confession of real and imaginary crimes. There were other times when he started out with the resolve of confessing nothing, when every word had to be forced out of him between gasps of pain, and there were times when he feebly tried to compromise, when he said to himself: 'I will confess, but not yet. I must hold out till the pain becomes unbearable. Three more kicks, two more kicks, and then I will tell them what they want.' Sometimes he was beaten till he could hardly stand, then flung like a sack of potatoes on to the stone floor of a cell, left to recuperate for a few hours, and then taken out and beaten again. There were also longer periods of recovery. He remembered them dimly, because they were spent chiefly in sleep or stupor. He remembered a cell with a plank bed, a sort of shelf sticking out from the wall, and a tin wash-basin, and meals of hot soup and bread and sometimes coffee. He remembered a surly barber arriving to scrape his chin and crop his hair, and business-like, unsympathetic men in white coats feeling his pulse, tapping his reflexes, turning up his eyelids, running harsh fingers over him in search of broken bones, and shooting needles into his arm to make him sleep.

The beatings grew less frequent, and became mainly a threat, a horror to which he could be sent back at any moment when his answers were unsatisfactory. His questioners now were not ruffians in black uniforms but Party intellectuals, little rotund men with quick movements and flashing spectacles, who worked on him in relays over periods which lasted—he thought, he could not be sure—ten or twelve hours at a stretch. These other questioners saw to it that he was in constant slight pain, but it was not chiefly pain that they relied on. They slapped his face, wrung his ears, pulled his hair, made him stand on one leg, refused him leave to urinate, shone glaring lights in his face until his eyes ran with water; but the aim of this was simply to humiliate him and destroy his power of arguing and reasoning. Their real weapon was the merciless questioning that went on and on, hour after hour, tripping him up, laying traps for him, twisting everything that he said, convicting him at every step of lies and self-contradiction, until he began weeping as much from shame as from nervous fatigue. Sometimes he would weep half a dozen times in a single session. Most of the time they screamed abuse at him and threatened at every hesitation to deliver him over to the guards again; but sometimes they would suddenly change their tune, call him comrade, appeal to him in the name of Ingsoc and Big Brother, and ask him sorrowfully whether even now he had not enough loyalty to the Party left to make him wish to undo the evil he had done. When his nerves were in rags after hours of questioning, even this appeal could reduce him to snivelling tears. In the end the nagging voices broke him down more completely than the boots and fists of the guards. He became simply a mouth that uttered, a hand that signed, whatever was demanded of him. His sole concern was to find out what they wanted him to confess, and then confess it quickly, before the bullying started anew. He confessed to the assassination of eminent Party members, the distribution of seditious pamphlets, embezzlement of public funds, sale of military secrets, sabotage of every kind. He confessed that he had been a spy in the pay of the Eastasian government as far back as 1968. He confessed that he was a religious believer, an admirer of capitalism, and a sexual pervert. He confessed that he had murdered his wife, although he knew, and his questioners must have known, that his wife was still alive. He confessed that for years he had been in personal touch with Goldstein and had been a member of an underground organization which had included almost every human being he had ever known. It was easier to confess everything and implicate everybody. Besides, in a sense it was all true. It was true that he had been the enemy of the Party, and in the eyes of the Party there was no distinction between the thought and the deed.

There were also memories of another kind. They stood out in his mind disconnectedly, like pictures with blackness all round them.

He was in a cell which might have been either dark or light, because he could see nothing except a pair of eyes. Near at hand some kind of instrument was ticking slowly and regularly. The eyes grew larger and more luminous. Suddenly he floated out of his seat, dived into the eyes, and was swallowed up.

He was strapped into a chair surrounded by dials, under dazzling lights. A man in a white coat was reading the dials. There was a tramp of heavy boots outside. The door clanged open. The waxen-faced officer marched in, followed by two guards.

'Room 101,' said the officer.

The man in the white coat did not turn round. He did not look at Winston either; he was looking only at the dials.

He was rolling down a mighty corridor, a kilometre wide, full of glorious, golden light, roaring with laughter and shouting out confessions at the top of his voice. He was confessing everything, even the things he had succeeded in holding back under the torture. He was relating the entire history of his life to an audience who knew it already. With him were the guards, the other questioners, the men in white coats, O'Brien, Julia, Mr Charrington, all rolling down the corridor together and shouting with laughter. Some dreadful thing which had lain embedded in the future had somehow been skipped over and had not happened. Everything was all right, there was no more pain, the last detail of his life was laid bare, understood, forgiven.

He was starting up from the plank bed in the half-certainty that he had heard O'Brien's voice. All through his interrogation, although he had never seen him, he had had the feeling that O'Brien was at his elbow, just out of sight. It was O'Brien who was directing everything. It was he who set the guards on to Winston and who prevented them from killing him. It was he who decided when Winston should scream with pain, when he should have a respite, when he should be fed, when he should sleep, when the drugs should be pumped into his arm. It was he who asked the questions and suggested the answers. He was the tormentor, he was the protector, he was the inquisitor, he was the friend. And once—Winston could not remember whether it was in drugged sleep, or in normal sleep, or even in a moment of wakefulness—a voice murmured in his ear: 'Don't worry, Winston; you are in my keeping. For seven years I have watched over you. Now the turning-point has come. I shall save you, I shall make you perfect.' He was not sure whether it was O'Brien's voice; but it was the same voice that had said to him, 'We shall meet in the place where there is no darkness,' in that other dream, seven years ago.

He did not remember any ending to his interrogation. There was a period of blackness and then the cell, or room, in which he now was had gradually materialized round him. He was almost flat on his back, and unable to move. His body was held down at every essential point. Even the back of his head was gripped in some manner. O'Brien was looking down at him gravely and rather sadly. His face, seen from below, looked coarse and worn, with pouches under the eyes and tired lines from nose to chin. He was older than Winston had thought him; he was perhaps forty-eight or fifty. Under his hand there was a dial with a lever on top and figures running round the face.

'I told you,' said O'Brien, 'that if we met again it would be here.'

'Yes,' said Winston.

Without any warning except a slight movement of O'Brien's hand, a wave of pain flooded his body. It was a frightening pain, because he could not see what was happening, and he had the feeling that some mortal injury was being done to him. He did not know whether the thing was really happening, or whether the effect was electrically produced; but his body was being wrenched out of shape, the joints were being slowly torn apart. Although the pain had brought the sweat out on his forehead, the worst of all was the fear that his backbone was about to snap. He set his teeth and breathed hard through his nose, trying to keep silent as long as possible.

'You are afraid,' said O'Brien, watching his face, 'that in another moment something is going to break. Your especial fear is that it will be your backbone. You have a vivid mental picture of the vertebrae snapping apart and the spinal fluid dripping out of them. That is what you are thinking, is it not, Winston?'

Winston did not answer. O'Brien drew back the lever on the dial. The wave of pain receded almost as quickly as it had come.

'That was forty,' said O'Brien. 'You can see that the numbers on this dial run up to a hundred. Will you please remember, throughout our conversation, that I have it in my power to inflict pain on you at any moment and to whatever degree I choose? If you tell me any lies, or attempt to prevaricate in any way, or even fall below your usual level of intelligence, you will cry out with pain, instantly. Do you understand that?'

'Yes,' said Winston.

O'Brien's manner became less severe. He resettled his spectacles thoughtfully, and took a pace or two up and down. When he spoke his voice was gentle and patient. He had the air of a doctor, a teacher, even a priest, anxious to explain and persuade rather than to punish.

'I am taking trouble with you, Winston,' he said, 'because you are worth trouble. You know perfectly well what is the matter with you. You have known it for years, though you have fought against the knowledge. You are mentally deranged. You suffer from a defective memory. You are unable to remember real events and you persuade yourself that you remember other events which never happened. Fortunately it is curable. You have never cured yourself of it, because you did not choose to. There was a small effort of the will that you were not ready to make. Even now, I am well aware, you are clinging to your disease under the impression that it is a virtue. Now we will take an example. At this moment, which power is Oceania at war with?'

'When I was arrested, Oceania was at war with Eastasia.'

'With Eastasia. Good. And Oceania has always been at war with Eastasia, has it not?'

Winston drew in his breath. He opened his mouth to speak and then did not speak. He could not take his eyes away from the dial.

'The truth, please, Winston. *Your* truth. Tell me what you think you remember.'

'I remember that until only a week before I was arrested, we were not at war with Eastasia at all. We were in alliance with them. The war was against Eurasia. That had lasted for four years. Before that—'

O'Brien stopped him with a movement of the hand.

'Another example,' he said. 'Some years ago you had a very serious delusion indeed. You believed that three men, three one-time Party members named Jones, Aaronson, and Rutherford—men who were executed for treachery and sabotage after making the fullest possible confession—were not guilty of the crimes they were charged with. You believed that you had seen unmistakable documentary evidence proving that their confessions were false. There was a certain photograph about which you had a hallucination. You believed that you had actually held it in your hands. It was a photograph something like this.'

An oblong slip of newspaper had appeared between O'Brien's fingers. For perhaps five seconds it was within the angle of Winston's vision. It was a photograph, and there was no question of its identity. It was *the* photograph. It was another copy of the photograph of Jones, Aaronson, and Rutherford at the Party function in New York, which he had chanced upon eleven years ago and promptly destroyed. For only an instant it was before his eyes, then it was out of sight again. But he had seen it, unquestionably he had seen it! He made a desperate, agonizing effort to wrench the top half of his body free. It was impossible to move so much as a centimetre in any direction. For the moment he had even forgotten the dial. All he wanted was to hold the photograph in his fingers again, or at least to see it.

'It exists!' he cried.

'No,' said O'Brien.

He stepped across the room. There was a memory hole in the opposite wall. O'Brien lifted the grating. Unseen, the frail slip of paper was whirling away on the current of warm air; it was vanishing in a flash of flame. O'Brien turned away from the wall.

'Ashes,' he said. 'Not even identifiable ashes. Dust. It does not exist. It never existed.'

'But it did exist! It does exist! It exists in memory. I remember it. You remember it.'

'I do not remember it,' said O'Brien.

Winston's heart sank. That was doublethink. He had a feeling of deadly helplessness. If he could have been certain that O'Brien was lying, it would not have seemed to matter. But it was perfectly possible that O'Brien had really forgotten the photograph. And if so, then already he would have forgotten his denial of remembering it, and forgotten the act of forgetting. How could one be sure that it was simply trickery? Perhaps that lunatic dislocation in the mind could really happen: that was the thought that defeated him.

O'Brien was looking down at him speculatively. More than ever he had the air of a teacher taking pains with a wayward but promising child.

'There is a Party slogan dealing with the control of the past,' he said. 'Repeat it, if you please.'

' "Who controls the past controls the future: who controls the present controls the past",' repeated Winston obediently.

' "Who controls the present controls the past",' said O'Brien, nodding his head with slow approval. 'Is it your opinion, Winston, that the past has real existence?'

Again the feeling of helplessness descended upon Winston. His eyes flitted towards the dial. He not only did not know whether 'yes' or 'no' was the answer that would save him from pain; he did not even know which answer he believed to be the true one.

O'Brien smiled faintly. 'You are no metaphysician, Winston,' he said. 'Until this moment you had never considered what is meant by existence. I will put it more precisely. Does the past exist concretely, in space? Is there somewhere or other a place, a world of solid objects, where the past is still happening?'

'No.'

'Then where does the past exist, if at all?'

'In records. It is written down.'

'In records. And—?'

'In the mind. In human memories.'

'In memory. Very well, then. We, the Party, control all records, and we control all memories. Then we control the past, do we not?'

'But how can you stop people remembering things?' cried Winston again momentarily forgetting the dial. 'It is involuntary. It is outside oneself. How can you control memory? You have not controlled mine!'

O'Brien's manner grew stern again. He laid his hand on the dial.

'On the contrary,' he said, '*you* have not controlled it. That is what has brought you here. You are here because you have failed in humility, in self-discipline. You would not make the act of submission which is the price of sanity. You preferred to be a lunatic, a minority of one. Only the disciplined mind can see reality, Winston. You believe that reality is something objective, external, existing in its own right. You also believe that the nature of reality is self-evident. When you delude yourself into thinking that you see something, you assume that everyone else sees the same thing as you. But I tell you, Winston, that reality is not external. Reality exists in the human mind, and nowhere else. Not in the individual mind, which can make mistakes, and in any case soon perishes: only in the mind of the Party, which is collective and immortal. Whatever the Party holds to be truth, *is* truth. It is impossible to see reality except by looking through the eyes of the Party. That is the fact that you have got to relearn, Winston. It needs an act of self-destruction, an effort of the will. You must humble yourself before you can become sane.'

He paused for a few moments, as though to allow what he had been saying to sink in.

'Do you remember,' he went on, 'writing in your diary, "Freedom is the freedom to say that two plus two make four"?'

'Yes,' said Winston.

O'Brien held up his left hand, its back towards Winston, with the thumb hidden and the four fingers extended.

'How many fingers am I holding up, Winston?'

'Four.'

'And if the Party says that it is not four but five—then how many?'

'Four.'

The word ended in a gasp of pain. The needle of the dial had shot up to fifty-five. The sweat had sprung out all over Winston's body. The air tore into his lungs and issued again in deep groans which even by clenching his teeth he could not stop. O'Brien watched him, the four fingers still extended. He drew back the lever. This time the pain was only slightly eased.

'How many fingers, Winston?'

'Four.'

The needle went up to sixty.

'How many fingers, Winston?'

'Four! Four! What else can I say? Four!'

The needle must have risen again, but he did not look at it. The heavy, stern face and the four fingers filled his vision. The fingers stood up before his eyes like pillars, enormous, blurry, and seeming to vibrate, but unmistakably four.

'How many fingers, Winston?'

'Four! Stop it, stop it! How can you go on? Four! Four!'

'How many fingers, Winston?'

'Five! Five! Five!'

'No, Winston, that is no use. You are lying. You still think there are four. How many fingers, please?'

'Four! Five! Four! Anything you like. Only stop it, stop the pain!'

Abruptly he was sitting up with O'Brien's arm round his shoulders. He had perhaps lost consciousness for a few seconds. The bonds that had held his body down were loosened. He felt very cold, he was shaking uncontrollably, his teeth were chattering, the tears were rolling down his cheeks. For a moment he clung to O'Brien like a baby, curiously comforted by the heavy arm round his shoulders. He had the feeling that O'Brien was his protector, that the pain was something that came from outside, from some other source, and that it was O'Brien who would save him from it.

'You are a slow learner, Winston,' said O'Brien gently.

'How can I help it?' he blubbered. 'How can I help seeing what is in front of my eyes?' he blubbered. 'How can I help seeing what is in front of my eyes? Two and two are four.'

'Sometimes, Winston. Sometimes they are five. Sometimes they are three. Sometimes they are all of them at once. You must try harder. It is not easy to become sane.'

He laid Winston down on the bed. The grip of his limbs tightened again, but the pain had ebbed away and the trembling had stopped, leaving him merely weak and cold. O'Brien motioned with his head to the man in the white coat, who had stood immobile throughout the proceedings. The man in the white coat bent down and looked closely into Winston's eyes, felt his pulse, laid an ear against his chest, tapped here and there; then he nodded to O'Brien.

'Again,' said O'Brien.

The pain flowed into Winston's body. The needle must be at seventy, seventy-five. He had shut his eyes this time. He knew that the fingers were still there, and still four. All that mattered was somehow to stay alive until the spasm was over. He had ceased to notice whether he was crying out or not. The pain lessened again. He opened his eyes. O'Brien had drawn back the lever.

'How many fingers, Winston?'

'Four. I suppose there are four. I would see five if I could. I am trying to see five.'

'Which do you wish: to persuade me that you see five, or really to see them?'

'Really to see them.'

'Again,' said O'Brien.

Perhaps the needle was at eighty—ninety. Winston could not intermittently remember why the pain was happening. Behind his screwed-up eyelids a forest of fingers seemed to be moving in a sort of dance, weaving in and out, disappearing behind one another and reappearing again. He was trying to count them, he could not remember why. He knew only that it was impossible to count them, and that this was somehow due to the mysterious identity between five and four. The pain died down again. When he opened his eyes it was to find that he was still seeing the same thing. Innumerable fingers, like moving trees, were still streaming past in either direction, crossing and recrossing. He shut his eyes again.

'How many fingers am I holding up, Winston?'

'I don't know. I don't know. You will kill me if you do that again. Four, five, six—in all honesty I don't know.'

'Better,' said O'Brien.

A needle slid into Winston's arm. Almost in the same instant a blissful, healing warmth spread all through his body. The pain was already half-forgotten. He opened his eyes and looked up gratefully at O'Brien. At sight of the heavy, lined faces, so ugly and so intelligent, his heart seemed to turn over. If he could have moved he would have stretched out a hand and laid it on O'Brien's arm. He had never loved him so deeply as at this moment, and not merely because he had stopped the pain. The old feeling, that at bottom it did not matter whether O'Brien was a friend or an enemy, had come back. O'Brien was a person who could be talked to. Perhaps one did not want to be loved so much as to be understood. O'Brien had tortured him to the edge of lunacy, and in a little while, it was certain, he would send him to his death. It made no difference. In some sense that went deeper than friendship, they were intimates: somewhere or other, although the actual words might never be spoken, there was a place where they could meet and talk. O'Brien was looking down at him with an expression which suggested that the same thought might be in his own mind. When he spoke it was in an easy, conversational tone.

'Do you know where you are, Winston?' he said.

'I don't know. I can guess. In the Ministry of Love.'

'Do you know how long you have been here?'

'I don't know. Days, weeks, months—I think it is months.'

'And why do you imagine that we bring people to this place?'

'To make them confess.'

'No that is not the reason. Try again.'

'To punish them.'

'No!' exclaimed O'Brien. His voice had changed extraordinarily, and his face had suddenly become both stern and animated. 'No! Not merely to extract your confession, not to punish you. Shall I tell you why we have brought you here? To cure you! To make you sane! Will you understand, Winston, that no one whom we bring to this place ever leaves our hands uncured? We are not interested in those stupid crimes that you have committed. The Party is not interested in the overt act: the thought is all we care about. We do not merely destroy our enemies, we change them. Do you understand what I mean by that?'

He was bending over Winston. His face looked enormous because of its nearness, and hideously ugly because it was seen from below. Moreover it was filled with a sort of exaltation, a lunatic intensity. Again Winston's heart shrank. If it had been possible he would have cowered deeper into the bed. He felt certain that O'Brien was about to twist the dial out of sheer wantonness. At this moment, however, O'Brien turned away. He took a pace or two up and down. Then he continued less vehemently:

'The first thing for you to understand is that in this place there are no martyrdoms. You have read of the religious persecutions of the past. In the Middle Ages there was the Inquisition. It was a failure. It set out to eradicate heresy, and ended by perpetuating it. For every heretic it burned at the stake, thousands of others rose up. Why was that? Because the Inquisition killed its enemies in the open, and killed them while they were still unrepentant: in fact, it killed them because they were unrepentant. Men were dying because they would not abandon their true beliefs. Naturally all the glory belonged to the victim and all the shame to the Inquisitor who burned him. Later, in the twentieth century, there were the totalitarians, as they were called. There were the German Nazis and the Russian Communists. The Russians persecuted heresy more cruelly than the Inquisition had done. And they imagined that they had learned from the mistakes of the past; they knew, at any rate, that one must not make martyrs. Before they exposed their victims to public trial, they deliberately set themselves to destroy their dignity. They wore them down by torture and solitude until they were despicable, cringing wretches, confessing whatever was put into their mouths, covering themselves with abuse, accusing and sheltering behind one another, whimpering for mercy. And yet after only a few years the same thing had happened over again. The dead men had become martyrs and their degradation was forgotten. Once again, why was it? In the first place, because the confessions that they had made were obviously extorted and untrue. We do not make mistakes of that kind. All the confessions that are uttered here are true. We make them true. And above all we do not allow the dead to rise up against us. You must stop imagining that posterity will vindicate you, Winston. Posterity will never hear of you. You will be lifted clean out from the stream of history. We shall turn you into gas and pour you into the stratosphere. Nothing will remain of you; not a name in a register, not a memory in a living brain. You will be annihilated in the past as well as in the future. You will never have existed.'

Then why bother to torture me? thought Winston, with a momentary bitterness. O'Brien checked his step as though Winston had uttered the thought aloud. His large ugly face came nearer, with the eyes a little narrowed.

'You are thinking,' he said, 'that since we intend to destroy you utterly, so that nothing that you say or do can make the smallest difference—in that case, why do we go to the trouble of interrogating you first? That is what you were thinking, was it not?'

'Yes,' said Winston.

O'Brien smiled slightly. 'You are a flaw in the pattern, Winston. You are a stain that must be wiped out. Did I not tell you just now that we are different from the persecutors of the past? We are not content with negative obedience, nor even with the most abject submission. When finally you surrender to us, it must be of your own free will. We do not destroy the heretic because he resists us: so long as he resists us we never destroy him. We convert him, we capture his inner mind, we reshape him. We burn all evil and all illusion out of him; we bring him over to our side, not in appearance, but genuinely, heart and soul. We make him one of ourselves before we kill him. It is intolerable to us that an erroneous thought should exist anywhere in the world, however secret and powerless it may be. Even in the instant of death we cannot permit any deviation. In the old days the heretic walked to the stake still a heretic, proclaiming his heresy, exulting in it. Even the victim of the Russian purges could carry rebellion locked up in his skull as he walked down the passage waiting for the bullet. But we make the brain perfect before we blow it out. The command of the old despotisms was "Thou shalt not". The command of the totalitarians was "Thou shalt". Our command is *"Thou art"*. No one whom we bring to this place ever stands out against us. Everyone is washed clean. Even those three miserable traitors in whose innocence you once believed—Jones, Aaronson, and Rutherford—in the end we broke them down. I took part in their interrogation myself. I saw them gradually worn down, whimpering, grovelling, weeping—and in the end it was not with pain or fear, only with penitence. By the time we had finished with them they were only the shells of men. There was nothing left in them except sorrow for what they had done, and love of Big Brother. It was touching to see how they loved him. They begged to be shot quickly, so that they could die while their minds were still clean.'

His voice had grown almost dreamy. The exaltation, the lunatic enthusiasm, was still in his face. He is not pretending, thought Winston; he is not a hypocrite; he believes every word he says. What most oppressed him was the consciousness of his own intellectual inferiority. He watched the heavy yet graceful form strolling to and fro, in and out of the range of his vision. O'Brien was a being in all ways larger than himself. There was no idea that he had ever had, or could have, that O'Brien had not long ago known, examined, and rejected. His mind *contained* Winston's mind. But in that case how could it be true that O'Brien was mad? It must be he, Winston, who was mad. O'Brien halted and looked down at him. His voice had grown stern again.

'Do not imagine that you will save yourself, Winston, however completely you surrender to us. No one who has once gone astray is ever spared. And even if we chose to let you live out the natural term of your life, still you would never escape from us. What happens to you here is for ever. Understand that in advance. We shall crush you down to the point from which there is no coming back. Things will happen to you from which you could not recover, if you lived a thousand years. Never again will you be capable of ordinary human feeling. Everything will be dead inside you. Never again will you be capable of love, or friendship, or joy of living, or laughter, or curiosity, or courage, or integrity. You will be hollow. We shall squeeze you empty, and then we shall fill you with ourselves.'

He paused and signed to the man in the white coat. Winston was aware of some heavy piece of apparatus being pushed into place behind his head. O'Brien had sat down beside the bed, so that his face was almost on a level with Winston's.

'Three thousand,' he said, speaking over Winston's head to the man in the white coat.

Two soft pads, which felt slightly moist, clamped themselves against Winston's temples. He quailed. There was pain coming, a new kind of pain. O'Brien laid a hand reassuringly, almost kindly, on his.

'This time it will not hurt,' he said. 'Keep your eyes fixed on mine.'

At this moment there was a devastating explosion, or what seemed like an explosion, though it was not certain whether there was any noise. There was undoubtedly a blinding flash of light. Winston was not hurt, only prostrated. Although he had already been lying on his back when the thing happened, he had a curious feeling that he had been knocked into that position. A terrific, painless blow had flattened him out. Also something had happened inside his head. As his eyes regained their focus he remembered who he was, and where he was, and recognized the face that was gazing into his own; but somewhere or other there was a large patch of emptiness, as though a piece had been taken out of his brain.

'It will not last,' said O'Brien. 'Look me in the eyes. What country is Oceania at war with?'

Winston thought. He knew what was meant by Oceania and that he himself was a citizen of Oceania. He also remembered Eurasia and Eastasia; but who was at war with whom he did not know. In fact he had not been aware that there was any war.

'I don't remember.'

'Oceania is at war with Eastasia. Do you remember that now?'

'Yes.'

'Oceania has always been at war with Eastasia. Since the beginning of your life, since the beginning of the Party, since the beginning of history, the war has continued without a break, always the same war. Do you remember that?'

'Yes.'

'Eleven years ago you created a legend about three men who had been condemned to death for treachery. You pretended that you had a piece of paper which proved them innocent. No such piece of paper ever existed. You invented it, and later you grew to believe in it. You remember now the very moment at which you first invented it. Do you remember that?'

'Yes.'

'Just now I held up the fingers of my hand to you. You saw five fingers. Do you remember that?'

'Yes.'

O'Brien held up the fingers of his left hand, with the thumb concealed.

'There are five fingers there. Do you see five fingers?'

'Yes.'

And he did see them, for a fleeting instant, before the scenery of his mind changed. He saw five fingers, and there was no deformity. Then everything was normal again, and the old fear, the hatred, and the bewilderment came crowding back again. But there had been a moment—he did not know how long, thirty seconds, perhaps—of luminous certainty, when each new suggestion of O'Brien's had filled up a patch of emptiness and become absolute truth, and when two and two could have been three as easily as five, if that were what was needed. It had faded out before O'Brien had dropped his hand; but though he could not recapture it, he could remember it, as one remembers a vivid experience at some remote period of one's life when one was in effect a different person.

'You see now,' said O'Brien. 'that it is at any rate possible.'

'Yes,' said Winston.

O'Brien stood up with a satisfied air. Over to his left Winston saw the man in the white coat break an ampoule and draw back the plunger of a syringe. O'Brien turned to Winston with a smile. In almost the old manner he resettled his spectacles on his nose.

'Do you remember writing in your diary,' he said, 'that it did not matter whether I was a friend or an enemy, since I was at least a person who understood you and could be talked to? You were right. I enjoy talking to you. Your mind appeals to me. It resembles my own mind except that you happen to be insane. Before we bring the session to an end you can ask me a few questions, if you choose.'

'Any question I like?'

'Anything.' He saw that Winston's eyes were upon the dial. 'It is switched off. What is your first question?'

'What have you done with Julia?' said Winston.

O'Brien smiled again. 'She betrayed you, Winston. Immediately—unreservedly. I have seldom seen anyone come over to us so promptly. You would hardly recognize her if you saw her. All her rebelliousness, her deceit, her folly, her dirty-mindedness—everything has been burned out of her. It was a perfect conversion, a textbook case.'

'You tortured her?'

O'Brien left this unanswered. 'Next question,' he said.

'Does Big Brother exist?'

'Of course he exists. The Party exists. Big Brother is the embodiment of the Party.'

'Does he exist in the same way as I exist?'

'You do not exist,' said O'Brien.

Once again the sense of helplessness assailed him. He knew, or he could imagine, the arguments which proved his own non-existence; but they were nonsense, they were only a play on words. Did not the statement, 'You do not exist', contain a logical absurdity? But what use was it to say so? His mind shrivelled as he thought of the unanswerable, mad arguments with which O'Brien would demolish him.

'I think I exist,' he said wearily. 'I am conscious of my own identity. I was born and I shall die. I have arms and legs. I occupy a particular point in space. No other solid object can occupy the same point simultaneously. In that sense, does Big Brother exist?'

'It is of no importance. He exists.'

'Will Big Brother ever die?'

'Of course not. How could he die? Next question.'

'Does the Brotherhood exist?'

'That, Winston, you will never know. If we choose to set you free when we have finished with you, and if you live to be ninety years old, still you will never learn whether the answer to that question is Yes or No. As long as you live it will be an unsolved riddle in your mind.'

Winston lay silent. His breast rose and fell a little faster. He still had not asked the question that had come into his mind the first. He had got to ask it, and yet it was as though his tongue would not utter it. There was a trace of amusement in O'Brien's face. Even his spectacles seemed to wear an ironical gleam. He knows, thought Winston suddenly, he knows what I am going to ask! At the thought the words burst out of him:

'What is in Room 101?'

The expression on O'Brien's face did not change. He answered drily:

'You know what is in Room 101, Winston. Everyone knows what is in Room 101.'

He raised a finger to the man in the white coat. Evidently the session was at an end. A needle jerked into Winston's arm. He sank almost instantly into deep sleep.

# 3

'There are three stages in your reintegration,' said O'Brien. 'There is learning, there is understanding, and there is acceptance. It is time for you to enter upon the second stage.'

As always, Winston was lying flat on his back. But of late his bonds were looser. They still held him to the bed, but he could move his knees a little and could turn his head from side to side and raise his arms from the elbow. The dial, also, had grown to be less of a terror. He could evade its pangs if he was quick-witted enough: it was chiefly when he showed stupidity that O'Brien pulled the lever. Sometimes they got through a whole session without use of the dial. He could not remember how many sessions there had been. The whole process seemed to stretch out over a long, indefinite time—weeks, possibly—and the intervals between the sessions might sometimes have been days, sometimes only an hour or two.

'As you lie there,' said O'Brien, 'you have often wondered—you have even asked me—why the Ministry of Love should expend so much time and trouble on you. And when you were free you were puzzled by what was essentially the same question. You could grasp the mechanics of the Society you lived in, but not its underlying motives. Do you remember writing in your diary, "I understand *how*: I do not understand *why*"? It was when you thought about "why" that you doubted your own sanity. You have read *the book*, Goldstein's book, or parts of it, at least. Did it tell you anything that you did not know already?'

'You have read it?' said Winston.

'I wrote it. That is to say, I collaborated in writing it. No book is produced individually, as you know.'

'Is it true, what it says?'

'A description, yes. The programme it sets forth is nonsense. The secret accumulation of knowledge—a gradual spread of enlightenment—ultimately a proletarian rebellion—the overthrow of the Party. You foresaw yourself that that was what it would say. It is all nonsense. The proletarians will never revolt, not in a thousand years or a million. They cannot. I do not have to tell you the reason: you know it already. If you have ever cherished any dreams of violent insurrection, you must abandon them. There is no way in which the Party can be overthrown. The rule of the Party is for ever. Make that the starting-point of your thoughts.'

He came closer to the bed. 'For ever!' he repeated. 'And now let us get back to the question of "how" and "why". You understand well enough *how* the Party maintains itself in power. Now tell me *why* we cling to power. What is our motive? Why should we want power? Go on, speak,' he added as Winston remained silent.

Nevertheless Winston did not speak for another moment or two. A feeling of weariness had overwhelmed him. The faint, mad gleam of enthusiasm had come back into O'Brien's face. He knew in advance what O'Brien would say. That the Party did not seek power for its own ends, but only for the good of the majority. That it sought power because men in the mass were frail cowardly creatures who could not endure liberty or face the truth, and must be ruled over and systematically deceived by others who were stronger than themselves. That the choice for mankind lay between freedom and happiness, and that, for the great bulk of mankind, happiness was better. That the Party was the eternal guardian of the weak, a dedicated sect doing evil that good might come, sacrificing its own happiness to that of others. The terrible thing, thought Winston, the terrible thing was that when O'Brien said this he would believe it. You could see it in his face. O'Brien knew everything. A thousand times better than Winston he knew what the world was really like, in what degradation the mass of human beings lived and by what lies and barbarities the Party kept them there. He had understood it all, weighed it all, and it made no difference: all was justified by the ultimate purpose. What can you do, thought Winston, against the lunatic who is more intelligent than yourself, who gives your arguments a fair hearing and then simply persists in his lunacy?

'You are ruling over us for our own good,' he said feebly. 'You believe that human beings are not fit to govern themselves, and therefore—'

He started and almost cried out. A pang of pain had shot through his body. O'Brien had pushed the lever of the dial up to thirty-five.

'That was stupid, Winston, stupid!' he said. 'You should know better than to say a thing like that.'

He pulled the lever back and continued:

'Now I will tell you the answer to my question. It is this. The Party seeks power entirely for its own sake. We are not interested in the good of others; we are interested solely in power. Not wealth or luxury or long life or happiness: only power, pure power. What pure power means you will understand presently. We are different from all the oligarchies of the past, in that we know what we are doing. All the others, even those who resembled ourselves, were cowards and hypocrites. The German Nazis and the Russian Communists came very close to us in their methods, but they never had the courage to recognize their own motives. They pretended, perhaps they even believed, that they had seized power unwillingly and for a limited time, and that just round the corner there lay a paradise where human beings would be free and equal. We are not like that. We know that no one ever seizes power with the intention of relinquishing it. Power is not a means, it is an end. One does not establish a dictatorship in order to safeguard a revolution; one makes the revolution in order to establish the dictatorship. The object of persecution is persecution. The object of torture is torture. The object of power is power.

Now do you begin to understand me?'

Winston was struck, as he had been struck before, by the tiredness of O'Brien's face. It was strong and fleshy and brutal, it was full of intelligence and a sort of controlled passion before which he felt himself helpless: but it was tired. There were pouches under the eyes, the skin sagged from the cheekbones. O'Brien leaned over him, deliberately bringing the worn face nearer.

'You are thinking,' he said, 'that my face is old and tired. You are thinking that I talk of power, and yet I am not even able to prevent the decay of my own body. Can you not understand, Winston, that the individual is only a cell? The weariness of the cell is the vigour of the organism. Do you die when you cut your fingernails?'

He turned away from the bed and began strolling up and down again, one hand in his pocket.

'We are the priests of power,' he said. 'God is power. But at present power is only a word so far as you are concerned. It is time for you to gather some idea of what power means. The first thing you must realize is that power is collective. The invididual only has power in so far as he ceases to be an individual. You know the Party slogan: "Freedom is Slavery". Has it ever occurred to you that it is reversible? Slavery is freedom. Alone—free —the human being is always defeated. It must be so, because every human being is doomed to die, which is the greatest of all failures. But if he can make complete, utter submission, if he can escape from his identity, if he can merge himself in the Party so that he *is* the Party, then he is all-powerful and immortal. The second thing for you to realize is that power is power over human beings. Over the body—but, above all, over the mind. Power over matter—external reality, as you would call it—is not important. Already our control over matter is absolute.'

For a moment Winston ignored the dial. He made a violent effort to raise himself into a sitting position, and merely succeeded in wrenching his body painfully.

'But how can you control matter?' he burst out. 'You don't even control the climate or the law of gravity. And there are disease, pain, death—'

O'Brien silenced him by a movement of his hand. 'We control matter because we control the mind. Reality is inside the skull. You will learn by degrees, Winston. There is nothing that we could not do. Invisibility, levitation—anything. I could float off this floor like a soap bubble if I wish to. I do not wish to, because the Party does not wish it. You must get rid of those nineteenth-century ideas about the laws of Nature. We make the laws of Nature.'

'But you do not! You are not even masters of this planet. What about Eurasia and Eastasia? You have not conquered them yet.'

'Unimportant. We shall conquer them when it suits us. And if we did not, what difference would it make? We can shut them out of existence. Oceania is the world.'

'But the world itself is only a speck of dust. And man is tiny—helpless! How long has he been in existence? For millions of years the earth was uninhabited.'

'Nonsense. The earth is as old as we are, no older. How could it be older? Nothing exists except through human consciousness.'

'But the rocks are full of the bones of extinct animals—mammoths and mastodons and enormous reptiles which lived here long before man was ever heard of.'

'Have you ever seen those bones, Winston? Of course not. Nineteenth-century biologists invented them. Before man there was nothing. After man, if he could come to an end, there would be nothing. Outside man there is nothing.'

'But the whole universe is outside us. Look at the stars! Some of them are a million light-years away. They are out of our reach for ever.'

'What are the stars?' said O'Brien indifferently. 'They are bits of fire a few kilometres away. We could reach them if we wanted to. Or we could blot them out. The earth is the centre of the universe. The sun and the stars go round it.'

Winston made another convulsive movement. This time he did not say anything. O'Brien continued as though answering a spoken objection:

'For certain purposes, of course, that is not true. When we navigate the ocean, or when we predict an eclipse, we often find it convenient to assume that the earth goes round the sun and that the stars are millions upon millions of kilometres away. But what of it? Do you suppose it is beyond us to produce a dual system of astronomy? The stars can be near or distant, according as we need them. Do you suppose our mathematicians are unequal to that? Have you forgotten doublethink?'

Winston shrank back upon the bed. Whatever he said, the swift answer crushed him like a bludgeon. And yet he knew, he *knew*, that he was in the right. The belief that nothing exists outside your own mind—surely there must be some way of demonstrating that it was false? Had it not been exposed long ago as a fallacy? There was even a name for it, which he had forgotten. A faint smile twitched the corners of O'Brien's mouth as he looked down at him.

'I told you, Winston,' he said, 'that metaphysics is not your strong point. The word you are trying to think of is solipsism. But you are mistaken. This is not solipsism. Collective solipsism, if you like. But that is a different thing: in fact, the opposite thing. All this is a digression,' he added in a different tone. 'The real power, the power we have to fight for night and day, is not power over things, but over men.' He paused, and for a moment assumed again his air of a schoolmaster questioning a promising pupil: 'How does one man assert his power over another, Winston?'

Winston thought. 'By making him suffer,' he said.

'Exactly. By making him suffer. Obedience is not enough. Unless he is suffering, how can you be sure that he is obeying your will and not his own? Power is in inflicting pain and humiliation. Power is in tearing human minds to pieces and putting them together again in new shapes of your own choosing. Do you begin to see, then, what kind of world we are creating? It is the exact opposite of the stupid hedonistic Utopias that the old reformers imagined. A world of fear and treachery and torment, a world of trampling and being trampled upon, a world which will grow not less but *more* merciless as it refines itself. Progress in our world will be progress towards more pain. The old civilizations claimed that they were founded on love or justice. Ours is founded upon hatred. In our world there will be no emotions except fear, rage, triumph, and self-abasement. Everything else we shall destroy—everything. Already we are breaking down the habits of thought which have survived from before the Revolution. We have cut the links between child and parent, and between man and man, and between man and woman. No one dares trust a wife or a child or a friend any longer. But in the future there will be no wives and no friends. Children will be taken from their mothers at birth, as one takes eggs from a hen. The sex instinct will be eradicated. Procreation will be an annual formality like the renewal of a ration card. We shall abolish the orgasm. Our neurologists are at work upon it now. There will be no loyalty, except loyalty towards the Party. There will be no love, except the love of Big Brother. There will be no laughter, except the laugh of triumph over a defeated enemy. There will be no art, no literature, no science. When we are omnipotent we shall have no more need of science. There will be no distinction between beauty and ugliness. There will be no curiosity, no enjoyment of the process of life. All competing pleasures will be destroyed. But always—do not forget this, Winston—always there will be the intoxication of power, constantly increasing and constantly growing subtler. Always, at every moment, there will be the thrill of victory, the sensation of trampling on an enemy who is helpless. If you want a picture of the future, imagine a boot stamping on a human face—for ever.'

He paused as though he expected Winston to speak. Winston had tried to shrink back into the surface of the bed again. He could not say anything. His heart seemed to be frozen. O'Brien went on:

'And remember that it is for ever. The face will always be there to be stamped upon. The heretic, the enemy of society, will always be there, so that he can be defeated and humiliated over again. Everything that you have undergone since you have been in our hands—all that will continue, and worse. The espionage, the betrayals, the arrests, the tortures, the executions, the disappearances will never cease. It will be a world of terror as much as a world of triumph. The more the Party is powerful, the less it will be tolerant: the weaker the opposition, the tighter the despotism. Goldstein and his heresies will live for ever. Every day, at every moment, they will be defeated, discredited, ridiculed, spat upon—and yet they will always survive. This drama that I have played out with you during seven years will be played out over and over again, generation after generation, always in subtler forms. Always we shall have the heretic here at our mercy, screaming with pain, broken up, contemptible—and in the end utterly penitent, saved from himself, crawling to our feet of his own accord. That is the world that we are preparing, Winston. A world of victory after victory, triumph after triumph after triumph: an endless pressing, pressing, pressing upon the nerve of power. You are beginning, I can see, to realize what that world will be like. But in the end you will do more than understand it. You will accept it, welcome it, become part of it.'

Winston had recovered himself sufficiently to speak. 'You can't!' he said weakly.

'What do you mean by that remark, Winston?'

'You could not create such a world as you have just described. It is a dream. It is impossible.'

'Why?'

'It is impossible to found a civilization on fear and hatred and cruelty. It would never endure.'

'Why not?'

'It would have no vitality. It would disintegrate. It would commit suicide.'

'Nonsense. You are under the impression that hatred is more exhausting than love. Why should it be? And if it were, what difference would that make? Suppose that we choose to wear ourselves out faster. Suppose that we quicken the tempo of human life till men are senile at thirty. Still what difference would it make? Can you not understand that the death of the individual is not death? The Party is immortal.'

As usual, the voice had battered Winston into helplessness. Moreover he was in dread that if he persisted in his disagreement O'Brien would twist the dial again. And yet he could not keep silent. Feebly, without arguments, with nothing to support him except his inarticulate horror of what O'Brien had said, he returned to the attack.

'I don't know—I don't care. Somehow you will fail. Something will defeat you. Life will defeat you.'

'We control life, Winston, at all its levels. You are imagining that there is something called human nature which will be outraged by what we do and will turn against us. But we create human nature. Men are infinitely malleable. Or perhaps you have returned to your old idea that the proletarians or the slaves will arise and overthrow us. Put it out of your mind. They are helpless, like the animals. Humanity is the Party. The others are outside—irrelevant.'

'I don't care. In the end they will beat you. Sooner or later they will see you for what you are, and then they will tear you to pieces.'

'Do you see any evidence that that is happening? Or any reason why it should?'

'No. I believe it. I *know* that you will fail. There is something in the universe—I don't know, some spirit, some principle—that you will never overcome.'

'Do you believe in God, Winston?'

'No.'

'Then what is it, this principle that will defeat us?'

'I don't know. The spirit of Man.'

'And do you consider yourself a man?'

'Yes.'

'If you are a man, Winston, you are the last man. Your kind is extinct; we are the inheritors. Do you understand that you are *alone*? You are outside history, you are non-existent.' His manner changed and he said more harshly: 'And you consider yourself morally superior to us, with our lies and our cruelty?'

'Yes, I consider myself superior.'

O'Brien did not speak. Two other voices were speaking. After a moment Winston recognized one of them as his own. It was a sound-track of the conversation he had had with O'Brien, on the night when he had enrolled himself in the Brotherhood. He heard himself promising to lie, to steal, to forge, to murder, to encourage drug-taking and prostitution, to disseminate venereal diseases, to throw vitriol in a child's face. O'Brien made a small impatient gesture, as though to say that the demonstration was hardly worth making. Then he turned a switch and the voices stopped.

'Get up from that bed,' he said.

The bonds had loosened themselves. Winston lowered himself to the floor and stood up unsteadily.

'You are the last man,' said O'Brien. 'You are the guardian of the human spirit. You shall see yourself as you are. Take off your clothes.'

Winston undid the bit of string that held his overalls together. The zip fastener had long since been wrenched out of them. He could not remember whether at any time since his arrest he had taken off all his clothes at one time. Beneath the overalls his body was looped with filthy yellowish rags, just recognizable as the remnants of underclothes. As he slid them to the ground he saw that there was a three-sided mirror at the far end of the room. He approached it, then stopped short. An involuntary cry had broken out of him.

'Go on,' said O'Brien. 'Stand between the wings of the mirror. You shall see the side view as well.'

He had stopped because he was frightened. A bowed, grey-coloured, skeleton-like thing was coming towards him. Its actual appearance was frightening, and not merely the fact that he knew it to be himself. He moved closer to the glass. The creature's face seemed to be protruded, because of its bent carriage. A forlorn, jailbird's face with a nobby forehead running back into a bald scalp, a crooked nose, and battered-looking cheekbones above which the eyes were fierce and watchful. The cheeks were seamed, the mouth had a drawn-in look. Certainly it was his own face, but it seemed to him that it had changed more than he had changed inside. The emotions it registered would be different from the ones he felt. He had gone partially bald. For the first moment he had thought that he had gone grey as well, but it was only the scalp that was grey. Except for his hands and a circle of his face, his body was grey all over with ancient, ingrained dirt. Here and there under the dirt there were the red scars of wounds, and near the ankle the varicose ulcer was an inflamed mass with flakes of skin peeling off it. But the truly frightening thing was the emaciation of his body. The barrel of the ribs was as narrow as that of a skeleton: the legs had shrunk so that the knees were thicker than the thighs. He saw now what O'Brien had meant about seeing the side view. The curvature of the spine was astonishing. The thin shoulders were hunched forward so as to make a cavity of the chest, the scraggy neck seemed to be bending double under the weight of the skull. At a guess he would have said that it was the body of a man of sixty, suffering from some malignant disease.

'You have thought sometimes,' said O'Brien, 'that my face—the face of a member of the Inner Party—looks old and worn. What do you think of your own face?'

He seized Winston's shoulder and spun him round so that he was facing him.

'Look at the condition you are in!' he said. 'Look at this filthy grime all over your body. Look at the dirt between your toes. Look at that disgusting running sore on your leg. Do you know that you stink like a goat? Probably you have ceased to notice it. Look at your emaciation. Do you see? I can make my thumb and forefinger meet round your bicep. I could snap your neck like a carrot. Do you know that you have lost twenty-five kilograms since you have been in our hands? Even your hair is coming out in handfuls. Look!' He plucked at Winston's head and brought away a tuft of hair. 'Open your mouth. Nine, ten, eleven teeth left. How many had you when you came to us? And the few you have left are dropping out of your head. Look here!'

He seized one of Winston's remaining front teeth between his powerful thumb and forefinger. A twinge of pain shot through Winston's jaw. O'Brien had wrenched the loose tooth out by the roots. He tossed it across the cell.

'You are rotting away,' he said; 'you are falling to pieces. What are you? A bag of filth. Now turn round and look into that mirror again. Do you see that thing facing you? That is the last man. If you are human, that is humanity. Now put your clothes on again.'

Winston began to dress himself with slow stiff movements. Until now he had not seemed to notice how thin and weak he was. Only one thought stirred in his mind: that he must have been in this place longer than he had imagined. Then suddenly as he fixed the miserable rags round himself a feeling of pity for his ruined body overcame him. Before he knew what he was doing he had collapsed on to a small stool that stood beside the bed and burst into tears. He was aware of his ugliness, his gracelessness, a bundle of bones in filthy underclothes sitting weeping in the harsh white light: but he could not stop himself. O'Brien laid a hand on his shoulder, almost kindly.

'It will not last for ever,' he said. 'You can escape from it whenever you choose. Everything depends on yourself.'

'You did it!' sobbed Winston. 'You reduced me to this state.'

'No, Winston, you reduced yourself to it. This is what you accepted when you set yourself up against the Party. It was all contained in that first act. Nothing has happened that you did not foresee.'

He paused, and then went on:

'We have beaten you, Winston. We have broken you up. You have seen what your body is like. Your mind is in the same state. I do not think there can be much pride left in you. You have been kicked and flogged and insulted, you have screamed with pain, you have rolled on the floor in your own blood and vomit. You have whimpered for mercy, you have betrayed everybody and everything. Can you think of a single degradation that has not happened to you?'

Winston had stopped weeping, though the tears were still oozing out of his eyes. He looked up at O'Brien.

'I have not betrayed Julia,' he said.

O'Brien looked down at him thoughtfully. 'No,' he said; 'no; that is perfectly true. You have not betrayed Julia.'

The peculiar reverence for O'Brien, which nothing seemed able to destroy, flooded Winston's heart again. How intelligent, he thought, how intelligent! Never did O'Brien fail to understand what was said to him. Anyone else on earth would have answered promptly that he *had* betrayed Julia. For what was there that they had not screwed out of him under the torture? He had told them everything he knew about her, her habits, her character, her past life; he had confessed in the most trivial detail everything that had happened at their meetings, all that he had said to her and she to him, their black-market meals, their adulteries, their vague plottings against the Party—everything. And yet, in the sense in which he intended the word, he had not betrayed her. He had not stopped loving her; his feeling towards her had remained the same. O'Brien had seen what he meant without the need for explanation.

'Tell me,' he said, 'how soon will they shoot me?'

'It might be a long time,' said O'Brien. 'You are a difficult case. But don't give up hope. Everyone is cured sooner or later. In the end we shall shoot you.'

## 4

He was much better. He was growing fatter and stronger every day, if it was proper to speak of days.

The white light and the humming sound were the same as ever, but the cell was a little more comfortable than the others he had been in. There was a pillow and a mattress on the plank bed, and a stool to sit on. They had given him a bath, and they allowed him to wash himself fairly frequently in a tin basin. They even gave him warm water to wash with. They had given him new underclothes and a clean suit of overalls. They had dressed his varicose ulcer with soothing ointment. They had pulled out the remnants of his teeth and given him a new set of dentures.

Weeks or months must have passed. It would have been possible now to keep count of the passage of time, if he had felt any interest in doing so, since he was being fed at what appeared to be regular intervals. He was getting, he judged, three meals in the twenty-four hours; sometimes he wondered dimly whether he was getting them by night or by day. The food was surprisingly good, with meat at every third meal. Once there was even a packet of cigarettes. He had no matches, but the never-speaking guard who brought his food would give him a light. The first time he tried to smoke it made him sick, but he persevered, and spun the packet out for a long time, smoking half a cigarette after each meal.

They had given him a white slate with a stump of pencil tied to the corner. At first he made no use of it. Even when he was awake he was completely torpid. Often he would lie from one meal to the next almost without stirring, sometimes asleep, sometimes waking into vague reveries in which it was too much trouble to open his eyes. He had long grown used to sleeping with a strong light on his face. It seemed to make no difference, except that one's dreams were more coherent. He dreamed a great deal all through this time, and they were always happy dreams. He was in the Golden Country, or he was sitting among enormous glorious, sunlit ruins, with his mother, with Julia, with O'Brien—not doing anything, merely sitting in the sun, talking of peaceful things. Such thoughts as he had when he was awake were mostly about his dreams. He seemed to have lost the power of intellectual effort, now that the stimulus of pain had been removed. He was not bored, he had no desire for conversation or distraction. Merely to be alone, not to be beaten or questioned, to have enough to eat, and to be clean all over, was completely satisfying.

By degrees he came to spend less time in sleep, but he still felt no impulse to get off the bed. All he cared for was to lie quiet and feel the strength gathering in his body. He would finger himself here and there, trying to make sure that it was not an illusion that his muscles were growing rounder and his skin tauter. Finally it was established beyond a doubt that he was growing fatter; his thighs were now definitely thicker than his knees. After that, reluctantly at first, he began exercising himself regularly. In a little while he could walk three kilometres, measured by pacing the cell, and his bowed shoulders were growing straighter. He attempted more elaborate exercises, and was astonished and humiliated to find what things he could not do. He could not move out of a walk, he could not hold his stool out at arm's length, he could not stand on one leg without falling over. He squatted down on his heels, and found that with agonizing pains in thigh and calf he could just lift himself to a standing position. He lay flat on his belly and tried to lift his weight by his hands. It was hopeless, he could not raise himself a centimetre. But after a few more days—a few more meal-times—even that feat was accomplished. A time came when he could do it six times running. He began to grow actually proud of his body, and to cherish an intermittent belief that his face also was growing back to normal. Only when he chanced to put his hand on his bald scalp did he remember the seamed, ruined face that had looked back at him out of the mirror.

His mind grew more active. He sat down on the plank bed, his back against the wall and the slate on his knees, and set to work deliberately at the task of re-educating himself.

He had capitulated, that was agreed. In reality, as he saw now, he had been ready to capitulate long before he had taken the decision. From the moment when he was inside the Ministry of Love—and yes, even during those minutes when he and Julia had stood helpless while the iron voice from the telescreen told them what to do—he had grasped the frivolity, the shallowness of his attempt to set himself up against the power of the Party. He knew now that for seven years the Thought Police had watched him like a beetle under a magnifying glass. There was no physical act, no word spoken aloud, that they had not noticed, no train of thought that they had not been able to infer. Even the speck of whitish dust on the cover of his diary they had carefully replaced. They had played sound-tracks to him, shown him photographs. Some of them were photographs of Julia and himself. Yes, even. . . . He could not fight against the Party any longer. Besides, the Party was in the right. It must be so: how could the immortal, collective brain be mistaken? By what external standard could you check its judgments? Sanity was statistical. It was merely a question of learning to think as they thought. Only–!

The pencil felt thick and awkward in his fingers. He began to write down the thoughts that came into his head. He wrote first in large clumsy capitals:

FREEDOM IS SLAVERY

Then almost without a pause he wrote beneath it:

TWO AND TWO MAKE FIVE

But then there came a sort of check. His mind, as though shying away from something, seemed unable to concentrate. He knew that he knew what came next, but for the moment he could not recall it. When he did recall it, it was only by consciously reasoning out what it must be: it did not come of its own accord. He wrote:

GOD IS POWER

He accepted everything. The past was alterable. The past never had been altered. Oceania was at war with Eastasia. Oceania had always been at war with Eastasia. Jones, Aaronson, and Rutherford were guilty of the crimes they were charged with. He had never seen the photograph that disproved their guilt. It had never existed, he had invented it. He remembered remembering contrary things, but those were false memories, products of self-deception. How easy it all was! Only surrender, and everything else followed. It was like swimming against a current that swept you backwards however hard you struggled, and then suddenly deciding to turn round and go with the current instead of opposing it. Nothing had changed except your own attitude: the predestined thing happened in any case. He hardly knew why he had ever rebelled. Everything was easy, except–!

Anything could be true. The so-called laws of Nature were nonsense. The law of gravity was nonsense. 'If I wished,' O'Brien had said, 'I could float off this floor like a soap bubble.' Winston worked it out. 'If he *thinks* he floats off the floor, and if I simultaneously *think* I see him do it, then the thing happens.' Suddenly, like a lump of submerged wreckage breaking the surface of water, the thought burst into his mind: 'It doesn't really happen. We imagine it. It is hallucination.' He pushed the thought under instantly. The fallacy was obvious. It presupposed that somewhere or other, outside oneself, there was a 'real' world where 'real' things happened. But how could there be such a world? What knowledge have we of anything, save through our own minds? All happenings are in the mind. Whatever happens in all minds, truly happens.

He had no difficulty in disposing of the fallacy, and he was in no danger of succumbing to it. He realized, nevertheless, that it ought never to have occurred to him. The mind should develop a blind spot whenever a dangerous thought presented itself. The process should be automatic, instinctive. *Crimestop*, they called it in Newspeak.

He set to work to exercise himself in crimestop. He presented himself with propositions—'the Party says the earth is flat', 'the Party says that ice is heavier than water'—and trained himself in not seeing or not understanding the arguments that contradicted them. It was not easy. It needed great powers of reasoning and improvisation. The arithmetical problems raised, for instance, by such a statement as 'two and two make five' were beyond his intellectual grasp. It needed also a sort of athleticism of mind, and ability at one moment to make the most delicate use of logic and at the next to be unconscious of the crudest logical errors. Stupidity was as necessary as intelligence, and as difficult to attain.

All the while, with one part of his mind, he wondered how soon they would shoot him. 'Everything depends on yourself,' O'Brien had said; but he knew that there was no conscious act by which he could bring it nearer. It might be ten minutes hence, or ten years. They might keep him for years in solitary confinement, they might send him to a labour-camp, they might release him for a while, as they sometimes did. It was perfectly possible that before he was shot the whole drama of his arrest and interrogation would be enacted all over again. The one certain thing was that death never came at an expected moment. The tradition—the unspoken tradition: somehow you knew it, though you never heard it said—was that they shot you from behind: always in the back of the head, without warning, as you walked down a corridor from cell to cell.

One day—but 'one day' was not the right expression; just as probably it was in the middle of the night: once—he fell into a strange, blissful reverie. He was walking down the corridor, waiting for the bullet. He knew that it was coming in another moment. Everything was settled, smoothed out, reconciled. There were no more doubts, no more arguments, no more pain, no more fear. His body was healthy and strong. He walked easily, with a joy of movement and with a feeling of walking in sunlight. He was not any longer in the narrow white corridors in the Ministry of Love, he was in the enormous sunlit passage, a kilometre wide, down which he had seemed to walk in the delirium induced by drugs. He was in the Golden Country, following the foot-track across the old rabbit-cropped pasture. He could feel the short springy turf under his feet and the gentle sunshine on his face. At the edge of the field were the elm trees, faintly stirring, and somewhere beyond that was the stream where the dace lay in the green pools under the willows.

Suddenly he started up with a shock of horror. The sweat broke out on his backbone. He had heard himself cry aloud:

'Julia! Julia! Julia, my love! Julia!'

For a moment he had had an overwhelming hallucination of her presence. She had seemed to be not merely with him, but inside him. It was as though she had got into the texture of his skin. In that moment he had loved her far more than he had ever done when they were together and free. Also he knew that somewhere or other she was still alive and needed his help.

He lay back on the bed and tried to compose himself. What had he done? How many years had he added to his servitude by that moment of weakness?

In another moment he would hear the tramp of boots outside. They could not let such an outburst go unpunished. They would know now, if they had not known before, that he was breaking the agreement he had made with them. He obeyed the Party, but he still hated the Party. In the old days he had hidden a heretical mind beneath an appearance of conformity. Now he had retreated a step further: in the mind he had surrendered, but he had hoped to keep the inner heart inviolate. He knew that he was in the wrong, but he preferred to be in the wrong. They would understand that—O'Brien would understand it. It was all confessed in that single foolish cry.

He would have to start all over again. It might take years. He ran a hand over his face, trying to familiarize himself with the new shape. There were deep furrows in the cheeks, the cheekbones felt sharp, the nose flattened. Besides, since last seeing himself in the glass he had been given a complete new set of teeth. It was not easy to preserve inscrutability when you did not know what your face looked like. In any case, mere control of the features was not enough. For the first time he perceived that if you want to keep a secret you must also hide it from yourself. You must know all the while that it is there, but until it is needed you must never let it emerge into your consciousness in any shape that could be given a name. From now onwards he must not only think right; he must feel right, dream right. And all the while he must keep his hatred locked up inside him like a ball of matter which was part of himself and yet unconnected with the rest of him, a kind of cyst.

One day they would decide to shoot him. You could not tell when it would happen, but a few seconds beforehand it should be possible to guess. It was always from behind, walking down a corridor. Ten seconds would be enough. In that time the world inside him could turn over. And then suddenly, without a word uttered, without a check in his step, without the changing of a line in his face—suddenly the camouflage would be down and bang! would go the batteries of his hatred. Hatred would fill him like an enormous roaring flame. And almost in the same instant bang! would go the bullet, too late, or too early. They would have blown his brain to pieces before they could reclaim it. The heretical thought would be unpunished, unrepented, out of their reach for ever. They would have blown a hole in their own perfection. To die hating them, that was freedom.

He shut his eyes. It was more difficult than accepting an intellectual discipline. It was a question of degrading himself, mutilating himself. He had got to plunge into the filthiest of filth. What was the most horrible, sickening thing of all? He thought of Big Brother. The enormous face (because of constantly seeing it on posters he always thought of it as being a metre wide), with its heavy black moustache and the eyes that followed you to and fro, seemed to float into his mind of its own accord. What were his true feelings towards Big Brother?

There was a heavy tramp of boots in the passage. The steel door swung open with a clang. O'Brien walked into the cell. Behind him were the waxen-faced officer and the black-uniformed guards.

'Get up,' said O'Brien. 'Come here.'

Winston stood opposite him. O'Brien took Winston's shoulders between his strong hands and looked at him closely.

'You have had thoughts of deceiving me,' he said. 'That was stupid. Stand up straighter. Look me in the face.'

He paused, and went on in a gentler tone:

'You are improving. Intellectually there is very little wrong with you. It is only emotionally that you have failed to make progress. Tell me, Winston—and remember, no lies: you know that I am always able to detect a lie—tell me, what are your true feelings towards Big Brother?'

'I hate him.'

'You hate him. Good. Then the time has come for you to take the last step. You must love Big Brother. It is not enough to obey him: you must love him.'

He released Winston with a little push towards the guards.

'Room 101,' he said.

# 5

At each stage of his imprisonment he had known, or seemed to know, whereabouts he was in the windowless building. Possibly there were slight differences in the air pressure. The cells where the guards had beaten him were below ground level. The room where he had been interrogated by O'Brien was high up near the roof. This place was many metres underground, as deep down as it was possible to go.

It was bigger than most of the cells he had been in. But he hardly noticed his surroundings. All he noticed was that there were two small tables straight in front of him, each covered with green baize. One was only a metre or two from him, the other was farther away, near the door. He was strapped upright in a chair, so tightly that he could move nothing, not even his head. A sort of pad gripped his head from behind, forcing him to look straight in front of him.

For a moment he was alone, then the door opened and O'Brien came in.

'You asked me once,' said O'Brien, 'what was in Room 101. I told you that you knew the answer already. Everyone knows it. The thing that is in Room 101 is the worst thing in the world.'

The door opened again. A guard came in, carrying something made of wire, a box or basket of some kind. He set it down on the further table. Because of the position in which O'Brien was standing, Winston could not see what the thing was.

'The worst thing in the world,' said O'Brien, 'varies from individual to individual. It may be burial alive, or death by fire, or by drowning, or by impalement, or fifty other deaths. There are cases where it is some quite trivial thing, not even fatal.'

He had moved a little to one side, so that Winston had a better view of the thing on the table. It was an oblong wire cage with a handle on top for carrying it by. Fixed to the front of it was something that looked like a fencing mask, with the concave side outwards. Although it was three or four metres away from him, he could see that the cage was divided lengthways into two compartments, and that there was some kind of creature in each. They were rats.

'In your case,' said O'Brien, 'the worst thing in the world happened to be rats.'

A sort of premonitory tremor, a fear of he was not certain what, had passed through Winston as soon as he caught his first glimpse of the cage. But at this moment the meaning of the mask-like attachment in front of it suddenly sank into him. His bowels seemed to turn to water.

'You can't do that!' he cried out in a high cracked voice. 'You couldn't, you couldn't! It's impossible.'

'Do you remember,' said O'Brien, 'the moment of panic that used to occur in your dreams? There was a wall of blackness in front of you, and a roaring sound in your ears. There was something terrible on the other side of the wall. You knew that you knew what it was, but you dared not drag it into the open. It was the rats that were on the other side of the wall.'

'O'Brien!' said Winston, making an effort to control his voice. 'You know this is not necessary. What is it that you want me to do?'

O'Brien made no direct answer. When he spoke it was in the schoolmasterish manner that he sometimes affected. He looked thoughtfully into the distance, as though he were addressing an audience somewhere behind Winston's back.

'By itself,' he said, 'pain is not always enough. There are occasions when a human being will stand out against pain, even to the point of death. But for everyone there is something unendurable—something that cannot be contemplated. Courage and cowardice are not involved. If you are falling from a height it is not cowardly to clutch at a rope. If you have come up from deep water it is not cowardly to fill your lungs with air. It is merely an instinct which cannot be destroyed. It is the same with the rats. For you, they are unendurable. They are a form of pressure that you cannot withstand, even if you wished to. You will do what is required of you.'

'But what is it, what is it? How can I do it if I don't know what it is?'

O'Brien picked up the cage and brought it across to the nearer table. He set it down carefully on the baize cloth. Winston could hear the blood singing in his ears. He had the feeling of sitting in utter loneliness. He was in the middle of a great empty plain, a flat desert drenched with sunlight, across which all sounds came to him out of immense distances. Yet the cage with the rats was not two metres away from him. They were enormous rats. They were at the age when a rat's muzzle grows blunt and fierce and his fur brown instead of grey.

'The rat,' said O'Brien, still addressing his invisible audience, 'although a rodent, is carnivorous. You are aware of that. You will have heard of the things that happen in the poor quarters of this town. In some streets a woman dare not leave her baby alone in the house, even for five minutes. The rats are certain to attack it. Within quite a small time they will strip it to the bones. They also attack sick or dying people. They show astonishing intelligence in knowing when a human being is helpless.'

There was an outburst of squeals from the cage. It seemed to reach Winston from far away. The rats were fighting; they were trying to get at each other through the partition. He heard also a deep groan of despair. That, too, seemed to come from outside himself.

O'Brien picked up the cage, and, as he did so, pressed something in it. There was a sharp click. Winston made a frantic effort to tear himself loose from the chair. It was hopeless; every part of him, even his head, was held immovably. O'Brien moved the cage nearer. It was less than a metre from Winston's face.

'I have pressed the first lever,' said O'Brien. 'You understand the construction of this cage. The mask will fit over your head, leaving no exit. When I press this other lever, the door of the cage will slide up. These starving brutes will shoot out of it like bullets. Have you ever seen a rat leap through the air? They will leap on to your face and bore straight into it. Sometimes they attack the eyes first. Sometimes they burrow through the cheeks and devour the tongue.'

The cage was nearer; it was closing in. Winston heard a succession of shrill cries which appeared to be occurring in the air above his head. But he fought furiously against his panic. To think, to think, even with a split second left—to think was the only hope. Suddenly the foul musty odour of the brutes struck his nostrils. There was a violent convulsion of nausea inside him, and he almost lost consciousness. Everything had gone black. For an instant he was insane, a screaming animal. Yet he came out of the blackness clutching an idea. There was one and only one way to save himself. He must interpose another human being, the *body* of another human being, between himself and the rats.

The circle of the mask was large enough now to shut out the vision of anything else. The wire door was a couple of hand-spans from his face. The rats knew what was coming now. One of them was leaping up and down, the other, an old scaly grandfather of the sewers, stood up, with the other his pink hands against the bars, and fiercely sniffed the air. Winston could see the whiskers and the yellow teeth. Again the black panic took hold of him. He was blind, helpless, mindless.

'It was a common punishment in Imperial China,' said O'Brien as didactically as ever.

The mask was closing on his face. The wire brushed his cheek. And then—no, it was not relief, only hope, a tiny fragment of hope. Too late, perhaps too late. But he had suddenly understood that in the whole world there was just *one* person to whom he could transfer his punishment—*one* body that he could thrust between himself and the rats. And he was shouting frantically, over and over.

'Do it to Julia! Do it to Julia! Not me! Julia I don't care what you do to her. Tear her face off, strip her to the bones. Not me! Julia! Not me!'

He was falling backwards, into enormous depths, away from the rats. He was still strapped in the chair, but he had fallen through the floor, through the walls of the building, through the earth, through the oceans, through the atmosphere, into outer space, into the gulfs between the stars—always away, away, away from the rats. He was light-years distant, but O'Brien was still standing at his side. There was still the cold touch of a wire against his cheek. But through the darkness that enveloped him he heard another metallic click, and knew that the cage door had clicked shut and not open.

# 6

The Chestnut Tree was almost empty. A ray of sunlight slanting through a window fell yellow on dusty table-tops. It was the lonely hour of fifteen. A tinny music trickled from the telescreens.

Winston sat in his usual corner, gazing into an empty glass. Now and again he glanced up at a vast face which eyed him from the opposite wall. BIG BROTHER IS WATCHING YOU, the caption said. Unbidden, a waiter came and filled his glass up with Victory Gin, shaking into it a few drops from another bottle with a quill through the cork. It was saccharine flavoured with cloves, the speciality of the café.

Winston was listening to the telescreen. At present only music was coming out of it, but there was a possibility that at any moment there might be a special bulletin from the Ministry of Peace. The news from the African front was disquieting in the extreme. On and off he had been worrying about it all day. A Eurasian army (Oceania was at war with Eurasia: Oceania had always been at war with Eurasia) was moving southward at terrifying speed. The midday bulletin had not mentioned any definite area, but it was probable that already the mouth of the Congo was a battlefield. Brazzaville and Leopoldville were in danger. One did not have to look at the map to see what it meant. It was not merely a question of losing Central Africa: for the first time in the whole war, the territory of Oceania itself was menaced.

A violent emotion, not fear exactly but a sort of undifferentiated excitement, flared up in him, then faded again. He stopped thinking about the war. In these days he could never fix his mind on any one subject for more than a few moments at a time. He picked up his glass and drained it at a gulp. As always, the gin made him shudder and even retch slightly. The stuff was horrible. The cloves and saccharine, themselves disgusting enough in their sickly way, could not disguise the flat oily smell; and what was worst of all was that the smell of gin, which dwelt with him night and day, was inextricably mixed up in his mind with the smell of those—

He never named them, even in his thoughts, and so far as it was possible he never visualized them. They were something that he was half-aware of, hovering close to his face, a smell that clung to his nostrils. As the gin rose in him he belched through purple lips. He had grown fatter since they released him, and had regained his old colour—indeed, more than regained it. His features had thickened, the skin on nose and cheekbones was coarsely red, even the bald scalp was too deep a pink. A waiter, again unbidden, brought the chessboard and the current issue of *The Times,* with the page turned down at the chess problem. Then, seeing that Winston's glass was empty, he brought the gin bottle and filled it. There was no need to give orders. They knew his habits. The chessboard was always waiting for him, his corner table was always reserved; even when the place was full he had it to himself, since nobody cared to be seen sitting too close to him. He never even bothered to count his drinks. At irregular intervals they presented him with a dirty slip of paper which they said was the bill, but he had the impression that they always undercharged him. It would have made no difference if it had been the other way about. He had always plenty of money nowadays. He even had a job, a sinecure, more highly paid than his old job had been.

The music from the telescreen stopped and a voice took over. Winston raised his head to listen. No bulletin from the front, however. It was merely a brief announcement from the Ministry of Plenty. In the preceding quarter, it appeared, the Tenth Three-Year Plan's quota for bootlaces had been over-fulfilled by 98 per cent.

He examined the chess problem and set out the pieces. It was a tricky ending, involving a couple of knights. 'White to play and mate in two moves.' Winston looked up at the portrait of Big Brother. White always mates, he thought with a sort of cloudy mysticism. Always, without exception, it is so arranged. In no chess problem since the beginning of the world has black ever won. Did it not symbolize the eternal, unvarying triumph of Good over Evil? The huge face gazed back at him, full of calm power. White always mates.

The voice from the telescreen paused and added in a different and much graver tone: 'You are warned to stand by for an important announcement at fifteen-thirty. Fifteen-thirty! This is news of the highest importance. Take care not to miss it. Fifteen-thirty!' The tinkling music struck up again.

Winston's heart stirred. That was the bulletin from the front; instinct told him that it was bad news that was coming. All day, with little spurts of excitement, the thought of a smashing defeat in Africa had been in and out of his mind. He seemed actually to see the Eurasian army swarming across the never-broken frontier and pouring down into the tip of Africa like a column of ants. Why had it not been possible to outflank them in some way? The outline of the West African coast stood out vividly in his mind. He picked up the white

knight and moved it across the board. *There* was the proper spot. Even while
he saw the black horde racing southward he saw another force, mysteriously
assembled, suddenly planted in their rear, cutting their communications by
land and sea. He felt that by willing it he was bringing that other force into
existence. But it was necessary to act quickly. If they could get control of the
whole of Africa, if they had airfields and submarine bases at the Cape, it would
cut Oceania in two. It might mean anything: defeat, breakdown, the redivision
of the world, the destruction of the Party! He drew a deep breath. An
extraordinary medley of feeling—but it was not a medley, exactly; rather it was
successive layers of feeling, in which one could not say which layer was
undermost—struggled inside him.

The spasm passed. He put the white knight back in its place, but for the
moment he could not settle down to serious study of the chess problem. His
thoughts wandered again. Almost unconsciously he traced with his finger in
the dust on the table:

$$2 + 2 =$$

'They can't get inside you,' she had said. But they could get inside you.
'What happens to you here is *for ever*,' O'Brien had said. That was a true word.
There were things, your own acts, from which you could not recover.
Something was killed in your breast: burnt out, cauterized out.

He had seen her; he had even spoken to her. There was no danger in it. He
knew as though instinctively that they now took almost no interest in his
doings. He could have arranged to meet her a second time if either of them had
wanted to. Actually it was by chance that they had met. It was in the Park, on a
vile, biting day in March, when the earth was like iron and all the grass seemed
dead and there was not a bud anywhere except a few crocuses which had
pushed themselves up to be dismembered by the wind. He was hurrying along
with frozen hands and watering eyes when he saw her not ten metres away
from him. It struck him at once that she had changed in some ill-defined way.
They almost passed one another without a sign, then he turned and followed
her, not very eagerly. He knew that there was no danger, nobody would take
any interest in them. She did not speak. She walked obliquely away across the
grass as though trying to get rid of him, then seemed to resign herself to having
him at her side. Presently they were in among a clump of ragged leafless
shrubs, useless either for concealment or as protection from the wind. They
halted. It was vilely cold. The wind whistled through the twigs and fretted the
occasional, dirty-looking crocuses. He put his arm round her waist.

There was no telescreen, but there must be hidden microphones: besides,
they could be seen. It did not matter, nothing mattered. They could have lain
down on the ground and done *that* if they had wanted to. His flesh froze with
horror at the thought of it. She made no response whatever to the clasp of his
arm; she did not even try to disengage herself. He knew now what had changed
in her. Her face was sallower, and there was a long scar, partly hidden by the
hair, across her forehead and temple; but that was not the change. It was that

her waist had grown thicker, and, in a surprising way, had stiffened. He remembered how once, after the explosion of a rocket bomb, he had helped to drag a corpse out of some ruins, and had been astonished not only by the incredible weight of the thing, but by its rigidity and awkwardness to handle, which made it seem more like stone than flesh. Her body felt like that. It occurred to him that the texture of her skin would be quite different from what it had once been.

He did not attempt to kiss her, nor did they speak. As they walked back across the grass she looked directly at him for the first time. It was only a momentary glance, full of contempt and dislike. He wondered whether it was a dislike that came purely out of the past or whether it was inspired also by his bloated face and the water that the wind kept squeezing from his eyes. They sat down on two iron chairs, side by side but not too close together. He saw that she was about to speak. She moved her clumsy shoe a few centimetres and deliberately crushed a twig. Her feet seemed to have grown broader, he noticed.

'I betrayed you,' she said baldly.

'I betrayed you,' he said.

She gave him another quick look of dislike.

'Sometimes,' she said, 'they threaten you with something—something you can't stand up to, can't even think about. And then you say, "Don't do it to me, do it to somebody else, do it to So-and-so." And perhaps you might pretend, afterwards, that it was only a trick and that you just said it to make them stop and didn't really mean it. But that isn't true. At the time when it happens you do mean it. You think there's no other way of saving yourself, and you're quite ready to save yourself that way. You *want* it to happen to the other person. You don't give a damn what they suffer. All you care about is yourself.'

'All you care about is yourself,' he echoed.

'And after that, you don't feel the same towards the other person any longer.'

'No,' he said, 'you don't feel the same.'

There did not seem to be anything more to say. The wind plastered their thin overalls against their bodies. Almost at once it became embarrassing to sit there in silence: besides, it was too cold to keep still. She said something about catching her Tube and stood up to go.

'We must meet again,' he said.

'Yes,' she said, 'we must meet again.'

He followed irresolutely for a little distance, half a pace behind her. They did not speak again. She did not actually try to shake him off, but walked at just such a speed as to prevent his keeping abreast of her. He had made up his mind that he would accompany her as far as the Tube station, but suddenly this process of trailing along in the cold seemed pointless and unbearable. He was overwhelmed by a desire not so much to get away from Julia as to get back to the Chestnut Tree Café, which had never seemed so attractive as at this moment. He had a nostalgic vision of his corner table, with the newspaper and the chessboard and the everflowing gin. Above all, it would be warm in there.

The next moment, not altogether by accident, he allowed himself to become separated from her by a small knot of people. He made a half-hearted attempt to catch up, then slowed down, turned, and made off in the opposite direction. When he had gone fifty metres he looked back. The street was not crowded, but already he could not distinguish her. Any one of a dozen hurrying figures might have been hers. Perhaps her thickened, stiffened body was no longer recognizable from behind.

'At the time when it happens,' she had said, 'you do mean it.' He had meant it. He had not merely said it, he had wished it. He had wished that she and not he should be delivered over to the—.

Something changed in the music that trickled from the telescreen. A cracked and jeering note, a yellow note, came into it. And then—perhaps it was not happening, perhaps it was only a memory taking on the semblance of sound—a voice was singing:

> 'Under the spreading chestnut tree
> I sold you and you sold me—'

The tears welled up in his eyes. A passing waiter noticed that his glass was empty and came back with the gin bottle.

He took up his glass and sniffed at it. The stuff grew not less but more horrible with every mouthful he drank. But it had become the element he swam in. It was his life, his death, and his resurrection. It was gin that sank him into stupor every night, and gin that revived him every morning. When he woke, seldom before eleven hundred, with gummed-up eyelids and fiery mouth and a back that seemed to be broken, it would have been impossible even to rise from the horizontal if it had not been for the bottle and teacup placed beside the bed overnight. Through the midday hours he sat with glazed face, the bottle handy, listening to the telescreen. From fifteen to closing-time he was a fixture in the Chestnut Tree. No one cared what he did any longer, no whistle woke him, no telescreen admonished him. Occasionally, perhaps twice a week, he went to a dusty, forgotten-looking office in the Ministry of Truth and did a little work, or what was called work. He had been appointed to a sub-committee of a sub-commitee which had sprouted from one of the innumerable committees dealing with minor difficulties that arose in the compilation of the Eleventh Edition of the Newspeak Dictionary. They were engaged in producing something called an Interim Report, but what it was that they were reporting on he had never definitely found out. It was something to do with the question of whether commas should be placed inside brackets, or outside. There were four others on the committee, all of them persons similar to himself. There were days when they assembled and then promptly dispersed again, frankly admitting to one another that there was not really anything to be done. But there were other days when they settled down to their work almost eagerly, making a tremendous show of entering up their minutes and drafting long memoranda which were never finished—when the argument as to what they were supposedly arguing about grew extraordinarily involved and abstruse, with subtle hagglings over definitions, enormous digressions, quarrels—threats, even, to appeal to higher authority. And then suddenly the life would go out of them and they would sit round the table looking at one another with extinct eyes, like ghosts fading at cock-crow.

The telescreen was silent for a moment. Winston raised his head again. The bulletin! But no, they were merely changing the music. He had the map of Africa behind his eyelids. The movement of the armies was a diagram: a black arrow tearing vertically southward, and a white arrow tearing horizontally eastward, across the tail of the first. As though for reassurance he looked up at the imperturbable face in the portrait. Was it conceivable that the second arrow did not even exist?

His interest flagged again. He drank another mouthful of gin, picked up the white knight and made a tentative move. Check. But it was evidently not the right move, because—

Uncalled, a memory floated into his mind. He saw a candle-lit room with a vast white-counterpaned bed, and himself, a boy of nine or ten, sitting on the floor, shaking a dice-box, and laughing excitedly. His mother was sitting opposite him and also laughing.

It must have been about a month before she disappeared. It was a moment of reconciliation, when the nagging hunger in his belly was forgotten and his earlier affection for her had temporarily revived. He remembered the day well, a pelting, drenching day when the water streamed down the window-pane and the light indoors was too dull to read by. The boredom of the two children in the dark, cramped bedroom became unbearable. Winston whined and grizzled, made futile demands for food, fretted about the room pulling everything out of place and kicking the wainscoting until the neighbours banged on the wall, while the younger child wailed intermittently. In the end his mother had said, 'Now be good, and I'll buy you a toy. A lovely toy—you'll love it'; and then she had gone out in the rain, to a little general shop which was still sporadically open near by, and came back with a cardboard box containing an outfit of Snakes and Ladders. He could still remember the smell of the damp cardboard. It was a miserable outfit. The board was cracked and the tiny wooden dice were so ill-cut that they would hardly lie on their sides. Winston looked at the thing sulkily and without interest. But then his mother lit a piece of candle and they sat down on the floor to play. Soon he was wildly excited and shouting with laughter as the tiddlywinks climbed hopefully up the ladders and then came slithering down the snakes again, almost to the starting-point. They played eight games, winning four each. His tiny sister, too young to understand what the game was about, had sat propped up against a bolster, laughing because the others were laughing. For a whole afternoon they had all been happy together, as in his earlier childhood.

He pushed the picture out of his mind. It was a false memory. He was troubled by false memories occasionally. They did not matter so long as one knew them for what they were. Some things had happened, others had not happened. He turned back to the chessboard and picked up the white knight again. Almost in the same instant it dropped on to the board with a clatter. He had started as though a pin had run into him.

A shrill trumpet call had pierced the air. It was the bulletin! Victory! It always meant victory when a trumpet call preceded the news. A sort of electric thrill ran through the café. Even the waiters had started and pricked up their ears.

The trumpet call had let loose an enormous volume of noise. Already an excited voice was gabbling from the telescreen, but even as it started it was almost drowned by a roar of cheering from outside. The news had run round the streets like magic. He could hear just enough of what was issuing from the telescreen to realize that it had all happened as he had foreseen: a vast seaborne armada secretly assembled, a sudden blow in the enemy's rear, the white arrow tearing across the tail of the black. Fragments of triumphant phrases pushed themselves through the din: 'Vast strategic manœuvre–perfect co-ordination–utter rout–half a million prisoners–complete demoralization–control of the whole of Africa–bring the war within measurable distance of its end–victory– greatest victory in human history–victory, victory, victory!'

Under the table Winston's feet made convulsive movements. He had not stirred from his seat, but in his mind he was running, swiftly running, he was with the crowds outside, cheering himself deaf. He looked up again at the portrait of Big Brother. The colossus that bestrode the world! The rock against which the hordes of Asia dashed themselves in vain! He thought how ten minutes ago–yes, only ten minutes–there had still been equivocation in his heart as he wondered whether the news from the front would be of victory or defeat. Ah, it was more than a Eurasian army that had perished! Much had changed in him since that first day in the Ministry of Love, but the final, indispensable, healing change had never happened, until this moment.

The voice from the telescreen was still pouring forth its tale of prisoners and booty and slaughter, but the shouting outside had died down a little. The waiters were turning back to their work. One of them approached with the gin bottle. Winston, sitting in a blissful dream, paid no attention as his glass was filled up. He was not running or cheering any longer. He was back in the Ministry of Love, with everything forgiven, his soul white as snow. He was in the public dock, confessing everything, implicating everybody. He was walking down the white-tiled corridor, with the feeling of walking in sunlight, and an armed guard at his back. The long-hoped-for bullet was entering his brain.

He gazed up at the enormous face. Forty years it had taken him to learn what kind of smile was hidden beneath the dark moustache. O cruel, needless misunderstanding! O stubborn, self-willed exile from the loving breast! Two gin-scented tears trickled down the sides of his nose. But it was all right, everything was all right, the struggle was finished. He had won the victory over himself. He loved Big Brother.

THE END

# APPENDIX

# The Principles of Newspeak

Newspeak was the official language of Oceania and had been devised to meet the ideological needs of Ingsoc, or English Socialism. In the year 1984 there was not as yet anyone who used Newspeak as his sole means of communication, either in speech or writing. The leading articles in *The Times* were written in it, but this was a *tour de force* which could only be carried out by a specialist. It was expected that Newspeak would have finally superseded Oldspeak (or Standard English, as we should call it) by about the year 2050. Meanwhile it gained ground steadily, all Party members tending to use Newspeak words and grammatical constructions more and more in their everyday speech. The version in use in 1984, and embodied in the Ninth and Tenth Editions of the Newspeak Dictionary, was a provisional one, and contained many superfluous words and archaic formations which were due to be suppressed later. It is with the final, perfected version, as embodied in the Eleventh Edition of the Dictionary, that we are concerned here.

The purpose of Newspeak was not only to provide a medium of expression for the world-view and mental habits proper to the devotees of Ingsoc, but to make all other modes of thought impossible. It was intended that when Newspeak had been adopted once and for all and Oldspeak forgotten, a heretical thought—that is, a thought diverging from the principles of Ingsoc—should be literally unthinkable, at least so far as thought is dependent on words. Its Vocabulary was so constructed as to give exact and often very subtle expression to every meaning that a Party member could properly wish to express, while excluding all other meanings and also the possibility of arriving at them by indirect methods. This was done partly by the invention of new words, but chiefly by eliminating undesirable words and by stripping such words as remained of unorthodox meanings, and so far as possible of all secondary meanings whatever. To give a single example. The word *free* still existed in Newspeak, but it could only be used in such statements as 'This dog is free from lice' or 'This field is free from weeds'. It could not be used in its old sense of 'politically free' or 'intellectually free', since political and intellectual freedom no longer existed even as concepts, and were therefore of necessity nameless. Quite apart from the suppression of definitely heretical words, reduction of vocabulary was regarded as an end in itself, and no word that could be dispensed with was allowed to survive. Newspeak was designed not to extend but to *diminish* the range of thought, and this purpose was indirectly assisted by cutting the choice of words down to a minimum.

Newspeak was founded on the English language as we now know it, though many Newspeak sentences, even when not containing newly created words, would be barely intelligible to an English-speaker of our own day. Newspeak words were divided into three distinct classes, known as the A vocabulary, the B vocabulary (also called compound words), and the C vocabulary. It will be simpler to discuss each class separately, but the grammatical peculiarities of the language can be dealt with in the section devoted to the A vocabulary, since the same rules held good for all three categories.

*The A vocabulary.* The A vocabulary consisted of the words needed for the business of everyday life—for such things as eating, drinking, working, putting on one's clothes, going up and down stairs, riding in vehicles, gardening, cooking, and the like. It was composed almost entirely of words that we already possess—words like *hit, run, dog, tree, sugar, house, field*—but in comparison with the present-day English vocabulary their number was extremely small, while their meanings were far more rigidly defined. All ambiguities and shades of meaning had been purged out of them. So far as it could be achieved, a Newspeak word of this class was simply a staccato sound expressing *one* clearly understood concept. It would have been quite impossible to use the A vocabulary for literary purposes or for political or philosophical discussion. It was intended only to express simple, purposive thoughts, usually involving concrete objects or physical actions.

The grammar of Newspeak had two outstanding peculiarities. The first of these was an almost complete interchangeability between different parts of speech. Any word in the language (in principle this applied even to very abstract words such as *if* or *when*) could be used either as verb, noun, adjective, or adverb. Between the verb and the noun form, when they were of the same root, there was never any variation, this rule of itself involving the destruction of many archaic forms. The word *thought,* for example, did not exist in Newspeak. Its place was taken by *think,* which did duty for both noun and verb. No etymological principle was followed here: in some cases it was the original noun that was chosen for retention, in other cases the verb. Even where a noun and verb of kindred meaning were not etymologically connected, one or other of them was frequently suppressed. There was, for example, no such word as *cut,* its meaning being sufficiently covered by the noun-verb *knife.* Adjectives were formed by adding the suffix *-ful* to the noun-verb, and adverbs by adding *-wise.* Thus for example, *speedful* meant 'rapid' and *speedwise* meant 'quickly'. Certain of our present-day adjectives, such as *good, strong, big, black, soft,* were retained, but their total number was very small. There was little need for them, since almost any adjectival meaning could be arrived at by adding *-ful* to a noun-verb. None of the now-existing adverbs was retained, except for a very few already ending in *-wise*: the *-wise* termination was invariable. The word *well*, for example, was replaced by *goodwise*.

In addition, any word—this again applied in principle to every word in the language—could be negatived by adding the affix *un-*, or could be strengthened by the affix *plus-*, or, for still greater emphasis, *doubleplus-*. Thus, for example, *uncold* meant 'warm', while *pluscold* and *doublepluscold* meant, respectively 'very cold' and 'superlatively cold'. It was also possible, as in present-day English, to modify the meaning of almost any word by prepositional affixes such as *ante-*, *post-*, *up-*, *down-*, etc. By such methods it was found possible to bring about an enormous diminution of vocabulary. Given, for instance, the word *good*, there was no need for such a word as *bad*, since the required meaning was equally well—indeed, better—expressed by *ungood*. All that was necessary, in any case where two words formed a natural pair of opposites, was to decide which of them to suppress. *Dark*, for example, could be replaced by *unlight*, or *light* by *undark*, according to preference.

The second distinguishing mark of Newspeak grammar was its regularity. Subject to a few exceptions which are mentioned below all inflexions followed the same rules. Thus, in all verbs the preterite and the past participle were the same and ended in *-ed*. The preterite of *steal* was *stealed*, the preterite of *think* was *thinked*, and so on throughout the language, all such forms as *swam, gave, brought, spoke, taken*, etc., being abolished. All plurals were made by adding *-s* or *-es* as the case might be. The plurals of *man, ox, life*, were *mans, oxes, lifes*. Comparison of adjectives was invariably made by adding *-er, -est* (*good, gooder, goodest*), irregular forms and the *more, most* formation being suppressed.

The only classes of words that were still allowed to inflect irregularly were the pronouns, the relatives, the demonstrative adjectives, and the auxiliary verbs. All of these followed their ancient usage, except that *whom* had been scrapped as unnecessary, and the *shall, should* tenses had been dropped, all their uses being covered by *will* and *would*. There were also certain irregularities in word-formation arising out of the need for rapid and easy speech. A word which was difficult to utter, or was liable to be incorrectly heard, was held to be *ipso facto* a bad word: occasionally, therefore, for the sake of euphony, extra letters were inserted into a word or an archaic formation was retained. But this need made itself felt chiefly in connexion with the B vocabulary. *Why* so great an importance was attached to ease of pronunciation will be made clear later in this essay.

*The B vocabulary.* The B vocabulary consisted of words which had been deliberately constructed for political purposes: words, that is to say, which not only had in every case a political implication, but were intended to impose a desirable mental attitude upon the person using them. Without a full understanding of the principles of Ingsoc it was difficult to use these words correctly. In some cases they could be translated into Oldspeak, or even into words taken from the A vocabulary, but this usually demanded a long paraphrase and always involved the loss of certain overtones. The B words were a sort of verbal shorthand, often packing whole ranges of ideas into a few syllables, and at the same time more accurate and forcible than ordinary language.

The B words were in all cases compound words.* They consisted of two or more words, or portions of words, welded together in an easily pronounceable form. The resulting amalgam was always a noun-verb, and inflected according to the ordinary rules. To take a single example: the word *goodthink,* meaning, very roughly, 'orthodoxy', or, if one chose to regard it as a verb, 'to think in an orthodox manner'. This inflected as follows: noun-verb, *goodthink*; past tense and past participle, *goodthinked*; present participle, *goodthinking*; adjective, *goodthinkful*; adverb, *goodthinkwise*; verbal noun, *goodthinker*.

The B words were not constructed on any etymological plan. The words of which they were made up could be any parts of speech, and could be placed in any order and mutilated in any way which made them easy to pronounce while indicating their derivation. In the word *crimethink* (thoughtcrime), for instance, the *think* came second, whereas in *thinkpol* (Thought Police) it came first, and in the latter word *police* had lost its second syllable. Because of the greater difficulty in securing euphony, irregular formations were commoner in the B vocabulary than in the A vocabulary. For example, the adjective forms of *Minitrue, Minipax,* and *Miniluv* were, respectively, *Minitruthful, Minipeaceful* and *Minilovely,* simply because *-trueful, -paxful,* and *-loveful* were slightly awkward to pronounce. In principle, however, all B words could inflect, and all inflected in exactly the same way.

Some of the B words had highly subtilized meanings, barely intelligible to anyone who had not mastered the language as a whole. Consider, for example, such a typical sentence from a *Times* leading article as *Oldthinkers unbellyfeel Ingsoc.* The shortest rendering that one could make of this in Oldspeak would be: 'Those whose ideas were formed before the Revolution cannot have a full emotional understanding of the principles of English Socialism.' But this is not adequate translation. To begin with, in order to grasp the full meaning of the Newspeak sentence quoted above, one would have to have a clear idea of what is meant by *Ingsoc.* And in addition, only a person thoroughly grounded in Ingsoc could appreciate the full force of the word *bellyfeel,* which implied a blind, enthusiastic acceptance difficult to imagine today; or of the word *oldthink,* which was inextricably mixed up with the idea of wickedness and decadence. But the special function of certain Newspeak words, of which *oldthink* was one, was not so much to express meanings as to destroy them. These words, necessarily few in number, had had their meanings extended until they contained within themselves whole batteries of words which, as they were sufficiently covered by a single comprehensive term, could now be scrapped and forgotten. The greatest difficulty facing the compilers of the Newspeak Dictionary was not to invent new words, but, having invented them, to make sure what they meant: to make sure, that is to say, what ranges of words they cancelled by their existence.

---

*Compound words, such as *speakwrite*, were of course to be found in the A vocabulary, but these were merely convenient abbreviations and had no special ideological colour.

As we have already seen in the case of the word *free*, words which had once borne a heretical meaning were sometimes retained for the sake of convenience, but only with the undesirable meanings purged out of them. Countless other words such as *honour, justice, morality, internationalism, democracy, science,* and *religion* had simply ceased to exist. A few blanket words covered them, and, in covering them, abolished them. All words grouping themselves round the concepts of liberty and equality, for instance, were contained in the single word *crimethink*, while all words grouping themselves round the concepts of objectivity and rationalism were contained in the single word *oldthink*. Greater precision would have been dangerous. What was required in a Party member was an outlook similar to that of the ancient Hebrew who knew, without knowing much else, that all nations other than his own worshipped 'false gods'. He did not need to know that these gods were called Baal, Osiris, Moloch, Ashtaroth, and the like: probably the less he knew about them the better for his orthodoxy. He knew Jehovah and the commandments of Jehovah: he knew, therefore, that all gods with other names or other attributes were false gods. In somewhat the same way, the Party member knew what constituted right conduct, and in exceedingly vague, generalized terms he knew what kinds of departure from it were possible. His sexual life, for example, was entirely regulated by the two Newspeak words *sexcrime* (sexual immorality) and *goodsex* (chastity). *Sexcrime* covered all sexual misdeeds whatever. It covered fornication, adultery, homosexuality, and other perversions, and, in addition, normal intercourse practised for its own sake. There was no need to enumerate them separately, since they were all equally culpable, and, in principle, all punishable by death. In the C vocabulary, which consisted of scientific and technical words, it might be necessary to give specialized names to certain sexual aberrations, but the ordinary citizen had no need of them. He knew what was meant by *goodsex*—that is to say, normal intercourse between man and wife, for the sole purpose of begetting children, and without physical pleasure on the part of the woman: all else was *sexcrime*. In Newspeak it was seldom possible to follow a heretical thought further than the perception that it *was* heretical: beyond that point the necessary words were non-existent.

No word in the B vocabulary was ideologically neutral. A great many were euphemisms. Such words, for instance, as *joycamp* (forced-labour camp) or *minipax* (Ministry of Peace, i.e. Ministry of War) meant almost the exact opposite of what they appeared to mean. Some words, on the other hand, displayed a frank and contemptuous understanding of the real nature of Oceanic society. An example was *prolefeed*, meaning the rubbishy entertainment and spurious news which the Party handed out to the masses. Other words, again, were ambivalent, having the connotation 'good' when applied to the Party and 'bad' when applied to its enemies. But in addition there were great numbers of words which at first sight appeared to be mere abbreviations and which derived their ideological colour not from their meaning, but from their structure.

So far as it could be contrived, everything that had or might have political significance of any kind was fitted into the B vocabulary. The name of every organization, or body of people, or doctrine, or country, or institution, or public building, was invariably cut down into the familiar shape; that is, a single easily pronounced word with the smallest number of syllables that would preserve the original derivation. In the Ministry of Truth, for example, the Records Department, in which Winston Smith worked, was called *Recdep*, the Fiction Department was called *Ficdep*, the Tele-programmes Department was called *Teledep*, and so on. This was not done solely with the object of saving time. Even in the early decades of the twentieth century, telescoped words and phrases had been one of the characteristic features of political language; and it had been noticed that the tendency to use abbreviations of this kind was most marked in totalitarian countries and totalitarian organizations. Examples were such words as *Nazi, Gestapo, Comintern, Inprecorr, Agitprop*. In the beginning the practice had been adopted as it were instinctively, but in Newspeak it was used with a conscious purpose. It was perceived that in thus abbreviating a name one narrowed and subtly altered its meaning, by cutting out most of the associations that would otherwise cling to it. The words *Communist International*, for instance, call up a composite picture of universal human brotherhood, red flags, barricades, Karl Marx, and the Paris Commune. The word *Comintern*, on the other hand, suggests merely a tightly knit organization and a well-defined body of doctrine. It refers to something almost as easily recognized, and as limited in purpose, as a chair or a table. *Comintern* is a word that can be uttered almost without taking thought, whereas *Communist International* is a phrase over which one is obliged to linger at least momentarily. In the same way, the associations called up by a word like *Minitrue* are fewer and more controllable than those called up by *Ministry of Truth*. This accounted not only for the habit of abbreviating whenever possible, but also for the almost exaggerated care that was taken to make every word easily pronounceable.

In Newspeak, euphony outweighed every consideration other than exactitude of meaning. Regularity of grammar was always sacrificed to it when it seemed necessary. And rightly so, since what was required, above all for political purposes, was short clipped words of unmistakable meaning which could be uttered rapidly and which roused the minimum of echoes in the speaker's mind. The words of the B vocabulary even gained in force from the fact that nearly all of them were very much alike. Almost invariably these words—*goodthink, Minipax, prolefeed, sexcrime, joycamp, Ingsoc, bellyfeel, thinkpol*, and countless others— were words of two or three syllables, with the stress distributed equally between the first syllable and the last. The use of them encouraged a gabbling style of speech, at once staccato and monotonous. And this was exactly what was aimed at. The intention was to make speech, and especially speech on any subject not ideologically neutral, as nearly as possible independent of consciousness. For the purposes of everyday life it was no doubt necessary, or sometimes necessary, to reflect before speaking, but a Party member called upon to make a political or ethical judgment should be able to spray forth the correct opinions as automatically as a machine-gun

spraying forth bullets. His training fitted him to do this, the language gave him
an almost foolproof instrument, and the texture of the words, with their harsh
sound and a certain wilful ugliness which was in accord with the spirit of
Ingsoc, assisted the process still further.

So did the fact of having very few words to choose from. Relative to our own,
the Newspeak vocabulary was tiny, and new ways of reducing it were
constantly being devised. Newspeak, indeed, differed from most all other
languages in that its vocabulary grew smaller instead of larger every year. Each
reduction was a gain, since the smaller the area of choice, the smaller the
temptation to take thought. Ultimately it was hoped to make articulate speech
issue from the larynx without involving the higher brain centres at all. This
aim was frankly admitted in the Newspeak word *duckspeak,* meaning 'to quack
like a duck'. Like various other words in the B vocabulary, *duckspeak* was
ambivalent in meaning. Provided that the opinions which were quacked out
were orthodox ones, it implied nothing but praise, and when *The Times*
referred to one of the orators of the Party as a *doubleplusgood duckspeaker* it was
paying a warm and valued compliment.

*The C vocabulary.* The C vocabulary was supplementary to the others and
consisted entirely of scientific and technical terms. These resembled the
scientific terms in use today, and were constructed from the same roots, but
the usual care was taken to define them rigidly and strip them of undesirable
meanings. They followed the same grammatical rules as the words in the other
two vocabularies. Very few of the C words had any currency either in everyday
speech or in political speech. Any scientific worker or technician could find all
the words he needed in the list devoted to his words occurring in the other lists.
Only a very few words were common to all lists, and there was no vocabulary
expressing the function of Science as a habit of mind, or a method of thought,
irrespective of its particular branches. There was, indeed, no word for
'Science', any meaning that it could possibly bear being already sufficiently
covered by the word *Ingsoc*.

From the foregoing account it will be seen that in Newspeak the expression
of unorthodox opinions, above a very low level, was well-nigh impossible. It
was of course possible to utter heresies of a very crude kind, a species of
blasphemy. It would have been possible, for example, to say *Big Brother is
ungood*. But this statement, which to an orthodox ear merely conveyed a self-
evident absurdity, could not have been sustained by reasoned argument,
because the necessary words were not available. Ideas inimical to Ingsoc could
only be entertained in a vague wordless form, and could only be named in very
broad terms which lumped together and condemned whole groups of heresies
without defining them in doing so. One could, in fact, only use Newspeak for
unorthodox purposes by illegitimately translating some of the words back into
Oldspeak. For example, *All mans are equal* was a possible Newspeak sentence,
but only in the same sense in which *All men are redhaired* is a possible Oldspeak
sentence. It did not contain a grammatical error, but it expressed a palpable

untruth—i.e. that all men are of equal size, weight, or strength. The concept of political equality no longer existed, and this secondary meaning had accordingly been purged out of the word *equal*. In 1984, when Oldspeak was still the normal means of communication, the danger theoretically existed that in using Newspeak words one might remember their original meanings. In practice it was not difficult for any person well grounded in *doublethink* to avoid doing this, but within a couple of generations even the possibility of such a lapse would have vanished. A person growing up with Newspeak as his sole language would no more know that *equal* had once had the secondary meaning of 'politically equal', or that *free* had once meant 'intellectually free', than for instance, a person who had never heard of chess would be aware of the secondary meanings attaching to *queen* and *rook*. There would be many crimes and errors which it would be beyond his power to commit, simply because they were nameless and therefore unimaginable. And it was to be foreseen that with the passage of time the distinguishing characteristics of Newspeak would become more and more pronounced—its words growing fewer and fewer, their meanings more and more rigid, and the chance of putting them to improper uses always diminishing.

When Oldspeak had been once and for all superseded, the last link with the past would have been severed. History had already been rewritten, but fragments of the literature of the past survived here and there, imperfectly censored, and so long as one retained one's knowledge of Oldspeak it was possible to read them. In the future such fragments, even if they chanced to survive, would be unintelligible and untranslatable. It was impossible to translate any passage of Oldspeak into Newspeak unless it either referred to some technical process or some very simple everyday action, or was already orthodox (*goodthinkful* would be the Newspeak expression) in tendency. In practice this meant that no book written before approximately 1960 could be translated as a whole. Pre-revolutionary literature could only be subjected to ideological translation—that is, alteration in sense as well as language. Take for example the well-known passage from the Declaration of Independence:

> *We hold these truths to be self-evident, that all men are created equal, that they are endowed by their creator with certain inalienable rights, that among these are life, liberty, and the pursuit of happiness. That to secure these rights, Governments are instituted among men, deriving their powers from the consent of the governed. That whenever any form of Government becomes destructive of those ends, it is the right of the People to alter or abolish it and to institute new Government. . . .*

It would have been quite impossible to render this into Newspeak while keeping to the sense of the original. The nearest one could come to doing so would be to swallow the whole passage up in the single word *crimethink*. A full translation could only be an ideological translation, whereby Jefferson's words would be changed into a panegyric on absolute government.

A good deal of the literature of the past was, indeed, already being transformed in this way. Considerations of prestige made it desirable to preserve the memory of certain historical figures, while at the same time bringing their achievements into line with the philosophy of Ingsoc. Various writers, such as Shakespeare, Milton, Swift, Byron, Dickens, and some others were therefore in process of translation: when the task had been completed, their original writings, with all else that survived of the literature of the past, would be destroyed. These translations were a slow and difficult business, and it was not expected that they would be finished before the first or second decade of the twenty-first century. There were also large quantities of merely utilitarian literature–indispensable technical manuals, and the like–that had to be treated in the same way. It was chiefly in order to allow time for the preliminary work of translation that the final adoption of Newspeak had been fixed for so late a date as 2050.

# FOR THE BEST IN PAPERBACKS, LOOK FOR THE

In every corner of the world, on every subject under the sun, Penguin represents quality and variety – the very best in publishing today.

For complete information about books available from Penguin – including Pelicans, Puffins, Peregrines and Penguin Classics – and how to order them, write to us at the appropriate address below. Please note that for copyright reasons the selection of books varies from country to country.

---

**In the United Kingdom:** Please write to *Dept E.P., Penguin Books Ltd, Harmondsworth, Middlesex, UB7 0DA*

If you have any difficulty in obtaining a title, please send your order with the correct money, plus ten per cent for postage and packaging, to *PO Box No 11, West Drayton, Middlesex*

**In the United States:** Please write to *Dept BA, Penguin, 299 Murray Hill Parkway, East Rutherford, New Jersey 07073*

**In Canada:** Please write to *Penguin Books Canada Ltd, 2801 John Street, Markham, Ontario L3R 1B4*

**In Australia:** Please write to the *Marketing Department, Penguin Books Australia Ltd, P.O. Box 257, Ringwood, Victoria 3134*

**In New Zealand:** Please write to the *Marketing Department, Penguin Books (NZ) Ltd, Private Bag, Takapuna, Auckland 9*

**In India:** Please write to *Penguin Overseas Ltd, 706 Eros Apartments, 56 Nehru Place, New Delhi, 110019*

**In Holland:** Please write to *Penguin Books Nederland B.V., Postbus 195, NL–1380AD Weesp, Netherlands*

**In Germany:** Please write to *Penguin Books Ltd, Friedrichstrasse 10–12, D–6000 Frankfurt Main 1, Federal Republic of Germany*

**In Spain:** Please write to *Longman Penguin España, Calle San Nicolas 15, E–28013 Madrid, Spain*

**In France:** Please write to *Penguin Books Ltd, 39 Rue de Montmorency, F-75003, Paris, France*

**In Japan:** Please write to *Longman Penguin Japan Co Ltd, Yamaguchi Building, 2–12–9 Kanda Jimbocho, Chiyoda-Ku, Tokyo 101, Japan*

# BY THE SAME AUTHOR

## DOWN AND OUT IN PARIS AND LONDON

After an Etonian education and service in the Imperial Police, George Orwell embarked on his first attempt to confront the world of poverty and failure, to defy the money values of the predatory world and of his own privileged background. In Paris and in London, working as a *plongeur* or spending nights with the tramps in the 'spike', Orwell mingled with the victims of modern society to produce the vivid account of the first steps on the road that led him to Wigan Pier and Catalonia.

## THE DECLINE OF THE ENGLISH MURDER AND OTHER ESSAYS

A collection of some of the less accessible essays by the author of *Animal Farm*. Including his lament for the inferior quality of modern murders and his comments on the changing face of fictional crime; his long essay on Dickens, and his shrewd critical remarks on Kipling and on the peculiar genius of Salvador Dali; eyewitness accounts of a hanging in Burma and a lazar-house in Paris; with notes on nationalism, on seaside postcards, and on his own ambition – surely realized – to make political writing into an art.

*and*

### THE LION AND THE UNICORN
#### Socialism and the English Genius

### HOMAGE TO CATALONIA

### INSIDE THE WHALE AND OTHER ESSAYS    THE ROAD TO WIGAN PIER

*also published, the celebrated biography by Bernard Crick*

### GEORGE ORWELL: A LIFE